1 MONTH OF
FREE
READING

at

www.ForgottenBooks.com

By purchasing this book you are eligible for one month membership to ForgottenBooks.com, giving you unlimited access to our entire collection of over 1,000,000 titles via our web site and mobile apps.

To claim your free month visit:

www.forgottenbooks.com/free776854

ISBN 978-0-483-12460-8
PIBN 10776854

BARCLAY.

Apology for the true Christian Divinity, &c., by
ROBERT BARCLAY, *Prop.* xv. §. 13—15.
p. 556, *&c. 8th Edit.*

AFTER representing revenge and war as an evil not
less opposite to the spirit and doctrine of Christ than
is light to darkness, and lamenting that, through
contempt of the law of Christ in this respect, the
world is filled with violence, oppression, and all
manner of lasciviousness and cruelty, unbecoming
mankind as creatures endued with reason, and still
more reproachful to men professing themselves the
disciples of Him, who by excellency is called the Prince
of Peace, this eminent author thus proceeds:

" Hear then what this great Prophet saith, whom
every soul is commanded to hear under the pain of
being cut off. Matt. v. from verse 38 to the end
of the chapter. For thus he saith: 'Ye have heard
that it hath been said, An eye for an eye, and a tooth
for a tooth: but I say unto you, That ye resist not
evil: but whosoever shall smite thee on thy right
cheek, turn to him the other also. And if any man
will sue thee at the law, and take away thy coat, let
him have thy cloak also. And whosoever shall compel thee to go a mile, go with him twain. Give to
him that asketh thee; and from him that would borrow of thee, turn not thou away. Ye have heard that
it has been said, Thou shalt love thy neighbour, and
hate thine enemy: but I say unto you, Love your
enemies, bless them that curse you, do good to them

that hate you, and pray for them which despitefully
use you, and persecute you, that ye may be the children of your Father which is in heaven. For he maketh
his sun to rise on the evil and on the good, and sendeth
rain on the just and on the unjust. For if ye love
them which love you, what reward have ye? Do not
even the Publicans the same? And if ye salute your
brethren only, what do ye more than others? Do not
even the Publicans so? Be 'ye therefore perfect, even
as your Father which is in heaven is perfect.'

" These words, with respect to revenge, as the
former in the case of swearing,* do forbid some things
which in time past were lawful to the Jews, considering their condition and dispensation; and command
unto such as will be the disciples of Christ, a more
perfect, eminent, and full signification of charity, as
also patience and suffering, than was required of them
in that time, state, and dispensation, by the law of
Moses. This is not only the judgment of most, if not
all, the ancient fathers, so called, of the first three
hundred years after Christ, but also of many others,
and in general of all those who have rightly understood and propagated the law of Christ concerning
swearing.

" And truly the words are so clear in themselves,
that, in my judgment, they need no illustration to
explain their sense, for it is as easy to reconcile the
greatest contradictions, as these laws of our Lord Jesus
Christ with the wicked practices of wars; for they are
plainly inconsistent. Whoever can reconcile this,
Resist not evil, with Resist violence by force: again,
Give also thy other cheek, with Strike again; also
Love thine enemies, with Spoil them, make a prey of
them, pursue them with fire and sword——whoever,
I say, can find a means to reconcile these things may

* Of which Barclay treats in the Part of his Apology immediately
preceding this.

5

be supposed also to have found a way to reconcile God with the devil, Christ with Antichrist, light with darkness, and good with evil. But if this be impossible, as indeed it is, so will also the other be impossible; and men do but deceive themselves and others, while they boldly adventure to establish such absurd and impossible things.

"Nevertheless because some, perhaps through inadvertency, and by the force of custom and tradition, do transgress this command of Christ, I shall briefly show how much war doth contradict this precept, and how much they are inconsistent with one another; and consequently that war is no ways lawful to such as will be the disciples of Christ. For,

"Christ commands, That we should love our enemies: but war, on the contrary, teaches us to hate and destroy them.

"James testifies, that wars and strifes come from the lusts, which war in the members of carnal men; but Christians, that is, those that are truly saints, have crucified the flesh with its affections and lusts; therefore they cannot indulge them by waging war.

"The prophets Isaiah and Micah have expressly prophesied, that in the mountain of the house of the Lord, Christ shall judge the nations, and then they shall beat their swords into ploughshares, &c. And the ancient fathers of the first three hundred years after Christ did affirm these prophecies to be fulfilled in the Christians of their times, who were most averse from war; concerning which Justin Martyr, Tertullian, and others may be seen: which need not seem strange to any, since Philo Judæus abundantly testified of the Essenes,* that there was none found among them that would make instruments of war. But how much more did Jesus

* The Essenes or *Esseni* were a Jewish Sect, the origin of which is supposed to have been prior to the time of the Maccabees.

come, that he might keep his followers from fighting, and might bring them to patience and charity?

"The prophet foretold (Isa. xi. 9.; lxv. 25.) that
there should none hurt nor kill in all the holy
mountain of the Lord; but outward war is appointed for killing and destroying.

"Christ reproved Peter for the use of the sword
saying, 'Put up again thy sword into its place
for all they that take the sword shall perish with
the sword.' Concerning which Tertullian speaks
well (lib. de Idololat.), 'How shall he fight in
peace without a sword, which the Lord did take
away? For although soldiers came to John, and
received a certain rule of conduct, and though the
centurion believed, yet by disarming Peter he dis-
armed every soldier afterwards.' And (lib. de
Coron. Mil.) he asketh, 'Shall it be lawful to use
the sword, the Lord saying, that he that useth the
sword shall perish by the sword?'

"The apostle admonisheth Christians, That they
defend not themselves, neither revenge, by rendering evil for evil; but give place unto wrath, because
vengeance is the Lord's. Be not overcome of evil
but overcome evil with good. If thine enemy
hunger, feed him; if he thirst, give him drink
But war throughout teacheth and enjoineth the
quite contrary.

"Christ calls his children to bear his cross, not
to crucify or kill others; to patience, not to revenge; to truth and simplicity, not to fraudulent
stratagems of war, or to play the sycophant, which
John himself forbids: to flee the glory of this world,
not to acquire it by warlike endeavours: therefore
war is altogether contrary unto the law and Spirit
of Christ.

"But it is objected, that it is lawful to war, because
Abraham did war before the giving of the law, and
the Israelites after the giving of the law.

" I answer as before, That Abraham, offered sacrifices at that time, and circumcised the males; which evertheless are not lawful for us under the Gospel.

"That neither defensive nor offensive war was lwful to the Israelites of their own will, or by their wn counsel or conduct; but they were obliged, at all imes, if they would be successful, first to enquire of he oracle of God.

[Further,] " Something is expressly forbidden by Jhrist (Matt. v. 38, &c.), which was granted to the ews, in their time, because of their hardness; and on he contrary, *we* are commanded that singular patience nd exercise of love which Moses commanded not to lis disciples."

Secondly, " It is objected, that defence is of natural ight, and that religion destroys not nature.

" I answer, Be it so; but to obey God, and commend ourselves to him in faith and patience, is not to lestroy nature, but to exalt and perfect it; to wit, to elevate it from the natural to the supernatural life, by Christ living therein, and comforting it that it may do all things and be rendered more than conqueror.

Thirdly, " It is objected that Cornelius, and that Centurion of whom there is mention made, (Matt. viii. 5.) were soldiers, and there is no mention that they laid down their military employments.

" I answer, Neither read we that they continued in them. But it is most probable that if they continued in the doctrine of Christ (and we read not anywhere of their falling from the faith) that they did not continue in them; especially if we consider, that [for] two or three ages afterwards, or at least a long while after that time, Christians altogether rejected war.

Fourthly, " It is objected, that the Scriptures and old fathers so called, did only prohibit private revenge, not the use of arms for the defence of our country, body, wives, children, and goods, when the magistrate commands it, seeing the magistrate ought to be obeyed; therefore, although it be not lawful for private men to do it of themselves, nevertheless they are bound to do it by the command of the magistrate.

" I answer, If the magistrate be truly a Christian, or desires to be so, he ought himself, in the first place, to obey the command of his Master, saying, Love your enemies, &c., and then he could not command us to kill them; but if he be not a true Christian, then ought we to obey our Lord and King, Jesus Christ, whom he ought also to obey: for in the kingdom of Christ all ought to submit to his laws, from the highest to the lowest, that is, from the king to the beggar, and from Cæsar to the clown. But alas! where shall we find such an obedience.

" But lastly, as to what relates to this thing, since nothing seems more contrary to man's nature, and seeing of all things the defence of one's self seems most tolerable; as it is most hard to men, so it is the most perfect part of the Christian religion, as that wherein the denial of self and entire confidence in God doth most appear; and therefore Christ and his apostles left us hereof a most perfect example. As to what relates to the present magistrates of the Christian world, albeit we deny them not altogether the name of Christians, because of the public profession they make of Christ's name, yet we may boldly affirm that they are far from the perfection of the Christian religion; because in the state in which they are, (a in many places before I have largely observed,) the have not come to the pure dispensation of the Gospel And therefore while they are in that condition, w shall not say, that war, undertaken upon a just*

---

* The context renders the meaning clear:—*An occasion relativel just, one which would be just on the* SUPPOSITION *of the lawfulness (War.* The Author, it may be remarked, appears to have looked for ward to a *gradual* prevalence of the doctrine he was defending; pro gressive in proportion as the love of God, the love of our neighbour and that faith which overcomes the world should more and mo

occasion is altogether unlawful to them. For even as circumcision and the other ceremonies were for a season permitted to the Jews, not because they were either necessary of themselves, or lawful at that time; after the resurrection of Christ, but because that Spirit was not yet raised up in them, whereby they could be delivered from such rudiments; so the present confessors of the Christian name, who are yet in the mixture, and not in the patient suffering spirit, are not yet fitted for this form of Christianity, and therefore cannot be undefending themselves until they attain that perfection. But for such whom Christ has brought hither, it is not lawful to defend themselves by arms, but they ought over all to trust to the Lord."

TUKE.

Principles of Religion, as professed by the Society of Christians, usually called Quakers, by HENRY TUKE, ch. viii. p. 143—149. 6th Edit.

" Having said what appears to be sufficient on the subject of oaths, we come next to consider the arguments used in defence of war. Of these the principle one is, that it is unavoidable and necessary. In reply to this we say, that so long as mankind are disposed to live under the influence of their passions, and to sacrifice their dearest interests to their avarice, or their ambition, this plea will not be wanting. But let us consider what proofs have been given that war is really unavoidable. Has any nation fairly made the experiment, and failed? Where is the country that

influence mankind. How encouraging the progress that *is* observable, in the present day; when not a few among different religious denominations are coming forward, as advocates of the glorious cause of Peace, on the sure basis of Christian principle.

has regulated its conduct by that justice, that libera
lity, that love, that humility, and that meekness
which Christianity requires, and yet has found wa
unavoidable? Can we contemplate the characters o
the individuals, who have been the rulers of nations
and say, that such have been the dispositions which
regulated their public and private conduct; an
that still they have not been able to preserve thei
country from war and bloodshed! Till all this can b
clearly proved, the argument from necessity is of n
weight.

" If, then, it cannot be shown that men, living an
acting in a truly Christian spirit, have found war t
be necessary and unavoidable, the argument assume
must be considered as destitute of foundation. But
that I may not be thought to reason chimerically
I shall show that a people have existed, who, act
ing upon these Christian principles, preserved thei
country from war and bloodshed, even while thei
neighbours were frequently involved in them. Penn
sylvania, it is generally known, was originally th
property of one called a Quaker, who filled most o
the offices of the government with persons of his owr
persuasion. Had not the conduct of this people to
wards their neighbours, both Indians and Europeans
been recorded by men totally unconnected with th
Society, my relation might appear partial and inter
ested; but history, impartial history, has transmitted
the conduct of this people to posterity in such a manner, as renders it unnecessary for me to say more
than that, so long as they retained their ascendency
in the state, which was about sixty or seventy years
neither internal nor external war was permitted to
disturb their peaceful habitations. We do not say
that occasions of difference never occurred: but other
means of settling their differences, than those generally
resorted to, were pursued, and, if not found successful,
submission was wisely preferred to the precarious and
violent decision of the sword.

"Great pains are taken to make a distinction between offensive and defensive war; and whilst the former is generally reprobated, the latter meets with many advocates. It must, I suppose, be admitted, that in almost every war, both parties profess to act on the principle of defence: and where is the criterion which accurately determines the difference? But suppose an extreme case, and that without any provocation, one man or one nation, is attacked by another, is there no dependence to be placed on a superintending Providence? and have religion and virtue no resources, but in the arm of flesh? Were our minds brought into a true Christian state, the protection of Divine Providence would be humbly and safely relied upon; so far, at least, as to prevent us from seeking redress by means destructive of the lives of our fellow-creatures.

"Such is the natural state of mankind, that 'offences must needs come;' but it ought to be remembered 'that wo is to him by whom the offence cometh.' Were those dispositions recommended by our blessed Lord, cherished by that which considers itself the offended party, it would soon appear that war is not so necessary and unavoidable, as is by many imagined.

"If sound policy were adopted, it would unite with true Christianity in eradicating this distressing evil. Can anything in this world compensate for the desolation and misery which war occasions on the earth? To the loss of life and property, with almost all worldly comforts, let us add the still more important loss which religion and virtue sustain from a state of war, and from the military life in general. Will it not then be difficult to conceive how men, who really have what they think the good of their country at heart, and who also consider themselves entitled to the denomination of Christians, can promote a practice, which is productive of so many, both natural and moral evils? In contemplating this distressing subject we find it necessary to have recourse to that

Christian charity, which it is our duty to extend to those who differ from us in principle and practice. I wish, however, for myself and my fellow-professors, that we may faithfully maintain our principles on this subject; being at the same time careful to support the doctrine of peace, in the spirit of peace : then we may be made instrumental in promoting the increase of the government of the Son of God, whose introduction into this world was announced by an angel, accompanied with a multitude of the heavenly host, praising God, and saying, ' Glory to God in the highest, and on earth Peace, good-will towards men.' Luke ii. 13, 14.

" There are a few arguments brought forward in favour of war, from some passages in the New Testament, which it will be proper to consider. Of these the principal one is, the expression of our Lord to his disciples : ' He that hath no sword, let him sell his garment and buy one.' Luke xxii. 36. This passage is generally considered to be of doubtful signification; and some, who do not agree with us in our sentiments on war, consider this expression of our Lord as allegorical.* When the disciples replied, ' Here are two swords,' he gave this short answer, ' It is enough.' Verse 38. This seems to imply that they did not understand his meaning; for if he had intended the external sword how could two be sufficient for the number of the disciples, and at a time when they were about to be attacked by a multitude, that came out as against a thief, with swords and staves? But what seems clearly to show that our Saviour did not intend to recommend the use of the sword in a literal sense is, the circumstance which occurred very soon after he had used the expression under consideration : for we find that when Peter, on the very same day, made use of a sword in defence of his Master, he was reproved

* "See Dr. Edwards on the Style, &c., of the Scripture, page 126."

by him in this manner : 'Put up again thy sword into his place ; for all they that take the sword shall perish with the sword.' Matt. xxvi. 52. It may also be added, that it was on the same, or the succeeding day, that our Lord said to Pilate, 'My kingdom is not of this world. If my kingdom were of this world, then would my servants fight, that I should not be delivered to the Jews.' John xviii. 36. Now, when these important and concurring circumstances are considered, can it be supposed, that our Lord intended to recommend to his disciples the use of the sword, either in defence of him or themselves, or on any other occasion?"

Another circumstance brought forward as an argument in favour of war, is the conversion of Cornelius, a centurion in the Roman army, and no account given of his having relinquished a military life.* As we have not any further account of this pious centurion, than that of his conversion, and the circumstances attending it, no argument of any weight can be drawn from this relation. Some ancient writers inform us, that the primitive Christians did not fight; and we may therefore reasonably suppose, that if the centurion continued firm in his attachment to the Christian religion, he abandoned his military life. At any rate, the silence of the sacred historian cannot, with propriety, be brought forward as an argument in support of war; or as showing it to be consistent with the Christian dispensation.

"It is further, argued, that the expression of the apostle Paul, who says respecting the magistrate : 'He beareth not the sword in vain' (Rom. xiii. 4.), is an implied acknowledgment of the propriety of using the sword in a military manner. This argument, I conceive, arises from a misapplication of the passage. The sword here alluded to, we have reason

* "Acts x. The remarks on this case apply to that of the centurion mentioned Matt. viii. 5."

to suppose, was only an emblem of civil power. We
are informed that one of the chief magistrates in
Rome, and it is to the Romans the Apostle uses this
expression, had a sword hung up in his court, as an
emblem of his power;* and we know that in this
country, especially in corporate towns, the chief ma
gistrates have a sword borne before them on particular
occasions, as an emblem of office. But if the sword
was even used in the punishment of offenders, it would
be no fair argument in favour of using it for the pur
poses of war, and those devastations attendant on this
lamentable evil.

"These, and such as these, are the arguments ad
vanced by many in support of an evil, which, in its
consequences, shocks humanity, destroys morality
weakens the influence of religion, and entails on man
kind miseries incalculable and indescribable. Was
the ingenuity of man as much exercised to put an
end to this calamity, as his ambition is to support it
we should soon find the benefits resulting from this
disposition. But it is religion, it is the Christian
religion, which alone provides an adequate remedy
for this malignant disorder; and when mankind are
willing to receive, in the purity, the love, the meekness
and the humility which its Divine Author inculcated
this, with other similar predictions respecting him
will be fulfilled: 'He shall judge among the nations
and work convictions† among many people; and they
shall beat their swords into ploughshares, and their
spears into pruning hooks: nation shall not lift u
sword against nation; neither shall they learn wa
any more.'" Isa. ii. 4.

* "Godwin's Roman Antiquities, p. 164."
† "See Lowth's Translation of Isaiah."

MARTIN.

*A Defence of some Principles held by the People
called Quakers, by J. M. (JOSIAH MARTIN),
∴ appended to Pearson's Great Case of Tithes.
London, 1733, p. 138, &c.*

After quoting Tertullian, Origen, and others, this
writer adduces the remarkable narrative of the martyrdom of a young man named Maximilian, "to
prove," as he affirms, "that it was held unlawful for
a Christian to bear arms and to fight, not only in the
days of Tertullian and Origen, but later down, even
to the emperor Diocletian's time," it being under his
reign that Maximilian suffered. The narrative, with
some notes by the Author, and an observation of his
subjoined, is as follows:—

"Maximilian being brought before the tribunal,
*Dion the proconsul said, What is thy name? Max-
imilian answered, Why wouldest thou know my name,
I must not fight, for I am a Christian. Dion the
proconsul said, let him be enrolled: And when he
was enrolled, it was recited out of the register, that
he was five feet ten inches high. Dion bid the officer
mark him; and when Maximilian refused, saying, I
cannot fight, Dion said, Bear arms, or thou shalt die.

* "Dion proconsul dixit; Quis vocaris? Maximilianus respondit:
Quid autem vis scire nomen meum? Mihi non licet militare, quia
Christianus sum," &c. This narrative is entitled Passio S. Maximi-
liani, and is printed at the end of a small book of Lactantius, De
Mortibus Persecutorem, Oxonii, Anno Dom. 1680. And also in
Rumart's Acta Primorum Martyrum, at Paris, in quarto, Anno 1689.
In Rumart's book the reader will find instances of others who suffered
martyrdom for refusing to bear arms, particularly one Marcellus, a
centurion, who went and laid down his arms before the ensigns of the
legion, and declared before all the soldiers, that he was a Christian;
for which he was put to death. "Rejecto cingulo militari coram sig-
nis legionis, Christianum se esse testatus est coram omni populo."

Maximilian answered, I cannot fight if I die; I figh
not for this world, but for my God.

" Dion the proconsul said, who has persuaded thee
Maximilian answered, My own mind, and he wh
called me. Dion spoke to his father, and bid hin
persuade his son. His father replied, He knows hi
own mind, and what is best for him to do. Dion the
said to Maximilian, Take thy arms, and receive th
mark.* He answered I can receive no such mark,
have already the mark of Christ. Dion the proconsu
said, I shall send thee quickly to thy Christ. He an
swered, I would have thee, for that will be my praise

" Dion bid the officer mark him, but he, still re
fusing, said, I cannot receive the mark of this world
and if thou shouldst mark me, I shall break it, for i
will avail nothing: I am a Christian, and it is no
lawful for me to wear such a mark about my neck
when I have received the saving mark of my Lor
Jesus' Christ, the son of the living God, whom tho
art ignorant of; who died to give us life, and who
God gave for our sins; Him all we Christians obe
Him we follow as the restorer of our life, and t
author of our salvation. Dion said, Take thy arm
and receive the mark, or thou wilt perish miserabl
Maximilian answered, I shall not perish, my name
already enrolled with my Lord; I cannot fight. Dic
said, Consider thy youth, and bear arms, for it is wh
becomes a young man. Maximilian replied, My ar
are with my Lord, I cannot fight for this world, I a
now a Christian. Dion the proconsul said, Amor
the life-guards of our masters, Diocletian and Ma
imianus, and Constantius and Maximinus, there a
Christian soldiers, and they fight. † Maximilian r

* " It is said the mark was made in the hand, and they wore
leaden ring about the neck."

† " The modest and Christian-like answer which Maximili
gave Dion when he told him there were Christian soldiers in t
life-guard of his masters, is worthy of our greatest notice, " I
sciunt," says he, " quod eis expediat: ego tamen Christianus su
et non possum male facere." They know what is expedient f

plied, They know what is expedient for them, but I am a Christian, and cannot do evil. Dion said, Take thy arms, despise not the business of a soldier, lest thou perish miserably. Maximilian replied, I shall not perish, and if I leave this world my soul will live with Christ my Lord.

"Dion then said, Strike his name out; and when t was done, Dion said, Because with a rebellious mind thou hast refused to bear arms, thou shalt be punished according to thy deserts, for an example to others! And then he read his sentence: Maximilian, because thou hast with a rebellious mind refused to bear arms, thou shalt die by the sword. Maximilian replied, Thanks be to God.

" He was twenty years three months and seventeen days old. And when he was led to the place of execution, he spake thus: ' My dear brethren, endeavour with all your might, that it may be your lot to see the Lord, and that he may give you such a crown. And then with a pleasant countenance he said to his father, Give the executioner the soldier's coat thou hadst got for me, and when I shall receive thee in the company of the blessed martyrs, we may also rejoice together with the Lord;' and thus he suffered.

" His mother, Pompeiana, obtained his body of the judge, and carried it to Carthage, and buried it near the place where the body of Cyprian the martyr lay; and thirteen days after, the mother died and was buried in the same place. Victor, his father, returned to his habitation rejoicing, and praising God, that he had sent before such a gift unto the Lord, himself expecting to follow after.

them; but I am a Christian and cannot do evil. This is truly the very language of a disciple of Christ; but what sort of Christians those were that Dion spoke of, that could fight, we can only guess it: they might indeed bear the name of Christians, as multitudes do now-a-days, but certainly they were not so well convinced, or at least not such strict followers of Christ's doctrine, as this Maximilian and some others whose names are upon record, who chose rather to die than to bear arms and fight for this world; which they could not do without transgressing the precept and command of Christ.—Matt. v. 44."

"The reader has now a testimony against bearing
arms and fighting, remarkable both for its antiquity
and the tokens it bears of the courage and fortitud
so conspicuous in the primitive Christians; we shal
therefore leave him to decide which were the true servants and disciples of Christ, who said to Pilate, M
kingdom is not of this world, if my kingdom were o
this world, then would my servants fight—whethe
such Christians as this Maximilian was, or such a
Dion said were of Diocletian's guard and did fight."

For further information respecting the doctrine an
practice of the primitive Christians in relation t
war, the reader may be referred to *Clarkson'.
Portraiture of Quakerism,* vol. iii. p. 41—75
2nd edition.

AN AUTHOR UNDER THE SIGNATURE OF

ECCLETUS.

*Notes on a letter to the Archbishops and Bishops o
the Church of England, &c. London,* 180
pp. 24—26. 30.

" War is surely proscribed by many precepts, an
by the whole example of Christ. Three words
his convey its death warrant—LOVE your ENEMIE
(Matt. v. 44. Luke vi. 27. 35) and the execution
this waits, in each of us, only our full surrender t
the Gospel. That is the perfection of Christian lov
which leaves no room for fear; and enables a man t
dismiss that sense of insecurity which is the true m
tive for holding out threats to another. Aspiring t
no less an end, we are willing to set out at once i
our practice from the precept and the example, leavin
the consequences to follow; not without looking f

ability, both to obey and to suffer, to the grace of God strengthening us, who otherwise could do nothing. We dare to oppose this conduct and this way of reasoning to that discriminating doctrine which would justify the Christian in disobeying any of his Lord's precepts, because of the possible consequences of his obedience. This would have provided very well for the ease of the primitive advocates for Christianity, in this and other testimonies against the religion of the lords of the world, who impugned them with no gentler arguments than fire and sword. They might have shunned the reply, and have pleaded that at that juncture it was not convenient. But in the mean time what would have become of the cause?

"The present state of the world undoubtedly affords an awful prospect; yet the Christian, confirmed in the true faith, is enabled to face it. Let us anticipate for him the worst that can happen to himself. He is plundered and oppressed. But his goods and his person were his servants; and their master, if he retain his integrity, may yet look on free. Yet more —he suffers ignominy, pain, and death. But he can suffer neither without the permission of his Almighty Protector, who has numbered the hairs of his head, who loves him beyond measure, and therefore consults his best interests in the event. He is banished however—from whence? From a scene of probation and suffering—and whither? To a kingdom of peace and glory, where, far from being enslaved, he reigns rejoicing! Such is the personal view of the subject to the magnanimous, that is to say, to the faithful follower of Christ in every age. A nation so constituted, could no more fight, than it could be enslaved. In the very improbable event of its being threatened by another with immediate violence, such a nation would appeal not only formally but really to Providence. Is not Povidence, the faithful Christian would say, one in being with Omnipotence; and does Omnipotence, want the feeble aid of forbidden violence on my part, to redress my wrong or establish my

right? · Having used every possible means for rea
sonable accommodation, I shall now wait his decision
That decision will be right and just, and more
cannot ask.

·" That the principle of peace will spread in th
world at large we can no more doubt, than tha
the Gospel will be preached in all nations : and whe
the time arrives for this, we have grounds in the histor
of the primitive church for the opinion, that sea
rivers, and mountains will not be barriers to its pro
gress, or circumscribe and determine the sphere of it
tranquillizing influence. The tumultuous course o
violence is easily marked by the world. When it
sudden and impetuous movements have been accom
plished, it ceases by the collision of its opposed part
The world then proclaims peace, while the laten
cause of war subsists as before. It is not so with th
peace of the Gospel. Those changes, in the mora
and intellectual state of mankind, which prepare th
way for this, have proceeded for ages, like the growt
of solid timber, slowly, silently, irresistibly; and
future age will undoubtedly witness their consum
mation.

---

*Such are some at least of the arguments by whic
the members of the Society of Friends justify thei
refusal to bear arms, or fight in any case; and b
which also they are willing to promote among thei
fellow-professors of the peaceable religion of JESUS
the coming of that day so clearly foretold by th
prophets, when "nation shall not lift up sword agains
nation, neither shall they learn war any more."*

END.

Printed by E. Couchman and Co., 10, Throgmorton Street, London.

MEMOIR

OF

THOMAS CHALKLEY,

CHIEFLY

EXTRACTED FROM A JOURNAL

OF HIS

LIFE, TRAVELS, AND CHRISTIAN EXPERIENCES,

First published in America.

~~~~~~~~~~~~~~~

LONDON:

Printed for the TRACT ASSOCIATION of the SOCIETY of FRIENDS.

Sold at the DEPOSITORY, 12, Bishopsgate Street, Without.

—

1862.

No. 23. [*Price* 1s. 3d. *per dozen.*]

MEMOIR, &c.

THE Christian experiences of the faithful serving to dir
and animate those who are willing to follow them in the p
of virtue and true religion, and their example shining wi
the greater brightness when they have, with the flesh, put
human infirmity, it becomes the duty of survivors to prese
and render useful to posterity, the memorials of their li
and actions which they may leave behind them. Such app
to have been the motives of the Friends of Philadelphia, w
published, in the year 1749, a Testimony to the religio
worth of THOMAS CHALKLEY.

"He was (say they) a member of our Monthly Meetii
above forty years; so that some of us had opportunities
being intimately acquainted with him, and of knowing
fidelity and diligence in promoting the cause of Truth, a
the edification of the Church of Christ; this having been t
principal engagement and concern of his mind, and which
preferred to any other consideration, as will appear to tho
who, with an honest and unprejudiced intention, peruse l
Journal of his Life and Travels."

The circumstances attending the formation of the chara
ter of this Friend, under the discipline of the cross of Chri
happily extended to him in his early years, will be best giv
(as far as the required brevity of a Tract will permit) in l
own expressions.

"I was born on the third day of the third month 1675,
Southwark, and descended of honest and religious paren
who were very careful of me, and brought me up in the fe
of the Lord; and oftentimes counselled me to sobriety, a
reproved me for wantonness; and that light spirit, which
incident to youth, they were careful to nip in the bud:
that I have cause to bless God, through Christ, on t
behalf of my tender parents.

And I may not forget the dealings of God with me in n
very tender years. When between eight and ten years
age, my father and mother sent me near two miles to scho
to Richard Scoryer, in the suburbs of London. I went most
by myself to the school; and many and various were t

xercises I went through, by beatings and stonings along the
treets, being distinguished to the people (by the badge of
lainness which my parents put upon me) of what profession
. was; divers telling me, it was no more sin to kill me, than
t was to kill a dog.

About this time the Lord began to work strongly on my
nind by his grace, insomuch that I could not forbear reprov-
ng those lads who would take the name of the Lord God in
heir mouths in vain; reminding them of the third command-
nent, 'Thou shalt not take the name of the Lord thy God in
ain, for the Lord will not hold him guiltless that taketh his
lame in vain;' and of Christ's saying, 'Every idle word that
nen shall speak, they shall give an account thereof in the
lay of judgment;' for which I was mocked and derided by
ome, and others would sometimes refrain from such bad
vords when I reproved them.

One time I remember I was amongst some men, one of
vhom I had reproved, and he told the rest of it, and turned
o me and said, that I was no Christian, and asked me, when
: said the Lord's prayer? I asked him, if he said it: he said
es. I then asked him how he could call God Father, and
)e so wicked as to swear and take God's name in vain, which
: had heard him often do; and I told him what Christ said
o the Jews, 'You are of your father the devil, because his
vorks ye do;' and that those that did the devil's work, could
lot truly call God Father, according to Christ's doctrine. So
)eing convicted in their consciences that what I said was
rue, they were all silent, and wondered that I being so young,
hould speak in such a manner; in which I remember I had
;reat peace and good satisfaction: and from thenceforth
hese men let me alone.

Notwithstanding I hated to hear wicked words, I loved
)lay exceedingly, being persuaded that there was no harm in
hat, if we used no bad words. One time I was at play at a
leighbour's house with the children, and in the midst of my
port I was reached to with strong convictions, insomuch that
: could not forbear weeping. The children's mother observ-
ng that I wept, said, 'Why do you weep, Tommy?' I told
ler I could not tell, except it was because I was a naughty
)oy. 'Oh?' said she, 'do not believe him, for that is the
levil tells you so, for you are the best boy in all our street.'
3ut I knew I was told the truth by conviction, and that she
vas mistaken, for I plainly understood by clear conviction,
ind by the Holy Scriptures (which I had been trained up in
he reading of) that I was too vain and wanton; for I loved
nusic, dancing, and playing at cards, and too much delighted

therein betimes, and was followed with the judgments of God therefore in the secret of my soul.

What I did in those sports and games, I always took care to do out of the sight, and without the knowledge of my tender parents; for I was afraid of their reproofs and correction, the which I was sure to have, if they had any intelligence of it.

I remember that unknown to my parents, I had bought a pack of cards, with intent to make use of them when I went (at the time called Christmas) to see my relations in the country, where there was liberty in the family so to do, and five miles on my way went to a meeting at Wanstead; at which a minister of Christ declared against the evil of gaming, and particularly of cards; and that the time which people pretend to keep holy, for Christ's sake, many of them spent mostly in wickedness, sports, and games; even some pretending to be religious: and, generally speaking, more sin and evil is committed in this time, than in the like space of time in all the year besides: so that the devil is served, instead of honouring Christ. From this meeting at Wanstead I went to the house of my relations, and the time drawing near that we were to go to our games, my uncle called to the [company present] to come and take a game at cards; at which motion I had strong convictions upon me not to do it, as being evil; and I secretly cried to the Lord to keep me faithful to him; and lifting up my eyes, I saw a Bible lie in the window, at the sight of which I was glad. I took it, and sat down, and read to myself greatly rejoicing that I was preserved out of the snare. Then my uncle called again, and said, 'Come, doctor, you and I, and my wife and daughter, will have a game at cards, for I see my cousin is better disposed.' Then he looked upon me, and said, he was better disposed also. So their sport for that time was spoiled, and mine in that practice for ever; for I never (as I remember) played with them more, but as soon as I came home, offered my new and untouched pack of cards to the fire.

I very well remember the work of God upon my soul, when I was about ten years of age, and particularly at a certain time when I had been rebelling against God and my parents, in vanity and lightness: and as I had offended both, so I was corrected by both: for I had not only the anger of my parents, but the Lord frowned upon me, insomuch that I trembled exceedingly, and was as though I heard a vocal voice say to me, 'What will become of thee this night, if I should take thy life from thee?' at which I was amazed, and in great fear. Then I covenanted with God, that if he would be pleased to spare my life (for I thought God would have taken my life from me that very moment), I would be more sober, and mind his fear more than I had done before.

Nevertheless I broke covenant with God my Maker, my adversary tempting me so to do, telling me I was but a child, and that it was natural for children to be brisk and to play, and that God would wink at my childhood and youth, and it was time enough for me, when a man, to become religious. But still God followed me with his chastising rod, and often put me in mind of my covenant that I made with him in my distress; and that he had granted my request which I then made to him; and unless I would take up a cross to my own corrupt will and inclinations, he should take me out of the world. Then, oh then! I cried, 'Lord help, or I die! save me, or I perish for ever! I cannot keep thy covenant, nor do thy will, without thy help and assistance!' and indeed if the Lord had not helped, I had been undone for ever.

And I then began to delight in reading and sobriety, which before were irksome to me: and when I read the Holy Scriptures, I desired that God would open them to my understanding, which he did to my edification many times. I also begged earnestly of the Lord, that he would be pleased to be with me, and make me like to those his children and servants, of whom I read in the Holy Scriptures, who faithfully served him all their days. And when I read of the crucifixion of our blessed Lord and Saviour Jesus Christ, it would break my soul into tenderness. I thought it was enough to awaken and humble my soul that was well-meaning, and had any sense of the power, love, and grace of Christ. Thus I went on for several years, feeling that peace which passeth natural understanding, which many times accompanied my poor and needy soul."

About the twentieth year of his age, his religious principle was put to the test by his being impressed for the sea-service. After a night passed in the hold of a tender, among other victims of this practice, whose conversation was of a nature tending greatly to distress him, he was brought up, and asked if he were willing to serve his majesty. "I answered, (he relates,) that I was willing to serve him in my business, and according to my conscience: but as for war or fighting, Christ had forbid it in his excellent sermon on the mount, and for that reason I could not bear arms, nor be instrumental to destroy or kill men. The lieutenant looked on me, and on the people, and said, 'Gentlemen, what shall we do with this fellow? he swears he will not fight.' The commander of the vessel made answer, 'No, no, he will neither swear nor

fight.' Upon which they turned me on shore. I was thankf
that I was delivered out of their hands; and my tend
parents were glad to see me again."

Having attained to a good degree of stability and exper
ence in religion, he found his mind engaged, in the love
God, to desire the spiritual welfare of others, and to beco
the instrument of promoting it. "In this concern (he o
serves) I felt the Gospel power of our Lord Jesus Christ
work upon my soul, and the word of God was as a seed
my heart, growing and opening in me, speaking to me, a
making my understanding fruitful in the things of his kir
dom; and in that ability which was given me of God, throu
his grace and Holy Spirit, I exhorted people to repentan
and amendment of life; and I always humbly desired t
help and divine influence of God's eternal Word therei
Oh! I did fervently pray that I might minister the Gosp
in the power of Jesus: for I clearly discerned in the light
the Son of God, that all ministering out of Christ's powe
was neither edifying nor efficacious unto souls: therefore
did earnestly beseech God for the continuance of the gift
his Spirit, that I might be enabled to preach the Gospel,
the power of Christ Jesus. The concern that was upon m
on this account at that time, is hard to be expressed i
words."

He was well received, in this new and important characte
by his Friends, and we must henceforth consider him as alte
nately engaged in dispensing to his brethren and to stranger
the free Gospel of Christ, and in ministering, according t
the practice of the Apostle Paul, with his own hands to hi
own necessities, and to those that were with him. His fir
labours in each sense, were performed in his native countr
but during the year 1698, he was occupied in a religiou
visit to the meetings of the Friends in America: in returr
ing from which service he witnessed the following remark
able and awful occurrence.

"After we had been almost seven weeks at sea, we though
that we were near the land, but we sounded several days, an
found no bottom. About this time our doctor dreamed
dream, which was to this effect, himself relating it to me
'He went on shore at a great and spacious town, the buil
ings whereof were high, and the streets broad; and as h
went up the street he saw a large sign, on which was writtei
in great golden letters, SHAME. At the door of the hous
(to which the sign belonged) stood a woman with a can i
her hand, who said unto him, 'Doctor, will you drink?' h
replied, 'With all my heart, I have not drunk anything bu

water a great while;' and he drank a hearty draught, which he said made him merry; so he went up the street reeling to and fro, when a grim fellow coming behind him, clapped him on the shoulder, and told him that he arrested him in the name of the governor of the place. He asked him for what; he answered for stealing the woman's can; the can he had indeed, and so he was had before the governor, which was a mighty black dog, the biggest and grimest that ever he saw in his life; and witness was brought in against him by an old companion of his, and he was found guilty, and his sentence was, to go to prison, and there to lie for ever.'

He told me this dream with such an emphasis, that it affected me with serious sadness, and caused my heart to move within me (for to me the dream seemed true, and the interpretation sure). I then told him he was an ingenious man, and might clearly see the interpretation of that dream, which exactly answered to his state and condition, which I thus interpreted to him: 'This great and spacious place, wherein the buildings were high and the streets broad, is thy great and high profession: the sign, on which was wrote shame, and the woman at the door, with the can in her hand, truly represent that great, crying, and shameful sin of drunkenness, which thou knowest to be thy great weakness: the grim fellow who arrested thee, is Death, who will assuredly arrest all mortals: the governor which thou sawest, representing a great black dog, is certainly the devil, who after his servants have served him to the full, will torment them eternally in hell.' So he got up, as it were in haste, and said, 'God forbid; it is nothing but a dream.' But I told him it was a very significant one, and a warning to him from the Almighty who sometimes speaks to men in dreams.

Some days after the doctor's dream, we met with a Dutch vessel in Lime-bay, a little above the Start, hailed her, and she us. They said they came from Lisbon, and were bound for Holland. She was loaded with wine, brandy, fruit, and such commodities; and we having little but water to drink (by reason our passage was longer than we expected) therefore we sent our boat on board, in order to buy us a little wine to drink with our water. Our doctor and a merchant that was a passenger, and one sailor, went on board, where they staid so long until some of them were overcome with wine, although they were desired to beware thereof; so that when they came back, a rope being handed to them, they were not capable of using it dexterously, insomuch that they overset the boat, and she turned bottom upwards, having the doctor under her. The merchant caught hold of a rope called the main sheet, whereby his life was saved. The sailor not getting so much drink as the other two, got nimbly on the bottom of the boat, and floated on the water till such time as our other boat was hoisted out, which was done with great speed, and we took him in; but the doctor was drowned before the boat came. The seaman that sat on the boat saw him sink, but could not help him. This was the greatest exercise that we met with in all our voyage; and much the more so, as the doctor was of an evil life and conversation, and much given to excess of drinking. When he got on board the aforesaid ship, the master sent for a can of wine and said 'Doctor, will you drink?' he replied, 'Yes, with all my heart, for I have drunk no wine a great while.' Upon which he drank a hearty draught that made him merry, (as he said in his dream,) and notwithstanding the admonition which was so clearly manifested to him but three days before, and the many promises he had made to Almighty God, some of which I was a witness of, when strong convictions were upon him, yet now he was unhappily overcome, and in drink when he was drowned. This is, I think, a lively representation of the tender mercy, and just judgment of the Almighty to poor mortals: and I thought it was worthy to be recorded to posterity, as a warning to all great lovers of wine and strong liquors. This exercise was so great to me, that I could not for several days get over it; and one day while I was musing in my mind on these things, it was opened to me, that God and his servants were clear, and his blood was on his own head; for he had been faithfully warned of his evil ways."

In his twenty-fourth year Thomas Chalkley entered into the married state, and soon afterwards emigrated with his family to the rapidly increasing colony of Pennsylvania. A remarkable preservation at the commencement of the voyage is thus related. "When the ship was at Gravesend, and ready to sail, several of our dear relations and friends accompanied us to the ship, on board of which we had a good meeting, and took our solemn leave of one another, as never expecting to see each other any more in this world. It was a solemn time indeed; we prayed for one another and so parted, our ship sailing that evening, and we got to Margate-Road, where we anchored, and the wind sprung up very fresh, and blew tempestuously, so that we broke our cable, and lost our best bower anchor, and drove violently towards the Goodwin Sands. We let go our sheet anchor, and three more, which were all we had, but they did not stop her. The people were in great consternation, expecting nothing but death: but for my part, being exceedingly sea-sick, and having been in many storms, I was not so much surprised with this. One of the passengers came weeping, and said our case was very bad. The doctor also came in the same manner, and cried, ' Oh ! Mr. Chalkley, we are all dead men!' then I thought with myself, I would go out on deck, and see what the matter was ; and when on deck, I went to the pilot, who had the lead in his hand, and he sounded and cried out, ' Lord have mercy upon us ! she is gone, she is gone, she is gone !' by which I perceived that we were very near the Goodwin Sands, on which many ships have been lost with all their crews. In this sense of danger, I sent for the passengers into the cabin, and told them that I thought it would be well for us to sit still together, and look unto, and wait upon God, to see what he would please to do for us ; that, if death came, we might meet him in as good a frame of mind as we could, and that we might not be surprised beyond measure ; and as we were thus composed in our minds, a concern came upon my dear wife, and she prayed to God the Father, in the living power and sense of his Son, and he heard from his holy habitation, and answered the prayer ; for immediately after the wind abated, and our anchors held us. This was a great deliverance, which is not to be forgotten. When we saw the longed-for morning, we were very near the sands, and the sea ran prodigiously high, and broke upon them mightily, so that we were forced to leave our cables and anchors, and make the best of our way to Deal, as well as we could. One of the owners, being on shore, and seeing us in distress, sent off a cable and anchor to us ; and we anchored before Deal with our new cable and anchor, and sent a boat for our other anchors and cables when it was calm, which brought them to us. And after we had supplied ourselves with what we wanted, we put to sea again, and had fair winds till we got as far as the Western Islands."

Having here encountered another storm, which greatly delayed their course, they at length entered the mouth of Patuxent river and landed in Maryland : the emigrant family having spent the winter in this province proceeded in the spring to Philadelphia. "I bought a lot of ground (he proceeds) upon the river Delaware, and there I followed my calling that summer, and in the fall I had an inward call to visit Friends in Barbadoes, which I proposed to our monthly meeting, and they certified on my behalf that they had unity with me in my proposal, conversation, and ministry : so I took ship at Philadelphia, about the 20th of the seventh month, 1701, and was about a month on the voyage ; Josiah Langdale was with me. We had several good meetings in the ship to our satisfaction; and were well received, and had many meetings at Barbadoes, which were often very large and open, and some of the people loving and tender. We had several meetings at Bridge-Town, Speight's Town, the Spring, and the Thickets, and at Pumpkin-Hill; and after being there about six weeks, we went in a sloop to Bermudas, where we found but very few Friends, yet had meetings in several places, and at the houses of some people who were not of our profession; and the longer we tarried, the larger our meetings were; and many began to be affected, and spoke well of us and our devotion; but some were disturbed and spoke to the governor to break up our meeting, which, at the desire of one of the inhabitants, we had appointed at his house; upon which he sent orders by one of his colonels to break up our meeting, which troubled divers sober people. After this I met with the governor at the house of Judge Stafford; and he being a moderate man, we had the following discourse, viz.

Gov. How do you like our country? We are but a little spot in the sea.

T. C. I like it well for its moderate climate. If the people were moderate also, it would be well.

Gov. Doth it answer your end in coming?

T. C. My end in coming, was to visit the people in Christian love.

Gov. Do you think the people will be brought over?

T. C. If they are brought to truth and righteousness, it will be well with them. That is the end of our coming.

Gov. If you had acquainted me with your design, when first you came, you had done well. It was your duty.

T. C. If we had known the governor's will herein, or that thou wouldst have spoken with us, we should readily have answered it: but knowing nothing of it, we could not tell but that it might be taken for rudeness in us, considering our homely way and manner of addressing such men.

Gov. Then your design in coming here was to preach. Had you no other end?

T. C. Yes. As we found a concern upon us to preach, and a desire in the people to hear.

Gov. Why do you not tarry with them? That looks strange. Here the people are affected with you, and you go away and leave them: upon my word I blame you for that.

T. C. We do not direct them to man, but to the Lord Jesus Christ, their Teacher and Bishop of their souls. And why should our leaving them look strange to the governor? for it was the practice of the apostles of our Lord Jesus

Christ, and his own practice, and command to his followers: And further, the apostles (which word signifies ambassadors or messengers) say, 'Follow us, as we are followers of Christ.' And they travelled up and down the world preaching the Gospel; and our great Lord himself had not whereon to lay his head.

Gov. The apostles were inspired men: inspired by the Holy Spirit to preach the Gospel. I suppose you do not pretend to be inspired.

T. C. Every true Christian ought to pray for the pouring out of the Holy Spirit, or Holy Ghost upon him; the church of England* also, prays for it, the receiving of which is inspiration.

Gov. Your reasons being grounded on Scripture, you are well grounded; for no man can deny the Scriptures. Then you say you are inspired?

T. C. I hope I am. I pray for it with great earnestness.

Gov. Then it is but ask and have, you think?

T. C. If we ask in faith, without wavering, we shall receive, according to the doctrine of Christ and his apostles in the New Testament.

Gov. Well, if any have a desire to hear you, you may preach and welcome."

Meeting now with no further obstruction, he finished his service and returned home.

Passing over some similar engagements in different provinces, we may next notice a visit, in company with other Friends, to the Indian natives, in the year 1706. "When I was travelling in those parts, (of Maryland,) I had a concern on my mind to visit the Indians living near Susquehannah, at Conestogoe; I laid it before the elders of Nottingham meeting, with which they expressed their unity, and promoted my visiting them. We got an interpreter, and thirteen or fourteen of us travelled through the woods about fifty miles, carrying our provisions with us, and on the journey sat down by a river, and spread our food on the grass, and refreshed ourselves and horses, and then went on cheerfully, and with good will, and much love to the poor Indians; and when we came, they received us kindly, treating us civilly in their way. We treated about having a meeting with them in a religious way, upon which they called a council, in which they were very grave, and spoke one after the other without any heat or jarring; and some of the most esteemed of their women do sometimes speak in their councils. I asked our interpreter, 'Why they suffered or permitted the women to

* Of which church the Governor was a member.

speak in their councils ? ' his answer was, 'That some wom
were wiser than some men.' Our interpreter told me, th
they had not done anything for many years without the cou
sel of an ancient grave woman; who, I observed spoke mu
in their council; for I was permitted to be present at it; a
I asked what it was the woman said: he told me she was
empress; and they gave much heed to what she said among
them, and that she then said to them, She looked upon o
coming to be more than natural, because we did not come
buy or sell, or get gain, but came in love and respect
them, and desired their well-doing both here and hereafte
and further continued, that our meetings among them mig
be very beneficial to their young people. She advised the
to hear us, and entertain us kindly; and accordingly th
did. Here were two nations of them, the Senecas and t
Shawnese. We had first a meeting with the Senecas, wi
which they were much affected; and they called the oth
nation, viz., the Shawnese, and interpreted to them what
had spoken in their meeting, and the poor Indians, partic
larly some of the young men and women, were under a sol
exercise and concern. We had also a meeting with the oth
nation, and they were all very kind to us, and desired mo
such opportunities; the which, I hope Divine Providence wi
order them, if they are worthy thereof. The Gospel of Jes
Christ was preached freely to them, and faith in Christ, wl
was put to death at Jerusalem, by the unbelieving Jews; ar
that this same Jesus came to save people from their sins, ar
by his grace and light in the soul, shows to man his sir
and convinceth him thereof, delivering him out of them, ar
gives inward peace and comfort to the soul for well-doir
and sorrow and trouble for evil-doing; to all which, as the
manner is, they gave public assent; and to that of the lig
in the soul, they gave a double assent, and seemed mu
affected with the doctrine of truth: also the benefit of't
Holy Scriptures was largely opened to them.

After this we returned to our respective habitations, than
ful in our hearts to the God and Father of our Lord Jes
Christ. Several of the Friends that went with me express
their satisfaction in this visit, and offered themselves free
to go again on the like service.

After these several journeys were over, and I had clear
myself, I was some time at home, and followed my busine
with diligence and industry, and throve in things of the wor
the Lord adding a blessing to my labours. Some people wou
tell me that I got money for preaching, and grew rich by
which being a common calumny cast upon our minist

that are travellers, I shall take a little notice of it, and leave it to posterity, that it is against our principle, and contrary to our known practice and rule, to take money for our preaching the Gospel of Christ, and the publishing of salvation through his name unto the people; for according to Christ's command, we receiving it freely, are to give it forth freely, and I can say without vanity or boasting, I have spent many pounds in that service, besides my time, which was, and is, as precious to me as to other people: and rising early, and lying down late; many days riding forty, fifty, and sixty miles a-day, which was very laborious and hard for my flesh to endure, being corpulent and heavy from the 27th year of my age: and I can truly say, that I never received any money or consideration on account of these services, either directly or indirectly; and yet if any of our ministers are necessitous or poor, we relieve them freely, not because they are preachers, but because they are needy; and when we have done those things, we have done but our duty: and well will it be for those who have discharged themselves faithfully therein; such will, besides the earnest of peace in their own souls in this world, have a blessed reward in the glorious kingdom of the Lord and his Christ in that world which is to come."

In the middle of 1707, this laborious and disinterested minister engaged in a religious visit to the Friends in the West Indies, Ireland, Great Britain, and some parts of the continent of Europe. While at sea in his various passages he was often "in perils of robbers," the sea swarming with those predatory vessels, which civilized governments, when at war with each other, have not even yet refused to licence. "In our way to Jamaica we saw a small privateer, that gave us chase, and it being calm, she rowed up towards us. The master prepared the vessel to fight, hoisting up his mainsail and putting out our colours. In the interim some were bold, and some sorrowful. One came to me, and asked what I thought of it? and what I thought of the Quakers' principles now? I told him I thought I was as willing to go to heaven as himself was; to which he said nothing, but turned away from me. Another asked me, what I would do now? I told him I would pray that they might be made better, and that they might be made fit to die. Then in the midst of their noise and hurry, in secret I begged of the Almighty, in the name, and for the sake of his dear Son, that he would be pleased to cause a fresh gale of wind to spring up, that we might be delivered from the enemy without shedding blood, (well knowing that few of them were fit to die,) and even whilst I was thus concerned, the Lord answered my desire and prayer, for in a few minutes the wind sprung up, and we soon left them out of sight, our vessel sailing extraordinarily well, and the next day we got to Jamaica, and had divers meetings; viz., at Port Royal, Kingston, and Spanish Town," &c., &c.

Another time, in a high wind and sea, the pursuing vessel making too much sail, her three top masts came down at once. Lastly, when near the port, he had before him the hard alternative of capture or shipwreck. "We saw two French privateers, that gave us chase about four o'clock in the morning and pursued us vigorously; but sailing better than they, we ran them out of sight by eight o'clock the same morning; and in about two hours after we saw the land of Ireland; it being misty weather, with rain and wind, our master thought it best to lay by and forbear sailing, that coast being rocky and dangerous, by which means the two ships that gave us chase, came up with us, and found us not in sailing order, and were within gun-shot of us, before we were aware of it. What to do now we could not tell, until they began to fire at us; but in this emergency and strait, our master resolved he would rather run the vessel on shore than they should have her, she being richly laden with indigo, silver, and gold, reckoned to the value of fifty thousand pounds. In this strait, we must either fall into the hands of the French, who were our enemies, or run against the rocks; and we thought it best to fall into the hands of the Almighty, and trust to his providence; so towards the rocks we went, which looked with a terrible aspect. The native Irish seeing us, they came down in great numbers, and ran on the rocks, and called to us, saying, that if we came any nearer we should be dashed to pieces. Then our master ordered the anchor to be let go, which brought her up, before she struck; and, with much ado, he put his boat out into the sea, and put in all the passengers, in order to set them on shore, the waves running very high, so that it looked as if every wave would have swallowed us up; and it was a great favour of Providence that we got to land in safety. The privateers not daring to come so near the shore as we did, after firing at us, went away; and our master carried the ship into the harbour of Kinsale in Ireland. Thus through many perils and dangers we were preserved, and got safe on the Irish shore, for which, and all other the mercies and favours of the Most High, my soul and spirit did give glory and praise!"

The particulars of his religious service, as detailed in the Journal, are incompatible with the plan of this memoir; but on his return to America, he writes thus: "I was from my family and habitation in this journey and travel for the space of three years, within a few weeks: in which time, and in my return, I had sweet peace to my soul, glory to God for evermore! I had meetings every day when on land, except second and seventh days, when in health, and nothing extraordinary hindered; and travelled by sea and land fourteen thousand three hundred miles, according to our English account. I was kindly and tenderly received by my friends, who longed to see me, as I did them, and our meeting was comfortable and pleasant."

Having in the interval between 1710 and 1716, buried his wife, and entered into a second marriage, he began to make voyages to the West Indies, and other parts, as a trader. This was a life to which he was led rather by circumstances than from inclination: and it undoubtedly contributed both to strengthen his Christian virtues by exercise, and to extend his usefulness as a monitor and example to others. In what disposition he was accustomed to move about on his outward affairs may be seen by the following extracts:—

"After some little stay at home, I went the second time that summer, [1716] to Bermudas, and then also I had some meetings, and did some business on the island. It was my constant care, that my worldly affairs should not hinder me in my religious concern for the good of souls. It happened at this time there was a mighty hurricane of wind, so that it blew many houses to the ground, and very many trees up by the roots, and rent divers rocks asunder, which I was an eye-witness of: though it is to be observed, that those rocks in the Summer-Islands, are not so hard as in some other parts of the world, particularly to the northward; for here they saw them with saws, and cut them with axes like wood. I was told there were sixty sail of vessels then at these islands, and all driven on shore, but three, and ours was one of the three that rode out the storm; for which I was truly thankful. In this great storm, or hurricane, several sloops, there being no ships, were driven upon dry land, so that after the storm was over, one might go round them at high water, and several were blown off the dry land into the water. One that was ready to be launched, though fastened on the stocks with two cables and anchors put deep in the ground, yet the violence of the wind blew her into the water, and dashed her to pieces.

About this time the Bermudas people had got a vast treasure of silver and gold out of the Spanish wrecks; and at a meeting which I had with a pretty many people on the first day of the week before the hurricane, or storm of wind, it came weightily on my mind to exhort them not to be lifted up therewith, nor exalted in pride: for I declared to them, that the same hand that took it from the Spaniards, could take it from those who now had got it out of the sea; and if he pleased, by the same way; which was a storm that cast away the ships going for Spain. And indeed so it happened the same week; for it was reckoned by men of experience and judgment, that they had lost more by the storm, than they had gained by the wrecks of the Spaniards.

A sober old man, not of our profession, told me the next day after the hurricane was over, that what I spoke in the meeting was soon come to pass: and he added, I was a true prophet to them. Many houses that were not blown down were uncovered. My landlord's house being old, several thought it would be down: but by the good providence of God, it was one of them which stood. I was in my store, which stood also; though I expected every minute it would have been blown down. It was by the mercy of God we were preserved, and not for any merit of ours. I entreated the Lord in the midst of this great wind, that he would please to spare the lives of the people: for many of them being seafaring men, were very unfit to die; at which time I thought I was sensible of the answer of my prayer, and he was pleased to be entreated for them: for notwithstanding the violence of the storm, and the great destruction it made, yet not one man, woman, or child, was lost, that I heard of, in all the island, which was to me very admirable. The friend of the house came to me after the storm abated, and said, the Lord had heard my prayers for them; although they could not by any outward knowledge, know that I had prayed for them, yet they had a sense given them, that I was concerned for them before the Almighty; which indeed was true. Oh! that we may never forget the merciful visitations of that high and lofty One, who inhabiteth eternity!

After I had finished my concerns, I embarked in the sloop Dove, for Philadelphia, she being consigned to me in the former and this voyage. It being often calm and small winds, our provisions grew very scanty. We were about twelve persons in the vessel, small and great, and but one piece of beef left in the barrel; and for several days the winds being contrary, the people began to murmur, and told dismal stories about people eating one another for want of provisions; and the wind being still against us, and for aught we could see, like to continue, they murmured more and more, and at last, against me in particular, because the vessel and cargo were consigned to me, and were under my care, so that my inward exercise was great about it; for neither myself, nor any in the vessel, did imagine that we should be half so long as we were on the voyage; but since is was so, I seriously considered the matter; and to stop their murmuring, I told them they should not need to cast lots, which was usual in such cases, which of us should die first, for I would freely offer up my life to do them good. One said, 'God bless you, I will not eat any of you.' Another said, 'He would die before he would eat any of me,' and so said several. I can truly say, on that occasion, at that time, my life was not dear to me, and that I was serious and ingenuous in my proposition: and as I was leaning over the side of the vessel thoughtfully considering my proposal to the company, and looking in my mind to Him that made me, a very large dolphin came up towards the top or surface of the water, and looked me in the face; and I called to the people to put a hook into the sea and take him, for here is one come to redeem me, said I to them; and they put a hook into the sea, and the fish readily took it, and they caught him. He was longer than myself; I think he was about six feet long, and the largest that ever I saw. This plainly showed us that we ought not to distrust the providence of the Almighty. The people were quieted by this act of Providence, and murmured no more. We caught enough to eat plentifully of until we got into the Capes of Delaware. Thus I saw it was good to depend upon the Almighty, and rely upon his eternal arm, which, in a particular manner, did preserve us safe to our desired port, blessed be his great and glorious name through Christ, for ever!

In the tenth month, 1717, divers considerations moving me thereto, I took a voyage to Barbadoes, and from thence to Great Britain and London; partly on account of business, and hoping once more, if it pleased God, to see my aged father, my brother, relations, and friends: which voyage I undertook in the solid fear of God. I desired the concurrence of my wife, and my friends and brethren of the meeting to which I did belong, in this undertaking; the which I had in a general way, and the good wishes and prayers of many particulars, with a certificate from our monthly meeting, signifying their unity with my conversation and ministry and present undertaking.

In this our voyage we saw several ships, but spoke with none; and in twenty-seven days from our Capes, we arrived at Barbadoes, and came to an anchor in Carlisle Bay.

I was sent for to Bridge-Town, to the burial of a master

of a ship, a young man who was very fresh and well a few days before. There was a great appearance of people, and I was pretty largely open in the meeting, on the words of the prophet, where he says, 'All flesh is grass, and all the goodliness thereof is as the flower of the field. The grass withereth, the flower fadeth! because the Spirit of the Lord bloweth upon it, surely the people is grass. The grass withereth, the flower fadeth; but the word of our God shall stand for ever.' (Isa. xl. 6, 7, 8.) And I treated of this Word, its wonderfulness, its duration, and its work in man, as also of the fading constitution of mortal man, though young and strong, as that young man was a few days before, whose corpse was then before us.

I was at divers other burials on this island, which indeed, doth prove a grave to many new-comers: it being a hot climate, makes those who are not accustomed to it very thirsty, and by reason of the extreme heat, it is not easy to quench their thirst; so that what is called moderate drinking, throws many strangers into a violent fever, and oftentimes is the cause of their death. I note this as a caution to any who may transport themselves thither, that may see this, that they may shun that danger, which might be avoided by drinking cool drinks, of which they have many sorts very pleasant, viz., cane, sugar-reed and white sorrel, pine, orange, and divers others: and I advise such, as they love their health, to refrain from drinking much hot drinks or spirits.

I saw several curiosities of nature in this island, which among the great numbers of the works of God, do show forth his praise and glory. One to the leeward part of the island, which is called the Spout, sends up a vast body of water into the air, occasioned by a great cavity in the rocks under the water, which may be seen in calm weather, when the sea is low; but when the wind blows, a great body of water being pent in a large hallow place, it forces it up into the air, sometimes ten, fifteen, and twenty yards high, according as the strength of the wind is more or less, and makes a report like a cannon or thunder a great way off. I believe I have seen it ten or twelve miles out at sea. I was also at a place called Oliver's Cave, which we got to with some difficulty, in going down the steep and craggy rocks. There is on the outward part next the sea, a very large vaulted place, in the form of a half circle, about one hundred feet high, as near as I could guess. In this large vault, behind a rock, is the mouth of the cave, not the height of a man at the first entrance; after one is in a few yards, one may walk upright comfortably, the bottom being pretty plain and smooth for about a hundred yards, and then we came into a large cave which is formed archwise, and about ten or fifteen yards high, as we thought, being much higher in the middle than the sides, but almost as regular as if it had been done by art; which we beheld with admiration, by the help of wax candles, and other lights, that we made and carried for that purpose.

When I had done my business in Barbadoes, having been about thirteen weeks there, our vessel being loaded, we sailed from thence the 10th of the second month, 1718, for London. We had a good passage, being five weeks and two days from Barbadoes to Great Britain.

After visiting my relations, and some meetings of Friends, in and about London, and having finished my business, being ready to return homeward, divers Friends accompanied us from London to Gravesend: and the wind not being fair, we went to Rochester, and had a meeting there; and then back to Gravesend, and there took a solemn farewell of our friends, recommending one another to the grace of Christ; having this time made but little stay in Britain.

In the fifth month, 1718, we sailed from the Downs, divers Friends in company with us; after about nine weeks' passage from land to land, having had meetings on first days and fifth days on board, all the voyage, we came all safe and well to Philadelphia, through the blessing of God, where I stayed with my family a few months, and then took another voyage for Barbadoes and Britain. I was under some concern more than ordinary, as to the support and well being, or accommodation of my family, the circumstances thereof being a little changed by the increase of children, remembering the words of the apostle, that those who had not that care and concern were worse than infidels. I also had in my eye a hope, through the blessing of God, to obtain wherewith to accommodate my friends who were strangers and pilgrims in this world for Jesus' sake, as I also had been myself; and that they might find a place or home and refreshment under my roof; not to excess, but to comfort and edification; which, in sincerity, is all the grandeur I covet or desire in this world. So after due consideration, on the 2nd day of the eleventh month, 1718, we set sail from Philadelphia, many friends taking their farewell of us for that voyage. Thus with hearts full of love and good-will, we parted with our friends, and went down the river about five miles, where we run aground, but got off next tide; and next day came to an anchor at Chester. On the 4th day of the month we set sail, and got to Newcastle about the eleventh hour; it being meeting-day, we went to meeting, where our great Lord was pleased in

some good measure to own us with his living presence, and
comfort us with his love! blessed be his holy name! In the
morning we sailed to Reedy Island, where we stayed for the
tide, and in the night our cable parted, which we knew not
of till the morning, and then we had gone from the place
where we anchored about a league: but though the vessel
drove about the river, yet she did not go on ground. We
dropped our other anchor, and sent the boat to seek for that
which was parted from us, but could not find it until the next
tide, and then could not get it up, and were unwilling to go
to sea without it; which occasioned us to stay several tides
before we could get it: at last with much difficulty we
weighed it, our men's clothes being much frozen; for it was
very cold and froze extremely hard. After this we went down
to Bombay-Hook, where was also another vessel going out to
sea. Next day the wind was against us, and it snowed much
and froze hard; and that night the river and bay were filled
with ice as far as we could see, and it drove very hard against
our vessel, so that we wished for day; for we thought some
times it would have torn our bows in pieces; but our anchor
and cable held us, we thought to a miracle, for which we
were thankful to the great keeper of all those who put their
trust in him. When the tide turned for us we got up the
anchor, and so let her drive with the ice down the bay; the
other vessel did the same. It was now dangerous moving,
go which way we would. The vessel in company with us
attempted to go back again, but seeing that we did not, as
we supposed, came to an anchor again, and we both went
down the bay together; and the wind springing up fair, we
got clear of the ice in a few hours' time; but by this hindrance
we could not get to sea that day, but were obliged to come
to anchor near the middle of the great bay of Delaware,
and the night being fair and calm, we rode it out safely,
which if it had been windy weather, would have been
dangerous. Early in the morning of the 9th day of the
month, we got to sea, and soon left sight of the land. Next
day the wind was high, and the weather proved stormy for
several days, insomuch that our main-deck was under water
most of the time, so that we were forced to go before it for
several days together. We also shut up our cabin windows,
and were tossed exceedingly, and I was very sea-sick; and we
began in this storm to fear falling on the rocks of Bermudas,
which we were near, as we imagined, and the wind set right
on the island. But when we had passed the latitude of Bermudas, we met with fair weather and winds, all the remaining
part of our passage being pleasant and comfortable: by which

I was led to consider the vicissitude which mortals may expect while on this unstable terraqueous globe, which is full of changes, and I strongly desired to be rightly prepared for that world which is eternal, and its joy and felicity permanent; at which blessed port, I hope in God's time, through his grace, safely to arrive. Thus through storms, tempests, ice, and snow, we left those frozen climes, and crossed the tropic of Cancer, between which and that of Capricorn, there is neither frost nor snow at sea, at any time of the year and the wind always, within a small matter, one way, viz., easterly, except in hurricanes and violent storms, which sometimes they have in those parts of the world. We arrived at Bridge-Town, in Barbadoes, in one and twenty days, which was the quickest passage that ever I had, this being the fourth time of my coming hither, where I was always kindly received by my friends.

In about five weeks I finished my business in this island, having no small satisfaction in coming to it; and our vessel being now laden, we took our solemn leave, and with the good wishes of many, departed for England.

Our Friends there signified to their brethren, they were glad of my company, and that I was serviceable to them, though I came upon business. My hand when need required, was to my business, but my heart was, and I hope is, and ever shall be, freely given up to serve the Lord, in that work whereunto I believe he has called me. We have liberty from God, and his dear Son, lawfully and for accommodation's sake, to work or seek for food and raiment; though that ought to be a work of indifferency, compared to the great work of salvation. Our Saviour saith, 'Labour not for the meat which perisheth, but for that which endureth for ever, or to eternal life:' by which we do not understand that Christians must neglect their necessary occasions, and their outward trades and callings; but that their chief labour, and greatest concern ought to be for their future well-being in his glorious kingdom. The great apostle of the Gentiles, wrought with his hands, even while he was in his travels, and in the work of the Gospel: and others tasted of the benefit of his labour naturally, as well as spiritually. It is also written that he that will not work shall not eat. By this and much more, which might be noted, it appears that we not only have liberty to labour in moderation, but we are given to understand, that it is our duty so to do. The farmer, the tradesman, and the merchant do not understand, by our Lord's doctrine, that they must neglect their calling, or grow idle in their business, but must certainly work and be industrious

in their callings. We ought all to understand that our
hearts and minds ought to be out of the world, or above the
nature and spirit of it. It is good and profitable for both soul
and body, rightly to distinguish between earthly and heavenly
things, and to be careful how they mix the one with the other
for it is an eternal truth, that God and mammon cannot dwell
together, or join together in the heart. If our love is more
to God than the creature, or to heaven than earth, then will
he dwell in us and with us: but if our love is more to the
creature than to Christ, or to earth than heaven, then will
he not dwell with us; but will leave us to ourselves; for the
Lord Omnipotent will not admit of any rival.

We had in this voyage weekly meetings for worshipping
the Almighty, in which the great Lord both of sea and land
was pleased greatly to manifest his name and truth amongst
us, for which my soul often secretly and openly blessed and
praised his Divine and glorious name and truth; for he bore
up my drooping spirits, so that I could truly say with the
royal Psalmist, not because he spoke it only, but also being
an experimental witness thereof, ' The floods have lifted up,
O Lord, the floods have lifted up their voice: the floods lift
up their waves. The Lord on high is mightier than the
noise of many waters, yea, than the mighty waves of the sea.'
Ps. xciii. 3, 4. This the king wrote of his own experience
in a spiritual sense; but I may say without boasting, I have
witnessed the rage and noise of mighty waves and waters
both natural and spiritual: the one, as though it would swallow up my reputation among men, and the other, as though
it would swallow up my person, in this my watery peregrina-
tion: but blessed be the name of Him that is holy and eternal,
who indeed is stronger than the noise of many waters, or than
the mighty waves of the sea, either inwardly or outwardly, I
will, through his strength, magnify his name, because he is
worthy; and may I do it for ever!

After some months' stay among my relations and friends
in London, we sold our vessel, the Snow Hope, and bought
another ship, which we called the Trine Hope, Warner Holt,
master; and when I had done my business, I sailed in the
same ship for Pennsylvania.

We met with rough seas and high winds in the latter part
of our passage till we came to the Capes of Delaware, which
we all rejoiced to see, and we had a pleasant passage up
the bay and river to Philadelphia, where I had once more a
comfortable meeting with my dear wife and family, which
I gratefully acknowledge as a high favour from the hand of
the Almighty."

A period of about seven years now ensued, in which T. Chalkley remained chiefly on shore, making frequent journeys in the exercise of his gift among his friends. He seems likewise in this interval to have contemplated an entire retreat from mercantile business, and had removed his residence, with this view from Philadelphia, to a small farm, not far from that city, at Frankfort. But a life of ease does not seem to have been consistent with the will of Providence respecting him; it appears rather that he was to remain an exercised servant of the Lord, enduring hardships, as a good soldier of Jesus Christ. Before entering upon the account of a more trying season, we must however detain the reader with the following most remarkable anecdote, the date of which is 1722. "In this year also I was at the burial of our friend, Jonathan Dickinson, at which we had a very large meeting; he was a man generally well-beloved by his friends and neighbours. In this meeting a passage he had often told me in his health, was brought to my remembrance, I think worthy to be recorded to the end of time, which is as follows: It happened at Port Royal, in Jamaica, that two young men were at dinner with Jonathan and divers other people of account in the world, and they were speaking about earthquakes, there having been one in that place formerly, which was very dreadful, having destroyed many houses and families. These two young men argued that earthquakes, and all other things came by nature, and denied a supernatural power or Deity; insomuch, that divers, surprised at such wicked discourse, and being ashamed of their company, left it; and at the same time the earth shook, and trembled exceedingly, as though astonished at such treason against its sovereign and Creator, whose footstool it is: and when the earth thus moved, the company which remained were so astonished, that some ran one way, and some another; but these two atheistical young men stayed in the room, and Jonathan with them, he believing that the providence of Almighty God could preserve him there if he pleased, and if not that it was vain to fly; but the hand of God smote these two young men, so that they fell down; and as Jonathan told me, he laid one on a bed, and the other on a couch, and they never spoke more, but died soon after. This was the amazing end of these two young men; a dreadful example to all Atheists, and dissolute and wicked livers. Oh! that young people might be warned, that the hand of God might be upon them for good, and that they would tenderly be concerned for their salvation."

"In this year, 1724, I met with various trials, afflictions,

and tribulations: and had not the secret hand of the Lord
which I felt underneath, bore up my spirit from sinking
I think I could never have waded through them.

I was now removed, as already related, into the country
for retirement, which I greatly loved and delighted in; but,
as soon as I was a little settled there, the enemy of all good
endeavoured to disquiet my repose, by stirring up some bad
people against me; who lived near, and in time past had
fawned upon me; and to add to my afflictions, I lost a vessel, in which I suppose, I had upwards of five hundred
pounds; and another vessel came in almost a wreck, in which
I suffered in my interest several hundreds more, and a third
I heard of, in which I had the like loss; and about the same
time I had also a good new barn burnt to the ground in
a few minutes, so that I was exceedingly stripped that way;
and to add yet more to my exercise, I was sorely afflicted
with sickness, having a swelling in my jaws, mouth, and
throat, to that degree, that I could neither speak nor swallow
for some time, nor eat nor sleep for about seven days, as
I remember, without great difficulty. What the distemper
was we could not be certain; some supposed it to be the
quinsy, others an imposthume;—also my little and only
daughter at the same time was likely to die; and as for my
own part, I was very willing to go, if it so pleased God; for
I saw through the deceit of the world, and that the friendship
of it was not permanent; and in my sore afflictions in body,
mind, and interest, it fared with me as with Job; for divers
of my pretended friends added to my afflictions by undue
reflections: whom I pray the Lord to forgive for his Son's
sake! At these times the remembrance of that saying of
Christ, ' But the very hairs of your head are all numbered,'
(Matt. x. 30) at times supported me, in hopes that all would
work together for good.

When I got a little well, so that I could go to meetings, I
went to German-Town, Abingdon, Philadelphia, and Derby.
My first going abroad was to Philadelphia, where, on a first-
day, we had a large meeting, and divers things were opened
in my mind. I told them they had Moses and the prophets,
and Jesus Christ, who was risen from the dead; for neither
death, hell, nor the grave, could detain the Lord of life and
glory. And I was open to declare to them, that they had
a great advantage of the coming of Christ, not only in his
appearance at Jerusalem, but as he came to and spoke to
the heart, by his inward and spiritual appearance; and that
this Gospel dispensation was, by his coming, made more
conspicuous, bright, and glorious, than that which went be-

fore. Friends were very glad to see me abroad again, they having expected daily to hear I was dead, and there was tenderness over the meeting, and God over all, through his dear Son our Lord Jesus Christ, was praised and glorified, who is worthy for ever."

Together with these circumstances of affliction, the reader must take into account the recent death of his tenth child (having before lost nine) and the suffering (neither unusual, nor unfruitful of good, to the Christian) of poverty of spirit and inward desolation. Of the latter he writes thus: "I had often been tried that way, and found by experience, that I must wait upon God my Saviour, for fresh and renewed visitations from above: in which exercise I had always, in the Lord's time, comfort from him, as by the same exercise I had now the same comfort also; but I thought it very long, and the enemy did greatly endeavour to break in upon my patience now more than usual: but my heart still depended in faith and hope upon the Lord my Redeemer and Saviour, and in his time he was pleased to help me, blessed be his holy arm and power for ever! Many blessed saints and servants of Jesus were brought to my mind, who were in the like condition, so that I had a secret joy in their company, who met with the like in their travels to the holy city."

What privileges has the sincere, though afflicted believer; and in what an awful state are they, whose earthly supports are failing, while everything within and around them proclaims, Ye have received your consolation!

In the course of an active life, this Friend met with several serious accidents: in 1725, he was run over by his own horse and cart, by which his shoulder was dislocated, and he was otherwise much hurt, so as to be confined to the house: "I was obliged (he writes) to keep at home some time, and thought it long, because I could not go to meetings as usual; but many friends came to see me, which was a comfort to me One day upwards of thirty persons came from several parts of the country to see how I did, and were glad I was like to recover. The day before I was so hurt, being the first of the week, I was at meeting at Philadelphia, and was concerned to speak of the uncertainty of life, and the many accidents we are incident to in these frail bodies, and exhorted Friends to live so, that they might have a conscience serene, and clear of offence towards God and man, and then they might expect the comforts of the Holy Ghost, which in such seasons of difficulty would be a great help and benefit to them: of which I had the sweet experience the next day, under great extremity of pain; and though the pain of my

body was such, that I could not for several nights take in
natural rest, yet I had comfort through the sweet influenc
of the Holy Spirit, which Christ promised his follower
John xiv. 16—26."

Nor was he himself wanting in the Christian duty of visi
ing the sick, which he performed often, to the comfort of th
party. Thus he relates, in travelling the same year in Lon
Island, "from Westbury, in the evening, we went to vis
a young woman who had been in a despairing condition fo
several years. The family came together, and we put ou
prayers to the Almighty, in the name of his dear Son; i
was a good time to us all: and the young woman and som
others expressed their satisfaction. This evening we we
to see another young woman, who was in a deep consum
tion, but in a very comfortable state of mind; having a grea
desire to see me before she died, she sent for me to come t
her, and her desire was answered, her spirit being revive
with a fresh visitation of the love of Jesus Christ, the hol
Physician of value, and our supplications were, that th
Lord would be pleased to be with her, and support her t
the end, and grant her an easy passage from this life to hi
glorious kingdom, when it should please him to remove her
which prayer we have cause to hope was answered."

A succession of mercantile voyages, with religious service
at intervals, as before, now occupied Thomas Chalkley fo
about ten years together.

"As I now found it necessary to continue my busines
and go to sea for a livelihood, I undertook the charge of th
ship New Bristol Hope, as master, though it was a way o
living to which I did not incline. I took care in our vessel tha
there should be no swearing in my hearing, nor drunkennes
to my knowledge, without reproof, and if I could not b
instrumental that way to break them from swearing, an
drinking to excess, my manner was to put them away, s
that we generally had a pretty quiet ship." Our limits wil
permit only some extracts from his account of these voyages

"In the ninth month [1730] I proceeded on a fifth voyage
as master, to Barbadoes. This voyage we were on our pas
sage about thirty-three days before we arrived at Barbadoes
when, after doing my business, and visiting our Friends' meet
ings, in about five weeks, we put to sea the 10th of the twelft
month, and sailed along to leeward of divers islands, till w
came to Anguilla, where we landed in expectation to get salt
but at this time not any was to be had there. We cam
to an anchor here in the night, hoping to get to a harbou
before it was dark; but it soon being very dark and comin

nto shoal water, we saw a large rock, and came to by the
side of it, in about five or six fathoms water; taking it to be
a ship, and when it was day we saw our mistake and that
instead of a vessel, we were too nigh a rock, and the wind
coming about tailed our ship towards it so near, that, we
were sensible of touching twice; I ordered the men to heave
a little further a-head and so we lay clear till morning.
When morning came, of which we were glad, several boats
with a cable, came to us, and the people advised us to put a
spring on our cable, and cut it, that she might cast the right
way; which accordingly we did, and it had the desired
effect; so that we soon got into a very fine harbour, it being
about a mile off. Many thanks were given by many of the
people for this deliverance to the Almighty. George Leo-
nard, the governor of this island, heard in the morning, that
a vessel was on the rocks, and the people were running with
saws and axes, in order to break her up, if she should not
be got off; the governor seeing them, sent a lieutenant with
orders, that let her belong to what nation soever, they
should help to get her off if it could be, and if she was
likely to be made a wreck, he charged them at their peril
not to meddle with her, nor anything belonging to her, until
they had first come to terms with the master: which is worthy
to be recorded.

We stayed several days before we could get our anchor;
for after we were in the harbour, it blew very hard for four
or five days: so that with our four oars we could not row
our boat a-head, but watching for a calm one night, our people went and got it, and then we went into the principal road
and harbour in the island, called Croaker's-Bay, the name
of that we came from was Rendezvous-Bay, where lived a
very kind friend of ours, named John Rumney, who, with
his wife and family, treated us with great love, and courte-
ously received us into their house, and he went with me to
the governor's, who was my old acquaintance and friend,
who with much love and tenderness, when he knew me took
me in his arms, and embraced me, and lovingly saluted me
with a kiss of charity, and thanked God for our deliverance,
and that he had lived to see me once more (I having been
there some years before); he was about seventy years old,
and had more than eighty who called him father: they living
much on roots and pulse, are very healthy in this island.
I was here nine days, and had seven meetings with the
people; the longer I stayed, the larger the meetings were: so
that I had some difficulty to leave them. Through the Grace
and gift of God I was helped to preach the Gospel of Christ

freely, and they received it both freely and thankfully, divers
if not all; for their hearts and mine were very open one to
another, the Lord's holy name be praised for ever.

On the 10th of the first month, we departed from the island
of Anguilla, with a pleasant gale: and had fair weather and
winds for several days; I spent some time of this voyage
in reading, and met with a passage of or concerning Friend
ship; the comfort and beauty of it therein was notably set
forth, yet, most who treat upon that noble subject, place, too
generally, the felicity thereof in humanity; whereas true
and lasting friendship is of a divine nature, and can never
be firmly settled without divine grace: Christ Jesus is the
prime friend of mankind, and from whom all true and lasting
friendship springs and flows, as from a living fountain, him
self being the head spring thereof: out of which holy foun
tain hath sprung as followeth, 'Henceforth I call you no
servants;' and, 'Ye are my friends, if ye do whatsoever
command you.' And again, 'By this shall all men know
that ye are my disciples, if ye have love one to another
O holy expressions! much to be admired, and worthy ever
true and good man's and woman's imitation and practice
Observe, that when they had done whatsoever Christ had
commanded them, then they were to be his friends, and they
were not only to be his friends, but one another's friends, as
he was theirs, and if occasion were, as he died, so they would
die for one another. By this mark and truest seal of the
truest friendship, all the world should know they belonged
to Christ, that they were united to him, and in him united
to one another. Nothing but disobedience and sin can ever
separate this friendship.

Against this friendship, which is in Christ, and grounded
and founded upon him, the gates of hell can never prevail
all friendship, upon any consideration, merely human, is
brittle and uncertain, and subject to change or mutability
as experience hath taught in all ages.

If any person hath a desire to have a particular friend, let
that person be sure to make choice of Christ; and such a
choose him, have a friend in whom all lasting peace, comfort
and delight, joy and pleasure is, and in him alone is to be
enjoyed for ever.

The 20th of the first month, being the first of the week
we had a comfortable meeting for divine worship, in which
the goodness of God was extended to us as we were rolling
on the mighty waters of the great deep, after which we had
pleasant weather, and a fair wind for several days.

On the 26th, the wind sprung up at east north-east, a hard

gale, which lasted several days; and having but little sea-room, for about thirty hours it blew so hard, that we could dress no victuals; I then thought on the words of Job, when he spoke to his impatient wife, saying, ' Shall we receive food at the hand of God, and shall we not receive evil also?' or that which is accounted or looks like evil in the eye of man. In this time of exercise, the love and heavenly life of God, in his beloved Son, filled my heart, and caused an overflowing of praises to his holy, glorious, and blessed name. Oh! it was exceeding precious to my soul at that time!

The 1st of the second month we saw land, being driven to the southward near two hundred and fifty miles in this last hard weather; but we soon after arrived at our desired port.

I again took shipping for the island of Barbadoes, being the sixth voyage, in the New Bristol Hope, and left the Capes of Delaware the 8th day of the 4th month, 1731. The 22nd of the said month, I being weary, laid me down to rest, and fell asleep, and was awakened out of my sleep with these words, O heart in heaven! it is an excellent thing to have a heart in heaven! Which words were comfortable to me, and left a sweetness on my mind all the day after, for which I was thankful, and greatly desired that my heart and mind might be set and fixed more and more on heaven and heavenly things, and that my treasure might be in heaven, that my heart might be there also, according to the doctrine of my Saviour (Matt. vi. 6. 20, 21.) 'Lay up for yourselves treasures in heaven: for where your treasure is, there will your heart be also.'

The 27th day, being the first day of the week, we had a comfortable meeting, the weather being moderate; and on the 7th of the fifth month, we arrived at Bridge-Town, in Barbadoes, where we unloaded part of our cargo, and from thence we went to Speight's-Town, where, after a stay of about five weeks, we accomplished our affairs. I also visited all our Friend's meetings, and some several times, in which we were edified and comforted, and divers of us had occasion to bless the holy name of God for his mercy to us: before we left the island, there happened a great storm or hurricane, which did much damage to the ships, and to the island, blowing down many houses, and spoiling much provisions, destroying almost all the plantain trees on the island, which is a very wholesome and pleasant fruit and much used by many instead of bread.

. - I was clearing out our vessel when this storm happene
and being twelve miles off, could not hear of or concernir
her, but thought it altogether unlikely that she should ri
out so great a storm, in so bad a harbour or road, it bein
open to the sea ; and such a storm as had not been know
for many years ; and some said never but one to the
knowledge. When I had cleared our ship, I set forward i
order to see what was become of her ; but the floods were s
out, and the ways so bad, I could not without some dange
get to her that night ;- but next morning, to my admiratio
from the top of a hill, on which a house in the storm w
blown flat to the ground, I saw our ship at an anchor, havin
rode out the storm, with one sloop by her, from which caus
my soul was humbly thankful.

On the 17th of the said month, with some more th
ordinary fatigue, we got up our anchor, and took in our boa
and got our passengers and provisions on board, the se
breaking high on the shore, so that several of our peopl
and our boat were in jeopardy of being lost; but at lengt
being all on board, we set sail, and having sailed slowl
about six or seven miles, we met with a sloop which ha
lost her mast in the storm, and next morning we met wit
two large London ships, which had put out to sea, no
venturing to ride it out.

. .We had fine pleasant weather for several days after w
left the island, and on the 22nd of the sixth month, being
the first day of the week, we had a meeting for the worship
of God, which was comfortable and satisfactory to us. The
4th and 5th of the seventh month, we had very fresh gale
from the north-east to the north, and were near a water
spout, about a stone's throw off, which surprised some for
board, on which I came out of my cabin, and saw the wate
run up out of the sea into the cloud, as plain as ever I saw
the water run into the river, till it filled the cloud with
blackness, and then it would break in great quantities into
the sea, which is dangerous when falling on vessels. The 5t
of the month, being the first day of the week, we had a good
religious meeting for Divine worship, wherein our peopl
were earnestly exhorted to a holy life, and to be earnestl
concerned for the true faith, which is in Christ : that fait
which works by love, and is the evidence of things no
visibly seen, being manifest by works of piety and virtue
In this voyage we were twenty-two days from the island o
Barbadoes to the sight of Cape Henry in Virginia, and ha
a pleasant passage in the main to Philadelphia, where, in th

seventh month, was held our yearly meeting, at which I had a desire to be, my watery employment having hindered my being at a yearly meeting for several years.

The 2nd of the second month (1733), I proceeded on a voyage to Barbadoes, it being the first in the Snow Barbadoes Packet, a vessel built on purpose for me. We got to the Capes the 20th of the second month in the evening, where we were obliged to come to an anchor; and the 21st we put out to sea, but the wind being against us, and looking like windy weather, I concluded to come to under our Cape, and wait for a fair wind: as soon as our Snow came to, we got our boat out and went to Lewis-Town; and next day, being first day, we had a meeting in the court-house. In this town, is an Episcopal and a Presbyterian meeting-house; but neither of their teachers was that day in town, and divers of the people were glad of a meeting, and I had a good opportunity with them. After meeting I went on board, and weighed anchor, and had a fair wind for above a week after. Near the latitude of Bermudas we had smart gales of wind, which obliged us to carry our topsails double reefed; and, after having been at sea twenty-seven days, in which time we had several meetings, we saw the island of Barbadoes; though for the most part, we had contrary winds, but all was well and God blessed, who is for ever worthy.

The 20th of the fourth month, having done my business, and also visited Friends' meetings, we sailed for Philadelphia; and on the 25th of the fourth month, being first-day, we had a seasonable and serviceable meeting, wherein the Almighty was worshipped and praised, and the people exhorted to sobriety and temperance. We were about twenty days from Barbadoes to Philadelphia.

After having stayed at home about six weeks, and visited the meetings of Friends in divers places, to mine and their satisfaction, on the 28th of the sixth month, I proceeded on another voyage for the island of Barbadoes. We left sight of our Capes on the 31st of the said month. The winds were for the most part contrary, and, before we got into the trade wind, we met with two hard gales: the last of which was a kind of hurricane, in which we could carry no sail at all; but let the vessel lie to the mercy of the seas, or rather to the mercy of Him that made the seas, and all that is therein, and in the earth also. In this storm we lost a spare top-mast, and divers other utensils belonging to the vessel; but all our people were well and safe. This voyage we had several comfortable religious meetings on board, in which we were exhorted to prepare for another and better world,

this being so very uncertain and momentary, and full o
various exercises, temptations, and afflictions.

I had on board three Whitehaven sailors, William Towe
son, William Tremble, and William Atkinson, and I do no
remember that I heard either of them swear an oath durin
the whole voyage, which I thought worthy to stand o
record, because it is so rare in seafaring men. About th
beginning of the eighth month, being in the latitude of Ba
badoes, the thoughts of my leaving my family and habitatio
and many of my loving relations, and near and dear friend
as at divers other times also, made me pensive and sorro
ful; but it being on a principle of justice, and sometim
meeting with the presence and goodness of God, I was e
abled to do my affairs and business, and forbore to appea
sorrowful as much as possibly I could, or be of a sad cour
tenance in the sight of men; but to Him who knew all thing
and sees in secret, I poured out my soul in all my affliction
for he only is able to help me. In this voyage, as usual,
read in the Holy Scriptures, and met with strong consolatior
therein, especially in the New Testament; I also read muc
in the works of that eminent judge and good Christian
Matthew Hale.

The 7th of the eighth month, we arrived at Barbadoes
stayed three weeks and one day, and had divers religious
meetings. I hastened to accomplish my affairs before win
ter, it coming on, and the time of the year dangerous fo
sailing on our coasts. On the 30th of the eighth month we
left the island of Barbadoes, bound for Philadelphia; and or
the 11th of the ninth month, it pleased God to favour us
with a gracious opportunity to worship him; wherein was
declared to the ship's company, the nature and advantage o
good, and the fountain from whence it flows, or springs; as
also the nature and disadvantage of evil; the one being on
springing from God, and the other proceeding from satan
or the devil, who is the root of all evil; and that man might
be left without excuse, God hath sent the divine and super
natural light of his Holy Spirit, to show to mortals what is
good, and what is evil; in order that they might embrace
the good and refuse the evil.

The 21st of the ninth month, we had a very hard gale o
wind at north-west, which blew so hard that it put us by
from sailing, so that we were obliged to lay the ship to the
wind; for, by the violence thereof, we could not carry any
sail; and it was so dark, that we could neither see stars, nor
one another; nor hear one another without we were very
near; the seas rising very high; indeed the long, stormy,

and dark nights were very dismal; and some of our goods got loose in the hold. In the beginning of the night, about the seventh hour, Philip Kearney, my apprentice, fell into the sea and was lost, which was a deep affliction to us on divers considerations.

The 25th we saw the land, and next day we came to an anchor in Delaware-Bay. The loss of this lad was a cause that we were not so joyful as is usual for people to be when come to the shore."

On returning from his next voyage, he met with the sorrowful news of the death of his only son, a youth of ten years old, particularly endeared to his friends by his sweetness of disposition and early piety. "In his sickness, (says the deeply afflicted, but through grace resigned, parent,) he behaved himself more like a wise man, than a youth of that age, bearing his pain and sickness with a great deal of patience. I being in another part of the world, he would gladly have seen me, but said, he should never see me any more, and therefore desired his mother to remember his dear love to his father, and tell him, that he was gone to his heavenly Father. He was very fervent in prayer in the time of his sickness, and prayed that God would preserve his people all the world over. His heart was full of love to his relations, acquaintance, and friends, who came to see him in his illness; and full of tender sweetness and divine love, he took his last leave of them, which greatly affected many.

"I undertook another voyage to Barbadoes, and from thence intending for London, in order to settle my affairs there, which I intended some years before, but losses and disappointments hindered me. Wherefore, the 7th of the tenth month, I proceeded on a fifth voyage in the Barbadoes Packet, and left Philadelphia, and was at a meeting the next day at Chester, (being first day,) and in the evening we had a large meeting at Grace Lloyd's, where I met with my dear friend Joseph Gill, who had good service in the said meeting; we rejoiced in Christ to see each other. We left Chester the 9th, and got that tide down the river to Newcastle, and, after visiting those few friends there, we set sail the 12th in the morning; the wind being high and the weather very sharp, freezing hard; our sails were so frozen, that we had hard work to get the vessel under sail. The 13th day weighed anchor, and sailed down the bay, and the 14th we were clear of the Capes. The first-day following we had a good, seasonable meeting, for the worship and service of God, and, in the said meeting, as I was treating of disobedience to parents, and disobedience to almighty God our great Parent

and heavenly Father, a youth, who was a passenger in t
vessel, went out hastily and abruptly, as I was showing t
ungratefulness of the first, much more than of the last. Whe
I asked the reason of his going out, he said, It was becau
he could not forbear crying; and thinking I spoke so becau
of him, he said he could not hear me any more. Afterwar
I understood that he was a youth who was very ungratef
and disobedient to his parents; the which I knew not of, f
his mother told me and himself also, that he went to sea (
account of his health.

The 23rd of the eleventh month, we saw the island
Barbadoes, at the breaking of the day, having been from th
Capes of Delaware forty days and one night; and I was trul
thankful, that, at last, we through Divine favour, got well t
our desired port, where we were lovingly received by ou
friends at Speight's-Town, who were joyful at our arriva
From thence I went to Bridge-Town, and so on to th
governor's, in order to enter our vessel; but, staying a littl
too late, the governor, who was the Lord Howe, was com
from his house on his way to Bridge-Town, with his coac
and six, and his attendants; but he, seeing me, courteousl
stopped his coach, and did my business as he sat therein,
and though I made an essay towards an excuse, he would
not admit of it, saying, There was no need of any excuse.
He was indeed an extraordinary courteous man: he died
soon after, much lamented, as he was much beloved.

My stay at Barbadoes this time was the longest I ever
stayed, believing it to be the last time I should go there, and
that I should see them no more. My so saying troubled
some of them; but growing in years, being then turned of
threescore, I thought it would be too hard for me to undertake such another voyage; therefore I was at all the meetings of our Friends on the island.

Several Friends had a large meeting at John Gibson's
where were many people, not of our persuasion, who generally were sober; but as I was recommending charity to the
people, according to the doctrine of the apostle Paul, as the
most excellent gift, I advised them to show it forth to all
people of all professions, and also to their negroes, telling
them, that some of the gentry of this island had observed
to me, that the more kind they were to their slaves, they had
their business the better done for it; though I observed also
that I had been at some places, where I had watched to hear
some expressions that might look like charity; but in divers
houses, and some of note, I could not hear any Christian-
like expressions to their slaves or negroes, and that with

orrow I had seen a great deal of tyranny and cruelty, the
which I dissuaded them from: this doctrine so exasperated
ome that were there, that they made a disturbance in the
meeting; one of which persons meeting me on the king's
highway, shot off his fowling-piece at me, being loaded
with small shot, ten of which made marks on me, and several drew blood; by which unfriendly action, the man got a
great deal of disgrace, it being highly resented by all who
were acquainted with me. Many were for prosecuting him;
for the people generally took notice of it with abhorrence;
but he sending for me, and signifying, he would not do so
again, I forgave him; and I pray it may not be laid to his
charge in the great day, and that he may be forgiven, he
being ignorant of the love I had and have for him, and all
men, even them whom I know to be mine enemies. It would
be too great a scandal and reproach to expose his name and
station in the world. Some thought I did well in forgiving
him, and some thought I did ill in it; but I spoke my mind
to him alone freely, in which I had satisfaction and peace.

After I had visited my friends, and settled my affairs as
well as I could, and loaded our vessel with sugars, for London, (being willing, once more to see my native land, and
to settle my affairs there, and see my relations and friends,)
on the 6th of the third month we set sail from Barbadoes to
London, and had pleasant weather. The 16th being the
first day of the week, we had a religious meeting for the
worship of God, in which I was concerned to speak on the
government of the tongue, having on board several hands
which did not sail with us before that voyage, that were
much used to swearing. After that meeting, we had not so
many bad words and oaths as before. I was thankful in my
soul to the Lord, and blessed his holy name, for his goodness to us that day; and, in the night, my sleep was very
sweet and comfortable, being sensible of the love of God in
the visions of the night: so that I witnessed the fulfilling of
the prophecy of Joel, chap. ii. 28.

The 23rd, being the first day of the week, we had a meeting, in which the grace of God, that comes by Jesus Christ,
was magnified, and a blessing begged for all who love and
serve God, throughout the world, by sea and land; also a
tender petition was put up to Almighty God, that, as he was
graciously pleased to look down on those eight persons in
Noah's ark, so he would please to look upon us in our
vessel; and that, as, by his Divine Providence, they safely
landed on the earth, so we, if it were his will, might safely

land at our desired port; yet not that our wills, but his
might be done; which supplication was put up with gr
submission,

The 8th of the fourth month, being the first day of t
week, we had a meeting, in which acquaintance with G
was exhorted to, showing the benefit of it, and of lovi
him above all things, and delighting in his law, and me
tating therein day and night. The 19th, in the morni
a strong northerly wind came up, and blew so hard, that
could not carry sail, but lay to the wind, under our miz
which was split or torn with the violence, of the wind, a
the sea rose so high that it came into the windows of o
great cabin; it was very rugged for the time, and though
was midsummer, it was so cold, that we were obliged
clothe ourselves as in winter. The 22nd being first day,
had a comfortable meeting after the storm, wherein the gr
benefit of true religion was a little opened to our small co
pany, and the Lord, most High, was praised for our deliv
ance and preservation. The 26th we sounded and fou
about seventy fathom depth of water. The 29th, we we
a-breast of the Isle of Wight. From the time we left t
island of Barbadoes, to the time we found ground, was seve
weeks. Thus through many perils and dangers, we came t
Great Britain; for all which mercies and providences, le
my soul bless and praise the holy name and mighty power (
the Most High.

In London I sold my vessel, the Barbadoes Packet, an
settled all my affairs to general satisfaction, so far as I know
on which account I had laboured for several years and wa
joyful that Providence had favoured me so far as to see i
accomplished; so that I now wholly intended to leave trac
ing by sea, the which I never inclined to, only on a principl
of justice: for I was fully resolved in my mind, that my cre
ditors should be paid their just debts though I might los
my life in the pursuit of it, about which I had no anxiou
guilt, because I never was extravagant nor indolent, but me
with divers casualties by fire and water; by the latter I los
many hundreds of pounds for several years together. An
I would persuade all in their undertaking for a livelihood i
this world, to be sure to have an eye to Divine Providence
who will not suffer us, (if we do well,) nor so much as
sparrow, to fall to the ground, without he thinks it best fo
us, he knowing what is for our good better than we know
ourselves. Thus, when I had paid my debts, and in a goo
degree settled my affairs, I visited several of my relations

and when I had visited meetings in and about London I
went towards the north, in order to visit some places where
I had never been, and some that I had been at."

A pretty extensive journey on a religious service is next
detailed; in the course of it, having returned from the north
and being at Colchester, he found his mind suddenly restricted from consenting to any further appointment of meetings
on his account: and almost immediately afterwards found
that he had been, by the new owners made master of the
ship he had brought from America and sold in London, in
order to her proceeding for Philadelphia. Embracing this
agreeable offer he repaired to London, took the command of
the vessel, and after a tedious passage by contrary winds,
reached home; when he thus closes the account of his mercantile labours:

"After many exercises and large travels by sea and land,
my brethren, and divers others not of our Society, expressed
their gladness to see me, rejoicing that I was likely to spend
my time more on the land, hoping that I would go no more
to sea; the which (God willing) I determined, having so
settled my affairs, that I could stay on shore; and was truly
and humbly thankful to the Almighty, that He, by his good
hand of Providence, in His due time, had favoured and
helped me so to do."

In 1733 travelling in Virginia, and finding that a new and
flourishing settlement of Friends on the frontier had not
adopted the preliminary step, so wisely taken by William
Penn, of purchasing the land from the Indian natives, he
addressed to them a letter of advice, in their collective capacity at the monthly meeting, earnestly pressing them (as it
seems they had manifested some reluctance) to the performance of this act of prudence as well as justice.

Several journeys in religious service in the succeeding
years must be passed by—and we now approach to the termination of the labours together with the life of this unwearied advocate for righteousness.

"On the last day of the fifth month [1741] old style, I
acquainted my Friends of the monthly-meeting of Philadelphia, with a concern I had some time been under, to visit
the people in the Virgin Islands, and more particularly in
Anguilla and Tortola, in order to preach the Gospel of our
Lord Jesus Christ freely, to those who might have a desire
to hear, as the Lord should be pleased to open my way; and
my Friends having unity with me therein, at their next
meeting gave me a certificate of their concurrence: soon after
which, having settled my affairs, and taken leave of my dear

wife and daughter, and the rest of my family and friends, o
the 19th day of the seventh month, I embarked at Philade
phia, in the sloop John, Peter Blunder, master, bound fo
the island of Tortola.

.We sailed down the river, and came to an anchor nea
Christine-Creek that night, in which there was a violen
storm, which drove several vessels on the marshes, so th
when the tide ebbed, one might walk round them. Ne2
day we sailed to Reedy-Island, where we waited for a fa
wind. We sailed down the bay in company with two sloop
one bound for Bermudas, the other for the island of Christ
pher's, and left the Capes on the 23rd day of the month, an
in eighteen days from that time fell in with the island c
Thomas, and in one day more turned up to Tortola.

In this voyage we saw nine sail of vessels, but spoke wit
none of them: had a rough passage, the wind being hig
and contrary above a week, and much rain: yet, through tl
mercy and grace of God, I was preserved above all fea
except the holy fear of the living Lord, in which I blesse
his holy name.

On the 12th day of the eighth month, John Pickerin
the owner of the sloop, who was likewise governor of th
island, with his spouse, met me at the waterside, and loving]
embraced me, and led me up to their house, and the same
evening had a meeting at his house; and on the 15th of the
month, being the fifth day of the week, we had a large satisfactory meeting, at which were many people, divers of them
not of our profession, and I think, the good hand of the
Lord was with us. I was concerned in this meeting to show
that the last dispensation of God to mankind, in and throug!
his dear Son, was a spiritual dispensation; a dispensation o!
pure divine love, which is to last and be with the true
believers in Christ for ever, according to his own doctrine
in the New Testament.

· On the first day of the week, and the 18th of the month,
we had another meeting larger than the former, and the
governor told me, he had never seen so large a gathering on
the island on any occasion. My spirit was much set a1
liberty in this meeting, and great openness and brokenness
was among the people, so that the Gospel was freely and
largely declared to them. The case of Cornelius, and of the
apostle Peter going to his house, was treated of, with divers
other matters, tending to edification. I was so affected with
the power, spirit, and grace, of our Lord Jesus Christ, that
when the meeting was over, I withdrew, and, in private,
poured out my soul before the Lord and begged that he

would be pleased to manifest his power and glorious Gospel more and more. At this meeting there was a woman who had suffered much for her going to meetings; her husband being a proud, haughty man, had beat her to the drawing of blood, he also drew his sword, and presented his pistol, with threatenings to kill her; but she thanked God, that she was resigned to lose her life for Christ's sake: this woman expressed some words in supplication in this meeting, in a broken manner. There was also another, a beautiful young woman, whose father had turned her out of doors for coming to Friends' meetings.

I went with the governor and his wife, to visit a few families, up in the mountains, and had a meeting, in which was great brokenness and tenderness in the time of prayer.

On the second day we visited several families in the division called the Road, to which we went by water in a coble, somewhat like our canoes: there were four of these in company, five persons in two of them, and seven in the other two. In this visiting of families, the people came and filled the rooms, and we had seasonable meetings, in which the people were so loving, and well affected, that we could seldom go in a friendly way to visit our friends, but they would presently fill their little rooms; and we scarcely could depart, without having a time of worship.

Next day we went to visit a young man's habitation, who had not yet finished his house, and the neighbours coming in, as usual, we had a good meeting.

I cannot but note, that the hand of the Lord God was with us, and I felt his visitation, as fresh and lively as ever, for which I was truly thankful, and thought if I never saw my habitation again, I was satisfied in this Gospel call, and religious visit; though, being in years, it was sometimes a little troublesome to the flesh, being in the 66th year of my age, and stiff in my limbs from hurts, with many falls and bruises; but as to my health, I had it better now, than for several years past: for which I am humbly thankful to Him, in whom we live and have our being; glory to his name, through his dear Son.

Third-day and fourth-day, visited several families, and had divers good opportunities; in one of those meetings a young man, named Jeremiah Martin, spoke a few words in prayer; in which season, we were, I think, all broken into tenderness, so that in truth we might say, that the power and Spirit of Christ was with and among us, and his great name was praised.

Fifth-day, being the week-day meeting, it was larger th
was ever known of a week-day at that place there bei
divers Friends, who came from an island called Jos. Va
dike's, and many neighbours and sober people were ve
attentive.

Sixth-day was at several people's houses, and had r
ligious meetings, which we could not well avoid, the peop
were so loving and desirous to hear what might be spok
to them, they being many of them like thirsty groun
wanting rain, and our good and gracious Lord gave
celestial showers, which were refreshing to us, and than
fully received.

Seventh-day, I went, with several Friends, to the hou
of one, who, with his wife, had been at our meeting on fift
day; he kindly invited me to his house, though he h
formerly wrote against Friends: he was now better informe
From his house I went to Townsend Bishop's, and the
being many Friends there from another island, we had a mo
comfortable, tender evening-meeting, in which we offered i
an evening sacrifice of high praises and thanksgivings to t
holy name of the living eternal God and his dear Son o
Lord and Saviour Jesus Christ, through the influence of t
Holy Spirit, one God over all, blessed for ever.

On the first day of the week, being the 25th of the montl
we had a larger meeting than ordinary; and in expectatio
of larger meetings than usual, the governor, John Pickerinε
had made several new forms to accommodate the people a
his own house, which he sent six miles on men's heads, th
roads not being passable for carriage by carts, &c. This
think worth noting, that their zeal may be had in remem
brance, and that others may be stirred up to a more re
ligious concern, who will scarce go six steps to a religiou
meeting, or will not go at all. In this meeting I was cor
cerned to speak of and set forth the doctrine of Christ, whic
he preached on the mount, contained in the 5th, 6th, and 7t
chapters of Matthew; and to press the people to come to th
practice of what is there commanded by the great Author c
the Christian religion; and to show that the despised Quaker
had learned out of that excellent sermon, much of their re
ligion, which displeases many people, and divers of the grea
men of the world; and to urge them to regard the grace c
God which bringeth salvation, and hath appeared to al
men. In this meeting, Dorcas, the wife of John Pickerinε
spoke to the people in public testimony, to which they gav
good attention.

After meeting we returned by water from the Road Harbour, to Fat-Hog Bay, where John Pickering lives, being upwards of twenty of us in company, in three cobles.

These two weeks I spent in the island of Tortola, to my great satisfaction."

Here the Journal ends. Thomas Chalkley being seized after a few days with a fever, apparently of the remittent kind, which in a week's time carried him off. After the first attack, he attended a religious meeting at a friend's house, "in which (says the friend) he spoke to us first concerning temptations, and how Christ was tempted, and how to withstand them; and afterwards on the parable of the great supper, and other subjects; ending his testimony with the words of the apostle Paul, 'I have fought a good fight, I have finished my course, I have kept the faith, henceforth there is laid up for me a crown of righteousness:' which words, and most part of this last sermon, were delivered in great brokenness; from whence I judged that he was sensible that he had not long to live, though I believe he was not afraid to die."

He was buried on the island, in a piece of ground, which being afterwards given to the Society of Friends for a burial-place, a meeting house was also built for them thereon by the governor.

The character with which the reader has now been made acquainted will probably have appeared to him to be no common one. To have chosen so early, to have loved so decidedly, to have advocated so constantly the way and the doctrine of the cross, are effects which could be produced only by the prevalence of the power of Christ in the heart, that field of the true Christian's struggle and victory, where having first yielded up himself to his rightful Lord, and undergone *His* discipline, he is endued with *His* strength, to engage in *His* cause and service.

And this Christian preacher, and example of meekness and piety, was a seafaring man, and a merchant; a man, who encountered many afflictions and reverses in life, probably also many close temptations in his intercourse with others. His meekness had not the advantage of meeting with but little to forgive; nor was he disinterested with every outward want provided for, nor virtuous in situations remote from the example of the profligate and the allurements of vice. On the contrary, during a great part of his time, he was tossed to and fro in the world, obliged to maintain the conflict against its spirit, having his faith and his integrity put very often to the proof. He was tried with

the "acceptable men in the furnace of adversity." Eccle
ii. 5. If that which is compared in Scripture to the gol
came at length purified out of this furnace, so that he cou
say, when near his end, in the words of the great apostle, ar
while endeavouring to follow his footsteps, "I have foug
a good fight, I have kept the faith; henceforth there is lai
up for me a crown of righteousness," we must acknowledg
in all this the abundant mercy, and loving-kindness of th
Lord, by which he was qualified to stand amongst the "clou
of witnesses;" in himself, a lively instance of the power
Grace, and to many others, an instructor, and example
their most important duties.

That which is to believers their "all in all" (Col. iii. 11
the Life of Christ, and power of godliness,—that which is i
them as "treasure in earthen vessels," (encompassed wit
human infirmities,) "that the excellency of the power ma
be of God," (2 Cor. iv. 7) was, then, the ground of his co
version and perseverance, as it was received and adhered 1
through faith. Yet there were outward helps and advantage
which, in the ordering of Providence, were made to co-op
rate to this end, and which may be often visibly traced i
the early part of a life devoted to religious usefulness. O
these we may notice, in the present case, first, the care an
restraint of pious parents, tending, as Thomas Chalkley ha
expressed it, to nip in the bud the light spirit incident't
youth; then, the planting in the mind of sound Christia
instruction. He was trained up, he says, in the reading o
the Holy Scriptures; when he came towards manhood, th
voluntary perusal of these, with secret earnest prayer, wa
blessed to him: and in after life, he appears to have devoted
much time to the study of the Bible; not as a critic, for h
had but little of human learning, but with a practical an
devotional intent; so that the plain and comprehensive pre
cepts and doctrines of Christ and his apostles, and especiall
those to be found in that excellent discourse of our Saviou
on the mount (Mat. v., vi., vii.), became the habitual subjec
of his meditations, and, as it were, the model of his ministry
But, how difficult would this attainment have been to him
had he been suffered in his youth to neglect the Scriptures
and to squander his time (as is too commonly the case wher
young persons are left to their own choice) on trifling, if no
licentious publications!

There is one class of readers to whom this Tract will pro
bably be interesting in the perusal—may it also be profita
ble to them in the remembrance! We mean, such as like
Thomas Chalkley, have the command of vessels, and spen

their time mostly on the seas. It is certainly a great mistake that this profession can only be carried on by the exercise of a harsh unfeeling authority: or that it requires or admits of an indifference to religion, and the use of phrases, by which the sacred name is profaned.

The present memoir affords a striking instance of the contrary, and we doubt not, many ship-masters and commanders now living, might be brought as additional examples. As this subject is an important one, we shall bestow, in concluding these remarks, a few sentences upon it, both as it regards the person invested with absolute authority on board a ship, and those whose place it is, implicitly to execute his commands.

The most solid ground of obedience, next to engagement and duty, is certainly respect, and a consciousness of real superiority in the commander. Now in reference to conduct, or the disposition of the mind, what, it may safely be asked, can confer this authority in a higher degree than Christian integrity, or recommend it like Christian meekness? If the commander would be obeyed from principle, and have the affections of his people, and their service, as well when he is absent, as while his presence induces the fear of correction, let him strive through Divine assistance to be a *Christian* in his command. Let him be found sober, chaste, temperate, true to his word and promise; let him treat the unskilful with mildness, instructing them in their duty, and repress the unruly with steady firmness: above all things, let him never lightly or profanely utter that holy name, which in the well-regulated mind is on all occasions connected with a feeling of serious reverence. There would result from such conduct, an influence over the minds and consciences of a ship's company, which would have the full support of the well inclined, and which it would be difficult for the most hardened to despise or resist.

On the other hand, viewing the subject as it regards the sailors, does not the constant dwelling in the same abode, and sharing the same toils and watchings, the same dangers and enjoyments with their commander, entitle them to be considered in a certain sense as his family—and are there no duties which, in this case, if he be a Christian indeed, will devolve upon him? "I took care in our vessel, (says Thomas Chalkley,) that there should be no swearing in my hearing, nor drunkenness to my knowledge, without reproof; and if I could not be instrumental that way to break them from swearing and drinking to excess, my manner was to put them away, so that we generally had a pretty quiet ship." It is not

every one who would feel himself authorized, or qualified,
he appears to have been, to call a ship's company togeth
and preach to them: but surely to admonish the profane a
immoral, reasoning with them at proper intervals on th
duty, endeavouring to draw their minds to faith in Chri
· their Redeemer, and the fear of God their Creator, is with
the province of the Christian head of such a family. If
this were added the help of a sufficient supply of the Ho
Scriptures, with encouragement to peruse them at suitab
times, we might surely anticipate in many instances a mo
happy effect.

A ship's company might thus come to constitute a lit
community of Christians, who would live together in pea
and harmony, serving instead of dishonouring God: who
indeed they would thus be led to seek unto and worshi
both privately and publicly, in Spirit and in Truth. Suc
having a peaceful conscience, and the strength of true fait
would be found like the subject of this memoir, firm
temptations and calm in danger; in the former, craving a
relying upon the secret help of the Almighty; in the latt
committing themselves to his protection; and in the roughe
trials and most adverse dispensations of His Providenc
holding fast their hope in His mercy, through Jesus Chri
our Lord. Amen.

END.

Printed by E. Couchman and Co., 10, Throgmorton Street, London.

THE LIFE OF

JOHN LILBURNE.

THE remarkable individual, whose life is briefly
sketched in the following pages, lived in troublous
times, when ecclesiastical and political tyranny both
struggled for ascendancy. Against these he contended
with a degree of firmness that excited the admiration of many; and as a bold opposer of oppression,
his character is brought prominently forward in the
Pictorial History of England.* But it is to the very
remarkable change produced in him by the power of
divine grace, that the attention of the reader is principally invited in this little Tract :—that change of heart
which must be known before a man can judge rightly
even of his own actions, and without which he labours
in vain to find peace or satisfaction, even in opposing
that which is evil. This change, when experienced,
brings the stout-hearted into subjection to the Prince
of Peace, and leads him in humility to seek the glory
of God in the highest, by means in harmony with
peace on earth and good will to men.

According to an account published in the Biographical Dictionary of 1798, this singular man was
born in the county of Durham, in the year 1618.
His father was possessed of a valuable estate, and
resided at Thickney Purcharden, the family seat, in

---

* Published by C. Knight and Co., London, 1840.

No. 105.   [*Price 6d. per dozen.*]

the county of Durham. John was a younger son, and being placed out as an apprentice to a clothier, or woollen draper, in London, when only twelve years of age, he must have acquired a very small stock of learning. The master was a Puritan, and the apprentice had been educated in the same religious sentiments. His deficiency in learning was supplied by a precocity of parts, and forwardness of disposition, which rendered his situation, as an apprentice uneasy to him, and he complained to the Chamberlain of the city of his master's ill usage. Thus early did he manifest a disposition impatient of control, which he carried with him through the greatest part of his life.

The times in which Lilburne lived were such as were likely to find employment for his active and enterprising mind. When his apprenticeship expired, instead of prosecuting his trade, he attached himself to the discontented party of that day, and in the year 1636, was sent to Holland by Dr. Bastwick, who was a prisoner by order of the Star Chamber, in the Gatehouse, London. Lilburne's errand was to obtain the printing of some pieces in Holland, unfavourable both to the civil and ecclesiastical government of this country, the principal of which, was Bastwick's "Merry Liturgy." For the distribution of these and other similar publications, he was brought before the High Commission Court, and sentenced to be whipped at a cart's tail, from the Fleet Prison to the Old Palace Yard; there to stand two hours on the pillory; to remain in the Fleet Prison till he conformed to the rules of the court; to pay a fine of £500 to the king, and to find security for his good behaviour.

He bore his punishment with so much fortitude and spirit, that he acquired the name of " Freeborn John" from his enemies, while his friends esteemed him as a saint. These circumstances occurred in the year 1637, and it appears that he continued a prisoner in the Fleet till 1640' part of the time

loaded with double-irons on his arms and legs, and
confined in one of the worst wards. Here he was
suspected of setting the prison on fire, but probably
without cause. The fear of him, however, produced
some amelioration of his situation, by which means
he found opportunity to publish a piece of his own,
entitled "The Christian Man's Trial."

The party to which Lilburne was attached, gaining
the ascendancy, he was liberated, but his restless
spirit soon brought him again into difficulties. Early
in the year 1641, he was arraigned before the House
of Lords for an assault upon the Governor of the
Tower, Colonel Lunsford, but was soon dismissed;
and in 1646, and some succeeding years, he obtained
decrees for a pecuniary remuneration on account of
his sufferings, out of the estates of those who were
attached to the royal party.

The civil wars now broke out with great violence,
and Lilburne, of course, attached himself to the
Parliament. He entered the army as a captain,
under the Earl of Essex, and was taken prisoner in
an engagement at Brentford, but after being tried
at Oxford for high-treason, was exchanged for one
considerably above his rank. When the Earl pressed
the Scotch Covenant upon his followers, Lilburne
differed with him, and through Cromwell's interest,
was advanced in the army. In this station he
signalized himself on various occasions, particularly
in the battle of Marston Moor, near York; and was
advanced to the station of lieutenant-colonel, under
the Earl of Manchester. This appears to have been
the termination of his military career; for quarrelling
with the Earl, he consequently lost his station under
him, and he was also committed, first to Newgate,
and afterwards to the Tower, for his improper
conduct to the Earl, as speaker of the House of
Lords. He continued prisoner till the year 1648;
when an order was made to discharge him from his
imprisonment, and to make him compensation for
his sufferings.

In the year 1649, he was again brought to trial for high-treason, against Oliver Cromwell and the House of Commons; both of whom he had represented, in divers publications, as destroying the liberties of the people of England. The expressions which he used in these publications, manifest the most undaunted courage in the support of those principles of liberty in which he had engaged. One of the publications was entitled, "An Impeachment of High-Treason against Oliver Cromwell, and his Son-in-law, Henry Ireton, Esquires, late members of the late forcibly dissolved House of Commons, presented to Public View by Lieutenant-Colonel John Lilburne, close prisoner in the Tower of London, for his real, true, and zealous affection to the Liberties of this Nation." The bold title of this piece will convey an idea of the spirit in which it was written, and both Cromwell, and the whole government as then constituted, are represented in such a degrading point of view, as must have been very galling to their feelings; and considering the point and ability with which Lilburne wrote, very injurious to their power.

In the course of his trial he manifested that undaunted spirit, and genuine love of liberty, which had always characterized him. So low was the opinion which he entertained of the then existing government, that he declared that what he had done was not only no high-treason, but that the government was such that no high-treason could be committed against it, and that, therefore, all true Englishmen were obliged to oppose the tyranny that was exercised.

The trial lasted three days, during which Lilburne pleaded his own cause with so much force of argument that the jury unanimously acquitted him of the charges brought against him.

When the verdict was pronounced, the people in Guildhall, where he was tried, shouted for joy for about half-an-hour. The judges, who had used all the means they could to condemn the prisoner, felt much chagrined with the verdict, and with the demonstrations of joy which it produced. It appears from this trial, as well as from various other circumstances, that much dissatisfaction existed with the ruling powers, who had disappointed the expectations of the people in various matters, which they had given reason to suppose would be reformed, in case they came in power: and this disappointment so operated upon Lilburne's irritable mind, as to produce the violent conduct and expressions for which he was tried.

Lilburne was no doubt a man of turbulent spirit; so much so, that it was sarcastically said of him, that if he only were left in the world, John would be against Lilburne, and Lilburne against John. He however, possessed an honest independence of mind, with a consistent love of liberty. Many as well as himself had risked their lives in opposing the monarchy and hierarchy of the preceding rulers; and they vainly hoped that, after demolishing a government which was disagreeable to them, and of which they had many just causes of complaint, they should be able to erect one that would be perfect. In this, however, as is commonly the case, they were sorrowfully disappointed; and according to their own representations, they were much more dissatisfied with the new than with the old state of things.

It rarely happens that those who are instrumental in the destruction of existing governments, are qualified to supply their places with better. But in all these commotions, the eye of the Christian is directed to that over-ruling Providence, who makes them ultimately conducive to his own glory, and the benefit of mankind. " His way is in the whirlwind and in the storm, [political as well as natural,] and the clouds are as the dust under his feet."

In 1651, Lilburne involved himself in fresh contention, in consequence of which, the Parliament fined him £7,000, and banished him from the nation.

Before the act of banishment could pass, he fled to Amsterdam, and returning without leave, he was again arrested and imprisoned. Dover Castle was, in 1655, the place of his confinement; and it was during his residence there, that he was visited by Luke Howard, a Friend, of that town. By his religious conversation, and the reading of several of the published writings of William Dewsbury and some other Friends, he was not only convinced of the truth of the principles held by the Society to which these people belonged, but his mind became settled in a degree of calmness, to which he had before been a stranger. His wife had manifested much affectionate attachment to him in his sufferings, as he had also done to her, and knowing, it may be presumed, the alteration which had taken place in her husband's mind, she endeavoured to strengthen him with the following advice, in a letter which she wrote to him.

"My dear,—Retain a sober, patient spirit within thee, which I am confident thou shalt see will be of more force to recover thee, than all thy keen metal hath been. I hope God is doing a work upon thee and me too, such as shall make us study ourselves more than we have done."

This advice was so grateful to her husband, that in replying to her, he repeated it, with these observations :—

"Oh, my dear love! I am deeply entered into my part of it. The mighty power of God enable thee to get in too, and also to go through thine; and effectually to go cheerfully and willingly along, hand in hand with me; which would render thee much more amiable, lovely, and pleasant in my eyes, although thou wert clothed in rags, than thou couldst be to me in thy drawing back, or standing still where thou wast, when I last saw thee, though therein thou wast clothed all over with rich and outwardly glistering earthly diamonds, and in the greatest of earthly prosperity.

"I am sorry thou art so straightly put to it for money; but to live on God by faith, in the depth of straights, is the lively condition of a Christian. O! that thy spirit could attain to this, according to thy desire in thy letter, and my own present frame of spirit. I now can contentedly feed upon bread and cheese and small beer alone.

"And for my liberty, about which thou so weariest and spendest thyself, as thy letter acquaints me thou dost, I can say to thee, that I am in my present temper of spirit, really ready, with Peter, at the sight of the glorious transfiguration of Christ, to say: 'It is good being here;' for here in Dover Castle, through the loving-kindness of God, I have met with a more clear, plain, and evident knowledge of God and myself, and his gracious outgoings to my soul, than ever I had in all my life-time, not excepting my glorying and rejoicing condition under the bishops. And now submissively and heartily I can say, the will of my Heavenly Father be done in me, by me, and for me, in whose will I leave thee and thine, with all thy and my friends, and rest thine, in the strength of renewedness of true love.

"JOHN LILBURNE.

"From Dover Castle, the place of the present enjoyed, delightful Dispensation of the eternal everlasting Love of God to my soul, the 4th of the 10th month, 1655."

Although Lilburne had imbibed the principles of Friends in general, it seems to have required considerable time to convince him that fighting was inconsistent with the spirit and precepts of the Gospel. This prevented him, for some time, from signing a declaration never to draw the sword against Cromwell's Government, which would probably have earlier obtained his freedom: for Cromwell seems to have entertained fears that his professing to have become a quaker, was merely a politic movement, in the hope of obtaining liberty. But Lilburne continuing faithful to the discoveries of the Light of

Christ, he became so fully convinced of the peaceable nature of the Gospel, that he gave forth a paper in print, of which the following is an extract.

"The true occasion of all outward war not being [then] taken away, or absolutely crucified, or subdued at the very root of my soul; if I had then signed such an engagement, I had clearly gone beyond my soul's real attainments, and thereby run presumptuously, and so had tempted the Lord, my then present leader, and abominably sinned against him.

"But now, I have the witness of God within myself, that I have really attained, with the young men in Christ spoken of by the apostle John, in a good degree, to overcoming the wicked one within me; so that now I am able to witness in truth and righteousness, that the true grounds or real occasions of all wars and fleshly strivings, is in a very large measure become dead, or crucified within me! Which true grounds and real occasions of all the outward war in the world, and all the wicked forerunners of it, and dependents upon it, truly rise from its fountain,—the raging power of sin or lust, in carnal, unregenerated, unsanctified, and unjustified men's hearts; as is plainly witnessed by the apostle James. 'From whence come wars and fighting among you? Come they not hence, even of your lusts, that war in your members? Ye lust and have not; ye kill, and desire to have, and cannot obtain. Ye fight and war, yet ye have not, because ye ask not: ye ask and receive not, because ye ask amiss, that ye may consume it upon your lusts.' 'Know ye not that the friendship of the world is enmity with God. Whosoever therefore will be a friend to the world is the enemy of God.' And therefore Christ the true Lord of the soul, and the true King of that heavenly and spiritual kingdom that he hath provided for all redeemed and righteous souls, declares, at his very answer for his life, before Pilate, and says: 'My kingdom is not of this world.

If my kingdom were of this world then should my servants fight, that I should not be delivered to the Jews. But now is my kingdom not from hence.' And therefore it was when Judas betrayed this spiritual king—Christ—into the hands of his murdering enemies, and that his servant Simon Peter drew his sword, and struck a servant of the high-priest, and smote off his ear, that this spiritual king cured the wounded man, although he was his enemy, and commanded his servant Peter to put up his sword again in its place. Saying further to him: 'All they that take the sword shall perish with the sword.' The whole laws of his inward and spiritual kingdom, are made quite in opposition against the laws of the mere outside glories of the god and prince of this world. It is impossible for any man in the world to be a servant to both these masters or kings at one and the same time. He that commits sin is the servant of sin, and so of the devil; and he that is the servant of sin, is free from righteousness, and not subject to Christ. This spiritual king having purchased all his subjects and servants with the glorious price of his own blood, by his spiritual command requires them 'not to be conformed to this world—the kingdom of the prince of darkness—but to be transformed by the renewing of their mind, that they may prove what is that good and acceptable and perfect will of God.'

"I have now the faithful and true witness in my own soul, that the Lord himself is become within me, the teacher of my soul, and enabler of me to walk in a measure of his pure ways and paths; yea, and so clear a teacher within me, he is already become unto me, as that I, with confidence, believe my inward teacher shall never now more be removed into a corner; but is, and shall be, as a continual voice speaking in my ears; 'This is the way, walk in it.' By this divine teaching, I am now daily taught to die to sin, and led up by it into living power, to be raised up and enabled to live in a pure measure of righteousnes; and by which inward and spiritual teachings, I am, I say again, led up into power in Christ, by which I particularly can, and do hereby witness, that I am already dead or crucified to the very occasions and real grounds of all outward wars, and carnal sword fightings, and fleshly bustlings and contests; and that, therefore, confidently, I now believe I shall never hereafter be a user of a temporal sword more, nor a joiner with those that do.

"And this I do here solemnly declare, not in the least to avoid persecution, or for any political ends of my own, or in the least for the satisfaction of the wills of any of my great adversaries, or for satisfying the carnal will of my poor afflicted wife; but by the special movings and compulsions of God, now upon my soul, am I in truth and righteousness compelled thus to declare; that so I may take away from my adversaries all their fig-leaf covers or pretences, for their continuing of my every way unjust bonds; and that thereby, if I must yet be an imprisoned sufferer, it may this day forward be, for the truth as it is in Jesus; which truth I witness to be truly professed and practised by the savouriest of people called Quakers.

"And to this my present declaration, which I exceedingly long and earnestly desire to have in print, and for which I know that I can cheerfully and assuredly lay down my life, if I be called to witness the truth of it, I subscribe my name.
"JOHN LILBURNE.

"From my innocent and every way causeless captivity, in Dover Castle, the place of my soul's delightful and contentful abode, where I have really and substantially found that which my soul many years has sought diligently after, and with unsatisfied longingness, thirsted to enjoy; this present 1st day of the week, being the 4th of the 3rd month, 1655."

From Sewell's account, it appears that Lilburne continued a prisoner till after the death of Cromwell; when he was released. But it is said, in the Biographical Dictionary, already noticed, that he

settled at Eltham, in Kent, passing the remainder
of his days in undisturbed and undisturbing tranquillity: and ,that he died there in 1657. However,
Sewell, whose account is probably correct, says, that
he died in London in 1660, continuing steadfast to
the doctrines he had embraced.

In this instance we have a striking proof of the
influence of true Christianity. Naturally of a turbulent and irritable disposition, fostered by circumstances which led to the continued indulgence of his
inclinations, the entire change in Lilburne's habits
and views, during the prime of life, affords a
remarkable example of that conversion which the
apostle describes under the figure of becoming a
*new man.**

Happy would it be if Christian belief were more
generally thus influential! It would lead mankind
to submit their wills to the government of Christ;
under whose rule alone true happiness can be
enjoyed. And while this submission would by no
means stand in the way of the performance of their
duty as subjects of the State, in maintaining just
laws and government, and opposing tyranny and
oppression, it would lead them, in performing their
part in these things, to do it as unto the Lord, and
not unto men. Thus they would feel themselves
restrained from the use of any means, in aiming to
obtain good or prevent evil, that are not sanctioned
by the Gospel; which breathes no other language
than "glory to God in the highest, on earth peace,
good will to men." While endeavouring faithfully
to discharge their civil duties, they would leave the
result, without anxiety, to their Lord and Master:
to whom all power in heaven and earth is committed
of the Father; and who still "bringeth the counsel
of the heathen to nought, and maketh the devices of
the people of none effect:" and who must ultimately
reign over all, how long soever He may bear with

---

* See Ephes. iv. 31; also Titus iii. 1 to 6.

12

those that oppose his peaceable government, giving them space to repent.

Were those who profess Christianity, unreservedly to "walk in the light of the Lord," can it be doubted that "He would teach them of his ways?" or, that "at his rebuke, they would beat their swords into ploughshares and their spears into pruning-hooks," and become redeemed both from the spirit of revenge, and from the practice of war, and conform themselves to the example of Him whom they acknowledge as their Lord and Saviour? "Who, when he was reviled, reviled not again, and when he suffered, threatened not, but committed himself to Him that judgeth righteously; who himself bare our sins in his own body on the tree, that we being dead to sins, should live unto righteousness," to the praise of "Him who hath called us to glory and to virtue."

END.

London: Printed by Edward Couchman, 10, Throgmorton Street; for the TRACT ASSOCIATION *of the* SOCIETY OF FRIENDS. *Sold at the Depository,* 84, *Houndsditch.*—1860.

A
BRIEF ACCOUNT

OF

WILLIAM BUSH,

LATE

CARPENTER ON BOARD THE "HENRY FREELING;"

INCLUDING HIS CORRESPONDENCE WITH

DANIEL WHEELER,

A MINISTER OF THE SOCIETY OF FRIENDS.

"It is written in the prophets, And they shall be all taught of God. Every man therefore that hath heard, and hath learned of the Father, cometh unto me."
—JOHN vi. 45.

LONDON:

Printed for the TRACT ASSOCIATION of the SOCIETY OF FRIENDS.

Sold at the DEPOSITORY, 12, Bishopsgate Street Without.

—

1862.

No. 106

[*Price 7d. per dozen.*]

A

BRIEF ACCOUNT

OF

WILLIAM BUSH, &c.

WILLIAM BUSH was born at Woolwich, in 1794. H
was the son of honest parents; and his mother especiall
was anxiously concerned for the spiritual welfare of he
children. Very little is known of his early life; but, a
a boy, he is said to have been of an amiable and quie
disposition: his education was very limited. Whe
thirteen years old, he was apprenticed to a shipwrigh
at Woolwich; and although during his apprenticeshi
he was industrious and attentive to business, yet
became gay, frequented ale-houses, associated with b
company, and indulged in the debasing pursuits commo
among sailors. On the expiration of his apprenticeshi
he began his sea-faring life, sailing mostly, as ship
carpenter, in vessels employed in the whale-fisher
In this occupation he lived in forgetfulness of Go
and plunged more deeply into sin: he was a bold a
daring seaman; for, as he stated, the absence of "t
fear of the Lord" banished the fear of death from h
mind, so that in the midst of storms, when others we
afraid, he would not hesitate to undertake the mo
perilous duties.

In the latter part of 1833, he was engaged as carpente
on board the Henry Freeling, a small vessel in whi
the late Daniel Wheeler, a Minister of the Society
Friends, paid a religious visit to the islands of t
Pacific Ocean. At first, William Bush's conduct w
occasionally a cause of uneasiness to his employer; an
at Rio Janeiro, he joined some of the crew in intr
ducing spirituous liquors into the vessel; but bei

truck with admiration at the kind, yet firm and judicious
reatment of Daniel Wheeler, he resolved never to be
uilty of a similar offence.

The crew of the vessel was regularly assembled, when
he weather permitted, for reading the Holy Scriptures,
nd for the purpose of divine worship, according to the
manner of Friends. These seasons were doubtless pro-
table to William Bush; but it was not until he had
een about nine months in the ship that any striking
hange took place in his character. He was first power-
ully impressed by the words, " I wonder whether any of
ou think of your future state," which Daniel Wheeler
vas led to express towards the close of one of their
meetings.

These may seem common-place words, but they were
vidently given to the preacher by the good Spirit of
he Lord, being brought with such power to the soul of
he hearer, that his peace in the broad way was entirely
roken. When alluding to this circumstance, W. Bush
ntimated that his stout heart, which had known no
ear during many alarming storms, by which the Henry
'reeling had been followed, was now brought down
nd made to tremble. His feelings were indescribably
hanged—the words he had heard rung continually in
is ears; for the four following days and nights he was
n a state of great mental agony—a new life seemed to
ave begun in him, and his thoughts, whether sleeping
r waking, were almost constantly turned to the momentous subject. In a letter written to Daniel Wheeler
t this time, he says, that during the watches upon deck
is mind had of late dwelt much upon the "goodness of
is great Protector," whose preserving power he had so
ften experienced; and that he now daily read a portion
f the New Testament, adding, " I find I am in dark-
ess;" and then, alluding to the time passed in his
erth, he says, " in hopes to get light, instead of sleep,
is prayer and tears."

The day after, he wrote again to Daniel Wheeler, as
llows:—" Since God has been pleased to strike the
low with my flinty heart, and the tinder is kindling,
hope to catch with the match, that I may light the

lamp—the lamp which will keep me in everlasting ligl
out of darkness; as it says in John, 'Yet a little whi
is the light with you. Walk while ye have the light, le
darkness come upon you: for he that walketh in darl
ness knoweth not whither he goeth.' And again, 'I a
come a light into the world, that whosoever believeth i
me should not abide in darkness.' I know that I have
to fight that great fight against Satan and his temptation
If I conquer, I am sensible I shall be happy."

Daniel Wheeler replied as follows:—" The lett
which thou handed to me on the morning of the 25t
instant, although altogether unexpected, was truly we
come, causing a tribute of humble thanksgiving to ari
in my heart to the God and Father of our Lord Jesu
Christ, 'whose mercy endureth for ever,' that He hat
laid his hand on thee. It is indeed a merciful visitatio
from the Lord to thy poor soul, extended in the greatne
of his love and strength; and therefore, it is my mo
earnest desire that thou may'st not trifle with it, (
endeavour to set it aside; for, if thou art not four
opposing the designs of Omnipotence by rebellion, di
obedience, and unbelief, He will save thee with an eve
lasting salvation. That, which now convinceth t
understanding and reproveth thee for sin, is nothing le
than the strivings of the Holy Spirit, unto which th
couldest never have come, or have been in any degi
sensible of, unless the Father had drawn thee by t
cords of his everlasting love. ' No man cometh to m
said Christ, ' except the Father draw him.' Again, '
man cometh unto the Father but by me.' He al
graciously declares, that ' him that cometh unto me
will in no wise cast out.' Now I would have thee ke
close to this blessed and holy principle of light in t
own mind, and patiently endure its searching, cleansi
operations; and be assured that that which is alo
able to convince thee and reprove thee for sin, is al
able to convert thee to God. Thou wilt then be turn
' from darkness to light, and from the power of Sat
unto God.' ' Be thou faithful unto death—to t
death of every sensual and carnal appetite and desi
and of the natural life also, if required for the sake

he Lord Jesus—and He will give, thee a crown of Life.'
ls thou may'st have dishonoured the Lord God in days
hat are past, so now thou may'st be called upon to
nake a return, and bring glory to his name by bringing
orth the fruits of repentance, and forsaking of sin.
Thou canst not tell what good effects thy example in
uture may have upon the rest of the ship's company;
rho, beholding thy good works, may be brought also
o glorify God on thy behalf. Repentance towards God,
nd faith towards our Lord Jesus Christ, is the only
ray towards the kingdom of heaven, that blessed place.
Jut there must be a patient submission and willingness
o endure the various turnings and overturnings of the
Lord's holy hand upon thee to make thee meet to be
artaker of such a glorious inheritance.

"My advice is, that thou consult no man; 'confer not
rith flesh and blood,' but let the Lord be thy only
eacher; for He teacheth as never man taught; there-
ore keep close to Him; keep on the watch constantly
owards Him, and He will lead thee to the place of true
rayer; and I have no doubt but the day will come,
rhen thou wilt be able to say, from heartfelt experience,
the Lord hath heard the voice of my weeping; the Lord
ath heard my supplication; the Lord will receive my
rayer.' Then that, which is now the convincer and
eprover of sin in thee, which judgeth the prince of this
rorld and casteth him out, will be found to be the
Ioly Spirit of Truth, which leadeth out of all error and
uideth into all truth; the blessed and promised Comforter.

"I can feel for thy situation, as one that has been
imself under the same condemnation, and knows what
e says,—that it is the Lord that hath visited thee with
he day-spring from on high.

"Thy sincere friend and soul's well-wisher,
"DANIEL WHEELER."

Soon after receiving the above, William Bush again
rote to D. Wheeler: his letter manifests that his
wakened conscience was in active operation, urging
im to an attentive consideration of the past; and that,
eing brought to see the nature of sin and to feel its
urden, he was led both to crave for forgiveness, and with

a measure of lively gratitude to perceive that sparir
mercy; which had not cut him off in the days of h
darkness and rebellion against God.

In another letter, he says :—" The Lord has bee
kindly with me, bringing to mind my youthful wicke
ness, such as playing at cards in ale-houses, going hon
at all hours of the night, finding my poor mother sittir
by the fire-place, with sometimes a little fire, at othe
none, after a hard winter day's work, waiting for h
wicked son, to let him in. This had no small work c
my conscience. I am happy that you are acquainte
with my feelings as to sin, but not with the weight
my sins and wickedness. I am sensible how grateful
ought to be to my blessed Redeemer, who has snatche
me from the claws of hell, and brought me to the blesse
light of life, for He has had compassion upon me. Th
is a fine morning to me, though cloudy weather. M
heart feels light, and more reconciled, thanks be to tl
Lord.

" I feel confidence that the Lord will forgive me; ar
pardon my sins. Sir, if you have any old books th
will afford one glimmer to this precious light, I shou
be very thankful for them."

The following is extracted from Daniel Wheele
reply :—" I am very thankful that the work of r
pentance is still going on in thy heart, and that t
Lord, in the riches of his tender mercy and compassic
is setting thy sins in order before thee, that so they m
go beforehand to judgment, and through the precio
blood of the ' Lamb of God,' Christ Jesus, be wash
away, and blotted out for ever. I am fully aware, th
the remembrance of thy past conduct, in the waste
time, which is graciously bestowed upon us for the gre
purpose of working out the salvation of our never-dyi
souls with fear and trembling, and not to spend in si
ning against the Lord, in cards and other wicked practic
in the very haunts of Satan, such as ale-houses, &
must now fill thy heart with shame, and remorse, a
sorrow; these painful conflicts stir thee up to repentan
and amendment of life—yet thine is not the sorrow
those who have no hope, but it is that sorrow whi

worketh repentance, not to be repented of, because it
will ultimately be found to be the forerunner of endless
joy in the Lord. I do not wonder at thy being desirous
to read any book that would be likely to add ' one glimmer to that precious light,' but I should be very sorry
to contribute to cause that precious light to be neglected,
by lending thee any book at the present time, lest it
should unhappily be withdrawn or darkened. 'If the
light that is in thee be darkness, how great is that darkness.' I know of no book whatever, suitable for thee to
read, in the present state of thy mind, but the Holy
Scriptures. This would be safe, because the main object
and bent of the Scriptures is to turn the people to Christ
Jesus. I consider thy desire to read is a very plausible
snare, laid by thy soul's great enemy to draw the attention of thy mind *without* thee, from the light of Christ
within thee; and then his crafty purpose would be fully
answered: for Satan well knows that he will soon lose
all his power over thee, if thou steadfastly follow this
light, because it makes manifest his works of sin and
darkness to thy mind. Now I believe that a man may
read, even in the Scriptures, the best of all books, until
he neglects this precious light of Christ, and goes away
from it, although, at the same time, these very Scriptures
direct and point to the Saviour. It was the exact case
of the Jews, who crucified him—they had the Scriptures,
and thought themselves secure of eternal life. But
what saith the Prince of Life, Christ Jesus, unto these
Jews? 'Search the Scriptures, for in them ye think ye
have eternal life; and they are they which testify of
me: and ye will not come to me, that ye might have life.'
There is no eternal life but for those who believe and
come to Jesus. See his own gracious invitation, 'Come
unto me all ye that labour and are heavy laden (with
the weight of sin and iniquity), and I will give you rest.
Take my yoke upon you, and *learn* of me, for I am
meek and lowly in heart, and ye shall find rest unto
your souls, for my yoke is easy, and my burden light.'
We must come to Him, and *learn* of Him, who alone can
give rest unto our souls. Now, any book or thing which
is suffered to divert the attention of thy mind from the

precious light of Christ within thee, would be taking
thee away from Him, and not bringing thee to Him,
who alone can show thee thy sins, and save thee from
them. If thou neglect this light that is in thee, the
work of repentance will cease, and Satan will again
prevail over thee. I hope thou wilt see the tempting
snare which is laid for thee, and therefore ' watch in
this light.' "

William Bush, in reply to this letter, says:—". I received your letter, and was very thankful for it. I.was
very happy that you showed me my error. This showed
me my darkness: ' The light shineth in darkness, and
the darkness comprehended it not.' Your letter shows
me that I must not refrain from the Scriptures, but seek
the Light of God more abundantly. I pray to God to
keep me in the way of Truth, and from the power of
Satan, and that I may return again to my friends. What
a happy hour it will be. When I took a last farewell
of my brother, and promised him he would see a change
in me, he in a flood of tears replied, ' Your poor mother,
if possible, would leap out of her grave to witness it,
though she said always you would be rich; and I hope
it will be in the kingdom of heaven.' "

Whilst the Henry Freeling was at Hobart Town,
W. Bush attended diligently the little meeting of persons
in that place professing with Friends; and on these
occasions his deportment bespoke a mind reverently
waiting upon the Lord: and he sometimes conversed
with persons with whom he met, and whom he believed
to be walking in the fear of God, upon the great mercy
which had been shown to him.—He was remarkably
careful for the welfare of the vessel, on board of which
he usually kept the captain's watch: on the passage
from Hobart Town to Sydney, on a dark, foggy evening,
he felt an inclination to take a look out upon deck out
of his regular course, and quickly discovered the glimmering of the fires of the natives on the shore. It
proved that the vessel had been driven by a current too
close to the land, and, from the direction in which she
was standing, would have been on the rocks in a few
minutes, but for this circumstance.

When in Sydney, he had leave of absence for a short time. Whilst on shore, a secret impression on his mind induced him to follow a woman of respectable appearance to a chapel, where he heard a sermon preached by Dr. Marshall, at that time surgeon on board the Alligator, sloop of war. The discourse was very applicable to the state of William Bush's mind, and was quite a comfort to him. He wrote to Daniel Wheeler on this subject, and the following is extracted from his reply:—

" Thy letter conveyed information which is very comforting, because I think the circumstance of thy going to the chapel, and meeting with Dr. Marshall, in the manner that thou describes, must be very confirming to thy mind; and, in tender mercy, permitted to encourage thee and strengthen thee to draw nearer and nearer to that good and gracious God, who hath done such great things for thee. He is, indeed, a Spirit, and must be worshipped in spirit and in truth; and what we go to meeting for, is to wait upon God in spirit. If we are diligently persevering to wait upon Him in reverent stillness, watching unto prayer, He will, in due time, enable us to silence all our own thoughts, bringing them into captivity to the obedience of Christ, who shall then rule and reign, whose right it is. And having, by the mighty working of his glorious power in our hearts, cleansed us from all sin, we shall indeed come to know Him to be, ' the Lamb of God, that taketh away the sin of the world.' And He will, at seasons, fill us with joy and peace in believing, to his own praise, and the glory of God the Father, who is God over all, blessed for ever.

" It is the great privilege of the Christian, who believes in the Spirit of Christ within him, that there is at all times an opportunity of seeking for a better acquaintance with this heavenly, in-dwelling principle of light, life, and love; not only when we go to meetings, but when we lie down, and when we rise up, when we are walking by the way, or during the WATCHES upon deck, day and night; even in the midst of our work, or when amongst other men, we can at all times turn the attention of our minds to this blessed Spirit; and God, who seeth in secret, will reward us openly, of whom it is written, ' He that believeth on Him shall not be ashamed,' and who hath graciously declared, ' They shall not be ashamed that wait for me.' For if we are faithful in seeking Him, and in patiently waiting for Him, He will not fail, from time to time, to renew our spiritual strength, and finally make us more than conquerors over all our souls' enemies, through ' Him who loved us, and washed us from our sins in his own blood.' "

The following is extracted from a letter of William Bush's to Daniel Wheeler, written about three months after :—" When we were at Hobart Town, James Back-house preached on the coldness that came over young beginners in the belief of God, which I have witnessed and been sensible of. I have stirred and aroused myself from it. It has been shown me that I have thought too much on the things of this world, and not of the world to come. I find great benefit in reading ' Piety Pro-moted;' and being sensible you lent me that book for the good of my poor sinful soul, I, sir, return my most humble thanks." He then goes on to state, how much he had been impressed with a portion of Scripture, which Daniel Wheeler had read to them on the preceding First-day, so much so, that he had left his berth and told a fellow-sailor his opinion respecting it ; and, in conclusion, says :—" I felt the Lord blessed me in spirit, and I had a fine night. Oh, that I may live to worship the Almighty God in spirit and in truth."

Daniel Wheeler wrote the following reply :—" I am glad to find, by thy note of this morning, that the good work of the Lord is going on in thy heart, and I hope thou wilt be strengthened to see the difference between the two powers at work in thee ; so that thou may'st more and more cleave to the one and turn thy back on the other; for assuredly, that which has a tendency to bring coldness and indifferency over thy mind towards God, is the power of Satan, the grand enemy of thy soul, and if not resisted, will lead to the way of death and darkness ; but that which shows thee and makes thee sensible, that thou hast thought too much about the things of this world, is the power of God, through his saving grace, shed abroad in thy heart in the greatness of his love towards thee, and which, if attended unto, will rescue from death and darkness, and lead thee to light and life. So that if thou faithfully maintain a strict watch over thy thoughts as they arise, thou wilt be led to pray more and more in thy spirit; and the Lord most High, who is a God ever hearing and answering prayer of his own begetting, will enable thee, by the light of his Holy Spirit, to discover from whence every thought springs, whether from a good or evil root, so that thou may'st trace unto what it would lead. If thy thoughts have a tendency to lead to coldness and indifference towards things of eternal consequence, and to fill thy mind with desires after the things of this perishing world, or to the gratification of self-ends and self-interest, or any worldly object whatever, so as to cause thee to overlook and neglect the Lord's mercies, which have been great towards thee, then thou may'st be sure that this is the work of the power of darkness; but if, on the contrary, thou art shown that thou thinks, or hast thought, too much about the things of this perishing world, then thou may'st depend upon it that this is the visitation of Divine Love, in order to save thy soul. To this, therefore, cling as for thy life, with all thy might; and as thou perseveres thou wilt in time be favoured to find, that the temptations of the enemy grow weaker and weaker, and that the power to resist them is stronger and stronger. * * * As we thus ' walk in the Spirit we shall not fulfil the lusts of the flesh:' therefore ' Watch and pray,' (the only sure protection against the wiles of the devil, which our Lord himself enjoined,) ' lest ye enter into temptation.'"

About five months after this, when off the island of Tahiti, William Bush's health became seriously affected, and it was thought needful to leave him on shore, although his own wish was to continue the voyage, without regard to the result.

It appears, from a letter of W. B.'s, as well as from his remarks in conversation, when alluding to this period, that there had been a decline from the fervour of first love, and that a coldness and indifference to those things that make for salvation had insensibly stolen over his

mind.   Such a state of feeling could scarcely exist,
without some external manifestation of it in his daily
walk and conversation.   Daniel Wheeler's fear for the
stability of this new convert is evident in the last letter
he wrote to him, and which was handed to him soon
after parting.   In it, D. W. forcibly sets before him the
awfulness of backsliding, after the great and manifold
mercies which he had experienced at the Lord's hand
and "entreats him to watch and pray, and to fast from
the gratifying things of time and sense, to take up the
cross, the daily, hourly cross, to his corrupt will and
inclination, or he could never follow Christ, or be where
He is."   Daniel Wheeler and William Bush only met
once after this : the interview was a deeply interesting
one.   W. B.'s heart was too full to communicate all he
wished, but enough was said and felt to satisfy his friend
that he had not laboured in vain; indeed, so convinced
was he of his heavenward progress, that he afterwards
remarked, that had he " gone to the South Seas for the
gathering of that man only, he should have thought
himself richly repaid."

To return to the time of W. B.'s illness at Tahiti : he
was in one sense left to himself, and although at th
time he felt it a severe trial, yet he afterwards had grate
fully to acknowledge, that all things were rightly ordered
by infinite wisdom.   The individual who had been made
instrumental of so much good to him, and on whom he
might otherwise have improperly leaned, being take
away, he was brought to feel the necessity of a more
entire reliance on the Lord alone, who graciously con
descended to guard, guide, and teach him.   It appear
to have been about two months before his health was s
far re-established as to enable him to take passage in
homeward-bound vessel.   During the time of his sickness
on the island his mind was seriously concerned in re
ference to his future course of life; he knew how sinful
it had hitherto been, and he, who felt no fear when
engaged in folly and wickedness, and who, under the
influence of the god of this world, became blind and
obdurate, was now tremblingly alive to his own weakness, and earnestly craved to be kept from all evil; he

longed for the time when he should be able to lead a quiet life on shore, and, instead of joining with the wicked, unite with Christian brethren in the public worship of his God.

On the first day after his return, he called on a female acquaintance, whom he had known from his childhood, and towards whom his mind had been directed during his passage homeward, as one suited to be the companion of his future path. She enquired where he was going; he replied, ". *To meeting ;*". and being asked where, answered, "*In my own room.*" This was the first time she had any reason to think a work of religion had been begun in his mind. It subsequently became more clear to him that she was his allotted helpmeet, and they soon after married, and settled at Blackwall, where he resided, and followed the occupation of shipwright till his decease. Their union was a happy one, because they were both led to "seek first the kingdom of God and his righteousness," and all things needful were added unto them.

In 1840, the writer of this Memoir informed W. Bush of the death of Daniel Wheeler, when he received the following reply :—

" DEAR SIR,—After reading your kind letter, it caused a tribute of thanksgiving to arise in my heart, when I thought that thou shouldest take knowledge of a poor sinful creature like me. When I read of my dear friend's decease, I felt sorrow at heart; but, God be thanked, I am able to testify that his labour was not in vain in the Lord, forasmuch as he was made instrumental in the hands of the Lord, to snatch, as it were, my poor soul from going down into the pit. I attended Friends' Meeting at Houndsditch, on First-day morning; but I cannot express what I felt in my heart towards all Friends for what they have done for me. Sir, should next First-day be convenient, and God willing, I should be very happy to wait upon you. I remain your humble servant, WILLIAM BUSH."

He came as proposed, and was deeply affected by hearing what was communicated, in reference to one so justly dear to him. He dwelt with evident pleasure on

the many deliverances he had experienced, and on th
abundant mercies of the Lord towards him, especiall
those which were associated in his memory with hi
departed friend, the influence of whose mind he h
himself powerfully felt, and seen to be so great in others
during their memorable voyage together. Serene an
tranquil in the assurance that all things would wor
together for his good, Daniel Wheeler was preserved i
a holy quietude, which enabled him to encourage thos
around him in the midst of the most violent storm:
This influence was felt by William Bush, who the
knew but little of the operation of that power whic
so signally sustained this devoted man. He used
relate that he had seen him, when they were in the most
imminent danger, with a smiling countenance, pat one
of the ship's boys, when in tears, on the cheek, tellin
him "not to be frightened, for he was as safe as if he
was in a king's palace." Indeed the voyage in th
Henry Freeling appeared to be a favourite topic of con
versation with him, and it was interesting to hear hi.
detailed description of many of its remarkable occurrences.

In the autumn of 1840, W. B. was visited by an
illness, which threatened his life, at which time the
following letter was received from him:—

"Blackwall, October 14th, 1840.

" DEAR FRIEND,—Having been afflicted with a rapid
fever, I write to inform you of the state of my mind,
seeing it is sweeping me away to that place appointed
for all living. The attack commenced on the 7th. I am
now examining myself. I cannot find the weight of any
of my sins remain—no, not the weight of a feather on
my mind. I feel that the blood of Jesus has cleansed
me from all sin, and has given me that peace of mind
that passeth knowledge. I find it good to wait on the
Lord, and how true it is, I renew my strength; and
being able to take hold of the hope that is set before me
in the Gospel, I rejoice with joy unspeakable and full of
glory. O, may the Spirit of Truth be with you, and
all your dear family. WILLIAM BUSH.

" May the Lord bless you all for his own name's sake.

Farewell all; if you see me again in the flesh it must be quick."

After such an account I hastened to see him, and never shall I forget the peaceful, the joyful state of his mind; indeed, his letter had but simply pourtrayed what was then witnessed, and what was the ground of his rejoicing. He related, that the evening before, when in a peculiarly happy frame of spirit, it occurred to him—" I'll pray;" but the thought arose—" I have nothing to pray for;" it then seemed to be said within him—" Glorify God;" and truly he was enabled to do so; for never during twenty-five years in which I have frequented the bedsides of the sick and dying, have I met with an instance in which this was more conspicuously done.

Before leaving him, it was thought right to express that, in case of his recovery, he must not expect always to have the sun thus above the horizon. He replied, " I do not, but I must enjoy it whilst it is so." From a letter received two days after, the following is extracted; being very weak, he had written it in pencil:—

" DEAR FRIEND,—Having, through divine power, strength this morning to write to you, I feel very thankful to Him who does all things well. *   *   * Two hours after you left me, my sister and her husband came to see me. The Lord opened my mouth, and I was supported to declare, ' the truth as it is in Jesus;' and my poor sister was, as [one] broken-hearted all the time. I also wrote a long letter to my brother and sister at Woolwich, upon the truths of religion, and was wonderfully borne up at this time. I all night felt the presence of the Lord, and was, with much resignation, enabled to wait the Lord's appointed time. At one time I thought it very near, and then again fell into a sweet sleep, and when I awoke, I had to declare it was like sleeping in the arms of Jesus. *   *   * No more at present; but praise the Lord, oh my soul, and all that is within me, praise His holy name!

" The Lord be with thy whole house."

W. Bush recovered from this illness, but the sensible enjoyment of the presence of his Lord, at whose spiritual table he had been permitted to sit, and to eat and drink, to the satisfying of his hungry and thirsty soul, did not continue without intermission; but he had again to experience the hiding of God's countenance, that he might know that all his fresh springs were in Him alone. This subject is alluded to in the following extract from one of his letters :—

"I received thy kind letter, for which I was truly thankful, inasmuch as it caused that light to shine which for two days has been hid from my eyes. Feeling liberty, I will tell thee what I felt, although it was called the Sabbath, it was not a Sabbath to me, for I was made to cry out, ' Why art thou cast down, oh my soul, and why art thou disquieted within me?—hope in God, for I shall yet praise Him, who is the health of my countenance, and my God.' Dear friends, I cannot find words to describe my dark feelings. I took up the Scriptures, but could not read them but with that cloud of darkness before my eyes, which grieved my poor soul. But when I look at Job's saying, ' Shall we receive good at the hand of the Lord, and shall we not receive evil?' This is, indeed, a lesson for me, to know the believer's path is not all sunshine. * * * I must again thank thee for that little treasure, called ' Shewen's Meditations,' after reading which, and studying for myself, I feel convinced we can, with God's help, and must, before we can enter the kingdom, live without sin. Last week, two of my friends came to see me—our discourse was upon sin. I said, is it impossible to live without sin? They answered, If you can, you are the first man. I said—I believe I can do all things, through Christ strengthening me, and that we must live without sin before we can enter the kingdom. * * * I think next week, if God be willing, to go to my work. I believe that my heavenly Father will answer my prayer, and my Saviour's—not that He would take me out of the world, but keep me from the evil."

William Bush, one day, called on a Friend, for the express purpose of knowing what was the belief of the Society on the doctrine of freedom from sin, manifesting great astonishment at having *unexpectedly* found, that any who had felt the power of religion in his own soul could entertain even a doubt on the subject. On being told what were the views of Friends, his countenance seemed to beam with a hallowed joy, and he exclaimed, with an emphasis to which no description can do justice, " What! am I, who served the devil so many years, to continue to do so till the end of my days? Cannot my Lord and Master make me as much *His* servant as I have been that of the devil? I cannot argue on the subject, but I do not find such a thing in the Scriptures [as that we must continue in sin]; neither am I told so *here*," laying his hand on his breast. He quoted the passages, " I press towards the mark for the prize of the high calling of God in Christ Jesus," and " His servants we are to whom we obey," &c.

He again writes, under date of January 4, 1841.

" DEAR FRIEND,—I received your kind letter and parcel. Please to excuse me for not writing before. I have to work from dark to dark—and when, in the right mind to write to thee, lacked opportunity. I thank God, for He has restored me to perfect health; and I am able to say, my affliction was not grievous, as it was a time of refreshing from the presence of the Lord. * * * I was invited to a meeting held for spiritual conversation, and being lately afflicted, I was called upon to speak. I said, I found the Lord a very present help in every time of need. That is all I had to say. I had not sat long before these words came to my mind, ' As every man hath received the gift even so minister the same one to another, as good stewards of the manifold grace of God.' I had to tell them what the Lord had done for my poor soul, that it was not in preaching, or in much talking, [that I was awakened unto righteousness,] but in silent waiting on the Lord, with the exception of these words, ' I wonder whether any of you think of your future state.' I had to tell them, I was for days and nights in prayers and in tears, under the weight of all my sins."

By the foregoing letter, we see that William Bush was advancing in the spiritual life, trusting in the Lord more and more, and encouraging others to trust in Him, whom he had found to be a very present help in trouble. For some time after his marriage, although he had a decided preference for the meetings of Friends, yet, not knowing of one within his reach, he usually attended the Independent chapel, of which his wife was a member; he gladly took his share in visiting the sick, and never allowed the idea of danger from infection to weigh with him, so as to prevent his cheerfully going to any of this class. He could speak well of the name of the Lord from heartfelt experience, and was never more happy than when testifying of what He had done for his soul. Knowing of a truth, that every one who thirsteth may " come to the waters," and he that hath no money may " come, buy, and eat," he earnestly desired that all should come and partake " without money and without price." On one occasion, having at the request of his wife gone to a " prayer-meeting," he was asked to take part in it; it was then he felt how widely his own views differed from theirs, and he replied, " No, I cannot do it. I have but little religion, and," placing his hand on his heart, " it is all here." When referring afterwards to this circumstance, he said, " But sometimes, when b the sick-bed of those I visit, I am enabled to pray, an the words come almost faster than I can utter them." The above and similar occurrences caused him to become increasingly dissatisfied with a ministry which was exercised at an appointed time, in the will of man, and without waiting on the Lord for renewed qualification. It was a great trial to him to separate from his beloved wife in public worship, but, feeling more and more drawn from the teachings of men, and that, however consistent the matter expressed might be with the truths of Scripture, yet that these ministrations did not tend to his edification and comfort, but even sometimes kept him from that communion with God which his soul longed for, he was best satisfied to leave this mode of worship; and having heard of the meeting of Friends at Ratcliff, which was about three miles from his home, he usually attended it twice on First-days until his death.

The following are extracts from a letter received from him, dated " Fifth Month 21st, 1842." " This brings to my mind the declaration of our blessed Lord; ' I say unto you, if ye have faith as a grain of mustard-seed ye shall say unto this mountain, remove hence, and it shall obey you.' I believe this faith will remove mountains of difficulty out of our path heavenward; but I believe these are for our trial. I have at times very smooth and quiet seasons, and I have been made to examine myself to see if I had been in the faith or no; for the word declares, ' It must be through much tribulation we must enter the kingdom.' Dear friend, may thou and thy dear partner, and thy tender offspring, be enabled with me to give ourselves up as clay in the hands of the potter; then shall we go on our way rejoicing in that peace and joy in believing, and [have] that peace of mind which passeth all understanding. Now to Him, who only hath immortality, dwelling in the light, which no man can approach unto; to Him be honour and power everlasting."

William Bush's religion was, as he stated, one of the heart; what he knew he knew experimentally; and it was very evident that he was steadily advancing in his heavenward journey, rejoicing in the possession of " the peaceable fruits of righteousness," so that it may be truly said, that his path was that of the " just man, which shineth more and more unto the perfect day." He was much attached to Friends, and was looking towards joining them at some future period; the rectitude of their views and practices was increasingly opening to his mind, and he latterly used the plain language for the most part, and had mentioned to his wife the prospect of making the external appearance of a Friend. There was, however, nothing sectarian in his mind; he loved all those who loved the Lord Jesus Christ in sincerity, and who showed before men that they were his disciples, by the love they had one to another.

Whilst in vigorous health, it appears that he had repeatedly spoken on the subject of sudden death, as rather to be desired than dreaded by the children of God; being permitted to feel in the assurance of living faith, that the change would be unspeakably glorious. Four days only before his own death he attended the

funeral of his brother-in-law ; and then expressed to hi
wife his belief, that he should not long survive, saying
he supposed he should be laid by the side of his mothei
in the grave-yard at Woolwich. On the 8th of Secon
Month, 1844, he was seized with apoplexy when a
work, and died in about twelve hours, not havin
spoken after he was brought home. We may res
assured that, sudden as was the stroke, it met him full
prepared; and that he, who whilst amongst us, rejoice
in commemorating the Lord's multiplied mercies, is nov
among the ransomed and redeemed, " singing the son
of Moses, the servant of God, and the song of the Laml
saying, Great and marvellous are thy works, Lord Go
Almighty; just and true are all thy ways thou King c
saints. Who shall not fear thee, O Lord, and glorif
thy name ?"

END.

Printed by E. Couchman and Co., 10, Throgmorton Street, London.

PIOUS WORKMAN:

A MEMOIR OF JOHN GRAY.

HE subject of the following little memoir was a working
an, gifted with no extraordinary talents, and not placed
ider any peculiar circumstances in life. His story is
fered to the consideration of the reader as not unworthy
notice, from the freshness with which it exhibits the
atures of a simple-minded follower of the lowly Saviour.
ith very limited means, and with but little command of
s own time, the subject of this narrative administered
rgely to the wants of the destitute, and to the relief of
iman suffering. Of him it may be truly said, that he lived
)t unto himself, but unto Him who died for him, and that
: strove to manifest his love to his Redeemer by keeping
s commandments.

John Gray was born at Brentford, in the County of Mid-
esex, in the year 1755. His father, William Gray, was a
azier and tin-plate worker; having a family of eleven
ildren to support on slender resources, he was subjected
many cares and difficulties; his children, nevertheless,
ceived an education suited to their circumstances, and
ere brought up in the principles of Christianity, as pro-
ssed by the religious Society of Friends.

When about five years of age John was sent to school at
ealand, in Lancashire. His disposition was cheerful, his
anners meek and quiet, and his habits domestic. Hus-
ndry and gardening formed his favourite pursuits, and
peared peculiarly to harmonize with his unsophisticated
ind. He would employ his half-holidays in assisting, as
r as he was able, in his master's farm, while his school-
lows were amusing themselves at a distance.

No. 107.   [*Price* 3d. *per dozen.*]

After leaving Yealand, John went to school at Gildersome in Yorkshire, where he remained but a few months ; at the age of about fifteen he was apprenticed to a respectable firm of pewterers, in Spitalfields, London ; in their employment he spent the remainder of his life, though the occupation but ill accorded with his taste for rural pursuits.

It was a disappointment to John Gray not to be permitted to follow the bent of his inclination, but those who knew the large amount of good that was effected through his humble instrumentality, in one of the poorest parishes in the metropolis, cannot doubt but that his wishes were over ruled by an all-wise Providence for purposes of mercy. For let us ever remember, that the soul of the most wretched wanderer through the streets is as precious and as immortal as that of the greatest prince.

In the life of an obscure journeyman, passing day after day, and year after year, in the same unvaried course, but few incidents occur worthy of record, and little is left to detain the pen of the biographer. In the present instance the narrative of the spiritual journey is equally barren. Of that great change of heart and mind which every true fol lower of Christ must experience, in taking upon him the yoke of his master and learning of his ways, we have no written record. But the fruits of the Spirit, which we manifested in the life and conversation of John Gray, a forded conclusive evidence that through the mercy of God in Christ Jesus he had passed from death unto life. His in tegrity, temperance, and respectful manners, won the estee of his employers ; whilst his cheerful piety, his kindness heart, and his unresisting patience under every untoward circumstance endeared him to all, and gradually obtaine for him a remarkable influence over his fellow-workmen. an oath or an evil word chanced to reach his ear, a sig from John Gray would often produce immediate silence and amongst all his companions, there was not an individua old or young, who would wilfully wound his feelings.

He was a faithful servant to the same employers for nearl fifty years ; his leisure time and much of his earnings wer devoted to works of benevolence, many of which, there reason to believe, are known only to Him who seeth i secret.

He might often be seen passing along in his peculiar gai half running, half walking, with a basin in his hand, co taining food for some poor object of his charity. Few knew whence he came, or whither he went ; for as far as his own resources could reach, he extended his kindness, without soliciting aid from others. At times, however, he was constrained to call upon his fellow-workmen and friends, to raise subscriptions for the more urgent claims of temporary destitution. The extreme simplicity of his mode of living enabled him not only to lay by sufficient for his own wants in time of need, but to afford pecuniary assistance to others, to an extent of which few had any idea. John did not, however, deny himself the comforts of life; he was neither extravagant, nor grudging, but lived righteously, soberly, and godly in the sight of all men; always presenting a neat and respectable appearance; his clothing was good and simple, after the fashion of the seventeenth century, such as is mostly worn by the religious Society of Friends, of which Society he continued through life a consistent and exemplary member.

Before proceeding further, it will be necessary to say a few words for the information of those not connected with his religious Society, into whose hands this Tract may possibly fall. Besides the meetings for divine worship on the First day of the week, and once in the middle of the week, the members in each district assemble monthly, for the transaction of the discipline of the Society. These meetings are called Monthly Meetings; and hence by a common figure, the individuals residing in each district are said to belong to such a Monthly Meeting, the whole Society being thus divided into Monthly Meetings. By the rules of the Society, certain queries, respecting the moral and religious condition of its members, are required to be periodically answered by these meetings. There are also Quarterly and Yearly Meetings, but of these we need not speak.

John Gray regularly attended the meetings for worship on the week-day, as well as on the Sabbath, besides many of those for exercising the discipline of the Society, and in so doing he sacrificed no inconsiderable portion of his wages; or, being paid so much for the day's work, of so many hours, he conscientiously deducted from the amount, for the time he was absent from work; thus, while faithfully discharging the duties of the day, he showed how justly he estimated the relative value of temporal and eternal things, and made his light to shine before men, as an example of sincere love to God, and of firm reliance on his protecting providence. The pecuniary sacrifice made in this and other religious pursuits, was equal to a fifth part of John Gray's whole earnings, which were by this means reduced to about twenty-five shillings per week. Yet out of this sum, he for many years allowed seven shillings a week to a widowed sister! he also contributed liberally to the funds of the Society for the support of their poor. On one occasion, having subscribed two guineas towards the maintenance of the Friends' School at Ackworth, it was suggested to him that one guinea would be quite as much as could be reasonably expected, but he replied that he should feel most easy to give two.

The widow of an old blind workman, with whom he had formerly lodged, he employed as a washerwoman: his consideration for her was very characteristic: John used frequently to wear paper gaiters, while at work, and the reason he assigned for doing so was, That the small pieces of metal falling from his work-bench on his stockings, would otherwise fasten in them, and cut the poor woman's hands when washing them! Every week he took this poor woman a supply both of food and money.

A poor lad frequented the neighbourhood of Spitalfields, who, from his deplorable appearance and the nick-name he obtained, was the object of continual persecution from the swarms of ragged children, whom idleness, intemperance, and vice had deprived of parental control. This poor creature was frequently relieved by our kind-hearted friend, who, one day seeing him pelted by his merciless enemies, went out and reprimanded the boys, and then proceeded to remonstrate with their parents, telling them how improper such cruelty was, and how great their own responsibility, in not bringing up their children in a more becoming manner. He returned from this kind mission, and, with a smile on his countenance, said, "They only laughed at me." Indeed, so little was he vexed by such disappointments, that one of his brothers said he never knew him moved upon any cross occurrence.

Though he gave away much in proportion to his income, yet he was not lavish, nor did he think it right to risk his own subsistance, in case of illness or old age, for the temporary relief of others. On the contrary, to meet these exigencies he laid by a portion of his earnings in the savings' bank. He never spent his money in spirits, tobacco, or in any other foolish or sensual indulgence; but what was not really required for his own or others' comfort he wisely laid up "against a rainy day."

Thus John Gray appears to have hit that happy medium between two extremes which is so rarely found. Heaven was ever uppermost in his mind, but earth was not despised. His neighbour was loved and benefitted, but his own future wants were not forgotten : and while he placed his trust for daily bread, both spiritual and temporal, on the Lord's all-seeing Providence, he never neglected the means which that Providence has wisely ordained : but learned of the ant to gather his food in the harvest, and to provide, in the time of strength and vigour, for the claims of age and decrepitude. Thus he was enabled, when accidentally deprived for some weeks of the use of his hand, to decline the customary subscription for the sick, tendered him by his fellow-workmen. He thanked them for their kindness, but assured them he had sufficient, and observed they might want it themselves.

It has been already said that John Gray was a consistent member of the religious Society of Friends, and it is well known that they have always held, and publicly borne testimony to the unchristian character of war, and of slavery. His employer has been heard to mention, as an instance of John Gray's conscientiousness, that he would never assist in executing Government contracts for supplying the army and navy, regarding it as giving an indirect sanction to war ; nor would he consent to put his hand to any goods designed for the negroes, until satisfied that it could not, in any way, encourage slavery or the slave trade.

He conscientiously disapproved of a hireling ministry, believing that the true ministers of Christ, having freely received, are bound freely to give. On one occasion, a young friend, in speaking on the subject of tithes, questioned the propriety of refusing to pay them, as is done by the Society of Friends, to which John simply replied, "Thou knowest we have a testimony to support." For he seldom gave his own opinion, but preferred referring to the Scriptures, or to the "testimonies" of the founders of the Society, whom he believed to be true ministers of the Lord, raised up to declare his name to a blind and rebellious generation.

Perhaps nothing was more remarkable in the character of John Gray than his modesty and humility. Being once requested by the Monthly Meeting to accept of some appointment, he expressed the genuine feeling of his mind, when he said, in his artless manner, "I feel as a little child." His demeanour towards those placed in stations above him was becoming and exemplary, and was especially shown when he felt it his duty to extend a word of remonstrance or caution to his masters, who did not conform so strictly to the rules of the Society as John conscientiously believed to be required. His usual remark on such occa-

sions was, "I do not know how we can answer the queries
if we are aware of an exception;" an argument evincing
much simplicity of heart, as well as integrity in the discharge
of what he regarded as his duty.

But though he believed it right to maintain the principles
and practices which he conscientiously approved, there was
none of that narrowness in the character of John Gray, which
would set limits to the power and goodness of God, by excluding from the kingdom of heaven all who differed from
him in religious profession. Our humble-minded friend
entertained happier ideas of divine love, and could acknowledge as a fellow-disciple every man who loved the Lord
Jesus Christ in sincerity, however mistaken his religious
opinions might seem.

He was always welcome at the house of his master's
family, who esteemed him highly, and in them he in return
felt a kind and friendly interest. He said little, but there
was an indescribable influence about the man, which drew
others towards him, and which added to his meek and respectful manners, made it impossible to help loving him,
or feeling that he was no ordinary character.

He was a man of few words, and his speeches were generally the imperfect expression of considerable thought, and
of a deeper wisdom than many gave him credit for. He
enjoyed cheerful conversation, so long as it was innocent;
but anything bordering upon the profane, or calculated in
any way to injure or offend, he sedulously shunned and
discouraged. Mindful of his own duty to God and man, he
was very careful not to under-rate the character of others,
and to avoid tale-bearing and detraction. Whenever he
heard others spoken against, he would endeavor to palliate
their conduct; for he well knew, from his acquaintance with'
the wretched and degraded, who became, from time to time,
the objects of his charity, how much the human mind is
influenced, both in disposition and sentiment, by early education, and after-association; he would often say, "We
must make great allowance for the way in which persons are
brought up, and not think too harshly of those who have not
been favoured with the advantages we enjoy, lest, in the end,
we should be found no better stewards than they, though
entrusted with more talents."

He did not, however, connive at evil in others, any more
than in himself; and once during his apprenticeship, having
had reason to suspect the conduct of a workman in the
manufactory, he felt it his duty to state his suspicions to his

master. They proved but too well founded; but the affair is said to have had a serious effect upon the tender mind of John Gray.

Thus far we have only enumerated the virtues of our friend; if he had his counteracting evils, it can only be said, that his meekness and humility concealed them. That he was subject to the infirmities of humanity, needs not to be questioned; but his irreproachable life affords satisfactory evidence that, through the infinite mercy and almighty power of Him who was manifested to destroy the works of the devil, he had well nigh attained to that state of purification in which, by the submission of the human will, the Lord and Saviour reigns supreme.

There is something so beautiful and so impressive in the character of a consistent Christian, that he must be depraved indeed who cannot in some degree appreciate it. Even those who will not acknowledge its excellence often feel its power; for there is connected with every man's temper, spirit, and daily walk, an influence which he silently exerts on those around him; and it was probably this influence which operated, more than anything external, on the minds of those associated with John Gray. He was a man beloved of all. His sincerity no man could question. The purity of his purpose, his charity, and kindness none could doubt. No envious spirit dared to speak, nor bigot to think evil of him; and thus he was the means of warming many a cold and stubborn heart, which no remonstrance or verbal eloquence could move.

But the time drew nigh when the earthly pilgrimage of our beloved friend was to terminate. On the evening of the 1st of 12th month, 1838, having received his wages, and distributed his customary alms, including a subscription for a poor workman, he retired to his lodging, and while he was seated by the fire-side, probably communing with his Maker, in gratitude for mercies during the past week, the undeniable message was sent, "Steward give up thy stewardship." The summons was sudden; but we reverently believe that he was graciously prepared to hear the joyful language, "Well done, good and faithful servant: thou hast been faithful over a few things, I will make thee ruler over many things, enter thou into the joy of thy Lord."

In the morning, as soon as the event became known, many poor creatures who had looked to him for maintenance, congregated about the humble abode of the departed, mourning the loss of their best or only friend upon earth. Numerous other persons who had known his virtues, with such of his fellow-workmen as resided in the neighbourhood, paid a last visit to his remains. Everywhere the name of John Gray was heard coupled with all that is good and excellent.

His remains were interred in the Friends' burial-ground at Whitechapel, in the presence of a numerous circle of friends. A veil of peaceful solemnity spread over the group, and, to repeat the words uttered upon the occasion, "There seemed, as it were, a voice from the grave, saying, 'Follow me, as I have followed Christ.'"

> His steadfast piety shall claim
> A lasting favour for his name ;
> The sweet remembrance of the just
> Shall flourish when he sleeps in dust.
>
> His name the poor shall learn to bless,
> Who oft hath succour'd their distress ;
> And many an humble mourner's tear
> Shall grace the good man's honour'd bier.

END.

London: Printed by E. Couchman & Co., 10, Throgmorton Street; for the TRACT ASSOCIATION of the SOCIETY OF FRIENDS. Sold at the Depository, 12, Bishopsgate Street Without.—1863.

THE

WORK OF RIGHTEOUSNESS.

The substance of the following pages is chiefly taken from a Tract entitled "A Salutation of Pure Love," by Thomas Colley.

WHEN Cornelius, the Centurion, was favoured with a visit from a holy angel, by whom he was instructed where to apply for the knowledge of those things by which both he and his household might be saved, he convened his kinsmen and near friends. His good-will not being circumscribed within the narrow bounds of his own family, he wished his friends might also be partakers with him; and since it pleased the Almighty to open mine eyes to see into my own state, and into the excellency of that salvation which he hath prepared before all people, I have felt disposed to offer a salutation in gospel love to my kindred after the flesh, desiring that grace, mercy, and peace may abound amongst them, whilst in this state of probation, and that they may finally witness an everlasting salvation. My mind has also been enlarged in love toward the human race in general; it desires that the God of all grace may be mercifully pleased so effectually to visit their souls, as to turn their feet into the way of peace, and bring their minds to a settlement on that foundation which standeth sure, which is Jesus Christ.

The soul of man, which was designed by the author of its existence for a participation in heavenly

No. 108.   [*Price 3d. per dozen.*]

happiness, can never attain to this happiness in the mere possession of the things of this world; for though people may seek happiness in the gratifications of sense, in pleasures, or in amusements, yet, in the seeming enjoyment of these, they frequently witness disappointment, and reflection upon them is often attended with bitterness. All real happiness centres in God. It is the work of Satan, the adversary of human happiness, to draw the attention and desires of mankind after those things which are inconsistent with the will of God, to make forbidden things appear desirable, and to represent transgression with respect to them as of small moment; and when Satan has once gained his point, the next temptation comes with greater strength. It is in vain for men to propose limits to themselves, or to think that they will go so far and no farther; for though in the early part of life, by turning the mind to the grace of God, temptations may be more easily overcome than in after-life, yet, by disregarding the secret checks of the Holy Spirit, which occasioned a struggle against sin, and by joining in with temptation, evil propensities gain strength, and sin becomes a habit. Hence we sometimes hear men say, when overcome by sin, and reproved for it, We know these things are wrong, but we cannot help doing them; and thus mankind, until they come to experience redemption by Jesus Christ, continue to yield to temptation.

What I earnestly desire is, that all may happily become partakers of this redemption. For though men have departed from God, and their understandings have become darkened, and their affections have been alienated from him, yet there is a time afforded to them wherein they may be saved. In this time God mercifully visits them, and strives with them by his grace, to bring them to repentance, and to faith in Christ, who died for the sins of mankind, in order that they might become reconciled unto God, and live to his glory.

The work of salvation which all ought to be engaged in, is not to be accomplished by man through his own power. Nothing can deliver a soul from sin but the grace of our Lord Jesus Christ. The apostle Peter said, "Of whom a man is overcome, of the same is he brought in bondage;" and it must be something superior to himself that can make him free. The apostle Paul, describing a state, sensible of the corruptions and evil propensities of fallen nature, expresses himself thus, "I know that in me, that is, in my flesh, dwelleth no good thing; for to will is present with me, but how to perform that which is good, I find not; for the good that I would, I do not; but the evil which I would not, that I do." He also says, "I see another law in my members, warring against the law of my mind, and bringing me into captivity to the law of sin;" and he afterwards exclaims, "O wretched man that I am! who shall deliver me from the body of this death?" and he presently gives the answer himself; "I thank God, through Jesus Christ our Lord;" he also informs us how this was effected: "For the law of the Spirit of life, in Christ Jesus, hath made me free from the law of sin and death."

The work of redemption is a work in which the heart must be engaged; for it is in the heart that the opposite powers of sin and grace strive. To which soever of these two powers contending within us for the mastery we yield obedience, that will have the government; as it is written, "Know ye not that to whom ye yield yourselves servants to obey; his servants ye are to whom ye obey, whether of sin unto death, or of obedience unto righteousness."

It will be in vain for us to bear the name of Christians, unless we repent of our sins, obtain their forgiveness through Jesus Christ, and experience the regenerating power of the Holy Spirit so to operate in us, as to deliver us from the power of sin, and reduce our hearts into obedience to God.

When Paul wrote his epistle to Titus, he used

these words, "The grace of God that bringeth salvation hath appeared to all men, teaching us that, denying ungodliness and worldly lusts, we should live soberly, righteously, and godly, in this present world." This grace meets, detects, and counteracts all the evil propensities of fallen nature, and lifts up a standard against all the temptations of the wicked one. There are no recesses of the heart so dark, as that its light does not penetrate them; there is no root of "the corrupt tree" so deep, as that this axe of God is not laid to it; so that a mind which is rightly directed to this grace, this Holy Spirit, this Spirit of Truth or Spirit of Christ, will find therein all-sufficient strength, as a reverent trust and confidence, is placed in it, and the soul is resigned to its power. For as this gift of God is in itself pure, it condemns all sin, and as it is accepted, it weakens the power of temptation, and enables a man to resist everything which defiles. But from the soul which is in subjection to sin, this Spirit of Truth, which proceedeth from the Father and cometh in the name of Christ, withdraws himself, for he dwelleth not in an unclean temple, and yet he follows the defiled with his reproofs and secret calls, during the time that his gracious visitations are extended.

God, in great mercy, has not only provided means for the recovery of mankind out of the fall, which are adequate to the great end proposed; but in much long-suffering, he waiteth to be gracious, stretching forth his arm, as it were, all the day long; not being willing that any should perish, but that all should be brought to true repentance and to salvation. Thus to those who reject his grace, he may say, as he did to the men of Judah and the inhabitants of Jerusalem concerning his vineyard; "What could have been done more to my vineyard that I have not done in it?"—It must be an awful situation for any poor soul to be in, at the close of time, when nature fails, and visible objects yield no relief, to have this language sounded in it, or to hear one like that which Christ uttered over Jerusalem, when he beheld her state, and wept as he considered the misery that was coming upon her, with this lamentation; "If thou hadst known, even thou, at least in this thy day, the things which belong unto thy peace! but now they are hid from thine eyes."

It is not the ordinary way of God's working, to force men into happiness, nor to save them against their knowledge and consent; but to exercise them under the influence and assistance of his grace, and as they willingly receive it, to enable them to "work out their salvation with fear and trembling; knowing that it is he that worketh in them, both to will and to do of his good pleasure."

Great and precious promises, and declarations of the kindness and good-will of the Almighty toward the children of men, are contained in the Holy Scriptures; such as, "I will sprinkle clean water upon you; and ye shall be clean. From all your filthiness, and from all your idols will I cleanse you. A new heart also will I give you, and a new spirit will I put within you." But he plainly declared, "I will yet for all this be inquired of by the house of Israel, to do it for them." Surely nothing is more worthy of our inquiry, especially seeing that our labour will not be in vain; for the declaration of Christ himself was, "Ask and ye shall receive, seek and ye shall find, knock and it shall be opened unto you:" but if we do not ask, there is little reason to expect that we shall receive, or if we do not seek, that we shall find, or if we do not knock, that the door will be opened unto us. And yet there may be an asking and not receiving, a seeking and not finding, and a knocking without being opened to, when the mind is insincere, and not directed to Christ, who is the door, the way, the truth, and the life. Many may be repeating prayers made ready to their hands, and which do not represent their real state, or attending on what they erroneously imagine to be ordinances of God, expecting them to minister to their sanctification, whilst their hearts are wandering after earthly objects, or they may be seeking, in some other formal or insincere way, while they are strangers to the state of their own souls. The state of the soul can only be known by attention to the teaching of the Lord's Spirit; and some knowledge of our own state is needful, in order that we may ask, seek, and knock in sincerity. It is well to remember the solemn declaration, "This people draweth nigh unto me with their mouth, and honoureth me with their lips, but their heart is far from me; but in vain do they worship me, teaching for doctrines the commandments of men."

In seeking the Lord we should not forget the declaration of the Apostle, "That which may be known of God is manifest in them," that is in men: "for God hath shewed it unto them;" nor the answer of Christ to the Pharisees, when they demanded of him when the kingdom of God should come: "The kingdom of God cometh not with observation: neither shall they say, Lo here! or Lo there! for behold the kingdom of God is within you."—"God," saith the Apostle, "who commanded light to shine out of darkness, hath shined in our hearts, to give us the light of the knowledge of the glory of God in the face of Jesus Christ." He has brought his salvation near, and hath caused his righteousness to be revealed, so that none need say, "Who shall ascend into heaven, to bring Christ down from above? or who shall descend into the deep, to bring up Christ again from the dead;" for "the word is nigh thee, even in thy mouth and in thy heart; that is the word of faith which we preach," said the Apostle Paul to the Romans.

As this "word of faith," or "engrafted word," is received into the heart, and the attention is turned to Christ, and obedience is yielded to the manifestations of the Holy Spirit, much benefit will be found from settling down frequently into a state of solemn silence before the Lord. In this state, having the mind gathered to him, waiting upon him, and being

willing to understand our own state before him, we
shall be enabled to pray to him in sincerity, and to
worship him in spirit and in truth. This profitable
state of silence was commanded by the Almighty:
" Be still and know that I am God;" " Be silent,
O all flesh before the Lord; for he is raised up out
of his holy habitation;" " Keep silence before me,
O islands, and let the people renew their strength.
Let them draw near, then let them speak." When
the mind is gathered into a state of quietude, under
the feeling of that divine power which can stay the
wanderings of the imagination, and give an understanding of the language, " The Lord is in his holy
temple, let all the earth keep silence before him,"—
when an awful solemnity covers the spirit, under
which true contrition of heart is experienced, this is
a desirable situation. In this state the love of Christ
is felt, and the language is understood, " I sat down
under his shadow with great delight, and his fruit
was sweet to my taste; he brought me to the banqueting house, and his banner over me was love."
In this state of quiet attention, sound instruction
is sealed on the understanding, and the mind becomes clothed with spiritual strength, consistently
with the testimony of the prophet; " Even the
youths shall faint and be weary, and the young men
shall utterly fall; but they that wait upon the Lord
shall renew their strength." Yea such as wait upon
him will find, by comforting experience, that there
is no joy to be compared with the joy of God's salvation. As those who wait upon God come to obtain redemption through Jesus Christ, witnessing
" the washing of regeneration and the renewing of
the Holy Ghost," they will feel experimentally that
" there is no condemnation to them that are in
Christ Jesus, who walk not after the flesh but after
the Spirit;" that there is in Christ, not only a well-
grounded hope of eternal life, but a peace far surpassing all the satisfaction that can be derived from
the perishing things of this world.

Though various conflicts may have to be passed through, before arriving at these attainments, the flesh lusting against the spirit, and the spirit against the flesh; yet as the Lord is sought unto as a refuge, and the God of Israel as a habitation, he will afford shelter as in his pavilion, he will forgive the transgressions of his children, and will save them as in the hollow of his hand; and though those who seek him may become " the song of the drunkard," or a by-word among their acquaintance, yet these light afflictions will be but as for a moment, and they are not worthy to be compared with the glories which are hereafter to be revealed. The apostles testified that " through much tribulation the righteous must enter the kingdom." But the Lord is not a hard master; his yoke is a cross to the carnal mind, but it is easy to the true disciple of Christ, and his burden light. Be persuaded to make trial for yourselves; and you who in time past may have been as sheep without a shepherd, shall know Christ to be the shepherd and bishop of your souls; your Saviour from sin, and your only hope of glory; and that, abiding in him, " the work of righteousness will be peace, and the effect of righteousness quietness and assurance for ever."

END.

London: Printed by E. Couchman & Co., 10, Throgmorton Street; for the TRACT ASSOCIATION of the SOCIETY OF FRIENDS. Sold at the Depository, 12, Bishopsgate Street Without.—1863.

OF THE

LIFE OF JOB SCOTT:

A MINISTER OE THE GOSPEL IN THE RELIGIOUS SOCIETY OF FRIENDS.

ABRIDGED FROM HIS JOURNAL.

LONDON:

Printed for the TRACT ASSOCIATION of the SOCIETY OF FRIENDS.

Sold at the DEPOSITORY, 12, Bishopsgate Street Without.

1863.

No. 109.   [*Price 7d. per dozen.*]

A MEMOIR

OF THE

LIFE OF JOB SCOTT.

———

I WAS born on the 18th day of the tenth month, 175]
at Providence, in the state of Rhode Island. Almost a
early as I can remember anything, I well recollect th
Lord's secret workings in my heart, by his Grace or Hol
Spirit; very sensibly bringing me under condemnation fc
my evil thoughts and actions, which, over and beyon
all outward instruction, I was made sensible were ev
and sprang from a real root of evil in me. Before I w
ten years old, I took up several resolutions to amend
ways, and live a serious and religious life. My mind beca
exceedingly disquieted when I went contrary to Divi
manifestation, though I had not yet a clear sense that
was the very power and Spirit of God upon me that
condemned and distressed me for sin, and strove to redee
my soul from the bondage of corruption.

I began to take notice of what I heard respecting religio
and among other things, the frequent mention in books a
conversation of the Spirit of God; that good people
former times had it in them, and by it learned the will
God, and were enabled to perform it. I perceived it w
often spoken of in both the Old and New Testament, a
many other writings. I understood that true converts
these days also have it. But, like many others, I overlook
its lively checks and calls in *myself;* had no idea that I h
ever known anything of it; longed to be favoured with
but supposed it was some extraordinary appearance, differe
far from anything I ever yet had been acquainted with.

Oh! that children and all people would be careful
their very early years, and, as they grow up and advance

life, to mind the "reproofs of instruction" in their own breasts; they are known to be "the way of life," divine life to the soul. This *something*, though they know not what it is, that checks them in secret for evil, both before and after they yield to the temptation, warning them beforehand not to touch or taste, and afterwards condemning them if they do so; and inwardly inclining them to a life of religion and virtue—this is the very thing, dear young people, whereby God worketh in you, to will and to do; and by which he will, if you cleave to it and work with it, enable you to work out your own salvation with fear and trembling before him. Had I steadily obeyed the truth in my inward parts, had I attended singly and faithfully to this divine monitor, my portion had been peace; my cup, a cup of consolation! I might have rejoiced and sung, whereas I have had to mourn and weep! For as I grew to fifteen and upwards, in violation of clear inward convictions, in opposition to the dictates of the Holy Spirit, I began to run into company, learned to dance, and play cards, and took great delight therein. I was often deeply condemned, and often strove to stifle the witness, and persuade myself there was no harm in any of these things.

My father sometimes reproved me in those days for my conduct; but sinning against Divine light and visitation, hardened me against his advice. I grew more and more vain, proud, airy, and wanton. I put myself in the way of much evil communication; and it mournfully corrupted good manners. My taste for pleasure and amusement grew keen, my spirits were low and languid when alone, and I rushed into company and merriment for alleviation.

Thus I went on frolicking and gaming, and spending my precious time in vanity. Often at night, and sometimes near break of day, I have returned home from my merry meetings grievously condemned, distressed, and ashamed; wishing I had not gone into such company, and resolving to do so no more; but soon my resolutions failed me, and away I went again and again, and thus continued making greater strides in folly than before. The Lord followed me close, in mercy, and often brake in powerfully upon me, turning all my mirth into mourning; yet I still got over the holy witness, did despite to the Spirit of Grace, and repaired again to my haunts of diversion and merriment. Sometimes when I have stood upon the floor to dance, with a partner by the hand, before all were quite ready, God has arisen in judgment, and smitten me to the very heart. Oh! I still feelingly remember his appearance within me, when none knew the agony of my soul. I felt ready to sink under the weight of condemnation and anguish; but resolutely mustering all the stoutness I was master of, I brazened it out, until the music called me to the dance, and then I soon drowned the voice of conviction, became merry, and caroused among my companions in dissipation, until time urged a dismission of our jovial assembly, and caused me to return, often lonely, to my father's house. Oh! me, how fared it with me then? I assure thee, reader, I have not forgotten those sad and mournful walks at the conclusion of my midnight revellings. I have been broken down in deep abasement and self-abhorrence; have come to a full stand, stopt and sat down on a stump, stone, or log, by the way; wrung my hands, strewed my tears before the Lord, in sorrow and extremity of anguish, bordering almost on desperation. I have begged forgiveness; implored assistance; vowed amendment; obtained some relief; and returned home in hope of reformation. But alas, alas! my resolutions were written as it were in sand; the power of habit had enslaved me; and almost the next invitation of my associates overcame all my engagements; the eager desires for diversion and pastime broke through all the sanction of vows, and violated the solemnity of sacred promises to my God.

Adored for ever be the name of the Lord; he forsook me not, but sounded the alarm louder and louder in mine ears. When I turned at his reproofs, he smiled upon me, and relieved my soul's anxiety; but when I again revolted, his rod was lifted up in fatherly correction. The " still small voice" was uttered in my dwelling, as in the cool of the day, " *Adam, where art thou?*" There was no hiding from him whose penetrating eye no secret can escape, and whose aim in reproving was only to save. He still reproved my wanderings, and pointed out the right way, according to Scripture declaration, " Thou shalt hear a voice behind thee, saying, This is the way, walk in it." Indeed the way was shown me; it was often plainly cast up before me; but I would not walk in it. I knew my Lord's will, but did it not; my *own* I still delighted in the indulgence of. Sometimes I spent nearly all the first day of the week, when I should have been at meeting, in playing cards, idle, if not dissolute conversation, and other vain amusements; returning home at night in condemnation, and sometimes sighing and crying; yet through all this the Lord preserved me from hard drinking, though often in the way of temptation and solicitation to it. Swearing I also mostly refrained from. Jesting, joking, and vain conversation, I went considerable lengths in; then again great shame and self-abhorrence would overwhelm me; again I vowed, promised, and renewed my covenant; but all in vain—I had not got deep enough; nor were my covenants made or renewed in the right ability, but too much in my own strength and creaturely resolutions; so they soon were broken. Sometimes I held out a week or two; other times only a day or two. Thus time passed on; and with an increase of years, I found an increasing propensity to wantonness and dissipation. But, blessed be the God of my salvation, he proportionally increased my sense of guilt and condemnation.

I had seasons of very serious consideration upon religion. What instructions I had outwardly received were mostly in the way of Friends; but when I came near to man's estate, falling in company with some of another society, I was drawn to attend their meetings in Providence. Friends' meetings were oftener held in silence than suited my itching ear. I loved to hear words, began to grow inquisitive, and to search pretty deeply into doctrines and tenets of religion; and, in my most religious seasons, I began to think of being baptized in water; though I have since seen, that water-baptism was but a forerunning, preparatory, and decreasing institution, and has long since done its office, and ceased in the church in point of obligation; and that there is now to the true church but "one Lord, one faith, and one baptism," that of the Holy Ghost, which only can purify and make clean the inside. Oh! my heart, my very soul is fully satisfied in this matter; having felt the living efficacy of this one saving baptism, and known its full sufficiency, without any other.

I had not yet fully given up to the motions of Divine life in my own heart. My mind was too much turned outward; and the preaching of those I sometimes went to hear, who preached in their own time, had a powerful tendency to keep it outward. In this state of outward attention and inquiry I found nothing that could give me power over sin and corruption; but notwithstanding all my serious thoughtfulness, and frequent ardent desires to become truly religious, I still, at times, broke loose, and launched forth into as great degrees of vanity and wickedness as ever: and then again a turn of seriousness would come over me. One time, under deep exercise, after reasoning and hesitating great part of a day, whether I had best give up with full purpose of heart, to lead a religious life or not, at length I gave up, and entered once more into solemn covenant, to serve God, and deny myself, according to the best of my understanding. Almost as soon as I had thus given up, and come to this good conclusion, in stepped the great adversary, and distressed my mind exceedingly with the doctrine of predestination; powerfully insinuating that a certain number were infallibly ordained to eternal salvation, the rest to inevitable destruction; and that not all the religious exercises of my mind could possibly make any alteration in my final destination and allotment. If God had damned me from all eternity, I must be damned for ever; if he had chosen me to eternal salvation, I might set my heart at rest, and live just such a life as would most gratify my natural inclinations; for what advantage could there be in religion and self-denial, if an eternal, unalterable decree secured my final end? I felt willing to hope I was a chosen vessel; and for a short time these ideas so crowded into my mind, that I was ready even to conclude a God all goodness had doomed the far greater part of mankind to never-ending misery, without any provocation on their part! I now view the doctrine of unconditional election to eternal life, and reprobation to eternal destruction, with abhorrence. I almost marvel that, under a cloud of darkness, my rational faculties could ever be so imposed upon, as to assent to so erroneous a sentiment. I know of no doctrine in the world that more shockingly reflects on the character of the Deity.

I did not indeed so drink down this false doctrine as to relinquish my purpose of amendment all at once; I held out a few weeks: when, mournful to relate, the influence of young company, and my vehement desires for creaturely indulgence, through the tolerating influence of the aforesaid insinuations, broke through all my most solemn engagements, threw down the wall and fortifications, and exposed me an easy prey to the grand enemy of my soul's salvation. Again I took my swing in vanity, amusements, and dissipation. This, however, was but a short race. The Lord, in lovingkindness, followed me with his judgments inwardly revealed against sin. The prince of darkness also followed me, with temptation upon temptation to evil; and with various subtle insinuations and dark notions, to rid me of all fear, restraint, or tenderness of conscience. At length, notwithstanding all I had felt of the power of God upon me, in reproof for sin, and invitation to holiness; yea though I had some true relish of divine good, the holy Witness became so stifled that

I began to conclude there was *no God;* that all things came by chance, by nature, by the fortuitous jumble and concourse of atoms, without any designing Cause, or intelligent arrangement: that it was idle, chimerical, and delusive, to think of serving or fearing a Being who had no existence but in imagination! Here let it be well considered, what a powerful influence the admission of one false doctrine, and the violation of Divine manifestation and conviction, has in paving the way for other false doctrines. Not much sooner had I received and cherished one of the grand falsehoods of the father of lies, the doctrine of irresistible necessity and predestination, than, in the mist of darkness which spread over my mind, I even dared to deny the eternal Deity; and, horrible to the last degree to think of, I began to rejoice in the idea of unbounded, unrestrained licentiousness and carnality; and that I was unaccountable for my conduct; not considering that, on my atheistical scheme, I was unprotected, and had no more to *hope* than to fear; none to look up to for defence and succour: but must be left a prey to violence, and all kinds of adversity attendant on this life. Oh! the depravity of taste and inclination, as well as of understanding, into which I was plunged!

I went on a few months after this, much in the same manner; my days I spent in vanity and rebellion; my nights frequently in horror and distress! Many a night I scarcely durst enter my chamber, or lay me down in bed. I have the most unshaken ground to believe it was the immediate power of God upon me, that thus terrified my guilty soul; and that, in the most fatherly goodness, condescension, and mercy, in order to prevent my going on to endless perdition, to which I seemed to be swiftly posting. Day after day, and night after night, I was distressed! the Lord setting my sins in order before me, and pleading with me to return unto him and live. At last I fled again to religious engagement for relief, betook myself to prayer, and cried to the Lord, in the bitterness of my spirit. Sometimes I begged and interceded for mercy, and power to make a stand and overcome sin, with such vehemency as if my very heart would break! Tears gushed from my eyes! My soul was overwhelmed with anguish! Oh! young man, whoever thou art, that readest these lines, I warn thee, I beseech thee, shun such misery, by obedience; such unutterable anxiety, by cleaving to the Lord. Yet, after all this, young company, music, gaming, pleasure, again rallied their forces, and had such influence over my resolutions, as evidenced them written as in dust, though mingled with tears, with wormwood, and gall; and I abandoned all again, to enjoy the pleasures of sin for a season. But God, rich in mercy and long-suffering kindness, still interrupted my career, disturbed my carnal satisfaction, and blasted all my joys. Once more a sense of just and holy indignation kindled up in my breast for transgression and grievous revolt. Awfulness took hold on me; amazement swallowed me up. I knew not which way to turn. The wrath of an offended, long-suffering God, seemed closing upon me on every side. I felt myself in thraldom, and almost without hope. I knew myself a prisoner, and yet I hugged my chains.

Thus I continued still in vanity and folly, with intervals of deep distress and mourning, until about nineteen years of age, when I became more fully and clearly convinced, and that very much by the immediate operations, illuminations, and openings of Divine light in my own mind, that this inward something, which had been thus long and powerfully striving with me, disturbing my every false rest, confuting every false and sin-flattering imagination of flesh and blood, or of the grand adversary, and enjoining me to give up all, and walk in the ways of virtue and true self-denial, was the true and living Spirit and Power of the eternal God; the very same that strove with the old world, influenced the patriarchs, prophets, and apostles; and visits, strives with, and at seasons more or less influences, the hearts of all mankind. I now saw this the only principle of all true conversion and salvation; that so long as *this* was resisted and rejected, separation must infallibly remain between God and the soul; but that, whenever this is received, and in all things thoroughly submitted to, a thorough reconciliation takes place.

It was through the eternal Spirit, this very Spirit that visits and strives with all, that Christ offered up that prepared body. It is through, and only through, the influence of the same Holy Spirit, that any soul was ever converted to God, or savingly benefited by the redemption that is in Jesus. Whatever way, O soul, or by whatever means thou art benefited in a spiritual sense, it is by this Holy Spirit, that is the immediate operative power and principle within thee.

Having thus, at length, become livingly convinced that it was nothing short of the eternal Power and Spirit of God that so forcibly wrought in me, in order for my deliverance from the power of darkness and seduction, I gave up to the holy requirings of God as inwardly made known to me—and clearly known were many things thus made. Nothing else could ever so have opened my mind, and made known my duty to me.

I gave up very fully to serve the Lord in the way of his leadings; I forsook rude and vicious company, withdrew into retirement, attended the meetings of Friends, and often sought the Lord, and waited upon him alone, in solemn, reverential silence, for his counsel, direction, and preservation; and he was graciously pleased to point out and cast up the way for me, one thing after another, with sufficient clearness. First, he showed me *negatively*, what I ought not to do in various particulars, breaking me off from my vicious practices and associations. This was *forsaking evil*. And then he taught and enjoined me the practice of several things *positively*, wherein he engaged me to choose and cleave unto that which is good. I saw clearly it was his will, and my indispensable duty, reverently to assemble for divine worship, and therein to *wait* upon him, draw inwardly near unto him, and, according to the apostle's language, *feel after him*, in order to find and enjoy him. I also found it my duty often to wait upon him alone, in awful, silent retirement, not approaching him in supplication, but when he influenced my heart thereto, with the true spirit of prayer and intercession. He also showed me that Religion was an internal life in the soul; that great attention, sincerity, and punctuality were necessary to the growth and prosperity of it; that I must not be content with attending meetings, and sitting in silence, though ever so reverently and properly: I must live continually in an inward watchfulness and dedication of heart; watch all my thoughts, words, and actions, and know all brought to judgment; and allow nothing to pass unexamined, nor willingly unapproved; that I must observe the most upright honesty and sincerity in my dealings among men, as in the presence of God. He taught me that men generally rely too much on external performances; and thus guarding my mind against thinking too much of anything outward, he opened my understanding to behold my duty in regard to outward plainness; that a plain, decent, and not costly dress and way of living, in all things, was most agreeable to true Christian gravity and self-denial: that rich, showy, or gaudy dress, house, food, or furniture, fed and fostered pride and ostentation, robbed the poor, pleased the vain, and led into a great deal of unnecessary toil and solicitude, to obtain the means of this way of life and appearance: that it could not afford any true and solid satisfaction; but

B

must unavoidably divert the mind from inward watchfulness; retard the work of mortification and true self-denial; and facilitate unprofitable acquaintance with such as would rather alienate the affections from God, than unite the soul to him.

Thus instructed, I bowed in reverence; and as it became from time to time necessary to procure new clothing, endeavoured to conform my outward appearance in this respect to the dictates of Truth, in which I found true peace and satisfaction. Also he instructed me to use the plain Scripture language, THOU to one, and YOU to more than one. The cross greatly offended me in regard to these things. This of language, in particular, looked so trifling and foolish to the worldly-wise part in me, and the fear of " the world's dread laugh" so powerfully opposed it, that it was very hard and trying to my natural will to give up to this duty. I thought if my right hand would excuse my compliance, I would gladly sacrifice it, rather than give up to use such a despised language, and submit to be laughed at, as viewing religion concerned in such things as these! This may seem incredible to some, but it is true, and as fresh with me as any past exercise. This exercise beset me day and night for some time, during which I shed many sorrowful and bitter tears, pleaded many excuses, and greatly wished some substitute might be accepted instead of the thing called for; but he who called me into the performance of these foolish things, (to this world's wisdom) was graciously pleased to show me, with indubitable clearness, that he would choose his sacrifice himself; and that neither a right hand, nor a right eye, neither thousands of rams, nor ten thousands of rivers of oil, would by any means answer instead of his requirings. If he called for so weak or so foolish a thing as the words *thou* and *thee* to a single person, instead of *you*, nothing else of my substituting would do instead of it; for " the foolishness of God is wiser than men." Let none dispute the ground with Omnipotence, nor confer with flesh and blood; lest, therein, *despising the day of small things*, they *fall by little and little.*

For be assured, O! thou *called* of the Lord, thou canst never become his *chosen*, unless thou *obey* his call and come out of all he calls thee from. If thou art not *faithful in a little*, thou wilt not be made *ruler over much.* Perhaps few will believe the fulness of heavenly joy which sprang in my bosom, as a well-spring of living waters, after my giving up in faithfulness to this requisition. And yet this flow of

Divine consolation lasted not long at this time; for, though I gave up to whatever the Lord required of me, yet as I had so long and so stubbornly rebelled against him, he saw meet, in his infinite wisdom, soon to hide his face from me again, and close me up in almost utter darkness, which rendered my days truly tedious, and my nights wearisome to my soul.

Oh! my God, thou leddest me through the desert, thou weanedst me from the world, and alluredst me into the wilderness: there thou didst hide thy face from me for a season, until the longings of my soul after thee were intensely kindled; then liftedst thou up my head, and spake comfortably to me; blessed be thy holy name for ever!

Many and varied afflictions are necessary to our refinement. Hence the place of this refinement is called, "the furnace of affliction." Through the purifying operations of these fiery trials, the soul is gradually redeemed from the pit of pollution. It is a precious work of Divine power to hide pride from man. And he who becomes thoroughly acquainted with the corruptions of human nature in its alienation from God, will find, if ever true humiliation and renovation be effected in him, that nothing short of the baptism of fire can rightly cleanse the corrupt, and humble the proud heart of fallen man.

Under the refining hand of God's power, whereby he thus humbled and abased my soul, I was given clearly to see the need I should have of this excellent qualification—*humility*, in my further progress in religious life. I saw pretty clearly, in the midst of my deepest depression, that if I should be favoured with unremitted tranquillity and divine enjoyment, I should be in danger of spiritual pride and exaltation. Blessed be the name of the Lord for this among his many other favours, that he taught me the necessity of humility, and forewarned, and therein fore-armed me against the wiles of Satan, which I afterwards became more fully acquainted with. Oh! with what ardency of desire did my prayers ascend before him, that he would rebuke the proud, luciferian spirit, and appoint my dwelling in the low valley, where the grass is green, and where the fragrant flowers give forth a pleasant smell. I saw that on the lofty mountains often reign barrenness and desolation. My mind was almost constantly impressed, in those days, with the love and desire of deep HUMILITY. I saw something of its real beauty, and craved it as one of the greatest blessings. Oh! said I, that I may put it on as a garment, and wear it for ever: yea, even appear in it before my Judge, in the assembly of saints and angels, in a future state. " Oh! Lord my God," (was then my language, and my heart now joins it) " suffer me never to forget my tribulations, nor to cease my supplications to thee, for the continuance of this precious blessing; let it be the first and the last in the catalogue of my requests."

Thus the great Leader of Israel led me on from step to step, not by any means through a constant and uninterrupted enjoyment of his presence; but, which for me has been far better, by frequent withdrawings, strippings, and deep-felt emptiness, poverty, and want; and that again and again repeated, even after large overflowings of his love—in my soul, as a river overflowing all its banks. Had he not, after such seasons of rejoicing, veiled his presence, and clothed my soul with mourning, I might, like ancient Israel, have " sang his praise and soon forgot his works." But now, through the many tribulations, and wise turnings of his holy hand upon me, my soul remains bowed, and to this day sensible of the tendering impressions of his love and good-ness. The savour of life is still fresh within me. He has led me about and instructed me, and (with reverence I speak it) hath kept and preserved me. May I still be preserved, and henceforth, for ever, kept safe under his all-powerful protection; walking worthy of the same to the end of my days.—Amen.

During a great part of the foregoing exercises, I had fre-quent openings and lively prospects respecting the Christian warfare, and the mysteries of the kingdom of heaven. I often believed that if I stood faithful, it would be required of me to declare to others what the Lord had done for me, and to entreat my fellow-creatures to seek an habitation in that kingdom that cannot be shaken or fade away. This concern began now to grow upon me considerably, even to that degree, that I felt at times in meetings a living engagement to communicate somewhat to the people; but, fearing I should begin in that great work before the right time, I kept back; and even divers times, when I was almost ready to stand up, I have concluded I would keep silence this once more; considering within myself, that if my so doing should be displeasing to the Lord, he would manifest his displeasure to me; but if I should presume to speak a word in his name, and it should prove to be without his holy requirings, or too soon, I should not only displease him, but also burden his people; and perhaps get into, and become entangled in a way of speaking from too small motions or impressions felt, or mournfully mistake the sparks of my own kindling for

Divine impressions; which might, in consequence of my giving way thereunto, be suffered to increase upon me to my great loss in the substantial and Divine life, if not to my utter ruin. In this guarded frame of mind I passed on for some time, often seeking to the Lord for counsel and direction. He who laid the concern upon me, well knowing the integrity of my heart, and that I was bent faithfully to serve him, without going too fast, or yet tarrying behind my Guide, dealt graciously with me, passed by my little withholdings, favoured with fresh and increasing incomes of his love, and from time to time cast up my way with still greater clearness; and at length in a manner so clear and confirming, as erased doubt and hesitation from my mind. In the fresh authority whereof I uttered a few words in our meeting at Providence, on the first day of the week, and 10th of the fourth month, 1774, to my own and I believe my friends' satisfaction. I felt the returns of peace in my own bosom, as a river of life, for a considerable time afterwards, sweetly comforting my mind, and confirming me in this solemn undertaking.

At divers times I had lively impressions to say a few words more, in public testimony; but still waited to be well assured. Not being, by once succeeding, encouraged to run too fast, I was favoured to know the fire of the Lord rightly kindled upon his altar; and to witness an offering of *his own preparing;* and I am well assured that such, and such only, are the offerings which will find acceptance with him. He never will reject these, any more than accept those of human obtruding.

My second public appearance in the ministry was at the lower meeting-house in Smithfield, 19th of the tenth month, 1774, when I found a living concern to encourage a careful engagement before the Lord, out of meetings; and to press it upon friends to draw nigh unto him from day to day, that strength may be renewed, and the divine savour of life retained; lest we lose the sense of what we often graciously enjoy in our religious meetings. Life, divine life, attended me in this little testimony, as in the former; and after meeting I enjoyed the sweet influence of him who is the God of my salvation, in a degree that was greatly to my confirmation and encouragement. After this I still continued seeking unto and waiting upon God for counsel and direction; in which frame of mind I was favoured to renew and increase a living acquaintance with him, and witness fresh instruction to my mind. Blessed be the name of the

Lord my God! I bow awfully before him, for his directing and preserving presence through many deep probations. He hath been with me in the heights and in the depths; has strung my bow and covered my head in the day of battle. May I serve him faithfully all the days of my stay here, until I go hence, and be seen of men no more.

I have been renewedly confirmed in the great advantage to families, and even to small children, that results from sitting down in solemn silence, and therein waiting upon God. I have seen the children much broken and tendered in such seasons, so that, even when there has not been a word spoken, tears have rolled down their cheeks, and their looks have been evidently expressive of heart-felt sensations.

I have also seen much advantage to whole families from the practice of a solemn pause at meals; and, where it is done in a feeling manner, with minds rightly turned to feel after God, and experience his blessing, and is not practised in a slight formal manner, it tends to season and solemnize the minds of young and old. I am morally certain, that I have many a day gone through the cares and concerns of life with much more composure, stability, satisfaction, and propriety, for the strength and assistance I have found, in drawing near to God in solemn silence in my family; and I wish the practice of reverently adoring him in this way may increase more and more.

1784. I have divers times lately very clearly seen the great folly of thinking ourselves of much importance, either in religious society, or in the world. O may my soul dwell ever in true abasement; for blessed and happy is he that knows a being brought down, yea down low, and there abiding: for until all self-exaltation is entirely rooted out of our minds, we are not what God would have us to be; and his turning and overturning in us, is in order, if not resisted, thus to make us; and until we do, from the centre of our souls, give him *all* the glory, there remains in us a source of unhappiness, disorder, and confusion.—O man! how great is the work of thy salvation; how many deaths thou hast to die, before that comes to reign in thee, which lives for ever! Know thou, that thou canst never fully enjoy that life which is "hid with Christ in God," until thou diest to thy own selfish life. It is he that loses his life for Christ's sake, that shall *find* it: yea, our blessed Saviour declares, if any man *hate* not his own life, he cannot be my disciple.* Lord God Almighty, carry on the great work in my soul; bow every

* Luke xiv. 26.

exalted imagination, and lay all that is not of thy own immediate begetting in me level with the dust!

Let him that thinketh he standeth be not high-minded, but
fear. Let none think themselves safe off the watch, because
of any degree of attainment and favour; the watch-tower
remains to be our place of safety: neither let any honest
mind be too much disheartened at the assaults of Satan.
There is a power above him, and he that cleaves close to it
shall know a victory over all the powers of darkness! This
I think my soul has a right to set its seal to, as I have ever
come off victorious when I have not turned my back upon
the Light, our divine Leader. Sing, O ye heavens! and
O ye pilgrims on the earth rejoice and triumph! for strong
and invincible is the God of our salvation; and abundantly
sufficient for our help is the grace afforded us. Let all but
keep to it and then safe are their steppings, and sure their
preservation.

[Having been entrusted with a gift in the ministry, in
which he was acceptably exercised among his friends at
home, under the influence of Gospel love, Job Scott visited
meetings in different parts of the United States; evidencing
that in the school of Christ he had been instructed in the
mysteries of the kingdom, and like the good scribe, was
enabled to bring forth out of the treasury, things new and
old, in the authority and demonstration of the Spirit.

In the year 1792, with the concurrence of his brethren,
he embarked from Boston on a religious visit to Friends in
Great Britain. During his stay in England, he laboured
diligently, and in the seventh month, 1793, sailed from
Liverpool for Ireland. In the course of his travels through
these islands he penned a number of impressive remarks,
among which are the following:—]

Oh! the deadness of professors! Oh! the flat formality
that too generally reigns! " Yet once more I shake not the
earth only, but also heaven." One stone must not be left
upon another, of mere creaturely performances, where God
is known to be " *all in all;*" and so he *is* known, where
Christ has reigned in the heart until he has " put down all
rule and all authority" but that of the pure Truth; for this
is the state in which is fulfilled the precious prediction and
promise, that " the Lord alone shall be exalted in that day."
That the professors of Christianity may be shaken from
their dead forms and lifeless images, and come to know
" that day," and therein God's exaltation over all that is of
man, is the travail and prayer of my soul to the God and

Father of our Lord Jesus Christ. And, O my God, if it be thy will, I pray thee hasten the more general coming and knowledge of that day among the nations. Amen.

What dreadful wars have raged through almost all ages and nations! What rivers of blood have human beings drawn from human beings! and what havoc are men still making of human lives, who say they are Christians! Will the state of mankind never be meliorated? Will the sword devour for ever, and the glorious and benign influence of the Gospel, by the wrath of men for ever be defeated? Forbid it, gracious heaven!—Indeed, I firmly believe, the time will yet come when "nation shall not lift up sword against nation, neither shall they learn war any more." O blessed day! O precious state of peace, harmony, and happiness! My spirit breathes unto God, that he may arise and hasten this great work of reformation on the earth; that the king-doms of this world may become the kingdoms of God and of his Christ. Amen, saith my soul.

Oh the mischiefs of the theatre! what dissipation it pro-motes! It operates directly against the life of religion, and tends to the destruction of morals; yet, sorrowful to say, too many great professors of Christianity, and some of the pre-tended ministers of the Gospel, are not ashamed openly to plead for and promote the destructive practice of stage-playing! False religion and worship shall be shaken, a well as earthly-mindedness, in order to make way for tha which cannot be shaken, the work of God's Holy Spirit i men's hearts, and that worship and religion which the hol operation thereof enables man to persevere in, to his ow unshaken peace, and the exaltation of the Divine glory.

At——there was so much lightness and irreverence amon, the people, that no way opened in the spring of the Gospe to preach Jesus and the resurrection among them; so th meeting was necessarily silent, for we preach not ourselves and not being able rightly to call Jesus, Lord, but by th Holy Ghost, durst not attempt to preach his Gospel withou that Divine unction and influence, well knowing it cannot be done; and that so many thousands attempting to do it, has been the means of overrunning the nations with the dead formal image of worship, consisting of words without life, and sounds without substance. God will not give his glory to another, nor his praise to graven images, or the work o men's hands of any kind, however specious or refined. He will indeed "glorify the house of his glory," where his honour dwelleth; where his Holy Spirit is the spring o action, and where he is the " worker of all things ;" where his people will be still, and know that he is God; where they patiently *wait* for him, and " let him arise," not arising themselves before him or without him. But alas! alas! who and where are these ? Truly not all who are professing so to do. But this is the standard unto which the true and thorough Gospel-worshipper must be reduced.

Ninth month 27th. Oh, my God, thou art weaning me still more and more, and much more than I once thought necessary, from the world, and from all that is in it. Well, good is thy will, and thy counsel is excellent. Do with me what thou wilt; form, fashion, and reduce me as thou pleasest. Thou hast given me clearly to see, that many who had even been in thy furnace came out too soon, and remained drossy and impure all their days by not abiding thy judgments, and not enduring the turnings of thy holy Hand upon them, and not following thee fully into all that separates and weans from all that flesh and blood delights in, which thou callest for, and art graciously leading such as will follow thee into. Oh! redeem my soul from all that hinders its full and unimpeded access to thee, the Fountain of living waters : set my affections wholly on things divine, and make me entirely thy own in the heavenly image and fellowship for ever.

[After having visited a number of meetings in Ireland, on the 9th of the eleventh month, Job Scott reached Ballitore, and the following night was taken unwell. His indisposition continuing to increase, on the 14th an irruption appeared that proved to be the small-pox. His mind was preserved in calmness and resignation, and being kindly attended through his illness by several friends, a daily account of his expressions and of the progress of the disorder was kept by one of them, from which the following is selected.]

Fifth day 14th. He said, " There is an eternal Arm underneath each of us which is sufficient to bear up and support ; and will do it, as far as is needful we should be supported. I have long been confirmed in the sentiment, that nothing could possibly happen that would harm me while I keep under the Divine influence."

In the evening, he said, " Though I am not without considerable bodily pain, yet I feel such a portion of that good which is infinite, that it does not seem worth mentioning ; and if there was no greater enjoyment hereafter, the present would be a state truly desirable, through a never-ending eternity ; yet the fulness is still more desirable.

In a letter dictated to his relations and friends at home, h
says—". My desires for my children's substantial growth i
the Truth, and strict adherence to all its discoveries, to th
close of their days, is by far the principal wish I have f(
them. Out of the enjoyment of a good degree of this pr(
cious inheritance I know of nothing in this world worth livin
for! Ye that know it, suffer nothing, I most cordially beseec
you, ever to divert your minds from an increasing and fervei
pursuit after the fulness of it, even unto the measure of tl
stature and fulness of Christ.

" Many and painful have been the probationary exercise
of this life to me. Ah! were there probability of strengtl
how I could enlarge, for my heart seems melted within me i
retrospective view; but all the former conflicts, howeve
grievous in their time, are lighter now than vanity, except ɛ
they are clearly seen to have contributed largely to th
sanctification of the soul; as they are remembered wit
awfulness and gratitude before Him who has not been wantin
to preserve through them all; and as they seem likely. t
introduce either very shortly, or before a very long time, t
an exceeding and eternal weight of glory. I have no kind ⸱
self-complacency on account of any good works properl
mine. My *own* works I have long seen the necessity
cease from; and trust, through the grace of God, by whi
I am what I am, I have been enabled in some precio
degree to do so. It is the Lord who worketh my works
me; and magnified be his Name for ever, he has oft
worked in me mightily, to my own humbling admiratio
and I trust, at times, to the thankful acknowledgment
many others; and as certainly as he liveth, he would wo
mightily in many thousands, if they would but let him ari
over all in them. Indeed he worketh in all as far as th
give way to his arising. This doctrine is to me as clear a
certain at this moment as ever it has been, and I have oft
been constrained to proclaim it to the nations, sometim
with almost invincible authority; and sometimes under
great deal of weakness and obstruction. The last has tend
much to keep the creature rightly dependant and humbl
and through every dispensation, the Leader of Israel h
seen best what was best for me.

" Let my children be engaged in some innocent emplo
ments, as much as may be, out of the way of a great deal
temptation, and, if I had need to add it, out of the way
very great accumulation; and yet through industry and pe
severance moderately productive. My very soul abhors t

dea that a Christian can ever be at liberty, whilst under the
nfluence of heavenly good, to seek, or even desire, much
wealth: though this disposition, in direct opposition to the
ife and doctrine of Christ, has gone far towards the destruction of true and spiritual religion, I believe in almost
every religious society in the world."

16th. During the course of the day he said to A. T.,
"I have seen the magnanimity of a true Believer, and how
one that is really so would bear all the trials permitted to
attend him;" adding very forcibly, "Dost thou believe in
God? thou must also believe in the justness of all his dispensations."

17th. He continued all this day under much oppression
from the disease, but no alarming symptoms appeared. He
requested that if he were removed, some further particulars
might be transmitted to his friends at home, adding, in substance, "The Lord's will is blessed, and I feel no controversy with it. It is the Lord that enables us to coincide
with his will, and say Amen to all the trials and conflicts he
permits to attend us. My mind is centred in that which
brings into perfect acquiescence; there is nothing in this
world worth being enjoyed, out of the Divine will. It is his
will that brings us into a state of existence, and it is for
a purpose of his glory."

19th. This night he patiently and quietly suffered much.
In the evening, he remarked the efforts to support nature
ailing; and added, "There are many resources in nature,
but if the great Author of nature does not think fit that any
of them should be for me, all is well." At another time,
much oppressed and worn down with this grievous malady,
he observed, " I have *no fear*, for perfect love casteth out
all fear, and he that feareth is not perfected in love!"

20th. On fourth-day morning he supplicated thus: " O
Lord my God, thou that hast been with me from my youth
to this day; if a man who hath endured with a degree of
patience the various turnings of thy holy Hand, may be
permitted to supplicate thy name; cut short the work in
righteousness, if consistent with thy will. Thou who hast
wrought deliverance for Jacob, evince that thou art able to
break my bonds asunder, and show forth thy salvation, that
so my soul may magnify thy Name for ever and ever." And
after a pause, wherein he seemed to feel the earnest of his
petition, added, " So be it saith my soul."

21st. At three o'clock this morning, he said, "You have
seen the awful progress of the disorder; as to me, it matters

little, only present pain—may the Lord release me shortly. To a person who came to see him he said, " Oh! Charles Charles! an inheritance in the eternal Truth is infinitely infinitely superior to all the enjoyments this world can afford Remember it as long as thou livest." Some time afte: " I do not wish hastily to make my escape : but if the Lor will be pleased to release me from the bonds of mortality an the struggles of life, and to cut the work short, considerabl short, in righteousness, I think I shall be willing to enrol in the list of his unspeakable favours." To the aforesaic " Farewell Charles! let no possible consideration divert the from a close attention to *that*, without which life must be live in vain." At another time he said, " Some of my wishes fc myself are centred in as speedy a release as may be consister with the will of our Heavenly Father, and an admission, whic I have no doubt at all, not in the least degree, of obtaining into that glorious kingdom, where the wicked cease froi troubling, and the weary soul is eternally at rest." 'And while after, " I think I have not, for several years past, know much or anything of boasting ; I have known something (that law of grace, whereby all boasting is entirely excluded but I may say, through that which has supported me under a the trials and conflicts which have attended my passage throu life, to you, my beloved friends, as to dear children, follo me, as I have endeavoured to follow Christ Jesus, the Lo of life and glory, and the rock of my eternal salvation."

22nd. On sixth-day morning, after suffering great u easiness, and getting little or no rest, he supplicated, " Lord! if it be consistent with thy holy will, let loose bands, and send the moment of relief to my poor body a soul." Afterwards said, " We cannot approve or disappro by parts the works of Omnipotence rightly ; we must appro the whole and say, Thy will be done in all things."

About five he appeared to be dying ; and at seven o'clo his purified spirit was gently released from its earthly ten ment, and we doubt not, ascended with joy to its heaven mansion, and the glory of an incorruptible inheritance wi the saints in light.

END.

E. Couchman & Co., Printers, 10, Throgmorton Street, London.

OF

JULIA MOORE,

𝔄 𝔓enitent 𝔉emale,

WHO DIED IN THE EASTERN PENITENTIARY OF PENNSYLVANIA,
IN THE YEAR 1843.

———

" Come now and let us reason together, saith the Lord; though your sins be as
carlet, they shall be white as snow; though they be red like crimson, they shall
be as wool." Isa. i. 18.

" Wherefore, I say unto thee, her sins, which are many, are forgiven; for she
loved much. And he said to the woman, Thy faith hath saved thee, go in peace."
Luke vii. 47—50.

PUBLISHED BY " THE FEMALE PRISON ASSOCIATION OF FRIENDS

IN PHILADELPHIA."

LONDON:

Printed for the TRACT ASSOCIATION of the SOCIETY OF FRIENDS.

Sold at the DEPOSITORY, 12, Bishopsgate Street Without.

———

1862.

No. 110.   [Price 4d. per dozen.]

AN ACCOUNT

OF

JULIA MOORE.

JULIA MOORE, the subject of the following narrative
was in early life exposed to the temptations and snares
of " a world that lieth in wickedness;" and having been
regardless of that wisdom which would have preserved
her in the fear of the Lord, she became easily entangled
in the wiles of the enemy; and following the multitude
to do evil, she forsook the paths of virtue, plunged into
a vortex of iniquity, and involved herself in ignominious
guilt.

Her companions in vice did not, however, prove to be
" friends in need;" for when overtaken by poverty and
sickness, comfortless and without a home, she was
impelled by necessity to seek a shelter in the Alms
House of Easton; where, while suffering from wounds
previously inflicted by a ruffian, she was visited by a
benevolent individual, and prevailed upon to accept of a
situation in this city, calculated to promote in the heart
of this poor unhappy woman a change which she then
professed to desire. But how truly was it verified in her
experience, that " the heart is deceitful above all things
and desperately wicked," as, in a few short months, she
gave evidence of her instability, by turning a deaf ear to
the reproofs of instruction, voluntarily forsaking the path
marked out for her recovery. Determined to have her
own way, she trampled upon the advice of her friends
and boldly took the road which leadeth down to destruction and death. Short, however, was her iniquitous
career; for being again exposed to temptation, she proceeded from one vice to another, until hardened in guilt

"she joined hands with the workers of iniquity," and participating in a cruel robbery, was arrested, and sentenced to seven years' imprisonment, before she had completed her twenty-eighth year. At this period it may be truly said that, viewed both physically and mentally, she was but a wreck of human nature. Sins of the deepest die had polluted her mind, and a succession of vices, hardships, and sufferings had impressed upon her features an image of disgusting wretchedness.

It was in the summer of 1839 that Julia entered her cell; not with subdued and contrite feelings, but loaded with guilt, impenitence, and disgrace. To an individual who saw her at this time, and manifested a desire to awaken her attention to her spiritual interests, she said in an assumedly pious and resigned spirit, that though misfortune frowned upon her here, her hope of happiness was in a future and better world; which quickly prompted the reproof, "that notwithstanding such pretended piety, a guilty criminal like her must be a stranger to such a hope." But need we marvel if "like the heath in the desert that knoweth not when good cometh," she should be slow to mark the judgments of an offended God, or discern in this chastisement the hand of out-stretched mercy? for though she had often experienced "the way of the transgressor to be hard," yet her cup of suffering had not until now, been fully measured. Having wasted the strength and vigour of her life; having buried, in worse than idleness, the precious moments of her youth; with broken health she had now come to reap in solitude the bitter fruits of folly and of crime. But the depravity of her mind, and the darkness that pervaded her spirit, rendered her not less an object of especial interest; and efforts were soon made to convince her of the enormity of her sins, and her need of sincere repentance. A member of the visiting committee, who saw her shortly after her commitment, observed that, even at that early interview, she evinced some tenderness, and appeared to be interested in the religious conversation she had with her; but upon entering her cell a few weeks afterwards, she perceived that her mind was somewhat agitated, and upon her remarking that she had passed some sleepless nights since their last interview, the friend inquired the

cause; to which Julia replied, " That a minister had been
in her cell and told her she was a lost, undone creature.
That she had been bolstering herself up, and sewing
pillows under her arm-holes, which would not do, for she
was a hardened, guilty creature." And though at the
time she seemed to be much exasperated, and had been
wickedly premeditating an act of revenge, if he should
repeat the charge, yet He who could open the eyes of the
blind, soon enabled her to behold her vileness, and she
afterwards remarked to this friend, that although the
minister's remarks above alluded to, were at first unwel-
come tidings, she had been favoured to recognise the
mercy that was mingled with such an exposure of her
real situation. The subject pressing heavily upon her
feelings, she was permitted to see the depravity of her
heart, and loathing her condition, she endured the most
bitter conflicts of mind, until that passage was brought
to her recollection by the Good Remembrancer, " though
your sins be as scarlet, they shall be white as snow;
though they be red, like crimson, they shall be as wool."

Being thus aroused to reflection, she had strong convictions of sin, and the gross immoralities of her lif
became burthensome to her awakened conscience. Sh
read her Bible attentively, and though the light of Truth
shone at times with brightness, yet the sins of her yout
pressed weightily upon her spirit; disease was makin
rapid progress; suffering days and wearisome nights wer
appointed her, and alternate seasons of hope and despai
were her permitted portion, until He, who was thus gra
ciously refining her in the furnace of affliction, saw mee
to administer the consolations of the Gospel *immediately*
as well as *instrumentally*, to her anguished soul.

In one of the many favoured opportunities with Julia
a friend found her mourning over her burden of sin, an
her own fruitless efforts to lighten it. She entreated he
to delay no longer, but to go just as she *was*, to the Savi
our of Sinners, who by his death had opened a perpetua
fountain for sin and for uncleanness, reviving the text
" *Now* is the accepted time, *now* is the day of salvation;'
which appears to have operated as a brightening glea
upon her trembling faith, as, in frequent allusion to th
period, she always designated it as " *her birth day*."

Upon another occasion, as she lay ill upon her bed, during an opportunity of public preaching to the prisoners, the words " *yet there is room,* arrested her attention, and contir 'd with her through the remainder of the day, as well as t. following night, which was one of extreme bodily suffering; when suddenly she was inspired with hope; and the query arose in her mind, "May there not be, room *even for me?*" and the possibility of such a mercy filled her soul with joy.

The work of grace thus marvellously begun in the heart of this poor creature, was increasingly manifest in the gratitude, patience, and resignation evinced throughout the course of her protracted illness, enforcing upon our minds the truth of the sentiment,

> " The Holy Spirit must reveal
> The Saviour's work and worth;
> 'Tis then the heart begins to feel
> A new and heavenly birth."

Remarkable indeed was the display of infinite mercy to this poor wanderer; for scarcely had one year of her imprisonment expired, before the mists of doubt and darkness began to vanish from her benighted soul, and she seemed to enjoy a perpetual sunshine. Upon one occasion, alluding to her situation, she said, that she was happy and thankful in her allotment, believing that it was a great mercy that she had been stopped short in her career of infamy, and cast into prison. For there her spiritual eyes had been opened to see herself as she really was; and there the precious Saviour had been manifested in her heart; " and now," (continued she,) " I give myself no uneasiness as to the time I may have to serve here; all is right; I know I deserve it all; and if my sufferings are only in this life, I shall be very thankful. The dry bread I eat here, is sweeter than the best meal I ever ate anywhere else, for I now can feel gratitude in my heart for it; and can sometimes pray that your labours may not be lost upon me."

At this period she was very ill; and in view of the prospect before her, remarked, "That if it was her Heavenly Father's will to raise her again, she would like to live a little longer, that she might know more of his word in her heart; but if it was his will to take her away, she believed that the wonderful mercy he had extended to her would be continued to the end. She knew that no power but His could have made such a change in her, and that she could do nothing herself, but *He* had heard her prayers, had taken away her stony heart and given her a heart of flesh.

On being asked if she had at all times felt comfortable, she cautiously answered; "The enemy is sometimes permitted to come in and trouble me; but then I look at my Saviour, and I feel his power running through me, and driving him away." Upon her friend exclaiming, "Oh! Julia, what a monument of mercy!" She looked up, with eyes overflowing with tears, and replied, "Oh, I know it! I feel it! Eternity will be too short to express my gratitude."

The very feeble state of her health made her sensible of her dependence upon those who daily administered to her bodily comforts, and she expressed great thankfulness for the unwearied attentions of the Physician and Matron of the Penitentiary, saying, that all her former acquaintances had been so hard-hearted, that it was very unexpected to her to meet with such kindness in a prison, where she wanted for nothing; adding, that if a reprieve were brought to her, and she was told that she might have her liberty again, it would not be good tidings to her. "For *here*," continued she, "I have found my Saviour! and *here* I want to enjoy him. Oh! if my poor fellow-prisoners would only believe in what you say, and feel His love as I do, they would be so full of happiness, they would not care for anything else. I often feel so sorry for them, that I try and pray your instructions may be blessed to them all." The subject of regeneration being adverted to, her visiter inquired whether she understood the meaning of "old things being done away, and all things becoming new?" to which she answered, "Oh, yes! God has changed me. I know I am changed! All my old thoughts are done away. I take no pleasure in them now. My only pleasure is in thinking of *Him!* Being reminded, that "we should not only believe on him when comforted by his smiles, but we must keep fast hold of our faith if he should hide himself from us," she replied, that sometimes she could not feel that there was any love in her heart; and then observed, "But I. think he sends sickness and pain upon me, to try my. patience, and see whether I would go to anything else, or. whether my dependence is on Him alone. But I go to Him, for I n't want any other help; and he comforts me by his word in my soul."

She spoke of herself with much humility, and great abhorrence of the wickedness of her former life; how long she had lived the child of the devil, participating in almost every kind of sin, till in mercy she was arrested and thrown into prison. Here her sufferings were for a season indescribable, until a dawn of hope arose—a glimmering of mercy appeared. "Now (she continued) I want no better home upon earth than I have here, though the prison walls are around me, and the doors fastened upon me. Oh! how willingly would I tell all the world the riches of redeeming love."

Through most of the year 1840, Julia continued to be fluctuating between life and death; yet her mind was generally tranquil and happy; and she assured us that her *lonely cell* had become to her "a happy, happy home!" It being remarked to her that it was not so when she first entered it; "Oh, no," she replied, "I had nothing until I was brought out; my sins were so great." Allusion being made to a remarkable view she had had of the depravity of her heart, "Yes," said she, "it was so dreadful, it frightened me, and I could not forget it." On being asked what had cleansed it, she immediately replied, "Nothing but that blessed blood; *He* died that we might live." On being reminded that in her weak state she had better not talk too much, "Oh!" said she, "I cannot be still. I would like the whole world to know what my Saviour has done for me, and how happy *He* makes me in my cell."

She said that in her life she had been a great swearer; and for some time after her imprisonment, even in her sleep, the most dreadful words would come into her mind, which troubled her so much that she tried to put them away, but she could not help herself; and she had cried unto the Lord that He would take such a spirit from her, and by His power He had done it. The nurse then inquired whether she had not some such suggestions

a few evenings before, when she suddenly turned her
head, and asked her, "whether Satan ever slumbered
or slept?" Upon which she remarked that, at the time,
she was lying very happy, communing with her Maker,
when all at once an expression passed through her mind
that frightened her, which she said led to the question;
but afterwards added, that she looked to the Lord, and
he took it away.

During the last three years of Julia's imprisonment,
she enjoyed but little bodily comfort, her pain being at
times so acute that she found it difficult to restrain her
tears; which led her to desire, that if it was her master's
will, she might retain her senses to the last; but meekly
added, "Let his will be done." "Oh," said she, "it
often comes into my mind,

> 'Thou hast chastened me I know,
> Thou hast wounded me in love;
> To wean my heart from things below,
> That it might soar above.' "

One of her visiters remarking, that it was wonderful
her mind was kept so clear of doubts; and another observing, that it might be, because she had given herself
up so entirely into the Divine hand; Julia added, "Oh,
yes! I want my dear Saviour to have all. I would
keep nothing back. I give myself to *Him* entirely."
And in alluding to the critical state of her health, she
said, that she might be here one hour, and in another
far away beyond the trials of time; but she had a well-
grounded hope that in the end all would be well, which
hope was founded alone upon the precious Saviour of
sinners. She spoke in the most humiliating manner of
her own condition without this unfailing Helper; and a
friend asking if she could now understand the passage,
"we are the temples of the Holy Ghost," reminding her
that we can do nothing but yield ourselves unto his
Spirit within us, which must carry on, and perfect the
work; "Oh, yes!" she replied, "I do indeed understand
it, for all was dark without Him."

Again, as a friend approached her bed-side, Julia said
to her, "Oh, what a night I have had since I last saw
you! my sufferings were so extreme. Our lamp had
gone out, and we were in utter darkness. Anne helped

me to my chair, and I went from one fainting fit to another, so great was the agony. But my dear Saviour was so near me—words cannot express how near he was to me. I felt that I could then willingly breathe out my life into his h—   s, as I lay in dear Anne's arms. Daylight was long coming, but I got easier;" then added, "afflictions do us good; they bring us to our senses; particularly for such miserable offenders as I have been all the days of my life. Poor weak creature that I am! *nothing but nothingness!*"

These repeated attacks of illness generally left her much reduced, and rendered it necessary to have another prisoner in her cell to wait upon her; and though the attentions of such were gratefully acknowledged, yet when she was sufficiently recovered to admit of it, she preferred being alone, feeling, as she expressed herself, well convinced that solitary confinement was the very best thing for her that could be, having found that a companion diverted her mind from a train of useful meditation and communion; and that she never felt lonely in her cell. That sometimes she would awake in the night, and think, "How very dark it is here; but then, in another world, all is bright;" and she said that she seemed to forget her present situation whilst dwelling upon the future, when a thousand years would be but as one day.

One of her visiters being indisposed, Julia sent her the following message: "Give her my kind and dear love, and tell her the sea is calm; all is peace! the soul is anchored on a rock that has a real foundation. And that is the hope—of me—a poor dying object—that sure foundation."

Upon another occasion, when a female minister assured her, that in her case it might be truly said, "Great and marvellous are thy works, Lord God Almighty, just and true are all thy ways, thou King of Saints," she appeared much tendered during the opportunity, and wept aloud.

The following week she was very low, apparently on the borders of the grave; at which time she observed that she would like to see once more all the dear friends who had been so much interested for her, and given her much good advice; after which she remarked, "I have a

comfortable hope; (a hope, I trust, not founded on my
own strength,) that when this tabernacle is dissolved, I
have a home prepared eternal with my Father in heaven! Oh, what have I not undergone? What have I
not seen? But blessed for ever be His name; He has
plucked me as a brand from the burning. I do not think
it would be a kindness in any one to assure me that
I should get well."

But though thus willing to depart, she was, beyond
the expectation of all who then saw her, brought back
again, doubtless for the trial of her faith in the patient
endurance of not only weeks, but months of agonizing
pain, a distressing cough and great oppression being
almost constant attendants upon her suffering complaint;
so that the winter of 1842 found her still an invalid;
though at intervals able to be out of bed, and even engaged in knitting or some light sewing. Though long
indisposed, Julia was not indolent. She felt very sensibly her dependent situation, and remarked at one time
to a visiter, that she knew she did not earn her salt; and
had resolved, on regaining her strength, that she would
work constantly, and complete as much as possible (for
the Institution); but after pursuing her plan a few days,
at night she did not feel comfortable, and her Bible was
present to her mind both waking and sleeping. At length
she became more uneasy, and concluded she would read
in it daily, and had found by doing so, she was happier,
and accomplished more work than when she felt burdened and distressed." Besides the value which Julia
thus attached to the perusal of the Holy Scriptures,
many pages of which she committed to memory, she also
took much pleasure in the reading of religious tracts and
hymns, which she said were often very refreshing to her
mind during her many painful and sleepless nights.
With much feeling she would sometimes repeat in our
hearing those expressive lines of Newton:

> "How tedious and tasteless the hours
> When JESUS no longer I see;"—

> "While blessed with a sense of his love,
> A Palace a toy would appear,
> And *Prisons* would palaces prove
> If JESUS should dwell with me there.'

A member of the committee, to whom she was much attached, being prevented by sickness from visiting the prison as usual, Julia wrote to her several times. One of these letters, written about two weeks previous to her death, may be properly introduced, to evince the strength of her affection, and the gratitude which filled her heart, whilst contemplating the goodness of the Lord to "*one so vile.*"

We give it precisely in her own language.

April 27th, 1843.

"I improve this opportunity to inform my sincere friend that I am very feeble at present. I hope that these lines may find your health gaining. I long to hear your instructions once more. I feel thankful that I have been spared to express the sense of gratitude I feel for those benefits you have all been pleased to confer upon me; I thank Almighty God for all his kind mercies to me. Experience plainly shows me He has made strangers my mother, father, sisters, and friends. I have reason to bless the day I entered this prison. I feel that I am a great sinner. Oh that I may feel more humble and lowly in heart. In the night when all is asleep, I think I sometimes hear a voice saying, "Be of good cheer; your sorrows shall be turned to joy." How sweet to my mind is this, "There is room for the chief of sinners." Here is my hope; Jesus is my refuge. He has heard me in a time accepted, and in the hour of great trouble *He* removed my burden. Blessed be God! I hope what few days I have here below, that the Lord will give me courage, strength, and faith, that my soul may be saved, and his name be glorified.

"Almighty God! unto whom all hearts are open, all desires known, and from whom no secrets are hid, cleanse the thoughts of my heart by the inspiration of thy Holy Spirit, that I may perfectly love thee, and worthily magnify thy Holy name, through Jesus Christ our Lord."

I sincerely thank you for the present you gave me, 'The Sinner's Friend."

I remain your truly afflicted scholar,

JULIA MOORE.

A few days after the date of this, she was attacked with erysipelas, which, proceeding to her head, rendered her situation alarming, and her appearance truly affecting; her face being greatly swollen, and her eyes entirely closed. Much as she suffered at this time, her mind appeared to be preserved in peaceful resignation. To an individual who conversed with her, she observed, "I am in darkness, but I can see Jesus, and feel that my hope in Him is sure. I suffer greatly, but oh! how merciful the Lord is to me."

A female friend, taking her by the hand, and expressing a desire that, under this load of accumulated suffering, she might keep fast hold of that faith which had hitherto been her support, she replied with a faltering voice, " The blessed Saviour suffered for me!"

The progress of disease producing insensibility, she survived but two days after this, when her purified spirit left its afflicted tenement, on the 10th of the fifth month, 1843, when she had been a prisoner nearly four years.

Having thus followed Julia to the borders of the unseen world, whilst contemplating her as a redeemed and happy spirit, let us reverently and thankfully admire the compassion and long forbearance of a merciful Saviour, who, as she herself declared, had plucked her as "a brand from the burning," and so marvellously supported her in seasons of conflict and dismay. And should this memoir meet the eye of any who have in a similar way wandered from the paths of virtue, may it lead them seriously to retrace the crooked paths of her misguided youth, and whilst with trembling they view the awful gulph into which her spirit had nearly plunged, ma it awaken in their bosoms the sincere desire, that they too may be brought to see themselves as they really are, and, struggling for the blessing, *like her* be led, by prayer and repentance, to *Jesus*, the Sinner's Friend.

END.

Printed by E. Couchman & Co., 10, Throgmorton Street, London.

EXPOSTULATORY REMARKS

ON THE USE OF

WATER BAPTISM;

ON

THE SPRINKLING OF INFANTS;

AND

ON THE SOLEMN RESPONSIBILITY UNDERTAKEN BY THOSE CALLED SPONSORS.

BY S. T.

LONDON:

Printed for the TRACT ASSOCIATION of the SOCIETY OF FRIENDS.

Sold at the DEPOSITORY, 84, Houndsditch.

1857.

No. 111.   [*Price 4d. per dozen.*]

EXPOSTULATORY REMARKS,

&c.

W<small>HEN</small> I was at Yarmouth, in the Isle of Wight, last summer, I had a religious meeting in the Wesleyan Meeting House. After it closed, when I came out into the street, a person (who was supposed to be an Episcopal minister) enquired of me, Whether I had ever been baptized? I replied, yes, with the Holy Spirit. And, on further enquiry, Whether I had been baptized with water; I replied in the negative. Whereupon he roughly queried with me:—Then how *dare* you to stand up and harangue the people, when you never were made a member of Christ's Church by baptism, and consequently have no right to the ministry of the Gospel?

Now, I have to query, whether, If water-baptism be, as it is acknowledged by the Church of England to be, "an outward and visible sign of an inward and spiritual grace;" whether is of greater efficacy, the sign or the substance; the outward type, or the inward and spiritual grace; the shadow, or the real thing? I suppose that all candid men and women will allow, that the substance is far better than the shadow; that the real thing is far better than the type; that the inward and spiritual grace is far better than the mere outward sign; that the baptism of the Holy Ghost is far better than the baptism of water! The latter is performed sometimes by unholy and sinful men; the former by Christ himself through the Holy Spirit.

And does not the bishop enquire, when candidates for the public ministry come forward before him, Whether they believe themselves called of the Holy Ghost to preach the Gospel? and can we suppose that the Holy Spirit would call *any* that are baptized with water *only*? Was it not said by Christ to his disciples, just before his ascension into heaven, " John truly baptized with water, but *ye* shall be baptized with the Holy Ghost?" which was to be the true qualification for the Gospel ministry.

Again, Can the sprinkling of water in the faces of little children be baptism? This was no practice of Christ, nor of the apostles; no precedent can be found for it in the New Testament. And can a human invention be the proper means of making members of Christ's Church, and qualifying men for the ministry? Can such means ever effect that great change of heart which is necessary to renovate the soul of man? Is it possible that the sprinkling of a little water in the face of an infant, while in a state incapable of knowing good from evil, can ever effect that great change which is necessary for us all, and by which alone we are made acceptable to God through Jesus Christ? Can such an empty ceremony ever effect anything of a spiritual nature? Are there not very many of those who have been thus sprinkled by the priest, who are never brought to the truth as it is in Jesus?

But although this rite of man will not do without the Holy Spirit, will not the baptism of the Spirit do without the sprinkling of water? Are not the commandments of God more to be regarded than the commandments of men? And is not the operation of the Holy Spirit effectual without the performances of men? And as the practice of sprinkling infants has no sanction from Holy Scripture, surely it must be a commandment of men! If so, then, may not the words adopted by our blessed Lord (Matthew xv. 8, 9.) be applied, "This people draweth nigh unto me with their mouth, and honoureth me with their lips; but their heart is far from me. But in *vain* they do worship me, *teaching* for *doctrines* the commandments *of men*."

I am fully persuaded, that multitudes have been deceived in believing that infant sprinkling is the means whereby people become members of Christ's Church! We find that the performance of this ceremony produces no change of heart: as they grow up, the evil propensities of their fallen nature grow with them; no evil is subdued thereby, and the soul is not regenerated; and how then can it make them members of Christ's mystical body, of which He is the Holy Head?

It is my belief, that there is a mystical washing of regeneration, and renewing of the Holy Ghost, which was shed on the believers formerly, and is shed on the believers now abundantly, through Jesus Christ our Saviour: that, being justified by his grace, we should be made heirs according to the hope of eternal life. If so, we are spiritually washed, sanctified, and justified, in the name of the Lord Jesus, and by the Spirit of our God; we are become new creatures, old things are passed away, all

hings are become new, and all things are of God, who
ath reconciled us to Himself by Jesus Christ; who of
God is made unto us wisdom, and righteousness, and
anctification, and redemption. Having an High Priest
ver the house of God, we can draw near with a true heart,
a full assurance of faith, having our hearts sprinkled
from an evil conscience (through sanctification of the
Spirit, unto obedience and sprinkling of the blood of
Jesus Christ), and our bodies washed with pure water.
The Priests and Levites under the Law were to wash
hemselves with water, in order to be cleansed and puri-
ied; which was an emblem of the purification of the
soul by the grace and Spirit of Christ; and the apostle
Paul said to the Corinthian believers, " Having therefore
hese promises, dearly beloved, let us cleanse ourselves
from all filthiness of the flesh and spirit, perfecting holiness in the fear of God."

The apostle Paul expressed his thankfulness that he
had baptized (with water) but very few, and further said
" Christ sent me not to baptize, but to preach the Gospel."
Now, if the commission (Matthew xxviii. 19.) included
baptism with water, and Paul was not sent to baptize
with water, then this commission was not a command to
ill the divinely anointed ministers of Christ's Gospel
to baptize with water. And upon what authority, then,
do the man-appointed ministers of the present day profess
to have received *their* commission? As this eminent
apostle had no command from Christ to baptize with
water, and thanked God that he had baptized but few,
I have no doubt that many of his converts never were
baptized *with water,* and yet they became members of
Christ's Church *by faith in Him.*

I do consider the sprinkling of infants derives no authority from the New Testament; that it can neither make a man a member of Christ's Church, nor have any part in that spiritual work; that the washing of regeneration is a spiritual process in the soul of man; that it is the work of God through Christ; and that those only whom the Lord Jesus baptizes with the Holy Spirit are members of his body, and that none others have a right to the Christian ministry.

I have also to query as follows:—Can it be right for persons to come forward and become bound as sureties, or what are called godfathers and godmothers, for infants; and to promise, in a solemn manner, as before God and the congregation, that their infant charge, as they grow up to maturer age, "Shall renounce the devil and all his works, the pomp and vanities of this wicked world, and all the sinful lusts of the flesh; that they shall keep God's holy will and commandments, and walk in the same all the days of their lives?" If all that have passe through this ceremony were to become thus far perfect we should have a different world from what we hav now! The lives of multitudes of those who have bee sprinkled by the priest, and even after what is calle *confirmation* by the bishop, are a continual evidenc of the inutility of these ceremonies. Our streets, our lanes, our prisons, and the various haunts of vice and dissipation, proclaim that man-made members of the Church of Christ are still the children of wrath, even as others who have not had anything of the kind done for them! there is no difference. If so, does it not appear to be a grand mistake; a great error; and a serious evil too? because the little children are taught to believe what is not true: that they are by this process *born again*, made *members* of Christ, *children of God*, and *inheritors* of the kingdom of heaven, when it is not so. We are told by higher authority (the apostle Paul),—It is by grace we are saved, *through faith*, and that *not of ourselves*, it is the *gift* of God; not of works, lest any man should boast. It is not of the law of Moses, neither of the works of *man*. No man can make children saints; for all that are made saints are of God's workmanship, created in Christ Jesus unto good works, which God hath before ordained, that we should walk in them. Can the episcopal priest, if he be a conscientious man, be easy to suffer any one that is not religious to come forward as a sponsor on such occasions? And how can a conscientious man or woman undertake such an *awful* responsibility upon themselves, for how can they fulfil it? And if the most conscientious cannot fulfil these engagements, then surely those who are not religious, who have no pretensions to religion, they cannot! And are there not thousands in this nation who are utterly unmindful of these solemn promises? But are we not told by an eminent apostle, that we must all appear before the judgment seat of Christ, that every one may receive the things done in his body, according to that he hath done, whether it be good or bad? As one that hath known the terrors of the Lord for sin, but who has been permitted to find mercy, I would persuade men and women to ponder the path of their feet when they come forward to make such solemn engagements, and never to promise to do that for another which they do not do themselves. I have no doubt but very many undertake to stand sureties without consideration, thoughtless of the consequences, and some even through ignorance! But let them solemnly consider, whether they can any longer be justified in pleading ignorance on these important subjects.

But there was no occasion for this contrivance of man; which, according to history, was got up in the dark night of apostacy from the true faith, in order to save (as they pretend) little children from the effects of the fall of Adam. It certainly is unnecessary; for if Christ tasted death for *all* men, then doubtless little children are included—they whom Christ set in the midst of the people, and of whom He said, of such is the kingdom of heaven. He died for them as much as for any; and the blood of atonement was shed as much for little children as for grown persons; for He gave himself a ransom *for all;* and it is the blood of Jesus Christ that cleanseth from *all* sin. ·   A

S. T.

1*st Month*, 29*th*, 1847.

END.

Printed by E. Couchman, 10, Throgmorton Street, London.

A

FRIENDLY CALL,

TO ALL PEOPLE,

TO COME OUT OF DARKNESS TO THE TRUE LIGHT;

OR,

A TENDER EXHORTATION
TO CEASE TO DO EVIL, AND LEARN TO DO WELL;
THAT SO PEOPLE MAY BE DELIVERED FROM THE POWER OF
SATAN, BY THE POWER OF GOD,
AND THE OPERATION OF HIS SPIRIT, IN CHRIST JESUS
OUR LORD.

———

WRITTEN IN YORK CASTLE BY A PRISONER FOR THE TRUTH'S SAKE,

IN THE YEAR 1677:

THOMAS THOMPSON.

Printed for the TRACT ASSOCIATION of the SOCIETY OF FRIENDS.
Sold at the DEPOSITORY, 12, Bishopsgate Street Without.

—

1866.

No. 112.   [*Price 3d. per dozen.*]

The Author of the following Address was a minister of
the Gospel in the Society of Friends, in the early days of
its history, when its members were exposed to grievous persecutions; and was one to whom it was given, in behalf of
Christ, not only to believe in Him, but also to suffer for His
sake; for he endured long imprisonments for the faithful
maintenance of his religious principles. The Address from
which the present is drawn was, as he states, when under
confinement on account of his conscientious refusal to comply with the demands made upon him for an ecclesiastical
state provision; believing, as he did, that such a provision
was in opposition to the injunction of the Great Head of
the church, "Freely ye have received, freely give." H
was a diligent labourer in the Gospel, and was the instru
ment, in the Divine hand, of gathering many souls unt
Christ; his engagement being to set before his hearers the all
important truth, that religion does not consist in forma
ceremonies, but that the heart must be changed, and becom
regenerated under the transforming power of the Spirit o
Christ.

He died at his house at Skipley, in Yorkshire, in the yea
1705. His dying bed was memorable for the heavenly peac
and joy which were with him in his last moments; saying
"My heart is filled with the love of God." "The Lor
Jesus Christ hath shed his precious blood for us; hath lai
down his life; and was made sin for us, who knew no si
Oh! praises, high praises and Hallelujahs," &c.

A FRIENDLY CALL, &c.

FRIENDS AND PEOPLE,

I, in my measure, being sensible of the terrors of the Lord against the wickedness and ungodliness of this world, and that they who now trifle away their time in folly, shall in the end come to sorrow and mourning, under the heavy wrath and displeasure of the Almighty, and that none know how suddenly it may come upon them, which my soul desires all may escape; therefore, in good will to the souls of mankind, especially to you my neighbours and acquaintance, was I moved in my spirit to write this unto you; which I desire you may read with soberness of mind, and consider with coolness, whether ye are in the way of the Lord which leadeth to life eternal, or following the pleasures of the flesh, in the broad way that leadeth to destruction.

"Blessed is the man that walketh not in the counsel of the ungodly, nor standeth in the way of sinners, nor sitteth in the seat of the scornful. But his delight is in the law of the Lord, and in his law doth he meditate day and night." Ps. i. 1, 2.

Thus the Prophet begins the Psalms, showing the blessed state of those whose delight is in the law of the Lord. Consider it well, dear people, of what quality or degree soever, and see where your hearts are, and what you are delighting in; for know assuredly that the Lord hath caused his day to dawn and his light to shine, even the light of Christ Jesus, who is "the true light which lighteth every man that cometh into the world," as the blessed apostle testifies. John i. 9. So in the light search your hearts; and see what is the delight of your minds; whether your delight be in the law of the Lord, and your meditations thereupon, or ye delight in earthly and perishing things, for surely they who delight in vanity cannot partake of the blessing.

Do not some of you delight in gaming and sporting yourselves, spending many hours in vain and unprofitable pleasures, which do not become people professing themselves christians, seeing we are exhorted to redeem the time, and not to spend or trifle it away in vanity, or fulfilling the lust of the flesh?

Others there are who delight in drunkenness, feasting, or banqueting; in music, singing, and dancing; not considering that they must come to judgment.

O! how can ye whose life is in these things, delight your souls in the law of the Lord, or partake of the blessings which the Lord hath in store for the righteous? Verily my heart relents to think upon the misery that will come upon you except ye repent. "Wo unto them that rise up early in the morning, that they may follow strong drink, that continue until night, till wine inflame them. And the harp and the viol, the tabret and pipe, and wine are in their feasts, but they regard not the work of the Lord." Isa. v. 11, 12. Therefore, dear people, turn and repent, and give ear to the voice of the Spirit of God within you, which at some times ye feel checking and reproving you for the evil of your doings; discovering to you what is contrary to the mind and will of God; and giving you to see your need of salvation through our Lord and Saviour Jesus Christ. So that divers times when ye have spoken rashly, or taken God's name in vain, i has shown you such profaneness is evil, and ye have been read to cry at the very next word "Lord have mercy upon me;' so quick and sharp have been the reproofs of the good Spirit in your heart. Now, if you would give diligent heed to this and weigh and try all your words and actions before hand, thi would be a guide unto you, and let you see the evil as it firs arises in your hearts, before it come forth into words or actions As for example, if any one of you are tempted to steal, swear or lie, the same good Spirit would persuade you that you d not right in so doing. Now, if you at that time would obe this manifestation, which persuades you to forsake the evil and do that which is right, you would be kept from thes sins: and out of every other sin, this light leads all who ar willing to follow and obey it. So that truly it may be said even as it was in days past, "Oh! Israel, thou hast destroye thyself, but in me is thine help. Hosea xiii. 9.

No longer glory in your shame, O ye sons of men! no delight in vanity; but "commune with your own heart o your bed, and be still:" Ps. iv. 4; that ye may learn the fea of the Lord which is to depart from and hate evil. And know ye that the Lord hath set apart him that is godly for himself. The Lord will hear when I call unto him: "But He is not a God that hath pleasure in wickedness, neither shall evil dwell with him; the foolish shall not stand in his sight, for he hateth the workers of iniquity; and will destroy them that speak leasing: for the Lord abhorreth the bloody and deceitful man." Ps. v. 4, 5, 6.

Wherefore all people, whether learned or unlearned, mind the light of Christ in your consciences, that you may be brought out of darkness and ignorance, and taught in the way of the Lord, and have your understandings enlightened in the things of God, that so your souls may partake of blessings from the Lord. But surely there must be a forsaking of the evil, before peace with God is witnessed. Therefore none rest yourselves contented in the performance of any outward ceremonies, while the root of iniquity remains and lodgeth in the heart: for a profession without possession will not serve to justification; neither will it excuse you before the Lord; for now He commands men everywhere to repent. I beseech you be persuaded to forsake the evil of your ways, and turn to the Lord with your whole heart: for I cannot but plainly declare unto you that 'tis not saying over the Lord's prayer, and other things used by many of you, that will serve you to obtain salvation, whilst the heart is not changed —for *in Him alone* is salvation known, who testified that he was the light, and that those who followed him should not walk in darkness: John viii. 12; who also said, "except your righteousness exceed the righteousness of the scribes and Pharisees (who said much but practised not accordingly) ye cannot enter the kingdom of heaven." Matt. v. 20: so your saying ye hope that through the merits of Christ you will be received to mercy at the closing up of your days, though ye continue in sin while ye here remain, is not sufficient. It is not the true hope of the people of God, which 'whosoever hath in him, purifieth himself even as He is pure:" is it not rather the hope of the hypocrite which will perish? Job viii. 13. But I testify that the Lord God of

heaven and earth is not only able, but willing also, to free a
forgive all those that will forsake their iniquities, and tru
come unto him in the way that he hath appointed, which
Jesus Christ. So unto him alone let all come, and he w
give you rest. He will ease you that are weary and hea
laden, of the heavy burdens of sin and corruption, and bri
you if ye mind his leadings, into a land of rest, which t
Father hath prepared for all that love him.

But the kingdom of heaven cometh not with observatio
of this or that or the other thing of man's inventions; bu
saith He, in whom is life—"If ye love me keep my comman
ments"—so reject not the call of his Spirit, but obey it. ?
may know it near you in your hearts, moving against s:
and drawing unto peace and holiness, without which "no m
shall see the Lord." Heb. xii. 14. But they that fear a:
serve the Lord "shall be girded with strength and their w
made perfect." Ps. xviii. 32. Here's a promise of streng
to them that fear the Lord, even that their way shall be ma
perfect. Must there not then be an overcoming of sin?
I do not say that 'tis by the power, or working, or stren
of man, nor by anything that he can do in any performanc
but by the strength; power, and love of God, in Christ Je
our Lord. And laying hold on this, and waiting to be gui
by that Spirit of truth, which shows what is that good
acceptable will of God, they come to take up the daily cr
to their corrupt inclinations; and thus a restoring of the s
comes to be witnessed, and a leading in the paths of righteo
ness. So come out of transgression, dear people, that y
souls, that have been long sick and ready to faint, ma
restored to strength: for is it not a certain truth, that w
your delights are in sinful pleasures, your minds feed u
dust, which was said to be the serpent's meat; and so lon
ye continue in that state, your souls pine and grow lean
want of food. So, dear people, be not deceived, such a
sow, such must ye reap: "if ye sow to the flesh ye sha
the flesh reap corruption; but he that soweth to the S
shall of the Spirit reap life everlasting." Gal. vi. 7, 8.
is no light matter—eternal happiness or everlasting w

nisery is before you. The selfish reasoner—fleshly wisdom, will tell you, if ye consult therewith, that ye are in a good state of Christianity; ye observe the ordinances; go and hear divine service; and hope to be saved by the merits of Christ Jesus, when ye are dead; though while ye live ye do many things which ye know in your consciences are contrary to his will and commandments; who hath said, "not every one that saith Lord, Lord, shall enter into the kingdom of heaven, but he that doeth the will of my Father which is in heaven." Matt. vii. 21. For it is the heart which God requires, and righteousness there wrought through faith in Christ Jesus, is alone accepted with Him; therefore may every one of you see that your hearts be changed by the operation of the Spirit of the Lord, and corruption purged therefrom by the blood of Jesus. And this, I am bold to affirm, as a certain truth, that where a thorough change is wrought in the heart, and the mind truly given up to serve the Lord, there holiness of life and conversation follow as the fruits of the Spirit. Henceforth "keep thy tongue from evil, and thy lips from speaking guile, depart from evil and do good, seek peace and pursue it: for the eyes of the Lord are upon the righteous, and his ears are open to their cry; but the face of the Lord is against them that do evil, to cut off the remembrance of them from the earth." Ps. xxxiv. 13, &c.

It is the Lord alone that delivers his people from the power of the enemy that would keep them in the bondage of sin, that so he might triumph over them as he doth over many at this day, who are held in his chains; but the Lord delivers out of his power all that will come unto him, and also preserves his chosen ones; praises be given unto him, over all for ever. Those that abide in his counsel he enableth to persevere in the straight way of self-denial, and to such his commandments are not grievous, but joyous; yea, they feel and experience of His goodness. "'Tis he alone who setteth the solitary in families, and bringeth out those who are bound with chains; but the rebellious dwell in a dry land," where the streamings forth of the love of God are not known.

So press forward, ye that have any desire to walk in the way of the Lord; stick not at anything which the witness for God

shows to be evil; but be ye faithful to the Lord, in forsakin
every thing that would defile, how goodly or pleasant soeve
it may seem in your own eye or reason; then shall ye com
to "understand the loving-kindness of the Lord," and be le
on in his way.

Mark the blessed state of the righteous, and the woful stat
of the wicked, described in the Scriptures of truth: for surel
all those words and writings of the holy men of God were lef
upon record for our admonition, edification, and instruction
and if ye do slightly read them over, and refuse to come t
the life which they testify of, then great will be your condem
nation; and those faithful testimonies which the servants c
the Lord have given forth and declared will rise up in judg
ment against you, and the witness for God in your hearts wil
unite in the condemnation of those that do evil.

Therefore, I cannot but exhort you once more to hearke
to the counsel of the Lord. I even beseech you to forsak
the evil of your ways, and break off your sins by repentance
for though your hearts may cheer you, and ye may follo
the sight of your eyes, yet know assuredly that for all thes
things, God will bring you to judgment; for the tim
hasteneth, that the daughters of music shall be brought lo
and the desire (after vanity) shall fail; and the dust sha
return to the earth as it was, and the spirit to God wh
gave it. Eccles. xii. 4. 7·

So the desire of my heart is, that the understandings of a
people may be opened to the things which belong to the
eternal peace, and that all may come to the knowledge of tl
truth in which they are made free indeed. The hope
Israel is in the Lord, "with whom is mercy and plenteous r
demption, who will redeem his people from all their troubles
To him alone be honour, praises, and pure obedience given f
ever more. So, as saith the preacher, the conclusion of tl
whole matter is, "Fear God and keep his commandments, f
this is the whole duty of man: for God will bring every wo
into judgment, with every secret thing, whether it be goo
or whether it be evil." Eccles. xii. 13, 14.

Printed by E. Couchman and Co., 10, Throgmorton Street, London.

THE SWISS PEASANT.

A SKETCH OF THE LIFE

OF

JOHANN RICKLI.

The following Sketch of the life of Johann Rickli has been selected from a printed Tract of ninety pages, written by himself, and presented to the translator when on a visit to Berne, in Switzerland, in the year 1843.

The christian experience of this pious man affords a striking testimony to the operation and guidance of the Holy Spirit. The narrative appeared to contain so much of Gospel truth, and so many incidents of a practical nature, related in simplicity, and with apparent sincerity, that it was thought an abridgment might prove acceptable and instructive to many English readers.

Stamford Hill, 5th Month, 1848.   J. Y.

I was born in the year 1756, in the Canton of Berne. My parents were of the Lutheran reformed church; and were accounted religious people. I was their only surviving child, and they were anxious that I should receive a religious education, and taught me early to read, and accustomed me to prayer. They were afraid of sending me to school, lest through the bad example of other children, I should learn more evil than good.

At home I read diligently the Heidelburgh Catechism; and having a quick and retentive memory, I soon learned it by heart; and could repeat the answers, and also give the names of the authors and passages referred to with readiness.

From my early youth, I was very susceptible of good impressions, and while reading the Holy Scriptures and other religious books, I was often melted to tears; but from unwatchfulness these impressions did not prove real and abiding.

No. 113.   [Price 4d. per dozen.]

In the ninth year of my age, my parents were obliged, according to the law of the Canton, to send me to school, and I had not been long there, before the time came for me to undergo a preparation to receive the Holy Supper, Here I again found the advantage of my ready memory: for I was soon able to repeat all the necessary questions put to me by the minister.

I wish here to remark, that great danger often arises to young persons, blessed with gifts and talents, from being too early and improperly put forward by their parents and teachers, in a manner that tends to fill the youthful mind with self-conceit and vanity. This might have proved a lasting injury to myself, had not God, in mercy, preserved me from it.

After the usual examination, I was found suitable to partake of this rite, but my preparation consisted only in a knowledge according to the letter; I knew nothing of heartfelt repentance, although my father, according to his own religious views, had taken great care that I should undergo a strict preparation; and also to myself, the subject appeared of great importance, much more so perhaps, than it did to any of my school companions. But I soon found that the vows and promises, entered into at the time of my baptism, were not sufficient to enable me to renounce the vanities of a wicked world; yet I passed on in a pretty orderly walk, until about the eighteenth year of my age: when sorrowful to relate, I was led away by evil companions, to lightness of conduct, and to hurtful things of almost every kind. Yet my Heavenly Father, by the convictions of His Spirit, knocked at the door of my heart, so that when I returned from my nightly revellings with my companions, I almost always formed resolutions never to accompany them again to the like excess: but these resolutions being made in my own strength, they only lasted till another temptation offered. My Heavenly Father, in His mercy, ceased not to knock still harder at the door of my heart and conscience; and the inwardly written law threatened me with judgment and hardness of heart. This made me a little more careful; I was frightened; and my stubborn will became more yielding to the gentle leading of the Spirit; and a strong desire sprung in my heart, to give myself up to follow my crucified Saviour.

It was in the twenty-fifth year of my age when I experienced this happy change. As this blessed light began to shine in my dark heart, it brought my sins to remembrance: and the righteousness of God passed strict judgment on my youthful levity and dissipation; and I had bitterly to lament over many of those follies, practised by young people, and too often considered as innocent; keen was the sting of conscience for time misspent that could never be recalled.

I have seen the danger to which young persons are subject in this respect; and that the example of parents too often gives to their children liberty to run into excesses; and in every station in life to depart from the simplicity of the Gospel. I observed so much moral deadness in the professors of Christianity in general, that it gave me great uneasiness; and I felt constrained to warn young people of the danger of trusting to a name of religion, without living under its power. I thought that if any one had, from his own experience, set before me the danger that I was in, when under similar temptation, I should not have gone so far astray. My counsel, though given in love, met with but little reception; yet, as a matter of duty, it brought peace to my own mind.

At the time of my awakening, I had no acquaintance with the different religious professors in the neighbourhood; and I thought it better for me to dwell much in retirement, that the work of repentance might be carried on through the operation of the Spirit of God alone, without the intervention of man; and that I might bear the hand of my God upon me, until I became reconciled to Him, through the pardoning mercies of His Son, my Redeemer.

When pardon for sin is experienced, there is a danger of considering the work of regeneration as completed, when it is only just commenced. On this rock my soul's enemy had nearly caused me to split, by telling me the work was now done; that I was a child of God, and safe; and that it was no more needful so strictly to watch, in order to lead a godly life. The subtle enemy directed me to an outward righteousness that was flattering to my old nature, which I felt was still alive; and I received the representation with joy, and as coming from a good spirit. I was not, however, suffered to remain under this delusion; but was given to see that faith in Christ saved the soul by regenerating it, and by leading to a life of prayer, and to a humble walk before God.

The lives and examples of the apostles and holy men of early times, rcorded in the Scriptures, were made precious to me in seasons of spiritual conflict. I also became acquainted about this time with some serious people, and was induced to frequent their assemblies; but I found among them much less of vital religion than I expected. Yet I could fully appreciate the fruits of the Spirit, in whomsoever I found them.

As I was an only son, and my parents were already in years, the care of providing for the family, and the management of our little farm, devolved on me; under these anxieties I felt the want of a housekeeper, and was induced to look out for a partner, that might be a help-meet through life. I had always considered marriage an important act; and upon being rightly guided in this step would depend my earthly happiness, and, by which also, my eternal welfare might be greatly promoted or retarded. I cried unto the Lord for direction, and have reason to believe he heard my prayer.

Through the aid of Divine Grace I had entered into covenant to follow my Saviour wherever he might be pleased to lead; and as I had to expect suffering and persecution in my future pilgrimage, I deemed it to be my duty, to make known my religious views to my intended partner; and left it for her consideration, whether she could feel it right to become united to me under such a prospect. We were ultimately joined to each other, in the promise to be faithful unto death.

After our marriage we lived in the family with my parents. My father had a single brother, a high professor, and learned in the Scriptures; but a man of such a pharisaical spirit, that he became our bitterest enemy; and also excited my father against us. After the death of my mother, our persecution increased. For conscience sake, we could no longer conform to many religious customs; neither could we condescend to the selfish practices of men, in our dealing, but endeavoured to act uprightly, and to walk in accordance with the spirit of the Gospel.

Our conduct displeased my uncle, and drew from him many bitter reproaches. He proceeded so far as to threaten us with dismission from the family. In this trying position, I prayed to my Heavenly Father for direction; and felt an inward assurance, that it would be right for me to wait until we should be turned out of doors; but that it must not be my own act.

When reasoning on the subject, I was anxious to know to what place I should go when driven from my father's house; but my fears were abated, when I reflected on the many difficulties over which I had been helped in past times; my troubled spirit was calmed, and I became resigned, patiently to wait for the opening of Providence, which was soon made manifest in a remarkable manner; for it was in this state of suspense that my aged father was suddenly removed by death; and I became heir to the one-half of his property. While reflecting on the dealings of Providence with me, and the need I had to seek after and rely on Divine guidance; it occurred to me, that great care was necessary to discern that which proceeded from a right spirit. For want of this discrimination, I have known many upright souls misled, in taking that for revelation, which was only the working of the imagination. The apostle John exhorts us "to try the spirits, whether they be of God."

Some time before the Revolution, I was chosen director of the choir (chorrichter) in the church, the performance of which office required an oath; but as the command in the New Testament, "Swear not at all" was weighty on my spirit, I could not take any oath, but give my yea, yea, and my nay, nay. Such a declaration was, at that time, quite a new thing: and the magistrate was greatly surprised to find me determined to abide by the Scripture command, but he did not deal severely with me. The same requirement was repeated by his successor; who, finding me firm in my resistance, the matter ended with a slight punishment.

Among my acquaintance with pious people, some were considered as fathers in the church. I am free to mention one particular in which these well-disposed persons would have led me into religious exercises beyond my strength and experience, had not my Heavenly Father preserved me. Private assemblies had existed before my conversion; and as some of the individuals who frequented them considered me a converted character, and possessed of some ability, and a considerable knowledge of the Bible, they appointed me to exhort in their public assemblies. But this appeared to me such a serious matter, that I could not accept of it through the appointment of man: for, according to my conviction, I believed that the exercise of such an office in the church required a divine apostolic *call*.

I prayed earnestly for direction how to act, and received, as I believe, an intimation in my heart that I must dwell deeper in humility before the Lord, to receive power from on high.

I continued to attend the meetings; but was not easy to be put forward to speak in them at the instigation of others; yet when I felt the constraining influence of the Spirit, I uttered what was in my heart, mostly in few words, and the Lord caused his blessing to rest upon them.

I was entreated by different sects and parties to join them in church fellowship, but I could not feel freedom to unite myself exclusively to any religious body. I saw much in all of them with which I could not conscientiously unite; and was sometimes tempted to absent myself from their assemblies altogether. But this did not bring peace to my own mind; I therefore continued to meet with the people, and as I believed myself called to minister among them, I was also called to imitate the example of our great High Priest, and patiently bear with the failings of others, from an humiliating sense of having many imperfections of my own. I may have erred, in looking for too much perfection in the members of Christ's church on earth; but I have ever found that to violate my religious principles never failed to wound my conscience.

When I sometimes looked at the corrupt state of professing Christendom, and contrasted it with that love to God and purity of heart which are essential to a right union of the church in the Holy Head, the passage in the prophet Hosea appeared instructive to me, " I will betroth thee unto me in righteousness, and in judgment, and in loving-kindness and in mercies; I will even betroth thee unto me in faithfulness, and thou shalt know the Lord."

This language sets forth the close union of Christ with His church, and, consequently, with each individual member of it. The ground of this union is the unchanging loving-kindness and righteousness of God, who requires that His judgment should pass on the transgressing nature, until the penitent receives pardoning mercy, through Jesus Christ, the bridegroom of souls: who of God, is "made unto us wisdom and righteousness, and sanctification and redemption."

Since the first of my awakening, I have had to experience much of the righteous judgment of God; not only on the evil, but also on that which bore the semblance of good, in order that it should be tried as gold in the fire. Earnest were my cries to the Father of Mercies, that the work of redemption might be perfected in me by the Spirit of my Redeemer; and that my experience in the things of God might be real; it was the substance that my soul longed for; shadows could no longer satisfy me. I saw with regret, that professors rested too much in the outward form, without seeking after vital religion; and that the soul once awakened had need to be doubly watchful, not to fall back into a state of ease and unwatchfulness.

As the Holy Spirit that convicted me of sin in the days of my awakening continued to enlighten and instruct me, I had precious openings regarding christian doctrine. The Scriptures of the Old and New Testaments appeared to me in a new light; all in beautiful harmony connected together as one chain of Gospel Truth. I delighted to meditate on them, and to wait before God in silence, and longed that christians in general might come to experience that blessed declaration, " All thy children shall be taught of the Lord, and great shall be the peace of thy children."

I became uneasy with my former method of prayer, whether from books, or from what I had learned by heart; and as I had heard speak of men, who could pray through the aid of the Spirit, without the help of books, I earnestly desired to be enabled to do the same; when it was inwardly intimated to me: "thou must *first* persevere in waiting before God, in the spirit of prayer."

After this experience, my words were few in vocal prayer, until the gift of supplication was enlarged in my heart; so that I could pray for myself and family, and for the people in various circumstances, in a way that brought peace and comfort to my own soul.

In the year 1800 commenced a new period in my history. Freed in great measure from many of the persecutions to which I had long been subjected, trials of another nature awaited me; and arising too, in a quarter from whence I might have expected comfort. The children we had now living were five sons and four daughters, who, while young, were all hopeful; and it delighted our hearts to observe in their opening minds a desire after heavenly things. I had seen the error that many pious parents commit, in being more anxious to have their children well settled in outward circumstances, than for their religious welfare. For my own I sought not earthly riches.

Through the help of Divine Grace, we endeavoured to discharge the relative duties towards them that devolved on us as parents; but when they came to be of an age to judge for themselves, they cast off parental restraint, and gave way to temptation; their own wills became strong, and the spirit of the world took hold of their affections; they stumbled at the cross of Christ; and despising the lowly appearance of his followers, contracted habits detrimental to our outward circumstances, which, together with some other causes, brought us, for awhile, into pecuniary difficulties. As I was not conscious of any wilful neglect on my part, I felt resigned to suffer all that my Heavenly Father might permit to befal me; and to His praise be it spoken, in the midst of judgment he remembered mercy, and helped me through this long and painfully afflictive dispensation.

After we had in some measure been delivered from a long and painful state of perplexity, relating to our outward affairs, we believed it right to give ourselves up more entirely to the leadings of Providence, and to labour for the spread of the Saviour's kingdom: but our dear children could not appreciate our motive; they thought our manner of acting would militate against their worldly interest, and subject them to scorn and derision; not having submitted to the transforming grace of God in the heart, they were not prepared to suffer for His sake. As we could not forfeit the approbation of our Heavenly Father, nor turn from the path into which He had led us, to gain the good will of our children, we endeavoured to commit them to Him who alone can change the heart—conversion is not the work of man, otherwise our beloved children would not have remained unconverted. The sorrow of heart it costs us on their account none can tell, but those who have passed through the like experience.

Many may think it strange that believing parents should have ungodly children. There was a time when I thought this almost impossible, but experience has convinced me to the contrary. So long as parents content themselves with an empty form of religion, and a cold morality, pleasing to the old nature, things, (as to a life of godliness,) may go on smoothly in their family; but when they obey the call, and take up the cross, deny themselves, and follow their Saviour, and earnestly press the same necessity upon the objects of their care, then comes the proof of their love and zeal to His cause.

For fifteen years we experienced a close trial of faith and patience on this account in our own children; and it is the prayer of my soul, that the mercy of God may be extended unto them and their offspring; and that they may experience forgiveness of sins, through the blood of Jesus Christ our Redeemer, and become prepared, through His grace, to inherit eternal life.

On the first day of the year 1816, and near the sixtieth year of my age, in reviewing a long and eventful life, I had to admire the boundless love and mercy of the Lord, in that he had not cast me off for my many wanderings from and unfaithfulness to Him, but was still waiting to be gracious. Gratitude filled my heart; and I desired to renew my covenant, and to commit myself, my wife and children, and all that concerned me, into the hands of my God and Saviour. Grant me, Heavenly Father, the necessary wisdom to walk according to thy will. Purify me from all evil, that whatsoever I do may tend to thy glory. Enlighten and guide me by the Spirit of thy Son, who has bought me with His own blood. Give me childlike obedience to follow thee faithfully. Grant me a new heart, that thy poor instrument may be enabled to speak of thy truth to the edification of the people, when assembled in thy name. Do thou Lord, by thy own power break the hard heart of sinners, that they may be converted unto thee.

Since the year 1818 nothing very remarkable occurred in our outward circumstances. My wife and I were favoured to live in our advanced age, in comparative happiness; despised and laughed at by the scoffers of religion, but respected and esteemed by those who loved the Saviour and His cause. We experienced the goodness of God both inwardly and outwardly, thanks be to His great name.

My acquaintance would often try to persuade me that a christian might enjoy, uninterruptedly, the gratifications of this world, and at the same time be heir to the kingdom of heaven. An art that I could never learn nor should I ever be able to learn it, were it permitted me to live my course over again. If we love the world the world will love its own; but let us remember, the love of the world is enmity with God; and our blessed Lord Himself said: "If any man will come after me, let him deny himself, take up his cross and follow me."

I have now brought this imperfect sketch of my history to a close. It was undertaken in an advanced period of my life, at the request of many of my friends and in thus presenting it to my brethren and sisters in Christ, I desire that the simple relation it contains of the dealings of the Lord with an unworthy servant, may be applied by His Spirit, and blessed to the edification of those who may read them.

The 23rd day of November, 1827, in the 72nd year of my age.—"I am crucified unto the world, and the world unto me."

ACCOUNT OF JOHANN RICKLI'S LAST DAYS, WRITTEN
BY ONE OF HIS FRIENDS.

For a long time I had much intercourse with Johann Rickli, and can testify that he and his wife were self-denying christians, and devoted their spiritual energies and much of their worldly substance to the good of their fellow creatures, and for the promotion of the Saviour's kingdom in the earth. Often have I been instructed, when travelling with J. R., to observe the remarkable influence his affectionate manner had in drawing souls unto God. So great his love and warm his zeal for the holy cause in which he was engaged, that his abundant charity led him at times to bestow his love on objects who proved unworthy; and when occasionally thus deceived, he remarked, "I would rather that the *love* should be *deceived*, than that I should live *without love* towards them."

On our journeys together I occasionally remarked, on seeing his bodily weakness, and his cheerful countenance, "That it was his habit of inward retirement, in waiting before the Lord, that enabled him to endure the fatigue of travelling, and the visits that he paid;" and he always answered with yes and amen. On behalf of the truth I can say that his was a real conversion; and that his spirit co-operated with the Spirit of God, and enabled him to obtain one victory after another, and through watchfulness and prayer, he attained to great steadfast-ness in the life of religion, which, through grace, was evident to the end of his days.

The 14th of September, 1833, he undertook a journey with his wife, to Shur, where he was to have spent some time, on a visit to their friends. But he had not been here many days, when he received an impression that he must return home, which he did, leaving his wife to prolong her visit;—but she had soon to be sent for to her husband, who believed his time would not be long in this world. On the 29th he had held a meeting, which had been a time peculiarly blessed. This was his last journey, and it was one of much benefit to those souls, who were permitted to enjoy his company, but on account of his bodily weakness, he was only able to visit a few of his friends.

When he was asked if he had any fear of death, he replied with joy, "No, I feel, thank God, that perfect love has cast out fear: but when the time of trial comes I know not how it may be, all that I have is not my own, it belongs to the Lord my God, and is all of grace!" October 3rd he busied himself a little with some out-door work, but soon returned into the house, saying to his daughter, he could work no longer. He received a *stroke* and fell on the floor. His daughter asking him if she should fetch the doctor, he replied, "No, I have a Physician who will do all things well. Now I shall go home." He comforted his sorrowing wife by telling her she would soon follow him. During his last illness she held him almost constantly by the hand, whereby it was remarked how this couple of seventy years loved one another in the Lord.

He was called to his eternal rest October 4th, about 10 o'clock in the evening; and interred on the 7th of the same month, 1833, at Goutenschroyl.

May my life be like his life, and my end like his end

A. R.

END.

London: Printed by E. Couchman & Co., 10, Throgmorton Street: for TRACT ASSOCIATION of the SOCIETY OF FRIENDS. Sold at the Deposito 12, Bishopsgate Street Without.—1864.

A SHORT ACCOUNT

OF

CLARA POPPLESTONE,

WHO DIED AT KINGSBRIDGE,

IN THE YEAR 1841.

———

" And they that know thy name will put their trust in thee; for thou Lord,
ast not forsaken them that seek thee." Ps. ix. 10.

LONDON:

rinted for the TRACT ASSOCIATION of the SOCIETY OF FRIENDS,
Sold at the DEPOSITORY, 12, Bishopsgate Street Without.

———

1866.

No. 114.   [*Price 3d. per dozen.*]

A SHORT ACCOUNT

OF

CLARA POPPLESTONE.

In attempting to record a brief sketch of the early visitations of divine grace on the mind of Clara Popplestone, its subsequent fruits, and its sufficiency to support the mind under suffering and trial, encouragement has been derived from the words of our gracious Redeemer, "Gather up the fragments that remain, that nothing be lost."

She was a native of Salisbury: her parents, though poor as to this world, and much occupied in the care of a numerous family, were honestly concerned to train up their children in the nurture and admonition of the Lord, frequently assembling them together for the purpose of reading the Holy Scriptures, and sometimes engaging with them in prayer.

Their little daughter Clara was, at a very early age, mad to feel the love of her Heavenly Father, drawing her t himself; He gave her to see the blessedness of rememberin her Creator in the days of her youth, and that in loving an serving Him, He would be her God. But being fearful o talking to others about her religious feelings, she did no open her mind to any of her own family; and it was onl to a poor elderly woman who lived near that she ventured t speak of the love of her Heavenly Father. With this age Christian friend she had frequent opportunities of speaking c the interests of her soul; and in after years she thankfull acknowledged that this poor woman had been a blessed ii strument in the Lord's hand in bringing her more perfectl to understand His ways.

During her early years, she took great pleasure in reading the Bible; but she shrank from doing it in the presence of her family, choosing to be alone at such times. On one of these occasions the 7th and 8th verses of the 54th chap. of Isaiah were so applied to her mind, that she was broken into tears, under an humbling sense of the condescension of her Heavenly Father, being particularly impressed with the words, "With everlasting kindness will I have mercy on thee, saith the Lord thy Redeemer." When laid on her bed of sickness and of death, she recurred to this instance of divine favour, in the thankful acknowledgment that this promise had been remarkably fulfilled in her experience through life; His "everlasting kindness" had gently drawn her feet into the paths of peace, when she had been prone to stray as from her Father's house; he had been her joy, her hope, and her confidence; when about the age of twelve, she had been led to a heartfelt acceptance of the Saviour's love, and believing in Him as the author of her faith, she felt that life was a privilege, and that if she were willing wholly to become His, a hope full of immortality would be given her.

At night before retiring to sleep, it became her delight to wait upon the Lord, to feel after the presence of his Spirit. And, as she learned subjection to his teachings, she knew this blessed Spirit not only to be a swift witness against sin, but also as a heavenly Comforter, when through the day it had been her concern simply to obey his monitions. She used to lie awake until her sisters were asleep, and frequently concluded by repeating her favourite hymn, beginning

And now another day is gone,
    I'll sing my Maker's praise;
My comforts, every hour make known
    His providence and grace.

In due time she went to live with a master and mistress,
who, themselves leading godly lives, became ensamples to
her, and the watchful, judicious restraint of the latter was a
peculiar benefit, which in advancing years she felt to be
a cause for gratitude. At about the age of twenty-five, she
was married to a young man, who, through the grace of
God, sought to serve Him; hence they became true helpers
to each other, sharing the cares and the comforts of life in
the bond of fellowship and affection during a period of ten
years: they had committed to their trust six children, one
of whom died young.

Owing to the prevalence of sickness, the depression of
trade, and other circumstances, they became very poor, and
in the autumn of 1840 they removed from Salisbury to
Kingsbridge, in Devonshire. Clara undertook the journey in
very delicate health, with an infant three months old. Soon
after their arrival at Kingsbridge, symptoms of confirmed
consumption were obvious, and it was during the progress of
this disease that the power of vital religion became more and
more evident, triumphing over the feelings of nature, the
temptations of Satan, and the sting of Death.

In the early part of her confinement to bed, she passed
through several trials of faith, under the apprehension that
her sins had been too great to be forgiven; being tempted
almost to believe that she had no part in the promises.
During one of these seasons of conflict, this language of the
Redeemer was brought to her remembrance, "Him that
cometh to me I will in no wise cast out:" and she was from
that time enabled confidingly to believe that, through unmerited mercy a place of rest was prepared for her; adopting
this language, "Though he slay me, yet will I trust Him."
In the thought of parting from her fondly-loved husband and
her dear children, to whom she was a most tender mother,
she was enabled to say, "I feel I can leave them, believing

hey will be cared for ; and this passage of Scripture comforts
me : 'Leave thy fatherless children, &c.' " Jer. xlix. 11.
Another time she said, with a heart melted under a grateful
sense of the Lord's chastening providence, " Oh sweet affliction, it is this shows us the anchor for trouble, and that
everything here below passes away." She frequently expressed her sense of the reality of the teaching of the Holy
Spirit, as having proved to her a guide and Comforter. As
she approached her end she had clearer views of the holiness
of God, and of the nature of sin, as opposed to his kingdom,
obstructing the reign of the Messiah, and separating from an
union with the Father through his beloved Son. Under
these feelings she remarked, " I am so happy when I can
think of Jesus ; I long to have a brighter view, to see Him
as He is—to be out of the world where sin and Satan harass—
this is such a sinful place—I long to be free from sin." At the
same time, it was deeply instructive to mark the patience in
which her spirit was sustained : after expressing her wish to
be dissolved and be with Christ, she would frequently add,
' But I desire to remain here as long as He sees fit ; His time
will be the best—Jesus is very precious ; He is my only
comfort, I am resting on Him." Her grateful heart abounded
in thankfulness to the Author of all her mercies, as well as
to those who administered to her bodily need. Under the
feeling whereof she said, " The Lord is gracious to me ; He
will not only give me grace and glory at the end, but He is
caring for me now, in supplying all my wants : for He has
raised me up so many kind friends, I cannot help loving you
all." One morning on a visitor entering her chamber who
was affected in beholding her extreme weakness, but who
felt deeply interested in her sweet and peaceful appearance,
she extended her trembling hand, and looking at it pathe-
tically, said, " Ah, what poor creatures we are, this body of
mine will soon be laid in the grave, but that cannot hold

the soul,"—and with a countenance beaming with delight
added, " Christ is precious to me !—but I feel the tempte
very busy sometimes, and I long for the time to come whei
I shall be taken home—I can lie in the night, and thin]
about my happy home—I hope I shall have patience–
patience to wait—I have been thinking why I am kept her
so long, and have been longing to go to my home."   On it
being remarked that this exercise of her patience was ii
wisdom and in love, she replied, " Oh yes not my will—no
my time—but Thine is what I hope to feel unto the end—
I do not wonder that people who are afflicted should be ver
miserable if they have no religion, because *then they have n*
Christ—no hope—and all beside is as nothing ; it is religioi
only that can comfort us when we are on a death bed."

During the last three or four weeks of her life, she wa
often too ill to utter more than a few short sentences ; bu
they were full of sweetness and unction, and testified of th
holy joy which was her experience in the felt presence of he
Saviour, saying " Oh my dear Redeemer is so precious t
me now, He comforts me—His power is with me—He is s
gracious—so good—that words fail to speak his goodness
what a privilege to be a child of God—I can lean upon Jesu
through all."   She many times adverted to the assuranc
He left with his disciples, as remarkably fulfilled in her sou
" I will not leave you comfortless."   Thus the faithfulnes
of her God and Saviour was with her an absorbing and sup
porting theme, and she frequently said, " I hope I have no
murmured against my God who is so good to me."

About two weeks before her death, when reduced to a stat
of extreme bodily weakness and suffering, her respiratio
being so difficult that she panted rather than breathed—th
covering of heavenly peace still attended her sick bed—an
on a friend expressing the comfort it was to be with her, i
the consoling belief that, to the end the " everlasting arms

would be underneath for her support, she replied with an earnestness and animation quite remarkable, "I know it— I know it—there is no doubt; my precious Redeemer is so good to me, no one knows, He comforts me—He is my dear Redeemer—He is my all—but I must seek for patience—patience to wait." In a few moments her countenance glowed with its peculiar expression of joy, innocence, and peace, and raising her voice, said with fervour, "When I can lift my eyes on high, and raise my thoughts to heaven, to think on Jesus the dear Redeemer, I seem almost transported there—and, oh! to think 'that if we believe that Jesus died and rose again, those also that sleep in Jesus will God bring with him'—how surprising—that He who is now in heaven should have died for us." Her powers shortly failed, and she again sank into the state of weakness from which she was thus raised, to speak of her hope and consolation in the beloved of her soul.

Still more might be added of the interesting expressions of this dear sufferer, who so manifestly rejoiced in tribulation, and who spoke of her sufferings as those only which her Heavenly Father saw fit to dispense, to prepare her for her mansion above, and which she frequently called "My happy home."

On the 8th of the 2nd mo., 1841, she passed a very restless night, and about five o'clock the following morning fever was followed by coldness, which her affectionate husband saw was the harbinger of death; she soon became herself sensible of it, and said, "Now I shall be quickly in heaven—it seems as though I saw angels, ministering spirits, waiting to take me to glory, where I shall ever be with God, and never sin any more; if I could speak I could tell you very much of the love of Jesus *now*—of His great goodness." She lay in this happy state until between seven and eight o'clock, uttering praises, and making melody in her heart, when the immortal

spirit was released from its afflicted tabernacle, to enter, v
may undoubtingly believe, the fruition of endless happines
evincing the truth of the sacred language, "Death is swa
lowed up in victory,—Oh, Death, where is thy sting? C
Grave, where is thy victory? The sting of death is sin: ar
the strength of sin is the law. But thanks be to God, whi(
giveth us the victory through our Lord Jesus Christ."

END.

Printed by E. Couchman & Co., 10, Throgmorton Street, London.

THOUGHTS

ON

BOOKS AND READING.

HE who duly reflects on the exquisite delicacy and susceptibility of the human mind, and its vast capacity either for
good or evil, will not easily overrate the importance of its
right culture, or the desirableness of having the influences
which are brought to bear upon it of a pure and healthful
character. Among the agents affecting it, few are more
powerful or constant than books. The choice and character
of our reading may, therefore, profitably form a frequent
subject for reflection.

Some persons are anxious to be thought great readers;
but it is well for such to remember that it is not what we
read, but what we digest, that nourishes the mind. "It
matters not," says an old writer, "how *many* books thou
hast, but how *good*: multitude of books do rather burden
than instruct; and it is far better thoroughly to acquaint
thyself with a few authors, than to wander through many."

The mind requires nourishing food. Trifling reading
enfeebles it. Lord Bacon wisely says, "Read not to contradict and confute, nor to believe and take for granted, nor to
find talk and discourse, but to WEIGH AND CONSIDER."
This is undoubtedly the great secret both of reading to profit
and of making the best choice of what we read. If books
were more commonly judged by their real weight, how many
popular works would at once shrink into insignificance. It
is melancholy to think of the millions of immortal minds,
that accustom themselves to reading, which, when weighed
in the balance is found to contain little else than the lightness
of vanity. How many that might have attained the stature
of full grown men have thus become enervated, dwarfish,
deformed, or crippled. With desires formed for the highest
enjoyments, and understandings capable of the noblest im-

No. 115.   [*Price 3d. per dozen.*]

provement, the reading of trifling and pernicious books, th
habit of mental association with low, mean, and unworth
thoughts, has prostrated the energies of thousands and de
based them below themselves.

As an intimate friend has sometimes been styled a second
self, so our favourite books may be justly called the mirror o
our minds. It may be well for us to look at ourselves in thi
glass. It is to be feared that some would have reason to b
ashamed of their own reflected image. The vast accumula
tion of trifling publications of late years, makes it needful t
be especially on our guard against them. The plain truth is
we have no time for such reading: and we must be bol
enough to say so and act accordingly. Let none of ou
young friends be ashamed to confess that they have neve
read much which the world loudly applauds. Let ther
beware of being lead astray by a vain desire to keep pac
with the literature of the age. Let them not imagine tha
any reading is necessary to their character or standing i
general society, which is inconsistent with Christian purit
of taste or feeling. Some of them have very little tim
for reading of any kind; such ought to be especially carefu
that the little which is granted them be duly improve
Let not the precious moments be squandered upon trifle
Lay out the little that you have to spend upon the best i
vestments. Remember that that which costs nothing is n
worth the buying. The book that can be read witho
thinking will be read without improvement.

Let it not be thought hard and uncharitable thus su
marily to dismiss the crowd of inferior authors. All that
asked is that they should be treated according to their meri
No one ought surely to think it unreasonable, that the b
and worthiest should be first entertained. And it may
safely affirmed that he who takes the trouble to READ A
DIGEST the good books first, will not only be amply reward
but will have neither time nor inclination for any othe
"A good book," says Milton, in characteristic language, '
the precious life-blood of a master spirit, embalmed and tr
sured up on purpose to a life beyond life." And when
may enjoy the privilege of communion with such spirits;
intellectual companionship with the wisest and best men
all ages; is it not surprising that any should seem to pre
mean and low-lived acquaintances? Here are those wh
characters are well known, who have stood the severest tes
who come recommended to us by the best judges, who ha
proved themselves worthy of our esteem and confidence; tl

nvite us to partake of their choicest gifts, and, as it were, ourt our society and friendship; and shall we be so unwise as to reject their favours, and rather choose associates that vill degrade instead of ennobling us, who intrude upon us vithout suitable recommendations, and leave us unimproved, or it may be disgraced and polluted by their idle, worldly, or ensual conversation?

But in making choice of our favourites, we should beware of being dazzled by the splendour of genius. It is not the possession, but the right employment of talent, that gives real worth to the character; and they who have perverted and abused their gifts and opportunities, however abundant, are surely more worthy of our just aversion, than of being reated as familiars and friends. The man who employs vealth not his own, for his own purposes and enjoyments, who openly sets at nought the most express declarations of rust, and makes himself great by the shameless fraud: such an one is accounted a disgrace to society. And shall they be hought worthy of our confidence and regard, who having received all their boasted knowledge, illuminations, and wisdom, from "the Father of Lights," have indeed magnified hemselves in them, but Him they have not glorified?

Even apart from the question of profit, if we desire the greatest amount of enjoyment, we must accustom our intelectual appetites to wholesome food, and in so doing, we shall quickly lose our relish for any other. The more our hearts re seasoned with divine grace, the less pleasure shall we have in writings which give evidence that the talents of their authors, however great or brilliant, have not been consecrated o the service of Him who gave them. The true disciple of he Lord Jesus knows the unspeakable privilege of an abiding in Him; and made sensible that communion with such a Saviour is altogether opposed to any allowance of "corrupt communications," he is prepared not merely to breathe forth he fervent petition, "Incline not my heart to any evil way," but feelingly to adopt the subsequent language referring to he worldly and depraved, in a sense applicable to the present subject, "Let me not eat of their dainties." (Ps. cxli. 4.) His joys spring from the pure fountain of Divine wisdom and onsolation, and he ceases to long for the polluted streams. He feels how much is implied in the solemn injunction, "Grieve not the Holy Spirit of God, whereby ye are sealed o the day of redemption," and is often reminded while yet a stranger and a pilgrim upon earth, that "that which is highly steemed among men is abomination in the sight of God."

It is not intended to be implied by the above remarks, that
our reading can be always confined to books that are wholly
unexceptionable. But if, as must be admitted, the tares and
the wheat are not seldom found together, how important does
it become that the senses should be in constant and lively
exercise rightly to discern them. And yet compared with
the multitude of readers, how rare are the instances in which
this is fully the case. How many are there, naturally bright
and intelligent, who, it is·to be feared, if they examined
themselves strictly, would find that vanity has far too large a
place in their motives for reading; who read, in short, not so
much for use as for display. And are there not others endowed with literary and refined tastes, who give themselves
up without restraint to the varied fascinations of taste or
imagination, and by habitual indulgence in mental stimulants
gradually lose their relish for that which is really wholesome?
Others again, and some of them with good intentions, allow
their moments of leisure to be wasted in a kind of "busy
idleness;" they look over a great variety of books, but for
want of settled diligence, their unsteady wanderings, in prose
or poetry, are attended with no satisfactory result. While
there is a yet larger class of listless triflers, who give way to
lounging and indolent habits of mind, wholly unworthy of
intelligent and responsible beings. If they take up a book
after the labours of the day, it is too often a feeble attempt
to think, as it were by proxy; and even this seems, not
unfrequently, too great an exertion, and the future can alone
fully disclose how many are the precious hours, now never to
be recalled, which have been thoughtlessly trifled away in
idly wandering over a newspaper, a review, or other publication of the day, with scarcely an object besides that of whiling
away the time.

For these and many other kindred evils there is no remedy
more efficacious than a sound and healthy PURPOSE, rightly
directed, and steadily maintained. This is the magnet that
can discover and gather to itself, even from the dust, all the
scattered particles within the range of its attraction, that are
to be found there. With this all our reading will be improved to the greatest advantage: whilst without it the
perusal of the best books will be desultory and comparatively
unimproving; the best materials may be collected, but they
will be in rude heaps that incumber, rather than adorn the
ground. And how great is the danger where there is no
fixed aim, that life may be frittered away in empty and
profitless, because purposeless occupation. Time passes on

the mind still idly roaming over the vast fields of fact, or imagination without restraint and without an, object, until the end comes, in which the soul, on looking back, " can find no purpose, that now she can abide by ;" nothing laid up in store, talents unimproved, opportunities irretrievably lost:— and *then* how bitter the reflection, that it might have been otherwise.

And it is from a deeply felt desire that it may be otherwise with the readers of these pages, that they, and especially the younger portion of them, are now earnestly called upon to seek after and cherish an honest, and healthy, and steadily decided purpose in all their pursuits. Where this is maintained the faculties become invigorated; the mind rouses itself for the attainment of its object; in reading, the most suitable books relating to the particular subject are sought out and carefully perused; and as others are occasionally consulted, whatever in them is found to bear upon the chosen pursuit, attaches itself upon the mind. And if some of them, as may at times be the case, are of a mixed character, he who most diligently maintains a sound and healthy purpose will be the best prepared watchfully to exercise a right discrimination, by which the unwholesome will be rejected without injury to the mind.

With such a purpose, it cannot easily be expressed how abundant a store of true entertainment and delight will be found under the comprehensive head of improving and profitable reading. Let the reader who doubts, fairly give it a trial. Let him recollect the preciousness of time, the necessity for improving it, and his own deep responsibilities. Whatever others may do, he, at least, cannot afford to indulge in vague and indolent ramblings from page to page of vacant common-place, or even brilliant trifling. Feeling that he was born for worthier objects, he will rather seek to apply himself, in moments of leisure, to some one department of useful learning. He may perhaps have a relish for Astronomy, Natural History, or other kindred subjects. The study of these will not be denied him, only let him pursue with diligence whatever he undertakes, not failing earnestly to desire that in surveying the works of the great Creator, his heart may be more and more filled with His love. Do his tastes or his circumstances lead him to prefer the pursuit of some practically useful art or science? Let him make himself master of it, not shrinking from the difficulties he will find in his way, but rather doing his best to surmount them; and thence proceeding gradually onwards to other branches, as his leisure and opportunities admit. If these pursuits are not to his taste, there are others which may be followed, not less interesting or important. In the department of History, for instance, it would not be easy to enumerate the many volumes that may be not unsuitably read or consulted of the history, both ancient and modern, of our own and of other countries; embracing books on Chronology, the study of Geography in connection with History, some of the best accounts of important voyages and travels, and, if leisure permit, an inquiry into the origin and progress of the laws and institutions of his native country. Biography is another department of reading, from which, with suitable care, a judicious selection may be easily made of many books full of deep interest, and calculated to be eminently serviceable, as affording examples and encouragements in honest diligence, noble-minded exertion, or patient suffering. Besides the books associated with his more regular pursuits, the occasional perusal of the works of some of our best prose writers, and of such poets as Milton and Cowper may be suitably intermingled with severer study; and he will relish them the more as his mind becomes braced by habits of connected and usefully directed reading; as he enjoys them, not to the neglect of duty, but by way of relaxation from it. He may perhaps be ready to think that enough has been already chalked out, but interesting and important as are many of the subjects above adverted to, there are yet others, more or less connected with still higher considerations, that invite his attention. He who takes a just view of his position, while not mistaking knowledge for experience, will assuredly not overlook as things of little moment the dealings of our Heavenly Father, whether with himself individually, or with the whole family of man. And how wide and rich is the field that is here open to his view. A knowledge of the history of the Jewish Church and People, a sound and discriminating acquaintance with the history of Christianity, more especially during the first three or four centuries, and the period onwards from the dawn of the Reformation, in the age of our own Wickliffe; embracing, as opportunity admits, the more valuable of the contemporary writings and of the lives or journals of the devoted servants of Christ, in various ages;—this is but a part of that which must present itself to the enlightened mind. Whatever else is omitted, *one book* must not be neglected; and oh! that each reader may be duly concerned to seek after and abide in that state of mind in which his delight will be in the careful and diligent reading of the Holy Scriptures, with frequent meditation, in humility and prayer.

In calmly considering the above review, the reader will not forget that it is but an outline of much that may, and of some things that ought, legitimately to occupy an intelligent and rightly concerned mind. And yet, brief and imperfect as it is, where, it may be seriously asked, with such an array of important and inviting subjects, is the ground for complaining of any lack of real pleasure, delight, or profit, within the comprehensive range of useful reading? They who think themselves stinted cannot surely have sufficiently explored the extent of the treasures laid open to them. Is there not here enough for all; not only that which as it is of universal import, all are called richly to enjoy, but also an abundant variety sufficient to satisfy every healthy taste.

But to all readers, especially those who are young, it may be emphatically said, take heed that the *variety* of pursuits become not a snare. Recollecting your own limited powers, and that the human mind cannot compass every thing, be careful not to grasp at too many subjects, but rather confine yourselves to those within reach, which more immediately concern you, and of which you are capable. If your tastes are not decided, prefer subjects which are important and useful to those which are less so. Study not from motives of vanity or from the love of display. Be earnest diligently to seek for Heavenly wisdom, not only to choose your pursuits aright, but to follow them out, when chosen, steadily and usefully, with true singleness of heart. Ever bear in mind the apostolic injunction to "avoid foolish and unlearned questions," which are indeed "unprofitable and vain." If we duly consider the uncertainty and shortness of life, we shall think it needful to put a check upon many curious but useless inquiries, that may be often suggested to our minds, and be even content to remain ignorant of many things, because we have neither time nor opportunity here upon earth adequately to search them out. And if our first and greatest concern be, as it ought to be, "to give diligence to make our calling and election sure," we shall not be idle. Our talents will find abundant occupation in the plain path of practical holiness, and in the comprehensive duties of "pure and undefiled religion." And in this work of faith and labour of love, we may often be cheered with the recollection that the period of our intelligent existence is not limited by the bounds of time; that, on the contrary, this present life is but, as it were, the childhood of the soul (1. Cor. xiii. 11, 12), and that in the eternity which awaits the faithful believer, all his desires for improvement, so far as they accord with Divine wisdom, will be abundantly satisfied, infinitely beyond his present conceptions. An eternity of love, light, and wisdom, shall fill his cup to over-flowing. Freed from the contagion of sin and the weakness of mortality, with an understanding renovated and enlarged, and capacities fitted for his new enjoyments, he will be prepared for all the glorious discoveries that may be then unfolded of the wisdom and knowledge of God, and the mysteries of His kingdom, which in this world it is not possible he should ever apprehend or even conceive. " Then shall he know even as he is known."

END.

London: Printed by E. Couchman and Co., 10, *Throgmorton Street, for the* TRACT ASSOCIATION *of the* SOCIETY OF FRIENDS. *Sold at the Depository,* 12, *Bishopsgate Street Without.*—1864.

POPULAR CUSTOMS

QUESTIONED,

AND COMPARED WITH

GOSPEL PRECEPTS AND EXAMPLES.

—

"Why call ye me, Lord, Lord, and do not the things that I say?"

LUKE vi. 46.

LONDON:

Printed for the TRACT ASSOCIATION of the SOCIETY of FRIENDS.

Sold at the DEPOSITORY, 12, Bishopsgate Street, Without.

—

1862.

No. 116.   [*Price 3d. per dozen.*]

PREFACE.

ALL Christian people appeal to Holy Scripture as the standard of their faith and practice; and it is of importance, therefore, that we frequently compare our individual practice with the rule thus laid down for the government of our conduct, in order to judge for ourselves, whether or no we are acting up to this standard. To assist in this inquiry, the queries which follow are proposed for the consideration of the candid reader.

It may be urged that we are at liberty to adopt the customs and manners of the age we live in. But, let us enquire, is it consistent for a Christian to follow indiscriminately the fickle fashions of the day? for although some customs may be lawfully modified or changed when they can be obviousl improved, it becomes us first to ascertain that, in so doing, n sacrifice of principle is involved. Simplicity of manners i dress and address, in conduct and conversation, and sincerit in all our intercourse with each other, are characteristics o the Gospel.

The moral law of Moses pruned the branches, whilst th Gospel lays the axe to the root of the corrupt tree. Of ol time it was said, An eye for an eye, a tooth for a tooth but the Gospel forbids all retaliation. By this rule we ma not resist evil, nor resent injuries; on the contrary we ar required to forgive those who trespass against us. It wa written in the Law, "Thou shalt not kill;" whilst th Gospel proclaims every man a murderer who *hates* hi brother. It was said aforetime, "Thou shalt not steal;' whilst the Gospel pronounces every covetous desire to b sin. "Thou shalt not commit adultery" is another of th commandments of the law of Moses; whereas Christ ha declared that the unlawful desire of the heart is sinful

t was said of old time, Thou shalt not forswear thyself, but
halt perform unto the Lord thine oaths; but Christ and his
apostle James positively prohibit all swearing.

It was requisite, under the old dispensation, for the people
f Israel, *when divinely directed,* to go to war with their
enemies; whilst under the new covenant, our Lord commands his followers to *love* their enemies—to do good to
those that hate them—to overcome evil with good.

Lying lips were always an abomination to the Lord; but
the Gospel declares that for every idle word that men shall
speak they shall give account thereof on the day of judgment.

Courteous manners, and giving to our superiors the honor
which is their due, are quite consistent with the simplicity
and sincerity characteristic of the Gospel; but far otherwise
are all adulation and the use of flattering epithets, which are
hypocrisy. Neither may the disciples of Christ deck their
persons with useless and unnecessary appendages, which tend
to provoke pride and ostentation, and frequently rob the
poor of their due. In short, the religion of the New Testament is a religion of principle. If the ground of action be
good it will produce the fruits of the Spirit; it will lead us
to fear God and work righteousness; enable us, by God's
grace to renounce the devil and all his works, the pomps
and vanities of this wicked world, and all the sinful lusts of
the flesh, and thus fulfil the law of Christ.

J. P.

POPULAR CUSTOMS

QUESTIONED.

1. Where, in the New Testament, do we read that Jesu
Christ or his apostles, either by example or precept, taught
the doctrine so universally allowed amongst professin
Christians, that men may hate their enemies, may do unt
others as they would not wish to be done unto; that the
are at liberty to do them harm instead of good: that they ma
plunder their fellow men of their property and take the
lives, and yet be accounted disciples of Christ?

Compare Matt. v. 44; vii. 12. Luke vi. 27—35; Rom. xii. 17—21.

2. When did Christ permit His followers to swear at a
or take any oath whatever, instead of simply and honest
speaking the truth, every man to his neighbour? Did
not say they were to let their communication be Yea, Ye
and their Nay, Nay?

Compare Matt. v. 34—37. Jas. v. 12.

3. Where do we read that our Lord authorised his f
lowers to call any man Master, or any woman Mistress, w
did not stand in these relations to them? Can we belie
that Christ or his apostles ever gave or allowed of a
flattering titles to men, such as, Your Majesty—your Ho
ness—Your Grace—Your Lordship—Your Worship?
And on what occasion did the apostles, as Ministers of t
Gospel, address each other by the title of Reverend—Rig
Reverend? &c. Is is not an act of insincerity for a man
subscribe himself "Your most obedient Servant"—"Yo
humble Servant," and the like, when his condition and
feelings are far from harmonizing with these expressions?

Compare Matt. xxiii. 8—12. Psal. cxi. 9. Job xxxii. 21, 22.

4. Where do we find in the New Testament, anything which justifies the parade and expense of modern funerals? Can we imagine that coachmen, mutes, plume-bearers, really mourn on these occasions? Is it not then inconsistent with Christian truthfulness to furnish such with black coats, cloaks, and hat-bands, as emblems of grief which they do not feel?

5. When did our Lord or his disciples address themselves, to a single person, in the plural language? Did they not invariably speak to every individual, however high in rank or excellent in character, without flattery, and in accordance with simple truth, in the singular number? On what ground does a professing Christian address our Heavenly Father in the singular number, and yet take offence on being so addressed himself?

Compare Matt. vi. 9—13. Acts xxiv. 10—14. and *passim*.

6. Whenever did they call the months of the year by the heathen names, January, February, &c., or the days of the week, Sunday Monday? &c. And when did they deviate, in these particulars, from the simple and natural mode of designating those periods of time in their numerical order, as First Month, Second Month, &c. First Day, Second Day? &c.

Compare Gen. chap. i. 5—8. and *passim*, and ii. 2, 3; viii. 13—14. Luke xxiv. 1. John ii. 1.

7. When and where did any disciple uncover his head, or bow his body, or bend his knee in token of reverence to any man or any place, but to the Lord alone? Is not He the same now as ever he was, a jealous God who will not give his glory to another?

Compare Eph. iii. 14.

8. Where do we read in the New Testament, that the apostles allowed their converts to trifle away their time in vain amusements, or to indulge in the pomps and vanities of this wicked world, or to be conformed to the fashions of it, or to be curious in adorning their persons, in dressing the hair, or putting on of apparel?

Compare Matt. vi. 25—34. John xvii. 15, 16. 1 Tim. ii. 9, 10.

9. Where do we read that the apostles of our Lord instituted the observance of any particular days or times, as Shrove-Tuesday—Ash-Wednesday—Holy Thursday—Good Friday,—Lent and Easter? And do not the very names given to them, such as—Christ-mass—Lam-mass—Michael-mass, &c., denote their origin?

Compare 2 Cor. vi. 2. Gal. iv. 9—11.

10. Where do we read that the upper chamber, or the other places where Christ or his apostles ministered, or the place where prayer was wont to be made, or whatsoever house the disciples assembled in for divine worship, was previously consecrated for that service, by any form or ceremony? Or the parcel of land where they buried their dead, was it pronounced to be, "Holy Ground?" Is not the whole earth the Lord's and the fulness thereof?

Compare Matt. chap. xiv. 23; xxvi. 36. Acts i. 13—15; ii. 1.
1 Cor. xvi. 19. Luke xxiii. 50—53. Mark vi. 29.

11. Where do the ministers of religion find, in the New Testament, that Christ or his apostles ever preached for money; or appealed to the authority of the magistrate to obtain for them a maintenance from the people? Are not all true preachers of the Gospel now, as ever, "inwardly moved thereto by the Holy Ghost?" Does not the love of Christ and a concern for his flock, over which they are called to be overseers, constrain them? Yea, is not a wo unto them, if they preach not the Gospel? Did not the apostles and disciples of our Lord, formerly, preach the Gospel to the people, as they had received it, without money and without price? Did they not work at their own trades and callings: and did not their own hands minister to their necessities that they might not be burthensome to others, or make the Gospel chargeable?

Compare Luke ix. 2, 3. Acts xviii. 3; xx. 33—35.
2 Thess. iii. 8—10.

12. Where do we find in the Bible that a college or classical education is essential to the true Gospel ministry? Does not the Holy Spirit now, as heretofore, send by whom He will send, anointing and moving, here one and there another, to preach the glad tidings of the Gospel, not in the enticing words of man's wisdom, or after the learning of this world, but in demonstration of the Spirit and with power? Were not some of the most eminent of the apostles chosen of the Lord from amongst the poor and unlearned of this world? and was there not given them, in the same hour, without any previous study, that which they should speak to the people? Where do we find that any of the primitive churches had one appointed minister, and only one; or, on what occasion did the people choose their own pastor? Is not the true anointing and appointing to the ministry now, as heretofore, the prerogative of Christ, the only head of His Church?

Compare Matt. iv. 18—22. John i. 35—49. Mark x. 28. Acts iv. 13; xiii. 2—4. 1 Cor. ii. chap. Gal. i. 15—19. Ephes. iii. 1—12. 1 Cor. xiv. 13.

Lastly. Taking the Holy Scriptures for our rule, does not there appear in the practices here brought under review much inconsistency with the purity and simplicity of the Gospel of Christ, and consequently with true Protestantism? Candidly and carefully weighing the precepts and example of our blessed Lord and his immediate followers, must we not acknowledge that the genuine principles of Christianity appear to lead out of all these practices; practices which superstition has engendered, and which education and example and want of consideration have sanctioned amongst those who wish to be considered as followers of Him, whose kingdom is not of this world.

None who profess to take the sacred volume for their rule, can refuse to acknowledge that they *ought* to "Renounce the devil and all his works, the pomps and vanities of this wicked world, and all the sinful lusts of the flesh;" and many even publicly engage to do so. How then can such practise the things which have been brought under notice, and yet consider themselves consistent Christians? How, consistently with this solemn covenant, can they indulge in intemperance or excess of any kind—spending a short and uncertain mortality in visiting theatres, or other places of vain amusements—in playing at cards—in music and dancing—in horse racing, hunting and shooting for diversion, or in other similar pursuits? Let the considerate reader judge.

"Enter ye in at the strait gate. ***** because strait is the gate, and narrow is the way, which leadeth unto life." Matt. vii. 13, 14.

"Whosoever doth not bear his cross, and come after me, cannot be my disciple." Luke xiv. 27.

"Be not conformed to this world: but be ye transformed by the renewing of your mind, that ye may prove what is, that good, and acceptable, and perfect will of God." Rom. xii. 1, 2.

"Finally, brethren, whatsoever things are true, whatsoever things are honest, whatsoever things are just, whatsoever things are pure, whatsoever things are lovely, whatsoever things are of good report; if there be any virtue, and if there be any praise, think on these things. Those things, which ye have both learned, and received, and heard, and seen in me, do: and the God of peace shall be with you." Phil. iv. 8, 9.

END.

Printed by E. Couchman and Co., 10, Throgmorton Street, London.

COMPENDIOUS VIEW

OF

THE TITHE SYSTEM,

ITS ORIGIN AND PROGRESS;

THE CONVERSION OF TITHES INTO TITHE-RENT-CHARGE, &c.

IT is the duty of all Christians to contribute liberally, according to their ability and consciences, for purposes of a religious and charitable nature, as need requires. No claim for tithe, or an exact tenth part of produce, profit, or income, is to be deduced from the law of nature; nor is there any moral or universal reason for contributing that or any other specific part. Religious and charitable objects, being many and various, are to be conscientiously estimated by each individual who contributes; there being no inherent and absolute claim in any one such object, to the exclusion of others. Abraham's gift of a tithe of the spoils to Melchizedek, and Jacob's vow to give the tenth of his increase to God, were spontaneous acts of special devotion. Similar consecrations were practised occasionally among the ancient heathen.

Under the dispensation of the Mosaic Law, the Israelites rendered tithes of the increase of their land to the Levites, who performed the common manual or personal offices of the tabernacle and temple; the priests, the sons of Aaron, having only a tenth of the tithes, with the first-fruits, first-born, &c.[*] The tribe of Levi had not any share allotted to them, in the territory of Canaan, as each of the other tribes of Israel had; as a substitute for this privation, and for other reasons, tithes were given to them. Another tenth or tithe appears to have been devoted for two successive years to sacred feasts, and every third year to poor Levites, the strangers, the fatherless, and the widows, who were to eat and be satisfied.[†] Among the Israelites, no legal provision existed for the recovery of tithes, as for debts from one man to another; but he that did not bring them robbed God, and was subject to punishment from him alone. Tithes were due by the Mosaic Law, being part of the Jewish polity; which law and polity, together with the Levitical

---

[*] Numb., xviii. 26—28. Neh., x. 30. Josephus Antiq., 4—8. Selden, 2—2.

[†] Selden, 2—3. Septuagint, Deut., xxvi. 12.

[*Price 6d. per dozen.*]

priesthood, were entirely abrogated by the coming and death of Christ; and, consequently, tithes as dependent on them. Therefore, to assert the claim of tithes now, on the ground of the Jewish practice, would be, as some eminent reformers have observed, to re-enact one of the ceremonial or typical observances of the law, which were to continue only till the Messiah came; and would be virtually a denial of his coming.*

We do not find that Jesus Christ commanded tithes under the Gospel dispensation, neither were they received by himself or by any of his apostles. There is no direction in the apostolic epistles for the payment of them, nor are they named in the New Testament, as a provision for the maintenance of Gospel ministers. Christ described himself, as not come to be ministered unto, but to minister; saying that it was enough for the disciple to be as his master and the servant as his Lord, and pointing their attention chiefly to a reward in heaven: and when he sent forth his disciples to preach and to do good to those among whom they came, he commanded them, as they had received freely, to give also freely to others. Nevertheless, he ordained that they who preach the Gospel should live of the Gospel; eating and drinking such things as should be given them, because the labourer is worthy of his reward. He also directed that, if any would not receive them, they should depart from thence, and shake the dust off their feet as a testimony against such. Paul, while he asserted the power of himself and his fellow-labourers to receive temporal things of those to whom they ministered spiritual things, declared that he had not used even this power, but that himself and others wrought with their hands for their support, and that if any would not work, neither should they eat. Therefore we feel warranted in concluding that the system of tithes, or of other stipulated payments for the preaching of the word, is not sanctioned under the Gospel dispensation, by the authority of Christ or of his apostles. On the contrary, the early believers were strictly cautioned to beware of covetousness, and the elders were commanded to feed the flock; the apostles especially foretold that grievous wolves should enter in among them, "not sparing the flock;" and, that "false teachers should, through covetousness, make merchandise" of the people, "teaching things which they ought not, for filthy lucre's sake."

* See the language of W. Brute, W. Thorpe, W. Swinderby, and others in Fox' Acts and Monuments, vol. I.; also W. Fulk, on Heb. vii.; Willett's Synopsis, &c.

So complete was the abolition of the Jewish law and usages after·the death of Christ, that, in the early succeeding days of the Christian church, and even for the first 300 years, tithes were neither demanded nor paid; although certain pretended apostolical constitutions assert the contrary.* But as the purity and simplicity of Christianity were departed from and corrupted—as "the mystery of iniquity" which had been foretold, began to work—and as avarice, ignorance, and superstition, with other evils, obtained the ascendancy, the practice of receiving pecuniary payments, in express return for the exercise of the ministry, was gradually introduced. These payments were at first drawn from the common funds of the several local churches, raised by voluntary contributions of the people, and by donations of houses, lands, &c., from individuals; which funds had been specially provided for the use of the poor and helpless. In the 4th and 5th centuries, when such demands increased, some of the ecclesiastical authorities pressed the people to contribute more largely, and not to be less generous than the ancient Jews, who gave a tenth of their increase.†

Avarice and corruption making further inroads, the clergy, as they were now called, urged the payment of tithes to be due by the example of the Mosaic law; and introduced the idea that such payments, and transfers of larger property to the church, or rather to its officers, were acts of the greatest piety and merit. Yet the priests among the ancient Israelites, as already observed, received only a tenth of the tithes, or a hundredth part of the increase of the land, with the first-fruits, &c. Christian ministers, therefore, assuming to stand in their place, could not claim tithes by virtue of any analogy or example from them; the tithes having been anciently possessed by the Levites, of whom the family of Aaron alone were priests, no others being permitted to exercise that holy office on pain of death.

Yet, in process of time, many of the superstitious priest-ridden monarchs of ancient Britain, and of other nations, misled by those false notions, and blinded by the delusive expectation of thus atoning for past sins, and obtaining salvation for themselves and their ancestors, decreed that tithes should thenceforward be paid by their subjects, and devoted

* See Selden's History of Tithes, chap. 4, and the authorities quoted by him. Eusebius, in his Ecclesiastical History to the 4th century, frequently mentions church lands, but says nothing of tithes; also the other historians of that age.
† Ambrose, Augustin, Jerome, Chrysostom, &c.

much of their property to ecclesiastical purposes. The grant
of Ethelwolf, king of the West Saxons, or of England, about
the year 855, is the principal one, as respects this country.*
Tithes being the tenth of the produce and fruits of every
man's industry, these princely donors, who undertook to bind
the people to the payment of them in after ages, manifestly
exceeded their legitimate powers, and acted unjustly; each
man having a natural and inherent right to the fruits of his
own honest exertions. Strong resistance was made in many
countries to the fulfilment of these oppressive decrees; but so
great were the power and avarice of the clergy, and the superstition and ignorance of the reigning princes, that the yoke
was at length generally enforced on the people. This was not
effected till after the year 1000, when the pope had usurped
dominion over the greatest part of Europe, and almost all
emperors, kings, and princes, were brought under his arbitrary and galling sway. Thus the system was introduced
in the night of apostacy and superstition; and was, like the
inquisition, transubstantiation, image-worship, purgatory,
and other false and absurd doctrines and practices, set up
in a dark and grossly degenerate age. Most of the popes,
who were chief instruments in establishing it, were men of
great superstition, sordid avarice, vast ambition, and criminal lives; it gains, therefore, no moral authority and
weight from its authors; but is open to great suspicion
and doubt, in proceeding from such impure and corrupt
sources.

In early periods, tithes were not possessed by the ministers
alone; but were variously distributed, in payments to them,
allowance to the bishops, relief of the poor, and repairs of the
places of worship.† A claim to some such partition is recognised by many of the original grants, by the declarations of
both papists and reformers, and is more or less acknowledged in numerous documents, down to the time of the
reformation.‡ Since then, it has been very much overlooked,
and abandoned; the tithes being wholly absorbed by the clergy
and impropriators, while the support of the poor, and the
repairs of the places of worship have been thrown on the
public, to be provided for by distinct and burdensome rates.

For several centuries, it had been the common practice, for
all to pay their tithes where they pleased; and hence, they

* See William of Malmesbury, Fox' Acts and Monuments, Rapin, and
other historians.
† Blackstone's Commentaries, book 1, chap. 11, sect. 5 and 2—3—2.
‡ Fox' Acts and Monuments, vol. 3. Selden, chap. 5.

were often bestowed on abbeys and monasteries, giving rise to great contentions; but in the year 1200, it was decreed by the pope, that every one should pay them to the priest of his own parish.* Thus the sacred work of the ministry was rendered more and more a species of property, a thing to be bought and sold, an occupation to be pursued for a livelihood. The first general council that established tithes, was one held in the Lateran, at Rome, in 1215, under Pope Innocent III.†

The removal of ecclesiastical causes from civil tribunals, and the establishment of ecclesiastical courts, was a privilege granted by William the Conqueror to the popish clergy, in order to conciliate their favour.‡

The demand of First-Fruits and Tenths was originally made by the pope on the English clergy, in the reigns of, John and Henry III., about 1200. The first-fruits consisted of the whole profits of each benefice, for the first year, according to a certain low rate. The tenths were a tenth part of the annual produce of each benefice, by the same valuation. Both these tributes were claimed by the popes, and enforced by them during many centuries, through a pretended analogy to the right of Aaron, the high priest of the Jews, who received from the Levites the first-fruits and a tenth part of the tithes; these and other papal exactions were, however, loudly complained of.§ At the time of the reformation, King Henry VIII., instead of extinguishing these tributes, transferred them from the pope to himself, as supreme head on earth of the English church, and to his successors, under a new valuation. This continued till the reign of Queen Anne, 1704, when the first-fruits and tenths were vested in trustees for the augmentation of poor livings, under the name of Queen Anne's Bounty, which has been confirmed and regulated by more recent statutes.||

Other large and vexatious exactions of money, drawn from the people by the popish ecclesiastics, for various pretended religious services, were gradually restricted by the civil power, and at length were generally abolished about the time of the reformation.¶ The payments, however, for sprinkling, marriage, burial, &c., called surplice fees, which were objected to from early periods, by many enlightened men, and are evidently of popish origin, are still upheld.**

---

* Blackstone, 2—3—2—2. Selden, chap. 7, sect. 1.
† Selden, 6—7.   ‡ Blackstone, 4—33—2.   § Blackstone, 1—8—4.
|| 2 Anne, c. 11. 26 Hen. VIII. c. 3. 27 Hen. VIII. c. 20. 1 Eliz. c. 4.
¶ Blackstone, 4—8.
** Blackstone, 3—7—1. Fox' Acts and Mon. Wickliffe, Tyndal, &c.

The validity of the claim to tithes under the present dispensation was often questioned, even by papists;[*] while many of the most distinguished reformers maintained that they were "pure alms," might be withheld altogether, and ought not to be paid to ministers of corrupt doctrines or immoral lives. For these and other sentiments opposed to the abuses of the age, many of those excellent Christians were committed to the flames. Among those who objected to them were John Wickliffe, John Huss, Jerome of Prague, John Zisca, Walter Brute, William Thorpe, and John Milton, as their writings testify.

Tithes, being the tenth part of the annual increase, arising from the land, the stock, and the industry of the people, were either prædial, as of corn, grass, &c.; or mixed, as of wool, milk, pigs, &c.; or personal, as of manual occupations, trades, fisheries, &c.; the gross produce being tithed under the first two heads, and the net profits under the last.[†] The claim was generally small at first, but was at length largely increased, through successive encroachments made by the clergy, and on the plea of the improvement of the land, this burthen has long operated as a great oppression and discouragement to the laborious cultivators of the soil. Tithes, being considered an ecclesiastical claim, were judged and tried by ecclesiastical courts, on the presumption that they were "due to God and the church."[‡] The old laws for the payment of them take this for their ground, and not any civil property or right possessed by the claimant; the base, therefore, being proved to be unsound, that which is built upon it loses its moral authority.

When the monasteries and other similar establishments were broken up by King Henry VIII., as head of the English church, in 1538, &c., he sold the greater part of their property, consisting of tithes, lands, jewels, plate, furniture, &c.; and with a small part of the large funds thus produced, he instituted six new bishoprics, also additional colleges, and professorships in the universities.[§] Other parts of their property he bestowed on his own favourites; from these sources arose impropriate tithes.[||] Therefore, all tithes whether claimed by a rector, vicar, religious house, or private individual, have the same objectionable origin; and the differ

* Hales, Aquinas, Henry de Grandavo, Cajetan, &c.
† Blackstone, 2—3—2.
‡ Blackstone, 3—7—1. 32 Henry VIII. c. 7.
§ See Clarendon, Smollett, and other English historians.
|| Blackstone, book 2, chap. 3, sect. 2. Idem 1—11—5.

ence consists chiefly in the party now claiming them. Some ecclesiastical duty or payment is still frequently attached to those who receive them, even in cases where they have been alienated from the church.*

Having thus been introduced among Christians by designing ecclesiastics and ignorant princes, tithes were first paid to the popish priests, who performed the mass, and conducted their other superstitious rites; which appropriation continued in England for several centuries, until the time of Henry VIII., about 1538. On the reformation in the British dominions, then nominally commenced, and gradually carried farther, most of the clergy, following the king, threw off the pope's supremacy, embraced that of the monarch, and thus continued to hold their benefices, and receive the tithes; while some who resisted were displaced, and other ministers appointed in their stead. This payment to the Protestant episcopal clergy continued for about fifteen years, until the death of Edward VI., in 1553.

Queen Mary, at the commencement of her reign, having restored papacy, transferred the tithes again to popish priests; that large majority who consented to conform to her religious notions, still retaining them. But this application to the Roman Catholic clergy, and to the sustaining of their superstitions, lasted only through her reign of about five years, until 1558.

On Queen Elizabeth's accession to the throne, she removed such of the priests as would not adopt her views, and replaced protestant episcopal ministers, re-investing them with the tithes, which continued in their possession through several reigns for about 88 years, till 1646, being nearly the time of the Commonwealth.

At an early period of the English revolution, the presbyterians came into power; and the episcopal ministers, who refused to yield, were ejected by authority of the Long Parliament; further reformations and changes were made; the titles of bishop and archbishop were abolished; and presbyterians being invested with the vacant benefices, the tithes were paid to them for some years; till the independents, obtaining the upper hand, with a profession of still greater reformations, to some extent supplanted the presbyterian ministers, and shared many of the pulpits and the tithes. In these latter changes, when many pious men sincerely desired to bring back the profession of Christianity to ancient

* Report of Governors of Queen Anne's Bounty, published by J. Ecton, 1721. 34 and 35 Henry VIII., cap. 19.

purity and simplicity, it was often seriously contemplated and discussed by them, and by the nation generally, whether tithes ought not to be altogether extinguished, as well as many other corrupt institutions; but, unhappily, motives of covetousness and expediency prevailed, and the system was still retained.

The restoration of the monarchy and the bishops, after an interval of about fourteen years, took place with that of Charles II., in 1660. From that time to the present, being a period of 190 years, the tithes have remained in the possession of protestant episcopal ministers. But little opposition or serious question has been raised with respect to them in Britain, except the steady passive refusal to comply with the demand, on the part of the members of the Society of Friends. George Fox, from an early date, denounced the prevailing practices of trading in holy things, and among his followers the freedom of the Gospel ministry has always been a prominent tenet. Their sufferings, on this and other grounds, were for a long time very severe, under different governments; and have doubtless been the means, under the Divine blessing, of procuring greater liberty of conscience for the nation at large.

In 1832 was passed the tithe-commutation act for Ireland, and in 1836 that for England and Wales; both of which introduced great changes in the system, by abolishing the term and principle of tithes, with many of the former usages, and establishing instead a permanent tithe-rent-charge, to be paid annually in money by the owners of the soil, to the previous claimants. In England and Wales the payments are made dependent in each year, not on the degree of culture bestowed on the land, but on the average prices of corn for the seven preceding years. Some few of the most arbitrary regulations are annulled; but the application of the receipts for the support of a state-church remains the same; and therefore the decided objections of conscientious dissenters still exist. In pursuance of former oppressive precedents, the burden on the English agriculturist was again increased, in some cases by as much as a fourth; and it was made, as far as possible, a civil instead of an ecclesiastical claim.

These various changes evidently show that the government or parliament, has repeatedly assumed to itself the authority to deal with tithes; either by appropriating the income to different purposes or parties, by introducing new principles, by altering the amount of the demand, or by abolishing it entirely. It cannot therefore be doubted that the legislature still possesses that power, and has a liberty and right to exercise it whenever it may think proper, in either of these ways, for the owners of the land or for the public.

Notwithstanding this power, the tithe system continues to be maintained, in a new shape, and has even spread its roots more deeply and widely, in the British dominions. Many of the other nations of Europe, where revolutions have taken place, have long since embraced the opportunity to shake off the yoke altogether, and have thus freed the consciences of many of the people from much serious difficulty. They have, however, generally placed the ministers of religious denominations on an equality, not by withholding payment from all, but by giving to each a moderate salary out of the national funds, either raised by the taxes, or received as rents from the former ecclesiastical property. The latter constitutes a very large proportion in many countries. It is not of course assumed that even this is a satisfactory arrangement, as it still proceeds on the principles of state-maintenance, and of stipulated pecuniary compensation; both which are clearly at variance with apostolical practice and precepts. In the United States of America, it was found vain to attempt to introduce the tithe-system, and it is consequently unknown there, as well as in all the British colonies.

Such having been the dark, superstitious origin and progress of tithes, their transfers and changes; and the objections to them having been so long and conscientiously upheld by enlightened reformers of different ages, in conformity to the great principles of the Gospel of Christ; a very serious duty devolves on the professors of the present day, to consider well the grounds of this ancient Christian testimony. It is closely connected with a sound scriptural view of the spiritual, sincere, and free nature of the Gospel ministry; and bears strongly against those many corruptions of the professing churches of Christ, which have greatly defaced their character, and lessened their usefulness.

Sincerely is it to be desired, that the evil effects produced in the interests of true religion by a system of endowments for upholding certain doctrines and practices, and the suspicious circumstances under which it was introduced, in the light of apostasy, may excite a deep and general concern in our own comparatively happy land—and it cannot be doubted that this will be the case as the light of truth increases. Thus, under the divine blessing, the reformation of religion will be advanced still further, and protestant Britain will not long remain almost the only exception to the abolition of the tithe-system; but, by moral and constitutional means, he generally free and fair institutions will be purged in this respect, and our beloved country at length be freed from the yoke.

May, then, the nature of true, disinterested, Gospel ministry and worship be more clearly understood, and Christianity more pure, free, and spiritual, spread generally among the nations of the earth.

Some have alleged that the various owners of land through out the country dedicated the tithe or tenth part of the produce to religious purposes for ever, and that they had right to do so. This, however, is not only improbable, bu an entire mistake. From the language of many of the earl grants, and contemporary writers, it is evident that larg numbers were unwilling to contribute, and that they wer threatened with punishment, human and divine, for disobe dience. In fact, so averse were many of the people to th imposition, that they resisted it in some parts for very long periods, and it was only by the protracted efforts of the civ and ecclesiastical authorities, that they were finally brough to submission.*

In general it appears to have been the bigoted, arbitrar monarchs, urged on and aided by the bishops and priest who enacted the payment of tithes in Britain; but at time the Parliament lent its sanction to the measure. The di ference in this respect is not material. Early history full of complaints against the oppressions which were the introduced in ecclesiastical affairs; the governing power, how ever constituted, overstepped its proper limits, in the enforce ment of perpetual tithes for sectarian objects, by invadin the rights of conscience and the divine prerogative. All tho who dissent from the religious views, which tithes or tithe rent-charge are employed to maintain, are called upon for distinct and onerous payment, without receiving any equiva lent. For rates and taxes to the government, or to loc purposes of a civil or charitable nature, they have a fair retur in the protection of their rights, the maintenance of orde and the general welfare and comfort of the people. But f payments to uphold certain religious ministers, tenets, ar forms, from which they conscientiously differ, no recognise or substantial recompense is made to them; and, therefor from time to time, a measure of great injustice is committe

* Krantz Hist. Selden, 6—4.

on all such. This would have been more palpable, had the demand been for the support of heathen idolatry; but the principle violated is the same in both cases, and the difference. is only in the degree.

It is alleged, again, that the payment of tithe or tithe-rent-charge is not more objectionable than the payment of rent for land to an ecclesiastical body. Very slight reflection, however, is sufficient to show that there is no valid ground for this position. The dissenter who pays the rent, has the use of the land as a fair compensation for his money; but for the tithe, or tithe-rent-charge, he has no compensation whatever, nor can he have any without violating his conscience; with respect to him, therefore, it is an unreasonable and inequitable demand.

It has been said that the owners had as much right to give the tithes for ever, as they had to give the estates for ever. It has, however, already been shown that the owners generally did not give the tithes, and that the surrender was a compulsory one, forced upon them by despotic princes and ecclesiastics. But they had an acknowledged and perfect right to give their estates for any purpose, according to their own conscientious views, provided they did not thereby injure, in purse or conscience, the just claims of their families, their friends, or the public.

Still the question may arise, whether the owners themselves had a right to bind their successors to pay tithes in perpetuity, for certain religious purposes. It is contended, in reply, that they had not, because, in so doing, they actually granted the labour of their descendants. Had they chosen to give the whole land, or a tenth of the land, they might doubtless have done so, with the provision already mentioned. The alienation would then have been complete, their successors would not have been parties, nor their consciences burdened. But the tenth of the land would not have satisfied the tithe claimant; the successive *nominal* owners must cultivate it for him, by employing their labour, skill, and capital; they must manure, sow, and reap it; they must pay the rates and taxes, stock it with cattle, incur the risk of failures and losses, and yield to him and to his successors the produce of the tenth, or an equivalent in money. All this makes every one of them a party in the matter, and an upholder of an object of which he may entirely disapprove. The imposition is so oppressive in its bearing, so unjust in its character, and so interfering with the privileges of conscience, that it is evident no owner has a natural and just right to enforce it on future generations, thus making them parties to his own religious opinions, and depriving them of the free exercise of private judgment and individual conscience, and of the fruits of their toil.

It is sometimes said that the original titles to land are, in many cases, very doubtful and questionable, as well as the title to tithes; that the commutation of these having taken place, the objectionable features of the impost are done away, and that it is now simply a money payment, into the application of which it is not necessary for us to inquire. This, however, is a very superficial view of the case. With respect to land, there is in general no other known claimant;—if there be, any question of disputed title may be fairly settled by legal tribunals. But with regard to tithe-rent-charge, the case is very different. The representative of the original owner is always known, being the person in actual posses-sion of the soil; or there are many objects of common and indisputable interest, to which the proceeds may be applied, if such an application be deemed advisable, in con-sequence of the long severance from the owners of the soil Though mitigated in some of its characters, and altered in name and form, it is still substantially the same with tithes and, with every desire to judge and to speak charitably, it is to be regarded as one of the main props of an unequal and unscriptural church establishment, of an oppressive system o religious partiality and exclusiveness, which shows itself a every corner, dips its hand, under various pretences, into the pockets of its neighbours, pervades almost every public institu tion, influencing, and, in some degree, perverting great nationa objects. It is not, therefore, as a mere money paymen for public purposes that the conscientious dissenter mus regard the tithe-rent-charge; but as a material part of th foundation of an enormous national encumbrance, the same i principle and application as the original anti-christian tribut He must, consequently, while he respects many of th receivers, bear a decided and uncompromising testimon against the system, and especially against this payment as it chief support; and he will do so on this clear simple groun that it is entirely at variance with the principles of th New Testament, and with the example and doctrine of ou Lord and his apostles.

London: Printed by Edward Couchman, 10, Throgmorton Street; for t TRACT ASSOCIATION of the SOCIETY OF FRIENDS. Sold at the DEPOSITOR 84, Houndsditch.—1854.

A

TENDER VISITATION

IN

THE LOVE OF GOD:

ONTAINING A PLAIN TESTIMONY TO THE ANCIENT AND APOSTOLICAL
LIFE, WAY, AND WORSHIP.

———

By WILLIAM PENN.

———

FRIENDS,

IN that love wherewith God, the Father of all mercy, and
our Lord Jesus Christ hath loved and visited my soul, I
likewise love and visit you; wishing in the same love
that you with all the saints might come to experience,
what is the knowledge, faith, hope, worship, and service,
that is of and from God, and which alone is truly acceptable unto him. John iv. 23, 24. And that you might so
run, that you may obtain: and that you being armed with
the spiritual weapons, may so fight as you may gain the
prize, and inherit the crown; so that the great God, the
Lord of heaven and earth, he who shall judge the quick
and the dead, he may be known by you, to be your God,
and you may know yourselves to be his children; born
not of *blood*, nor of the *will of the flesh*, nor of the *will of
man*, but born again of his *holy* and *incorruptible seed;*
by the word of God, born of his *Spirit* (John i. 13.;
i. 6. and 1 Pet. i. 23.), and joined unto him in an everlasting covenant; that while you live here, you may not live
yourselves, but to the *glory of God:* and when you
have finished your course here below, you may lay down
your heads in peace, and enter into everlasting rest with
the faithful; here all tears shall be wiped away from your
eyes, and everlasting joy and gladness shall be the portion
of your inheritance. Rev. xxi. 4.

No. 1.   [*Price 8d. per dozen.*]

Let me, therefore, friends, speak freely, and be open-hearted unto you, and consider you my words in the fear of God, for I am pressed in spirit to write to you.

First, Have you all turned yourselves to God, who was the Teacher of *Adam*, (while in his innocency,) who was the Teacher of the *Israelites*, through his prophets and of the *true Christians*, through his Son Jesus (Heb. i. 2.); through whom he speaks his will in the hearts of all true Christians? if not, then are you yet erring from his Spirit, and going astray from the Lord who is the Teacher of the New Covenant.

Secondly, Know you the *end* and *design* of the coming of Christ? are you come to an inward experience of what the same is? Hearken to the words of his beloved disci-ple, who has said, *For this purpose the Son of God was manifested, that he might* (put an end to sin, and) *destroy the works of the devil.* 1 John iii. 8. Do you know this by your own experience? Ah! deceive not yourselves where, pray, does sin dwell? and where are the works o the devil? are they not in the hearts of men and women is not that the seat of *wickedness*, the tabernacle of *si* the temple of the *devil?* have not men there worshippe his spirit? (Rev. xiii.) have not men there bowed dow before him? and are not all such born of his evil seed Must not Christ, who is the Seed of God, bruise his *hea* there destroy his work, and take his kingdom from him The soul, which by Satan is defiled, and kept in captivit must not Christ redeem it, purify it, and save it; that may be changed, and seasoned with the Divine Seed, an so come to bear the holy image of the same: to that en that Christ may come to dwell in a *pure heart*, and th God may be worshipped in his own *evangelical* templ in his own Spirit in man and woman! What of the things are you truly come to know? and what have y yet felt hereof? Christ is therefore come into the wor even for that very end is he called JESUS, viz., that should *save his people from their sins* (Matt. i. 21.): a to that end has *John* directed all to him by these wor *Behold the Lamb of God, which taketh away the sin the world.* John i. 29.

Look now to yourselves, O inhabitants of *Christendom !* whether he has taken away your sins, and what those sins are. Examine and try yourselves by his holy light, from what evil things you are now redeemed, which you were before subject unto: for Christ saves no man from the wrath of God, whom he hath not first redeemed from sin: for, *the wages of sin is death* (Rom. vi. 23.); *and whatsoever men sow, that they shall reap in the great and last day of judgment.*

To whom then do you live, my friends, and in what life? Do you live in the life of God and Christ, wherein the saints of old did live, *whose lives were hid with Christ in God* (Col. iii. 3.): and who did live, because Christ *lived in them?* Is the old wine, and also the old bottles put away? Is the old man with all his deeds put off? The old evil and corrupt ground, which brings forth all evil and corrupt fruits; is that burnt up by the fire of God? *for his Word is like a fire.* Jer. xxiii. 29. The old heavens, the old service of God, are they *rolled up as a scroll and vesture,* and *melted through the strong heat of the burning and judging Spirit of God?* Are you become as *new bottles,* which receive the *new wine* of the kingdom of God which endures for ever? Have you, my friends, *put on the new man, which after God, is created in righteousness* and *in true holiness?* Eph. iv. 24. Can you feel that there is brought forth in you the *new heaven* and the *new earth,* wherein righteousness dwelleth? Consider, you who truly and sincerely seek to know the Lord and his works in you, and *spend* not *your money for that which is not bread, nor your labour for that which satisfieth not* (Isa. lv. 2.), nor will profit anything in the day of account: that your souls be not deceived, but that you may be saved in the day of the Lord.

Come, you that are *weary* and *heavy-laden* and you that *hunger* and *thirst* after *righteousness,* and desire to walk in the purity and righteousness of the saints: be it known unto you, that Jesus Christ, who can discharge, ease, help, and save you all, he is near you, and stands at the door of your hearts, and that he waits to be *gracious* to you: he knocks that you may open unto him. Rev.

iii. 20. and Isa. xxx. 18. It is he who has visited you with his saving light, whereby he has manifested your state and condition to you, and begotten a holy feeling in you, whereby you are become weary of your evil doings, and raises up a holy thirst in you after better things. Now then, if you desire and expect ever to be filled and satisfied from him, then must you receive him as he is revealed, and as his holy will is made known in your hearts: and keep yourselves under his holy judgments and reproofs: for *the reproofs of instruction are the way of eternal life*. Prov. vi. 23. Love, therefore, that which reproves you for evil, and turn from those evils for which you are reproved; *for Zion shall be redeemed through judgment, and her converts with righteousness*. Isa. i 27; iv. 4. Love, I say, the judgments of Christ, and submit thereunto, and wait for him, to feel him yet more and more, that you thus may say, with one of old, *In the way of thy judgments, O Lord, have we waited for thee ; and with our souls have we desired thee in the night season ; and with our spirits within us, will we seek thee early ;* for *when thy judgments are in the earth, the inhabitants of the world will learn righteousness*. Isa xxvi. 8, 9. *For judgment*, said Christ, *am I come into this world* (John ix. 39.): that is, as a holy light to make manifest; and as a righteous judge to condemn all unrighteousness of men : and all those that love his reproofs and willingly suffer his chastisings and fatherly rebukes they shall see *judgment brought forth unto victory* (Matt xii. 20.), and that the *prince of this world*, the corrupt root, the corrupt nature, ground, or origin in you, as well as the evil fruits and ungodly works thereof shall be *judged.* And when this is done, and is fulfilled, then you shall know what it is to sing his high praises in truth and righteousness: then you shall come to sing the song of the Lamb; and know that you by that Lamb, are redeemed and saved. Rev. v. 9.

But it may be some will ask, Who is able to perform so great and blessed a work? Fear not, you that seek the kingdom of God and his righteousness with all your hearts: for God has laid *help* upon one that is *mighty* viz., upon Jesus Christ, and he shall make your sin

known unto you, and redeem you from all unrighteousness, if you will walk in his light, as his beloved disciple
speaks, saying, *If we walk in the light, as he is in the
light, we have fellowship one with another, and the blood
of Jesus Christ his Son cleanseth us from all sin.* 1 John
i. 7. And, therefore, friends, if you will be saved by the
blood of Christ, then must you leave and forsake all
which the light of Christ does condemn in you: yea, you
must watch against your own thoughts, words, and
deeds, that you at unawares may not be overcome by the
enemy of your souls; for he comes as a *thief* in the night
to destroy you. Do not live, nor act, so as to *grieve the
Holy Spirit of God* (Eph. iv. 30.); but turn your minds
from all evil, in *thoughts, words, and deeds;* yea, if you
love the *light of Christ,* then *bring your deeds* every day
to the *light, and see whether they are wrought in God,
or no:* for *all things that are reproved* or justified *are
made manifest by the light, for whatsoever doth make
manifest is light* (Eph. v. 13.): and that light *burns as
an oven against all unrighteousness;* yea, *it is like a
refiner's fire.* Mal. iii. 2. For it is the fiery part of the
baptism of Christ, and therefore it is called the *brightness
of his coming, the consuming spirit of his mouth* (2 Thess.
ii. 8. and Isa. x. 17.), whereby that wicked one shall be
revealed, and burnt up, and rooted out; the thorns and
briars shall be burned up and devoured, and the filthiness
both of the flesh and spirit purged away. If now your sins
are become a burthen to you: if you thereby are wearied,
and if you heartily desire that they may be weakened
in you, and at last conquered also; then let *the holy
watch of Jesus* be sincerely and earnestly kept in your
hearts; which *watch* is in the *light;* for in darkness is
no safe nor true watching. Watch therefore with the
light of Christ wherewith you are enlightened: watch
(I say) against every unfruitful *thought, word,* and *work*
of darkness. Stand upon your guard in the blessed
light, and be you armed therewith like the saints of old,
that you may discern the enemy, and resist him, when
and howsoever he does appear and approach unto you;
that so he may not overcome you, but that you may obtain victory over him; for when he sees his allurements

ineffectual, his snares discovered and broken (as this is
done in the light of Christ), then is he weakened in his
attempts, and your souls grow stronger to resist him,
until at last he is wholly defeated and conquered. 'For
this was the way of the ancients, who were more than
conquerors (Rom. viii. 14. 37.), who, walking after the
light and Spirit of Jesus, were redeemed from condemnation, which will come upon all those that live after the
flesh. O this *light* and this *grace* bringeth *salvation!*
for it teacheth us *to deny ungodliness and worldly lusts,*
which bring condemnation, *and to live soberly, righteously, and godly in this present world.* Tit. ii. 11, 12:
And this is the only living way to the everlasting rest
and peace of God. This was the teacher of the saints,
this was *Paul's* refuge and comfort in his greatest temptations. *My grace* (said the Lord) *is sufficient for thee.*
2 Cor. xii. 9. And as it has been in time past, so is it in
this our day, to all them that come to receive it, embrace
it, and love it; and who are willing to be guided by it
and follow it; and to them said the Lord, *Depart you
from all evil ways, from all vain uses and customs, a
from the vanities of this world.* See Isa. lii. 11. Re
ceive you my counsel, which is the living oracle, or th
voice of God and the fountain of all wisdom; and d
not hew out to yourselves *cisterns, broken cisterns, tha
can hold no water.* Prov. viii. 1., &c. Jer. ii. 13.

Thirdly, Are your preachers and teachers sent by Go
or by men? Gal. i. 1. How are they come to be yo
teachers? consider of this seriously. Are they of thos
that have accompanied with Jesus? are they instructe
and sanctified by him? are they born again? have the
received their commissions and are they sent forth b
him? Matt. xxviii. 19, and Acts i. 4, 5. 8. Are th
true and faithful witnesses? have they *heard, seen, tast*
and *handled* that which they speak and deliver unto yo
1 John i. 1. Is it the living Word which they prea
unto you? or do they by their own spirit and understan
ing, in their own time and will, explain and interp
those matters, which the saints of old, and the primiti
Christians spake forth as they were moved by the Ho

Ghost? 2 Pet. i. 21. If it be so, then have they not received such work, or such victory,—through the Holy Spirit in themselves, as the saints had experience of.

Fourthly, Do your preachers turn your minds to the light of Christ, (that is, the life in him,) which *shines in our hearts* (Acts xxvi. 18.); which alone discovers *sin to the creature,* and shows every man what the Lord *doth require of him?* Mic. vi. 8. Do they direct you to that light which did lead the saints of old, and by their *believing in the light* made them *children of light* (John xii. 36.), wherein the *nations of them that are saved shall walk?* Rev. xxi. 23, 24. Do they turn you, (I say) to his *light,* to this *grace* and *spirit* in yourselves, which cometh by *Jesus Christ?* Does your knowledge, feeling, experience, and worship, consist in the revelations and works of this blessed principle of God's begetting in you? so that your faith and hope consist not in words only though they may all be true in words,) nor in the education of an outward religious persuasion by vain teachers; but that your *faith* and *hope* are grounded and builded upon the *power of the living God,* who gives victory over the world (1 John v. 4.), unto all those, who in their hearts *believe in the light of Jesus;* and this blessed hope *purifies* the heart, and *fortifies* the soul.

Fifthly, When you come to your meetings, both preachers and people, what do you do? Do you then gather together bodily only, and kindle a *fire,* compassing yourselves about with the *sparks* of your own kindling, and so please yourselves, and walk in the *light of your own fire, and in the sparks which you have kindled* (Isa. l. 11.); as those did in the time of old, whose portion it was to *lie down in sorrow?* or rather do you sit down in *true silence,* resting from your own *will* and *workings,* and *waiting upon the Lord* (Lam. iii. 25, 26. 28.), fixed with your minds in that *light* wherewith Christ has *enlightened you* (John i. 9.), until the Lord *breathes* life in you, refresheth you, and prepares you, and your spirits and souls, to make you fit for his service, that you may offer unto him a pure and spiritual sacrifice? For *that which is born of the flesh is flesh* (John iii. 6.); and *he that soweth to his flesh shall of the flesh reap corruption : for flesh and blood cannot inherit the kingdom of God : but he that soweth to the Spirit, shall of the Spirit, reap life eternal* (Gal. vi. 8. 1 Cor. xv. 50.), through Christ who has quickened him.

What have you felt, then, my friends, of this work in your hearts? has Christ there appeared? what has he done for you? have you bowed down before him, and received him in your hearts? Is he *formed* in you? Gal. iv. 19. Do you live *no more*, but does Christ live *in* you? for if you know not Christ to be *in* you, then are you yet *reprobates* (2 Cor. xiii. 5.), though you confess him in words; as the apostle said of old.

All you, therefore, that hunger and thirst after the righteousness of God's kingdom, which is an everlasting blessed kingdom, *turn in*, my friends, and come to *Christ,* who stands at the door of your hearts and *knocks.* Rev. iii. 20. He is the *light of the world*, and it concerns all true servants of the Lord, to direct all men to this light: else have they not a right discerning, nor true sight or taste of the things of God, viz., *to turn men from darkness to light, from the* kingdom *of Satan to the power*, and kingdom *of God ;* from the dark inventions, and human traditions of men, to Christ the great *light of God*, the *High Priest*, and *Holy Prophet*, whom all men must hear, and out of whose mouth, the law of the *spirit of life* must be received. Rom. viii. 2. By this he judges men in righteousness, and in him are hid all the *treasures of wisdom and knowledge.* Col. ii. 3. This is the High Priest of all true Christians, and their *chief treasure.*

Happy therefore are all those that receive him in their hearts, those that know him to be their *light*, their *guide*, their *king*, their *lawgiver*, their *bishop*, and their *heavenly shepherd*, who follow him through all things, and through all persecutions and sufferings, and that steadfastly love his cross, (the power of God,) and with all gladness embrace the approach thereof: who have experienced that *without* Christ (John xv. 5.) they can do *nothing :* and therefore wait for his Divine power, strength, and wisdom to govern and guide them. For such can receive no testimony from any preachers, except that testimony which is given from the *holy unction* (1 John ii. 20.), in and through them : because men, without Christ can do nothing, as he has said : for men cannot preach, men cannot pray, men cannot sing as it ought to be ; yea, men, without him, can do nothing to the praise and glory of God. For it is only the Son of God that glorifies the Father through his children.

And therefore let him kindle the fire with the pure coals from his holy altar : and do you not offer to him in your self-will ; no, Jesus did not do his *own will,* but the *will of his Father.* John vi. 38. So let us not do our *own,* but *his will.* He has done nothing but what his Father had made known unto him ; and we must all witness what Christ has declared unto us, and what he has wrought in us (John iii. 11. 1 John i. 3.), or else we should be false witnesses. *Woman,* said Christ, to his mother, *mine hour is not yet come.* So that he did wait his Father's time, in whose hands the times and seasons are. We must *wait,* but God *orders* and happy are those who do his will. *My sheep,* said Christ, *hear my voice and follow me ; but they will not hear the voice of strangers.* John x. 27. Now those that speak, if their voices and conversations are not with the life, the power, and with the Spirit of Christ, they are strange voices, (I pray you observe well,) and Christ's sheep will not sit under *such voices,* nor under *such shepherds ;* who do but steal (Jer. xxiii. 30.) the words of the prophets and apostles, but do not experience them, nor succeed them in their spirits and conversations : for Christ's sheep do discern those that *so teach,* from *his,* for he has given that spiritual gift to *see* them : which is not to be had, nor found in the crafty wisdom of the world, with all its human learnings, arts, and sciences : but stands in the innocent nature of the *true sheep ;* and for them it is like *natural,* viz., souls that are become harmless, and are arrived at the state of *a little child ;* for to such doth God reveal his secrets ; because, by the work of regeneration, they are become his own begotten ; and to such belongs the kingdom of God, and the knowledge of the mysteries thereof.

Wherefore, pray take notice, how it is with you. Is sin revealed? Yes. Through what? By the *light of Christ*. But is sin likewise judged? Have you submitted yourselves to *his light?* And are you therewith united? Is your old self-righteousness thereby judged? and are thereby all your false judgments judged? Is the prince of this world judged in you? Does Christ *go before you?* John x. 4. And does he give you eternal life? Examine and search yourselves; for thus he deals with his sheep: *I go before them, they follow me, and behold I give them life eternal.* Does Christ go before you, and lead you in all your worship, which you do as your bounden duty to God? Do you wait for his leadings? Is it the religion of Christ wherein you walk? Read his holy sermon on the mount. Or else, do you *go before* him, and do you *climb up another way* (John x. 1. 8.), before he stirs in you, before he moves you, before he gives you power and ability to approach his throne? Ah! True silence before the Lord is better abundantly than *forward prayers and self-willed offers,* or any traditional and formal perform- ances; for consider, that it is *life eternal to know God.* John xvii. 3. Now, no man can know him, who has not heard his voice. And no man can hear his voice who is not silent in himself, and waits not *patiently* for him, that he may *hear what God will speak to his soul* (Ps. lxxxv. 8.) through Christ Jesus, the great, holy, and heavenly *High Priest* of God to mankind, who is the heavenly prophet also, unto all them that believe in his name. But, my friends, do you know the *fellowship* of his *holy life,* of his blessed *cross, death,* and *resurrection?* Phil. iii. 10, 11. Do you confess him inwardly in your- selves, as well as outwardly before men? If so, then has he given you life eternal. Again, if you feel not in you *life* and *immortality* (2 Tim. i. 10.) brought to *light,* then are you yet in your sins, and know not the *Lamb of God who taketh away the sin of the world.* John i. 29. For *as many as received him, to them gave he power to become the children of God.* John i. 12. And they know by the witness of God in themselves, that they are *of God* as said the beloved disciple *John, and the whole world lieth in wickedness.* 1 John v. 19.

Beloved friends, beware therefore of *idolatry*, and *worshipping of images*, I mean the worship of *inward images*, which is an *inward idolatry:* for if you show a great aversion against all outward idolatry, yet if you worship God after the imagination you have of God, and which you conceive in your own minds, without the inspiration of the Almighty, you worship images of your own framing, and so come to commit idolatry. And therefore take heed that your worship does not consist in your own imaginations and self-conceits of God; and do not bow down to such, (which is indeed to yourselves,) and then think or presume that you are bowing down to God and Christ: when, on the contrary, it is nothing else but a mere picture of your own making. And this is the great abomination and loss of poor Christendom, viz., that the spirit which deceives man, sits in the place of God, and is worshipped as God (Dan. xii. 11. and Thess. ii. 4.), by those that know not the true and living God, who is as a consuming fire, and as everlasting burnings in the soul against sin, righteousness, and judgment of the world. John xvi. 8.

Now he that revealeth the Father is the Son, the true light; for he has said, *No man knoweth the Father but the Son, and he to whom the Son will reveal him.* Matt. xi. 27. Has Christ revealed the Father unto you? Are you come to Jesus? If so, then you have known the godly sorrow, the true mourning, and that repentance which men need never to repent of. But if you have not known this day of judgment and contrition, then are you not come to Christ. Wherefore come you to Jesus, viz., to his appearance in you, by his divine Light and Spirit, which every way discovers and judges the world's nature, spirit, and image in you; for to him is all judgment committed, and he will reveal the Father; yea, he that has seen the Son, has likewise seen the Father; for he is in the Father, and the Father is in him. John xiv. 9, 11. If now the manifestation of Jesus in you, as well of the Father, as of the Son, is the *foundation* of your knowledge; so that God and Christ, *whom to know is life eternal,* are become the holy object of your worship; then are you real worshippers in the Spirit and truth

(John iv. 24.).; then are you come out from the workmanship, from the will and imaginations of your own spirits,
and from all human worship, and are come to the worship
of the Spirit of the living God, and to live in him, be led
and moved by him in all godly performances, for the
spirit of man only knows the *things of man*, but the
Spirit of God knows and reveals the *things of God.*
1 Cor. ii. 11. (And this worship (John iv. 23.) of his
kingdom and church has Christ raised up again in these
our days, which was set up by Christ sixteen hundred
years ago.) And in this worship have the true followers
worshipped the Father, before the great apostacy from
the Spirit and power of the Lord broke in upon the
primitive ages of the church. And after such a glorious
manner shall it be restored; yea, so it is already with
many thousands, whom God through the appearance of
Christ in the heart, has gathered, both in our, and other
countries, whereby he has judged them as men in the flesh
(in their *fleshly lusts*, in their *fleshly worships)* that they
might live unto God and Christ, who quickened them by
the death of the cross, and justified them as men in the
spirit risen from the dead.

Glory be therefore to God, who lives and reigns on
high, that *that dark and sorrowful night is vanishing*, and
that the sun rising of the eternal day has already appeared
and is arising more and more over the nations in the
world; in which day *Babylon, the mother of harlots,*
[*false worshippers*] shall come in *remembrance* (Rev. xvi.
19.), before the God of the whole earth, viz., that *Babylon*
which has followed *merchandizing* with the *Scripture;*
and with the *souls of men*, (Rev. xviii. 13.) and has *persecuted* the spiritual seed, the children of God, and faithful witnesses of Jesus (although clothed in *sackcloth)*
(Rev. xi. 3.); because they would not receive *her marks*
(Rev. xiii. 16.), and *her fine linen too*, nor submit to her
fleshly birth, invention, profession, worship, and *dominion.*

This *Babylon* lives but too much yet in every one
of all sorts of people, or professors, by whom the truth is
held in *unrighteousness;* when they see not through the
light of the Spirit of Christ, and when their knowledge
and worship of God is not received and performed by

hat same blessed Spirit. ...There, I say, is *Babylon*, that
s, *confusion*. *Oh, come out of her, my people !* saith the
Lord, *and I will receive you.* .

He that calls God his father, and is not *born of God ;*
he that calls Christ Lord, and not *by the Holy Spirit,* but
meanwhile is serving another master; those that attribute to themselves the words of the *regenerated,* their
revelations and experiences, when they are yet *unregenerated,* and have no part therein, but endeavour in all
these things to make themselves a fair covering; they
shall experience in the day of the Lord that it shall profit
them nothing; for *Wo to those,* saith the Lord, *that cover
with a covering, and not of my Spirit : that take counsel,
but not of me.* Isa. xxx. 1. Let, therefore, all those
that are yet in *Babylon,* hasten out of her speedily, and
you that are in the *suburbs* of that great city, hasten you
away; yea, make haste with all speed! Prepare yourselves to meet the Lamb, your bridegroom ; who comes
now to you (who are *mourning, hungering,* and *thirsting*
after him) to lead you out of your bewildered states, to
his saving light and blessed appearance : for now he
sees you, and now he calls you, and knocks at your doors
to come in unto you. And therefore open ye unto him,
and let him in; let him no longer lie in the manger
(Luke ii. 7.), nor at your doors ; but rather give him your
hearts, and let him *reign* over you as a *King,* for he has
bought us with his own *precious blood,* and is therefore
worthy that we serve and honour him, and that he reign
over us : and that he be our *King* and *Lawgiver,* who
*gave his own life for us, that we should not perish, but have
everlasting life* (John iii. 16.) *in him.* He has laid down
his life for you, and can you not lay down your sins for
his sake; yea, for your own sakes? Consider, that he
descended from the glory of his Father to bring you to
glory; and can you not depart from the *withering* glory
of this world, that you may inherit his glory which is
everlasting? It is that wrong false self in man which
only hinders it; it is *that* only which objects against it,
that consults, and endeavours to avoid the cross.

This *self* has in all times been desirous to be in great
esteem, and has, therefore, in all ages, hindered men from

doing the will of God *on earth, as it is in heaven:* but where self is disannulled, and men have had no great esteem for the selfish part, but have humbled themselves to the death of the cross of Christ, that he might deliver them from the *wrath to come*, and give them *an inheritance in the kingdom of his Father*, there the will of God will be done on earth, as it is in heaven, and therein will the heavenly Father be glorified. On the contrary, those that live in sin, they are in communion with the devil, and drink his cup of unrighteousness; which, however it is sweet in the mouth, is afterwards *bitter in the belly.* And though it be sweet here for a time, it shall afterwards be crabbed and distasteful. Again, the cup of Christ is *here* bitter in the mouth, but sweet hereafter in the belly; here *sour,* but hereafter *pleasant: You,* said he, *shall weep and lament, but the world shall rejoice:* but observe the end hereof, *your sorrow shall be turned into joy* (John xvi. 20.), but their rejoicing into weeping.

And this is therefore the word of truth, no man shall enjoy the cup of blessing, or drink out of the cup of salvation, but he that has first drunk of the cup of tribulation; he that has first known his fellowship with the sufferings of Christ, and of his holy mystical cross: for those that suffer with him, shall reign with him, and *no cross, no crown.*

Lean then upon his breast, for so does the *Bride in spirit.* Cant. viii. 5. Trust in *him* and not in *man* (Jer. xvii. 5.), nor in yourselves, for he will guide you best, because he is given you of God, to be your heavenly guide. And if it should be in a way under the cross, (which way is proper to him,) yet it is, notwithstanding, a way of joy and pleasantness, and all his holy paths are peace to those that love him. O, therefore, feel his holy drawings, and wait in his light upon his holy movings in your souls; *Stand still and see his salvation* wrought in you, by his *own arm* (Exod. xiv. 13, 14.); that you may know him to be Jesus indeed, viz., *a Saviour,* as well from your *sins here,* as from the *wrath to come;* and that he may preserve you from vain thoughts, vain words, and vain conversations, yea, from the voluntary worship of this world, and from the slavish fear of man; to the end that he may work his own work in you, and make you conformable to his own blessed image; and that you may be made free by the Lord, through the power of his everlasting Gospel, which is now again sounded forth by his own Angel, to the inhabitants of the earth, calling with a loud voice, *Fear God and give glory to him; for the hour of his judgment is come.* Rev. xiv. 6, 7. And you must feel this judgment in your hearts, that the prince of this world, with all *his evil seed,* with all his *wrong plants* (Matt. xv. 13.), and *appearances* may be judged in you: and that you may be witnesses upon earth for God, and the Lamb, that sits upon the throne, against all *darkness* of men and devils: nay, against death, hell, and the grave: and that God may bless you with all sorts of blessings in Christ Jesus.

But yet I find myself pressed in spirit, to give you one warning more, viz., that you would no longer use vain words, (though true in themselves,) because they are worth nothing; for they take God's name in vain, that use it without life and power. And I entreat all those that endeavour to know God, and come up to the true life of his dear Son, that you make no profession of worship, without the feeling, preparing, and ordering of the true and overcoming power of God: for such worship is not of God: and such professors are *poor, lean, naked, and miserable* people: yea, they are only as chaff among the corn. And therefore beware you of that woman *Jezebel,* the *false prophetess,* of whom the early Christians were warned (Rev. ii. 20.), who has the *words* but not the *life* of the Son of God. Her preaching tends to death, she makes a talk of the sound and fame of wisdom, (but will not afterwards harbour her when she cries in her streets,) she awakens none, she brings no man to God; she does not build up in the heavenly work, nor administer the right spiritual bread to the soul. For Christ only is the bread which gives life eternal and those that will eat of this bread must first come to him (John vi. 32, 33. 35. 51.); let him into your hearts as Lord and Master, to provide and order his, to his praise, and as such must he be received, when he appears in the souls, even as a refiner's fire, and as a fuller's soap, to purify and refine from all unrighteousness (Mal. iii. 2.); yea, to reveal unto men their sins, and destroy the same with the brightness of his coming, and with the spirit of his mouth, in which no deceit is found. He is that light in the brightness of his coming, which you must love, and whose testimony you must keep, and he is the quickening Spirit, whose breath of his mouth revives the soul, and destroys the sin that slays it: for all those that come to receive him in this office, in this way, and in this work, shall also know that he is the *Lamb of God, which taketh away the sin of the world* (John i. 29.), the spiritual passover, the heavenly bread, the true vine, which bringeth forth the new wine of the kingdom, the blessed olive tree (1 Cor. v. 7. John vi. 51.; xv. 1. Rom. xi. 24.); yea, the tree of life, and eternal salvation, which grows in the midst of the paradise of God (Rev. ii. 7.), whose leaves are for the healing of the nations.

This is a salutation to you all, from the holy and fervent love which God has poured into my heart and soul; who am in a travail to help the nations to be gathered to Christ, the light and salvation thereof (Isa. xl. 3.), that Zion may be the joy and Jerusalem the praise (Isa. lxii. 7.) of the whole earth. Amen, Amen.

END.

London: Printed by E. Couchman and Co., 10, Throgmorton Street; for the TRACT ASSOCIATION of the SOCIETY OF FRIENDS. Sold at the DEPOSITORY 84, Houndsditch.—1861.

ON THE

Great Love of God to Mankind,

THROUGH

JESUS CHRIST OUR LORD.

———

By THOMAS CHALKLEY.

Extracted from a Treatise in the Collection of his Works.

———

" For God so loved the world, that he gave his only begotten Son, that whosoever believeth in him should not perish, but have everlasting life." John iii. 16.

———

In sincerity and unfeigned love, both to God and man, were these lines penned. I desire thee to peruse them in the same love, and then, peradventure, thou mayst find some sweetness in them. Expect not learned phrases, or florid expressions; for many times heavenly matter is wrapped up in plain expressions. It sometimes pleases God to reveal the mysteries of his kingdom, through the grace of his Son, our Lord Jesus Christ, to babes and sucklings, and he oftentimes ordains praises out of their mouths; one of which, Reader, I desire thou mayst be.

My intent in writing these sheets is, that they, through the help of God's grace, and the good Spirit of Christ, may stir up true love in thee; first to God and Christ, and then to man. Then thou wilt be fit to be espoused to Him who is altogether lovely (that is, Christ); which is the desire of him that is thy friend, more in heart than word.

[A.D. 1697.]   T. CHALKLEY.

———

HAVING been concerned for the good and welfare of the children of men, and having in my youthful days tasted of the infinite love of God in and through his dear Son the holy Lamb Jesus, who laid down his life for the sins of the world, and in my tender years reaped great benefit, through faith in, and obedience unto him; I have found, by experience, that one without the other, namely, faith without works, will not answer the end of the great love of Christ Jesus our Lord; in that he offered himself a sacrifice for all mankind, not for people to live in sin, but to take away the sin of the world: in a word, "Faith without works is dead." Jas. ii. 20.

No. 2.   [*Price 6d. per dozen.*]

Christ first loved us, and paid that debt for us, that of ourselves we were not able to do. Oh, his infinite love! it hath oftentimes melted my soul into tenderness. Oh! that ever the sons of men should requite evil for good, or disobedience for such gracious obedience! I would to God, that all believers in Christ would live in that fear of God, and that love to Christ, that keepeth the heart clean; because nothing unclean can enter the kingdom of heaven. I do not mean a slavish fear, but fear that is wrought by love; for they that love the Lord, the great, everlasting God, will fear to offend him.

This is the matter that chiefly beareth stress on my mind at this time; the necessity of love to God and Christ, and one another; "Eye hath not seen, nor ear heard, neither have entered into the heart of man, the things which God hath prepared for them that love him." 1 Cor. ii. 9. It is joy unspeakable, and full of glory: but then we must love him *so* as to keep his commandments. This is the work that I am very earnest in pressing people to, whether youth or aged. It is not too soon for the young, neither too late for the aged to begin this work of obedience, through faith and love to God and Christ, if his Spirit is reproving or striving in them.

So that, in that ability which God hath given me, I would endeavour to stir up all to serve him, and to be in good earnest, and not to put the day of God, even of the mighty Jehovah, afar off: but to love the Lord unfeignedly, and with true obedience: since it is that sacrifice that is only acceptable to God: that is to say, To love him in deed and in truth, more than in word and with tongue: for against such a people, the Lord, by his servant, complained in old time; They (saith the Lord "draw near me with their mouth, and with their lips do honour me:" but oh! their great misery was, their hearts were far from him; they did not love him with their whole hearts; that was their great fault. What lamentation shall be taken up for such as do so mock the Lord the great God of Love? Surely he will render vengeance, [or punishment,] as in flames of fire, upon all the wicked and ungodly, and those that forget him It is not by saying, but by doing, that we are justified through faith in Christ: not he that saith Lord, Lord only; but he that doeth his will also, shall enter the kingdom.

Now the will of God and Christ his Son, is, That we should love him above all; and in loving him, we shall love one another; "Thou shalt love the Lord thy God with all thy heart, and with all thy soul, and with all thy mind." Matt. xxii. 37. "This is the first and great commandment; and the second is like unto it, Thou shalt love thy neighbour as thyself: on these two commandments hang all the law and the prophets." Ver. 38—40.

If these two great commandments were obeyed, it would answer God's great love to us, in sending his Son, to bless us. Oh! the glory of God, how it would shine! it would make the young men as valiants of Israel, and the old men as captains of thousands: then Christ would reign gloriously indeed, in the hearts of the children of men. Here the Lamb, and his followers (that walk in the light, and in that commandment that burns as a lamp), would get the victory over the devil and his followers. But, on the contrary, this is the great error of mankind, they talk of God and Christ in words, but deny him in works: nay, some will not stick to say, It is impossible to keep the commands of Christ: there is no perfection on this side the grave: contrary to the saying of Christ, "Be ye perfect even as your Father which is in heaven is perfect." Matt. v. 48. Yet say they, it is impossible; which is as much as to say, Christ is a hard master, in commanding what cannot be done. Consequently out of their own mouths they will be condemned. Oh! that people would but so love God, and his dear Son, as to strive to do his commands; for it is impossible they should obey, if they do neither believe nor endeavour; but let such know, that many shall seek and shall not enter; much less enter if they do not seek: but we must of necessity strive, in obedience to his will, and by his assistance, (not in our own natural will,) to enter in at the strait gate: a man would enter in with all his pleasant things: but God's will is, that he should be brought low, that he might exalt him.

My intention is to awaken people out of the sleep of sin, which is death; and to stir them up to righteousness, and love to the Lord, and their neighbour, even with their whole heart; this is what my heart breathes to and supplicates the Lord of heaven for; then would the end of my labour, in his love, be answered; for great is the love of God in sending his Son, and also in sending his servants and stirring them up to rouse people out of the sleep of security, that they might see the danger they are in, and how near they lie to the brink of the pit of burning. Oh! that people would but seriously consider that which is shown and told them in the love of the Lord. Oh! that it might be laid to heart! However, whether they will hear, or forbear, God will be clear, and his servants also will be clear. But if we not only hear but also obey, that peace that our Lord giveth to his followers, which passeth the understanding of men, will be our portion, and the lot of our inheritance for ever; but this is on condition of obedience, and keeping the commands of God. "If ye love me, keep my commandments" (John xiv. 15.), saith the Lord. So, if people live in saying, and not in doing; in professing and confessing, yet still live in pride and high-mindedness, and in sin; it is apparent they do not love Christ Jesus, according to his own words; neither doth he justify them; it is only the doers, that he will justify. The apostle John says, "If a man say I love God, and hateth his brother, he is a liar" (1 John iv. 20.), and by plain Scripture testimony, such are not of God: moreover, if he says, he loves Christ, yet doeth not his sayings, he is also a liar, and the truth is not in him, o Christ is not in him; who said, I am the Truth; and thus man becomes reprobated; for Paul writing to the brethren saith, "Examine yourselves whether ye be in the faith prove your ownselves: know ye not your ownselves how that Jesus Christ is in you, except ye be reprobates." 2 Cor. xiii. 5. Which indwelling of Christ is a grea mystery to many; although Christ within, which the apostles preached, was the hope of the saints' glory. Col i. 27. And how earnest was Christ in prayer to hi Father, that his followers might be one in him, and tha they might be united together in one ! 'John xvii. : Such was the love of Christ to his church; now, what remains on the church's part? surely it is, that we love him again; for saith John, "He that loveth not, knoweth not God; for God is love." I John iv. 8. They that dwell in enmity, are not the children of God, but the children of Satan; who always hated the appearance of Christ, the Light of the world, and yet stirreth up those that are led by his dark spirit, to war against him, and his seed in his children.

But indeed it is as Christ hath said men love darkness rather than light; and how strange is it, seeing the one is so glorious, and the other so miserable; but the reason is, as Christ hath shown, because their deeds are evil. John iii. 19. That is indeed the very cause; for if their deeds were good, they would love the Light, which is Christ Jesus, the Lord of Life and Glory, and bring their deeds to him that he might judge them; who will give righteous judgment to every man according to his works. John v. 29. The righteous will have their portion in the resurrection of life, joy, and peace in the Holy Ghost; but the wicked in the resurrection of damnation! Oh! that I might be instrumental, in the hand of the Lord, to open the eyes of some that are spiritually blind, that they might see the splendour, the beauty, and the great glory of the dear Son of God, that most excellent Light which God hath prepared, according to good old Simeon's testimony of him, "Thou hast," says he, "prepared" him "a light to lighten the Gentiles, and the glory of thy people Israel." Luke ii. 32. A glorious light indeed! He is *my* chiefest joy: I would not part with him for all the pomp and vain glory of the world: neither would I have the shining beams and glorious rays (which comfort me for well-doing, and reprove me for, and discover the contrary) clouded from my sight and understanding, for the finest gold or choicest rubies. The universal love of Christ is everlasting to them that are open-hearted unto him, and to all that will hear his voice, so as to obey it; or, he says, "I stand at the door and knock," that is, at the door of the heart of man; "if any man hear my voice, and open the door, I will come in to him, and will sup with him and he with me." Rev. iii. 20. And John says, "We have known and believed the love that God hath to us: God is love, and he that dwelleth in love, dwelleth in God, and God in him." 1 John iv. 16. A heavenly habitation, and glorious dwelling-place! Who would but endeavour to dwell in love, and forsake enmity, that they might attain unto such eternal happiness, as to have their abode with the Lord!

This fulfils the words of Christ, "For he dwelleth with you, and shall be in you." John xiv. 17. How was he to be in them? A comforter for well-doing, that they might have the hope of glory: and a reprover for sin, self-righteousness, and wrong-judgment. Indeed it was the great love of God, in thus sending his beloved Son a light into this dark world, to show people their evil deeds, and to condemn sin in the flesh: for he is the sinful world's condemnation, as well as a Saviour and Justifier of the righteous and holy believer. The Jews of old hated him, and many of them did intend to darken his bright and shining light, but some of the Jews believed on him, and after they came truly to believe on his name, spread his Gospel of Truth and glad tidings amongst the children of men, and also suffered for his name's sake. It is also said, "He came unto his own, and his own received him not; but as many as received him, to them gave he power to become the sons of God, even to them that believe on his name." John i. 11, 12. But what say such to him, as account themselves spiritual Jews? See Rom. ii. 28. I mean those that call themselves by his name? Why, many of them trample upon his light and appearance, and despise the Spirit of his grace, which is a swift witness against evil, and lets men see what is good and what is bad; comforts for the one, and brings judgment and condemnation for the other. By this we may know Christians from Anti-Christians, and lovers of Christ from them that love him not: if we love him, we become subjects to him, subject to do his will. And if we love him thus unfeignedly with all our might and mind and our neighbours as ourselves, and with the sword of the Spirit valiantly encounter with the devil, or Satan then shall we be his subjects, and he will receive us into his warfare, and through him we shall be victorious;. for the Lamb and his followers will have the victory.

. I would have all to cast down that which they glory in (that is not right in his sight) at his footstool, and do like the poor penitent woman, that lay and wept at his feet. Luke vii. 38. She thought all little enough to get into his favour. Christ himself also was meek and lowly; " Learn of me," said he, "for I am meek and lowly in heart." Matt. xi. 29. [Yet] all power in heaven and earth was given unto him.—Take me, said he, for "an example," when he washed his servants' feet. Seeing his love was so great to them, and is also to us, let us love him again, not with feigned love, but with love that may manifest us to be his followers, and in this love let us love one another. "A new commandment," said our Lord, "I give unto you, that ye love one another; as I have loved you, that ye also love one another; by this shall all men know that ye are my disciples: if ye have love one to another." John xiii. 34, 35. Christ's love was unfeigned to his disciples, nay, to all the world in general: for what greater love can there be, than for a man to lay down his life for his friend; and he not only laid down his life for his friends, but for his enemies also. Rom. v. 10. So that his love was great and unfeigned. We ought with the same love to love him again, since that he loved us first; and this cannot be without obedience to his commands. Thus undoubtedly we should with true love, love him, and one another. This love is exceeding precious, it thinks no evil, and we may be sure will not do any willingly and knowingly. If a man seeth his neighbour or brother in that which is not right, he prayeth to the Lord to help him and tenderly admonisheth him; yea, if having this love he woundeth, his wounds are faithful, for "Faithful are the wounds of a friend." Prov. xxvii. 6. He that is thus endued with love, is not hindered from reproving his brother, but if there be a cause, it rather stirs him up to be faithful therein, without respect of persons. Oh! the love that is raised in them that love the Lord above all; it is great to the sons and daughters of men; it doeth wonderful things; it is valiant for God: it overcomes its enemies; it is not overcome with evil, but it often overcomes evil with good; it smiteth sin in the gate (that is, in its first appearance) before it be entered into man, so as to subject him thereunto; it gets victory over the devil, for he cannot stand before God's love. I would to God that people did but know the virtue of love to Christ, and one another in him; it would cause them, for the enjoyment thereof, to forsake all manner of enmity one against another, and all things else, how near or dear soever: yea, though they were as a right hand, or a right eye, they would be forsaken for its sake, and for the sake of him that first loved us.

If all people would obey these two commandments, (Matt. xxii. 37—40.) the whole Law and the Prophets, yea, and the Gospel too, would be all obeyed.

But self is a great enemy unto man, and doth very much hinder his eternal happiness; it shutteth the ear from hearing the cause of the widow and fatherless or of the needy, and drowns the cry of the oppressed; to whom we ought not only to lend an ear, but also to administer relief according to their necessity and our ability. But mankind are too apt to despise the base or low things of the world, and to join with that which is pleasant to the eye, and agreeable to the lusts of the heart, (like Dives the rich glutton of old, who loved self better than poor Lazarus,) but not to consider that which is lasting, and would do them good for ever. How shall I express the excellent glory and eternal sweetness of this love to the Lord and our neighbour.

Now I would show some of the many snares of death and Satan.

First, some are too apt to judge one another, and to speak evil of things they know not, except by report and supposition, which too often lets in enmity, and is not according to the mind of Christ, but is a snare of the enemy of man's salvation. Surely, if people were sensible thereof, they would not so hardly censure one another for indeed, we ought to be well satisfied before we give judgment, and then it ought to be in love and not in enmity. It is better to suffer than to censure, or to be judged than to judge. " Judge not that ye be not judged,'

(Matt. vii. 1.) said the Judge of heaven and earth. To forgive one another is every Christian's duty, and without which we cannot justly expect God to forgive us our trespasses, as Christ taught. Matt. vi. 14, 15.

Secondly, Many are rebelling against God, and doing despite to the Spirit of Grace in their own hearts, and trespassing one against another, not living in love, but in enmity against God and one another. The judgment of man is terrible to the rebellious; how much more, if men rebel against God our Saviour, will his judgment be just and dreadful, as he hath not only power to kill the body, but can afterwards cast the soul into hell? Oh, that the sons and daughters of men would but fear to offend him, the King of eternal glory!

Thirdly, I have also many times been grieved, when I have heard cursing and swearing, and the Lord's name taken in vain, which many much abound in, by sea and land, and too little consider, that God will not hold them guiltless. Exod. xx. 7. Oh! the deep sense of this great sin, it hath been, and is of great moment, and is a great concern on my mind. Vengeance from heaven is and will be the portion of all such, as thus violate the mind and will of God. Judgment, Judgment, is the lot and inheritance of all the wicked, who remain and live in wickedness. Although the Lord is slow to anger, and of great loving-kindness, and his mercy endureth for ever to them that truly repent of evil, and do that which is good; yet he has also prepared weeping, wailing, and gnashing of teeth, for them that continually live in sin. But those that are willing to put the day of God afar off, are ready to say, Christ is our advocate with the Father; he maketh intercession for our sins, (very well,) but it is conditionally; it is, if thou wilt repent and sin no more. Mark that well—Repentance, without sinning no more, will not do. John viii. 11. Confession is very good, but confession without forsaking will stand in little stead in the day of account.

Fourthly, Also being drunk with wine, or with strong drink.—Drunkenness is a great sin against God, and an abuse of God's mercies and good creatures. And by this frame of drunkenness, men are often fitted for any business that their master the devil may call them to; so that this great sin ought to be strictly watched against. Surely if men had any good desires in their hearts, or any love to God, they would refrain from such great wickedness. I admire how people can expect mercy from God, or the intercession of Christ, when they are piercing his sides, and putting him to open shame : for those that are sinning against him, are piercing him. But he that loveth Christ Jesus, the lord of life and glory, so as to keep his commandments, the Lord will love him, and intercede for him, and make himself known unto him; according to his words, which he spake, " He that hath my commandments, and keepeth them, he it is that loveth me, and he that loveth me shall be loved of my Father; and I will love him, and will manifest myself unto him." John xiv. 21.

. Fifthly, Covetousness, which is idolatry, is also another great snare of the enemy, and many are caught therein: It is in vain for the covetous to say, he hath a share in the love of God; for he hath neither love to the Lord nor to his neighbour. A poor naked man might ask him long enough for relief, or for his coat, before he would give him his hand to help, or coat either, or any manner of relief although Christ expressly commanded it, " Give to him that asketh thee, and from him that would borrow o thee turn not thou away." Matt. v. 42. How can any b so hard-hearted, as to see his brother's or his neighbour' poverty, and not administer of his ability to the needful' necessity? But, says the covetous or miserable man, have children, or a family to take care of: but too ofte covetousness brings a curse, and not a blessing, upo family and children also. Perhaps one that is covetou may say, that charity begins at home : but let hir remember, that if it doth begin there, the consequenc most commonly is very bad when it ends there. Ever Christian hath need to have charity in his breast, in two-fold sense, or else there is no proper pretence t Christianity; in short, covetousness is out of the lov either to God or man. All these, with abundance mor that I shall forbear to mention, are eminent snares of th devil; and Satan layeth them according to the propensi

of man and woman, and suits them with their nature.
O! I will warrant thee he will colour them finely, and
put a pleasant gloss upon them, to betray thy soul, and
keep it in bondage for ever.

Sixthly, It is he that tells the murderer, that it is better
to live a merry life and short, than to take pains and care
all his life-time! and the thief likewise, with the robber.

Seventhly, It is he also that tells the whoremongers
and drunkards, that so many people are in these practices,
because it is natural for people to be so overcome: but
he doth not tell them, that by nature all are children of
wrath, (Ephes. ii. 3.) and that without this lustful nature
be overcome there is no salvation.

Eighthly, It is he that tells the swearers, they are so
used to it, that it is impossible for them to leave it off.
He never bids them repent and forsake, that they might
find mercy with God and Christ that died for them; but
died not that they should live in sin.

Ninthly, It is he that tells the covetous, it is good to be
saving, and not to spend all his substance in gluttony and
pride; no: he will bid him hate pride, and that he should
not give much alms, though rich in this world; for the
devil will tell him, that it is proud people do it only in
ambition, and to be seen of men; but he will not tell him,
it is a sin to be covetous. He also tells the proud that
they are counted happy, and that pride is counted good
for promoting the commonwealth, and that it is as good to
be out of the world as out of the fashion: he tells them
that pride is neatness; and how many pretty excuses he
has, to keep people in pride is admirable. He doth not
tell them that Christ the Lord was meek and lowly, and
that they should take him for an example. He, the Lord,
did not come in splendour and glory outwardly; but
clothed and adorned with the robes of righteousness and
love. This is my beloved! may he be thine also, gentle
reader! I entreat you, O ye children of men, both sons
and daughters, do not offend Christ by disobeying him:
but, (I beseech you, in his sweet and tender love,) if you
have offended him by sinning against him, oh! for the
Lord's sake, and your own soul's sake, do so no more, but
unfeignedly repent.

Now if the poor creature did but love the Lord its Maker above all, and its fellow-creature as itself, the enemy of mankind would be overcome, and we made more than conquerors, through him that hath loved us, even Christ Jesus our Lord. Self would then be abhorred as in dust and ashes, and the Lord would be loved and glorified above all, for which end he created mankind; but certain it is, that this end cannot be answered, nor the Lord so loved, unless sin be forsaken and hated; for the devil is the author of sin, and Christ of righteousness.

"I," says Christ, "am the way, and the truth, and the life," (John xiv. 6, and John viii. 12.) "I am the light of the world." Oh! saith my soul, in abundance of love and good-will unto the sons and daughters of men, that they would but walk in the way of truth, and the true light of the world, then they would see clearly the snares of Satan; which, that every one, male and female, (especially those that profess Christianity,) might do and escape the same, is the very desire of my soul.

T. CHALKLEY.

END.

London: Printed by Edward Couchman and Co., 10, Throgmorton Street; f the TRACT ASSOCIATION of the SOCIETY OF FRIENDS. Sold at the Depositor 84, Houndsditch.—1861.

THOUGHTS

ON THE

IMPORTANCE

OF

RELIGION.

~~~~~~

LONDON:

Printed for the TRACT ASSOCIATION of the SOCIETY of FRIENDS
Sold at the DEPOSITORY, 84, Houndsditch.

—

1865.

No. 3.

[Price 3d. per dozen.]

THOUGHTS, &c.

EMBARKED on the stream of time, and carried forward with uniform and irresistible force, how many thousands do we see amusing themselves in the pursuit of shadows, or gliding along in stupid unconcern, notwithstanding their surrounding companions daily disappear, and are gone they know not whither. We also, fellow-traveller, are making rapid progress in our course, and it will surely be wise to devote a few moments to reflect upon the most important of all subjects which can possibly occupy our attention:— the purpose of our existence, and the end of our voyage.

If we consider our animal frame, composed of parts essential to the well-being of the whole, and put together with inimitable skill, or survey the means that have been appointed to sustain this fabric, during the limited period of its existence; if we look upon the inferior animals, or study the structure of the vegetable tribes: if by means of the faculties we possess, we endeavour to understand a little of the laws which appear to regulate the operations incessantly taking place in this lower world; or if we lift our eyes to those luminous bodies scattered through the immensity of space, all proceeding harmoniously in the paths prescribed to them,—should not our souls be filled with awe and reverence? Nothing short of Infinite Wisdom could have effected this; nothing short of Infinite Power could sustain it for a moment.

This Wisdom and this Power, O fellow-traveller, is God, even *thy* God. He has condescended to create thee what thou art. Kind and benevolent, as unlimited in power. He has provided for thy comfort, thy accommodation, thy pleasure even here. He has furnished thee with suitable food, has enamelled the fields with flowers, and instructed every warbler of the grove in his peculiar song. He has endowed thee with reason, whereby thou mayest understand a little portion of his wonders; and to crown the whole, has given thee a capacity to acquaint thyself with Him, the Author of them all. Everything proclaims that the object of the Creator is the happiness of his creatures; and if thou be not happy the fault is in thyself. Do not suppose that thou art placed in this transitory scene, merely to eat, to drink, and to sleep, and after a few years, to vanish away like a dream or a vision of the night. No;—thy great Creator has called thee into existence, at that period which was consistent with his Supreme Will; and though thy frame shall go to decay when it may please him to call for the spirit which animates it, yet be assured, that this spirit shall exist for ever. When the present life ceases thou must enter upon eternity, which will be either miserable beyond description, or unspeakably happy. The few and uncertain moments of thy present state are all that are allowed thee to prepare for it. Be aroused, then, to a just consideration of thy condition; venture not to sleep on the brink of a precipice, but apply thyself in earnest to the great work before that awful proclamation is made,—"He which is filthy, let him be filthy still." Rev. xxii. 11.

The only means of becoming happy here and hereafter, is by earnestly endeavouring to know and to

perform the Divine will. This we cannot do of
ourselves; man by nature is a fallen creature, continually prone to evil; but God is graciously pleased
to extend to every one of his rational creatures
the visitations of his Holy Spirit, which, secretly
operating upon the soul, convince it of sin, and if
yielded to, produce a true repentance, and that change
of heart without which no man can see the kingdom
of God. Thus the Divine Being communicates with
his creatures in order to draw them to Himself;
and in proportion as they attend to these secret
attractions, He manifests Himself more and more
clearly to them, and they become more closely united
to Him. In this way the holy men of old were
inspired (2 Pet. i. 21.); and were employed as mediums
to convey the most important truths to the rest of
mankind. Their writings, collected together, are
called the Holy Scriptures, and clearly point out that
conduct which will be acceptable to God. 2 Tim. iii.
15—17. But above all, they inform us that "God so
loved the world that he gave his only begotten Son,
that whosoever believeth in him should not perish but
should have everlasting life." The Lord Jesus Christ,
who is one with the Father, in whom "dwelleth all
the fulness of the Godhead bodily," is the only
Mediator between sinful man and the source of purity.
In him the means of redemption and union with God
were most clearly and affectingly displayed; and
having accomplished his mission in the flesh, and
offered up himself upon the cross as "a propitiation
for the sins of the whole world," all who feel the
weight of their transgressions must seek through
him, for pardon and reconciliation. He is spiritually
present in the hearts of all those who, above all

things desire to know and to perform the Divine Will. He is influencing them to good thoughts and good actions; enabling them to overcome their perverse natural inclinations, and to subdue their wills; and thus he is *purifying*, and rendering them, acceptable, through himself, to his Heavenly Father. "Behold I stand at the door and knock: if any man hear my voice and open the door, I will come in to him, and will sup with him, and he with me." Rev. iii. 20. And again, "If a man love me, he will keep my words, and my Father will love him, and we will come unto him, and make our *abode* with him." John xiv. 23. Infinite condescension! Unutterable love! His knocks are the monitions of his grace and good Spirit in the heart; and to attend to these and follow them is to *open* unto him. This leads to our purification, and consequent fitness for a closer communion with him. The Heavenly Visitor will now be no longer "as a wayfaring man who tarrieth only for a night," but "We will make our *abode* with him." This is the essence of true religion; and let our denominations in this world be what they may, if this be our happy experience, we shall belong to "the general assembly and church of the first-born," whose names "are written in heaven." Heb. xii. 23.

But this Divine Spirit, which strives with man for his good, if neglected, or resisted, will be gradually withdrawn; we may harden our hearts against it, despise its reproofs, and silence its voice *for a time*. We shall then be left to ourselves, and permitted to follow our own evil propensities; our souls will be in a state of defilement and alienation from the source of true happiness, and if we die in this state, dreadful indeed will be our portion. *That* witness for God which we have refused to hear, will then speak out in a voice not to be silenced, and from which we shall be no longer able to escape.

Now is the acceptable time: now, while we have health and strength, let us use all diligence to acquaint ourselves with God that we may be at peace; for though he desires the salvation of all, (1 Tim. ii. 4.) he *will* be sought unto, and he has graciously promised to be found of those that seek him aright.

We ought diligently to peruse the Holy Scriptures, humbly seeking for divine assistance, in order that the blessed truths contained therein, may be made the means of strengthening our good desires, comforting us under trial, and fixing our souls in living faith on our Lord and Saviour. As our dependence is thus singly placed on the Shepherd and Bishop of souls, He will enable us to comprehend those eternal truths which are hid from the wise and prudent of this world, but revealed to the babes in Christ. Matt. xi. 25. And we shall be made partakers of that most blessed privilege, communion with God in prayer. We should watch for opportunities frequently to retire from the hurry and bustle of life, that we may pour out our souls to our Heavenly Father, beseeching Him that He would manifest unto us *His will*, help us to subdue *our own*, and bring us into conformity with His holy law. Every secret aspiration to God, even if no words be uttered, is prayer; and we may be in the exercise of it even when our hands are engaged in our lawful occupations. This is the prayer which our Lord enjoined to his disciples, that they might not enter into temptation. Matt. xxvi. 41. Many awakened souls have suffered great loss, and made for themselves a long wilderness, by consulting with those who were as much at a loss as themselves, and going from one learned man to another, to seek that *without*, which can only be found *within*. The kingdom of God, said Christ (Luke xvii. 21.), is within you; his constant reference was to *this;* his constant aim, to turn men from a dependence upon the ceremonies of religion to the essence of it. When we are so far convinced of these great truths as to give up ourselves wholly to God, and can say with sincerity, "Thy will and not mine be done;" then we shall enjoy that heavenly communion which constitutes the happiness of the blessed above. Narrow prejudices will no longer exist; our souls will expand with love to our fellow-creatures; and we shall consider all mankind as branches of the same family, having one common Father. We shall feel a real interest in the happiness of all within our influence, and endeavour to promote it to the utmost of our power. These are the effects which would be produced by submitting to the operation of Divine grace in the heart. "We shall then experimentally know that God is good. We shall be qualified to taste and see *how* gracious he is, by his influence upon our minds, by those virtuous thoughts, which he awakens in us, by those secret comforts and refreshments, which he conveys into our souls, and by those ravishing joys and inward satisfactions which are perpetually springing up and diffusing themselves among all the thoughts of good men. He is as a soul within the soul, to irradiate its understanding, rectify its will, purify its passions, and enliven all the powers of man. How happy is an intellectual being [who has experienced this communication to be opened] between God and his own soul! Though the whole creation frown upon him, and all nature look black about him, he has his light and support within him, that are able to cheer his mind, and bear him up in the midst of all those horrors which encompass him. He knows that his Helper is at hand, and is always nearer to him than anything else can be which is capable of annoying or terrifying him. In the midst of calumny or contempt he attends to that being who whispers better things within his soul, and whom he looks upon as his defender, his glory, and the lifter up of his head. In his deepest solitude and retirement, he knows that he is in company with the Greatest of Beings; and perceives within himself such real sensations of his presence, as are more delightful than anything that can be met with in the conversation of his creatures. Even in the hour of death, he considers the pains of his dissolution to be nothing else but the breaking down of that partition which stands betwixt his soul and the sight of that Being who is always present with him, and is about to manifest Himself to him in fulness of joy." *Addison.*

If we duly ponder these things, fellow-traveller, and give up our hearts to the guidance of the Holy Spirit, the end of *our* voyage will be the beginning of a new existence, inconceivably glorious and eternally happy!

END.

Printed by E. Couchman and Co., 10, Throgmorton Street, London.

AN ADDRESS

TO THOSE IN

LOW CIRCUMSTANCES.

"All things work together for good, to them that love God." Rom. viii. 28.

MY DEAR BRETHREN AND SISTERS,

WHOM I salute in that love which ought to unite the families of the whole earth, since we are all the children of one common parent; all subject to the same feelings; all partakers of the mercies of God, and invited by our Heavenly Father to become inhabitants of his kingdom of glory, when we have done with the things of time, and death hath closed our mortal eyes upon all that now surrounds us; I have often thought of you with desires that you may know where to seek support and comfort, in those difficulties and trials you sometimes meet with. I have desired you may believe that the goodness of God, the gracious Lord of the Universe, is not confined to any rank of men. Do not think he loves you less than others because you often feel the want of the conveniences, and sometimes can scarcely procure the necessaries of life. Every station has trials belonging to it, and they who abound in riches, and appear to be the happiest, are often feeling in secret, griefs and anxieties to which you are strangers.—They do not always enjoy their possessions. Riches and power bring cares along with them, and expose to temptations which do not attack the poor. Such as are in high stations, and feel they are not happy, would be willing to exchange places with the poor if they could know real peace: while the poor are thinking how truly they should enjoy life, could they procure the possessions of their wealthy neighbours. But the truth is, happiness is equally offered to every body by that Almighty Being, who is called the Father of the Universe. The advice which is given us in the Bible is this: Acquaint thyself with God, and be at peace. This is the one sure means of comfort, whether for rich or poor. It is only for want of knowing God, that so many in the world are unhappy; for if they were willing to follow this counsel, they would know that he is graciously disposed to bless every one whom he hath created.

No. 4.   [*Price 3d. per dozen.*]

Perhaps some of you may be ready to say, "If Go
loves me, why do I feel so many pains, so much distress an
anxiety?" But, dear people, it is not by the design of a graciou
God that we are miserable : on the contrary, he designed u
for happiness ; and though none of us can pass through lif
without pain and sorrow, these pains and sorrows are fre
quently the effects of sin, and spring originally from our own
errors, and the disorders of human nature in its fallen state
Our Heavenly Father, like a good physician, intends that al
the troubles of this life shall prove as good and wholesome
medicines to cure us of our faults, which are like a sickness o
the soul; and if we were but willing to learn the lessons he
would teach, we should know that help is laid upon One who
is mighty to save, and able to deliver to the uttermost, al
that come unto God by him. Heb. vii. 25.

O! you that have many difficulties to encounter; you who
sometimes think there is nobody so unhappy as yourselves
consider, I entreat you, have you not always been more ready
to think of your troubles than to remember the blessings and
mercies of God? Try to find out what is the cause of you
greatest affliction. I think I may safely say, there are no
people so unhappy as those who are forgetful of God. How
frequently do poor families suffer through the bad conduct
a man, who spends in intemperate drinking the price of h
labour, which should provide for his helpless little ones. Ho
many young people are not able to get forward in life becaus
they are known to have been bred up under parents who hav
set them an ill example, and too frequently encouraged the
to tell lies, steal, and keep idle company! Now if the hear
of people were more generally inclined to do what they kno
to be right, they would avoid the greatest miseries of life : f
religion would teach them to do justly, love mercy, and wa
humbly with their God. Micah vi. 8. It would make the
industrious and sober, desirous to bring up their families
the love and fear of Almighty God, and thus remove t
greatest of their real troubles. They would learn to ask f
the blessing of God upon their honest labours, and surely
would give them everything he saw needful for their sou
and bodies. Religion would teach them to bless him if th
were favoured with health and strength : and if they we
visited by sickness, enable them to bear it with patien
and then they would learn many useful lessons from su
afflictions, and know what solid peace is given to them w
patiently submit to their Heavenly Father's will; for t
apostle Paul says, "All things work together for good,

hem that love God " (Rom. viii. 28.) ; I know that those who
have large families to provide for, have often many cares, but
I know also that our Heavenly Father encourages us to cast
our cares upon him, for He careth for us. 1 Pet. v. 7.

I hope there is not one amongst those I now address, who
is so ignorant as not to know that " God so loved the world,
that he gave his only begotten Son, that whosoever believeth
in him should not perish but have everlasting life." John
ii. 16. Know you not " the grace of our Lord Jesus Christ,
that though he was rich, yet for your sakes he became poor,
that ye through his poverty might be rich ? " 2 Cor. viii. 9.
Rich in those treasures which are laid up for all his obedient
followers, where neither moth nor rust doth corrupt, nor
thieves break through and steal. The history of this gracious
Saviour of the world, and the account of his wondrous acts of
love towards poor perishing souls, with the doctrines he and
his apostles taught, expressive of the nature of the Christian
religion, are contained in that part of the Scripture called the
New Testament; which, my dear friends, if you have any
love for your dearest and best interests, I do most earnestly
recommend to your perusal. But if you would read it to
profit, do so with your hearts raised to God, beseeching him
to enable you so to read that you may understand the sacred
truths which it contains.

In one of the sermons our Lord Jesus Christ preached to
the people, he told them to seek first the kingdom of God
and his righteousness, assuring them that all things needful
should be added. Matt. chap. vi. He directed them to consider the fowls of the air, and the lilies of the field, adding,
" Wherefore if God so clothe the grass of the field, &c., shall
he not much more clothe you ? " This then ought to convince
us that the want of true religion is the cause of the miseries of
which we complain. Religion will indeed prove as a sovereign
balsam to sweeten every bitter cup, and strengthen us to pass
with patience the days of our mortal course. It will discover
to us many comforts in every situation, and we shall know
that it is the true pearl of great price more precious than
silver or gold.

Perhaps some of you may be ready to say, " What have
I to do with religion, I who am so much taken up with my
family; I have scarcely time to take a little rest. They who
have nothing to do, may indeed think of religion, but as for
me, I am obliged to work like a slave to earn a little bread."
Should any of you think something of this kind, let me answer,
you have a very wrong notion of religion, if you suppose

none can attend to its dictates but they who have much leisure. Neither the wisdom of this world, nor much leisure is absolutely necessary for the exercise of true religion. The more time we have, the more indeed we ought singly to devote to the worship and service of our greatest and best friend, for such the Almighty is to us:—but religion consists in a state of heart which loves God above all things, and looks up to him as our Father, our Friend, the Teacher of man, who waits to be gracious, who invites us to learn of himself. Let us consider this, and we shall know that, in the midst of unavoidable business, we can lift up our thoughts to him, and he will accept the prayers of the heart; these will arise before him when our lips cannot utter a petition. But, alas! it is for want of desiring to know God, that so many are strangers unto him, and to the state of their own hearts; and Oh what a pity it is, that any should miss of the happiness of knowing this great and good, this holy and glorious Being; for, This (said the Saviour of mankind) is life eternal, to know thee the only true God, and Jesus Christ whom thou hast sent. John xvii. 3.

What a comfort, what a consolation it is to know him as the God of love; and such the Scriptures declare him to be "God is love, and he that dwelleth in love, dwelleth in God and God in him." 1 John iv. 16. This is the reason why he requires us to seek and serve, to honour and obey him. And Oh! there is every reason to love him above all. He crowns our days with tender mercies, with abundant loving-kindness he is a kind and compassionate Father, the Fountain of Light, of Life, and Love. You, who are mothers, hear the words of tender mercy with which he condescends to speak to all who have put their trust in him: "Can a woman forget her sucking child, that she should not have compassion on the son of her womb? Yea, they may forget, yet will I not forget thee." Isa. xlix. 15. Such is the love and watchful care of God, our Heavenly Father, of whom it is declared "He shall feed his flock like a shepherd." Isa. xl. 11 "Behold, he that keepeth Israel, shall neither slumber nor sleep." Ps. cxxi. 4.

From the very beginning of time to the present day, he has made himself known to the world by unbounded unmerited mercy, goodness, and love, declaring that he afflicts not willingly nor grieves the children of men; for like as a father pitieth his children, so the Lord pitieth them who fear him. And will you then live in forgetfulness of Him who never forgets you? Will you remain in bondage to sin and satan, when you are called by the Gospel of Jesus into the glorious liberty of the sons and daughters of God? Will you obey satan, the enemy of your souls, rather than serve that gracious God in whom you live, and move, and have your being? O! think how great and holy He is, who is Lord of heaven and earth; before whom bright and glorious angels fall prostrate in adoration. Think how he created all things by the word of his power, and upholds them continually.

If he were to command the sun to depart from the heavens it would vanish away: if he were to forbid the earth to bring forth fruit we must perish from off it. And will you, who breathe his air, and partake of the benefits of his creation, will you complain you have had no proof of his love? Will you, to whom he has given life for such glorious purposes, be so ungrateful as to forget him, your kind benefactor? Well might king David the Psalmist say, "When I consider thy heavens, the work of thy fingers, the moon, and the stars, which thou hast ordained; what is man that thou art mindful of him, and the son of man that thou visitest him?" Ps. viii. 3, 4. Above all, remember we have immortal souls dwelling in these bodies;—souls which are a spark of life and must exist to all eternity.

The day will soon arrive, when we shall feel that the chief business of this life is to prepare for another and a better world. Then we shall find it signified little whether, in this life, we were rich or poor, learned or ignorant, as to this world's wisdom: but the only thing worth our attention will be, whether we have come to the saving knowledge of God in Christ Jesus our Lord. I believe there never was, nor ever will be a person born into the world, whom our Almighty Father is not willing to teach the nature of true religion: and if multitudes pass through life without knowing it, it is because they have rebelled against that inward conviction which would have led them to a knowledge of themselves, and awakened desires after an acquaintance with God. If then so many may be said to be ignorant of their duty, the fault is their own: for if they have but a sincere desire of knowing what is right, that gracious God, who knows our most secret thoughts, will lift up the light of his countenance on their souls. The Saviour himself sufficiently assured his followers, that none, at last, would be able to plead ignorance as an excuse for the neglect of their duty. The apostle tells us, "The grace of God that bringeth salvation hath appeared to *all* men, teaching us that denying ungodliness and worldly lusts, we should live soberly, righteously, and godly, in this present world." Tit. ii. 11, 12. Now all who obey these *first* teachings, will find an increasing wish to be more and more taught of God: and, as they yield to this inward something, which pleads with and admonishes them in the secret of their hearts, they will discover that they have been mercifully visited by God, with his "Day-spring from on high." They will know what the apostle meant, when he declared, "The word is nigh thee, even in thy mouth and in thy heart." Rom. x. 8. And what the blessed Redeemer meant by "The kingdom of God is within you." Luke xvii. 21.

It is indeed the privilege of the religion of Jesus Christ, (the Gospel dispensation under which we live,) that there is not an absolute *necessity* for the teaching of men, in order to comprehend those truths which relate to the salvation of our souls. The prophet Jeremiah, who lived many hundred years before the appearance of our Saviour amongst men, was commanded by the Almighty to describe the Gospel-day in this manner, "Behold, the days come, saith the Lord, that I will make a new covenant with the house of Israel, and with the house of Judah; not according to the covenant that I made with their fathers, in the day that I took them by the hand to lead them out of the land of Egypt. But this shall be the covenant that I will make, saith the Lord; I will put my law in their inward parts, and write it in their hearts, and will be their God, and they shall be my people: and they shall teach no more every man his neighbour, and every man his brother, saying, Know the Lord; for they shall all know me, from the least of them unto the greatest of them, saith the Lord." Jer. xxxi. 31—34. If when you feel the secret checks of that Divine teacher, who reproves you whenever you do wrong, you would yield to what he requires, you would feel the reward of peace in your hearts: a peace promised by the Saviour of the world to his obedient children—"Peace I leave with you, my peace I give unto you; not as the world giveth, give I unto you," &c. John xiv. 27.

This will be putting the precepts of the Christian religion in practice. But though it is a great favour to read or to hear the instructive proofs contained in the Scriptures, yet this will be to no purpose if you do not *obey* as well as hear them. The apostle Paul tells us (2 Cor. iv. 6.), that "God who commanded the light to shine out of darkness, hath shined in our hearts, to give the light of the knowledge of the glory of God in the face of Jesus Christ." The more we attend to the discoveries of this Divine Light, the more we feel that there is much in our hearts which wants to be enlightened, and cleansed from evil. Then we shall learn that the soul stands in need of something to support and nourish it, as well as the body: and that as the soul is immortal, its food must be spiritual. We shall then hear and joyfully understand, what the holy Redeemer said formerly, when he declared, "I am the bread of life: he that cometh to me shall never hunger, and he that believeth on me shall never thirst." John vi. 35. And again, "I am the light of the world: he that followeth me shall not walk in darkness, but shall have the Light of Life." John viii. 12.

This then is the condemnation, that light is come into the world, but men love darkness rather than light, because their deeds are evil. John iii. 19. The evil deeds of men make them prefer darkness to light. They are not desirous, in general, to accept of, and benefit by, the remedy provided by the infinite love of God; they are not sufficiently concerned to walk while *they* have the light. It ever was and ever will be the language of the gracious Redeemer, "Look unto me and be ye saved all ye ends of the earth." Isa. xlv. 22.

"Come unto me all ye that labour and are heavy laden, and I will give you rest." Matt. xi. 28. Do not then, I earnestly and affectionately entreat you, do not deceive yourselves by thinking, since God is merciful, and Jesus Christ is willing to be the saviour of all men, that you need not be anxious about your present conduct, or future state. This would be a dreadful error indeed. It is true that Jesus, the Redeemer of his people, has laid down his life for us, that we might depart from evil, and stand accepted in the divine sight: that we may be delivered from the bondage of sin and satan, and brought into the glorious liberty of the sons and daughters of God; but if we would profit by these proofs of his love, we must accept of his salvation on the terms he offers it; we must be his true disciples by *forsaking sin*, and endeavouring to do the will of God upon earth as it is done in heaven. Remember, we cannot enter the kingdom of everlasting rest, to join the celestial company of saints and angels, till we have learnt to lament our past transgressions, and have suffered the blessed Saviour of the world to cleanse our hearts from evil, that they may be filled with the graces of his Holy Spirit. He has given us all a time for repentance; he has offered us the means of being saved in him, with an everlasting salvation; but if we neglect these means, if we suffer this day of gracious visitation to pass away unimproved, dreadful indeed will be our state.

Recollect you are *now in time*, *to-morrow* you may be in

eternity! Work then while it is day: for the night cometh wherein no man can work. The blessed Jesus himself declared, in effect, to the Jews, If ye believe not that I am he, and die in your sins, whither I go ye cannot come. John viii. 21. 24.

Do not think that you are sufficiently prepared for eternity, if you go to some place of worship, and abstain from gross sins; for if you become acquainted with your own hearts, through that grace with which the Almighty mercifully visits the children of men, you will be humble under a sense of his goodness, and your own unworthiness; you will then become of the number of those whom he hath blessed, saying, "Blessed are they that mourn, for they shall be comforted; blessed are the poor in spirit, for theirs is the kingdom of heaven." Matt. v. 3, 4.

And you, dear young people, who may read these lines, let me, in real desire for your happiness, invite you to remember your Creator in the days of your youth; remember that he sees all your actions, and knows all your thoughts, that without his blessing, you cannot really prosper; you could not be happy even if you possessed all this world contains. It is only by knowing and serving the Lord that you can have peace: for, "There is no peace, saith my God, to the wicked." Isa. lvii. 21. Be encouraged then, to look up to your Heavenly Father as your best friend. He hath assured us, They that seek wisdom early shall find her. Prov. viii. 17. "Ask and ye shall receive, seek and ye shall find, knock and it shall be opened." Matt. vii. 7.

The blessed Jesus received little children saying, "Suffer the little children to come unto me, and forbid them not; for of such is the kingdom of God." at the same time he declared, "Whosoever shall not receive the kingdom of God as a little child, he shall not enter therein." Mark x. 14. 15. Be humble, then, be simple, be obedient to the teachings of Him, who will be as a Shepherd to the little ones of his flock. Do not continue in the practice of anything which, when you have done it, brings uneasiness over your minds, but follow those things that make for your peace; this attention to *small* things is the way to grow in grace, and in the knowledge of our Lord and Saviour Jesus Christ. He that is faithful in the *little*, will be made ruler over more. To-day, then, O! to-day, if you will hear his voice, harden not your hearts; hear and obey, and your souls shall live!

London: Printed by E. Couchman & Co., 10, Throgmorton Street; for the TRACT ASSOCIATION of the SOCIETY OF FRIENDS. Sold at the Depository, 12, Bishopsgate Street Without.—1862.

EXTRACT

FROM THE

DVICE OF WILLIAM PENN

TO HIS CHILDREN.

PART I.

LONDON:

d for the TRACT ASSOCIATION of the SOCIETY OF FRIENDS.

Sold at the DEPOSITORY, 84, Houndsditch.

—

1861.

5.   *[Price 4d. per dozen.]*

EXTRACT, &c.

MY DEAR CHILDREN,

NOT knowing how long it may please God to continue me amongst you, I am willing to embrace this opportunity of leaving you my advice and counsel; and I both beseech you and charge you, by the relation you have to me, and the affection I have always shown to you, and indeed received from you, that you lay up the same in your hearts, as well as your heads, with a wise and religious care.

I will begin with that which is the beginning of all true wisdom and happiness,—the holy fear of God.

Children fear God:—that is to say, Have a holy awe upon your minds to avoid that which is evil, and a strict care to embrace and do that which is good. The measure and standard of which knowledge and duty, is the Light of Christ in your consciences, by which (John iii. 20, 21.) you may clearly see if your deeds, and your words, and thoughts too, are wrought in God or not, for they are the deeds of the mind, and for which you must be judged: I say, with this divine light of Christ in your consciences, you may bring your thoughts, words, and works to judgment in yourselves, and have a right, true, sound, and unerring sense of your duty towards God and man. And as you come to obey this blessed light in its holy convictions, it will lead you out of the world's dark and degenerate ways and works, and bring you unto Christ's way of life, and to be of the number of his true self-denying followers; to take up your cross for his sake, who bore his for yours; and to become the children of the light, putting it on as your holy armour; by which you may see and resist the fiery darts of Satan's temptations, and overcome him in all his assaults.

I would a little explain this principle to you : It is
called Light (John i. 9.; iii. 19, 20, 21.; and viii. 12.
Eph. v. 8. 13, 14. 1 Thess. v. 5. 1 John i. 5, 6, 7.
Rev. xxi. 23.) because it gives a man a sight of his sin.
And it is also called the quickening Spirit; for so He
is called, and the Lord from heaven (1 Cor. xv. 45.
47.), who is called and calls himself, the light of the
world. John viii. 12. And why is he called the
Spirit? Because he gives man spiritual life. Christ
promised to send his Spirit to convince the world of
their sins (John xvi. 8.) : wherefore, that which convinces you and all people of their sins, is the Spirit of
Christ. This is highly prized, Rom. viii. (as you may
read in that great and sweet chapter), for the children
of God are led by it. This reveals the things of God
that appertain to man's salvation and happiness
(1 Cor. ii. 10, 11, 12.); it is the earnest God gives his
people. 2 Cor. v. 5. It is the great end, and benefit,
and blessing of the coming of Christ, viz., the shining
forth of this Light, and pouring forth of this Spirit.
Yea, Christ is not received by them that resist his
Light and Spirit in their hearts; nor can they have
the benefit of his birth, life, death, resurrection, intercession, &c., who rebel against the Light. God sent
his Son to bless us, in turning us from the evil of our
ways; therefore have a care of evil, for that turns you
away from God; and wherein you have done evil, do
so no more. But be ye turned, my dear children,
from that evil in thought, as well as in word or deed;
or that will turn you from God your Creator, and
Christ, whom he has given you for your Redeemer;
who redeems and saves his people *from* their sins
(Tit. ii. 14.), not *in* their sins. Read Acts ii. and
Heb. viii., and the Christian dispensation will appear
to be that of the Spirit; which sin quencheth, hardens
the heart against, and bolts the door upon.

This holy, divine principle is called Grace too (Tit.
ii. 11, 12.); there you will see the nature and office of
it, and its blessed effects upon those that were taught
of it in the primitive days. And why grace? Because

it is God's love, and not our desert; his good-will, his kindness. He "so loved the world, that he gave his only-begotten Son, that whosoever believeth in him should not perish, but have everlasting life." John iii. 16. And it is this holy Son, that is declared to be "full of grace and truth," and that of his grace we "receive grace for grace" (John i. 14. 16.) : that is we receive of Him, (the fulness,) what measure of grace we need. And the Lord told Paul in his great trials, when ready to stagger about the sufficiency of the grace he had received to deliver him, "My grace is sufficient for thee." 2 Cor. xii. 9. O Children, love the grace, hearken to this grace; it will teach you, it will sanctify you, it will lead you to the rest and kingdom of God; as it taught the saints of old, first, what to deny; viz., To deny "ungodliness and worldly lusts;" and then what to do; viz., To "live soberly, righteously, and godly in this present world." Tit. ii. 11, 12. And he that is full of grace, is full of light, and he that is full of light is the quickening Spirit, that gives a manifestation of his Spirit to every one to profit with (1 Cor. xii. 7.) ; and he that is the quickening Spirit is the truth. "I am the way, and the Truth, and the Life," said he to his poor followers. John xiv. 6. And, if the Truth make you free, said He to the Jews, then are you free indeed. John viii. 32. 36. And this Truth sheds abroad itself in man, and begets Truth in the inward parts; and makes false, rebellious, hypocritical man, a true man to God again. Truth in the inward parts is of great price with the Lord. And why called Truth? Because it tells man the Truth of his spiritual state; it shows him his state, deals plainly with him, and sets his sins in order before him. So that, my dear Children, the Light, Spirit, Grace, and Truth, are not divers principles, but divers words or denominations given to one eternal power and heavenly principle in you, though not of you, but of God, according to the manifestation or operation thereof in the servants of God of old time; Light, to discover and give discerning; Spirit, to quicken and enliven; Grace, to wit, the love of God: Truth, because it tells man the truth of his condition, and redeems him from the errors of his ways; that as darkness, death, sin, and error are the same, so Light, Spirit, Grace, and Truth are the same.

This is that which is come by Christ; and a measure of this Light, Spirit, Grace, and Truth is given to every man and woman to see their way to go by, which leads out of the vain honours, compliments, lusts, and pleasures of the world.

O my dear Children! this is the pearl of price; part with all for it; but never part with it for all the world. This is the Gospel leaven, to leaven you; that is, sanctify and season you in body, soul, and spirit, to God your heavenly Father's use and service, and your own lasting comfort. Yea, this is the divine and incorruptible seed of the kingdom, of which all true regenerate men and women, Christians of Christ's making, are born. Receive it into your hearts, give it room there: let it take deep root in you, and you will be fruitful unto God in every good word and work. As you take heed to it, and the holy enlightenings and motions of it, you will have a perfect discerning of the spirit of this world, in all its appearances, in yourselves and others: the motions, temptations, and workings of it, as to pride, vanity, covetousness, revenge, uncleanness, hypocrisy, and every evil way; you will see the world in all its shapes and features, and you will be able to judge the world by it, and the spirit of the world in all its appearances. You will see, as I have done, that there is much to deny, much to suffer, and much to do; and you will see, that there is no power or virtue but in the Light, Spirit, Grace, and Truth of Christ, to carry you through the world to God's glory, and your everlasting peace. Yea, you will see what religion is from above, and what is from below; what is of God's working, and what of man's making and forcing; also what ministry is of his Spirit and giving, and what of man's studying, framing and imposing. You will, I say, discern the rise, nature, tokens, and fruits of the true from the false ministry; and what worship is spiritual and what carnal: and what honour is of God, and what that honour is which is from below, of men, yea, fallen men, that the world so generally loves, and which is spoken against in John v. 44. You will see the vain and evil communication that corrupts good manners, the snares of much company and business, and especially the danger of the friendship of this present evil world.

Having thus expressed myself to you, my dear Children, as to the things of God, his Truth, and kingdom, I refer you to his Light, Grace, Spirit, and Truth within you, and the Holy Scriptures of Truth without you, which, from my youth, I loved to read, and were ever blessed to me, and which I charge you to read daily: the Old Testament for history, chiefly, the Psalms for meditation and devotion, the Prophets for comfort and hope, but especially the New Testament for doctrine, faith, and worship; for they were given forth by holy men of God, in divers ages, as they were moved by the Holy Spirit; and are the declared and revealed mind and will of the Holy God to mankind under divers dispensations; and they are certainly able to make the man of God perfect through faith, unto salvation; being a true and clear testimony to the salvation that is of God, through Christ the second Adam, the Light of the world, the quickening Spirit, who is full of Grace and Truth; whose Light, Grace, Spirit, and Truth bear witness to them in every sensible soul, as they frequently, plainly, and solemnly bear testimony to the Light, Spirit, Grace, and Truth both in himself, and in and to his people, to their sanctification, justification, redemption, and consolation, and in all men to their visitation, reproof, and conviction, in their evil ways; I say, having thus expressed myself in general, I refer you, my dear children, to the Light and Spirit of Jesus that is within you, and to the Scriptures of Truth without you.

O THAT children and people would be careful in their very early years, and as they grow up and advance in life, to mind the reproofs of instruction in their own breasts! they are known to be the way of life, divine life to the soul.

This *something*, though they know not what it is, that checks them in secret for evil, both before and after they yield to the temptation; warning them before-hand, not to touch or taste, and afterwards condemning them if they do so, and inwardly inclining them to a life of religion and virtue; this is the very thing, dear young people, whereby God worketh in you, to will and to do: and by which he will, if you cleave to it, and work with it, enable you to work out your own salvation, with fear and trembling before him.—Despise it not, do no violence to its motions, love it, cherish it, reverence it, hearken to its pleadings with you: give up without delay to its requirings, and obey its teachings. It is God's messenger for good to thy immortal soul: its voice in thy streets, is truly the voice of the living God.—Its call is a kind invitation to thee, from the Throne of Grace.

Hear it, and it will lead thee; obey it, and it will save thee from the power of sin and Satan; it will finally lead to an inheritance incorruptible in the mansions of rest, the house not made with hands, eternal in the heavens.

Journal of JOB SCOTT, *p.* 15.

END.

Printed by E. Couchman and Co., 10, Throgmorton Street, London.

WILLIAM PENN'S

LETTER

TO HIS

WIFE AND·CHILDREN.

~~~~~~~~~~~~~~~~~~~~~~~~~~

LONDON:

ted for the TRACT ASSOCIATION of the SOCIETY of FRIENDS.

Sold at the DEPOSITORY, 84, Houndsditch.

—

1860.

6.   *[Price 6d. per dozen.]*

ADVERTISEMENT.

The Author of the following Letter is well known as the founder of the colony of Pennsylvania; which Charles II. granted to him in consideration of debts due to his father, Admiral Penn, at the decease of the latter. On being lately re-published in a life of William Penn, in two volumes 8vo, by Thomas Clarkson, it attracted notice as a performance fraught with instructive counsel; and is now, for the convenience of those who may not possess the above work, reprinted in a separate form.

London, 1814.

W. PENN'S LETTER.

My love, which neither sea, nor land, nor death itself, can extinguish or lessen toward you, most endearedly visits you with eternal embraces, and will abide with you for ever; and may the God of my life watch over you and bless you, and do you good in this world and for ever! Some things are upon my spirit to leave with you in your respective capacities, as I am to one a husband, and to the rest a father, if I should never see you more in this world.

My dear wife; Remember thou wast the love of my youth, and much the joy of my life, the most beloved, as well as most worthy of all my earthly comforts: and the reason of that love was more thy inward than thy outward excellencies, which yet were many. God knows, and thou knowest it, I can say it was a match of Providence's making, and God's image in us both, was the first thing, and the most amiable and engaging ornament in our eyes. Now I am to leave thee, and that without knowing whether I shall ever see thee more in this world; take my counsel into thy bosom, and let it dwell with thee in my stead while thou livest.

First: Let the fear of the Lord, and a zeal and love to his glory dwell richly in thy heart; and thou wilt watch for good over thyself and thy dear children and family, that no rude, light, or bad thing be committed; else God will be offended, and he will repent himself of the good he intends thee and thine.

Secondly : Be diligent in meetings for worship and discipline : stir up thyself and others herein ; it is thy duty and place : and let meetings be kept once a-day in the family to wait upon the Lord, who has given us much time for ourselves ; and, my dearest, to make thy family matters easy to thee, divide thy time and be regular : it is easy and sweet ; thy retirement will afford thee to do it : as, in the morning, to view the business of the house, and fix it as thou desirest seeing all be in order : that by thy counsel all may move, and to thee render an account every evening. The time for work, for walking, for meals, may be certain, at least as near as may be : and grieve not thyself with careless servants ; they will disorder thee ; rather pay them and let them go, if they will not be better by admonitions : this is best to avoid many words, which I know, wound the soul, and offend the Lord.

Thirdly : Cast up thy income, and see what it daily amounts to ; by which thou mayest be sure to have it in thy sight, and power to keep within compass : and I beseech thee to live low and sparingly, till my debts are paid, and then enlarge as thou seest it convenient. Remember thy mother's example, when thy father's public spiritedness had worsted his estate (which is my case). I know thou lovest plain things, and art averse to the pomps of the world ; a nobility natural to thee. I write not as doubtful, but to quicken thee, for my sake to be more vigilant herein ; knowing that God will bless thy care, and thy poor children and thee for it. My mind is wrapt up in a saying of thy father's : " I desire not riches, but to owe nothing :" and truly *that* is wealth : and more than enough to live, is a snare attended with many sorrows. I need not bid thee be humble, for thou art so : nor meek and patient for it is much of thy natural disposition ; but I pray thee be oft in retirement with the Lord, and guard against encroaching friendships. Keep them at arm's end, for it is giving away our power, aye, and self too, into the

possession of another; and that which might seem
engaging in the beginning, may prove a yoke and
burden too hard and heavy in the end. Wherefore
keep dominion over thyself; and let thy children, good
meetings, and friends be the pleasure of thy life.

' Fourthly: And now my dearest let me recommend
to thy care my dear children; abundantly beloved of
me, as the Lord's blessing, and the sweet pledges
of our mutual and endeared affection. Above all
things, endeavour to breed them up in the love of
virtue, and that holy, plain way of it which we have
lived in, that the world in no part of it get into my
family. I had rather they were homely than finely
bred, as to outward behaviour; yet I love sweetness
mixed with gravity, and cheerfulness tempered with
sobriety. Religion in the heart leads into this true
civility, teaching men and women to be mild and
courteous in their behaviour, an accomplishment
worthy indeed of praise.

Fifthly: Next, breed them up in a love one to
another; tell them it is the charge I left behind me;
and that it is the way to have the love and blessing
of God upon them; also, what his portion is who hates
or calls his brother fool. Sometimes separate them
but not long, and allow them to send and give each
other small things, to endear one another with. Once
more I say, tell them it was my counsel they should
be tender and affectionate one to another. For their
learning be liberal. Spare no cost, for by such parsimony all is lost that is saved; but let it be *useful*
knowledge, such as is consistent with truth and godliness, not cherishing a vain conversation or idle mind;
but ingenuity mixed with industry, is good for the
body and mind too. I recommend the useful parts of
mathematics, as building houses or ships, measuring,
surveying, dialling, navigation; but agriculture is
specially in my eye. Let my children be husbandmen and housewives; it is industrious, healthy, honest,
and of good example, like Abraham and the holy
Ancients who pleased God, and obtained a good

report. This leads to consider the works of God and
nature; of things that are good; and diverts the mind
from being taken up with the vain arts and inventions of a luxurious world. It is commendable in the
princes of Germany, and the nobles of that empire,
that they have all their children instructed in some
useful occupation. Rather keep an ingenious person in
the house to teach them, than send them to schools; too
many evil impressions being commonly received there.
Be sure to observe their genius, and do not cross it as
to learning. Let them not dwell too long on one
thing; but let their change be agreeable and all their
diversions have some little bodily labour in them.
When grown big have most care for them; for then
there are more snares both within and without. When
marriageable, see that they have worthy persons in
their eye, of good life, and good fame for piety and
understanding. I need no wealth, but sufficiency;
and be sure their love be dear, fervent, and mutual,
that it may be happy for them. I choose not they
should be married to earthly covetous kindred; and
of cities and towns of concourse beware; the world is
apt to stick close to those who have lived, and got
wealth there; a country life and estate I like best for
my children. I prefer a decent mansion of an hundred pounds per annum, before ten thousand pounds
in London, or such like place, in a way of trade.
In fine, my dear, endeavour to breed them dutiful to
the Lord, and his blessed light, truth, and grace in
their hearts, who is their Creator, and his fear will
grow up with them. Teach a child (says the wise
man) the way thou wilt have him to walk, and when
he is old he will not forget it. Next, obedience to
thee, their dear mother, and that not for wrath, but
conscience' sake; liberal to the poor; pitiful to the
miserable; humble and kind to all. And may my God
make thee a blessing, and give thee comfort in our
dear children; and in age, gather thee to the joy and
blessedness of the just (where no death shall separate
us) for ever.

And now, my dear children, that are the gifts and mercies of the God of your tender father, hear my counsel and lay it up in your hearts; love it more than treasure, and follow it; and you shall be blessed here, and happy hereafter. In the first place, remember your Creator in the days of your youth. It was the glory of Israel, in the second of Jeremiah; and how did God bless Josiah, because he feared him in his youth! and so he did Jacob, Joseph, and Moses. O, my dear children, remember and fear and serve him who made you, and gave you to me and your dear mother, that you may live to him, and glorify him in your generation!

. To do this in your youthful days seek after the Lord that you may find him; remembering his great love in creating you: that you are not beasts, plants, or stones, but that he has kept you and given you his grace within, and substance without, and provided plentifully for you. This remember in your youth, that you may be kept from the evil of the world; for, in age, it will be harder to overcome the temptations of it.

.. Wherefore, my dear children, eschew the appearance of evil, and love, and cleave to that in your hearts, which shows you evil from good, and tells you when you do amiss and reproves you for it. It is the light of Christ, that he has given you for your salvation. If you do this, and follow my counsel, God will bless you in this world, and give you an inheritance in that which shall never have an end. For the light of Jesus is of a purifying nature; it seasons those who love it and take heed to it; and never leaves such till it has brought them to the City of God, that has foundations. O that ye may be seasoned with the gracious nature of it! Hide it in your hearts, and flee, my dear children, from all youthful lusts; the vain sports, pastimes, and pleasure of the world: redeeming the time because the days are evil;—You are now beginning to live.—What would some give for your time? Oh! I could have lived better, were I, as you, in the flower of youth.—There-

fore love and fear the Lord; keep close to meetings,
and delight to wait on the Lord God of your father
and mother, among his despised people, as we have
done; and count it your honour to be members of that
Society, and heirs of that living fellowship which is
enjoyed among them; for the experience of which
your father's soul blesseth the Lord for ever.

Next: be obedient to your dear mother, a woman
whose virtue and good name is an honour to you; for
she has been exceeded by none in her time for her
plainness, integrity, industry, humanity, virtue, and
good understanding; qualities not usual among women
of her worldly condition and quality. Therefore honour
and obey her, my dear children, as your mother, and
your father's love and delight! nay, love her, too; for
she loved your father with a deep and upright love,
choosing him before all her many suitors: and though
she be of a delicate constitution and noble spirit, yet
she descended to the utmost tenderness and care for
you, performing the painfullest acts of service to you
in your infancy, as a mother and a nurse too. I
charge you before the Lord, honour and obey, love
and cherish your dear mother.

Next: betake yourselves to some honest, industrious,
course of life, and that not of sordid covetousness, but
for example, and to avoid idleness. And if you change
your condition and marry, choose with the knowledge
and consent of your mother if living, or of guardians,
or those who have the charge of you. Mind neither
beauty nor riches, but the fear of the Lord, and a
sweet and amiable disposition; such as you can love
above all this world, and that may make your habitations pleasant and desirable to you.

And being married, be tender, affectionate, patient,
and meek. Live in the fear of the Lord, and he will
bless you and your offspring. Be sure to live within
compass; borrow not, neither be beholden to any.
Ruin not yourselves by kindness to others; for that
exceeds the due bounds of friendship; neither will
a true friend expect it. Small matters I heed not.

Let your industry and parsimony go no further than for a sufficiency for life, and to make a provision for your children, (and that in moderation,)-if the Lord give you any. I charge you help the poor and needy; let the Lord have a voluntary share of your income, for the good of the poor, both in our Society and others; for we are all his creatures; remembering that "he that giveth to the poor lendeth to the Lord."

Know well your in-comings, and your out-goings may be better regulated. Love not money nor the world; use them only and they will serve you; but if you love them, you serve them, which will debase your spirits as well as offend the Lord.

Pity the distressed, and hold out a hand of help to them; it may be your case; and as you mete to others, God will mete to you again.

Be humble and gentle in your conversation, of few words, I charge you; but always pertinent when you speak; hearing out before you attempt to answer; and then speaking as if you would persuade, not impose.

Affront none, neither revenge the affronts that are done to you; but forgive, and you shall be forgiven of your Heavenly Father.

In making friends consider well first; and when you are fixed, be true, not wavering by reports, nor deserting in affliction, for that becomes not the good and virtuous. Watch against anger, neither speak nor act in it; for, like drunkenness, it makes a man a beast, and throws people into desperate inconveniences.

Avoid flatterers, for they are thieves in disguise, their praise is costly, designed to get by those they bespeak; they are the worst of creatures; they lie to flatter, and flatter to cheat; and, which is worse, if you believe them you cheat yourselves most dangerously. But the virtuous, though poor, love, cherish, and prefer. Remember David, who asking the Lord, who shall abide in thy tabernacle, who shall dwell upon thy holy hill? answers, He that walketh uprightly, worketh righteousness, and speaketh the truth in his heart; in whose eyes the vile person is contemned, but honoureth them who fear the Lord. Next, my children, be temperate in all things; in your diet, for that is physic by prevention; it keeps, nay it makes people healthy and their generation sound. This is exclusive of the spiritual advantage it brings. Be also plain in your apparel. Keep out that lust which reigns too much over some. Let your virtues be your ornaments; remembering life is more than food, and the body than raiment. Let your furniture be simple and cheap. Avoid pride, avarice, and luxury. Read my " No Cross no Crown." There is instruction.

Make your conversation with the most eminent for wisdom and piety; and shun all wicked men as you hope for the blessing of God, and the comfort of your father's living and dying prayers. Be sure you speak no evil of any, no, not of the meanest: much less of your superiors, as magistrates, guardians, tutors, teachers, and elders in Christ.

Be not busy bodies; meddle not with other folk's matters, but when in conscience and duty pres$_t$: for it procures trouble, and is ill manners, and very unseemingly to wise men.

In your families, remember Abraham, Moses, and Joshua, their integrity to the Lord; and do as you have them for your examples.

Let the fear and service of the living God be encouraged in your houses; and that plainness, sobriety, and moderation in all things, as becometh God's chosen people; and as I advised you, my beloved children, do you counsel your's, if God should give you any. Yea, I counsel and command them as my posterity, that they love and serve the Lord God with an upright heart; that he may bless you and yours, from generation to generation.

And as for you who are likely to be concerned in the government of Pennsylvania, and my parts of East Jersey, especially the first, I do charge you

before the Lord God and his holy Angels, that you be
lowly, diligent, and tender, fearing God and loving
the people, and hating covetousness. Let Justice
have its impartial course, and the law free passage.
Though to your loss, protect no man against it; for
you are not above the law, but the law above you.
Live therefore the lives yourselves, you would have
the people live, and then you have right and boldness
to punish the transgressors. Keep upon the square,
for God sees you; therefore do your duty; and be
sure you see with your own eyes and hear with your
own ears. Entertain no lurchers; cherish no informers
for gain or revenge; use no tricks; fly to no devices
to support or cover injustice; but let your hearts be
upright before the Lord, trusting in him, above the
contrivances of men, and none shall be able to hurt
or supplant.

Oh! the Lord is a strong God, and he can do whatsoever he pleases; and though men consider it not, it
is the Lord that rules and overrules in the kingdoms
of men, and he builds up and pulls down. I, your
father, am the man that can say, He that trusts in the
Lord shall not be confounded; but God in due time,
will make his enemies be at peace with him.

If you thus behave yourselves, and so become a
terror to evil doers, and a praise to them that do well,
God, my God, will be with you in wisdom and a
sound mind, and make you blessed instruments in his
hand, for the settlement of some of those desolate parts
of the world, which my soul desires, above all worldly
honours and riches, both for you that go, and you that
stay; you that govern and you that are governed;
that in the end you may be gathered, with me, to the
rest of God.

Finally, my children, love one another, with a true
endeared love, and your dear relations on both sides;
and take care to preserve tender affection in your
children to each other, often marrying within themselves, so as it be without the bounds forbidden in
God's law, that so they may not, like the forgetting,

12

unnatural world, grow out of kindred, and as cold as strangers; but, as becomes a truly natural and Christian stock, you, and yours after you, may live in the pure and fervent love of God towards one another, as becometh brethren in the spiritual and natural relation.

So my God, that hath blessed me with his abundant mercies, both of this and the other and better life, be with you all, guide you by his counsel, bless you, and bring you to his eternal glory! that you may shine, my dear children, in the firmament of God's power, with the blessed spirits of the just, that celestial family, praising and admiring him the God and Father of it, for ever and ever. For there is no God like unto him; the God of Abraham, of Isaac, and of Jacob, the God of the Prophets, the Apostles, and Martyrs, of Jesus, in whom I live for ever.

So farewell to my thrice dearly beloved wife and children!

> Yours, as God pleaseth, in that which no waters can quench, no time forget, nor distance wear away, but remains for ever.
>
> WILLIAM PENN.

Worminghurst,
4th of Sixth Month, 1682.

Printed by E. Couchman, 10, Throgmorton Street, London.

A

CHRISTIAN EXHORTATION

TO

SAILORS,

AND PERSONS ENGAGED IN A SEA-FARING LIFE.

———◆———

"They that go down to the sea in ships, that do business in great waters;
"These see the works of the Lord, and his wonders in the deep.
"For he commandeth and raiseth the stormy wind, which lifteth up the waves hereof.
"They mount up to the heaven, they go down again to the depths: their soul is melted because of trouble.
"They reel to and fro, and stagger like a drunken man, and are at their wit's end.
"Then they cry unto the Lord in their trouble, and he bringeth them out of their distresses.
"He maketh the storm a calm, so that the waves thereof are still.
"Then are they glad because they be quiet; so he bringeth them unto their desired haven.
"Oh, that men would praise the Lord for his goodness, and for his wonderful works to the children of men."   Ps. cvii. 23—31.

〰〰〰〰〰〰〰〰〰

LONDON:

Printed for the TRACT ASSOCIATION of the SOCIETY of FRIENDS.

Sold at the DEPOSITORY, 12, Bishopsgate Street Without.

——

1866.

No. 7.   [*Price 3d. per dozen.*]

A

CHRISTIAN EXHORTATION.

———

I HAVE often meditated upon the nature of a sea-faring
life; and in considering the dangers and difficulties, to
which many of my fellow-creatures employed upon the
seas are exposed, my heart has been warmed with strong
desire, that they may be more generally acquainted with
the consolations of true religion. In this desire, I have
wished to remind them of the love of our Heavenly
Father; and, in a few words, to beseech them to consider, how far they are endeavouring to live in love to
Him, and to walk in the way of His commandments.

It is a very precious truth, which we find recorded in
the Holy Scriptures, that " God is no respecter of per
sons." Acts x. 34. Our Almighty Creator has mad
of one blood all the nations of men that dwell upon th
face of the earth; and in His love He makes no dis
tinction between the rich and the poor, the learned an
the unlearned;—between the inhabitants of one natio
and those of another; but all are children of the sam
family, created with the gracious design that they shoul
enjoy peace with Him while here, and everlasting ha]
piness hereafter. The great work of true religion, 1
which I now desire to direct your attention, my de
brethren, appears to me to consist in knowing this gre
and gracious Being, in loving Him, in doing His will, ar
living in His fear. This is the principal business of lif
this would make us truly happy. It is for want
knowing and loving God, that there is so much mise
and wretchedness in the world, that so many are livin
without peace, and as we have reason to fear, dyin
without hope.

It is from God that we receive all our blessings : it
He who hath clothed and fed us : his fatherly eye ha

been watching over us for good. It is He who hath delivered us in danger; and it is of His mercy that our lives are lengthened out to the present day. Oh! how great is His goodness! how much do we owe to Him, from whom we have received all these favours! But He has not only provided for us in those things which concern our present outward condition: He has placed His good Spirit in our hearts, to instruct us in His holy law; and it is by this that, as a kind and tender Father, He is reproving us for our disobedience; and inviting us to forsake every wicked way, and to walk in the path of peace. It is thus that He has made himself known to the children of men in all the former generations of time; and He is in the same manner manifesting His gracious regard to the inhabitants of the earth, at the present day.

This is the voice of His Wisdom, the invitation of Divine Love. It is the grace of our Lord Jesus Christ, and the power of God unto salvation. In our early childhood, this Holy Spirit visits our minds, and reproves us for evil; and as we advance in life it continues to follow us, pleading with us, and persuading us to turn unto the Lord, and serve Him with our whole hearts, But if we resist its power, if we refuse this invitation of the love of God, and do that which we *know* to be evil, it condemns us, it brings us into sorrow, and heaviness, and distress. We are afraid of His displeasure, and instead of looking up to Him, as to a merciful and tender Father, which His obedient children can do with humble confidence, our hearts are filled with terror, and we look to Him, as to a just and righteous Judge, who will punish those that rebel against His law.

Now, do you not know something of this divine power? Have you not heard this voice of heavenly wisdom, and been favoured, after this manner, with the invitation of divine love? Consider then the goodness and mercy of God, and be entreated to receive the visitation of His Holy Spirit. Hear its reproofs, and listen to its instructions. Let it bring to your remembrance the sins of your early lives. Be willing to behold yourselves as you are seen in the sight of Almighty God, and if you feel that you have transgressed his law, and that you are

sinners in His holy presence, suffer his righteous judg
ment, endure the fatherly correction of His powerfu
hand. But do not despair of His mercy and forgiveness
remember that Jesus Christ our Lord, " came into th
world to save sinners" (1 Tim. i. 15.) ; to save the chie
among sinners, to save them from sin, and to give then
hope in the great mercy of God.

He has given himself for us; yes, He has tasted deatl
for every man. He died for us that He might redeen
us from all iniquity, and that we might be purified t
Him, and by Him. For He came into the world, an
fulfilled all righteousness in obedience to His Father'
will, not only that He might be a perfect pattern unto u
in holiness, humility, meekness, and love; but He ha
borne our infirmities, and victoriously endured the temp
tations with which we are tried, that He might manifes
his tender compassion with the weakness of our nature
Now he who has done and suffered so much for poo
rebellious sinners, who was crucified by the hands o
cruel men, and who is now ascended into the glory whicl
He had with the Father before the world began, is stil
waiting to receive those that seek Him ; the language o
His love is still the same; " Him that cometh to me
will in no wise cast out." Jonh vi. 37. If we embrac
the invitation of His love, and come unto Him, we shal
find all that we want, to render us acceptable to tha
pure and holy Being, who is, through his beloved So
seeking our happiness and everlasting peace.

Christ will then be our Light and our Leader. H
will be our strength and our defence. Through His Hol
Spirit we shall become more thoroughly instructed i
the way of righteousness and peace : we shall not onl
be more fully convinced of the necessity of denying ou
selves of much to which our evil inclinations are pron
but we shall see, that the way of the cross is a patl
attended with the purest joys, and most substantial con
solations, of which we can possibly partake in this lif
Through our Redeemer our hearts will be strengthened
and we shall be endued with holy courage to acknow
ledge ourselves his disciples, even in the presence of hi
enemies. If we thus faithfully follow Him, He wi
defend us in the hour of temptation, and give us th

victory over the many lusts of our flesh, and the love of this present world. He will not only deliver and preserve us from that which is evil; but if we live in obedience to his good Spirit, we shall delight in the law of God; we shall love him with all our heart, and with all our soul, and with all our strength, and with all our mind; and we shall love our neighbours as ourselves. Luke x. 27. In every nation, and amongst all the different people we meet within the world, we shall do unto others as we would that they should do unto us. Matt. vii. 12. We shall take no unjust advantage in our dealings, we shall not oppress our fellow-creatures, when we have it in our power;—but we shall fulfil the law of kindness unto all; loving our enemies, doing good to them that hate us, and blessing them that curse us, and praying for them that despitefully use us and persecute us. Matt. v. 44. And in our daily conduct and deportment among men, we shall approve ourselves true disciples of the Lord Jesus, in chastity, humility, meekness, sobriety, temperance, and patience. It is thus that Christ becomes all in all to them that believe in Him, come unto Him, and obediently follow his blessed guidance. And thus shall we know Him as He is described to be "the Lamb of God which taketh away the sin of the world." John i. 29. We shall rejoice in Him as *our* Redeemer, because He has saved us from our sins, and settled our minds in hope of obtaining through the goodness of God, an inheritance in his glorious kingdom in the world to come.

This is pure Religion and true Christianity. It is attainable by all of every class, whatever may be their situation or condition. So that although a sea-faring life may subject those who follow it to many difficulties and discouragements, and may be attended with some temptations peculiar to itself; yet through the condescending mercy of our Heavenly Parent, the consolations of the Gospel, that message of glad tidings of mercy and redemption to poor, sinful man, which is freely offered through our Lord and Saviour Jesus Christ, are as certainly within the reach of the sailor and fisherman, as of those in any other station or employment in life. He who is God of the whole earth, is also God of the great seas; all is the workmanship of his hand; his all-seeing

eye beholds us everywhere, in all circumstances, and i
every land. When we are in peril of our lives, an
ready to perish with cold and hunger,—when our heart
fail us through fear, and we may think that sudde
destruction is coming upon us, though we may be out c
the reach of help from our fellow-men, yet He sees us
and if it please Him, He will deliver us. But if in Hi
wisdom, He suffers the continuance of all these hard
ships, until we even lose all hope of life, He can mak
us content in all our many troubles, and comfort us i
the assurance that when we leave this world, we sha
have peace with him for ever. His ear is always ope
to our petitions; and though we may not be able t
express our wants to him in words; yet as He searche
our hearts, and knows our wants, if we ask in submissio
to his will, He will help us. True prayer is the languag
of the heart, the breathing of the soul to God; so tha
whether we express our wants in words, or secretly pou
forth our souls in sighs and groans before Him, we hav
cause to hope that our prayers will meet with his gra
cious regard. If we have none to give us the instructio
which we feel we want, if we have no outward minist
to remind us of our duty to God and our fellow-creature;
yet if we take heed to the teaching of the Spirit of Chri
in our hearts, we shall never want a teacher, for that wi
make us wise unto salvation; it will be as a word behin
us, when we turn to the right hand, or to the left, sa
ing, "This is the way, walk ye in it." Isa. xxx. 21.
we had the opportunity of frequently attending on t
teaching of men, their help might fail us; but this w
never fail us; it is in us, and it will abide with us.

Thus might the Lord Almighty be worshipped in spir
and in truth by the poor seaman, day by day, while he
toiling upon the deep waters. And thus would the ho
religion of the blessed Jesus bring forth acceptable frui
so that the great name would be praised by many of o
fellow-creatures, who seem to be living in forgetfulne
of God, and without concern for their latter end. Th
would be sober and temperate in their lives and conduc
there would be no more quarrelling or discord amoi
them; they would speak the truth every man to
neighbour; the tongues of those who had once bl

phemed the holy name of God, and cursed their fellow-
creatures, would be governed by the fear of offending
their Maker; and instead of cursing, and wicked wanton
words, they would often speak one to another in meekness and kindness, and persuade one another in brotherly
love, to join with them in serving the Lord Jesus Christ.
The Holy Bible, which it is to be feared, is now too much
neglected by many among them, would meet with more
frequent and serious perusal; and to this profitable employment we may hope that the Divine blessing would
be graciously added, by increasing their love to God, and
their acquaintance with the promises of the Gospel.

Being thus preserved in the fear of the Lord, in their
daily occupations on the sea, the poor mariners, when
temptations assail them on shore, would be also helped
to resist the devil in all his devices, to flee the wicked
and deceitful company of those who in almost every
sea-port are trying to lead them into wantonness and
drunkenness, and endeavouring to spoil the youth of
their innocency, and to rob them of the wages, which
they have earned through so many toils and dangers.

But alas! where at the present day shall we find
greater wickedness and more abominable vice than in
some of these places, among our sailors and their companions in riotous mirth; and how are they, in foreign
lands, even where the religion of Christianity is hardly
known, violating the law of God's righteousness, and
causing his name to be blasphemed among the heathen!
Consider these things I entreat you. Listen to the voice
of God, and flee while you have opportunity to return.
Time is short and uncertain to all; but to you it seems
more particularly uncertain. Remember how many of
your companions have been called at an unexpected hour:
how many who partook with you of the same mess,
perhaps but a few months ago, have found a watery grave
in the mighty deep. How little do you know, but the
next storm may sweep you off this stage of life, and bring
you to the bar of the great Judge! Oh! then, that he
that reads may be brought to fear, and to trust in the
Lord.

I would now address a few words more particularly
to you, *young men:*—to you who are now healthy and

strong, full of courage, and perhaps, looking for man
more days. Let me entreat you to remember you
Creator now in the days of your youth. It is not to
soon for you to seek the Lord, and to think of you
latter end. Have you not already heard the voice of hi
Holy Spirit? has it not reproved and pleaded with you
and do you not now feel the power of its convictions?
would hope that the minds of many of you are not so fa
hardened, that you can sin against God without remorse
Are not your ears shocked when you hear the name c
the great Preserver of men openly profaned: and do no
your tender hearts now shudder at what offends you
eyes almost every day! If this be your happy case, Oh
beware that no man rob you of this heavenly treasure,—
the fear of God. Do not forget that you are constantl
under the notice of our Almighty Parent, that He hear
your words, and sees your actions, by night as well as b
day; on the sea, as well as by land; and that althoug
much may be concealed from man, yet nothing can b
hid from his all-seeing eye.

Let not any example among your elder associates, o
even superiors, induce you to transgress the law of th
Lord. Turn a deaf ear to their enticements, and loo
unto God, and He will help you to bear their reviling
and reproach without anger or impatience. He will giv
you that sweet peace which will make your hearts joyfi
in the midst of all the sufferings you can endure fro
wicked men for his name's sake. Thus, dear your
people, would you be preserved in the fear and love
God, in a life of many temptations, and find Him
strong hold in every time of trouble. He would be wit
you in all your many difficulties and dangers, and if yo
were called from this world in early life, you might ho
that you would be permitted to enter into his kingdo
of rest and peace.

END.

Printed by E. Couchman & Co., 10, Throgmorton Street, London.

THE

ANCIENT CHRISTIANS'

PRINCIPLE, OR RULE OF LIFE,

REVIVED, OR SET FORTH,

WITH A DESCRIPTION OF TRUE GODLINESS, &c.

Extracted from the Writings of Hugh Turford.

———◆———

Recommended to the serious perusal of the professors of Christianity of every denomination; who may be assisted by it in discovering whether they are coming up in the vital and essential part of true religion, or too much resting in a mere profession of godliness; a point of the utmost importance for all to be ascertained of; as, without the former, no profession will avail to the cleansing of the soul from sin, and preparing it for an inheritance in that kingdom, into which all, doubtless, must desire at last to obtain an admission.

———◆———

PAUL, an apostle of Jesus Christ, writing to Titus, had this saying, "The grace of God that bringeth salvation, hath appeared to all men; teaching us that, denying ungodliness and worldly lusts, we should live soberly, righteously, and godly in this present world."

From which weighty saying, these following questions arise:—

QUEST. I. What is the grace of God?

ANSW. The grace of God that bringeth salvation, is no less than a divine inspiration, the gift of God to the sons and daughters of men. It is under the Gospel administration, the fulfilling of that covenant which God, by the mouth of his prophet Jeremiah, promised to make with the house of Jacob; which was, that he would write his law in their hearts, and put it in their inward parts.

No. 8.   [*Price 7d. per dozen.*]

For as God made man in the beginning humble, lowly, meek, merciful, pure, peaceable, just, and faithful: *so* he would have all men to be. But forasmuch as nothing less than the good Spirit of God, in the inward parts of man, can reduce any of us to such a qualification [or state]. God hath given to every man a measure thereof to enlighten his understanding, and to guide him in the path of life and salvation; and this measure being the free gift of God, is, by the apostle in the text, and in many other places of Scripture, called Grace.

In our present age, light within, a law within, Spirit within, Christ within, is the scoffing of some, and little regarded by many; but I must tell them they scoff and slight the chiefest treasure that ever the soul of any man was possessed of: they slight the talent that God hath given to every man to improve, in order to our rising from our fall, and [coming] to live under the government of the eternal Spirit.

The converted heathens* walked by this rule: they took the eternal Spirit of Christ in themselves for their guide; they confided therein, and became followers thereof; and that brought them to be a holy nation, an a peculiar people. And we should be the same, did w turn to this eternal Spirit in our own hearts, and orde our conversation according to the leadings and guiding thereof.

We cannot conclude that the kingdom of Christ, tha then appeared in power, did (as the sun in the firmamen sometimes doth) show itself in a morning, to be no mor seen all day: for the kingdom of Christ is an everlastin kingdom, and the new covenant that was made with th house of Jacob, an everlasting covenant. Neither ma we conclude that God hath withdrawn himself from th children of men: for he never forsakes us, unless we firs forsake him.

Why [then] are not we, who are called Christian grown to the stature of them that were born heathen and brought up in blindness and ignorance? Why are n we sanctified and made a holy people, as well as they Why are not our bodies cleansed, and made an habitatio for the eternal Spirit, as theirs were? Why is not ou

---

* [The author is speaking of the early converts to Christianity.]

conversation in heaven, or at least more heavenly than it is? If we would be as the primitive Christians were, we must begin where they did: we must turn to the light of righteousness in our own hearts, and walk in that light until we become children of the light.

QUEST. II. Where doth the grace of God that bringeth salvation appear?

ANSW. The great God, in his infinite wisdom and everlasting love, hath placed his royal seed and plant of renown in the hearts of the sons and daughters of men: there the grace of God that bringeth salvation may be found: there, until it come to be veiled by clouds of iniquity, it shows itself a witness against all unrighteousness and ungodliness.

As every evil motion and temptation that leads to sin, appears within; so the grace of God that is given to men, to save from sin, appears also within.

There is not a man born into the world, if he has lived to commit sin, but hath felt and known in himself rebukes for sin; and these rebukes are the appearances of grace, and called in Scripture, "light," and "true light:" for it manifests every work of darkness: it shows us both when and wherein we have done amiss; and this it hath done in all ages.

God hath not in any age left himself without a witness in the hearts of men, to declare his righteousness, truth, and faithfulness. But there is as much difference between the appearance of grace, and the power of grace to salvation; the light of righteousness, and that fulness which enables us to lead a life of righteousness; as between a seed that is sown, and the herb when it is come to full growth: but the one leads to the other; and it is he that attains to the fulness of grace, that comes to lead a sober, righteous, godly life in this present world.

Every man hath, as I may say, life and salvation before him, death and destruction behind him; he hath also a good Spirit to conduct him in the way of life and salvation, and an evil spirit waits to lead him in paths of death and destruction. The preaching of the Gospel was, and ought still to be, for the opening of the eyes of those that are blind, to see the working of these two spirits in themselves, and the leadings thereof, that they might turn from the evil, and become followers of that which is good : that He whose right it is, might come to have the rule in them and over them.

And certain I am, many may be found that [would confess they] have some sight, some sense, and some feeling of the eternal Spirit of Jesus : that they have the knowledge of something in themselves that calls for just weights and an equal balance; for doing unto all men as they would be done by : for truth in their words, and faithfulness in their promises. Did they keep to this, they would follow a right guide, and the seed of grace would grow: truth and faithfulness would grow; knowledge, temperance, patience, brotherly-kindness, and charity would grow; and we should find in ourselves, that an entrance into the kingdom of Christ would be abundantly ministered.

The proud, the covetous, the envious, and other ungodly persons may, for a time, and a long time, have the appearances [or visitations] of grace; they may have rebukes for sin; but if by such rebukes they do not learn righteousness, they grow not in grace, neither doth grace grow in them. All such hide their talent, and in time, for want of improvement, [may] come to have it quite taken from them.

Quest. III. If the grace of God appears unto all, and if there is a sufficiency therein to make them godly, how comes it to pass that there are so many ungodly?

Answ. As the grace of God that bringeth salvation appears unto all men, so motions of sin that lead to destruction appear unto all men; and the work of the devil is to make forbidden things appear desirable, the world, and the vanities thereof to be full of pleasantness. And as our affections come to be taken therewith, as we make the world our delight, and pursue after it, we depart from God; and though grace may make many appearances, though the good Spirit of God may long strive with us, though we have in ourselves many checks and rebukes, and are thereby made sensible that our ways and our doings displease God, yet are we prone to persever therein; and through a continued perseverance, sin grow and comes to have dominion over us.

QUEST. IV. What manner of salvation doth the grace of God bring?

ANSW. As the appearances of grace are rebukes for sin, so the salvation that grace brings is a saving *from sin.*

If grace teacheth men to live soberly, righteously, and godly in this present world, grace saves good men *from sin* in this present world.

We read of an angel that appeared to Joseph, saying, "Fear not to take unto thee Mary thy wife, for that which is conceived in her is of the Holy Ghost; and she shall bring forth a Son, and thou shalt call his name Jesus, for he shall *save* his people *from their sins.*"

Nothing defaceth the image of God in man but sin; nor can anything recover that image again, but our being saved from sin.

Saving from sin on this side the grave may, to such as are strangers to God's salvation, seem an incredible thing; but were they so well acquainted with the power of grace as too many are with the strength of sin, they would say, "Christ's yoke is easy."

I grant, that the shining of an inward light, which is the first manifestation of Christ to the sons and daughters of men, seems at first small and powerless; and so do our first motions to sin; but follow such sinful motions as far as they will lead, and we shall find them powerful enough. May not many be found at this day, even amongst us who are called Christians, so captivated under the power of sin, that a bond slave who is held in chains of iron, can more easily break his bonds, arise, depart, and return unto his native country, than they can cease from iniquity, rise from their fall, and lead a sober, righteous, godly life? And if the seed of sin comes by our following the motions thereof, to have such power over us, why may not the seed of grace, if we return thereunto, and become followers thereof, have as much.

Undoubtedly John, who had travelled "from death unto life," and was an eye witness of things as they were in the beginning, felt in himself such a power when he said, "Whosoever is born of God doth not commit sin; for his seed remaineth in him, and he cannot sin." 1 John iii. 9. And many living witnesses may be found at this day, who can say, from a sensible experience, that where this

righteous seed is risen and comes to have dominion, it is
so powerful and restraining, that they cannot be unjust in
their dealings nor unfaithful in their promises; they cannot tell an untruth, though ever so much to their outward
advantage; they cannot be intemperate, wasting the good
creatures that God hath given for their nourishment, by
excessive eating and drinking; they cannot oppress the
poor, the widow, and fatherless, nor take by violence that
which they have no right unto. The small seed in them
is become the tallest of herbs, and hath as much power
over them as sin hath over those who dwell therein.

These are, as the Colossians were, delivered from the
power of darkness; these have, as the Philippians had,
their conversation in heaven; these glorify God in their
lives, and so answer the end of their creation.

By grace the ear of man is shut from hearkening to
fables and evil reports; his eye is turned aside from gazing
upon vanity; his tongue is not suffered to curse, swear,
lie, or to be employed in any idle communication; his
hand is limited from taking bribes to pervert justice, and
from taking by violence, or otherwise, anything that is
not his own; his feet are restrained from going with the
drunkard to excess, or with a lewd woman to the chamber
of wantonness, or with rude persons to rioting, revelling,
or any other rude exercise. By this dominion that grace
comes to have over us, the Lord saves His people from
their sins. As we live in subjection to this power, we
are servants to another Prince: sin and Satan have lost
their dominion over us. This is God's salvation: by
this we come to "live soberly, righteously, and godly, in
this present world."

Quest. V. Whom did the apostle mean when he
said "Teaching us:" was it the world in general or only
some particulars?

Answ. Grace appears unto *all* men: every one tha
is born into the world hath a light in his soul, that show
him the motions of sin; and rebukes him when and a.
oft as he yields thereunto.

Quest. VI. We must confess that we have know
inward rebukes for sin; we have been checked, reproved

and convicted in ourselves after we have done amiss; but we have not found anything in and of ourselves, when strong motions and temptations have arisen in our minds, to restrain us from doing amiss; and to deny ungodliness and worldly lusts in our own strength seems too hard for any mortal. What can we do in such a case?

ANSW. Could man, in his own strength, deliver his soul from under the power of sin and Satan, return unto God, and lead a sober, righteous, godly life in this present world, there would have been no need of a Redeemer, no occasion for a Saviour; no use of a quickening Spirit, to give life to our souls; no necessity of God's writing his law in our hearts, for a rule to guide our steps by; no want of a light in our souls to show us where the devil spreads his net, casts his bait, lays his gin, and displays his false colours; but man can no more deliver his soul from the power of sin and Satan without the help of the Lord, than Israel, when they were in Egypt, could go free from the servitude of Pharaoh without his help; therefore grace appears unto all men for their aid. And though the appearance of grace may seem but small aid to set our souls free from the servitude of sin and Satan, and to conduct us in the way of life and salvation; it is not smaller than Israel's aid was, to bring them from under the servitude of Pharaoh, and conduct them to the promised land.

Israel's aid was but two aged men, (the younger of them being about eighty years old,) having no weapons but a rod in one of their hands; yet by this small means, God being with them, they brought from under the power and servitude of Pharaoh six hundred thousand men, besides women and children; and grace, being a Divine inspiration, is aid enough to bring six hundred thousand millions from under the servitude of sin and power of Satan, did men but confide therein, and give themselves up to be guided thereby.

Inward rebukes, if we have regard thereunto, beget a fear; and as "the fear of the Lord is the beginning of wisdom," so it is the beginning of a reformation of our lives.

If I am checked in myself for making a lie, and have regard to that which checked me, I shall be afraid of making another; or, if I find in myself rebukes for not

keeping my promise, or for doing anything amiss, and
have regard to such rebukes, I shall be afraid to do the
like, lest the next rebukes be sharper; and as this holy
fear abides in us, we come to deny ungodliness, and in
denying ungodliness, we learn righteousness; but such
as find in themselves rebukes for sin, and have no regard
thereunto, are no scholars in the school of grace.

If one plague will not make Pharaoh willing to let Israel
go, he shall have another, and another, until he be willing;
and if one rebuke will not make us willing to part with a
beloved sin, we shall have another, yea, trouble and terror.

Paul knew terror before he came to find peace with
God, and peace in his own conscience: he was acquainted
with judgment before he came to obtain victory. Nothing
hath power to break the bonds of captivity, and set us
free from the law of sin and death, but the law of the
Spirit of life in our own hearts.

QUEST. VII. What may truly and properly be called
a sober, righteous, godly life?

ANSW. A sober life, many may, in some measure, be
acquainted with; but a righteous, godly life is [too]
rarely considered.

That devotion which consists in hearing sermons,
reading good books, performing family duties, &c., hath
been accounted godliness, and the practitioners thereof
righteous people.

These things are not to be discommended, where they
are done in sincerity; but these are not the true character
of righteousness and godliness.

This [or] more might be found amongst the Scribes
and Pharisees, yet Jesus told his disciples, that "Except
their righteousness exceeded the righteousness of the
Scribes and Pharisees, they should in no case enter into
the kingdom of heaven."

One way to know what is righteous and godly, is to
consider what is unrighteous and ungodly, for the one is
opposite to the other, as light to darkness; and these
things that follow, most will acknowledge to be unrighteous and ungodly; namely, drunkenness, whoredom, theft,
envy, hatred, bloodshed, swearing, cursing, lying, extor-
tion, fraud, double-dealing, tale-bearing, and whispering

(which is the seed of strife): all these things are unrighteous, and pride, above many evils, most ungodly.

These are not fruits proceeding from the good Spirit of God, but from the evil spirit of this world: not issues of life, but streams that flow from a corrupt spring: these come not from the teaching of grace in our hearts, but from evil motions that arise in our minds: these make us sinners before the Lord; and as long as we live in the practice of any of them, we shall not be righteous in his sight.

These are infirmities of the soul, that millions of money have been given to physicians to cure, but behold, health hath not been by them restored—these are weeds that thousands have been hired to pluck up, but who to this day have not ma e clean gardens, nor ever will by all the art they have. Christ is the Physician of souls: none can take away the sins of the world, but he alone.

Whosoever thinks to attain to a righteous, godly life, but by the teachings of grace in his own heart, deceiveth his own soul.

Men may lop or hinder the growth of many branches of iniquity that appear outwardly, but cannot take away the cause which is within, and until the cause is removed, there can be no thorough cure.

"Walk in the Spirit," said Paul, "and ye shall not fulfil the lust of the flesh." Gal. v. 16. *That* is the only remedy; *that* is the soul-healing salve; and what is the walking in the Spirit, but following the leadings of grace in our own hearts? Grace, as it comes to have the rule over us, brings down all exalted thoughts, abaseth pride, shuts out covetousness, gives no place unto wrath, reduceth us to a cool, quiet frame of spirit, in which frame we can bear and suffer. Grace will not suffer us to do any unjust thing, nor allow us to speak an ill word, much less to be drunk, steal, or commit whoredom, or any such abominable vices; for it is the promised Spirit of truth that leads into all truth, leads out of all error, and so brings salvation indeed.

As God in his unlimited love to mankind "maketh his sun to rise on the evil and on the good, and sendeth rain on the just and on the unjust;" so he that hath good-will to all, which proceeds out of the heart, when the good Spirit of God comes to make its abode there, will not wrong any, oppress any, show violence to any, or speak evil of any, but be ready to serve all men in love and faithfulness.

And since this reformation is only and alone by the grace of our Lord Jesus Christ, give me leave to say with the prophet, (Isa. lv. 1.) " Ho, every one that thirsteth, come ye to the waters," and drink; every one that hath a desire in his soul after righteousness, turn in to the grace of God in his own heart. The water that the prophet invited all thirsty souls unto, is no other than that which Christ giveth; and whosoever drinketh thereof thirsteth no more, but hath (as many at this day can witness) a well in himself, not only issuing, but flowing up to eternal life.

The grace of God is a free gift, without money, and without price: nothing is required on man's part but to hearken thereunto, and take counsel therefrom: " Hear," said the prophet, " and your soul shall live."

Adam, hearkening to evil motions died unto righteousness, and so do all ungodly men; but he that hearkens to the voice of grace lives unto righteousness, and from the flowings of that spring that he hath in himself, leads a sober, righteous, godly life in this present world.

Hearing and reading, at the best, tend to instruct us in what we ought to do: but godliness is doing what grace teacheth.

QUEST. VIII. Were not the Scriptures written for our learning, and are not they a sufficient rule of righteousness?

ANSW. The Scriptures are a rule; but who can walk by that rule, unless he is inspired with the good Spirit of God? The Christian's rule of righteousness is Christ's direction. Let us, who say the Scripture is our rule, examine our abilities to walk by our rule. Are we lights to the world? Do our good works glorify God, or shame our Christian profession?

If ever we think to walk by Scripture rules, if ever we intend to keep our Lord's command, and if we would lead a righteous godly life in this present world, we must turn in to the grace of God in our own hearts, for that gives us power to keep to our rule.

OBJ. But some may say, our dependence for life and salvation is not on works of righteousness, but on faith; we believe, and therefore hope to be saved.

ANSW. I know that is most men's dependence; and faith we all think we have; but is it a faith that purifies the heart, and makes our bodies fit temples for the Holy Ghost?

Paul put the Corinthians on an examination of themselves, on a trial and proof of their faith, and it would not be amiss, if all that account themselves believers, did prove their faith, by the same touchstone: "Know ye not," said Paul, "your ownselves, how that Jesus Christ is in you, except ye be reprobates!" (2 Cor. xiii. 5.) This is life eternal, not only to hear of a God, and a Saviour, but to know him; to feel the power of God, and to be witnesses of Christ's salvation.

Faith and works of righteousness go together; he that hath the one hath both, and grace is the spring from whence both proceed.

A DESCRIPTION OF TRUE GODLINESS: OR, A TRIAL OF OUR CHRISTIANITY.

THE life and nature of Christ, all true Christians, who have the Spirit of Christ, may find in themselves; and others may have some sense thereof by reading and well considering the contents of the fifth, sixth, and seventh chapters of Matthew, where it is said, that Jesus "seeing the multitudes, went up into a mountain, and when he was sat, his disciples came unto him, and he opened his mouth and taught them." What he taught his disciples *then*, he teacheth all true Christians *now*: though he ascended, the Holy Spirit that dwelt in him descended, and did then, doth now, and to the end of the world will, tabernacle with all the Lord's redeemed, to be their Teacher; and as many as walk after this Spirit are taught of Christ, and walk in his footsteps; for as no vine beareth one kind of grape, and the branches another, so all the members of Christ answer the life of Christ in

their conversation; they are humble, lowly, meek, mer
ciful, patient, peaceable, just, upright, honest, and faithful
A Christian is not known by his words or his devotion
but by his works, his nature, his life, and his conversa
tion.

I shall not insist on all the particulars contained in the
fore-mentioned chapters, but chiefly on the five following
exhortations or commands of our Lord.

The true trial of [our] Christianity is to be found in
the life and nature of Christ. If the Spirit of Christ
hath the rule in us, these following fruits will be brough
forth by us.

First. In all our communication, our yea will be yea
and our nay, nay: the word that goeth out of our lips
will be sure.

He that is a Christian indeed hath no necessity in
himself, nor need to be urged by others, to bind his sou
with an oath to perform his word! for the law of the
Spirit of life in his own heart constrains him so to do.

Christians in their communications weigh their words
before they utter them, with their capacities to perfor
them; knowing that a promise cannot be broken withou
violating the righteous law of God in their own hearts
Whenever such violence is done, terror ensues; and thi
makes good men, who live under the government o
Christ dread much more to break their words, tha
others do to forfeit their bonds. This holy dread make
our yea to be yea, and our nay to be nay; this makes u
cautious in our promises, and careful in our performances
The exhortation may be read in Scripture, but the bind
ing tie must be known in our own hearts. All that hav
the Scripture have this rule: but unless we have
principle of life in ourselves, we cannot walk by thi
rule; and we must not only have such a principle, bu
we must also improve it by a continued practice, befor
it comes to be our life, our centre, and our nature. Ti
then we may say, "These things we *should* do;" bu
cannot say, "These things we *do,*" and so witnes
against ourselves, that though we have the Scripture
we walk not according to the Scriptures: though we hav
the words of Christ, we are not in the life and nature

Christ; our yea is not yea, and our nay, nay, in our communication : our words and our promises are not steadfast and sure.

A second exhortation or command of our Lord was this, "Resist not evil;" and this was not only His doctrine, but His life and nature, as we may plentifully read in Scripture. Though He met with revilings, reproaches, buffetings, and cruel usage, we do not find that He was once moved thereby, much less that ever He resisted; but gave His face to the smiter, and His cheeks to them that plucked off the hair; and when He was led as a lamb to the slaughter, "He was as a sheep dumb before the shearer; He opened not his mouth."

Now the fruits of the Spirit in the Head and members are one in nature; for, as Christ was humble, lowly, meek, patient, peaceable, under all His sufferings, so are Christians, if Christians indeed; they render not evil for evil, they desire not an eye for an eye, nor a tooth for a tooth: revenge of any kind is far from them; but as patience and forbearance was the life and nature of Christ, so it is the life and nature of all Christians, as they grow in grace.

And by this also professors of Christianity may prove themselves, whether they are Christians indeed; for it is the deed that manifesteth all things; bad men may have good words; forms may be imitated, but the patience, the meekness, the forbearance that dwelt in Christ, and may be found [in degree] in all true Christians, cannot be imitated.

A third exhortation or command of Christ was this, 'Love your enemies, bless them that curse you, do good to them that hate you, and pray for them which despitefully use you and persecute you."

This also was not only the doctrine, but the life and nature of Christ; and as it is the life and nature of Christ, so it is the life and nature of Christians, who are thoroughly leavened with the Spirit of Christ.

No man having the spirit of Jesus, and living under the government thereof, can hate the person of any man; for by creation we are all the workmanship of God's hands; and all true Christians know that enmity, hatred cursing, spite, and persecution, proceed not from men, a they are the Lord's creation, but, as they have lost thi image, and thereby become emptied of good, and fille with all evil; for, as an evil spirit comes to have the rul over us, evil fruits will be brought forth by us.

Could we but see ourselves, did we but observe ou own natures, with the fruits we bring forth in our live: we might easily judge of ourselves whether we wer converts or not: whether the Spirit of Christ, or th spirit of this world, had the rule in us and over us; fo the course of our lives, especially in times of tria declares who are led by the meek spirit of Jesus, an who are not; who are leavened with the leaven of right ousness, and who are not; who lead a sober, upright godly life, and who do not: it is not our words, but ou conversation [or lives] that manifest what spirit hath th rule in us and over us.

For until, by conversion, our natures come to b changed, we cannot love enemies, having as much enmit against them as they have against us; we cannot ble: them, we cannot pray for them; we shall be forward t do them hurt, but far from doing them good.

Come, professors of Christianity, lay aside your forn that you have long contended about; measure yourselv by this line, try yourselves by this touchstone; are yo reduced to such a frame of spirit as to "love your ene mies, bless them that curse you, do good to them th: hate you, and pray for them that despitefully use you an persecute you?"—This is a true character of Christianit

A fourth branch of the life, nature, and doctrine Christ was manifested in these words.

"Take no thought* for your life, what ye shall eat, what ye shall drink, nor yet for your body, what ye sha put on; but seek ye first the kingdom of God, and h righteousness."

As many as have found the kingdom of God and h righteousness, and are come to live under the rule ar government of a right spirit, have the mind of Chris

* [Rather, *Be not anxious.* This is a more correct translation.]

though they live in the world, their thoughts run not out after the world. A true Christian is diligent in his calling, moderate in his expenses, content in his state; takes but little thought what he shall eat, or what he shall drink, or wherewithal he shall be clothed; he delights in justice, equity, truth, and faithfulness, and his thoughts are exercised therein; and resting on God's providence, his honest endeavours are attended with a blessing.

Ungodly men seek the world first, I may say first, and last; the riches of the world, the honour of the world, the pleasures of the world, and the praise of the world; "what they shall eat, or what they shall drink," to please their appetites; "what they shall put on," to be accounted great in the world, and to have the pre-eminence above and before their fellow-creatures: their thoughts run far more, how they shall be conformable to the fashions of the world, than how they shall be conformable to the life, nature, and doctrine of Christ.

This is the natural state of the sons and daughters of men, whilst they continue in a state of degeneracy, aliens to the commonwealth of Israel, and strangers to that covenant of promise that the Lord made with the house of Jacob. And to a better state none can come, but by seeking and finding the kingdom of God and his righteousness, or the rule and government of Christ, by his eternal Spirit in their own hearts. There the seed is sown; there the leaven is laid; there the pearl of great price is found, but not without digging deep: for whilst vice is uppermost, virtue is lowermost; whilst sin reigns, the power [or dominion] of grace is not felt: the bringing down of the one is the exaltation of the other. There must be a death unto sin before there can be a new birth unto righteousness; and there must be a new birth unto righteousness, and a growth in righteousness, before we can centre in that content, as to "take no thought what we shall eat, what we shall drink, or wherewithal we shall be clothed." And so it is every man's principal concern first to seek the kingdom of God and his righteousness; first, to know the rule and government of a right spirit in himself; for this makes him capable of leading a Christian life, and of performing Christian duties both to God and man.

The fifth and last branch of the life, nature, an
doctrine of Christ, that I shall here insist upon, is this
" All things whatsoever ye would that men should do t
you, do ye even so to them; for this is the law an
the prophets."

This doing is accounted by many zealous professors o
Christianity, in our present age, a moral righteousness
and so but a small part, or rather no part of true godli
ness; but, rightly considered, all actual righteousness
if it proceeds from a right spirit, is in itself the tru
righteousness of faith.

Were the understandings of all who are called Christian
enlightened to see themselves as they are, to prove them
selves by this Christian rule, weigh themselves in thi
equal balance, the following sorts of men and women
with many others would no more pass for true Christians

As first, all who in suits of law, by perverting justice
or other subtle contrivances, possess themselves of house
lands, or goods, that they have no right unto.

Secondly, all such as by violent robbing, or privat
stealing, take that which is not their own.

Thirdly, all such as detain the wages of the hireling, c
grind the poor, by beating down the value of their labou
till they cannot live thereby.

Fourthly, all such as in trade or dealing use ligh
weights, short measure, or any other kind of deceit.

Fifthly, all such as either give or take bribes.

Sixthly, all such as take wages to serve, and are n
faithful to their trust.

Seventhly, all such as make contracts, and perform n
the same; or engage themselves by promises, and ha
no regard to their word.

Eighthly, all such as by evil reports, whisperings,
backbitings, sow the seeds of strife, create prejudice,
quench charity.

None of these abide in the doctrine of Christ, no
of these do as they would be done unto; though th
bear a Christian name, they are strangers to a Christia
life.

[To conclude,] By what way may the proud becor
humble, the wild become sober, the covetous becor

ontent, the fraudulent become just, the intemperate
ιecome moderate, the incontinent become chaste, the
ιnfaithful become faithful? I know many will say, By
ιearing good ministers, reading good books, and con-
erring with good men. But these things have been
ried, and that for several years, by many, yet no such
hange hath been thereby wrought.

By hearing good ministers, reading good books, and
onferring with good men, we may be convicted, but not
horoughly converted; for as virtue hath a spring, so
ice hath a root that [mere] words will not reach. The
trength of sin is the growth of that seed which the
vicked one hath sown in the inward parts of the sons
nd daughters of men: and forasmuch as the cause is
vithin, it is impossible it should be wholly removed by
hings without: as the cause is within, so the cure must
e within, by mortifying the body of sin, or bringing
own the strength thereof; which is thus effected:

There is no unrighteous thing done, but there is an
nward motion before there is any outward action; and,
y that light which enlighteneth every man that cometh
nto the world, if our eyes are inward, we may see those
notions; and the way to mortify the body of sin, is to
eny and turn from every such motion in the rising
hereof; for in their rising they are weak and powerless,
nd may be easily turned back. If we do not suppress
ice in the risings thereof, it will continue our lord:
ut by every such denial, we bring down that which
ould arise and reign in us and over us, whether it be
ride, covetousness, envy, falsehood, or any other vice
hatever: for the more denials are given to vice, the
wer assaults it will make: the stronger the opposition,
ie weaker the attempt. As yielding gives vice ground
ɔ grow from a seed to a body, denials bring it down from
body to a seed; so that though something thereof may
ɔide in us, it doth not reign over us.

The axe is never laid to the root of the tree till a
formation begins within; the life of righteousness
ands [or has its rise] in the mortification of sin, which
an inward work. The spirit of this world must
ɔ brought down, before the Spirit of the Lord can be
alted in us.

And as they that live after the flesh, have less life,
less light, less grace, less fear; so such as walk after the
Spirit, doing such things as are upright, honest, and of
good report, from a principle in their own hearts, find an
increase: they come to have more life, more light, more
grace, more fear of offending God, or their neighbour;
and this increase is a living unto righteousness. As
the one goes further from, so the other draws nearer to
the kingdom of heaven.

Now a talent is not improved by lying hid in a
napkin: if we would have more grace, we must exercise
the measure we have attained unto: we must live in the
continual practice of right things; we must keep in lowliness, meekness, temperance, patience, and other virtues;
we must be just in our dealings, as well in the smallest
concern, as in those which are more weighty; for a small
matter turns the balance, and if that small matter
be wanting, things are not just, we do not as we would
be done by.

And this just dealing, as righteousness comes to reign,
will be no hard thing, for as we accustom ourselves
thereunto, it will be uppermost; it will be as a diligent
handmaid, ready to offer her service; and every act of
righteousness, performed in a right spirit, hath its reward
which is not only an answer of peace, but joy in the
Holy Ghost.

The way of life is the way of pleasantness, all her paths
are peace. At the beginning of our journey, it will seem
a strait and narrow way; but after we have travelled
on a while, we shall run therein with great delight. For
the kingdom of heaven, or Christ's government by His
eternal Spirit in the hearts of His people, doth not consist
of righteousness alone: the righteousness that proceeds
from a right spirit is accompanied with peace and joy.
As ill-doing is attended with trouble and sorrow, well
doing is attended with peace and joy. All the pleasure
of wickedness, that the whole world affords, are not to
be compared to the joys of a righteous life. Every evil
motion we deny, in obedience unto Christ, affordeth
superior joy to that which a warrior hath in battle, when
his enemy fleeth before him.

I cannot recommend myself, or any other, to any

etter way for the reforming of our lives, than to turn in
ar eye to the gift of God in ourselves, that by His
andle [or light] we may see the risings of vice, and so
eny it: that the contrary, which is grace and truth, may
se and reign in us; for that is our help, that is our
strength, and that is our defence. .

Many have been awakened from the sleep of sin, and
ave had in themselves a true hunger and thirst after
righteousness, who being awakened by an outward min-
try, from *that* expected to have their hunger and thirst
atisfied: but "it is the Spirit that quickeneth." What
an satisfy a soul that thirsteth after righteousness, but
that which is in very truth the spring of righteousness?
this in ourselves the well is to be found, that whosoever
rinketh of shall never thirst; *there* is the spring that
oweth up unto everlasting life.

As the kingdom of heaven stands not in words, but in
ower; so it is not words, but the power of God that can
ortify the deeds of the body, change our nature and
ake us new creatures.

Should we enter into reasoning with any motions of
n, it is much if we are not overcome thereby, for it is
he nature of sin, not to turn back at a small denial,
pecially if it be a sin that hath prevailed over us before;
at in turning therefrom we give it the repulse; if it be
ot hearkened unto, it goes back.

And what can show us the rising of evil motions?
Preachers cannot; books cannot; nothing that is without
an effectually show us what is within: it must be an
ward light; it must be the eternal Spirit, that was in
he beginning given unto man for an Instructor.

As the seed of sin grows and waxeth strong in us by
ur yielding to evil motions, so the seed of grace grows
ad waxeth strong in us by the denying of evil motions.
s the old man is put off, the new man is put on; as
ce is denied, virtue is embraced; and this new man
akes us new creatures: that which is created after God
news in us the image of God: and bearing that image
holiness and righteousness, our conversation will de-
are us to be Christians indeed.

But if this old man with his deeds of darkness be not
t off, the new man that is created after God's image in

righteousness and true holiness will not be put on; an
though we have been awakened unto righteousness, w
shall fall asleep again, some in one form and some i
another, feeding on words without any sense of power o
life: and this second sleep appears to be a dead sleep
for that though we may hear much spoken against pride
covetousness, envy, &c., we are not so much as touche
therewith, but live in the open show thereof.

Did the sons and daughters of men who are calle
Christians, make it their concern to be Christians indeed
by mortifying in themselves the spirit of this world
which is the origin of all vice, they would be not onl
a happy, but a lovely people: for by mortifying the bod
of sin, oppression would cease; all wrongs and injurie
would be at an end; love would spring both to God an
man; grace would grow; humility, meekness, modera
tion, and all other virtues would show themselves. The
would be another manner of people in their conversation
their words and their works would be just, upright, an
honest; they would confide in one another without an
scruple or doubt.—What is more lovely than to be a
all times, and on all occasions, just, upright, honest, an
faithful, doing to all men, in all things whatsover, eve
as we would that they should do unto us? Living und
the rule and government of a right spirit qualifies us f
performing every Christian duty:—We shall love t
Lord our God with all our hearts, and our neighbou
as ourselves; which is the sum of all godliness, and tl
true character of Christianity.

END.

London: Printed by E. Couchman & Co., 10, Throgmorton Street; for Tract Association of the Society of Friends. Sold at the Deposito 12, Bishopsgate Street Without.—1864.

RELIGIOUS DUTIES.

CONSISTING CHIEFLY OF EXTRACTS FROM THE HOLY
SCRIPTURES.

*Selected from " The Duties of Religion and Morality, as inculcated in
the Holy Scriptures, with preliminary and occasional Observations,
by* HENRY TUKE."

CHAP. I.

ON FAITH AND HOPE IN GOD.

THE first duty which we owe to the Divine Being, is Faith; or, a belief in the existence of God, in his power, and in his goodness. It is called Faith, because these great and important truths do not admit of that kind of demonstration by which many other truths may be proved; and yet all around us, and all within us, so fully evince the existence, the power, and the goodness of a Divine Being, that this may be considered a just and reasonable duty. On a subject so much above our comprehension, we must be content, in some degree, to walk by faith and not by sight. We need not, therefore, stumble at this first principle of religion, to which our implicit acquiescence is required. "Without faith it is impossible to please God; for he that cometh unto him, must believe that He is, and that He is a rewarder of all those that diligently seek him." When these principles have their proper influence on the heart, they are of great service to us in our passage through life; and tend greatly to reconcile our minds to those various circumstances, which are, by an all-wise Providence, permitted or dispensed to us. It is by the eye of faith that we see Him, who is, to every other eye, invisible; and by this eye of faith we are enabled to look beyond the things which are seen, and are temporal, to those things which are not seen, and are eternal. It was under the influence of this faith, that "Moses chose rather to suffer affliction with the people of God, than to enjoy the pleasures of sin; seeing Him who is invisible, and having an eye to the recompense of reward."

                    [*Price* 1*s. per dozen.*]

From faith in the Divine Being and Providence proceeds that "Hope which is an anchor to the soul, both sure and steadfast." In the storms and tempests attendant on this probationary state of existence, an humble hope and trust in the mercies and providence of God are essentially necessary to the preservation of the vessel, from being driven on the rocks or quicksands which surround our coast; and on which shipwreck is sometimes made of everything that renders life valuable, or eternity desirable.

This hope or trust may be divided into two parts; first, as it relates to the providence of God in reference to the things of this life; and secondly, as it relates to his mercy in respect to those things which pertain to that life which is to come. With respect to the first, our blessed Lord strengthens his disciples in their confidence in the Divine Providence by many apt allusions, and pressing exhortations; " I say unto you, take no thought (or rather, be not anxious) for your life, what ye shall eat or what ye shall drink; nor yet for your body what ye shall put on.—Behold the fowls of the air; for they sow not, neither do they reap, nor gather into barns; yet your Heavenly Father feedeth them.—Consider the lilies how they grow; they toil not, neither do they spin and yet I say unto you, that Solomon in all his glory, was not arrayed like one of these. Wherefore, if God so cloth the grass of the field, which to-day is, and to-morrow is cast into the oven, how much more will he clothe you, O ye of little faith; Therefore seek ye first the kingdom of God and his righteousness, and all these things shall be added unto you." We have, in the prophet Habakkuk, an eminent instance of resignation to Divine protection, and of confidence therein. After foreseeing some impending calamities, he expresses himself in this animated and animating language "Although the fig tree shall not blossom, neither shall fruit be in the vines; the labour of the olive shall fail, and the fields shall yield no meat; the flocks shall be cut off from the fold, and there shall be no herd in the stalls; yet I will rejoice in the Lord, I will joy in the God of my salvation."

It sometimes happens that religiously disposed minds fall into a state of depression and discouragement, respecting their inward or their future state. This, so far as it excites vigilance and exertion, may be beneficial; but when its tendency is to lead to despair of the mercies of God, and to carry away our confidence in his goodness and loving-kindness, becomes a disposition to which we ought not to give way but should carefully guard against its attacks. This situation mind is strongly described by the Psalmist in the 77th salm: "In the day of my trouble I sought the Lord: my nd was stretched out in the night and ceased not; my soul fused to be comforted. I remembered God, and was trou ed, and my spirit was overwhelmed. Will the Lord cast off r ever? will he be favourable no more? Is his mercy clean me for ever? doth his promise fail for evermore? hath God rgotten to be gracious? hath he in anger shut up his tender ercies?" Here the Psalmist seems to recollect his own culiar weakness and turns his reflections another way. "I id, this is my infirmity; but I will remember the years of e right hand of the most High. I will remember the works the Lord; surely I will remember thy wonders of old. will meditate also of all thy works, and talk of thy doings. iy way, O God! is in the sanctuary: who is so great a God our God!" In another Psalm, we find the pious David nsoling himself in this encouraging soliloquy: "Why art ou cast down, O my soul? and why art thou disquieted thin me? Hope thou in God; for I shall yet praise him o is the health of my countenance and my God." Here see the benefit of attending to that Apostolic exhortation: ast not away, therefore, your confidence, which hath great ompense of reward."

The following passages point out the necessity and advan es of a proper trust or confidence in God, on all occasions: rust in the Lord with all thy heart, and lean not unto own understanding. In all thy ways acknowledge him, he shall direct thy paths. Commit thy works unto the rd, and thy thoughts shall be established. Commit thy y unto him, trust also in him, and he shall bring it to pass. dgment is before him, therefore trust thou in him."

CHAP. II.

ON THE LOVE OF GOD.

When we consider the attributes which are ascribed to Divine Being, and the relation in which we stand to him, hing can be more reasonable, nothing more becoming that tion, than the tribute of Love; it is a disposition of mind ch we ought peculiarly to cultivate, as being, in an espe manner connected both with our duty and happiness. en this feeling predominates in the mind those religious raints which are aptly described by "the yoke of Christ,"

become easy, and his burthen is made light. The ways o
righteousness come to be "ways of pleasantness, and all it
paths are peace."

When our Saviour was insidiously asked, "Which is th
great commandment of the law?" the reply was, "Thou sha
love the Lord thy God, with all thy heart, and with all th
soul, and with all thy mind. This is the first and great con
mandment." Did we place this duty sufficiently before us, a
the most desirable object of our attainment, and frequentl
examine ourselves respecting it; considering at the sam
time the many reasonable motives which we have for fulfillin
it; we should be likely to witness an increase of this love i
our hearts, and feelingly to unite with the expressions of Hol
Writ: "I love thy commandments above gold, yea, above fir
gold. Thy word is very pure, therefore thy servant loveth i
Let them that love thy name be joyful in thee, for tho
Lord! wilt bless the righteous. Let such as love thy sa
vation say continually, the Lord be magnified! The Lo
preserveth all them that love him."

But of all the inducements to the love of God, there
none so powerful as that which the Apostle mentions: "Go
commendeth his love towards us, in that, while we were y
sinners, Christ died for us." In the enjoyment of this co
soling faith, Christians can say, "The love of God is sh
abroad in our hearts by the Holy Ghost which is given un
us." Such was the prevalence and the establishment
this love in the heart of the Apostle, and some of his fello
believers, that he could confidently declare; "I am persuad
that neither death nor life, nor angels, nor principalities, n
powers, nor things present, nor things to come; nor heigl
nor depth, nor any other creature, shall be able to separa
us from the love of God, which is in Christ Jesus our Lord

The principal proof of our love, arises from our obedience
what we know to be the Divine will concerning us, or his co
mandments to us. "If ye love me," says our Saviour "ke
my commandments." Consistent with this language, is th
of the Apostle John: "This is the love of God, that we ke
his commandments; and his commandments are not grievou

In order to guard us against the loss of that love which
so important a part of our duty, the following advices a
cautions are given: "Set your affections on things abo
and not on things on the earth; love not the world, neith
the things which are in the world; If any man love t
world, the love of the Father is not in him; for all that is
the world, the lust of the flesh, the lust of the eyes, and t

ride of life, are not of the Father, but of the world. The world passeth away and the lust thereof. Whosoever will be friend of the world, is the enemy of God, for the friendship of the world, is enmity with God." Let not these interesting cautions and observations be forgotten; and then the following salutations of the Apostle may be verified in our experience: "The Lord direct your hearts into the love of God, and into the patient waiting for Christ.—Grace be with all them that love our Lord Jesus Christ in sincerity."

CHAP. III.

ON THE FEAR OF GOD.

The next duty which we owe to the Divine Being, and which may probably be considered by many as previous to that of Love, is the fear of offending him. This has been, in all ages, the disposition of the righteous, by which they have been, in a great measure, preserved from falling into those religious and immoral practices, which draw down Divine displeasure on men. When we consider the Omnipotence, the Omniscience, and the Justice of God, we shall find abundant cause for cherishing this Fear, accompanied with an awful reverence of spirit towards him. So forcibly was this duty impressed on the mind of one of the Patriarchs, that the Divine Being was styled, "The fear of Isaac." Joseph was an eminent example of the beneficial effects of this fear. He says of himself, "I fear God," and he gave a striking proof of it, when, under a peculiar temptation, he resisted it with this memorable language, "How can I do this great wickedness, and sin against God?"

When we attend to all the beneficial consequences which are described in Scripture, as the result of this virtue, its importance must forcibly impress our minds, and should stimulate us to the attainment of it. "Thou shalt fear the Lord thy God," was a precept early given to the Jewish nation, and was added to many of their legal institutions, as an incentive to duty. In the book of Job, we have a grand description of the inestimable value of true wisdom; which is, after all that is said of it, reduced to this simple, but important point: "The fear of the Lord, that is wisdom, and to depart from evil, is understanding." Solomon concludes his no less fine description of wisdom in similar words: "The fear of the Lord is the beginning of wisdom; and the knowledge of the

Holy is understanding." In this description of wisdom, h
also says, "The fear of the Lord is to hate evil: pride, an
arrogancy, and the evil way, and the froward mouth, do
hate." Again, "By the fear of the Lord, men depart fror
.evil. It is a fountain of life, to depart from the snares of deatl
By humility and the fear of the Lord are riches, and honou
and life."

The Psalmist inculcates the Divine fear, in this invitin
language: "Come, ye children, and I will teach you th
fear of the Lord. What man is he that desireth life, an
loveth many days, that he may see good? Keep thy tongu
from evil, and thy lips from speaking guile. Depart fror
evil, and do good, seek peace, and pursue it. The eyes (
the Lord are upon the righteous, and his ears are open t
their cry. The face of the Lord is against them that do evi
to cut off the remembrance of them from the earth." W
have many other incitements to this duty in the Scripture
particularly in the Psalms: "God is greatly to be feared i
the assembly of the saints, and to be had in reverence of a
them that are about him. He is to be feared above all god
Thou, even thou, O God of Jacob! art to be feared: ar
who may stand in thy sight, when once thou art angry? B
there is forgiveness with thee, that thou mayest be feare
Stand in awe and sin not. Serve the Lord with fear, ar
rejoice with trembling. Let all the earth fear the Lord. L
all the inhabitants of the world stand in awe of him. Tl
Lord reigneth, let the people tremble. He sitteth betwee
the Cherubims, let the earth be moved. Who would n
fear thee, O King of Nations! for to thee doth it appertain

Our blessed Redeemer gave his disciples some particul
instructions on this subject: "I say unto you, my frienc
be not afraid of them that kill the body, and after that ha
no more that they can do. But I will forewarn you who
you shall fear. Fear Him, who, after he hath killed, ha
power to cast into hell; yea, I say unto you, fear Him."

Thus we find in every dispensation the fear of God was
necessary attainment. It formed a prominent part in th
message, delivered by the angel, who was seen to fly in t
midst of heaven, having the everlasting Gospel to prea
unto them that dwell on the earth; saying with a loud voi
"Fear God, and give glory to him, for the hour of his juc
ments is come; and worship him that made heaven a
earth, and the sea, and the fountains of waters."

CHAP. IV.

ON RELIGIOUS MEDITATION.

By Religious Meditation, is meant that inward retirement f mind from the cares and concerns of this world, in which e may contemplate the works of God, both in creation and redemption: and consider the duties which we owe to him, ad one to another.

To have the mind frequently engaged in this manner, is f no small importance to the religious improvement of a hristian. For this purpose as well as for that of inward stirement and private prayer, some persons set apart partiilar times of the day; whilst others find it practicable when iey are engaged in their outward employments, inwardly to stire from the world's concerns, secretly to meditate upon ie law of the Lord, to wait upon him for the renewal of heir spiritual strength, and to pour out their supplications nto him. To prescribe the mode of performing these uties, is not my business; and indeed it is a point in which e cannot well prescribe one for another. That they are ities, important and beneficial, will, no doubt, be generally lmitted; and we have reason to believe, that they have sen practised by the righteous of all generations. We are ld that Enoch walked with God: and we may reasonably ippose, that this was by secret communion with him, and editation upon his works and commands.

Of religious meditation we have an example in the case ' Isaac; and from the incidental mention of his "going to the field at eventide to meditate," a presumptive proof, least, is afforded that the practice was not uncommon ith the Patriarchs. To Joshua, the successful leader of e children of Israel into the promised land, this command is given: "This book of the law shall not depart out of y mouth; but thou shalt meditate therein day and night, at thou mayest observe to do according to all that is ritten therein; for then thou shalt make thy way prosrous, and then thou shalt have good success." We have t little left on record in the Scriptures, of the private, ligious exercises of those concerning whom they are writa, previously to the book of Psalms. Here we find in the st Psalm, religious meditation represented as a material part the employment of the man who is styled blessed. "His light," says the Psalmist, "is in the law of the Lord, and

in his law doth he meditate day and night." It was, no
doubt, to this duty that the Psalmist alluded, when he gave
this exhortation: "Commune with your own heart upon
your bed; and be still." The benefits which result from
religious meditation are thus described: "My soul shall be
satisfied as with marrow and fatness, and my mouth shall
praise thee with joyful lips, when I remember thee upon my
bed, and meditate on thee in the night watches." Again we
find this employment excellently and profitably illustrated
and its benefits under close conflicts strongly described: "I
have considered the days of old; the years of ancient times
I call to remembrance my song in the night, and my spirit
made diligent search. Will the Lord cast off for ever, and
will he be favourable no more?" After various considerations of this kind the Psalmist concludes in this manner:
"Surely I will remember thy wonders of old. I will meditate also of all thy works, and talk of thy doings. Thy way,
O God, is in the sanctuary: Who is so great a God as our
God!"

But the inspired writers did not confine their meditation
to the law of their God, or to his providential dealings with
his people. They saw him, and they adored him, in the
works of creation. From these they drew many beautiful
similes, and inculcated much important and humbling instruction. "The heavens declare the glory of God, and the
firmament showeth his handy-work. Day unto day uttereth
speech, and night unto night showeth knowledge. There is no
speech nor language where their voice is not heard." Again,
"When I consider thy heavens the work of thy fingers, the
moon and the stars which thou hast ordained, What is man
that thou art mindful of him? and the son of man, that thou
visitest him?"

Our duties also afford very copious subjects for our meditation. Thus the Apostle Paul enumerates many particulars
of a very comprehensive nature, and recommends them to
the contemplation of his favourite Philippians: "Whatsoever
things are true, whatsoever things are honest, whatsoever
things are just, whatsoever things are pure, whatsoever things
are lovely, whatsoever things are of good report; if there be
any virtue, if there be any praise, think on these things.
To this exhortation he adds these memorable words: "Those
things which ye have both learned, and received, and heard
and seen in me, do; and the God of peace shall be with you.

CHAP. V.

ON WATCHFULNESS AND WAITING UPON GOD.

When we consider how we are surrounded in this world y temptations to evil; how much our own propensities icline us to comply with it; and that, in addition to these iducements, there is also an unwearied enemy and evil oirit, who is seeking our destruction; watchfulness will ppear to be an indispensable duty. The world, the flesh id the devil, are all represented in Holy Writ as enemies, ʒainst which it is necessary to be upon our guard. The orld lieth in wickedness, and its friendship is enmity with ʰód. "The flesh lusteth against the spirit;" and so powerful that enemy who has these weapons to war with against ir happiness, that an Apostle formerly gave this important ʰhortation to the early believers: "Be sober, be vigilant, ʰr your adversary the devil, as a roaring lion, goeth about ʰeking whom he may devour." When these considerations ʰve taken place in our minds, we shall be convinced of the ʰopriety of that universal command given by our blessed ʰviour: "What I say unto you, I say unto all; watch." ʒain, "Watch and pray that ye enter not into temptation." ʰus also the Apostles: "Watch ye, stand fast in the faith, ʰit you like men, be strong. Let us watch and be sober. ʰ ye sober, and watch unto prayer."

The truly humble-minded Christian, is frequently brought ʰ feel his own incapacity for every good word and work. ʰ is often made sensible of that important truth inculcated ʰ his Divine Master: "No man can come unto me, except ʰ Father which hath sent me, draw him." From this ʰse and feeling, he finds the necessity of patiently waiting ʰon God for help and strength in the performance of his ʰigious duties. The benefit of this state of mind is freʰently described in Holy Writ, and its duty strongly ʰforced: "Wait on the Lord, be of good courage, and he ʰll strengthen thy heart: wait, I say, on the Lord." ʰain, "I waited patiently for the Lord, and he inclined ʰo me, and heard my cry. He brought me up also out of ʰorrible pit, out of the miry clay: and set my feet upon a ʰk, and established my goings; and he hath put a new ʰg in my mouth, even praise unto our God. Many shall ʰit and fear, and shall trust in the Lord." Thus does the ʰal Psalmist describe the beneficial consequences of waiting ʰn God, and Solomon represents wisdom, no doubt the

wisdom which is from above, speaking in this manne
" Blessed is the man that heareth me, watching daily at n
gates, waiting at the posts of my doors."

The prophet Habakkuk appears to have been sensible of t]
importance of this duty, both for his own particular benef
and for the fulfilment of his prophetical office; " I will sta
upon my watch, and set me upon the tower, and will wat
to see what he will say unto me, and what I shall answ
when I am reproved." In this state of mind he received t
Divine communication and commission to " write the visio
and make it plain upon tables, that he may run that reade
it." Thus also we find the Apostles were commanded by the
Heavenly Master, previously to their entering upon the
Apostolical office, " to wait at Jerusalem for the promise
the Father; which," saith he, " ye have heard of me."

I shall conclude this subject with the lively descripti
given by the evangelical prophet, of the benefits arising fro
this exercise of mind: " Even the youths shall faint a
grow weary, and the young men shall utterly fall; but th
that wait upon the Lord, shall renew their strength, th
shall mount up with wings as eagles : they shall run, and n
be weary; they shall walk, and not faint."

CHAP. VI.

ON PRAYER.

Of all the duties which Religion requires, there is not
more clearly obligatory, or more interestingly important, tl
that of Prayer. This is a duty which we may be said to o
to ourselves as well as to God. When we consider
manifold wants, our infirmities, and our dangers, with
incapacity to supply or relieve ourselves; and when
reflect that the Divine Being alone is capable of affording
that supply and assistance which are necessary for our
sent and future well-being; the importance of this duty
ourselves, or for our own benefit, must be obvious. Ag
when we consider that God is the giver of every good
perfect gift; that the earth is his, and the fulness there
that in him are hid all the treasures of wisdom and kn
ledge; these considerations show, that prayer is a duty wl
we owe to his Omnipotence and Goodness : but in addi
to these reasonable considerations, the commands which
given us in the Holy Scriptures, impose prayer upon u

eing indispensably due to the Almighty. We have various recepts and examples, respecting this duty in the Old 'estament; all tending to incite us "to lift up our hearts with ur hands to God in the heavens;" but in the New Testament he directions are most full and particular. Our blessed Lord 1culcated this duty very forcibly among his disciples: and /è are told, "that he spake a parable to them to this end, hat men ought always to pray and not to faint." The Apostle 'aul is very earnest in his injunctions on this head; "Be areful (or anxious) for nothing; but in everything by prayer nd supplication, with thanksgiving, let your requests be 1ade known unto God. Continue in prayer, and watch in he same with thanksgiving. Pray without ceasing. I will herefore that men pray everywhere, lifting up holy hands, rithout wrath and doubting: that supplications, prayers, 1tercessions, and giving of thanks, be made for all men; for ings and for those that are in authority; that we may lead a uiet and peaceable life, in all godliness and honesty; for this s good and acceptable in the sight of God our Saviour."

But there are some circumstances necessary to be attended o, in order to make our prayers acceptable, and such as will e likely to procure a favourable answer to them. The first f these is sincerity of heart, in the abhorrence of sin, and 1 desires after holiness and purity. Of this the Psalmist ppears to have been fully sensible, when he says, "If I egard iniquity in my heart, the Lord will not hear me." .gain, "I will wash my hands in innocency, so will I com- ass thine altar, O Lord!" Solomon also makes a memorable bservation on this subject: "He that turneth away his ear 'om hearing the law, even his prayers shall be an abomina- on to the Lord." In another place he says, "The sacrifice f the wicked is an abomination to the Lord: but the prayer f the upright is his delight." In the answer which the young an who had been blind made to the cavilling Jews, we have 1 instructive remark on the qualification for true prayer: We know that God heareth not sinners; but if any man be worshipper of God, and doeth his will, him he heareth." he Apostle John also inculcates a similar doctrine: "Be- ved, if our hearts condemn us not, then have we confidence wards God; and whatsoever we ask we receive of him, cause we keep his commandments, and do those things at are pleasing in his sight."

The direction and caution which were given by our viour on this subject, should also be remembered, in order avoid that ostentatious disposition which mars, in the

sight of God, all our otherwise good words and works:
"When thou prayest, thou shalt not be as the hypocrites are:
for they love to pray standing in the synagogues, and in the
corners of the streets, that they may be seen of men. But
thou, when thou prayest, enter into thy closet; and when
thou hast shut thy door, pray to thy Father who is in secret;
and thy Father who seeth in secret, shall reward thee openly."

Our Lord having thus cautioned his disciples against a
desire to be seen and praised of men, proceeds to correct
another false apprehension which some had entertained, that
they should be heard for their much speaking. Of this notion
he exposes the folly; and, in order to exemplify the doctrine
which he taught, he gives his disciples a most comprehensive, and, at the same time, concise specimen of prayer.

"Our Father, who art in heaven, hallowed be thy name:
thy kingdom come: thy will be done in earth as it is in
heaven. Give us this day our daily bread; and forgive us
our debts as we forgive our debtors: and lead us not into
temptation, but deliver us from evil, for thine is the kingdom, and the power, and the glory, for ever. Amen."

On one part of this excellent prayer, our blessed Lord makes
a short comment, to show the importance of a disposition of
mind, which, through Divine grace, it is in our power, and
is certainly our duty, to attain. "If ye forgive men their
trespasses, your heavenly Father will also forgive you; but if
ye forgive not men their trespasses, neither will your Father
forgive your trespasses." Of how great importance is this
duty of forgiveness! and, may it not be added, how little is
it attended to!

Our approaches to the throne of Divine grace, ought also
to be accompanied with a trust in the mediation and intercession of Jesus Christ: to which he himself holds out this
and other encouraging promises: "Verily, verily, I say unto
you, whatsoever ye shall ask the Father in my name, he will
give it you." We are also directed to "ask in faith, nothing
wavering."

There is another important requisite necessary to be
attended to, in the performance of the solemn duty of prayer
This is, the assistance of the Holy Spirit; the necessity
of which the Apostle Paul clearly sets forth, when he says
"The Spirit also helpeth our infirmities: for we know no
what we should pray for, as we ought: but the Spirit itsel
maketh intercession for us with groanings which cannot b
uttered: and he that searcheth the hearts knoweth what i
the mind of the Spirit, because he maketh intercession fo

the saints according to the will of God." The same Apostle, in another place, describes true prayer in this manner: "Praying always, with all prayer and supplication in the Spirit, and watching thereunto with all perseverance."

But notwithstanding these requisites for the performance of true prayer, let not any be discouraged from an attention to this important duty from a sense of their own imperfections. If we are sincerely desirous of being brought into a state of perfect acceptance with our Maker, we may approach him, with an humble dependence on the Spirit and mediation of his Son, putting up our prayers unto him, and "watching thereunto with all perseverance." Thus the penitent sinner will meet with that gracious acceptance which is mercifully held out to him, and the truth of the language of the Psalmist, will be verified in his experience :—" As the heaven is high above the earth, so great is his mercy towards them that fear him. As far as the east is from the west, so far has he removed our transgressions from us. Like as a father pitieth his children, so the Lord pitieth them that fear him: for he knoweth our frame, he remembereth that we are dust."

Great is the importance of a due attention to the duty on which we are now treating, and to the various circumstances necessary for its acceptable performance. Of this the Psalmist appears to have been deeply sensible, when he preferred this petition to the Divine Being : " Let my prayer come up before thee as incense, and the lifting up of my hands as an evening sacrifice." For want of a due attention to those circumstances, there is reason to fear that many at this time may be subject to the same remark, which the Apostle James makes concerning some in his day : " Ye fight and war, yet ye have not, because ye ask not; ye ask and receive not, because ye ask amiss; that ye may consume it upon your lusts." On the other hand, we are told by the same Apostle, that " the fervent prayer of a righteous man availeth much." This we have good reason to believe, is the prayer which ascends like incense, before the throne of God, and of the Lamb.

CHAP. VII.

ON THANKSGIVING AND PRAISE.

Thanksgiving is an expression of our gratitude to the Divine Being for favours received. Praise may convey a sense of admiration, as well as of gratitude, and is applicable to the power and wisdom as well as to the goodness of God.

Thus says the Psalmist: "Oh that men would praise the Lord for his goodness, and for his wonderful works to the children of men!"

The reasonableness of these duties, and the obligations to perform them, are so self-evident to every considerate mind that believes in a Divine Being and Providence, that, if we had no injunctions to the practise of them, they would unavoidably become an almost involuntary effusion from every feeling heart. But it is to be regretted that, either from want of consideration, or from want of sensibility, there are among those who are surrounded with blessings on every hand, many who are inattentive to the favours which they enjoy or ungrateful for them. Ingratitude to the Divine Being for temporal or spiritual blessings, is a sin which is peculiarly marked by his displeasure. Of this we have a strong proof in the instance of the Israelites, of whom, after recapitulating the peculiar favours by which they had been distinguished, it is said: "But Jeshurun waxed fat and kicked; then he forsook God who made him, and lightly esteemed the Rock of his salvation. They provoked him to jealousy with strange gods, they sacrificed unto devils and not to God. And when the Lord saw it he abhorred them, because of the provoking of his sons, and of his daughters."

Here we see the idolatry of the Jews described as the consequence of their ingratitude for the blessings which were conferred upon them; and the Apostle, in describing the depraved state of the heathen world, both in its religion and morality, traces it to the same source: "Because that when they knew God, they glorified him not as God, neither were thankful, but became vain in their imaginations, and their foolish heart was darkened: professing to be wise they became fools; and changed the glory of the incorruptible God, into an image made like to corruptible man; and to birds, and to four-footed beasts, and creeping things. Wherefore God also gave them up to uncleanness, through the lusts of their own hearts, to dishonour their own bodies between themselves; who changed the truth of God into a lie, and worshipped and served the creature more than the Creator, who is blessed for ever. Amen."

Numerous are the examples, as well as the exhortations, which are contained in the Holy Scriptures, and particularly in the book of Psalms, relating to this subject, from which it may be sufficient to extract the following: "It is a good thing to give thanks unto the Lord, and to sing praises unto thy name, O most High; to show forth thy loving-kindness in the morning, and thy faithfulness every night. Let the people praise thee, O God; let all the people praise thee. Bless the Lord, O my soul! and all that is within me, bless his holy name. Bless the Lord, O my soul! and forget not all his benefits; who forgiveth all thy iniquities; who healeth all thy diseases; who redeemeth thy life from destruction; who crowneth thee with loving-kindness and tender mercies. Oh! that men would praise the Lord for his goodness, and for his wonderful works to the children of men."

The inspired writers of the New Testament likewise furnish us with many incitements to this duty. Christianity itself was introduced with, "Glory to God in the highest," as an acknowledgment previously necessary to the promotion of "peace on earth and good-will towards men." We find the mother of our Lord pouring out her soul, in a grateful song of praise, which begins with this pious language: "My soul doth magnify the Lord, and my spirit hath rejoiced in God my Saviour—for he that is mighty hath done to me great things; and holy is his name." The Apostle Paul very pressingly inculcates an attention to these duties. "In every thing," says he, "give thanks, for this is the will of God in Christ Jesus. And be not drunk with wine, wherein is excess, but be ye filled with the Spirit; speaking to yourselves in psalms, and in hymns, and in spiritual songs; singing and making melody in your heart to the Lord, giving thanks always, for all things, unto God and the Father, in the name of our Lord Jesus Christ. By him, therefore, let us offer the sacrifice of praise to God continually, that is, the fruit of our lips, giving thanks to his name."

It is not, however, a formal performance of this duty that will meet with Divine approbation. It must, like prayer, be the produce of an humble and sanctified heart. When this is attained to, thanksgiving and praise will frequently become involuntary effusions, and ascend with acceptance before Him who is the giver of every good and perfect gift; and, as this state of mind is continued in, qualification will finally be experienced to join with that innumerable multitude, mentioned in the book of Revelations, "who stood before the Throne and before the Lamb, clothed with white robes, saying, Salvation to our God, who sitteth upon the Throne, and unto the Lamb;" to which sacred anthem the whole angelic host returned this responsive language: "Amen. Blessing, and glory, and wisdom, and thanksgiving, and honour, and power, and might, be unto our God, for ever and ever. Amen."

CHAP. VIII.

ON PUBLIC WORSHIP, AND THE APPROPRIATION OF ONE
DAY IN THE WEEK FOR THIS PURPOSE.

The Public Worship of the Almighty is a special duty of
all men, who have opportunity and ability for it. This results
from the relation in which we all stand to God, as our Creator,
Preserver, and Benefactor. Common benefits demand united
thanksgiving and praises. A social acknowledgment of these
mercies and blessings, not only become us as dependent
beings, but is attended with various advantages. The rich
and prosperous, when thus assembled with the poor and
afflicted, and acknowledging their dependence on the same
great Benefactor, may learn humility, and be led to sentiments of charity towards their fellow-creatures. The children
of poverty and distress, whilst assembled with the opulent,
and joining them in solemn worship, may feel that they are
all the offspring of one gracious Parent; all equally dependent on his bounty and goodness; and from those feelings
they may learn to support, with resignation and hope, that
allotment which the Father of Mercies has assigned to them.
In the one class, sentiments of pride and contempt for others
are likely to be suppressed; and in the other, envy, discon-
tent, and murmuring are discouraged. Whatever differences
may elsewhere exist among men, in the presence of the Divine
Being, "the rich and the poor meet [equally] together; for
the Lord is [equally] the maker of them all."

The Holy Scriptures inform us, that this duty had been
practised in all ages, by those who had been distinguished
for piety and virtue. In early times the sacrifices of animals
or offerings of the fruits of the earth, were the most common
mode of publicly acknowledging a dependence on the Divine
Being, and were most probably of Divine institution; but
when it pleased the Almighty to separate from the rest
of mankind a people, whom he distinguished by peculiar
precepts and favours, it appears that in addition to those
offerings, they met together for the performance of Divine
worship: "Ye shall keep my sabbaths, and reverence my
sanctuary; I am the Lord." This precept points out the
institution of a time and place for public worship; and they
were both religiously observed by the pious among the
Jews; though there is reason to believe they were much
neglected by many of another description.

The Psalmist, with that humble piety which peculiarly distinguishes his character, is an eminent instance of public, as well as private devotion: "As for me, I will come into thy house in the multitude of thy mercy, and in thy fear will I worship towards thy holy temple." Again, "we will go into his tabernacle; we will worship at his footstool." And, in order that he may perform this service acceptably, he forms an excellent resolution: "I will wash my hands in innocency; so will I compass thy altar, O Lord, that I may publish with the voice of thanksgiving, and tell of all thy wondrous works." Nor was it merely as an obligation, that he performed this important duty; "His delight was in the law of the Lord;" and this made the performance of religious worship a grateful, not an irksome task. "Lord, I have loved the habitation of thy house, and the place where thy honour dwelleth. How amiable are thy tabernacles, O Lord of Hosts; I was glad when they said unto me, let us go into the House of God,—for a day in thy courts is better than a thousand [elsewhere]. I had rather be a door-keeper in the house of my God, than dwell in the tents of wickedness."

Although the Christian dispensation exempted its professors from the ceremonious part of the Jewish law, it did not, by any means exempt them from the duty of public worship. We have the examples of our Saviour and his Apostles, in support of this practice. The Apostle Paul is indeed very strenuous in inculcating it: "I beseech you, brethren, by the mercies of God, that ye present your bodies a living sacrifice, holy, acceptable unto God, which is your reasonable service;" and in the Epistle to the Hebrews, public worship is thus excellently illustrated and enforced: "Having, therefore, brethren, boldness to enter into the holiest, by the blood of Jesus; by a new and living way, which he hath consecrated for us through the veil, that is to say, his flesh; and having a High Priest over the House of God, let us draw near with a true heart, in full assurance of faith;—not forsaking the assembling of ourselves together, as the manner of some is; but exhorting one another, and so much the more, as ye see the day approaching."

The Christian religion has, however, freed its professors from being confined to particular places, for the performance of religious worship. Thus our Saviour taught his disciples; "Where two or three are gathered together in my name, there am I in the midst of them;" and in the memorable conversation which he held with the Samaritan woman, he showed that public worship was not to be confined to any

particular place: for when she enquired of him, whether
Jerusalem, or the mountain of Samaria, was the true place of
worship, he set them, and, by consequence, all other particular places aside, as being exclusively appropriated to this
purpose. "Woman, believe me, the hour cometh, when ye
shall neither in this mountain nor yet at Jerusalem, [exclu-
sively] worship the Father. But the hour cometh, and now
is, when the true worshippers shall worship the Father in
spirit and in truth; for the Father seeketh such to worship
him. God is a spirit, and they that worship him, must worship him in spirit and in truth." Here we see the fulfilling
of the evangelical prophecy: "In every place incense shall
be offered unto my name, and a pure offering."

Though no place is exclusively essential to the performance of public worship; yet some place is necessary for "the
assembling of ourselves together:" and some time must be
peculiarly appropriated to this purpose. Under the Jewish
law, and most probably prior to that time, the seventh day
of the week was set apart for this service; but when that
dispensation was abrogated, the primitive Christians thought
proper to alter the time from the seventh to the first day
of the week. Although the ceremonial part of the Jewish
sabbath is not obligatory upon Christians, yet several of the
reasons assigned for its institution, apply to us equally with
them. Christians in all ages have, therefore, agreed in the
appropriation of a seventh day, or one day in the week to
be particularly set apart for public worship, and for other
means of religious improvement; as also for a time of relaxation and rest from bodily labour to those who are subject
to it. This indulgence was extended, under the Law, to the
animal creation, as well as to those persons who were in a
state of servitude and bondage: "That thine ox and thine
ass may rest; and the son of thy handmaid, and the stranger,
may be refreshed."

The religious observance of one day in the week, is of so
much importance to the preservation of piety and virtue;
and the neglect of it is so evidently marked with irreligion,
and, in general, with immorality, that however necessary it
is to avoid the superstitious observance of it, which our
Saviour had occasion to censure, in the time of his personal
appearance on earth; yet every reasonable consideration
conspires to press the practice closely upon us, as affording
an opportunity, which many could not otherwise easily obtain,
of acquiring religious instruction and improvement; and of
publicly performing that worship, which is due unto "Him

that made heaven and earth, the seas, and the fountains of waters."

The pious Christian does not, however, confine his public devotions to one day in the week. Sensible of the obligation, and feeling the benefit of a more frequent performance of this religious service, he embraces opportunities, when afforded to him, of attending on public worship, on some other day, or days, than that which is specially set apart for this purpose: and although this may, in some instances, require him to leave his temporal concerns; and may seem to be attended with some worldly disadvantages; yet the views which he entertains of religious obligations, induce him to follow the example of the good king David, when, on a certain occasion, he made use of this disinterested language: "Neither will I offer burnt offerings unto the Lord my God, of that which doth cost me nothing."

CHAP. IX.

ON OBEDIENCE AND PATIENCE.

When the mind is impressed with the belief of the power and goodness of God, and brought under the influence of that love and fear which we owe to him, obedience to the manifestations of his will, becomes the necessary result of this impression and influence. But, as the operation of these principles is generally slow and gradual, and the Christian traveller has many temptations and difficulties to encounter, before he has reason to believe that, "in him verily is the love of God perfected;" it is of importance to know, that simple obedience to the Divine will is an indispensable obligation: "To obey is better than sacrifice, and to hearken than the fat of rams: for rebellion is as the sin of witchcraft, and stubbornness is as iniquity and idolatry."

Fear and love are, however, motives which are essential to true obedience. We find them in the Holy Scriptures used to excite the minds of the people to the service of God, and to an attention to his commands: "Thou shalt fear the Lord thy God and serve him. Thou shalt love the Lord thy God, and keep his charge and his statutes, and his judgments, and his commandments alway. Ye shall observe to do as the Lord your God hath commanded you: ye shall not turn aside to the right-hand or to the left; that ye may live, and that it may be well with you. Thus saith the Lord of Hosts, the God of Israel:—Obey my voice, and walk ye in all my ways, that I have commanded you, that it may be well unto you."

In the New Testament, the importance of obedience to the Divine will and commands is very strongly enforced. Our blessed Redeemer manifested how little he sought the praise of men, and how much he desired the glory of his Father, and the real good of mankind, when he gave this salutary caution to his hearers: "Not every one that saith unto me, Lord! Lord! shall enter the kingdom; but he that doeth the will of my Father who is in heaven." Again, he saith; "Ye are my friends, if ye do whatsoever I command you." And it was the observation of his beloved disciple, "He that doeth the will of God, abideth for ever."

Besides the particular instructions given by the Apostles of Christ, the general duty of obedience or keeping the Divine commands, is thus enforced: "Not the hearers of the law are just before God, but the doers of the law shall be justified. Be ye doers of the word, and not hearers only, deceiving your ownselves. This is the love of God, that we keep his commandments: and his commandments are not grievous. Hereby we do know that we know him, if we keep his commandments. He that saith, I know him, and keepeth not his commandments, is a liar: and the truth is not in him. But whoso keepeth his word, in him, verily, is the love of God perfected." When we consider these various testimonies to the importance of the practical part of religion, in which is necessarily involved a belief of its doctrines, because these are likewise Divine commands; we shall see the propriety of that conclusion, to which Solomon, after all his researches, was brought: "Fear God and keep his commandments, for this is the whole duty of man."

Intimately connected with Obedience, is the duty of Patience, by which is understood the bearing, with fortitude o mind and resignation to the Divine will, whatever is permitted to befal us in this probationary state of existence. Obedience and Patience, or to do and suffer the whole will of God, may be said to comprehend the whole of those duties, which religion and virtue require. Patience therefore holds an important place among the duties of a Christian. His life is aptly compared to a state of warfare, in which he has not only much to do, but much to bear. He must in commo with other men, submit to many privations and trials; an sometimes his religion will subject him to more; for which however, it affords an ample compensation. But as this com pensation is not always immediate, we are called upon by our faith, our hope, and our love to the Supreme Being, without whose providential attention, we are told, not a hair of our heads falleth to the ground, to bear with holy resignation whatever he permits to befal us; and, in conformity to those excellent examples which are transmitted to us in Holy Writ, to say, when sufferings and trials are our lot: "The Lord gave, and the Lord hath taken away; blessed be the name of the Lord. Not my will but thine be done."

When our Lord was apprising his disciples of the afflictions which would befal them, he gave them this seasonable exhortation: "In your patience possess ye your souls." And the Apostle Paul says, "We glory in tribulations: knowing that tribulation worketh patience; and patience, experience; and experience, hope; and hope maketh not ashamed, because the Love of God is shed abroad in our hearts, by the Holy Ghost, which is given unto us. For which cause we faint not; for though our outward man perish, yet the inward man is renewed day by day: for our light affliction, which is but for a moment, worketh for us a far more exceeding and eternal weight of glory; while we look not at the things that are seen, but at the things which are not seen; for the things which are seen are temporal; but the things which are not seen are eternal." The author of the Epistle to the Hebrews, gives the following instructive exhortations on this subject: "My son, despise not thou the chastening of the Lord, nor faint when thou art rebuked of him; for whom the Lord loveth he chasteneth, and scourgeth every son whom he receiveth. We have had fathers of our flesh who corrected us, and we gave them reverence; shall we not much rather be in subjection to the Father of spirits, and live? For they, verily, for a few days chasteneth us, for their own pleasure; but he for our profit, that we might be partakers of his holiness. Now no chastening for the present seemeth to be joyous, but grievous: nevertheless, afterward it yieldeth the peaceable fruit of righteousness unto them who are exercised thereby."

The Apostle James, among other exhortations to the duty of Patience, gives the following: "Take my brethren, the prophets, who have spoken in the name of the Lord, for an example of suffering affliction and patience. Behold, we count them happy who endure. Ye have heard of the patience of Job, and have seen the end of the Lord; that he is very pitiful, and of tender mercy."

As affliction is more or less the lot of humanity, it is of the utmost importance that we endeavour to have our minds fortified by patience, which may be called the strong-hold of religion and virtue. To this end it may be beneficial to us to consider, how much we enjoy, or may enjoy, and of how little we are worthy. Humility is the ground-work of patience. It gives light to the mind, and strength to the heart. "But if thou faint (says Solomon) in the day of adversity, thy strength is small." The humble, resigned mind knows that all things shall work together for good; and in times of affliction is enabled to say with the prophet: "Although the fig-tree shall not blossom, neither shall fruit be in the vine: the labour of the olive shall fail, and the fields shall yield no meat; the flock shall be cut off from the fold, and there shall be no herd in the stalls; yet I will rejoice in the Lord; I will joy in the God of my salvation."

CHAP. X.

ON REPENTANCE TOWARDS GOD AND FAITH IN OUR LORD JESUS CHRIST.

When we consider the number and extent of our duties to God, on the one hand; and the depravity and frailty of human nature, on the other; we must suppose that the neglect or violation of these duties will, at times, take place, even with those who may make the most early and regular advances in the way of holiness; but with respect to the generality of mankind, this neglect and violation are so prevalent and self-evident, that any attempt to demonstrate them would be superfluous. If, therefore, it is as it ought to be, a matter of concern to us, to live and die in the Divine favour, Repentance, united with amendment of life, becomes a most important duty.

The very first sermons which were preached both by our Saviour, and his forerunner, the Baptist, were on the subject of Repentance; and in a few energetic expressions they enforced this first principle of the doctrine of Christ; "Repent, for the kingdom of heaven is at hand. Bring forth fruits meet for repentance." With these precepts was laid, as it were, the foundation of that religion, with which the world has been blessed through Jesus Christ. Repentance was, no doubt, always a necessary duty, since the transgression of our first parents: but the Gospel dispensation being more particularly applied to the depraved state of human nature, this first work of true religion is primarily inculcated. We also find, that when the disciples went forth to preach and to teach, this appears to have been the first and principal part of their mission: for we are told by one of the Evangelists, that "they went out and preached that men should repent." After the ascension of our Lord, and the pouring forth of the Spirit on the Apostles and Disciples, we find the doctrine of Repentance was preached in this powerful language: "Repent ye, and be converted; that your sins may be blotted out, when the times of refreshing shall come from the presence of the Lord: and he shall send Jesus Christ, who before was preached unto you."

In that excellent relation of his Gospel labours, which the Apostle Paul gave to the elders of Ephesus, we may perceive that Repentance formed a very prominent part in the doctrines which he taught, "testifying (says he) both to the Jews, and also to the Greeks, Repentance towards God, and faith toward our Lord Jesus Christ."

The connection of Repentance with Faith in Christ, forms a peculiar excellence of the Gospel dispensation, and to which it is of the utmost importance to attend. How consoling is this consideration! "If any man sin we have an advocate with the Father, Jesus Christ the righteous: and he is the propitiation for our sins; and not for ours only, but for the sins of the whole world." Numerous are the testimonies in Holy Writ to this gracious design of our merciful Redeemer. The Evangelical prophet strongly and clearly speaks of it: " He was wounded for our transgressions; the chastisement of our peace was upon him, and with his stripes we are healed. All we, like sheep, have gone astray: we have turned every one to his own way; and the Lord hath laid on him the iniquity of us all." This passage was opened to the Ethiopian Eunuch, and applied to Christ by Philip the Evangelist.

The doctrine of Faith in Christ, as the means of reconciliation with God, is forcibly inculcated in the writings of the Apostles. To repeat all that they say on this subject, would be to transcribe a large portion of their Epistles. We are told by our Saviour himself, when some inquired of him, "What shall we do, that we may work the works of God? This is the work of God, that ye believe on him, whom God hath sent." The importance of this belief, or faith, is thus inculcated by the Apostle Paul, in his Epistle to the Romans: "Now the righteousness of God without the law, is manifested, being witnessed by the law and the prophets: even the righteousness of God, which is by faith of Jesus Christ, unto all and upon all them that believe; (for there is no difference; for all have sinned and fallen short of the glory of God;) being justified freely by his grace, through the redemption that is in Christ Jesus; whom God hath set forth to be a propitiation through faith in his blood, to declare his righteousness for the remission of sins that are past through the forbearance of God."

The author of the Epistle to the Hebrews largely exemplifies the doctrine of Christian redemption. The eighth, ninth, and tenth chapters are particularly forcible and interesting in the manner in which this subject is treated: and it will be proper to recite, in this place, some of the pertinent exhortations and observations with which he closes the subject: "Having, therefore, brethren, boldness to enter into the holiest by the blood of Jesus, by a new and living way which he has consecrated for us through the veil,—that is to say, his flesh; and having a High Priest over the house of God: let us draw near with a true heart, in full assurance of faith. He that despised Moses' law died without mercy under two or three witnesses: of how much sorer punishment, suppose ye, shall he be thought worthy, who has trodden under foot the Son of God, and hath counted the blood of the covenant wherewith he was sanctified, an unholy thing, and done despite to the Spirit of Grace? For we know him, who hath said, Vengeance belongeth unto me: I will recompence, saith the Lord: and again, the Lord shall judge his people.—It is a fearful thing to fall into the hands of the living God."

Seeing then, that our duty and interest are both intimately connected with our possessing faith in Christ; let us embrace it with full purpose of heart, and hold fast the profession of it without wavering. Yet let us not forget that "faith without works is dead, being alone;" and that we ought therefore to "add to our faith, virtue;" and to hold it in conjunction with a good conscience: thus we may entertain a well-grounded hope, that when this probationary state shall terminate, we shall "receive the end of our faith, even the salvation of our souls."

END.

London: Printed by E. Couchman and Co., 10, Throgmorton Street; for the TRACT ASSOCIATION of the SOCIETY OF FRIENDS. Sold at the DEPOSITORY 84, Houndsditch.—1861.

ON

THE INCONSISTENCY

OF

TITHES AND TITHE RENT CHARGE

WITH THE

GOSPEL DISPENSATION.

ISSUED BY THE YEARLY MEETING OF THE RELIGIOUS SOCIETY
OF FRIENDS, HELD IN LONDON, 1851.

IN this day, in which the minds of men are greatly agitated by the pretensions of an earthly priesthood, we have been led renewedly to contemplate the beauty and simplicity of the worship of the New Covenant as practised in the primitive Church. Few as are the particulars concerning it which are furnished by the inspired penmen in the Holy Scriptures, they are sufficient to show that it was a worship not of form, but in power; not of carnal ordinances and outward ceremonies, but "in spirit and in truth."* Those who had been brought, through faith in their Lord and Saviour, from under the law of sin and death to the law of the spirit of life in Christ Jesus, were wont to meet together in his name; and whether it was in an upper chamber, or in the house of a convert, or by the sea-shore, or by the river-side, we cannot doubt it was in single dependence upon Him who had graciously declared, "Where two or three are gathered together in my name, there am I in the midst of them."† Before his ascension to the right hand of the Father, he had owned such gatherings with his bodily presence, coming in amongst his

* John iv. 23.   † Matt. xviii. 20.

No. 119.   [*Price 6d. per dozen.*]

disciples when they were assembled with closed doors, for fear of the Jews; and after He had "ascended up on high and led captivity captive," He, their heavenly President, ruled in their assemblies; and in the plenitude of his power and love, shed forth upon them his gifts, varied in kind and degree, but all proceeding from "one and the self-same Spirit,"* and directed to the accomplishment of the same blessed objects, "the perfecting of the saints," and "the edifying of the body of Christ."† In accordance with the precept and declaration of our Lord, "Be not ye called Rabbi, for one is your Master, even Christ,"‡ it is abundantly evident that, amongst the primitive believers there was a liberty as well as a brotherhood in the truth, which, under the guidance of their Divine Head, was perfectly consistent with the fulfilment of the injunction, "Let all things be done decently and in order."§ For, at the very time when the Apostle was restraining some of the irregularities which appeared in the Church of Corinth, he says expressly, "Ye may all prophesy" (or "speak with the Spirit") "one by one, that all may learn and all may be comforted."|| In this liberty and in this order, whilst "all" were to be "subject one to another," those who were over their brethren in the Lord, were men whom the Holy Ghost had made overseers¶ and "stewards of the manifold grace of God,"** not lords over his heritage, but "ensamples to the flock"†† which He had purchased with his own most precious blood. Those who ministered, ministered as of the ability which God gave them.‡‡ From Christ they "freely received"§§ their gifts, and in obedience to his express precept, they "freely" (that is, gratuitously)|||| exercised them. The law, with its priesthood and its tithes and offerings (set apart for the support of one tribe,

* 1 Cor. xii. 11.
† Eph. iv. 12.
‡ Matt. xxiii. 8.
§ 1 Cor. xiv. 40.
|| 1 Cor. xiv. 31.
¶ 1 Pet. v. 5.—Acts xx. 28.
** 1 Pet. iv. 10.
†† 1 Pet. v. 3.
‡‡ 1 Pet. iv. 11.
§§ Matt. x. 8.
|||| δωρεὰν.

which, under the peculiar national theocracy of the Jewish people, was excluded from its proportional inheritance in the land of promise), had given place to the Gospel, in which the Lord Jesus Christ is the only High Priest, and the entire company of believers a holy priesthood, to offer up spiritual sacrifices, acceptable to God by Him.* No other priesthood is spoken of in Scripture as pertaining to the New Covenant.

Though it may not be easy to trace the successive steps by which, as vital Christianity declined, the departure from this blessed primitive order was brought about, yet we can at once perceive the contrast between the simplicity, the spirituality, and the liberty which prevailed in the early Christian Church, and the costly and cumbrous appendages, the outward ceremonies, and the ecclesiastical domination which mark the church in the apostacy, in which the exercise of the spiritual gifts of the many, for the good of the whole, was superseded by the exclusive services of one man, the sole and the humanly-appointed minister, and, as he came at length to be called, the person or parson of the church.† And whilst he thus usurped the ministerial duties of the whole congregation, the body of ministers came to be designated the church or clergy (that is, heritage),‡ to the virtual exclusion of the great company of believers, who, as a whole, are throughout the New Testament spoken of as the church, the "heritage"§ of the Lord,—the bishops or overseers, presbyters or elders, and deacons, being only officers or servants therein.

One of the most striking of the corruptions which crept into the church in its decline was the reconstruction of an outward priesthood, appointed, amongst other functions, to offer, on a material altar, a pretended sacrifice of Christ afresh in the gross superstition of the *mass*, whereby was set at nought, or obscured through human inventions, the glorious and ever-blessed truth, that He had, " by one

* 1 Pet. ii. 5.　† *Persona ecclesiæ.*　‡ οἱ κλῆροι.
§ 1 Pet. v. 3, and compare Rom. viii. 16, 17; Eph iii. 6.; Tit. ii. 14.

offering, perfected for ever all them that are sanctified." *
And having raised an unauthorised imitation of a priesthood which God had abolished, and given to it functions
which He never sanctioned, the next step, at least in the
Church of Rome and the churches derived therefrom † was
to provide for the payment of these services by the revival
of the Levitical tithes, which having ceased with the *Old*
Covenant, to which they belonged, have no place whatever in the *New*. At first, indeed, the payment of tithes
was voluntary,‡ and the objects to which they were appli-

* Heb. x. 14.

† Tithes do not appear to have been paid in the *Eastern* Church.
Selden's History of Tithes, chapters 5 and 6; History of Benefices,
by Paolo Sarpi, chapter xi.

‡ Eagle on the Law of Tithes, vol. i. p. lviii. Compulsory payments
were, in fact, unknown in the Christian Church for many ages.
"Whatsoever we have in the treasury of our church," says Tertullian
in the beginning of the third century, "is not raised by taxation, as
though we put men to ransom their religion, but every one amongst
us contributes a moderate sum monthly, or whensoever he will, and
only if he will, and only if he can, for none is compelled, but each
contributes freely." Tertullian's Apology, chapter 39. So even in
the work called the 'Apostolical Constitutions,' supposed to be a com-
pilation of the fourth or fifth century, in which the traces of growing
corruptions are largely apparent, the contributions to the church are
styled *free gifts* (see book ii. chapter 36), and it is remarkable that
the officers of the church are forbidden to receive even these from the
vicious or impenitent, or from those who offered them without a good
conscience toward God (book iv. chapters 6, 7, 8). "In the early
ages of Christianity," to use the words of a late eminent judge,
"there were no compulsory payments; no tithes were paid; the
whole of the funds depended upon voluntary donations and oblations
made from time to time, or the produce of lands which had been
given to the church." Justice Littledale in his Judgment in Rennell
v. Bp. of Lincoln, Barnewall and Cresswell's Reports, vol. vii. p. 153.
It is also remarkable that, so far, at least, as we have observed, the
early writers previously to the age of Cyprian (about the year 250),
make no mention of *Ministers*, as such, having any share in the
funds thus freely collected. They appear to have been distributed
solely among the widows, the orphans, the prisoners, or other necessitous members of the church. Tertullian's Apology, chapter 39;
Justin Martyr's first Apology, chapter 67. The ministry of spiritual
gifts, it was considered, must be strictly gratuitous. "Doubtless,"
says Irenæus, writing about the year 180, "the gifts are innumerable
which the church throughout the whole world has received of God,
and daily exercises for the good of the nations, in the name of Jesus
Christ, who was crucified under Pontius Pilate; neither defrauding
any, nor seeking gain of any, for as the church has freely received
them from God, so it freely dispenses them." Irenæus on Heresies,

cable included the duties of hospitality, the provision for the poor, and the maintenance of the buildings for worship, as well as the support of the minister; but as the mystery of iniquity continued to work, they were at length claimed and enforced as " due unto God and holy Church,"* and with very little exception appropriated exclusively to the priest.

After a long night of apostacy, when the day of reformation began to dawn, not a few of those who were raised up to testify against the spiritual despotism, the superstitious ritual, and the corrupted doctrines of Rome, bore testimony also against its priesthood of man's appointment, and the Levitical system of tithes, whereby it was supported.† We

book ii. c. 57. So Lactantius, more than a century later, "These things are done gratuitously." 'Divine Institutes,' book iii. chapter 26. Hence we find in those early days, the receiving of money objected against some who made high pretensions to spiritual gifts. "Does not all the Scripture," says a Christian, writing to a correspondent, in a letter preserved by Eusebius, "seem to thee to forbid a prophet to receive gifts and money? When, therefore, I see a prophetess receiving gold and silver and costly garments, how can I fail to reject her?" "If, however," he adds, "they deny that their prophets took presents, let them, at least, acknowledge that if they should be proved to have received them they are no prophets." Eusebius's Ecclesiastical History, book v. chapter 18. So late as the eighth century the well-known Bede could thus plainly address the then Archbishop of York:—"Freely ye have received, freely give; provide neither gold nor silver. If, therefore, Christ ordered the apostles to preach the Gospel freely, and did not permit them to receive gold or silver, or any temporal payment of money, from those to whom they preached, what hazard, I would ask, must hang over those who do the contrary?" Bede's Minor Historical Works, by Giles, vol. ii. p. 142.

* Statute 27th of Henry VIII. chapter 20.

† Amongst others, the Vaudois Christians taught that "all good men, as such, are priests." See Ricchinius's 2nd Dissertation, chapter 3, section 4, prefixed to his edition of Moneta's 'Five Books against the Cathari and Waldenses.' Reinerus says, "They teach that we ought not to pay tithes because they were not paid in the primitive Church, * * * and that all the clergy ought to work with their hands like the apostles." Ricchinius, as quoted above. See also Moneta, book v., chapter 7. Wycliffe asserted that tithes are pure alms, and ought not to be exacted by the arm of the law. See Wycliffe's Dialogues, book iv., chapter 17; also Vaughan's 'Life of Wycliffe,' chapter 8. Though not to be placed amongst the Reformers of the Church, the opinion of Milton is striking, on account of the reasoning by which it is supported. He says:—"That tithes were ceremonial is plain, not being given to the Levites till they had been

feel deeply thankful to the Lord for the work of reformation, which in many instances not without the blood of his
servants and witnesses, was then accomplished in various
parts of professing Christendom. It was, nevertheless, a
very imperfect work, and in some places, and especially in
our own beloved country, a work of compromise; one of
the strong evidences of which is the retention of the priesthood and tithes in the Reformed Church of England, as
by law established.

When, in process of time, it pleased the Lord, by the
breaking forth of his Spirit, to bring our early Friends to
a clear view of the primitive purity and spiritual privileges
of the Gospel of Christ, no part of their testimony was
more clear and explicit than that which, in the obedience
of faith, they bore against the human priesthood and its
offices, and against the system of tithes, which forms so
striking a feature of its antichristian character. To acknowledge this priesthood, and to render to it the tithe of
the beasts of the field and of the produce of the earth, was,
in their view, to be unfaithful in their allegiance to Him
who, having come a " High Priest for ever, after the order
of Melchisedec," had put an end to the priesthood of Aaron,
and abolished also the tithes and offerings that pertained
thereto. Their refusal to pay tithes was thus intimately
connected with their heartfelt homage to their Lord and
Saviour, and with their deliverance from that yoke of bondage which had so long oppressed the professing but apos-
tate Church. It was connected also with the clear and
scriptural views which the Lord, by the light of his Spirit,
gave them of the true nature of Christian worship and
Gospel ministry : for He who taught them not to call any
man master in spiritual matters, gave them also, in the

first offered a heave-offering to the Lord. He then, who by that law
brings tithes into the Gospel, brings in withal a sacrifice and an altar,
without which tithes, by that law, were unsanctified and polluted,
and therefore never thought on in the first Christian times, till ceremonies, altars and oblations by an ancienter corruption were brought
back long before."—Milton's Prose Works, 4to, vol. i. p. 618.

blessed experience that he was himself their Master, and that they were all brethren, to know that he still distributed spiritual gifts among them, for their mutual edification and comfort. To pay tithes therefore, was, for them, like circumcision for the Judaizing Galatian converts, a virtual return to the bondage of the Law, and renunciation of the spiritual privileges of the Gospel. Clear and scriptural as are these grounds for their refusal of the demand, the course which they pursued was that which they felt to be required of them by the Spirit of the Lord, as well as by his written revelation. The will of their God was the root of this, as of all their distinguishing testimonies; and feeling it to be laid upon them by their Lord, in proof of their allegiance to Him, to withhold the payment of these claims, can we wonder at the faithfulness and uncompromising firmness with which, sustained by His power, through fines and imprisonments, even unto death, they meekly yet valiantly testified against that which they, with such emphatic propriety designated "the antichristian yoke of tithes!"

In their resistance to ecclesiastical as well as military demands, Friends have acted upon the broad and palpable distinction which exists between payments made specifically for objects inconsistent with the law of Christ, or directly to an authority which they cannot conscientiously recognize, and payments into the National Treasury for the general purposes of the State, though some of the purposes may be objectionable. Thus, in obedience to the clear command of our Saviour and the precept of his Apostle, they have been careful to "render unto Cæsar the things which are Cæsar's;" "tribute to whom tribute is due;" "custom to whom custom:" whilst, on the other hand, they have regarded the payment of a tax specifically applied to military purposes, or the payment of tithes to a humanly-appointed priesthood, and for services inconsistent with the freedom and spirituality of the New Covenant, as a violation of the duty enjoined upon them by the same high authority, of rendering "unto God the things which are God's." In the case of ecclesiastical tithes, not only is the money specifically appropriated to the objectionable purpose, but the payment is made directly to one whose only title to it depends upon his filling an office which we cannot recognize as having any true place in the Church of Christ. As *Priest* he claims his tithes, and whoever pays them to him virtually admits his claim in that character. Were he to cease to be a priest, even his legal title to them would be at an end.

In the mind which, under the operation of the Holy Spirit, is brought to appreciate the paramount importance of a religious testimony, all considerations of expediency, and even human law, when opposed to the divine, at once give place. Not that we are on this account precluded from taking landed property, by devise or by descent, or from purchasing or hiring it, even when it is sold or let for less than would otherwise have been its value, on account of its being subject to this antichristian impost. Else, we might almost say, in the language of the Apostle, we "must needs go out of the world,"—prevented, as we should be, by reason only of our desire to maintain a good conscience in religious matters, from occupying that place in civil society, as owners or cultivators of the soil, to which our Creator in his providence may have called us, or from bearing that testimony to the law of Christ which, in the fulfilment of his purposes, he requires from his faithful obedient followers. And though the members of our Society have refused actively to comply with the direct pecuniary payment of tithes and other ecclesiastical demands, they have nevertheless deemed it right passively to submit to the operation of the law, which takes from them the full value of the claim, often augmented by costs and expensive proceedings; and by this submission, the difficulty which might otherwise have existed, by reason of any supposed conflict between the law of God and the alleged rights of property in the subject-matter of these unrighteous imposts, is removed. We appeal to two centuries of consistent faithfulness in the main body of the Society, especially in those who have been most distinguished for sterling integrity towards their fellow-men, and spiritual-mindedness, and piety towards God, as a practical evidence that that which has been uniformly professed to be a Christian testimony was no fanatical or hasty conceit, and was dictated by no desire to avoid any just pecuniary burden.

We should hardly be doing full justice to the subject of our refusal to pay all ecclesiastical demands, were we not to allude to our uniform practice in relation to the ministry amongst us, as a Church, from our first rise to the present day. This, we need hardly say, has been in strict accordance with the principle that the Gospel should be free, that there should be no pay for preaching. For, though in conformity with the directions of the Apostle Paul, in the 9th chapter of his 1st Epistle to the Corinthians, our ministers, when engaged from home in their Lord's work, are accustomed, so far as regards the supply of their present wants, to receive " carnal things" from those to whom they sow " spiritual things ;"* yet not only is this supply of their needful wants wholly of free will and not a matter of compulsion or of bargain, but when they are at home or resident in a fixed place of abode, they pursue their respective outward callings, considering that, when able under such circumstances to maintain themselves, they are excluded from receiving support by the plain and explicit doctrine of many passages in the New Testament, and especially by the obvious import of the language used by the same Apostle to the elders or bishops of Ephesus, whilst exhorting them to feed the flock,—" I have coveted no man's silver or gold or apparel, yea, ye yourselves know that these hands have ministered to my necessities and to them that were with me. I have showed you all things, how that so labouring, ye ought to support the

* 1 Cor. ix. 11.

weak, and to remember the words of the Lord Jesus, how he said, 'It is more blessed to give than to receive.'"* The Apostle's language and conduct are thus seen to be perfectly consistent; and it has ever been our concern to endeavour herein to be found walking in his steps.

In offering to our dear brethren the foregoing view of the origin and history of this our ancient testimony against tithes, we cannot refrain from expressing our belief that, under the Divine blessing, the testimony itself and the consequences which have flowed from it, have tended in no small degree to preserve unimpaired our distinguishing views of ministry and worship, and to prevent our being led into those religious rites and observances with which many, even of the sincere professors of the name of Christ in other denominations, are to a greater or less degree entangled.

We think it right in this place, with thankfulness to the Lord, and with grateful acknowledgment to the legislature of our country, to allude to the mitigations which have progressively taken place in the processes for the recovery of tithes and other claims of an ecclesiastical nature, both in the simplifying of proceedings and in the diminution of expenses, and finally, in the entire abolition of imprisonment in respect of such claims, so far as the members of our Society are concerned.

At length, in the year 1836, the legislature passed an Act for effecting the commutation of all tithes in England and Wales into a tithe-rent charge, issuing out of the lands previously subject to them. This Act, by taking away the jurisdiction of the Ecclesiastical Courts, and most of the other costly processes for the enforcing of the demand, and creating a direct and inexpensive mode of recovering it, lessened the amount of pecuniary suffering inflicted by this oppressive system. But although it has thus removed some of the branches, it has left the root untouched. The title by which the tithe was claimed, was, in every particu-

* Acts xx. 33—35.

lar, impressed upon the substituted rent-charge; and the demand for the support of a priesthood is still a compulsory demand, and in payment of services which we believe to be inconsistent with the freedom and spirituality of the New Covenant. Whilst, therefore, we feel for our members, who, in many places, have been exposed to some new difficulties and perplexities in reference to this alteration in the law, more especially during the state of transition, we believe it to be our duty, as the result of repeated deliberations on the subject on various occasions, during the fifteen years which have elapsed since the passing of the Tithe Commutation Act, to express our solid judgment that the Christian testimony which our forefathers had to bear against tithes, we, their successors in religious profession, are called upon, in meekness, consistency, and firmness, to support, against the payment of the impost secured to the priesthood, under the altered name, and with the somewhat modified incidents of tithe rent-charge.

In conclusion, we would remind you that the present is a day of peculiar, we might almost say of critical, importance to the members of our religious Society, in relation to its testimony against all ecclesiastical demands. On the one hand, the greater mingling with those of other religious denominations, and with the world at large, in the affairs of business, of philanthropy, of science and literature, as well as in social intercourse, tends, without great watchfulness of spirit, to the admission into our own minds of opinions, views, and feelings which may insensibly modify and weaken our attachment to the root of all Christian testimony, and to the various yet consistent branches of Christian profession, which have, we reverently believe, under the fostering hand of the good Husbandman, sprung from that root, and formed the distinguishing characteristics of our religious Society. On the other hand, to say nothing of the more obvious assaults and covert encroachments of superstition, the Church of England, as by law established, has, during the last quarter of a century, been in various ways extending its arms and strengthening its power over the consciences and property of the people. Amongst the evidences hereof we may mention the grants out of the National Treasury towards the building of new places for worship, already in some instances repaired and supported by general rates; the arrangements for the appointment of Chaplains of the Established Church for prisons and union-houses, compulsorily paid for by all denominations, and in many instances the exclusion from them in a greater or less degree of other religious teachers, as well as the payments by Government for ecclesiastical purposes in the colonies. Whilst, therefore, we desire to be preserved in charity towards all men, and to recognize and unite with that which is good in all, it is our earnest desire that, unworthy as we may be of so great a mercy, we may be enabled to stand fast in that liberty wherewith Christ has made us free, and not become entangled in any yoke of bondage; but that faithfully upholding our principles, and, through Divine assistance, walking consistently therewith in humility and watchfulness in all things, we may yet be strengthened of the Lord to fulfil the end for which we believe our religious Society was raised up by Him, and has been preserved to this day, even to promote the revival and extension of pure and primitive Christianity, to the praise of his most Holy Name.

Signed in and on behalf of the Meeting, by

JOHN HODGKIN,

Clerk to the Meeting this year.

END.

London: *Printed by Edward Couchman, 10, Throgmorton Street; for the* TRACT ASSOCIATION *of the* SOCIETY OF FRIENDS. *Sold at the* DEPOSITORY, 84, *Houndsditch.*—1852.

A SKETCH OF THE LIFE

OF

THOMAS SHILLITOE.

~~~~~~~~~~~~~~~~~~~~~~

THE declaration of the Most High "Them that honour me, I will honour," was strikingly fulfilled in the case of Thomas Shillitoe. The brief sketch of his life, contained in this little Tract, is chiefly taken from his Journal, published in two volumes, in 1839; a work which will well repay the reader for a careful perusal.

Thomas Shillitoe was born in London, in 1754; and while he was quite young, his father became landlord of the Three Tuns public-house at Islington. Here, from the age of twelve to sixteen, Thomas was pot-boy, and exposed to the influence of evil company, by which he was nearly ruined. After this he was apprenticed to a grocer, who was a tippler and a bad example in other respects. This place being unfavourable to his best interests, and promising nothing valuable in regard to business habits, he wished to be liberated from it, and for this purpose, induced his parents to have his indentures cancelled. His master had removed to Portsmouth; and there, as well as while living in London, Thomas had felt the benefit of the example of religious young men with whom he became acquainted. On leaving Portsmouth, he returned to London, took another situation, and formed an acquaintance with a relative, with whom, on the First day of the week, he attended the meetings for worship of the Society of Friends; not however from religious motives, but that he might dine with his young and ungodly relative, who took him in the

No. 120. [Price 4d. per dozen.]

afternoons to fashionable tea-gardens and other places of amusement, where they spent the remainder of the day in that which, for want of knowing better, the world calls Pleasure. The retrospect of time thus spent was not comfortable. The rebuke of God's Spirit was felt by the conscience of the transgressor; and happily, he bowed under it, and was brought to consider the misery into which the road he was taking would eventually lead, if he continued to pursue it. With a different object, he now attended the meetings of Friends diligently, morning and afternoon, earnestly seeking, in deep repentance, an acquaintance with God, and that peace which comes by Jesus Christ. His prayers were earnest that the Lord would not leave him, nor suffer him to become a prey to his soul's adversary; and as, in the exercise of faith, he yielded to the purifying power of the Holy Spirit—the Baptism of the Holy Ghost and of fire—corresponding good fruits were brought forth, and shown in his conduct.

After a time, he believed it to be his duty to use the simple and truthful language adopted by the Society of Friends; but to do this in the situation he then occupied was so great a cross to him, that he flinched from it, and brought himself into difficulty by giving up his place. His father, who seems to have been much a stranger to true religion, and to have had little consideration for the conscience of his son, was greatly offended at his attending the meetings of Friends; and now he was unwilling to afford him an asylum till he could meet with another situation, telling him, after a visit of a few days, that he must quit the house, and go to those whom he had joined in religious profession.

In these circumstances, Thomas was not forsaken by Him who cares for the very sparrows. A situation was obtained by the day his father had fixed for his departure from his house. It was in the banking-house of a Friend; and here the inexperienced convert "hoped to be more secure, and out of the way of much temptation." "But alas!" he says, "I soon found my mistake; and that no situation is safe, without the daily, unremitting watch is maintained." Few of those with whom he was associated were acquainted with the work of grace, the increase of which he longed after; and some of them were much given up to the world and its delusive pleasures. "Here," he says, "I had nearly made shipwreck of faith. But, oh! the mercy of God, who snatched me again as a brand out of the burning, and opened mine ear to counsel."

Not feeling comfortable in the occupation he was engaged in, he became very desirous to know what business it would· be best for him to pursue, and was earnest in prayer for direction on this subject. The answer in the secret of his soul was such as to convince him, that he ought to learn the business of a shoemaker. He was now about twenty-two years of age, and the prospect of learning a new business was formidable to him. At first his earnings in it were very small; but by diligent application, he acquired so much knowledge of shoemaking as enabled him to commence that business at Tottenham, where he carried it on successfully for many years. About the age of twenty-four he believed it would be of advantage to marry; and he besought the Lord to guide him in this important step. In reference to it he says "I thought I had good ground to believe the Lord was pleased to grant my request, and to point out to me one who was to be my companion in life." Thomas Shillitoe was married to this individual, whose name was Mary Pace, in 1778; and she was his faithful companion to old age, and survived him nearly two years.

As he grew in grace, his interest in the welfare of others increased, and at times he believed it required of him to speak as a minister of the Gospel of Christ in the meetings for worship of the society which he had joined. After affording him ample time to make proof of his ministry, the Society recorded him as

one of its acknowledged ministers, and gave its sanction to his going into Norfolk, to discharge some
religious service which he believed the Lord required
of him. In the prospect of leaving his family and
business for a time, in order to pay this visit, great
discouragement came over him; but he says: "One
day when I was standing cutting out work for my
men, my mind being under the weight of the concern,
these discouragements again presented themselves, if
possible, with double force; but in adorable mercy,
I was so brought under the influence of Divine help,
as I had not often, if ever before known. And as
I became willing to yield to it, the power of the
mighty God of Jacob was mercifully manifest, subduing the influence and power of the adversary;
holding out for my acceptance this encouraging promise, which was addressed to my inward hearing, in
a language as intelligible as ever I heard words
spoken to my natural ear,—I will be more than bolts
and bars to thy outward habitation; more than a
master to thy servants, for I can restrain their wandering minds; more than a husband to thy wife, and a
parent to thy infant children. At this, the knife I
was using fell out of my hands; and I no longer
dared to hesitate, after such a confirmation." On
returning from this service, he had to acknowledge
the Lord's faithfulness, and that his temporal concerns
were in as good order as they could have been under
his own superintendence.

From this period he often left his business and
family, to travel in the Lord's service. His visits
were chiefly to members of the Society of Friends;
but his Christian concern for the welfare of others
embraced all classes, from the throne to the dungeon.
Under what he believed to be the pointing and guidance of the Holy Spirit, and with the sanction of the
religious community to which he belonged, he visited
many parts of Great Britain and Ireland, France,
Germany, Holland, Norway, Russia, Prussia, Switzerland, and North America. He obtained personal

interviews with George the Third and William the
Fourth of Great Britain, the King and Royal Family
of Denmark, the King of Prussia, and the Emperor
Alexander of Russia, as well as with many persons
high in office in their respective governments, and
those of several other countries; with these he
laboured to promote their own personal subjection
to the government of Christ, and to excite their
interest in the extension of the Redeemer's kingdom
among their subjects, as being that alone under which
solid peace and true prosperity can flourish. Failing
to obtain similar interviews with George the Fourth
of Great Britain, he twice presented him with written
addresses, in which he faithfully reasoned with him of
" temperance, righteousness, and judgment to come."

On the continent of Europe, as well as in our own
country, under the constraining influence of the love
of Christ, he frequently visited prisons, seeking to turn
the attention of the prisoners to those convictions of
sin which they had slighted, and by which the Lord
had striven with them, to turn them from the evil of
their ways, and bring them to repentance; he also
encouraged them to submit patiently to the chastisement they had brought upon themselves, and to be
willing to turn to the Lord with full purpose of heart,
that they might obtain mercy and forgiveness through
Jesus Christ. On some of these occasions the prisoners were much softened, so that many of them
wept; and on parting from them, under the feeling of
Divine influence, which had spread over them, he shook
hands with each of them, as the token of his love.—
In Ireland he visited the drinking-houses in several of
the towns and cities, and expostulated with the people
who resorted to them; directing their attention to the
evil of their practices, and the inevitable misery into
which these would lead, if persisted in; and exhorting
them to repent and turn to the Lord, that they might
obtain mercy. He also, in several places, visited
magistrates and the ministers of various religious
denominations, and endeavoured to stir them up to

do their duty in the fear of the Lord. On these occasions, he was generally accompanied by one or more of his friends.

Many of the people whom he met with in the drinking-houses were living in open sin; yet, when he counselled them to repent and turn from their sins, that they might find peace with God through Jesus Christ, they replied, that their priests would forgive them their sins. Thomas Shillitoe was brought into great sorrow for these deluded people; for he knew that Christ himself warned people to repent or they should perish; that he also called those a "generation of vipers" who hoped to be saved without bringing forth fruits meet for repentance; and that he neither remitted the sins of any who did not repent, nor ever gave even to his apostles authority to remit the sins of the impenitent.—At Kilkenny, Thomas visited a Roman Catholic Bishop, and pointed out to him his awful responsibility to God in connection with this matter, and the duty which lay upon him, to strive to undeceive the people; he also counselled the bishop to seek help from God to discharge his duty, by directing the people to God and Christ who only can forgive sin. The bishop, who died soon after, appeared to feel the force of this exhortation, and when they parted, he expressed thankfulness for the visit.

In 1812, Thomas Shillitoe joined his friend Ann Fry in a visit to the colliers and miners in the neighbourhood of Kingswood, near Bristol, and to a lawless class of people called "the Gang" then living in that neighbourhood; they held some meetings among these people, and visited many of them in their own houses. In the course of this visit, the language of afflicted women, "My husband, my sons were killed in the pit," almost daily met their ears, and they were brought into deep sympathy with these widows and with their fatherless children. They were much affected at the indifference shown by some of the men to the dangers to which they were exposed; and they laboured to awaken in their minds a right sense of these dangers, and to persuade them to seek help from God, to live in his fear; that through his mercy in Christ Jesus, they might become prepared to leave this world with a well-grounded hope of eternal life, if suddenly called away.

Their visits and honest expostulations, under the feeling of Christian love and interest, were well taken and made a remarkable impression on many of the lawless, as well as of the sober minded, whom they visited; and the solemn feeling which came over them, often bringing the most untoward into serious thoughtfulness, proved to them afresh, that when the Good Shepherd puts forth any in such services, he still condescends to go before them, and by his own good Spirit to help and protect them.

In the spring of 1813, Thomas Shillitoe united with his friend Joseph Wood, of Highflats, in a visit of Christian sympathy, to the widows and fatherless children of seventeen men, who had been executed at York, for outrageous conduct and murder, in the neighbourhood of Huddersfield. These visits were paid from house to house; some of them were of a very heart-rending character; but "being willing," says Thomas Shillitoe, "as I humbly hope I may say we were, to sit where the surviving sufferers sat, we were helped to go down into suffering with them, and thereby became qualified through the renewal of Divine aid to administer suitably to the need of those we sat with." The visited were in deep distress, and the Christian sympathy and counsel conveyed, while it soothed some minds bordering on despair, directed them to " the grace of God which brings salvation" through a crucified and glorified Redeemer, and which warns against sin and reproves for it, in the secret of the heart; and which, if it had been attended to, would have preserved the deluded men from the crimes for which they had suffered.

When at Altona in 1821, he was sorrowfully affected with the levity of the people, and with the manner in which they pursued their ordinary business and attended places of amusement on the " Sabbath ;" and under the feeling of religious duty, he wrote an address to them upon the subject, expostulating with them, and reminding them of the judgments of the Most High denounced against those who live in iniquity. This address he sent to England to be translated and printed, and he then distributed it with his own hands. For this act of Christian love and disinterestedness he was cast into prison, but was discharged the next day, his labours being more correctly appreciated by some others than they had been by the police-master.

While in Petersburgh in 1824, Thomas Shillitoe was permitted to have two interviews with the Emperor Alexander. In the first of these he presented an address to the natives of Great Britain residing in Russia, and which he had found he could not circulate among them in that country without imperial sanction. The Emperor received him with Christian kindness and condescension; and before they parted, expressed himself in substance as follows: "Before I became acquainted with your religious Society and its principles, I frequently, from my early life, felt something in myself, which, at times, gave me clearly to see that I stood in need of a further knowledge of Divine things than I was then in possession of; this I could not then account for; nor did I know where to look for that which would prove availing to my help in this matter, until I became acquainted with some of your Society, and with its principles. This I have since considered to be the greatest of all the outward blessings the Almighty has bestowed upon me; because hereby I became fully satisfied in my own mind, that that which had thus followed me, though I was ignorant of what it meant, was that same Divine Power inwardly revealed, which your religious Society have, from their commencement, professed to be actuated by in their daily walk through life ; and my attention became turned with increasing earnestness, to seek after more of an acquaintance with it in my own soul. I bless the Lord that he thus continues to condescend to send his true Gospel ministers, to keep me in remembrance of this day of his merciful awakening to my soul." He then added, " My mind is, at times, brought under great suffering, to know how to move along ; I see things necessary for me to do, and things necessary for me to refuse complying with, which are expected from me. You have counselled me to an unreserved and well-timed obedience in all things. I clearly see it to be my duty; and this is what I want to be more brought into the experience of: but when I try for it, doubts come into my mind, and discouragements prevail; for although they call me an absolute monarch, it is but little power I have for doing that which I see to be right for me to do."

In the subsequent interview, the manner in which the " Sabbath" was disregarded in Russia, was brought under the Emperor's notice ; also the restrictions on the circulation of the Holy Scriptures ; the debasing state of vassalage existing among the people, and the barbarity of the punishment of the knout, the Emperor desiring that he would not hesitate to open his mind fully. Before parting, Thomas Shillitoe says, " Opportunity having now been afforded me, to relieve my mind of all that I apprehended was required of me to express, in the line of religious duty, a pause took place; and feeling myself constrained to kneel down in supplication, the Emperor went on his knees by my side. After rising from our knees, and sitting awhile quietly together, the time for my departure being come, I rose to go; and after holding each other most affectionately by the hand, he saluted me, and we took a heart-tendering Farewell."

In the prime of life Thomas Shillitoe had given up taking animal food, finding he had not power to digest it ; and as the effort to remove the difficulty, by using stimulating liquors, only increased the malady it was proposed to cure, he became an habitual abstainer from such beverages. He went through a large amount of bodily and mental exercise, and "endured hardness as a good soldier of Jesus Christ." Many of his journeys in the service of his good Lord and Master were taken on foot, with a view of "not making the Gospel chargeable." In 1805 he diminished his business, and in 1806 gave it up, in order to be more fully at liberty for those Gospel labours which he believed the Lord required of him. When about eighty years of age he walked from Tottenham to Exeter Hall, a distance of about six miles, to attend a meeting of the British and Foreign Temperance Society. His address on this occasion exhibited the beneficial effects of Temperance in his own experience; it was afterwards published as a tract, and entitled, "Health and Comfort in Old Age."

Toward the latter part of his life he felt the infirmities of declining years. His bodily sufferings were often considerable; but living near Friends' meeting-house, he regularly attended all the meetings, and continued earnestly to exhort those who assembled there, to let their obedience to the law of God keep pace with the knowledge of its requirements; he also urged them to press after holiness of life, and a thorough surrender of their wills to the Divine Will. He was earnest that he might be found ready to meet his Lord, often adverting to the necessity of watchfulness, lest, after having long professed the truth, he should in the end become a castaway. In the retrospect of his lengthened but active life, he said, "I feel I have nothing to depend upon but the mercies of God in Christ Jesus. I do not rely for salvation upon any merits of my own; all my own works are as filthy rags. My faith is in the merits of Christ Jesus, and in the offering he made for us. I trust my past sins are all forgiven me,—that they have been washed away by the blood of Christ who died for my sins;" and he added, that such had been his faith during the whole course of his religious life.

On the 5th of 6th month, 1836, he was taken

alarmingly ill. Early in the morning of the following
day, he became much worse, from increased debility;
and his breathing being difficult, he said, "It is
labour, but not sorrow. Oh! deliver me, if consistent
with Thy blessed will. I am in the hands of a merciful God: take me; I can give up all in this world.
O come; come blessed Jesus! if it is consistent with
Thy blessed will.—Into Thy careful keeping,—into
Thy merciful hands, I commend my dear children
and grandchildren."

On the following day, he exclaimed, "O, Heavenly
Father! be pleased, if consistent with Thy blessed will,
to say, It is enough. Lend help, O merciful Father!
that I may not let go my confidence.—O! assist
me in your prayers, that I may be released from the
shackles of mortality.—O! take me, holy Jesus, I
pray thee, to thyself. O! have mercy, have mercy.—
I truly know sorrow as to the body, but not as to the
mind. Oh! my head aches, but not my heart."

The next day, he said, "Oh! what should I have
been now, if I had not submitted to Christ's baptism,
—to the baptism of fire." He enquired if he was not
weakening fast. The doctor replied, "I fear thou
art;" Thomas responded, "O do not fear, but rejoice,
rejoice on my account; O! pray for me and with me,
that my faith fail not.—O, good Lord Jesus! cast a
crumb of help, and deliver me; I earnestly pray thee
to come; come quickly, if I dare claim to be Thy
servant."

On a subsequent day, he said, "I have passed a
better night than I could have expected, but it has
been through my Redeemer sustaining me. I hope
I am kept from murmuring; I desire a cheerful submission, for I cannot help myself, nor can any man
help me. O! the balm, the oil poured into my
wounds caused by my shortcomings. I desire to
submit, and say, Thy blessed will be done."

The next day, he said, "I will try to sing of mercy;
mine eyes hath seen Thy salvation, and Thy glory.
When shall I feel Thy presence?—My friends must

not think more highly of me than they ought to think. If I have been anything it has been of grace, not of merit." He had previously expressed a wish that he might go out of the world, with a clear head, and a clean heart.

He afterwards exclaimed, "O, holy, blessed Jesus! be with me in this awful moment! Come!—Oh, come, and receive me to thyself; and of thine own free mercy, in thine own time, admit me into Thy heavenly kingdom!"

About two o'clock on the following morning, he was moved into a more comfortable position; after this he became faint, and from that time gradually sank away, so that those about him could only discover by close watching, when he ceased to breathe.

Thus lived Thomas Shillitoe, and thus he died, at the age of about eighty-two, on the 12th of the 6th month, 1836; full of days, and full of peace; beloved and honoured for his work's sake; and leaving a bright example of the comfort and benefit of serving the Lord.

END.

London: Printed by E. Couchman & Co. 10, *Throgmorton Street; for the* TRACT ASSOCIATION *of the* SOCIETY OF FRIENDS. *Sold at the Depository,* 12, *Bishopsgate Street Without.*—1864.

CHRISTIAN'S CROSS.

EXTRACTED CHIEFLY FROM

PENN'S "NO CROSS NO CROWN."

"If the righteous scarcely be saved, where shall the ungodly and the sinner appear?" If the thoughts, words, and works of the righteous must come under scrutiny before the impartial Judge of heaven and earth, how then shall the ungodly be exempted? We are told by Him who cannot lie, that many shall even say unto Him, Lord! Lord! and recount the works that they have done in his name, and yet be rejected with this direful sentence, "I never knew you; depart from me, ye that work iniquity." As if he had said, Get you gone, you evil doers: though you have professed me, I will not know you; your vain and evil lives have made you unfit for my holy kingdom: get you hence, and go to the gods whom you have served; your beloved lusts which you have worshipped, and the evil world which you have so much coveted and adored; let them save you if they can, from the wrath to come upon you, which is the wages of the deeds you have done.

Christ came to save man from sin, and from death, and wrath as the wages of it; and those who are not delivered by him from sin, can never be saved from the death and wrath that are the assured wages of sin. "There is mercy with the Lord, that he may be feared;" he delighteth not in the death of poor sinners, but rather that they should come to know the

No. 94.   [*Price 3d. per dozen.*]

Truth, and be saved. For this purpose he hath set forth his Son, a propitiation for sin, and hath given him to be a Saviour, that those who believe in him and follow him, may feel the mercy of God, in the remission of their sins, for Jesus' sake. Behold the remedy, an infallible cure of God's appointing.

But perhaps some may say, Where is Christ to be found? How is he to be received, to effect this mighty cure? He suffered on the cross for the sins of the world. "Behold the Lamb of God, which taketh away the sin of the world." He is also the great spiritual "Light that enlightens every man that cometh into the world." He manifests to men their deeds of darkness and wickedness, and reproves them for committing them. He says, "Behold, I stand at the door and knock; if any man hear my voice, and open the door, I will come in to him, and will sup with him, and he with me." What door can this be, but that of the heart of man?

Thou, like the inn of old, mayest have been full of other guests; thy affections may have entertained other lovers; there may have been no room for thy Saviour in thy soul; wherefore salvation may not yet have come into thy house, though it may be come to thy door, and may often have been offered to thee. But if Christ still call and knock; that is, if his light still shine into thy heart and reprove thee, there is hope that thy day of visitation is not yet over. Wherefore believe in him, and receive him. This is of absolute necessity, in order that thy soul may live with him for ever. He said to the Jews, "If ye believe not that I am he, ye shall die in your sins; and whither I go ye cannot come." And because they believed him not, they did not receive him, nor any benefit by him. But they that believed, received him: "and *as many as received him, to them gave he power to become the sons of God.*" To such, Christ was ever made Propitiation, Reconciliation, Salvation, Righteousness, Redemption, and Justification.

'He, who, by his Spirit, stands at the door of thy heart and knocks, and sets thy sins in order before thee, and calls thee to repentance, is the Saviour of the world. If thou believe not in him, thou wilt die in thy sins; it is impossible that he should do thee good, or effect thy salvation, unless thou believe in him, for Christ works not against faith, but with it. It was said of old, "He did not many mighty works" in some places, because the people believed not in him. If thou truly believe in him, thou wilt open the door of thine heart to his knocks; thou wilt yield to the discoveries of his light, and the teachings of his grace or good Spirit will be very dear unto thee.

It is the nature of true faith to produce a holy fear of offending God, a deep reverence for his precepts, and a most tender regard to the inward testimony of his Spirit; as to that, by which his children have, in all ages, been safely led to glory. For as they that truly believe, receive Christ, in all his tenders to the soul; so those who thus receive him, receive with him power to become the sons of God, ability to do whatever he requires, strength to mortify their lusts, control their affections, deny themselves, and overcome the world in its most enticing appearances. This is the CHRISTIAN's CROSS which thou, O man, must take up, if thou intend to be the disciple of JESUS. Nor canst thou be said to receive Christ, or to believe in him, whilst thou rejectest this cross. For as receiving Christ is the means appointed of God for salvation, so bearing the daily cross after him is the only true testimony of receiving him; and therefore it is enjoined by him, as the great token of discipleship, "If any man will come after me," said Christ, "let him deny himself, take up his cross, and follow me." Nothing short of this will do. No crown, but by the cross; no life eternal but through death to sin. To speak of the Christian's cross is to use a figurative speech, borrowed from the outward tree, or wooden cross, on which Christ submitted to the will of God, in suffering death for sinners, at the hands of evil men.

The work of apostleship, we are told by an eminent labourer in it, was "to turn people from darkness to light, and from the power of Satan unto God." And for this blessed work, Christ endued the apostles with power, and so blessed their faithful labours, that in a few years, many thousands that had lived without God in the world, were inwardly quickened by his Spirit, and made sensible of the coming of the Lord Jesus Christ, as a Judge and Lawgiver in their souls; by whose light, or Holy Spirit, the hidden things of darkness were condemned in them, and they were brought to a true repentance, and knew their sins to be blotted out for Christ's sake, and received ability to serve the living God in newness of spirit. Thenceforward they lived not to themselves: but unto God, and the "law of the spirit of life in Christ Jesus," by which they overcame the "law of sin and death," was their delight. They quitted their old masters, the world, the flesh, and the devil; and delivered themselves up to the guidance of the Holy Spirit, or "grace of God," that taught them "to deny ungodliness and the world's lusts, and to live soberly, righteously, and godly in this present world."

The light with which Christ had enlightened them, discovered Satan in all his approaches, and the power which they received enabled them to resist and vanquish him in all his stratagems. Thus where once, nothing was examined, nothing went unexamined; the thoughts were brought to judgment before they were allowed any room in their minds; a strict guard being kept upon the very wicket of the soul. Now the old heavens and earth, that is, the old, carnal, or Jewish and typical worship, and the old earthly conversation passed away apace, and all things became new. He was no more a "Jew, that was one outwardly, nor was that circumcision, that was in the flesh: but he was the Jew that was one inwardly, and *that* circumcision, which was of the *heart*, in the spirit, not in the letter, whose praise is not of man, but of God." Indeed the glory of the cross shined so conspicuously through the self-denial of the lives of those who daily bore it, that it struck the heathen with astonishment, and in a short time so shook their altars, discredited their oracles, struck the multitude, invaded the court, and overcame their armies, that it led priests, magistrates, and generals in triumph after it, as the trophies of its power and victory.

While this integrity dwelt with Christians, the power that attended them was invincible. It quenched fire, daunted lions, turned the edge of the sword, outfaced instruments of cruelty, convicted judges, and converted executioners. In fine, the very ways their enemies took to destroy them, increased them; and by the deep wisdom of God, those, who in all their designs endeavoured to extinguish the Truth, were made great promoters of it. The care of Christians was not now, how to sport away their precious time, but how to redeem it, that they might "work out their salvation with fear and trembling." To make sure of their heavenly calling and election, was much dearer to them than the poor and trifling joys of mortality.

The Christian's cross is a submission to that Holy Spirit, that divine grace and power, which crosseth the carnal minds of men. And as the heart of man is the seat of sin, and where he is defiled, there he must be sanctified! so where sin lives, there it must be crucified and die. But in what way is the cross to be borne? When evil presents to the mind, that Spirit which shows the evil, shows also that it should not be yielded to; and if its counsel be closed in with, and God be looked unto for help, he gives power to escape: but they that gaze upon the temptation, at last fall in with it, and are overcome by it; and come under condemnation.

The Son of God is gone before us, and has left us an example, that we should follow his steps: he, by the eternal Spirit, led a life of self-denial, and suffered death upon the cross, for man's salvation, and we by the same Spirit, ought to offer up our-, selves to do or suffer the will of God, for the service and glory of Christ, who came in the greatness of his love to save man from sin. Though clothed with the infirmities of a mortal man, yet being within fortified by the Almightiness of an immortal God, he travelled through all the straits and difficulties of humanity, and opened "the new and living way" to eternal blessedness. O come, let us follow him, the most unwearied, the most victorious captain of salvation! to whom all the great Alexanders and mighty Cæsars of the world are infinitely less than the poorest soldiers of their camps could be to them. True, they were great princes of their kind, and conquerors too, but on very different principles. For Christ made himself of no reputation to save mankind, but these plentifully ruined people to augment their kingdoms. They vanquished others, not themselves; Christ conquered self; self ever vanquished them: of merit, therefore, he is the most excellent prince and conqueror. They advanced their empire by rapine and blood, but he his by suffering and persuasion: he never by compulsion, they always by force, prevailed. Misery and slavery followed all *their* victories; *His* brought greater freedom and felicity to those he overcame. In all *they* did, they sought to please themselves; in all *He* did, he aimed to please his Father, who is God of gods, King of kings, and Lord of lords. It is this most perfect pattern of self-denial that we must follow, if ever we would come to glory.

When God is pleased to try our affections by calling on us to part with the temporal blessings that he has given us, they must not be preferred to his will. Christ himself descended from the glory of his Father, and willingly "made himself of no reputation" among men; he humbled himself to the poor form of a servant, yea, to the ignominious death of the cross, that he might deliver us from sin, and set us an example of true humility, and entire submission to the will of our heavenly Father; and he said, "He that loveth father or mother, son or daughter, more than me, is not worthy of me." Again, "whosoever he be of you, that forsaketh not all that he hath, he cannot be my disciple."

This made those honest fishermen, whom the Lord called, to quit their lawful trades, and others to offer up their estates, reputation, liberty, and lives, to the displeasure and fury of their kindred, and of the governments under which they lived, for the spiritual advantage that accrued to them, by their faithful adherence to his holy doctrine. But many excused themselves from following him, as in the parable of the feast. Some had bought land, some had married wives, and others had bought oxen, and could not come. That is, an immoderate love of the world hindered them; their lawful enjoyments, from being their servants, became their idols; and they worshipped them more than God, and would not quit them, to come to God. But this is recorded to their reproach; and herein we may see the power of self upon the worldly man, and the danger that comes to him by the abuse of lawful things. What, thy wife dearer to thee than thy Saviour; and thy land and oxen preferred before thy soul's salvation! O beware, that thy comforts prove not snares first, and then curses! Wo to them that have their hearts in their earthly possessions! for when they are gone, their heaven is gone with them!

Reader, be not thou one of these; but come, take up thy cross and follow Him that giveth life eternal to the soul.

B.

END.

FORSAKING ALL TO FOLLOW CHRIST.

Jesus, I my cross have taken,
   All to leave, and follow Thee:
Naked, poor, despis'd, forsaken,
   Thou, from hence my all shall be.
Perish every fond ambition,
   All I've sought, or hoped, or known:
Yet how rich is my condition,
   God and heaven are still my own!

Let the world despise and leave me,
   They have left my Saviour too;
Human hearts and looks deceive me,—
   Thou art not, like them, untrue:
And whilst Thou shalt smile upon me,
   God of wisdom, love, and might,
Foes may hate, and friends disown me,
   Show thy face and all is bright.

Go then earthly fame and treasure:
   Come disaster, scorn, and pain;
In thy service pain is pleasure;
   With thy favour loss is gain.
I have called thee, Abba, Father;
   I have set my heart on Thee:
Storms may howl, and clouds may gather,
   All must work for good to me.

Men may trouble and distress me,
   'Twill but drive me to thy breast;
Life with trials hard may press me;
   Heaven will bring me sweeter rest.
Oh! 'tis not in grief to harm me,
   While thy love is left to me;
Oh! 'twere not in joy to charm me,
   Were that joy unmixed with Thee.

Soul! then know thy full salvation;
   Rise o'er sin, and fear, and care;
Joy to find, in every station,
   Something still to do or bear.
Think what Spirit dwells within thee;
   Think what Father's smiles are thine;
Think that Jesus died to win thee;
   Child of heaven canst thou repine?

London: Printed by E. Couchman & Co., 10, *Throgmorton Street; for the*
TRACT ASSOCIATION *of the* SOCIETY OF FRIENDS. *Sold at the* DEPOSITORY,
12, *Bishopsgate Street Without.*—1862.

CHRISTIAN'S PATHWAY.

Extracted principally from a Letter by Stephen Crisp, dated 1668.

MY spirit has been deeply exercised concerning many who feel something which is good stirring in their hearts, and striving to bring them into a serious consideration of their course of life, and of the true condition of their immortal souls; but who, when they have begun to turn their minds to this good thing, have had many doubts about its nature, and fears lest they should be misled or deluded by it. They have been tempted to slight it, and not knowing that it was the Spirit of the Lord, the same that convinces mankind of sin, in order to lead them to repentance, and to faith in Christ, the propitiation for sin, they have even imagined it to be a work of the evil one, designed to deprive the soul of its peace.

But, Reader, when thou slightest the strivings of this good Spirit, and thus gettest ease for a little while, and takest liberty to act against it, and both to do and to say that which it condemns in secret, does it not arise again, and destroy thy peace, and bring trouble and anguish upon thy soul? Sometimes thou fearest that thou withstandest thy convictions to thy own destruction, and sometimes that thou art under a delusion. Thus thou art in a great strait. The flesh warreth against that which comes to disturb it, and the Spirit against that which resists and rebels

No. 96.   [*Price 3d. per dozen.*]

against it, for these two are contrary. Now, in this
state, how acceptable might a messenger be, to show
unto such an one, that which might deliver his soul
from going down to the pit (Job xxxiii. 23, 24), and
save his life from the destroyer.

For the sake of such as are in this state, I am often
drawn into deep exercise, by day and by night; and
my cry to God for them is, that he may bring forth
their imprisoned spirits out of the prison-house, and
dispel their darkness.

"Every good gift and every perfect gift is from
above, and cometh down from the Father of lights"
(Jas. i. 17.), who willeth not the death of a sinner,
but would rather that he should turn, repent, and
live. Ezek. xxxiii. 15. Therefore hath He, in His
infinite love and tender mercy to the children of men,
prepared a way of deliverance, even through Jesus
Christ, the Mediator of the New Covenant (Heb.
xii. 24.) ; whom He hath freely given, to be a ransom
for man, and a light unto a dark world, and that He
should, by the gift of the Holy Spirit, freely offered
to all, "enlighten every man that cometh into the
world" (John i. 9.)—of which number, remember,
that thou art one.

But if thou rebel against that light wherewith
Christ hath enlightened thee, whither will thy rebellion lead? It was said of old, "They that rebel
against the light, know not the ways of it." (Job
xxiv. 13.) ; and the more thou rebellest, the more
dark thou wilt daily grow; and as darkness increases
in thee, so the power of it will bind thee down as a
chain, and smother every good desire. For by rebellion, men grow past feeling : and the custom of sin
taketh away the sense and burden of it.

But to thee I write, who art not yet come to this
state of hardness of heart, but who art ready to say :
"If I were but sure that it is the Spirit of God which
shows me my sins, I would follow it, and love it, and
own it. Thou well knowest this Spirit hath power
to condemn thee, and to break thy peace when thou

disobeyest it, therefore try and prove what it can do
for thee when thou obeyest it. Thou can'st not obey
this heavenly Spirit, except by taking up the daily
cross to thy own will, lusts, and affections; but if
thou do not oppose it, but give thyself up to be
guided by it, thou wilt come to know, that it is able
to deliver thee when thou art tempted, as well as to
judge thee when thou hast yielded to the tempter.

The way then to the answering of thy doubts about
this inward manifestation of the Spirit is to be found
by obeying it, and yielding to it. They that do evil
grow into hatred against the Spirit that judges them;
and thus, coming under its condemnation, they grow
afraid of it. But this only proves that it is sent of
God; for it doeth God's work, which is a righteous
work. He hath placed this witness in thy conscience,
to bear witness for Him, concerning all thy actions,
whether they be good or evil; and thou thyself whosoever thou art, whether high or low, rich or poor,
professor or profane, shall confess that this Spirit
hath never condemned thee for that which was good,
nor borne witness against thee for that of which thou
wast not guilty.

Come, then, thou that hast been tossed with doubts
and questionings about the Truth; hearken to counsel.
Obey, and walk in the Christian's pathway, and thou
shalt daily see more of the light of the Spirit, till it
break forth as the morning unto thee, and till it shine
unto the perfect day: yea, a day of gladness and
rejoicing to thy poor distressed soul.

Arise, O thou that sittest sorrowing and crying
out in secret, because of the bonds and fetters that
are yet upon thee! Arise, arise, in the Name of the
Lord God of Zion, who draws nigh to thee by His
quickening Spirit! Hearken unto the voice of Him
who saith to the prisoner, "Come forth" (Isa. xlix.
9.); and to the bowed down, "Arise;" and to the
feeble ones, "Put on strength and follow me; I will
confound thy foes, and break the strength of thine
enemies. As I have done for my people who have

forsaken all to follow me and obey me, so will I do for thee; and if thou wilt walk before me in uprightness, and keep my covenant, as they have done, no power nor strength of the enemy, within or without, shall be too hard for thee."

When the Lord Almighty thus ariseth in thy soul, and His pure light shineth in thee, how shalt thou see thy vain doubtings dispelled and know a clear conviction prevail in thy spirit concerning the way of God! A secret joy will then be felt by thee; and the seed of the kingdom, that hath long been buried in thy heart, will begin to spring up in thee; in which seed, thy soul will feel some touches of that heavenly life and peace, which exceed all that this world can ever afford or bestow. When, therefore, thou feelest this as refreshing dew upon thy soul, then dwell singly in the sense of it. Keep thine eye to the joy set before thee in Christ Jesus. For if thou allow thy mind to wander, there are objects on every hand, to lead thee from thy soul's Beloved, and to defile thy heart, and make it unfit for the dwelling of Him who is holy and pure, and will not abide in a polluted temple.

Thou can'st not serve two masters (Matt. vi. 24.), nor partake of the Lord's table, and of the table of devils. 1 Cor. x. 21. Feed not, then, that which hungers after evil things, and delights in them; but what is for famine, let it be famished; and what is for the sword, let the two-edged sword that goeth out of the mouth of the faithful and true Witness cut it down. —Rev. i. 16. and iii. 14. And so thou shalt see the giants in the land slain before thee by One that is mighty to deliver, and able to bring thee out of spiritual Egypt with a high hand; but this thou can'st not witness, except by believing in Him, and diligently following Him. If thou willingly yield to His gentle drawings, when thou feelest them in thy heart, thou wilt find them to be profitable and effectual to thy soul; and the more thou followest Him, the more thou wilt feel His goodness break in upon thee for thy encouragement; and the less thou wilt doubt of His love and mercy in leading thee still further, even unto the end, and unto that rest which will satisfy thy soul.

Thus walking and dwelling in the light, thy conversation will be in heaven (Phil. iii. 20.), as was that of the saints of old; and like them, thou wilt witness thy unity to be with the Father and with the Son. For "If we say that we have fellowship with Him, and walk in darkness, (which all sinners do, sin being the work of darkness,) we lie and do not the Truth. But if we walk in the light, as He is in the light, we have fellowship one with another : and the blood of Jesus Christ, His Son, cleanseth us from all sin." 1 John i. 6, 7.

And as thou art faithful in bearing thy daily cross, which crucifies that nature in thee that hath resisted the Lord, and kept thy soul in bondage—as thy old nature comes to die, and thou art buried by spiritual baptism into Christ's death, thou wilt be made a partaker of the new life, and the true resurrection, which is in Christ.—Rom. vi. 3—5. All that are in Him, are in the resurrection and in the life, for He said, "I am the resurrection and the life : he that believeth in me, though he were dead, yet shall he live." John xi. 25. This living to God in His Son is, "the first resurrection;" and over those who witness it, "the second death hath no power." Rev. xx. 5, 6. Those who are partakers of this resurrection will be delivered from doubt or fear about the way of salvation, and will be given up to do and to suffer according to God's blessed will; and here is true and perfect rest to the soul. But the more thou reasonest against obeying God's witness in thy heart, the less able thou art to obey it. The way to obtain more light, is to be obedient to the little which thou hast received. It is thy own unfaithfulness which makes thee to go daily with a burden upon thy shoulders, and guilt upon thy conscience, so that thou can'st not come before the Lord with an open face, but art covered with thine own iniquities.

In this state, thou knowest neither sabbath, new moon, nor holy-day to the Lord; but all is labour, toil, and wearisomeness of spirit.

Oh, how my soul pities those who are in this state! I have deep sympathy with their sorrows, and in tender love am drawn to extend a hand of help, as having myself obtained mercy, and to testify of the goodness of the Saviour to poor and needy souls; for He is willing to relieve and comfort them. ―My desires is, that thy bonds may be broken, and thy soul escape; but, in the name of the Lord, I tell thee, there is no other way for deliverance, but by giving up, in simple obedience to that faithful and true witness of God which moves in thee against sin. Therefore repent, believe in Christ who died for thy sins, and wait to feel thy mind and will subjected to His power, that thou mayest become of the blessed number of His willing people, who walk in the Christian's path. Cease from thy reasonings against obeying the Truth, and from saying thou can'st not do it, thou wantest power, and that when God gives thee grace, then thou wilt obey; for such sayings are vain.

It is true that none can obey the Lord but by His grace and power given unto them; but He hath caused His grace, even that which bringeth Salvation, "to appear unto all men" (Tit. ii. 11.); and it hath appeared in thee, and is a reprover in thee. Turn then to that Spirit which smiteth thee, and thou wilt turn to the grace of God; for it is His grace, or good Spirit, that strives with thee, to lead thee out of the evil, which it reproves, and to bring thee to God, from whom the grace cometh. If thou give up to obey the drawings of this good Spirit, and in obedience thereto deniest thyself of thy lusts and pleasures, and of following thy own will, thou shalt not want power; but shalt feel Him near, who worketh in thee, first the willingness, and then the deed, according to His own good pleasure. Phil. ii. 13. Thus is the glory His alone.

Now thou knowest the mystery of the spiritual cross, and how it is the power of God, for want of which all that reject Christ and the power of this cross complain, and do not "walk as He walked." 1 John ii. 6. So long, therefore, as thou livest in the cross, thou livest in the power; thy obedience becomes more easy, and all things are possible to thee through Christ, who died for thee. Whilst "dying daily" (1 Cor. xv. 31.) to that which is evil in thyself, thou feelest more life, joy, and pleasure in that which is good and acceptable to God; and thy desires become more and more fervent after a full and perfect enjoyment of His presence in thy soul, in the pure unity of the Spirit. As good desires grow stronger in thee, it becomes easier to part with those things which hinder thy spiritual progress. Though these be even thy bosom sins, they must all be parted with for the love thou bearest to Christ, who first loved thee, and gave Himself for thee (Gal. ii. 20.); for such only as have this love, and continue in it, are counted worthy to be heirs of the kingdom of God.

Think it not strange, therefore, to be brought through manifold trials (1 Pet. iv. 12.), that thy soul may thereby be prepared as a bride, for Christ her husband (Rev. xxi. 2.); for there are many who desire an acquaintance with Him, but are not willing to be fitted for Him; they must first put off the vile raiment, or be washed from their sins in His blood, and then put on the white linen of the righteousness that is wrought out by His power. But while this work is going forward, what need there is of patience and quietness of spirit! what need of subjection to the working of the Holy Spirit in all things! that thou mayest not be setting bounds to that which must limit thee, nor be saying in thy heart, "If my trials were but so," or, "my exercises so and so, I could then bear them." No! rather submit in all things, willing to do and suffer, to be tried and exercised, as it pleaseth the Lord to order or to permit

8

for thy good; and under all His dispensations say, "It is the Lord, let Him do what seemeth to Him good." 2 Sam. xv. 26. Whosoever thus give up to Him, will find that though He wound, yet He will heal them again; though He slay them, yet shall they live by Him.

Learn, therefore, to exercise patience and faith. Remember the Israelites of old, who in their greatest straits were commanded to "stand still and see the salvation of God" (Exod. xiv. 13.); and they were a figure to thee. O, wait, therefore, for the knowledge of Christ, that He may lead thee in the Christian's path, establish righteousness in thy heart, and bring peace and everlasting rest to thy immortal soul.

END.

London: Printed by E. Couchman and Co., 10, Throgmorton Street; for the TRACT ASSOCIATION of the SOCIETY OF FRIENDS, Sold at the Depository, 12, Bishopgate Street Without.—1864.

THE

LIBERTY OF GOSPEL MINISTRY

EXEMPLIFIED,

IN A SHORT ACCOUNT OF

THOMAS AND JANE COLLEY,

~~~~~~~~~~~~~~~~~

THOMAS COLLEY was a native of the village of Smeaton, near Pontefract, in Yorkshire, where he was born in the year 1742. Of his early life little more is known than that he was educated in the principles of the Episcopal Church. While residing at Sheffield as an apprentice, he became awakened to a sense of the sinfulness of sin, and to his need of a Saviour, and associated himself with some pious people, among whom he subsequently became a preacher.

He married in 1764, and his wife proved a true help-meet to him, both in things temporal and spiritual. She had been led to compare closely with the doctrines of the New Testament, the practices which are common amongst most denominations of Christians, and some of these she had perceived were not in accordance with the precepts of Christ and his apostles.

It was customary among the people with whom her husband was associated, to make a collection at the conclusion of their meetings, and to hand it to the preacher; and on one occasion, when he returned home, and extended his hand to give her a small sum which he had received in this way, she drew back her hand, and addressed him thus :—"Thomas is it the Gospel you have been preaching? If it be, the command is, 'Freely ye have received, freely give;' but if it be not the Gospel, then how could you take money for pretending to preach that which you have not preached."

This address made a deep impression on the mind of Thomas Colley : he became greatly burdened in spirit, under the conviction that he had acted in a way which was contrary to the precept of his Lord and Master, and he felt restrained from preaching again in the same manner. In the forenoon of the First-day of the following week, about the time at which people were going to their various places of worship, he went out, thinking that he would go to some one of these places, but unresolved as to which. In proceeding along the streets, he noticed some persons belonging to the Society of Friends going to their meeting, and came to the conclusion that he would follow them : for having understood that their meetings were often held in silence, he thought that he should find a quiet opportunity of reflecting upon those subjects which now weighed so heavily upon his spirit.

Soon after taking his seat in this meeting, with his mind turned to the Lord, and desiring to be given to see what was in accordance with the divine will, he became sensible of the influence of the Holy Spirit bringing a feeling of solemnity over the congregation, under which his own mind was reverently bowed before the God of heaven and earth, and greatly contrited. His understanding became at this time much more clearly enlightened than it had previously been, to perceive the nature of that worship of the Father which is in spirit and in truth, and to apprehend the accordance of the practice of silent waiting upon God in religious assemblies, with this true Gospel worship; and he came to the conclusion, that in whatever manner others might assemble to worship God, the way in which he should be enabled most acceptably to perform this solemn duty was that adopted by the Society of Friends.

Jane Colley soon joined her husband in attending the meetings of Friends; and as their attention was directed to the state of their own hearts before the Lord, and "to feeling after him, if haply they might find him,' they found these occasions blessed to their souls; their strength in the Lord was renewed, and they witnessed the promise of Christ respecting the Holy Spirit, "He shall take of mine and shall shew it unto you," more abundantly fulfilled in their experience. They were received into membership with Friends in 1766.

As Thomas Colley bore patiently the baptisms of the Holy Spirit, by which he was made sensible of his help-lessness to perform the divine will in his own strength, and was brought to trust in the Lord alone, he grew in grace; and in process of time, he felt constrained by the love of Christ to speak as a minister of the Gospel in the meetings of Friends. His first communication in this line of service was in the year 1768. Being careful in humility and watchfulness, to occupy the talents committed to him, his services were acceptable and edifying, and in due time he was acknowledged by his Friends as one of their approved ministers. Not long after this, he felt himself called upon, by Him who "putteth forth his own sheep and goeth before them," to travel in the service of the Gospel, and way was made for him in the discharge of this duty, according to the good order established among the Society of Friends, by which their ministers, though not receiving any pecuniary remuneration for preaching the Gospel, but conscientiously adhering to the precept, " Freely ye have received, freely give," are nevertheless carefully provided for in regard to travelling and other needful expenses, while from home in the service of the Gospel.

As the Society does not restrict the services of its ministers to any particular places, but when those who are approved amongst them, believe themselves called to particular services, and bring the subject before their Monthly Meetings, which are held for the care of their congregations, these meetings weightily deliberate upon such subjects before the Lord; and if they feel unity with the ministers in regard to the service they have in prospect, they give them certificates of their unity, and set them at liberty to proceed in the performance of their apprehended duty. In this way, Thomas Colley performed many journeys in Great Britain, Ireland, and some more distant countries, with the concurrence of that church with which he had become united.

In 1779, in company with his friend Philip Madin, an Elder, also of Sheffield, he paid a religious visit in the island of Barbadoes, and in a few of the other British West India Islands. Being favoured to return home in safety, he penned the following reflections :—" Under a grateful remembrance of the many favours of the Almighty, graciously extended to us, through the course of this long and perilous journey, in preserving us in the midst of a raging and tumultuous war; in opening our way in the service in which we were engaged, and affording ability and strength to discharge the duty of the day, our spirits are humbly bowed in deep reverence and thankfulness to the Father and Fountain of all our mercies."

A few years after his return from this voyage, he again left his near connections, and travelled extensively in North America, where his Gospel labours were well received, and made a deep and instructive impression on the minds of many of those whom he visited; for he was eminently qualified to set forth the blessings of salvation through our Lord Jesus Christ, who came as the light of the world, and offered himself as a sacrifice for the sins of mankind; and to turn the attention of his hearers to the teachings of the Holy Spirit, in the secret of the soul; in order that they might not only know this blessed Teacher as a witness against sin, but as the Comforter of those who, being reconciled unto God through the death of his Son, follow him in the regeneration.

In reference to one of his visits to London, he writes; " I have laboured many weeks in this populous place— visited all the meetings [of Friends] in this city, and most of them on First-days, and have had public meetings in all their meeting-houses, and in many other places. In this service, I may with reverence acknowledge that the Lord has been near, and has fulfilled his ancient promise, "As the day, so shall thy strength be." The meetings have generally been large; neither unfavourable weather, nor snow on the ground, has prevented people from attending them; and that living Power, which is both ancient and new, has been the crown and diadem of our religious assemblies." *

---

* The meetings styled in this paragraph "public meetings," were meetings for worship held by public notice, such as are frequently held at the particular request of ministers of the Society of Friends, when they feel it their duty to engage in such service; but notwithstanding such meetings are sometimes held by public notice, all the meetings for worship of the Society are open to the public at all times.

When not engaged in religious service, this devoted man was diligent in attention to his business, which was that of a cutler; herein following the example of the apostles, and especially that recorded of Paul, who laboured with his own hands as a tent-maker, and thus ministered not only to his own necessities, but to the necessities of those who were with him, "that he might make the Gospel of Christ without charge." *

Toward the latter end of the year 1810, Thomas Colley's health began to decline, and he said to one of his friends "I have for a considerable time apprehended I should have a lingering illness, and have never desired it might be otherwise. I do not, as some have done, wish for a sudden removal, as I think divine providence, as well as divine grace is as much manifested in times of sickness as in times of health. It now yields me great consolation that I worked while health and ability were afforded. I now see but little to be done. It is cause of great satisfaction that I was enabled to pay my last religious visit in London." In the meeting at Sheffield, at this period of his life, he spoke with increasing frequency both in testimony and in supplication; manifesting with clearness, and in the power and love of the Gospel, as a father in the church of Christ, that he longed with increasing solicitude for the spiritual progress of those amongst whom he had long and faithfully laboured.

In the 7th month, 1811, he was seized with violent illness, which he expected to survive only a few days; but being a little revived, he said to a friend who visited him, "I am a poor weak creature, uncertain how this attack may terminate; nor am I anxious about it:" and referring to his labours as a minister, he added, "For

* Acts xviii. 3; xx. 32, 34, 35. 1 Cor. iv. 12.

some time past, I have been concerned to use, the strength afforded, in discharging manifested duties; and on retrospect, I do not see one religious duty or service left undone."

After this he gradually declined; and in the sixth month, 1812, he became very weak. On the 10th, when one of his friends who had called on him, was about to take his leave, having to attend the meeting of ministers and elders that evening, he said with a calm and expressive countenance, "The Lord bless thee; and may he be with you in all your movements in the promotion of his work." Then referring to his own situation, he added, "How long the taper may glimmer in the socket is uncertain; I think it will not be long. My love to Friends. Farewell!"

He spoke but little after this, but appeared to be patiently waiting the summons to join the "innumerable multitude who have washed their robes and made them white in the blood of the Lamb;" and on the 12th of the sixth month, he expired, in the 70th year of his age, having been a minister forty-four years.

Jane Colley survived her husband about seven years: she was one of the many evidences which have occurred in the Society of Friends, that where the restrictions of man do not interfere with the work of the Lord, he still continues to fulfil that prediction of the prophet Joel, respecting the preaching of women, to which the apostle Peter referred on the day of Pentecost: "And it shall come to pass in the last days, saith God, I will pour out of my spirit upon all flesh; and your sons and your *daughters* shall prophesy;" "and on my servants and on my *handmaidens* I will pour out in those days of my Spirit, and they shall prophesy." She became a minister in 1779. Her labours were edifying to her friends, but were chiefly confined to the meeting to which she belonged. While health permitted, she attended diligently to her husband's business when he was absent on religious service, but during many of her latter years she was confined to her room by a painful disease. In this season of trial she testified that her love for her friends, and for the prosperity of truth and righteousness was amongst her greatest comforts in life, and that she was mercifully favoured with an undoubted evidence, that a place of rest and peace with her Saviour would be allotted her in his eternal kingdom. A few hours before her death, which occurred when she was about 77 years of age, she said, " My sufferings are very great; but in the end all will be well;" and soon after putting up the prayer, " Holy Father, if consistent with thy will, grant me a release, and take me to thyself," her spirit quitted its tenement of clay, to join the glorious company in heaven in everlasting praises to Him who died for them; whom not having seen on earth they loved, and in whom believing, they rejoiced with joy unspeakable and full of glory.

END.

London: Printed by E. Couchman & Co. 10, Throgmorton Street; for the TRACT ASSOCIATION of the SOCIETY OF FRIENDS. Sold at the Depository, 12, Bishopsgate Street Without.—1863.

NECESSITY OF HOLINESS

IN THIS LIFE.

ABRIDGED FROM AN ESSAY

By JOSEPH STORRS FRY.

" Not as though I had already attained, either were already perfect."
PHIL. iii. 12.

WE are informed by the sacred historian, that after the Almighty had finished the inferior parts of the creation, as a consummation of his work, he made man: and. that he said, "Let us make man in our image, after our likeness: so God created man in his own image; in the image of God created he him. And God gave man dominion over the fish of the sea, and over the fowl of the air, and over the cattle, and over all the earth, and over every creeping thing that creepeth upon the earth."[a] He created man after his own image, and made him lord over his own creation.

It is not for us to conceive any outward or personal form to the Creator of the universe, but we may suppose that the likeness of Himself, which he was pleased to stamp on man, was in the endowment of a portion of his own divine nature. He breathed into his nostrils the breath of life, and man became a living soul. The Psalmist, speaking of man, exclaims, " Thou hast made him a little lower than the angels, and hast crowned him with glory and honour. Thou hast made him to have dominion over the works of thy hands: thou hast put all things under his feet."[b]

It pleased Infinite Wisdom to endow all the other parts of the animal creation with instincts suited to their several natures, and quite adequate to their wants; whereby they are directed in the choice of their food, and in all their necessary functions. By this principle, they are implicitly led through life without reasoning, and without being accountable for good or evil actions. But man who is made in the image of God, is not thus to walk blindly through

[a] Gen. i. 26—28. [b] Ps. viii. 5.

  [Price 3d. per dozen.]

life; because, as a blind, instinctive obedience to the Divine commands, on the part of man, would not have been sufficient in the sight of God, from the noblest work of his creation, on which he had stamped his own image, it pleased him in his inscrutable wisdom, to subject man to trial, by giving him the choice between good and evil; graciously affording him ability to resist temptation, yet leaving him completely a free agent.

When God placed Adam and Eve in the garden of Eden, it pleased him to prove their fidelity and obedience, by forbidding them to taste of the fruit of one particular tree, which was properly called the tree of the knowledge of good and evil. The good or evil in this case is not to be measured by the seeming importance of the thing; neither is it important what was the nature of the fruit; but the good or evil consisted in obedience or disobedience; because God had said, "Thou shalt not eat of it; for in the day that thou eatest thereof, thou shalt surely die."c   Here obedience was required as an act of free-will. Adam had power to obey; but giving way to the temptation, he disobeyed, and then first experienced the knowledge of *evil*. We, the offspring of Adam, well know, that whenever we give way to evil temptations, our power to resist the next temptation is lessened, and we feel ourselves further removed from the Divine nature and life, and more under the dominion and influence of evil. Adam did not then die as a man, for we know that he lived many hundred years after this act of disobedience; but he experienced a death to the nature and image of God: and indeed the eventual death of the body may be considered as involved in the above awful denunciation. Thus, by one man sin entered into the world, and death by sin; and so death passed upon all men, for that all have sinned; but thanks be to God, that not as the offence, so also is the free gift; through the offence of one, though many be dead; much more the grace of God by Jesus Christ hath abounded unto many: the judgment was by one to condemnation; but the free gift is of many offences unto justification. For if by one man's offence, death reigned by one, much more they which receive abundance of grace, and of the gift of righteousness, shall reign in life, by one, Jesus Christ.

We have abundant evidence in the sacred pages, that since the fall of Adam, God in his grace has dispensed such means to his creature man, as were at all times sufficient to restore him to Divine favour; to enable him to resist the tendency to violate the Divine law by committing evil; and

c Gen. ii. 17.

to walk in the paths of righteousness and obedience: of which we have an instance in Abel, the son of Adam. "By faith, Abel offered unto God a more excellent sacrifice than Cain, by which he obtained witness that he was righteous."[d] This faith must have been a faith in the revealed will of God. And that God did reveal himself to man in those early times through the same channel as he is graciously pleased to do in these Gospel days is also evident:—namely, by his grace, which the Apostle Paul declares "was given us in Christ Jesus before the world began, but is now made manifest by the appearing of our Saviour Jesus Christ."[e]

In the fulness of time, it pleased God to send his Son Jesus Christ into the world, in the likeness of man; to put away sin by the sacrifice of himself (Heb. ix. 26.), and to bring in that righteousness of faith, of which all true believers are the partakers and the heirs: for by one offering hath he perfected for ever all them that are sanctified. By living faith in his blood we become partakers of his own divine nature: for this faith works by love to the purifying of the heart: and that efficacious baptism whereby the conscience becomes purged from dead works to serve the living God, is to be found only in this most precious blood of Christ; who through the Eternal Spirit offered himself without spot to God. He came as that Divine Word, which was in the beginning, to proclaim the Gospel of peace and salvation to all nations, in a more glorious and manifest manner than it had ever been before proclaimed. He came "a Light to lighten the Gentiles, and the Glory of the people Israel."[f] He was "The *True Light* which lighteth *every man* that cometh into the world."[g] The burthen of his ministry was to testify against the sins of the world; and to proclaim the sufficiency of Divine Grace, in and through himself for the purpose of cleansing the heart of man from all sin. "Blessed (says he) are they who hunger and thirst after righteousness, for they shall be filled."[h] "Blessed are the pure in heart, for they shall see God."[i] "Whosoever committed sin is the servant of sin."[j] These expressions, from this high authority, ought to be sufficient to satisfy all who are called by his name,—Christians,—that it is necessary that in this life we should be purged from all sin. The pure in heart are to see God; what then is to become of the impure, which is the state of every sinner? He that committeth sin, is the servant of sin; consequently not the servant of God: for a man cannot serve God and mammon.

This is abundantly confirmed by the apostles whom the

[d] Heb. xi. 4.   [e] 2 Tim. i. 9.   [f] Luke ii. 32.   [g] John i. 9.
[h] Matt. v. 6.   [i] Matt. v. 8.   [j] John viii. 34.

Lord Jesus sent forth to preach, and to promulgate his Gospel of peace and salvation; who in their exhortations and epistles insist on this as a primary doctrine of christian divinity: namely, the redemption and preservation of the soul of man from sin, by Jesus Christ, the Word of God, which lighteth every man that cometh into the world.

The Apostle Paul addresses the Romans in the following language: "Likewise reckon ye also yourselves to be dead indeed unto sin, but alive unto God, through Jesus Christ our Lord. Let not sin, therefore, reign in your mortal body, that ye should obey it in the lusts thereof; neither yield ye your members as instruments of unrighteousness unto sin; but yield yourselves unto God as those that are alive from the dead; and your members as instruments of righteousness unto God."[k] "But now being made free from sin, and become servants to God, ye have your fruit unto holiness, and the end everlasting life: for the wages of sin is death, but the gift of God is eternal life, through Jesus Christ our Lord."[l] "I would have you wise unto that which is good, and simple concerning evil; and the God of peace shall bruise Satan under your feet."[m] He exhorts the Corinthians to "awake to righteousness and sin not:"[n] to cleanse themselves "from all filthiness of the flesh and spirit, perfecting holiness in the fear of God."[o] He tells the Ephesians that God hath chosen them in Christ, that they should be holy and without blame before him, in love.[p] He then enumerates many duties that they are to fulfil; that so the church might be glorious, "not having spot or wrinkle, or any such thing; but that it should be holy, and without blemish."[q] He exhorts the Philippians to such a course of conduct, that they may be blameless and harmless, the sons of God, without rebuke, in the midst of a crooked and perverse nation; among whom they shine as lights in the world.[r] To the Colossians he says, God "hath delivered us from the power of darkness, and hath translated us into the kingdom of his dear Son; in whom we have redemption through his blood even the forgiveness of sins."[s] "And you that were sometimes alienated, and enemies in your mind, by wicked works; yet now hath he reconciled in the body of his flesh, through death; to present you holy and unblameable in his sight."[t] "That we may present every man perfect in Christ Jesus."[u] "That ye may stand perfect and complete in all the will of God."[v] He tells the Thessalonians

[k] Rom. vi. 11—13.   [l] Rom. vi. 22, 23.   [m] Rom. xvi. 19, 20.
[n] 1 Cor. xv. 34.   [o] 2 Cor. vii. 1.   [p] Eph. i. 4.   [q] Eph. v. 27.
[r] Phil. ii. 5.   [s] Col. i. 13, 14.   [t] Col. i. 21, 22.   [u] Col. i. 28.
[v] Col. iv. 12.

that "God hath not called us unto uncleanness, but unto holiness," [w] exhorting them to abstain from all appearance of evil. "And (he adds) the very God of peace sanctify you wholly; and I pray God, your whole spirit and soul and body be preserved blameless, unto the coming of our Lord Jesus Christ. Faithful is he that hath called you, who also will do it." [x] To Timothy he says, "Let every one that nameth the name of Christ depart from iniquity." [y]

The Apostle Peter, writing to the strangers scattered abroad, says, "As he which hath called you is holy, so be ye holy, in all manner of conversation: because it is written, Be ye holy; for I am holy." [z]

The heart of man is compared to a garden, or a field; which, to produce an abundant and clean crop, requires constant vigilance to extirpate the weeds. If the weeds are cleared, a healthy luxuriant crop, with the blessing of "God who giveth the increase," [a] may in due time be expected: but if the soil be neglected, an abundant crop of weeds and thistles will ensue. Our Saviour, in his exposition of his parable of the sower, says, "He that received seed among thorns, is he that heareth the word; and the care of this world, and the deceitfulness of riches, choke the word, and he becometh unfruitful; but he that received seed into the good ground, is he that heareth the word and understandeth it; which also beareth fruit, and bringeth forth; some an hundred fold, some sixty, some thirty." [b]

Was our Saviour, and were the Apostles unreasonable, in recommending this sort of Holy Life to us? Would they have given forth such counsel, such exhortations, unless they had known that it was in the power of man through the light and grace of the Holy Spirit, to observe and keep them? Certainly not. We may then conclude that it was reasonable in them to recommend the holy life they have described, to both Jews and Gentiles; and that it is possible for mankind thus to live.

But some may perhaps argue that those to whom the Apostles wrote, were men of higher religious attainments than any of the present day. This, however, was not the case; for to the church of Ephesus the Apostle Paul says, "And you hath he quickened who were dead in trespasses and sins; wherein, in time past, ye walked, according to the course of this world; according to the prince of the power of the air, the spirit that now worketh in the children of disobedience: among whom also, we all had our conversation in times past, in the lusts of our flesh, fulfilling the desires of

[w] 1 Thess. iv. 7.　　[x] 1 Thess. v. 23; 24.　　[y] 2 Tim. ii. 19.
[z] 1 Pet. i. 15, 16.　　[a] 1 Cor. iii. 7.　　[b] Matt. xiii. 22, 23.

the flesh and of the mind; and were by nature the children of wrath, even as others; but God, who is rich in mercy, for his great love wherewith he loved us; even when we were dead in sins, hath quickened us together with Christ; (by grace ye are saved) and hath raised us up together, and made us sit together in heavenly places in Christ Jesus." [c] Surely, mankind of the present day are not worse than these Ephesians were, who were dead in trespasses and sins; gratifying the lusts of the flesh and the mind: yet these sinners were raised up, to sit in heavenly places in Christ Jesus. And so may sinners now, if they will receive him who alone giveth power to become the sons of God; and this only unto them who believe on his name.

We have abundant testimonies in Scripture of the *sufficiency* and *excellency* of Divine Grace to enable man to resist and to overcome sin. The Apostle Paul says, "Where sin abounded, grace did much more abound; that as sin hath reigned unto death, even so might grace reign, through righteousness, unto eternal life, by Jesus Christ our Lord." [d] "There has no temptation taken you, but such as is common to man; but God is faithful, who will not suffer you to be tempted above that ye are able; but will, with the temptation, also make a way to escape, that ye may be able to bear it." [e] "The grace of God that bringeth salvation, hath appeared to *all men*, teaching us that, denying ungodliness and worldly lusts, we should live soberly, righteously, and godly in this present world." [f] And when addressing the Jews or Hebrews, in order to show them the superiority of the spiritual dispensation of the Gospel over the ceremonial dispensation of the law, he says, "But now hath he (Jesus Christ) obtained a more excellent ministry, by how much also he is the mediator of a better covenant, which was established upon better promises; for if that first covenant had been faultless, then should no place have been sought for the second; for, finding fault with them, he saith, Behold the days come, saith the Lord, when I will make a New Covenant with the house of Israel, and with the house of Judah; not according to the covenant that I made with their fathers, in the day when I took them by the hand, to lead them out of the land of Egypt; because they continued not in my Covenant; and I regarded them not, saith the Lord: for this is the Covenant that I will make with the house of Israel after those days, saith the Lord; I will put my laws into their mind, and write them in their hearts, and I will be to them a God; and they shall be to me a people. And they

[c] Eph. ii. 1—6.   [d] Rom. v. 20, 21.   [e] 1 Cor. x. 13.
[f] Tit. ii. 11, 12.

shall not teach every man his neighbour, and every man his brother, saying, Know the Lord: for all shall know me, from the least to the greatest."[g] The Apostle James says "If any of you lack wisdom, let him ask of God, that giveth to all men liberally, and upbraideth not; and it shall be given him; but let him ask in faith, nothing wavering."[h] "Resist the devil, and he will flee from you; draw nigh to God, and he will draw nigh to you. Cleanse your hands, ye sinners; and purify your hearts, ye double-minded."[i] And the Apostle John, in his first general epistle, says, "If we walk in the light as he is in the light, we have fellowship one with another; and the blood of Jesus Christ his Son cleanseth us from all sin." "If we confess our sins, he is faithful and just to forgive us our sins; and to cleanse us from all unrighteousness." "Whosoever abideth in Him sinneth not; whosoever sinneth hath not seen him, neither known him. Little children, let no man deceive you, he that doeth righteousness is righteous, even as he is righteous. He that committeth sin is of the devil; for the devil sinneth from the beginning. For this purpose the Son of God was manifested, that he might destroy the works of the devil. Whosoever is born of God doth not commit sin, for his seed remaineth in him; and he cannot sin, because he is born of God."[j]

It is our interest as well as our duty, to obey the divine law, as much as in us lies: for if we be disobedient, we most justly incur the displeasure of him whose favour is better than life. Yet obedience is to be considered as the native element of the new creature, rather than as something constituting a title to salvation: as that sure result and evidence of justifying faith, which makes us meet for heaven, although it cannot entitle us to it. May we be qualified reverently to adopt the language of the Apostle: "Not by works of righteousness which we have done; but according to his mercy he saved us, by the washing of regeneration, and renewing of the Holy Ghost."[k]

A pure life is not less man's own interest, than it is his duty to God; for we may be assured that sin and happiness are never united in the same person. "There is no peace, saith the Lord, unto the wicked."[l] They may indeed acquire riches; but unless the enjoyment of these riches be accompanied by that of a truly blameless life, it may be said of them in the words of king Solomon, "What good is there to the owners thereof, saving the beholding of them with their eyes."[m] "There is that maketh himself rich, yet hath

[g] Heb. viii. 6—11. [h] Jas. i. 5, 6. [i] Jas. iv. 7, 8. [j] 1 John iii. 6—9.
[k] Tit. iii. 5. [l] Isa. xlviii. 22. [m] Eccles. v. 11.

nothing; there is that maketh himself poor, yet hath great riches." But the upright in heart possess "durable riches," that peace of mind and heavenly enjoyment which the world cannot give, neither can it take them away. As the prophet Isaiah exclaimed, "Thou wilt keep him in PERFECT PEACE whose mind is stayed on thee, because he trusteth in thee."[p]

Many will readily assent to the assertion of the Apostle, that "The unrighteous shall not inherit the kingdom of God, neither idolaters, adulterers, thieves, covetous, drunkards, revilers, nor extortioners."[q] But they please themselves with a hope, that although they go on in sin, yet that God, in his mercy will pardon them at last. But we are assured that "There shall in no wise enter into the New Jerusalem, anything that defileth, neither whatsoever worketh abomination, or maketh a lie; but they which are written in the Lamb's book of life."[r] How important! How awfully important! that every individual, of whatsoever religious denomination he may be, should endeavour, by Divine grace, to keep God's holy commandments, and to walk therein all the days of his life. For although the mercy of God in Christ Jesus to truly penitent sinners is infinite; how know we that, when the awful moment of death arrives, we may have time to repent, or even to cry out, "God be merciful to me a sinner?"[s] that we may not be taken away by a sudden and instantaneous stroke, either by disease or accident, as is the lot of thousands! If then we have not experienced the great work of redemption effected in us, by the blood of Jesus Christ cleansing us from all our sins, what ground have we to hope that our names will be found written in the Lamb's book of life; God having declared, "Whosoever hath sinned against me him will I blot out of my book;" and the sentence will be a sentence of wo: "He that is unjust let him be unjust still; and he which is filthy let him be filthy still; and he that is righteous let him be righteous still. And, behold, I come quickly, and my reward is with me, to give to every man according as his works shall be. I am Alpha and Omega, the beginning and the end, the first and the last. Blessed are they that do his commandments, that they may have right to the tree of life; and may ENTER IN through the gates of the city: for WITHOUT are dogs, and sorcerers, and whoremongers, and murderers, and idolaters, and whosoever loveth and maketh a lie."[t]

[n] Prov. xiii. 7. [o] Prov. viii. 18. [p] Isa. xxvi. 3. [q] 1 Cor. vi. 9, 10. [r] Rev. xxi. 27. [s] Luke xviii. 13. [t] Rev. xxii. 11—15.

A MEMOIR

DEBORAH BACKHOUSE,

WHO DIED AT THE AGE OF 34 YEARS.

DEBORAH BACKHOUSE was the daughter of Richard and Elizabeth Lowe, of Worcester, and was born the 29th of 8th month, 1793. She lost her father when between two and three years of age; but the pious care of her mother, to train up the children with whom she was left, in the nurture and admonition of the Lord, greatly made up to them the loss which they had sustained, by the removal of a parent sincerely concerned for their spiritual welfare.

Elizabeth Lowe was diligent in instructing her children in the principles of Christianity, and careful to train them in the practice of those things, into which true Christian principles lead. This carefulness led her to caution them against indulging feelings or habits which would be likely to foster pride or vanity, and thereby hinder the growth of religion in the soul; and the subject of this memoir sometimes mentioned feelingly the condemnation she experienced, when but young, in making some small alterations in her dress, in order to gratify a disposition to have it less simple than was the wish of her beloved mother.

In the early part of the year 1818, while residing at Tottenham, in Middlesex, Deborah Lowe had an attack of illness, which confined her to her chamber for several months. In the course of it she evinced that she was not uninstructed in the school of Christ; and on one occasion, on a hope being expressed that she was recovering, she replied, that she had been thinking, that to depart and to be with Christ would be far better. Many times, after her recovery, with expressions of thankfulness to God, she recurred to the seasons of Divine favor, which she had been permitted to enjoy in the time of her great weakness.

In the course of the following summer she regained her usual health; and keeping her attention to the teachings of

No. 99.   [Price 3d. per dozen.]

the Holy Spirit, her religious experience increased; and submitting patiently to the baptisms of the Holy Ghost and of fire in her own heart, she became prepared to labor for the religious edification of others. She first spoke as a minister of the Gospel in a meeting at Tewkesbury, when on a visit there, in the autumn of the year 1819. Her communications in this line of labor were neither frequent nor long, but were clear and edifying; and in the exercise of Gospel ministry, she felt deeply the importance of submitting to those baptisms of the Holy Spirit by which the minister is made to feel, that the natural powers of man, however cultivated, if unassisted by the grace of God, are insufficient for this important work; and that if any minister aright in the church of Christ, whether male or female, it must be " as of the ability that God giveth."*

In 1822 she became the wife of James Backhouse, of York. It was her fervent desire to act in accordance with the divine will in regard to marriage; and on this important subject she sought the counsel of God in prayer, with becoming christian earnestness.

The great delicacy of her health necessarily secluded her much from the society of her friends; but seldom entirely prevented her attending to the state of her own family. She was a very affectionate wife and parent, and was exemplary in the management of her children, in whom she was careful to suppress, from the earliest periods, the appearances of self-will. She was of the judgment, that children ought to be taught very early to pay attention to those convictions of good and evil, of which they are often so sensible as to be uncomfortable when they yield to the evil, and comfortable when they resist it. She believed that these convictions were from God, and drew to Christ; and as such she endeavoured to direct the attention of her eldest child to them, who was only about four years of age when her mother died.

She was industrious and orderly in the management of her household affairs, and kind to her servants, but she preserved

---

* It may be proper to state, that the Society of Friends, of which Deborah Backhouse was a member, believe that, under the Gospel dispensation, spiritual gifts, (without which there can be no true ministry,) are not confined to men; but that, in accordance with ancient prophecy, the Holy Spirit is poured forth for the edification and refreshment of the church of Christ, upon daughters as well as upon sons. (See Acts ii. 16—18; Eph. iv. 7—12.) They look to the spiritual qualification, not to the distinction of sex, believing that in Christ Jesus there is neither male nor female, but that all are one in Him. (Gal. iii. 28.) And they consider this to be in accordance with primitive practice. (Acts xxi. 9; 1 Cor. xi. 5.)

with firmness a proper authority over them, and endeavoured to promote their spiritual as well as their temporal welfare. She was diligent in reading the Holy Scriptures, and careful to have them read daily, in the presence of her family and servants.' She felt much for the poor, and encouraged her servants to be careful not to waste anything that might be useful to them. She retired to rest as well as rose early, often saying she had observed things thrown much out of proper order, and much time lost, by the heads of families sitting up to an unseasonable hour, and rising late.

In the summer of 1827, she was obliged to give up joining with her friends in publicly testifying her dependence upon the Most High, by joining with them in meetings for worship. She was confined in the seventh month, and for a few weeks after appeared to be recovering strength. Her infant daughter died when about five weeks old. She bore this trial with christian resignation; often saying she believed it unsafe for her to dwell much upon her loss. Her health from this period ceased to improve; in a few weeks she became evidently weaker, and often intimated an apprehension of her continuance being very doubtful; but she remarked, that it was a duty to try suitable means for promoting recovery. With this view she accompanied her family to Scarborough.

Whilst at Scarborough she was introduced into a very trying baptism of spirit, under a sense of the withdrawing of the supporting influence of Him whom her soul loved; and without whose help she felt it to be impossible to be resigned to that separation from the nearest ties of life, which she apprehended might be fast approaching. She sometimes remarked, that she felt as if she could give up to anything rather than to die. In this state she patiently waited upon the Lord for strength to bow to His holy will; and He was pleased, after permitting this season of deep proving, to enable her cheerfully to adopt the language; "Not as I will, but as Thou wilt." She returned home after a few weeks, without witnessing any amendment. From about the middle of the 11th month her strength declined rapidly, and towards its close she was so much reduced as to be confined to her room; but while her bodily strength was fast wasting, her liveliness of spirit increased, and she felt additional interest in things around her.

In the evening of the 3rd of 12th month, her mind was sweetly contrited under a sense of her Heavenly Father's love. Under this feeling she earnestly enjoined her friends to be very careful not to say one single word that should possibly attribute any merit to her; and emphatically said, " I am nothing at all but a poor worm. I have not one scrap of my own to trust to. It is of Divine grace and mercy, that I am permitted to feel such a portion of inexpressible peace. For some time past I have seemed free from condemnation, I have felt comfort in having endeavoured to serve the Lord, and in doing the little I have been enabled to do for the cause of truth."

She then expressed an earnest desire, that no shade might be brought upon this precious cause through her, adding, "But O! I am so very poor and unworthy." On being reminded that an apostle has testified that, it is "Not by works of righteousness that we have done, but according to his mercy He saveth us," &c., and a belief being expressed, that she would thus be "accepted in the Beloved," and all would redound to the praise of the Lord, she sweetly assented, and said, "Yes! that is it. All to the praise and glory of the Lord."

After this she spoke of a deep concern she was under, that her children might be trained up in the fear of the Lord, and instructed in Divine things; that their tender minds might be closely watched, and everything withheld from them, which might encourage pride or any other wrong disposition. She then remarked, that she viewed children as a very important charge; and that a great weight of responsibility attached to parents and others, to whom they were committed. She said she longed, that if her dear children should live to grow up, they might be made as lights in the world; that she had never desired much of this world's goods for them, but only a sufficiency to live in a plain way: that she even dreaded the idea of riches, knowing they were often a great snare and temptation.

On the 4th she saw most of the family, imparted to them counsel, instruction, and warning, adapted to their different states; and endeavoured, in a particular manner, to impress upon them the importance of an attention to the light, or manifestation of the Holy Spirit, in their own minds; which, she said, would very clearly direct them in all things; and, if obeyed, lead to that peace which passeth all human understanding.

She afterwards gave suitable advice to the young woman who had the care of her children, reminding her of the necessity of a daily attention to the dictates of the Spirit of

Truth in her own heart, as essential to prepare her for rightly doing her part, in watching over and instructing them.

Again adverting to the important station of parents, she said she had never felt it so weighty before;—that much, very much, depended upon their endeavors to bring up their children in the fear of the Lord, setting them a good example, and not only closely watching over them, but checking and restraining them, in everything that had a tendency to injure their minds, or to lead them from the simplicity of the truth. She mentioned, with humble gratitude, the care of her own dear mother; and how remarkably it had been blessed to all her family, and had been a means of great preservation to herself she having had strong inclinations toward many things of a wrong tendency, which would have led her from the truth; adding, that she considered the care, counsel, and restraint of her dear parent, had been an unspeakable favor to her, and a great help in turning her to the right way. She appealed to her sisters, who stood by, saying, "My precious sisters can, I know, add their testimony to her excellent example, watchful concern, and prayers on our behalf; and that she desired for us heavenly riches, far before anything of a worldly nature."

She was then led to make thankful acknowledgment to her gracious Lord, for his goodness, mercy, and love, so variously manifested; saying, it was all of his rich, unmerited mercy, and that she had nothing good of herself. "No! nothing at all. All is of thy goodness, O Lord! and what shall I render unto thee for all thy benefits! Unto thee is all the praise and the glory."

On the 7th, she slept little during the night; but had much interesting conversation with her husband, mentioning, amongst other things, that she could scarcely have believed it possible, that a separation from him and their dear children could have been made so easy to her as it then felt, and that there was now no object for which she wished to remain.

Early on the morning of the 9th she wished to have her brother and sisters called, apprehending the time of her departure was at hand. On their coming into the room she embraced them affectionately, saying: "I know you all very well, and wished to see you again whilst I could speak, for I apprehend the time will now be very short." She then requested them, with her husband, to sit down around the bed, and be still.

In about an hour after she exclaimed: "What; am I in

the body still? I thought I had been gone; and it seems like coming to life again!" During most of the day, and till midnight, she seemed as if on the confines of eternal glory; and her hands and eyes were frequently raised in an attitude of adoration.

Having taken nothing for several hours, she was asked by one of her sisters to take a tea-spoonful of toast-water, when she replied, "No, my love! My mouth does not feel dry; neither am I faint. My soul has been refreshed with showers of heavenly dew, which have descended around me, and I have also felt them refresh this poor tabernacle so much, that I want nothing more; and I wish you could all have been refreshed as I was." She then expressed a belief, that she should be sustained to the end; for she was sensible of an Arm underneath, not only supporting her spirit, but her poor body also.

Some time after this several of her relations, and a few other friends coming in, a solemn silence ensued, which she broke by the following expressions, in an audible voice: "Surely I believe that the everlasting arms of God, through Jesus Christ my Saviour, are stretched forth to receive me. I feel the showers of heavenly love falling around us. What can be comparable unto this! O, inexpressible! inexpressible!"

After another pause she said, "I have a clear view of the outward sufferings of our blessed and holy Redeemer." She then spoke of his bleeding on the cross, and exclaimed, "O, let me adore! All this for poor, fallen, lost man, that he may be saved."

Another friend coming in, silence again ensued, and, after a while, she said, that the view of the outward sufferings of the Redeemer had a little returned, but was withdrawn, and her mind turned to the inward work of Christ, which was a great and necessary work. She then spoke of the importance of faithfulness, repeating, "Nothing else will do; I hope the words will go to those for whom they are intended."

Soon after this she supplicated thus: "Now, Holy Father! if the work be fully finished, be pleased to take me to thyself; if that be fully finished which thou hast given me to do."

Being requested soon after to take a little water, and finding great difficulty in swallowing it, she said, with a sweet and animated countenance: "I shall soon be led to living fountains of water, where I shall drink everlastingly, without fear of difficulty."

After this she was brought under considerable exercise of

mind, and said, there were some little things in her own house and family, which were not enough in the simplicity that truth requires; which, had she been sufficiently attentive to the light which makes manifest reprovable things, would not have been given way to. She appeared closely to scrutinize every little thing: and testified that, if the light were attended to, it would show clearly what was or was not in conformity to the Divine will. She acknowledged, in an humble affecting manner, her regret at not having been more faithful in these things, saying, " Yes, Lord! I see; and if I had paid more attention to the light I should have seen long since; and I do most sincerely repent and implore thy forgiveness." Some time after she remarked to her husband, that though a little shade had been permitted, it was all withdrawn, and that she again felt the showers of heavenly love descending as before.

In the course of the night she said she felt that all wisdom and knowledge were nearly departing from her, and fervently prayed thus : " O gracious Father! be Thou pleased to help me in this trying hour; and be near to support and preserve me from bringing any shade upon Thy holy Truth ;" adding soon after, "I believe Thou wilt not leave me, nor forsake me, unto the end."

During the night she seemed, at times, unable to collect her ideas in conveying what she wished; but remarks made, even under these circumstances, were fraught with instruction, and gave abundant evidence where her mind and hopes were centred.

Toward the morning of the 10th she again became perfectly clear, and spoke of several circumstances connected with her own situation. She also alluded to the language of the apostle John: " Greater is He that is in you, than he that is in the world:" and referred also to that passage of Scripture : "The Seed of the woman shall bruise the serpent's head ;" and remarked, that the enemy had been permitted to buffet her almost to the end. She then petitioned that the promises might be fulfilled to her; and afterwards expressed a belief that they would be fulfilled, both in her own experience, and in the experience of all those who trusted in the Lord with all the heart.

Soon after this, stretching forth her hand to one of her husband's sisters, who stood by her, she said: " O, my dear sister! help me to praise the Lord; for he has given me the victory over death, hell, and the grave ;" and during the remaining time of her continuance in this state of existence, it appeared as if all was joy and peace, not interrupted even by bodily suffering.

The whole of this day she was sweetly cheerful, and said she quite enjoyed the company of her relations; and when asked if she had any pain, she replied she had nothing worth calling pain. Scarcely an hour passed without her making some reference to her change, feeling assured that it was near, and remarking, she did not wish to stay, even in that comfortable state; that she was nearly ready for her narrow bed, and would not need any attention much longer.

In the afternoon she lay very quietly, conversing now and then a little, while circulation was gently retiring from the extremities. Between five and six o'clock, when so weak that articulation was difficult, she bore a last testimony to her love for the truth as it is in Jesus; after which, inquiring what time it was, and being told that it was six o'clock, she emphatically said: "In two hours the end will be come." Soon afterwards she fell into a slumber, from which she did not arouse; she gradually became weaker, till about a quarter past seven o'clock, when she ceased to breathe, and her redeemed and liberated spirit ascended, no doubt, to the place prepared for it, in that glorious kingdom, of the joy of which she had had so precious a foretaste; there to unite with the general assembly and Church of the First-born, in songs of everlasting praise, to the Lord God and the Lamb.

END

London: Printed by E. Couchman & Co., 10, Throgmorton Street: for the TRACT ASSOCIATION of the SOCIETY OF FRIENDS. Sold at the Depository, 12, Bishopsgate Street Without.—1863.

A

SHORT MEMORIAL

OF

JUDITH HILL.

~~~~~~~~~~~~~~~~~~~

LONDON:

Printed for the TRACT ASSOCIATION of the SOCIETY of FRIENDS,

Sold at the DEPOSITORY, 12, Bishopsgate Street Without.

—

1865.

No. 100.   [*Price 3d. per dozen.*]

SHORT MEMORIAL, &c.

JUDITH HILL was the only daughter of Andrew and Judith Leaner, of the city of London, who educated her in profession with the established Church of England, yet she was allowed to follow many of the vain customs of the world; though often in her youthful days she was made sensible, by the convictions of the Holy Spirit on her mind, that she was not living as became a disciple of the blessed Jesus. About the twenty-third year of her age she yielded obedience to the visitations of the love of the Almighty to her soul, and believing it to be her duty to join herself in religious profession with the Society of Friends, she frequented diligently their meetings for divine worship, and became a consistent and valuable member of that community. The alteration in her appearance, the christian simplicity that she felt it right for her to assume in dress and behaviour, brought upon her the displeasure of her parents, particularly that of her mother. These not having been undertaken in her own will, but, as she apprehended, being called for by Him who had brought her out of darkness to walk in the light of His Gospel, she was supported under this trial with christian fortitude and patience, being blessed therein with a portion of that peace which the world can neither give nor take away. She gained the esteem and regard of her friends, and her mother eventually became, not only reconciled, but encouraged her in her religious course.

She entered into the marriage state with John Hill, and they had a numerous family of children, whom she was piously concerned to train up in the nurture and admonition of the Lord. Her religious care was not confined to her own but largely extended to the offspring of others, having accepted, with her husband, the superintendence of a girls' school on the Surrey side of London, which was established by a Committee of members of the Society of which she was so bright an ornament,—seeking no other recompense herein, than a desire to be found in the way of her duty; and her disinterested labours were abundantly rewarded, not only with peace of mind, but she had the comfort of witnessing the fruit of her pious labours in some of her interesting charge.

In the year 1779, the educational institution was established at Ackworth, in Yorkshire, a seminary which continues to the present day in the Society, and which has been greatly blessed of the Lord; and to herself, and husband, was committed the superintendence of this large family, which important station she filled to the satisfaction of her friends, and eminently to the lasting benefit of many of those who had the privilege of partaking of her christian counsel and care.

After some years her health began to decline, and for the last three months of her life she was mostly confined to her chamber, experiencing much suffering from bodily affliction; but she was strengthened to endure it with exemplary patience and resignation to the divine will.

During her illness she uttered many striking expressions; many of which were preserved, evincing to those around her, that having been engaged to build her hopes for salvation on the alone true foundation, Jesus Christ, she had experienced that He was indeed an unfailing refuge,—one in whom she could trust. In the early part of her illness, her husband and daughter and some friends being present, she said, " How it may please the Lord to deal with me I know not; but if He should see meet to remove me this night, I am freely resigned to His divine will;—come what may, I can truly say, I have not desired either for myself, or my children, riches or length of days; but that they might be nurtured in the admonition and fear of the Lord, and inherit a portion in the blessed Truth."

At another time she said to her husband: "The Lord brought us together, and hath supported us through many deep trials and afflictions; when, to look back to my childhood and education, I have cause to acknowledge, with great thankfulness, His preserving hand in the time of ignorance. I have often felt a pity for those who are brought up in the follies and vanities of this world to their great loss; who perhaps would not have deviated so widely if they had had a different education; but this has not been the case with any of ours. I don't speak these things boastingly." Further adding, " From the time that the Lord was pleased to visit me, and to call me out of the fashions of the world, and the vain customs thereof, I don't remember that I ever revolted from that which was made manifest to be my duty: but as I gave up to the requiring of Truth, I found peace; though I was made a reproach and a by-word when in my father's house, yet was I made willing to leave all for truth's sake,—and I have always found liberty enough in the Truth for all that is necessary."

Her husband coming in again to take leave of her before he went to meeting, said, " he had been a witness, that He who had been with her in the prime of youth had not left her in the decline of life." She answered, " No, my dear, that He hath not; for He hath been mercifully pleased to be with me, and to bear me up under every trial and affliction; to whom be rendered praises and adoration, saith my soul, for evermore. Farewell, my dear love, and remember me, and pray for me, that I may have an easy passage out of this world." After a little pause, (addressing herself to her daughter and grand-daughter,) " Though you are not outwardly gathered with them for worship, yet remember the declaration of our blessed Lord, who said, ' Where two or three are gathered in my name, there will I be in the midst of them.'"

In the afternoon a young man of the family came to see her; after a time in silence she said, " I am pleased to see thee; I have been very ill indeed since I saw thee last; but through mercy have enjoyed a calm and peaceful mind, which is a great favour, and I hope to be thankful for it. Be thou careful to live and govern in the spirit of meekness, for like will beget its like." Then taking her leave said: " Farewell—farewell—I am pleased with thy company; and I wish thou may'st be so preserved through life, that we may be favoured to meet hereafter, if we should never see each other's faces more in mutability."

Her husband and one of her daughters sitting by her bed-side one evening, after lying a considerable time still, she said, " I have not been asleep; but whilst I lay thus quietly, this passage of Scripture arose in my mind—' They that wait upon the Lord shall renew their strength.' I often did, when in health, retire to my chamber, and have found great satisfaction in so doing, being many times so favoured, that I could say with David, ' Lord, one hour in thy pre-sence is worth a thousand elsewhere.' I have not sought popularity, or desired the praise of men; but that the Lord would be pleased to lead me quietly along in the way of my duty, which He hath been mercifully pleased to do."

One time, finding great difficulty in breathing, on one of her daughters going hastily to the bedside, she said, " My dear, I am not worse, though very weak, and according to my feelings seem drawing very fast towards my conclusion: don't mourn for me, but rather rejoice with thanksgiving, that the Almighty is pleased to favour with His presence in this time of sore conflict, who maketh the afflicted bed com-fortable; and endeavour to follow me as I have endeavoured to follow Christ."

One night enquiring of her daughter, who sat up with her, what it was o'clock, on being told, she said, " So my time passes on,—painful days, and wearisome nights: but I murmur not, for I am fully resigned to the will of the Lord; believing a time of rest will come, when all sorrow and pain will be at an end;"—adding,—" The Lord is worthy to be served; be thou faithful unto Him."

The same morning two Friends came to visit her, who

expressed the satisfaction and peace they felt in sitting with her, having an evidence that she had fought the good fight, and kept the faith, and had now nothing to do but to wait the Lord's time, to put off mortality, and put on immortality, and be crowned with life eternal: After which she broke forth in manner following: "My soul cannot sufficiently magnify and adore thy excellent name, O Lord! for all thy gracious dealings towards me; who hast been my guide and support through many deep conflicts and probationary seasons: and for this also, that Thou hast been pleased to send thy servants to visit me. It has been my earnest desire if there was any secret sin lurking in me, that I had not seen, that Thou wouldst be pleased to manifest it unto them. Thou, who hast been with me in six troubles, hast not left me in the seventh; but even in this time of great bodily affliction, Thou hast been pleased to be near for my support and help; for which, and all Thy mercies, I beg to be enabled to render unto Thee thanksgiving and praise."

One morning, her two grandsons coming to her bedside, she looked very affectionately, and said, " Jacob blessed the lads—I also have desired that the blessing of the Lord might rest upon you, my dear children. This perhaps may be the last advice I shall have to give you. Be careful on all occasions to speak the truth,—nothing that loveth, or maketh a lie, or doeth any wicked thing can enter the kingdom of heaven. Therefore, if you hope for an admittance into this glorious kingdom, you must become as little children; for our dear Lord said, of such is the kingdom of heaven. If you are careful to live thus, ye need not fear to die; for if you are taken away in childhood, the Almighty will receive you into His pure rest; you will become as the holy angels, to dwell for ever in His glorious presence. Above all things, be concerned to live in the fear of the Lord; then will the God of Abraham, Isaac, and Jacob, be your God." Then, taking them by the hand, kissed them, and said, " Farewell in the Lord." After breakfast, her daughter and others of the family being present, being asked how she was, she replied, "Still struggling hard for breath; but a time of rest will come. Our dear Lord told His followers, that in His Father's house were many mansions, if it had not been so He would have told them. I hope, and believe, I shall, when the Lord is pleased to remove me, be favoured to have a place in one of these glorious mansions. I can truly say, if I die now, I die in peace with all men. Our blessed Lord said to His followers, ' By this shall all men know that ye are my disciples, if ye love one another.' Love is a distinguishing mark of a christian, therefore dwell in love, and the God of Peace be with you."

The morning before her departure, her daughter hearing her speak, went to the bedside; she said, "Didst not thou hear what I said? I said the sting of death (which is sin) is taken away. The pale horse and his rider will have no victory, for the guardian angel of the Lord's presence encampeth about me, ready to convey my soul when He shall see meet to release it to the celestial regions of immortal bliss." The same evening, the masters of the school came into her room, and she gave them much valuable counsel, as to their conduct towards the children, and the influence of Christian example upon them; mentioning that this, with mild treatment in love, was the best way of maintaining right authority over them, saying, "Let your banner over them be love, as the banner of Christ is love over you: for neither grace, nor glory, nor any good thing, will the Lord withhold from them that love and serve Him."

On awaking out of her sleep the same night, she said to her daughter, "I have had a sweet sleep, and in a dream it hath been told me, the Lord saith thy work is finished,—I will cut it short in righteousness, for this morning shall thy soul be released." Adding "I think I am not mistaken,—'tis not a vain imagination; therefore should like to have my dear husband called." When he came she said: "I was loath to have thee disturbed, yet could not be so well satisfied without taking a final leave of thee, and my dear children." Then mentioned the above intimation of the time of her departure, and expressed the great satisfaction she felt in that they had been true helpmates, and that they had been favoured with many very comfortable evidences that the Lord joined them together; and said, " He who gave had a right to take away when He saw meet. We have been enabled, with industrious care, to maintain and educate our children with but little substance; yet that, with the blessing of the Lord, has been sufficient. My mind is covered with the love of God. 'There is more joy in heaven over one sinner that repenteth, than over ninety and nine just persons that need no repentance.' ' Christ came not to call the righteous, but sinners to repentance.' " And again she said she felt His love flow in her heart towards all mankind. " I feel my little strength weaken apace, but my faith in the Lord grows stronger and stronger. I have a firm hope, and an unshaken assurance of entering into everlasting happiness." A solemn pause ensued, then she broke forth in manner following: " Awful, solemn silence! how comfortable! how acceptable! It has been refreshing to my mind at this time. O seek after it, dear children, and keep low and humble; for all that is exalted shall be brought down; yea the sturdy oaks of Bashan, and the tall cedars of Lebanon will the Lord lay low." Then taking her husband and children individually by the hand, kissed them, bidding them " Farewell—farewell in the Lord." She continued till about eight o'clock in the morning, and then quietly departed this life, without sigh or groan, the 26th day of the 10th month, 1785, aged nearly 66 years. Her remains were interred in Friends' burial ground at Ackworth, in Yorkshire.

END.

Printed by E. Couchman & Co., 10, Throgmorton Street, London.

TO THE
RAILROAD EXCAVATORS.

————◆————

MY FRIENDS,

I have often looked on with interest while you have been at your work; and as I have watched you loosening the earth with the pickaxe, and wheeling it away in barrows, or filling the waggons, or laboriously employed in various other ways, I have wished to know what was in the hearts of some of you, and what provision you were making for the world to come. You are the means by which those great works, the Railroads, are being executed; and many of you labour upon them early and late. But the grandest Railroad that ever will be made, with all its hollows and embankments, its tunnels, and its bridges, is a very little work in comparison with the salvation of one of your souls. You think your work is a lasting one; but, even supposing it to last as long as the world itself endures, what is that to Eternity? What will become of the Railroads when, "the heavens shall pass away with a great noise, and the elements shall melt with fervent heat, the earth also, and the works that are therein shall be burned up?"[a] And what will become of your souls in that day? Will you be of the number of those who shall rejoice when they shall see "the Son of man coming in the clouds of heaven with power and great glory?"[b] or will you be of those who shall "say to the mountains and rocks, fall on us, and hide us from the face of him that sitteth upon the throne, and from the wrath of the Lamb; for the great day of his wrath is come, and who shall be able to stand?"[c]

"There is but a step between us and death," is a saying which you, of all men, know to be true. How many among you have met with a sudden and dreadful death whilst at their work! the very relation of which makes those shudder who are not exposed to the danger. But thou who reads this may be the next to be so taken away. Thy body may be scarred by powder, or crushed into a frightful mass; that will not then concern thee. What will become of thy soul?

[a] 2 Pet. iii. 10.   [b] Matt. xxiv. 30.   [c] Rev. vi. 16.

To which of the two abodes of our never-dying spirits dost
thou expect to go? To a Heaven of Joy and Peace and
Glory, to behold for ever, the face of God and of the Lamb?
or to a dreadful Hell, to "everlasting destruction from the
presence of the Lord,"[a] to the hopeless company of the devil
and his angels, " where their worm dieth not, and the fire is
not quenched?"[b] " There is no work, nor device, nor knowledge, nor wisdom, in the grave whither thou goest."[c] God
is in mercy prolonging thy life, and gives thee, it may be,
this day to repent in. He has declared that " his Spirit
shall not always strive with man:"[d] therefore harden not
thy heart, nor put off the work for a moment; for "now
is the accepted time, now is the day of salvation."[e]

: You labour in the sweat of your brow to earn your wages.
Your employers give you, in return for your labour, that
which is needful for the support of your bodies; but which
cannot feed your immortal souls. But it is not thus that
God giveth. " The gift of God is eternal life through Jesus
Christ our Lord."[f] This is his free gift, offered to every one
of you. What! you may exclaim, does the great and holy
God, whom I have offended so many times, and lived in open
transgression of his laws, freely offer me everlasting life?
Oh! yes. " Believe on the Lord Jesus Christ, and thou
shalt be saved."[g] " Christ died for every man."[h] " I came
not," said that blessed Saviour, ". to call the righteous, but
sinners to repentance."[i] You must work before you can eat
and drink bodily food: you must have money to pay for it.
But hear the gracious word of the Lord: " Ho! every one
that thirsteth, come ye to the waters, and he that hath no
money; come ye, buy and eat, yea, come, buy wine and
milk without money and without price."[k] " This is a faithful saying, and worthy of all acceptation, that Christ Jesus
came into the world to save sinners."[l] " He became poor,
that we, through his poverty, might be rich;"[m] " he was
despised and rejected of men," though he is Lord of all;
" he was wounded for our transgressions, he was bruised for
our iniquities, the chastisement of our peace was upon him,
and by his stripes we are healed: all we, like sheep, have
gone astray: we have turned every one to his own way; and
the Lord hath laid on him the iniquity of us all."[n] He died
upon the cross for us, that we might live. " For God so

[a] 2 Thess. i. 9.
[b] Mark ix. 44.
[c] Eccles. ix. 10.
[d] Gen. vi. 3.
[e] 2 Cor. vi. 2.
[f] Rom. vi. 23.
[g] Acts xvi. 31.
[h] Heb. ii. 9.
[i] Luke v. 32.
[k] Isa. lv. 1.
[l] 1 Tim. i. 15.
[m] 2 Cor. viii. 9.
[n] Isa. liii. 3. 5; 6.

loved the world, that he gave his only begotten Son, that whosoever believeth on him should not perish, but have everlasting life."[a] Oh! what a great salvation is here! make haste, repent, and believe, I beseech you, that you may obtain it. Does God so love us? does Christ so love us? and shall we love anything better than him? Shall we love our sins—our sins of the heart and of the flesh—better than him who gave himself for us, "the just for the unjust, that he might bring us to God?"[b] You cannot go to heaven in your sins. When he said, "I will give unto him that is athirst of the fountain of the water of life freely: he that overcometh shall inherit all things; and I will be his God, and he shall be my son:" he said also, "But the fearful and unbelieving, and the abominable, and murderers, and whoremongers, and sorcerers, and idolaters, and all liars shall have their part in the lake which burneth with fire and brimstone, which is the second death."[c] Some of you, also, are, I fear, profane swearers, and dishonest, and drunkards: the like portion is prepared for you, except you repent. Oh! "let the wicked forsake his way, and the unrighteous man his thoughts; and let him return unto the Lord, and he will have mercy upon him; and to our God, for he will abundantly pardon."[d]

I must not conclude without a word of encouragement to those both of yourselves and your families, and I hope there are many such, who have seen something of the exceeding sinfulness of sin, and who do hunger and thirst after righteousness. "Blessed are the poor in spirit for theirs is the kingdom of heaven."[e] I beseech you not to let the mockery or persecution of others make you ashamed of the Lord Jesus Christ. He was not ashamed of you when he suffered for your sakes; "he gave his back to the smiters, and his cheeks to them that plucked off the hair, he hid not his face from shame and spitting;"[f] "who, when he was reviled, reviled not again, when he suffered, he threatened not, but committed himself to him that judgeth righteously."[g] And shall not we, children of his unspeakable mercy, rejoice to "follow him withersoever he goes?"[h] "In the world," said he, "ye shall have tribulation, but be of good cheer, I have overcome the world."[i] "Blessed are ye when men shall hate you, and when they shall separate you from their company, and shall reproach you, and cast out your name as evil for the Son of man's sake. Rejoice ye in that day, and leap for joy: for behold, your reward is great in heaven."[k]

a John iii. 16. d Isa. lv. 7. g 1 Pet. ii. 23.
b 1 Pet. iii. 18. e Matt. v. 3. h Rev. xiv. 4.
c Rev. xxi. 6. 8. f Isa. l. 6. i John xvi. 33.
  k Luke vi. 22, 23.

Take heed when opportunity arises, faithfully to warn others to flee from the wrath to come. And for yourselves, watch and pray, and be patient; remembering that "our light affliction which is but for a moment, worketh for us a far more exceeding and eternal weight of glory; while we look not at the things which are seen, but at the things which are not seen; for the things which are seen are temporal, but the things which are not seen are eternal."[a] "And now, brethren, I commend you to God and to the word of his grace, which is able to build you up, and to give you an inheritance among all them which are sanctified."[b]

[a] 2 Cor. iv. 17, 18.   [b] Acts xx. 32.

RULES OF CONDUCT.

1. Lift up your hearts to God every morning and evening. Pray without ceasing; that is, always desire he may be with you in spirit.

2. Read your Bible to yourselves often; to your families daily.

3. Make a right use of the first day of the week (called Sunday); neither work nor buy in it. Let no excuse hinder you from attending a place of worship morning and afternoon.

4. Never take the name of God in vain; never curse or swear, or use any bad language.

5. Keep away from the beer and spirit shops: and avoid needless association with those who will lead you astray.

6. Send your children to school, if you possibly can.

7. Live in love with your fellow labourers, and with all your neighbours.

Grace, mercy, and peace be unto you from God our Father, and Jesus Christ our Lord.—1 Tim. i. 2.

END.

London: Printed by E. Couchman and Co., 10, Throgmorton Street, for the TRACT ASSOCIATION OF THE SOCIETY OF FRIENDS. Sold at the DEPOSITORY, 12, Bishopsgate Street, Without.—1862.

CHARACTER AND DOCTRINE

EARLY FRIENDS.

~~~~~~~~~~~~

THE religious Society of Friends dates its rise from about the year 1647. This was, in England, a period in which many of the props, on which men had long been accustomed to lean, both in civil and religious matters, were shaken or removed. The fears, troubles, and heart-stirring thoughts connected with the domestic commotions, which then prevailed in the nation, led many into a deep search, as to the grounds of their opinions and the real stability of their religious hopes; but the movement of this period must be traced to a much earlier date.

The English Reformers who fled into Switzerland, during the persecution in the reign of Queen Mary, and who returned from their exile on the accession of Elizabeth to the throne, were far from being content with the point to which the Queen allowed the reformation to be carried. Many of them, however, appeared to satisfy their consciences with the hope, that they were doing more good by taking offices under her auspices, than by leaving them to be filled by those who were less attached than themselves to the Protestant cause; but others could not be persuaded thus to compromise their religious judgment, and chose rather to remain without office and profit than to conform to all the rites and ceremonies which the Queen had chosen to impose upon the nation. Uniformity in matters of religion was at this time the favourite doctrine of all parties, and was hardly less espoused by Elizabeth than it had been by her sister Mary: for very severe laws were made in the reign of Elizabeth, under which both Papists and Protestant Dissenters were cruelly persecuted, and some of them even put to death.—A religious move-

No. 102.   [*Price* 4*d. per dozen.*]

ment deep and inward, though not very active, was going on during the subsequent reign of James the first: and it may fairly be said, that the continued denial of the right of private judgment to the people in religious matters and the unchristian efforts which were made by his successor, Charles the first, to force conscience, contributed not a little to that convulsion of the state, in which the monarchy was for a time overthrown.

The proceedings of Archbishop Laud and his party, during the reign of this monarch, in endeavouring to assimilate the Episcopal Church of England more closely to the church of Rome, excited a strong feeling of revulsion in the minds of many Episcopalians, and led the way for that extraordinary ascendency which the Scotch Presbyterians suddenly obtained in England in those days. There was among this people, at that time, much high religious profession united with the bitterest intolerance towards all who could not accept their Directory of Faith. There was, however, also to be seen much deep and practical religious conviction, and in not a very few, an earnest search after truth. The strictness of their lives, and the earnestness of their preaching, doubtless recommended them to the more serious part of the nation of various classes; but in connection with the power which they obtained, it is evident that they sought primarily, the absolute ascendancy of their own church polity and doctrine. Though they had denounced strongly, popish and prelatical impositions upon conscience in their own case, they did not scruple in the case of others, to attempt to rule in that seat of God; and they were no less ready than their predecessors, to punish those who could not bow down to their authority. Thus it was evident that presbyter and prelate alike sought to be lords over God's heritage, and that amidst the earnest discussions respecting church-government, and the forms of religious worship, the essential, experimental work of the Holy Spirit on the heart, and the true liberty of the Gospel, were in great measure overlooked. All the chief religious parties of the day so mistook the nature of Christianity as to endeavour to obtain their objects by the power of the sword; and many of the individuals who were extensively engaged in the enterprise of reformation, if sincere, in the outset, became corrupted by success, and sought selfish ends, under the guise of patriotism and religion.

There was, however, a large number who were constant and earnest in their desire for the establishment of truth and righteousness; and these, grieved with the versatility and hypocrisy which prevailed, were led into a deeper search into things within them and around them. Many prayers ascended to heaven from individuals and from little communities scattered about in various places, that they might see more clearly the path in which they ought to walk, and be strengthened to follow Christ wherever he should lead them. The deep cries of these, made in living faith were not in vain; they came to see, that they had been too much engaged in discussions about outward forms, and had too much depended upon man, in the great work of religion, and for its establishment in the earth. They continued steadfast in the great doctrine, that the door of God's mercy was freely opened to sinful man, through the propitiatory sacrifice of Christ alone; but their minds were awakened to see themselves and the condition of things around them in a new light: the requirements of a disciple,—the denial of self,—the transforming power of the Spirit,—the restoration into the divine image, that they might really become sons of God and brethren of Christ;—these things, though they had heard them discoursed about, now took possession of their minds with the force and energy of new truths: and as they dwelt upon them, they were led to believe that there was to be known, a fuller deliverance from sin and a closer union with Christ than they had hitherto found. They were told, indeed, that a state was not to be attained here, in which man walks before the Lord in entire allegiance to his will, and therefore without disobeying him; but they believed, that though man's knowledge is imperfect, and that from weakness he may slip or fall, his heart may nevertheless be so renewed by grace, as that his love shall be pure and simple; and his eye being single to the Lord, his whole mind may be enlightened to see truly and to pursue steadily, the things which belong unto his peace. They felt, and deeply lamented, how short they were of this experience, which they believed to be the privilege of the Christian, and they sought help from many quarters; for nothing less than this experience could satisfy their inward cravings, or their thirst after the knowledge of the very truth as it is in Jesus.

These seeking people found, however, but little help from those who were esteemed the most eminent religious teachers, and they came to place less and less dependance upon man, and to look to the Lord only for light and strength. Such appears to have been, with different degrees of clearness, the state of many minds in various parts of England, when George Fox, who had himself been similarly led and deeply instructed in the school of Christ, went forth preaching the truth as he had found it to his own peace. Many received his message, as the expression of their deepest thoughts, and as an answer to their fervent prayers. He preached Christ crucified for the sins of all men: opening the way of reconciliation to all who believe in him, and receive him into their hearts, as their rightful Lord; Christ come in the flesh, and Christ, according to his promise, come in the Spirit, to be with his disciples in their individual and collective character, to the end of the world.

These were the fundamental doctrines which George Fox preached; and it was no way in disparagement of the doctrine of Christ having come in the flesh, that he dwelt more conspicuously upon that of Christ being come in the Spirit; seeing the latter was that which, in the professing church, Satan had been most busy in restricting and perverting. "I was glad," says George Fox, "when the Lord God and his Son Jesus Christ sent me forth into the world, to preach his everlasting gospel and kingdom, that I was commanded to turn people to that inward light, spirit, and grace, by which all might know their salvation and their way to God, even that Divine Spirit which would lead them into all truth."

The knowledge of Christ dwelling in the heart by faith, ruling there, and subjecting everything to himself, by the power of his Spirit, was the experience to which George Fox called men. This, he declared, was the state of liberty which Christ had promised to give to his followers, and which they only know who believe in and accept that "light, spirit, and grace," which convicts of sin, and leads, through deep repentance and living faith, into righteousness. The Lord Jesus promised to be "with his disciples alway, even to the end of the world." And these words, in George Fox's view, referred to his spiritual presence in the soul, as the teacher, bishop, and prophet of his people: superseding all the Jewish priesthood, and excluding all those corrupt imitations of it, by which man, in various ages, had sought to exalt himself and to evade that spiritual rule of Christ, to which the flesh and the devil ever were and still are so strongly opposed. He travelled unweariedly throughout England, from place to place, calling men to repentance, and to come to God through Christ their Saviour, who had died for them, and who, by his Spirit within them, was enlightening, convicting, and seeking to convert them.

There were many who heard this call with gladness of heart, and who came to sit under Christ's teaching, and to learn in all humility, in his school. These when deserted by kindred and friends, and persecuted on every hand, yet not forsaken by their gracious Lord, felt that it was "enough for the disciple to be as his Master." And indeed their sufferings were grievous and long. For when the Presbyterians had been superseded in power by those who had complained so heavily of church tyranny, and who had spoken so well of liberty of conscience, and of the evils of state impositions in religious matters, these were not proof against the temptations of power; it was soon apparent that they also but too generally "loved the uppermost seats in the synagogues, and to be called of men Rabbi." They were ready not only to take the pulpits of the ejected ministers, but also to extort from others, who conscientiously differed from them, that forced maintenance for preaching, which had been galling to many of themselves, when it was imposed by prelatical or presbyterian authority. It is due to the cause of truth, as maintained by the Early Friends, to remark that they upheld liberty of conscience, not only when suffering under persecution, but also when they were raised to power in the province of Pennsylvania.

Those who united with George Fox, in his views of the presence of Christ in the Church, and in its individual members, and who believed in his spiritual guidance and teaching, could not conform to the customary modes of worship. They met together to worship God, who is a spirit, in spirit and in truth. They could not offer to Him words which did not truly express their feelings. They believed that, in true worship, all acts must be performed in the abasement of self, and under the influence of the Holy Spirit. When assembled they were often strengthened and comforted together in silent waiting before the Lord; whilst, individually, they breathed their secret aspirations unto God, and realized that Christ was amongst them by his Spirit, uniting their hearts together in mutual love to him and his great cause. And when any amongst them, under this deep feeling of true worship, were constrained in spirit to speak the word of exhortation, prayer, or praise, they gratefully accepted it, as from the Lord, and as drawing to him. But preconcerted, human arrangements for preaching or prayer,—the setting up of one man as the sole teacher in the congregation,—the establishment of a body of such ministers by the state,—the imposition of their maintenance upon those who differed from them,— all these were, in their view, violations of great Christian principles, interfering with Christ's authority and government in his church, and excluding the free exercise of the various gifts bestowed by him for its edification. They admitted freely the preaching of women, as well as that of men, according to the practice of the apostolic age, when sons and daughters prophesied, and the Spirit of the Lord was poured out upon "servants and handmaidens," not limiting the number in any church.

But though the Early Friends maintained the right and duty of the members of a Christian Church to exercise the spiritual gifts with which they were severally endued, they held that the authority to judge of the offered services of the members rested with the assembled body of the church, under the direction of its spiritual Head. Entire individual independence in society is a contradiction in terms. In the primitive church, though there was the utmost liberty of prophesying, it is declared that "the spirits of the prophets are subject to the prophets, for God is not the author of confusion, but of peace, as in all the churches of the saints." The members were "subject one to another in the fear of God," and this subjection, as well as the duty of caring for and watching over one another for good, were clearly recognized by the Early Friends, and formed the basis of that system of discipline which was established among them, and under which, as members of the body, they enjoyed so large a measure of liberty in connection with true order. Under this discipline the poor were cared for, the education of the youth was promoted, religious efforts were used to reclaim the wandering and delinquent members, and when Christian labour had failed, the ultimate proceeding was the declaration of the Society's disunity with the offender as one of its members. This proceeding carried with it no prescription from its religious worship or the ordinary intercourses of human kindness, and the Society was open at all times to receive the disowned person again into fellowship, on the evidence being afforded of a changed mind. As the Society declined conscientiously the usual rites in connection with marriages, births, and deaths, the registration of these events was under the special care of the meetings for discipline. After nearly 200 years from its establishment, the original system of discipline is with much benefit steadily acted upon, and those principles which, at its rise, united the members of the Society in Christian fellowship, continue to be upheld by, and to distinguish their successors in religious profession.

Although the Early Friends maintained that immediate spiritual guidance was still granted to the Children of God, they fully recognized the divine authority of the Holy Scriptures, and were ever ready to have their doctrines and practices tried by them: they accepted them indeed unequivocally, as given by inspiration of God, and loved and valued them as the genuine records of his dealings with his creature man, and as communicating to him the knowledge of that Gospel covenant by which life and immortality were brought to light; they read and quoted them freely, referred to them for the proof of the soundness of their own faith and doctrine, and recommended them strongly to the perusal of others; but they warned men against fancying themselves in a state of salvation, because of possessing a knowledge of the Scriptures, whilst remaining strangers to that true faith in Christ, through which alone they make wise unto salvation.

Believing that no typical or ceremonial rites were appointed by Christ, or his Apostles, for the continual or universal observance of the church, and in connection with the views which these christian people entertained of the spirituality of the Gospel dispensation, they abstained from the use of Water Baptism, and from what is called the Sacrament of the Lord's Supper.—In the declaration of Christ, that the time was at hand when "they that worship the Father must worship Him in spirit and in truth," they saw the essential abolition of all ritual religious services, and the opening of that real spiritual relation and intercourse between man and his Creator, which is the glory of the Gospel of Christ. Under the Christian dispensation there is one, and but one, baptism. "I indeed," said the forerunner of Christ, "baptize you with water unto repentance; but he that cometh after me is mightier than I, whose shoes I am not worthy to bear, he shall baptize you with the Holy Ghost and with fire." Matt. iii. 11. This baptism of the Spirit, by which conversion of heart is known, and the repentant sinner is brought, through living faith in Christ, into his adopted family, was fully asserted by the early Quakers; as was also that spiritual communion with Christ, whether alone, or in fellowship with the brethren, in which the benefits of his death, resurrection, and ascension are appreciated and appropriated, by the power of the Holy Spirit. This they believed to be the true Supper of the Lord,—the spiritual eating of his flesh and drinking of his blood.

The imposition of tithes on the people, they esteemed to be a virtual recognition of the continued authority of Judaism, and a practical denial, that Christ had come, had superseded the whole Judaical economy, and had placed upon the site of its departed glories, the spiritual temple, in which he was the great High Priest. He said to his disciples, "Freely ye have received, freely give." Those

vhom he sent to minister to his flock in spiritual things
were entitled to partake of the carnal things of those
who received their message : but this natural claim gave
no authority, they asserted, to the imposition of payment. Such an imposition, in the view of the Early
Friends, was utterly opposed to the liberty and nobility
of the Christian system, and was an evidence of corruption in the church which practiced it, whatever name
that church might bear. They called men, therefore, to
come out of it; to leave hireling priests and mere lip
services; and to come to Christ alone for the supply of
their spiritual necessities. They believed it would be
on their part, a virtual recognition of an unchristian
system, if they were to pay the ecclesiastical demands
imposed upon them, esteeming it a case in which they
must act upon the apostolic rule, "to obey God rather
than men."

In obedience also to Christ's command, "Swear not
at all," they refused all judicial, as well as other oaths :
and in like accordance with Christ's commands, of love
to enemies, and of not returning evil for evil, they
believed that all war was unlawful to the Christian.—
They did not seek to be singular; but in the maintenance
of strict truth, and the avoidance of pride and flattery,
they were led into great simplicity in their dress, manners, and language.

These various testimonies brought much contumely,
from the high professors as well as from the profane,
upon the Early Friends. They were said to be "against
ministry, magistracy, and ordinances :" but being brought
into an entire submission to whatever, in their enlightened consciences, they believed to be the will of
their Lord, they acted simply and decidedly upon their
convictions of duty, and gave up all that they counted
dear, in faithful allegiance to him; and many of them
went forth, as into the highways and hedges, to proclaim
the truth, believing themselves called to invite others to
come and enjoy the Gospel liberty which they had found.
—Great were their sufferings when the high professors
of Oliver Cromwell's days had the rule in England; and
still greater were they under the government of the
second Charles, when the old Episcopalian was again

instated in power, and when the prominent members of "Church and State" seemed to vie with each other, both in licentious indulgence aud in cruelty. A systematic legalized effort appears, at this period, to have been made to exterminate the Quakers! Cruel laws of Henry the Eighth and Queen Elizabeth, made originally against Papists, were revived, especially those for the regular attendance "at church," and the taking of the oath of allegiance, and were executed with severity upon the Quakers.

The Conventicle Act, passed in the year 1664, pro- hibited the meeting together of five or more persons for the exercise of religion, in other manner than is allowed by the liturgy or practice of the Church of England, under pain of being committed to prison for the first offence, and transported beyond the seas for the second! An act had previously been passed, against those, who "on the ground that it was contrary to the word of God," refused to take an oath before a lawful magis- trate; or who should, "by printing, writing, or other- wise, go about to maintain and defend, that the taking of an oath is in any case whatsoever altogether unlaw- ful;" and this offence was in the Conventicle Act also made punishable by transportation!

With these and similar legal engines, bishops, clergy, judges, and magistrates, with the aid of a host of wicked informers, set themselves to work to hunt down these Christian people. At one period more than 4,200 of them were shut up in close and noisome prisons, chiefly for meeting together to worship God in such manner as they believed he required of them, and for refusing to swear, in accordance with the positive command of their Lord and Saviour, "Swear not at all." When the plague was raging in London, in 1665, the persecutors were busily engaged in committing the Quakers to infected prisons, and putting them on board vessels for transportation. Many died in prison, and out of fifty-five put on board one vessel, which was designed to transport them to the colonies, twenty-seven died of the plague, rescued from the hands of cruel men, and, as we reverently believe, taken to be with their Lord.

All the trials, however, which were permitted to attend

hem did not shake their faith and constancy. Though he world hated them, they were heartily united in love o God and one to another. At the hazard of their own iberty, those who were at large, visited their brethren who vere in prison and ministered to them. And at a time vhen many of them were sick and dying, from their con- inement in filthy holes and dungeons, a large number of heir friends entreated, that if their afflicted brethren could iot be otherwise relieved, themselves might be allowed o take, body for body, the places of the most suffering risoners. The government, unmoved, rejected the offer, iut the love which directed it was not without its in- luence on the minds of the people, who could not avoid bserving how largely the despised Quakers evinced the harity, as well as the zeal and constancy, of the primitive Christians.

Many persons were led by the treatment and by the onduct of the Early Friends to look more inquisitively nto their doctrines and manners : they remembered that, ieretofore, the way of truth had been everywhere spoken gainst ; and when they found that these objects of ;eneral reproach were industrious in their callings, and xemplary in all the duties of social life ; and that they vere also ready to forsake houses and lands, parents and hildren, rather than disobey what they believed to be he law of Christ, the enquirers were often led to con- lude, that these much despised people were indeed true ollowers of Him, who, with his disciples, was not of this vorld, and therefore the world hated them.

It is worthy of remark, how much this kind of conviction iot founded on minute reasoning, but resting chiefly on he practical and internal evidence for the truth, whether urnished by the lives of its converts, or by the convictions f the Spirit in the hearts of those to whom it is preached, ias marked the course through which Christ, the great Iead of his own Church, has, in all ages, thought fit to ;ather his people out of the world. In the opening of he Gospel day, though then accompanied by extraordi- iary miracles, there was much of this process to be bserved ; and in the subsequent revivals of divine truth, vhether in Germany, Switzerland, or England, a large najority of the converts were drawn by a sense of

Truth—by finding a conformity of the doctrine preached both with Scripture, and with the testimony of the Holy Spirit, the witness for God in their own hearts.

Many among the early converts to the Truth, who had been wise and great in this world, were made willing to become fools in the sight of men. In deep humility, they sat as at the foot of the cross, seeking to learn of that promised Comforter, who, the Saviour declared, should "teach" his disciples "all things," and bring to their "remembrance whatsoever he had said unto them." Their delight was in the law of the Lord, and they gloried in nothing save in the cross of Christ, by whom the world was crucified unto them, and they unto the world.

They found, as one of them has said, that it was the nature of true faith to produce a holy fear of offending God, a deep reverence for his precepts, and a most tender regard to the inward testimony of his Spirit. They proved that those who truly believe, receive Christ in all his offers to the soul; and that to those who thus receive him, is given power to become the sons of God,—ability to do whatsoever he requires; strength to mortify their lusts, control their affections, deny themselves, and overcome the world in its most enticing appearances.—This is the true bearing of that blessed cross of Christ, which, according to his own words, is the great and essential characteristic of his disciples; and that the Early Friends were among these true cross-bearing disciples was abundantly evidenced before the world in their life and conversation; and by these as well as by their preaching, they held out to mankind the apostolic invitation, "Come and have fellowship with us; for truly our fellowship is with the Father, and with his Son Jesus Christ."

END.

London: Printed by E. Couchman & Co., 10, Throgmorton Street; for the TRACT ASSOCIATION of the SOCIETY OF FRIENDS. Sold at the Depository, 12, Bishopsgate Street Without.—1866.

SOME

OBSERVATIONS,

PRINCIPALLY ON THE SUBJECT

OF

RELIGIOUS WORSHIP;

AFFECTIONATELY SUBMITTED

TO THE

CONSIDERATION

OF THE

PROFESSORS OF CHRISTIANITY.

———

LONDON:

Printed for the TRACT ASSOCIATION of the SOCIETY OF FRIENDS.

Sold at the DEPOSITORY, 12, Bishopsgate Street Without.

———

1863.

No. 103.   [*Price 4d. per dozen.*]

SOME OBSERVATIONS, &c.

In turning my most serious thoughts and considerations to the weighty and deeply important subject of Religious Worship—the worship of that almighty and incomprehensible Being, before whom "the nations are as a drop of a bucket, and who taketh up the isles as a very little thing"—they naturally recur to the solemn declaration of our Holy Redeemer in reference to it, and to the state of mind in which alone it can be acceptably performed, under the dispensation then about to be ushered into the world—"Our fathers worshipped in this mountain," said the inquiring woman at Jacob's Well, to our blessed Lord, "and ye say that in Jerusalem is the place where men ought to worship"—Jesus saith unto her "Woman, believe me, the hour cometh, when ye shall neither in this mountain, nor yet at Jerusalem, worship the Father—ye worship ye know not what; we know what we worship: for salvation is of the Jews.—But the hour cometh, and now is, when the true worshippers shall worship the Father in spirit and in truth: for the Father seeketh such to worship Him. God is a Spirit, and they that worship Him must worship Him in spirit and in truth."

This language assuredly embodies all that is essential in the nature and character of public, as well as private worship, and hence whatever acts may take place in the assemblies of professing Christians, they must, in order to their acceptance in the divine sight, harmonize with the great fundamental principle thus laid down—they must be spiritual, emanating from the Spirit, and subject to His guidance and direction—they must be in Truth, springing from the fountain of Truth, —"the fulness of Him who filleth all in all."—This language moreover, "God is a Spirit, and they that worship Him must worship Him in spirit and in truth," implies a capability on man's part, as he is divinely influenced, of entering into union and communion with God; and of maintaining whilst thus influenced, a spiritual intercourse with Him —and seeing that God is a Spirit—omnipresent—omnipotent—and omniscient, it follows that all man's need is both intimately known, and abundantly provided for, in his holy communion and intercourse—that in this exercise, his ignorance is enlightened—

his weakness strengthened—his hope enlarged and invigo-rated, and his faith in the Lord Jesus Christ, and in the efficacy of His grace, confirmed and established.

With these views it has appeared to me, that in gathering together for the worship of Almighty God, it should never be lost sight of, that is worship is essentially an inward work —a spiritual exercise—a prostration of soul—individually and collectively—man ceasing from his own works, yea, from his own thoughts, and in the "silence of all flesh," waiting "to hear what God the Lord will speak"—a position highly becoming a poor, weak, dependent creature, seeking the notice and favour and approbation of a pure and holy God; and thus abiding in this state of reverent watchfulness, the spiritual worshipper shall assuredly know the Lord Jesus, as He is believed in and obeyed, to be in him by His Spirit, an all powerful Redeemer, working in him by the communi-cation of His grace, the ability "both to will and to do of His own good pleasure."

Man, as he stands alienated from God, is not merely prone to evil, but is essentially evil—evil is his element, and the commission of evil is at all times within his power; not so, good—this springs only from the source and fountain of good—is not within man's reach, otherwise, than as it is freely and graciously communicated.

Too much importance has, I fear, been attached to what is termed "mental energy" in the performance of divine wor-ship, for it has appeared to me, that man, as man, and of his own capacity, is without energy as to things spiritual and divine—he may possess physical and intellectual energy, and may put forth these where and when he will, but the reverse of this is true as it respects spiritual things—here his strength consists in the knowledge and sensible experience of his weakness—his riches in the consciousness of his poverty—his wisdom in the knowledge of his ignorance; and this view is clearly in accordance with scriptural testimony, beautifully set forth as characteristic of apostolic conviction and expe-rience—"when I am weak then am I strong"—"If any man think he knoweth anything, he knoweth nothing yet as he ought to know."—"As poor, yet making many rich—as having nothing and yet possessing all things." Man's place, especially as it regards divine things, is to lie low before the Lord, and to move only as power is communicated from on high. I am aware that all cannot receive these sayings, ne-vertheless there are those to whom it is given, not only to understand them, but to rejoice in the knowledge of them, as constituting their highest privilege and their truest wisdom.

In connection with these sentiments, and as bearing on the same subject, I would here introduce a few remarks on some passages in the Epistle of James, i. 17. 21. "Every good gift and every perfect gift is from above, and cometh down from the Father of lights, with whom is no variableness, neither shadow of turning—of His own will begat He us with the word of truth, that we should be a kind of first fruits of His creatures—wherefore, my beloved brethren, let every man be swift to hear, slow to speak, slow to wrath, for the wrath of man worketh not the righteousness of God. Wherefore lay apart all filthiness and superfluity of naughtiness, and receive with meekness the engrafted word which is able to save your souls "—" The word of truth," spoken of in the 18 v. is doubt-less the same "word" as that referred to in the 21 v. under the appellation of "the engrafted word," and which the apostle says "is able to save your souls."—Now it is of deep importance that we attach a right meaning to these terms, "word of truth" and "engrafted word," and I may confess that to my apprehension they are capable of but one inter-pretation—Jesus, by His grace and spirit and power, is the " Word of truth "—the " engrafted Word "—" the Word quick and powerful "—the Word that was in the beginning with God—the Word that" " was" and is " God"—and this " Word "—unchangeable—incorruptible and eternal, is, I undoubtingly believe, the " engrafted Word " to which the apostle here refers, and which he declares " is able to save the soul." To apply these terms to any power short of this power, would be manifestly unsafe, seeing that " there is no other name under heaven, given among men, whereby they may be saved, but the name of Jesus"—and this " Word" it is, that men are to be " swift to hear "—the spiritual voice of the " great shepherd of the sheep," speaking intelligibly to the spiritual ear, (" my sheep hear my voice ") and com-municating such lessons of grace and salvation, as will in vain be looked for from the teachings of men.

Again, " If any man among you," says the same apostle, " seem to be religious, and bridleth not his tongue, but deceiveth his own heart, this man's religion is vain "—this saying of the apostle appears to me fraught with important instruction ; surely it may be said, that an unguarded use of the tongue in religious matters, is calculated to deceive the heart, by inducing those thus disposed, to draw inferences, as to their religious standing and experience, at once dangerous and delusive—the more this subject is contemplated, the more important, I believe, it will appear ; seeing that the essence of " pure and undefiled religion," consists in the renewal and regulation of the heart, and that this interior work, involves much of watchfulness and prayer—much of self-denial and bearing the daily cross. Now, if instead of this "dying daily" unto self—this daily bearing of the cross of Christ, the free use of the tongue is indulged in, irrespective of the state of the heart, and men draw conclusions favorable to their religious state on this ground, the danger of such a course must be obvious—" Not every one that saith unto me Lord, Lord, shall enter into the Kingdom of Heaven, but he that doeth the will of my Father who is in heaven"—now, how pointedly and significantly does this language of our Holy Redeemer apply to the subject before us—to use the tongue and to say, "Lord, Lord," how easy—how familiar—but this may be, and much more than this, and yet be utterly unavailing as to any spiritual advantage to the soul. Such acts may pass for prayer amongst men, but if unaccompanied by the spirit of prayer, (and for this holy and divine gift, man is entirely dependent on the free mercy and love of God in Christ Jesus,) they reach not the ear of the Majesty on High, and are consequently unprofitable and vain. The preceding declaration of our Lord should be here brought into view, "by their fruits ye shall know them." Bad men may bring forth good words, but they cannot bring forth fruits really good and holy.

To what lengths a profession in words may be carried, our Holy Redeemer shows in the following verse, "Many will say unto me in that day, Lord, Lord, have we not prophesied in thy name? and in thy name have cast out devils? and in thy name done many wonderful works?" and yet notwithstanding all this profession, what was His judgment respecting them—" I never knew you ; depart from me all ye that work iniquity"—now the fruits which men are to bring forth, are the fruits of the Spirit, and these the apostle tells us are "love, joy, peace, long-suffering, gentleness, goodness, faith, meekness, temperance," and " against such " he adds " there is no law."

In returning, however, from this lengthened digression, I would that none should misunderstand me, as though I limited worship to mere passiveness of soul—not so—in this holy silence—this waiting upon God, the gifts and graces of the Holy Spirit are mercifully shed forth, not only for the illumination and consolation of the individual worshipper, but for the instruction, edification, and strength of the body— thus "to one is given by the Spirit the word of wisdom—to another the word of knowledge by the same Spirit—to another faith by the same Spirit—to another prophecy. But all these worketh that one and the self-same Spirit dividing to every man severally as He will, for the manifestation of the Spirit is given to every man to profit withal." Here there is no restriction or limitation, whether we speak in reference to age, or sex, or mental capacity, but a liberty commensurate with the revelation of the divine will—agreeably with that saying of the same apostle, 2 Cor. iii. 17, "Now the Lord is that Spirit; and where the Spirit of the Lord is, there is liberty." Here, too, he that speaketh, speaketh "as the oracles of God"—"He that ministereth, does so in the ability which God giveth"—and in this is true and real edifying—precious edifying; the building up of the body in holiness and love.

In looking into the records of the Old Testament, we find, even in those earlier periods of the world, evidences of spiritual worship (before and after the promulgation of the Law by Moses) both numerous and impressive; a worship obviously the result of an unpremeditated, inward, and spiritual emotion; and irrespective of an appointed time, or place, or mode. In the beautifully affecting case of Abraham's servant, when he went to Padan Aram to find a wife for his master's son—in the prospect of attaining his object, his heart became evidently affected, and it is said, that out of its fulness, "the man bowed down his head and worshipped the Lord"—and again, when his anticipations were fully realized, it is added, that "he worshipped the Lord, bowing himself to the earth." When Moses and Aaron were sent to deliver their brethren from Egyptian affliction and bondage, it is declared that "Moses and Aaron went and gathered together all the elders of the children of Israel: and Aaron spake all the words which the Lord had spoken unto Moses, and did all the signs (commanded) in the sight of the people. And the people believed: and when they heard that the Lord had visited the children of Israel, and that he had looked upon their affliction, then they bowed their heads and worshipped." Again at the institution of the Passover, when the Israelites understood its object and its end, it is said, "the people bowed the head and worshipped." On another occasion we learn that "as Moses entered into the tabernacle, the cloudy pillar descended, and stood at the door of the tabernacle, and the Lord talked with Moses. And all the people saw the cloudy pillar stand at the tabernacle door, and all the people rose up and worshipped, every man in his tent door." On that awfully interesting and affecting occasion, when "the Lord descended in the cloud, and stood with Moses on Mount Sinai," and there proclaimed the name of the Lord, passing before him and proclaiming, "The Lord, the Lord God, merciful and gracious, long-suffering, and abundant in goodness and truth," then "Moses made haste, and bowed his head towards the earth, and worshipped." When the Moabites, in the reign of Jehoshaphat, invaded Judea, and great consternation prevailed amongst the people on that account, it is recorded that the Spirit of the Lord came on Jahaziel, in the midst of the congregation —" and he said, Hearken ye, all Judah, and ye inhabitants of Jerusalem; and thou, King Jehoshaphat—Thus saith the Lord unto you, be not afraid nor dismayed by reason of this great multitude; for the battle is not yours but God's." "And Jehoshaphat bowed his head with his face to the ground: and all Judah, and the inhabitants of Jerusalem fell before the Lord, worshipping the Lord." It is said in Nehemiah, that when Ezra "opened the book" of the law "in the sight of all the people" that "all the people stood up:" and "Ezra blessed the Lord, the great God.—And all the people answered, Amen, Amen, with lifting up their hands: and they bowed their heads, and worshipped the Lord with their faces to the ground."

This bowing of the head in connection with worship so affectingly and so beautifully set forth in the passages which have been brought under review, sometimes as the act of an individual, and at other times as that of the assembled multitude; sometimes in connection with vocal utterance, and at other times without it, pourtrays, it appears to me, on the part of those thus exercised, an inward sense of the divine presence and goodness and power—an acknowledgement of His spirituality and holiness, and a consequent bowing of the head and worshipping before Him.

In referring to the cases which have been adverted to, my object is to establish the fact, that in these early and less enlightened days, the inwardness and spirituality of worship was understood and recognised; and that in its essential character—its divine and living principle, it has been the same in all ages.

This view, moreover, is strengthened in my mind by certain passages scattered throughout the writings of the prophets, indicative of that prostration of soul in which it becomes man to appear before God, and in which he is best prepared to realize the divine presence. "Be silent O all flesh before the Lord," is the language of Zechariah, "for He is raised up out of his holy habitation." Habakkuk expresses his sense of the divine presence and majesty in similar terms: "The Lord is in His holy temple, let all the earth keep silence before Him." The Almighty, speaking through David, uses these words, "Be still and know that I am God; I will be

exalted amongst the heathen, I will be exalted in the earth."
On another occasion the Psalmist says, "Stand in awe and
sin not : commune with your own heart, upon your bed, and
be still." In accordance with these sayings are the words of
the wise man, used by him in reference to the Jewish worship:
"Keep thy foot when thou goest to the House of God, and
be more ready to hear, than to give the sacrifice of fools :
for they consider not that they do evil.—Be not rash with
thy mouth, and let not thine heart be hasty to utter anything before God ; for God is in heaven, and thou upon the
earth ; therefore let thy words be few." These passages
must have a meaning—must be applicable to man's condition
and circumstances as he stands related to his Heavenly
Father ; and this meaning and this applicability one would
suppose not of difficult apprehension.

There is, however, another class of passages which bear on
this subject, and to these I would now refer :—"My soul,"
says David, "wait thou only upon God, for my expectation
is from Him—He only is my rock and my salvation : He
is my defence, I shall not be greatly moved : in God is
my salvation and my glory : the rock of my strength, and my
refuge is in God."—And again he says, "I wait for the
Lord, my soul doth wait, and in his word do I hope—my
soul waiteth for the Lord, more than they that watch for the
morning : I say more than they that watch for the morning."
Again "I waited patiently for the Lord ; " or as the margin
reads it—"In waiting I waited," and "He inclined his ear
unto me and heard my cry." "They that wait upon the
Lord," says Isaiah, "shall renew their strength ; they shall
mount up with wings as eagles ; they shall run and not be
weary ; and they shall walk and not faint." Again he says,
"they shall not be ashamed that wait for me." "The Lord
is good," says Jeremiah, "unto them that wait for Him, to
the soul that seeketh Him." "Turn thou to thy God " is
the language of Hosea: "keep mercy and judgment, and
wait on thy God continually." Passages of similar import
might be greatly multiplied, but these are sufficient for my
purpose, and it has appeared to me, that if, under that
preparatory dispensation of "meats and drinks, and carnal
ordinances," under which, as the apostle testifies, "the way
into the holiest was not yet made manifest:" the saints of old
were deeply sensible of the advantages of this holy exercise,
(and that they were so cannot, I think, be doubted ;) surely
not less advantage would result from it now, when Christ,
the eternal substance, has come, through whom a door of
access is opened both for Jew and Gentile, "by one Spirit

into the Father," and through whom also is freely and graciously communicated, in this His Gospel day, a larger measure of spiritual illumination, and blessing, and grace.

Here, however, it may not be unsuitable to observe, that notwithstanding this "greater measure of spiritual blessing," yet such are the deceitfulness and depravity of the human heart, and so slow are men to learn the lessons of wisdom, and of grace, that the experience of even the devout and sincere worshipper, may, in the dispensations of an all-wise and ever-gracious Providence, be, for a season, yea, for a long-season, marked with deep and varied conflicts of spirit; but as these inward baptisms are borne in meekness, the truth of the apostle's language will, in due time, be witnessed, where he says, "tribulation worketh patience; and patience experience; and experience, hope; and hope maketh not ashamed, because the love of God is shed abroad in our hearts by the holy Ghost given unto us"—while in resignation of soul, we love and wait for the appearance of our God and Saviour.

In looking into the New Testament, we find the apostle John addressing the first Christian churches in this language —" Ye have an unction from the Holy One and ye know all things." This declaration was unquestionably understood by those to whom it was addressed, and it became alike their privilege and their duty, fully to apply it in their daily walk and experience. The same may be said of the kindred passage of the same apostle, "The anointing which ye have received of Him abideth in you, and ye need not that any man teach you: but as the same anointing teacheth you of all things, and is truth and is no lie, and even as it hath taught you, ye shall abide in Him." Now the "unction," and the "anointing" of which the apostle speaks, cannot be supposed to refer to anything of an outward character, and must therefore undoubtedly apply to the inward operations of the Holy Spirit—the sacred writer well knowing that these operations are as "the savour of life unto life" to all those who believe in and obey them, and are clearly distinguishable by the sincere and enlightened worshipper, not only from the workings of the natural mind, but also from all the devices of Satan, although "transformed into an angel of light." And here I would seriously put it to the thoughtful reader, whether any position of the human soul is so adapted to the full and entire reception of this spiritual teaching as that of silent waiting upon God? Here the soul, abstracted from all outward things, is permitted to realize the divine presence; to feed on "the bread which cometh down from heaven;"

to drink of the wine of the kingdom; to participate spiritually, by faith with thanksgiving, of that "flesh and blood" which, our Holy Redeemer declares, is to the believing soul, in a sense incomprehensible to the unenlightened mind, both "meat indeed and drink indeed."

I am however, well aware that there is an unwillingness on the part of man, even when in some sense awakened to the importance of eternal things, and when measurably renewed by divine grace, to come into actual communion with the Almighty: it was so in the days of the Jewish Lawgiver; it is so in these days—"Speak thou to us," said the Israelites to Moses, "and we will hear: but let not God speak to us, lest we die." And why is this? Man not fully recognising the reality of this communion, nor the greatness of its privilege, and being at the same time deeply conscious of the divine purity and holiness, and equally sensible of his own degeneracy and impurity, shrinks from the humiliating condition into which such an intercourse necessarily places him. —Moreover, in these circumstances, he finds nothing to gratify the outward eye; nothing to entertain the outward ear; nothing to engage the intellectual sense; and hence he turns away from a position, which those alone can appreciate or desire who are made willing to bear the cross of Christ, and who, in the denial of self, are resigned in humility of soul to the all-wise appointments of His inscrutable wisdom; —but men generally, averse to this high and holy privilege, are well satisfied to have to do with their fellow-men; to give ear to their words, and deference to their sayings; but to stand with God on his holy hill of Zion (let him that readeth understand), and to maintain with Him, by His freely-communicated aid, a spiritual intercourse there, is a privilege for which they have neither capacity nor desire; and hence too it is, that most men are so averse to silent waiting upon God, and to that spiritual worship so intimately connected with it, and so almost necessarily springing out of it.—Let the preacher speak, is a sentiment loudly expressed by the conduct of professing christians generally, and we will hear; but that God should speak to us, that is indeed a matter which we do not understand, and for which we have neither inclination nor desire.

Nevertheless, seeing that the testimony of prophets and apostles, and of Christ himself, unite in the establishment of the great truths, that "God is a Spirit"—and that the Gospel dispensation is emphatically the dispensation of the Spirit—may we not safely assert, that the worship coincident therewith must, not only in its leading characteristics, be necessarily spiritual, but that its life and vitality—its efficacy on earth, its acceptance in heaven—depend wholly on its being so.

Moreover, "The law of the Spirit of Life in Christ Jesus," is pre-eminently a spiritual law, "written not with ink, but with the Spirit of the living God: not in tables of stone, but in the fleshy tables of the heart"—does it not, therefore, become us deeply to consider, whether a practice thus commended to our acceptance (that of silently waiting upon God) can be WHOLLY disregarded, in their public assemblies, by professing christians in these days, without great detriment to the cause of truth, and great and afflicting loss to the universal Church of Christ? I believe, and am deeply persuaded, that it cannot. And here, lest any should suspect me of undervaluing the ministration of the Gospel through human agency, I would, in addition to what has already been expressed on the subject, assert my high value, I may say, reverence and love, for true and living ministry; a ministry exercised in wisdom and power from on high; and for those other vocal engagements, whether of prayer, thanksgiving, or praise, so often and so consolingly associated with it. But I desire my fellow-creatures to become sensible of the unwise and dangerous substitution of the "means" for the end; and of that resting in outward things, so inimical to the attainment of true spirituality of mind.

It is nevertheless true that men may conscientiously differ as to the sentiments intended to be conveyed by the sacred writers, in the language so frequently used by them in reference to "silence," and to that "waiting upon God," to which they bear such repeated testimony: but I cannot doubt but that it generally, if not always, implies a state in which the workings of the natural mind are silenced, and the whole soul reverently prostrated before God. But man is no longer silent before God; no longer simply waits upon Him; when, without the sensible guidance and influence of the Holy Spirit—that Spirit which quickeneth and giveth life, and which alone can qualify men to offer "spiritual sacrifices acceptable unto God through Jesus Christ," he prays, or preaches, or exhorts as in his own judgment, or in conformity to the arrangements of his fellow men, the occasion may seem to require.

In pursuing the consideration of the very important subjects, which, in the preceding pages, have been presented to the view of my fellow-professors of the christian name (subjects, the right understanding of which, involves the spiritual and eternal interests of all men), I trust that nothing of a sectarian spirit has influenced my pen—on the contrary, unless I deceive myself, my single aim and only object has been the edification of my fellow candidates for eternity, in as far as it may please my Heavenly Father to make this feeble effort conducive to so good an end. Of this great and important truth I am fully persuaded, and with the expression of it, I would bring my little work to its close, that the greater the sincerity of men in cherishing a deep and hallowed acquaintance with the light and life and grace and power of the Lord Jesus Christ, as revealed by His Holy Spirit unto the soul—an exercise so fully, so clearly, and so frequently testified of in the Scriptures of Truth—the more will they know of the true creation of God in Him, and of the apostle's meaning, where he speaks of being "changed from glory to glory, as by the Spirit of the Lord"—an experience doubtless attained by the first christians, and as assuredly attainable by us. But in order to the consummation of this great end, we must "draw nigh in spirit unto God" having the spiritual eye open; the spiritual ear unstopped; the spiritual senses, in the obedience of faith, preserved lively and fresh—thus should we "watching unto prayer" and "walking in the light of the Lord," be favored as were the saints of old, to "sit in heavenly places in Christ Jesus;" and that this may be the blessed experience of both the reader and the writer, is indeed his earnest desire and prayer; and with this expression of his love and good will, he bids the reader farewell in the Lord.

END.

Printed by E. Couchman & Co., 10, Throgmorton Street, London.

THOMAS LEE TAYLOR.

"Mark the perfect man, and behold the upright; for the end of that man is peace." From these words of the royal Psalmist, it is evident that there were, under the dispensation of the Law, men who were esteemed perfect and upright. And beyond all doubt, such men lived to the glory of God, and received the end of their faith, even the salvation of their souls.

And if, under "the Law, which was weak," and which in itself "made nothing perfect," there were men who were perfect and upright, much more may we expect to find such under the dispensation of the Gospel; respecting which the Apostle Paul says, "God sending his own Son in the likeness of sinful flesh, and for sin, condemned sin in the flesh, that the righteousness of the Law might be fulfilled in us, who walk not after the flesh but after the Spirit."

Perfection is indeed the standard of attainment set before the Christian by his Lord and Master, whose command is, "Be ye therefore perfect, even as your Father which is in heaven is perfect;" and it is a question of vast importance, how this state of perfection is to be attained. No man can claim it of works, for "all have sinned and come short of the glory of God." But is not the man, who, through "repentance toward God, and faith toward our Lord Jesus Christ," has received the forgiveness of sins;

No. 104.   [*Price 3d. per dozen.*]

and who in humble dependence upon God, seeks help from him day by day, to "perfect holiness in the fear of the Lord," to be esteemed a perfect and an upright man, in the true scriptural sense of these terms?

If a man who has attained to such a state, should be overtaken with a fault, being in the habit of watching over his own soul, he will quickly perceive his error, and humble himself before God, and in renewed repentance, will seek forgiveness through Christ, who offered himself on the cross, a sacrifice for our sins, and who is the "fountain set open for sin and for uncleanness." Thus his condition will be restored; and walking before God with increasing love and fear, he will become increasingly established in holiness—The man who has faith in the promise, "Ask and ye shall receive;" and who believes in the power of God to sanctify his believing children "wholly, in body, soul, and spirit," will not rest until he knows deliverance through Christ, both from the guilt and power of sin; until by the help of the Holy Spirit, he is enabled to take up the cross, deny himself and follow Christ.

If such a man be called to leave this world, even in the meridian of life, he is found, with his treasure in heaven, and his heart there also. Far from being surprised or dismayed, he has lived under a sense of the uncertainty of time, and is sustained by that peace of God which passeth the understanding of man in his unregenerate state, and which keeps the hearts and minds of the righteous, through Jesus Christ. Such a one may have been closely attached to the nearest connexions in life; but even these he is enabled to commit resignedly unto the Lord; and he knows, that though he would willingly have cared for them longer, had this been in accordance with the divine will, yet, as regards himself, "to depart and to be with Christ is" indeed "far better."

Among numberless witnesses to the truth of these observations, was Thomas Lee Taylor, of Pontefract,

in Yorkshire, who died at the age of forty-two, and
to whose character and last hours the attention of
the reader is here invited. He was born at Wood-
bridge, in Suffolk, in 1802, and was brought up in
connexion with the Episcopal Church. While a
young man, he became awakened to the importance
of true religion, and to its spiritual and experimental
character; and leaving the forms and ceremonies in
which he had been educated, he sought to become
one of those worshippers who "worship the Father
in spirit and in truth." In this state of mind, after
some search into the principles of other religious
professors, he united himself with the Society of
Friends, under the conviction, that their views of the
Gospel were in true accordance with the New
Testament.

In the year 1826, he settled at Pontefract, where
he became well known as an industrious tradesman,
remarkable for his meek and agreeable manners, for
his conscientious integrity, and for his labours to
promote the best welfare of his fellow-men. He
was regular in attending the meetings for divine
worship of the Society to which he had become
united; and in these meetings his deportment in waiting upon God in silence, was remarkably reverent.
As he grew in grace, he became deeply concerned
for the spiritual welfare of his fellow-men, and especially that of his fellow-professors; to the latter he
sometimes addressed a word of exhortation, not only
privately, but also in their religious assemblies, to
their comfort and edification. He was diligent likewise in giving religious counsel to his neighbours:
and such was the kindness of his manner, and his
consideration for the feelings of others, that he
generally secured their respectful attention and their
esteem. If he heard any using profligate language,
he would watch for opportunities to expostulate with
them, when they were free from irritation, and he
would often accompany his expostulation with an
appropriate Tract.

He appeared through life, to entertain a low estimate of his own spiritual attainments, and great
distrust of himself. He several times remarked that
in an early stage of his Christian experience, the
words of Scripture were powerfully impressed on
his mind, " Let him that thinketh he standeth, take
heed lest he fall;" and that during the progress of
his religious course, this caution having been frequently revived, especially in seasons of retirement,
it had been an incitement to watchfulness, and had
led him to seek with increased earnestness for grace
and preservation.

In the autumn of 1844, he took the Small-pox,
and though he had this disease mildly, it was succeeded by another, which in a few days terminated
his valuable life. In the course of his illness, he
spoke freely of his state and prospects; and from
his remarks, the following are selected : " How wonderful the love and condescension of the Father, in
providing a sacrifice available for all !" " What
poor creatures we are !—In so short a time, how
much I am reduced? Wisely ordered no doubt !"—
Being answered, " By Him who doeth all things
well," he emphatically said, " Yes, by Him who
doeth all things well. Pray for me."—To a person
who had been called in, he said, " However lightly we
may, in time of health, esteem Christian principles,
I find in this time of trial, inexpressible support
and comfort from them, and earnestly recommend
them to thee."—The same morning, he inquired
particularly, if it were thought that he would recover;
and on being informed that his was a very critical
case, he sweetly replied, that whichever way it terminated, all would be well; but that, had it pleased
the Almighty to prolong his life, he should have
enjoyed being with his family and friends a few
years longer. He also said to a friend, " I think
the struggle will soon be over; but how delightful,
to contemplate joining Abraham, Isaac, and Jacob,
with dear Christian friends, in the kingdom of heaven,

and to be for ever singing praises to God and the Lamb!"

Speaking to a near relative, he said, that if he had leaned on his own strength he should have fallen: that divine aid alone had enabled him to stand; and he recommended his relative to devote a portion of each day to private retirement, for the purpose of communing with his own heart before the Lord; saying that he had himself derived much comfort and strength from this practice.

Notwithstanding the care he had manifested from early life, " to keep a conscience void of offence toward God and toward man," he many times during his illness, expressed the deep sense he felt of his own unworthiness; and that it was alone through the merits and intercession of his dear Redeemer, that he hoped to be admitted to those glorious mansions, where no sin or sorrow can ever enter,— that this hope was as an anchor to the soul, both sure and steadfast, and which entereth into that within the vail; whither the forerunner is for us entered, even Jesus made an high-priest for ever.—Very frequently he said, that it was no merit of his own, that it was all grace,—free, unmerited grace,—by which he was favoured with such clear evidence that all would be well: repeating,

" Nothing in my hand I bring
Simply to thy cross I cling."

He strove with great earnestness, to impress upon his eldest son, the necessity there is for all to experience a change of heart, dwelling very particularly on the love of the Father, in sending his beloved Son into the world, that whosoever believeth in Him should not perish, but have everlasting life. He also alluded to the influence of the Holy Spirit; reproving for sin, and when obeyed, giving that peace, which cannot be felt while pursuing mere earthly pleasure.

Early one morning, he requested the family might

be collected for the purpose of taking leave of them.
He first addressed his young men; after that his
wife, sons, and other relatives, also a friend who had
attended upon him, each separately, and in a very
affectionate and impressive manner.—It would be
difficult to portray the sweet and solemn feeling that
accompanied these addresses, or the earnest solicitude
which he evinced, that all might be found faithful,
and humbly endeavouring, through divine grace, so
to live, that they might be prepared to meet again in
heaven. He then wished the 7th chapter of Revelations might be read, and dwelt particularly on the
text which speaks of the white robes of the glorified
righteous. The 103rd Psalm was also read; and
after a short address, which could not be distinctly
understood, he concluded with the lines of Cowper: -

"To Jesus, the crown of my hope,
My soul is in haste to be gone;
O bear me, ye cherubim, up,
And waft me away to his throne!"

On some of the family returning from meeting,
he inquired, "Have you had a good meeting?" and
said, "Pray for me, that mercy may be extended in
the hour of trial."—To a friend he said, "O to
meet where there is no more sorrow!" and on her
expressing an earnest desire that this might be the
case, he added, "Glorious things are spoken of thee,
O Zion, the city of the Great King. God is known
in her palaces for a refuge."

On a message of love being delivered to him from
some of his friends, he said, "Mine to them, and say
that I am happy, happy, happy! The sting of death
is taken away.—O death! where is thy sting? O
grave! where is thy victory?"

On the morning of the 11th of the 11th month, the
day on which he died, he prayed for patience, as he
had often done in the course of his illness, and entreated those present to pray for him; and soon after,
his purified spirit quitted its earthly tenement, in the
enjoyment of that peace with God through Jesus

Christ, which is the blessed inheritance of the redeemed of the Lord.

READER, art thou one of those who are daily seeking help from God, to perfect holiness in his fear, and who are in the enjoyment of an evidence of their past sins being blotted out, through faith in Christ, who offered himself upon the cross, a propitiatory sacrifice for our sins? If this be thy happy state, may the Lord enable thee, in watchfulness and prayer, to hold out to the termination of thy life, and crown thee with that peace which marks the end of the man who is perfect in Christ, and upright before the Lord, the Judge who cannot be deceived.—But if thou art one of those who are hoping to be saved by Christ, whilst neglecting the convictions of the Holy Spirit, by which sin is reproved in the heart; and who are not bringing forth fruits meet for repentance? If this be thy state, be alarmed! lest He whom thou callest thy Saviour, but whom thou art not serving as thy Master, nor suffering to rule over thee as thy Lord, should call thee to his judgment-seat in this state, and reject thee; for his solemn declaration is, "Not every one that sayeth unto me Lord, Lord, shall enter into the kingdom of heaven; but he that doeth the will of my Father which is in heaven."—Or if thou art one of those who mourn over their sins, but still go on transgressing against the light which cometh by Jesus Christ, which is the witness of the Spirit in thy own bosom? If this be thy state, mayst thou learn to apply in faith unto God for strength; mayst thou believe that He is both able and willing to help thee to turn away from temptation; and that, as thou art humbled before him, under the conviction of thy own helplessness and unworthiness, and therefore askest of him nothing in thy own name, but only in the worthy name of Jesus, our great and merciful high-priest and advocate with the Father, he will be faithful to his promises, and will deliver thee, and crown thee with his loving-kindness and tender mercy. Then thou shalt know in thy own experience, that though the power to be perfect and upright is not of man, the grace of God is sufficient to make those who wait upon him for it in faith, both perfect and upright, and to crown their end with peace;—But if thou be one of those who are heedlessly living in sin, then hearken to the voice of Christian love, lest the day of thy visitation pass by, and thou reap thy reward in outer darkness, with those who will not have Christ to rule over them.—Give heed to the light, which at times shines into thy heart, and by which, in spite of thy unwillingness to attend to it, God has often convinced thee of sin. Be willing to understand thy lost condition, and that thou art yet a servant of the devil and an enemy of God, lest the Lord rise up against thee, and close against thee for ever, the door of mercy, which, in his long-suffering and forbearance, has long stood open before thee. Repent and believe on the Lord Jesus Christ, that thou mayest receive through him the forgiveness of thy sins, and the gift of the Holy Ghost, by the help of which, the love of evil may be conquered, and the love of righteousness may be established in thy heart. Thus thou will be enabled to perfect holiness in the fear of the Lord, and end thy days in the peace of the perfect and the upright man, even that peace which the righteous partake of in this world, and which, in the presence of God and of Christ and of all the redeemed children of the Lord, they will enjoy for ever, in the world to come.

END.

London: Printed by E. Couchman & Co., 10, *Throgmorton Street; for the* TRACT ASSOCIATION *of the* SOCIETY OF FRIENDS. *Sold at the* DEPOSITORY, 12, *Bishopsgate Street Without.*—1863.

W A R,

IS IT LAWFUL

UNDER

THE CHRISTIAN DISPENSATION?

LONDON:

Printed for the TRACT ASSOCIATION of the SOCIETY OF FRIENDS.

Sold at the DEPOSITORY, 84, Houndsditch.

—

1860.

No. 144.   [*Price* 10*d. per dozen.*]

ADVERTISEMENT.

———

The following pages are extracted from a Work entitled, " Observations on the Distinguishing Views and Practices of the Society of Friends.*" By* J. J. Gurney.

WAR,

IS IT LAWFUL UNDER THE CHRISTIAN

DISPENSATION?

———◆———

Of all the practices which disturb the tranquillity and
lay waste the welfare of men, there is none which operates
to so great an extent, or with so prodigious an efficacy,
as *war*. Not only is this tremendous and dreadfully prevalent scourge productive of an incalculable amount of
bodily and mental suffering,—so that, in that point of
view alone, it may be considered one of the most terrible
enemies of the happiness of the human race,—but it
must also be regarded as a moral evil of the very deepest
dye. "From whence come wars and fightings among
you?" said the apostle James, "come they not hence,
even of your lusts which war in your members? Ye lust
and have not; ye kill and desire to have, and cannot
obtain; ye fight and war, yet ye have not, because ye
ask not." Chap. iv. 1, 2. War, therefore, has its origin
in the inordinate desires and corrupt passions of men;
and as is its origin, so is its result. Arising out of an
evil root, this tree of bitterness seldom fails to produce,
in vast abundance, evil fruits—malice, wrath, cruelty,
fraud, rapine, lasciviousness, confusion, and murder.

Although there are few persons who will dispute the accuracy of this picture of war—although every one knows
that such a custom is evil in itself and arises out of an
evil source—and although the *general position*, that war
is at variance with the principles of Christianity, has a
very extensive currency among the professors of that
religion—it is a singular fact, that the religious Society of
Friends is almost the only class of Christians who hold it
to be their duty to God, to their neighbour, and to themselves, absolutely and entirely to abstain from that most
injurious practice. While the views of the Friends on
the subject are thus comprehensive and complete, the

generality of professing Christians, and many even of a reflecting and serious character, are still accustomed to make distinctions between one kind of war and another. They will condemn a war which is oppressive and unjust; and in this respect they advance no farther than the moralists of every age, country, and religion. On the other hand they hesitate as little in expressing their approbation of wars which are defensive, or which, in their opinion, are undertaken in a just cause.

The main argument, of a scriptural character, by which the propriety and rectitude of warfare is defended and maintained, is *the divinely sanctioned example of the ancient Israelites.* That the Israelites were engaged in many contests with other nations; that those contests were often of a very destructive character; and that they were carried forward, on the part of the Israelites, under the direct sanction, and often in consequence of the clear command of the Almighty, are points which no one who is accustomed to peruse the history of the Old Testament, can pretend to deny. But we are not to forget that the wars of the Israelites differed from wars in general (even from those of the least exceptionable character in point of justice,) in certain important and striking particulars. That very divine sanction which is pleaded as giving to the example of that people an authority of which other nations may still avail themselves in the maintenance of a similar practice did, in fact, distinguish their wars from all those in which any other nation is known to have been ever engaged. They were undertaken in pursuance of the express command of the Almighty Governor of mankind: and they were directed to the accomplishment of certain revealed designs of his especial providence. These designs had a twofold object: the temporal preservation and prosperity of God's peculiar people, on the one hand, and the punishment and destruction of idolatrous nations, on the other. The Israelites and their kings were, indeed, sometimes engaged in combating their neighbours without any direction from their divine Governor, and even against his declared will; and these instances will not of course be pleaded as an authority for the practice of war: but such of their military operations as were sanctioned and ordered of the Lord (and these only are adduced in the argument in favour of war) assumed the character of a work of obedience and faith. They went forth to battle, from time to time, in compliance with the divine command, and in dependence upon that Being who condescended to regulate their movements, and to direct their efforts, in the furtherance of his own providence. These characteristics in the divinely-sanctioned warfare of the Hebrews, were attended with two consequences of the most marked and distinguishing character. In the first place, the conflicts in which this people were thus engaged, and which so conspicuously called into exercise their obedience and faith, were far from being attended by that destruction of moral and pious feeling, which is so generally the effect of war; but on the contrary were often accompanied by a condition of high religious excellence in those who were thus employed in fighting the battles of the Lord—an observation very plainly suggested by the history of Joshua and his followers, of the successive Judges, and of David. And secondly, the contests which were undertaken and conducted on the principles now stated, were followed by uniform success. The Lord was carrying on his own designs, through certain appointed instruments; and under such circumstances, while failure was impossible, success afforded an evidence of the divine approbation. Now it cannot be predicated even of the justest wars, as they are usually carried on among the nations of the world, that they are undertaken with the revealed sanction, or by the direct command of Jehovah—or that they are a work of obedience and faith—or that they are often accompanied with a condition of high religious excellence in those who undertake them—or that they are followed by uniform success. On the supposition, therefore, that the system of Israelitish morals is still in force without alteration and improvement, it is manifest that we cannot justly conclude from the example of God's ancient people, that warfare, as it is generally practised, even when it bears the stamp of honour or defence, is consistent with the will of God.

In addition to the example of the Hebrews, the defenders of modern warfare are accustomed to plead the authority of John the Baptist.* It is recorded in the Gospel of Luke, that when that eminent prophet was

* See *Grotius de Jure Belli ac Pacis*, lib. i. cap. ii. § vii. 5.

preaching in the wilderness, various classes of persons resorted to him for advice and instruction. Among others, "the soldiers demanded of him, saying, And what shall we do? And he said unto them, Do violence to no man, neither accuse any falsely; and be content with your wages;" chap. iii. 14. Since the precept of John to these soldiers, that, *they should do violence to no man*, probably related to their deportment among their friends and allies, it may be allowed that he did not, on this occasion forbid the practice of fighting. On the other hand, it must be observed, that the expressions of the Baptist afford no direct encouragement to that practice. On the supposition that the soldiers would continue to be soldiers, he confined himself to recommending to them that gentle, orderly, and, submissive demeanour, which was so evidently calculated to soften the asperities of their profession.

But, although John the Baptist was engaged in proclaiming the *approach* of the Christian dispensation, he belonged to the preceding institution, and his moral system was that of the law. The objection of the Friends to every description of military operation, is founded principally *on that more perfect revelation of the moral law of God, which distinguishes the dispensation of the Gospel of Christ.* They contend that all warfare—whatever are its peculiar features, circumstances, or pretexts —is wholly at variance with the revealed characteristics and known principles of the *Christian* religion.

In support of this position, we may, in the first place, adduce the testimony of the prophets; for these inspired writers, in their predictions respecting the gospel dispensation, alluded both to the superior spirituality and to the purer morality of that system of religion, of which the law with all its accompaniments was only the introduction. In the second chapter of the book of Isaiah we read the following prophecy: "And it shall come to pass in the last days, that the mountain of the Lord's house shall be established in the top of the mountains, and shall be exalted above the hills; and all nations shall flow unto it. And many people shall go and say, Come ye, and let us go up to the mountain of the Lord, to the house of the God of Jacob; and he will teach us of his ways, and we will walk in his paths; for out of Zion shall go forth the law, and the word of the Lord from Jerusalem.

And he shall judge among the nations, and rebuke many people; *and they shall beat their swords into ploughshares, and their spears into pruninghooks: nation shall not lift up sword against nation, neither, shall they learn war any more;*" ver. 2—4. The prophet Micah repeats the same prediction, and adds the following animating description: "But they shall sit every man under his vine and under his fig-tree; and none shall make them afraid: for the mouth of the Lord of hosts hath spoken it; Micah iv. 1—4. It is allowed by the Jews that the "last days" of which these prophets speak, are the "days of the Messiah;" and the unanimous consent of Christian commentators confirms the application of those expressions to the period of that glorious dispensation which was introduced by our Lord and Saviour, Jesus Christ. Accordingly, the actual predictions of his coming are elsewhere accompanied with similar descriptions. In Isa. ix. 6, the Messiah is expressly denominated the "Prince of Peace." In Isa. xi. the reign of Christ is painted in glowing colours, as accompanied by the universal harmony of God's creation. Lastly, in Zech. ix. 9, 10, we read as follows: "Rejoice greatly, O daughter of Zion; shout, O daughter of Jerusalem; behold, thy King cometh unto thee: he is just, and having salvation; lowly, and riding upon an ass, and upon a colt the foal of an ass. *And I will cut off the chariot from Ephraim, and the horse from Jerusalem, and the battle-bow shall be cut off: and he shall speak peace unto the heathen: and his dominion shall be from sea even to sea, and from the river even to the ends of the earth.*" Comp. Ps. xlvi. 9.

It is undeniable that, in these passages, a total cessation from the practice of war is described as one of the most conspicuous characteristics of Christianity. Such a consequence is represented by Isaiah as arising from the conversion of the heathen nations,—as resulting from their being led into the ways, instructed in the law, and enlightened by the word of the Lord. Whoever, indeed, were to be the members of the true Church of God, she was no longer to participate in the warfare of the world. The chariot was to be cut off from Ephraim, and the war-horse from Jerusalem. It is true that, for the full accomplishment of these glorious prophecies, we must look forward to a period yet to come. But let us not deceive ourselves. The inspired writers describe this complete and uninterrupted peaceableness, as a distinguishing feature of the dispensation under which Christians are living—as the result of obedience to that law which they are, at all times, bound to follow: and we may therefore infer that, if the true nature of the Christian dispensation were fully understood, and if the law by which it is regulated were exactly obeyed, a conversion to our holy religion, or the cordial and serious holding of it, would be uniformly accompanied with an entire abstinence from warfare. Thus the prevalence of the law of peace would be found commensurate, in every age of the church, with the *actual* extent of the Messiah's kingdom over men. As the language of prophecy clearly suggests this doctrine, so it will be found that, on the introduction of Christianity, there were promulgated certain moral rules which, when fully and faithfully obeyed, infallibly lead to this particular result.

The distinction which men are accustomed to draw between just and unjust warfare is, in a great plurality of instances, entirely nugatory; for there are few wars, however atrocious, which are not defended, and not many perhaps which the persons waging them do not *believe* to be justified by some plea or other connected with self-preservation or honorable retribution. In addition therefore to the laws which forbid *spontaneous* injury, some stronger and more comprehensive principles were obviously needed, in order to the accomplishment of this great end; and these principles are unfolded in that pure and exalted code of morality which was revealed, in connection with the Gospel. They are, *the non-resistance of injuries, the return of good for evil, and the love of our enemies.*

It was the Lord Jesus himself who promulgated these principles, and promulgated them as distinguishing his own dispensation from that of the law. "Ye have heard that it hath been said, An eye for an eye, and a tooth for a tooth: but I say unto you, *That ye resist not evil*: but whosoever shall smite thee on thy right cheek, turn to him the other also.—Ye have heard that it hath been said, Thou shalt love thy neighbour, and hate thine enemy. But I say unto you, *Love your enemies, bless them that curse you, do good to them that hate you, and pray for them that despitefully use you, and persecute you;* that ye may be the children of your Father which is in heaven; for he maketh his sun to rise on the evil and on

the good, and sendeth rain on the just and on the unjust.
For if ye love them which love you, what reward have ye?
do not even the publicans the same? And if ye salute
your brethren only, what do ye more than others? do
not even the publicans so? *Be ye therefore perfect,
even as your Father which is in heaven is perfect."*
Matt. v. 38—48; comp. Luke vi. 27—29. So also, the
apostle Peter commands the believers not to render
"evil for evil, nor railing for railing, but contrariwise,
blessing." 1 Pet. iii. 9. And Paul, in the following
lively exhortation, holds up the very same standard of
Christian practice: "Dearly beloved, avenge not yourselves, but rather *give place unto* wrath: for it is written,
Vengeance is mine; I will repay, saith the Lord. Therefore if thine enemy hunger, feed him; if he thirst, give
him drink: for in so doing thou shalt heap coals of fire
on his head. Be not overcome of evil, *but overcome evil
with good."* Rom. xii. 19—21.

In the delivery of that holy law, by obedience to which
Christians may be brought, in their small measure (*and
yet with completeness according to that measure,*) to a
conformity with the moral attributes of their Heavenly
Father, *our Lord has laid his axe to the root.* He has
established certain principles which, as they are honestly
observed in conduct, must put an end to every evil
practice; and thus is the tree which bears the fruit of
corruption cut down and destroyed. Of this nature, precisely, are the principles which we are now considering,
and which, when followed up with true consistency,
cannot fail to abolish warfare, whether offensive or defensive, whether aggressive or retributive, whether unjust
or just. The great law of Christ, which his disciples are
ever bound to obey, is the *law of love*—love complete,
uninterrupted, universal, fixed upon God in the first
place, and afterwards embracing the whole family of man.
And, since war (of whatsoever species or description it
may be) can never consist with this love, it is indisputable that, where the latter prevails as it ought to do,
the former must entirely cease.

It is observed that our Lord's precepts, which have now
been cited, are addressed to *individuals.* Since this is
undeniably true, it follows that it is the clear duty of individual Christians to obey them; and to obey them
uniformly, and on every occasion. If, during the common

course of their life, they are attacked, insulted, injured, and persecuted, they ought to suffer wrong, to revenge no injury, to return good for evil, and love their enemies. So also, should it happen that they are exposed to the more extraordinary calamities of war, their duty remains unaltered; their conduct must continue to be guided by the same principles. If the sword of the invader be lifted up against them, the precept is still at hand, that they resist not evil. If the insults and injuries of the carnal warrior be heaped upon them, they are still forbidden to avenge themselves, and still commanded to pray for their persecutors. If they be surrounded by a host of enemies, however violent and malicious those enemies may be, Christian love must still be unbroken, still universal. According, then, to the law of Christ, it is the duty of *individuals* to abstain from all warfare; nor can they avoid such a course if they follow his law. We are informed by Sulpitius Severus, that when the Roman Emperor Julian was engaged in bestowing upon his troops a largess, with a view to some approaching battle, his bounty was refused by Martin, a soldier in his army who had been previously converted to Christianity. "Hitherto," said he to Cæsar, "I have fought for thee: permit me now to fight for my God. Let those who are about to engage in war accept thy donative; I am the soldier of Christ; *for me*, the combat is unlawful."* Where is the solid, the sufficient, reason, why such, under similar circumstances, should not be the expressions of every true Christian?

The man who engages in warfare, retains his private responsibility; and, whatever may be the proceedings of his countrymen, whatever the commands of his superiors, he can never dispossess himself of his individual obligation to render to the law of his God a consistent and uniform obedience. But, secondly, the unlawfulness of war, under any of its forms, is equally evident when it is regarded as the affair of nations. Doubtless there may be found in the Scriptures a variety of injunctions relating to the particulars of human conduct, and applicable to men and women only as individuals; but it is one of the excellent characteristics of the moral law of God, that its *principles* are of universal application to mankind,

---

* *De Vita B. Mart. Ed. Amst.* A. D. 1665, p. 445.

whatever be the circumstances under which they are placed; whether they act singly as individuals, or collectively as nations. No one, surely, who has any just views of morality, will pretend, for a moment, that those fundamental rules of conduct, which are given to guide every man in his own walk through life, may be deserted as soon as he unites with others, and acts in a corporate capacity. The absurd consequence of such a system would be manifestly this—that national crimes of every description might be committed without entailing any national guilt, and without any real infraction of the revealed will of God.

Now among these fundamental rules—these eternal, unchangeable principles—is that of *universal love*. The law of God, which is addressed without reservation or exception to all men, plainly says to them, Resist not evil: revenge not injuries: *love your enemies*. Individuals, nations consisting of individuals, and governments acting on behalf of nations, are all unquestionably bound to obey this law; and whether it is the act of an individual, of a nation, or of a government, *the transgression of the law is sin*; 1 John iii. 4. Nations or governments transgress the Christian law of love, and commit sin, when they declare or carry on war, precisely as the private duellist transgresses that law, and commits sin, when he sends or accepts a challenge, and deliberately endeavours to destroy his neighbour. It ought also to be observed that, through the medium of the nation, the case is again brought home to the conscience and responsibility of the individual. The man who takes a part, either himself or by a substitute, in the national warfare, takes a part also in the national sin. He aids and abets his nation in breaking the law of Christ. So far then is the example of his countrymen—the authority of his legislature—the command of his monarch—from being sufficient to justify his engagement in warfare, that he cannot follow that example, avail himself of that authority, or obey that command, *without adding, to his private transgression, the further criminality of actively promoting the transgression of the state.*

For the reasons now stated, I consider it evident that a total abstinence from warfare, on the part both of individuals and of nations, would be the necessary result of a strict adherence to the principles of the law of Christ.

But it will not be difficult to carry the argument a step further, and to show that one of the precepts now cited from the Sermon on the Mount, appears to bear a specific and peculiar allusion to the subject of war. " *Ye have heard that it hath been said, Thou shalt love thy neighbour and hate thine enemy ; but I say unto you, Love your enemies.*" In the first part of his discourse, our Lord has instituted a comparison between the system of morality, which, under the sanction and influence of the Mosaic institution, prevailed among the Israelites, and that purer and more perfect law of action, of which he was himself both the author and the minister. In calling the attention of his hearers to the sayings uttered " by them of old time " on the several moral points of his discourse, such as killing, adultery, divorcement, perjury, and retaliation —he has uniformly quoted from the law of Moses itself. It was with the principles of that law, as they were understood and received by the Jews, that he compared his own holier system, and he improved, enlarged, or superseded, the introductory and more imperfect code of morals (as was in each particular required) in order to make way for one which is capable of no improvement, and must endure for ever. Now the precepts of ancient times to which he last refers—the precepts respecting love and hatred—formed, in all probability, like the whole preceding series, a part of those divine edicts which were, delivered to the Israelites by Moses. That which related to the love of their neighbour is recognized at once, and is as follows : " Thou shalt not avenge nor bear any grudge against the *children of thy people*, but thou shalt love thy neighbour as thyself;" Lev. xix. 18. The reader will observe that the love here enjoined was to be directed to the *children of the people of Israel*. The neighbour to be loved was the fellow-countryman ; or if a stranger, the proselyte : and the precept in fact commanded no more than that the Israelites—the members of the Lord's selected family—should *love one another*. So also the injunction of old, that the Israelites should hate their enemies, was exclusively *national*. They were not permitted to hate their private enemies, who belonged to the same favoured community. On the contrary, they were enjoined to do good to such enemies as these : " If thou meet thine enemy's ox or his ass going astray," said the law, " thou shalt surely bring it back to him again."

Exod. xxiii. 4. But they were to hate* their national enemies—they were to make no covenant with the foreign and idolatrous tribes, who formerly possessed the land of Canaan. "When the Lord thy God shall bring thee into the land whither thou goest to possess it," said Moses to the assembly of his people, "and hath cast out many nations before thee, the Hittites, and the Girgashites, and the Amorites, and the Canaanites, and the Perizzites, and the Hivites, and the Jebusites, seven nations greater and mightier than thou; and when the Lord thy God shall deliver them before thee, thou shalt smite them, and utterly destroy them; thou shalt make no covenant with them, nor show mercy unto them." Deut. vii. 1, 2; comp. Exod. xxxiv. 11—13.

It is to these edicts, delivered in the times of old, and under the peculiar circumstances of the dispensation then existing, that the law of Christ is placed in opposition: "But *I* say unto you, *Love your enemies.*" How much soever, then, we may be justified by the undoubted universality of this law, in applying it to the circumstances of private life, we can scarcely fail to perceive that it was principally intended to discountenance these *national* enmities; and that the love here enjoined was specifically and peculiarly such as would *prevent the practice of war.* The Israelites were commanded to combat and destroy with the sword the nations who were their own enemies, and the enemies of God. But Christians are introduced to a purer and more lovely system of moral conduct: and the law which they are called upon to obey, is that which proclaims peace upon earth and good-will to men: they are commanded to be the friends of all mankind. If they are sent forth among idolatrous nations, it is as the ministers of their restoration, and not as the instruments of their punishment; and as they may not contend with the sword against the enemies of their God, much less may they wield it for any purpose of their own, whether it be in aggression, retribution, or defence. Armed with submission, forbearance, and long-suffering, they must secede from the warfare of a wrathful and corrupt world;

---

* The verb "to hate," as used in the Holy Scriptures (Heb. שנא. Gr. μισέω) does not imply *malignity of mind* so much as *opposition and enmity in action*; as the reader may be fully convinced on a reference to the Concordances; see *Schleusner, Lex. voc.* μισέω, *No.* 1.

and whatever be the aggravations to which they are exposed, must evince themselves, under the softening influence of universal love, to be the meek, the harmless, the benevolent followers of the PRINCE OF PEACE.

I know of nothing in the New Testament which has any appearance of contravening the force of these divine precepts, or of the deductions now made from them, but a single passage in the gospel of Luke. We are informed by that sacred historian, that after our Lord's paschal supper, and immediately before he was betrayed into the hands of his enemies, Jesus thus addressed his disciples: "When I sent you without purse, and scrip, and shoes, lacked ye anything? And they said, Nothing. Then said he unto them, But now, he that hath a purse, let him take it, and likewise his scrip: *and he that hath no sword, let him sell his garment and buy one.* For I say unto you, That this that is written must yet be accomplished in me, 'And he was reckoned among the transgressors:' for the things concerning me have an end;" chap. xxii. 35—37. The words employed by the Lord Jesus on this occasion may, when superficially considered, be deemed to inculcate the notion that his followers were permitted and enjoined to defend themselves and their religion with the sword; but the context and the circumstances which followed after these words were uttered, evidently decide otherwise. The disciples appear, after their usual manner, to have understood their Lord literally, and they answered, "Here are two swords," and Jesus replied, *It is enough.* Now in declaring that two swords were *enough*, although they were then exposed to aggravated and immediately impending danger, he offered them an intelligible hint that he had been misunderstood— that the use of the sword in defence of their little company, was neither consistent with his views, nor really implied in his injunction. But the opportunity was at hand on which the disciples were to be completely undeceived. The enemies of Jesus approached, armed and caparisoned as if they were in pursuit of some violent robbers. When the disciples saw what would follow, they said unto Jesus, "Lord, shall we smite with the sword?" and Peter, the most zealous of their number, without waiting for his Master's reply, rushed forward and smote the servant of the High Priest, and cut off his ear. Then were he and his brethren clearly instructed by their Lord, that it was their duty, not to fight, but to suffer wrong. "Suffer ye thus far," said he to Peter; and immediately afterwards he confirmed his doctrine by action: he touched the wounded man and healed him. Then, in expressions of the greatest significancy, he cried out to Peter, "Put up thy sword into the sheath: the cup which my Father hath given me, shall I not drink it?" See John xviii. 11: and as an universal caution against so antichristian a practice as that of using destructive weapons in self-defence, he added, "*All they that take the sword shall perish with the sword:*" Matt. xxvi. 52. Lastly, when soon afterwards he was carried before Pilate the Roman governor, he plainly declared that his kingdom was of such a nature, that it neither required nor allowed the defence of carnal weapons. "My kingdom," said he, "is not of this world: if my kingdom were of this world, *then would my servants fight, that I should not be delivered to the Jews; but now is my kingdom not from hence.*" John xviii. 36.

It is sufficiently evident, therefore, that when our Lord exhorted his disciples to sell their garments and buy swords, his precept was not to be understood *literally.* Such, indeed, is the explicit judgment of the generality of commentators. We may, therefore, either conclude, with Erasmus, that the sword of which our Lord here spake, was the sword of the Spirit—the word of God (see *Com. in. loc.*), or we may accede to the more prevalent opinion of critics, that the words of Jesus imported nothing more than a general warning to the disciples, that their situation was about to be greatly changed—that they were soon to be deprived of the personal and protecting presence of their divine Master—that they would be exposed to every species of difficulty, and become the objects of hatred and persecution—that they would no longer be able to trust in their neighbours, and would, therefore, be driven to a variety of expedients in order to provide for their own maintenance and security.*

In order to complete the present branch of the argument, it must be remarked, that the doctrine of the Society of Friends respecting the absolute inconsistency of warfare with the moral code of the Christian dispen-

* See *Estius, Vatablus and others, in Poli Syn, Gill, &c.*

sation, was one which prevailed, to a very considerable extent, during the early ages of the Christian church. Justin Martyr, (A.D. 140) in his First Apology, quotes the prophecy of Isaiah, (already cited in the present Essay,) respecting the going forth of the law and of the word of God from Jerusalem, and the consequent prevalence of a state of peace. "That these things have come to pass," he proceeds, "you may be readily convinced: for twelve men, destitute both of instruction and of eloquence, went forth from Jerusalem into the world, and by the power of God gave evidence to every description of persons, that they were sent by Christ to teach all men the divine word: *and we who were once slayers of one another* (that is to say, commonly engaged in warfare) *do not fight against our enemies.*"[*]   Irenæus, Bishop of Lyons, (A.D. 167) discusses the same prophecy, and proves its relation to our Saviour, by the fact, that the followers of Jesus had disused the weapons of war, and no longer knew how to fight.[†]   Tertullian (A.D. 200) in one part of his works, alludes to Christians who were engaged together with their heathen countrymen in military pursuits;[‡] but on another occasion, he informs us that many soldiers who had been converted to Christianity, quitted those pursuits in consequence of their conversion; and he repeatedly expresses his own opinion, that any participation in war was unlawful for believers in Jesus—not only because of the idolatrous practices enjoined on the soldiers of the Roman armies, but because Christ had forbidden the use of the sword and the revenge of injuries.[§] Origen, (A.D. 230) in his work against Celsus, says of himself and his brethren, "We no longer take up the sword against any nation, nor do we learn any more to make war. We have become, for the sake of Jesus, *the children of peace.*"[||]   In another passage of the same work he maintains that Christians are the most useful of subjects, because they pray for their monarch. "By such means," says he, "we fight for our king abundantly: *but we take no part in his wars, even though he urge us:*"[¶]

---

[*] *Apol.* i. cap. 39, p. 67, Ed. Ben.
[†] *Adv. Hær.* lib. iv. cap. 34, Ed. Ben., p. 275.
[‡] *Apol.* cap. 42, Ed. Semler, v. 102.
[§] *De Idol.* 19; Ed. Semler, iv. 176; *De Coron. Mil.* 12, iv. 355.
[||] Lib. v. 33, Ed. Ben., i. 602.
[¶] Lib. viii. 73, Ed. Ben., i. 797.

Here we have not only this ancient and eminent father's declaration of his own sentiment, that war is inconsistent with the religion of Christ; but a plain testimony, (corresponding with that of Justin and Irenæus), that the Christians of those early times were *accustomed* to abstain from it. Traces of the same doctrine, and practice are very clearly marked in the subsequent history of the church. Under the reign of Dioclesian (A.D. 300) more especially, a large number of Christians refused to serve in the army, and in consequence of their refusal many of them suffered martyrdom.* Now, although the conduct of these Christians might partly arise, as Grotius suggests, from their religious objections to the idolatrous rites at that time mixed up with the military system, it is probable that the unlawfulness of war itself for the followers of Christ was also a principle on which they acted. Thus Lactantius, who wrote during the reign of this very emperor, expressly asserts that " *to engage in war cannot be lawful for the righteous man, whose warfare is that of righteousness itself.*† And again, in the twelfth canon of the Council of Nice, held under the reign of Constantine (A.D. 325), a long period of excommunication is attached, as a penalty, to the conduct of those persons who, having once in the ardour of their early faith renounced the military calling, were persuaded by the force of bribes to return to it—"like dogs to their own vomit."‡ The circumstances particularly alluded to in this canon, might indeed have taken place during the tyranny of the idolatrous Licinius, whom Constantine had so lately subdued; but the canon itself was, I presume, intended for the future regulation of the church; and such a law would scarcely have been promulgated under the reign of the converted Constantine, had not an opinion been entertained in the council, that *war itself*, however prevalent and generally allowed, was inconsistent with the highest standard of Christian morality.

The *visible* effects of a mighty battle are sufficiently appalling—multitudes of the wounded, the dying, and the dead, spread in wild confusion over the ensanguined plain! But did Christians fully know the *invisible* consequences

---

* Vide *Grot. de Jure Bell.*, lib. vi. cap. ii. §8; *Ruinart, Acta Martyrum; de S. Maximiliano*, Ed. Amst., p. 300.
† *De Vero Cultu*, lib. vi. cap. 20.
‡ Vide *Mansii Coll. Concil.*, tom. ii., p. 674.

of such a contest—could they trace the flight of thousands
of immortal souls (many of them disembodied, perhaps,
while under the immediate influence of diabolical passions)
into the world of eternal retribution—they would indeed
shrink with horror from such a scene of destruction, and
adopt, without further hesitation, the same firm and
unalterable conclusion.

Notwithstanding the clearness and importance of those
principles which evince the utter inconsistency of the
practice of war with the Christian dispensation, it is continually pleaded that wars are often expedient, and
sometimes absolutely necessary for the preservation of
states. To such a plea it might be sufficient to answer
that nothing is so expedient, nothing so desirable, nothing
so *necessary*, either for individuals or for nations, as a
conformity, in point of conduct, with the revealed will of
the Supreme Governor of the universe.

Let reflecting Christians take a deliberate survey of the
history of Europe during the last eighteen centuries, and
let them impartially examine how many of the wars waged
among Christian nations have been, on their own principles, really expedient or *necessary* on either side, for the
preservation of states. Would not the result of such an
examination be, a satisfactory conviction that by far the
greater part of those wars are so far from having truly
borne this character, that, notwithstanding the common
excuse of self-defence, by which, in so many cases, they
have been supposed to be justified, they have, in point of
fact, even in a political point of view, been much more
hurtful than useful to all the parties engaged in them.
Where, for instance, has England found an equivalent
for the almost infinite profusion of blood and treasure,
which she has wasted on her many wars? Must not the
impartial page of history decide that *almost the whole* of
her wars, however justified in the view of the world by
the pleas of defence and retribution, have, in fact, been
waged against imaginary dangers—might have been
avoided by a few harmless concessions—and that they
have turned out to be extensively injurious to her in
many of their results?

For true Christians—for those who are brought under
the influence of vital religion—for those who would
"follow the Lamb *whithersoever* he goeth,"—war is *never*
right. It is *always* their duty to obey his high and holy

law—to suffer wrong—to return good for evil—to love their enemies. If, in consequence of their obedience to this law, they apprehend themselves to be surrounded with many dangers—if tumult and terror assail them—let them still remember that "cursed" is "the man that trusteth in man, and maketh flesh his arm;" let them still place an undivided reliance upon the power and benevolence of their God and Saviour. It may be his good pleasure that they be delivered from the outward peril by which they are visited; or he may decree that they fall a sacrifice to that peril. But whatever be the result, as long as they are preserved in obedience to his law, so long are they safe in his hands. They "*know* that ALL THINGS work together for good to them that love God." Rom. viii. 28.

Godliness, however, has the promise of this life, as well as of that which is to come; we may, therefore, entertain a reasonable confidence that our temporal happiness and safety, as well as our growth in grace, will, in general, be promoted by obedience to our Heavenly Father. It is not in vain, even in an outward point of view, that God has invited his unworthy children to cast their cares upon him; and to trust him for their support and protection; for though he may work no miracles in their favour, the very law which he gives them to obey is adapted, in a wonderful manner, to convert their otherwise rugged path through life, into one of comparative pleasantness, security, and peace. These observations are applicable, with a peculiar degree of force, to those particulars in the divine law, which, as they are closely followed, preclude all warfare. No weapons of self-defence will be found so efficacious as Christian meekness, kindness, and forbearance; the suffering of injuries; the absence of revenge; the return of good for evil; and the ever-operating love of God and man. Those who regulate their life and conversation with true circumspection, according to these principles, have, for the most part, little reason to fear the violent hand of the enemy and the oppressor. Having on the breastplate of righteousness, and firmly grasping the shield of faith, they are quiet in the centre of storms, safe in the heart of danger, and victorious amidst a host of enemies.

Such, in a multitude of instances, has been the lot of Christian individuals, and such might also be the experience of Christian, nations. When we consider the still degraded condition of mankind, we can hardly, at present, look for the trial of the experiment; but, was there a people who would renounce the dangerous guidance of worldly honour, and boldly conform their national conduct to the eternal rules of the law of Christ—was there a people who would lay aside the weapons of a carnal warfare, and proclaim the principles of universal peace; suffer wrong with condescension; abstain from all retaliation; return good for evil, and diligently promote *the welfare of all men*—such a people would not only dwell in absolute safety, but would be blessed with eminent prosperity, loaded with reciprocal benefits, and endowed, for every good, and wise, and worthy purpose, with irresistible influence over surrounding nations.

END.

Printed by R. Couchman, 10, Throgmorton Street, London.

AFFLICTION SANCTIFIED.

A SHORT MEMOIR

OF

SARAH GILKES.

"The Lord redeemeth the soul of his servants, and none of them that trust in Him shall be desolate."—Ps. xxxiv. 22.

"No chastening for the present seemeth to be joyous, but grievous: nevertheless afterward it yieldeth the peaceable fruit of righteousness unto them which are exercised thereby."—Heb. xii. 11.

THESE declarations of Holy Scripture were remarkably fulfilled in the experience of SARAH GILKES; and the following brief account of her has been prepared with the hope that it may afford instruction and encouragement to others.

She was born in Essex, in the year 1803.

Her father was a person of property but lost it all by gambling; her mother bore a good moral character, and required of her children a strict observance of their religious duties. Her father dying when she was very young, she was placed under the care of her grandfather, who, at his decease, left her a considerable sum of money; but of this she was unjustly defrauded, and was consequently left much to her own resources. When old enough, she engaged herself as lady's-maid in the family of a Roman Catholic nobleman. Of this family she always spoke with the greatest respect, believing that, while exemplary in the performance of their religious ceremonies, they possessed more than the *form* of religion: she especially estimated the kind and affable, though dignified conduct of her mistress. After having lived in this family several years, she became the wife of

[*Price 4d. per dozen.*]

a merchant in Manchester, and was, in consequence, for a time, placed in easy circumstances; but her husband, by unsuccessful foreign speculations and the failure of some of his associates in trade, became involved in great pecuniary difficulties. He then removed to London, and notwithstanding his earnest desires to satisfy the demands of his creditors, he was, for a short time, placed in the King's Bench prison. Here his devoted and energetic wife did not leave him, but firmly resisted the solicitations of her friends to return to them, saying, as she had shared with him in prosperity, she would not forsake him in adversity. She used the utmost exertions to procure a respectable maintenance both for her husband and self; and it was in such seasons of peculiar difficulty that the energies of her mind were most conspicuous. Persevering industry, cheerful self-reliance, united with a firm faith and trust in her never-failing Helper, were remarkable traits in her character.

Her husband's health gradually declined under the pressure of his afflictions; her attentions to him were indefatigable, both in nursing and in procuring for him the support which his enfeebled state required. A short time before his peaceful close, he expressed to his wife his firm belief that although she would have much trial to pass through, yet the Lord would be with her and support her to the end.

The expense incurred by her husband's funeral greatly added to her difficulties; and the extraordinary exertions she used to defray it, proved the integrity of her character. She was afterwards engaged by a lady as companion, and continued to reside in London, though in a poor state of health. During this period she was obliged frequently to avail herself of the gratuitous assistance of an eminent surgeon, whose disinterested attention to her, she ever gratefully remembered.

Her various trials were, under the divine blessing, made the means of awakening her to a deeper interest in eternal things.

After having been a widow for six years, she married a person in an humble station in life, but one whom she highly esteemed.

They had many difficulties to encounter, and in course of time, were reduced to great poverty, being chiefly lependent for their support upon her earnings as a dressmaker, of which business she had acquired a good knowledge previous to her second marriage. They removed from London to Hemel Hempstead, on account of their health; here she continued her unremitting exertions, often far beyond her strength. In about four years they went to reside at Luton, where she became known to many kind and sympathizing friends. By these she was much esteemed, and they assisted her in obtaining the surgical aid which the increase of her disorder (the dropsy) required. A Christian friend, who once visited her while there, remarked, she believed her to be one of those described by the prophet, "All thy children shall be taught of the Lord; and great shall be the peace of thy children:" and that being *so* taught she had been led to Jesus as her Saviour and her only hope of glory.

Endowed with a comprehensive mind, capable of deep reflection and discrimination, her conversation was interesting and instructive. She was fond of reading, especially works of a religious character; and the prayerful perusal of her Bible was greatly blessed to her seeking mind. When reading a celebrated work on the Doctrines of the Christian Religion, and comparing it with the contents of the New Testament, with earnest prayer for the knowledge of the truth, she was enabled to see the spirituality of the Gospel Dispensation, and the inefficacy of all forms and ceremonies, especially with regard to those called the Sacraments. Although she had been, as she said, baptized when an unconscious infant, and thus constituted a member of the Established Church, she did not continue in fellowship with that body, but for a time united with the Primitive Methodists, by whom she was highly esteemed; but not finding all she desired amongst them, she sat alone and sought the Lord in retirement.

The fear lest she might become burdensome to her friends, induced S. G. to avail herself of the advantage of the Hitchin Infirmary. By earnest prayer she sought the Lord for direction therein, not venturing to take this step in her own will. It had long been her constant practice to seek for divine guidance in all her undertakings.

. She keenly felt the separation from her friends at
Luton, not so much as to pecuniary assistance, (as they
continued their liberality to her to the last,) but especially as it deprived her of their Christian sympathy and
social intercourse. This discipline, she apprehended, her
naturally affectionate heart peculiarly needed, to lessen
her dependence on earthly objects, and to stimulate her
to lean more entirely on the Lord. It was her invariable
practice to breathe a prayer for her friends on receiving
assistance from them, saying that, although she felt
much difficulty in expressing her gratitude, yet she believed it was all registered on high; and she appeared to
refer all to the goodness of the Lord in disposing their
hearts to help her.

As her disease was pronounced incurable, and she could
not be retained for any length of time in the Infirmary,
a private lodging was procured for her. Her little
chamber was remarkable for neatness, though very scan-
tily furnished, and was often decorated with beautiful
flowers supplied by the kindness of her friends : of such
objects she was a great admirer, viewing them as the
work of an Almighty hand. Her personal appearance
was prepossessing, and her dress, from principle, neat
and simple. She was admitted an out-patient of the
Infirmary: one of the Surgeons of the Institution most
kindly attended upon her to the last, and while endeavouring to alleviate her sufferings, he bore ample testimony
to the fortitude and patience which she evinced; and
her gratitude for his services was beyond expression.

The following particulars, which are furnished by the
Town Missionary, refer to this period.

"My first visit to Mrs. G. was at Hitchin Infirmary.
I was much pleased with the state of her mind. On
putting some questions to her respecting the safety of
her soul, she gave me to understand that she had an
interest in Christ, and a good hope of eternal life. This
she did in such a clear and intelligent manner, that I was
led to conclude she was one of God's children, notwithstanding the very heavy affliction from which she was
suffering. On removing from the Infirmary to her
humble dwelling, she sent for me to visit her; I did so,
and must say my visits were attended with a blessing
to my own soul. She was at this time somewhat con-

erned how provision for this life was to be obtained; but although the path of Providence was dark, her trust in God was firm. She said, 'I know the Lord will provide, I believe He will never suffer me to want. When I look back upon His past care over me, it would be wicked to doubt.' Our conversations were sometimes on the doctrines of Scripture, at others on the experience of believers; upon either of these subjects she was at home. If she spoke of doctrine, her views were intelligent and well defined; if on experimental religion, there was a fulness of expression to which none but a matured saint could give utterance. On one occasion she expressed her attachment to all who love the Lord Jesus Christ, by whatever name they are called; at the same time she said, 'My views are rather peculiar; do you know I hold with the Friends in many things—I do think there is something so delightful in silently waiting upon God.' Once on my entering her room, she said, with a smile upon her countenance, 'I have been, in imagination, placing myself in my coffin and shroud, and I feel no fear.' At another time, 'I wish the time was come.'"

"Though Mrs. G. was one of the greatest sufferers I ever visited, yet upon this subject she never dwelt, but would converse upon heavenly things, until she appeared to forget that her soul was confined in such a body; proving the truth of these beautiful lines—

'Labour is rest, and pain is sweet,
If thou, my God, art near.'

"Towards the close of her life, she told me how good the Lord had been, and in a very touching manner said, 'In my first husband's lifetime we were at one period in comfortable circumstances, in fact we had all that heart could wish, but when he died I had nothing to bury him with; but the Lord raised me friends, and from that time to this I have lived upon His bounty. Oh I cannot tell His goodness!' At another time I called upon her as I was going to conduct a religious service, and said, shall I tell the people from you, that the religion of Jesus is able to support upon a dying bed? 'Yes, tell them it *can*,' she replied, 'but tell them it must be *true* religion, nothing else will do—no *form* can save.'"

To a kind female attendant, who was with her during the surgical operations, she said, "I am happier in this humble room than when surrounded by all the luxuries money could purchase; I did not then think of God, or that I had a never-dying soul, until I was visited with disappointments and bereavements, and brought to see what a poor and vain thing this world is, with all its fading pleasures—it only elevates to depress; and I also found friendship a very precarious thing indeed; and that if I did not give up all, I should be a lost creature. I *did* give up all, and sought peace with God, and obtained and enjoy it without measure. So you see, my dear friend, God has various ways in bringing us to His fold. His strokes are fewer than my crimes, and lighter than my guilt. I feel God does not willingly afflict, nor without some wise purpose. His correction is delightfully mixed with mercy—my burthen is not too heavy for me to bear—He tempers the wind to the shorn lamb, and when the *need-be* has accomplished its end, then the load is removed. Oh how precious I feel God to my soul! He is altogether lovely—the chief of ten thousand. Not one drop in all my bitter cup but what a God of love saw to be absolutely necessary. I now stand like a rock in a raging torrent with sunshine on its brow; the sky is only decked with stars in the night, so the Christian shines most in the darkness of affliction. Oh the delightful hours I spend in this humble room, in communion with my God! I have fought with heavenly weapons—I have kept my course, depending upon Him who does not fail to perform His promises; and I feel I shall soon wear a crown of righteousness at His right hand. My soul will soon be in the hands of its covenant God. The messenger of death is fast approaching to call me home. To die is gain."

While preparing to undergo the surgical operation for the last time, she thus addressed the same individual, "My dear, this is the last time I shall have to go through this operation, but I am as happy as a lamb. I often compare myself to a lamb. Although you may think my sufferings great, *I do not feel* them as such. God does all things well—I am confident He has done all things well for me. I feel, were I called to appear before Him this night, He would meet me with a smile." Her firm belief that the Lord never forsakes those who truly trust in

Him, supported her in all her trials, feeling assured that though he might permit their faith to be closely tried; yet, in His own time and way, He would help His dependent children.

It was affecting and interesting to visit her after she was confined to her bed, which was the case for some months previous to her decease,—to witness the sweet serenity of her emaciated countenance lighted up with a smile, though often in great bodily extremity, and longing to be released, and to hear her tell of the bright prospects for the future—the crown of glory that awaited her, but especially the consolation that was afforded her in secret communion with her dear Saviour. She earnestly recommended one of her friends to seek after retirement before God, saying, "It is far more profitable than going to hear the most popular preacher;" and remarked that she had been striving to get deeper in religion for some years,—that when thus waiting upon God, and looking to him for direction, the Holy Spirit is known at times to descend with a mighty influence; and that she had experienced Christ to be in her "a well of water springing up unto everlasting life." She observed, with regard to true Gospel Ministry, that the impression is deep and lasting, while that which proceeds from mere human wisdom soon fades from the memory.

On one occasion, being reminded of the language of the Saviour, "All power is given unto me in heaven and on earth," she earnestly repeated, "Yes, *all power.*"

About this time S. G. appeared to have been favoured with a divine visitation, of which she spoke with awfulness and fear;—during the night, while her husband thought her asleep, she was inwardly retired, and was permitted to enjoy sweet communion with her Saviour. From this time an increased solemnity was observable in her deportment. Once, when too ill to listen to the reading of the Scriptures, she said, she had been thinking much on the 84th Psalm; and at another time she realized the comfort contained in the following stanza, which has soothed many a departing saint—

> " Jesus can make a dying bed
>   Feel soft as downy pillows are;
>   While on His breast I lean my head,
>   And breathe my soul out sweetly there."

8

On being asked whether she felt comfortable, she said, "*Staid on the Rock.*" A similar query being put on another occasion, raising her hands and eyes, she exclaimed, "My Jesus has done all for me."

She deeply felt the prospect of separation from her husband, who had been her affectionate attendant by day and night, but was strengthened to resign him, exhorting him to live to the Lord, and then He would take care of *him* as He had done of *her* all her life long. A few days before her departure she listened attentively to the reading of the 21st chapter of Revelation, so beautifully descriptive of that city of which she hoped soon to become an inhabitant.

The day before she died she requested to be raised in her bed; and whilst supported by her husband and another person, she with great difficulty articulated, "I have got all through retirement, meditation, and secretly waiting upon God." Her kind nurse, who called on her at this time, says, "I found her very, very low, hardly strength to speak; still she was perfectly conscious, and knew me: she kissed my hand and told me she felt she was about to be released from all suffering, and that all was *peace, peace;* and added, 'My dear, I hope your end may be like mine; if so, we shall meet in everlasting happiness, never to be separated.'"

The Town Missionary, who also visited her that evening, remarks, "I heard some of the last accents from her lips,—she lifted her dying hands and exclaimed, 'There is my mansion,—I am ready to be offered;' and on my leaving said, 'We shall meet above.'" She continued sensible, though gradually sinking, till the next evening, when she peacefully expired; and we humbly trust, through the mercy of her Saviour, was permitted to enter that city "Whose walls are salvation and whose gates are praise." Her countenance in death was beautiful to look upon, and conveyed the idea of perfect rest and peace. She died the 9th of the Seventh month, 1855, aged 52 years.

END.

London: *Printed by Edward Couchman,* 10, *Throgmorton Street; for the* TRACT ASSOCIATION *of the* SOCIETY OF FRIENDS. *Sold at the* DEPOSITORY, 84, *Houndsditch.*—1860.

A
PROTESTANT MINISTER
IN A
ROMAN CATHOLIC CHAPEL
AT
NAPLES.

FROM THE LIFE OF STEPHEN GRELLET.

To-DAY I visited the Foundling Hospital, which is a very large establishment. About eighty nuns have the principal charge of it. In one part there are about four hundred girls, most of whom have attained the age of young women. It is a kind of convent. As I was going through a long corridor, accompanied by several of the nuns and priests attached to this extensive institution, we passed the door of their chapel, which was open. I saw the girls, with several nuns, on their knees before a large Madonna, or representation of the Virgin Mary, very richly and finely dressed. Wax candles were burning before it. They were singing to the image, but at the same time their faces were towards us, laughing. My soul was sorrowful on beholding them, and their superstition and idolatry. The chief of the priests who were with me asked if I did not wish to go into the church to see the girls at their devotions. I told him I should like to do so

No. 147.   [*Price* 1½*d. per dozen.*]

if it were proper. I felt a strong inclination to go in, but, as from religious principle I do not uncover my head in any place as if it was holy ground, I was unwilling to give offence to any one by going in. The nuns said, nobody here would be offended at it. The priests also said, "we have on our heads our cassocks; your hat is to you no more than these are to us, especially as it is from religious principle that you act." Then I told them I would go in, on condition that, if I apprehended it was required of me by the Lord to communicate anything to the young women thus assembled; he, the chief priest, who spoke good French, would interpret for me. He very readily agreed to do so. We all went in. Besides the girls, most of the nuns were in the church, about their great Madonna. When they had concluded singing their hymn, I told them how greatly my heart had been pained, as I passed by, on seeing the lightness of their conduct whilst engaged in what they call a devotional act; that I could not however be surprised at it, if they truly looked on that image before them as what it really is,—nothing but a piece of wood, carved by man's device, which can neither hear, nor see, neither do good nor evil to any. Our devotion, I said, is to be to Him who sees the secret of our hearts, hears not our words only, but knoweth our every thought; from Him we have everything to fear if we do not serve, obey, and honour Him; and the richest blessings to hope for if we love, fear, and serve Him. The worship acceptable to Him is to be performed in spirit and in truth, from the very heart; this is the temple in which He is to be found, and in which He revealeth Himself. Here, at noon-day, they have lighted tapers, which cannot enable them to discover the sinfulness of the heart; but the light of Christ, which enlightens every man that cometh into the world, and by which everything with which He has a controversy is made manifest, showeth us our sins, that we may look upon Him whom, by our sins, we have pierced. He is the Saviour of all those that come to him in faith and true repentance. Then I proceeded to proclaim to them the Lord Jesus Christ as the only Saviour of sinners, the only hope of salvation, the way, the truth, and the life, without whom no man can come to God the Father; all that pretend to enter by any other way than by Him, the door, are accounted as thieves and robbers. The priest interpreted faithfully into Italian, of which I could judge. The nuns and the other priests said, several times, "this is the truth," or "it is so." The countenances of the girls had much altered; they hung down their heads, and tears flowed from some of their eyes. Thus did my blessed Master enable his poor servant, in a Popish church, assisted by priests, to bear testimony to his blessed truth, and against the superstitious worship that those poor girls were offering to a carved piece of wood. After we came out, some more of the nuns collected about us, and, in answering some of their questions, I further unfolded to them what acceptable worship to God consists in, and also what is the only hope of salvation. No man can save his brother, or give to God a ransom for his soul; that, therefore, it is great presumption for any to attempt to take upon themselves to pronounce absolution from sin on a sinner. After opportunities of this sort I sometimes marvel that they do not lay their hands upon me; but here, on the contrary, they parted from me with expressions of their satisfaction with my visit. Surely this is the Lord's doing; blessed and reverend is his name!

END.

London: Printed by E. Couchman and Co., 10, Throgmorton Street; for the TRACT ASSOCIATION of the SOCIETY OF FRIENDS. Sold at the Depository, 12, Bishopsgate Street Without.—1866.

LORD BROUGHAM,

ON

THE DUTY OF HISTORIANS AND PUBLIC INSTRUCTORS IN RELATION TO WAR;

Being an Extract from his Address on his Installation as Chancellor to the University of Edinburgh.

ELOQUENCE, however, can only in these times be worthily employed in furthering objects little known to, and, if dimly perceived, little cared for, by the masters of the art in ancient days—the rights of the people, the improvement of their condition, their advancement in knowledge and refinement—above all, in maintaining the cause, the sacred cause, of peace at home and abroad. Suffer me to dwell somewhat upon the intimate connection of this last-mentioned important subject with the education of youth, the formation of their opinions, the cherishing of right feelings on the merits of those whose history is taught, or who are known as contemporaries, at least as having flourished in times near our own. Historians and political reasoners, the instructors of the people, have ill-discharged their duty in this most important respect, partaking largely in the illusions of the vulgar which they were bound to dispel : dazzled by the spectacle of great abilities, and still more of their successful exertion, they have held up to admiration the worst enemies of mankind, the usurpers who destroyed their liberties, the conquerors who shed their blood—men who in the pursuit of power or of fame made no account of the greatest sufferings they could inflict on their fellow-creatures. The worst cruelty, the vilest falsehood, has not prevented the teachers of the world from bestowing the name of " great" upon those scourges, and to this must be ascribed by far the greater part of the encouragement held out to unprincipled, profligate conduct, in those who have the destinies of nations in their hands. It is not, however, by merely dwelling with disproportionate earnestness upon the great qualities and passing over the bad ones of eminent men, and thus leaving a false general impression of them, that historians err and pervert the feelings and opinions of mankind. Even if they were to give a careful estimate of each character, and pronounce just judgment upon the whole, they would still leave by far the most important part of their duty unperformed, unless they also framed their narrative so as to excite an interest in the *worthies* of past times, to make us dwell with delight on the scenes of human improvement, to lessen the pleasure too naturally felt in contemplating successful courage or skill, whensoever these are directed to the injury of mankind; to call forth our scorn of perfidious designs, however successful, our detestation of cruel and bloodthirsty propensities, however powerful the talents by which their indulgence was secured. Instead of holding up to our admiration the " pride, pomp, and circumstance of glorious war," it is the historian's duty to make us regard with unceasing delight the ease, worth, and happiness of blesse peace. He must remember that—

> " Peace hath her victories
> No less renowned than war's ;"

and he must not forget to celebrate these triumphs the progress of science and of art, the extension an security of freedom, the improvement of national insti tutions, the diffusion of general prosperity—exhaustin on such pure and wholesome themes all the resources o his philosophy, all the graces of his style, giving honou to whom honour is due, withholding all incentives to mis placed interest and vicious admiration, and not merely b general remarks on men and events, but by the manner o describing the one and recording the other, causing us t entertain the proper sentiments, whether of respect o interest, or of aversion or indifference, for the variou subjects of the narrative. Consider for a moment wha the perpetrators of the greatest crimes that afflic humanity propose to themselves as their reward fo over-running other countries and oppressing their own t is the enjoyment of power, or of fame, or of both,

> " He can requite thee, for he knows the charms;
>   That cull fame in such martial acts as these;
> And he can spread thy name on lands and seas,
>   Whatever clime the sun's broad circle warms."

Unquestionably the renown of their deeds, their names eing illustrious in their own day, and living after them n future ages, is, if not the uppermost thought, yet one hat fills a large place in their minds. Surely if they vere well assured that every writer of genius, or even of uch merit as secured his page from oblivion, and every eacher of youth, would honestly hold up to hatred and ontempt acts of injustice, cruelty, treachery, whatever alents they might display, whatever success they might chieve, and that the opinions and the feelings of the vorld would join in thus detesting and thus scorning, it s not romantic to indulge a hope that some practical iscouragement might be given to the worst enemies of ur species. That in this as in everything else there is ction and reaction cannot be doubted. The existence of he popular feeling in its strength beguiles the historian, nd instead of endeavouring to reclaim, he panders to it. ounder and better sentiments might gradually be dif- used, and the bulk of mankind be weaned from this fatal rror, of which the heavy price is paid by themselves in he end. It is not to be denied that the degree of re- robation due to such crimes must practically depend pon the age in which they have been committed, and he nation to which the offender belongs. But one onsideration oftentimes referred to is never to be ad- nitted as an extenuation, much less a defence, of unjust ostilities—the propensity of man to war, called the ncurable propensity by those who make no attempt to pply a remedy. This is the very worst and most vulgar orm of necessity, or denying man's free will, and im- iously making Heaven the author of our guilt. But he absurdity is equal to the wickedness of the pretext. he self-same topic might be used in excuse or in pallia- ion of the ordinary crimes of pillage and murder—nay, night be applied as well to physical as moral evil, and ;iven as a reason against using the lightning rod to rotect us from the storm, or against taking precautions to escape the venom of the snake when his rattle warns us, or the fury of the tiger when he howls in the forest. . . . The multitude are in a measure the accomplices, if not the instigators, of those who, for selfish objects, betray their interest, and work their misery or their ruin. Seduced by the spectacle of triumphant force, stricken with wonder at the mere exercise of great faculties with great success, men withdraw their eyes from the means by which the ends are attained, and lose their natural hatred of wicked- ness in their admiration of genius and their sense of power. It is truly a disinterested admiration, for they themselves pay the price; and their oppression, with every suffering that misgovernment can inflict, is the result of the cruelty which they did not abhor, the meanness which they did not scorn, when dazzled with the false lustre shed over de- testable or despicable deeds by brilliant capacity crowned with victory. Napoleon knew how safely he might rely on their delusion; and he knew that the people whom he enslaved and ruined were intoxicated with the glory which he gained, and for which they so heavily paid. In one respect at least he was less to blame than they; *he* faced the danger, if he witnessed the miseries of war; while *they* in perfect safety upheld him in his course, to make their country unprofitably powerful by the slaughter of thou- sands and the misery of millions. Surely a most sacred duty is imposed upon the teachers of mankind, whether historians who record or reasoners who comment upon events, to exert all their powers for weaning them from this fatal delusion; to mark as their worst enemies those who would cherish the feelings of mutual aversion or jea- lousy between nations connected by near neighbourhood, which makes hostility most pernicious, and friendly inter- course most beneficial; and, above all, unceasingly to impress upon their minds the contrast between the empty renown of war, with its unspeakable horrors, and the solid glory of peace, as real as its blessings are substantial.

END.

London: Printed by E. Couchman & Co., 10, Throgmorton Street; for the TRACT ASSOCIATION *of the* SOCIETY OF FRIENDS. *Sold at the Depository,* 12, *Bishopsgate Street Without.*—1863,

ON

THE READING

OF THE

HOLY SCRIPTURES.

~~~~~~~~~~~~~~~~~~~~~~~

EXTRACTED FROM A WORK ENTITLED "THOUGHTS ON HABIT
AND DISCIPLINE," BY J. J. GURNEY.

~~~~~~~~~~~~~~~~~~~

LONDON:

Printed for the TRACT ASSOCIATION of the SOCIETY OF FRIENDS.

Sold at the DEPOSITORY, 12, Bishopsgate Street Without.

—

1862.

No. 131.   [*Price 3d. per dozen.*]

READING OF THE HOLY SCRIPTURES.

THE BIBLE is not given to us as a sealed book which we have no right to open when we please, or to study without the intervention of some ecclesiastical guide. It is a treasure which was never placed by Divine Providence under the key of a priesthood, but is one of the free gifts of God to man, graciously adapted by the Author of our being, to the whole of our fallen race. It is indeed an admirable evidence of the truth and divine origin of the Sacred Volume, that for its most important practical purposes—especially for the great end of the soul's salvation—it is just as intelligible to the humble but pious cottager, as it is to the most learned and cultivated among mankind.

Among good religious habits, the frequent and careful perusal of this best of all books assumes a highly important place. Young people cannot be habituated to a more profitable line of acquaintance, than that which leads to an intimacy of soul with prophets, evangelists, and apostles, and above all, with the Lord Jesus, whose example, character, and doctrine, are brought before us in the most vivid manner in the four Gospels. The daily *private* reading of Scripture ought, therefore, to be a primary object in Christian education. In following this pursuit, we shall find it a great advantage to peruse the Sacred Volume in its original languages. The Hebrew of the Old Testament is accessible, without difficulty, to every persevering student, and the Greek, which is so commonly taught in our schools, cannot be better applied, as we advance in life, than in the use of that precious volume, the Greek Testament. Independently of the consideration of its divine origin, the writings which it contains are of unrivalled force, beauty, and simplicity. Yet, doubtless, it *is* its divine origin which imparts to it the sweetness of its savour, and the strength of its charm. Here are the morals, and here the doctrines of heaven; here is a history most graphical in its touches, and most teaching in its tendency; here are prophecies which develop that mighty struggle between good and evil, between light and darkness, which has been going on, in this world of alternations, during the last eighteen centuries, and which is destined to result in the final triumph of truth and holiness. Here, above all, is presented to us the Lord Jesus Christ, the man of sorrows, the herald of peace, the pattern of virtue, the one great sacrifice for sin, suffering and triumphant, dying and living again, and now for ever exalted at the right hand of the Father, to be our Advocate with Him.

Let not those, however, who do not enjoy the privilege of reading the Scriptures in their original form, imagine for a moment that they are *at fault* with only the common English version in their hands. It is an admirable translation, dignified, clear, forcible, and generally accurate. Well may we be thankful to that Divine Providence, which has led to its being so far established by custom, rather than authority, as to have become, in effect, the one version used by all who speak the language of this country. Such a provision is far more favourable to the cause of religion, than the distraction which would be occasioned by the competition of many translations of the Bible into our language, however excellent any of them might be.

The young and well-trained member of a household, who is accustomed to the private perusal of Scripture on rising in the morning, and before he retires to rest at night, and who hears it read, or reads it himself daily in the family circle, is in the way of obtaining an *accurate* knowledge of its contents, a knowledge which he has been led to acquire by a love of the truth, and by which that love cannot fail to

be confirmed. Here, however, I would advise my young
friends, of every name and class, never to pass a day without
committing a small portion of the Sacred Volume to memory
The records of the Bible Society contain many accounts of
great attainments in this line of divine learning. It has
sometimes happened, that young persons among the poor in
Ireland, have learned by heart whole books of the New
Testament, and thus, when afterwards deprived by their
ecclesiastical guides of the Sacred Volume, they have found
themselves in happy possession of a large part of its contents. The Abyssinian Scriptures are said to have been
used in the same manner, and with the same success; and
certainly it ought to be a very general practice. Those who
thus learn the Scriptures, make them their *own* in a double
degree; and passages well committed to memory in earl
life, will generally remain in it, even to old age. Early lif
is the period for such exercises of a faculty, which is almos
sure to lose its power of retention as business multiplies
and the *brain grows old*.

There are two points which ought to be habitually
observed in the reading and interpretation of the Sacred
Volume. The first is that *broad impartiality* which prefers
simple truth to any preconceived opinions, and to any
human system. The second is a reverent dependence on
the illuminating influence of the Holy Spirit. "I have
long pursued the study of Scripture," said an aged and
revered friend of mine, long since deceased, "with a desire
to be impartial. I commit myself to the teaching of the
inspired writers, whatsoever complexion it may assume.
One thing I know assuredly, that in religion, of myself, I
know nothing. I do not, therefore, sit down to the perusal
of Scripture, in order to *impose* a sense on the prophets and
apostles, but to *receive* one as they give it me. I pretend not
to teach them; I wish, like a child, to be taught *by* them."

This principle of childlike submission to divine authority,
and of an even-handed equity in the reception and appreciation of the contents of Holy Scripture, has no more
important application than to those cardinal subjects, *justi-*

cation and sanctification. It has always appeared to me
hat the glad-tidings of salvation, which are declared to us
i Scripture, and especially in the New Testament, prin-
ipally consist of two leading and essential parts, equal to
ach other in magnitude and importance, and although
istinct in their nature and character, yet perfectly ac-
ordant, and combined by an inseparable union, in God's
wn mighty plan for the redemption of mankind.

The first of these parts finds its centre in the doctrine of
he Atonement, and relates to that which our Lord Jesus
Jhrist has already done for us of his own voluntary love
nd mercy, and wholly independently of ourselves. He hath
trodden the winepress ALONE, and of the people there was
one" with him. "He is the propitiation (or expiatory
acrifice) for our sins;" and through the all-availing offering
f Jesus on the cross, we, who are "by nature the children
f wrath," receive the forgiveness of our sins, and are recon-
iled to a just and holy God. The second grand constituent
f the Gospel of Christ, is the promise of the Holy Spirit,
nd the whole doctrine of his enlightening, enlivening, and
anctifying influences. It is by these influences that the
ving and reigning Saviour visits our dark hearts, convinces
f sin, bestows the grace of repentance, converts to a living
aith in Himself, and carries on that necessary work of
nward purification, which can alone prepare us for a state
f eternal holiness, peace, and joy.

If, in the perusal of Holy Writ, we dwell on the former
f these subjects to the exclusion of the latter, we shall
oon fall into antinomianism; and if on the latter, to the
xclusion of the former, we shall be in danger of being
veighed down, even unto destruction, by the burden of our
ast sins. We stand in absolute need of the pardon of
ur past transgressions through the atoning sacrifice of
esus; and equally do we require a deliverance from present
in, by the power of the Holy Spirit. Let us then cleave,
vith equal love, and zeal, and reverence, to both these
ranches of divine truth. Justification and sanctification
re joined together by the hand of our God, and must never

be dissevered. If one of them occupy a less space in ou
minds and feelings than the other, our Christianity will soo:
become defective or distorted, just in the degree in whic.
the holy balance between them is sacrificed and lost. Ca:
anything be more clear or more emphatic than the numerou:
passages of Scripture, in which the sacred writers, and ou:
Saviour himself in his ministry, set forth the doctrine of hi:
mediation and expiatory death? Is there anything mor:
lucidly stated, or more carefully insisted on in the Bible
than the gracious work and offices of the Holy Spirit? Th:
foundation will be of no use to us, if we build nothing upo:
it; and our building is a cloud or a shadow—a mere castl:
in the air—if it does not rest on Christ, the Rock of ages.

Persons may entertain very different, and sometimes eve:
opposite views on some other doctrines of religion, whic.
are by no means destitute of importance; and they may b:
very far from agreeing one with another, either in opinio:
or practice, in relation to church government and modes o:
worship; and yet if they thoroughly embrace the sacre:
truths now adverted to, and hold them in even balances
tracing both these lines of mercy to the fathomless depth o:
the love of God the Father, they are severally in the wa:
of experiencing the blessed effects of Christianity, so fa:
as relates to its main purpose—the salvation of the soul
Being baptised by the one Spirit into the one needful faith
and being followers of one and the same Lord, they ar:
fellow-members of the one Church of Christ upon earth
and may look forward to the perfection of their union i:
the world to come.

> " Yes, let the future smile or mourn,
> To us a glorious place is given,
> With the great church of the first-born,
> Whose names are registered in heaven.
> Beyond the bounds of time's expansion,
> Where change and sorrow never come,
> We're journeying to the promised mansion,
> Made ready in our Father's home.

Friends, kindred, loving and beloved,
That wont on earth our lot to cheer,
Thither are, one by one, removed,
And we shall find them *settled there.*
Enough! though sin, and pain, and death,
This transitory world infest,
They who attain to Abraham's faith,
Shall be with faithful Abraham blessed.". . . .

. . . . . HANKINSON.

The points on which Christians differ are unquestionably
not to be disregarded. It is greatly to be desired that on
these points also, light and truth should spread, and that the
simple, broad, spiritual views held out to us in the Holy
Scriptures, should be accepted in their native fullness, and
primitive strength. Nevertheless, it is an excellent habit of
mind—one which we cannot too carefully cherish in ourselves and others—to view the various parts of the fabric
of truth *in their right proportions;* not allowing secondary
points, however interesting they may be to ourselves, to
occupy a larger portion of our field of vision, than properly
belongs to them in the order of the Gospel. Such a habit of
mind will never discourage us in the faithful support and
diligent pursuit of truth; at the same time it will greatly
aid us in the maintenance of that Christian love which is
the badge of discipleship. The good old motto was never
more important than in the present-day of polemical strife
and sectarian prejudice, "In essentials, UNITY; in non-
essentials, LIBERTY; in all things, CHARITY."

It is abundantly evident that we shall never comply with
these principles, or form the habit now recommended,
while we lean to our own understandings, and follow the
counsels of our own hearts. Man is by nature prone to
dark and distorted views, and there is nothing more common even among persons who make a high profession of
religion, than a zeal which is "not according to knowledge."
It is only as we are favoured with the help and guidance
of the Holy Spirit, and submit to his influence, that we
can correctly perceive, and rightly appreciate the various
parts of divine truth. There can be no saving knowledge of

the Gospel of Christ without this influence. "For wha man knoweth the things of a man, save the spirit of mar which is in him? even so the things of God knoweth no man, but the Spirit of God. Now we have received, not the spirit of the world, but the Spirit which is of God; that we might know the things that are freely given to us of God. . . . . . The natural man receiveth not the things of the Spirit of God . . . . . neither can he know them because they are spiritually discerned. But he that i spiritual judgeth (or discerneth,) all things, yet he himsel is judged (or discerned,) of no man. For who hath kno the mind of the Lord, that he may instruct him? But w have the mind of Christ." 1 Cor. ii. 11—16.

It is indeed our duty to avail ourselves of every mean within our reach, for ascertaining the meaning of Scripture, and for developing its almost endless riches. History, geography, the records of ancient customs, and the testimony of modern travellers—not to mention the critical study of the original languages, and philology in all its legitimate applications—have a very important place, as means of an accurate acquaintance with the volume which contains the ever blessed charter of the liberty of souls. Yet that charter may be effectually read and understood by those who have little or no access to these various sources of information; and whether we be numbered among the learned or ignorant of mankind, it is only as we are *habituated*, in the reading of Scripture, to a watchful dependence on the influences of the Spirit—correcting our dispositions and enlightening our vision—that we shall obtain that true and experimental knowledge of religion, on which the value of the book depends.

END.

Printed by E. Couchman and Co., 10, Throgmorton Street, London.

BRIEF MEMOIR

FRANCIS HOWGIL,

OF TODHORNE, NEAR GRAYRIGG, WESTMORELAND.

~~~~~~~~~~~~~~~~~~~~

FRANCIS HOWGIL was born about the year 1618. He received an university education, and being of a serious turn of mind, became a teacher among several bodies of professing Christians successively, until about the thirty-fourth year of his age; when he united with the religious Society of Friends, among whom he became a devoted minister of the Gospel.

He has left upon record an interesting account of his early religious experience. He tells us, that when twelve years of age, he earnestly sought "to know that God whom the world professed," of whom he read in Holy Scripture, and whom Abraham, Moses, the Prophets, and Apostles, served and worshipped. He became very strict in his religious observances; he often sought retirement, and gave himself to reading and meditation. He began to perceive that the sports in which youth so much delights "are vanity, and last but for a moment." When he had indulged in folly, he found afterward that he was condemned in himself for what he had done, and this sense of judgment for sin often caused him to weep. Then, for some time he would refrain: but again the temptation offered, and again he was overcome. He therefore, endeavoured to abstain from the company of those, who, by their conduct and conversation, allured him into evil; and, he says, he did not go to the former excesses, although "something in him hankered after them;" but as he obeyed the checks of conscience, he had peace.

No. 132.   [*Price 4d. per dozen.*]

He now devoted himself to reading the Holy Scriptures and other religious works; engaged in vocal prayer, "often three or four times a day;" yet, he says, he "knew not where God was, but imagined a God at a distance." Being still condemned for yielding to frivolity and conduct unbecoming a professor of religion, he adopted a course yet more strict, and would go five or six miles to hear the discourse of some noted minister, or as they phrased it, "some more excellent means." Nevertheless, he only grew in words; he found himself still the same, nay, worse—for knowledge puffed him up.

Such continued to be his condition for several succeeding years; when at length his attention was turned *within.* Then it was shown him that his heart was corrupt; and as he kept the eye of his mind directed to the light in his conscience, he was restrained from many things he would otherwise have yielded to: for often in the very instant when about to commit sin, either in word or deed, he was stopped. Thus he saw himself preserved out of the error to which he had been in danger to yield, and great joy arose in him and peace; but when, through disobedience to that which thus checked him, he did anything forwardly or rashly, he was judged in himself for his deed. But his teachers persuaded him it was only his "natural conscience;" and hearkening to them, he slighted that heavenly light which *illuminated* his "natural conscience," as being too low a thing, only "common grace." They told him, that the saints had "a peculiar grace and faith." So listening to those who darkened counsel by words without knowledge, he suffered loss; but, he says, he was still convicted of sin.

Again, Francis Howgil observes, they said that the saints believed in Christ, and therefore, His righteousness was imputed to them, and sin was not imputed; "so that I must seek Him in the means, as prayer and receiving the sacrament, (as they called it) and they judged me a worthy communicant; and I was in great fear lest I should eat unworthily; and none could instruct me what the body of Christ was."

He continues: "At one time I read all the Scriptures that spake of Christ's sufferings. The teachers said I must believe that He suffered for *me;* and I believed it all, yet I could not see how he died for *me,* and had taken away *my* sin: for the witness for God in my conscience told me I was the servant of sin while I committed it. They told me I must not omit that ordinance, (the sacrament so called) or thereby faith was confirmed and strength added. On he one hand, they pressed it as a duty; on the other, I saw hat the Scriptures said, 'He that eateth unworthily, eateth lamnation to himself.' I was in fear, though none from vithout could accuse me. I thought I had sinned against he Holy Ghost, and great trouble fell upon me. Then hey said I had not come prepared; yet I had all the pre- paration they had spoken of; but they were physicians of 10 value."

Francis Howgil informs us that, at this period, he fasted, nd prayed, and walked mournfully, and thought surely 1one were like him, buffeted and tempted on every hand. He ran from one man to another for help, and they re- ninded him of the promises; but he could not apply them, or he knew that the body of sin was whole, and that the 'oot of iniquity remained within him. When he told them hat he felt there was guilt in him, they replied that our sin vas taken away by Christ, but that the guilt will remain as ong as we live. So he would say within his heart, this is a niserable salvation, that the guilt and condemnation of sin hall still remain! Thus, though preserved from gross evil, orrow continued to encompass him, and he was led to ques- ion all he had ever experienced, which he had been led to believe was grace, repentance, or faith.

At length he came to the conclusion, that surely these could not belong to the ministry of Christ! He withdrew iimself from their teaching, and retiring into solitude, poured but his soul before the Lord, and wept. All that he had ever done, seemed then to be brought to his remembrance, nsomuch that even every thought was judged. His heart vas tendered and greatly broken. When he could sorrow nost, he had most peace; for something spake within him rom the Lord, though he fully knew Him not then. He ays, he "was told that it was heresy to expect 'the word of he Lord' to be spoken in these days," for that it was "only o be found in the Scriptures," so he was induced not *much* o regard it; yet he was, nevertheless, led to do many ighteous things by the immediate power and word of God. Then peace and joy sprang up in him, and the promise was. pplied to him, that God himself would be his Teacher and iis God. And he often obeyed the immediate guidance of God's Holy Spirit, though the attraction might be in a lirection contrary to his own will, and in doing so, denied iimself; but this he was told was "legal," and was "slavery." He therefore tried to get above fear, and united in what are

termed "ordinances,"* which they said was son-like obedience, because "Christ had done *all* without us."

Yet he was not at rest. Though he had joined one society
of religionists after another, he found no peace, no guide.
Some preached the doctrine of free grace, as they termed
it; namely, that all sin is done away by Christ, past, present,
and future; and said that it is only necessary to believe this
doctrine, and all is finished. To this, he hearkened a little,
and so lost strength. But which ever way he turned, this
language was spoken in him, "His servant thou art whom
thou dost obey;" and knowing that he was overcome by sin,
he says, he had no justification witnessed in him, but condemnation.

Then some preached Christ within, who were themselves
without. And these spoke of redemption and justification
within, and of God appearing in man, and overcoming the
power of the devil. He tells us, "The light in my conscience bore witness that it must be so; and I was exceedingly pressed to wait and find it so; and something in me

---

* In reference to the observance of those ceremonial usages termed
"ordinances," which Francis Howgil was led to apprehend it was no
longer his place to unite in, it may be proper to remark, for the information of sincere Christians, into whose hands this brief memoir may
come, that the religious Society of Friends have always declined to make
use of outward symbols in worship, because they believe that all *types*
were done away in Christ, when by His "one offering" He abrogated
the Law of Moses for ever. It is expressly declared in the New Testament, that when the Lord Jesus cried out upon the cross "It is finished,"
the vail of the Temple was rent in twain, and the way into the holiest of
all made manifest. Thus the Law with its types and shadows passed
away, and the New and Last Dispensation of Sonship was brought in,
under which "the good things themselves to which the shadows of the
Law had pointed, were freely offered to the acceptance of every believer
in Christ." Entertaining this clear conviction, Friends deem it incon-
gruous, and therefore, unsuitable for them, as Christians, still to adhere
to the use of "shadows," *as if the time were not yet arrived when the*
good things foreshadowed could be obtained. They hold that the time
has arrived, when all who are fully brought into the Gospel Dispensation,
are permitted to sit down in heavenly places with Christ Jesus, and to
drink of "new wine" with Him in His Father's kingdom; that such do eat
His flesh, do drink His blood, and grow thereby to the stature of men
in Him. For they have been regenerated, not by the baptism of John,
who only baptised with water unto repentance, and which was intended
merely as a type,) but by that inward and spiritual baptism which now
saveth,—the baptism of the Holy Ghost and fire. Their hearts thus
purified and made clean, Christ condescends to make them His temple;
there He dwells, and there He teaches them by His Spirit. These are
not designed to continue under the Law, as under a schoolmaster, but
under Christ; and such possessing Christ, "possess all things."

breathed after the living God. And I had a true love to all that walked honestly, of what profession soever; and I hated their reviling one another, or that they should persecute one another, and I always took part with the sufferer. But I saw that though these spoke of things *within*, and of a power to come, they enjoyed not what they spake of; for the same fruits were still brought forth. At last, I saw that none walked as the ministers of Christ; none that pretended to the ministry had any such gift, nor were any of them such members as were in the Apostles' times: and I got myself rid of them, for always as I dissented from their judgment, they hated and persecuted me."

"Now it was revealed in me, that the Lord would teach His people Himself. So I waited. And the word of the Lord was in me, that the time was at hand, when the dead should hear the voice of the Son of God. And it burned in me as a fire that the day was near, when it should not be said, 'Lo, here! nor Lo, there!' but all the Lord's people should be taught of Him. Still, my mind ran out into carelessness; for I knew not (an abiding under) the cross of Christ. Yet I had ever, as my mind was turned to the Light, pure openings; and a belief that I should see the day, and bear witness to His name. So when things opened so fast, the wisdom of the flesh caught them, and I went up, and down preaching against all the ministry. I also ran out with that which was revealed in myself, and preached up and down the country out of the fulness that was in the old bottle, and was wondered after and admired by many who had waded up and down like myself: and we fed one another with words, and healed up one another in deceit, and all laid down in sorrow when the day of the Lord was made manifest. For I was overthrown, and my foundation swept away, and my righteousness and my unrighteousness were judged, and weighed, and found too light."

At this period, 1652, George Fox was the means of convincing the teachers of the congregation accustomed to meet at Firbank Chapel, Westmoreland, who joined in Christian profession with him; and among them, was the subject of this brief sketch.

Francis Howgil thus refers to the important change which then took place in his religious views. "As soon," he says, as "I heard one declare, that the Light of Christ in man, is the way to Christ, I believed the eternal word of truth, and the Light of God in my conscience sealed to it. I saw it was the true and faithful witness for Christ Jesus.

My eyes were opened; the dreadful day of the Lord fell upon me, sorrow, pain, fear, terror, for the sight that I saw with mine eyes. In the morning I wished it had been evening, and in the evening I wished it had been morning: I sought death in that day and could not find it; it fled from me. I became as a fool and a man distracted. All was overturned! I suffered the loss of all; for all that ever I did, I saw was in the accursed nature."

"But as I bore the indignation of the Lord, [I found] the serpent's head began to be bruised. And as I gave up all to judgment, the captive came forth out of prison, and my heart was filled with joy. I came to behold Him whom I had pierced. Then I saw the cross of Christ, and stood by it; and the enmity was slain by it, the new man was made, (so making peace;) and eternal life was brought in, through death and judgment. I received from God the perfect gift; the holy law of God was revealed unto me, and was written in my heart; and His fear and His word which did kill, now made alive."

"Thus it pleased the Father, to reveal His Son in me through death, and I came to witness cleansing by His blood, which is eternal. I have peace in doing the will of God, and am entered into the true rest, and lie down with the lambs in the fold of God, where the sons of God rejoice together, and the saints keep holiday."

Such is the substance of Francis Howgil's account of his own religious experience. And now, introduced into the glorious liberty of the Gospel, and prepared and ordained by Christ, the Head of the Church, to preach that Gospel to others, he was concerned to do so *freely*, without receiving wages for his preaching; and we are told that, no longer satisfied to retain the money he had formerly received for his services as a teacher, in the parish of Colton, in Furness Fells, Lancashire, he believed himself "commanded of the Lord to go and return that money to the parish and people from which he had received it;" which he accordingly did.

In 1652, the year in which he became a "Friend," he travelled, in company with James Naylor, in the work of the ministry, through portions of his native county of Westmoreland; and though from the arbitrary and intolerant spirit of that, comparatively, unenlightened day, they were both subjected to an unjust imprisonment of nearly five months, in Appleby gaol, for their preaching; yet, after his liberation, he continued to journey up and down on foot, boldly declaring the word of the Gospel, and directing the attention of the people to Christ Jesus, as their Teacher and their Saviour.

In 1654, he laboured extensively in London, along with Edward Burrough, and other ministers; and large meetings of Friends were in consequence established in the city. In the following year they visited Ireland, and after establishing meetings of Friends in Dublin, and other places, they were expelled the nation by order of Henry Cromwell, Lord Deputy of Ireland.

In 1661, he was imprisoned in London, on the false accusation of being concerned in the insurrection made by the "Fifth Monarchy Men;" and in 1663, he was arrested in the market at Kendal, where he was peaceably engaged in the affairs of his business. He was at once brought before the bench of magistrates; who, having no transgression wherewith to charge him, gratuitously tendered to him the oath of allegiance and supremacy, (well knowing that, for conscience' sake, he could not swear at all;) and upon his refusal, committed him a prisoner to Appleby gaol. Tried at the assizes, he was sentenced to a "præmunire," which was then considered to comprehend, imprisonment for life; and the forfeiture of his goods and chattels to the king. On judgment being pronounced, Francis Howgil observed, "A hard sentence for my obedience to the commands of Christ! The Lord forgive you all."

He never recovered his liberty, but bore his prolonged imprisonment with fortitude and much patience; indeed, he dates one of his letters of counsel to Friends, "From Appleby gaol, the place of my rest, where my days and hours are pleasant unto me." His meekness and Christian resignation, gained him the esteem of the gaoler and his family; as well as of the inhabitants of Appleby, many of whom were wont to refer their differences to his arbitration.

After nearly five years' detention, he was seized with his last illness, which was only of about nine days' duration. He continued very fervent in prayer, and uttered many sweet expressions, to the refreshment of those who were with him.

On one occasion he observed, " God will own His people, even those who are faithful. As for me, I am well, and content to die; and truly one thing I have observed, which is, that this generation passeth fast away. We see many precious Friends within these few years have been taken from us; therefore Friends had need to watch and be very faithful, so that we may leave a good, and not a bad savour to the succeeding generation; for it is but a little time that any of us have to stay here."

At another time he remarked, "This was the place of my first imprisonment for the Truth; and if it be the place of my laying down the body, I am content."

Several respectable inhabitants of Appleby, (among them the mayor) not of the Society of Friends coming to see him, some of them prayed that God might speak peace to his soul; to whom he sweetly observed, "God hath done it."

A few hours before his death, he said, "I have sought the way of the Lord from a child, and lived innocently as among men; and if any enquire concerning my latter end, let them know that I die in the faith which I lived and suffered for."

After this, he uttered words of prayer to God, and peacefully finished his course, a prisoner for the testimony of Jesus.

He died in 1669, in the fiftieth year of his age; having been a minister among Friends for about seventeen years.

[Caton MSS.: G. Fox's Journal: Francis Howgil's Works: Sewel's History of Friends: Besse's Sufferings: Biographical Memoirs of Friends.]

END.

London: Printed by Edward Couchman, 10; *Throgmorton Street: for the* TRACT ASSOCIATION *of the* SOCIETY OF FRIENDS. *Sold at the Depository,* 84, *Houndsditch.*—1857.

A

SHORT ACCOUNT

OF

JOHN STICKLAND.

LONDON:

Printed for the TRACT ASSOCIATION of the SOCIETY OF FRIENDS.
Sold at the DEPOSITORY, 12, Bishopsgate Street Without.

—

1865.

No. 133.   [*Price* 5½ *per dozen.*]

JOHN STICKLAND.

TRUE religion is the work of the Holy Spirit upon the soul. It does not consist in a subscription to creeds or confessions of faith, or in any outward observances, however good in themselves; but in the dedication of the heart to God, and the entire surrender of the will and affections to his government.

John Stickland was born near Worth, in Dorsetshire, in the year 1753. His life, though not passed in an exalted station amongst men, presents another testimony to the power of Divine Grace to preserve from evil, amid great temptations and under many disadvantages; and also of its efficacy to instruct in the knowledge of those things which belong to the salvation of the soul.

He was brought up in the profession of the Established Church, and attended the place of worship of the parish where he lived. But falling into the company of wicked boys, he gradually became much corrupted, and indulged in singing songs and other idle pastimes. The good Spirit of God, however, did not fail to warn him of his evil practices, and reprove him for them. About his fourteenth year he was more powerfully visited, and, being awakened to a sense of his sinful condition, he sought, even with tears, for a state of redemption. Still, however, the force of temptation again overcame him, and he fell back into his former practices. When about eighteen, he was again awakened and alarmed under a sense of his sins, but no effectual change seems to have been wrought in him. He sought to fly from conviction, and to drown his sorrow, by frequenting the company of young persons, and indulging in music and dancing, and went farther in folly than he had before done. But he could not stifle the pure Witness in his conscience. His convictions grew deeper and more poignant, until he became hateful in his own eyes, and feared lest the earth should open and swallow him up, as he had read it did some wicked men in ancient days.

About this time the Lord was pleased to visit him with a fever, which brought him, apparently, to the borders of the grave. In this reduced state, the Holy Spirit again opened his condition to him, and he was awfully affected at the sight of it. For some time he seemed destitute of all hope of salvation; but at length he experienced a state of contrition, in which his heart was broken, and his spiritual eye opened to look, in a degree of faith, upon Christ Jesus as the Saviour of sinners, who could not only forgive his past transgressions, but make him holy in heart and life.

Speaking, in after life, of the work of the Holy Spirit in his heart, he says, " I am a witness of the grace of God. I was one of the most vain and wicked, and lived among the wicked. I saw myself going to destruction. I felt my sins a heavy burden. I cried out, ' Mercy! mercy! O what shall I do to be saved?' I was led to Jesus Christ for redemption through his blood. I obtained pardon, and went on my way rejoicing."

He now felt it to be his duty to be very circumspect in all his conduct and conversation; and the preacher of the parish where he lived, being an irreligious man, he left him and went to a dissenting meeting. These things drew upon him the censure of his relations and neighbours. He says, " After I was awakened, when I went to church and saw the irreverence, and heard the superficial sermons of our parish minister, my heart was filled with grief, so that I thought I could suffer the cutting off of my arm, to open the eyes of one of them, if that would do it. But, alas! I found them, even my own relations, like a fox in a trap, which will bite you, if you attempt to liberate him, thinking you are an enemy. Instead of attending to my admonitions, they said I was beside myself; that I worshipped the moon and stars, and prayed to hayricks and trees, because I went out to meditate in the fields, and in summer evenings walked in private places to read my Bible. When I went to church, I was noticed for my devotion, and the minister said I was not now like any one of his people, and he thought the devil was in me, and that I should become an enthusiast."

In a manuscript account which he left, of some incidents of his life, he says, " When my father left East Holme, I was retained by my master on the farm, and soon became a servant in the house. At this time he had taken a housekeeper, who had lived with the late clergyman of Winfrith in a very unchristian manner. She, with my master's footman and housemaid, were living in a very loose and extravagant manner, drinking, gambling, &c., which I took the liberty to reprove and counteract, as I had begun to seek the favour of God, and live up to my profession. But my conduct was highly displeasing to [the housekeeper,] because I could not drink, dance, and play cards with them. On one occasion she said to me, ' Thou hast no taste for a game of cards, or a dance, or a merry song, or jest, but *the Bible—the Bible*—is all with thee. I would not that thou shouldst visit me on a deathbed for all the world, for fear I should die in despair.' ' But,' said I, ' if reading my Bible gives me as much pleasure as your cards give you, I am not behindhand with you, even in this life ; and I am certain it will give me more comfort, on a deathbed, to reflect on reading the Bible, than it will give you to remember your waste of time in cards.' ' I think that, too,' said she, ' and then I shall be on the wrong side. But how is it that I can sing songs, dance, and play cards, and yet go to church on Sundays, and all is well with me, and I can enjoy myself and be happy ? But I have observed that if thou dost only join with us to laugh and jest *a little*, I see in thee afterward a look of grief and a shyness of our company. I see no harm in a merry jest.' ' No,' said I, ' your mind is like a dark room. The window is closed—you cannot see what is in your heart. But the curtain is drawn, in a degree, from my window, and I can see the evil of sin, and what sin is in the sight of the Lord, so as to hate and avoid it, or else to become a miserable soul.' "

Finding both his precepts and example to be a constant testimony against their wickedness, and an obstacle to the license which they desired, the other servants, and especially the housekeeper, endeavoured to prejudice his master against him, and get him turned away. His absenting himself from the national worship, to which his master was attached, was used as one means for this purpose.

On this subject he remarks :

" The housekeeper stirred up my master against me because I could not go to church. Once in two weeks I went to Corfe Castle, by eight o'clock in the morning, to hear a Methodist preacher, and thence to Wareham. My master called for me, and threatened to discharge me, if I would not go to church, and asked me why it was ? I told him the church minister was a wicked man, and his doctrine very superficial and false in its application, and therefore I could not hear him. ' Then,' said he, ' we must part ; there are your wages.' I answered, ' My soul is of more value to me than all you have in the world is to you ; nor will I sell it for money, nor suffer your blind teacher to lead me to destruction. Liberty of conscience is my birthright, and I will not sell it for the world.' So I took up my money, and, with my best wishes for his salvation, left the room. Soon after, he called for me again, and said, ' You shall have your birthright, if you will stay with me; and I will give you more wages, and you shall go where you wish to a place of worship. Will you stay with me ? ' ' Yes,' said I, ' on such terms, except a rise of wages. Let that be as you please. I do not ask it.' He then said ' I will make my observations on you and on your enemies, to see who behave most properly.' So I went on in my duty to my God, and to my master, and to my aged and afflicted mother; my soul prospered, and I enjoyed good health."

"The housekeeper continued to speak against me to my master, and told many false things, but I never spoke against them to him, but reproved them to their faces, going on in my duty to him and to the Lord. I was as a Mordecai in the gate. It came to pass, however, that their conduct became known to him, and it fell upon their own heads, as was the case with Haman. The Lord prospered my undertaking on the farm. I took care of the young cattle. As I was feeding the calves, at the end of a field, I saw my master coming to me in great haste, and looking angry. When he came near me, he said in a loud voice, ' John, I have found out your enemies. They fear not God, nor care for my interest. I will discharge them all, and you shall be over all my business, for you only have I found faithful. * * * * has been making a gallows for you these three years, and now she shall be hanged on it herself. I will go home and give them all notice to go, then I will come to you again.' "

Soon after this, he saw his master coming to him again, who said to him, " I now give you the choice of two things : one is to look after my farm and pay my people, with a rise in your wages; or, secondly, to attend on me and keep accounts, both within and without, and I will satisfy you for your services. Let me know in two weeks. * * *

" When I do not ride my horse on Sunday, you take it out of the stable, and ride it to Wareham [to meeting]. I will give you this coat from my back, which is almost new, and will make you a fine Sunday dress."

The servants, who had been plotting to effect John's ruin, were soon discharged, and he became the writer and accountant of his employer, conducting himself with such strict propriety and uprightness as to obtain a large place in his affection and confidence. Having neither wife nor child to be his companion, he conversed the more freely with John, who had thus opportunities of conveying religious views to his mind, and, there is reason to believe, was made useful to him.

Another enemy, however, sprung up in a gardener, who was sometimes employed on the premises, and, being in the habit of smoking tobacco, used to call for frequent draughts of strong beer with his pipes. This John refused to give him, when the keys came into his hands, because it was his master's property. Offended at his refusal, he sought to prejudice his master against John; but his efforts turned to his own disadvantage, and he was himself discharged from the premises.

Keeping a single eye to his inward Guide, John prospered in his undertakings, and found favour with his employer.

At the expiration of nearly fourteen years his master was affected with paralysis, and on John's going to him, remarked, " I am soon to leave this world, of which I know little, and am going to the world of which I know nothing ; for which change I am unprepared. I am sorry that I ever discouraged you in religion. I now see there is no such thing as happy living or dying without true religion—I say *true religion*."

" As my master drew near his end, he became more and more attached to me. He was deeply convinced of his fallen state. I feel happy in reflecting on my conduct towards him. There is indeed no real happiness, except we are in Christ, and live to him and not to ourselves. Reader! may you so live as to die in the Lord, and be for ever happy in His presence. After his interment, and all charges paid, I gave up to my new master the book and balance of all accounts, and had the blessing of a good conscience. He then committed [the farm] East Holme, and all the people and stock into my hands, and I became his bailiff, and had the care of it for about fourteen years after. He came there only occasionally, for a few weeks at a time."

The book of expenses, above alluded to, was placed in the hands of an attorney to copy. This man had drawn the will of John Stickland's former master, and persuaded him to let the farm and make him (the attorney) the steward for it; but after the will was executed, he became so uneasy, that he had the attorney called, and altered it so as to provide for J. S., as has already been stated. This circumstance irritated the mind of the attorney, who sought occasion against him, as will be seen by the following narrative.

" When the parliament ended that year, J. Bond came to Holme, and informed me of a deficit in my accounts ; saying he had taken the book to his chamber, and had searched it with great care and diligence for two weeks, and found that more than £ 100 were missing, and that his brother, my master, had likewise examined and found it so. Yet, said he, we do not really suspect you of swindling. I said, ' If there be a fraud, I am the man [who have committed it], for I took and paid all, without the help of any other person, and I have a good conscience.' He said, ' My brother will come soon, when the circuit ends ; ask him for the book, and examine it for yourself.' This report raised fears and perturbation of mind, and I cried unto the Lord for wisdom and direction how to find out the embezzlement; for I could appeal to him for my innocence in the affair."

" In a few weeks my master came, and I asked him for the book, which he kindly gave into my hand. I took it aside to trace the copy, and found it right. I then cast up the columns, and found them correct. Then I feared and cried in my heart, Lord ! What shall I do ? The Red Sea is before me, and the Egyptians behind me. I then felt a strong impression of mind, as though a voice said audibly, *Carry over—carry over.* I began at once to carry over the columns, and soon found one that was *four* hundred pounds, but the attorney had carried over only *three.* Then I proceeded to carry over the other sums, and found another where £ 14 12s. 7½d. was left back. I went to my master and said, ' I have found it out.' ' You have not—you cannot,' said he. I replied, ' I have.' ' I cannot give you credit for it,' said he. ' Please to see; here are £ 400, and the attorney has carried only £ 300.' ' Ah! so it is,' he said. ' See again: here is £ 14 12s. 7½d. left out of the sum carried over.' ' So it is,' said master, ' and you are wiser than all of us. Here are five guineas for you, and I will never mistrust you as long as I live.' Soon after, my master's sisters came to see him, and when they saw me, said, ' We wish you joy ; you have sustained your character.' In like manner every one of the worthy family addressed me, at the first interview after my innocence was proved.

" But what was yet more gratifying, was a letter my master sent me from London, to say he was not coming into the country at this season, and that I was to receive his rents, and if I wanted money on the farm account, I was to keep it, and send him only what I could spare. He also stated that the attorney was indebted to him such a sum, and I was to call upon him for it. I carried the letter to show the aforesaid attorney my authority; at the sight of which he was greatly agitated, and paid me the money. ' You thought, I suppose,' said I, ' to hang or transport me for cheating my master. But you did not know that I had a Counsellor to teach me, wiser than all the attorneys in the world.' At this he muttered something, and I came away, singing, in my heart, the song of Moses :—' The enemy said I will pursue ; I will overtake ; I will divide the spoil ; my hand shall destroy them ! Thou didst blow with thy wind ; the sea covered, them—they sank as lead in the mighty waters. Who is like unto Thee, O Lord ; among the gods, who is like unto Thee ! '

"My master, by his abilities and talents, became a great man. I lived under him thirty-three years in all good conscience. For a few years before his death he suffered much, and declined by slow degrees. I cannot recollect a word or action that will plant a thorn in my dying pillow respecting him. For his salvation, I sent up my cries to God, especially when near his end."

In his diary he says :

" At Bath I became acquainted with a poor man, a member of the Society of Friends. He said to me, I compare the relating of religious experience, too freely, to a bottle in which is a precious perfume. If the cork be drawn often, the scent will evaporate, and the sweet savour be lost."

During the early religious exercise of John Stickland, and before he had attained to an abiding sense of Divine counsel and favour, a person placed in his hands a Popish book, the reading of which brought him into much conflict and distress. His mind was greatly agitated with doubts and difficulties which he found himself unable to resolve. But as he honestly endeavoured to seek for a knowledge of the Truth as it is in Jesus, He who teacheth as never man taught, was pleased to open his understanding, and enable him to see clearly into the errors of that dark delusion. The exercises he had passed through on these subjects prepared him to be useful to others in after life, an instance of which is as follows :

About the 24th year of his age, he accompanied his first master, Nathaniel Bond, to a meeting of custom-house and excise officers at West Lulworth. At the inn where they quartered he saw some tracts in favour of Popery, which the landlady told him belonged to a person who lodged there, and was eagerly endeavouring to propagate his opinions among the neighbours. " We are all such fools here," said she, " that we cannot answer him, but I think you could; and I hope you will. He'll be in by and by, and will be sure to have something to say to you."

This brought J. S. under deep concern. He retired to a solitary place among the rocks near the cove, where he earnestly sought the Lord, and asked counsel of Him who has promised both wisdom and utterance to his dependent children in every time of need. "I felt myself," said he, "but a youth and a stripling, unaccustomed to war, while this priest appeared as Goliath. At length I felt assured that the God of Israel, in whom alone I trusted, would be with me to teach me what to say." On his return to the inn, he found the priest in company with several of the officers, and he soon challenged J. S. to dispute with him relative to the Popish and Protestant faith. J. S. proposed that they should have their conversation in some more private and quiet place; but the priest said, "No place is more suitable than this, that all the company may hear the arguments on both sides."

The persons present seemed deeply interested in the discussion; and, by keeping watchful and attentive to the openings of Truth, John was enabled to answer the priest in a satisfactory manner. About the middle of the conversation, one of the officers arose and said: "I wish I was not obliged to leave—but must beg to offer one remark, which is, that our friend Stickland has both reason and Scripture on his side; but as for you, (turning to the priest,) you have neither." Chagrined at this unlooked-for address, the priest seemed troubled, and, before the close of the debate, was quite confounded. The landlady said afterward, that from that day the priest left off trying to persuade people into Popery, and never held up his head again while amongst them, saying he was tired of his religion, which, in a little while, he entirely renounced.

In his thirty-sixth year, John Stickland was married to Elizabeth Gwyer, a native of Downton, in Wilts. In partnership with Hannah Beauchamp, she had previously entered into the drapery and grocery business at Wareham. Though he embarked in this business, he still retained his situation on the farm at East Holme, going and returning daily. His prospects of domestic happiness, in his humble sphere of life, were bright, but it pleased his heavenly Father soon to cloud them; for in about eleven months his wife was taken from him. Deeply as he was stricken by this unexpected bereavement, he was afterward prepared to acknowledge the wisdom and mercy of the dispensation, saying, "I loved her too well; therefore the Lord took her from me." The flail that strikes hard separates the wheat from the chaff.

In 1792, John Stickland was married to Hannah Beauchamp, and they united in endeavouring to seek first the kingdom of heaven. They had five children, whom they were concerned to train up in the fear of the Lord. John had long seen the inconsistency of wearing gay and fashionable attire, with the simplicity of true religion ; and both he and his wife laboured to instil into the minds of their children the duty of self-denial in this respect, adopting for them, upon principle, a plain and simple dress. J. Wesley remarks: "You who are fond of dress, know in your hearts, that it is with a view to be admired that you thus adorn yourselves, and that you would not be at the pains, were there none to see you but God and His holy angels. O stop, then! aim at pleasing God alone, and all these ornaments will soon drop off."

No less concerned was J. S. to watch against other things, the tendency of which is to inspire pride and vanity. On sending one of his daughters to school, he charged the governess never to call her *Miss,* observing, " Pride comes fast enough without that."

About the year 1794, he believed that his Divine Master called him to engage in the solemn work of the ministry of the Gospel. This brought him into much exercise of soul, under a sense of his own weakness, and the awfulness of the engagement. He was not hasty to enter upon it, but rather disposed to put it by. He had providentially been brought into an acquaintance with Richard C. Brackenbury, a person of considerable estate, from another part of England, who having received, as he believed, a gift in the ministry, thought it right to leave all and travel from place to place, without any view to outward gain, to preach Christ to the people.

This good man was impressed with the belief that the Lord was calling John Stickland into the Gospel vineyard, and being led to his house, was brought into much feeling with him. He embraced every opportunity of urging upon him his conviction that the Lord had thus called him ; but he greatly shrunk and seemed as if he could not be obedient. Sometime after, he had a great desire to see this friend of his, whom he felt to have been made to him an instrument of good ; and, going for this purpose to Poole, attended his preaching, as he thought unobserved ; but Richard C. Brackenbury, at the close of the meeting, gave notice that a friend from the country would hold a meeting there that afternoon. They dined together, and in the course of conversation John asked who the friend was that was to hold the meeting in the afternoon. " *You,*" said the other ; " I knew you were coming before I saw you." As this was not known to him by any outward information, it struck J. S. with so much force, that he turned pale, and could eat no more. Seeing his conflict of mind, Richard said to him, ". Go into my chamber, and there tell thy great Master what His servant Brackenbury has said to you; and if He says you are not to go this afternoon, *don't* go." J. S. retired, accordingly, to wait on the great Head of the Church, to know His will; and, after a season of sweet, silent contrition of heart, in which he poured forth many tears, he felt it his duty to go. On his way to the meeting-house, these words were powerfully spoken in his mental ear, Be not afraid of their faces, lest I confound thee before them. After entering it, he says, " All fear of man was taken from me, and the people appeared to me no more than grasshoppers." These words also were brought to his remembrance, " Behold, I have made thee this day a defenced city, and an iron pillar and brazen walls." Speaking, in another place, of going to this meeting, he says, it " was with much previous trembling and fear of man, until the Lord delivered me from it, and then I was bold in spirit."

About this time he wrote these lines in his pocket Bible:

" How ready is the man to go,
  Whom God hath never sent;
How timorous, diffident, and slow,
  His chosen instrument.
Lord ! if from Thee this mark I have
  Of a true messenger;
By whom Thou wilt, Thy people save,
  And let me always fear."

A minister one day said to J. S., " Some people say they find it difficult to preach or pray; for my part, I find no difficulty in it, but can pray or preach at any time." He mentioned this to his friend Brackenbury, who replied, " Were such my experience, I should call my whole state in question."

John Stickland having engaged in the important work of the ministry, it may not be uninteresting to trace some of his views on the subject. He says, " Christ is the Head of the Church, which is His body. He therefore has the sole prerogative, or right and power to call and send whom He pleases to qualify for His work. He calls godly men by His Spirit and by His people to be bishops and deacons in His church. I think such are sometimes called elders, and I read of no other officers appointed by Him. As God is a Holy Spirit, He requires us to worship Him with our spirits, taught and assisted by His own Spirit, whether with or without words. But words can never please God, except when they are the language of the heart, therefore wicked men can never worship him acceptably. And pious men, I think, are in danger of falling into lip service and bodily exercise, which profit nothing, but may deceive the unguarded soul."

"True Gospel ministry may not inaptly be represented as a coin of pure gold from the heavenly treasury, of great value, having on one side the memorable words of our blessed Lord, *Without me ye can do nothing*; and on the other, Jonah's commission, *Preach the preaching that I bid thee.*

" I think I have never read in the Bible of any person who read his prayers. I believe Jacob did not. Neither did Abraham's servant, for he spake to God in his heart; nor did Hannah in the temple, for she also spake in her heart. The publican said, God be merciful to me a sinner; and the poor woman only said, Lord help me. None of these had a book to pray from, yet God heard and answered them. The Lord's prayer is very short but comprehensive, I read of some who made long prayers and received the greater condemnation on that account. I remember, when my eyes were opened to see that I was in the high road to destruction, nothing troubled me more than my mocking the Almighty at church, saying about twenty times in one service, 'Lord have mercy upon us'—'Christ have mercy on us'—'We beseech thee hear us, good Lord,' &c.

"I would be careful, too, not to take his name in vain, by too frequent mention of it. I have felt quite shocked, under some people's prayers, by their boldness and vain repetition of the Divine name.

"Christ is wise enough to be our Teacher, and he has promised to be with his people to the end of the world. Why then should we not trust him. Unbelief is the root of formality in worship, deadness in preaching, and dulness in hearing. Yea it opens the heart to error. For as without faith it is impossible to please God in our conduct, how much more in our worship."

On one occasion, and one only, "wishing to be more methodical in his sermon," he studied it beforehand; but when he went to deliver it, he says he felt like David in Saul's armour, and prayed to be forgiven for the attempt, and he would never do so again. Attending a Friends' meeting at Poole, the silence was broken by a woman, who repeated only a short passage of Scripture. The strength and light imparted to his mind were such that he often afterward referred to this precious opportunity, as a proof that a few words, with life accompanying, are more profitable than a long discourse without it; and also that the ministry of women may tend greatly to establish the soul.

In vindicating and encouraging the ministry of women, he stood much alone in his neighbourhood; few, if any, of the preachers agreeing with him. He relates the following anecdote: "I was conversing with a dissenting minister on the ministry of women, when he told me that, some time before, he delivered a discourse against it, from the passage, 'I suffer not a woman to teach.' When the family were called to dinner that day, one of his daughters tarried behind, being engaged in reading the Bible. He asked her why she came not? She said, 'O, father, I am reading something so pretty. What is it? said he. She replied, 'Paul went into Philip's house, and *he had four daughters that did preach.*' The word in our version is 'prophesied;' but, said he, I looked at the Greek, and found it should be translated *preached.* I felt mortified that my own little child should pull down my sermon; but I perceived my error, and hope I shall never speak against women preaching any more."

Speaking of preaching, a Friend asked him how he managed about going out to hold meetings.

I consider first what is my duty;—next, how it will look on my dying bed;—and then I trust in the Lord to give me what to say.

It was John's maxim to return good for evil. If he was told, Such an one is your enemy, his reply was, Then I'll try and do him some good.

Meeting with a stranger one day, whilst riding on the road, they fell into conversation on the planting of trees, a subject with which J. S. was very familiar. Ever watchful to mind the pointings of duty, he felt his mind drawn to refer to the beautiful passage in Isaiah lix. 13: "Instead of the thorn shall come up the fir tree, and instead of the briar shall come up the myrtle tree," &c.; and to illustrate the two states it represented, and the necessity of a change from the first, or fallen nature, to that of a regenerated Christian. Some time after, he received, from an unknown hand, a fine myrtle tree, carefully packed, which he set out in a favourite spot in the shrubbery at East Holme, and prized highly. From whom it came remained a mystery, till one day he received a message from the principal inn at Wareham, informing him that a person there wished to speak with him. The stranger asked if he had received a myrtle. "Yes," replied he, "but I never knew whence it came." "I sent it," returned the other. "Do you remember seeing me on the road, and speaking to me about the briar and the myrtle? I was then as a thorn and a briar, but now, through grace, I am become a myrtle." It appeared that the communication had left a deep and lasting impression on the mind of the stranger, and produced a happy effect.

On one occasion, when John Stickland was preaching at Portland, he felt a stop to that Divine liberty and authority with which he had been favoured, and a gentle intimation that it was the proper time to close. But the idea occurred, "What will the people think of my ending so soon?" He was induced to go on longer, and when the meeting closed, a woman said to him, "If you had left off about the middle of your sermon, I should have got some good—*but I lost in the last part all I had gained in the first.*" "Ah," said John, with a heavy sigh, which showed that his conscience was already smiting him, "if I have not preached to you, you have preached to me."

John Stickland bears testimony to the upright conduct of members of the Society of Friends, in their transactions with him in his secular calling; and he also says, "I have ever felt an attachment to that body of Christian people, so opposed to bloody wars, and, like my late dear friend Brackenbury, can say, as he once did to me, 'I have one foot amongst the Quakers and another amongst the Methodists;'" J. S. adding, "I always feel (as he said) my soul refreshed whenever I read their writings." Consistently with such sentiments he was very cordial towards those of his family who embraced their views.

Concerning "that time," at which, says he, "the Lord called me to go to and fro amongst so many people of different names called Protestants, [it] now yields me pleasure to review;" and he adds "my call was to all people who would open their doors and say 'Come in and speak to us.' The Methodists did so most readily, dissenters, and Baptists." But his narrative recites that the risk was not small which he incurred, neither his sacrifice of personal ease and comfort, for the sake of the people more at large; nor did he find that advancing age and infirmity excused the continuance of his efforts for the good of souls. The account which he gives of the renewal of his qualifications for Gospel labour would seem to justify the application of those words of the Psalmist—"my youth is renewed like the eagle's."

In the year 1832, his second wife died, a loss which he deeply felt; but he says, "My comforts under this trouble are, that she is fallen asleep in Christ, and my hope soon to go to her, and to have our part with the meek followers of the Lamb. Full of concern for her children's eternal happiness, she followed them with her prayers and tears to the latest hour."

"Her death was almost sudden. She was very cheerful on the evening of her decease, and we went to bed at our usual hour, but neither of us felt disposed to sleep. She said, 'We cannot sleep; but if I ever sleep again, I hope to dream of heaven and heavenly things, as I shall not be much longer in this world.' Soon after these words, she became very restless, and desired to dress and go down and sit in her chair, which was complied with. I helped her down, and she directly closed her eyes, and fell asleep in Christ, without a sigh or groan."

The death of his wife left him very solitary; he had reached that period of life when temporal enjoyments yield but little satisfaction, yet he had within himself an unfailing source of comfort. The blessed Comforter, promised by our Lord to come to and abide with his disciples, graciously condescended to be present with him, and to solace and sweeten his lonely moments.

About this time, he removed into a very lowly cottage, containing only three small rooms, all on the ground floor. But he possessed an humble and contented mind, and had learned how to receive with cheerful and resigned feelings, all that his Heavenly Father saw meet to dispense, adopting, as his own, these words:

> " The little room for me designed,
> Will suit as well my easy mind,
> As palaces of kings."

The following extracts from letters were written by J. Stickland, near the close of life.

" Oh! what a comfort to look back on sixty years of my eighty, and call the Almighty the God of my youth too, and to retaste the comfort of my first love, and to be a child in my old age."

" Yet I want a deeper work of faith, love, and every grace of the good Spirit of the Lord. 'To be holy and without blame before him in love.' "—Eph. i. 4.

" If any man worship God, and do his will, him he heareth. This, by the help of the Holy Spirit, every Christian can do."

Gradually ripening for heaven, this humble servant of the Lord was now descending to the borders of the grave; and, though the infirmities of age were stealing upon him, yet the fervour of his spirit did not abate. He knew that the daily bread must daily be wrestled for, and he was earnest not to fall into a state of listless ease or cool indifference. His views of the spiritual nature of true religion, and the insufficiency of all outward observances, were strengthened. There was an evident deepening in religious experience, and an increased meetness for the kingdom of heaven. His heart seemed replenished with love to all, and he delighted in that communion of spirit with the Source of all good, and with his fellow believers, which is the privilege and the joy of Christians.

His last sickness continued eight months. He was desirous to be released from his earthly tenement, and often prayed his Heavenly Father to take him home. Shortly before his decease, his daughter asked him if he was quite happy. He replied, "Yes; I have nothing upon my conscience. Remember, my dear, these words, 'I will never leave thee, nor forsake thee.' Remember that word *never*." He was quite cheerful, but spoke little of the things of this world, his mind seeming almost constantly employed in prayer, or in exhortation to those around him. In the seventh month, 1836, he quietly departed; and, in contemplating his circumspect, watchful life, and his peaceful death, we may well adopt the language, "Let me die the death of the righteous, and let my last end be like his."

END.

Printed by E. Couchman and Co., 10, Throgmorton Street, London.

A MEMOIR

OF

JOHN BARLOW,

LATE PROFESSOR OF ANATOMY AND PHYSIOLOGY IN THE VETERINARY COLLEGE,

EDINBURGH.

OHN BARLOW, who died in the fortieth year of his age, was born in the year 1815, at the Oak Farm, Chorley, Cheshire, an estate which had been in the possession of the family for about two hundred years. He was from childhood of a sedate and grave demeanor, and there is reason to believe that he very early became susceptible of religious impressions. When only nine years of age he went to Ackworth School, in Yorkshire, and remained there four years. He was a most affectionate and dutiful son, and one of the kindest of brothers; and during the few years he remained at home, after his return from school, he maintained a consistent character as a member of the Society of Friends, and was greatly beloved by those who knew him. In his boyish days he evinced a strong love for animals, and the cows on his father's farm became the objects of his special attention. This youthful predilection doubtless influenced his choice of a profession, and tended to induce him to devote much of his time to obtaining a knowledge of the diseases to which domestic animals are liable. When he removed to Edinburgh, to pursue his professional studies, in the Verterinary College, his parents' anxieties were awakened lest is mixing so much with general Society, as he did at one time, should have the effect of drawing him aside from the path of Christian self-denial, in which it was their earnest desire that he should walk. He evidently felt the danger himself, and in adverting to this kind of association, he says, in writing to a friend: "I did not seek this for the sake of spending time, and far less for the sake of simply forming connexions; I sought it for the quality of the people, intellectually estimated. Still, all things considered, I feel best satisfied to forego the associations just alluded to, for I was

No. 134.   [Price 3d. per dozen.]

often compelled to countenance customs to which I am in reality averse."

It was a critical period of his life; his attachment to the Christian profession, in which he had been trained, and which his judgment approved, was closely tried; and his mental conflict was sometimes great. For a time he was not regular in his attendance of meetings for public worship, but the refiner was at hand, the power of Divine grace was near to help. "I do not attempt to vindicate" he says, in allusion to this period, "my seclusion from Friends, I have been the loser, and intend, by right assistance, to do what I can to retrieve myself. * * * I do not want conviction, but resolution to be more faithful—I must endeavour, however unworthily, to be more consistent. I have of late had much to endure, but I believe it has had its use, and I am thankful for it." In further allusion to his attendance of meetings for Divine worship, he adds : " On returning home there arises a degree of satisfaction, which poor as I am, would probably, I think, be withheld, did I absent myself from these gatherings ; and I have the conscious, heart-felt satisfaction afforded me, of having done rightly, and of having more closely walked up to what I ever knew was a religious and spiritual obligation."

It would be interesting and instructive to be able to trace the successive steps by which, under the presence and power of the Holy Spirit, John Barlow was conducted in his onward course, to that beautiful appreciation and appropriation of the Truth as it is in Jesus, which so much brightened the horizon of his early setting sun ; but, at this juncture, the work that was going on between his soul and his God was, to a great extent, a hidden one. Yet the following remark respecting a change of residence which, at one time, he contemplated, clearly shows how, amidst all his intellectual pursuits, he was accustomed humbly to recognise the Divine hand, even in the ordinary occurrences of life. "I was wondering where Providence might dispose my lot, and I did feel, I humbly confess, a tender thankfulness that, thus far, the trials I have sustained have, I trust, had their use. I further felt somewhat of an assurance that, if I did my part, in consistence with what I am given to believe is required of me, a blessing will rest even upon my temporal undertakings. Oh, that I may be enabled to trust that all will be for the best."

He did not remove from Edinburgh, but after having obtained his diploma, he continued his professional engagements in connection with the College at which he had been

student, to the end of his days. To follow him through
the various phases of his professional life is not the object of
this brief notice—yet it may be interesting to the reader, to
know how he was looked upon by those who were best
acquainted with him as a professional man. One of these,
after alluding to his being a member of the Society of
Friends—adds; "His career has ever been marked by the
principles which distinguish that body of professing Christians. Modest, gentle, and unassuming in his manners, he
obtained the respect of all who came in contact with him.
Moral worth, and a delicate susceptibility towards the feelings of others, secured to him the warm attachment of a
circle of intimate friends." Dr. J. W. Gairdner remarks:
' It was impossible to be brought into connection with him
without admiring the thoroughly scientific spirit which
entered into all his labours. In his own department he was
always well informed, and even (without the least pretension
or dogmatism) an original thinker, who rarely failed in
forming a decided opinion, where the matter admitted of it.
His opinions, however, were always stated with a moderation
and care which showed that they were only advanced after
the most careful consideration. The display of his knowledge
was distasteful to him ; and although his information was
always yielded up readily to a friendly question, it was
rarely put into such a shape as to appear to claim anything
for himself. These qualities of his mind led him to frequent
the Physiological Society, the meetings of which he regularly
attended, much more as a hearer than a speaker; and I have
often been conscious that this subordination of his scientific
ambition to the desire of learning and aiding the inquiries of
others was, as regards the result, a misfortune. The very
reserve which he imposed upon himself gave an additional
value to everything that he said. The slightest affirmation
of a truth was in him to be respected as much as the most
dogmatic assertion. The habitual guard which he maintained,
not over his words alone, but over his thoughts and feelings,
prevented much of that self-deception to which even good
men are liable ; and he would as studiously have avoided the
appearance of a hollow or treacherous friendship as he did
the over-statement of a fact or an opinion. To say that
such a man was greatly loved wherever he was thoroughly
known, is to say what necessarily follows from a character so
simple, so truthful, so unselfish." To the foregoing we add
the testimony of Professor Simpson: "His character was
indeed of a very high order, both intellectually and morally.
He was wonderfully informed on many of the most intricate

modern questions in anatomical science; and I seldom or never conversed with him on such questions without deriving much information from his conversation. It often appeared to me, that he was a man destined to advance and elevate veterinary medicine; and we must all deplore his loss, the more so, as he has been removed from among us while scarcely yet in his prime. I believe that all who knew him well respected him deeply, not less for his amiability and kindliness of heart, than for his great talents and high intellectual cast of mind." Such was the estimate, which while scarcely yet in his prime, his professional associates themselves of high standing as men of science, formed of John Barlow.

His professional career was successful and distinguished— and great hopes were entertained of his future usefulness. A happy matrimonial connexion, and the added comfort of an interesting group of children, seemed to render his domestic enjoyments complete,—when towards the end of 1855, he was seized with an illness which gradually assumed the character of a severe spinal affection, and after some weeks of intense suffering his system yielded to the pressure of excruciating pain, which the ablest medical skill failed to subdue.

In the early stages of his illness there was but little allusion to his spiritual state; but, from what he said afterwards, it was evident that he had thought and felt much, during this season of suffering and of humiliation. When at last his lips were opened to tell of the power and mercy and the pardoning love of his Saviour, his whole thoughts and conversation seemed fixed on his own immortal interests, and on that which tended to the eternal welfare of all within his reach,—and indeed of the whole human family. On one occasion he alluded forcibly to the passage: "The lofty looks of man shall be humbled, and the haughtiness of men shall be bowed down, and the Lord alone shall be exalted in that day," adding, "There have been growing convictions for some time past, that greater faithfulness should be mine. I feel that I have not occupied all the talents committed to me, and if permitted to recover, I must, through His grace, dedicate myself to the service of my Heavenly Father. I have dearly loved science and my profession, and have followed it with a too exclusive devotion—have perhaps made it somewhat of an idol. The pursuits in which I have been engaged are laudable and useful; and I believe I have been considered successful—though I do not say this with any self gratulation—but now I feel they have too often

)een permitted to take the place of higher_things, when
hey should have been lawfully pursued, in subjection to
:oncerns of eternal moment."

This view he frequently dwelt upon, saying, "I have made
ntellect and human knowledge too much the one object—
his has been my weakness;—though at one time I would
iot have acknowledged it a weakness. Pecuniary success
ias not been my point of ambition; the *snare* has been in
.n over ardent desire for the advancement of science; and
)erhaps some corresponding care for scientific reputation.
3ut in all these things there is no anchor or refuge for the
mmortal soul; and nothing to satisfy the cravings of in-
:reasing spiritual perceptions. Oh no! nothing but the free
nercy of God in Christ Jesus will avail—Christ, the only
loor of reconciliation provided by God—oh, to think of it!
.o think of His sending His beloved Son into the world, to
edeem man from his lost and fallen state! And on this
oundation we must all stand for the redemption of the soul.
Jreeds and systems are nothing—this is what all must come
.o. If persons could but view eternity in the light in which
 now see it, how would they think upon it—dwell upon it
-and make its interest the first and all-important business
.f their lives!"

The principal feature of his disease was the *intense* and
inremitting bodily suffering which accompanied it, often-
imes amounting to agony; but in this painful discipline, he
ecognized the chastening of a Father's love, saying,—" Oh,
 do believe that the Lord, the Almighty God has prescribed
 right remedy for every disease; and I feel that this intense
uffering is the means peculiarly adapted to bring me to this
amedy. Even, in the first temple, the veil had to be lifted
.p, before the priest was permitted to enter the Holy of
Iolies; and in the second Temple,—in Christ Jesus,—the
.ew and living way,—there, too, a veil must be taken away
:om the heart, before we can fully comprehend the mys-
aries of the kingdom."

To one of his affectionate watchers, he said, "May I beg
.f thee to ask for me, at the common place of union, if
onsistent with His holy will, a little relief from pain?" but
dded, after a moment's pause, "Yet, not my will, but Thine
.e done!"

He frequently acknowledged with thankfulness, that he
elieved, within the last few hours—even within the last
.our—he had been permitted to make some spiritual advance-
ient; and felt increasingly sensible of the application to
.is soul of the great work of redemption; that it was not

merely an outward belief and acknowledgment of the Gosp
that would do: "Oh, no, it is the word, the power of Christ
Spirit in the heart." At another time, he said, "Nothii
earthly will do; if anything earthly would do, it would n
be all to the Lord's glory. He is the beginning and th
end—only think of that—the beginning and the end
Then, expressing thankfulness for the joy and comfort th
were granted to him, he earnestly prayed that he "migh
never be permitted to speak of these things with unsan
tified lips."

He dwelt much, about this time, on the necessity
coming to the cross—"the very foot of the cross." Aga
adverting to the value of natural endowments, when sanctifi
and dedicated to the service of Christ, he said that tho
thus gifted, were doubtless fitted for more extended usefu
ness; but he continued, "It is a simple way—a child m
walk in it, but it is a narrow way."

Under the pressure of severe pain, he said, "But o
what are my sufferings compared to my blessed Saviour
who not only endured the depth of physical suffering, b
also bore the load of the sins of the whole world, and all t
for me—and not for *me* only—but for the whole world."

At this time he seemed to be made a rich partaker of t
joy of believing, expressing his fervent adoration in the l
guage of Scripture:—"Wonderful Counsellor, the Migh
God, the Everlasting Father, the Prince of Peace." Feeli
at the same time, the depths of unworthiness, he said, "It
no merit of my own—no merit of my own!"

The work that was going forward was the more striking,
it did not appear to be from the anticipation of his bei
near his end; for, within a short time of his decea
he expressed the feeling of probability that he would
through mercy, raised up again to his tenderly-loved wife a
three little ones; and if so, the hope and prayer of his he
was often poured forth, that if such were the will of
Heavenly Father, he might be enabled to dedicate his wh
talents and life to the service of his God and Saviour, and
made as "a pillar in the temple of the Lord." At the sa
time, if it were the Divine will that it should be otherwise,
felt an assurance that all would be well, and entreated
dear wife not to grieve; endeavouring to comfort and cons
her tenderly sorrowing spirit. Then, after a while, he m
touchingly added; "I think I have reached the depth of t
lowest valley. But through infinite mercy, a full assura
of pardon and acceptance is granted; and if my life shou
terminate this night, my peace is made with God." Twi

ter nights of severe suffering, his remark in the morning
as: "What a blessed night—what a short night;" and on
le occasion he uttered most impressively: "The finished
ork! the finished work!"

His whole soul seemed absorbed in the stupendous thought
eternity, and the mighty importance of its interests: and
it of the abundance of his heart, he was almost constantly
ving utterance to prayer and praise in short sentences,
ten interrupted by the anguish of his suffering, and then
commenced after a partial relief from pain.

He breathed the atmosphere of love towards all—to those
ound him—to his medical attendants—and to a few stu-
nts who saw him, at their own request. It seemed his
ission to urge upon them the importance of keeping the
ought of eternity always before them, and uppermost, and
erything else in due subordination; by which alone a
essing could rest upon any earthly pursuit or enjoyment.

On being asked by his kind medical attendant, how he
d passed the night, he replied, "I trust I have made some
iritual advancement, and perhaps have not lost ground in
her respects." He then with gratitude expressed his belief
at the best of human skill had been exerted in his case,
d added: "You are but instruments in the hand of a
gher Power;" and when the physician responded, "Yes,
e must leave it to Him," he replied, "I trust Him; I trust
im."

In sending messages of dear love to his absent friends he
id, "Tell them, that although they may not have exactly
e same road to travel, yet they have all the same end to
tain, and that I am not ashamed now publicly to confess
y Lord and Saviour."

Within the last twenty-four hours he began to feel, that
cording to all human probability, his close drew near; but
ain expressed the fullest assurance that all would be well.
I believe it is not presumptuous now to say these things,
r it is a moment in which there is no deception—no
lusion."

He desired to see the servants; addressed them as his *dear
rvants*, and said to them: "Though their positions might
different, and theirs a life of daily toil, yet that all were
ke regarded in the eyes of their Heavenly Father." He
anked them for their labours on his account. It was met
a grateful acknowledgment of his kindness to them, as
e of the best of masters: to which he replied, It was
ly my duty—my course is nearly run—but do not grieve
me, for I die the death of the Christian."

On more than one occasion he had remarked "It woul
be very hard to leave my dearly loved wife and children;
yet when his dear children, whom he had, according to h
own confession, loved almost to idolatry, were brought t
him, he was perfectly calm, having, it is thankfully believe
committed his precious ones to the care of the heaven
Shepherd.

Observing that his wife was looking with much feeling an
earnestness, on something which she held in her hand, I
enquired: "What is that my darling?" On the reply, tha
it was a likeness of himself, he sweetly and impressively sai
"Registered elsewhere, for eternity—eternity!"

On a wish being expressed, that his death-bed experien
might be a blessing and stimulus to those left behind, ar
that we might all meet above, he rejoined, "A company
saints in glory;" frequently saying, as if dwelling on th
anticipation of coming joy, "Sing praises, sing praises;" ar
once adding, "with the saints in light."

Near the close, he said, "I am ready to go now, or a litt
later—any moment—all is peace, peace, peace!"

In the course of the evening, he said, "I have had ver
great pleasure in my professional pursuits and studies, ar
was progressing in them—and my reputation was perha
a little dear to me—but now, through marvellous mercy,
have no anxieties—now I look to the full fruition in glor
where I believe I shall soon sing praises, sing praises, si
praises." In a little while after, he said cheerfully, "I ha
had a sleep— I do not know that I could call it a dream-
but I saw happy, happy people:" then, after a pause, I
added, "I believe it to be one of those manifestations, som
times permitted to those who are near entering into glory.'

These were nearly his last words, and, in a short tim
after, his spirit gently passed away.

END.

London: Printed by E. Couchman & Co., 10, *Throgmorton Street; for*
TRACT ASSOCIATION *of the* SOCIETY OF FRIENDS. *Sold at the* DEPOSITO
12, *Bishopsgate Street Without.*—1862.

THE

AUSTRALIAN YOUTH.

LONDON:

inted for the TRACT ASSOCIATION of the SOCIETY of FRIENDS.

Sold at the DEPOSITORY, 12, Bishopsgate Street Without.

—

1862.

No. 135.

THE AUSTRALIAN YOUTH.

THE following short and unadorned narrative is presente
to the reader as affording a striking evidence of th
power of Divine Grace, and furnishing an encouragin
instance of what may be effected by Christian kindnes
and care in training and educating the children of thos
who have been regarded as holding the very lowest plac
in the family of man.

Edward Warrulan was the son of one of the chief
amongst the natives of South Australia, residing not fa
from Adelaide. When a mere child he was brought t
England by Edward Eyre, the Australian traveller. H
accompanied his kind patron almost wherever he went
and his orderly conduct was very remarkable. Not lon
after his arrival in this country he went with his frien
to Windsor, to be presented to the Queen, and th
"Illustrated London News" published some account c
him and his visit, with a portrait, giving a pretty accurat
idea of his personal appearance.

When Edward Eyre was appointed, by the Secretar
of State for the Colonies, to be the Assistant-Governor c
New Zealand, an arrangement was made at the Coloni
Office for defraying the expense of maintaining an

ducating Edward Warrulan in this country, out of the
and set apart for the benefit of the South Australian
atives; and Dr. Hodgkin was requested to act as his
uardian in carrying out the plan. Admission was
btained for him into the Friends' agricultural school
t Sibford, in Oxfordshire, where he remained four
ears. He had there the advantage of a guarded and
eligious education; and, besides the ordinary school
earning, he received some instruction in farming and
orticulture. Whilst he had much observation, and an
xcellent memory for persons, places, and things, as well
s for historical facts, he had great difficulty in under-
tanding the grammatical construction of sentences, and
nore particularly everything relating to numbers; and
till greater difficulty in retaining that which he had
eemed to master in respect to these subjects. It may
e inferred, from the great want of numerals in the
Australian languages, that defect in arithmetical power is
 characteristic of the Australian natives; and yet two
ouths, brought to this country from West Australia by
Dr. Madden, were reported by their teacher to have no
lifficulty of this kind.

Of Edward's conduct at Sibford school, the Master
tates, "We found him of a peaceable and inoffensive
haracter, and we do not remember, at any period, his
ver having intentionally done wrong. In meetings for
vorship, at Scripture readings, and other religious
ngagements, his deportment was thoughtful and suited
o the occasion. He committed to memory, weekly,
ortions of the Sacred Volume, and, in a severe attack
f indisposition, which he had whilst at school, the re-
nembrance of these texts gave him great comfort; and

THE AUSTRALIAN YOUTH.

THE following short and unadorned narrative is presented to the reader as affording a striking evidence of the power of Divine Grace, and furnishing an encouraging instance of what may be effected by Christian kindness and care in training and educating the children of those who have been regarded as holding the very lowest place in the family of man.

Edward Warrulan was the son of one of the chiefs amongst the natives of South Australia, residing not far from Adelaide. When a mere child he was brought to England by Edward Eyre, the Australian traveller. He accompanied his kind patron almost wherever he went, and his orderly conduct was very remarkable. Not long after his arrival in this country he went with his friend to Windsor, to be presented to the Queen, and the "Illustrated London News" published some account of him and his visit, with a portrait, giving a pretty accurate idea of his personal appearance.

When Edward Eyre was appointed, by the Secretary of State for the Colonies, to be the Assistant-Governor of New Zealand, an arrangement was made at the Colonial Office for defraying the expense of maintaining and educating Edward Warrulan in this country, out of the fund set apart for the benefit of the South Australian natives; and Dr. Hodgkin was requested to act as his guardian in carrying out the plan. Admission was obtained for him into the Friends' agricultural school at Sibford, in Oxfordshire, where he remained four years. He had there the advantage of a guarded and religious education; and, besides the ordinary school learning, he received some instruction in farming and horticulture. Whilst he had much observation, and an excellent memory for persons, places, and things, as well as for historical facts, he had great difficulty in understanding the grammatical construction of sentences, and more particularly everything relating to numbers; and still greater difficulty in retaining that which he had seemed to master in respect to these subjects. It may be inferred, from the great want of numerals in the Australian languages, that defect in arithmetical power is a characteristic of the Australian natives; and yet two youths, brought to this country from West Australia by Dr. Madden, were reported by their teacher to have no difficulty of this kind.

Of Edward's conduct at Sibford school, the Master states, "We found him of a peaceable and inoffensive character, and we do not remember, at any period, his ever having intentionally done wrong. In meetings for worship, at Scripture readings, and other religious engagements, his deportment was thoughtful and suited to the occasion. He committed to memory, weekly, portions of the Sacred Volume, and, in a severe attack of indisposition, which he had whilst at school, the remembrance of these texts gave him great comfort; and

when too poorly to read for himself, he took great pleasure in listening to others. He also expressed a great
desire that his parents might be brought to a knowledge
of their Saviour."

Amongst his school-fellows he contracted warm friendships, which were maintained until his decease; and
letters from two of these juvenile correspondents, received
after his death, proved the strong attachment that existed
between them.

When E. Warrulan was of an age to make it desirable
that he should apply himself to some useful occupation
by which he might both maintain himself and become
serviceable to others, on his return to his own country, it
was evident that he had neither strength nor inclination
for agriculture; and he tried carpenter's work with the
same result.

It was then suggested by a kindly interested friend,
who, in his extensive travels, had become well acquainted
with colonial life and with the habits and dispositions of
several native races, that the business of a saddler would
be very likely to suit Edward's capacity and inclination,
and also to afford him the most certain means of profitably employing himself. The idea was happy and judicious, and, in acting on this plan, he evinced a perseverance and industry which, it is believed, he had never
shown before.

Whilst following his occupation his right hand was
severely mutilated by a machine, but was restored by the
kind and able treatment of his medical attendant. The
confinement to his room for several weeks, and the necessarily painful dressings attending the cure, had no preju-
dicial effect on his patience or temper, and his sense of

thankfulness, expressed both to the doctor and kind mistress of the family, amply proved his gratitude to man, whilst he was equally sensible of the source from whence, as he often acknowledged, all his blessings flowed.

This illness may, in the appointment of Divine Wisdom, have been permitted as a fitting means to introduce his mind to that further purification which he was favoured to experience prior to the unexpected and rather sudden termination of his youthful career.

After spending some years at Banbury in learning saddlery and harness work, he removed in the spring of the year 1855 to Birmingham, where an advantageous position had been obtained for him in a large harness manufactory, and where he remained until his death.

The testimonies of both his employers to his good conduct and general docility are highly satisfactory. Without losing its child-like simplicity, his character, which, from its native gentleness and politeness was truly prepossessing, gradually unfolded; and though he was often subject to irritating circumstances, he was scarcely ever known to repel them, except by mild expostulation, or shrewd replies, which, as he advanced in years, were mostly couched in Scripture language, singularly applicable and unanswerable.

It will prove a lasting satisfaction to those generous friends who were interested in his welfare, that their intercourse with him tended to foster that propriety of conduct which formed a native element in his character; and, further, that they had impressed him with the knowledge and love of his Heavenly Father and Redeemer, which became, in his last moments, both a solace to himself and a rich legacy to survivors.

In the autumn of 1855 a pleasure trip to London was granted to their work-people by his employers at Birmingham, affording the subject of this memoir, an opportunity of partaking of the kindness of his friends in that city. His health was not more feeble than usual, but, on returning to Birmingham, he mentioned that one of the passengers in the railway train had refused to close the window, though respectfully urged to do it. From this circumstance his susceptible frame received a shock which it never overcame, and a severe cold was the consequence. It obtained the immediate care of his kind hostess, and that of a medical friend, whose skill was assiduously and gratuitously afforded to the last. Their combined efforts mitigated the severity of the attack; but the termination of his life, about six weeks after, proved how difficult it is for foreigners to bear the varying climate of Great Britain.

Many attentions and delicacies which his feeble health required were furnished during his illness by his numerous friends, and Dr. Hodgkin kindly paid him a visit, E. Warrplan was delighted to see his kind friend, and anxiously inquired when he might return to Australia, where now all his affection appeared to centre. He had long been desirous of forwarding, for his father's acceptance, a copy of the sacred writings; and now he was more than ever earnest to communicate personally to him that sense of his Saviour's love, which, it is believed, he had for many years found to be his comforter during his separation from his kindred, and which now in his illness he felt to be doubly precious.

To his own family, and perhaps to many of the natives of the Australian continent, it is difficult, to estimate the oss which they may have sustained in the removal of this truly interesting youth. His dying sympathies were with his "brethren according to the flesh;" and though prevented from personally communicating to them the unsearchable riches of Christ, strong is our desire that the utterances of the interesting sufferer, on his dying bed, may reach some of those for whom his last words and his closing thoughts were intended.

He frequently alluded to his father, and wished to go to Australia to tell him how good his Saviour was to him, and his desire that he, too, should come to Jesus, and partake of his love.

Once, putting his arms round his attendant, with much affection, he said, "What shall I call you—mother,—step-mother? *No, mother!*" and from that time he used no other designation in addressing her.

During his illness, he was asked what his hopes then were. He replied, "My hope is in the Saviour and His *promises.* My Saviour is always around me; I am happy on my bed; I am happy on my couch; my Jesus strengthens me:" and he energetically asked those around him, "Are you happy?"

A few days before his death, on its being said to him "Then you know that Christ died for you?" "Yes," he answered, "and not for me only, but for the whole world."

The evening previous to his decease, he looked smilingly on his kind attendant, and said, "I have had some sweet sleep. Yes, I have been asleep in Jesus."

Not unfrequently his hands were clasped, as though he was in prayer, when it could not be understood what he said.

Not long before his death, he exclaimed, "The angels are around my bed; I want to soar away." "The white robe; oh, the white robe!" and shortly after he passed away as in a sweet sleep.

May this little narrative of the life and death of this Australian youth be to the praise of that Divine grace, which, at times, is remarkably displayed in those who, though ranking among the weak of this world, are strong in faith, and heirs of eternal blessedness. His early training and his knowledge of the Holy Scriptures were greatly blessed to him, and the encouraging language may be held forth to all instructors of youth, "In the morning sow thy seed, and in the evening withhold not thy hand: for thou knowest not whether it shall prosper, either this or that, or whether they both shall be alike good." And may those dear children, into whose hands this Tract may come, be encouraged early to seek the Lord for their portion and to yield up their hearts to the precious influence of his love towards them in Christ Jesus.

END.

Printed by E. Couchman and Co., 10, Throgmorton Street, London.

LETTER TO CHRISTIAN WOMEN,

ON

ORNAMENTAL DRESS,

BY

ADONIRAM JUDSON,

Baptist Missionary in Burmah, originally addressed to the Female Members of Christian Churches in the United States.

DEAR SISTERS IN CHRIST,

Excuse my publicly addressing you. The necessity of the case is my only apology. Whether you will consider it a sufficient apology for the sentiments of this letter, unfashion able, I confess, and perhaps unpalatable, I know not. We are sometimes obliged to encounter the hazard of offending those whom of all others we desire to please. Let me throw myself at once on your mercy, dear sisters, allied by national consanguinity, professors of the same holy religion, fellow pilgrims to the same happy world. Pleading these endearing ties, let me beg you to regard me as a brother, and to listen with candour and forbearance to my honest tale.

In raising up a church of Christ in this heathen land, and in labouring to elevate the minds of the female converts to the standard of the Gospel, we have always found one chief obstacle in that principle of vanity, that love of dress and display (I beg you will bear with me), which has, in every age, and in all countries, been a ruling passion of the [female] sex, as the love of riches, power, and fame, has characterized the other. That obstacle lately became more formidable, through the admission of two or three fashionable females into the church, and the arrival of several missionary sisters, dressed and adorned in that manner, which is too prevalent in our beloved native land. On my meeting the church, after a year's absence, I beheld an appalling profusion of ornaments, and saw that the demon of vanity was laying waste the female department. At that time, I had not maturely considered the subject, and did not feel sure what ground I ought to take.—I apprehended also, that I should be unsupported and perhaps opposed by some of my coadju-

No. 136.   [*Price 3d. per dozen.*]

tors. I confined my efforts, therefore, to private exhortation, and with but little effect. Some of them out of regard to their pastor's feelings, took off their necklaces and ear ornaments before they entered the chapel, tied them up in a corner of their handkerchiefs, and, on returning, as soon as they were out of sight of the mission house, stopped in the street to array themselves anew.

In the meantime, I was called to visit the Karèns, a wild people, several days' journey to the north of Maulmain. Little did I expect to encounter the same enemy in those "wilds, horrid and dark with o'ershadowing trees."—But I found that he had been there before me, and reigned with peculiar sway, from time immemorial. On one Karèn woman, I counted between twelve and fifteen necklaces of all colours, sizes, and materials. Three was the average. Brass belts above the ankles, neat braids of black hair tied below their knees, rings of all sorts on the fingers, bracelets on the wrists and arms, long metal instruments perforating the lower part of the ear, and reaching nearly to the shoulders, fancifully constructed bags, enclosing the hair, and suspended from the back part of the head, not to speak of the ornamental parts of their clothing, constituted the fashions and the *ton* of the Karènesses. The dress of the female converts was not essentially different from that of their countrywomen. I saw that I was brought into a situation that precluded all retreat—that I must fight or die.

For a few nights I spent some sleepless hours, distressed by this and other subjects, which will always press upon the heart of a missionary, in a new place. I considered the spirit of the religion of Jesus Christ. I opened to 1 Tim. ii. 9. and read those words of the inspired apostle, " I will also that women adorn themselves in modest apparel with shamefacedness and sobriety, *not with broidered hair, or gold, or pearls, or costly array.*" I asked myself, Can I [receive into the church] a Karèn woman in her present attire? No. Can I [give her the privileges of fellowship] in that attire? No. Can I refrain from enforcing the prohibition of the apostle? Not without betraying the trust that I have received from him. Again, I considered that the question concerned not the Karèns only, but the whole Christian world; that its decision would involve a train of unknown consequences; that a single step would lead me into a long and perilous way. I considered Maulmain and the other stations; I considered the state of the public mind at home. But " *What is that to thee? follow thou me;*" was the continual response, and weighed more than all. I renewedly offered myself to

Christ, and prayed for strength to go forward in the path of duty, come life or death, come praise or reproach, supported or deserted, successful or defeated, in the ultimate issue.

Soon after coming to this conclusion, a Karèn woman offered herself [to be admitted into the church]. After the usual examination, I inquired whether she could give up her ornaments for Christ? It was an unexpected blow! I explained the spirit of the Gospel. I appealed to her own consciousness of vanity. I read to her the apostle's prohibition. She looked again and again at her handsome necklace (she wore but one), and then with an air of modest decision, that would adorn beyond all outward ornaments, any of my sisters whom I address, she took it off, saying *I love Christ more than this.* The news began to spread. The Christian women made but little hesitation. A few others opposed, but the work went on.

At length the evil which I most dreaded came upon me. Some of the Karèn men had been to Maulmain, and seen what I wished they had not. And one day, when we were discussing the subject of ornaments, one of the Christians came forward and declared, that at Maulmain, he had actually seen one of the great female teachers wearing a string of gold beads around her neck!!!

Lay down this paper, dear sisters, and sympathize a moment with your fallen missionary. Was it not a hard case! However, though cast down, I was not destroyed; I endeavoured to maintain the warfare as well as I could; and when I left those parts, the female converts were, generally speaking, arrayed in modest apparel.

On arriving at Maulmain, and partially recovering from a fever which I had contracted in the Karèn woods, the first thing I did was to crawl out to the house of the patroness of the gold beads. To her I related my adventures; to her commiseration I commended my grief. With what ease and truth too, could this sister reply, "Notwithstanding these beads, I dressed more plainly than most minister's wives and professors of religion in our native land. These beads are the only ornament I wear; they were given me when quite a child, by a dear mother, whom I never expect to see again (another hard case); and she enjoined it on me never to part with them, as long as I lived, but to wear them as a memorial of her!" O ye Christian mothers, what a lesson you have before you. Can you give instructions to your daughters, directly contrary to the apostolic commands? But to the honour of my sister be it recorded, that as soon as she understood the merits of the case, and the mischief done by such example, off went the gold beads; and she gave decisive proof that she loved Christ more than father or mother. Her example, united with the efforts of the rest of us, at this station, is beginning to exercise a redeeming influence in the female department of the church.

But, notwithstanding these favourable signs, nothing, really nothing, is yet done. And why? This mission, and all others, must necessarily be sustained by continued supplies of missionaries, male and female, from the mother countries. Your sisters and daughters will come out, to take the place of those who are removed by death, and to occupy numberless stations still unoccupied. And, when they arrive, they will be dressed in their usual way, as Christian women at home are dressed. And the female converts will run around them, and gaze upon them, with the most prying curiosity, regarding them as the freshest representations of the Christian religion from that land where it flourishes in all its purity and glory. And, when they see the gold and jewels pendant from their ears, the beads and chains encircling their necks, the finger rings set with diamonds and rubies, the breast pins, the rich variety of ornamental head dresses; "the mantles and the wimples, and the crispin-pins," (see the rest in Isaiah iii.*), they will cast a bitter, reproachful, triumphant glance at their old teachers, and spring with avidity to repurchase and resume their long-neglected elegancies—the cheering news will fly up the various settlements—the Karènesses will reload their necks and ears, and arms, and ancles—and when, after another year's absence, I return and take my seat before the Burmese or the Karèn Church, I shall behold the demon of vanity enthroned in the centre of the assembly more firmly than ever, grinning defiance to the prohibitions of apostles, and the exhortations of us who would fain be their humble followers.

And thus you, my dear sisters, sitting quietly by your firesides, or repairing devoutly to your places of worship, do, by your example, spread the poison of vanity, through all the rivers, and mountains, and wilds of this far distant

---

* In that day the Lord will take away the bravery of *their* tinkling ornaments *about their feet*, and *their* cauls, and *their* round tires like the moon, the chains, and the bracelets, and the mufflers, the bonnets, and the ornaments of the legs, and the head bands, and the tablets, and the ear-rings, the rings, and nose jewels, the changeable suits of apparel, and the mantles, and the wimples, and the crispin-pins, the glasses, and the fine linen, and the hoods and the veils. And it shall come to pass, *that* instead of sweet smell there shall be stink; and instead of a girdle a rent; and instead of well-set hair baldness; and instead of a stomacher a girding of sackcloth; *and* burning instead of beauty.

land; and, while you are sincerely and fervently praying for the upbuilding of the Redeemers kingdom, are inadvertently building up that of the devil. If, on the other hand, you divest yourselves of all meretricious ornaments, your sisters and daughters, who come hither, will be divested of course ; the further supplies of vanity and pride will be cut off, and the churches at home being kept pure, the churches here will be pure also.

Dear Sisters,—Having finished my tale, and exhibited the necessity under which I lay of addressing you, I beg leave to submit a few topics to your candid and prayerful consideration :—

1. Let me appeal to conscience, and enquire what is the real motive for wearing ornamental and costly apparel ? Is it not the desire of setting off one's person to the best advantage, and of exciting the admiration of others ? Is not such dress calculated to gratify self-love : to cherish the sentiments of vanity and pride ? And is it not the nature of those sentiments to acquire strength from indulgence ? Do such motives and sentiments comport with the meek, humble, self-denying religion of Jesus Christ ? I would here respectfully suggest that these questions will not be answered so faithfully in the midst of company, as when quite alone kneeling before God.

2. Consider the words of the apostle quoted above, from 1 Tim. ii. 9 : "I will also that women adorn themselves in modest apparel, with shamefacedness and sobriety, *not with broidered hair, or gold, or pearls, or costly array.*" I do not quote a similar command recorded in 1 Peter iii. 3, because the verbal construction is not quite so definite, though the import of the two passages is the same. But, cannot the force of these passages be evaded ? Yes; and nearly every command in Scripture can be evaded; and every doctrinal assertion perverted, plausibly and handsomely, if we set about it in good earnest. But, preserving the posture above alluded to, with the Inspired Volume spread open at the passage in question, ask your hearts, in simplicity and godly sincerity, whether the meaning is not just as plain as the sun at noon-day. Shall we then bow to the authority of an inspired apostle, or shall we not ? From that authority, shall we appeal to the prevailing usages and fashions of the age ? If so, please to recall the missionaries you have sent to the heathen; for the heathen can vindicate all their superstitions on the same ground.

3. In the posture you have assumed, look up, and behold the eye of your benignant Saviour ever gazing upon you,

with the tenderest love,—upon you, his daughters, his spouse, wishing above all things, that you would yield your hearts entirely to him, and become holy as he is holy, re-joicing when he sees one and another accepting his pressing invitation, and entering the more perfect way : for, on that account he will be able to draw such precious souls into a nearer union with himself, and place them at last in the higher spheres, where they will receive and reflect more copious communications of light, from the great Fountain of Light, the uncreated Sun.

4. Anticipate the happy moment, hastening on all the wings of time, when your joyful spirits will be welcomed into the assembly of the spirits of the just made perfect. You appear before the throne of Jehovah ; the approving smile of Jesus fixes your everlasting happy destiny ; and you are plunging into " the sea of life and love unknown, without a bottom or a shore." Stop a moment ; look back on yonder dark and miserable world that you have left; fix your eye on the meagre, vain, contemptible articles of ornamental dress, which you once hesitated to give up for Christ, the king of glory—and on that glance, decide the question instantly and for ever.

Surely, you can hold out no longer. You cannot rise from your knees, in your present attire. Thanks be to God, I see you taking off your necklaces and ear-rings, tearing away your ribbons, and ruffles, and superfluities of head-dress ; and I hear you exclaim, What shall we do next ? An important question, deserving serious consideration. The ornaments you are removing, though useless and worse than useless, in their present state, can be disposed of to feed the hungry, clothe the naked, relieve the sick, enlighten the dark-minded, disseminate the Holy Scriptures, and spread the glorious Gospel throughout the world. Little do the inhabitants of a free Christian country know of the want and distress endured by the greater part of the inhabitants of the earth. Still less idea can they form of the awful darkness which rests upon the great mass of mankind, in regard to spiritual things.

During the years that you have been wearing these useless ornaments, how many poor creatures have been pining in want ! How many have languished and groaned on beds of abject wretchedness ; how many children have been bred up in the blackest ignorance, hardened in all manner of iniquity ! How many immortal souls have gone down to Hell, with a lie in their right hand, having never heard of the true God and the holy Saviour ! Some of these miseries might have been mitigated ; some poor wretch have felt his pain relieved ; some widow's heart been made to sing for joy ; some helpless orphan have been rescued from hardened depravity, and trained up for a happy life here and hereafter. Some, yea many, precious souls, might have been redeemed from the quenchless fire of Hell, where now they must lie and suffer to all eternity, had you not been afraid of being thought unfashionable, and not "like other folks!" had you not preferred adorning your persons, and cherishing the sweet seductive feelings of vanity and pride.

O Christian sisters, believers in God, in Christ, in an eternal Heaven and an eternal Hell! can you hesitate and ask what you shall do? Bedew those ornaments with the tears of contrition; consecrate them to the cause of charity —hang them on the cross of your dying Lord. Delay not an instant. Hasten with all your might, if not to make reparation for the past, at least, to prevent a continuance of the evil in future.

Unite, Christian sisters of *all denominations*, and make an effort to rescue the Church of God from the insidious attacks of an enemy, which is devouring her very vitals. Be not deterred by the suggestion, that in such discussions you are conversant about *small* things. Great things depend on small: and in that case, things which appear small to short-sighted men, are great in the sight of God. Many there are, who praise the principle of self-denial in general, and condemn it in all its peculiar applications, as too minute, scrupulous, and severe. Satan is well aware that if he can secure the minute units, the sum total will be his own. Think not anything small, which may have a bearing upon the kingdom of Christ, and upon the destinies of eternity. How easy to conceive, from many known events, that the single fact of a lady's divesting herself of a necklace, for Christ's sake, may involve consequences which shall be felt in the remotest parts of the earth, in all future generations to the end of time; yea, stretch away into a boundless eternity, and be a subject of praise, millions of ages after this world and all its ornaments are burnt up!

Beware of another suggestion made by weak and erring souls, who will tell you that there is more danger of being proud of plain dress, and other modes of self-denial, than of fashionable attire and self-indulgence. Be not ensnared by this last, most finished, most insidious device of the great enemy. Rather believe, that he, who enables you to make a sacrifice, is able to keep you from being proud of it. Believe, that he will kindly permit such occasions of morti-fication and shame, as will preserve you from the evil threatened. *The severest part of self-denial consists in en-*

countering *the disapprobation of one's dearest friends.* All who enter the strait and narrow path in good earnest, soon find themselves in a climate extremely uncongenial to the growth of pride.

The gay and fashionable will, in many cases, be the last to engage in this holy undertaking. But let none be discouraged on that account. Christ has seldom honoured the leaders of worldly fashion, by appointing them leaders in his cause. Fix it in your hearts, that in this warfare, *the Lord Jesus Christ expects every woman to do her duty!* There is, probably, not one in the humblest walks of life, but would, on strict examination, find some article, which *might* be dispensed with, for purposes of charity, and *ought* to be dispensed with, in compliance with the apostolic command. Wait not, therefore, for the fashionable to set an example; wait not for another; listen not to the news from the next town; but *let every individual go forward*, regardless of reproach, fearless of consequences. The eye of Christ is upon you. Death is hastening to strip you of your ornaments, and to turn your fair forms into corruption and dust. Many of those for whom this letter is designed will be laid in the grave before it can reach their eyes. We shall all soon appear before the judgment-seat of Christ, to be tried for our conduct, and to receive the things done in the body. When placed before that awful bar, in the presence of that Being, whose eyes are as a flame of fire, and whose irrevocable fiat will fix you for ever in heaven or in hell, and mete out the measure of your everlasting pleasures and pains, what course will you wish you had taken? Will you then wish, that, in defiance of his authority, you had adorned your mortal bodies with gold, and precious stones, and costly attire, cherishing self-love, vanity, and pride? Or will you wish that you had chosen a life of self-denial, renounced the world, taken up the cross *daily*, and followed him. *And as you will then wish you had done*, DO NOW.

Dear Sisters,

Your affectionate brother in Christ,

A JUDSON.

Maulmain, 1831.

In this reprint a few expressions have been altered for others of similar purpose, and noticed by being enclosed thus [ ].

London: *Printed by E. Couchman & Co.* 10, *Throgmorton Street; for the* TRACT ASSOCIATION *of the* SOCIETY OF FRIENDS. *Sold at the Depository,* 12, *Bishopsgate Street Without.*—1863.

ON THE DUTY

OF

Christian Simplicity and Plainness

IN

LANGUAGE, DRESS, AND BEHAVIOUR,

ACCORDING TO THE VIEWS OF

THE SOCIETY OF FRIENDS.

BY JOHN ALLEN.

LONDON:

Printed for the TRACT ASSOCIATION of the SOCIETY OF FRIENDS.

Sold at the DEPOSITORY, 84, Houndsditch.

—

1860.

No. 137.   [*Price 6d. per dozen.*]

ON THE DUTY OF

CHRISTIAN SIMPLICITY & PLAINNESS.

THE early Friends were mostly plain, simple-hearted people, whose minds had long been set upon heavenly things, and seeking a more excellent way than they had known. Many of them had made trial of various modes of religious profession, as well as of the pleasures of the world, but were dissatisfied with them all. Retired and self-denying in their habits, moderate in their views, and desiring to have their citizenship in heaven, they looked on this life as a pilgrimage to a better. In their language, mode of dress, and behaviour, as well as in their habits, pursuits, and enjoyments, they differed but little, if at all, from the more plain and serious part of those around them; yet their whole conduct was marked by a truthfulness and simplicity, which they believed to be required by the teachings of the Holy Spirit, emphatically termed the "Spirit *of Truth.*" In this respect, as well as in upholding the great, simple, spiritual doctrines of the Gospel, they considered that the work of reformation from the evils of the apostacy had not yet been carried far enough. In the following pages are set forth some of the reasons for their external simplicity and plainness.

First, As to Language :—

Their words were few, and were those of truth and soberness, bespeaking a deep concern for the salvation of their souls. Brought under strong convictions by the power of the Lord, and very conversant with Holy Scripture, they highly valued the examples of the prophets, of our Holy Redeemer, and of his early followers,

as therein set forth, and as contrasted with the vanity
and pride of the world. To those examples they desired
to be wholly conformed. Finding the singular pronouns
thou, thee, &c., invariably used in the sacred volume
and throughout antiquity, when correctness required
them; living also mostly in the country, and accustomed
to this mode of expression in conversation one with
another; they believed that they ought not to depart
from it when addressing their superiors; since they
looked upon the use of the plural number in such cases
as an obvious deviation from simple truth, adopted in
compliance with corrupt custom. Inquiries into the subject showed them that the practice in question had been
introduced in a degenerate and dark period, to flatter
the extravagant vanity of emperors, popes, and other
potentates; some of whom, not content with the indi-
viduality assigned them by nature, and professing to
be superhuman, claimed for themselves divine honours,
and actually wished to be regarded as more than one.
The word *thou*, till then always used in addressing
a single individual, conveyed, in their estimate, too
slender a degree of honour; and therefore, wishing to be
more exalted than became sinful mortals, they required
a flattering untruthful style, suited to their ambition,
and even more deferential than was addressed to the
divine Majesty of Heaven. When we endeavour to lay
aside the prejudice of custom, and reflect seriously and
impartially on this puerile assumption, can we do otherwise than acknowledge the folly, and even the sinfulness,
in which it originated? Yet, absurd as the fiction was,
it gratified the empty ambition of the vainly great; and
by imitation the custom gradually made way downwards,
through the several classes of society, till it came at
length into common use, and was generally expected
as a necessary mark of civility. Though sometimes
ridiculed by satirists, as Erasmus, or condemned by
reformers, as Luther and others, it continued to be the
usual practice to the time of our early Friends, who
found the plain original phraseology nearly confined to
the country people, and even disused by many of them.
  George Fox and his coadjutors were convinced that
there was nothing really uncivil or indecorous in the

correct ancient style of address, and that it ought not to give offence to any, since it was used to the Deity himself. They therefore adhered invariably to the singular number, in addressing each person without distinction; and after a time published a work,* showing incontestably that this practice agreed with the grammatical rules of ancient and modern languages. But though it did not then, nor does now, displease even the highest personages to be *spoken of* in the singular number, yet to be *spoken to* in so simple and novel a mode was, as Fox remarks, " a sore cut to proud flesh," deeply wounding the pride of those in authority, and bringing down on the heads of the poor but conscientious speakers, abuse, menaces, imprecations, and blows.

This, however, was not the only deviation from common parlance which they believed to be required of them. They declined, on very similar grounds, to adopt the merely complimentary epithets of Master, Mistress, and all others of that description. Forbidden by the highest authority to call any man master who did not really stand in that relation to them, and feeling the native equality and dignity of all men as joint partakers of the benefits of Christ's death, and as called to be brethren in Him, they adhered to the simple name; and, while giving honour to those to whom honour was due, they were courteous to all, but not servile to any, plain in their words, but free alike from flattery and rudeness. Knowing that many were accustomed to be addressed with titles of honour and sanctity, who had no just pretensions to them, they felt called on by Christian truthfulness and duty to abstain from using such, as terms of mere form; believing them to give countenance to insincerity and hypocrisy, and feeling the force of the words of Elihu, " Let me not accept any man's person, neither let me give flattering titles to man; for in so doing my Maker would soon take me away." And they were confirmed in these conclusions by the complaint of Christ himself against the Jews, that their seeking honour one from another, and not that alone

* Entitled "A Battledoor."

which came from God, was an obstacle to their belief in Him.

Another departure from the usual mode of expression was early adopted by Friends, in respect to the names of the months and days. The common terms of *July, August, Sunday, Thursday*, &c., appeared to them objectionable, as derived from the deified heroes of paganism, or the natural objects of its idolatrous worship. Finding in Holy Scripture no such terms, but the plain numerals, *First, Second, Third*, &c., they concluded it right for them to observe the same simple and much more convenient Christian nomenclature.

The Emperor Constantine, as history informs us, having been a great worshipper of the sun, and desiring, by blending heathenism with Christianity, to conciliate both parties, was the earliest who enacted that the first day of the week, which was religiously observed by the Christians, should be called *Dies Solis*, or *Sunday*, in honour of his favourite Apollo, or the sun. Other days, and some of the months, were also named, on similar grounds, after the objects of pagan worship, many of them abominably corrupt; and thus the holy Christian profession was lowered to suit an idolatrous standard.

To place this measure and its evil consequences more clearly in view, let us suppose that an extensive conversion to Christianity should take place in India, and that the converts, pleading European example, should propose to name the days and months, Vishnoo day, Juggernaut month, &c. This would doubtless be generally felt to be an unjustifiable concession to heathenism, and highly inconsistent with Christian purity; yet it would rest on very much the same grounds as our own practice, so inconsiderately and commonly adopted. We find that the Jews were commanded not even to take the names of the heathen gods into their mouths, and it was prophesied that the Lord's people should be turned to a pure language. Can consistent Christians do less than follow such a course?

Popery too, as well as heathenism, left deep traces of superstition in the language and practices of professed Christians, calculated to convey erroneous sentiments and to foster a superstitious spirit. To one or other of these sources may be attributed various usages and terms, which have derived force from habit, and the origin of which is little considered. Among them are the old festivals of pretended saints, and even of pagan deities, still observed in many places as times of idleness, revelry, and profaneness; while saintship is often transferred to the names of parishes, towns, and ships, and holiness falsely ascribed to offices, buildings, &c., even among Protestants. These were considered as relics of deep-seated error by the early Friends; who felt called upon to testify against them, as departures from Christian principle, and to carry out the great work of reformation, so as to purify the language, the usages, and notions, as well as the tenets and religious observances prevailing. In endeavouring closely to conform to truth and principle in these respects, the consistent believer will be brought to set a guard on his lips in other matters; he will feel that extravagant or profane expressions, used in compliment or thoughtlessness, are condemned by the Spirit of Truth; and will humbly desire to be enabled to observe the exhortation of the apostle; that his "speech may be alway with grace, seasoned with salt."

These and other reasons for plainness and truthfulness in language, not only influenced the early members of the Society of Friends, but have been felt by their consistent successors in religious fellowship to be founded on Christian integrity and truth, and have therefore been recognised and acted on to the present day.*

Secondly, As to Dress :—

Another branch of Christian simplicity is plainness in attire, resulting, as in language, from that seriousness of mind which, intent on heavenly things, shuns the vanities and allurements of the world as destructive snares. Faithful Christians, in successive ages of the church, from Christ and his apostles downward,—distinguishing between useful clothing to promote comfort and health, and useless ornaments to gratify personal vanity—have testified against outward adorning and pride

* It is to be regretted that many Friends, in the use of the singular number, depart from correctness by using *thee* for *thou*, thus lessening the beauty and force of the simple style of address, and depriving themselves of one of the arguments for its adoption.

of apparel, as tending to foster worldly-mindedness and sin; and have felt it their duty to observe habits of simplicity and moderation, in obedience to the restraints of the Spirit of Truth.

Our predecessors were marked by the weightiness of their spirits, and the seriousness of their behaviour; but it does not appear that, when they united together in religious fellowship, they adopted any particular costume, or dressed differently from other sober people of the day. They were not charged with singularity in dress, as they were in language; hence it may be concluded that in personal appearance they were very similar to those around them: they declined, however, the use of needless ribbons, of lace, gaudy colours, and mere ornaments, which were worn largely by fashionable persons: it was the absence of these, and not any peculiar cut of the clothes, which, as George Fox says, distinguished them as Quakers. He recommended plainness, frugality, usefulness, and decency, in opposition to their contraries, but nothing more; and he himself, perhaps from motives of economy, often wore a leather dress. When William Penn joined the Society, he seems not to have made any sudden change of garb, but to have left off its ornamental appendages one after another.

But though the clothing of Friends was at first not unlike that of other serious persons in the same circumstances of life, yet, since they were restrained by principle from following the changes of fashion, they soon became singular, not designedly, but of necessity, being left behind by the capricious career of novelty, finery, and vanity. When a change has been recommended by convenience, simplicity, or economy, it has been adopted; consequently the general attire of friends in the present day is not just what it was even fifty years ago. Industry too has led to affluence, and affluence to indulgences, which have produced among many, it must be admitted, more costliness of attire, and closer assimilation to the prevailing habits of the world, than true Christian simplicity would justify. It is evident, however, that the avoiding of mere ornament is by no means inconsistent with some variety in the quality and cost of garments, according to the means and station of individuals, or with that cleanliness and neatness, so becoming intelligent and sensitive beings. Many of the fashions in dress are inconvenient, absurd, and even immodest, and therefore have nothing to excuse, much less to recommend them.

If then the simple attire of Friends has become singular, the fault, if such it be, is chargeable to those who have followed the guidance of changeful fashion, and not to themselves who have remained comparatively stationary. While they feel that there is no virtue in any particular form of dress, they believe that plainness, as a testimony against a vain and inconstant world, is a highly important duty. Were they now to conform to the present usual mode, and adhere to it, there is little or no doubt that in a few years there would again be a marked difference in appearance, between them and the major part of the community; so that they could only escape singularity by adopting the ever-changing fashion of the day.

If we look at some of the results of such a course, we shall find them to be evil in many respects. Time is thus wasted, which ought to be employed in works of philanthropy and charity, in intellectual improvement, in social duties, in religious reading and meditation; for all which time, an account will be required from each of us at last. Money is misused, by being expended in articles of ornament, as costly as they are useless, and in frequent changes in order to keep pace with the prevailing modes, instead of being applied to feed the hungry, cover the naked, and comfort the distressed; for, as William Penn truly remarked, the expense of the trimmings of the vain world would suffice to clothe the naked one. But above all, the thoughts and affections, instead of being set on the adorning of the mind, on objects worthy of intelligent and immortal beings, are degraded and misapplied to merely personal adorning; in order to gratify vanity, and to attract the regard of the worldly-minded, producing many evil results.

Indulgence in gay attire is condemned by the general tenour and spirit of the New Testament, and by some of its direct precepts. How much is embraced in the command, " Be not conformed to this world, but be ye transformed by the renewing of the mind!" And we are assured that " the lust of the flesh, and the lust of the eye, and the pride of life, are not of the Father, but of the world." The apostles Paul and Peter, in very particular terms, forbade the female believers from using plaited or embroidered hair, gold, pearls, and costly array; and recommended, in their stead, good works, and a meek and quiet spirit,—ornaments of great and intrinsic value. While gay clothing frequently leads into great temptations, and further departures from the narrow path of self-denial; a plain attire, on the contrary, proves to many persons an early and encouraging step in that path, a check against hurtful company and vain amusements, and is to some extent a safeguard to the youthful and inexperienced, from much that is frivolous, dissipating, and sinful. Though often felt to be a trial and sacrifice of the feelings and will; yet if it be borne in the service of Him who endured the cross and despised the shame for the sake of his followers, it proves a wholesome discipline to the mind; and, when maintained in a proper spirit, strengthens it against yielding to self-gratification, thus serving as an important accessory to high Christian principle.

The Redeemer's yoke is declared to be easy, and his burden light,—a truth which is confirmed by the simple-hearted Christian in every age;—while the yoke and burden of the vain, fashionable, dissipated world, to say nothing of the overt sins which often follow, are harassing to the mind and conscience, destructive of true peace, encouraging to evil passions, and at the end are found to be insupportable.

Thirdly, as to Behaviour :—

Plainness of behaviour is understood by Friends to imply principally a non-compliance with the customary practices, of taking off the hat, bowing the body, or using other complimentary tokens of honour and submission to our fellow-creatures, so generally observed in the world. While to uncover the head, and to bow the knee, in devout reverence to the Divine being, are acts of obeisance due from every one; our faithful predecessors felt that, as in the case of words, so in this of actions, it was decidedly improper to pay the same marks of respect to mortal man as to the Supreme Majesty on high.

"Stand up, I myself also am a man," was the impressive language by which the apostle Peter rebuked Cornelius, who showed him undue reverence. And the angel described by John said to him, under similar circumstances, "See thou do it not, I am thy fellow-servant; worship God." The example of Mordecai, who bowed not nor did reverence to Haman, is a striking example of obedience to duty, in firmly refusing to pay insincere marks of honour to the vainly great.

While a testimony against insincerity and servility in behaviour is maintained by the watchful Christian, he will also feel the pleasure and the obligation to be courteous to all men. True courtesy, whether of language or behaviour, does not consist in complimentary phraseology or bodily obeisances: it carries the evidence of its own sincerity to the heart of the thoughtful and candid.

Plainness of behaviour is not confined to abstaining from the practices already noticed; it embraces also that seriousness of deportment, contrasted with levity and trifling, which becomes a responsible being; it is the effect of sincerity of mind on the daily life, instead of the flattering dissimulation, which the mere worldly man expects and shows. He whose heart is actuated by the love of God and his neighbour, can neither fail to be courteous, nor stoop to be adulatory, to his fellow-man. He who feels that he is a feeble being, surrounded by powerful temptations, and assaulted by an unwearied adversary, but contending for a glorious immortal prize,—and who is there that ought not so to feel?—may well be thoughtful and serious, lest he fail in the conflict. But, if faithful, he will often be filled with a heavenly peace, and an innocent cheerfulness, which the world can neither give nor destroy; as far removed from levity and flattery as from melancholy and incivility,—Christian simplicity and love, simple-hearted kindness, and true courtesy being the natural fruits.

In taking this brief review of the manner in which the Society of Friends has been led to adopt the practices referred to, we have no wish to judge our fellow Christians, but rather to invite their candid and serious consideration to the subject. To our own Master each of us must stand or fall. Religious societies, as well as individuals, may have their special missions and lines of service to perform; and we, believe, that the mission or service of our religious body has been, and still is, both marked and useful in many respects, and not the least so in this. That we may make an exhibition of our simplicity, as well as perform other duties, in a pharisaical and self-righteous spirit, is sufficiently obvious; yet this affords no reason for conformity to the world, its vanity and insincerity.

It was doubtless in reference to the testimony of the whole life and conduct, and not to the mere words, that our Lord used that remarkable language, "Whoso shall confess me before men, him will I also confess before my Father which is in heaven;" "but whoso shall be ashamed of me and of my words, of him shall the Son of Man be ashamed when he cometh in glory."

If it should be thought by any that too much stress has been laid on the points under consideration, the writer may remark, that he has no desire to give them more than their due weight. Though not pleaded for as among "the weightier matters of the law," they are believed to have an important bearing on those weightier matters, and to be among the things which "ought not to be left undone," by the self-denying disciple of the lowly Jesus. While other branches of Christian duty are often enforced, these are rarely brought under notice; yet all, whether esteemed more or less important, which are truly based on the ground of conformity to the holy pattern and precepts of Christ and his apostles, are integral parts of the system of christian morals, and, as such, have strong claims on our faithful and consistent adoption.

Consistency is a word of extensive import, which may well lead many of us to examine what characters we maintain under different circumstances of daily occurrence. "Happy is he who condemneth not himself in that thing which he alloweth." If our simplicity be sincere and of real value, proceeding from a sense of duty and from the fear of the Lord, it will be carried out into our general conduct and habits of life. It will influence our desires, and appear in the character of our houses and furniture, our provision for the table, our establishments, and even our enjoyments. Truthfulness and sincerity will regulate our conversation, our reading, and correspondence. Our "moderation would be known unto all men," and show itself in every position,—in business and in recreation, at home and abroad, whether in prosperity or adversity, in the domestic circle, or on the platform of public life; and each of us would be enabled, in all humility, to adopt the words of the apostle Paul, "My rejoicing is this, the testimony of my conscience, that in simplicity and godly sincerity, not with fleshly wisdom, but by the grace of God, I have had my conversation in the world."

END.

Printed by E. Couchman, 10, Throgmorton Street, London.

ON THE

WORSHIP OF GOD.

~~~~~~~~~~~~~~~~~~~~~

LONDON:

Printed for the TRACT ASSOCIATION of the SOCIETY OF FRIENDS.

Sold at the DEPOSITORY, 12, Bishopsgate Street Without.

1865.

No. 138.　．　　　　　　　　　[*Price 3d. per dozen.*]

ON THE

WORSHIP OF GOD.

"GOD is a spirit, and they that worship him must worship him in spirit and in truth." These were the words of the Lord Jesus, in his memorable conversation with the woman of Samaria, recorded in the fourth chapter of the Gospel according to John; and they ought always to be kept in mind, in considering the subject of worship, whether public or private.

Man in his fallen state, living carelessly and willingly in sin, is not in a condition to worship God in spirit and in truth; for in such a state, man is living in the service of the devil; and the Holy Scriptures declare, that "the sacrifices of the wicked are an abomination to the Lord." The question therefore naturally arises, In what way may a sinner come to "worship God in spirit and in truth?"

The words of the Saviour, "I came not to call the righteous, but sinners to repentance," convey an answer to this question. This subject is also illustrated by the Lord Jesus, in the parable of the Pharisee and the Publican, by placing the offensive self-right-eousness of the Pharisee, in contrast with the humility of the penitent Publican, who, in the depth of his contrition, "would not lift up so much as his eyes to heaven, but smote upon his breast and said, God be merciful to me a sinner;" and who, the Saviour tells us, "went down to his house justified, rather than the other." Luke xviii. 9.—14.

When the sinner attends to the convictions of the Holy Spirit, by which God, in mercy, enlightens his heart, and shows him his sins, in order to lead him to repentance, then he begins to worship God in spirit and in truth. God accepts the heartfelt prayers of repenting sinners, as they cry to Him for mercy, and for deliverance from the power of Satan. The pardon of past sin is granted to the penitent for Jesus' sake. who laid down His life a sacrifice for our sins; "the just for the unjust, that he might bring us to God."

The sincere offerings of the penitent believing soul, in all the stages of its Christian progress, are acceptable worship to God, being "in spirit and in truth." The watchfulness of such souls over their thoughts, their words, and their actions, in the fear of the Lord, lest they should sin; their trust in the mercy of God, extended to them through Jesus Christ, and their good works, the fruit of the Holy Spirit, working in them to will and to do of the Lord's good pleasure, are also acceptable to God as worship performed "in spirit and in truth;" for the worship of God is honour or service rendered unto Him, in the temple of their own hearts, whether in solitude, or in their daily walk in life, or when believers are met together with their hearts turned to the Lord.

There are few particular directions in the New Testament respecting public worship, but in the tenth chapter of the Epistle to the Hebrews, we are admonished to " consider one another, to provoke unto love and to good works : not forsaking the assembling of ourselves together, as the manner of some is; but exhorting one another." There are also directions in the twelfth chapter of the First Epistle to the Corinthians, respecting the orderly exercise of spiritual gifts in the assembled church.

It is the privilege of believers in Christ to unite in worship, and that in great simplicity : for He has said, " Where two or three are gathered together in my name, there am I in the midst of them." Matt. xviii. 20. This is without any reference to the nature of the place where they are met, or to the presence of any man to teach them, or to preach to them. It may be in a house, or in a field, or in a ship, or on a mountain : but be it wheresoever it may, when believers are so met, the presence of their Lord sanctifies the place. The provision of a suitable place for public worship is a matter of reasonable convenience, but the idea that worship must necessarily be in some building, set apart for the purpose, and conducted by an appointed minister, is without authority from Christ or His apostles. The martyr Stephen plainly tells us that " the most High dwelleth not in temples made with hands"—Acts vii. 48 ; and the Apostle Paul said to the men of Athens, " God that made the world and all things therein, seeing that he is Lord of heaven and earth, dwelleth not in temples made with hands : neither is worshipped with men's hands, as though he needed anything." Acts xvii. 24, 25.

The religion of the Gospel, the worship which the Gospel prescribes, and that which alone is acceptable to God, is adapted to all the situations in which man can be found; for, as said the apostle Peter, when he first preached -the Gospel to a company of Gentiles, in the house of Cornelius the centurion, "God is no respecter of persons, but in every nation he that feareth him and worketh righteousness is accepted with him." Wheresoever two or three or more such persons are met together in the name of Christ, there is an assembly for the worship of God. God accepts the worship of these, because their Mediator, Intercessor, and High Priest, Jesus Christ the Lord, is present with them. He bows their hearts before his Father; He causes "his Holy Spirit to help their infirmities," and to "make intercession for them with groanings which cannot be uttered," and draws forth their spirits in silent reverence, or in prayer, thanksgiving, or praise.

If such companies remain in silence all the time in which they are so met, God is nevertheless worshipped by them, "in spirit and in truth;" and He at seasons gives them a solemnizing sense of His presence, by His love spread over them, and shed abroad in their hearts, to their great comfort and encouragement. Seeing Him through faith, who is invisible to sight, they feel the blessedness of this united worship. Their hearts are warmed with renewed love to their Heavenly Father, their Redeemer and their Sanctifier. Their unity one with another is increased. They rejoice in their experience of the communion of Saints. They feed together on Christ the living bread from heaven. They realize the declaration of the Saviour, "If any man hear my voice and open the door, I will come in to him and sup with him, and he with me." Rev. iii. 20.

If at other times they are permitted to feel their own helplessness and unworthiness, it is in order that they

may be deepened in that poverty of spirit on which
Christ pronounced the blessing: " Blessed are the
poor in spirit, for theirs is the kingdom of heaven;
and that that holy condition of soul may be promoted,
in which they can "worship God in the spirit, and
rejoice in Christ Jesus, and have no confidence in
the flesh." Christ is the minister of the sanctuary
to such worshippers; and through His mediation as
their High Priest, they are enabled unitedly " to offer
up spiritual sacrifices, acceptable to God by Jesus
Christ." 1 Pet. ii. 5.

When the Lord's believing children meet before
Him in silence with their attention turned to the
teaching of His Spirit, if He influence any of them to
preach or vocally to pray, these acts, being then performed in spirit and in truth, are acts of acceptable
worship: and as the hearts of those who hear are
humbled before the Lord, under the power of His
Spirit attending such ministry, that worship of God,
which is " in spirit and in truth," is not interfered
with, but on the contrary is promoted.

If there be assembled with such worshippers, those
who are not yet turned to the Lord, the ministry of
the Gospel, under the power of the Holy Spirit, is
often so blessed as to turn them to repentance toward
God and faith toward our Lord Jesus Christ; and by
thus " baptizing them in the name of the Father, the
Son, and the Holy Ghost," to lead them also, to
worship the Father, " in spirit and in truth; for
thus by instrumental means, as well as by the direct
power of the Holy Spirit, does the Father still condescend to seek such worshippers to worship Him.

Howsoever Christian ministry may be exercised,
whatever in it is effectual in bringing sinners to
repentance and to the exercise of faith in Christ, is to

be esteemed as partaking of the character of that spiritual baptism, with which Christ sent his disciples to baptize, when he commanded them, saying, "Go ye therefore and teach all nations, baptizing them in the name of the Father, and of the Son, and of the Holy Ghost: teaching them to observe all things whatsoever I have commanded you: and lo, I am with you alway, even unto the end of the world." Matt. xxviii. 19, 20. And whensoever assembled Christians are reverently bowed in spirit before the Lord, whether under the baptizing power of such ministry, or under the immediate baptism of the Holy Spirit administered by Christ Jesus, the ever living head of the universal Church, which he hath purchased with his own blood, there also, "God" who "is a spirit, is worshipped in spirit and in truth."

The habitual attendance of a place of worship, the listening to the preaching of the Gospel or to the prayers of others, or the utterance of words in the form of prayer ourselves, will not constitute true worship, unless our hearts are turned to the Lord, with the desire that we may be delivered from the guilt and power of sin, and be enabled to walk before God in holiness of life

As our true happiness, both in this world and in the world to come, is inseparably connected with our being worshippers of God "in spirit and in truth," let us consider what we know, in our own experience, of this worship. If we be strangers to it, let us be willing to see our dangerous condition, lest God call us to judgment unexpectedly, and we be found to have wasted in sin, that time which he gave us so to employ, as that we might be trained to love and serve Him; and let us repent and seek reconciliation with Him through Jesus Christ. But if we have tasted that the Lord is gracious, and have already known His love in Christ Jesus to warm our souls, and excite love to Him in return for His love, let us cherish this love, and in daily communion with Him, seek the help of His Spirit to enable us to serve Him. Then those encouraging sayings of Christ will be fulfilled in our experience, " He that hath my commandments and keepeth them, he it is that loveth me: and he that loveth me shall be loved of my Father, and I will love him and manifest myself to him." " If a man love me, he will keep my words; and my Father will love him, and we will come unto him and make our abode with him." John xiv. 21—23. May we then be among the blessed number who worship God " in spirit and in truth," in the public congregation, in our families, in our closets, and in the secret temple of our own hearts; and thus, when He calls us from this state of existence, be found, with our robes washed and made white in the blood of the Lamb, and prepared to unite in everlasting worship with those who are " before the throne of God, and serve him day and night in his temple."

END.

Printed by E. Couchman & Co., 10, Throgmorton Street, London.

OLD JOHNSON,

REFORMED POACHER.

~~~~~~~~~~~~~~~~~~~

LONDON:

Printed for the TRACT ASSOCIATION of the SOCIETY OF FRIENDS.

Sold at the DEPOSITORY, 12, Bishopsgate Street, Without.

—

1866.

No. 139.   [*Price 4d. per dozen.*]

OLD JOHNSON,

THE REFORMED POACHER.

JOHN JOHNSON, a short account of whose life is given in this Tract, was born about the year 1760. When of an age to work, he was employed in the slate quarries at Swithland, near Leicester. Here he worked for many years, but at the same time became a great poacher; and when forty years old, and having a wife and four children, he was sentenced to transportation for seven years for robbing a fish-pond.

Some time before this occurred, he attended a religious meeting, to which the people of the neighbourhood were invited, at the request of Ann Burgess, a minister in the Society of Friends. She directed her hearers to the convictions of the Holy Spirit, condemning them for sin in the secret of their own hearts, and leading those who attend to these convictions to repent, and to seek forgiveness through Jesus Christ, and strength through Him to forsake their sins. Johnson's heart was touched, and desires after salvation were awakened in his mind: but not acting in faith on what he then felt, he again yielded to temptation, and fell into the sin which cost him his liberty, and as it proved in the end, made him an exile for the remainder of his days.

While he was in prison, the same Friend visited him and gave him much good advice, and presented him with a Bible which he often read. When on board of the Cornwallis, the ship in which he was sent to

New South Wales, he was so ill that his life was despaired of; and he felt that he was unfit to die, and to "stand before the judgment seat of Christ;" he therefore determined to reform; and on landing in New South Wales he gained a good character for honesty and industry. At that time prisoners of good conduct were allowed the benefit of their own labours on their arival in New South Wales, but this privilege has not been granted them for many years past, until by several years of orderly, unpaid labour, they have gained tickets-of-leave. In the course of a few years Johnson earned £300, and he hoped by means of this to return to his family when the time of his sentence should expire. In the mean time tidings of his wife's death reached him and distressed him greatly. A doctor and a lawyer professed great sympathy for him: they were men whom he considered much better educated than he was, and he felt greatly flattered by their friendship. They advised him not to mourn over the dead, but to rejoice with the living; and they promised to do great things for him if he would drink with them. He yielded to their solicitations, and they drank freely, and kept him intoxicated, till £70 were spent, which they left Johnson to pay! When he was again sober, the bitterness of his circumstances rankled in his bosom; and having once stifled his painful feelings by strong drink, he returned to it again and again for relief, till the remainder of his £300 was gone, and a craving appetite for strong drink set up, which he did not overcome for many years.

When Norfolk Island was occupied with a view to raising Indian corn for the supply of New South Wales, Johnson was sent there; and while there he became free; but both there and while in New South Wales the influence of bad example told fearfully upon him, and he sank deeper into sin.

The experiment of raising Indian corn for New South Wales on Norfolk Island did not prove successful; many of the people were therefore removed from that Island to Van Diemen's land, and among these was John Johnson. Here he continued to feel the bitterness of his exile, but now he had not the means to pay his passage home, and the Government makes no provision for the return of those who have been transported. Sometimes he also felt bitterly his sore bondage to sin, and prayed that the Lord would send him deliverance.

At this period Van Diemen's Land was much infested by Bush-rangers; these were convicts who had run away from their masters or from the Government works, and had taken to a life of plunder. Johnson's hut was attacked by a party of these robbers, who tied his hands behind him, and set him on his knees to pray, before a large fire, in which they told him they would burn his body, to prevent detection. By the overruling of the Most High they were prevented from carrying their threat into execution; but they set fire to his hut and burnt it with all his household effects, including his Bible. This was a great loss to him, and it was many long years before he obtained another. A party of these marauders compelled him, at another time, to go with them to a house they were about to rob; they placed him in front to receive any shots, should any be fired to repel them; but they got quiet possession, the people being out; they then compelled Johnson to drink a large quantity of rum, which made him helplessly drunk; and in this state they put him into a bed in the house, and left him there, for the double purpose of preventing him from giving an alarm before they escaped, and of throwing suspicion upon him in connection with the robbery; but the character he had gained for honesty and truth-speaking, saved him from such suspicion.

Thus time passed on with a variety of trials till 1830, when Johnson was 70 years old. At this time a Wesleyan Tract Distributor found him a few miles from Hobart Town, "three parts drunk," on a sabbath morning, in a room where several others were in bed, completely intoxicated; and where some of them had been fighting in the night, and the floor was smeared with their blood! Hopeless as this state of things appeared, the messenger of " good tidings" left them some Tracts: Johnson read these, and under the blessing of God, they were the means of reviving his desires after salvation. He went in consequence, with one of his companions, to hear some of the Wesleyans, who about that time began to preach at O'Brien's Bridge, a village near to which he resided. These two men now became awakened to 'a sense of their awful condition, in living in the service of the devil through sin; and they groaned under the burden of their sins, desiring deliverance. Confiding in the declaration, that "the effectual fervent prayer of a righteous man availeth much," Johnson and his friend went to the Wesleyan Chapel in Hobart Town, and asked the prayers of the congregation. By their own account and that of others, this was a time of great excitement, but the Lord who condescends to the weakness of the sincere hearted, was pleased to grant an answer of peace to their fervent supplications; and these two true penitents returned home under a sense of the pardoning mercy of God, granted to repenting sinners through Jesus Christ, who offered himself on the cross, a sacrifice for the sins of the whole world. The future life of Johnson and his friend proved that they had really turned from following Satan to following the Lord.

From this time they joined a Wesleyan congregation, who soon erected a little chapel at O'Brien's Bridge; and meetings for prayer and mutual edification were often held in a cottage belonging to John Leach, a pious Wesleyan, in the neighbouring settlement of Glenorchy. Two rooms in this cottage Johnson occupied; and when age and infirmity rendered him incapable of paying rent, he was permitted by the pious owner, whose own means of support were very slender, to live in them rent free.

For a few of the latter years of the life of old Johnson, as he was now generally called, he suffered much from a bleeding cancer, and this in the end brought him to his grave.

In the year 1834, he was visited by James Backhouse and George Washington Walker, when he gave them much of the information here already noted down: he also informed them, that from long want of practice he had almost lost the power of reading; that after his conversion he got a Testament; but as he could not follow the lines without a pointer, and he had used the shank of a tobacco-pipe for that purpose, the print was nearly worn out. A Bible of a larger type was soon after obtained for him; and by the aid of a quill pointer, he read it easily to his great comfort.

Speaking of poaching, he said it was a bad practice, and he did not think anybody could follow it with a good conscience; and to this cause he attributed his transportation. It had separated him from his family, of whom he had not heard for many years.

In a visit paid to him the same year, he spoke of being very feeble, and compared himself to an old, cracked, earthen vessel, kept together by being bound about; but he was full of thanksgiving to the Lord for all his mercies, and of admiration that he should be so regarded of the Most High: he said, "What am I, a poor bit of dust, that the Lord should so regard me? I who lived so long in sin and rebellion against God; he has had mercy upon me, but I can never forgive myself, nor love him sufficiently. What am I, or what are we all, that the Lord should thus regard us?" In an illness from which he had scarcely recovered at this time, he said, he cast himself upon his Saviour, and felt quite willing to die. In the violence of his pain, he prayed that if it was consistent with the Lord's will he might be eased, and permitted, before he was taken away, to speak a few words on the Lord's goodness; and immediately his pain abated. He said that he had for four years, been in the practice of getting out of bed every night and kneeling down to pray, in addition to praying at other times; that he was now getting so weak that it was with difficulty he could do it, and he began to question whether it was necessary. The feeble old man was reminded that "God is a spirit, and that they that worship him, must worship him in spirit and in truth;" and that it is the sincere prayer of the heart which he will accept, whether such prayer is put up on bended knees or in any other posture, or whether it is expressed in words or only in the secret language of the heart. Johnson said he was comforted by this view of the subject, and remarked, that he saw the matter more clearly, than he had before done; that when he was first turned to the Lord, he was so igno-rant as to think he must necessarily go into the bush 'to pray, where he could make a great noise. Since that time he had often gone with his friend John Leach, to a retired spot in his garden, which was beautifully situated on the side of the Derwent, and there had joined with him in prayer; and to this spot he con-tinued daily to go, to pour out his soul to his God and Saviour; but he was now growing so weak that he did not think he could go there much longer. He also said, that when he was newly turned to seek salvation, he thought he must do something which was difficult, to prove his love to God; and that for this purpose he left his house three times at midnight, and climbed into a difficult place among the mountains to pray; but he had long seen that this was a mistake; that God accepts a sincere heart for Christ's sake, and not for the sake of any of our own works.

When J. Backhouse and G. W. Walker were in New South Wales in 1835, they received the following letter from John Johnson.

Glenorchy, Van Diemen's Land,
Feb. 19th, 1835.

Dear Friends,
My affectionate concern for your welfare and prosperity in the good cause constrains me to write a few lines to you, in the fervent hope they will find you quite well in health, and strong in the mighty power of the God of Jacob. With regard to my poor infirm body, I am not well, nor do I suppose I shall ever more be so; but blessed be my Saviour who graciously strengthens me to bear the infirmities of the flesh. I can truly say that my mountain stands strong; and my faith and hope grow stronger and stronger; and I hope they will continue to do so unto the perfect day. Bless the Lord, O my soul, and help me to show forth Thy praise.

The pain in my breast is increasing daily; if, there-fore, you could please to advise me of something to relieve me I should be truly thankful, for the pains are now frequent and most excruciating; but as my will is swallowed up in the Lord's most holy will, I am enabled to bear all, with that resignation which is so much his due.

Remember me, if you please, to Daniel Wheeler and his son; and though 'tis very probable they will never see my face in the flesh, still I am persuaded we shall all reap the harvest of eternal felicity, if we endure to the end. May the Lord help us onward; and to his glorious name be the praise for evermore.

I trust the time is fast approaching when I shall have the pleasure to hear from my friends in England, before I give up the ghost; and as soon as I hear from them I will be sure to let you know; and if you should hear before me, do let me know.

And now to conclude, I heartily wish to hear from you, to know how you are getting on, both with things spiritual and temporal. Now "may the good will of Him that dwelt in the bush," rest upon you both, and abide with you for ever.

From your affectionate friend,
JOHN JOHNSON.

The much desired information from England was soon after obtained. A nephew of Johnson's old friend, Ann Burgess, had made out his relations, who were glad to hear of his conversion. Death had made inroads in his family, but three of his children were still living; and one of Johnson's brothers said he hoped and trusted that if it should not be his lot to meet his brother again on earth, they might meet in heaven, and added, "Which may the God of all grace grant, for his name and mercy's sake."

In 1837, J. Backhouse and G. W. Walker were again in Van Diemen's Land; and visited John Johnson, whose strength had failed greatly; his speech had also become very feeble; but he was in a sweet state of mind. In his simple way, he described himself as often feeling as if heaven broke over his head, with such an overflowing as he could not give an idea of; he said he was endeavouring to wait patiently;

knowing that he should be called when the Lord saw that he was prepared, and feeling quite willing to go. He said also that he had now many comfortable "blanket prayers," not being able to kneel at all. He also spoke of the wonderful change which the Lord had wrought in him, by his grace; so that he who was before an old sinner, whose very thoughts were corrupt, was now turned from evil thoughts and brought to think on his God and Saviour, and to feel his love and mercy continually supporting him. This great change continued to show itself, when, in a fit of illness, he was often delirious; for then he was almost constantly singing hymns of thanksgiving and praise, or talking as if expostulating with persons who were living in sin, and advising them to turn to the Lord.

In the year 1837, J. Backhouse found Old Johnson almost confined to bed; he remarked that he could not now kneel in prayer; that if he were on his knees he could not get up again; but he said, he often prayed in secret, in his heart, particularly when in bed; that sometimes he felt the Lord's presence, but sometimes did not; that he felt it good to wait upon the Lord in silence; and he commemorated the goodness of his Heavenly Father in causing his temporal wants to be supplied. He sent messages of love to many of his acquaintance, and desired that they would pray for him. At this time he expressed a doubt of the propriety of bad people using the Lord's prayer, and said he thought it could not be right for them to say "Our Father which art in heaven," when by the showing of Holy Scripture, they were "of their Father the devil;" he also said he feared many people talked of religion and being born again, who knew nothing of such a work.

On the 20th J. Backhouse again visited him and found him weaker, but full of love: he said he felt more and more, in seasons of emptiness, a fear lest he should fall, and that it was only by Divine grace that he could be preserved to the end; but that he was often sensible of the Lord's presence, and that he believed he should soon see his Saviour.

On the 26th, G. W. Walker and another Friend

found the good old man far gone, but still able to speak; hoping in the Lord and anticipating a happy change.

Early in the morning of the 27th, Old Johnson peacefully breathed his last, while one of his neighbours was reading to him the 31st Psalm, upon which he had dwelt much, with great comfort for several days. A few minutes before his departure, on being asked if he felt comfortable, he replied, "Yes, I shall soon be happy in heaven," and added something about his friend, John Leach, whom he hoped to join in everlasting praises to their Saviour.

"Is not this a brand plucked out of the fire," a monument of the long-suffering of God, reminding us of his own solemn declaration, by the mouth of the prophet Ezekiel, "As I live, saith the Lord God, I have no pleasure in the death of the wicked, but that the wicked should turn from his way and live."

We have no information of the early training of Old Johnson, but it is evident from his own account, that in the prime of manhood, a merciful visitation of Divine grace was granted him. Being unfaithful to the convictions of this grace, to which his attention had been directed, he again yielded to temptation, and reaped the bitter fruits of sin, in bondage and exile from his native land. In this condition, after giving some evidence of a desire to reform, he fell into the company of educated drunkards; and being carried away by the flatteries of these servants of Satan, he was brought, in addition to all his other misery, under the curse of a drunken appetite; and but for the renewed mercy of a long-suffering God, would, at last, in all likelihood, have filled a drunkard's grave. But God, in his mercy, regarded him in his bondage to sin, and heard his cries for deliverance, and sent to him another messenger, with the invitation to repent, to believe on the Lord Jesus and live; and Johnson now exercised faith and obeyed the message; the torrent of sin and consequent misery under which he had reached seventy years of age, was stayed; and he was made a partaker of that peace which flows as a river in the heart cleansed by the blood of Christ, and sanctified by the Holy Spirit given of the Father to all who truly repent and believe in the Lord Jesus. Being thus turned from darkness to light, and brought from under the power of Satan to God, Johnson was taught of the Lord, and grew in grace, and in the knowledge of God and of the Lord Jesus Christ, and became an heir of eternal life.

May the reader examine himself as to what he knows of "the grace of God that bringeth salvation." If, unhappily, he be a stranger to its converting power, let him seek after it as diligently as they that dig for gold, being assured that God is waiting to be gracious even unto him. In the Saviour's promise, "Ask and ye shall receive; seek and ye shall find; knock and it shall be opened unto you," every encouragement is offered to the poor contrite sinner. Such an one will not ask in vain; the promise will be fulfilled; this grace will be given him; and joining in with it, through Divine mercy, he will be favoured to escape the misery that follows in the train of sin. If, happily, he knows something of this grace—if in the secret of his heart he hears a voice saying, "This is the way, walk in it," when tempted to turn to the right hand or to the left;—if whilst reading the Holy Scriptures, or whilst listening to the preaching of the Gospel, or in silent meditation before the Lord, he feels his spirit tendered, a hatred of sin, and a longing after holiness kindled in his heart, O let him cherish these feelings as evidences of the 'love of God in Christ Jesus our Lord. Let him wait on the Lord daily for a renewal of these favours; let him watch and pray lest he enter into temptation.

Had Old Johnson, at an earlier period, listened to and obeyed the heavenly call, how different might have been his condition! Instead of spending thirty years, from the prime of manhood till he was three score years and ten, in the service of sin and Satan, with nothing but the miserable wages of these bad masters,—exile, shame, and suffering,—he might have been a happy man, blessed himself, and a blessing to those around him; "reconciled to God by the death of his Son;" a servant of Christ, reaping the blessed fruits of that service; love, joy, and peace; and realizing on earth a foretaste of the happiness of heaven. As a brand plucked out of the fire in the eleventh hour, poor old Johnson partook of these blessings, but his thirty years of sin were irrecoverably and miserably lost.

Reader, "Now is the accepted time; Now, is the day of salvation;" "To-day, if ye will hear His voice, harden not your hearts;" "Work while it is called To-day, for the night cometh when no man can work." Accept the offers of Divine mercy; take heed to that grace which teaches us in the secret of our own hearts, that "denying ungodliness and worldly lusts, we should live soberly, righteously, and godly, in this present world; looking for that blessed hope and the glorious appearing of the Great God and our Saviour Jesus Christ, who gave himself for us, that he might redeem us from all iniquity, and purify unto himself a peculiar people, zealous of good works."

END.

Printed by E. Couchman, & Co. 10, Throgmorton Street, London.

MARY CASSON;

OR

OLD THINGS PASSED AWAY.

~~~~~~~~~~~~~~~~

In the following short account of Mary Casson, we read he history of one who in the days of health and vigour liligently performed many of her outward duties, but vho failed in giving her heart to God, and was thus inprepared for the hour of trial and suffering, or for the iolemn realities of a death bed. To trace the blessed nd happy change that took place in her views and eelings after she had seen herself to be a sinner, and had xperienced the pardoning mercy of God in Christ Jesus, nay be helpful and encouraging to others, who whilst ving in forgetfulness of God, or trusting to a life of noral propriety, are still dissatisfied, still find there is omething which the soul longs for, and which the vorld cannot give.

Mary Casson was born in the North of England, and ft her parents' roof at the early age of twelve years, to nter upon domestic service. From this time she knew ttle of a mother's care; and in after life she remarked ow mercifully she was preserved from the dangers that urrounded her youth and inexperience in her first place.

She was active, clever, and industrious, of strict ntegrity and propriety of conduct; and became a horoughly good servant, very attentive to the comforts

No. 140.   [*Price 3d. per dozen.*]

and devoted to the interests of those with whom she
lived. She was many years in service, having entered it
so young, though she lived scarcely to middle age; and
being experienced as well as capable, she was much
valued, especially in her two last places.

Her connections were respectable; mostly small farmers
Before leaving home she had received a little education
and she improved the advantages within her reach
whilst living in respectable well-ordered families. Thu
she deservedly obtained the regard of her employers
two of whom left her small legacies; these, with he
own careful savings and some additional helps, amounter
to a considerable sum for one in her station, when sh
entered on her last situation in the early part of th
year 1837. The possession of this money, however, dir
not prevent her from cheerfully performing the humble
kinds of work, although it was her great delight to b
occupied in those higher services which gave scope t
her talents.

Having so many good qualities, Mary's mistre
thought she should find in her a really valuable help
and was only discouraged by her having a hard cougl
which she said she generally had in winter, and a
this lessened with the coming on of spring, it cease
to give much uneasiness. Yet it was not very lon
before it was perceived, that with all her exceller
qualifications, it might still be said to her, as to tl
young man who had done so well from his youth :-
"One thing thou lackest."

Her heart was not humbled: she had not yet give
way to the working of that power which is as a fire ar
hammer, to break the rock in pieces. This was shov
by the manner in which symptoms of more serious illne
were received. Instead of submitting to her alter
circumstances, and attending to the cautions given h

respecting her health, she disregarded them, persisting in going through her accustomed work, when almost unable to do so, saying, " I will fight with it."

. At this time an almost painful independence of character was manifest. The thought of receiving wages and maintenance, while unable fully to perform her duties, was distressing to her. She became extremely anxious to go back to the north to her own relations (having removed with the family to their house near London), rather than remain where she could imagine herself a burden. In the course of this spring, she was placed for two months in that excellent institution, " The Invalid Asylum for respectable Females," at Stoke Newington, where she was well cared for, both medically, and in all other respects. She came out, apparently much better ; but the complaint had become too deeply fixed upon the lungs, probably for a considerable time before, for this improvement to be more than temporary. She always looked back with satisfaction on the time spent at the Invalid Asylum, where she had the privilege of association with some pious inmates ; and where there is reason to believe some progress was made in preparation of heart to receive and obey the truth.

During the summer she had the advantage of medical advice, both in the neighbourhood of London, and at Leamington, where she passed two or three months with her mistress. But while at Leamington, disease evidently advanced, and she became unable to do more than attend to herself.

While struggling with the risings of impatience, under her increasing trial, she went to her own chamber, and taking up her Bible, it opened at the 51st Psalm, when the text, " Against thee, thee only have I sinned, and done this evil in thy sight," struck her eye, and was powerfully applied to her heart. She saw at once that these few emphatic words described her own case. Her conscience was smitten under the sense of her guilt before God. She felt that she was vile. She abhorred herself and repented in dust and ashes. She received a broken heart and a contrite spirit. From the powerful application of this text, she herself was accustomed to date her conversion. Undoubtedly it was made as a sharp arrow within her, bringing her more deeply under the work of "repentance towards God."

With the subject of this little memoir, there was from that hour a marked change. It was a change as evident as it was blessed; and might be seen, especially, in her grateful submission to those very circumstances which had lately so deeply tried her. Thankfulness took the place of impatience; and every murmur was lost in the accents of confession, prayer and praise. She could now see that her Heavenly Father was afflicting her in love, in order to draw her nearer to himself.

Her love of the Scriptures became ardent, from thi period to the close of her life. She perceived how the testified of Him in whom her contrite but believing sou had found peace. The depth of her humiliation unde the mighty hand of God had prepared her to receive with gladness the gospel of his Son. She had looked on Him whom her sins had pierced, and mourned; and was thus brought near that kingdom which belongs to the poor in spirit. She had mourned, and she was comforted with the hope of the gospel, through "faith in our Lord Jesus Christ."

In the humble trust that her sins were forgiven her for his name's sake, and of her adoption through grace she could now rejoice in Him; and was made a blessed partaker of the Holy Spirit, which, it is said, "they who believe on Christ should receive." Her delight in having the Bible read to her, when unable to join the family fo this purpose, will long be recollected with lively interest, by those engaged on these occasions. These readings were gratefully alluded to when near her end. The free conversation to which they led, afforded very satisfactory evidence of the gradual opening of her mind, to perceive divine truths as she advanced in holiness.

Late in the autumn of 1838, on leaving Leamington, she removed to the house of a relation in Kendal, where her master and mistress had repeated opportunities of visiting her, and of thankfully observing her steady growth in grace, and preparation for that world toward which she was hastening.

Her respect to the feelings and her regard to the interests of others, continued in lively exercise, though she was so ill. This was shown by her anxiety respecting her mistress, then in poor health; and her fears lest she should give way to too much concern on her account.

She felt much interested for the spiritual welfare of her fellow-servants, and when she could no longer speak to them on these subjects, she endeavoured to write to them, though it was too late for her to complete the letter.

She mourned over those who were living in sin, and when roused in the night by noise in the streets, the condition of the souls of those who through intemperance, made such disturbances, seemed to press heavily on her heart. She awoke on one of these occasions from a sort of sleep, and found herself saying,

"Stop poor sinner, stop and think."

She lamented over a relation who had fallen into this vice. Yet "Who maketh thee to differ?" was the language of her heart when speaking of these things.

She would observe how she had been watched over by a merciful God all her life; and though often careless and not alive to his goodness, how she had been kept from those great transgressions into which many others had fallen; and what a privilege she considered it was to have been placed, during later years, in religious families.

Alluding to the time she spent at a place where she lived many years, she described how she used to lead a very quiet orderly life, attending a place of worship regularly, and liking to hear religion talked of; but how different things now appeared to her. "There was no taking up the cross there." She now wished to invite others to seek that peace and happiness which she had found, in giving up her heart to serve the Lord; but when her acquaintance seemed little moved, she said, "Perhaps, it is just as I should have done myself, some time ago."

She had made a judicious will, disposing of her little property, in the earlier part of her illness; and though naturally of an anxious turn in worldly matters, her mind seemed perfectly at rest concerning them after this time.

Her heart at times overflowed in the feeling of the goodness of God to her. She repeatedly spoke with great humility of her hope of eternal happiness, whenever the end should come. She was ready to depart and be with Christ, but her mind was stayed in that quietness and confidence which the Lord alone can give, and she desired patiently to wait his time. She gave directions as to her funeral with great calmness, and with the same consideration for the convenience of others, which had before been so striking.

She spoke one day sweetly of her sick bed, as her place of prayer, and she greatfully acknowledged her ability to pray in her wakeful and wearisome nights, and the many beautiful and comforting texts which were brought to her recollection, and which she was enabled to turn into prayers and praises. On one occasion she said to a friend, "You are fond of good reading, and so was I before I became so very weak; but when you come to such a time as this, I believe you will find that nothing but the Scriptures will do; and even that in a very small compass, just a few texts." She was then very much reduced, and could only speak a few sentences at a time, and those word by word; yet she generally appeared comfortable and confiding. About this time she observed to a friend, that though her feelings varied, her faith was never permitted to fail, and that she thought it would be wrong to doubt, after having had her Saviour's love and mercy so graciously made known to her. In conversation with an old fellow-servant, she expressed her thankfulness for her change of views and the comfort she now experienced, which she said was of greater value than the brightest things she had known when in health. She told her, it was the passage in the 51st Psalm, already mentioned, which first seemed to bring home the truths of religion to her soul. She said she had outwardly respected the Scriptures before, and stood up for them, if spoken against in her presence, yet did not inwardly feel their value : but that the words, "Against thee, thee only, have I sinned," and "Create in me a clean heart," came with power to her heart, and melted it into deep repentance. At another time she said in reference to this Psalm, perhaps she ought not to prefer one part of the Bible to another, but her own experience in connection with it had made her value it particularly.

To one who visited her she related, as a proof of her former thoughtless state, how she would come into the morning family reading, and perhaps have her whole attention engrossed by some article of furniture, which she had forgotten to dust or clean; and her thoughts were thus led away from the most important things.

How needful is it to watch, even by those who have tasted the Lord's goodness, against the attention being diverted when professedly employed in holy things.

Humble trust in the mercy of her Saviour continued to mark her course to the close of her sufferings. The day before her death, a kind friend suggested that a few passages of Scripture would suit her better than much reading. "Yes," she replied, "she could not do with anything in a large way now, she was so very weak." Her visitor was unwilling to induce her to speak much, but mentioned some comforting texts, and alluded to the hymn—

"The Saviour has pass'd thro' its portals before thee ;"—

reminding her also of Baxter's dying expression, that he was "almost well." She seemed quite able to listen, and expressed no doubts or fears.

She sunk rapidly at last, but without much apparent increase of suffering; and her dismissal was truly peaceful. Thus, in answer to prayer, was the way made easy to this convert of grace; whom the regenerating power of the Holy Spirit had made as a little child, and taught to lean on her Redeemer, the Beloved of souls. Brought nigh by his blood unto the Father, the eternal God was her refuge, and underneath were the everlasting arms.

END.

London: Printed by E. Couchman and Co., 10, Throgmorton Street, for the TRACT ASSOCIATION of the SOCIETY OF FRIENDS. Sold at the Depository, 12, Bishopsgate Street Without.—1866.

ADRIFT ON A RAFT;

OR,

THE WRECK OF THE ARCTIC.

THE American Mail steam-ship, the Arctic, with more than two hundred passengers, left Liverpool on the 20th of ninth month (Sept.), 1854, and on the 27th of the same month, when 65 miles N.E. of Cape Race, New-foundland, she was run into by a French iron steamer, and in four hours disappeared beneath the waves. Of the passengers and crew, about forty were saved in one of the boats, a few others were picked up from rafts by passing vessels. The following personal narrative is given by James Smith, of Mississippi, who, after passing two nights and part of three days floating alone on a few planks lashed together, was saved by Captain Russell, of the Cambria.

But before introducing this striking narrative, we invite the reader's attention for a few moments to a brief mention of Mahlon Day a fellow-passenger of James Smith, and a member of the Society of Friends, known to many in this country, and to many more in his native land, America, as an experienced and exemplary christian. He with his wife and daughter perished in the waves.

Captain Luce, commander of the Arctic, and one of the few who survived the wreck, informs us that five minutes before the ship went down, Mahlon Day asked his opinion as to the probability of safety. On being told by Captain Luce that there was now no hope, Mahlon Day shook hands with him, bade him farewell, and said, "We shall meet hereafter." He then rejoined his wife and daughter, and was seen to go down clasping them in his arms. Captain Luce, who was on the Arctic whilst she was sinking, says, that on rising again to the surface, he seized upon a piece of a wheel-house, and

No. 141.   [*Price 4d. per dozen.*]

with eleven others, succeeded in getting on it. Presently he saw some one on a door, paddling towards them with his hands. It was Mahlon Day, who soon joined them, and stood with them for more than an hour, cheering them and turning their thoughts upon their only hope. Observing at length that the little craft was rapidly becoming water-logged, he turned to Captain Luce and said, "I see we are too many here, and I endanger the rest, I will take to my door again;" which he did, and was soon hidden from their view by the fog and the darkness. Just before leaving, he exclaimed, "My wife and child! they are gone!" His whole demeanour through this scene of trial, betokened resignation to the will of his Divine Master, and implicit reliance on Him who alone can save. His last act was one of self-sacrifice for the safety of others. Such, in Mahlon Day, were some of the results of a real reception of the Gospel of Christ. It does not extinguish the love of life, nor the conjugal and parental affections, but gives nobler and higher motives for the preservation of the one and a richer sense of enjoyment of both these blessings. By the grace of God, Mahlon Day had been found a faithful servant of Christ amidst life and its duties. The same grace was found equal to his needs in this hour of extremity, and thus he was prepared to meet his Saviour amidst the tumult of the waves. To him "The Lord on high was mightier than the noise of many waters, yea, than the mighty waves of the sea."

James Smith thus commences his narrative :—" I was a passenger in the Arctic. We had been out from Liverpool seven days, and were in about longitude 52° W. and somewhere about 50 or 60 miles off Cape Race, on the coast of Newfoundland, when the dreadful occurrence took place on Wednesday, September 27th.

"During the day, up to the time of the accident, the weather had been quite foggy, and I was somewhat astonished and alarmed several times, when on deck, seeing the weather so thick that I fancied not more than three or four of the ship's lengths ahead could be seen, and she going on at full speed, without any alarm-bell steam-whistle or other signal being sounded at intervals, in some such manner as I had been accustomed to in a

fog, on other vessels. At about 15 minutes after the
meridian eight bells had been struck, and while sitting
in my state-room in the forward cabin, the earnest cry
of a voice on deck (which I at the moment took to be
that of the man on the look out) to 'stop her, stop her—
a steamer ahead!' was heard with alarm by myself and
all others in the cabin; at the same time the man giving
the alarm could be heard running off towards the engine-
room, and before he had reached it, we were made aware
of the concussion by a somewhat slight jar to our ship,
accompanied by a crashing noise against the starboard
bow. It was a moment of awe and suspense, but I think
we all seemed to satisfy ourselves that the shock was
slight, and that, as we were on so large and strong a
vessel no serious damage had happened or could well
happen to such a ship, in an occurrence of such a nature.
With such a reliance on my own mind, at any rate, I
was very quickly on deck, and, in detached accounts from
other passengers, learnt that a screw steamer, with all
sail set, had struck us on the starboard bow, and glancing
aft our starboard wheel-house, struck her again, and she
passed off astern of us, out of sight, immediately, in
the thick fog. I on the first glance at our bulwarks
thought that all was right with us, but instantly began
to get alarmed from our careening over on the side we
had been struck upon, as well as from the call to the
passengers to keep on the port side. I saw Captain Luce
on the paddle-box, giving orders in one way and another,
and most of the officers and men running here and there
on the deck, getting into an evident state of alarm without seeming to know what was to be done, or applying
their energies to any one thing in particular, except in
getting the anchors and other heavy articles over on to
the port side of the ship. I looked over the starboard
bow, and saw several large breaks in the side of our ship,
from 8 to 12 or 14 feet abaft the cutwater, and I was
convinced that in the 10 or 15 minutes' time our wheels
were further submerged in the water than usual. Our
ship seemed to right herself somewhat after getting the
deck weight upon the larboard, but it was too evident
that Captain Luce himself, as well as all hands, was
becoming aware of our danger; and, from the tremendous

volume of water being thrown out from our steam pumps I was convinced we were making water at a fearful rate A deep-seated, thoughtful look of despair began to settl upon every countenance—no excitement, but ladies an children began to collect on deck with anxious and en quiring looks, receiving no hope or consolation : wif and husband, father and daughter, brother and sister would weep in each other's embrace, or kneel togethe imploring Almighty God for help. Men would go abou the decks in a sort of bewilderment as to what was bes to be done ; now laying hold of the hand-pumps wit redoubled energy, or with sickening effort applying thei power to the hauling up of freight out of the forwar hold, already floating in water before the lower hatches were opened. System of management or concentration of effort was never commenced or applied to any one object. Two separate ineffectual attempts to stop the leaking by dropping a sail down over the bow were made, and the engines were kept working the ship a-head toward the land ; but in the course of an hour, I should think, from the time of the collision, the lower furnaces were drowned out and the steam pumps stopped. Then it seemed to become only a question of how many hours or minutes we should be above water. The first officer, with his boat's crew, we had left behind from the first. The second officer, with a lot of the sailors, had lowered another boat, and left the ship, and a general scrambling seemed to be going on as to who should have places in the only two remaining boats that I saw on deck. One of those still remaining was a large one on the quarter-deck, occupied by ladies and children and some few gentlemen. The other was on the upper deck forward, and in the possession of a lot of firemen. Things were in this condition at about two hours after the accident. Captain Luce was superintending the lowering of spars and yards, aided mostly by passengers, for the purpose of making a raft, and complaining that all his officers and men had left him. Most of the women and children were collected round the boat on the quarter-deck, seemingly resigned to their fate. Some few gentlemen exerted all their powers to prevail on others to work on at the pumps, but all to no purpose ; the ship kept on gaining in quantity as steadily as time progressed. The engines had stopped working, and I, seeing that the chief engineer, with some of his assistants and firemen, had got the forward boat in the water over by the bow, under the pretence of working at the canvas which was hanging over the bow, so as to sink it down over the leaking places, but seeing, as I thought, symptoms of their real intention to get off from the ship without too many in the boat, I dropped myself down near by them on a small raft of three planks about a foot wide each, and 10 or 12 feet long, and an inch in thickness, lashed together with some rope and four handspikes, and which I had just previously helped to lower into the water, for the purpose of working from about the bow of the ship. Finding it bore me up, I shoved off, intending to get alongside of the engineers' boat, but as I shoved off, several firemen and one or two passengers dropped down into the boat, the engineer protesting against their doing so, and at the same time pushed off and pulled well away from the ship, with about 12 or 15 persons in his boat, declaring to those on board, at the same time, that he was not going off, but would stay by the ship to the last. At the same time he, or those in the boat with him, continued to pull away in what I considered was the direction of the land, and were in a few minutes lost in a fog. I now saw there was no probable chance for me but to remain where I was on my frail little raft, until I could see some better chance after or before the ship went down. She had now settled down to the wheel-houses. The upper furnaces had for some time been drowned out. People on board were doing nothing but firing signal guns of distress, trying to get spars overboard, and tearing doors off the hinges—nothing else seemed to present itself, as a means of saving the lives of some three hundred souls still on board. I have crossed the Atlantic nine times, and nearly every previous time have had in my charge one or more of my family or near relatives, but now I thanked my God that I had not even an acquaintance with me in this my adversity. I tightened up my little raft as well as I could, so as to make it withstand the buffetings and strainings of the heavy rolling sea, and with the aid of a long narrow piece of plank, which I tore up off the others, using it a a paddle. I kept hovering within about 200 or 300 yard of the sinking ship, watching operations there, an keeping myself from being drifted out of sight, so as t have what company there might be left on rafts like m own, after our doomed vessel had sunk beneath th surface. In this position I saw three different smal rafts like my own leave the ship, one of them with three and another with two of the firemen standing erect o them, the third with an old Frenchman we had alread picked up, and one of the mess boys of the ship sittin on it. Those three rafts all drifted close by me, so nea that I was hailed by one and another of them, with th request for us all to keep near together, to which I as sented, but told them we had all better try and keep b the ship till she went down. And this time I notice that the large boat, which had been on the quarter-deck was in the water, and was being freighted pretty full t all appearance with several women, and a good numbe of men, and that the raft of spars was at the same tim being lashed together and several getting on it. noticed also a couple of large empty water casks, lashed together with five men on them, apparently passengers. leave the ship, and drifting towards me ; while within about 50 yards, they capsized with the force of a heavy swell, giving their living freight an almost immediate watery grave. Three of them I noticed regained the top side of the casks only to be immediately turned over again, and the casks separating I saw no more of them. My heart sickened at so much of immediate death, and still I almost longed to have been one of them, for at the same instant, and as near as I can judge, at about half-past four, the ship began to disappear ; stern fore-most she entered under the surface, her bow rising a little as she slowly went under, and I distinctly heard the gurgling and rushing sound of the water filling her cabins from stem to stern as she went under, taking, I should think, from 30 seconds to a minute in disap-pearing, with a large number of people still upon her deck. Thus went down the noble Arctic, leaving nothing behind but a mixture of fragments of the wreck, and struggling human beings. I saw one large half-round ragment burst above the surface, and several of the struggling fellow-mortals get on it; this and the raft of spars with several on it, and the boat full of people, was all that I could distinctly make out as being left in the neighbourhood of where the ship went down to windward: and the three small rafts to leeward along with my own were left to pass the night, now beginning to close in upon and hide away from my sight—I wish I could say from my memory—this dreadful day; but such a night of extreme melancholy, despair, and utter loneliness, I hope I shall never again experience. I had, it is true, become familiarized with death, and felt as if it would be great relief to go immediately like the rest; but oh! how unprepared was I to see my God, and for my family's sake how necessary I felt it was for me still to live a while longer. The night was cold and chilly, the dense fog was saturating my already wet clothing: I was standing up to the ankles in the water, with the waves every now and then washing me up above the knees—all circumstances seemed to say it is but a question of how long the physical frame can endure this perishing state, or how long before a more boisterous sea turns over or separates the slightly fastened planks. Thus reflecting, I offered up to Him who ruleth the winds and the waves—to Him unto whom we all flee in our deepest distress—a sincere petition for mercy, that, as I had now been called to account, I might, notwithstanding my unworthiness, find an acceptance through the merits of Him who suffered for us, and who stands ready to aid, and who says, 'Knock and it shall be opened unto you.' Unto whom can we look, oh, our God, but unto Thee? Our whole life is, after all, but as this hour—a mere question of a few short days; and what are all the mere vanities transpiring during an ambitious and short existence, compared to an assurance which maketh our latter end a fearless one? Relieved and consoled by this petition, I was somewhat calmly resigning myself to await my time as long as my strength and power of endurance could hold out, when I discovered close by me a large square basket, lined with tin, floating lightly by me—one of the steward's dish baskets it proved to be, and paddling up to it, I got it on board, and with the help of a piece of small rope I had round my shoulders, I lashed it pretty fimly on the top of the plank, thus not only tending to make my raft more secure, but affording me a comparatively dry place to sit, on the edge of it, and with my feet inside, forming a shelter for my legs up as high as my knees. After getting this all arranged, and while sitting watching the water every now and then washing over the top of it, and becoming convinced that it would soon be partly filled and add to my discomfort, as well as to the weight of the raft, I was again surprised to hear a distinct rattle against the side of the raft, which, proving to be a small air-tight tin can—a part of a set of such used as a life preserver—I seized hold of it as an additional token of the presence of a protecting Providence. I cut one end of it with my pocket-knife, and found it answer the purpose of what above anything else I then needed—a baling pot—and by which I was enabled to keep my little shelter clear of water; and so acceptable as a protection from the cold, damp blast did I find this little willow house, that I soon found myself cramped down into the inside, thus keeping not only my feet and legs, but the lower part of my body somewhat warm. In this sort of situation I wore away the tedious night, and the breaking dawn revealed to my sight nothing but thick mist, the unceasing rolling waves, and my own little bark; not a single vestige of all else that the night closed upon was now to be seen. About mid-day the sun cleared away the mist, and the heat of his rays was truly grateful, but, oh, how desolate in its very cheerfulness seemed the prospect he thus unfolded. Over the whole broad expanse of waters not a sail could be seen, not a thing save the figures of the two firemen, about half a mile distant, still standing erect, and show-ing themselves at intervals, as every swell raised them on its crest. I had not yet felt either hunger or thirst, for which I was truly thankful, for I had but a handful of dry, broken crackers in my hat, which I felt determined to save to the last, and of course no water. I dreaded the craving of either.

"The day wore on still clear until about an hour before nightfall, when the two firemen (within hailing distance of whom I had worked my way again) discovered ship under full sail broadside towards us, but it was with faint hopes of success that I hoisted my handkerchief, tied to the end of the strip of wood I was using as a paddle, the firemen doing the same with a shorter piece of wood in their possession. The ship at one time, we noticed, lay to, or altered her course for a moment, giving us a hope that she had discovered something, but the night closed in again, and with it all hopes of a rescue.

"The morning dawned again, and with it a horrid scene of despair, at the gloomy prospect of the same dense, foggy atmosphere, now and then fully developing to view the same two erect figures dancing about on the rolling surf, and in my selfish liberality, I bargained with myself that I would endure still during this day, seeing that my two companions, who were obliged to be on their feet, supporting each other, in a very precarious-looking, back to back attitude, were able still to exist. I felt a little hungry this morning, and ate half a biscuit. While warming myself by about two hours' paddling up towards them, during which the fog partially cleared away, and while close to them, we all became excited at the sight of a sail far to the south, as I thought, but broadside towards us. Like the one on the previous evening, I had little hope of her coming much nearer, but being determined to leave no effort untried which might possibly attract their notice, I stripped myself, and taking off my shirt, tied it by the sleeves to the end of my paddle, and, with my handkerchief on a small strip of wood tied on above it, I thought I had a tolerably conspicuous signal, and waved it to and fro for more than an hour, until the ship was nearly out of sight; and just as I had lowered it in utter hopelessness, we all descried at the same instant, in the opposite direction, another sail. When within three miles of us, and about an hour and a half after she first hove in sight, we were relieved by her backing her sails, altering her course, and lying-to for a while; then, hoisting a signal on her spanker-gaff, she put about and bore away, on and on far in the distance, on the opposite tack, until my heart began to fail again, doubting whether she was beating to windward for us, or had gone on her way, rejoicing in the discovery and rescue of only a portion of the unfortunate wretches within range of her. But again, how light and buoyant was the joy, as she at last put about, and stood directly for us; and on and on she advanced like a saving angel, until we could see her noble-looking hull distinctly rise and fall within little over a mile distant from us, when she backed her sails again and waited for some time in the prosecution of her mission of mercy, no doubt relieving some of our scattered companions from a like precarious state. Soon she filled away again, and at last, lying-to close by the two firemen, I saw her boat lowered, with five men in it, who, picking up the two firemen in their course, came dashing along direct for my raft, and, soon bounding alongside, I allowed myself to tumble on board of them, unable, physically, to adopt anything of a graceful action, and morally overpowered with gratitude to God and to those His instruments. I remained speechless until I got on board the ship. Before getting on board, however, the boat went away off some distance to windward, and picked up the three other firemen whom I had seen leave the Arctic, but who had been ever since out of view. We all got huddled upon the deck somehow, although rather awkwardly, and making my way down to her neat little cabin, as well as my stiff feet and legs would allow, I had the pleasure of paying my respects to Captain John Russell, and found myself on board the ship Cambria, of Greenock, bound from Glasgow for Quebec. Captain Russell, and several of the passengers, paid us every attention that I could have desired; Captain Russell kindly giving me up the berth which he had been using himself, and putting everything on board in requisition that might tend in the least to relieve and make us comfortable. I was surprised to learn that the old Frenchman, whom we had picked up from the Vesta, was our good genius on this occasion. Being directly in the track of the approaching Cambria, he was picked up by the second mate, Mr. Ross, jumping overboard with a line, and seizing hold of the old man, they were both pulled on board, and the rescued Frenchman in the best English he could muster, made Captain Russell aware that others were near. He then went to the masthead, and with his glass made out the other four pieces of wreck which we were all on, and, making his long tack

o windward, came back in the midst of us, picking up
irst, from that half-round piece of wreck that I saw
ourst above the surface at the time of the ship going
under, Captain Luce, Mr. George F. Allen, of the Novelty
Works, and a young German, a passenger of the Arctic,
by the name of Ferdinand Kaye. They, along with
eight others of those who went down with the ship, had
gained this piece of wreck, which turned out to be a
egment of one of the paddle-boxes; and singular it
seems that Captain Luce, who had stuck by his sinking
ship to the last minute, was thus saved at last on the
very boards which, as commander, were his post of duty.
The same thing, however, had caused the death of an
nteresting son, by striking or falling on him as it burst
above water. The eight others who had gained it with
hem, had from time to time perished on it.

"In the course of a few days we all began to get
round and feel pretty well, with the exception of the
severe pains in our feet, which continue with very little
ntermission, and at the same time it is most congenial
o our feelings, that we have the daily opportunity of
endering praises and thanksgiving to a gracious God
or His mercy and goodness towards us."

Perhaps we might leave the reader of this striking
arrative to draw from it the lesson which it appears
alculated to convey, and yet we may be permitted a few
arting words. Though we only know James Smith
hrough the medium of his letter, we infer from it that
e is one, who not only believes in the superintending
rovidence of God, but who places his hope of acceptance
nd salvation in his Saviour alone. We would remind
he reader, that so believing in Christ as to have the
ssurance of reconciliation with God through Him, and
o living, as to know his Spirit witnessing with our
pirit that we are His, is the best stimulus to exertion
n times of peril; the best preparation for cool, prompt,
fficient, and self-denying action. Such it would seem
as the case with Mahlon Day, and to him when action
t length became fruitless, and patient endurance was his
only remaining duty, then he doubtless found this faith
in Christ the best preparation so to endure; and finally,
when action and endurance were over, this faith was to

him the sure guarantee for a glorious exchange. If, as in the instance of James Smith, patient endurance should end in restoration to life and home, and family and friends, then the result should be renewed devotedness of life and love and service to our God and Saviour.

ADRIFT UPON A RAFT, clouds and darkness above, and fathomless gulfs of destruction below, is but too true a picture of poor lost man, when he knows not or believes not the glorious Gospel of our Lord Jesus Christ. But to such as these, even in the hour of extreme peril, an ark of safety is offered : for He who commandeth and raiseth the stormy wind, which lifteth up the waves,* will, if they cry unto Him in their trouble, bring them out of their distresses.† The gracious promise belongs even to them, " Believe on the Lord Jesus and thou shalt be saved." And the Saviour himself assures them, " Him that cometh unto me I will in no wise cast out."

> Let not conscience make you linger,
> Nor of fitness fondly dream,
> All the fitness he requireth,
> Is to feel your need of him :
> This he gives you,
> 'Tis his Spirit's rising beam.

Yield your mind to the convictions of the Holy Spirit. Meditate much on the love of Christ your Saviour. Be constant in your attendance on public worship : love the Holy Scriptures, read them in the morning to renew your confidence in God, in the evening to excite gratitude to Him for His fatherly care. Be fervent and frequent in prayer. Pray for the help of God's Holy Spirit to enable you to pray aright. Press after holiness of life as evidence of your love. Thus, then, no longer ADRIFT UPON A RAFT, but safe in the ark, a member of the one universal church of Christ, which He hath purchased with His own blood, when the end comes death will have no sting, the grave no victory; and " so an entrance shall be ministered unto you abundantly, into the everlasting kingdom of our Lord and Saviour Jesus Christ."‡

* Ps. cvii. 25.   † Ps. cvii. 19.   ‡ 1 Pet. i. 11.

London: Printed by E. Couchman and Co., 10, Throgmorton Street, for the TRACT ASSOCIATION of the SOCIETY OF FRIENDS. Sold at the Depository, 12, Bishopsgate Street Without.—1865.

REST FOR ALL.

HE Saviour of the world has said, "Come unto me all ye
that labour and are heavy-laden, and I will give you rest."
So I hear some heart murmur, "I am tired, and burdened,
and long for a little rest for my spirit, but *how* can I go to
Jesus? I have so little knowledge or feeling on these subjects, that though I believe He says *come*, I cannot go."
  Whoever thou art that hast had such a thought, wilt thou
hear and deeply ponder this truth?—the very first feeling of
dissatisfaction with the vanities of the world, the first sigh,
the first look, the first feeble desire towards God—each and
all is an approach to Him. The turning from the world
shows a sense of weariness,—the sigh, or the look, denotes
a want, a desire for help in bearing the burden; and it is to
those who are thus weary and heavy-laden that Christ says,
Come unto me." It is the weary that are refreshed; those
who *feel* burdened that are in need of rest: rejoice then,
whoever thou mayst be, that art trembling under thy load;
thou art in the state to receive the welcome of Jesus and
his sweet and sure promise "I will give you rest." But
how will He give this rest? "Take my yoke upon you and
learn of me, for I am meek and lowly in heart, and ye shall
find rest unto your souls; for my yoke is easy and my
burden is light." Under the yoke and teaching of Christ we
find rest, and *only* there; and though to the unrenewed nature of man this may seem a hard yoke, comprising as it does
the denial of self, and the taking up of our daily cross, yet
if we learn of Him, and receive from Him of his meekness
and lowliness, we shall feel a strength and calmness through
every event of life, which will impart a sense of safety and
repose in which we may realize the words of the Apostle,
"we which have believed, do enter into rest."
  Dear fellow-traveller, whatever be thy labour, whatever
thy burden, whether temporal or spiritual, whether sorrows or sins; know that that which in thee is longing for
release—that which is groaning, mourning in its path of
trial or toil, is that which must say, "I come to thee my
Saviour for rest!" Cease from thy own will and desires,
and let the meekness and lowliness of Jesus live and breathe

within thee, for in his spirit alone we find rest; *He is our rest*. In whatever circumstances we are placed, however prosperous, however adverse, Christ alone can be our rest. Let us look at the cases of two men, the one surrounded by all the luxury and fascination of the world, the other under the weight of extreme poverty, and we shall see that they stood equally in need of the same rest.

In the year 1609, there was born in Gloucestershire, a little boy who lost both his parents before he was five years old—the future Sir Matthew Hale, Lord Chief Justice of England. Much attention was paid to his education, and with great vigour and application he prosecuted his studies; but neither wealth nor learning imparted ease or quietness of mind; and as he grew older, he became restless, rushed into company and extravagances; and had not God, in mercy, called him, through a remarkable circumstance, rest and peace might long have been sought in vain. Being one day in company with other young men, one of the party, through excess of wine, fell down apparently dead at their feet. Young Hale was so affected on this occasion that he immediately retired into another room, and shutting the door, fell on his knees and prayed earnestly to God that his friend might be restored to life, and that he himself might be pardoned for having given countenance to so much excess: at the same time he made a resolution that he would never again join in such company, nor "drink a health" while he lived. His friend recovered, and after this event there was an entire change in Hale.

Subsequently, when he became a judge, he conducted himself in the duties of his office with the greatest integrity; the motives which influenced him were founded on the only firm basis—that of the fear and love of God. In one of his papers, entitled "Things to be had in continual Remembrance," he says, "That in the administration of justice I am entrusted for God, the king, and the country; and therefore that it be done uprightly, deliberately, and resolutely. That I rest not upon my own direction and strength; but implore and rest upon the direction and strength of God," &c. Towards the close of life he made the following reflections on the vicissitudes of human affairs:—"In the course of my life, I have been in as many stations and places as most men: I have experienced almost continual motion; and although of all earthly things I have desired rest, and a fixed private station, yet various changes, and the public employment put upon me, have made it literally my experience that I have no continuing city. When I had designed for myself a settled mansion in one place, and fitted it to my convenience and repose, I have had to repair to another, till my dwellings have been like so many inns to a traveller; yet this unsettledness has taught me that I must not expect my rest in this lower world, but consider it a place of journey and pilgrimage, or as a little nursery wherein we may be dressed and pruned, till we are fit to be transplanted into Paradise."

Sir Matthew Hale discerned the loving hand of an Almighty Father in all his trials, and was led to own that he could even rejoice in all this change and unsettledness; because it had shown him that he must not seek a resting-place in any earthly pursuits or enjoyments, and had enabled him through the grace of God, to find *that* true rest and peace which the world could never take away.

As an instance of the power of faith in Christ to give rest to the soul under the most depressed circumstances, I would tell you of William Kelly, who for years was one of the happiest of beings, though he lived in a garret cold and cheerless, with none of the external comforts of life, and no furniture but his bed, a chair, and the chest which contained his Sabbath garment; but here he held sweet communion with his God, and his Bible was to him more than meat and drink, or company. William Kelly was born in the Isle of Man in 1731. His parents were honest and very poor: at the parochial school he learnt to read, and his mother took pains with his religious education. He was apprenticed to a tailor, and afterwards travelled about England for improvement in his trade. On his return he was led into the company of idle and dissolute young men, and soon learned their vices, and proceeding from one degree of intemperance to another, he became an habitual drunkard. But before arriving at this, he felt the horrors of an accusing conscience, and often resolved to quit the haunts of drunkenness; but again and again he entered into temptation. One day, being unable to pay at the public-house, the landlady seized his hat as security for payment, and he hurried home bare-headed and mortified. This circumstance had a powerful effect on his mind, and for the first time he sought help and strength from Jesus the Saviour of sinners, to keep him from this great sin: from that time to the end of his life, a period of forty years, he never tasted beer or spirituous liquor: he now became a new man, and while his hands were engaged in honest labour, his heart was ascending to heaven in prayer and praise. During the latter years of his life, he was disabled from work by a complaint in his

back; and his small savings from former days afforded hi
a very scanty subsistence, but he was always thankful an
at rest in his spirit. His usual diet was bread and water
occasionally a pennyworth of milk, or a herring; and for th
last two years of his life, when his little funds were exhausted
it pleased that good Providence who never forsakes thos
who trust in Him, to raise up to him friends who neve
allowed him to want. His conversations with those aroun
him were very instructive; and with peculiar earnestness h
described the consequences of drunkenness. Speaking o
the subject of religion, he said, "Soul-work is the mos
important of all work: let us remember the story of a poo
man, who, when asked by his friends why he spent so man
hours in meditation and prayer, lifted up his hands and eye
to heaven and said, 'For ever! for ever! for ever!'"

To the busy, bustling, noisy world, such a man as this i
but little known; yet while *they* toil, *he* is at rest; an
though one of the lowliest upon earth, he may be one o
the highest in the Courts of Heaven. "As having nothin
and yet possessing all things," he waits patiently for that
Rest, in which he will partake of the river of God's pleasures
for evermore.

Reader, in both these cases, Rest was the thing longed for.
Sir Matthew Hale was not too wealthy to crave it, and
William Kelly was not too poor and miserable to obtain it.
Each had to become alike poor in spirit before he could
receive it; and each, in receiving it, obtained that blessing
of the Lord which maketh truly rich.

Oh! weary and heavy laden ones, above all things seek
and pray for this rest. Believe in the sympathy of Jesus
in times of trial: "He giveth power to the faint." In
loneliness and suffering we are peculiarly watched over by
Him who is "touched with a feeling of our infirmities;"
who has, for us, passed through all suffering, and who extends
the gracious invitation to every one of us, "Come unto me
and I will give you rest."

END.

London: Printed by E. Couchman & Co., 10, *Throgmorton Street; for the*
TRACT ASSOCIATION *of the* SOCIETY OF FRIENDS. *Sold at the Depository,*
12, *Bishopsgate Street Without.—*1866.

THE

SOWER AND THE REAPER.

A NARRATIVE.

" And herein is that saying true, One soweth and another reapeth."—
JOHN iv. 37.

" The wages of sin is death; but the gift of God is eternal life through
Jesus Christ our Lord."—ROMANS vi. 23.

LONDON:

Printed for the TRACT ASSOCIATION of the SOCIETY OF FRIENDS.

Sold at the DEPOSITORY, 12, Bishopsgate Street Without.

1863.

No. 143.   [*Price 3d. per dozen.*]

THE SOWER AND THE REAPER.

A NARRATIVE.

WHILST the happiness of mankind is greatly marred
by the prevalence of vice and impiety in the world,
the dark picture is much relieved by the impressive
example and benevolent efforts of those who, having
been taught in the school of Christ, know his love
to be shed abroad in their hearts. These, whether
learned or unlearned, rich or poor, are "the salt of
the earth:" and by diligently embracing opportunities
for usefulness, they do much to promote the welfare
of those around them.

Many, in pursuing their labours of love on behalf
of their benighted fellow men, have had to endure
much opposition, with taunts and ridicule. The following short narrative is calculated to encourage those
who may be thus circumstanced, to persevere; and to
stimulate others to engage in a similar course.

R—— Common is a secluded locality about four
miles from a market town, and at some distance from
any high road. The inhabitants, who are mostly of
the poorer class, have, therefore, but little opportunity
of benefitting by the example and oversight of those
whose stations in life are more favoured. Notwithstanding these disadvantages, that gracious Saviour
who came to call sinners to repentance, was pleased
to provide means for their help; and they became the
objects of christian care and instruction in the following remarkable manner. A benevolent gentleman in
the neighbouring town, had a dream, which made
much impression on his mind, and he felt strongly inclined to relate it to Charles H——, a poor, but pious
labourer, living in the same town. He called on him
accordingly, and after telling him the occasion of his
visit, proceeded thus: "I dreamt last night that some

person addressed me in a firm and somewhat imperative tone, with the words 'Go to Duck's Hill,' which command was repeated three times; I now come to ask, Where is Duck's Hill?". Charles replied, he did not know. The next day J. W., a journeyman mechanic, who was connected with the Wesleyans, called on Charles, and told him he had, for two or three weeks past, gone to R—— Common on the sabbath days, for the purpose of reading the Scriptures to the poor people there, and asked Charles if he would assist by taking turns with him in the engagement, to which the latter agreed. Charles went accordingly the following sabbath, and was directed to a room in a house that had been used as a workhouse. Some persons came to meet him who would have listened to him, but others were there who were determined to prevent his being heard; two of them in particular made great disturbance, stamping up and down the stairs, and beating upon a tea tray. After having thus encountered strong opposition in this his first attempt to instruct the poor people, before going away, he fell into conversation with a person, who remarked to him, "Ah! this Duck's Hill is a very depraved neighbourhood." Charles was forcibly struck on finding that *Duck's Hill* was the name of that part of R—— Common; and to be brought here in the way he was, so immediately after the dream had been related to him, without having before heard of the place, appeared to him to indicate a call of Divine Providence to service in that locality. He was much affected by observing the depravity and vice which prevailed, and the neglected state of the people, as to any endeavours to improve their condition. The men were so degraded, that the farmers of the neighbourhood were unwilling to employ them. In order to avoid being disturbed in future, Charles H—— and his humble audience met in a cottage; and here he repaired regularly every sabbath day, and also one evening in the middle of the week, for the engagement devolved exclusively upon him. It soon became evident that good impressions were made on some of the company, and particularly among the women, by means of C. H.'s readings and simple exhortations.

Although this change in their meeting place protected them, in some measure, from interruption, they were still occasionally disturbed. Sometimes a man would come in and tell one of the women that her husband was fighting, or on some other account, required her attention; and once a druken man was led.to the door of the cottage, and thrust in among them. However, the improvement which was manifest, encouraged Charles H—— to persevere. In a few months he had a company of serious persons in pretty constant attendance, and he was regarded by them with marked respect. It became necessary to seek a larger place to meet in, and two rooms in another cottage, opening into each other, and capable of seating about seventy persons, were engaged at seven shillings and sixpence per quarter. This expense would have pressed heavily upon Charles H. and his hearers, but the gentleman by whom he was employed, finding that his undertaking had assumed so interesting a character, kindly paid the rent, and by other means afforded him encouragement.

It was whilst matters were thus favourably progressing with these poor people, that a female minister of the Society of Friends attended one of their meetings. She addressed them from Rev. xiv. 7: "Fear God and give glory to him, for the hour of his judgment is come; and worship him that made heaven and earth, the sea and the fountains of waters." Her communication, delivered in a kind and feeling manner, seemed to find its way to their hearts, and to impress them very seriously. Much solemnity prevailed. When she left the house, the company evinced their gratitude for her christian interest on their behalf, by ranging themselves on each side of the path to shake hands with her.

This edifying occasion tended much to encourage Charles H—— to persevere in his labour of love, as well as to stimulate his hearers to a patient continuance in well doing. He now became thoughtful respecting the husbands of some of his female hearers; and finding that the love of intoxicating drinks was the chief obstacle, both to their temporal and spiritual well-being, he concluded to encourage them to abstain entirely from the use of them. Some of the poor men were the more easily persuaded to this, on account of having, from time to time, been sent to prison for poaching and other offences committed whilst under the influence of strong drink. After one or two of the men had been induced to make trial of this abstinence, many others soon followed their example; and this step tended to promote religious reflection and the attendance of the meetings.

The number of persons who met, now so much increased, that it was found needful to provide a still larger meeting-place; and after a fruitless search had been made for a building suited to their circumstances, a piece of ground was purchased and presented to them by a friend who was warmly interested in their proceedings. A sum of money was also raised by the contributions of other benevolent individuals, with which a house was built, capable of seating about one hundred and fifty persons, and which is not unfrequently filled. How pleasing, and how calculated to excite thankfulness to the Author of all good, are the facts, that many of these poor men and women, who, in the early part of their lives were dissolute characters, have been, for several years past, regular attendants of these meetings, and have brought their children with them; and that now there are sons and daughters of these reformed persons, conducting themselves respectably, uniting with their elders in sabbath school teaching and by other means stimulating their juniors and one another to good works.

Such is the improved condition of this neighbourhood, that those same men, who had been regarded as the very dregs of society, and who because of their depraved habits could scarcely obtain employment, are now preferred to others on account of their sobriety and general good conduct. There is, in this company, a patriarchal old man (W.L.), whose serious deportment is particularly striking. He has had nine children, who, with their children, numbering in all upwards of fifty persons, are mostly connected with this little community. This venerable disciple speaks thankfully of the comfort he derives from seeing his family reformed characters; and with feeling and energy, of the blessings appertaining to the Gospel.

It now remains for us to offer to the reader a remarkable account of the conversion, reformed life and peaceful death of one of these poor men.

Henry Lavender was a son of the above-mentioned W. L. He had been a ringleader in disturbing the meetings when they were first held, and was one of the two who beat upon the tea tray, as already related. He had a wife and five or six children, and his occupation was that of a woodman. This poor man was often to be seen in a fearful state of intoxication on the sabbath day; and when in that state he was apt to be very quarrelsome, and disposed to fight. Charles H——, the last time he saw him thus disgracefully employed, placed himself between the two fighting men, and with some difficulty prevailed on them to desist. Some time afterwards Henry confessed that what Charles said to him on that occasion, seemed so to paralyze him, that he had not power to lift his arm. Under the baneful influence of strong drink, Henry Lavender went on from bad to worse, till one evening, in company with another man of his own degraded caste, he stole a silver watch. For this offence he suffered six months' imprisonment in Cold-bath fields. Whilst there, he was brought to some serious reflection, and was prevailed upon to sign the pledge of abstinence from strong drink, to which he continued true through the remainder of his life. After his discharge from prison, he accepted the invitation of those whom he had before so wickedly opposed, to unite with them in their worship. He now became sensible of his lost condition, of his heavy load of sin and guilt, and was enabled in faith to flee to Christ as his only refuge and hope of reconciliation with an offended God. His habits, associations, and desires soon gave clear evidence of a real change of heart; and his daily walk was such as becometh the Gospel of Christ. His case, as a changed man, was regarded by his acquaintance, as most remarkable. After being thus reclaimed, he had many hard struggles, as his health and pecuniary circumstances were grievously undermined; yet by his own industry and the assistance of a few friends, he paid all his debts honourably, and became much respected by all who knew him. But soon after he had become, in a great measure, extricated from his difficulties, and had begun to enjoy the comforts of home, and a peaceful mind, the messenger of death was sent to summons him to another state of being. Charles H——, being informed of his illness, called one morning to see him; and after some serious conversation, and engaging in prayer with him, promised to call on him again in the afternoon. In this second visit, Charles asked him if he feared death, should he be called upon to meet it. He replied, "Stop! I must not answer in haste: I cannot say with Paul, 'I have fought the good fight;' but blessed be God, I can say, whereas once I was blind, so now I see—I *see* I am a great sinner and deserve hell; but Jesus has died for me." After describing his great bodily suffering, he said, "When I think of what Christ has done for me, I pray for patience, and I have it; amidst my agony Christ is precious, bless his holy name!" His friend then spoke to him on the nature of true worship, reminding him, that as God is a spirit, those who worship him, must worship him in spirit and in truth—that words were not always needful to constitute prayer; for—

> " Prayer is the burden of a sigh,
>   The falling of a tear,
> The upward glancing of an eye,
>   When none but God is near."

He said, "I thank God, I feel it." Charles then spoke of the work of Jesus, and of the all-sufficiency of his grace; assuring him that, by keeping a steadfast eye on Christ as the atonement made for sin, and resting only upon him as the foundation of all his hope, he would find that as the day, so would his strength be. Henry replied, "May the Lord help me so to do."

At the commencement of his illness, both himself and his friends entertained the hope of his recovery; but it soon became evident that the disease was too deeply seated to justify that hope. When he was apprised of his danger he said, "I am quite prepared to go, when the Lord is pleased to call me." Looking at his eldest son, a boy about fourteen years of age, he said, he hoped he would be a good boy, and assist his mother when he was gone; that, though as a father he loved his children, yet, if his Heavenly Father called him, he could freely resign them all: he hoped and trusted the Lord would provide for his wife and family, and that they would keep in the good way, and attend the house of prayer. He gradually grew worse; his friends saw he was sinking; but they had the satisfaction of observing, that he still kept in view the Rock of Ages. He continued quite sensible till the spirit left its earthly tenement. On being raised up, at his own request, to take a little water, he gently fell asleep in Jesus.

During his illness he was visited by most of his neighbours: they were desirous to hear his instructive remarks, and to watch and render him any assistance in their power. Thus, by giving heed to the grace and good Spirit of God, Henry Lavender, from an idle, quarrelsome drunkard, became a good neighbour, a kind father, an affectionate husband, and a sincere christian; and he died in the faith and hope of the Gospel. Forty-six persons followed his remains to the grave, having to walk a considerable distance in a heavy rain.

"Seek ye the Lord while he may be found, call ye upon him while he is near: let the wicked forsake his way, and the unrighteous man his thoughts; and let him return unto the Lord, and he will have mercy upon him, and to our God, for he will abundantly pardon."—Isa. lv. 6, 7.

END.

Printed by E. Couchman & Co., 10, Throgmorton Street, London.

SUMMARY

OF THE

PRINCIPAL EVIDENCES

FOR

THE TRUTH AND DIVINE ORIGIN

OF THE

CHRISTIAN REVELATION.

LONDON:

Printed for the TRACT ASSOCIATION of the SOCIETY OF FRIENDS.

Sold at the DEPOSITORY, 84, Houndsditch.

—

1859.

No. 125.   [*Price* 1*s.* 8*d. per. dozen.*]

A SUMMARY, &c.

THE method intended to be pursued in this Treatise, is to present to our readers the following series of propositions, and then to prove distinctly the truth of each.

I.   From considering the state of the heathen world, before the appearance of our Lord upon earth, it is evident that there was an absolute necessity for a revelation of God's will, and, of course, a great probability beforehand that such a revelation would be granted.

II.   At the very time when there was a general expectation in the world of some extraordinary personage making his appearance in it, a person called Jesus Christ did actually appear upon earth, asserting that he was the Son of God, and that he was sent from heaven to teach mankind true religion; and he did accordingly found a religion, which from him was called the Christian Religion, and which has been professed by great numbers of people from that time to the present.

III.   The books of the New Testament were written by those persons to whom they are ascribed, and contain a faithful history of Christ and his religion; and the account there given of both, may be securely relied upon as strictly true.

IV.   The scriptures of the Old Testament (which are connected with those of the New) are the genuine writings of those whose names they bear, and give a true account of the Mosaic dispensation, of the historical facts, the divine commands, the moral precepts, and the prophecies which they contain.

V.   The character of Christ, as represented in the Gospels affords very strong ground for believing that he was a divine person.

VI.   The sublimity of his doctrines and the purity of his moral precepts confirm this belief.

VII.   The rapid and successful propagation of the Gospel by the first teachers of it, through a large part of the world, is a proof that they were favoured with divine assistance and support.

VIII.   A comparison between Christ and Mahomet and their respective religions, leads us to conclude, that while the

religion of the latter was confessedly the invention of man,
that of the former was derived from God.

IX. The predictions delivered by the ancient prophets,
and fulfilled in our Saviour, show that he was the Messiah
expected by the Jews, and that he came into the world by
divine appointment, to be the great deliverer and redeemer
of mankind.

X. The prophecies delivered by our Saviour himself, prove
that he was endued with the foreknowledge of future events,
which belongs only to God and to those inspired by him.

XI. The miracles performed by our Lord, demonstrate
him to have possessed divine power.

XII. The resurrection of our Lord from the dead is a fact
fully proved by the clearest evidence, and is the seal and
confirmation of his divinity and of the truth of his religion.

These are the several points we shall undertake to prove in
the following pages; and if these are clearly made out, there
can be nothing more wanting to satisfy every reasonable man,
that the Christian Religion is a true Revelation from God.

PROPOSITION I.—*From considering the state of the
heathen world, before the appearance of our Lord upon
earth, it is evident that there was an absolute necessity
for a divine revelation of God's will; and, of course, a
great probability beforehand that such a revelation would
be granted.*

They who are acquainted with ancient history know perfectly well that there is no one fact more certain and more
notorious than this: that for many ages before our Saviour
appeared upon earth, and at the time he actually did appear,
the whole heathen world, even the politest and most civilized
and most learned nations, were, with a very few exceptions,
sunk in the most deplorable ignorance of everything relating
to God and to religion; in the grossest superstition and idolatry; and in the most abominable corruption and depravity
of manners. They neither understood the true nature of
God, nor the attributes and perfections which belong to him,
nor the worship that was acceptable to him, nor the moral
duties which he required from his creatures; nor had they
any clear notions or firm belief of the immortality of the soul,
and a state of rewards and punishments in another life. They
believed the world to be under the direction of a vast multitude of gods and goddesses; to whom they ascribed the worst

passions and the worst vices that ever disgraced human
nature. They worshipped also dead men and women, birds
and beasts, insects and reptiles, (especially that most odious
and disgusting reptile the serpent,) together with an infinite
number of idols, the work of their own hands, from various
materials, gold, silver, wood, and stone. With respect to
their own conduct, they were almost universally addicted
to the most shocking and abominable vices; even many of
their solemn religious ceremonies and acts of devotion were
scenes of the grossest sensuality and licentiousness. Others
of them were attended with the most savage and cruel superstitions, and sometimes even with human sacrifices.

The description given of the ancient pagans by St. Paul,
in the first chapter of his epistle to the Romans, is strictly
and literally true. " They were filled with all unrighteousness, fornication, wickedness, covetousness, uncleanness, ma-
liciousness, full of envy, murder, debate, deceit, malignity;
whisperers, backbiters, haters of God, despiteful, proud,
boasters, inventors of evil things, disobedient to parents,
without understanding, covenant breakers, without natural
affection, implacable, unmerciful."

These are not the mere general declamations of a pious
man against the wickedness of the times; they are faithful
and exact pictures of the manners of the age, and they are
fully and amply confirmed by contemporary heathen writers.
They are applied also to a people highly civilized, ingenious,
learned, and celebrated for their proficiency in all liberal arts
and sciences. What, then, must have been the depravity of
the most barbarous nations, when such were the morals
of the most polite and virtuous?

There were, it is true, among all the ancient nations, and
especially among the Greeks and Romans, some wise and
comparatively good men, called philosophers, who had juster
notions of morality and religion than the rest of the world,
and preserved themselves to a certain degree unpolluted by
the general corruption of the times. But these were few in
proportion to the great bulk of mankind, and were utterly
unable to produce any considerable change in the prevailing
principles and manners of their countrymen. They themselves had but very imperfect and erroneous notions respecting the nature and attributes of God, the worship he
required, the duties and obligations of morality, the method of
God's governing the world, his design in creating mankind,
the original dignity of human nature, the state of corruption
and depravity into which it afterwards fell; the particular
mode of divine interposition necessary for the recovery of the

human race; the means of regaining the favour of their offended Maker, and the glorious end to which God intended finally to conduct them. Even with respect to those great and important doctrines above mentioned, the immortality of the soul, the reality of a future state, and the distribution of rewards and punishments hereafter, they were full of doubt, uncertainty, and hesitation: and rather ardently wished and hoped for, than confidently expected and believed them. But even what they *did* know with any degree of clearness and certainty, they either would not condescend, or wanted the ability to render plain and intelligible to the lower orders of the people. They were destitute also of proper authority to enforce the virtues they recommended; they had no motives to propose powerful enough to overrule strong temptations and corrupt inclinations: their own example, instead of recommending their precepts, tended to counteract them; for it was generally (even in the very best of them) in direct opposition to their doctrines; and the detestable vices to which many of them were addicted, wholly destroyed the efficacy of what they taught.

Above all, they were destitute of those awful sanctions of religion, which are the most effectual restraints on the passions and vices of mankind, and the most powerful incentives to virtue, the rewards and punishments of a future state, which form so essential and important a part of the Christian dispensation.

There was, therefore, a plain and absolute necessity for a divine revelation, to rescue mankind from that gulf of ignorance, superstition, idolatry, wickedness, and misery, in which they were almost universally sunk; to teach them in what manner, and with what kind of external service, God might most acceptably be worshipped, and what expiation he would accept for sin; to give them a full assurance of a future state and a future judgment; to make the whole doctrine of religion clear and obvious to all capacities; to add weight and authority to the plainest precepts, and to furnish men with extraordinary and supernatural assistance, to enable them to overcome the corruptions of their nature. And since it was also plainly worthy of God, and consonant to all our ideas of his goodness, mercy, and compassion to the work of his own hands, that he should thus enlighten and assist and direct the creatures he had made, there was evidently much ground to expect that such information and assistance would be granted; and the wisest of the ancient heathens themselves thought it most natural and agreeable to right reason to hope for something of this nature.

You may give over, says Socrates, all hopes of amending men's manners for the future, unless God be pleased to send you some other person to instruct you; and Plato declares, that whatever is right, and as it should be, in the present evil state of the world, can be so only by the *particular interposition of God.* Cicero has made similar declarations; and Porphyry, who was a most inveterate enemy to the Christian Religion, yet confesses, that there was wanting *some universal method of delivering men's souls, which no sect of philosophy had ever yet found out.*

These confessions of the great sages of antiquity infinitely outweigh the assertions of our modern infidels, "that human reason is fully sufficient to teach man his duty and enable him to perform it; and that, therefore, a divine revelation was perfectly needless." It is true that, in the present times, a Deist may have tolerably just notions of the nature and attributes of the Supreme Being, of the worship due to him, of the ground and extent of moral obligation, and even of a future state of retribution. But from whence does he derive these notions? Not from the dictates of his own unassisted reason, but (as the philosophist Rousseau himself confesses) from those very Scriptures which he despises and reviles, from the early impressions of education, from living and conversing in a Christian country, where those doctrines are publicly taught, and where, in spite of himself, he imbibes some portion of that religious knowledge which the sacred writings have everywhere diffused and communicated to the *enemies* as well as the friends of the Gospel. But they who are destitute of these advantages, they who had nothing but reason to direct them, and therefore knew what reason is capable of doing, when left to itself, much better than any modern infidel; (who never was, and never can be, precisely in the same predicament;) these men uniformly declare, that the mere light of nature was *not* competent to conduct them into the road of happiness and virtue; and that the only *sure and certain guide* to carry men well through this life *was a divine discovery of the truth.* These considerations may serve to show that, instead of entertaining any unreasonable prejudices beforehand against the possibility or probability of any divine revelation whatever, we ought, on the contrary, to be previously prepossessed in favour of it, and to be prepared and open to receive it with candour and fairness, whenever it should come supported with sufficient evidence; because, from considering the wants of man and the mercy of God, it appears highly probable that such a revelation would *some time or other* be vouchsafed to mankind.

PROPOSITION II.—*At the very time when there was a general expectation in the world of some extraordinary personage making his appearance in it, a person called Jesus Christ did actually appear upon earth, asserting that he was the Son of God, and that he came from heaven to teach mankind true religion; and he did accordingly found a religion, which from him was called the Christian Religion, and which has been professed by great numbers of people from that time to the present.*

It was necessary just to state this proposition, as the foundation of all the reasoning that is to follow: but the truth of it is so universally acknowledged, that it requires but very few words to be said in support of it.

That there was, about the time of our Saviour's birth, a general expectation spread over the eastern part of the world, that some very extraordinary person would appear in Judea, is evident both from the sacred history and from pagan writers. St. Matthew informs us, that when Jésus was born in Bethlehem of Judea, there came wise men (probably men of considerable rank and learning in their own country) from the East, saying, "Where is he that is born King of the Jews; for we have seen his star in the East, and are come to worship him?" In confirmation of this, two Roman historians, Suetonius and Tacitus, assert that there prevailed at that time, over the whole East, an ancient and fixed opinion, that there should arise out of Judea a person who should obtain dominion over the world.

That at this time, when Augustus Cæsar was Emperor of Rome, a person called Jesus Christ was actually born in Judea; that he professed to come from heaven to teach mankind true religion, and that he had a multitude of followers; the sacred historians unanimously affirm, and several heathen authors also bear testimony to the same facts. They mention the very name of Christ, and acknowledge that he had a great number of disciples, who from him were called Christians. The Jews, though professed enemies to our religion, acknowledge these things to be true; and none even of the earliest pagans who wrote against Christianity ever pretend to question their reality.—These things are as certain and undeniable as ancient history, both sacred and profane, and the concurrent testimony both of friends and enemies, can possibly make them.

PROPOSITION III.—*The books of the New Testament were written by those persons to whom they are ascribed, and contain a faithful history of Christ and his religion : and the account there given of both may be securely relied upon as strictly true.*

The books which contain the history of Christ and of the Christian Religion, are the four Gospels and the Acts of the Apostles. That the Gospels were written by the persons whose names they bear, namely, Matthew, Mark, Luke, and John, there is no more reason to doubt than that the histories which we have under the name of Xenophon, Livy, or Tacitus, were written by those authors.

A great many passages are alluded to or quoted from the Evangelists, exactly as we read them now, by a regular succession of Christian writers, from the time of the Apostles down to this hour ; and at a very early period their names are mentioned as the authors of their respective Gospels ; which is more than can be said for any other ancient historian whatever.

These books have always been considered by the whole Christian world from the Apostolic age, as containing a faithful history of their religion, and therefore they ought to be received as such ; just as we allow the Koran to contain a genuine account of the Mahometan religion; and the sacred books of the Bramins to contain a true representation of the Hindoo religion.

That all the facts related in these writings, and the accounts given of everything our Saviour said and did, are also strictly true, we have the most substantial grounds for believing :—

For, in the first place, the writers had the very best means of information, and could not possibly be deceived themselves.

And, in the next place, they could have no conceivable inducement for imposing upon others.

St. Matthew and St. John were two of our Lord's Apostles; his constant companions and attendants throughout the whole of his ministry. They were actually present at the scenes which they describe: eye witnesses of the facts, and ear witnesses of the discourses which they relate.

St. Mark and St. Luke, though not themselves Apostles, yet were the contemporaries and companions of Apostles, and in habits of society and friendship with those who had been present at the transactions which they record. St. Luke expressly says this in the beginning of his Gospel, which opens with these words : " Forasmuch as many have taken in hand to set forth in order a declaration of those things which are most surely believed among us ; even as *they* delivered them unto us, which from the beginning were *eye witnesses and ministers of the word*, it seemed good to me also, *having had perfect understanding of all things from the very first*, to write unto thee, in order, most excellent Theophilus, that thou mightest know the *certainty* of those things wherein thou hast been instructed." St. Luke also being the author of the Acts of the Apostles, we have, for the writers of these five books, persons who had the most *perfect knowledge* of everything they relate, either from their own personal observation, or from immediate communications with those who saw and heard everything that passed.

They could not, therefore, be themselves deceived; nor could they have the least inducement, or the least inclination, to deceive others.

They were plain, honest, artless, unlearned men, in very humble occupations of life, and utterly incapable of inventing or carrying on such a refined and complicated system of fraud, as the Christian Religion must have been if it was not true. There are, besides, the strongest marks of fairness, candour, simplicity, and truth throughout the whole of their narratives. Their greatest enemies have never attempted to throw the least stain upon their characters ; and how, then, can they be supposed capable of so gross an imposition as that of asserting and propagating the most impudent fiction? They could gain by it neither pleasure, profit, nor power. On the contrary, it brought upon them the most dreadful evils, and even death itself. If, therefore, they were cheats, they were cheats without any motive, and without any advantage ; nay, contrary to every motive and every advantage that usually influence the actions of men. They preached a religion, which forbids falsehood under pain of eternal punishment, and yet, on this supposition, they supported that religion by falsehood ; and whilst they were guilty of the basest and most useless knavery themselves, they were taking infinite pains, and going through the greatest labour and sufferings, in order to teach honesty to all mankind.

Is this credible ? Is this possible ? Is not this a mode of acting so contrary to all experience, to all the principles of human nature, and to all the usual motives of human conduct, as to exceed the utmost bounds of belief, and to compel every reasonable man to reject at once so monstrous a supposition.

The facts, therefore, related in the Gospels, and in the Acts of the Apostles, even those evidently miraculous, *must* be true; for the testimony of those who *die* for what they assert, is evidence sufficient to support *any* miracle whatever. And this opinion of their veracity is strongly confirmed by the following considerations :—

There are, in all the sacred writings of the New Testament, continual allusions and references to things, persons, places, manners, customs, and opinions, which are found to be perfectly conformable to the real state of things at that time, as represented by disinterested and contemporary writers. Had their story been a forgery, they would certainly have been detected in some mistake or other concerning these incidental circumstances, which yet they have never once been.

Then, as to the facts themselves which they relate, great numbers of them are mentioned and admitted both by Jewish and Roman historians : such as the star that appeared at our Saviour's birth, the journey of the wise men to Bethlehem, Herod's murder of the infants under two years old, many particulars concerning John the Baptist and Herod, the crucifixion of our Lord under Pontius Pilate, and the earthquake and miraculous darkness which attended it. Nay, even many of the miracles which Jesus himself wrought, particularly the curing the lame and blind, and casting out devils, are, as to the *matters of fact*, expressly owned and admitted by several of the earliest and most implacable enemies of Christianity. For though they ascribe these miracles to the assistance of evil spirits, yet they allowed that the miracles themselves were actually wrought.

This testimony of our adversaries, even to the miraculous parts of the sacred history, is the strongest possible confirmation of the truth and authority of the whole.

It is also certain, that the books of the New Testament have come down to the present times without any material alteration or corruption; and that they are, in all essential points, the same as they came from the hands of their authors. That in the various transcripts of these writings, as in all other ancient books, a few letters, syllables, or even words, may have been changed, we do not pretend to deny; but that there has been any designed or fraudulent corruption of any considerable part, especially of any doctrine, or any important passage of history, no one has ever been able to prove. Indeed it was absolutely impossible. There can be no doubt but that as soon as any of the original writings came out of the hands of their authors, great numbers of copies were immediately taken, and sent to all the different Christian churches. We know that they were publicly read in the religious assemblies of the first Christians. We, know, also, that they were very, soon translated into a variety of foreign languages, and these ancient versions (many of which still remain) were quickly dispersed into all parts of the world; nay even several of the original manuscripts remained to the time of Tertullian, at the end of the second century. There are numberless quotations from every part of the New Testament by Christian writers, from the earliest ages down to the present, all which substantially agree with the present text of the sacred writings. Besides which, a variety of sects and heresies soon arose in the Christian church, and each of these appealed to the Scriptures for the truth of their doctrines. It would, therefore, have been utterly impossible for any one sect to have made any material alteration in the sacred books without being immediately detected and exposed by all the others. Their mutual jealousy and suspicion of each other would effectually prevent any gross adulteration of the sacred volumes; and with respect to lesser matters, the best and most able critics have, after the most minute examination, asserted and proved, that the holy scriptures of the New Testament have suffered less from the injury of time, and the errors of transcribers, than any other ancient writings whatever.*

PROPOSITION IV.—*The scriptures of the Old Testament, which are connected with those of the New, are the genuine writings of those whose names they bear, and give a true account of the Mosaic dispensation, as well as of the historical facts, the divine commands, the moral precepts, and the prophecies which they contain.*

That part of the Bible which is called the Old Testament, contains a great variety of very different compositions, some historical, some poetical; written at different times, and by different persons, and collected into one volume by the care of the Jews.

* The style, too, of the Gospel (says the amiable and elegant author of the Minstrel) bears intrinsic evidence of its truth. We find there no appearance of artifice or party spirit; no attempt to exaggerate on the one hand, or depreciate on the other; no remarks thrown in to anticipate objections; nothing of that caution which never fails to distinguish the testimony of those who are conscious of imposture; no endeavour to reconcile the reader's mind to what may be extraordinary in narrative: all is fair, candid, and simple. The historians make no reflections of their own, but confine themselves to matter of fact, that is, to what they heard and saw; and honestly record their own mistakes and faults, as well as the other particulars of the story.—*Beattie's Evidences,* v. 1, p. 89.

That these books were all written by those whose names they bear, there is not the least reasonable ground to doubt; they have been always considered as the writings of those persons by the whole Jewish nation (who were most interested in their authenticity, and most likely to know the truth) from the earliest times down to the present; and no proof to the contrary has ever yet been produced.

That these writings have come down to us in the same state in which they were originally written, as to all essential points, there is every reason to believe. The original manuscripts were long preserved among the Jews. A copy of the book of the law was preserved in the ark; it was ordered to be read publicly every seven years, at the feast of the tabernacles, as well as privately, and frequently, in every Jewish family.

There is a copy still extant of the five books of Moses (which are called the Pentateuch) taken by the Samaritans, who were bitter enemies to the Jews, and always at variance with them: and this copy agrees in every material instance with the Jewish copy.

Near three hundred years before Christ these scriptures were translated into Greek, and this version (called the Septuagint) agrees also in all essential articles with the Hebrew original. This being very widely spread over the world, rendered any considerable alteration extremely difficult; and the dispersion of the Jews into all the different regions of the globe made it next to impossible.

The Jews were always remarkable for being most faithful guardians of their sacred books, which they transcribed repeatedly, and compared most carefully with the originals, and of which they even numbered the words and letters. That they have not corrupted any of their own prophetical writings appears from hence: that we prove Jesus to be the Messiah from many of those very prophecies which they have themselves preserved, and which (if their invincible fidelity to their sacred books had not restrained them) their hatred to Christianity would have led them to alter or suppress. And their credit is still further established by this circumstance, that our Saviour, though he brings many heavy charges against the Scribes and Pharisees, yet never once accuses them of corrupting or falsifying any one of their sacred writings.

It is no less certain that these writings give a true and faithful account of the various matters which they contain. Many of the principal facts and circumstances related in them are mentioned by the most ancient heathen authors. The first origin and creation of the world out of chaos, as described by Moses; the formation of the sun, the moon, and

he stars, and afterwards of man himself; the dominion given
im over other animals; the completion of this great work
ı six days; the destruction of the world by a deluge; the
ircumstances of the ark and the dove; the punishment of
odom by fire: the ancient rite of circumcision; many par-
iculars relating to Moses, the giving of the law, and the
ewish ritual; the names of David and Solomon, and their
eagues with the Tyrians; these things, and many others of
he same sort, are expressly mentioned, or plainly alluded to,
n several pagan authors of the highest antiquity and the best
redit. And a very bitter enemy of the Jews as well as Christ-
ıns, the Emperor Julian, is, by the force of evidence, com-
elled to confess, that there were many persons among the
ews divinely inspired; and that fire from heaven descended
n the sacrifices of Moses and Elijah. Add to this, that the
eferences made to the books of the Old Testament, and the
assages quoted from them by our Saviour and his Apostles,
ı a plain proof that they acknowledged the authority of those
itings, and the veracity of their authors.

It is true, indeed, that in the historical books of the Old
Testament there are some bad characters and bad actions
recorded, and some very cruel deeds described; but these
things are mentioned as mere historical facts, and by no
means approved, or proposed as examples to others. And
excepting these passages, which are comparatively few in
number, the rest of those sacred books, more especially Deu-
teronomy, the Psalms, Proverbs, Ecclesiastes, and the Prophets, are full of very sublime representations of God and
his attributes; of very excellent rules for the conduct of life,
and examples of almost every virtue that can adorn human
nature. And these things were written at a time when all
the rest of the world, even the wisest and most learned and
most celebrated nations of the earth, were sunk in the grossest ignorance of God and religion; were worshipping idols
and brute beasts, and indulging themselves in the most
abominable vices. It is a most singular circumstance, that
a people in a remote, obscure corner of the world, very inferior to several heathen nations in learning, in philosophy,
in genius, in science, and all the polite arts, should yet be so
infinitely their superiors in their ideas of the Supreme Being,
and in everything relating to morality and religion. This can
no otherwise be accounted for than on the supposition of
their having been instructed in these things by God himself,
or by persons commissioned and inspired by him; that is, of
their having been really favoured with those divine revelations, which are recorded in the books of the Old Testament.

B

With respect to the prophecies which they contain, the
truth of a great part of these has been infallibly proved by
the exact fulfilment of them in subsequent ages, such as those
relating to our Saviour (which will be hereafter specified), to
Babylon, to Egypt, to Edom, to Tyre and Sidon. But those
which refer more particularly to the dispersion of the Jews
are so very numerous and clear, and the accomplishment of
them, in the present state of the Jews, is a fact which obtrudes
itself, at this moment, so irresistibly upon our senses, that I
cannot forbear presenting to the reader some of the most
remarkable of those predictions, as they are drawn together
by a most able writer.

" It was foretold by Moses, that when the Jews forsook the
true God, " they should be removed into all the kingdoms of
the earth, should be scattered among the heathen, among all
people, from one end of the earth even unto the other; should
become an astonishment, a proverb, and a by-word among all
nations'; and that among those nations they should find no
ease, neither should the sole of their foot have rest; but the
Lord should give them a trembling heart, and a failing of
eyes, and sorrow of mind, and send a faintness into their hearts
in the land of their enemies; so that the sound of a shaken
leaf should chase them." The same things are continually
predicted through all the following prophets: " That God
would disperse them through the countries of the heathen;
that he would sift them among all nations, like as corn is
sifted in a sieve; that in all the kingdoms of the earth, whither
they should be driven, they should be a reproach and a proverb, a taunt and a curse, and an astonishment and a hissing;
and they should abide many days without a king, and without
a prince, and without a sacrifice, and without an image, and
without an ephod, and without teraphim."

Had anything like this, in the time of Moses or of the
prophets, ever happened to any nation in the world? Or was
there in nature any probability that any such thing should
ever happen to any people? That when they were conquered
by their enemies, and led into captivity, they should neither
continue in the place of their captivity nor be swallowed up
and lost among their conquerors, but be scattered among all
the nations for many ages, and yet continue a distinct people?
Or could any description of the Jews, written at this day, be
a more exact and lively picture of the state they have now
been in for many ages, than these prophetic descriptions,
especially that of Moses, given more than three thousand
years ago.

PROPOSITION V.—*The character of Christ, as represented in the Gospels, affords very strong grounds for believing that he was a divine person.*

Whoever considers with attention the character of our blessed Lord, as it may be collected from the various incidents and actions of his life, (for there are no laboured descriptions of it, no encomiums upon it, by his own disciples,) will soon discover that it was, in every respect, the most perfect that ever was made known to mankind. If we only say of him what even Pilate said of him, and what his bitterest enemies cannot and do not deny, *that we can find no fault in him,* and that the whole tenor of his life was entirely blameless throughout, this is more than can be said of any other person that ever came into the world. But this is going a very little way indeed in the excellence of his character. He was not only free from every failing, but possessed and practised every imaginable virtue. Towards his heavenly Father he expressed the most ardent love, the most fervent yet rational devotion, and displayed in his whole conduct the most absolute resignation to his will, and obedience to his commands. His manners were gentle, mild, condescending, and gracious: his heart overflowed with kindness, compassion, and tenderness to the whole human race. The great employment of his life was to do good to the bodies and souls of men. In this all his thoughts and all his time were constantly and almost incessantly occupied. He went about dispensing his blessings to all around him in a thousand different ways; healing diseases, relieving infirmities, correcting errors, removing prejudices, promoting piety, justice, charity, peace, harmony among men, and crowding into the narrow compass of his ministry more acts of mercy and compassion than the longest life of the most benevolent man upon earth ever yet produced. Over his own passions he had the most complete command; and though his patience was continually put to the severest trials, yet he was never once overcome, never once betrayed into any intemperance or excess in word or deed, "never once spake unadvisedly with his lips." He endured the cruelest insults from his enemies with the utmost composure, meekness, patience, and resignation; displayed the most astonishing fortitude under a most painful and ignominious death, and, to crown all, in the very midst of his torments on the cross, implored forgiveness for his murderers, in that divinely charitable prayer, "Father, forgive them, for they know not what they do."

Nor was his wisdom inferior to his virtues. The doctrines he taught were the most sublime and the most important that were ever before delivered to mankind; and every way worthy of that God from whom he professed to derive them, and whose Son he declared himself to be.

His precepts inculcated the purest and most perfect morality; his discourses were full of dignity and wisdom, yet intelligible and clear; his parables conveyed instruction in the most pleasing, familiar, and impressive manner; and his answers to the many insidious questions that were put to him showed uncommon quickness of conception, soundness of judgment, and presence of mind, completely baffled all the artifices and malice of his enemies, and enabled him to elude all the snares that were laid for him. It appears, then, even from this short and imperfect sketch of our Saviour's character, that he was, beyond comparison, the wisest and most virtuous person that ever appeared; and even his bitterest enemies allow that he was so. If, then, he was confessedly so great and so good, it unavoidably follows that he must be what he pretended to be, a divine person; and of course his religion also must be divine; for he certainly laid claim to a divine original. He asserted that he was the Son of God; that he and his religion came from heaven, and that he had power of working miracles. If this was not the case, he must, in a matter of infinite importance, have asserted what had no foundation in truth. But is such a supposition as this in the smallest degree credible? Is it probable, is it conceivable, is it consistent with the general conduct of man, is it reconcileable with the acknowledged character of our Lord, to suppose, that anything *but* truth could proceed from him whom his very enemies allow to have been in *every* respect (and of course in point of veracity) the best and most virtuous of men? Was it ever known, is there a single instance to be procured in the history of mankind of any one so unblemished in morals as Christ confessedly was, persisting for so great a length of time as he did in assertions, which, if untrue, would be repugnant to the clearest principles of morality, and most fatal in their consequences to those he loved best, his followers and his friends? Is it possible that the pure, the upright, the pious, the devout, the meek, the gentle, the humane, the merciful Jesus could engage multitudes of innocent and virtuous people in the belief and support of a religion which he knew must draw on them persecution, misery, and death, unless he had been authorized by God himself to establish that religion; and unless he was conscious that he possessed the power of amply recompensing those who preferred his religion to every other consideration? The common feelings of mankind must revolt at such a preposterous idea.

It follows, then, that Christ was, in truth, a divine teacher, and his religion the gift of God.

PROPOSITION VI.—*The sublimity of our Lord's doctrines and the purity of his moral precepts confirm the belief of his divine mission.*

There is no where to be found such important information and such just and noble sentiments concerning God and Religion as in the scriptures of the New Testament.

They teach us in the first place, that there is one Almighty Being, who created all things, of infinite power, wisdom, justice, mercy, goodness; that he is the governor and preserver of this world, which he has made; that his providential care is over all his works; and that he more particularly regards the affairs and conduct of men. They teach us to worship this great Being in spirit and in truth; and that the love of him is the first and great commandment, the source and spring of all virtue. They teach us, more particularly, how to pray to him, and for that purpose supply us with a form of prayer called the Lord's Prayer, "which is a model of calm and rational devotion, and which, for its conciseness, its clearness, its suitableness to every condition, and for the weight, solemnity, and real importance of its petitions, is without an equal or a rival." They teach us, moreover, what we all feel to be true, that the human heart is weak and corrupt; that man is fallen from his original innocence; that he is restored, however, to the favour of God, and the capacity of happiness, by the death and mediation and atonement of Christ, who is the way, the truth, and the life; and that he will be assisted in his sincere, though imperfect endeavours after holiness, by the influence of God's Holy Spirit.

They assure us, in fine, that the soul does not perish with the body, but shall pass after death into another world; that all mankind shall rise from the grave, and stand before the judgment seat of Christ, who shall reward the virtuous and punish the wicked, in a future and eternal state of existence, according to their deserts.

These are the great, and interesting, and momentous truths, either wholly unknown, or but very imperfectly known to the world before; and they render the meanest peasant in this country better acquainted with the nature of the Supreme Being, and the relation in which we stand to him, than were any of the greatest sages of ancient times.

Equally excellent, and superior to all other rules of life, are the moral precepts of the Gospel.

Our Divine Master, in the first place, laid down two great leading principles for our conduct, love to God and love to mankind; and thence deduced (as occasions offered and incidents occurred, which gave peculiar force and energy to his instructions) all the principle duties towards God, our neighbour, and ourselves.

With respect to God, we are commanded to love, fear, worship, and obey him; to set him always before us; to do all things to his glory; to seek first his kingdom and his righteousness; to resign ourselves wholly to his pleasure, and submit, with patience cheerfulness, and resignation, to everything he thinks fit to bring upon us.

With regard to our neighbour, we are to exercise towards him the duties of charity, justice, equity, and truth; we are to love him as ourselves, and to do unto all men as we would they should do unto us; a most admirable rule, which comprehends the sum and substance of all social virtue, and which no man can mistake.

As to those duties which concern ourselves we are commanded to keep ourselves unspotted from the world, to be temperate in all things, to keep under our body, and bring it into subjection, to preserve an absolute command over all our passions, and live soberly, righteously, and godly in this present world.

These are the general directions given for our conduct in the various situations and relations of life. More particular injunctions are given in various parts of Scripture, especially in our Saviour's admirable sermon from the mount, where we find a multitude of most excellent rules of life, short, sententious, solemn and important, full of wisdom and dignity, yet intelligible and clear. But the principle excellence of the Gospel morality, and that which gives it an infinite superiority over all other moral instructions, is this: that it prefers a meek, yielding, complying, forgiving temper to that violent, overbearing, inflexible, imperious disposition, which prevails so much in the world; that it regulates not merely our actions, but our affections and our inclinations; and places the check to licentiousness exactly where it ought to be, that is, on the heart; that it forbids us to covet the praise of men in our devotions, our alms, and all our other virtues; that it gives leading rules and principles for all the relative duties of life;

of husbands and wives, of parents and children, of masters and servants, of Christian teachers and their disciples, of governors and subjects; that it commands us to be, as it were, lights in the world, and examples of good to all: to injure no man, but to bear injuries patiently; never to seek revenge, but to return good for evil; to love our very enemies, and to forgive others as we hope to be forgiven; to raise our thoughts and views above the present life, and to fix our affections principally on that which is to come.

But besides all this, the *manner* in which our Lord delivered all his doctrines and all his precepts; the concise, sententious, solemn, weighty maxims into which he generally compressed them; the easy, familiar, natural, pathetic parables in which he sometimes clothed them; that divine authority, and those awful sanctions with which he enforced them; these circumstances gave a weight, and dignity, and importance to the precepts of Holy Writ, which no other moral rules can boast.

If now we ask, as it is very natural to ask, who that extraordinary person could be, that was the author of such uncommonly excellent morality as this? the answer is, that he was, to all outward appearance, the reputed son of a carpenter, living with his father and mother in a remote and obscure corner of the world, until the time that he assumed his public character. "Whence, then, had this man these things, and what wisdom is this that was given unto him?" He had evidently none of the usual means or opportunities of cultivating his understanding or improving his mind. He was born in a low and indigent condition, without education, without learning, without any ancient stores from whence to draw his wisdom and his morality, that were at all likely to fall into his hands. You may, perhaps, in some of the Greek or Roman writers, pick out a few of his precepts, or something like them. But what does this avail? Those writers he had never read. He had never studied at Athens or at Rome; he had no knowledge of orators or philosophers. His fellow labourers, the persons who assisted him during his life, and into whose hands his religion came after his death, were a few fishermen on the Lake of Tiberias, as unlearned and uneducated, and, for the purpose of framing rules of morality, as unpromising as himself. Is it possible, then, that such men as these could, without any assistance whatever, produce such perfect and incomparable rules of life as those of the Gospel; so greatly superior in purity, solidity, perspicuity, and universal usefulness to all the moral lessons of all the philosophers upon earth put together? Every man of common sense must see that this is absolutely impossible;

and that there is no other conceivable way of accounting for this, than by admitting what these persons constantly affirmed, that their doctrines and their precepts came from the fountain of all perfection, that is, from God himself.

PROPOSITION VII.—*The rapid and successful propagation of the Gospel by the first teachers of it, through a large part of the world, is a proof that they were favoured with divine assistance and support.*

We find in the Acts of the Apostles, and in their Epistles, that the number of converts to the Christian Religion began to increase considerably almost immediately after our Saviour's ascension; and continued increasing to an astonishing degree through every age until the final establishment of Christianity by Constantine. The first assembly which we meet with of Christ's disciples, and that a few days after his removal from the world, consisted of one hundred and twenty. About a week after this three thousand were added in one day; and the number of Christians publicly baptized, and publicly associating together, was very soon increased to five thousand. In a few years after this the converts were described as increasing in great numbers, in great multitudes, and even in myriads, tens of thousands; and multitudes, both of men and woman continued to be added daily; so that within about thirty years after our Lord's death the Gospel was spread, not only throughout almost all parts of the Roman empire, but even to Parthia and India. It appears from the Epistles written to several churches by the Apostles, that there were large congregations of Christians, both at Rome and in all the principal cities of Greece and Asia. This account is confirmed by contemporary Roman historians; and Pliny, about eighty years after the ascension, complains that this *superstition*, as he calls it, had seized not cities only, but the lesser towns also, and the open country; that the pagan temples were almost deserted, the sacred solemnities suspended, and scarce any purchasers to be found for the victims. About twenty years after this, Justin Martyr, a Christian writer, declares that there was no nation of men, whether Greeks or barbarians, not excepting even those savages that wandered in clans from one region to another, and had no fixed habitation, who had not learned to offer prayers and thanksgivings to the Father and maker of all, in the name of Jesus, who was crucified. And thus the Church of Christ went on increasing more and more, till, under Constantine, he empire became Christian; at which time there is every reason to believe that the Christians were more numerous and more powerful than the pagans.

In what manner, now, can we account for this wonderful and unexampled progress of the Christian Religion?

If this religion had set out with flattering the corrupt passions of mankind, and held up to them the prospect of power, wealth, rank, or pleasure, as the rewards of their conversion; if it had soothed their vices, humoured their prejudices, and encouraged their ancient superstitions; if the persons who taught it had been men of brilliant talents, or commanding eloquence; if they had first proposed it in times of darkness and ignorance, and among savage and barbarous nations; if they had been seconded by all the influence and authority of the great potentates of the earth, or propagated their doctrines at the head of a victorious army, one might have seen some reason for their extraordinary success.

But it is well known that the very reverse of all this was the real truth of the case. It is well known that the first preachers of the Gospel declared open war against all the follies, the vices, the interests, the inveterate prejudices, and favourite superstitions of the world; that they were (with a few exceptions) men of no abilities, no learning, no artificial rhetoric or powers of persuasion; that their doctrines were promulgated in an enlightened age, and to the most polished nations, and had all the wit and learning, and eloquence and philosophy of the world to contend with: and that, instead of being aided by the authority and influence of the civil powers, they were opposed, and harassed, and persecuted by them, even to death, with the most unrelenting cruelty; and all those who embraced their doctrines were exposed to the same hardships and sufferings.

Is it now credible, that, under these circumstances, twelve poor illiterate fishermen of Galilee should be able, merely by their own natural powers, to spread their new religion in so short a space over so large a part of the then known world, without any assistance or co-operation from any quarter whatever? Did anything of the kind ever happen in the world before or since?

It is plainly unprecedented and impossible. As, therefore, all *human* means of success were against them, what else but *supernatural* means were left for them? It is clear almost to demonstration, that they must have been endowed with those miraculous powers, and favoured with that divine assistance to which they pretended; and which of course proved them to be the messengers of Heaven.

PROPOSITION VIII.—*A comparison between Christ and Mahomet, and their respective religions, leads us to conclude, that while the religion of the latter is confessedly the invention of man, that of the former is derived from God.*

There is a religion in the world called the Mahometan, which is professed in one part of Europe, and most parts of Asia and Africa. The founder of this religion, Mahomet, pretended to be a prophet sent from God; but it is universally allowed, by all who are not Mahometans, and who have searched very carefully into the pretensions of this teacher, that he was an enthusiast and an impostor, and that his religion was a contrivance of his own. Even those persons who reject Christianity do not think Mahometanism to be true; nor do we ever hear of a Deist embracing it from conviction.

Here, then, we have two religions co-existing together in the world, and both pretending to be revelations from heaven; one of these we know to be a fraud, the other we affirm and believe to be true. If this be so, upon comparing them and their authors together, we may expect to find a most marked and essential difference between them, such a difference as may naturally be supposed to exist between an imposter and a divine teacher, between truth and falsehood. And this, I apprehend, will appear to be actually the case with respect to Christ and Mahomet, and their respective religions.

Mahomet was a man of considerable rank in his own country; he was the grandson of a man of the most powerful and honourable family in Mecca, and, though not born to a great fortune, he soon acquired one by marriage. These circumstances would of themselves, without any supernatural assistance, greatly contribute to the success of his religion. A person considerable by his wealth, of high descent, and nearly allied to the chiefs of his country, taking upon himself the character of a religious teacher in an age of ignorance and barbarism, could not fail of attracting attention and followers.

Christ did not possess these advantages of rank and wealth, and powerful connexions. He was born of parents in a very mean condition of life. His relations and friends were all in the same humble situation; he was bred up in poverty, and continued in it all his life, having frequently no place where he could lay his head. A man so circumstanced was not likely, by his own personal influence, to force a new religion, much less a false one, upon the world.

Mahomet indulged himself in the grossest pleasures. He perpetually transgressed even those licentious rules which he had prescribed to himself. He made use of the power he had acquired to gratify his passions without control, and he laid claim to a special permission from heaven to riot in the most unlimited sensuality.

Jesus, on the contrary, preserved throughout life the most unblemished purity and sanctity of manners. He did no sin, but was perfectly holy and undefiled. Not the least stain was ever thrown on his moral character by his bitterest enemies.

Mahomet was violent, impetuous, and sanguinary.

Christ was meek, gentle, benevolent, and merciful.

Mahomet pretended to have secret communications with God, and with the angel Gabriel, which no other person ever saw or heard.

Jesus was repeatedly declared to be the Son of God by voices from heaven, which were plainly and distinctly heard and recorded by others.

The appearance of Mahomet was not foretold by ancient prophecies, nor was there at the time any expectation of such a person in that part of the world.

The appearance of Christ upon earth was clearly and repeatedly predicted by several ancient prophecies, which most evidently applied to him and to no other; and which were in the keeping of those who were professed enemies to him and his religion. And there was at the time of his birth a general expectation over all the East that some great and extraordinary personage would then manifest himself to the world.

Mahomet never presumed to foretell any future events, for this plain reason, because he could not foresee them; and had he foretold anything which did not come to pass, it must have entirely ruined his credit with his followers.

Christ foretold many things which did actually come to pass, particularly his own death and resurrection, and the destruction of Jerusalem.

Mahomet never pretended to work miracles; on the contrary, he expressly disclaimed any such power, and makes several laboured and awkward apologies for not possessing it.

Jesus, we all know, worked a great number of the most astonishing miracles in the open face of day, and in the sight of great multitudes of people. He made the deaf to hear, the dumb to speak, the lame to walk, the blind to see, and even the dead to rise from the grave.

Mahomet, during the first twelve years of his mission, made use only of argument and persuasion, and in consequence of that gained very few converts. In three years he made only fourteen proselytes, and in seven only eighty-three men and eighteen women.

In the same space of time our Saviour and his Apostles converted thousands and tens of thousands, and spread the Christian Religion over a great part of Asia.

Mahomet told the Jews, the Christians, and the Arabs that he taught no other religion than that which was originally taught to their forefathers by Abraham, Ismael, Moses, and Jesus. This would naturally prejudice them in favour of his religion.

Christ preached a religion which directly opposed the most favourite opinions and prejudices of the Jews, and subverted, from the very foundation, the whole system of pagan superstition.

Mahomet paid court to the peculiar weaknesses and propensities of his disciples. In that warm climate, where all the passions are ardent and violent, he allowed them a liberal indulgence in sensual gratifications; no less than four wives to each of his followers, with the liberty of divorcing them thrice.

In the same climate, and among men of the same strong passions, Jesus most peremptorily restrained all his followers from adultery, fornication, and every kind of impurity. He confined them to one wife, and forbade divorce, except for adultery only. But what was still more, he required them to govern their eyes and their thoughts, and to check the very first rising of any criminal desire in the soul. He told them, that whoever looked upon a woman, to lust after her, had committed adultery with her already in his heart; and he assured them that none but the pure in heart should see God. He declared open war, in short, against all the criminal passions and evil inclinations of mankind, and expressly required all his followers to renounce those favourite sins that did most easily beset them; nay, even to leave father, mother, brethren, sisters, houses, lands, and everything that was most dear to them, and take up their cross and follow him.

With the view of bribing men to embrace his religion, Mahomet promised to reward his followers with the delights of a most voluptuous paradise, where the objects of their affection were to be almost innumerable, and all of them gifted with transcendent beauty and eternal youth.

Christ entirely precluded his disciples from all hopes of sensual indulgences hereafter, assuring them that in heaven they should neither marry nor be given in marriage, promising them nothing but pure, celestial, spiritual joys, such as eye hath not seen, nor ear heard, nor the heart of man conceived.

Beside the powerful attractions of sensual delights, Mahomet had another still more efficacious mode of producing conviction, and gaining proselytes; and that was, force, violence, and arms. He propagated his religion by the sword; and till he made use of that instrument of conversion the number of his proselytes was a mere nothing. He was at once a prophet, a warrior, a general, and a conqueror. It was at the head of his armies that he preached the Koran. His religion and his conquests went on together, and the former never advanced one step without the latter. He commanded in person in eight general engagements, and undertook by himself and his lieutenants fifty military enterprises. Death or conversion was the only choice offered to idolators, and tribute or conversion to Jews and Christians.

Jesus employed no other means of converting men to his religion but persuasion, argument, exhortation, miracles, and prophecies. He made use of no other force but the force of truth; no other sword but the sword of the Spirit, that is, the Word of God. He had no arms, no legions to fight his cause. He was the Prince of Peace, and preached peace to all the world. Without power, without support, without any followers but twelve poor humble men, without one circumstance of attraction, influence, or compulsion, he triumphed over the prejudices, the learning, the religion of his country; over the ancient rites, idolatry, and superstition, over the philosophy, wisdom, and authority of the whole Roman empire.

The great object of Mahomet was to make his followers soldiers, and to inspire them with a passion for violence, bloodshed, vengeance, and persecution. He was continually exhorting them to fight for the religion of God: and, to encourage them to do so, he promised them the highest honours, and the richest rewards, in paradise. "They who have suffered for my sake, and have been slain in battle, verily I will expiate their evil deeds from them, and I will surely bring them into a garden watered by rivers, a reward from God, and with God is most excellent reward." This duty of warring against infidels is frequently inculcated in the Koran, and highly magnified by the Mahomedan divines, who call the sword *the key of heaven and hell*, and persuade their people that the least drop of blood spilt in the war of God, as it is called, is most acceptable unto him; and that defending the territories of the Moslems for one night is of more avail than a fast of two months. It is easy to see to what a degree of fierceness this must raise all the furious, vindictive passions of the soul, and what a horde of savages and barbarians it must let loose upon mankind.

The directions of Christ to his disciples were of a different temper. He positively forbade them the use of any violence whatever. The sword that was drawn by one of them in his defence he ordered to be sheathed; "Put up thy sword within the sheath: they that use the sword shall perish by the sword." He would not consent to bring down fire from heaven on the Samaritans who had refused to receive him: "The son of man," he told them, "came not to destroy men's lives, but to save them. Peace I leave with you; my peace I give unto you. Do violence to no man; resist not evil. Be ye merciful, even as your Father in heaven is merciful. Blessed are the merciful, for they shall obtain mercy."

The consequence was, that the first followers of Mahomet were men of cruelty and violence, living by rapine, murder, and plunder. The first followers of Jesus were men of meek, quiet, inoffensive, peaceable manners, and in their morals irreproachable and exemplary.

If now, after comparing together the authors of the two religions we have been considering, we take a short view of the sacred books of those religions, the Koran and the Gospel, we shall find a difference no less striking between them; no less strongly marking the truth of the one and the falsehood of the other.

The Koran is highly applauded, both by Mahomet himself and his followers, for the exquisite beauty, purity, and elegance of the language, which they represent as a standing miracle, greater than even that of raising the dead. But admitting its excellence (which yet has been questioned by several learned men) if beauty of style and composition is to be considered as a proof of divine inspiration, the writings of Plato and Xenophon, of Cicero and Cæsar, and a multitude of other inimitable writers in various languages, will have as just a claim to a miraculous origin as the Koran. But in truth these graces of diction, so far from being a circumstance favourable to the Koran, create a strong suspicion of its being a human fabrication, calculated to charm and captivate men by the arts of rhetoric and the fascination of words, and thus draw off their attention from the futility of its matter and the weakness of its pretensions. These are the artifices of fraud and falsehood. The Gospel wants them not. It disdains the aid of human eloquence, and depends solely on the force of truth and the power of God for its success. "I came not (as St. Paul sublimely expresses himself,) with excellency of speech, nor with the enticing words of man's wisdom, but in demonstration of the Spirit and of power, that your faith might not stand in the wisdom of men but in the power of God."

But, whatever may be the purity of the language, the matter and substance of the Koran cannot bear a moment's comparison with that of the Gospel. The narrative is dull, heavy, monotonous, uninteresting; loaded with endless repetitions, with senseless and preposterous fables, with trivial, disgusting, and even immoral precepts. Add to this, that it has very little novelty or originality to recommend it, the most material parts of it being borrowed from the scriptures of the Old Testament or the New; and even these are so disguised and deformed by passing through the hands of the impostor (who vitiates and debases everything he touches) that you can hardly know them to be the same incidents or transactions that you read with so much delight in the Bible.

The Gospel, on the contrary, is everywhere, concise, simple, original, animated, interesting, dignified; its precepts important, its morality perfect, its sentiments sublime, its views noble and comprehensive, its sanctions awful.

In the Koran Mahomet is perpetually boasting of his own merits and achievements, and the supreme excellence of his book. In the Gospel no encomiums are bestowed by the Evangelists, either on themselves or their writings. Even the virtues of their divine Master are not distinctly specified, or brought forward into a conspicuous point of view. It is from his actions only, and his discourses, not from the observation of his historians, that we can collect the various transcendent excellencies of his character. Here we plainly see the sober modesty of truth opposed to the ostentatious vanity of imposture.

In the description of future rewards and punishments the Koran is minute, circumstantial, and extravagant, both in painting the horrors of the one and the delights of the other. It describes things which cannot and ought not to be described, and enters into detail too horrible or too licentious to be presented to the human mind.

In the Gospel the pains and the pleasures of a future life are represented concisely, in strong but general and indefinite terms, sufficient to give them a powerful but not an overwhelming influence over the mind.

There is still another and a very material mark of discrimination between the Koran and the Gospel. Mahomet shows throughout the utmost anxiety to guard against objections, to account for his working no miracles, and to defend his conduct, in several instances, against the charges which he suspects may be brought against him. This is always the case with imposture. It is always suspicious, afraid of being detected, alive to every appearance of hostility, solicitous to anticipate, and eager to repel the accusations of enemies.

Truth has no occasion for such precautions, and therefore never uses them. We see nothing of this sort in the Gospel. The sacred historians show not the smallest solicitude, nor take the least pains to obviate cavils or remove difficulties. They relate plainly and simply what they know to be true. They entertain no doubt of it themselves, and seem to have no suspicion that any one else can doubt it; they therefore leave the facts to speak for themselves, and send them unprotected into the world, to make their way (as they have done) by their own native force and incontrovertible truth.

Such are the leading features of Mahomet and his religion on the one hand, and of Christ and his religion on the other; and never was there a stronger or more striking contrast seen than in this instance. They are, in short, in every essential article the direct opposites of each other. And as it is on all hands acknowledged that Mahomet was an impostor, it is fair to conclude that Christ, who was the very reverse of Mahomet, was the reverse of an impostor, that is, a real messenger from heaven. In Mahomet we see every distinctive mark of fraud; in Jesus not one of these is to be found; but, on the contrary, every possible indication and character of truth.

PROPOSITION IX.—*The predictions delivered by the ancient Prophets, and fulfilled in our Saviour, show that he was the Messiah expected by the Jews, and that he came into the world by divine appointment, to be the great Deliverer and Redeemer of mankind.*

The word Messiah signifies anointed; that is, a person appointed to some high station, dignity, or office; because originally among the eastern nations men so appointed (particularly kings, priests, and prophets) were anointed with oil. Hence the word Messiah means the person pre-ordained and appointed by God to be the great Deliverer of the Jewish nation, and the Redeemer of all mankind. The word Christ means the same thing.

Now it was foretold, concerning the Messiah, that he should come before the sceptre departed from Judah, that is, before the Jewish government was destroyed; and, accordingly, Christ appeared a short time before the period when the Jewish government was totally overthrown by the Romans.

It was foretold, that he should come before the destruction of the second temple. "The desire of all nations shall come, and I will fill this house with glory, saith the Lord of Hosts; the glory of this latter house shall be greater than that of the former." Accordingly Christ appeared some time before the destruction of the city and the temple of Jerusalem by the Romans.

It was foretold, by the prophet Daniel, that he should come at the end of 490 years after the rebuilding of Jerusalem, which had been laid waste during the captivity of the Jews in Babylon, and that he should be cut off; and that afterwards the city and sanctuary of Jerusalem should be destroyed and made desolate. And accordingly, at what time soever the beginning of the 490 years can, according to any fair interpretation of the words, be fixed, the end of them will fall about the time of Christ's appearing; and it is well known how entirely the city and sanctuary were destroyed by the Romans some years after he was cut off and crucified.

It was foretold that he should perform many great and beneficial miracles; that the eyes of the blind should be opened, and the ears of the deaf unstopped; that the lame man should leap as a hart, and the tongue of the dumb sing; and this we know was literally fulfilled in the miracles of Christ: the blind received their sight, the lame walked, the deaf heard.

It was foretold, that he should die a violent death; that he should be wounded for our transgressions, and bruised for our iniquities; that the chastisement of our peace should be upon him; and that with his stripes we should be healed; that God would lay on him the iniquity of us all. All which was exactly accomplished in the sufferings of Christ, "who died for our sins, the just for the unjust, that he might bring us to God."

It was foretold, that to him should the gathering of the people be: and that God would give him the heathen for his inheritance, and the utmost parts of the earth for his possession, which was punctually fulfilled by the wonderful success of the Gospel and its universal propagation throughout the world.

Lastly, many more minute circumstances were told of the great Deliverer, or Redeemer, that was to come.

That he should be born of a virgin; that he should be of the tribe of Judah and the seed of David; that he should be born in the town of Bethlehem; that he should ride upon an ass in humble triumph into the city of Jerusalem; that he should be a man of sorrows, and acquainted with grief; that he should be sold for thirty pieces of silver; that he should be scourged, buffeted, and spit upon; that he should be numbered with the transgressors (that is, should be crucified, as he was between two thieves); that he should have gall and vinegar given him to drink; that they who saw him crucified should mock at him, and at his trusting in God to deliver him; that the soldiers should cast lots for his garments; that he should make his grave with the rich; and that he should rise again without seeing corruption. All these circumstances, it is well known, were foretold, and, to the greatest possible exactness, fulfilled in the person of Christ.

What now shall we say to these things? Here are upwards of twenty different particulars, many of them of a very extraordinary nature, which, it was foretold, seven hundred years before our Saviour was born, would all meet in him, and which did all actually meet in his person. Is not this a most extraordinary consideration? There are but three possible suppositions that can be made concerning it: either that this was a mere fortuitous coincidence, arising entirely from chance and accident; or that these prophecies were written after the events had taken place; or lastly, that they were real predictions, delivered many years before these events came to pass, and all fulfilled in Christ. That any one should by chance hit upon so many things which should all prove true, and prove true concerning one and the same person, though several of them were of such a nature as were unlikely to happen *singly* to *any person whatever;* this exceeds all bounds of credibility, and all power of conjecture or calculation.

That these prophecies were not written or delivered after the things predicted had happened is most certain; because they are found in books which existed long before those events came to pass, that is, in the books of the Old Testament; and the Jews themselves, the mortal enemies of Christ and his religion, acknowledge that these prophecies were in those books exactly as we now see them many hundred years before Christ came into the world.

The books themselves were in their own keeping, in the keeping of our adversaries, who would undoubtedly take effectual care that nothing favourable to Christ should be fraudulently inserted into them. The Jews were our Librarians. The prophecies were in their custody, and are read in all their copies of the Old Testament as well as in ours. They have made many attempts to *explain* them away, but none to question their authenticity.

It remains then that these are all real predictions, all centring in our Saviour, and in him only, and delivered many centuries before he was born. As no one but God has the foreknowledge of events, it is from him these prophecies must have proceeded; and they show, of course, that Christ was

he person whom he had for a great length of time pre-deter-
mined to send into the world, to be the great Deliverer,
Redeemer, and Saviour of mankind.

PROPOSITION X.—*The prophecies delivered by our
Saviour himself prove that he was endued with the foreknowledge of future events, which belongs only to God
and to those inspired by him.*

He did very particularly, and at several different times,
foretel his own death, and the circumstances of it; that the
chief priests and scribes should condemn him to death, and
deliver him to the Gentiles, that is, to Pilate and the Roman
soldiers, to mock, and scourge, and crucify him: that he
should be betrayed into their hands; that Judas Iscariot
was the person who should betray him; that all his disciples
would forsake him and flee; and that Peter would particularly thrice deny him in one night. He foretold further, that
he would rise again the third day; that after his ascension
he would send down the Holy Ghost on his Apostles, which
should enable them to work many miracles. He foretold,
likewise, many particulars concerning the future success of
the Gospel, and what should happen to several of his disciples;
he foretold what opposition and persecution they should meet
with in their preaching; he foretold what particular kind of
death Peter should die, and intimated that St. John should
live (as he did) till after the destruction of Jerusalem; he
foretold, that, notwithstanding all opposition and persecution,
the Gospel should yet have such success as to spread itself
over the world; and, lastly, he foretold the destruction of
Jerusalem, with such very particular and minute circumstances, in the 24th chapter of St. Matthew, the 13th of St.
Mark, and the 21st of St. Luke, that no one who reads the
description of that event, in the historians of those times, can
have the smallest doubt of our Saviour's divine foreknowledge. We have a most authentic, exact, and circumstantial
account of the siege and destruction of that city by the
Romans, written by Josephus, a Jewish and contemporary
historian; and the description he has given of this terrible
calamity so perfectly corresponds with our Saviour's prophecy, that one would have thought, had we not known the
contrary, that it had been written by a Christian, on purpose
to illustrate that prediction.

This power of foretelling future events is a plain proof
that Christ came from God, and was endued with this power
from above.

PROPOSITION XI.—*The miracles performed by our Lord demonstrate him to have possessed divine power.*

Although the preceding propositions contain very con vincing proofs of the divine mission of Christ, and the divine authority of his religion, yet, undoubtedly, the stronges evidence of this arises from the wonderful and well attested miracles which he wrought from the beginning to the end of his ministry. He cured the most inveterate diseases ; he made the lame to walk ; he opened the eyes of the blind and the ears of the deaf ; he cast out devils ; he walked upon the sea ; he fed five thousand persons with a few small loaves and fishes, and even raised the dead to life again. These miracles were all wrought in open day, in sight of multitudes of wit nesses, who could not be imposed upon in things which they saw plainly with their own eyes, who had an opportunity of scrutinizing them as much as they pleased, and who did actu ally scrutinize them with a most critical exactness, as appears from the very remarkable instance of the blind man restored to sight by our Lord, in the ninth chapter of St. John, a transaction which is recommended very earnestly to the attention of our readers.

It is true that miracles, being very unusual and extra ordinary facts, they require very strong evidence to support them ; much stronger, it must be owned, than common events that are recorded in history ; and, accordingly, the miracles of Christ *have* this very strong and extraordinary evidence to support them ; evidence such as is not to be equalled in any other instance, and such as is fully competent to prove the reality of the greatest miracle that ever was performed.

Besides a multitude of other persons who were eye wit nesses to these miracles, and who were actually convinced and converted by them, there were twelve persons called Apostles, plain, honest, unprejudiced men, whom our Saviour chose to be his constant companions and friends, who were almost always about his person, accompanied him in his travels, heard all his discourses, saw all his miracles, and attended him through all the different scenes of his life, death, and resur rection, till the time of his ascension into heaven. These persons were perfectly capable of judging whether the works which they saw Jesus perform were real miracles or not ; they could tell whether a person whom they had known to be blind all his life was suddenly restored to sight by our Saviour's only speaking a word or touching his eyes ; they could tell whether he did actually, in open day-light, walk

on the sea without sinking, and without any visible sup-
rt; whether a person called Lazarus, whom they were well
quainted with, and whom they knew to have been four
ys dead and buried, was raised to life again merely by
hrist's saying, *Lazarus, arise!*
In these, and other facts of this sort, they could not pos-
bly be deceived. Now these, and many other miracles
ually astonishing, they affirm that they themselves actually
w performed by our Saviour. In consequence of this, from
ing Jews, and of course strongly prejudiced against Christ
d his outward appearance, which was the very reverse of
erything they expected in their Messiah, they became
s disciples; and on account of their conversion, and more
irticularly on account of their asserting the truth of his
iracles and his resurrection, they endured for a long course
years the severest labours, hardships, sufferings, and per-
cution, that human nature could be exposed to, and at last
bmitted to the most cruel and excruciating deaths; all
hich they might easily have avoided, if they would only
ive said that Christ was *not* the Son of God, that he never
se from the dead. Yet this they refused to say, and were
ntent to die rather than say it.*
Is not this giving the strongest proof of their sincerity
nd of the reality of Christ's miracles, that human nature and
uman testimony are capable of giving? The concurrent
nd uncontradicted testimony of twelve such witnesses is,
ccording to all the rules of evidence, sufficient to establish
he truth of any one fact in the world, however extraordi-
ary, however miraculous.
If there had been any powerful temptation thrown in the
ray of these men; if they had been bribed, like the followers
f Mahomet, with sensual indulgences; or, like Judas Isca-
iot, with a sum of money, one should not have been much
irprised at their persisting, for a time at least, in a preme-
itated falsehood. But when we know that instead of any
f these allurements being held out to them, their Master
retold to them, and they themselves soon found by expe-
ience, that they could gain nothing, and must lose every-
hing in this world, by embracing Christianity; it is utterly
npossible to account for their embracing it on any other
round than their conviction of its truth from the miracles
hich they saw. In fact, must they not have been absolutely
iad to have incurred voluntarily so much misery, and such
ertain destruction, for affirming things to be true which

* No man ever laid down his life for the honour of Jupiter, Neptune,
r Apollo; but how many thousands have sealed their Christian testimony
ith their blood.—*Beattie*, v. 2.

they knew to be false; more especially as their own religion taught them that they would be punished most severely in another world, as well as in this, for so wicked a fraud? Is it usual for men thus to sport with their own happiness, and their very lives, and to bring upon themselves, with their eyes open, such dreadful evils, without any reason in the world, and without the least possible benefit, advantage, credit, or pleasure resulting from it? Where have you ever heard of any instance of this sort? Would any twelve men you ever knew, especially men of credit and character, take it into their heads to assert that a certain person in the neighbourhood raised a dead man to life, when they knew that no such thing had ever happened; and that they would all, with one consent, suffer themselves to be put to death rather than confess that they had told a lie? Such a thing never happened since the world began. It is contrary to all *experience* and all credibility.

It is certain then (as certain as anything can be that depends on human testimony) that real miracles were wrought by Christ; and as no miracles can be wrought but by the power of God, it is equally certain that Christ and his religion drew their origin from God.

PROPOSITION XII.—*The resurrection of our Lord from the dead is a fact fully proved by the clearest evidence, and is the seal and confirmation of his divinity and of the truth of his religion.*

The resurrection of Christ being one of those miracles which are recorded in the Gospel, the truth of it is, in fact, already proved by what has been advanced respecting those miracles in the preceding article. But it is an event so singular in its nature, and so infinitely important in its consequences, that it well deserves to be made the subject of a distinct proposition.

After our Saviour's crucifixion, Joseph of Arimathea, we are told, laid the body in his own new tomb, hewn out of a rock, and rolled a great stone to the door of the sepulchre. In order to secure themselves against any fraud, the Jews desired the Roman governor, Pilate, to grant them a band of soldiers to guard the sepulchre, lest, as they said, the disciples should come by night and steal the corpse away. Pilate's answer was in these words, "Ye have a watch, go your way, make it as sure as you can: so they went and made the sepulchre sure, sealing the stone, and setting a watch." The Evangelist then proceeds to relate the great ent of the resurrection with that ingenuous and natural implicity which characterises the sacred historians, and which arries upon the face of it every mark of sincerity and truth.

"In the end of the sabbath, as it began to dawn towards he first day of the week, came Mary Magdalene, and the ther Mary, to see the sepulchre. And behold there was a reat earthquake; for the angel of the Lord descended from eaven, and rolled back the stone from the door, and sat upon t. His countenance was like lightning, and his raiment hite as snow. And for fear of him the keepers did shake, nd became as dead men. And the angel of the Lord anwered, and said unto the women, Fear not ye; for I know hat ye seek Jesus that was crucified. He is not here, for he s risen from the dead; and behold he goeth before you into Galilee, there ye shall see him. Lo! I have told you. And s they went to tell his disciples, behold Jesus met them; aying, All hail; and they came and held him by the feet, and worshipped him. Then said Jesus unto them, Be not afraid; o tell my brethren, that they go into Galilee, and there they hall see me. Now, when they were going, behold some of he watch came into the city, and showed unto the chief riests all that was done. And when they were assembled vith the elders, and had taken counsel, they gave large money unto the soldiers, saying, Say ye, his disciples came by night, nd stole him away while we slept; and if this come to the governor's ears, we will persuade him and secure you. So hey took the money, and did as they were taught; and this aying is commonly reported among the Jews unto this day."

Such is the relation of this wonderful fact given by St. Matthew, which comprehends not only his own account of it, rut that also which was circulated in opposition to it by the hief priests and rulers of the Jews. Here then we have airly before us the two different representations of this event y the friends and by the enemies of Christ; of which the ormer asserts that it was a real resurrection, the other that t was a fraud; and between these two we must form our pinions, for no third story has been set up, that we know of, y any one.

One thing is agreed on by both sides, viz., that the body ras not to be found in the sepulchre: it was gone, and the uestion is by what means? The soldiers gave out that he disciples "came by night, while they slept, and stole it way." But it is not very easy to understand how the oldiers could depose to anything that passed while they rere fast asleep; they could not possibly tell in what manner the body was stolen away, or by whom. Nor, considering he extreme severity of the Roman military discipline, is it credible that if they had been asleep they would have confessed it ? For it was certain death to a Roman soldier to be found sleeping upon guard. Nothing could have prevailed upon them to make such a declaration as that but a previous promise of impunity and reward from the Jewish rulers ; a plain proof that they had been tampered with, and that it was a concerted story.

In the next place, supposing the story true, of what use could the dead body be to the disciples ? It could not prove to them, or to others, that their Master was risen from the dead; on the contrary, it must have been a standing and visible proof of the contrary. It must convince them that he, instead of being the deliverer they expected, was an imposter, and they most cruelly deceived. And why they should choose to keep in their possession, and to have continually before their eyes, a lifeless corpse, which completely blasted all their hopes, and continually reminded them of their bitter disappointment, is somewhat difficult to be imagined.

The tale, then, told by the soldiers is, upon the very face of it, a gross and clumsy forgery. The consequence is, that the account given by St. Matthew is the true one. For if the body was actually gone (an acknowledged point on all sides) and if it was not, as we have proved, stolen away by the disciples, there are but two possible suppositions remaining ; either that it was taken away by the Jews and Romans, or that it was raised to life again by the power of God. If the former had been the case it could only have been for the purpose of confronting and convicting the disciples of falsehood and fraud by the production of the dead body. But the dead body was *not* produced. It was, therefore, as the Gospel affirms, raised from the grave and restored to life. There is no other conceivable alternative left.

And that this was actually the case is proved by our Lord's appearing, after his resurrection, not only to the two women who came first to the sepulchre, but to the two disciples going to Emmaus, and to the disciples assembled together at two different times, and to all the Apostles, and to about five hundred brethren, at once. And he not only appeared to them silently, but he talked and ate with them ; he showed them his hands and his feet ; he made them handle him : he held several long conversations with them ; and at last, ascended up into heaven in their sight.

These were things of which the plainest and most ignorant men could judge. It was impossible for them to be deceived in an object with which they were well acquainted, and which presented itself to all their senses.

But there is another most decisive proof, rising from their

n conduct, that they were perfectly convinced of the reality
our Lord's resurrection.

It appears that the Apostles were far from being men of
itural courage and firmness of mind. When our Lord was
prehended, all his disciples, we are told, forsook him and
d. Peter followed him afar off, and went into a hall in the
lace of the high priest, where the servants warmed them-
lves, and being there charged with being a disciple of Jesus,
peremptorily denied it three times with vehemence and
ith oaths. It does not appear that any of his disciples
tended in the judgment hall to assist or to support him.;
d when he was crucified, the only persons that ventured to
ind near his cross were his mother, and two or three other
men, and St. John. They all, in short, appeared dismayed
d terrified with the fate of their Master, afraid to acknow-
dge the slighest connection with him, and utterly unable
face the dangers that seemed to menace them. But, im-
ediately after the resurrection of the Lord a most astonish-
g change took place in their conduct. From being the
ost timid of men they suddenly became courageous, un-
ounted, and intrepid; they boldly preached that very Jesus
hom but a short time before they had deserted in his greatest
stress; and although his crucifixion was fresh before their
yes, and they had reason to expect the same or a similar fate,
et they persisted in avowing themselves his disciples, and
old the Jews publicly, "that God had made that *same* Jesus,
whom they had crucified, both Lord and Christ;" and when
hey were brought before the rulers and elders to be examined
especting the lame man whom they had cured at the gate
f the temple, "Be it known unto you all (said they) and to
ll the people of Israel, that by the name of Jesus Christ of
Nazareth, whom ye crucified, and whom God raised from the
lead, even by him does this man stand here before you all.
This is the stone that was set at nought of you builders,
which is become the head stone of the corner; neither is there
alvation in any other; for there is none other name under
heaven given among men, whereby we must be saved."

And when a second time they were brought before the
ouncil, and forbidden to teach in the name of Jesus, their
answer was, "We ought to obey God rather than man. And
when they were again reprimanded, and threatened, and
beaten, yet they ceased not in the temple, and in every house,
o teach and to preach Jesus Christ; and with great power
rave the Apostles witness of the resurrection of the Lord
Jesus."

In what manner now shall we account for this sudden
ind most singular change in the disposition, and as it were

in the very constitution, of the Apostles. If Christ had not risen from the grave, and his dead body was in the possession of his disciples, was this calculated to inspire them with affection for their leader, and courage to preach a doctrine which they knew to be false? Would it not, on the contrary, have increased their *natural timidity*, depressed their spirits, extinguished all their zeal, and filled them with indignation and horror against a man who had so grossly deceived them, and robbed them, under false pretences, of everything that was dear and valuable to them in the world? Most unquestionably it would. Nor is it possible to account in any rational way for the strange revolution which took place in their minds, so soon after their Master's death, but by admitting that they were fully persuaded and satisfied that he rose alive from the grave.

It may be said, perhaps, that this persuasion was the effect not of irresistible evidence but of enthusiasm, which made them fancy that some visionary phantom, created solely by their own heated imagination, was the real body of their Lord restored to life. But nothing could be more distant from enthusiasm than the character and conduct of these men, and the courage they manifested, which was perfectly calm, sober, collected, and cool. But what completely repels this suspicion is, that their bitterest adversaries never once accused them of enthusiasm, but charged them with a crime which was utterly inconsistent with it, fraud and theft; with stealing away the body from the grave. And if they did this, if that dead body was actually before their eyes, how is it possible for any degree of enthusiasm short of madness (which was never alleged against them) to mistake a dead body for a living man, whom they saw, and touched, and conversed with? No such instance of enthusiasm ever occurred in the world.

The resurrection of our Lord being thus established on the firmest grounds, it affords an unanswerable proof of the truth of our Saviour's pretensions, and consequently, of the truth of his religion; for had he not been what he assumed to be, the Son of God, it is impossible that God should have raised him from the dead, and thereby given his sanction to an imposture. But as he did actually restore him to life, he thereby set his seal to the divinity which he claimed, and acknowledged him, in the most public and authoritative manner, to be "his beloved Son, in whom he was well pleased."

And this evidence of our Lord's divine mission is of the more importance, because our Saviour himself appealed to it as the grand proof of his being sent from heaven to instruct and to redeem mankind. For when he cast the buyers and

llers out of the temple, and the Jews required of him a sign,
hat is, a miraculous proof, that he had the authority of God
or doing those things, his answer was, "Destroy this temple
meaning his body), and in three days I will raise it up.
When, therefore, he was risen from the dead, his disciples
emembered that he had said this unto them: and they be-
eved the Scriptures, and the word which Jesus had said;"
nd they themselves constantly referred to the resurrection
ore than to any other evidence as the great foundation on
hich their faith was built.

The reason for this, perhaps, was, that this great event
ontained in itself at once the evidence both of miracle and
rophecy. It was certainly one of the most stupendous
anifestations of divine power that could be presented to
he observation of mankind; and it was, at the same
me, the completion of two most remarkable prophecies:
hat of our Saviour's above mentioned, and that well known
ne of king David's, which St. Peter expressly applies to the
esurrection of Christ: "Thou wilt not leave my soul in hell,
either wilt thou suffer thy Holy One to see corruption.

CONCLUSION.

These are the principal proofs of the truth of the Christian
eligion. Many others of a very satisfactory nature might
e added, but the question may be safely rested on those that
ave here been stated.

And when we collect them all together into one point of
iew; when we consider the deplorable ignorance and incon-
eivable depravity of the heathen world before the birth of
Christ, which rendered a divine interposition essentially ne-
essary, and therefore highly probable; the appearance of
Christ upon earth, at the very time when his presence was
ost wanted, and when there was a general expectation
hroughout the East, that some great and extraordinary per-
onage was soon to come into the world; the transcendent
xcellence of our Lord's character, so infinitely beyond that
f every other mortal teacher; the calmness, the composure,
he dignity, the integrity, the spotless sanctity of his man-
ers, so utterly inconsistent with every idea of enthusiasm or
mposture; the sublimity and importance of his doctrines;
he consummate wisdom and perfect purity of his moral
recepts, far exceeding the natural powers of a man born in
he humblest situation, and in a remote and obscure corner
f the world, without learning, education, languages, or books;
he rapid and astonishing propagation of his religion, in a
ery short space of time, through almost every region of the

East, by the sole efforts of himself and a few illiterate fishermen, in direct opposition to all the power, the authority, the
learning, the philosophy, the reigning vices, prejudices, and
superstitions of the world; the complete and marked opposition, in every essential point, between the character and
religion of Christ and the character and religion of Mahomet,
exactly such as might be expected between truth and falsehood; the minute description of all the most material circumstances of his birth, life, sufferings, death, and resurrection,
given by the ancient prophets many hundred years before he
was born, and exactly fulfilled in him, and him only, pointing
him out as the Messiah of the Jews, and the Redeemer of
mankind; the various prophecies delivered by Christ himself,
which were all punctually accomplished, more especially the
destruction of Jerusalem by the Romans; the many astonishing miracles wrought by Jesus, in the open face of day,
before thousands of spectators, the reality of which is proved
by multitudes of the most unexceptionable witnesses, who
sealed their testimony with their blood, and was even acknowledged by the earliest and most inveterate enemies of the
Gospel; and, lastly, that most astonishing and well authen-
ticated miracle of our Lord's resurrection, which was the
seal and confirmation of his own divine origin, and that of
his religion; when all these various evidences are brought
together, and impartially weighed, it seems hardly within
the power of a fair and ingenuous mind to resist the impression of their united force. If such a combination of
evidence as this is not sufficient to satisfy an honest inquirer
into truth, it is utterly impossible that any event, which
passed in former times, and which we did not see with our
own eyes, can ever be proved to have happened, by any
degree of testimony whatever. It may safely be affirmed,
that no instance can be produced of any one fact or event,
said to have taken place in past ages, and established by
such evidence as that on which the Christian Revelation
rests, that afterwards turned out to be false. We challenge
the enemies of our faith to bring forward, if they can, any
such instance. If they cannot (and we know it to be impossible) we have a right to say, that a religion, supported
by such an extraordinary accumulation of evidence, must
be true; and that all men, who pretend to be guided by
argument and by proof, are bound, by the most sacred
obligations, to receive the religion of Christ as a real
revelation from God.

Printed by E. Couchman, 10, Throgmorton Street, London.

ANDREW PEARSON.

ANDREW PEARSON was born at Oakenshaw, near Bradford in Yorkshire, in 1798. He was of a thoughtful turn of mind, and while very young, felt the reproofs of the Holy Spirit in his heart for sin, and became interested about heavenly things. As he grew up he sought the company of pious people, and attended the places of worship of various denominations, but without obtaining the peace of mind which he thirsted after.

The inconsistencies which he saw in the conduct of many who professed to be religious, and in that of some of those who filled the office of ministers, stumbled him greatly: for he had not yet learned that a good cause has sometimes unworthy advocates, even as Judas was found among the apostles of Christ. The Saviour forewarned his disciples to take heed lest they should be offended, and told them, that "it was impossible but that offences would come;" and in order to make them watchful over their own conduct, he added, "But woe unto him by whom they come." Instead of looking to Christ, as the only perfect example for Christians, and observing that the Holy Scriptures condemn unfaithfulness, whether in priests,

No. 126.   [*Price 4d. per dozen.*]

apostles, ministers, or any other class of professors of religion, Andrew Pearson joined with such as regard the profession of religion as priestcraft; and, for a time, considered himself quite able to prove that those who believed in the divinity of Christ, were under a delusion. In this season of darkness he ceased to attend any place of worship, and determined to live according to what his own reason and judgment approved.

Andrew Pearson was early trained to earn his bread by weaving, and had but little schooling. While working at his loom, he was often visited by a young man, who laboured diligently, but in vain, to reason him out of his unbelief; but while striving in his own strength, to keep a conscience void of offence, he was often dismayed by finding himself overcome by temptations which his conscience condemned, and which he had determined to resist: and this experience at length convinced him that he stood in need of a Saviour.

While in this state of conflict, he heard that some persons of the Society of Friends had appointed a meeting for worship in a neighbouring barn, and had given a general invitation to the surrounding inhabitants to attend. He hastily left his loom, and went across the fields to the place. When he arrived, the late Ann Jones, of Stockport, a minister of that Society, was addressing the meeting, and it was with difficulty that he found a place within hearing of her voice. She was one of the Friends at whose request the meeting had been appointed; his attention soon became fixed by her ministry: and as she continued to speak, she was brought into sympathy with such a state as his, under what she believed to be the enlightening and constraining influence of the Holy Spirit. She spoke as to some individual in the company. Andrew Pearson felt her words come home to himself; and when afterwards relating this circumstance, he said, " She traced me through all the lanes of my life, till I was ready to think the people present would know that I was the person addressed."

In returning from this meeting, he was joined by a dissenting minister, who entered into conversation respecting the meeting, and who said, he did not believe any in the present day, had Gospel authority for addressing individuals in a congregation, in the way in which some one had been addressed that evening. Andrew Pearson maintained a contrary view, but without acknowledging that he felt himself to be the person to whom the address in question was applicable, and on whose mind it had been sealed by the Holy Spirit, as an evidence of the love and mercy of God in his dear Son, and of a ministry exercised " as of the ability that God giveth."

Ann Jones had cautioned her hearers against trusting unduly to the teaching of man in the things of God, and had directed them to the teaching of the Holy Spirit, promised by Christ, as the teacher of his disciples; and by which man is convinced of sin, and as he keeps under this conviction, is led to repentance, and brought to know Christ who died for sinners, to be also the Saviour from sin. Andrew Pearson had continued through all his days of darkness, to be a diligent reader of the Holy Scriptures: and now that his attention was turned to the enlightening of the Holy Spirit, by which holy men of old were moved to speak the things contained therein, these divine records were no longer to him as a sealed book; but he said, "They appeared to me like a rich cabinet of jewels just opened to my view, but of which I had before seen only the outside." His unbelief respecting the divinity of Christ, now vanished as a dream; for he felt an inward evidence of the divine character and power of Christ, as his crucified, risen, and glorified Lord, and of his own reconciliation with the Father through Him; and in the subjection of his heart to the government of Christ, and the guidance of the Holy Spirit, sent of the Father in the name of his dear Son, Andrew Pearson felt it to be his duty and his privilege, to render divine worship, in spirit and in truth, to the Father, the Son, and the Holy Spirit as one God, blessed for ever.

Having thus embraced the truth as it is in Jesus, in the love of it, Andrew Pearson's religious course was from this time very unwavering; for his soul was now nourished by feeding on Christ as "the bread of life, which cometh down from heaven," and in communion of spirit with Him, he partook of that living water which Christ giveth, and which became in him a well of water springing up into everlasting life. He lived a few miles from any of the meetings for worship of the Society of Friends, but on becoming thus changed by the grace of God, he at once commenced attending them; and as his mind was stayed upon the Lord, and his dependence was upon Him, he found comfort and edification in these meetings, whether the Gospel was preached in them, or whether they were held in silence. In order to be able to attend those also which were held in the middle of the week, he often took the webs which he had woven, to his employers in the town, on the day on which these meetings were held.

He was not in haste to seek membership with the Society of Friends; but was admitted on his own request, in 1827. About three years afterwards, he began occasionally to speak in the ministry in their meetings for worship, under the constraining of the love of Christ: his sermons were generally short, and spoken in great simplicity; they bore evidence of a humble mind, and of deep religious experience, and were often strikingly appropriate to the state of individuals; they also gave such evidence of his having received a gift in the ministry, that after having made full proof of his calling to this service, he was recorded by the Society as a minister of the Gospel. He was in the frequent practice of visiting individuals and families in their own houses, particularly the poor, the sick, and the afflicted, without regard to their religious denomination; and the word of Christian exhortation or counsel, spoken by him on these occasions, was often much blessed.

In the latter part of his life his residence was in Bradford, where, to provide things needful for himself and his family, and to avoid making the Gospel chargeable, he assisted in a hardware business, carried on by his brother. In the autumn of 1848, he had a paralytic attack, which, for a time, seemed to threaten speedy dissolution. To a friend who called on him soon after this attack, he said, " I am heavily afflicted, but I feel the foundation to be firm." A few weeks after this, being deprived of the power of writing, he dictated a letter to a friend, in which he says, " I am very poor, yet the Lord looks upon me. He does not suffer me to sink in deep waters; though they are permitted to rise very high, yet in mercy they do not overflow me. The Lord knows how to direct the storm. He says to the waves and the billows, 'Be still,' when the poor disciple may feel that he is sinking; and I think (and speak it reverently) that I have seen, with an eye of faith, Him whom I love, and wish to serve all the days of my life, and who, I trust, will bring me to the haven of rest."

From this time he was in a feeble state of body, and he appeared to be waiting the command of his Master as to life or death; nevertheless he made several calls on his friends, and dropped here and there a word of counsel or encouragement. His right arm being rendered nearly useless, he feared lest he should become a burden to others, and remarked, that if it pleased his Heavenly Father, he should be thankful if the work were cut short in righteousness.

In all his trials, whether from bodily affliction or other causes, the Lord was his refuge, and he could from deep experience testify to his goodness and faithfulness, and to the safety of following the guidance of the Holy Spirit. His dwelling place was as at the feet of his Saviour; and his solid countenance and instructive conversation, as well as his quickness of spiritual perception, bore testimony to the union and communion of his soul with his Lord and Master.

Few of Andrew Pearson's observations have been noted down: but at one time he remarked that it had never been a temptation to him, to desire this orld's goods beyond what was needful for the upport of the body; and added, "Even when I was ery young, I thought how much better it was to ive according to the Scriptures, than in what the vorld calls pleasure." At another time, he expressed he desire that those with whom he was united in eligious fellowship might live up to their Christian rinciples, keeping humble, and attentive to the uidance of the Holy Spirit, and remarked, "In seek-ng to be great, how dwarfish we become! In desiring o be rich, how poor we are! Let us look to the aster and follow Him."

In conversing respecting the Monthly Meetings f the Society of Friends, at which, meetings for rorship are held before entering upon the disciplinary ffairs of the Society, he observed that they had often been favoured seasons; that he had attended them as long as he could, and had found great comfort in so doing. He also spoke feelingly of the privilege enjoyed by those who were able to attend meetings for public worship, from which he was now precluded by bodily infirmity, though only fifty years of age; and he expressed regret that any should unnecessarily absent themselves from those meetings which are held in the middle of the week, adding, "We cannot serve two masters."

On First-day the 18th of 2nd month, 1849, some Friends on their way from meeting, called upon him and took him to dine with them. After dinner they spent a little time in religious reading; a solemn quiet came over them; Andrew Pearson addressed to these Friends a few words of exhortation and encouragement, speaking also of the need of taking

up the cross,—of "bearing about in the body the
dying of the Lord Jesus,"—of the peace granted to
his followers, and of "the good things in store for
them;" and concluded with the declaration of the
Apostle, that "neither death nor life should be able
to separate them from the love of God, which is in
Christ Jesus our Lord."

These were almost the last words spoken by this
heavenly-minded man. In the silence which ensued,
a feeling of the divine presence spread over the
company, as they sat in reverent stillness before the
Lord. While thus sitting, Andrew Pearson was seized
with apoplexy, and in less than two hours from the
time of his making the foregoing remarks, he quietly
passed away, to be for ever with the Lord.

END.

London: *Printed by Edward Couchman,* 10, *Throgmorton Street; for the*
TRACT ASSOCIATION *of the* SOCIETY OF FRIENDS. *Sold at the Depository,*
84, *Houndsditch.*—1860.

THE CAFFRE WARS

THE CHRISTIAN COLONIST.

THE anthem of the angelic host, announcing the birth of Christ, "The Prince of Peace," was, "Glory to God in the highest, and on earth Peace; Good will toward men." Consistent with this authoritative declaration of the design and character of the Gospel, are the injunctions of Christ, "I say unto you, Love your enemies; bless them that curse you; and pray for them that despitefully use you, and persecute you; that ye may be the children of your Father which is in heaven." The declaration of the Lord Jesus before Pilate, is in perfect harmony with the angelic anthem and with his own injunctions; "My kingdom is not of this world; if my kingdom were of this world, then would my servants fight,"—"but now is my kingdom not from hence."

But notwithstanding these plain statements of the principles of the Gospel, there are individuals professing to be christians, who question the applicability of these principles, who deny that war is prohibited in the Gospel; who defend the practice, and do not scruple to engage in it themselves.

Those who are prepared to obey the commands and to follow the example of Him who "when he suffered threatened not, but committed himself to Him who judgeth righteously," are frequently questioned as to

No. 128.   *[Price 4d. per dozen.]*

the course which they would pursue in carrying out their principles, were they placed amidst scenes of actual warfare.

The following account, taken from a " Narrative of a Visit to South Africa, by James Backhouse," is commended to the reader, as containing practical evidence of the applicability of a course of conduct resulting from implicit confidence in these principles, under circumstances of peculiar trial.

Fourth Month 9th, 1839.—" On arriving at the dwelling of Richard Gush, we received a hearty welcome. This individual objected to take up arms in the late Caffre war. He also refused to leave his own house and go to Graham's Town for protection, as most of the other inhabitants of Salem had done, their conduct appearing to him to imply a want of trust in God, and an undue leaning upon human help. On about 300 Caffres' appearing in the neighbourhood of Salem, he thought it is duty to go to them, notwithstanding the dissuasions of his wife and daughter. Accompanied by a person named Woest, and followed at a distance by his son-in-law, Philip Amm, and another young man, he went on horseback, having first put off his coat, that the Caffres might see that he was unarmed. In further proof of this, on approaching them, he and his companion held up their hands, and at about 150 yards distance called to them, desiring that if any one among them could speak the Dutch language he would come to them, with his hands also erect. When the Caffres saw that these intrepid men were unarmed, their captain and one of his men came near. Richard Gush then inquired why the Caffres came to steal the cattle of the Salem people, which they had that morning taken away as they were going out to feed, or to burn the village and kill the people, which they had threatened to do. Hearing Richard Gush speak in the Dutch language, they said that they were not come to hurt the Dutch, but to drive the English into the sea. Richard Gush told them that he was an Englishman, and that the village before them was English, and he inquired of the man who spoke Dutch, if he had ever lived in the colony. The man replied that he had lived twelve years near Bathurst. Richard Gush then said, 'Dost thou know any one amongst the settlers who has taken cattle from the Caffres, or done them any harm?' The man replied, 'No.' Then pointing to the Wesleyan Mission House, Richard Gush told him, that five missionaries had gone from that place to teach the Caffres, mentioning the names of William Shaw, Stephen Kay, Samuel Young, John Ayliff, and Samuel Palmer. The man said he knew none of them but John Ayliff, from which it was inferred that he belonged to Hintza, among whose people John Ayliff was labouring." Richard Gush then pointed to the Wesleyan Chapel, and said, 'There the inhabitants of Salem pray for you that you may become better men.' Both the Caffre, who spoke Dutch, and his captain, stood like men ashamed of their conduct, but said that it was hunger that drove them out to steal. To this Richard Gush answered, 'You cannot be hungry now, for you have nearly all the cattle in the bush behind you.' The number of these was considerable. The men then said they had no bread. Richard Gush then pointed to his house, at the door of which his wife and children were standing, and said; 'If you will send one of your men, my wife will give him some bread and tobacco, and I will stand security for him till he return." The man replied, 'If you will go yourself and fetch it, we will go away.' Richard Gush then rode back, and soon returned, bringing two loaves of bread, weighing about 15 lbs., a roll of tobacco of 10 lbs., and twelve pocket-knives. He told the captain to take some of the knives to his chief, and tell him that they were sent by one who could neither steal cattle nor kill his fellow-men, but who, with his fellow-settlers, had always been the best friends of the Caffres, and should not cease to pray that God would make them better men. He also expostulated with them on their great wickedness. The parties then shook hands, and the Caffres went away, and were no more seen in the vicinity of Salem, which might be justly regarded as given of the Lord into the hand of one who dared to trust him.

"Some years previous to this, some Caffres stole Richard Gush's whole team of bullocks when he was travelling, and when his circumstances were so adverse that he could not purchase others to replace them. He would not, however, lodge an information on the case before the authorities, lest any military should be sent after the Caffres, and human blood should be spilled. A kind Dutchman let him have more oxen on trust, hoping they might be payed for some time, but knowing all the circumstances. Thus Richard Gush kept his hands clean of the patrol system, which was one of petty reprisal utterly repugnant to justice, and to the peaceable spirit of the Gospel.

"During the war, Richard Gush had frequent occasion to travel to Graham's Town. The danger was so great that it was seldom that any one dared to accompany him. Before setting out he sought for the feeling of peace in the prospect, and when advanced upon the way, he often turned into some little copse

y the side of the road, and in retirement of spirit
efore the Lord, sought further confirmation as to
ontinuing his journey. On feeling peaceful in the
nticipation, he proceeded; and, thus trusting in
he Lord and seeking His counsel, he was preserved
in safety."

Caffre wars have subsequently occurred, and Richard
Gush, confirmed in his views of the peaceable nature
of the Gospel of Christ, has still been enabled to bear
a consistent testimony against war. Under date of
17th of 3rd month, 1854, in a letter to James Backhouse, Richard Gush, after thankfully recapitulating
many blessings and favours, which the Lord has
granted him, thus proceeds, "I have food and raiment; I have no doubt but He who has cared for me
for sixty-five years, will care for me till I shall hunger
no more, nor thirst any more. In 1841 I took my
family to Graham's Town, while I finished the works
I had contracted for. I afterwards put my house at
Salem in good repair, and bought twelve oxen and
seventeen cows. In 1845 the war broke out, when I
lost all my cows and most of my oxen; that was a
trying time to many. My sufferings were small when
compared with many, who were driven from their
homes, and their houses burnt. Webber, the aged
Baptist minister, whom thou called upon when coming
to Salem, being exposed to a camp, lived but a short
time. He was much pleased in reading ' Barclay's
Apology,' and told his children, if he was young he
should embrace the principles of Friends. It was
painful to see at night many houses on fire in every
direction. One night, about ten o'clock, I heard
firing about a mile from my house; as soon as it was
light I went to the place and found two Caffres shot;
their wicked countrymen came and asked them for

powder; they said they had none, and as they were coming out of their hut they were both shot. One lay dead in the doorway; the other was shot in the shoulder; he was alive. I brought him home on my horse; and dressed his wounds; after a few days he was sent to the hospital, where he got well. One day, when I was seeking my cattle, I saw two war-Caffres about 500 yards from me; at another time some Caffres were 200 yards from me. It is a comfort in such circumstances to see Him who is invisible, and to know that more are they that are for us than they who are against us. I was told that if I remained in the house, I and my family would be all killed. . . . While many have fallen around me, I and my dear children are still alive. We suffered a little in the war for want of meat. I might have had meat from the Government, but I thought it best to keep free. I was thankful that I was able to keep my family during the war without going into debt.

"The most awful war we have had was the last, I believe more were killed on both sides than in the two former wars. Three men were killed belonging to Salem, and two wounded not far from the village. I believe I was a wonder to many, while I minded my cattle without a gun for eight months. I made a kraal close to my house; the Caffres came one night and took them all; nine oxen, five cows and their calves; my wagon and fourteen oxen were with my sons, Joseph and William. While I had my cattle we had plenty of milk and butter. After this we were without any for sometime; but many poor families lost all at the beginning, and were without a home. I have no words to express the comfort I often felt, when alone, minding my cattle, and when they were taken from me by permission of Him who gave them. Since that time the Lord has blessed me with more than I had before. Thomas Peel was at my house some time since; he keeps himself from fighting, but could not trust himself in the field without a gun; he was thankful he had that trouble for nothing, as he never saw a Caffre. How many who believe that the Saviour is able to save their souls from the power of Satan, are afraid to trust Him with their natural life. They say, if all Christians refused to fight, that the Caffres would come and destroy them all. My reply to such is, that they talk like the wicked Jews, who knew the Saviour taught his followers to love their enemies; and seeing great multitudes following him, they said, 'If we let him thus alone, all men will believe on him' (he will disarm the nation), 'and the Romans will come and take away our place and nation.' What they did to save themselves brought destruction upon them; there is no safety but under the shadow of His wings; if the Jews had sought refuge there, the Romans could never have destroyed them, and they would have remained the joy of all nations to this day. When will the Christian world believe that Jesus 'will save unto the uttermost all that come unto God by Him?'

"The wars in Europe affect me much. I hope that every Friend will keep from being entangled in any way. . . . If thou will send me some Tracts, I shall be glad. If there are any peace Tracts in the Dutch language they may do good among the Boers." After several affectionate messages, he concludes, "Now I have finished this, I have not said half what I wish. Do not forget me in thy prayers; I often remember thee and Richard Barrett.—Farewell, my dear friend, "RICHARD GUSH."

It would be difficult to compress within the limits of a Tract, the refutation of the sophistries by which the force of the authority of Holy Scripture is evaded, in regard to the peaceable and peace-making spirit of the Gospel. "Love your enemies," "Resist not evil," "Live in peace," "See that none render evil for evil," "Avenge not yourselves," "Blessed are the peace-makers." Such are the precepts and principles commended and enforced by the whole tenor of the New Testament. It has been well observed, that an approval or allowance of war could not have been subjoined to these instructions without the most obvious and the grossest inconsistency. A process of explanation which attempts to justify war in the face of these, would serve to make Holy Scripture subservient to any system of error or of wickedness. If these precepts form part of the communicated will of God, and if his communicated will be the only ultimate standard of right and wrong wheresoever that will is made known, human duty is determined; and then, no views of supposed expediency, no apparent advantages; neither dangers, nor pleasures, nor sufferings, nor death itself, ought to have any opposing influence in regulating our conduct.

END.

London: Printed by E. Couchman and Co., 10, Throgmorton Street; for the TRACT ASSOCIATION of the SOCIETY OF FRIENDS. Sold at the DEPOSITORY, 84, Houndsditch.—1861.

JOHN EDE,

THE PENITENT MINER.

JOHN EDE, the subject of this Tract, was born at Helston in Cornwall, and worked in a mine there, till within about five years of his death, when he removed to Liskeard, where he continued in the same kind of employment. He scarcely ever went to a place of worship, and, as he said on his sick bed, he thought very little about religion; and yet, when in any danger, he always felt afraid. To use his own words, he "was very wicked, and used to swear, and to do every thing that was bad." He had also often given way to intoxication; but on his marriage, he left off this practice, because he thought he could not afford it.

Most of the mines of Cornwall are very deep; in the summer of 1851, he met with an accident in one of them; while he was climbing up the shaft, a large piece of timber fell on his back, and injured him so much, that he never recovered. He suffered great pain, especially in one leg, which afterwards became almost useless; a bad cough also came on, and he grew very weak.

For nearly a year, he continued in the same wilful neglect of religion as when in health: but as one attack of bleeding from the lungs followed another,

No. 129. [*Price 3d. per dozen.*]

he became alarmed, and now, yielding his mind to the convictions of the Holy Spirit, which showed him his sins, he felt how foolish and wicked his past life had been. He began to wish that his conduct might be different if he should get well again : but he soon saw that there was little hope of recovery; and very bitter and dreadful were his convictions for sin. He felt that he had been living in rebellion against God, and that now he must appear before Him though totally unprepared. He had walked in the ways of his own heart, and the sight of his own eyes ! and for these things God was bringing him to judgment. " It is a fearful thing to fall into the hands of the living God." The conflict was long and sore; but at last, the blessed Spirit, which had showed him his sins and led him to repentance, gave him to see that Jesus is the refuge for sinners; and to this refuge he was per-suaded to flee. One day, casting himself on Jesus, he felt that the burden of his sins was rolled away, that God had forgiven him for Christ's sake, and then he could sleep without fear.

The change was great and sudden; but it was wrought by Him who said, " Come unto me all ye that labour and are heavy laden, and I will give you rest." He now wondered at the mercy of God, who had spared him so long, while many around him were cut off without warning, and who had granted him such an evidence of forgiveness through the blood of Christ, that he could say, " If He should take me this minute, I feel I should go home to glory."

Though peace and joy were commonly his portion after this, there were times when the sense of his Heavenly Father's presence was withheld; old temp-tations assailed him, and with tears, he would speak of Satan doing all he could, to turn him aside. At one time, after two days of much trial, on lying down in bed, and beginning to pray, he said that such a flood of peace and joy filled his soul, it was sweeter than honey.

He continued for some time to get down stairs daily, and to sit in an easy chair: here he would enjoy listening while the Bible, or Tracts, or hymns were read to him by visitors whe pitied his ignorance, for he had never learned to read. This was a loss he often lamented; and he begged his wife to take care that his two little girls might be well taught. He listened with deep interest to the Tract about Richard Nancarrow, and frequently spoke of it.

On becoming much worse, he readily agreed to hear a hymn, saying, "Oh, there won't be many more now;" and as the last verse was read,

"The more we toil and suffer here,
The sweeter rest will be."

he smiled at the thought of the rest to which he was so near, but added, "Not yet, we must wait."

At another time, speaking of Jesus as our great Advocate with the Father, he said, "Ah! we've got a good lawyer; if we give up our case to him, we shan't lose the trial." One day he remarked that he had had but little reading for a day or two, and had not been so comfortable, and said, "We need some reading to stir us up when we are so weak." He spoke of the peace he had known since the day when he felt his sins rolled away; "but still," he said, "Old things that I don't wish will keep coming into my mind."

Some one had requested a doctor to visit him, who thought he might be helped; but he felt assured that no earthly physician could cure him; "I'm in the hands of a very good doctor," he said, "and when he pleases, he will come and take me to himself; I must wait patiently till then." He delighted to speak of the free gift of salvation, which he said, "Money cannot purchase, nor poverty prevent our having; it is free for all, without money and without price."

He was often much disturbed by the noise of people passing under his window, and on market nights greatly distressed, when he heard the drunken songs and profane language, so fearfully common amongst miners. He had a painful remembrance of his own misery while following the same wicked course, and was grieved at their disregard of the love and mercy of God, of which he was now so richly partaking. Having a great horror of intemperance from his own bitter experience, he was delighted to hear that the sale of strong drinks had been forbidden by law in one of the American States, as he knew well the difficulty of resisting continued temptation.

Once when a friend called to see him, he said, "I've had a very comfortable day. As I lay here this morning, I thought I could look up and say, 'I know that if my earthly house of this tabernacle be dissolved, I have a building of God, a house not made with hands, eternal in the heavens;'—eternal, not for a little while for a few days or years, but for ever. We're sent here for a few years on trial, as you may say; it won't be very long now, I must wait. I prayed last night, that if He was about to take me home, He would take me in his arms very easy; that there might be a joyful feeling in all round, that I was gone home to glory. If we can but get home to heaven, we shan't want to go out any more. I shan't have cough there, nor hort breath. What a beautiful word heaven is!" hen turning to his wife, who was standing by, and ho felt it very hard to give him up, he said, "Look) the Lord; he has promised to be a God to the idow, and a Father to the Fatherless; and we must elieve him." And when she spoke of feeling lonely fter he was gone, he said, "Never mind, He'll be ompany for you, you wont be alone," adding while is eyes were filled with tears, "Meet me in heaven, nd then we shall be together for ever."

For a short time he seemed better, the pain almost eased, and he was able to be down stairs for some ours each day; but afterwards, he said he believed e had thought too much about this little improve- ent: people came in and told him how much better e looked, and this threw him off his guard; the nemy was still so busy trying every way to overcome iim. A time of darkness and doubt followed, and he ven feared he should be lost; but again the Lord was oleased to reveal himself for his help, and to rebuke the tempter. He then said, "The Lord came in like ι flood upon my soul, and I could'nt tell what to do ;o praise Him enough."

His weakness now became extreme. One day he aid, "My little strength is gone; if I can but get vithin the gates of heaven, I shan't want to come out ιny more." He could not bear much reading, but vished to hear the 14th chapter of John, "My chapter" ιs he called it, "Let me hear it once more."

He was now sinking daily, and unable to speak nuch; but about a week before his death, having re- 'ived a little, he said, "Very weak,—praise the ιord! comfortable,—bless the Lord! a little longer, —I'm going home to heaven,—I cannot praise him

here,—I shall when I get home to heaven." When
some one said, that the valley would not be dark, he
answered with a smile, "I'm just at the bottom; I'm
happy, happy, as happy as possible; tell everybody
how happy I am. I have been thinking what a fine
thing it is for a man in health to be able to say, All
is well." At length, he was only able to whisper,
"All is well;" and this was confirmed by the peaceful
expression of his countenance. A few hours after
saying these words, the welcome messenger arrived to
call him home.

He died on the 4th of the 10th month, 1852, aged
only 26 years.

The declaration of our Lord and Saviour Jesus
Christ, "A good tree bringeth not forth corrupt fruit;
neither doth a corrupt tree bring forth good fruit,"
was strikingly illustrated in the life of John Ede. In
his unconverted state he brought forth the evil fruit
of wickedness,—"Swearing and everything that was
bad." Nevertheless, God followed him in mercy, and
reproved him by his Spirit, and these reproofs at times
alarmed him. When sickness came upon him, he
allowed his mind to dwell under the convictions of the
Holy Spirit. His evil course of life then afforded him
evidence that his heart was corrupt, that love to God
had no place there, and that he was not prepared to
stand before the judgment seat of Christ.

Through great and sore conflict, he was at length
led to repentance. He earnestly sought mercy of
God; and for the sake of Jesus Christ who laid down
his life a sacrifice for the sins of the whole world, God
gave him evidence of that forgiveness, which he will
not withhold from any who repent and believe in
Jesus.

When John Ede had experienced this great and glorious change, the remainder of his life, though short, illustrated the injunction of our Lord, "Make the tree good, and his fruit good,—for the tree is known by his fruit;" for he brought forth the good fruit of love to God, and of desire that others should likewise forsake their evil ways.

Cases like this, in which the sinner, when death is near, is led to repentance, display the long-suffering of God to those who, even at this late hour, repent and believe in Jesus. But to presume upon such mercy, and under this presumption to continue in sin, is a fearful and deadly delusion. How many are cut off in an instant by deadly accidents, without a moment's warning! and even if not thus hastily summoned, there is every reason to fear whilst men live in sin, that they will die in sin, and so have their portion in that awful state of future punishment, of which our Lord declares, that "their worm dieth not, and the fire is not quenched."

To those who, like John Ede, have spent their youth, health, and strength, in the service of sin, the parable of the labourers called into the vineyard, at the eleventh hour, offers encouragement, even then, to repent and turn to the Lord. But for these, the loss already sustained is very great. They can have no pleasant remembrances of youthful dedication to their God and Saviour, nor of the prime of manhood spent in the service of the Lord. During the long period which they have wasted in serving the devil through sin, they have been strangers to that peace of God which passeth the understanding of man in his unregenerate state; they have been without the heavenly delight which attends the feeling of being reconciled to God through Jesus Christ; and they must often have bitterly in recollection, the evil influence which their example has had on their own families, and on others by whom they have been surrounded.

Reader, what is the evidence afforded by the fruit which thou art bringing forth? If it be such as proves that the tree is not yet made good, remember the shortness and the uncertainty of time, and the awfulness of eternity, and accept, without delay, the gracious invitations conveyed by the prophet Isaiah: "Come now, and let us reason together, saith the Lord: though your sins be as scarlet, they shall be as white as snow; though they be red like crimson, they shall be as wool." "Seek ye the Lord while he may be found, call ye upon him while he is near: let the wicked forsake his way, and the unrighteous man his thoughts: and let him return unto the Lord, and he will have mercy upon him, and to our God, for he will abundantly pardon."

END.

London: Printed by E. Couchman & Co. 10, Throgmorton Street; for the TRACT ASSOCIATION of the SOCIETY OF FRIENDS. Sold at the Depository, 12, Bishopsgate Street Without.—1866.

ON

UBLIC WORSHIP

AND

PRIVATE DEVOTION.

EXTRACTED FROM A WORK ENTITLED "THOUGHTS ON HABIT
AND DISCIPLINE," BY J. J. GURNEY.

LONDON:

'rinted for the TRACT ASSOCIATION of the SOCIETY of FRIENDS.

Sold at the DEPOSITORY, 84, Houndsditch.

—

1860.

No. 130.   [*Price 4d. per dozen.*]

IT is an excellent custom—one which we cannot too steadily observe for ourselves, or too carefully promote in young persons under our care—*to retire into solitude*, from time to time, and especially at the commencement and conclusion of each passing day, for the purpose of close self-examination, and of communing, as ability may be afforded us, with our Father who is in heaven. "It is good for a man that he bear the yoke in his youth. He sitteth *alone* and keepeth silence, because he hath borne it upon him; he putteth his mouth in the dust, if so be there may be hope."[1] "Stand in awe and sin not: commune with your own heart upon your bed, and be still."[2] When, in times of solitude and stillness, we faithfully review our conduct, as rational and moral agents, and rigorously examine our mental and spiritual condition before the Lord, there can be no doubt that we shall be greatly humbled; and this state of prostration, connected, as it cannot fail to be, with a sense of our weakness and need, will often be accompanied by an earnest breathing of soul to God in prayer. Now although this contrite and devotional frame of mind is produced only by the influence of the Holy Spirit, and is far indeed from being at our own command; yet waiting upon the Lord *in retirement* is a Christian habit, which it is our bounden duty to cultivate both in ourselves and in our children.

Our Saviour's precept on the subject of prayer is clear to the point. "But thou, when thou prayest, *enter into thy closet, and when thou hast shut thy door*, pray to thy Father which is in secret, and thy Father which seeth in secret shall reward thee openly."[3] The Pharisees loved

[1] Lam. iii. 27—29.   [2] Psal. iv. 4.   [3] Matt. vi. 6.

o pray, "standing in the synagogues and in the corners of the streets," that they might be "seen of men;" but it is the privilege of the truly devotional Christian, frequently to retire into that privacy in which he us under the notice of no human eye, and there to seek for ability to *present his fervent petitions unto Him*, from whose all-penetrating sight we can no where and never be concealed. Not only is the observance of such a practice required by the precept of Jesus, but it is in conformity with his recorded example. It was his custom, at seasons, and especially on the near approach of duties or exigencies of peculiar importance, to separate himself from his disciples, to retire into the solitary places of the garden, the wilderness, or the mountain, and privately to commune with his God and Father in solemn awful prayer.[1]

It is an animating truth that He who commanded and taught his disciples to pray, and who set them the example of private devotional exercise, is himself the all-availing Mediator, in whose name we are freely invited to present our petitions to the Father. "If ye shall ask any thing in my name, I will do it."[2] "Verily, verily, I say unto you, whatsoever ye shall ask the Father in my name, he will give it you. Hitherto have ye asked nothing in my name. Ask and ye shall receive, that your joy may be full."[3] In dependence on the advocacy of our adorable Redeemer, the Christian, when all around him is silence and solitude, will find it his dearest delight to commune with the Author of his being, and "in every thing by prayer and supplication, with thanksgiving," to make his "requests known unto God."[4]

Let no one imagine, however, that I am pleading for the offerings of the lip, which are not accompanied by the feelings of the heart; for those who draw near to God

---

[1] Matt. xiv. 23; Luke vi. 12; xxii. 41.   [2] John xiv. 14.
[3] John xvi. 23, 24.   [4] Phil. iv. 6.

with their lips, while their hearts are far from him, are
so far from bringing down his mercy upon their souls,
that they are justly liable to his condemnation; like
children who come to their parents with professions of
regard and allegiance, which they do not feel, or, in other
words, with a lie in their mouths. Such children must
look, not for reward, but punishment; "the hope of the
hypocrite shall perish." Prayer, in order to be well-
pleasing to the Lord, and effectual for our benefit, must
be heartfelt and sincere. When our souls are truly
touched with a sense of our poverty, our need, our help-
lessness, nay, our very wretchedness by nature, then,
and then only, can we truly find access, through Christ,
and by one Spirit, unto the Father. Certain it is, that
we cannot pray aright, without the "Spirit of grace and
supplications." "The Spirit also helpeth our infirmities,
for we know not what we should pray for as we ought;
but the Spirit itself maketh intercession for us with
groanings which cannot be uttered; and he that searcheth
the hearts knoweth what is the mind of the Spirit,
because he maketh intercession for the saints according
to the will of God."[1]

While the habit of frequent retirement from society
for devotional purposes, is one of a highly salutary
character, we are not to forget that there is a solitude
of soul, into which we may habitually retreat before the
Lord, while we are engaged in the business of life, and
are surrounded even by a multitude of our fellow-men.
The watchful Christian, while he pursues his daily career
through the world, never forgets that the Lord is nigh;
he well knows where strength is to be found for every
duty, and comfort in every care, perplexity, and sorrow;
he is accustomed to introversion of mind, and is quick to
feel the visitations of the Spirit of prayer. These give
rise to frequent aspirations, which, though they be
nothing more than the secret sigh, or the momentary

[1] Rom. viii. 26, 27.

jaculation, ascend with acceptance into the ear of the
ord of Hosts, and bring down a blessing on the obe-
ient follower of a crucified Saviour.

> " Prayer is the soul's sincere desire,
> Uttered or unexpressed,
> The motion of a hidden fire,
> That trembles in the breast.
>
> " Prayer is the Christian's vital breath,
> The Christian's native air,
> His watchword in the hour of death—
> He enters heaven with prayer."
>
> MONTGOMERY.

Finally, it is a blessed evidence of the work of grace
n the soul, when Christians are found expressing prayer
nd praise by the whole tenor of their dispositions, their
emeanour, and their conduct. Such an expression of
prayer is found in that truly religious life, which affords
a palpable evidence that the individual is ever feeling,
and thinking, and acting as a child in leading strings,
fearing to take a single step alone, habitually depending,
in all things, on an Omnipresent, Omnipotent, and most
bountiful Father. And such an expression of *praise* is
made manifest by the cheerful, willing-hearted follower
of the Lamb, whose every word and action bespeak a
spirit filled with gratitude to the Author of all his
blessings. His heart glows and burns within him, and
there can be no wonder that he runs well, for his race is
the race of LOVE.

There are no persons to whom the habit of private
devotion is more important than the heads of families,
whose duty it is, like David, to walk before their house
" with a perfect heart." If such persons are themselves
acquainted with the benefit of communion with God,
they will unquestionably feel that it is incumbent upon
them to collect their children and servants together at

least once in the day, that the whole family may unite in hearing a portion of Scripture, and in drawing near in spirit to that Almighty Being, whose " mercies are new every morning," whose " compassions fail not." This is a practice which has happily become very general among serious Christians of all denominations, and there can be little doubt that the blessing of the Lord rests on his servants and children, who thus daily acknowledge Him in their family circles.

Among those good religious habits in which it is our bounden duty to train up our families by example as well as precept, is the diligent attendance of congregational worship; whatsoever may be the section of the professing Church of Christ, to which we are individually attached. This practice ought to be regarded, both by young and old, as a pleasure and a privilege, not a task. It is of the highest importance that our children should be imbued, from their very early years, with a relish for heavenly things—with a sense of their beauty and loveliness, as well as of their awful importance. A *devotional taste* may be formed in the young mind, through divine assistance, without much difficulty; and, when once formed, it will exclude the vitiated tastes of a world lying in wickedness. When a sense of enjoyment comes to be associated with public worship, the habit of assembling with our brethren for the purpose, is formed of course; and as it becomes more and more confirmed, the relish of this reasonable service, if not heightened in its flavour, is at least strengthened in its efficacy. The more constantly we attend to so sacred a duty, the more necessary will it become to our *comfort*—the more substantial will be our *delight*, when we enter into the "gates" of the Lord " with thanksgiving, and into his courts with praise." Nor is it to be forgotten that the religion of the closet—the persevering devotion of the private hour—is an important preparation for that fervency and heavenly mindedness in congregational worship, without which it will effect but little for the permanent benefit of our souls.

I have reason to be thankful that I was trained from very early years in the *habit* of uniting with my friends in public worship, some one morning in the middle part of the week, as well as on the sabbath day. Thus to break away from the cares and pursuits of business, at a time when the world around us is full of them, I have found to be peculiarly salutary; and can now acknowledge with truth, that the many hours so spent have formed one of the happiest as well as most edifying portions of my life. Sure I am that such hours will not be lost to any seriously disposed persons, but will lead to a better performance even of their temporal duties, than would otherwise have been the case. That the same remark applies, in full force, to the right observance of the sabbath itself, will be freely acknowledged by all who know and feel its value.

Far indeed am I from pleading for the actual sacredness of any one day of the week above another, or for that legal and ceremonial strictness with which this institution was observed, under the law of Moses. So far as that law was either civil or ceremonial, it is now abolished, and therefore not obligatory on Christians. Nevertheless, I am clearly of the judgment, that the setting apart of every seventh day, for the blessed purposes of rest and worship, is a divine institution—one which originated in God's own sabbath after the creation, when he blessed and hallowed the seventh day of rest after the six days of action—one which, in point of authority, pervades all time, and attaches to the whole family of man.

That no blessing rests on the desecration of this day, all experience proves. Those who have seen it, under the curse of West Indian slavery, wrested from its legitimate purposes, and turned into a day of traffic and dissipation; those who have watched the effect, among

both Protestant and Roman Catholic nations on the
continent of Europe, of the open shops on that day even
during the hours of worship and of the formal religious
service of the morning, followed up by the thronged
theatre of the evening; those who have known men of
great intellect, who, in consequence (in part at least) of
never allowing themselves the "seventh day's rest," have
at last been so shattered in mind as to commit suicide,
(and all these circumstances have come under my own
notice)—will be little disposed to undervalue this divine
ordinance, or to lower its position to the shelf of a *mere*
expediency.

Let us then carefully cherish, both in ourselves and
in those under our care, a reverent regard for the provision which the Creator has thus mercifully made for
the relief and help both of our bodies and souls—for the
winding up of a framework which may well be compared
to the delicate machinery of a watch or clock; and let
this weekly recurring day be *habitually* devoted to *waiting*
on the Lord. "Even the youths shall faint and be weary,
and the young men utterly fall; but they that wait on
the Lord shall RENEW THEIR STRENGTH; they shall
mount up with wings as eagles; they shall run and not
be weary; and they shall walk and not faint."[1]

[1] Isa. xl. 30, 31.

END.

Printed by E. Couchman, 10, Throgmorton Street, London.

A BRIEF MEMOIR

OF THE

LIFE OF GEORGE FOX,

AN EMINENT INSTRUMENT

THE DIVINE HAND, IN GATHERING THE RELIGIOUS SOCIETY
OF FRIENDS, COMMONLY CALLED QUAKERS.

CHAPTER I. 1624—1649.

EORGE Fox, a few particulars of whose extraordinary life
re recorded in the following pages, was an eminent in-
trument in the Lord's hand, in turning the attention of men
o the spiritual nature of the Gospel dispensation. He was
)orn at Drayton in the Clay, Leicestershire, in the year
1624, and appears to have yielded in very early life to the
risitations of the light of the Divine Spirit manifested in the
secret of his own heart; and by attention thereto, to have been
enabled, with remarkable clearness, to see through the vain
customs and corruptions abounding in the world; and which,
luring a long and dark night of apostacy, had been substituted in the place of pure religion, by the ingenuity of men.

His parents, Christopher and Mary Fox, were highly
esteemed by their neighbours for piety and uprightness, and
they endeavoured to bring up their family in an exemplary
manner, according to the profession of the Episcopal Church,
to which they belonged. But it suited neither their circumstances, nor situation in life, to give their children much
learning, so that George Fox enjoyed but few literary advantages. Yet his mother was tenderly watchful over him;
and perceiving his serious temper, his piety, and stability,
endeavoured to cherish his religious impressions, and to
strengthen his good resolutions. When very young, he
possessed an observing mind, and such gravity and innocency
of spirit, that his relations were desirous he should be educated for the ministry; he refused to join in vain and childish
sports, or to mingle in the company of the irreligious or
profane; but when he saw persons behaving themselves

 [*Price* 1s. *per dozen.*]

lightly, it excited sorrow, and occasioned him to say within himself, "If ever I come to be a man, surely I shall not do so; nor be so wanton."

Of his early life, he remarks, "While I was a child, I was taught how to walk, so as to be kept pure. The Lord taught me to be faithful in all things,—inwardly to God, and outwardly to man. For the Lord showed me, that though the people of the world have mouths full of deceit, and changeable words,—my words should be few and savoury, seasoned with grace; and that I might not eat and drink, to make myself wanton, but for health; using the creatures as servants in their places, to the glory of Him that created them."

His tender mind was often grieved with the inconsistent conduct of the professors of religion. On one occasion, when about nineteen years of age, having observed the light and unprofitable conversation and conduct of some of this description, his mind was deeply affected; and withdrawing from their company, he spent the greater part of the night alone, in prayer; mourning because of the wickedness which abounded in the world. In this situation the language was intelligibly addressed to his mind, "Thou seest how young people go together into vanity, and old people into the earth:—thou must forsake all, old and young, and be as a stranger unto all."

The exercises of his mind increasing, about the twentieth year of his age he broke off all familiarity with his former acquaintance, and leaving home, travelled into Northamptonshire and Buckinghamshire, and from thence to London. On this journey professors sought to become acquainted with him; "but," he remarks, "I was afraid of them, for I was sensible they did not possess what they professed." His distress of mind, at this time, was great, and the enemy of all righteousness, taking advantage of his sorrows, tempted him to despair of the mercy of God in Christ Jesus. Not succeeding in this snare, he tried to draw him into the commission of some sin. But it pleased the Lord, who saw the integrity of his heart, and knew his close trials, to support his mind, and eventually to deliver him out of them all.

Hearing that his relations were uneasy with his absence from home, he returned, and remained some time with them. They seem to have been, in great measure, strangers to the nature of his religious exercises; and proposed different remedies, to remove his deep thoughtfulness, respecting the everlasting welfare of his soul, and the things which belong to the kingdom of heaven; but their schemes were little suited to the state of his feelings. He sought lonely places,

here he poured out his cries to the Lord, from whom alone
e expected true comfort.

But though afflicted, he was not forsaken; and by the
aching of the Holy Spirit, which our blessed Saviour pro-
ised should lead His followers into all truth, his mind was
structed in many of the mysteries of Christian redemption.
e gave an evidence of this on one occasion, when Nathaniel
tephens, the priest of his native town, queried of him,
Why Christ cried out on the cross, 'My God, my God,
hy hast thou forsaken me?' and why he said, 'If it be
ossible let this cup pass from me, yet not my will but thine
e done?'" George Fox replied, "That, at that time, the
ns of all mankind were upon him, and their iniquities and
·ansgressions, with which He was wounded, which He was
ɔ bear, and be an offering for, as He was man, but He died
ot, as He was God; and so, in that He died for all, and
asted death for every man, He was an offering for the sins
f the whole world." Thus early in his Christian experience,
id this faithful servant of the Lord bear his testimony to
e·truth of that consoling and fundamental doctrine of the
ospel, that Christ came into the world to save sinners, and
id down his precious life, as a sacrifice and propitiation for
he sins of mankind.

In the year 1645, he went to Mansetter, in Warwickshire,
nd thence to Tamworth and Coventry. At each of these
ilaces he had conversation with those called ministers, re-
pecting the state of his mind; but their attempts to assuage
is grief, and the advice they offered, showed them to be
ery deficient in solid religious experience, and left him
rithout relief.

Of the opinions then generally prevalent among professors,
ne of the first which was clearly shown him to be an error,
ɣas the idea that persons were believers and Christians
nerely because they made a profession of religion. He was
aught that true Christians or believers were such only as
ɣere really born of God, and who had passed from death
into life, and no others, however high their pretensions to
eligion might be. The effect of this sentiment was to
trike at the root of a formal, ceremonial religion; to lead
nen to close self-examination, and to an earnest endeavour
ɔ experience the great work of regeneration, begun and
arried forward in the heart, that thus they might become
rue believers in Christ.

At one time, whilst walking in the fields, on a first-day
norning, the Lord gave him to see, that being educated at
ɔollege, or acquiring human learning, was not a sufficient

qualification for Gospel ministry; at which he greatly wondered, because of the prevailing idea that men could be
fitted by education for that sacred office. But he was now
convinced, that nothing short of an immediate call and
qualification from Christ, the head of His own church, was
a sufficient authority to preach in his name; and that, before
persons could properly declare to others the mysteries of life
and salvation, they must become, in measure, practically
acquainted with them in their own experience. That as
Christ called, commissioned, and sent forth his apostles, in
the beginning of the Christian dispensation, so, in these
latter days, all who have a part in the ministry must be
called and qualified by him.

These views were so clearly impressed on his mind, that
he was fully satisfied of their truth, and he greatly admired
the Lord's goodness in thus instructing him. He perceived
that they struck at the priests' ministry, and he could not go
any longer to hear their preaching; but took his Bible, and
retired alone into private places, waiting upon the Lord, in
silence. His relations were troubled at his conduct, and
endeavoured to persuade him to attend their public worship;
but he could not feel at liberty to do so, nor yet to join with
any class of dissenters, but became as a stranger to all,
relying wholly on the Lord Jesus Christ.

In the further progress of his religious experience he was
shown that God, who created the world, "did not dwell in
temples made with hands;" and that it was therefore improper to call the houses erected for the public worship
of the Almighty, "The temples of God," and "Dreadful
places;" or the land on which they were built, "Holy
ground;" terms which, at that time, were commonly applied
to them; both by priests and people.

He apprehended, that the use of such epithets kept the
minds of the people too much outward, and prevented them
from realizing the truth of the Gospel declaration, that the
hearts of sincere Christians are the temples of the Holy One;
and that, according to the new covenant of the Gospel, He
dwells and walks in his obedient children.

Thus divinely instructed, he could say with David, "Day
unto day uttereth speech, and night unto night showeth
knowledge." Yet he was frequently under great conflict of
mind, and many temptations beset him, insomuch that when
it was day, he wished for night, and when it was night,
he longed for the coming day.

Early in 1647, he felt his mind drawn to go into Derbyshire, where he met with some friendly people. From

ence, he went through parts of Leicestershire and Notghamshire, where he found a number of tender, seeking rsons, with whom he had meetings. Elizabeth Hooton, e of these, appears to have been the first person who enly joined in religious profession with him, and also the st minister in the Society of Friends, himself excepted.

The exercise of his mind was not so constant but that had intervals of consolation; and, at times, was brought to a state of heavenly enjoyment, which he compares to ing in Abraham's bosom. "As I cannot," he says, declare the misery I was in, it was so great and heavy on me, so neither can I set forth the mercies of God unto e, in all my misery. Oh! the everlasting love of God to y soul, when I was in great distress! When my troubles d torments were great, then was his love exceeding great. 10u, Lord, makest a fruitful field a barren wilderness, and a rren wilderness a fruitful field. Thou bringest down and ttest up. Thou killest and makest alive. All honour and ory be to thee, O Lord of glory."

Not finding in his intercourse with different professors of ligion that comfort and settlement which he longed for, he ntinued to live in retirement; and when all hope of help :om man was utterly gone, and he had nothing outward to)ok to, he writes, "Then, O! then, I heard a voice, which iid, 'THERE IS ONE, EVEN CHRIST JESUS, THAT CAN SPEAK O THY CONDITION.' And when I heard it, my heart did :ap for joy. Then the Lord let me see, why there was none pon the earth that could speak to my condition; namely, hat I might give him all the glory. For all were concluded under sin, and shut up in unbelief, as I had been; that esus Christ might have the pre-eminence, who enlightens, nd gives faith, grace, and power. Thus, when God doth rork, who shall let it? This I knew experimentally. My esires after the Lord grew stronger, and zeal in the pure nowledge of God and of Christ alone. For though I read he Scriptures that spake of Christ and of God, yet I knew Iim not but by revelation, as He who hath the key did pen, and as the Father of Life drew me to His Son by Iis Spirit. Then the Lord gently led me along, and let me ee His love, which was endless and eternal, surpassing all he knowledge that men have in the natural state, or can ver get by history or books."

After being thus highly favoured, he was again assailed rith temptation to despair, as though he had sinned against he Holy Ghost; by which he was in great perplexity and rouble, yet still he gave himself up to the Lord.

One day, after walking solitarily abroad, on his return home he was so absorbed in the love of God, that he could not but admire the greatness of that love; and it was opened to him by the Eternal Light and Power, "THAT ALL WAS DONE, AND TO BE DONE, IN AND BY CHRIST, and how he conquers and destroys this tempter, the devil, and all his works;" and he was enabled to see that all the troubles and temptations which had been permitted to befal him, were for the trial of his faith, and were good for him; and he remarks, "My living faith was raised, and I saw that all was done by Christ the Life, and my belief was in Him."

When he was about twenty-three years of age, he commenced his public labours, as a minister of the Gospel, at Duckenfield, Manchester, and places in the neighbourhood. The success accompanying his ministry was great; and the report of his piety and zeal having spread far, many came from different parts of the country to see, and converse with him, on religious subjects. This brought a fear upon his mind, lest he should be improperly drawn out into words, or elated by the attention shown him, which proved a preservation to him. But others were exasperated, at the reception which his doctrine met with. They could not endure to hear of perfection, and of living a holy and sinless life, and began to plead for sin and imperfection, by which the tender convictions and attractions of the Spirit of grace are quenched.

"Of all the sects of Christendom (so called) that I discoursed with," he says, "I found none could bear to be told, that any should come to Adam's perfection; into that image of God, that righteousness and holiness that Adam was in before he fell; to be clean and pure, without sin, as he was. Therefore, how should they be able to bear being told that any should grow up to the measure of the stature of the fulness of Christ, when they cannot bear to hear that any should come, whilst upon earth, into the same power and spirit that the prophets and apostles were in? Though it is a certain truth, that none can understand their writings aright without the same Spirit by which they were written."

The visitations universally of the light of Christ in the heart, by which he enlightens every man that cometh into the world, was a doctrine of which George Fox was early convinced, and which, like the primitive ministers of Christ, he and his fellow-labourers in the Gospel frequently declared to their hearers. His convictions of this truth are thus described : "The Lord God opened to me by His invisible power, that every man was enlightened by the divine light of Christ. I saw it shine through all; and they that believed in it, came out of condemnation to the light of life, and became the children of it; but they that hated it, and did not believe in it, were condemned by it, though they made a profession of Christ."

In describing his commission as a minister, he says, he was sent to turn people from darkness to light—to the grace of God, and to the truth in the heart, which came by Jesus, that "all might come to know their salvation nigh." "I saw that Christ died for all men; was a propitiation for all;" "and that the manifestation of the Spirit of God was given to every man to profit withal. These things I did not see by the help of man, nor by the letter, though they are written in the letter; but I saw them in the light of the Lord Jesus Christ, and by his immediate Spirit and power, as did the Holy men of God, by whom the Holy Scriptures were written. Yet I had no slight esteem of the Holy Scriptures, they were very precious to me, for I was in that Spirit by which they were given forth; and what the Lord opened in me, I afterwards found was agreeable to them. I could speak much of these things, and many volumes might be written; but all would prove too short to set forth the infinite love, wisdom, and power of God, in preparing, fitting, and furnishing me for the service he had appointed me to; letting me see the depths of Satan, on the one hand, and opening to me, on the other, the divine mysteries of His own everlasting kingdom."

"Now when the Lord God and His Son Jesus Christ sent me forth into the world, to preach His everlasting Gospel, I was glad that I was commanded to turn people to that inward Light, Spirit, and Grace, by which all might know salvation, and their way to God; even [through] that Divine Spirit which would lead into all truth."

"By this Divine Spirit of God, and Light of Jesus, I was to bring people off from all their own ways, to Christ, the new and living way; from their churches, which men had made and gathered, to the Church in God, the general assembly written in heaven, of which Christ is the head; from the world's teachers, to learn of Christ, of whom the Father said, 'This is my beloved Son, hear ye him.' I was to bring people off from all Jewish ceremonies, and from men's inventions; from all their images and crosses, and sprinkling of infants, with all their holy days (so called), and all their vain traditions, which had gotten up since the apostles' days, and which the Lord's power was against; in the dread and authority of which I was moved to declare against them all, and against all that preached, and not freely, as being such as had not received freely from Christ."

He now travelled more extensively, and laboured abundantly, in preaching the word. Many were convinced of the doctrines which he promulgated, and during the years 1647 and 1648 several meetings of Friends were settled.

"About this time," he remarks, "I was sorely exercised, in going to their courts, to cry for justice, and in speaking and writing to judges and justices, to do justly; in warning such as kept public-houses for entertainment, that they should not let people have more drink than would do them good; in testifying against wakes or feasts, their May-games, sports, plays, and shows, which trained up people to vanity and looseness, and led them from the fear of God; and the days they had set forth for holy days, were usually the times wherein they most dishonoured God by these things. In fairs also, and in markets, I was made to declare against their deceitful merchandize, warning all to deal justly, to speak the truth, to let their yea be yea, and their nay, nay, and to do unto others as they would have others do unto them; forewarning them of the great and terrible day of the Lord, which would come upon all. I was moved, also, to cry against all sorts of music, and against the mountebanks, playing tricks on their stages, for they burdened the pure life, and stirred up people's minds to vanity. I was much exercised, too, with schoolmasters and schoolmistresses, warning them to teach their children sobriety, in the fear of the Lord, that they might not be nursed and trained up in lightness, vanity, and wantonness." "I was made to warn masters and mistresses, and fathers and mothers, in private families, to take care that their children and servants might be trained in the fear of the Lord, and that they themselves should be examples of sobriety and virtue to them."

CHAPTER II. 1649—1657.

George Fox bore a decided and faithful testimony against the prevailing custom of receiving pecuniary compensation for preaching. He had been given to see that none were true Gospel ministers but those whom Christ called, gifted, and commissioned for the work; that these necessary qualifications were, without regard to human learning or ordination, riches, station, or sex; and that all who were thus anointed, were commanded by their Divine Master to give as freely as they had received. He therefore deeply deplored the covetous spirit, which was apparent among many who took upon

them that responsible office, which induced them to seek
for the highest salaries, leaving their flocks and places for
greater wages, and pleading a call from the Lord so to do.
Against this practice he testified, as an abomination, and
crying sin. "O," says he, "the vast sums of money that
are got by the trade they make of the Scriptures, and by
their preaching, from the highest bishop to the lowest priest!
What one trade else in the world is comparable to it? notwithstanding the Scriptures were given forth freely, and
Christ commanded his ministers to preach freely, and the
prophets and apostles denounced judgment against all covetous hirelings and diviners for money." In the "free spirit
of the Lord Jesus was I sent forth, to declare the word of
life and reconciliation freely, that all might come to Christ,
who gives freely, and who renews up into the image of God,
which man and woman were in before they fell, that they
might sit down in the heavenly places in Christ Jesus."

He inculcated, by example, as well as by precept, a plain
and simple mode of living, free from needless show and
expense, believing that the Christian religion led all those
who faithfully obeyed its requirings into simplicity and self-
denial; and that, instead of being conformed to the world,
they were to renounce its vain fashions and customs, and
avoid every thing which promoted pride or luxury. Convinced that the use of compliments and flattering titles,
bowing and putting off the hat, and of using the plural
number when speaking to one person, had their origin in the
pride of the human heart, which seeks honour from man, he
was conscientiously bound to refrain from the use of every
thing of the sort, and to keep to the Scripture language of
thou and thee, to one person, according to the correct rules
of grammar. "The Lord showed me," he says, "that it
was an honour, which he would lay in the dust and stain :
an honour which proud flesh looked for, but sought not the
honour which came from God only. That it was an honour
invented by men, who were offended if it were not given
them. But Christ saith, ' How can ye believe, who receive
honour one of another, and seek not the honour that cometh
from God only ?' O the blows, beatings, and imprisonments
that we underwent, for not putting off our hats to men !
The bad language and evil usage we received on this account
are hard to be expressed ; besides the danger we were sometimes in of losing our lives for this matter, and that by the
great professors of Christianity."

His first imprisonment for the cause of Truth seems to
have occurred in 1641, at Nottingham, where, in the house

for public worship, he spoke to the people on the subject of the Scriptures, showing that the Spirit of Christ, by which the holy men of old wrote the Scriptures, was that by which only they could be rightly understood. As he was speaking, the officers arrested him, and took him to a filthy prison, where he was detained, until the sheriff, taking compassion on his uncomfortable situation, removed him to his own residence. How long he remained a prisoner, does not appear, but he says it was "a pretty long time;" and, after being discharged, he travelled, as before, in the work of the ministry.

At Mansfield Woodhouse, he entered the place of worship, and attempted to address the assembly, but the people fell upon him, and cruelly beat him with their hands, Bibles, and sticks; they then put him into the stocks, where he remained some time, and finally, stoned him out of the town. By this unchristian usage, he was so injured as scarcely to be able to stand or walk; but meeting with some persons who pitied his situation, they administered to his relief, and, through the mercy of the Lord, he was soon healed.

In the year 1650 he visited Derby, where he preached at a great meeting; many officers of the army, priests, and teachers being assembled. For this, he and his companions were arrested, and taken before the magistrates, who enquired why they came thither? George Fox replied, "God moved us so to do;" he told them also, "That all their preaching, baptism, and sacrifices, would never sanctify them," and desired that they would look unto Christ as revealed in themselves, and not unto men; it being Christ that sanctifieth. Then they ran into many words, but he desired that they would not dispute respecting God and Christ, but obey Him. They put him in and out of the room often, hurrying him backward and forward, and, after an examination of eight hours' duration, committed him to the house of correction, where he was confined for six months. During this examination, the justices endeavoured to draw from him some expression, by which they might prove him guilty of holding blasphemous opinions. They asked him, If he had no sin? To which he replied, "Christ my Saviour has taken away my sin, and in Him there is no sin." They then queried, how Friends knew that Christ did abide in them; he replied, "By His Spirit that He hath given us." Finding nothing in this upon which to ground a charge, they ensnaringly asked, "Whether any of them were Christ?" To which George Fox promptly replied, "Nay—we are nothing—Christ is all." This full acknowledgment of their own nothingness, and of the all-sufficiency of the Saviour, defeated their design. But although he thus cleared himself, and his fellow-professors, from their imputations, they made out a mittimus, and sent him and one of his companions to prison, as persons charged with uttering and broaching divers blasphemous opinions.

His relations were much concerned at his imprisonment, and offered to be bound that he should come to the town no more, if the justices would discharge him. But he told them that, having done no wrong, he could not consent to have any one bound for him—a practice which he and his friends adhered to throughout all their long imprisonments. One of the justices was much enraged at his refusal; and as George Fox was kneeling down to pray for him, he ran upon him, and struck him with both his hands, crying out, "Away with him, gaoler,—take him away, gaoler." It was this justice, Gervas Bennet, who first called Friends "Quakers," because George Fox bid him tremble at the word of the Lord.

The time of his commitment being nearly out, and the Parliament engaged in raising troops, a commission, as captain of one of the new regiments, was offered to him by some of the officers of Government. But he objected to receiving it, on conscientious grounds. He believed that, instead of war and bloodshed, the Gospel of Christ breathed "peace on earth and good-will to men,"—that the Son of God came not to destroy men's lives, but to save them, and to teach mankind to love their enemies, instead of fighting with them,—to do good, rather than evil, to those who hate them, and to pray for those who despitefully use them. "I told them," he remarks, "I knew from whence all wars did arise, even from the lusts, according to James's doctrine, and that I lived in the virtue of that life and power that took away the occasion of all wars." * Still they endeavoured to persuade him to accept their offer; and finding they could not prevail, they became angry, and ordered him to be thrust into the common gaol. This was a most noisome, offensive place, infested with vermin; and there, among thirty felons, he was kept almost half a year; yet he was occasionally allowed to take some exercise in the garden, his keepers believing he would not go away.

* *Note.* Strange! that the professed followers of the Prince of Peace, whose weapons "should not be carnal but spiritual" (" for we," saith the Apostle, "do not war after the flesh"), should be so blind to the true character of the Saviour's kingdom, as that they should even make a trade of war; glorying in the destruction of their fellow-men, and hurrying them, too often unprepared, into the awful presence of their offended Judge.

The subject of the punishment of death, for crimes affecting property only, seems very closely to have engaged his attention during this confinement. He remarks, "I was under great suffering in my spirit, because of it, and under the very sense of death." While he was in the prison, a young woman was brought there for robbing her master; and when she was about to be tried for her life, he wrote to the judge and jury, showing how contrary it was to the law of God, in old time, to put persons to death for such offences. She was, however, condemned to die, and taken to the place of execution; but, when upon the ladder, she was reprieved; and being brought back to prison, and receiving a pardon, was afterwards convinced of the Truth, and became a Friend.

After being a prisoner almost a year, he was set at liberty, about the beginning of the winter of 1651; and immediately resumed his travels, going into Leicestershire, Nottinghamshire, and Yorkshire, preaching repentance and amendment of life, wherever he came. In several places he met with very cruel usage, being beaten and stoned, so as to endanger his life; but through the goodness of his gracious Lord, he was soon healed; and nothing daunted at the hardships he endured, he persevered, as a good soldier of Jesus Christ, in proclaiming the glad tidings of salvation and peace through Him.

He now became known to many of the justices, some of whom formed a favourable opinion of his doctrine, and treated him with much kindness.

Coming to Tickhill, he sat some time with Friends, at their meeting, and then went to the house of public-worship, and began to address the people. But they immediately fell upon him and beat him, the clerk striking him on the face with a Bible, so that the blood gushed out on the floor of the house: then they cried, "Let us have him out of the church;" accordingly they dragged him out, beat him, knocked him down, and threw him over a hedge: then they dragged him through a house into the street, stoning and beating him as they went, so that he was covered with blood and dirt. As soon as he could recover himself, and get upon his feet, he preached repentance to them, showing them the fruits of their false profession, and how they disgraced the Christian name. After some time, he got into the meeting of Friends; and the priest and his hearers coming by the house, he went with Friends into the yard, and again addressed them. They scoffed and called them Quakers; but such was the power accompanying his preaching, that the priest trembled, and one of the people called

at, "Look, how the priest trembles and shakes; he is
turned a Quaker also." In consequence of the abuse committed that day, two or three justices convened at the town
to examine into the matter; and though the person who
shed his blood was liable to a severe penalty, George Fox
forgave him, and would not appear against him.

Travelling onward, he came to Firbank Chapel, in Westmoreland, where Francis Howgill and John Audland had
been preaching that morning. While others were gone to
dinner, he went to a brook, got a little water, and then came
and sat down on the top of a rock, hard by the chapel. In
the afternoon, the people gathered about him, with several
of their preachers. It was judged there were above a
thousand persons present, to whom he declared God's everlasting truth and word of life, freely and largely, for about
the space of three hours, directing all "to the manifestation
of the Spirit of God in themselves, that they might be turned
from darkness to light, and believe in it, that they might
become the children of it, and might be turned from the
power of Satan unto God; and by the Spirit of truth, might
be led into all truth, and sensibly understand the words of
the prophets, and of Christ, and of the apostles, and might
all come to know Christ to be their teacher to instruct them,
their counsellor to direct them, their shepherd to feed them,
their bishop to oversee them, and their prophet to open
divine mysteries to them; and might know their bodies to
be prepared, sanctified, and made fit temples for God and
Christ to dwell in." In the openings of heavenly life, he
explained to them the prophets, and the figures and shadows,
and directed them to Christ the substance. The Lord's
power accompanied his ministry, and reached home to the
hearts of the people; whereby many were convinced, and all
the teachers of that congregation, who were many, received
God's everlasting truth, and subsequently some of them
became ministers among Friends.

At Carlisle, having preached at the market-cross, and in
the house for public worship, he was committed to prison
as a blasphemer, a heretic, and a seducer," and cruelly
used, being thrust into a common hole amongst the felons
and disorderly persons, without bed, fire, or other accommodation. He remained in prison until the assizes; when the
judges, finding that the high charges on which he was
committed could not be sustained, resolved not to bring him
to trial; and the magistrates, fearing the interference of the
Parliament, soon after released him, as the easiest method of
concealing their illegal conduct.

B

He now resumed his travels, going through Westmoreland, Cumberland, Northumberland, &c. "The everlasting Gospel and word of life," says he, "flourished, and thousands were turned to the Lord Jesus Christ, and to his teaching." The success of his labours provoked the envious opposers, who were vexed to see the principles of Friends spreading; and they not only invented and circulated many slanders against them, but prophesied the downfall of the Society. But, after awhile, they saw that the Lord blessed and increased Friends, as he did Abraham, both in the field and in the basket, and that all things prospered with them. Then they saw the falsehood of all their prophecies against them, and that it was in vain to curse where God had blessed.

"At the first convincement," says G. Fox, "when Friends could not put off their hats to people, nor say you to a single person, but thou and thee; when they could not bow, nor use flattering words in salutations, nor go into the fashions and customs of the world, many Friends that were tradesmen lost their customers; for the people were shy of them, and would not trade with them, so that, for a time, some Friends could hardly get money enough to buy bread. But afterwards, when people came to have experience of Friends' honesty and faithfulness, and found that their yea was yea, and their nay was nay; and that they kept to their word in their dealings, the lives and conversation of Friends did preach, and reached to the Witness of God in the people; then things altered so, that the inquiry was, 'Where was a draper, or shopkeeper, or tailor, that was a Quaker; insomuch that Friends had more trade than many of their neighbours. Then the envious professors altered their note, and began to cry out, 'If we let these Quakers alone, they will take the trade of the nation out of our hands.' This hath been the Lord's doing, to and for his people, which my desire is, that all who profess his holy truth may be kept truly sensible of; and that all may be preserved in and by his power and Spirit, faithful to God and man; first to God, in obeying Him in all things, and then in doing unto all men that which is just and righteous."

A change having taken place in the Government of England, King Charles being deposed, and Oliver Cromwell declared "Protector" of the Commonwealth, the disturbances and difficulties attendant on a state of civil warfare, reached the peaceable Society of Friends, though they meddled not with political affairs. In 1654, George Fox was arrested at Whetstone, by a company of troopers, and carried before Colonel Hacker, who, after a partial examiation, sent him to London to Cromwell. The Colonel was very desirous to extort from him a promise, that he would hold no more meetings, pretending that they were dangerous to the safety of the Government. But he was not free to come under such an engagement; and when he found the Colonel determined on sending him to the Protector, he knelt down by him, and besought the Lord to forgive him. He was brought before Cromwell, at Whitehall, and they had much conversation on the subject of religion. As he was turning to leave him, Cromwell caught him by the hand, saying, "Come again to my house; for if thou and I were but an hour of a day together, we should be nearer one to the other;" adding, that he wished George Fox no more ill than he did to his own soul." He was discharged from his confinement; and, by Cromwell's order, taken to the dinner-hall, and invited to dine with the company; but he declined accepting the offer, sending word to him, that "he would not eat his bread nor drink his drink." When Cromwell heard this, he said, "Now I see there is a people risen and come up that I cannot win, either with gifts, honours, offices, or places; but all other sects and people I can." It was told him again, that Friends had forsaken their own, and were not, therefore, likely to look for such things from him.

In the years 1654 and 1655, he continued travelling diligently in England, holding meetings both among his friends, and the people generally; and though occasionally arrested, or otherwise misused, yet the violence of persecution was in some degree mitigated. In describing the character of his Gospel labours among the people, he says, "I directed them to the light of Christ, by which they might see their sins, and their Saviour Christ Jesus the way to God, and their Mediator to make peace betwixt God and them; their Shepherd to feed them, and their Prophet to teach them. I directed them to the Spirit of God [revealed] in themselves, by which they might know the Scriptures, and be led into all truth; by which [Spirit] they might know God, and in it have unity one with another."

By this time some Friends were settled in the north of Ireland, to whom George Fox wrote the following brief but comprehensive epistle, the reading of which much tendered those assembled on the occasion:—

"Friends—

"In that [Power] which convinced you, wait; that you may have that removed, you are convinced of [as sin].

And all my dear friends, dwell in the life, love, power, and wisdom of God, in unity one with another, and with God; and the peace and wisdom of God fill your hearts, that nothing may rule in you but the life, which stands in the Lord God.   "G. F."

Near the close of the year 1655, George Fox, and his companion Edward Pyott, were arrested in Cornwall, and sent prisoners, under a guard of soldiers, to Launceston gaol.

In about nine weeks after their commitment, they were brought to the assizes, when the accusations against them being proved to be utterly false, the judge fined them twenty marks each for keeping on their hats, and ordered them to be detained in prison until it was paid.

To prison they were accordingly sent; and finding that there was little probability of soon obtaining a release, they determined to demand free quarters, and to cease paying the gaoler for their board. This so incensed him, that he put them into a hole, called Doomsdale, which was so filthy, damp, and unwholesome, that it was remarked, few who went into it came out in health. It was covered with mire and water in some places, as deep as the tops of their shoes, and they could not lie down, but were obliged to stand up constantly. For a long time the gaoler would not suffer them to cleanse it, nor to have any victuals, but what were handed to them through the grate; and on one occasion, when a little girl had brought them some meat, he arrested and prosecuted her for " breaking his house."

The sessions being at hand, they drew up a statement of their sufferings, and presented it to the court, at Bodmin. On reading it, the justices ordered the door of the prison to be opened, and that the prisoners should have liberty to cleanse it, and to purchase their provisions in the town. While George Fox was in confinement at Launceston, many persons visited him, to whom he preached the Gospel, and explained the nature of his religious principles; and so large a number were convinced by his faithful labours, that one of the Protector's chaplains remarked, " They could not do George Fox a greater service, for spreading his principles in Cornwall, than to imprison him there."

During his confinement, a Friend went to Oliver Cromwell, and offered himself to lie in prison, if the Protector would release George Fox, and accept of him instead. This struck Cromwell so forcibly, as an act of disinterested kindness, that he turned to his council and other attendants, and asked " Which of you would do so much for me, if I were in the same condition?" After being about half a year in gaol, they were discharged in the seventh month, 1656. The gaoler who had used them so cruelly, was not only turned out of his office, but came to poverty, and afterwards was himself a prisoner in the same place.

After accomplishing a visit to Friends in most parts of England, to the comfort and strength of his brethren, George Fox returned to London, where he remained some time. Diligently engaged in his Master's cause, he allowed himself but little rest; and when not travelling, much of his time was occupied in writing essays for publication, with a view of spreading a knowledge of the doctrines of the Society, correcting the false charges which were so often made against them, or checking the violence of persecution.

He was, indeed, an indefatigable labourer, scarcely allowing himself time to take sufficient food or sleep, and wholly giving up temporal business, that he might be more at liberty to serve the Lord.

The Society had now greatly increased in numbers, and meetings were settled in most parts of the kingdom, which Friends were concerned to attend with diligence, notwithstanding the cruel usage they often met with.

Persecution served but to strengthen the faith and constancy of the sufferers, who counted the testimony of truth, and the faithful support of their religious principles, dearer than any earthly consideration; freely surrendering their property, their bodies, and their lives, rather than neglect their duty to God. For many years, there were seldom fewer than one thousand of them in prison for their testimony to the truth.

In 1657, George Fox visited Scotland, where he found the people under the influence of the dark doctrine of unconditional election and reprobation. He preached the universal love of God to all mankind, and proved that reprobation was the consequence of sin committed, and not of a personal decree to irremediable perdition. He taught, that He who was a propitiation for the sins of the whole world, for reprobates as well as saints, commanded his ministers to preach the Gospel to all nations; that He died for all, and enlightens all, by the manifestation of his Spirit; that they who vex, quench, and grieve the Holy Spirit, are the reprobates; and the fault lies at their door, because they have rejected the grace of God, which brought the offer of salvation to them. But they who receive and obey Christ, become elected in him, and partakers of the blessings of his propitiatory sufferings and death.

At Edinburgh, the magistrates issued an order for him to

appear before them, which he readily obeyed. On being introduced, he paused a little, and then addressed them— " Peace be amongst you.—Wait in the fear of God, that ye may receive his wisdom from above, by which all things were made and created, that by it ye may all be ordered, and may order all things unto your hands, to God's glory." After inquiring into the cause of his coming into Scotland, and the nature of his business there, they issued an order commanding him to leave the country in one week form that time. But in the performance of religious duty, he believed it right to obey God rather than man; and apprehending himself called to further service there, he continued holding meetings and preaching the Gospel, in Edinburgh and its vicinity, for a considerable time ; and, although he returned again to that city, after visiting meetings in the country, yet he was suffered to pass unmolested.

Leaving Scotland, he came to Durham, where he met with a person, recently from London, who had come for the purpose of aiding in the establishment of a college, to prepare young men for the ministry. George Fox reasoned with him on the subject, showing that human learning, though prosecuted to the greatest extent, could never qualify for preaching the Gospel; that this could only be done through the power and assistance of Christ's Spirit, he being the great Minister of ministers, whose exclusive right it is, to call and qualify his servants to preach life and salvation in his name. He reminded him that Peter and John, though unlearned men, preached Christ Jesus to Jews and Gentiles, with great success; and that Paul declared he was made an apostle, not of man, nor by man, neither received he his Gospel from man, but by the revelation of Jesus Christ. The man assented to the truth of many of these arguments, manifested much tenderness of spirit, and, after further consideration, declined the prosecution of his intentions.

CHAPTER III. 1657—1669.

In those days there was a large number of serious, seeking persons, in the different religious societies, who were earnestly engaged for their soul's salvation, and could not find in the stated ceremonies and performances to which they were accustomed, that peace and satisfaction which they desired. Few, however, understood the operations of the Holy Spirit in their own hearts; or had faith to believe in

s sufficiency to lead them in the path of peace. They
elt it striving with them for sin, and inclining them to
oliness, but as yet knew not what it was. In this state
f mind, seeking the truth, yet not finding it, and tossed
ith doubts and fears respecting their spiritual condition,
ne preaching of George Fox came to them like a message
om heaven, directing them to the light of Christ Jesus in
ne conscience, the Comforter, or Holy Spirit, which he
romised to send his disciples, to bring all things to their
emembrance, and to guide them into all truth. They saw
hat they had depended too much upon men, and upon out-
ard performances, and had overlooked the teachings of this
lessed Spirit in their souls; and they now turned to it with
oy, and in faith received and obeyed its commands. They
erceived that, whilst partaking of the outward bread and
ine, they had rested therein, and had too much overlooked
hat true communion, in which Christ comes into the souls of
is obedient children, and sups with them, causing them to
artake of that living bread which cometh down from
eaven, and of that new wine of His kingdom, whereby
heir spiritual vigour is renewed. They also saw that the
aptism of water was a mere external thing, which could
ither wash the soul from pollution, nor initiate it into the
hurch of Christ; and that they must therefore experience
e one only true and saving baptism, by the Holy Ghost and
e;—"not the putting away of the filth of the flesh, but
e answer of a good conscience toward God, by the resur-
ction of Jesus Christ." It was the dawning of a new and
yful day to their souls; and as they attended, in simple
edience, to the discoveries of this Divine Light, they were
ought from under the bondage of sin into the glorious
erty of the children of God; wherein they knew Christ
be their Saviour and Redeemer, and that he had indeed
me to them a second time, without sin unto salvation.

At the time Charles II. was proclaimed King, there were
out seven hundred Friends in different prisons in England,
ho had been committed under the governments of Oliver
d Richard Cromwell. The King, on his accession to the
rone, set them all at liberty. It seemed to be, at that time,
s intention to grant liberty of conscience to his subjects; but
e rash and tumultuous behaviour of some disorderly persons,
efeated this desirable object. These were termed Fifth-
onarchy-men, who, making an insurrection in the city of
ondon, pretending religion in their wicked designs, the sus-
icions of the Government were excited, and persecution again
ll heavily upon all who dissented from the State religion.

Men and women, who were known to be Friends, could scarcely pass without violent abuse, through the streets and highways, on their lawful business, or to procure provision for their families. Many were hauled out of their houses and some, who were sick, were cruelly dragged from their beds to prison. Amid this storm of ill-usage, Friends continued steadfast to their principles, and faithfully attended their meetings, although they went to them with a full expectation of beatings, stonings, and imprisonment. The prisons were filled with the peaceable " Quakers," and many thousands were thrown into gaol in the space of a few weeks.

Although many of these were soon after set at liberty, as being entirely innocent of any connection with those wild enthusiasts, the Fifth-monarchy-men, yet the meetings of Friends continued to be disturbed by the soldiers and rude people. At one time, a company of Irishmen came to the meeting-house at Pall Mall, with the intention of causing a disturbance, but the meeting was over before they arrived, George Fox having gone into an upper chamber, overheard one of them, a colonel, say, " he would kill all the Quakers." He immediately went down, and reproved this blood-thirsty man, telling him " that the Law said, ' An eye for an eye and a tooth for a tooth;' but he threatened to kill all the Quakers, though they had done him no harm. But here,' said George Fox, " is Gospel for thee: here is my hair, and here is my cheek, and here is my shoulder," turning it to him. This address so surprised the man and his companions as to induce the remark that, if these were Quaker principles, they had never heard the like before. George Fox replied, that what Friends were in words the same they were in life. The man who made the threat became moderate and courteous, although one of his company, who staid without the house, said he was so desperate a character that he did not dare to go in with him, fearing he would have done Friends some mischief. Such is the powerful influence which a gentle and peaceable demeanour, under provocation, has over the spirits even of persecutors; furnishing strong evidence of the blessed effects of the meek and unresisting spirit of the Gospel, and of the truth of the declaration, that " a soft answer turneth away wrath."

Few persons possessed a more undaunted courage and firmness than did George Fox. No danger seemed to alarm or disconcert him, no perils to deter him from the performance of duty. He was ever ready to bear his full portion of suffering for the religion he espoused; and by example, as well as by precept, to encourage his brethren in the faithful maintenance of their principles. Hearing that Colonel Kirby had sent a lieutenant to the house of Margaret Fell, at Swarthmore to search for him, he went on the following morning to Kirby Hall, where the colonel resided. On being introduced to him, he observed, that "understanding he was desirous of seeing him, he had come to visit him, to know what he had to say, or whether he had anything against him." Colonel Kirby seemed taken by surprise, and said, before all the company, he had nothing against him. After much friendly conversation had passed, they shook hands and parted.

Soon after this Colonel Kirby went to London, and the other justices held a private meeting, and granted a warrant to apprehend George Fox. Information was given him over night, both of the meeting and the warrant, and he had ample opportunity to avoid it; but he chose rather to stay and meet the storm, hoping that he should thus shield his friends from its force. On the following morning an officer, armed with sword and pistols, apprehended him and carried him before the justices, when he was examined on various points. They then tendered the oath to him; and on his conscientiously refusing to swear, required him to appear at the next sessions. The time appointed approaching, George Fox repaired to Lancaster, and appeared before the judges, according to his engagement. The concourse was large, and the court-house very full; but he made his way to the bar, and there stood with his hat on. Silence being ordered, he addressed the company twice, "Peace be among you." The chairman asked him if he knew where he was. "Yes, I do," he replied; "but it may be my hat offends you. That is a low thing, that is not the honour that I give to magistrates, nor the true honour is from above. I hope it is not the hat that you look upon to be the true honour." After some further conversation, they bade one of the officers take his hat off, and then proceeded to examine him, respecting a pretended plot against the Government, of which he showed himself to be entirely clear. Not being able to find any other charge against him, they tendered him the oaths of allegiance and supremacy; and for his again refusing to swear, committed him to prison. He bid the judges and people take notice that he suffered for the doctrine of Christ, and for obedience to his command.

At the following assizes, he was again brought to the bar; but continuing to decline taking the oath, was remanded to prison.

At the next assizes, he was brought before Judge Turner. The indictment being read, George Fox stated that it con-

tained many errors, which he wished to show. These h
severally pointed out, and proved, to the confusion of th
court; and as he was continuing his exposure of thei
irregular proceedings, the judge desired him to stop, an
say no more, for he had heard enough. To which Georg
Fox replied, " If thou hast enough, I desire nothing but lav
and justice at thy hands: for I do not look for mercy."

JUDGE.—"You must have justice, and you shall hav
law."

G. F.—" Am I at liberty then, and free from all that hatl
been done against me in this matter."

JUDGE.—"Yes: you are free from all that hath beei
done against you. But then [standing up in a rage, h
added,] I can put the oath to any man here, and I wil
tender you the oath again;" and notwithstanding the unfair
ness of such a procedure was clearly laid before him, an
the hardship of the prisoner's case, who had been so long ii
gaol, without any cause whatever; yet he persisted in hi
unrighteous course. He ordered the clerk of the court t
give him the book. George Fox took it in his hand, an
looking into it, with great composure said, "I see it is a
Bible, and I am glad of it." The oath was then read, an
the judge asked him whether he would take it or not. T
which G. Fox replied, " You have given me a book here t
kiss and to swear on: and this book says, ' Kiss the Son
and the Son says in this book, ' SWEAR NOT AT ALL;' an
so says also the Apostle James. I say as the book say
and yet ye imprison me. How chance, ye do not impriso
the book for saying so? How comes it that the book i
at liberty amongst you, which bids me not to swear, and ye
ye imprison me for doing as the book bids me?"

On hearing this short but conclusive argument, the
snatched the Bible out of his hand again; and the judg
replied, " Nay, but we will imprison George Fox."

He reminded them of the oaths already taken to an in
dictment full of errors, and of his telling them as he ha
done, if any of them could convince him that Christ or hi
apostles had altered the command against swearing, the
should see that he would swear. He told the jury it wa
for Christ's sake he could not swear; and therefore warne
them not to act contrary to the witness for God in thei
consciences, for before his judgment-seat they must all b
brought. " As for plots, and persecution for religion, an
popery, I do deny them in my heart; for I am a Christiar
and shall show forth Christianity amongst you this day.]
is for Christ's doctrine I stand."

The jury found the indictment against him; and the dge calling him to the bar in the afternoon, asked him hat he had to say to it. He desired he might have a py of it, and time given him to examine it. After some scourse, they committed him to prison until the next size; and Colonel Kirby gave orders to the gaoler to keep him close, and suffer none to come to him, for he as not fit to be discoursed with by men." The gaoler cordingly put him into an apartment in the tower, where e smoke and damp from the rooms of the other prisoners me up so thick that it stood like dew upon the walls, and metimes a lighted candle could scarcely be seen. At times was almost suffocated; and the under-gaoler was so afraid breathing the smoke, that George Fox could hardly per- ade him to come and unlock one of the upper doors, to ntilate the room. " Besides," says he, " it rained in upon y bed; and many times, when I went to stop out the rain the cold, winter season, my shirt was wet with the rain at came in upon me; and the place being high, and open the wind, sometimes, as fast as I stopped it, the wind ew it out again. In this manner did I lie all that long, ld winter, till the next assize; in which time, I was so arved with cold and rain, that my body was greatly elled, and my limbs much benumbed."

At the assize, held the 16th of the month called March, 64–5, he was again brought before the court, Judge wisden being on the bench. Whilst he was showing the rors in this second indictment, the judge called to the oler, "Take him away—take him away," which was ac- rdingly done. After he was gone, the jury brought in a rdict of guilty, and the court recorded him as a pre- nired person, though he was not called to hear the rdict, nor was sentence pronounced, which was contrary law.

He was now laid by in prison; and from the bitterness of persecutors, there seemed little probability that he would n be released.

The justices were so incensed, at the manner in which had exposed them at the sessions, that they determined, possible, to get him removed from Lancaster. And in out six weeks after the assizes, obtaining an order from e King and Council to that effect, they forthwith pro- ded to execute it, but without letting him know whither ey intended carrying him. He was so weakened by the el usage he received, as to be scarcely able to walk or nd; and they offered him wine to drink, which he refused.

He remonstrated earnestly against their taking him away, because he had been illegally treated at the sessions. But remonstrance was in vain—they placed him on horseback, and though so stiff and feeble as scarcely to be able to keep his seat, they conveyed him to Scarborough Castle, which was to be the place of his imprisonment.

Continuing very weak, and subject to faintings, they sometimes, after he first came there, allowed him to walk out, under the care of a sentry; but this kindness was soon exchanged for a course of great severity. They removed him into an open room, where the rain came in, and the chimney smoked exceedingly. The governor coming to see him, he represented the cruelty of his case to him, but could obtain no improvement of it. After spending above fifty shillings of his own, in excluding the rain and smoke, his persecutors, finding the room was now tolerable, removed him from it to another far worse, open to the sea, and in which there was neither chimney nor fire-hearth. The rain drove in and ran over his bed, and on to the floor, so as to make it necessary to bale it up; and when his clothes were wet, he was not allowed fire to dry them. These hardships further impaired his health, his body was benumbed with cold, and his limbs swelled far beyond their natural size. In this suffering situation, they refused to allow his friends to come to him, or to bring him suitable food, so that he was obliged to hire a person to supply him, and it sometimes happened that the soldiers would take it away from her as she was bringing it.

At length, his meek and patient endurance of suffering, and the blamelessness of his conduct and conversation, softened the hearts of some of his keepers; considerable interest was excited in his favour; and his friends, John Whitehead and Ellis Hookes, drew up a relation of his case, which was laid before the King, and an order for his release obtained. This imprisonment lasted nearly three years. The day after his liberation the great fire broke out in London, and consumed a large part of the city. During his confinement in Lancester gaol, he had a remarkable vision of an angel of the Lord, with a glittering drawn sword in his hand, stretched out southward, toward the city, which he believed to be indicative of this calamity.

He now resumed his labours in the ministry of the Gospel, travelling through several of the counties of England, until he came to London, "having many large and precious meetings among the people. But I was so weak," he adds, " with lying almost three years in cruel and hard imprisonnents, and my joints and body were so stiff, and benumbed, that I could hardly get on my horse, or bend my joints, nor could I well bear to be near the fire, or to eat warm meat, I had been kept so long from it. Being come to London, I walked a little among the ruins, and took good notice of them. I saw the city lying, according as the word of the Lord came to me concerning it, several years before."

In the year 1666, George Fox recommended the establishment of Monthly meetings, for the close inspection into the state of the Society, and the conduct of its members, as well as to render suitable assistance to such as might be in necessitous circumstances. To use his own words, they were 'to take care of God's glory, and to admonish and exhort such as walked disorderly, or carelessly, and not according to truth." Hitherto they had had only Quarterly meetings; these embraced a considerable district of country, as well as a large number of members, so that it was difficult to oversee them with that vigilance which he thought requisite. Believing himself thus called to establish these meetings, he travelled through most parts of the nation, showing to Friends the necessity of a wholesome order and discipline in the church; that all might be preserved in unity and harmony, consistently with the profession they were making. The beneficial effects of the discipline were soon apparent, in preserving the members faithful in the support of the principles and testimonies of the Society, and in clearing it of the reproach of such as walked disorderly.

In 1667, his enlarged mind was engaged on the subject of education; and, pursuant to his recommendation, two schools were established, in the neighbourhood of London— one for boys, and one for girls—" for instructing them in whatsoever things were civil and useful in the creation;" thus embracing a wide range, and showing that he held no narrow views of the benefits of good instruction.

In 1669, he went into Ireland, visiting most of the principal towns, as well as the settlements of Friends; and although envy and ill-will stirred up some to persecute him, yet, through the goodness of the Shepherd of Israel, he escaped out of their hands. "The Lord," says he, " disappointed all their counsels, and defeated all their designs against me; by His good hand of providence, He preserved me out of all their snares, and gave us many sweet and blessed opportunities to visit Friends, and spread Truth through that nation. For meetings were very large, Friends coming to them from far and near, and other people flocking in. The powerful presence of the Lord was preciously felt

with and amongst us, whereby many of the world were
reached, convinced, and gathered to the Truth; the Lord's
flock was increased, and Friends were greatly refreshed and
comforted in feeling the love of God. Oh, the brokenness
that was amongst them, in the flowings of life! so that, in
the power and Spirit of the Lord, many broke out in singing
praises to the Lord, making melody in their hearts."

In the passage home a storm arose, which put the vessel in
great danger. "But the power of God went over the winds
and storms; he had them in his hand and his power bound
them."

Landing at Liverpool, he proceeded through Lancashire,
Cheshire, and Gloucestershire, to Bristol, where he met with
Margaret Fell, widow of Thomas Fell, one of the judges of
the Welch courts. He had long been intimately acquainted
with her; and had, for a considerable time, believed it would
be right that they should be united in marriage, which he
had formerly communicated to her, though not with an
expectation of proceeding in it at that time. "Wherefore,"
says he, "I let the thing rest, and went on in the work and
service of the Lord, as before, according as the Lord led me,
travelling up and down in this nation, and through the
nation of Ireland." But now, being at Bristol, and finding
Margaret Fell there, he believed it right that their marriage
should be accomplished.

Previously to taking this step, he was careful to ascertain
what were the feelings of her children respecting it; and
they "severally expressing their satisfaction therewith," he
queried whether their mother had fulfilled her husband's
will towards them, or whether they would in any way be
losers by her marriage. After giving him a clear reply on
this head, and desiring that he would not again mention the
subject, he told them, "that he was plain, and would have
all things done plainly, for he sought not any outward advantage to himself." Their intention of marriage being then
made public, and having the full approbation of their friends,
a meeting was appointed for its accomplishment; and they
were joined together in the Lord, in the honourable marriage
bond. Margaret Fox was a godly and devout woman, very
serviceable in the church, and endured many sufferings and
cruel imprisonments for the cause of Truth.

CHAPTER IV. 1669—1690.

The great increase of wickedness throughout the kingdom, after the restoration of King Charles the Second, was a source of much sorrow to Friends and other religious persons. Many of the latter, being driven away by the cruelties practised towards dissenters, expressed their belief that, if Friends did not stand their ground, the nation would be overrun with drunkenness, debauchery, and excess. The awful sense of this flood of sin, which as a mighty torrent was sweeping through the land, deeply affected George Fox; and such was the grief and exercise of his mind, that it seriously impaired his health, his sight and hearing being almost gone, and his body so enfeebled, that his friends thought he could not long survive. During this season of conflict, he was engaged in prayer to the Lord, that he would be pleased to prosper truth, and preserve justice and equity in the land, and bring down iniquity, oppression, falsehood, profanity, and licentiousness.

On his recovery, he went to London, and having been for some time drawn in spirit to visit his brethren in America, he embarked for Barbadoes, in the spring of 1671, a considerable number of ministers, who were engaged in the same service, accompanying him.

When they had been at sea about three weeks, they were chased by a Turkish man-of-war, which gained fast upon them; and the prospect of falling into their hands, put the captain and crew into great terror. It was on a seventh-day evening, and the moon shining clear, they could perceive the vessel nearing them;—when the captain came to George Fox to know what should be done, observing that, if the mariners had taken Paul's counsel, they would not have suffered the damage they did. He told them, "it was a trial of faith, and therefore the Lord was to be waited on for counsel." After a time of mental retirement, and waiting on the Lord, it was shown him, that the Lord's life and power was placed between them and their pursuers. He then told them to put out all the lights, except the one they steered by, and directed that all in the ship should be as quiet as possible, and that they should tack about and steer their right course. They did so, but still the vessel gained upon them, and was now so close that the passengers were alarmed. The watch cried out, "They are just upon us;" and rising up in his berth, George Fox looked through a port-hole, the moon being not quite down, and perceived it was so. He was about to get up and leave the cabin; but remembering it had been shown him, "that the Lord's life and power was between them," he returned again to bed. Soon after this, the moon went down, and a fresh breeze springing up, they escaped out of their hands, though they had come so close that it seemed almost impossible.

On arriving at Barbadoes, he held several large public meetings, to which most of the principal officers and persons of the island came, and many were convinced. His enslaved coloured brethren, as might be expected, claimed his compassionate care. His first concern for them was, that they should partake of religious instruction, and be trained up in the fear of God; in the next place, that they should be treated mildly and gently, and no cruelty exercised towards them; and lastly, that, after a certain term of servitude, they should be set free. [His Friends in religious profession subsequently saw further, and did not retain any in membership with them who persisted in holding their fellow-creatures in bondage.]

Some false reports having been industriously spread by the enemies of Friends, such as that they denied Jesus Christ, &c. After one of those meetings, Colonel Lyne, a sober, discreet man, remarked, "Now I can gainsay such as I have heard speak evil of you, who say you do not own Christ, nor that he died,—whereas I perceive you exalt Christ, in all his offices, beyond what I have ever heard before."

But these scandalous reports had been so widely circulated, that George Fox thought it his duty, in conjunction with some other Friends, to draw up a paper, in the name of the Society, to clear it of these charges. They accordingly prepared and published an address to the governor and council, which for soundness of doctrine, and clearness and force of expression, has rarely been surpassed, and of which the following is an extract:—

"Whereas many scandalous lies and slanders have been cast upon us, to render us odious; as that 'We deny God, Christ Jesus, and the Scriptures of truth,' &c. This is to inform you, that all our books and declarations, which for these many years have been published to the world, clearly testify [to] the contrary. Yet for your satisfaction, we now plainly and sincerely declare,

"That we own, and believe in the only Wise, Omnipotent, and Everlasting God; the Creator of all things in heaven and earth, and the Preserver of all that he hath made; who is God over all, blessed for ever; to whom be all honour and glory, dominion, praise, and thanksgiving, both now and for evermore!

"And we own, and believe in Jesus Christ, his beloved and only begotten Son, in whom he is well pleased; who was conceived of the Holy Ghost, and born of the Virgin Mary; in whom we have redemption through his blood, even the forgiveness of sins; who is the express image of the invisible God, the first-born of every creature; by whom were all things created, that are in heaven and in earth, visible and invisible, whether they be thrones, dominions, principalities, or powers: all things were created by him.

"And we own and believe, that He was made a sacrifice for sin, who knew no sin, neither was guile found in his mouth; that he was crucified for us in the flesh, without the gates of Jerusalem; and that he was buried, and rose again the third day, by the power of his Father, for our justification; and that he ascended up into heaven, and now sitteth at the right hand of God. This Jesus, who was the foundation of the holy prophets and apostles, is our foundation; and we believe there is no other foundation to be laid, than that which is laid, even Christ Jesus: who tasted death for every man, shed his blood for all men, is the propitiation for our sins, and not for ours only, but also for the sins of the whole world; according as John the Baptist testified of him, when he said, 'Behold the Lamb of God, which taketh away the sin of the world.' John i. 29.

"We believe, that He alone is our Redeemer and Saviour, even the Captain of our Salvation, who saves us from sin, as well as from hell and the wrath to come, and destroys the devil and his works. He is the Seed of the woman that bruises the serpent's head,—Christ Jesus, the Alpha and Omega, the First and the Last. He is, as the Scriptures of truth say of him, our wisdom and righteousness, justification and redemption; neither is there salvation in any other; for there is no other name under heaven, given among men, whereby we may be saved. He alone is the Shepherd and Bishop of our souls: he is our Prophet, whom Moses long since testified of, saying, 'A prophet shall the Lord your God raise up unto you of your brethren, like unto me; him shall ye hear in all things, whatsoever he shall say unto you: and it shall come to pass, that every soul that will not hear that prophet, shall be destroyed from among the people.' Acts ii. 22, 23.

"He it is, that is now come in Spirit, and hath given us an understanding, that we may know Him that is true. He

rules in our hearts by his law of love and of life, and make
us free from the law of sin and death. We have no life bu
by him; for he is the quickening Spirit, the second Adam
the Lord from heaven, by whose blood we are cleansed, an
our consciences sprinkled from dead works, to serve th
living God.

"This Lord Jesus Christ, the heavenly man, the Emmanuel
God with us, we all own and believe in; whom the high
priest raged against, and said, he had spoken blasphemy
whom the priests and elders of the Jews took counci
together against, and put to death; the same whom Juda
betrayed for thirty pieces of silver, which the priests gav
him as a reward for his treason; who also gave large mone
to the soldiers, to broach a horrible lie, namely, 'That h
disciples came and stole him away by night, whilst the
slept.' After he was risen from the dead, the history of th
Acts of the Apostles sets forth how the chief priests an
elders persecuted the disciples of this Jesus, for preachin
Christ and his resurrection. This, we say, is that Lor
Jesus Christ, whom we own to be our life and salvation.

"Concerning the Holy Scriptures, we do believe they were
given forth by the Holy Spirit of God, through the holy me
of God, who, as the Scripture itself declares, 2 Pet. i. 21,
'spake, as they were moved by the Holy Ghost.' We
believe they are to be read, believed, and fulfilled (he that
fulfils them is Christ); and they are 'profitable for doctrine,
for reproof, for correction, for instruction in righteousness,
that the man of God may be perfect, thoroughly furnished
unto all good works,' 2 Tim. iii. 16, and are able to 'make
wise unto salvation, through faith which is in Christ Jesus.' "

Having spent several months in Barbadoes and Jamaica,
he sailed for Maryland, visiting New England, and other
parts of the American Continent. In one place he heard
that they talked of hiring him for their minister, not understanding the principles of Friends; George Fox, therefore,
concluded it was time for him to be gone; for if their eye
was so much to him, or any other person, they would not
come to the great teacher, Christ Jesus. "Hiring ministers," he remarked, "had spoiled many, by hindering them
from improving their own hearts; whereas our labour is
to bring every one to his own teacher in himself."

Proceeding on their journey, he and his friends went into
Carolina, enduring great hardships from the extreme bad-
ness of the way; there being no open roads, but only paths
through the wilderness, and in many places deep bogs and
swamps, so that they were commonly wet up to the knees,

and lay out in the woods at night. Yet they were mercifully preserved from any serious injury from the exposure. There appeared to be great openness among the people to receive them, and they met with very little opposition. At one place, a doctor contended against the universality of the light of Christ, asserting that the Indians had it not. George Fox, therefore, called an Indian to him, and asked him whether, or not, when he spoke falsely, or did any wrong action, there was not something in him which reproved him for it. To which he readily answered, there was, and that it reproved him, and made him feel ashamed when he had done or spoken evil.

Having travelled through most of the provinces where there were Friends, and preached the Gospel of salvation to the people, he felt himself at liberty to return to his own country, where he arrived in the spring of 1673. "We had in our passage," he observes, "very high winds and tempestuous weather, which made the sea exceeding rough, the waves rising like mountains, so that both master and sailors wondered, and said they had never seen the like before. But though the wind was strong, it set for the most part with us, so that we sailed before it; and the great God, who commands the winds, who is Lord of heaven, earth, and the seas, and whose wonders are seen in the deep, steered our course, and preserved us through many imminent dangers. The same good hand of Providence that went with us, and carried us safely over, watched over us in our return, and brought us safely back again—thanksgiving and praises be to his holy Name for ever."

In 1677, accompanied by William Penn, Robert Barclay, and several other Friends, he visited Holland; and his service in those parts appears to have been well received, not only by the members of his own Society, but by serious people of other persuasions. In 1678, he reached his residence at Swarthmore. Whether at home or abroad, the care of the churches, and a righteous concern for the honour and promotion of the cause of Christ, daily rested upon him; and he spared not himself, but laboured diligently, as the Lord called him thereto. In his retirement at Swarthmore, where he remained nearly a year and a half, he wrote many excellent epistles to his brethren; some to warn them against dangers which he saw threatened the church; some to encourage them to be bold and valiant, in support of the testimonies of truth, and others to cheer and refresh them under suffering.

In an epistle which he addressed to the Yearly Meeting are the following excellent paragraphs :—

"My desire is, that all your lights may shine, as from a city set upon a hill, that cannot be hid; and that ye may be the salt of the earth, to salt and season it, and make it savoury to God, and [that] you [yourselves may] all be seasoned with it. Then all your sacrifices will be a sweet savour to the Lord, and ye will be as the lilies and roses, and [the] garden of God, which gives a sweet smell unto him, whose garden is preserved by its power, the hedge, that hedges out all the unruly and unsavoury, and the destroyers and hurters of the vines. Here all are kept fresh and green, being watered every moment with the everlasting holy water of life, from the Lord, the fountain. My dear friends, my desire is, that the heavenly Seed, that bruises the head of the serpent, both within and without, may be your crown and life; and ye in him, one another's crown and joy, to the praise of the Lord God over all, blessed for evermore. This holy Seed will outlast and wear out all that which the evil seed, since the fall of man, hath brought forth and set up. As every one hath received Christ Jesus the Lord, so walk in him, in the humility which he teaches. Shun the occasions of strife, vain janglings, and disputings, with me of corrupt minds, who are destitute of the truth; for th truth is peaceable, and the Gospel is a peaceable habitatio in the power of God; his wisdom is peaceable and gentle and his kingdom stands in peace. Oh! his glory shines ove all his works! In Christ Jesus, ye will have peace, yea a peace that the world cannot take away; for the peac which ye have from him, was before the world was; and wil be when it is gone. This keeps all, in that which is weight and substantial over all chaff. Glory to the Lord God ove all, for ever and ever! Amen.

"And now, my dear friends, the Lord doth require mor of you than he doth of other people, because he hath com mitted more to you. He requires the fruits of his Spirit, o the light, of the Gospel, of the grace, and of the truth; fo herein is he glorified, as Christ said, in your bringing fortl much fruit; fruits of righteousness, holiness, godliness, virtue truth, and purity; so that ye may answer that which is o God in all people. Be valiant for his everlasting, gloriou Gospel, keeping in unity, and in the Holy Spirit, light, anc life, which is over death and darkness, and was before deatl and darkness were. In this spirit, we have the bond o peace, which cannot be broken except ye go·from the Spirit and then ye lose the unity and bond of peace, which ye have from the Prince of Peace.

"The world also expects more from Friends than from other people, because you profess more. Therefore you should be more just than others, in your words and dealings, and more righteous, holy, and pure in your lives and conversations, so that your lives and conversations may preach. For the world's tongues and mouths have preached long enough; but their lives and conversations have denied what their tongues have professed and declared.

"And, dear friends, strive to excel one another in virtue, that ye may grow in love, that excellent way which unites all to Christ and God. Stand up for God's glory, and mind that which concerns the Lord's honour, that in no wise his power may be abused, nor his name evil spoken of by any evil talkers or walkers; but that in all things God may be honoured, and ye may glorify him in your bodies, souls, and spirits, the little time ye have to live. My love to you all, in the holy Seed of life, that reigns over all, and is the First and Last, in whom ye all have life and salvation, and your election and peace with God, through Jesus Christ, who destroys him that hath been betwixt you and God; so that nothing may be betwixt you and the Lord, but Christ Jesus. Amen."

Returning to London in 1680, he spent most of the winter there, assisting Friends in their endeavours to induce the Parliament to grant some relief from the hardships and grievances they endured in various parts of the kingdom, and labouring in other ways for the promotion of the cause of righteousness in the earth.

Persecution still continuing, Friends were frequently shut out of their meeting-houses. On one occasion, when the doors were guarded by constables with their staves, and they refused him and others entrance, they assembled in the yard. A Friend commenced speaking, whom they ordered to be silent, and grew angry at his persisting. George Fox laid his hand on the constable, and desired him to let the Friend alone. "After he had done," says G. Fox, "I was moved to stand up and speak; and, in my declaration, I said they need not come against us with swords and staves, for we are a peaceable people, and had nothing in our hearts but good-will to the King and magistrates, and to all people upon the earth. We did not meet, under pretence of religion, to plot and contrive against the Government, or to raise insurrections, but to worship God in spirit and in truth. We had Christ to be our Bishop, Priest, and Shepherd, to feed us, and oversee us, and He ruled in our hearts, so we could all sit in silence, enjoying our Teacher." He was also moved to pray, when the people, constables, and soldiers put off their hats, and the power of the Lord was felt to be over the assembly. Such was the influence of the solemnity, that, on parting, one of the constables took off his hat, and desired the Lord to bless them. Thus the Holy Spirit, at times, raised a testimony in the hearts of their opponents that Friends were "true men," and sought the welfare of all.

In the spring of 1684 he again visited Holland, where he remained for several weeks. He attended the yearly meeting at Amsterdam, and Friends had a refreshing time together, in the love of God.

Although, after his return to England, he ceased from much travelling, and principally resided in or near London, yet his enlarged and active mind was diligently engaged in labours of Christian love, writing epistles to his brethren, attending to the sufferings of those who were under persecution, visiting the sick and afflicted, and ministering to their consolation, besides being frequently engaged in public testimony in religious meetings; thus imitating the example of his Divine Master, in going about and doing good to the bodies and souls of men. At a time when the nation was much agitated by political contests and popular disaffection George Fox was concerned on account of his brethren, les they should be drawn into the spirit of the contendin parties, contrary to the known testimony of the Society, an to the neglect of their religious duties. He therefore wrot an epistle, "to caution all to keep out of the spirit of th world, in which the trouble is, and to dwell in the peaceabl truth."

His health and strength at length declined so much, tha he was scarcely able to sit a meeting through; and when h did, he often had to retire to a chamber contiguous, as soon as it was over, in order to lie down. "Yet," he says, "my weakness did not take me off from the service of the Lord, but I continued to labour in and out of meetings, in the work of the Lord, as he gave me opportunity and ability."

On the eleventh of the 11th month, 1690, he went to White Hart Court meeting, in which he was engaged, in testimony and prayer, in a powerful and affecting manner. As soon as the meeting was over, he withdrew to the house of Henry Goldney, a Friend who lived near, and remarked, that he felt the cold strike to his heart as he came out of the meeting: yet added, "I am glad I was there—now I am clear—I am fully clear." He laid down to rest himself; but finding the sensation of cold continue, he soon after went bed, with symptoms of increasing weakness. His mind which, for a long course of years, had been engaged under the influence of the universal love of God, in endeavouring to promote the everlasting welfare of mankind, and to draw souls to Christ, rose superior to the infirmities and pains of the frail tenement it occupied, and still evinced a lively and unabated interest in the promotion of this glorious cause.

He sent for several of his particular friends, and, at this awful crisis, communicated to them his mind, respecting matters connected with the welfare of the church, and his desire for the spread of Friends' books; that those principles which he had so long personally advocated, might thereby be diffused in the earth.

The triumphant state of his mind, amid the decay of expiring nature, was manifest by his expressions to those who visited him: saying, "All is well—the Seed of God reigns over all, and over death itself. And, though I am weak in body, yet the power of God is over all, and the Seed reigns over all disorderly spirits."

In this heavenly and prepared frame, his spirit quitted its earthly tenement, on third-day, the 13th of the eleventh month, 1690, between the hours of nine and ten at night; he being then in the 67th year of his age. His funeral was attended by a very large concourse of Friends and others; and after a solemn meeting, the corpse was interred in Bunhill-fields burial-ground, where testimony was borne to the all-sufficiency of that Divine Power which had raised up, and qualified this extraordinary man, for the work of his day, and eminently enabled him to adorn the doctrine of God his Saviour.

Thus lived and thus died George Fox,—and "he being dead yet speaketh." In person he was tall, and rather corpulent, his countenance manly, intelligent, and graceful; and his manners, says William Penn, were "civil beyond all forms of breeding."

The same author remarks, "above all he excelled in prayer: the inwardness and weight of his spirit; the reverence and solemnity of his address and behaviour; the fewness and fullness of his words, have often struck even strangers with admiration, as they used to reach others with consolation. The most awful, living, reverent frame I ever felt or beheld, I must say, was his in prayer." Truly, it was a testimony that he knew, and lived near unto the Lord; for they that know him most will see most reason to approach him with reverence and fear.

"Though God had visibly clothed him with divine authority, yet he never abused it, but kept his place in the church of God, with great meekness, and a most engaging humility and moderation: for upon all occasions, like his blessed Master, he was a servant to all, holding and exercising his eldership in the Power which had gathered them, with reverence to the Head, and care over the body:—And I can say; having been his companion for months together, both by night and day, by sea and by land, that I never saw him out of his place, or not a match for every service and occasion."

His ministry was deep, searching, and powerful; and though not ornamented with the elegancies of literature, yet he possessed the tongue of the learned, in another and a higher sense, and could speak a word in season to the conditions and capacities of the people, having a discernment thereof given to him of God.

The following anecdote is related of him by an ancient woman Friend :—

"And now, Friends, I will tell you how I was first convinced. I was young at that time, and lived in Dorsetshire, when George Fox came to that country; and he having appointed a meeting, to which people generally flocked, I went among the rest; and in my going along the road, this query arose in my mind : 'What is that I feel, which condemneth me when I do evil, and justifieth me when I do well? What is it?' In this state I went to the meeting. It was a large gathering, and George Fox rose up with these words: 'Who art thou that queriest in thy mind, What is it which I feel which condemneth me when I do evil, and justifieth me when I do well? I will tell thee what it is. Lo! He that formeth the mountains and createth the wind, and declareth unto man what is his thought; that maketh the morning darkness, and treadeth upon the high places of the earth: the Lord, the God of Hosts is his name. It is He by his Spirit, that condemneth thee for evil, and justifieth thee when thou doest well. Keep under its dictates, and it will be thy preserver to the end.'" To this narration the Friend added, "It was the truth, the very truth, and I have never departed from it."

END.

London: Printed by E. Couchman & Co., 10, Throgmorton Street; for the TRACT ASSOCIATION of the SOCIETY OF FRIENDS. Sold at the DEPOSITORY, 12. Bishopsgate Street Without.—1863

PREPARATION FOR DEATH.

WHEN the close of life is brought into view by sickness or distress, we often hear people say, "I wish I was prepared to die." But too frequently this wish is expressed in a way which denotes little idea of what a right preparation for death is.

Great is the folly of those who live in sin, deluding themselves with the thought that they will turn about at last, and settle their account with God, and thus prepare for death. They lose the greatest measure of happiness which can possibly be enjoyed in this life, and put in imminent peril their prospect of happiness in the life to come.

In order to arrive at correct views respecting preparation for death, let us consider the condition of mind needful for the enjoyment of heaven. Let us remember, that God and Christ, and the holy angels, and the spirits of just men made perfect, constitute the company of heaven; and that our feelings and pleasures must be like theirs, if we would love this company and be happy amongst them. What then are the scriptural evidences of the existence of this love in our hearts? Our Saviour says, "He that hath my commandments, and keepeth them, he it is that loveth me;" and He promises this blessed return to such love; "He that loveth me shall be loved of my Father, and I will love him, and manifest myself to him." And again, "If a man love me he will keep my words; and my father will love him, and we will come unto him and make our abode with him." The apostle John also says, "By this we know that we love the children of God, when we love God and keep his commandments," and "If we say we have fellowship with God and walk in darkness, we lie and do not the truth; but if we walk in the light, as he is in the light, we have fellowship one with another; and the blood of Jesus Christ his Son cleanseth us from all sin."

No. 122.   [*Price* 1½*d. per dozen*].

Great indeed is the claim which God has upon our love. "As I live, saith the Lord God, I have no pleasure in the death of the wicked." Ezek. xxxiii. 11. The goodness, mercy, and long-suffering of God, are largely extended toward us, in order to draw forth our love unto Him. He sent His beloved Son into the world to bless and to save us; and Christ has assured us, that "God so loved the world, that he gave his only begotten Son, that whosoever believeth in him should not perish, but have everlasting life; for God sent not his Son into the world to condemn the world; but that the world through him might be saved. The apostle Paul also tells us, that "God commendeth his love toward us, in that while we were yet sinners Christ died for us."

If therefore we would be rightly prepared for death, we ought not to be content with that imperfect evidence of our love which is marked by cold, inconstant, unfaithful service. Let us remember the declaration of our Saviour, "Many that are first shall be last," and that it applies to those who have been awakened to some sense of the sinfulness of sin, and who, it may be, have tasted of the goodness and mercy of God, in the evidence being given them by His Spirit, that their sins were blotted out for Jesus' sake; but who from unwatchfulness have lost their first love, and who yet remain in a halting state, rather proving God's long-suffering toward them, than giving evidence of their love to Him, by keeping His commandments.

There are others, and among them some who have had few advantages, or who have only been awakened at a late hour, who gave evidence of the strength of their love to God, by forsaking their evil ways, and by keeping His commandments. These are they who by yielding their minds to the convictions of the Holy Spirit, have become deeply sensible of the sinfulness of sin, and of their own want of power to withstand temptation, or to work righteousness, in their own strength; and who are therefore instant in prayer to God for strength to walk acceptably before Him.

Such have faith in the power of God to enable them
to keep His commandments, and in his willingness to
help them for Jesus' sake, deeply sensible as they may
be of their own unworthiness. They rejoice in realizing the evidence of God's love to them in the communion they hold with Him, agreeably to the experience of the early Christians, as set forth by the apostle
John: " Hereby know we that we dwell in God and
he in us, because he hath given us of his Spirit."
May we not believe that among these, there are of
the last who shall be first in the kingdom of heaven?

Vain indeed are all notions of settling an account
with God, by formal acts of self-denial or of assumed
devotion, in the closing scenes of a life voluntarily
spent in the service of the devil through sin. Truly
enlightened Christians, in every stage of their progress, feel that they have nothing to offer of their own
to make reconciliation with God. If their sins be
forgiven, it must be of the free mercy of God offered
to mankind on repentance and faith in Jesus Christ,
and for the sake of that great sacrifice which He made
upon the cross, when he laid down His life an offering
for the sins of the whole world. The true evidence
that they accept this mercy is, that they strive, if life
be prolonged, to love God and to keep His commandments. The happiness resulting from being reconciled
to God through Jesus Christ, and of having His love
shed abroad in the heart by the Holy Ghost, which
He giveth to His reconciled children, must, like most
other things, be experienced to be fully understood.
It is nevertheless a reality of unspeakable value to
those who possess it, and better worth seeking after
than anything else that is to be had in this life.
Those who partake of its sweetness, are willing to
follow Christ, denying themselves of all that is contrary to the will of God; they have also the evidence
of their sins being forgiven them for Jesus' sake, and
a well grounded hope of acceptance with God through
Him, when time to them shall be no longer.

But if this blessed work of true preparation for
death be not really carried on, and we rest in the vain

notion of settling our account at last, and thus remain insensible of the love of God, it would have been better for us had we never been born. Having neglected the striving of the Holy Spirit, by which God has often reproved us for sin, our time will have been wasted over self-gratification and worldly objects, and heaven will be lost to us. We shall be found at last, not only without any preparation for death, but without any capacity for the enjoyment of heaven. Our condition will only fit us for the company of fallen spirits, or in other words, for the company of the devil and his angels, in the burning anguish consequent on having neglected the love of God, until the power of loving Him was lost, and of having set our love on those things which, perishing with time, cannot be enjoyed in eternity.

O, beware of slighting the love of God! Quench not the strivings of His Spirit. "There is forgiveness with him that he may be feared." "Let the wicked forsake his way, and the unrighteous man his thoughts; let him turn unto the Lord, and he will have mercy upon him, and to our God and he will abundantly pardon." O, cherish the love of Christ, who in the greatness of His love, and in compassion to our fallen condition, left the glories of heaven, took upon Him our nature, sympathised with our infirmities, and laid down His life a sacrifice for our sins; let us hold frequent communion of spirit with Him, and prove our love by keeping His commandments. Then, though feeling unworthy of the least of the mercies of God, yet accepting them as being freely given to us for Jesus' sake, we shall be prepared to live to His glory in this world, His peace will keep our hearts and minds amidst the trials of time, and at the end of our days, we shall be found prepared to die, and to inherit everlasting happiness in the kingdom of heaven.

END.

London: Printed by E. Couchman & Co. 10, Throgmorton Street; for the TRACT ASSOCIATION of the SOCIETY OF FRIENDS. Sold at the Depository, 12, Bishopsgate Street Without.—1865.

SKETCH OF THE RISE

OF THE

SOCIETY OF FRIENDS:

THEIR

DOCTRINES AND CHARACTER.

LONDON:

·Printed for the TRACT ASSOCIATION of the SOCIETY of FRIENDS.

Sold at the DEPOSITORY, 12, Bishopsgate Street, Without.

1862.

No. 123.   [*Price 4d. per dozen.*]

THE religious Society of Friends dates its rise from about the year 1647. This was, in England, a period in which many of the props, on which men had long been accustomed to lean, both in civil and religious matters, were shaken or removed. The fears, troubles, and heart-stirring thoughts connected with the domestic commotions which then prevailed in the nation, led many into a deep search as to the grounds of their opinions, and the real stability of their religious hopes; but the movements of this period must be traced to a much earlier date. To go to their source, we must at least go back to the days of the enlightened Wickliffe and the persecuted Lollards; but this would lead us beyond our present space.

The English Reformers who fled into Switzerland, during the persecution in the reign of Queen Mary, and who returned from their exile on the accession of Elizabeth to the throne, were far from being content with the point to which the Queen allowed the Reformation to be carried. Many of them, however, appeared to satisfy their consciences with the hope, that they were doing more good by taking offices under her auspices, than by leaving them to be filled by those who were less attached than themselves to the Protestant cause; but others could not be persuaded thus to compromise their religious judgment, and chose rather to remain without office and profit than to conform to all the rites and ceremonies which the Queen had chosen to impose upon the nation. Uniformity in matters of religion was at this time the favorite doctrine of all parties, and was hardly less espoused by Elizabeth than it had been by her sister Mary; for very severe laws were made in the reign of Elizabeth, under which both Papists and Protestant Dissenters were cruelly persecuted, and some of them even put to death. A religious movement, deep and inward, though not very active, was going on during the subsequent reign of James the First; and it may fairly be said, that the continued denial to the people of the right of private judgment in religious matters, and the unchristian efforts which were made by his successor, Charles the First, to force conscience, contributed not a little to that convulsion of the State, in which the monarchy was for a time overthrown.

The proceedings of Archbishop Laud and his party, during the reign of this monarch, in endeavouring to assimilate the Episcopal Church of England more closely to the Church of Rome, excited a strong feeling of revulsion in the minds of many Episcopalians, and led the way for that extraordinary ascendancy which the Scotch Presbyterians suddenly obtained in England in those days. There was among this people, at that time, much high religious profession, united with the bitterest intolerance towards all who could not accept their Directory on matters of worship and other outward services. There was, however, also to be seen much deep and practical religious conviction, and in not a very few an earnest search after truth. The strictness of their lives, and the earnestness of their preaching, doubtless recommended them to the more serious part of the nation, of various classes; but, in connection with the power which they obtained, it is evident that they sought primarily the absolute ascendency of their own church polity and doctrine. Though they had strongly denounced, in their own case, popish and prelatical impositions upon conscience, yet they did not scruple, in the case of others, to attempt to rule in that seat of God; and they were no less ready than their predecessors to punish those who could not bow down to their authority. Thus it was evident that presbyter and prelate alike sought to be lords over God's heritage, and that amidst the earnest discussions respecting Church government and the forms of religious worship, the essential, experimental work of the Holy Spirit on the heart, and the true liberty of the Gospel, were in great measure overlooked. All the chief religious parties of the day so mistook the nature of Christianity, as to endeavour to obtain their objects by the power of the sword; and many of the individuals who were extensively engaged in the enterprise of reformation, if sincere in the outset, became corrupted by success, and sought selfish ends under the guise of patriotism and religion.

There was, however, a large number who were constant and earnest in their desire for the establishment of truth and righteousness: and these, grieved with the versatility and hypocrisy which prevailed, were led into a deeper search into things within them and around them. Many prayers ascended to heaven from individuals and from little communities, scattered about in various places, that they might see more clearly the path in which they ought to walk, and be strengthened to follow Christ wherever be should lead them. The deep cries of these, made in living faith, were not in vain: they came to see that they had been too much engaged in discussions about outward forms, and had too much depended upon man in the great work of religion, and for its establishment in the earth. They continued steadfast in the great doctrine, that the door of God's mercy was freely opened to sinful man, through the propitiatory sacrifice of Christ alone; but their minds were awakened to see themselves and the condition of things around them in a new light. The requirements of a disciple; the denial of self; the trans- forming power of the Spirit; the restoration into the Divine presence, that they might really become sons of God and brethren of Christ; were things which, though they had heard them discoursed about, now took posses- sion of their minds with the force and energy of new truths; and as they dwelt upon them, they were led to believe that there was to be known a fuller deliverance from sin, and a closer union with Christ, than they had hitherto found. They were told, indeed, that a state was not to be attained here, in which man walks before the Lord in entire allegiance to his will, and therefore with- out disobeying him; but they believed that, though man's knowledge is imperfect, and though from weakness he may slip or fall, yet his heart may nevertheless be so renewed by grace, as that his love shall be pure and simple, and his eye being single to the Lord, his whole mind may be enlightened to see truly and to pursue steadily the things which belong unto his peace. They felt and deeply lamented how short they were of this experience, which they believed to be the privilege of the Christian, and they sought help from many quarters; for nothing less than this experience could satisfy their inward cravings, or their thirst after the knowledge of the very truth as it is in Jesus. These seeking people found, however, but little help from those who were esteemed the most eminent religious teachers and they came to place less and less dependance upon man, and to look to the Lord only for light and strength.

Such appears to have been, with different degrees of clearness, the state of many minds in various parts of England, when George Fox, who had himself been similarly led and deeply instructed in the school of Christ went forth preaching the truth, as he had found it to his own peace. Many received his message as the expression of their deepest thoughts, and as an answer to their fervent prayers. He preached Christ crucified for the sins of all men; opening the way of reconciliation to all who believe in him, and receive him into their hearts as their rightful lord;—Christ come in the flesh, and Christ according to his promise, come in the Spirit, to be with his disciples in their individual and collective capacity to the end of the world.

These were the fundamental doctrines which George Fox preached; and it was no way in disparagement of the doctrine of Christ having come in the flesh, that he dwelt more conspicuously upon that of Christ being come in the Spirit; seeing the latter was that which, in the professing church, Satan had been most busy in restricting and perverting, "I was glad," says George Fox, "when the Lord God, and his Son Jesus Christ, sent me forth into the world, to preach his everlasting gospel and kingdom, that I was commanded to turn people to that inward light, spirit, and grace, by which all might know their salvation and their way to God, even that Divine Spirit which would lead them into all truth." Christ dwelling in the heart by faith, ruling there, and subjecting everything to himself by the power of his Spirit, was the experimental knowledge to which George Fox called men. This he declared, was the state of liberty which Christ had promised to give to his followers, and which they only know who believe in and accept that "light, spirit, and grace," which convicts of sin, and leads, through deep repentance and living faith, into righteousness. The Lord Jesus promised to be "with his disciples alway, even unto the end of the world." And these words, in George Fox's view, referred to his spiritual presence in the soul, as the teacher, bishop, and prophet of his people; superseding all the Jewish priesthood, and excluding all those corrupt imitations of it, by which man, in various ages, had sought to exalt himself, and to evade that spiritual rule of Christ, to which the flesh and the devil ever were, and still are, so strongly opposed.

He travelled unweariedly throughout England, from place to place, calling men to repentance, and to come to God through Christ their Saviour, who had died for them and who, by his Spirit within them, was enlightening, convicting, and seeking to convert them. There were many who heard this call with gladness of heart, and who came to sit under Christ's teaching, and to learn in all humility in his school. These, when deserted by kindred and friends, and persecuted on every hand, yet not forsaken by their gracious Lord, felt that it was "enough for the disciple to be as his Master." And indeed their sufferings were grievous and long. For when the Presbyterians had been superseded by those who had complained so heavily of church tyranny, and who had spoken so well of liberty of conscience, and of the evils of state impositions in religious matters, these were not proof against the temptation of power: it was soon apparent that they also, but too generally, "loved the uppermost seats in the synagogues, and to be called of men, 'Rabbi.'" They were ready not only to take the pulpits of the ejected ministers, but also to extort from others, who conscientiously differed from them, that forced maintenance for preaching which had been galling to many of themselves, when it was imposed by prelatical or presbyterian authority. It is due to the cause of truth as maintained by the early Friends, to remark that they upheld liberty of conscience, not only when suffering under persecution, but also when they were raised to power in the province of Pennsylvania.

Those who united with George Fox in his views of the presence of Christ in the Church, and in its individual members, and who believed in his spiritual guidance and teaching, could not conform to the customary modes of worship. They met together to worship God, who is a spirit, in spirit and in truth. They could not offer to Him words which did not truly express their feelings. They believed that, in true worship, all acts must be performed in the abasement of self, and under the influence of the Holy Spirit. When assembled, they were often strengthened and comforted together in silent waiting before the Lord; whilst, individually, they breathed their secret aspirations unto God, and realized that Christ was amongst them by his Spirit, uniting their hearts together in mutual love to Him and his great cause. And when any amongst them, under this deep feeling of true worship, were constrained in spirit to speak the word of exhortation, prayer, or praise, they gratefully accepted it, as from the Lord, and as drawing to him. But preconcerted human arrangements for preaching or prayer; the setting up of one man as the sole teacher in the congregation; the establishment of a body of such ministers by the State; the imposition of their maintenance upon those who differed from them; all these were, in their view, violations of great Christian principles, interfering with Christ's authority and government in his Church, and excluding the free exercise of the various gifts bestowed by him for its edification. They admitted freely the preaching of women, as well as that of men, according to the practice of the apostolic age, when sons and daughters prophesied, and the Spirit of the Lord was poured out upon "servants and handmaidens," not limiting the number in any church.

But though the early Friends maintained the right and duty of the members of a Christian Church to exercise the spiritual gifts with which they were severally endued, they held that the authority to judge of the offered services of the members rested with the assembled body of the Church, under the direction of its spiritual Head. Entire individual independence in society is a contradiction in terms. In the primitive church, though there was the utmost liberty of prophesying, it is declared that " the spirits of the prophets are subject to the prophets, for God is not the author of confusion, but of peace, as in all the churches of the saints." The members were " subject one to another in the fear of God," and this subjection, as well as the duty of caring for and watching over one another for good, were clearly recognized by the early Friends, and formed the basis of that system of discipline which was established among them, and under which, as members of the body, they enjoyed so large a measure of liberty in connection with true order. Under this discipline the poor were cared for, the education of the youth was promoted, religious efforts were used to reclaim the wandering and delinquent members, and when Christian labour had failed, the ultimate proceeding was the declaration of the Society's disunity with the offender as one of its members. This proceeding carried with it no proscription from its religious worship or the ordinary intercourses of human kindness, and the Society was open at all times to receive the disowned person again into fellowship, on the evidence being afforded of a changed mind. As the Society declined conscientiously the usual rites in connection with marriages, births, and deaths, the registration of these events was under the special care of the meetings for discipline. After nearly two hundred years from its establishment, the original systen of discipline is with much benefit steadily acted upon, and those principles which, at its rise, united the members of the Society in Christian fellowship, continue to be upheld by, and to distinguish, their successors in religious profession.

Although the early Friends maintained that immediate spiritual guidance was still granted to the children of God, they fully recognized the divine authority of the Holy Scriptures, and were ever ready to have their doctrines and practices tried by them: they accepted them indeed unequivocally, as given by inspiration of God, and loved and valued them as the genuine records of his dealings with his creature man, and as communicating to him the knowledge of that Gospel covenant by which life and immortality are brought to light; they read and quoted them freely, referred to them for the proof of the soundness of their own faith and doctrine, and recommended them strongly to the perusal of others; but they warned men against fancying themselves in a state of salvation, because of possessing a knowledge of the Scriptures, whilst remaining strangers to that true faith in Christ, through which alone they make wise unto salvation.

Believing that no typical or ceremonial rites were appointed by Christ or his Apostles for the continual or universal observance of the church, and in connection with the views which these Christian people entertained of the spirituality of the Gospel dispensation, they abstained from the use of Water Baptism, and from what is called the Sacrament of the Lord's Supper. In the declaration of Christ, that the time was at hand when "they that worship the Father must worship Him in spirit and in truth," they saw the essential abolition of all ritual religious services, and the opening of that real spiritual relation and intercourse between man and his Creator, which is the glory of the Gospel of Christ. Under the Christian dispensation there is one, and but one, baptism. "I, indeed," said the forerunner of Christ, "baptize you with water unto repentance; but he that cometh after me is mightier than I, whose shoes I am not worthy to bear, he shall baptize you with the Holy Ghost and with fire." Matt. iii. 11. This baptism of the Spirit, by which conversion of heart is known, and the repentant sinner is brought, through living faith in Christ, into his adopted family, was fully asserted by the early Quakers; as was also that spiritual communion with Christ, whether alone or in fellowship with the brethren, in which the benefits of his death, resurrection, and ascension are appreciated and appropriated, by the power of the Holy Spirit. This they believed to be the true Supper of the Lord,—the spiritual eating of his flesh and drinking of his blood.

The imposition of tithes on the people they esteemed to be a virtual recognition of the continued authority of Judaism, and a practical denial that Christ had come, had superseded the whole Judaical economy, and had placed upon the site of its departed glories the spiritual temple in which he was the great High Priest. He said to his disciples, "Freely ye have received, freely give." Those whom he sent to minister to his flock in spiritual things, were entitled to partake of the carnal things of those who received their message; but this natural claim gave no authority, they asserted, to the imposition of payment. Such an imposition, in the view of the early Friends, was utterly opposed to the liberty and nobility of the Christian system, and was an evidence of corruption in the church which practised it, whatever name that church might bear. They called men, therefore, to come out of it; to leave hireling priests and mere lip services; and to come to Christ alone for the supply of their spiritual necessities. They believed it would be, on their part, a virtual recognition of an unchristian system, if they were to pay the ecclesiastical demands imposed upon them, esteeming it a case in which they must act upon the apostolic rule, "to obey God rather than men."

In obedience also to Christ's commands "Swear not at all," they refused all judicial as well as other oaths; and in like accordance with Christ's commands of love to enemies, and of not returning evil for evil, they believed that all war was unlawful to the Christian. They did not seek to be singular; but in the maintenance of strict truth, and the avoidance of pride and flattery, they were led into great simplicity in their dress, manners, and language.

These various testimonies brought much contumely, from the high professors as well as from the profane, upon the early Friends. They were said to be "against ministry, magistracy, and ordinances;" but being brought into an entire submission to whatever, in their enlightened consciences, they believed to be the will of their Lord, they acted simply and decidedly upon their convictions of duty, and gave up all that they counted dear, in faithful allegiance to him; and many of them went forth, as into the highways and hedges, to proclaim the truth, believing themselves called to invite others to come and enjoy the Gospel liberty which they had found. Great were their sufferings when the high professors of Oliver Cromwell's days had the rule in England; and still greater were they under the government of the second Charles, when the old episcopalian was again instated in power, and when the prominent members of "Church and State" seemed to vie with each other, both in licentious indulgence and in cruelty. A systematic, legalized effort appears, at this period, to have been made to exterminate the Quakers! Cruel laws of Henry the Eighth and Queen Elizabeth, made originally against the Papists, were revived, especially those for the regular attendance at "church," and the taking of the oath of allegiance, and were executed with severity upon the Quakers.

The Conventicle Act, passed in the year 1664, prohibited the meeting together of five or more persons for the exercise of religion, in other manner than is allowed by the liturgy or practice of the Church of England, under pain of being committed to prison for the first offence, and transported beyond the seas for the second! An act had previously been passed against those who, "on the ground that it was contrary to the Word of God," refused to take an oath before a lawful magistrate; or who should "by printing, writing, or otherwise, go about to maintain and defend, that the taking of an oath is, in any case whatsoever, altogether unlawful;" and this offence was in the Conventicle Act also made punishable by transportation!

With these and similar legal engines, bishops, clergy, judges, and magistrates, with the aid of a host of wicked informers, betook themselves to the work of hunting down these Christian people. At one period more than 4,200 of them were shut up in close and noisome prisons, chiefly for meeting together to worship God in such manner as they believed he required of them, and for refusing to swear, in accordance with the positive command of their Lord and Saviour, "Swear not at all." When the plague was raging in London, in 1665, the persecutors were busily engaged in committing the Quakers to infected prisons, and putting them on board vessels for transportation. Many died in prison, and out of fifty-five put on board one vessel, which was designed to transport them to the colonies, twenty-seven died of the plague, rescued from the hands of cruel men, and, as we reverently believe, taken to be with their Lord.

All the trials, however, which were permitted to attend them, did not shake their faith and constancy. Though the world hated them, they were heartily united in love to God and one to another. At the hazard of their own liberty, those who were at large visited their brethren who were in prison, and ministered to them. And at a time when many of them were sick and dying from their confinement in filthy holes and dungeons, a large number of their friends entreated, that if their afflicted brethren could not otherwise be relieved, they themselves might be allowed to take, body for body, the places of the most suffering prisoners. The government, unmoved, rejected the offer, but the love which directed it was not without its influence on the minds of the people, who could not avoid observing how largely the despised Quakers evinced the charity, as well as the zeal and constancy, of the primitive Christians.

Many persons were led by the treatment and by the conduct of the early Friends to look more inquisitively into their doctrines and manners: they remembered, that heretofore, the way of truth had been everywhere spoken against; and when they found that these objects of general reproach were industrious in their callings and exemplary in all the duties of social life, and that they were also ready to forsake houses and lands, parents and children, rather than disobey what they believed to be the law of Christ, the inquirers were often led to conclude, that these much despised people were indeed true followers of Him who, with his disciples, was not of this world, and therefore the world hated them.

It is worthy of remark, how much this kind of conviction, not founded on minute reasoning, but resting chiefly on the practical and internal evidence for the truth, whether furnished by the lives of its converts, or by the convictions of the Spirit in the hearts of those to whom it is preached, has marked the course through which Christ, the great Head of his own Church, has, in all ages, thought fit to gather his people out of the world. In the opening of the Gospel day, though then accompanied by extraordinary miracles, there was much of this process to be observed; and in the subsequent revivals of Divine truth, whether in Germany, Switzerland, or

England, a large majority of the converts were drawn by a sense of Truth,—by finding a conformity of the doctrine preached, both with Scripture and with the testimony of the Holy Spirit, the witness for God in their own hearts.

Many among the early converts to the Truth, who had been wise and great in this world, were made willing to become fools in the sight of men. In deep humility they sat at the foot of the cross, seeking to learn of that promised Comforter, who, the Saviour declared, should "teach" his disciples "all things," and bring to their "remembrance whatsoever he had said unto them." Their delight was in the Law of the Lord, and they gloried in nothing save in the cross of Christ, by whom the world was crucified unto them, and they unto the world.

They found, as one of them has said, that it was the nature of true faith to produce a holy fear of offending God, a deep reverence for his precepts, and a most tender regard to the inward testimony of his Spirit. They proved that those who truly believe, receive Christ in all his offers to the soul; and that to those who thus receive him, is given power to become the sons of God,—ability to do whatsoever he requires; strength to mortify their lusts, control their affections, deny themselves, and overcome the world in its most enticing appearances. This is the true bearing of that blessed cross of Christ, which, according to his own words, is the great and essential characteristic of his disciples. That the early Friends were among these true cross-bearing disciples, was abundantly evidenced before the world in their life and conversation; and by these, as well as by their preaching, they held out to mankind the apostolic invitation,—"Come and have fellowship with us; for truly our fellowship is with the Father, and with his Son Jesus Christ."

END.

Printed by E. Couchman & Co., 10, Throgmorton Street, London.

HISTORICAL SKETCH

OF THE

ORIGIN OF THE

CHRISTIAN DISCIPLINE,

OR

CHURCH GOVERNMENT,

OF THE

SOCIETY OF FRIENDS.

LONDON:

Printed for the TRACT ASSOCIATION of the SOCIETY of FRIENDS,

Sold at the DEPOSITORY, 12, Bishopsgate Street Without.

—

1865.

No. 124.   [*Price 8d. per dozen.*]

CHRISTIAN DISCIPLINE.

THE discipline of a Christian church, taken in its widest sense, includes all the arrangements and regulations instituted for its maintenance, and for the religious and civil welfare of its members. The term is not unfrequently used more with reference to the proceedings of the church towards offending members, than to those more congenial parts in the office of discipline, which refer to the prevention of offences by judicious care and oversight, by the strengthening of the weak, the instruction of the ignorant, the preservation of right order in the affairs of the church, and the exercise of Christian sympathy in the relief of the necessities of poor or suffering brethren. It is in the comprehensive sense of the term discipline, that we shall consider it in the following pages.

It cannot be said that any *system* of discipline formed a part of the original compact of the Society of Friends. There was not indeed, to human appearance, anything systematic in its formation. It was an association of persons who were earnestly seeking after the saving knowledge of divine truth. Many of them could have said with the Psalmist, "As the hart panteth after the waterbrooks, so panteth my soul after thee, O God." They were men of prayer, and diligent searchers of the Holy Scriptures: and not a few of them had been highly esteemed for religious experience in the several societies with which they had been connected. Their trust, however, in outward rites and ceremonies, and human systems, was utterly broken up, and they longed to know more than they had hitherto experienced of that inward power and grace, conforming the heart to the Lord Jesus, which they believed was the privilege of the Gospel. Thus seeking rest, they believed they found it in a more full and experimental reception of Christ in all His gracious offices, not only as their one Mediator and Intercessor, but also as the living and ever-present Head of the church, and as the light and life, the spiritual ruler, teacher, and friend of every individual member.

They always asserted, that those views which distinguished them from other Christian professors, did not lead them to any disparagement of those great doctrines which they had heretofore held, and which have always been maintained by the Society of Friends, respecting the manhood of Christ, His eternal existence, and His propitiatory sacrifice, as the means of our reconciliation with the Father. But their views of His priestly office in the church, and of His gracious condescension in teaching His people himself, did lead them to a less dependance upon man, and to much inward retirement and waiting upon God, that they might know His will, and become "quick of understanding in the fear of the Lord." Yet were they very frequent in their meetings together for mutual edification and instruction, for the purpose of united worship in spirit and in truth, and for the exercise of their several gifts, as ability might be afforded by Him who has promised to be with the two or three disciples who are gathered together in His name.

From these meetings, in which the love of God was often largely shed abroad in the hearts of those who attended them, even when held in silence, most of those ministers went forth, who, in the earliest periods of the Society, proclaimed to others the truth as they had found it, and called them from dependance on man to that individual knowledge of Christ and of His teachings, which the Holy Scriptures so clearly and abundantly declare to be the privilege of the Gospel times. As these views struck at the very root of that great corruption in the Christian church, by which one man's performances on behalf of others had been made essential to public worship, and on which hung all the load of ecclesiastical domination and the trade in holy things; so it necessarily separated those who had, as they believed, found the liberty of the Gospel, from those who still adhered, either with conscientous regard, or from a mere ignorant and selfish attachment to that system which was upheld by the existing churches of the land.

RISE OF THE DISCIPLINE.

Being thus separated from others, and many being every day added to the church, there arose of course peculiar duties of the associated persons towards each other. Christianity has ever been a powerful, active, and beneficent principle. Those who truly receive it, no more "live unto themselves," and this feature and fruit of genuine Christianity was strikingly exhibited in the conduct of the early Friends. No sooner were a few persons connected together in the new bond of religious fellowship, than they were engaged to admonish, encourage, and, in spiritual as well as temporal matters, to watch over and-help one another in *love*.

The members who lived near to each other, and who met together for religious worship, immediately formed, from the very law of their union, a Christian family or little church. Each member was at liberty to exercise the gift bestowed upon him, in that beautiful harmony and subjection which belongs to the several parts of a living body, from the analogy of which the apostle Paul draws so striking a description of the true church; "Ye are the body of Christ and members in particular." Thus George Fox, writing to his friends in the year 1652, exhorts them :—"Be faithful to God, and mind that which is committed to you, as faithful servants labouring. in love; some thrashing, some ploughing, and some to keep the sheep; he that can receive this, let him, and all watch over one another in the spirit of God."*

Not only were there in very early times those individual spontaneous exercises of Christian love on the part of the members one toward another, which flowed naturally from their religious feeling and brotherhood, but in several of those parts where large convincements had taken place, there are stated to have been meetings held "concerning the poor, and to see that all walked according to the Truth."†

George Fox mentions in his Journal that some meetings for discipline were established in the North so early as 1653, and the memoirs of other worthies afford us instructive examples of the spirit and manner in which the discipline was exercised in very early times. We

---

* Collection of Epistles of George Fox, p. 15, fol. edit., 1698.
† Letters of Early Friends, p. 311.

shall select one of these examples. Stephen Crisp, in his Memoirs,* speaking of his own state soon after his convincement, which was in 1655, and within a few years of the establishment of a meeting at Colchester, the place of his residence, thus expresses himself:—"The more I came to feel and perceive the love of God and His goodness to me, the more was I humbled and bowed down in my mind to serve Him, and to serve the least of His people among whom I walked; and as the word of wisdom began to spring in me, and the knowledge of God grew, so I became a counsellor of those that were tempted in like manner as I had been; yet was kept so low, that I waited to receive counsel daily from God, and from those that were over me in the Lord, and were in Christ before me, against whom I never rebelled nor was stubborn; but the more I was kept in subjection myself, the more I was enabled to help the weak and feeble ones. And as the Church of God, in those days, increased, my care daily increased, and the weight of things relating both to the outward and inward condition of poor Friends came upon me; and being called of God and His people to take the care of the poor, and to relieve their necessities as I did see occasion, I did it faithfully for divers years, with diligence and much tenderness, exhorting and reproving any that were slothful, and encouraging them that were diligent, putting a difference according to the wisdom given me of God, and still minding my own state and condition, and seeking the honour that cometh from God only."

OF THE EARLIEST MEETINGS FOR DISCIPLINE.

But though each little community had thus the care of its own affairs, that love which bound its members together, and led them to watch over one another for good, also united them to all who were like-minded, wherever scattered. Some communities might be weak, others strong. Under their bitter sufferings, they might well seek the support which there is in the union and counsel of faithful brethren. And so we find that within a few years of the rise of the Society, many general meetings were held for the care and service of the body.

* Memoirs of Stephen Crisp, p. 51, 12mo. edit., 1824.

These were of two classes, viz., first, district meetings, and secondly, those which embraced the affairs of the whole community. How these meetings were constituted it is not easy to determine with precision. It is certain, however, that the "labourers in the Gospel," by whose instrumentality the church had been gathered, took the most prominent part in the proceedings, as it was natural for them to do at that period.

The first general meeting of which we are aware that any records are extant, was held at Balby, near Doncaster, in Yorkshire, in the year 1656, and from this meeting a number of directions and advices were issued, addressed "To the Brethren in the North." This document refers to most of the points which now form the chief subjects of our discipline. It contains instructions as to the Gospel order of proceeding with delinquents, offers advice to husbands and wives, parents and children, masters and servants, as to the discharge of their relative duties, and urges the duty of strict justice in trade, and a cheerful and faithful performance of civil offices in the commonwealth. This meeting was most probably a district one. George Fox mentions attending a general meeting in Bedfordshire, in 1658, which lasted three days; at which, he says, "there were Friends present from most parts of the nation, and many thousands of persons were at it." He also mentions attending a meeting at Skipton, in 1660, "for the affairs of the church, both in this nation and beyond the seas:" and he says, that he had recommended the establishment of this meeting several years before, when he was in the North, "for many Friends suffered in divers parts of the nation; their goods were taken from them contrary to law, and they understood not how to help themselves, or where to seek redress. This meeting," he adds, "had stood several years, and divers justices and captains had come to break it up; but when they understood the business Friends met about, and saw Friends' books, and accounts of collections for the use of the poor; how we took care one county to help another, and to help our Friends beyond sea, and to provide for our poor, so that none should be chargeable to their parishes; the justices and officers confessed we did their work, and would pass away peaceably and lovingly." A document has been preserved, issued by this meeting, addressed to friends and brethren, recommending a collection to be raised for the service of truth abroad.

Next to general meetings we must notice the establishment of quarterly meetings, which were constituted of Friends deputed by the several meetings within a county. These meetings, in several of the counties at least, had existed prior to the general establishment of district monthly meetings, and they appear to have had much the same office in the body as the monthly meetings now have amongst us. George Fox, in an epistle of an early date, writes thus respecting them :—" In all the meetings of the county, two or three may be appointed from them to go to the quarterly meetings, to give notice if there be any that walk not in the truth, or have been convinced and gone from the truth, and so have dishonoured God; and likewise to see if any that profess the truth follow pleasures, drunkenness, gaming, or are not faithful in their callings and dealings, nor honest; but run into debt and so bring a scandal upon the truth. Friends may give notice to the quarterly meeting (if there be any such), and some may be ordered to go and exhort them, and bring in their answers to the next quarterly meeting; and to admonish all them that be careless and slothful, to diligence in the truth and service for God, and to bring forth heavenly fruits to God, and that they may mind the good works of God, and do them in believing on his Son, and showing it forth in their conversation, and to deny the devil and his bad works, and not to do them; and to seek them that be driven away from the truth into the devil's wilderness by his dark power. Seek them again by the truth, and by the truth and power of God bring them to God again."*

CHRISTIAN CHARACTER OF THE SOCIETY'S DISCIPLINE.

Thus, then, we believe it may be safely asserted, that there never was a period in the Society when those who agreed in religious principles were wholly independent of each other, or in which that order and subjection which constitute *discipline* did not exist: but, as the number of members increased, those mutual helps and guards which had been in a considerable degree spontaneously afforded, were found to require some more regular arrangement for the preservation of order in the church.

* Collection of Epistles, p. 276, fol. edit., 1698.

The history of these proceedings affords no small evidence, that the spirit of a sound mind influenced the body in these early times ; contending, as its members did, for so large a measure of individual spiritual liberty, and placing the authority of man, in religious matters, in a position so subordinate to that of the one Great Head of the church, they nevertheless recognized the necessity of order and government in it, of arrangements, and of human instrumentality, under the direction of the Spirit of Christ. They disapproved alike of " persecution and libertinism ; that is, a coercive power to whip people into the temple ; that such as will not conform, though against faith and conscience, shall be punished in their persons and estates ; or leaving all loose and at large as to practice, unaccountable to all but God and the magistrate."*

The idea of a church in the minds of the early Friends appears to have been precisely in accordance with that presented to us in the New Testament. It was a family of which Christ was the ever-living Head, embracing members in various conditions, and endued with various gifts to be employed for the benefit of the whole. There are the young and ignorant to be cared for and instructed, the disorderly to be restrained, admonished, or corrected, the wants of each to be supplied, in that spirit of sympathy which is so strongly represented in the words of the Apostle, " If one member suffer all the members suffer with it."

"There are," says Robert Barclay, "fathers and children, instructors and instructed, elders and young men, yea, and babes—there are, that cannot cease, but must exhort, instruct, reprove, condemn, judge, or else for what end gave Christ the gifts mentioned."† Ephesians, iv. 11, 12 ? No one was to usurp authority over God's heritage, but having gifts differing according to the grace that was given, each member was to attend to his own calling and appointment in the family of Christ. There was room for all, liberty for all, to exercise the gifts bestowed upon them, and as each member was engaged to wait upon the Head, and seek alone to be guided by that wisdom which

---

* William Penn's Preface to George Fox's Journal ; p. 33, 8vo. edit. p. xxviii. See also Barclay's Anarchy of the Ranters, p. 11, edit., 1733.

† The Anarchy of the Ranters, p. 9, edit., 1733.

is from above, he would know his own place and sphere in the family, and whether more or less conspicuous, would be an important part of the body, ministering in his appointed place to the health and strength of the whole.

These views imply a belief in the spiritual presence and guidance of Christ in His church, a doctrine which is at the root of the Christian Discipline of the Society of Friends. Wherever this fundamental doctrine of Christ's immediate government is not, to a considerable extent, practically maintained, the liberty of all, and the subjection of all, are conditions incompatible with each other.

Christian men met together in the fear of God to promote the good of His people, having their own minds subjected to the government of Christ, and above all things desiring to glorify Him, are met together "in His name." He is "in the midst of them," and presides over them; no one sets up to be the chief, but each recognizes the gift of his brother, and exercises a full spiritual liberty in the use of his own. Wherever this liberty is withheld from the true members of the church, either in their smaller or larger assemblies, not only the form, but the very spirit of the primitive church, and of Christianity itself, are so far abandoned and violated. Wherever the exercise of spiritual gifts is restricted by mere human appointment, there man assumes lordship over God's heritage, and Christ's headship in the church is essentially denied. It was against this practical denial that the very mission of George Fox and his associates was directed. "Christ head over all things to His church," was the great fundamental truth which they were engaged to proclaim, and it was beautifully illustrated in their system of discipline. "It is needful," said they, "that we call to mind how long, and in what manner, the world has been distracted and divided about those things which the apostles practised, and what sad calamity (besides the loss and departure from the truth) has come upon many nations, about forms and ways of discipline and government of the church (so called),—some saying the apostles made bishops, and gave them power, and they ordained elders; others saying nay, it was by the laying on of the hands of the presbytery; and others pleading that it was the election and choice of the churches. And how have men gathered themselves into forms and sects, according to their divers persuasions; and how are others setting up committees to approve and send forth preachers, and given them maintenance, seeing into the errors of the former: but all being ignorant of the life or of the true power. And thus have men usurped, one over another, and intruded into the things they understood not; and by human policy and invention, set up a carnal, worldly religion and worship, which has for many hundred years overspread the whole face of the earth." *

OBJECTS OF THE DISCIPLINE.

1. It appears, by the account of the meeting at Skipton, to have been with our Society as it has been with the primitive church, that the care and provision for its poor members was amongst the earliest occasions of disciplinary arrangements. The occasion for this provision was much increased by the cruel persecutions and robberies to which, on their first rise, the Friends were almost everywhere exposed. It was no rare occurrence, at that period, for the father of a family to be thrown into a dungeon, and for the house to be spoiled of the very children's beds, and of all their provisions. Nor was it uncommon to seek their entire proscription and ruin, by refusing to deal with them. Well may we say, with reverent thankfulness, in reference to those times, "If it had not been the Lord who was on our side, when men rose up against us, then they had swallowed us up quick when their wrath was kindled against us." In the provision made for the care of the poor, we must include also the supply of the necessities of the Gospel labourers, who, with the concurrence of their friends, travelled abroad for the spread and advancement of the truth.

The members of the persecuted Society were far from opulent; but they proved themselves rich in charity as well as in faith and hope: and the illustration of these virtues, by the sacrifices which they made for the relief of their more afflicted associates, and their unbroken constancy in the sufferings which they endured for the

* From an Epistle prepared at a district meeting, held at Durham, in 1659; read and approved at the general meeting, held at Skipton, in the week following that at Durham.—*Letters of Early Friends,* p. 288.

testimony of a good conscience, were doubtless amongst the practical arguments which *at length*_extorted the commendation even of their enemies.

2. A second and perhaps contemporaneous object of the meetings for the discipline of the Society, was the obtaining of redress for those illegally prosecuted or imprisoned, as also appears from the extract relative to the meeting at Skipton. Though so patient in suffering, they deemed it their duty to apprize magistrates, judges, and the Government, of illegal proceedings, and to use every legal and Christian effort to obtain redress. Several Friends in London devoted a large portion of time to this object, and regular statements of the most flagrant cases were sent to them, and were frequently laid by them before the King and Government. Their constancy in suffering was hardly exceeded by their unwearied efforts to obtain relief for their suffering brethren, and for the alteration of the persecuting laws, and, through these means, the cause of religious liberty in general was essentially promoted.

3. A third object, which at a very early period of the Society pressed upon its attention, was the proper registration of births and deaths, and the provision for due proceedings relative to marriage. Their principles led them at once to reject all priestly intervention on these occasions, and hence the necessity for their having distinct arrangements in regard to them. In some of the meetings of earliest establishment, regular registers have been preserved from the year 1650 to the present time. Great care was taken in regard to proceedings in marriage; investigation as to the clearness of the parties from other marriage engagements, full publicity of their intentions, and the consent of parents, appear to have been recommended in early times as preliminaries to the ratification of the agreement between the parties; and this act took place publicly in the religious meetings of the Society. Marriage has always been regarded, by Friends, as a religious, not a mere civil, compact.

4. The right education of youth, the provision of suitable situations for them as apprentices or otherwise, and the settlement of differences without going to law one with another, were also among the early objects of the Society's care.

5. The last, though not least, object of the discipline in early times, which we shall enumerate, was the exercise of

spiritual care over the members. As the Society advanced it was soon reminded of our Lord's declaration, "It must needs be that offences come." United as they were, in the main, in true Christian fellowship, differences did arise. Evidencing, as the Society did, to a large extent, the fruits of the Spirit, there were those who fell away from their Christian profession, and walked disorderly; and sound as was the body of Friends in Christian doctrine, there were members who were betrayed into false doctrines and vain imaginations; and pure and spiritual, and consistent with true order and Christian subjection as were the principles of religious liberty advocated by the Society, there were those who appear to have assumed them under the false expectation of an unbridled independence.

To all these cases the discipline was applied in very early times. The duty of the church to oversee its members, to deal with, and, if needs be, to separate from or disown those who persisted in walking disorderly, was always asserted; yet the spirit of tenderness which breathes through the writings of George Fox, in regard to the treatment of delinquents, and which there is good reason to believe was practically illustrated to a large extent in the conduct of the Friends of those days, is worthy of especial notice. In one of his epistles he thus writes:—"Now, concerning Gospel order, though the doctrine of Jesus Christ requireth his people to admonish a brother or sister twice before they tell the church, yet that limiteth none, so as that they shall use no longer forbearance. And it is desired of all before they publicly complain, that they wait in the power of God, to feel if there is no more required of them to their brother or sister, before they expose him or her to the church. Let this be weightily considered, and all such as behold their brother or sister in a transgression, go not in a rough, light, or upbraiding spirit, to reprove or admonish him or her; but in the power of the Lord and Spirit of the Lamb, and in the wisdom and love of the truth, which suffers thereby, to admonish such an offender. So may the soul of such a brother or sister be seasonably and effectually reached unto and overcome, and they may have cause to bless the name of the Lord on their behalf; and so a blessing may be rewarded into the bosom of that faithful and tender brother or sister who so admonished them. And so keep the church order of the Gospel, according as the Lord Jesus Christ hath commanded; that is, 'If thy brother offend thee, speak to him betwixt thee and him alone; and if he will not hear, take two for three; and if he will not hear two or three, then tell it to the church.' And if any one do miscarry, admonish them gently in the wisdom of God; so that you may preserve him and bring him to condemnation, and preserve him from further evils, which it is well if such do not run into, and it will be well for all to use the gentle wisdom of God towards them in their temptations, and condemnable actions; and, with using gentleness, to bring them to condemn their evil, and to let their condemnation go as far as their bad action has gone and no farther, to defile the minds of Friends or others; and so to clear God's truth and people, and to convert the soul to God, and preserve them out of farther evils. So be wise in the wisdom of God."*

SYSTEMATIC ESTABLISHMENT OF MEETINGS FOR DISCIPLINE.

We now proceed to notice the more regular and systematic establishment of monthly and quarterly meetings, and of the yearly meeting. Though the history of those times bears ample testimony to the useful part which was taken in this important work by many faithful Friends, yet it is clear that George Fox was the chief instrument in the arrangement and establishment of these meetings. In the epistle from "Friends met in London," in the year 1673, it is said, " Though a general care be not laid upon every member, touching the good order and government in the church's affairs, nor have many travailed therein, yet the Lord hath laid it upon some in whom he hath opened counsel for that end, and particularly in our dear brother, and God's faithful labourer, George Fox, for the help of many."† But though the judgment of this eminent man had so much weight with his friends, it is worthy of notice how carefully he sought to keep the body from an improper dependence upon him. As in his preaching, he directed his hearers to Christ for themselves, as alike *their* and *his* teacher, so in the discipline of the Society, he

* Collection of Epistles, fol. edit., p. 284.
† Letters of Early Friends, p. 340.

laboured diligently that the body might be strengthened to act for itself, under the direction of its great Head.

He says in his Journal, under the date of 1666, "Then was I moved of the Lord to recommend the setting up of five monthly meetings of men and women Friends in the city (London), besides the women's meeting and the quarterly meetings, to take care of God's glory, and to admonish and exhort such as walked disorderly or carelessly, and not according to truth. For whereas Friends had had only quarterly meetings, now truth was spread and Friends were grown more numerous, I was moved to recommend the setting up of monthly meetings throughout the nation." In 1667 he laboured most diligently in this service, under much bodily weakness from his long confinements in cold and damp prisons. In 1668 he thus writes, concerning this service :—" The men's monthly meetings were settled through the nation. The quarterly meetings were generally settled before. I wrote also into Ireland, Scotland, Holland, Barbadoes, and several parts of America, advising Friends to settle their men's monthly meetings in those countries, for they had their quarterly meetings before." These monthly meetings, so instituted, took a large share of that care which had heretofore devolved on the quarterly meetings, and were, no doubt, the means of bringing many more of the members into a larger sphere of usefulness and the exercise of their respective gifts in the church, the free course for which he was so anxious to promote. With reference to this subject, he observes, in one of his epistles :—" The least member in the church is serviceable, and all the members have need one of another."

The quarterly meetings from this time received reports of the state of the Society from the monthly meetings, and gave such advice and decisions as they thought right ; but there was not, until some years after this period, a general yearly meeting, to which all the quarterly meetings sent representatives. Of the establishment of that meeting we come now to speak.

REPRESENTATIVE YEARLY MEETING OF LONDON.

There is reason to believe that, from the year 1661 to 1672, a meeting, chiefly, if not wholly, composed of "the labourers in the Gospel," was held, in London, at which the various affairs of the church were considered, and such advice or direction given, as its emergencies required. There has been preserved a very important document issued by the meeting held in the year 1666, chiefly referring to some dissensions then prevalent;* and we have also a record of the proceedings of a meeting of a similar kind, held in the year 1668, from which an epistle was issued, and the several quarterly meetings were requested to make a collection, for the service of truth beyond the seas, and the distribution of books.

. There can be no doubt that these annual meetings of the ministers, held in London and elsewhere, had great authority in the Society, and that the advices and regulations which issued from them were received by the several meetings, as expressing the judgment of the body. They were so far representative, that ministers from nearly all parts of England attended them : but it was not in accordance with the principles which those good men had taught, that such a meeting, governing, as we may say, the whole body, should be permanently composed solely of this class of the members; and it is very evident, from their proceedings that the ministers themselves did not think it desirable that the service of this meeting should be confined to them. There was no disposition on the part of those who had been instrumental in gathering the church to be lords over God's heritage; they desired that the fullest opportunity should be afforded to all faithful brethren for the exercise of their various gifts; and in accordance with these feelings, we find at the yearly meeting held in Devonshire House, London, in 1672, the following minute was adopted:—"It is concluded, agreed, and assented unto, by Friends then present, that for the better ordering, managing, and regulating of the public affairs of Friends relating to the truth and service thereof, that there be a general meeting of Friends held at London once a year, in the week called Whitsun-week, to consist of six Friends for the city of London, three for the city of Bristol, two for the town of Colchester, and one or two from each of the counties of England and Wales respectively. That the quarterly meetings in London, Bristol, Colchester, and all and every the counties of England and Wales respectively at the quarterly meetings immediately preceding the said

---

* See Letters of Early Friends, p. 318.

week called Whitsun-week in every year, do take care to nominate and appoint the number of Friends aforesaid, to be present at the general meeting aforesaid; there to advise about the managing of the public affairs of Friends throughout the nation. That the Friends so chosen for the purpose aforesaid, be desired to be at London by the second-day night of the Whitsun-week, so called, in every year at furthest. And upon their arrival there, the six Friends for the city of London, together with a competent number of the other Friends of the country, may then examine and appoint the time and place for the then meeting of the said general meeting, some time in the said week, called Whitsun-week, in every year, accordingly, until further order be taken therein. That as many Friends that labour in the truth as have freedom thereunto may be present at the said general meeting; that all others, except such as are nominated, appointed, and chosen, be desired to forbear to come to the said general meeting, except such Friends as they, when met together, shall see meet to admit." *

The representative yearly meeting, thus constituted, met at the time proposed, in 1673, and after much harmonious consideration of the state of the churches, issued an epistle, full of wise and Christian counsel, to all their "dear friends, brethren and sisters in this, and other nations." The Friends who had assembled on this occasion, however, did not think that the time was fully come for the establishment of a regular annual meeting of this description. They came to the conclusion, that the general meeting, constituted as it then was, "be discontinued till Friends, in God's wisdom, shall see a further occasion;" and it was further agreed, that the general meeting of Friends who labour in the work of the ministry, do continue as formerly appointed. This meeting of Friends in the ministry, for the general care of the church, which had now been so formally constituted and authorized, appears to have been regularly held annually from this time to the year 1677 inclusive.

In 1675 a series of important advices and instructions was agreed upon, and sent forth to the several meetings: they are contained in an epistle, and are thus introduced: —" At a solemn general meeting of many faithful friends and brethren concerned in the public labour of the

Gospel and service of the church of Christ, from the most parts of the nation." This document is signed by eighty-one Friends, most of whom are well known as having been conspicuous in the early history of the Society, and the spirit of fervent piety and charity which it breathes is well worthy of their character. In 1677 the general meeting of ministers, true to the principles which governed them in the minute which they made in 1672, agreed again to convene the meeting of representatives in the ensuing year, and then to advise respecting its continuance. Accordingly in 1678 the representative yearly meeting assembled in London, and after agreeing upon several matters, the substance of which was conveyed to the various meetings of Friends, in the form of an epistle, accompanied by much Christian counsel, concluded to meet again the next year after the same manner; and these representative meetings have continued to assemble once a year in London, with unbroken regularity, to the present time. Nor has any essential alteration taken place in the constitution of the meeting, which, though largely attended by other members, is declared in the last revised edition of the "Rules of Discipline," "to consist of representatives from every quarterly meeting in Great Britain and from the yearly meeting of Ireland, likewise of acknowledged ministers and appointed elders, and of the correspondents."*

OF THE RELATION OF THE SEVERAL MEETINGS TO EACH OTHER, AND OF THEIR PROCEEDINGS.

Thus was a series of representative meetings established, in the order and character of which very little change has since been made, so little, indeed, that the description given of them by William Penn, in his account of the rise and progress of the Society, may form a suitable concluding review of their past and present general offices and relation to each other. He says, that " George Fox exhorted that some out of every meeting of worship should meet together, once in the month, to confer about the wants and occasions of the church, and as the case required, so those monthly meetings were fewer or more

* Rules of Discipline, p. 124, No. 5.

in number in every respective county; and that these
monthly meetings should, in each county, make up one
quarterly meeting, where the most zealous and eminent
Friends of the county should assemble to communicate,
advise, and help one another, especially where any business
seemed difficult, or a monthly meeting was tender of
determining a matter. Also these quarterly meetings
should digest the reports of the monthly meetings, and
prepare one for the county against the yearly meeting,
in which the quarterly meetings resolve, which is held
yearly in London, where the churches of this nation,
and other nations and provinces, meet by chosen members
of their respective counties, both mutually to communicate their church affairs, and to advise and be advised
on any depending case to edification; also to provide a
requisite stock for the discharge of general expenses for
general services in the church. At these meetings any
of the members of the churches may come if they please,
and speak their minds freely, in the fear of God, to any
matter; but the mind of each meeting therein represented
is chiefly understood, as to particular cases, in the sense
delivered by the persons deputed or chosen for that
service."*

When thus met together for the service of the church,
one of their members, chosen by the body, acts as clerk
to the meeting, and endeavours to collect the real sense
and judgment of the members present. It is not usual to
determine any matter by the majority of voices; the aim
being to arrive at the truth in the matter proposed, and
knowing that there are different degrees of experience
among the members, as well as diversity of gifts, the
mere counting of numbers is not considered to be the
true method of decision in the affairs of the church. The
views of the early Friends as to the spirit and manner in
which the meetings for discipline should be conducted, are
so well expressed in the following passages from one of
their highly esteemed writers, that we cannot illustrate
the subject better than by extracting them :—

"It is not of absolute necessity that every member of
the church should have the same measure of understanding
in all things : for then, where were the duty of the strong
bearing with the weak ?—and then, where would be any
submitting to them that are set over others in the Lord?

* Preface to George Fox's Journal, 8vo. edit., p. xxvii.

—which all tend to the preserving of unity in the church, notwithstanding the different measures and different growths of the members thereof. For as the spirits of the prophets are subject to the prophets, so are the spirits of all that are kept in a true subjection to the sense of life given by the same spirit in the church, and by this means we come to know the one master, even Christ; and have no room for other masters in the matter of our obedience to God."

* * * * * *

"And whereas it may often fall out that among a great many, some may have a different apprehension of a matter from the rest of their brethren, especially in outward or temporal things, there ought to be a Christian liberty maintained for such to express their sense with freedom of mind, or else they will go away burdened; whereas, if they speak their minds freely, and a friendly and Christian conference be admitted thereupon, they may be eased; and oftentimes the different apprehension of such an one comes to be wholly removed, and his understanding opened to see as the rest see."

* * * * * *

"Seek not to drive a matter on in fierceness or in anger, nor to take offence into your mind at any time, because what seems to be clear to you is not presently received; but let all things in the church be propounded with an awful reverence of him who is the head and life of it; who hath said, 'Where two or three are gathered together in my name, I will be in the midst of them.' But he that follows his own spirit sees nothing as he ought to see it. Therefore, *let all beware of their own spirit and natural temper*, as they are sometimes called; but *let all keep in a gracious temper*. Then are ye fit for the service of the house of God."

* * * * * *

"It is no man's learning nor artificial acquirements, it is no man's riches nor greatness, it is no man's eloquence and natural wisdom, that makes him fit for government in the church of Christ, unless he, with all his endowments, be seasoned with the heavenly salt, and his spirit be subjected, and his gifts pass through the fire of God's altar, a sacrifice to his praise and honour, that so self may be crucified and baptized in death, and the gifts made use of in the power of the resurrection of the life of Jesus in him.

" And when this great work is wrought in a man, then all his gifts and qualifications are sanctified; then they are made use of for the good of the body, which is the church; and they are as ornaments and jewels which serve for the joy and comfort of all who are partakers of the same divine fellowship of life in Christ Jesus our Lord." *

OF THE MEETING OF MINISTERS.

When the general meeting of ministers transferred much of its duties to the representative yearly meeting, of which they formed a part, there were some portions of service which more particularly belonged to the ministers themselves.

Although the power to approve or disapprove of ministers, rested with the members of the church to which they respectively belonged, in the capacity of a monthly meeting, yet it was deemed fitting that the ministers should have an especial oversight of each other, and that they should meet together for mutual consultation and advice in regard to those of their own station.

George Fox, in 1674, writes thus :—" Let your general assemblies of the ministers, [in London] or elsewhere, examine, as it was at the first, whether all the ministers that go forth into the counties, do walk as becomes the Gospel, for that you know was one end of that meeting, to prevent and take away scandal, and to examine whether all who preach Christ Jesus do keep in his government and in the order of the Gospel, and to exhort them that do not." Meetings for these purposes, in which Friends in the station of elder are now united, continue to be regularly held.

OF WOMEN'S MEETINGS.

All the meetings which have been hitherto described were conducted by men; but one of the earliest features of our religious economy was the elevation of the position of women in the church, by recognizing them as helpers in spiritual as well as in temporal things; holding in the former, as well as in the latter, a distinct place, and having

* Epistle to Friends, by Stephen Crisp, 1690.

duties which more peculiarly devolve on them. For this purpose meetings were established among them, with a special regard to the care and edification of their own sex. A meeting of women Friends is mentioned at Bristol as early as 1668, and it appears from a passage already quoted from George Fox, that they had been held in London at a still earlier period. Their general establishment does not, however, appear to have taken place until after the settlement of the men's meetings. After speaking of these he says :—" Truth still spreading further over the nation, and Friends increasing in number, I was moved by the same eternal power, to recommend the setting up of women's meetings also." His views in regard to the establishment of these meetings are conveyed in the following passages :—" That faithful women, called to a belief of the truth, and made partakers of the same precious faith, and heirs of the same everlasting Gospel of life and salvation, as the men are, might in the like manner come into the profession and practice of the Gospel order, and therein be meet helps to the men in the restoration, in the service of truth, and the affairs of the church, as they are outwardly in civil and temporal things; that so all the family of God, women as well as men, might know, possess, and perform their offices and services in the house of God: whereby the poor might be better taken care of; the younger sort instructed, informed, and taught in the way of God; the loose and disorderly reproved and admonished in the fear of the Lord; the clearness of persons proposing marriage more closely and strictly inquired into in the wisdom of God; and all the members of the spiritual body, the church, might watch over and be helpful to each other in love."

Again, speaking of the important duties of women in the church, he says :—" The elder women in the truth were not only called elders, but mothers. Now a mother in the church of Christ and a mother in Israel is one who nourishes, and feeds, and washes, and rules, and is a teacher in the church, an admonisher, an instructor, an exhorter. So the elder women and mothers are to be teachers of good things, teachers of the younger, and to be trainers of them up in virtue, holiness, righteousness, in wisdom, and in the fear of the Lord in the church of Christ."

There is good reason to believe that these views of George Fox were practically carried out; and that the meetings of the women Friends, established for these Christian purposes, had a very salutary influence upon the body, both by the service which they directly rendered, and by the right opening which they gave to the exercise of the gifts of faithful women in the church. An instructive epistle " from the women Friends in London to the women Friends in the country, and elsewhere, about the service of women meetings," was written in the year 1674. The true character of that service is very clearly set forth in this document. It is stated, that though their service was distinct in some respects, it was in perfect unity with that of their brethren. " We being in that humility and subjection of spirit to the Lord, and therein preferring them (our brethren), it shuts out all usurpation, and the spirit of it; so that we in a sincere mind are workers together with them in the same faith, only distinct as to the place, and in those particular things which most properly appertain to us as women;—still eyeing the universal Head in whom male and female are one, where no division can be admitted of, so that the body is held entire, in Christ Jesus united.   *   *   *   *   Their services," they state, " have been and are to visit the sick and the prisoners that suffer for the testimony of Jesus; to see they are supplied with things needful; and relieving the poor, making provision for the needy, aged, and weak, that are incapable of work: a due consideration for the widows, and care taken of the fatherless children and poor orphans, according to their capacities; for their education and bringing up in good nurture, and in the fear of the Lord, and putting them out to trades, in the wholesome order of the creation. Also the elder women exhorting the younger in all sobriety, modest in apparel, and subjection to truth; and if any should be led aside by the temptations of Satan any way, to reclaim such; and to stop tattlers, and false reports, and all such things as tend to division amongst us; following those things which make for peace, reconciliation, and union. Chiefly," say they, " our work is to help the helpless in all cases, according to our abilities;" and " although more especially our provision is set apart for the supply of the household of faith and family of God, yet we cannot be limited; but as the universal bounty of the Lord maketh His sun to rise on the good and the bad, and sendeth rain on the just and on the unjust, so the same bounty, according to its measure in us, often finds the same object of charity, which cannot (as we find freedom) be sent empty away. But as on the Lord we wait, and our eye is single unto Him, from whom we daily receive our living supply for these our services, the Lord hath been and is with us, as oft as we meet together, answering abundantly with what his work calleth for, and his arm of power is over us, which at first gathered us; and in it is our preservation to this day; to which power we commend you, dear sisters." Few will deny that the objects here described are fitting occasions for the exercise of faithful women in the church, and that the spirit of love which the document breathes, marks the writers to have been like-minded with those women who, when the Lord Jesus was on earth, followed Him, and ministered to Him.

EFFECTS OF THE ESTABLISHMENT OF THE DISCIPLINE.

The persevering efforts of George Fox to establish a regular, uniform system of discipline, a work in which he was assisted by nearly all those who had been instrumental in gathering the Society, proved a great trial of spirits. To a large proportion of the members, the arrangements appear to have been quite satisfactory. There was, however, a considerable number of objectors. The self-willed and lawless opposed it with vehemence, and it must be admitted that not a few of a very different class were drawn aside by specious arguments, to oppose what was represented as an encroachment upon individual spiritual liberty. Certain it is that a schism to some extent took place on this occasion; which, however, there is reason to believe, left the Society in a more healthy state than it found it. The general meeting of ministers in 1677 issued a strong declaration on the subject. Robert Barclay wrote, upon this occasion, his "Anarchy of the Ranters," William Penn his "Liberty Spiritual," and Stephen Crisp an excellent tract, all of them endeavouring to prove the necessity of established order and discipline in the church of Christ.

They utterly disclaimed the idea that the doctrine which they had taught of individual illumination was opposed to order, government, and subjection in the church of Christ. They maintained that there was a perfect harmony between the ORDER of the Gospel and that blessed truth so constantly upheld by the Society of Friends, that " where the spirit of the Lord is, there is LIBERTY," not only from the thraldom of sin and Satan, but from the yoke of ceremonies, and from the unautho-rized domination of man in matters of religion. ".The Spirit of the Lord " can never lead into licentiousness, discord, or insubordination. It is the spirit of truth; it is also the spirit of meekness, forbearance, gentleness, and love. Utterly opposed to the notion of independence one of another in the church, this Holy Spirit binds together in one all the living members, provides for every one his right place, and qualifies for his right functions in the body of Christ. It teaches all the members of that mystical body to be subject one to another in love, and above all to be subject in all things to the Lord Jesus himself, who has bought us with a price of infinite value, and whose undoubted right it is to rule over His own church according to His will.

Such are the truly scriptural principles on which George Fox and his brethren were enabled to institute that system of discipline, the rise and establishment of which we have attempted to describe in the preceding pages, and which is still steadily maintained in our religious Society. Nor can it be denied that the wisdom manifested in its institution, affords a decisive evidence that those who were engaged in it were not given over, as some persons have imagined, to a wild and lawless enthusiasm, but were truly subjected to the yoke of Christ, and were eminently favoured with the practical experience of His gracious guidance and government.

N.B.—Free use has been made in this little work of the Introduction to the Rules of Discipline of the Society of Friends, published by the Society in the year 1834.

END.

Printed by E. Couchman and Co., 10, Throgmorton Street, London.

THE HAPPY EFFECTS OF RELIGION ON THE MIND IN HUMBLE LIFE.

Exemplified in Infancy and Old Age, in the cases of ISABELLA BROWN, aged Twelve years, and of URSULA COTTOM, aged Seventy-five years.

ISABELLA BROWN,

Was the daughter of Richard and Isabella Brown, of Llanidloes, in North Wales, and died at Ackworth School, in Yorkshire, in the year 1822, aged about twelve years. The father of this interesting child, when a lad, had been sent to the same school: and while there was attacked with the disease called *Gutta Serena*, by which he entirely lost his sight; notwithstanding which, as he was much attached to the School, he was suffered to remain there two years longer; from thence he was removed to the Blind School at Liverpool; where he learnt the art of basket-making; he afterwards went to the Asylum for the Blind at Bristol, and paid a visit, on his way, to his relations at Llanidloes. For a considerable time his earnings were very small, yet he managed to save a little, and was enabled when he became well acquainted with his trade, to commence basket-making on his own account, in his native place. The following year he married Isabella Pugh, of the same place, with whom he had been long acquainted; they then opened a small shop, in addition to the basket-making, and exhibited in the situation allotted them, a bright example of industry, integrity, and contentment. Isabella, the subject of this little memoir, from her very early infancy listened with great attention to the instructions of her father, and became so affectionately attached to him that she spent most of her time with him in the workshop, either reading to him, or rendering any little assistance

No. 65.   [*Price 3d. per dozen.*]

in her power; she often heard her father speak of Ackworth School with much interest and pleasure, notwithstanding the loss he had sustained while a scholar there; and as soon as she was old enough, she manifested a strong desire to go there, but being a delicate child, it was deferred till her health was somewhat improved: she accordingly went, accompanied by her father, in the year 1822. Previous to this, she had made considerable progress in her learning, under the instruction of her parents, being principally taught in the English language, though she could read the Bible in Welch with little difficulty.

Her active mind soon became acquainted with the business of the schools, and she appeared anxious to employ her time to the most advantage; and her amiable manners secured to her the society of girls of a similar disposition to her own, in whose company and that of her teachers, she appeared much to enjoy herself. But alas! how often are our fairest prospects blighted; this interesting child had not been five weeks in the school before she was taken ill with a sore throat, attended with pains in her feet and ankles, from which at first the medical attendant thought she would shortly recover, but he soon found it necessary to call for the assistance of a skilful physician, and the disease was hardly checked by all the means they could devise: a considerable degree of fever ensued, with a fixed pain in her left side, which was not removed till near her death; she continued little more than two weeks, during which her patience and resignation under great suffering, and her gratitude for every little attention to her, endeared her very much to those who were about her.

For a few days previous to Isabella's death, her nerves were in a state of great excitement, but her mind was clear, and clothed with uncommon sweetness: she several times wished to have portions of the Scriptures read, and at the conclusion she would remark, that the passages were excellent and very beautiful. During the last night she was extremely restless, and

early in the morning it was evident that life was fast
ebbing; her nerves for some hours were in a state of
such extreme agitation that almost every muscle in her
whole frame was in motion. When the agitation had
somewhat subsided, after a little solemn silence, she
broke forth, in the most impressive manner, saying,
" I shall die, I shall die very soon, and I shall go to
heaven and be happy :" and looking upwards she said
" I have seen the Almighty seated on His throne, and
I shall go to Him and sing praises to the Lord God
Almighty :. I am not afraid to die." Soon after these
expressions were uttered, she informed those who stood
round her bed, that she had one thing more to mention,
and desired to be raised up; she then proceeded—
"Before I left home, a relation told my mother, that
if I went to Ackworth School, I should die there; I
know this grieved my poor mother, but I hope she will
be comforted when she is told that I am going to heaven;
I had hoped to be useful at home, if I lived to return,
but now I am quite satisfied to die here; I have no
pain of body or of mind, which is a great favour."
She was asked if she had any further message to her
parents, she replied, " Nothing but love, and that I am
going to heaven :" she was then laid down again, and
appeared to be dying, but after slumbering awhile she
again revived a little and said, " The right time is
long coming; I am glad I have done; I am living as
it were after death." About two hours after this, she
died without groan or struggle; and we humbly trust
that her purified and redeemed spirit has been admitted
into those mansions which the Lord Jesus has prepared for all those who love Him.

The distance from Ackworth School to Llanidloes
being great, and not direct by post, communication
with her parents was slow, and as they awaited the
receipt of several letters, under the hope of receiving
better tidings before they determined to take so long
a journey, they did not reach Ackworth till the afternoon of the day on which their beloved child had died.
in the morning.

URSULA COTTOM.

THE subject of this memoir knew nothing of her early history, having been an inmate of the Foundling Hospital in London; and on enquiry, no clue to her relations could be found in the records of that institution.

When about twelve years of age, she was placed out as an apprentice with a man and his wife who were both pious people of the Methodist connexion; which she always considered as a providential circumstance in her life, and observed in her simple style, " that a watchful Providence had good things in store for her ;" she was taken with them to the Methodist meetings, and was soon favoured to become acquainted with the visitations of Divine love in her own mind; and before her apprenticeship was expired, she was united to the Society, and was a zealous and consistent member. After remaining a year over the term of her apprenticeship, as a servant in this family, she went to live as housekeeper with Richard Cottom, of Scarborough, a worthy man, also of the Methodist Society, and about four years afterwards became his wife, and was then an active member and class leader in the said Society.

Some time after this she felt her mind drawn towards the Society of Friends, and frequently attended their meetings; being convinced of the value and importance of silent waiting upon God, and of close attention to the manifestations of the Spirit in her own heart. Her husband at first strongly objected to her leaving the Methodist connexion; but being convinced of the propriety of granting full liberty of conscience, he complied: and in 1798, she became united to Friends, with whom she remained an upright and consistent member until the close of her life.

She contributed to the support of herself and her husband by keeping a small shop; in which situation she was a remarkable example of the strictest honesty and uprightness; and also showed by her life and conversation how much good may be done in the humblest sphere, if the heart is but influenced, and directed by the power of Divine grace.

She was an active distributor of tracts and other good books; and her company was often sought both by the rich and poor, particularly when labouring under doubt and discouragement, or groaning under the burden of a guilty mind, or an awakened conscience; and she was faithful in exhorting some, and consoling others amongst those who came to tell their sorrows, or to ask her advice.

Her husband lived till he was ninety-five years of age; and during the latter part of his life was quite dependent upon her exertions for his support. She appeared to do all in her power for him, and maintained the character of a faithful wife and kind nurse: but she now found her means so diminished, that she was glad to accept one of the residences provided by the benevolence of the late Joseph Taylor, who left £1,000 for that purpose, by which fourteen poor families are provided with a comfortable dwelling. In this residence she still carried on her little business; but being unable to do much, she found the advantage of having, by the strictest economy, laid up a little provision for old age; and the repugnance which she evinced to accept any assistance from a fund, which could be properly applied to lengthen out her little store, was truly praiseworthy, though almost carried to excess. This conduct evidently did not arise from pride, but from a spirit of independence and scrupulous honesty; and when she did accept of assistance, a most exact account was kept of the application of every part of it.

At this time her heart was filled with gratitude and thankfulness; and, placed in a small, but clean and comfortable apartment, she was led to exclaim, " Surely goodness and mercy have followed me all the days of my life." Her piety and contented cheerfulness exhibited an instructive lesson to all who visited her; one

Friend of great experience remarked, that when she was in affliction, a visit to Ursula Cottom was always a means of consoling her mind, and that she returned benefited by her instructive example and pious resignation.

She latterly suffered much from ill health: and in the first month, 1833, was taken very ill, and on being put to bed, expressed her belief that she should never rise from it again.

A friend calling to see her, asked her if she wanted anything? "Oh no!" she replied, "I have more done for me than any one could ask for or think of; I am surrounded by so many comforts, through the kindness of my heavenly Father. How can I be thankful enough?" On the Friend expressing a wish that she should not want anything, she said, "Dear Hearts! you are very kind; my heart overflows with love and gratitude. My heavenly Father has been merciful to me every way; my pain has been very great; but I trust that the rod which He sees meet for me, is intended to purify me from something that is left: and that in His own time, He will take me to His kingdom. My heart feels already united with those who are around the throne, ascribing to Him, and to the Lamb all glory, and honour, and praise, which are His due."

Another time awaking from a slumber, and taking the hand of one who sat by her, she said, "I have been favoured this morning with such a remarkable sight of the wisdom and goodness of God. O! it was beyond all expression! His marvellous goodness and mercy to His creature, man; how He provides for his comfort; and feeds both him and the beasts of the earth. And I bless and praise his Holy Name, that He has surrounded me with comforts—with every thing I want. Thou sees I am nearly a lump of clay; ' Dust thou art, and unto dust thou shalt return.' This was the sentence pronounced upon fallen man; and I am willing, very willing to die; my body feels like unto the grave, where it will soon be laid; but my spirit is filled with unspeakable love and mercy. I.

feel I shall be clothed with the nature of Christ, my Saviour, and for this my spirit shall praise Him."

On a belief being expressed that she would be sustained through the conflict, she said, "O yes; my Saviour is with me. He will sustain me through all: He will conquer all things for me, and give me the victory."

At another time, under a sensible feeling of the Divine goodness, she said, "I am endeavouring to clasp, by faith, my dear Redeemer, who has done, and will do much for me. It is said, 'the righteous hath hope in his death;' I have no merit of my own; ah, no! *it is the interest I feel in the all-atoning sacrifice.*"

A friend who called to see her, expressed a hope that she felt God to be near her. She replied, "Yes bless and praise Him! I am seeking after inward stillness."

The following morning she observed to the same Friend, "I am still here, a monument of love and mercy; after which she repeated the following lines :—

" ' Jesus! lover of my soul,
    Let me to thy bosom fly;
While the nearer waters roll,
    While the tempest still is nigh.

' Hide me, Oh! my Saviour hide!
    'Till the storm of life is past;
Safe into the haven guide;
    Oh! receive my soul at last.

' Other refuge have I none :
    Hangs my helpless soul on thee;
Leave, Oh! leave me not alone,
    Still support and comfort me.

' All my help on Thee is laid;
    All my wants to Thee I bring;
Cover my defenceless head,
    With the shadow of thy wing!' "

A short time after this she prayed thus: "Pure and Holy God! fit and prepare me for an entrance into that city, where nothing that is impure; nothing that worketh an abomination, or that maketh or loveth a lie, can ever enter.

A short time before her death, calling a Friend to her, she said, " I found in the night I had a strong city ; 'salvation has God appointed for walls and bulwarks' O ! thank God for all things ! 'He is my strength and my song—He also is become my salvation !' Blessed and everlasting God ! Thou wilt never leave me, nor forsake me. O mercy ! mercy ! I ever bless and praise Thee !—In the end everlasting righteousness." Here her voice failed her, from being exhausted. After this, although she continued a few days, she was not able to express much. A few hours before her close, on being asked if she was in much pain, she said, " Death ! death !" and after laying still some time, gently departed.

Her attendants bear witness to the patience and cheerfulness with which she was enabled to endure acute bodily pain. One of them observed the sting of death was taken away; as frequently during her illness, she burst forth into expressions of praise and thanksgiving, similar to the few which have been recorded.

She was indeed a remarkable instance of the expansive influence of Divine love—a theme on which she often dwelt—which enabled her to soar above all her sufferings, and caused her heart to overflow with praise and thanksgiving, though placed in a very humble station, and furnished with little more than the necessaries of life. What a lesson of instruction is this ! How empty, at such an hour, are the riches and pleasures and pursuits of this world ! when weighed in the balance they appear as less than nothing, and vanity. Hath not God chosen the poor of this world rich in faith, and heirs of the kingdom, which He hath promised to them that love Him ?

London : Printed by E. Couchman & Co., 10, Throgmorton Street ; for the TRACT ASSOCIATION of the SOCIETY OF FRIENDS. Sold at the DEPOSITORY, 12, Bishopsgate Street Without.—1864.

DISCRETION,

INDUSTRY, FRUGALITY,

AND

CHEERFULNESS,

CONSIDERED.

XTRACTED FROM THE THIRD PART OF A WORK ON THE DUTIES OF
RELIGION AND MORALITY:

By HENRY TUKE.

LONDON:

rinted for the TRACT ASSOCIATION of the SOCIETY OF FRIENDS.

Sold at the DEPOSITORY, 12, Bishopsgate Street Without.

—

1865,

No. 66.   *[Price 3d. per dozen.]*

DISCRETION, or PRUDENCE.

This is a virtue of high importance, in regulating the whole of our conduct through life. It is often applied to the management of our temporal concerns, as preventing us from engaging in unwarrantable undertakings, and as inducing us to keep our expenses within our incomes.—But this is not the whole of the objects it embraces. There is scarcely any concern in life, in which we do not need the aid of discretion,—When better motives are wanting, it may be profitably applied to the restraint of vice; and even our other virtues stand in need of its salutary restrictions. "A good man showeth favour and lendeth;" but, at the same time, "he guideth his affairs with discretion."

What we have on this subject in Holy Writ is principally contained in the Proverbs of Solomon. He represents Prudence as being the intimate companion of Wisdom. "I Wisdom dwell with Prudence. The wise in heart shall be called prudent." Wisdom and Prudence are distinct acquirements, and the former is very imperfect without the latter. "My son (says Solomon again) keep sound wisdom, and discretion. The discretion of a man deferreth his anger. A fool's wrath is presently-known; but a prudent man covereth shame. A prudent man concealeth [his own] knowledge but the mouth of fools proclaimeth foolishness. Every prudent man dealeth with knowledge; but a fool layeth open his folly. The simple believe every word; but the prudent man looketh well to his way. A prudent man foreseeth the evil, and hideth himself; but the simple pass on, and are punished."

This virtue we find recorded among the qualities, which the Evangelical Prophet foretold should distinguish the character of the Messiah: "My servant shall deal prudently;" and we find the Apostle, in his Epistle to Titus, recommending that the young women and young men should be advised to the exercise of discretion.

The following remarks on this subject, by an eminent writer,* are so excellent, as to induce me to give them a place here: "Discretion is like an under-agent of Providence,

* Addison.

to guide and direct us in the ordinary concerns of life. There are more shining qualities in the mind of man, but there is none so useful as discretion. It is this, indeed, which gives a value to all the rest; which sets them at work in their proper times and places; and turns them to the advantage of the person who is possessed of them. Without it learning is pedantry, and wit impertinence. Virtue itself looks like weakness; the best parts only qualify a man to be more sprightly in errors, and active to his own prejudice." Again, "Though a man have all other perfections, and want discretion, he will be of no great consequence in the world." To this I would add, that when Humility is united with Prudence, they produce, in my apprehension, more than any other virtues, comfort and reputation for us in this world; and are not without their use in preparing us for a state of happiness in that which is to come.

INDUSTRY, or DILIGENCE.

The importance of this virtue, for the reputable support of individuals and of families, is universally acknowledged. Indeed, employment is beneficial in every station of life. The want of industry, when circumstances require its exercise, is represented by the Apostle, as making a man worse than an infidel. Yet, perhaps, he did not mean to say, that idleness is worse than infidelity; but that when it prevails among Christians, it places their character, in this particular respect, below that of many who are infidels or heathens. The cause of Religion suffers much, when those who lay claim, and perhaps an extraordinary claim to it, neglect a proper attention to their temporal concerns. By this means they often fail of performing those engagements which they have entered into, become burdensome to others, and, by distress and perplexity, often lose the little religion that they once possessed. It was, I apprehend, to correct this error in religion, that the Apostle thus strongly represents the consequences of neglecting a proper care for ourselves and our families : " If any provide not for his own, and especially for those of his own house, he hath denied the faith, and is worse than an infidel." Very strenuously does Solomon recommend industry, or diligence in business; and as severely does he reprobate the opposite vice :—" The hand of the diligent maketh rich, and beareth rule : but the slothful shall be under tribute. The substance of a diligent man is precious. Seest thou a man diligent in his business? He shall stand before kings: he shall not stand before mean men. Be thou diligent to know the state of thy flocks, and look well to thy herds, for riches are not for ever; and doth the crown endure to every generation?" To the sluggard, and respecting him, the following passages are appropriate: "Go to the ant, thou sluggard, consider her ways and be wise; who, having no guide, overseer, or ruler, provideth her meat in summer, and gathereth her food in the harvest.—I went by the field of the slothful, and by the vineyard of the man void of understanding: and lo! it was all grown over with thorns, and nettles covered the face of it, and the stone wall thereof was broken down. Then I saw and considered it well: I looked upon it and received instruction. Yet a little sleep, a little slumber, a little folding of the hands to sleep: so shall thy poverty come as one that travelleth, and thy want as an armed man."

By the foregoing passages, we see the benefits of industry, and the evils consequent upon idleness. But let us be careful not to suffer the duty here recommended so to absorb our attention as to make us neglect any of those other duties which religion requires of us. At the same time that we are careful to be "not slothful in business," let us remember what immediately follows, but "fervent in spirit, serving the Lord."

FRUGALITY.

Frugality consists in a sparing use of what we possess, and the avoiding of unnecessary expense. Both frugality and industry are public as well as private virtues. They enrich nations as well as individuals. True frugality increases our enjoyments as well as our possessions. It makes a man of moderate circumstances, and sometimes even a poor man, more independent than one who possesses great affluence, if the latter is not bounded by prudence in his expenses. Although this virtue is not much inculcated in direct terms in the Holy Scriptures, yet it may be considered as necessarily included in that prudence or discretion of which we have already treated: and it is so unavoidable a consequence of many of the moral precepts which are inculcated both in the Old and New Testaments, that it may be considered a Christian virtue. That moderation which we are required to exhibit to all men cannot be fully exercised without it; and when

we abstain from all those indulgences and vices which the
Christian religion forbids, we are, at least, in the high road
to frugality.

But whilst we are paying proper attention to this virtue,
as well as to industry, we should beware of their extremes;
a parsimonious and a covetous disposition. Both these are
evils, against which we have many scriptural admonitions;
"There is that scattereth, and yet increaseth: and there is
that withholdeth more than is meet, and it tendeth to
poverty. He that soweth sparingly, shall reap also sparingly."
"Thou shalt not covet anything that is thy neighbour's " is
the substance of the tenth commandment. Covetousness is,
indeed, peculiarly marked with divine disapprobation. "The
wicked blesseth the covetous, whom the Lord abhorreth."
"Incline my heart to thy testimonies, and not to covetousness," was the prayer of the Psalmist: and Solomon saith,
"He that hateth covetousness shall prolong his days." This
vice is severely reprehended by the Jewish prophets: "For
the iniquity of his covetousness was I wroth. With their
mouth they show much love; but their heart goeth after
their covetousness. Wo unto him that coveteth an evil
covetousness."

Our blessed Lord frequently reproves this vice in the
Pharisees of his time: and gives this solemn charge: "Take
heed and beware of covetousness; for a man's life consisteth
not in the abundance of the things which he possesseth."

The following instructive exhortations of the Apostle ar
of great importance to us all: "Godliness with content
ment is great gain; for we brought nothing into this world,
and it is certain we can carry nothing out. Having food
and raiment let us be therewith content. But they that
will be. rich fall into temptation and a snare! and into
many foolish and hurtful lusts, which drown men in destruction and perdition: for the love of money is the root of
all evil (or rather of all these evils); which while some have
coveted after, they have erred from the faith, and pierced
themselves through with many sorrows. Therefore, let you
conversation be without covetousness; and be content with
such things as ye have; for he hath said, I will never leave
thee, nor forsake thee."

CHEERFULNESS.

Writers on Morality have not often given Cheerfulness place among the duties of men. It is, however, sufficiently culcated in the Scriptures, to induce us to notice it among ese duties; and it is the more needful, because the ene- ies, and even some of the friends of religion, are apt to clude it from the code of those virtues which Christianity quires.

Cheerfulness is a medium betwixt levity and gloominess. is compatible with seriousness: and its purest and most rmanent source is an humble, grateful consideration of the any favours and blessings which we enjoy from the Divine nd. A writer,* lately quoted, makes these, among other cellent observations upon it: "When I consider this eerful state of mind, I cannot but look upon it as a con- ant habitual gratitude to the great Author of nature. An ward cheerfulness is an explicit praise and thanksgiving to rovidence under all its dispensations. It is a kind of ac- iescence in the state wherein we are placed; and a secret pprobation of the Divine will, in His conduct towards man."

By numbering, or considering our blessings, the mind is revented from dwelling improperly on the deprivations hich we sustain, or think we sustain, in this probationary ate of existence. In this disposition, the propriety of the postolic exhortation is seen and felt: "Rejoice evermore, nd in everything give thanks."

It is of no small importance in our passage through life to aintain a cheerful state of mind. To this end an attention the foregoing exhortation of the Apostle, and a considera- on of the reasons for it will be beneficial. Correspondent ith this exhortation are some observations of the wise olomon, in which he shows the benefits of a cheerful dis- osition. These observations are, no doubt, intended to xcite that cheerful vivacity which is consistent with religion nd virtue; and it appears to have been particularly the bject of Solomon to guard against a fretful disposition, by rhich many persons needlessly distress themselves, and at he same time make those with whom they are connected ncomfortable. When sorrow proceeds from sufficient cause, nd is duly regulated, this writer, with others of the sacred enmen, shows its advantages, and excites sympathy with

* Addison.

it. He also exposes the folly of a light, airy disposition of mind. "Even in laughter the heart is [often] sorrowful; and the end of that mirth is heaviness. I said of laughter, it is mad: and of mirth what doeth it?"

Our blessed Lord was particularly careful to guard His disciples against a gloomy disposition and appearance. Even in the performance of a religious duty which, above all others, implies serious humiliation, he prohibits an appearance that might improperly expose the employment of the mind, or cause an impression of extraordinary sanctity: "When ye fast, be not as the hypocrites, of a sad countenance. But thou, when thou fastest, anoint thy head and wash thy face; that thou appear not unto men to fast, but unto thy Father who is in secret; and thy Father who seeth in secret shall reward thee openly." Notwithstanding the very serious importance of our Lord's mission, he affected no austerity, he practised no severity. He sympathized with the true mourners; but, at the same time, he encouraged and animated them with a prospect of a better day. He endeavoured to relieve His disciples from all anxiety respecting the things of this world: He taught them to be content with a little, and to be thankful for that little. His whole system (if I may so call it) was calculated to relieve the mind, and to give it a serenity and cheerfulness above that of any other religion in the world.

It should, however, be considered that, previous to the perfect operation of religion on the mind, and perhaps, even when the work is nearly completed, there will be many close conflicts and secret exercises, as well as outward trials, which will unavoidably, at times, depress the heart, and affect the countenance. We should also consider, that the minds and countenances of some persons are so formed by nature as to deprive them of that cheerful appearance which others possess: these circumstances should excite much caution in judging one another in this respect. It must, however, be admitted by those who consider the duties and prospects which Christianity presents, and particularly our blessed Lord's sermon on the mount, that gloominess and moroseness, as well as censoriousness and ostentation, form no part of the religion of Jesus Christ.

END.

Printed by E. Couchman and Co., 10, Throgmorton Street, London,

A CONCISE

AND

FAMILIAR EXPOSITION

OF THE

LEADING PROPHECIES

REGARDING

THE MESSIAH,

WITH THEIR ACCOMPLISHMENT;

INTENDED AS A

MANUAL FOR YOUNG PERSONS.

———◆———

"Art thou He that should come, or do we look for another!"

Matt. xi. 3.

～～～～～～～～～～～

LONDON:

Printed for the TRACT ASSOCIATION of the SOCIETY OF FRIENDS.

Sold at the DEPOSITORY, 84, Houndsditch.

——

1861.

No. 67.   [*Price 8d. per dozen.*]

A CONCISE

AND

FAMILIAR EXPOSITION, &c.

ONE of the most striking circumstances connected with th
Christian dispensation, is the long and singular train o
prophecy, by which it was ushered into the world. Thes
remarkable predictions, delivered in various ages, were com
mitted to the custody of a chosen people, whose whol
history and present condition have themselves been justl
accounted miraculous. The events foretold, though in som
instances of a most extraordinary nature, and, before their
actual occurrence, apparently irreconcileable with each other,
were all brought to pass, in the person of Jesus Christ,
hundreds of years after they were predicted,—at a time
when, in consequence of these prophecies, there was a strong
expectation of the promised Deliverer,—and by means of
agents not at all interested in their completion. The predictions relate to all the important circumstances in Messiah's
history,—his pre-existent state,—the family of which he was
to be born,—the time, place, and other circumstances of
his nativity,—his external rank and condition,—his being
anointed with the Holy Ghost,—his moral character,—his
offices,—his miraculous works,—his last sufferings, death,
and burial,—his resurrection and ascension,—and other remarkable events which were to follow his appearance.

I. With respect to Messiah's PRE-EXISTENT STATE, the
prophets tell us in the plainest manner, that the hour of his
earthly birth was not to be the commencement of his being.
Thus Micah declares that, out of the town of Bethlehem
Ephratah, "shall he come forth that is to be ruler in Israel;
whose goings forth have been of old FROM EVERLASTING."
They speak moreover of his equality with God. Thus Zechariah in a memorable passage, cited by our blessed Lord,
on the eve of his death, as applicable to himself, breaks out
in the following remarkable words; "Awake, O sword, against
my shepherd, and against the man that is MY FELLOW, saith

the Lord of Hosts." They tell us still further that he is God himself. Thus Isaiah announces, " Behold a Virgin shall conceive, and bear a son, and shall call his name IMMANUEL, which being interpreted," as the evangelist Matthew explains, is " God with us." And again, the same prophet declares, " Unto us a child is born, unto us a son is given; and his name shall be called Wonderful, Counsellor, THE MIGHTY GOD, the everlasting Father, the Prince of Peace."—When Jesus of Nazareth, accordingly, appeared upon earth, he spake of his own pre-existence. He told the Jews, " Before Abraham was, I am;" and in addressing his Father, he referred to " that glory, which he had with him, before the world was." He declared, that " all men should honour the Son, even as they honour the Father:" and it was imputed to him by the Jews as blasphemy, that he made himself equal with God. In still more express terms, he asserted his own divinity, saying, " I and my Father are one; he that hath seen me hath seen the Father." But it may naturally be asked, in what manner he established his claim to this high character, and by what signs he manifested his divinity. To this it is answered, that he exhibited every evidence and seal of his divinity, which imagination can suggest, or the nature of the claim can possibly admit,—by performing supernatural works,—by penetrating the secrets of the heart,—by teaching sublimer truths and purer doctrines, than had ever fallen from the lips of uninspired man,—by being the single individual, that ever appeared in the form of man, of whom it could be said, that " he was in all points tempted like as we are, yet without sin,"—by rising victorious from the grave,—by visibly ascending to that heaven whence he declared he came,—by the miraculous fulfilment of that promise, which he gave to his apostles, of extraordinary assistance from above, and of his other predictions, particularly those regarding the destruction of Jerusalem, the persecution of his followers, and the triumphant march of his religion. What stronger proof upon this subject, could have been demanded from our Lord, than what all these circumstances, taken together, afford; or would the Most High have vouchsafed so strong an attestation in favour of one, who had presumptuously usurped his own honour.

II. With regard to the FAMILY of which Christ was to be born, it is pleasing to observe the manner in which the light of prophecy, dim and feeble at first, breaks forth more and more unto the perfect day. In the first promise which was made to the mother of mankind, she was assured only in general terms that it was "HER SEED, which should bruise the serpent's head."—When ABRAHAM, the father of the chosen people, was providentially called to leave his own country, and his kindred, for a land that God would show him, he received the express promise, that "in him," or, as was afterwards more distinctly explained to him, "in his seed, all families of the earth were to be blessed."—This Patriarch had more than one son, and, in answer to his prayer, "O that Ishmael might live before thee," as well as on other occasions, he was expressly told, that the covenant was to be made, not with Ishmael, his first begotten, but with the son of Sarah, who was not yet born. "Sarah, thy wife shall bear thee a son indeed, and thou shalt call his name Isaac: and I will establish my covenant with him for an everlasting covenant, and with his seed after him. And as for Ishmael, I have heard thee: behold, I have blessed him, and I will make him a great nation. But my covenant will I make with ISAAC, which Sarah shall bear unto thee."—Isaac, in like manner, had two sons, Esau and Jacob; and here, again, the promise was limited to Jacob, to the exclusion of his elder brother. The Lord said unto Jacob, "I am the Lord God of Abraham thy Father, and the God of Isaac; in thee and in thy seed, shall all the families of the earth be blessed."— Jacob had twelve sons, and in the prophetic blessing, which he pronounces over them, on his death-bed, he distinctly marks out the chosen tribe. After warning Reuben, that though he "was his first born, his might, and the beginning of his strength, the excellency of dignity, and the excellency of power, yet, unstable as water, he should not excel,"—and declaring of Simeon and Levi, that "he would divide them in Jacob and scatter them in Israel,"—he, in rapturous and glowing language, hails the future glory of the more highly-favoured JUDAH. "Judah, thou art he whom thy brethren shall praise; thy hand shall be in the neck of thine enemies; thy father's children shall bow down before thee: the sceptre shall not depart from Judah, nor a lawgiver from between his feet until Shiloh come; and unto him shall the gathering of the people be"—It was lastly revealed, that the promised Deliverer should be of the stock of JESSE, and the house of DAVID. "There shall come forth," said Isaiah, "a rod out of the stem of Jesse, and a branch shall grow out of his roots, and the Spirit of the Lord shall rest upon him," &c. So, also Jeremiah declares, "Behold the days come, saith the Lord, that I will raise unto David a righteous branch," &c. —All this was fulfilled in the person of Jesus Christ, who was the seed of the woman; the seed of Abraham, of Isaac, and of Jacob; of the tribe of Judah; of the stock of Jesse; and of the house and lineage of David.

III. With regard to the TIME of Messiah's birth, it was announced by the patriarch Jacob, in the passage already quoted, that "the sceptre should not depart from Judah, nor a lawgiver from between his feet, UNTIL SHILOH COME;" which implied, that this tribe should continue a peculiar people, possessing its own laws, until the coming of the Deliverer. Every other tribe lost this distinction, long before the appearance of Christ. The ten revolting tribes never returned from Assyria. Benjamin became an appendage of the tribe of Judah. But Judah continued a distinct people, retaining, even under a foreign master, its own peculiar laws and customs. Thus, in our Saviour's trial before Pilate, the governor bade the Jews "take him and judge him, ACCORDING TO THEIR LAW." From the answer made to this proposal, it would appear, indeed, that their former rights, in this respect had begun to be curtailed, and that they had lost, in their own persons, the power of life and death; though, even in this matter, they seemed to have retained the right to call upon the foreign judge to administer "their" law. "We have a law," said they, "and by this law he ought to die." The sceptre was then on its departure; and not long thereafter, the Jews ceased to be a nation, and were scattered abroad over the face of the earth. Had Christ's appearance, accordingly, taken place at a period not much later than it actually did, the prophetic declaration of the patriarch could not have been accomplished.—With regard to the time of this appearance, also, a remarkable revelation was made to Daniel. "SEVENTY WEEKS are determined upon thy people, and upon thy holy city, to finish the transgression, and to make an end of sins, and to make reconciliation for iniquity, and to bring in everlasting righteousness; and to seal up the vision and prophecy, and to anoint the Most Holy. Know, therefore, and understand, that from the going forth of the commandment to restore and to build Jerusalem unto the Messiah the Prince, shall be seven weeks and threescore and two weeks. And after threescore and two weeks shall Messiah be cut off, but not for himself." Now, it has been shown by Sir Isaac Newton, as well as many other learned men, that by computing each day for a year, the seventy weeks were precisely accomplished at the time when Christ was *cut off*. On this subject, it seems proper to remark that the division of years, as well as of days, into weeks or portions of seven, was quite familiar to the Jews, with whom every seventh year was a sabbath for the land as every seventh day was for the people. It is also remarkable, that this comparison of years to days seems not to have been uncommon in their prophetic language. It was thus the Lord, by Moses, foretold to the children of Israel their forty years' detention in the wilderness: "After the number of the days, in which ye searched the land, even forty days, EACH DAY FOR A YEAR, shall ye bear your iniquities, even forty years." Thus also we read in the fourth chapter of Ezekiel, that the Lord enjoined this prophet to perform a certain observance for forty days, as typical of a period of forty years; saying, "I have appointed thee EACH DAY FOR A YEAR."— There yet remains one striking circumstance, by which the prophets still further limited the period of Messiah's advent namely, their declaration that it should take place during the subsistence of the second temple. "I will shake all nations," saith the Lord, by Haggai, "and the desire of all nations shall come, and I will fill THIS HOUSE with glory, saith the Lord of Hosts." So also Malachi announces, "the Lord, whom ye seek, shall suddenly COME TO HIS TEMPLE, even the Messenger of the covenant, whom ye delight in; behold he shall come, saith the Lord of Hosts." At a time, accordingly, when men were eagerly looking out for the "desire of all nations," Christ came to that temple, of which, within a few years, not one stone was to be left upon another, and there received the welcome greetings of those "who waited for the consolation of Israel."

IV. The precise PLACE of the Messiah's birth is distinctly pointed out in ancient prophecy. "Thou BETHLEHEM EPHRATAH," saith Micah, "though thou be little among the thousands of Judah, yet out of thee shall he come forth unto me, that is to be ruler in Israel." Had an uninspired penman ventured to predict, from probability alone, the birthplace of the promised King of Judah, he would hardly have fixed it at Bethlehem; which, though truly the city of David, was only the residence of his early years, under the lowly roof of his father Jesse. Such a writer would, on the contrary, have rather led his countrymen to look for this event at Sion, the royal residence. Relying, however, on the prophecy of Micah, the Jews appear to have had a universal expectation that their king was to be born at Bethlehem. So the priests and scribes expressly told Herod, when he, with jealous fear, made inquiry upon the subject. So also, on one occasion, some of the Jews, under the erroneous notion that Christ was a native of Nazareth, where he had been brought up, rejected him, saying, "Shall Christ come out of Galilee? Hath not the Scriptures said, that Christ cometh of the seed of David, and out of the town of Bethlehem, where David was?" It adds, moreover, much weight to the evidence of Scripture prophecy, that the ordinary residence of Christ's mother was at Nazareth; and that the providence of God so ordered, for the fulfilment of the prediction, that she should, notwithstanding, be at Bethlehem at the time of her son's birth. This too, was brought about, not by means of agents who had in view the accomplishment of prophecy, but in obedience to the decree of a Heathen Emperor.

V. Besides the family of which Messiah was to be born, and the time and place of his birth, there were OTHER RE-MARKABLE CIRCUMSTANCES connected with his nativity, which were the subjects of prophecy. Thus Isaiah, in a passage already referred to, declares, "Behold A VIRGIN shall conceive and bear a son, and shall call his name Immanuel;" and this accordingly was fulfilled in the person of Jesus, who was born of Mary, a virgin of Nazareth. Ancient prophecy also in more than one passage, and by the mouth of more than one prophet, foretold, that ere the Lord himself should come forth for the deliverance of his people, a messenger should go before him to prepare his way. Isaiah speaks of "THE VOICE of him that crieth in the wilderness, Prepare ye the way of the Lord; make straight in the desert a high-way for our God." So also Malachi, the last of the prophets, thus speaks in the name of the Lord, "Behold I will send MY MESSENGER, and he shall prepare the way before me, and the Lord whom ye seek, shall suddenly come to his temple." Accordingly, before Jesus Christ commenced his ministry, the voice of John the Baptist was heard in the wilderness of Judea, preaching the preparatory doctrine of repentance for the remission of sins,—declaring, that "there came one after him who was mightier than he, the latchet of whose shoes he was not worthy to stoop down and unloose;"—and expressly pointed out Jesus as the "Lamb of God which taketh away the sin of the World."

VI. The descriptions given by the prophets of Messiah's external RANK and CONDITION are very remarkable. In some of them he is described as a Prince endowed with all glory and power; in others, as placed in the lowest and most abject condition; and there are still others in which both conditions are at once ascribed to him. In the language of Jeremiah, "Behold the days come, saith the Lord, that I will

raise unto David a righteous branch; and a KING shall reig
and prosper, and shall execute judgment and justice on th
earth." "I saw," saith Daniel, "in the night visions, an
behold, one like the Son of Man came with the clouds o
heaven, and came to the Ancient of Days, and they brough
him near before him; and there was given him dominion
and glory, and a kingdom, that all people, nations, and lan
guages should serve him; his dominion is an everlastin
dominion, which shall not pass away, and his kingdom tha
which shall not be destroyed." "The government," sait
Isaiah, "shall be upon his shoulder; of the increase of hi
government and peace there shall be no end." On the othe
hand, the same prophet declares "He is DESPISED and RE-
JECTED of men, a man of sorrows and acquainted with grief;
and we hid, as it were, our faces from him; he was despised,
and we esteemed him not." But this description of the Messiah's humiliation, it ought to be particularly remarked, is
both preceded and closed by representations of his exaltation
and triumph. "Behold," saith the prophet in the preceding
words, "my servant shall deal prudently, he shall be exalted
and extolled and be very high. As many were astonished
at thee; (his visage was more marred than any man, and his
form more than the sons of men;) so shall he sprinkle many
nations, the kings shall shut their mouths at him; for that
which had not been told them, shall they see; and that which
they had not heard, shall they consider." So also in the
concluding words, the prophet, in the name of the Lord, triumphantly declares that, "he will divide him a portion with
the great, and he shall divide the spoil with the strong." In
the following remarkable passage, also, from the same prophet, the lowest humiliation is blended with the loftiest exaltation in the description of the future deliverer. "Thus
saith the Lord, the Redeemer of Israel, and his Holy One, to
HIM, WHOM MAN DESPISETH, to him whom the nation abhorreth, to a servant of rulers; kings shall see and arise, PRINCES
ALSO SHALL WORSHIP, because of the Lord that is faithful,
and the Holy One of Israel, and he shall choose thee." Zechariah likewise exclaims, "Rejoice greatly, O Daughter of
Sion! shout, O Daughter of Jerusalem; behold THY KING
cometh unto thee; he is just, and having salvation; LOWLY,
and riding upon an ass, and upon a colt, the foal of an ass."
The literal fulfilment of this prophecy on Christ's entrance
into Jerusalem is well known. The prediction itself plainly
implies, that Messiah, though a king, was to have none of
the pride and pomp of earthly monarchs. All these appa-

ently conflicting predictions have been strikingly fulfilled in the person of Jesus Christ, the Son of Mary. Who could be more "despised and rejected of men," than this reputed son of a carpenter of Nazareth; born in a stable, and cradled in a manger; the companion of lowly fishermen, and even the friend of publicans and sinners; the very outcasts of the people; the continual subject of scorn and false accusation; who had not where to lay his head; and who died at length the ignominious death of a malefactor on the cross? Yet this despised Nazarene have we seen "exalted to be a Prince and a Saviour, receiving the heathen for his inheritance, and the uttermost parts of the earth for his possession;" "him, whom man despised, whom" his own "nation abhorred," have we ourselves seen "kings and princes arise and worship;" and to him hath been given a "name, which is above every name, at which every knee" doth already begin "to bow, of things in heaven, and things in earth, and things under the earth."

V, VII. It was foretold that Christ should be in a particular manner endowed with THE HOLY SPIRIT. Thus Isaiah, speaking of the Rod of Jesse, says, "The Spirit of the Lord shall rest upon him, the spirit of wisdom and understanding, the spirit of counsel and might, the spirit of knowledge, and the fear of the Lord," &c. Again, he saith, "Behold my servant whom I uphold; mine elect; in whom my soul delighteth: I have put my Spirit upon him." And again "The Spirit of the Lord God is upon me, because the Lord hath anointed me to preach good tidings," &c. It was, accordingly, the boast of the apostles, that "God anointed Jesus of Nazareth with the Holy Ghost, and with power;" and, in proof of this assertion, they could refer not only to the doctrines which he taught, and to the works which he wrought, but also to the visible descent of the Spirit upon him, at the time of his baptism.

VIII. With regard to the MORAL CHARACTER of Messiah, he is described by the prophets as perfectly holy, guileless, humble, patient, gentle, merciful. Isaiah, speaking in the name of the Lord, calls him "My righteous servant." By Jeremiah, he is termed "THE LORD OUR RIGHTEOUSNESS:" and by Daniel, "the Most Holy." Isaiah says, "He had done no violence, neither was any deceit in his mouth." Zechariah, "He is just and having salvation, lowly," &c.— Speaking of his patience, Isaiah saith, "He was oppressed and he was afflicted, yet he opened not his mouth: he is brought as a lamb to the slaughter, and, as a sheep before her shearers is dumb, so he openeth not his mouth."—In reference to his gentleness, the same prophet declares, "He shall not cry, nor lift up, nor cause his voice to be heard in the streets: a bruised reed shall he not break, and the smoking flax shall he not quench." Again, "He shall feed his flock like a shepherd; he shall gather the lambs with his arm, and carry them in his bosom; and shall gently lead those that are with young."—With regard to his mercy, particularly as displayed in compassion to the poor and needy, it would be endless to multiply passages. Neither is it necessary to point out to any one at all acquainted with the life of our blessed Lord, as pourtrayed by the evangelists how eminently he, in all respects, sustained the character which had previously been given of him by the prophets.

IX. The prophets describe the various OFFICES which the Messiah was to execute, for the salvation of his people, viz., those of instruction, expiation, and government. We cannot here recite all the passages, in which the shedding abroad of LIGHT and KNOWLEDGE is ascribed to him. We shall mention only one circumstance connected with this subject, which is the peculiar boast of Christianity,—that its divine author, unlike former teachers, was to address his doctrine, not to the more highly favoured classes only of the community, but also to the poor and the lowly. In the language of Isaiah, "The Spirit of the Lord God is upon me, because the Lord hath anointed me to preach good tidings UNTO THE MEEK." So, also, Jeremiah, speaking in the name of the Lord, of the new covenant which he was to make with the house of Israel and of Judah, declares, "They shall teach no more every man his neighbour, and every man his brother, saying, know the Lord: for they shall all know me, FROM THE LEAST OF THEM, unto the greatest of them, saith the Lord." These predictions were fully accomplished. The first of them our Saviour himself recited, in the synagogue of the city where he was brought up, adding, "This day is this Scripture fulfilled in your ears;" and in answer to John's message, "Art thou he that should come?" he replied, "The poor have the Gospel preached to them."—The Redeemer's EXPIATORY OFFICE is no less clearly pointed out by the prophets. Isaiah declares, "Thou shalt make his soul AN OFFERING FOR SIN. He hath borne our griefs, and carried our sorrows; he was wounded for our transgressions; he was bruised for our iniquities; the chastisement of our peace was upon him; and with his stripes we are healed. The Lord hath laid on him the iniquity of us all. He was cut off out of the land of the living: for the transgression of ny people was he smitten. He hath poured out his soul into death, and he bare the sins of many, and made intercession for the transgressors." So, also, it was revealed to Daniel, that "Messiah should be cut off, but not for himself; and that he should finish the transgression, and make an end of sin, and bring in everlasting righteousness. How all this was fulfilled in the person of Jesus Christ, who, in the language of his apostles, "was made sin for us who knew no sin," it is unnecessary to state.—In treating of the external condition of the Messiah, we have already had occasion to notice some of the prophecies which relate to his KINGLY OFFICE, and the mode of their completion. Suffice it at present, to say, that, in every circumstance, which can be supposed to constitute a great and glorious prince, the fulfilment of prophecy is complete; by the wise and salutary laws which Christ has given to his church,—by the protection which, during so many ages, he has afforded it against all the assaults of its enemies,—and by the triumphant manner, in which, going forth conquering and to conquer, he continues to extend his victorious sceptre over the kingdoms of the earth.

X. The prophets speak of the MIRACULOUS WORKS which Messiah was to perform. "Then," saith Isaiah, "the eyes of the blind shall be opened, and the ears of the deaf shall be unstopped; then shall the lame man leap as an hart, and the tongue of the dumb sing." All this, and much more, it is needless to observe, was literally fulfilled in the person of Christ, who, in testimony of his divine mission, could say, "Go and show John again those things which ye do hear and see; the blind receive their sight, and the lame walk; the lepers are cleansed, and the deaf hear; the dead are raised up!"

XI. The prophetic accounts of the Messiah's LAST SUFFERINGS AND DEATH are delivered with a minute accuracy, which, (if we were not perfectly certain that they were given long before the event,) would lead us to believe that they were historical descriptions rather than predictions. The 53rd chapter of Isaiah, and the 22nd Psalm are particularly striking. With regard to the book of Psalms, we may take this opportunity of observing that, though it is not arranged in our Bibles among the prophetic Scriptures, it possesses all the characteristics of this species of writing, was viewed in this light by the ancient Jews, and is accordingly referred to very frequently, both by our Lord and his apostles, as belonging to this class. The writings of David, in particular, the progenitor and representative of Christ, while applicable to himself only in a remote and figurative sense, were, in many instances, literally fulfilled in the person of Jesus, and in his person only.—Following the order of events, we may notice upon this branch of the subject, in the first place, the singular prophecy of Zechariah, in which he says, "They weighed, for my price, THIRTY PIECES OF SILVER, and the Lord said unto me, CAST IT UNTO THE POTTER; a goodly price that I was prized at of them; and I took the thirty pieces of silver, and cast them to the potter, IN THE HOUSE OF THE LORD." Now, the evangelists tell us, that the price for which Judas covenanted to deliver up his master to the chief priests, was "thirty pieces of silver;" that the traitor, "when he saw that Jesus was condemned, repented himself, and cast down the pieces of silver in the temple;" and that the chief priests "took counsel, and bought with them the potter's field to bury strangers in."—The same prophet, speaking of "the man that is God's fellow," says, "Smite the shepherd, and the sheep shall be scattered." The evangelists inform us that, on the night on which Jesus was betrayed, he, referring expressly to this very passage, told his apostles, "All ye shall be offended because of me this night." The predictions, both of Zechariah and of Jesus, were that night fulfilled. "They all forsook him and fled;" and one of the most valiant actually thrice denied him.—"He was taken," says Isaiah, "from prison and from judgment." The evangelists tell us, that Christ was arrested by order of the chief priests, who kept him a prisoner all night, and delivered him over, next morning, to Pilate, the Roman governor, who sent him to Herod, and at length, upon his return, pronounced judgment against him.—"I gave my back," says Isaiah, "to the smiters." And again, "He was wounded for our transgressions; he was bruised for our iniquities; and with his stripes we are healed." The evangelists tell us, "Pilate took Jesus and scourged him."—Isaiah says, "he is despised and rejected of men;" and again, more particularly, "He hid not his face from shame and spitting." So also the Psalmist complains, "I am a worm, and no man, a reproach of men and despised of the people; all they that see me laugh me to scorn; they shoot out the lip, they shake the head, saying, He trusted on the Lord that he would deliver him; let him deliver him seeing he delighted in him." Compare this with the accounts given by the evangelists of the insults offered to our Lord. While he stood before the high priest, "they did spit in his face and buffetted him, and others smote him, with the palms of their hands. "Herod," also, "with his men of war set him at nought, and mocked him, and arrayed him, in a gorgeous robe." In leading him away from Pilate's judgment-seat, "the soldiers plaited a crown of thorns, and put it upon his head, and a reed in his right hand; and they spit upon him, and took the reed and smote him on the head and mocked him." On the cross too, "they that passed by reviled him, wagging their heads, and saying, if thou be the Son of God, come down from the cross. Likewise also the chief priests mocking him, with the scribes and elders, said, He trusted in God; let him deliver him now, if he will have him." One of the thieves also, "cast the same in his teeth." —The Psalmist says, "They pierced my hands and my feet;" and Zechariah, "They shall look upon me, whom they have pierced, and they shall mourn for him, as one mourneth for his only son," &c. The evangelists tell us of Jesus that "They crucified him," and that "one of the soldiers with a spear pierced his side."—Isaiah says, "He was numbered with the transgressors." The evangelists tell us that he died the death of a malefactor, and that "they crucified two thieves with him."—The cry of agony, which Jesus uttered upon the cross, was that of the prophetic Psalmist, "My God, my God, why hast thou forsaken me."—"They part," saith David, "my garments among them, and CAST LOTS upon my vesture. The evangelists tell us, that "the soldiers, when they had crucified Jesus, took his garments and made four parts, to every soldier a part; and also his coat; now the coat was without seam woven from the top throughout, they said therefore among themselves, Let us not rend it, but cast lots for it, whose it shall be."—"They gave me also," saith the Psalmist again in the same passage, "GALL for my meat, and in my thirst, they give me VINEGAR to drink." Now the evangelists inform us that, when our Redeemer was about to be nailed to the cross, "they gave him vinegar to drink mingled with gall, and when he had tasted thereof, he would not drink;" and that, in the very close of this awful scene, "Jesus saith, I thirst; and they filled a sponge with vinegar, and put it upon hyssop, and put it to his mouth: when Jesus, therefore, had tasted the vinegar, he said, IT IS FINISHED: and he bowed his head, and gave up the Ghost." §XII. The very BURIAL of Jesus is the subject of accomplished prophecy. "He made his grave," saith Isaiah, "with the wicked, and WITH THE RICH in his death." After the sad picture which the prophet had drawn, in the immediately preceding words, of Messiah's low condition, in point of ex-

ternal circumstances and worldly reputation, surely nothin
could be more unlikely, than that he should receive a buria
with the rich. Yet, however obscure and despised had bee
his life, and apparently ignominious his death, all the evan
gelists concur in expressly testifying, that, "there came t
Pilate A RICH MAN of Arimathea, named Joseph, and begge
the body of Jesus, and when Joseph had taken the body, h
wrapped it in a clean linen cloth, and laid it in his ow
new tomb."

XIII. The RESURRECTION of the "Holy One" from th
grave, ere his body should see corruption, and his subsequen
ASCENSION to the right hand of the Father, are thus spoke
of by David in the sixteenth Psalm; "My flesh also sha
rest in hope: for thou wilt not leave my soul in hell, neithe
wilt thou suffer thine Holy One to SEE CORRUPTION: tho
wilt show me the path of life; in thy presence is fulness o
joy: AT THY RIGHT HAND there are pleasures for ever
more." All this, as every Christian, on sure evidence
believes, was literally and fully accomplished in the person
of the Holy Jesus: and that it was thus fully accomplishe
in his person only, has been conclusively argued by two o
his apostles, Peter and Paul, in their discourses on differen
occasions. So, also, the whole of the 110th Psalm, "The
Lord said unto my Lord, sit thou at my right hand," &c.,
refers to Messiah's exaltation, as our blessed Lord himself
and his apostles have clearly shown; and received its accomplishment on the ascension of Christ.

XIV. The prophets foretold several remarkable events,
which were to follow the Messiah's appearance, such as, an
extraordinary and general effusion of the Holy Spirit, the
bringing in of the Gentiles, and the destruction of Jerusalem
with its temple. With regard to the effusion of the HOLY
SPIRIT, Isaiah led his countrymen to look forward to a remarkable era, when "the Spirit should be poured upon them
from on high." And Joel told them, in the name of the
Lord, in language which must to them have been far more
startling, "It shall come to pass afterward, that I will pour
out my Spirit upon ALL FLESH," &c. This promise, which
our Lord, in his last words to his apostles, assured them was
immediately to be accomplished, began to be confirmed on
the memorable day of Pentecost, by the visible and glorious
descent of that Spirit, who afterwards so signally displayed
his Almighty power by the wonderful gifts which he bestowed
on the apostles,—and his impartial goodness, by its being
shed abroad, not upon the Jews alone, but upon Cornelius

so, and other Gentile converts.—On the subject of the
ringing in of the GENTILES, it would be endless to recount
ll that has been written by the prophets. Suffice it, there-
re, to refer to that early declaration of Jacob, that "unto
Shiloh shall the gathering of the nations be ;" and to the no.
ss distinct assurance of Malachi, the last of the prophets,
"From the rising of the sun, even until the going down of
the same, my name shall be great among the Gentiles ; and
in every place incense shall be offered unto my name; and a
pure offering : for my name shall be great among the heaven, saith the Lord of Hosts." 'Of the manner in which
these predictions have been fulfilled, and are still daily fulfilling, the people of this remote land are at once witnesses
and living examples.—The last circumstance, which we have
mentioned, is the predicted DOWNFALL OF JERUSALEM AND
ITS TEMPLE. This event, the last which the mind of a Jew
would be inclined either to imagine or receive, is alluded to
in many passages of the Jewish Scriptures. But of these
the most remarkable is the revelation made to Daniel, in
which it is expressly disclosed, "that the people, of the
prince that shall come, shall destroy the city and the sanctuary," &c. This prophecy was afterwards, on different
occasions, more fully repeated and explained by our blessed
Lord himself, who, on "beholding the city wept over it,
saying, the days shall come upon thee that thine enemies
shall cast a trench about thee, and compass thee round, and
keep thee in on every side, and shall lay thee even with the
ground, and thy children within thee; and they shall not
leave in thee one stone upon another." The total destruction
of the city and temple by the Romans, under all the circumstances foretold in Scripture, is the subject no longer of
prophecy, but of undoubted history.

In reviewing the whole of this subject, the Christian may
triumphantly ask, whether any one of the vast multitude of
circumstances above enumerated "which God spake by the
mouth of his holy prophets, that have been since the world
began," has failed to be fully accomplished in the person of
Jesus Christ,—whether they have ever been accomplished
in the person of any other individual who has yet appeared,
or can be so fully accomplished in the person of any who
may yet appear ? Even if it should be imagined, that the
application of some of the above prophecies to Messiah is at
all doubtful, far more than enough will remain of undoubted
predictions, universally applied by the ancient Jews to their
great promised Deliverer, and all accomplished in the per-

son of Jesus Christ. Nor is it any good objection that th
prophecies, though undoubtedly fulfilled, have in some re
spects, received their accomplishment in a manner differen
from that which the Jews previously expected. This, in truth
adds strong additional weight to the prophetic evidence; a
utterly exclusive of the notion, that the fulfilment had bee
designedly brought to pass by the agents of Christianit
The most satisfactory, doubtless, of all prophecy, is tha
which is fulfilled by the agency either of men who had n
belief in the prophecy, or of those who neither looked fo
nor desired its accomplishment, in the manner which the
themselves have been instrumental in bringing to pass.
The application of this principle to the religion of Christ is
sufficiently obvious.—In conclusion, we shall only further
observe, that of the strong argument arising from prophecy,
the above is necessarily no more than a faint and imperfect
outline; and that the more the subject is considered, the
more shall we be led to exclaim with the eye witnesses o
our Saviour's miracles, "This is of a truth that prophet that
should come into the world."—" Him hath God exalted
with his right hand to be a Prince and a Saviour, to give
repentance unto Israel and the forgiveness of sins."

END.

Printed by E. Couchman and Co., 10, Throgmorton Street, London.

SOME

EXTRACTS

FROM

' *The True Christian's Faith and Experience:* "

By WILLIAM SHEWEN.

FIRST: CONCERNING THE *UNIVERSAL LOVE OF GOD* TOWARDS ALL MANKIND.

SECOND: CONCERNING THE DOCTRINE OF *ELECTION AND REPROBATION.*

In making the following Selections from the writings of an early member of the Society of Friends, it will be seen that the object proposed is *not controversy;* nor a desire to treat at large a point of Christian doctrine, which, perhaps, more than most others, has been made a fruitful source of debate, and, to say no worse, ' of vain jangling" Rather, it is designed practically to apply the truth most surely believed amongst us: "that God was in Christ reconciling *the world* unto himself"—that, " as in Adam all die, even so in Christ shall all be made alive."

LONDON:

Printed for the TRACT ASSOCIATION of the SOCIETY of FRIENDS.

Sold at the DEPOSITORY, 12, Bishopsgate Street Without.

1865.

No. 87.   [*Price 3d. per dozen.*]

EXTRACTS.

CONCERNING THE UNIVERSAL LOVE OF GOD TOWARDS
ALL MANKIND.

THE love of God is universal; his grace, which bringeth
salvation, hath appeared and doth appear unto all men
he hath given a manifestation of his spirit to every ma
to profit withal, even to the rebellious; God so love
the world that he gave his only-begotten Son, that who
soever believeth in him should not perish, but have ever
lasting life; he is the true light, that lighteth every ma
coming into the world; this light is saving, and sufficien
to lead all mankind that love it and walk in it, to him
from whom it comes, where they may inherit life and salvation. God wills not the death of him that dies, neither
doth he desire the death of a sinner, but rather that he
would turn and live: his call is to all men everywhere to
repent: and there is a possibility that all may hear his
voice, repent, and partake of his universal love; be saved
by his grace which hath appeared; profit by the manifestation which he hath given; and be guided out of rebellion by his good Spirit, to believe in him who saves from
perishing, and gives everlasting life. These things are
called for, and exhorted to, throughout the Holy Scriptures; and there is a possibility to obey them; otherwise
all is in vain, the call to all in vain, the appearance of
grace to all in vain, the gift and manifestation of the
Spirit to every one in vain, and the shining of the light
in vain, if men may not obey it and walk in it. So
man's destruction is of himself, and his sores remain un-
cured, and his soul unredeemed, not because there is no
balm in Gilead or because the arm of the Lord is shortened, or his love abated; neither because he hath decreed
any man's destruction from eternity; but because men

will not make use of the balm, nor be gathered by his arm, that is stretched out all the day long, even to the rebellious to save them, nor receive that love that is daily tendered : their eye is blind, and their souls poor, miserable, and naked; not because he hath not eye-salve, fine linen, and treasures of wisdom and knowledge to furnish them withal ;· but because men are taken up with other things, and have no mind to purchase gold tried in the fire, nor white raiment to be clothed : the forbidden fruit seems more beautiful and lovely to desire : the enemy having drawn out man's mind to look after it, he turns his back upon the other; his eye is blinded, and his ear stopped; he cannot see the glory of God to surpass the beauty and glory of all things visible and invisible, nor delight in the hearing of his voice and obeying it : but his stolen water is sweet, and the forbidden fruit is plea-sant to man in this his blind, deaf, and dead estate, wherein he walks in the broad way, and falls into every temptation, bait, and snare of the enemy, that old ser-pent, who, having drawn him thus far, takes him captive at his pleasure. Thus entered sin in the beginning, thus it increaseth, and thus the enemy prevails.

Now, no man in this estate can open that eye which was blinded through transgression, nor unstop that ear, nor save and deliver himself out of the hand of his ene-my, which holds him in sore captivity. Therefore, herein is the universal love of God manifest, that he hath laid help·upon one that is mighty, who is able to save to the uttermost : that he hath appointed and prepared a seed which is able to bruise the serpent's head; and that he hath sown this good and powerful seed in the hearts of all; in the bad ground, as well as in the good; that he hath caused his light to shine in the hearts of all, though in darkness; his rain to fall upon all, just and unjust; and hath called upon all men everywhere. If they will hearken to his voice, turn at his reproof, be gathered by his arm, which is stretched out to save, they shall not miss of salvation : but if they stop their ear, harden their heart, continue in rebellion, and refuse to be reconciled, their destruction is of themselves, and God will be just when he judgeth.

ELECTION AND REPROBATION.

Election and reprobation stand in the two seeds, called the seed of the woman, and the seed of the serpent; and all mankind are partakers of the one, or of the other; as either of these two seeds grows up in them, and as they grow up in the one, or in the other, or join to the one, or to the other; and are born of the one which is incorruptible, or of the other which is corruptible. This seed, which is incorruptible, and hath remained pure throughout all generations, is that in which all nations are blessed (Acts iii. 25), as they come to be born of it. This is it unto which all the promises of God are yea and Amen, which was not made unto seeds, as of many, (as Paul saith, speaking of the seed of Abraham), but of one seed, which is Christ; and they that are Christ's are Abraham's seed and heirs by promise. Gal. iii. 16. 29. The election or choice of God stands in this seed, and all the heavenly blessings, and evangelical promises, come to be enjoyed and inherited by mankind through faith, in this seed, through the growing up of it in them, and through the knowing it to remain in them, and becoming the greatest of all seeds. With this seed, and with all that are born of it, God's election stands sure, and his covenant is kept with it for ever; whom he loves here, he loves to the end; and to all that love this seed, he will be their God, and they shall be his people, the elect, which can never be deceived, nor the gates of hell prevail against.

And the true Christian, who is born of this incorruptible seed, obeys Peter's exhortation, giving diligence to make his calling and election sure: adding to his faith, virtue; and to virtue, knowledge; and to knowledge, temperance; and to temperance, patience; and to patience, godliness; and to godliness, brotherly kindness; and to brotherly kindness, charity: and as he doth these things he shall never fall, but have an entrance ministered abundantly into the everlasting kingdom of his Lord and Saviour Jesus Christ. 2 Pet. i. 5, 6, 7. 10, 11. And he lays aside all malice, and all guile, and hypocrisies, and envies, and all evil speakings, and becomes as a new born babe, desiring the sincere milk of the word, that he may grow up more and more, and increase with the increase of God thereby, until he grows up in the promised seed, in which his calling and election stands, unto the unity of the faith, and of the knowledge of the Son of God, unto a perfect man, unto the measure of the stature of the fulness of Christ, growing up in him in all things, which is the head, even Christ. 1 Pet. ii. 1, 2. This is the mark of the high calling of God in Christ Jesus; and these are the marks, tokens and signs, fruits and effects, which attend and accompany all those who are born of this incorruptible seed, in which their election stands: in, through, and by which their calling and election is made sure. And the true Christian, who is thus elected, being born of this seed, hath not only the witness in himself, and the Spirit of God bearing witness and sealing to his spirit, that he is a child of it; but the fruit of this seed also shows itself forth, and appears, that men may see and behold it, and glorify his Father which is in heaven.

Now the reprobation stands in the seed of the serpent: and all that are joined to it, and become children of it, are reprobate to every good word and work, and go upon their bellies, and dust is their meat; they dwell upon the earth where the wo is, and where the devil is come down among them; they walk upon that ground which is cursed, and inhabit the dark corners thereof; they hate the light, and are reprobate from the presence of God, and from the glory of his power; children of disobedience and wrath, in whom the old serpent rules, holding them in sore captivity.* And as in this state of reprobation, they abide, they are children of the devil, and his lust they do, his servants and slaves they are, and cannot cease from sin, nor enjoy the many glorious promises made to the seed of the woman, nor know the serpent's head in them bruised by it, being reprobate from that faith which gives victory over him. In whomsoever his seed grows up, enmity increaseth in them against

* Marks of reprobation.

the seed of the woman, against the promised seed, and all the children of it; hence arose Cain's envy, Ishmael's mocking, and Esau's rage; and the same is continued in that generation or birth, down to the present age; this is that birth which is after the flesh; which always did, and doth to this day, persecute him that is born after the Spirit: this is the seed of the wicked which shall be cut off, and of evil doers that shall never be renowned. Ps. xxxvii. 28. Isa. xiv. 20.

But out of this estate of reprobation and deep pit of misery, wherein a great part of mankind is held, the testimony of the true Christian is, that God hath appointed a means of deliverance, salvation, and redemption. There is, during the day of visitation, a possibility of being born again of the other seed, the incorruptible seed, wherein the election stands; children of disobedience and wrath may become children of God, and partake of his grace and mercy :* the seed of the serpent may be rooted out of the heart of man, though it hath grown there long and filled it with its fruit; and the good seed of the kingdom may spring up and grow there; and every thorn, briar, thistle, and plant, which our heavenly Father hath not planted, which hindereth its growth, may be pulled up; and they that have borne the earthly image, may bear the heavenly; and they that have yielded their members servants to unrighteousness, may yield them servants to righteousness; those that are foolish may become wise; those that are disobedient and deceived may become obedient and undeceived; those that serve divers lusts and pleasures, and live in malice and envy, hateful and hating one another, may come to witness victory over, and redemption from, all these things. This testimony is plentifully borne witness to in the Holy Scriptures: as Paul wrote to Titus, saying, We ourselves were sometimes foolish, disobedient, deceived, serving divers lusts and pleasures, living in malice and envy, hateful, and hating one another (Tit. iii. 3.) : these were all the fruits and effects of the evil seed; these were all fruits of the ground that is cursed; and in this estate

* A possibility that the reprobate may become elect.

ey were reprobate concerning the faith, and children of rath as well as others, but, saith he, after the kindness d love of God our Saviour toward man appeared; not r works of righteousness which we have done, but cording to his mercy he saved us, by the washing of generation, and renewing of the Holy Ghost, which he ed on us abundantly through Jesus Christ our Saviour. o, in the kindness, love, and free mercy of God, by the ashing of regeneration, or new birth, they became translanted out of the old into the new, out of the seed f the serpent into the seed of the woman, out of the probate state into the chosen and elected state; taken it of the wild olive, and planted or grafted into the true ne, that brings forth fruit, which glads the heart of od and man. And he is ready to do the same in this ge for all who love his appearance, and hearken to his oice and obey it, and who shut their ears against the oice of the serpent: which is possible to be done. These all enjoy God's salvation, and partake of his love and indness, which the saints enjoyed in former ages, and do n this age, and which are freely tendered *to all* for their verlasting good. For God hath not, as some affirm, redestinated or fore-ordained the greatest part of mankind, or any part, to everlasting perdition; nor made my fixed decree, that so many and no more, shall be aved, and all the rest damned, and that this decree vas established before mankind was brought forth, without having respect to either good or evil that they hould do.

This is a doctrine which is condemned, being contrary o the Gospel or glad tidings of peace and reconciliation! nd inconsistent with all the dispensations of God's love owards lost man: the end designed of the Lord in all iis promises, appearances, and dispensations before the aw, under the law, and in the days of the evangelical rophets, who saw and prophesied of glorious things, vhich God would bring to pass for the universal good of nankind: for Isaiah saw that day in which the Lord vith his sore, great, and strong sword, should punish eviathan, the piercing serpent, even leviathan that rooked serpent, and slay the dragon which is in the sea;

he saw that the abundance of the sea should be converted, and the forces of the gentiles should come unto him whom God hath appointed to be his salvation to the ends of the earth (Isa. xxvii. 1.; lx. 5) ; and he spake o a time wherein the Lord would gather all nations and tongues to come and see his glory, which he had given for a light to the gentiles, and for the glory of his people Israel, to finish transgression, and make an end of sin, and bring in everlasting righteousness (Dan. ix. 24.) ; to destroy the devil and his works, to repair the breach, and restore paths to dwell in, even paths of holiness, wherei the wayfaring man, though a fool, cannot err (Isa. lviii. 22 ; xxxv. 8.) : this is the end or substance of all the dispensations of God; and many have been, and are, living witnesses of the same; and no man is exempted, by any decree of God, from the enjoyment of these things.

Intending brevity, and hoping the light of the glorious Gospel will cause this destructive, pernicious doctrine, (which limits the efficacy of divine grace,) to vanish away, I forbear to enlarge, with a breathing to the Lord that people may come to know the fallow ground ploughed up, and the hard clods broken, and their hearts made tender and honest, that the good seed of the kingdom, wherein the election stands, may spring and grow up, and bear fruit in them to everlasting life, and the seed of the serpent rooted out, and he and all his works destroy- ed; this is the glorious liberty which the whole creation groans for, and which some already enjoy : praises to God for ever, whose love extends to all, whose arm is stretched out to help all, whose sceptre of salvation is held forth to all, whose desire is, that all may come to the knowledge of his truth, and be saved.

END.

Printed by E. Couchman and Co., 10, Throgmorton Street, London.

A TREATISE

CONCERNING

THOUGHTS AND IMAGINATIONS.

BY WILLIAM SHEWEN.

REVISED FROM THE THIRD EDITION PRINTED 1769.

EVIL thoughts and imaginations are great troublers of the world; and it is a great misery, when man is given up to follow his own evil thoughts and imaginations. A sore judgment was pronounced against the disobedient, rebellious Jews, by Jeremiah, who said, " Hear, O Earth! behold the Lord will bring evil upon this people, even the fruit of their own thoughts." And the Lord, by the prophet Isaiah, said, " I have spread out my hand all the day unto a rebellious people, which walked in a way that was not good, after their own thoughts;" these thoughts were thoughts of iniquity, and the act of violence accompanied them. It is written, also, " every imagination of the thoughts of man's heart was only evil continually." And very great is the misery, bondage, and slavery of man in this state; he is an enemy to God, to himself, to his neighbour, and to his brother; wasting and destruction are in his paths; and the way of peace he knoweth not."

Now, reader, that which is principally on my mind, is to set before thee a certain infallible way, by which thou mayest be saved from following or obeying thy own thoughts, and gain strength against, and get victory over all thy evil imaginations; and also, attain to good thoughts and heavenly meditations in the room thereof; and know " every thought brought into captivity to the obedience of Christ." And when thou art restored from thy fallen state, into the state that man was in before he transgressed, even as into the garden of God, thou must then dress and keep the garden,

No. 88.   *[Price 4d. per dozen].*

even the garden of thy heart. Thou must then watch over, and, in the wisdom and power of God, govern thy thoughts, lest the serpent beguile thee as he beguiled Eve.

Understand then, first, that out of the ground, from which evil thoughts and imaginations arise, spring all the briers, thorns, and thistles, and other hurtful weeds in man, in whose heart they began to spring, even as soon as he began to lose his faith in God his Maker, and to hearken to the voice of the serpent, and to give credit to his lies: these produced a vain thought; from which the false hope sprung, that he, by eating the forbidden fruit, should better his condition, and that they should be as gods, according as the serpent told the woman. By this false hope, grounded upon the thoughts and imaginations, the first transgression entered. Then, when the temptation was entered into, and sin committed, thoughts and imaginations began to multiply and to fill the disobedient, earthly heart of man; who, having now turned his back upon that which was heavenly, slighted the voice and command of God, who before was his teacher and lawgiver, and lent his ear to the wicked one, and gave up his mind and heart to obey him, even thinking this was all for the best. Thus poor man being deceived with vain thoughts and false hopes, lost his dwelling-place in paradise; in which, after he had transgressed, he still thought to remain. He was soon convinced he had done amiss in eating the forbidden fruit; and fear possessed his heart, when he heard the voice of God in the cool of the day; and, therefore, he sought means to cover and hide himself from the sight of God: but herein his thoughts were vain, and his endeavours to no purpose; the woman, the man, and the serpent, all received the fruit of their doings. Nothing but life; good, and blessing, were known before; now death, evil, and cursing, the fruit of disobedience, became the daily companions of mankind, who found, and still find by woful experience, that saying true, "when sin is finished it brings forth death."

Thus man lost his innocency and his place in the garden which God planted, through neglecting the work which God appointed him to do, which was to dress it, and to keep it. And I testify to all the wise in heart, that after they have found that which was lost, and witnessed a restoration into innocency—into spiritual Eden—they have work there to do. Dressing and keeping are two very significant words: they were the business of man in the beginning, in the state of innocency. If he had not neglected this work, and slighted the light, power, wisdom, and glory of God with which he was replenished, he had never fallen. When tempted in thought, if he had watched in the light and wisdom of God, he would have discovered the tendency of the temptation, and have prevented its coming to a desire and act; but, first giving place to a selfish thought, it soon sprang into a hunger or desire, and thence into an act. This is also the progress of sin at the present day; which mankind in innocency had, and still have, power and wisdom from God to prevent, if they abide in this power and wisdom, and keep in the light and strength of God, which are as near as the temptation can be, and sufficient to preserve: and where this work is neglected, men, yea, holy men, fall and sin after the simili-tude of Adam's transgression, and are beguiled as Eve was beguiled; and are drawn out of innocency, after they have attained to it. Therefore, let none be high-minded, but let all fear, and take Christ, the second Adam, for an example, who, when he was tempted, did not desire after the things presented though very specious in appearance, and accom-panied by very large promises; even as were those presented to the first Adam; but it is written that while the temptation lasted, Christ eat nothing: he gave no place to selfish thoughts, or to the enticements of the enemy. Let all the children of the light follow his example, and the powerful salvation of God shall surround them; "neither height nor depths, angels, principalities, nor powers, things present, or things to come, shall be able to separate them from the love of God in Christ Jesus."

Evil thoughts and imaginations are of a multiplying nature, and they increase and take root in the generality of mankind; who through evil works, are restrained from the life of God, and remain degenerate plants sprung from the seed of the evil doer, dwelling and labouring in that ground which God hath cursed. In this state, man knows not the Seed of the woman to bruise the serpent's head, and to redeem and preserve him from obeying his own thoughts and imaginations, which are evil; and which, indeed, in this state can be no otherwise, whether they lead into self-sinning or self-righteousness; both of which are abomination to the Lord, and destructive to the well-being of mankind, both temporally and eternally. All the wickedness that has been brought forth and acted in the world since the beginning, began first in thought; and the thought being cherished and joined to by the mind and will, it increased into words an actions. That which is clean cannot proceed from that whic is unclean; the heart of mankind in the fall is universall corrupt, and desperately wicked; and, the thoughts an imaginations thereof are evil continually: and before it ca be otherwise, there is an absolute necessity to experience th heart to be cleansed, and created anew. The ground mus be made good before the good seed can grow and flourish before good and heavenly thoughts and meditations ca spring and remain therein. But when this state is know and enjoyed, then abide with Him, dwell and walk with Him who hath wrought these mighty things in thee, and for thee and in his wisdom and power, dress and keep the garden o the heart with all diligence, that that which would defile ente not, as it did in the beginning, neither creep in again, for thi is possible. Therefore as God put man into Eden in th beginning when he was a noble plant, wholly a right seed, t dress and keep the garden; so the Son of God now, to thi age, saith, "Watch and pray lest ye enter into temptation;' and an apostle saith, "Take heed lest as the serpent beguile Eve, through his subtilty, so he could corrupt your minds from the simplicity that is in Christ."

This I testify from certain knowledge, that God hath ordained means, whereby man may come to experience his foul heart cleansed and sanctified, notwithstanding it should be so corrupt that nothing good proceeds out of it, neither anything that is heavenly springs up in it: his state may become like that of some of the Christians of the primitive times, of whom it was said, "Such were some of you, but ye are washed, ye are sanctified, ye are justified," &c. "The fallow ground may be ploughed up" and bear seed, "the wilderness may become a fruitful field," and "streams may break forth in the desert, which may come to rejoice and blossom as a rose;" "crooked things may be made straight, and rough places smooth;" "mountains may be brought down and removed, yea, melted at the presence of God;" and "the low valleys may be exalted; the wilderness may become like Eden, and the desert like the garden of the Lord." All these mighty works and wonders hath the Lord wrought in this age, in and for a remnant, who are come to the fulfilling of the prophecies, are living witnesses of the same, and in his Holy Spirit and power proclaim, that the love and mercy of God towards lost man is universal; that his hand is stretched forth to help him out of the snare, pit, ıd deep, dark dungeon, whereinto he has fallen; out of hich he cannot by all his strength, wisdom, and invention, elp himself; and to set him at liberty, that he may run in ıe ways of God's commandments with delight, and lay aside l his thoughts and inventions, wherein he corrupted ımself; and to bring him into such a state, as that he may e able to think good thoughts, speak good words, and do ood works; and to avoid the contrary.

Having received understanding of the means God hath rdained for the good and salvation of mankind; and being ›mewhat acquainted with the two great mysteries of godness and iniquity, and the way and working of each, my esire is, to impart something of the same in a few words; ıd to instruct those to whom this, my testimony, may come, ow they may be rid' of those troublesome companions, amely, evil thoughts and imaginations, that arise in their earts while corrupt; and how their hearts may be purified ıd made a holy habitation for God, as the heart of man was efore sin entered, and innocency was lost.

The way that leadeth thereto, I declare to be as follows: ıd whoever thou art that hast a desire to find that which as lost, observe, believe, and receive what I say as truth; ot to be received or learned by tradition, but by the experiıental, powerful work of the Spirit of truth in thy own ıind; and what I' have said or shall say, is, and shall be, ccording to the Holy Scriptures, and witnessed to by them; ›r I cannot write contrary to them, being in unity with ıem, and with the just men's spirits that wrote them. Then, now thou, O man! whoever thou art, and whatever thy ıoughts and imaginations may be; how far soever thou art ın in corruption, darkness, and degeneration from the state f innocency, purity, and holiness; that a measure of divine ght attends thee. Though thou be darkness, or in darkness, ; shines in thee, in order to show thee thy way out of the arkness. Though thou be degenerated and run from God ıto the earth, yet this pure Spirit of God follows thee, and ılls thee back; and thou mayest in this state hear it as a oice behind thee saying, "Return, return; this is the way; ʳalk in it." This is the kindness and love of God to thee in is Son, who died for the sins of mankind; who is the light f the world, and lighteth every one that cometh into the ʳorld. If thou obey the light of the Son of God, though ɦou wert dead in sin, and buried as in a grave, thou shalt ɾise and come forth and live before him; the bars and gates

of hell shall not be able to retain thee. But if thou sligh
and despise the light of God that visits thee, and shut thin
ear against his voice, and rebel against him, and follo\
thine own thoughts and imaginations, doing the thing tha
is evil, he will witness against thee; for "the eye of th
Lord runs to and fro through the earth, beholding the evi
and the good." "The word that is nigh in the mouth, an
in the heart, which is quick and powerful, sharper than an
two-edged sword, pierces even to the dividing asunder c
soul and spirit, and of the joints and marrow, and it discernet
the thoughts and intents of the heart." This is the candl
by which the Lord searcheth Jerusalem : from him th
shadow of death cannot hide, nor the rocks and mountain
cover or defend. The Spirit of truth convinceth the worl
of sin, and sets men's sins in order before them, and reprove
and smites in secret for evil, and brings to judgment th
hidden things of darkness. From the eye or light of th
Lord, thou canst no more hide thyself than Adam and Cai
could. Though thou shouldst hate the light which showet
thee thy thoughts, and love the darkness so as to dwell in it
yet the light or eye of God will pursue thee and find the
out. Neither hell, nor darkness, nor the uttermost parts o
the earth, can secure thee from the just condemnation of
God, if thou hate the shining of his light, and stop thine ear
against his voice and teaching. While thou doest so, thou
choosest the way of death, and neglectest the means of
salvation that God hath ordained : "for this is the condemnation of the world, that light is come into it, and men love
darkness rather than light, because their deeds are evil."

Now at the first step towards restoration and everlasting
happiness, thou art required to turn thy mind from the
darkness in which thou dwellest, to the light, or Spirit of
God, and to decline the power of Satan that works in the
darkness and to embrace the power of God ; and when thou
dost but begin to do so, thou wilt find the scales begin to fall
from thine eyes, and the veil to be taken off thy heart, and
the fetters and chains of darkness to be loosed, and the
prison-doors of sin to be opened. So when thy candle is
lighted, and thine eye opened, thou wilt discern thy way out
of darkness, and see, as it were, the angel of the Lord going
before thee, and guiding thee in the right way ; and thou
wilt also perceive what is in thy house, and clearly understand what hath lodged in the dark room of thy heart. And
when thou comest to see things as they are, thou wilt receive

wisdom to give them names according to their nature, and to judge righteously concerning them. And as thou lovest this light thou wilt be enabled by it to divide betwixt thought and thought, and will begin to make conscience of a thought; and to hate every vain thought. And when thou canst not be easily rid of vain thoughts, nor remove them from their old lodging-place, thou wilt breathe and cry to the Lord in the spirit, as one of old did, who was burdened and oppressed with their company:—" Search me, O God: and know my heart: try me, and know my thoughts; and see if there be any wicked way in me, and lead me in the way everlasting." This is the cry which the Lord hears and will answer.

Jeremiah said to Jerusalem, " Wash thy heart from wickedness that thou mayest be saved; how long shall thy vain thoughts lodge within thee ?" Now the only way to dislodge vain thoughts and to be rid of their company, is to show them no countenance, to make no provision for them, and to give them no entertainment; but by the light of God, which discovers them to be thy enemies, to judge them; and in thy thoughts and imaginations, to give them no regard: and though they do and may rise, pursue, and compass thee about like bees, yet, keeping thy eye fixed in the light and power of God, thou wilt see them in due time scattered as chaff before a fierce wind, and destroyed as stubble before a devouring fire.

As thou comest to believe in the light, and to trust in the power of God, thou wilt become a child of the light, and wilt soon be able to say, the darkness is past, and the true light now shineth, and wilt receive that primitive wisdom which man had in the beginning; but in which he abode not, through looking at the temptation and beauty of the thing presented to his eye. The woman was deceived in her thoughts; in her judgment and understanding was she beguiled, before she obeyed the tempter so far as to eat the fruit, which appeared good for food, pleasant and desirable, and able to make her wise; and being deceived, she hoped to find the serpent's words true; and to become more wise and more happy by taking the serpent's counsel; but instead thereof, she fell into the depth of misery. The same danger still attends the children of light; the sons and daughters of God. Adam was a son of God before the transgression; and it is only such as are in the restoration, children of the light and of the day, that are capable of falling as Adam and Eve did, and of sinning after the similitude of Adam's transgres-

sion, and of losing innocency, purity, holiness, and uprightness, as they did, and of being driven, as out of the garden,
of God, as they were. Such as were never in it spiritually,
and never dwelt in the state of restoration, innocency, purity,
and holiness, cannot be said to fall from, or to lose it.
Children of darkness, and of the devil, who, dwelling in the
region and shadow of death, never knew what the life of
purity and holiness was, nor what the simplicity of the Gospel
of Christ was, cannot be so beguiled of the serpent as was
Eve, nor lose that they never knew, nor had; yet such are
beguiled of the serpent in another sort; not of what they
have had, or did once enjoy, but of what they might have
had, and ought to enjoy; and this he effects by keeping
their eyes and minds abroad, and by persuading them to
follow any other thing, and to walk in any other way, rather
than to turn the eye of their minds inward, to the light,
word, power, and Spirit of God; which shines, speaks, and
works in man, in order to lead, to teach, to guide, and to
direct him in the way of life and salvation; and to bring him
into the glorious liberty of the sons of God; into a perfect
translation from darkness to light, and from the kingdom
and power of Satan to the kingdom and power of the Son of
God, and to "know Christ to be made unto him, wisdom
and righteousness, sanctification and redemption."

This is a blessed end for which God sent his Son, a light
into the world, even to enlighten the Gentile and the Jew,
the professor and the profane; that they through him might
believe, and receive eternal life, and enter into that blessed
rest which God hath prepared for his people; which the
primitive Christians, who believed, entered into; and in
which they did not speak their own words, nor think their
own thoughts, nor do their own works, but their Heavenly
Father spake in them; and their thoughts were of God, and
he wrought all their works in them and for them. This is a
blessed state indeed; and those who have entered into this
rest, which God hath prepared, have come to witness and
experience these things, in this age, as the primitive
Christians did in ages past.

While any are found thinking their own thoughts, speaking
their own words, and doing their own works, though under
a profession of Christianity, they cannot enter into the rest
which God hath prepared; but they may create to themselves false rests, and kindle a fire, and walk by the light of
their own sparks, but in the end they must lie down in sorrow.

True rest and peace are obtained through faith in Christ, nd a true self-denial : a dying to self-sinning, and to self-ghteousness, to self-thinking and working, to contriving nd inventing, to self-wisdom and understanding : all these iings must be denied, and brought to nothing. Feeding pon these things occasioned, and occasions the curse, and l the labour, trouble, sorrow, and torment that has attended, nd does attend mankind since the fall. To death they must l come; and man must cease from his own works, as God id from his, before a sitting down in the kingdom of God in be witnessed.

Now thou who art a child of light, understanding this one iing for thy comfort and encouragement, in thy warfare ʒainst evil thoughts : that, notwithstanding a multitude of iem arise in thee, and troops thereof attend thee, which are l themselves sinful ; yet if thou join not with them in thy ind, will, and understanding, they are not thy thoughts, either shall the evil thereof be imputed unto thee. If thou ɔvest the light, and keepest thy mind joined to it, even to ie Spirit of God, or appearance of Christ in thee, which iscovereth all temptations unto thee, in the very thought nd first appearance of them ; thou art becoming one with ie Lord in mind and spirit, notwithstanding in thy members iere is a law or power that wars against thee ; and, as thou bidest with the Lord, having thy soul waiting upon him, ven as the eye of a maid waits upon the hand of her iistress, he will save and deliver thee, and subdue all thine nemies, even those of thy own house, which are thy reatest enemies.

Though temptations may, and will attend thee, yet it is o sin to be tempted ; neither art thou to account thyself, or to be accounted a sinner, because sin and vain thoughts iay present themselves in thee, in thy state of warfare ; but hou mayest say as Paul did, " It is no more I, but sin that welleth in me ; and, that in me, that is in my flesh, dwells o good thing : " which flesh, as regards its affections and ists, thou art now in the way to know, to wither as the rass, and the glory of it to become as the faded flower of he field, and sin that dwelleth therein to be destroyed, and he creature of God's making to be preserved, the earthen essel that holds the heavenly treasure to be sanctified and aved, and delivered from the yoke of bondage under which he whole creation of God groans. And this thou shalt ertainly arrive at, as thou keepest thine eye upon thy

Saviour, thy light, thy way, thy captain, whom thou wilt perceive to go before thee, conquering, and to conquer, till all his and thy enemies be subdued and destroyed, and thou be made as a king and a priest unto God, and art able to say as the primitive Christians did, as he is, so are we, in this present world," being made pure, holy, righteous, harmless, and innocent, and in all things resigned to the will of God. When thou comest into this state thou wilt understand and receive what I say; but till then it will be as a mystery, and a hard saying unto thee.

Take heed of thinking, willing, and running; that obtains not the prize. Stand still and see the salvation of God. Mind, above all, the arm of his power in thee, which is able to suppress thy thoughts, to mortify thy will, to stop thy running, and to give thee strength to resist the devil, and make him flee, and to furnish thee to every good word and work, and, to give thee dominion over thy own spirit, whose property is to be swift in thought, eager in desire, and restless in the accomplishment thereof.

It is written, " he that hath rule over his own spirit is better than he that takes a city:" but he that hath no rule over his own spirit, is like a city broken down, and withou walls. These things are infallibly true. while the usurpe keeps the throne, the Prince of Peace, and his peaceabl government are not known. Tribulation and anguish com upon every soul of man that doeth evil, that thinketh an imagineth evil, and that yields his members servants t unrighteousness let his opinion, profession, and talk of religion, be what it may. Without turning from sin, and witnessing a finishing or ending of it, and righteousness being set up in its room, the wages and reward of sin will be received, and the fruit of evil thoughts and doings will be the possession.

To live under the Government of Christ, knowing him to sway his sceptre in the heart, and to be established in the throne thereof, is a heavenly state: but this none come to enjoy, till they have first known him to sit as a refiner with fire, and as a fuller with soap: and as a spirit of judgment and burning; and, as the stronger, to dispossess the strong man, spoil all his goods, sweep and cleanse the house, and to furnish it again with heavenly goods, thoughts, desires, and meditations, and in all things else that become the house of the Lord.

It is the duty of a Christian to watch in the light against

l thoughts, and to use the axe of God which is laid to the
t of them, that their springing again may be hindered,
the end of them prevented; so also, it is the duty of
ry one, when good thoughts and desires spring in the room
reof, to cherish them, and to join with them, in keeping
eye unto the Lord, that begat them, or raised them up
the heart: these being thoughts of purity, peace, righte-
ness, holiness, and joy in the inward man; such thoughts
thou of thyself canst not think—these are comfortable
ughts, justifying and excusing thoughts, thoughts that
l stand approved in the light; and the tendency and end
them are good, even as pleasant fruit to the soul: such
sed David to say, "How precious are thy thoughts unto
, O God! how great is the sum of them: if I would count
m, they are more in number than the sand; when I
ake I am still with thee." As thou lovest the light, and
ghtest in the law of God, and meditatest therein, these
d thoughts will multiply and increase in thee, to thy great
tent and satisfaction. But the thoughts of the wicked
sin; and sin brings trouble, anguish, and torment, men
accused or excused in their thoughts. It is said
elshazzar was so much troubled in his thoughts, that his
untenance was changed, and the joints of his loins were
osed, and his knees smote together. Many are the amazing,
rmenting thoughts that attend the wicked, "whose feet
n to do evil, and who make haste to shed innocent blood;
eir thoughts are thoughts of iniquity; wasting and
struction are in their paths; the way of peace they know
ot: and there is no judgment in their goings."
"The thoughts of the righteous are right, and those that
mmit their way to the Lord, their thoughts shall be
tablished:" and it is a blessed state indeed; to have good
oughts established in the heart. Those who enjoy such a
ate can go forth, and come in, in peace; lie down and
se up in peace; live and walk in peace; and praise the
od of peace, who is blessed for evermore. And this is the
eace—the inward peace—which the world with all its
easures and pleasures cannot give, nor by its frowns take
way; and this peace is the portion of all that get victory
ver their own thoughts, imaginations, lusts, desires, and
fections; and that keep in the wisdom and power of God,
hen good thoughts are established in them: and they are
us made partakers of the divine nature, so that they as
aturally think good thoughts—thoughts of love, peace, and

obedience in this state, as they did the contrary while in th
degenerate state. In this state of innocency and harmless
ness, it is, however, necessary to be diligent in the wisdor
of God, to dress and keep the garden of the heart, les
having found honey, thou feed thyself without fear, ea
and drink, and rise up to play; and so through plenty grov
idle and wanton, and forget the Lord, and let his benefit sli
out of thy mind; and slight his commandments, and le
pride, and exaltation, and a selfish spirit, grow up agair
as the first Adam, and others did, who are mentioned ir
the Holy Scriptures, "which are written for our learning
and admonition; upon whom the ends of the world are
come." Wherefore, "let him that thinketh he standeth
take heed lest he fall."

END.

London : Printed by E. Couchman & Co., 10, Throgmorton Street; for the
TRACT ASSOCIATION of the SOCIETY OF FRIENDS. Sold at the DEPOSITORY,
12, Bishopsgate Street Without.—1865.

A BRIEF NOTICE

OF

CHRISTIAN DOCTRINE,

AS HELD BY THE

RELIGIOUS SOCIETY OF FRIENDS.

In compiling this brief notice of Christian Doctrine, as held by the Society of Friends, several of the works of the Society on the subject have been consulted. Among these may be enumerated Barclay's Apology, Tuke's Principles of Friends, Gurney on the distinguishing Views and Practices of the Society of Friends, &c. —To these the reader is referred for further information.

THE religious Society of Friends have uniformly declared their belief in One only-wise, Omnipotent, and Eternal God: the Creator and Preserver of all things, infinite in every glorious attribute and perfection; the inexhaustible source of all good, as well as of all happiness : and the only worthy object of adoration, worship, and praise, from angels and from men.

They believe that the Holy Scriptures of the Old and New Testament were given by inspiration of God : and that they contain the perfect and authentic declaration of christian faith.

They believe that there is one God the Father, of whom are all things :

That there is one Lord Jesus Christ, the only begotten of the Father, the Redeemer and Saviour of men :

That there is one Holy Spirit, the promise of the Father and the Son, the Leader, Comforter, and Sanctifier of his people, and that these Three are one.

They believe that "the Word," who was in the beginning with God, and was God, "is the true light which lighteth every man that cometh into the world;" that, in the fulness of time, "the Word was made flesh," and dwelt amongst men; that He, the Lord Jesus Christ, was born

No. 89.   [*Price 3d. per dozen.*]

of the Virgin Mary; that he led a life of perfect holiness setting us an example that we should follow his steps; that He suffered under Pontius Pilate, the ignominious death of the cross: that he was crucified outside the gates of Jerusalem, the propitiation and expiatory sacrifice for the sins of the whole world; that he arose again from the dead, ascended up on high, and is set down on the right hand of God, "where he ever liveth to make intercession for us;" and all men are, by nature, through the fall of our first parents, in a state of spiritual death, naturally prone to evil, and enslaved by the power of Satan; that all are in a situation in which, without the salvation of Jesus Christ, they must be eternally lost; and that the remission of sins, of which any partake, is only through, and by virtue of the one "offering of the body of Jesus Christ;" "for there is none other name under heaven, given among men, whereby we must be saved."

And seeing that Jesus Christ "gave himself a ransom for all," the Society of Friends have always maintained the belief in the universality of that grace which comes by Him, and that all the families of the earth are, through Him, blessed with the offer of eternal life and salvation; that the forgiveness of sins, and the gift of the Holy Spirit are offered to all men through Him; and that, by the operation of this blessed gift, all are favoured with th visitations of the love of God, convincing them of sin and attracting them to a life of holiness. By this Spirit the Patriarchs and the holy men of old, who lived unde the Law, walked acceptably before God. The ancien prophets distinctly foretold its more plenteous effusion and its powerful and life-giving effects under the Gospe dispensation; and Christ himself declared, that it wa. expedient that he should go away, that He might send the Comforter, the Spirit of Truth, who should come in his name and guide them into all truth. Thus, the pardon of sin is obtained through Him whom God hath set forth to be a propitiation, through faith in his blood; and freedom from sin is experienced through the power o his Spirit working mightily in the heart.

A holy and constant watchfulness unto prayer is re quired to preserve the mind alive to the guidance of th

Holy Spirit; who is a swift witness for God in the soul, and who if diligently sought after and waited for, produces that tenderness of spirit, and that quickness of understanding in the fear of the Lord, which are essential to a growth in grace.

Apprehending that in the doctrine and practice of many professing Christians, there has been much departure from the purity and spirituality of the religion of Christ, as set forth in the New Testament, Friends have been led to adopt those important distinctions which characterize them as a body.

1. Knowing that the worship of God can only be rightly performed "in spirit and in truth," and feeling that God alone is acquainted with the spiritual condition of those assembled, Friends have been led, when met for the performance of public worship, (a duty which they have ever felt themselves called upon faithfully to perform,) to prefer a state of silent, inward communion with God, to any formularies, or to any words, however eloquent, unless uttered from the heart, and under the influence of the Holy Spirit. Hence they assemble together in silence, looking unto God who has promised to draw nigh unto those who draw nigh unto Him. The living members of Christ, when met in his name, know Him to minister to their several conditions, and to enable them to pour out their souls before God, in prayer and praise. They are favoured at times unitedly to feel that Christ is their heavenly president; and in the fellowship of the Holy Spirit, they are refreshed together in Him. The experience of Friends has proved that a state of silence is peculiarly adapted to promote that reverent dependence upon divine help, and that humiliation and contrition which prepare the heart to offer that homage due from frail, finite beings, to Him who is the " High and Lofty One, who inhabiteth eternity, whose name is Holy."

2. Friends believe that a right qualification for preaching the Gospel does not depend upon human learning; and that to subject any to a course of scholastic teaching as an essential preparation for the ministry, is to interfere with that work of the Spirit of God, which alone can render man a fit instrument for the promulgation of divine

truth; that as, in the earliest period of the Christia
church, the Holy Spirit was poured upon servants an
upon handmaidens, agreeably to ancient prophecy, s
the gift of the ministry is still bestowed, according t
the divine will, without respect to sex, or to any merel
external circumstances. Friends are also deeply im
pressed with the belief, that the qualification for th
ministry can be derived only from God, and that n
minister ought to address an audience, met for th
solemn purpose of worshipping the Almighty Creatoi
unless immediately influenced and assisted to do s
by the Holy Spirit. Our Lord Jesus Christ, whe
sending forth his disciples to proclaim the "coming o
his kingdom," in accordance with the free spirit of th
Gospel, commanded his disciples, saying, "Freely y
have received, freely give;" and the Society of Friend
have always believed it right to act upon this principle
and to bear a testimony against all pecuniary remune
ration for the preaching of the Gospel, and against al
demands for the support of a priestly establishment.

3. Friends believe that the ceremonial observances o
the Jewish Law were abolished, in point of obligation
when the New Covenant was established by the death o
Christ; they believe also that no ceremonial rites wer
instituted by Christ as parts of the Gospel dispensation
The rite of Baptism with Water, and that of the parti
cipation of Bread and Wine, usually denominated th
Sacrament of the Lord's Supper, are, therefore, in thei
estimation, not binding upon Christians. They believ
there is but one baptism belonging to the Christian dis
pensation, the essential baptism of Christ by the Hol
Ghost; they believe also that the only true Supper of th
Lord is the spiritual participation of his flesh and blood
with which he feeds and sustains those who freely ope
the door of the heart unto Him. It appears plain t
them, that the principle on which ceremonial rites ar
founded, appertains to the Old Covenant, and that suc
rites are not in accordance with that entirely spiritua
experience, which the Scriptures describe as so distin
guishing a feature of the Gospel: "For the kingdom o
God is not meat and drink, but righteousness, and peace

nd joy, in the Holy Ghost." In-consequence of this iew, Friends have always declined the use-of external ites; but they feel the absolute necessity of experiencing ommunion with Christ in spirit—of partaking of that oul-quickening nourishment; of which the bread and ine, dispensed by Christ at the last paschal supper of hich he partook with his disciples, were typical—and ? being baptised with that "baptism which now saveth," hich "is not the putting away of.the filth of the flesh, ut the answer of a good conscience toward God, by the esurrection of Jesus Christ."

4. They are strongly impressed with a conviction of he utter inconsistency of all war, with the spirit and recepts of the Gospel of Christ, which breathes "peace n earth, and goodwill to men." Our Saviour commanded is followers "to love their enemies;" and Friends are onvinced, that the fruits of his Spirit are utterly opposed o those dispositions which engender strife. It was fore-old, in ancient prophecy, that under the Messiah's reign, en should learn war no more; and in proportion to the extension of his dominion, is the blessed promise verified, "Violence shall be no more heard in thy land, wasting nor destruction within thy borders;" and surely it behoves those who utter the petition, "Thy kingdom come, thy will be done on earth as it is in heaven," to seek to promote universal righteousness and peace, and the temporal and spiritual well-being of every individual of the human family.

5. Friends conscientiously decline the taking of Oaths, believing that the positive command of Christ, "I say unto you, Swear not at all; but let your communications be Yea, yea; Nay, nay, for whatsoever is more than these cometh of evil," is applicable to judicial, as well as to profane swearing, and is binding upon all the disciples of Christ: and that Christians should, in all their transactions, diligently attend to the dictates of the Holy Spirit, which would lead them to a scrupulous observance of the truth, both in their words and in their actions.

6. Whilst Friends decline those practices which they thus hold to be contrary to the will of their divine Lord and Master, they are conscientiously concerned to demean

themselves as good citizens, and to yield that willing an
respectful obedience, in all lawful things, which is due t
those who are placed in authority over them; endeavour
ing, as much as in them lies, " to keep a conscience voi
of offence toward God and toward men." But believin
that God, who alone can rightly instruct and govern th
conscience, has reserved to Himself the power and do
minion over it, they esteem it not lawful for any persons
whatever may be their rank or station, or whatever th
authority they may hold in governments, to coerce th
consciences of men; and that, therefore, all fining o
imprisonment, inflicted for a conscientious adherence t
religious principle, or for different views respecting wor
ship or christian practice, is contrary to the will of God

7. The standard which the Gospel erects, is that o
" perfecting holiness in the fear of God," and the de
voted servant of the Most High knows, that it is his
blessed privilege, as it is also his most solemn duty, to b
continually endeavouring to " press toward the mark fo
the prize of the high calling of God, in Christ Jesus.'
His affections being set on things above, he feels it to be
utterly incompatible with the spirit of a true Christian,
to seek enjoyment in the vain and frivolous pursuits,
in which the corrupt and unregenerate heart is prone to
indulge, or in anything else that is contrary to the
Divine Will. On this ground, Friends, as a body, have
always believed themselves called upon to observe great
purity and circumspection in their conduct and conversation, and plainness and simplicity in their apparel,
and in the furniture of their houses.

8. They conscientiously object to every practice which
has had its origin in a spirit of flattery! such as the
complimentary bowing of the knee, and taking off the hat
and addressing persons with such titles as are merely
adulatory. They believe that, to apply to persons appellations, which do not correctly distinguish their station or
circumstances, is a departure from that law of sincerity
and truth, which ought in all things to govern the
conduct and language of the Christian. On this ground,
they also consider it right to adhere to the scriptural
language of Thou and Thee, when speaking to a single

rson; the substitution of the plural pronoun having
iginated in a disposition to administer to the vanity of
an, by ascribing to one, the qualities, dignity, and worth
many. The common method of distinguishing many
the months, and the days of the week, having had its
se in heathenish superstition, and these names being
erived from the names of imaginary deities, to the
onour and worship of which these months and days
ere originally dedicated, Friends have uniformly declined
e use of such appellations, and have adhered to the
mple numerical order of First, Second, Third, &c.

9. They also refrain from wearing mourning garments
r the dead, and from joining in those public demon-
rations of rejoicing which involve a culpable waste of
roperty, and are generally attended by a demoralizing
fluence. They likewise esteem it their duty, to testify
gainst every species of gaming, against theatrical amuse-
ents, and against all those diversions, whether public
r private, which, in their very nature, are more or less
pposed to the devout, circumspect, and self-denying life
f the follower of Jesus.

10. Being impressed with the serious responsibility,
ncurred by those, who, for the sake of a temporary gra-
ification, waste their time, that most precious treasure,
given for the high and holy purposes of glorifying the
Almighty Creator, and of becoming prepared for an
ternity of happiness, Friends cannot approve of those
ursuits which, however pleasing to the natural mind,
nd by a degenerate world esteemed as innocent, are
evertheless calculated to alienate the mind from the fear
f God, and to disqualify it for attention to the serious
nd important duties of life. Such pursuits are opposed
o that disposition of soul, in which alone we can obey
he sacred injunction, "See that ye walk circumspectly,
ot as fools, but as wise, redeeming the time."

Friends therefore esteem it highly important, that they
who class themselves amongst the followers of the Lord
Jesus should walk worthy of the high profession they are
making, and that they should turn a deaf ear to the derision of the world, patiently bearing this, as well as every

8

other fruit of its persecuting spirit. This spirit is eve opposed to the righteousness of Christ, who, when fore warning his disciples of the sufferings that awaited the for his holy name's sake, said, "These things have spoken unto you, that in me ye might have peace. I the world ye shall have tribulation, but be of good cheer I have overcome the world."

This true peace, this heavenly consolation, which th Lord alone can give, Friends know by experience to b the blessed portion of those, who, by living faith, ar united to Christ, and who bearing his yoke, obey his ow sacred injunction, "If any man will come after me, le him deny himself and take up his cross daily, and follow me." Where an implicit faith is placed in Divine guid-ance, and obedience keeps pace with the knowledge received, the spiritual ear becomes opened to distinguish the voice of the Good Shepherd, and the children of God experimentally know the Lord to be their Teacher, and that, by his Holy Spirit, they are led into all Truth; for the Lord's children are all taught of Him, and great is the peace of his children. He guides them through this life by his counsel, and finally receives them to glory.

END.

London: Printed by E. Couchman & Co., 10, Throgmorton Street; for the TRACT ASSOCIATION *of the* SOCIETY OF FRIENDS. *Sold at the Depository,* 12, *Bishopsgate Street Without.*—1866.

MEMOIRS

OF THE

LIFE AND RELIGIOUS EXPERIENCE

OF

WILLIAM LEWIS,

LATE OF BRISTOL.

I was born the 17th of the 9th month, 1753. Nothing *very remarkable* attached to my early days, that I can now recollect; I say, *nothing very remarkable*, because, unhappily, an early desire of, and pursuit after, all that is in the world, is (in a greater or lesser degree) the course of every natural man's heart, according to the complexional bias: my own, I remember, was strongly drawn after lying vanities, the participation of which, was limited only by slender means and parental authority, that imposed close confinement to business: into which I was introduced in my fourteenth year, possessing little from my previous education but writing and arithmetic, all that my father judged necessary for a plain mechanic; his designation respecting me. Previous to this period, the only effect of the inshining of divine light in my dark heart, now remembered, was the solemn impressive authority of the Holy Scriptures, and the beauty that appeared to my view in true holiness of life and entire dedication of heart unto Almighty God; leading me greatly to admire and even to take comfort concerning his ancient servants, whose lives were fully devoted to him; and to regret the falling short of some others who appeared to have a degree of zeal for his glory; but at the age of fourteen, the *convicting* power of the precious light was sensibly felt, and condemnation awfully witnessed, in the pursuit of sinful pleasures; none of which were ever indulged in, without a dread of that eye, from which I both knew and *felt*, nothing could be hid. To lessen this terror, faint resolutions were

No. 90. [*Price 8d. per dozen.*]

formed to resist when next tempted; but these being chiefly
the effect of fear, and resorted to, as the dip of a finger in
water, to cool the fiery indignation I felt burning in my
conscience, were generally broken in the hour of trial; *so*
feeling, notwithstanding, continued for a considerable time,
and a faint hope was cherished of emerging from the miry
clay, into which I had plunged my poor soul; but no *effort*
was made to break off from my evil ways, and the time
could command was mostly spent in reading plays and
novels.　Hereby an indolent, effeminate turn of mind was
excited and nourished; extreme fondness of dress, and everything gratifying to such a cast of spirit was more and mor
indulged in; useful and instructive literary productions wer
dry and tasteless; business, and, in a word, everything tha
required mental energy and uniform attention, became heav
and irksome: thus, even the *desire* to struggle for deliv
erance seemed, in great measure, extinct; and though drea
of the consequences of a continuance in such a course woul
at times awaken, yet I thought it next to an impossibility fo
anything to loosen my affections, short of the immedia
prospect of a removal out of the world; for so tenacious wa
my poor mind of *present* enjoyment, and so fearful of an
interruption thereof, that I well remember the alarm I felt,
lest the *doctrine*, inculcated by the clergyman of the parish
in which I resided at the time called Christmas, should be
at all impressive or convicting; namely, that it was set apart
by the Church for the purpose of *piously* commemorating
the mercy and love of our Heavenly Father, in sending his
dear Son into the world, in order, that by delivering us from
its corruptions, our spirits might be fitted and prepared for an
abode with him in the realms of light and purity: I knew
that if this doctrine were *acted upon* by his auditors, our
merry meetings, my chief joy, hitherto peculiarly marked
with indulgence at this much longed-for season, would
necessarily be discontinued; having, even in this dark state,
(witl nt recurring to doctrine or precept) an inward con·
viction f the incompatibility of a disposition to worldly
delights, vith true spiritual relish; and indeed the supposing
both can subsist together, involves an incongruity of the
greatest magnitude.　A refuge, however, from those fears,
was near at hand; I recollected that heretofore the same
doctrine had been *preached, heard,* and (if accompanied with
rhetorical embellishment) *admired;* but this all ended, both
preacher and hearers, each according to their ability, went
away, to throw in their *mite,* at *least,* for the promotion of

isting, dancing, singing, &c.; *thus* my *alarm* was quieted,
the hope that things would go on in their usual course,
d that we should continue to " chaunt to the sound of the
ol, drink wine out of bowls, and anoint with the chief
ntments," undisturbed by apprehensions of future wo for
esent ease. Such was my condition at this early period;
d which continued, without any material alteration until
e year 1775, (the 22nd of my life) when I was powerfully
rought upon, and *suddenly* formed an earnest purpose of
art to break off from my sins; and to seek peace with my
od, in a truly religious course. Immediately upon taking
is resolution, I acted upon it; threw off my gay apparel;
stricted myself to uniform moderation in satisfying *even the*
al wants of nature; cutting off everything like *indulgence*
eating, drinking, sleeping, &c., in a word, all of a recreative
st; and strictly endeavoured to redeem the precious time I
uld command, by retiring to my bed-room, or attending
me public place of worship, immediately on my release from
tward business: in private I prayed frequently, earnestly,
d at as much length as I could, knowing, at this time, little
ore of christian practice, than what was comprised in such
gagements and exercises; quite uninformed respecting
ctrines, I had no predilection towards any particular sect
account of their distinguishing tenets, or forms of public
orship; but having long entertained a high opinion of the
———, from their *daily* meeting together, I frequented
eir assemblies for a time; after which, at the persuasion
a friend, I became a hearer at ———, and hastily joined
membership there. I call it *hastily*, because there was no
evious deep examination of their opinions, nor earnest
plication to the fountain of wisdom for direction; both of
ich, such an important movement called for. But as much
I remember of my feelings at that time, they were so
rongly excited by the *main object* of my new course, viz.,
eace with God, and a well-grounded hope of being admit-
d to his heavenly kingdom at last, that very little room
as left in my mind to be occupied on points of doctrine.
ch sweetness, for a time, accompanied my religious ex-
cises, that it seemed enough for me to *hear* of God's
ercy in Christ Jesus, and that an *experimental partici-*
tion thereof was *attainable* in this present world; and
ese things being set forth in a lively manner by their
eachers, were so like marrow and fatness to my soul, that
atisfied therewith) other points, occasionally introduced,
ade but little impression, and consequently obtained very

slight consideration. But this state of mind was, little b
little, disturbed: on being questioned, as to the ground c
my selecting this body of professors from among the rest
and on what foundation I built my religious *doctrinal* opin
ions (naturally supposed to coincide with those of m
brethren) I became tenacious in these respects—a sectarian
spirit found an entrance, and under its influence I began t
search the Scriptures, with a view to collect all they con
tained that would bear a construction favourable to th
Calvinistic system; *labouring hard* against the force c
passages with which I found it impossible to reconcile tha
system, and struggling with an *inward conviction*, whicl
(do what I could) opposed the belief of partiality in God
and of a covenant of grace and mercy in Christ Jesus, whicl
extended to a *few only*, of his fallen creatures, leaving th
rest to perish eternally. Thus exercised, the good provi
dence of my Heavenly Father directed the attention of i
piously disposed neighbour to my state; who (much con
cerned at the danger I appeared to be in, of imbibing th
doctrines alluded to) put into my hand some deeply spiritua
writings, clearly and fully convincing to my mind; so tha
I soon desisted from an engagement which nothing bu
sectarian tenacity introduced me into; an engagement, i
which *conviction* was *resisted*, the plain doctrines and d
clarations of Prophets, Apostles, and Christ Jesus himse
were rejected, and, in fine, every thought of Almighty Go
reconcileable with the belief of his *goodness* and *justice*, w
almost totally abandoned. Oh! what a shocking idea t
cherish! that a *good* and *gracious* God, should permi
myriads of *myriads* of intelligent spirits, to come int
existence, with nothing before them but a wearisome painft
passage through a vale of tears, abounding with trouble an
sorrow, and to terminate only by their entrance into a stat
still more replete with suffering; where wo irremediable
horror and anguish at present inconceivable, must be thei
portion to all eternity!

Released from these shackles, my mind found swee
liberty in admitting the belief in the universal love of Go
in Christ, to his creature man; and I fully received th
apostolic testimony of his being "no respecter of persons:
and rejected every opinion and doctrine that was not buil
on this foundation.

With this view of things, and under these impression
the *manner of worship*, as well as the *communications* :
————, soon became unsatisfactory; the meetings of th

ciety of Friends were thought of, and resorted to, chiefly
the ground of their being conducted *exteriorly* in a way
re congenial to my convictions, than those of any other,
t I had knowledge of; but not without expectations from
ministry among them; believing that those who were
lly called to this work would receive *immediately*, what
s suitable to the states of those to whom they ministered.
e vocal communications I heard among them were mostly
se and convincing: clear also upon points I had been
rcised about; at times deeply spiritual, and enforced with
rgy, accompanied with something which evinced to my
lings, they were the result of living experience. This
vement tended to *deepen* my late impressions, and I
an to act in correspondence with them; instead of singing,
ering a long string of petitions, and much reading in my
urs of retirement; I waited in silence, with earnest desire
d labour of mind after inward solemnity and prostration of
rit before the Holy One; longing after that quickening
wer, which, contriting, prepares the heart to receive divine
munications, and, receiving them, to return of *his own*,
the Great giver of every perfect gift.
Ceasing, in this manner, from creaturely activity, and my
tention confined to what passed *within*, a painful con-
tion ensued of my being in *reality* (as to spirituals)
oor and miserable, blind and naked." That precious light
ich had previously visited with sweet drawings, and now
ured me into the wilderness, showed me "my desert
d;" and the dark workings of unbelief and impatience
ggested that it had left me there: my little experience
ior to this was called in question, and at length considered
mostly the effect of a heated imagination: *perturbation* and
en *anguish* of soul ensued: I wrote bitter things against
self almost continually, and refusing every hope of com-
rt, a door was opened for despondency; it entered my very
ins and I let go all my confidence; the bitter cup of *despair*
s tasted; and considering myself forsaken of my God, I
ied and sobbed aloud from disquietude of soul. In such a
ndition as this, I could not continue long; *relief* would
turally be sought *some way*: the cruel subtle one was
ar, and thoughts like these presented,—" I have deceived
soul in imagining myself a subject of divine grace, and
tributing my first feelings and hopes to its operation; my
art and affections are still earthly and sensual, though the
agination for a time fondly pictured a heavenly interior:
have (though undesignedly) deceived my brethren and the

world, in making religious profession: I am as other me
to whom I have *virtually* said, 'stand by thyself;' and no
seeing myself in the true light, I must appear hencefort
as I really am, and no longer continue as a wolf in sheep
clothing."

This bait of the enemy, to a mind weary and comfortles
was unhappily swallowed; and after some months' deep wa
ing, or rather *plunging* in dark waters, in an evil hour
yielded to the suggestion that "rest was good," *however o
tained*, from such painful and fruitless labour; that the lar
I had viewed as a howling wilderness and vale of tears w
(compared with my dreary spot) *pleasant;* and thus I aga
" bowed my shoulders to bear and became a servant
tribute." *Religious restraint* was in great measure throw
aside, although I kept for a time within the bounds of m
rality, and to such order as was common in my father
house; going with the family on the first day of the week
their place of worship, and hearing some of them read t
Scriptures. But, alas! these bounds soon became painf
narrow to my will and the workings of my natural prope
sities; the *one effectual restraining power* being departe
from, they awoke with force in my enslaved heart, ai
gradually took the reins, so that I was indeed led captive
the will of the cruel tempter of mankind; no desire to resis
temptation remained, but every new path that opened any
thing pleasant to my view, was eagerly pursued; in shori
sad as it is to relate, I became a mere libertine, and my las
state was now worse than my first.

In reciting the *consequences* of my vile apostasy, it ma
be best, in order to give a clear view of the leading an
concurrent circumstances, to go back a little to the *gloom
state and exercises* which preceded—As I have already sai
my first purpose of devoting myself to Almighty God wa
sincere—I really intended from that day forth, to take
hope in him for my portion; but the vow was made *hastil*
without counting, or indeed knowing, the cost; in conside
able ignorance also of myself, particularly of my instabilit
of spirit, and an effeminate mind, which shrunk from suffe
ing, and was very tenacious of present enjoyment, whateve
object was in view, humility, the main requisite for laying
sure foundation for stability and real advancement, was bu
little regarded; *great things* were desired and expected, an
fervidity of mind, cherished as a mark of true zeal, an
mistaken for a feature of the truly renewed and pure imag
When, therefore, I was led inwardly, and become more int

ately acquainted with myself, and to have some discern-
ent of the difference between creaturely heat and divine
ght, and was made to feel the convicting power of the latter;
d seeing *therein* my condition to be so far below what I
ad thought it to be, there was (in addition to the distress
have mentioned, as feeling on a *religious ground*) a con-
iderable portion from the *creaturely source*, which gradually
aining ground gave the enemy an advantage, and at length
triumph over me. Self-love having nothing to feed upon,
; soon became weary of privation, and heavy under its hu-
iliating fast. Retirement for religious exercises, divested
f all that had at first given a relish thereto, became irksome,
nd pretexts for the omission of it, were easily admitted, if
ot sought for: one, I well remember, viz., *conversation on
eligious subjects* with a neighbour, at the times formerly
llotted to private devotion; but conviction followed, of its
eing resorted to, as a relief from the weight of my own
roper exercise and burden; this brought condemnation and
ncreased discouragement; my confidence naturally dimin-
shed—acts of rebellion against conviction in other things
(comparatively little) followed, until, at length my hope was
et go; the heavens were as brass over my head, and having
no expectation of any prayer of mine passing through, it ultimately produced the effects already recited: thus, there was a
"drawing back" in the hour of tribulation, instead of keeping
the word of patience: divine love had allured me; brought me
into the wilderness; into the valley of Achor, (i. e. trouble,)
in wisdom the allotted spot to dwell in. If I had continued
there until all that hindered my progress towards victory
over my soul's enemies had died the appointed death;
hoping and quietly awaiting for the Lord's salvation; doubtless vineyards would in due time have been given me there,
and I should have sung the Lord's song indeed, which he
can give to his truly abased and "poor in spirit," even "in
the night." But, sorrowful to relate! I now became a slave
to my propensities; unable to bear reflection, company was
eagerly and continually sought, and every means used to
silence the voice of conscience, still awfully loud at times:
for although I thus sought to flee from the presence of the
Lord of heaven and earth, yet such was his pity and mercy
to my poor soul, that he forsook me not utterly. In secret
I was still pierced with the arrows of convicting light, and
pressed sore with horrible dread of death and judgment to
come. Oh! if there be on this side that state between which
and the realms of light the "great gulf is fixed," any anguish

like that felt by the soul, which, after once receiving, thus
rebels against the light!—any condition more replete with
internal horror and gloom, than that of *such* a backslider, it
exceeds all I can picture to my imagination, or stretch my
thoughts unto.

In the course of this long night of apostacy, some interesting events took place: I married, and had several children: formed a promising connexion in trade, in which there
was a fair prospect of providing for my family: but, not
sufficiently alive to the weight of the solemn and interesting
obligations I was now under, pleasure was followed with
eagerness. Thus I went on, *apparently* gay and happy, but
in *reality* miserable, until the year 1789, when it pleased my
long-suffering and merciful God to visit me with severe
illness; wholly confined by this, I was now left to my own
thoughts and reflections on my past course, and made *awfully
to feel* the state it had brought me to; even to be "without
hope and without God in the world." "Destruction and
misery (I knew) were in my paths," and the way of peace I
was convinced I could no otherwise know, than by turning,
with full purpose of heart, unto him from whom I had so
deeply revolted: *partial* reformation I viewed as odious in
the sight of Omniscience, particularly for such a one as myself;
my former views of a truly religious state, and the deep
inward work necessary to be passed through, in order to its
attainment, all returned, and the cost of real discipleship
with a crucified Master so counted, was terrific to my long
corrupted and debased spirit; the "world's dread laugh"
also, was no small thing to take into the account, for one
situated as I was; known to many of various classes in civil
society, and (from marriage connexions) in habits of intimacy
with some who were in much grandeur in their manners and
establishment in life; to all this were added, strong apprehensions that my natural instability would *ever* be prevalent,
and a faithful spirit too high for me to attain to. The
struggle was deep and painful, but at length, strength was
vouchsafed to renew my covenant with a good and gracious
God, who had long waited for my return, and now called
me so to exalt him as to become capable of a participation of his living mercies, and tender forgiveness of my
manifold sins. Accordingly, on the 26th day of the 9th
month, 1789, in the sight of a heart-searching God, I took
up a purpose, from that time, earnestly to seek for peace
with him; to break off from all my evil habits, and enter
upon a truly religious course: earnestly praying for strength

;o perform my vows, and dreading nothing so much as
unfaithfulness, or any abatement of the fervent desires which
I felt to be a true penitent, and (like the prodigal) a seeker
;o be received among such, in our Heavenly Father's house.
The Lord graciously regarded my petitions; delivered me
from that *horror* at the thought of death, which had long
been deeply felt in my soul; thus I gathered a *little* strength,
and my head was lifted up, at times in *hope;* and in the
beginning of the year 1790, I was favoured with a return of
bodily strength also, and matters both inward and outward,
wore an aspect more cheering than for many years past.

My views of religion and the worship of Almighty God
continued the same as under my first profession; consequently, the principles and practices of every society of
Christians, must be very distant from my sentiments, excepting those of *Friends*—yet looking upon the division of
the church into sects, as the consequence of a departure from
the pure spirit of Christ, I strongly questioned for a time the
propriety of my joining any one of them, exclusively; and
determined upon seeking to God in secret for his guidance
in this matter; occasionally attending the different assemblies, but mostly those of the Friends and Methodists. A
conduct so unusual, was likely to appear as the effect of an
unsettled judgment, and I believe, did so, to many; but the
case was not exactly so—still believing in the necessity of
a holy quickening power from God, to revive in man the
lost holy image in which he was first created, and that Jesus
Christ was this power, inwardly revealed in every man; consequently, that looking to anything short thereof for help,
was, at best, holding fast something founded on that dispensation which made nothing perfect, because it stood in
exterior observations, which could do nothing effectual as
pertaining to the conscience. The baptism, therefore, that
now saveth, was, (in my view) such an union with the world-
renouncing spirit of Christ, as gives the victory over things
present: thus the Apostle, "as many as were baptised into
Christ have put on Christ." "They that are Christ's, have
crucified the flesh, with the affections and lusts," &c., &c.
Respecting the supper of the Lord—all exterior acts appear
very insignificant, when he declared, that participation of his
flesh and blood was an union with him, of the same nature,
as was his with his Heavenly Father. John vi. 56, 57. Can
we then suppose he meant by anything he said, at partaking
of the passover with his apostles, to enjoin the observance of
some new outward and visible sign instead thereof? Could

he, as an High Priest, made "after the power of an endles
life," minister to his church in anything like the priests unde
the law, whose gifts and sacrifices, we read, could not mak
him that did such service perfect, because it stood only i
meats and drinks and divers washings, and carnal ordinance
imposed on them *until the time of reformation?*

Other cardinal points in which the Society of Friend
differs from most other bodies of christians, namely those o
war, oaths, and the ministry, I had early occasion of *publicl*
evincing my unity with, a considerable time before I becam
a member of the Society, or knew I ever should be; plain
ness and simplicity in apparel, manners, and speech also (t
a certain extent) appeared to me from my early conviction
to be quite accordant with the precepts and example of ou
holy Redeemer; and well knowing that the vanity of my o
heart was that which induced conformity to the world
these respects, whilst in my state of bondage thereto, sell
denial in *practice* extended in some degree to them, in
gradual manner.

Respecting *plainness of speech*, I have said that, *to
certain extent*, the propriety of it was accordant with m
judgment—it was so, but some time elapsed before I felt i
necessary to adopt it so fully as Friends do. What led to
close and deep consideration, concerning the ground on which
they believe it right to differ from others in this respect, was,
to the best of my recollection, nearly as follows: after two
years' seclusion from public places of worship, (except when
particularly invited to any,) in my hours of retirement, which
were then many and daily, it forcibly came to my view, that
a course so ascetic, was not accordant, either with the spirit
of the Gospel or the plain injunctions of the apostles, or the
practice of believers in any age of the church; brotherly
union and fellowship appearing to be of the very essence of
that spirit, which, breathing good will to all, and loving
without dissimulation, naturally cares for the spiritual welfare
of others, and bears their burdens. Opening my mind to
these considerations, they soon pressed weightily, and my
thoughts turned to religious fellowship; at the first glance
that way, the Society of Friends appeared to be the only one
I could possibly join myself to; but in order to this, it was
seen to be necessary that my judgment and practice should
be altogether in conformity with theirs; and excepting *language,* they were nearly so; but the very *idea* of a change
in this particular, caused such a shrinking, and almost dread
of mind, as induced an attempt to sift and prove groundless,

their arguments in proof of its being a genuine christian testimony, against that corruption in speech, which, as to the letter, I could not deny to be very evident, in that commonly adopted. How far I evaded the force of what they advanced on the subject, or how soon I passed from that, to what the Scriptures contained as applicable to the point in question, I cannot now recollect, only, that ultimately, a diligent search in them, concerning the matter, was exclusively resorted to. The first passage that met, and arrested my attention was the apostolic injunction, to be in the use of " sound speech that cannot be condemned." This pressed and pinched in some degree at first, but I got from under its weight, by reasoning after this manner—Sound! that is surely so, which proceeding from a heart without rottenness and divested of all deceit, seeks not to leave a false impression on the minds of hearers. But " hold fast the form of sound words " came from the same authority, and appearing to inculcate, that substantial rectitude of heart, with every other effect of the light of Christ therein, should shine forth in its native garb before others, and that in the real possession of truth *inwardly*, every appearance of evil must be abstained from *outwardly*. This, for a time, lay with more weight than the former; but at length, appeared to contain, in substance, nothing that added to its force. I came at last to the Lord's message unto his people through the prophet Malachi, charging them with such withholding, as was even robbery in his sight, and which was committed by keeping back " tithes and offerings:" reflecting upon this charge, and remembering that, in these offerings, mint, annise, &c., were included, things as insignificant in themselves, when compared with the weighty matters of the law, as a form of sound words could be to substantial truth in the inward parts, and yet, that divine wisdom made them of such importance as to condemn those who refused compliance with what was enjoined respecting them, in the awful manner noticed, I began to fear (I say, *to fear*) that Friends were right, and that it was my duty, as an individual, to join them in testimony against the corruptions crept into modern language, and to go back to the primitive simplicity and plainness of speech. A sure exercise of mind now took place, and whilst under it, falling in company with a ministering friend from America, a communication from his lips was as a seal thereto. He addressed the company, some of whom had dropt our peculiar testimonies, nearly in this manner, " Robbery, Robbery! it is a crime of no small magnitude with

respect to things pertaining to man: how great then is it
turpitude, when the rights of the Most High are invaded
and the creature holds back what is due to the Creator
Some of old were charged even with this atrocity: they ha
the impudence to query, Wherein? but an answer was
ready, in tithes and offerings." After this introduction, he
enlarged on the subject, and when the company were about
to separate, noticed me; asked who I was, &c.: on being
told my name and a few particulars, he parted with me, after
uttering these few words, "Well William! bring all the
tithes into the store house." The impression such an address
must naturally leave on my mind after my previous exercise,
may readily be conceived; it was powerful indeed, and im-
printed on it an indelible character. From this period,
(1793) I had a fixed apprehension that I should fall short of
divine requiring, if the cross was not submitted to, in respect
of language, yet continued shrinking therefrom, and struggling with that which imposed it, for nearly two years, during
which time, many prayers, with tears, were offered up to a
gracious God, for guidance in the matter, and for strength
to bear all he might see meet to lay upon me for the
reduction of my natural will, and the humiliation of my soul
before him, and in the sight of man also; until at length,
almost dreading to address him, in terms I feared to use
when speaking to my fellow-creatures, in much trepidation
of spirit I submitted to adopt, what Friends term, *the plain
language;* whereby, another stumbling-block was removed
out of my path. From this time (the year 1795) I attended
their meetings regularly, and about three years after, on
applying to be admitted a member of the Society, I was
received as such, by the Monthly Meeting of my native city.
W. L.

Before the reader proceeds, it may be well to pause, and
contemplate the contents of the preceding pages. There is
something very instructive in what he writes, respecting the
impressions made on his mind at a very tender age, by the
ray of light shed on those invaluable records, the Holy
Scriptures; proving the benefit which may accrue to the
young (although very inexperienced) mind, from a frequent
hearing, or perusal of them. But who, *without heart-felt
emotions,* can read his after conflicts with the strong propensities of fallen nature, and behold the dreadful state into

hich he was plunged by disobedience to his religious con-
ictions? Surely the description he gives of his state at that
ime should powerfully arrest the attention of those who, in
ke manner, are pursuing lying vanities and sinful gratifi-
ations: yet seeking, though in vain, to hide themselves
rom the all-seeing eye. Such was the case with our beloved
riend; but in the depth of unutterable distress, he happily
urned with full purpose of heart unto him from whom he
ad so deeply revolted, by whose gracious assistance he was
enabled to break off from his sins; made willing to bear the
consequent reproaches of his former companions, and openly
to take up his cross; following, in the way of self-denial,
his crucified Lord, and, in adorable mercy, partaking of the
pardoning love of God in Christ Jesus.

Although it does not appear that he kept, for any long
time, a regular diary, yet we find something of this kind for a
short space in the year 1807, which seems worthy of notice.
We therefore give the following extracts from his manuscripts.

"1807, 9th Mo. 23rd. In the house all the day, through
bodily indisposition—endeavoured to feel after him in whose
presence alone, not only the 'fullness of joy,' but every
degree of heavenly refreshment is experienced. What is
the reason, Oh my soul! thou enjoyest so little thereof? Is
not this the cause? The Lord is in his holy temple, but the
heart is infested with the thieves which rob him of his glory
and pollute the place, which, if pure, he would make his
sanctuary; so that thou canst partake of glances only, of his
tender favour and holy presence, which, in amazing condescension, he, at times, vouchsafes: Oh may the cry be
yet more earnest, to be purged, though with hyssop, that
I may be clean, and so pure in heart, as to see and walk
with my God!

"25th. At Thornbury meeting, and was engaged therein
to press the necessity of diligence and earnest search after
the pearl of great price—returned the next day, and was
providentially relieved from perplexity, respecting a secular
matter. How graciously doth the great Controller of events
manifest himself to those who trust in his wisdom and
power, even in things appertaining to this life! Opening
a way, where (to our view) we were encompassed as with a
hedge of thorns, and no prospect before us of an escape
without hurt.—'Trust in him at all times; ye people! pour
out your hearts before him.'

"30th. In the multitude of my thoughts, something soft-

ening was felt, and continued with me; went forth to my
worldly engagements in the spirit of supplication, and was
kept until the evening in a peaceful calm—at a friend's house
was enabled to offer an evening sacrifice, in which the
necessity of watching, in order to witness a qualification for
prayer, was (I trust in the love of truth) closely pressed on
some visited minds present; retired in the hope that I had
not been out of my place.

"10th Mo. 4th. O Thou that hearest prayer! most gracious and condescending Father of mercies! I desire to bless
and praise thy holy name for all thy goodness to my soul;
which thou hast redeemed with the precious blood of Christ
Jesus, whom I desire, in the obedience of faith, to call my
Lord, and to follow, as he is pleased to lead. Amen and
Amen!!—Thus far, under some sense of my last night's petition being answered, in that I had sweet access by prayer
this morning to the Fountain of Life—afterwards went to
meeting in a softened state, and heard a testimony in which
the query, "What manner of persons ought ye to be?" was
closely pressed upon all—may it be daily put to my soul
with piercing energy.

"After this, I allowed myself a little quiet retreat in the
country, where, disengaged from outward hindrances, I was
favoured with a degree of inward calm, and therein had sweet
access to the God of all consolation, who renews the strength
of all who wait humbly upon him; but in about two weeks
after my return, it pleased him in whose hand is the breath
of every living thing, in his inscrutable wisdom, to visit my
dwelling with a deeply affecting stroke, taking out of time
into eternity, after a short illness, the youngest of my family,
a promising youth in his nineteenth year: this was felt in
the creaturely part very acutely, but resignation to the
divine will was maintained, accompanied with thankfulness,
in the belief that he was taken from the evil to come; much
of which, it was obvious from peculiar circumstances, if he
had lived, would have assailed him, and have rendered his
path very slippery. Another cause of thankfulness, was the
nature of his disease (water on the brain) which in all human
probability, had he continued in existence, would have
caused great suffering, without hope of relief. Thus are we
given sometimes 'to see in part' the goodness of the Lord,
even in his painful dispensations to us his creatures. May
my soul deepen in reverent humility and gratitude before
him for all his goodness to me! After this I again had some
retirement from secular concerns; during which my hope

the redeeming, cleansing power of that 'blood which
eaketh better things than that of Abel,' was a little
ghtened, in the prospect of becoming thereby a companion
and partaker with, those who being washed therein from
eir sins, attain 'the white stone and new name,' which is
own only by those who overcome and receive it. Oh that
may henceforth so faithfully follow the great Captain of
lvation, and manfully fight under his banner against my
ul's enemies, as (through his strength) daily to experience
e house of Saul to become weaker and weaker, until all
thin me that is at enmity with the pure will of my God, be
bdued! so that his kingdom may indeed come; and the
ghteous government of his Christ be fully established, by
l his foes becoming his footstool. Amen! Amen!"

In his general deportment and engagements, civil and
eligious, he evinced marks of the real christian; redeemed,
a more than common degree from the love of earthly
ings, we believe it may be truly said of him, that he was
an example to the believers, in word, in conversation, in
harity, in spirit, in faith, and in purity." In private life, a
varm and faithful friend—a sympathizer with the afflicted
vhether in body or in mind, and ready to help them, as far
s in his power; of a truly catholic spirit, his love was far
rom being limited by the borders of his own religious pro-
ession—wherever sincerity of heart and a real desire after
hristian purity appeared, there went his heart also; to such
vas the hand of christian fellowship extended; nevertheless,
ie stood firm to his own religious principles, and when oc-
asion required, was bold in opposing, or declining, what he
ould not unite with.
Having experimentally known the operation of the word
f life in his own heart, he felt himself constrained to declare
into others what God had done for his soul; to invite them;
y those mercies which he had witnessed, to come, taste, and
ee, how good the Lord is; as also, by those *terrors*, of
vhich he had so largely partaken, to warn the rebellious;
ind for about nine years before his decease, he thus stood
imong his fellow members in the station of a minister.
His labours in the ministry were principally in and around
iis native city, but about nine months before his decease
after a remarkable recovery from extreme illness) he paid a
eligious visit, with the concurrence of his friends at home,

to the meetings of Friends in Lincolnshire, Derbyshire, and some parts of Yorkshire and Lancashire, much to the edification of those he visited and to his own peace. Among some memorandums made as he went along, are the following remarks which appear worthy of notice. In one place, feeling his mind oppressed, under an apprehension of the prevalence of a worldly spirit, he thus writes, " Oh what an oppressor of the precious seed is a worldly, trafficking spirit! How does it fetter the soul in its prison house of darkness, so that no living desires can burst the way to God on high! As I advance, I think I discover this spirit has carried into captivity, and holds in bondage. I fear the love of money is not seen to be so bitter a root as it really is; but that, on the contrary, it is too much indulged, even to the hardening of the heart."

On humility, he observes, " What a beautiful garment for the spirit of man is humility! true genuine humility! how invaluable the ornament of a meek and quiet spirit! Surely these are garments in which all should be clothed, and in some degree shine forth, who go in and out with acceptance, before the Lord's people; giving no offence in anything, that the ministry be not blamed, but even if defamed, to entreat."

After this, he was very little from home; for in about three months, symptoms of his former disease again appeared, and in the 5th Mo., 1816, had so increased, as to have assumed a very decided character, leaving little hope of his recovery. He was preserved in great patience under bodily sufferings; *fully* resigned to the divine will: and much engaged in inward retirement and secret supplication.

On the 7th day of the 6th Month, 1816, he was released from the troubles and conflicts of time, and his remains were interred in the Friends' burial ground at the Friars, Bristol, on the 15th of the same. The funeral was attended by many of his fellow citizens, in addition to those of his own Society; evincing their esteem for one whom they had long known and respected.

END.

London: *Printed by Edward Couchman,* 10, *Throgmorton Street; for the* TRACT ASSOCIATION *of the* SOCIETY OF FRIENDS. *Sold at the* DEPOSITORY, 84, *Houndsditch.*—1859.

SENTIMENTS

OF

THE SOCIETY OF FRIENDS

ON

DIVINE WORSHIP,

AND

GOSPEL MINISTRY.

~~~~~~~~~~~~~~~~

The following Treatise on Divine Worship and Gospel Ministry, forms the ifth Chapter of a work, entitled, " The Principles of Religion, as professed by e Society of Friends, usually called Quakers: written for the instruction of eir youth, and for the information of strangers, by Henry Tuke." As most ' the professors of Christianity, in the present day, admit, with the Society of riends, the necessity of conforming their religious sentiments and practices to e standard of Divine Truth exhibited in the Holy Scriptures, the following ges are commended to their serious perusal, in the hope that they may tend promote such conformity, with regard to the great objects which they are tended to illustrate.

~~~~~~~~~~~~~~~~

LONDON:

rinted for the TRACT ASSOCIATION of the SOCIETY OF FRIENDS,

Sold at the DEPOSITORY, 12, Bishopsgate Street Without.

—

1866.

No. 91.   [*Price* 5½*d. per dozen.*]

DIVINE WORSHIP,

AND

GOSPEL MINISTRY.

Worship an act of the Soul towards God.—Meetings for Worship may be held in silence.—Public Worship an indispensable duty: reasonable and beneficial.—Silent Worship adapted to all states: its advantages: Scripture arguments for it.—Prayer a necessary duty.—The qualifications of Ministers.—Human learning not essential to the Ministry.—No individual has a right exclusively to assume the exercise of it.—On women's preaching.—On preaching for hire.—Tithes.

WE consider that worship is an act of the soul towards God; that He is a Spirit; that the soul of man is spiritual; and, therefore, that, in the performance of the solemn duty of worship, words are not essentially necessary; because He, who is a Spirit, understands the language of the Spirit. Nevertheless, we do not disapprove the use of words in our religious meetings, whether in prayer, praises, or in the exercise of Gospel ministry; when they are delivered under the influence of the Holy Spirit, which only can, as we apprehend, rightly qualify for the performance of these important services. Hence, when we come to our places of religious worship, we think it right to sit down in silence, and wait therein upon God, for the assistance of that Spirit which helpeth our infirmities, and without which we know not what to pray for as we ought. Here we may be favoured, at times, to feel the Spirit itself making intercession for us; under the influence of which, we believe, a secret aspiration will ascend with more acceptance before the Father of Spirits, than any form of words which may be prepared for us, or that does not arise from a heart thus qualified for verbal expression.

Holding our meetings under these impressions, it very
quently happens that they are continued throughout
silence: a state which, when attended with a right
ercise of mind, we consider as best adapted to the
rformance of the solemn duty of Divine worship: for
re, every individual who feels his own condition and
cessities, can secretly pour out his soul unto God,
thout distraction or interruption; and here also we
freely partake of those Divine influences upon the
ıd which, when mercifully afforded, constitute the
hest enjoyment of man upon earth.
But we are sensible that these effects are not always
perienced in our religious meetings. We fear that
ne who attend them, have not their minds rightly
ercised; we know that Divine good is not at our
mmand; and we believe that the sensible enjoyment
it, is often withheld for a season, and sometimes for
ong season, from the truly exercised mind: " Verily
ıou art a God that hidest thyself, O God of Israel, the
viour!" Isa. xlv. 15. But even in this situation,
think it much safer to wait in a state of passive
lence, than, by the activity of the creature, to rush
ıprepared into those external acts of devotion, which
e believe are no further acceptable, than as they come
ɔm a heart rightly prepared to offer them. A state of
ımble, silent waiting, and dependence on Divine help,
so adapted to the relation in which man stands to his
reat Creator, that we believe it peculiarly likely to
eet with Divine acceptance and regard: " Blessed are
ose servants whom the Lord, when He cometh shall
ıd watching." Luke xii. 37. But to those who do
ɔt patiently abide in this state of mind, a very different
ınsequence is shown to result: " Behold! all ye that
ndle a fire, that compass yourselves about with sparks:
alk in the light of your fire, and in the sparks that ye
ıve kindled. This shall ye have of mine hand; ye
ıall lie down in sorrow." Isa. l. 11. And we ought
ɾ no means to forget the consequence, under the Law,
˙ offering strange fire to the Lord. Lev. x. 1—5.
We consider it an indispensable duty, publicly to
eet together for ˌthe worship of God; and " not to
rsake the assembling of ourselves together, as the

manner of some is." Heb. x. 25., It is both a reasonable and a beneficial duty;—reasonable, because it is a public acknowledgment of our dependence on the Supreme Being:—and beneficial, because we may, if rightly exercised in our minds, be favoured to draw nigh unto God, by the Spirit of his Son; and thus experience that communion, which is with the Father, and with his Son Christ Jesus; and which the true Christian travellers also have one with another in Him.

In a silent travail in spirit for this desirable experience, the spiritual strength of those who are thus exercised, is increased; they become helpful one to another, in promoting the circulation of that life in which their fellowship consists; and are, at times, so united in feeling one for and with another, as to attain to an experience similar to that which the apostle describes: " Whether one member suffer, all the members suffer with it; or one member be honoured, all the members rejoice with it." Cor. xii. 26.

It may be supposed by some, that, although this mode of worship may be adapted to adults in religious experience, it is too refined an attainment for those who are in a state of infancy in religion, or who are much strangers to it.—We, however, consider it as eminently adapted to every human being, who is desirous of being acceptable in the sight of his Creator. Where is the well-disposed mind, that has not occasion for an attention to that universal command : " What I say unto you, I say unto all, Watch !" Mark xiii. 37. This secret attention and exercise of mind is, therefore, necessary for all; and as man is willing to be reduced into it, the weak and erring mind may be brought to the discovery of its own state : and, feeling the necessity of Divine aid to overcome its evil propensities, and to secure eternal happiness, may thus feel also the necessity and the qualifications, to pray for forgiveness of past sins, and for ability so to live under the influence of Divine fear and love, as to experience preservation from those evils which abound in the world, or to which the mind may be naturally prone.

Many, therefore, we conceive, are the advantages which result from silent worship. It enables a number

Christians to meet together for the performance of
is important duty, without depending on any man to
sist them therein; a dependence, which deprives num-
rs of publicly discharging this duty, even once in the
eek. It also preserves from the dangerous situation,
 drawing nigh unto God with the mouth, and hon-
ring Him with the lips, whilst the heart is far from
im; and it is peculiarly adapted to the performance of
at worship in spirit and in truth, concerning which our
essed Redeemer has given this memorable testimony:
The hour cometh, and now is, when the true wor-
ippers shall worship the Father in spirit and in truth;
r the Father seeketh such to worship Him. God is a
irit; and they that worship Him, must worship Him
spirit and in truth." John iv. 23, 24.
In addition to the foregoing reasons, many passages
ay be adduced from the Scriptures, pointing out the
vantage of silent waiting upon God. In reading those
votional effusions, which have been transmitted to us
 the book of Psalms, we find this waiting strongly and
equently inculcated. The evangelical prophet, like-
ise, speaks frequently of the benefit of such a state of
aiting, in which silence is either expressed, or ne-
essarily implied. The latter part of the fortieth chapter,
nd the beginning of the forty-first, are so suited to the
resent subject, and, at the same time, so replete with
ligious instruction and consolation, that it may be
seful to give them at large: "Why sayest thou, O
acob! and speakest, O Israel! my way is hid from the
ord; and my judgment is passed over from my God?
[ast thou not known, hast thou not heard, that the
verlasting God, the Lord, the Creator of the ends of
e earth, fainteth not, neither is weary? There is no
arching of his understanding. He giveth power to the
int; and to them that have no might He increaseth
rength. Even the youths shall faint and be weary,
nd the young men shall utterly fall: but they that wait
pon the Lord shall renew their strength; they shall
ount up with wings as eagles; they shall run, and not
e weary; they shall walk and not faint. Keep silence
efore me, O islands! and let the people renew their
rength; let them come near, then let them speak;

let us come near together to judgment." Isa. xl. 27 to xli. 1.

But, whilst we are laying aside the outward forms, we are far, very far indeed, from desiring to discourage the practice of true prayer. It is a duty which we owe to our great Creator; and which the feelings of our own manifold wants and dangers will often draw from the rightly-concerned mind. It is indeed difficult to conceive how anything deserving the name of religion can be preserved without it.—" Watch and pray, that ye enter not into temptation," (Matt. xxvi. 41.) is an injunction delivered by our Holy Head and High Priest: who, in this, as in many other instances, has shown, that He was, as the author of the Epistle to the Hebrews expresses it, " touched with the feeling of our infirmities" (Heb. iv. 15); for he immediately adds: " The spirit indeed is willing; but the flesh is weak."

In this command, our blessed Lord sets forth both the necessity and the preparation for this great duty, which constitutes a very important part of religious worship. We are not to rush hastily or unpreparedly either into private or public prayer; but, having our minds engaged in true watchfulness, or waiting for the influence of the Holy Spirit upon the soul, we thereby become qualified to put up our petitions to the Father of Spirits, in such a manner as the impressions which He affords us of our wants shall indicate. And when we are brought into an humbling consideration of the many mercies and favours, of which we are unworthy partakers: as the objects of creation, of redemption, and of that bountiful provision which is made for us; we shall find abundant cause frequently to offer that praise, by which the Almighty is glorified! and of which He is, with the Son of his love, through the Eternal Spirit, for ever worthy.

After these remarks on religious worship, we proceed to the consideration of the subject of Gospel Ministry.

The right qualification of those who occupy the station of ministers, is of great importance to every religious society. It will, I presume, be universally agreed to be, in the first place, necessary, that the principles and practice of these, should correspond with their pro-

ssion and station : and next, that they be called and
alified, according to the nature and principles of that
ligion, which they stand forth to espouse. To apply
ese self-evident rules to the Christian religion, under
s various divisions, it must be deemed necessary for a
ospel minister, that he possess a heartfelt conviction of
e truths of Christianity, as well as of the principles of
at particular society, of which he is a member; also
at his moral conduct be such as the Gospel of Christ
quires. When there is any material deficiency, either
principle or practice, there is reason to fear, that such
ill do more injury than benefit to the cause of religion ;
well as render themselves objects of disgust and con-
mpt. " Unto the wicked God saith; What hast thou
do to declare my statutes; or that thou shouldst take
y covenant in thy mouth; seeing thou hatest in-
ruction, and castest my words behind thee?" Ps. l.
6, 17.
As to the further qualification for a Gospel minister,
though the definition given may be generally agreed
, yet, in the application of it, there exists some
iversity of sentiment. As the nature and principles of
he Christian religion are the same now as formerly, we
onceive that the same Divine call and influence, which
ualified the early ministers and promulgators of the
iospel, should be, in a degree at least, experienced by
s ministers to the end of the world : especially, as we
ave no other qualification pointed out in the Holy
criptures. This call was " not of men, neither by
ian; but by Jesus Christ, and God the Father." Gal.
1. We believe that the same is inwardly and im-
iediately received by the true Gospel ministers of the
resent day; and that, in the discharge of the duties of
his sacred office, the renewed influences of divine wis-
om and strength should be waited for and experienced.
hus ministers are qualified to speak to the state of their
earers; and to baptize them into the Name [or Power]
f the Father, the Son, and the Holy Spirit; thereby
ulfilling that true commission for Gospel ministry, given
y our Saviour.—Matt. xxviii. 19.
The foregoing qualifications correspond with the de-
cription which the apostle Peter gives of prophecy, and

which we conceive to be descriptive of the essentials of a Gospel minister. "Prophecy came not in old time by the will of man: but holy men of God spake as they were moved by the Holy Ghost." 2 Pet. i. 21. Thus we see that both ancient prophecy and Gospel ministry came " not of men, nor by man:" that they required those who exercised them to be holy men of God; such as could say to others: " Walk, as ye have us for an example" (Phil. iii. 17); and that, in performing the duties of these offices, they should speak " as they were moved by the Holy Ghost;" or in other words, as the " Spirit gave them utterance." Acts ii. 4. If ministers are not thus influenced and directed, we may expect the declaration respecting the prophets formerly, who ran and were not sent, to be verified: " They shall not profit the people at all." Jer. xxiii. 32. Nor should this serious language be forgotten: " Wo unto the foolish prophets, that follow their own spirit, and have seen nothing." Ezek. xiii. 3.

What is said respecting an inward call to the ministry, is by no means peculiar to our religious Society. However the doctrine of the Influence of the Spirit may be slighted by some, it is, in this instance, as well as in its general influence and operation, clearly maintained by the Church of England, as appears by the following question, put to those who apply to be admitted to the office of deacon: " Do you trust that you are *inwardly moved by the Holy Ghost*, to take upon you this office and ministration," &c. The answer required is, " I trust so." This doctrine is also consistent with the general observation on the priesthood, made by the author of the Epistle to the Hebrews: " No man taketh this honour unto himself, but he that is called of God, as was Aaron." Heb. v. 4. The writings of the apostles abundantly show, not only whence they derived their commission, but also the influence under which they exercised it: thus the apostle Paul says:—" Which things we also speak, not in the words which man's wisdom teacheth, but which the Holy Ghost teacheth." 1 Cor. ii. 13.

From all these considerations, we believe, as is already stated, that it is necessary, in the first call to the min-try, to be " inwardly moved by the Holy Ghost;" and that, in the various performances of this sacred office, the renewings of this Divine influence and ability should be waited for and experienced, as the most likely means to fulfil the apostolic exhortation: " If any man speak, let him speak as the oracles of God; if any man minister, let him do it as of the ability which God giveth; that God in all things may be glorified, through Jesus Christ: to whom be praise and dominion for ever and ever. Amen." 1 Pet. iv. 11.

From our views of this important subject, there arise few points in which we materially differ from most other professors of Christianity.

1. In not considering human learning essential to a Gospel minister.

2. In believing that no individual has a right to assume the exclusive exercise of this ministry, in a congregation of Christians; but that all, both male and female, who are rightly moved thereto, may exercise his gift.

3. That this ministry being, if rightly received, received freely and without pecuniary expense to qualify for it, it therefore ought to be freely communicated; and no further support expected by ministers, than what is authorized by Christ, and practised by his apostles.

Upon each of these points it seems proper to make a few remarks.

On the first, very little appears necessary; for if we consider the Holy Scriptures, and particularly the New Testament, as any guide to us in this matter, we shall not only find, that human literature is nowhere recommended for this office, but likewise, that many of the apostles were illiterate men. It is also clear, that the apostle Paul, though a man of learning, disclaimed the influence of it upon his ministry; as appears from various parts of his epistles, particularly, from the first and second chapters of the Epistle to the Corinthians, of which the first five verses of the second chapter, appear especially worthy of notice: " And I, brethren, when I came to you, came not with excellency of speech or of wisdom, declaring unto you, the testimony of God: for I determined not to know anything among you, save

Jesus Christ, and Him crucified. And I was with you in weakness, and in fear, and in much trembling: and my speech and my preaching was not with enticing words of man's wisdom, but in demonstration of the Spirit and of power; that your faith should not stand in the wisdom of men, but in the power of God." 1 Cor. ii. 1—5.

But, although we do not consider human learning as essential to a Gospel minister; yet we are so far from disesteeming or slighting its use, that we wish due attention to be paid to it by the members of our Society; for we believe that those who have it and are disposed to make a right use of it, may apply it to the promotion of religion and virtue, as well as to the benefit of civil society.

With respect to the second point, we have the practice of the primitive church so decidedly in our favour, that I am at a loss to conceive, how a practice so repugnant to it can have so generally prevailed as it has done, in almost all the Christian churches.

The practice alluded to, is that of an individual assuming the exclusive exercise of the ministry; which is directly contrary to what the apostle recommends, as well as declares to be the practice of the church in early times. This appears clear from the fourteenth chapter of the first Epistle to the Corinthians, where, first addressing the believers in general, the apostle thus expresses himself: "Follow after charity, and desire spiritual gifts; but rather that ye may prophesy." 1 Cor. xiv. 1. By this prophesying, he does not appear so much to mean the foretelling of future events, as the general purposes of Gospel Ministry; for in the third verse, he says: "He that prophesieth speaketh unto men to edification, and exhortation, and comfort." 1 Cor. xiv. 3. After this general advice and explanation, he proceeds to show the superiority of prophesying to speaking with tongues: and then of those who have received this divine gift, he says: "Let the prophets speak two or three, and let the others judge. If any thing be revealed to another that sitteth by, let the first hold his peace; for ye may all prophesy one by one, that all may learn, and all may be comforted." 1 Cor. xiv. 29—31.

After stating this unequivocal description of the rule
nd practice of the primitive church, I shall proceed to
1e consideration of another part of this head, from
hich it appears that we admit women, as well as men,
a participation and exercise of the gift of Gospel
inistry. We are aware of the objection which is made,
om the prohibition laid upon women's speaking and
aching in the Church, and usurping authority over
1e man. 1 Tim. ii. 11—15. But if, on every occasion,
here there is an apparent difference on one part of
cripture and another, it is admitted that Scripture is
he best interpreter of Scripture, I believe very little
ifficulty will arise in removing this objection. It should
e considered, that the words used by the apostle on
his occasion, cannot mean the exercise of the Gospel
inistry; because in the very epistle in which he first
entions this prohibition, he gives particular directions
especting the manner in which women are to exercise
hat gift, which he denominates, " praying or pro-
hesying" (1 Cor. xi. 5); and which he, no doubt, con-
idered as different from speaking, teaching, or usurping
authority: for it cannot, with any colour of reason, be
supposed, that the apostle would give directions for the
exercise of that which he thought should never be
exercised."*

In addition to the preceding argument, several other
passages in the Old and New Testaments may be advanced, which clearly show, that women, as well as men,
were engaged in the work of the ministry, or as prophetesses in early times. Passing over Miriam, Deborah,
and Huldah, we find Anna, a prophetess in the Jewish
church, publicly exercising her gift in the Temple; and
hailing the recent birth of the Messiah. The Samaritan
woman, with whom our Saviour held an interesting conversation at Jacob's Well, appears to have been the
irst of his disciples, who publicly preached the coming
of Christ; and remarkable was the success which at-
ended her ministry. Women were the first witnesses
of our Lord's resurrection, and were commissioned by
Him to proclaim this important truth to his disciples.

* See John Locke's note on 1 Cor. xi. 3, where he supports the
onstruction here given.

After his ascension, they were, equally with the men, partakers of the effusions of the Holy Spirit; and we find several females mentioned as being prophetesses, or fellow-labourers with the apostles in the Gospel of Christ. Luke, in speaking of Philip, the deacon, says: " The same man had four daughters, which did prophesy." Acts xxi. 9. In the Epistle to the Romans, the apostle says : " I commend unto you Phebe our sister, who is a servant of the church which is at Cenchrea.*—Greet Priscilla and Aquila my helpers in Christ Jesus."† " Salute Tryphæna and Tryphosa, who labour in the Lord. Salute the beloved Persis, which laboured much‡ in the Lord." Rom. xvi. 12. And in another epistle, he says, " Help those women that laboured with us in the Gospel." Phil. iv. 3.

These are passages which clearly evince the admission of the female sex, in early times, to the work and service of the Gospel; but what adds not a little to our argument is, that this was expressly foretold in such a manner, as would, if we had no precedent, fully warrant the practice; for on this subject we may use the words of the apostle Peter, and say : " This is that which was spoken by the prophet Joel : And it shall come to pass in the last days, saith God, I will pour out of my Spirit upon all flesh ; and your sons and your *daughters* shall prophesy ; and your young men shall see visions ; and your old men shall dream dreams ; and on my servants, and on my *handmaidens*, I will pour out in those days of my Spirit, and they shall prophesy." Acts ii. 16—18.

We come now to the third point, namely, the maintenance which is allowed to the ministers of the Gospel. On this subject, the directions of our blessed Lord are so particular, that with the practice of his apostles,

* Rom. xvi. 1. The Greek word in this passage rendered servant, is the same as in other places is rendered deacon or minister. It is rendered minister here in almost all other translations.

† Rom. xvi. 3. Priscilla is here, and in two other passages, placed before her husband; from which, and other circumstances, we may conclude she was a minister of no small eminence in the church.

‡ The adjective for " beloved," being in Greek in the feminine gender, shows that Persis was a woman. The Greek words here rendered " labour" and " laboured," are the same as the apostle uses when he speaks of himself labouring in the Gospel.

hey set the matter in a very clear point of view. The directions, so far as they relate to this subject, I shall transcribe from the tenth chapter of Matthew, when Christ sent forth the twelve apostles on their first mission: "Heal the sick; cleanse the lepers; raise the dead; cast out devils; freely ye have received freely give. Provide neither gold, nor silver, nor brass in your purses;—for the workman is worthy of his meat. And into whatsoever city or town ye shall enter, inquire who in it is worthy, and therein abide till ye go thence. And whosoever shall not receive you, nor hear your words; when ye depart out of that house or city, shake off the dust of your feet." Matt. x. 8—14.

In the foregoing passage, we have directions for the conduct of the ministers of Christ, both when their ministry is received, and when it is rejected. In the former case, all that is provided is temporary accommodation, whilst travelling in the work of the ministry; or so engaged therein, as to prevent their attention to their temporal occupations. In the latter case, they are by no means authorized to extort a forced maintenance; but, as a testimony against those who reject them, they are directed to shake off the dust that cleaveth to their feet. Well would it have been for the Christian Religion, had its ministers, under all denominations, adhered to their Lord's instructions on this subject, and acted with that noble disinterestedness which He inculcates, and which we find was practised by his immediate followers, so as to enable one of them to say: "I seek not yours, but you." 2 Cor. xii. 14.

And here I cannot well avoid expressing great regret for the wound which, there is reason to believe, Christianity has received, and still receives, from a lucrative establishment for ministers; a circumstance which holds out a temptation for unqualified, and even immoral men, to seek for, and get into, that office, with no better motive (I believe it will be generally allowed) than that which it was foretold would actuate the corrupted sons of Eli: "Put me, I pray thee, into one of the priest's offices, that I may eat a piece of bread." 1 Sam. ii. 36.

We are aware of the arguments advanced from some expressions of the apostle Paul, in favour of an established support for ministers, and which, I apprehend, are all comprised in the following words of the apostle: " Do ye not know, that they which minister about holy things, live of the things of the temple; and they which wait at the altar, are partakers with the altar? Even so hath the Lord ordained, that they which preach the Gospel, should live of the Gospel." 1 Cor. ix. 13, 14. Now all this only proves a support consistent with what " the Lord hath ordained," and which is already given in his own words. This we readily admit, and adopt in our practice; but surely no one can infer, from the fore-going passages, that ministers are to be provided with a settled maintenance; and are not to labour with their hands, or to be engaged in the usual occupations of life for their own support, and that of their families!

That we are justified in the construction given of our Lord's direction, and the apostle's reference to it, is abundantly clear from the practice which resulted from it; and which cannot be more completely or energetically described, than in the words of the same apostle, contained in his most excellent address to the elders of Ephesus, which he concludes in this memorable language; " I have coveted no man's silver, or gold, or apparel; yea, you yourselves know, that these hands have ministered unto my necessities, and to them that were with me. I have showed you all things, how that, so labouring, ye ought to support the weak, and to remember the words of the Lord Jesus, how He said, It is more blessed to give than to receive." Acts xx. 33—35.

These being our sentiments on this important subject, we make no provision for the support of our ministers, further than the discharge of those expenses, which travelling in their religious services necessarily occasions; and, if we make no provision for the support of our own ministers, whose ministry we approve, we think ourselves fully warranted in declining to contribute to the support of others, and of a worship connected with them, from both of which we conscientiously dissent. A ministry with a settled maintenance, forced even from those who so far disapprove of their establishment, as to withdraw from their teaching, is so evidently incompatible with the doctrine and practice of Christ and his apostles that,

I think it unnecessary to say more to justify our principles in this respect. But, although it appears to me to be a system so deeply injurious to the interests of true religion, I have no doubt that many, not seeing the subject in the same point of view, have seriously entered, under these circumstances, into this vocation, and are piously concerned to discharge the duties of their station. These should be left to their own master, to whom we must all, at last, either stand or fall.

After what has been said respecting the general maintenance of Gospel ministers, it appears superfluous to enter into argument against that most objectionable and anti-christian mode, of support by Tithes. Their divine right is generally exploded and abandoned; their impolicy is almost as universally acknowledged. How far the testimony which we have borne against them may have contributed to produce these effects, is not for me to determine; but it is hoped that, so long as this yoke remains, that testimony will continue to be maintained, with the firmness and meekness which should ever be united in the support of religious truths.

SILENT WORSHIP.

Though glorious, O GOD! must thy temple have been,
  On the day of its first dedication,
When the Cherubim's wings widely waving were seen
  On high, o'er the ark's holy station;

When even the chosen of Levi, though skill'd
  To minister, standing before Thee,
Retir'd from the cloud which the temple then fill'd,
  And thy glory made Israel adore Thee:

Though awfully grand was thy majesty then;
  Yet the worship thy Gospel discloses,
Less splendid in pomp to the vision of men,
  Far surpasses the ritual of Moses

And by whom was that ritual for ever repeal'd?
 But by HIM, unto whom it was given
To enter the Oracle, where is reveal'd,
 Not the cloud, but the brightness of heaven.

Who, having once entered, hath shown us the way,
 O Lord! how to worship before thee;
Not with shadowy forms of that earlier day,
 But in *spirit* and *truth* to adore thee!

This, this is the worship the Saviour made known,
 When she of Samaria found him
By the patriarch's well, sitting weary, alone,
 With the stillness of noon-tide around him.

How sublime, yet how simple the homage he taught
 To her, who inquir'd by that fountain,
If JEHOVAH at Solyma's shrine would be sought?
 Or ador'd on Samaria's mountain?

Woman! believe me, the hour is near,
 When HE, if ye rightly would hail him,
Will neither be worship'd *exclusively* here,
 Nor yet at the altar of Salem.

For GOD is a Spirit! and they, who aright
 Would perform the pure worship he loveth,
In the heart's holy temple will seek, with delight,
 That spirit the Father approveth.

And many that prophecy's truth can declare,
 Whose bosoms have livingly known it;
Whom GOD hath instructed to worship him there,
 And convinc'd that his mercy will own it.

The temple that Solomon built to his name,
 Now lives but in history's story;
Extinguish'd long since is its altar's bright flame,
 And vanish'd each glimpse of its glory.

But the Christian, made wise by a wisdom divine,
 Though all human fabrics may falter,
Still finds in his heart a far holier shrine,
 Where the fire burns unquench'd on the altar!

END.

Printed by E. Couchman & Co., 10, Throgmorton Street, London.

THE LAST DAYS

OF

HONOR JAGO.

"Neither is he that planteth anything, neither he that watereth; but God, that giveth the increase." 1 Cor. iii. 7.

In the following account of the change of an aged woman "from darkness to light, and from the power of Satan unto God," we have an illustration of the manner in which the Most High sometimes confers his blessing on an artless remark made in Christian good-will to a poor forlorn fellow-creature, or blesses the reading of a Tract to his own glory. Such instances are calculated to encourage those who are endeavouring to direct the attention of mankind, by these humble means, to that Saviour who died for them, and whom they may have long neglected or despised; and may also prove an incitement to others to seek that mercy and forgiveness which to the repentant sinner is freely offered through Him.

With this view the following extract is published from a letter written by a person residing in a village in Cornwall.

"While attending a Tract meeting a short time since, one of our distributors gave a very pleasing account of an old woman, who, as they termed it, had been convinced and converted, through the instrumentality of a come-by-chance Tract. When I heard this, I thought it not unlikely to be one of those you gave away while here. I took the earliest opportunity of calling on the old woman; and, on entering her room, was agreeably surprised by the manner in which she accosted me. She said: 'Oh, my dear, are you come! Sit down, and I will tell you all about it. My soul is happy in God now.

No. 92.   [Price 1½d. per dozen.]

I have no time to talk about the world, or anything i
it. I feel I must always be talking of, and praising th
Lord, for what he has done for me.' I then asked he
how long it was since she felt the change. She told m
that she had felt a concern for her soul ever since las
January; that she, with some others, was standing nea
her door, to see some Quaker ladies getting into thei
carriage, when one of the ladies stepped aside, and sai
to her, 'Wilt thou accept a Tract? I hope thou ar
not too old to read it.' That word pierced me to th
heart. What, thought I, does the lady think I am to
old to be saved? That impression never wore awa
from my mind; it sunk deeper and deeper, till I becam
completely sin-sick. For some months I kept all this t
myself, wishing I could see that dear lady again, to kno
what she meant by my being too old to read the Tract
for, still, I could not persuade myself but that she meant
I was too old to be saved; not thinking, she though
from my age and infirmities, I was too old to read it.
continued to read the Tract again and again; but stil
without any relief. Thus I went on for some time,
praying and reading, till, at last I came to the determina-
tion to throw myself on Jesus; and while reading the
Tract, entitled, 'Salvation by Jesus Christ,'* when I
came to that part, to look unto Jesus, the Lamb of God
that taketh away the sin of the world; through mercy,
I was enabled so to look as to have peace with God
through him. Then it was, that I was happy indeed in
Jesus. Old things passed away, and all things became
new.

"This was her statement, on my first visit: she was
then very ill, and had been so for some weeks. I continued to see her occasionally; and often thought it
would have been highly gratifying to you, could you
have seen her, and heard from her own lips what I had
the pleasure to hear. She was not ashamed to acknowledge to all around her, that the words you spoke, and
the Tracts you gave, were the instruments in the hand
of the Almighty, to the salvation of her soul. The last
time I saw her was the evening before her death. She

* No. 75 of the series published by Friends' Tract Association.

n desired me to give her dying love to you; and to
l you, that she believed she should know you in hea-
n. It was indeed good to be there. She died the
lowing morning: and her last words were, 'Victory,
tory. The port is in sight. I shall soon be there.
allelujah! Hallelujah!'

"Thus died Honor Jago, the 1st of this month, [11th
. 1841,] aged 83 years. A great number of persons
ited her during her illness, on hearing of the change
at had taken place in her. Previous to receiving the
acts, she was thought to be remarkably dark and
rdened; and had not attended any place of worship
· more than forty years. After receiving the Tracts
e began to attend meetings [for Divine Worship], and
ntinued to attend them as long as she was able."

In the instance here recorded, it pleased the Most
igh, in his long-suffering and tender mercy, to extend
e visitations of his grace to an advanced period of life,
d to call this individual as in the eleventh hour of her
y: but let none who read this Tract, be emboldened
ı that account, to put off answering the call of the Lord
ı a future day. The present time only is ours. The
ɔungest know not but the present may be their eleventh
ɔur. It may be said to any, how young soever they
ay be, "This night thy Soul shall be required of thee."
None can answer but when God calls, and none can
ɔmmand the visitations of his grace. "To-day," there-
re, if he calls by his good Spirit to your souls, "harden
ɔt your hearts," lest ye perish in your sins. There is
ason to believe, the long portion of Honor Jago's life
ɔent in estrangement from God, was not a time of peace
· comfort, but one of hopelessness and of darkness; and
ıough she could, at length, rejoice in the prospect of
ıture happiness, and in the present mercy which had
ıscued her from everlasting destruction, yet had she
ɔught and found that mercy in Christ Jesus in her early
ıys, which was so precious to her on the verge of the
ıave, and continued to walk in the light of the Lord,
ıe might have enjoyed the sense of his goodness and
ıve during the whole course of her long life: and have
ıen able to look back upon the time she had spent to
ıs glory, under similar feeling to that which led the

4

Psalmist to say: "A day in Thy courts is better than a thousand. I had rather be a doorkeeper in the house of my God, than to dwell in the tents of wickedness. For the Lord God is a sun and shield. The Lord will give grace and glory; no good thing will he withhold from them that walk uprightly."—Ps. lxxxiv. 10, 11.

~~~~~~~~~~

Too old to read! what, am I then
    Too old to be forgiven?
Too old to read! and am I then
    Too old to hope for heaven?

T'was thus I thought on what I'd heard,
    With feelings of dismay,
Till pointed to the Incarnate Word,
    The life, the truth, the way.

Ah! then I mourned my sinful course;
    Saw all was dark within;
But faith beheld Him on the cross,
    A sacrifice for sin.

And then, with ever-pitying eye,
    My soul he reconciled
By His own blood, my sins passed by,
    And own'd me for his child.

May I, then, join the saints above
    His goodness to adore;
Proclaim the wonders of His love;
    And praise Him evermore!

END.

London: Printed by E. Couchman & Co., 10, Throgmorton Street; for the TRACT ASSOCIATION of the SOCIETY OF FRIENDS. Sold at the Depository, 12, Bishopsgate Street Without.—1863.

A

SHORT ACCOUNT

OF

JOHN · SPALDING,

LATE OF READING.

~~~~~

WRITTEN BY HIMSELF.

~~~~~

I SHALL pass over the early part of my life, only observing I had been educated in a religious way. I mention this, as, at times, when I lived in London, where I served an apprenticeship, in the midst of my dissipation I frequently felt the reproofs of the Lord in mine heart, but which were soon smothered in the vortex of pleasure. After I had served my apprenticeship, I returned into the country to assist my father in his business of a farrier, at Reading, in the year 1786. A little time afterwards, as I attended the parish church, so called, where a celebrated preacher officiated, I found an awakening power, which produced not a little alteration in me. I more constantly attended the services, public and private; joined the more particular professors; and went on for several years as one of them. I also abstained from vain company and conversation which I had before been addicted to, so that I was one of the chief professors; but I found a gradual wearing off of the force of the impressions I had received; less dislike to worldly company; and the power of sin gaining the ascendancy; that I at times felt much uneasiness; particularly as on serious reflection, I felt the strength of my lusts and passions, and the evil propensities of my nature unsubdued; notwithstanding my knowledge of the truths of the Gospel, and the profession I made. Observing and conversing with my fellow professors; I found the same in them I lamented in myself; which brought at times

No. 77.   [*Price 8d. per dozen.*]

great anxiety of mind, and breathings to the Lord, that he would make me indeed what I professed to be; and what I was persuaded by the Scriptures of Truth, a true Christian might be; that is, free from the power, as well as the guilt of sin. . Thus I went on till about the year 1792, often feeling the dominion of sin, and desiring deliverance from it; when I sought the conversation of some of the people called Quakers, and desired to know their principles, and enquired for some of their writings. The first book, I think, that I read, was Penn's "No Cross, No Crown," which much tendered my spirit and removed some unfavourable opinions I had received respecting Friends. I then, in some measure, saw how far what I had known before fell short of what that work directed to; yet I continued attending at the parish place of worship; having the most favourable opinion of the minister there and a particular esteem for him as a man, who also frequently professed a particular affection towards me. Once, I remember, when I had so far deviated from my profession as to go to a horse race, he sent for me, and kindly admonished me as a friend and overseer. I mention this, as afterwards, when it pleased the Lord to enlighten my mind more clearly, and convinced me of the necessity of leaving the form of worship I had been accustomed to, it was a sore trial to me, to leave him, in a manner that I apprehended he would feel not a little concern about. The next book I read I think was Barclay's Apology, which opened many things so clearly to me, that I could not but consent to them; nevertheless there were some things that at first reading, I could not assent to, particularly respecting public worship. I thought it needfu there should be a time appointed, and somebody ready t officiate, that the ignorant might be instructed; and that man, taught, as I apprehended, of the Lord, and properly qualified, might at any time exhort or preach to the people. I still attended the old place, going occasionally to Friends' meetings on any particular occasions, when some strangers were expected; whose testimonies, though I could not but approve of them, yet were not able to draw me from my former society; but I found the work of the Lord going on by degrees.

At first, I think, I considered the ordinance of the Lord's supper, as it is called, and was sensible I had never found any profit in it, from the beginning of my partaking of it; and though I had often heard others speak very highly of it, as finding particular and extraordinary comfort and benefit in it and I often at the time earnestly desired to find the benefit o it as well as others : yet it still remained a dead, unprofitable service ; I therefore declined it entirely. The next thing, I think, I observed, was the public singing. I began to see a great inconsistency in that practice, particularly after sermon, I could feel it had in myself, as well as in others, a manifest tendency to lightness of spirit, and removing any serious impressions which might have been received from the foregoing discourse ; that I soon left the place, immediately after sermon was ended. It was not long, however, before I saw a gross inconsistency in the practice altogether, when I weightily considered the matter contained in what was sung, how impossible it was for a congregation of different kinds of people to join in singing whatever might be given out, whether suitable to their conditions or not ; much of which, I was persuaded, could not be said by any, without uttering gross falsehoods, which I could not believe could be acceptable in the sight of the Lord. I was in consequence constrained to give forth some observations on the subject in writing, addressed to the professors of religion, attending the place called St. Giles's Church.

"*A few observations concerning the custom of singing in public meetings of worship ; by one who has long been convinced of the inconsistency of it ; and now calls upon every one who professes to be a follower of the meek and lowly Jesus, to lay aside prejudice, and seriously consider the following remarks ; which are offered in the fear of the Lord.*"

" First, it ought ever to be considered that God is a Spirit, and they that worship him must worship him in spirit and in truth. In other words, it is the language of the heart which he regards, not words, however excellent of themselves. Now I appeal to the witness of God in every heart, considering the variety of conditions, the different subjects of praise, adoration, confession, petitioning, &c., &c., contained in every collection, whether in the fear of the Lord, any one, in whatever state or condition he may be in at the time, can with propriety be ready to sing whatever may be given out. It appears to me impossible that a whole congregation (even if we except the ignorant) can be in the same frame of mind, considering the various dispensations of the Lord's providence towards his people ; consequently if that is not the case, it follows of course that, if all sing, some must utter words with the mouth contrary to the language of the heart, which so far from being acceptable to the Lord, I am persuaded is hypocrisy and abomination in his sight.

"Again, it appears to me inconsistent also with regard to the other parts of worship: for if the language of the heart is spoken in prayer, which often precedes singing, and which implies a sense of our wants, doth it not show an indifference whether our prayers are heard and answered or not, to begin singing immediately, perhaps very different in matter as well as in manner, to what has been prayed for?

"Again, after preaching, if the Lord's power is known and felt under the word, is it not more likely to profit, if the mind is occupied in serious meditation, than singing, which, from my own experience, I can say has a tendency to divert the mind from solemn, serious reflection? I am now speaking more particularly concerning those who have attained to a measure of the grace of God. Ask yourselves seriously, is outward singing intended or calculated to please the carnal ears of men, or a holy God? Why such anxiety about tunes, voices, and music? Is the Lord to be pleased with such poor things? Oh no; you cannot suppose it. Consider from what root it springs, from the old man or the new; and remember, the axe is laid to the root, to destroy all that is of the earth, of our fleshly nature. I have considered those passages in the New Testament where the subject is mentioned, and am confirmed by them in my opinion of the inconsistency of public singing. The apostle speaks of singing with grace in the heart; of making melody in the heart to the Lord; not making a noise with the tongue, unless that proceeds from the heart; which how seldom it does in public singing I appeal to every considerate mind.

"I am convinced in my own mind, considering our situation here, the power and devices of the enemy, our own inbred corruptions, that it is more seasonable to watch and pray, to be ever on our guard, and waiting to feel the light and power of Christ, to discover and subdue the hidden things of darkness—that as children of the light we may walk in the light, and find the blood of Jesus Christ cleansing us from all sin—than evidencing that trifling, careless spirit too commonly, if not always, attending outward singing.

"I could say much more against it, but would not be tedious, particularly respecting those that are without. How seldom can such people, living in open and avowed opposition to God, join in singing without uttering gross, abominable lies—and are we not accessory thereto? Is it not expected, when a psalm or hymn is given out, all present who are capable will 'oin? Then let it not be said, how can we help the abuse of t. Ought we not rather to set them an example of truth d righteousness, and not countenance any practice that has tendency to promote lightness and irreverence. Oh! my riends, this cannot be acceptable to the Lord, who requireth ruth in the inward parts. I recommend to your serious consi- eration what the Lord says in the 1st of Isaiah, respecting the rdinances of his own appointing, when not done in a proper pirit. I perceive every day, more and more, an evident eparture from the simplicity of Christ. Where is the daily ross borne? Observe the appearance of professors? What fference is there from the world? Sure, my friends, these hings ought not to be. Bear with me, I beseech you. I m much concerned for the honour of our profession. If the ross is truly borne, all self-seeking and self-pleasing will be one away, and the fruits of the Spirit more evidenced; which am persuaded will not be in the present practice of public utward singing, often of words, as to the matter, scarce thin the bounds of probability; and I am convinced if eople would seriously consider the matter, it would appear ery inconsistent with the gravity and solemnity of the true Christian profession.

"May the Lord set these things home upon every heart, that there may be a concern to offer unto him acceptable sacrifice; which more than once is said to be a broken and contrite spirit.

" 'Blessed are ye that mourn,' says Christ (not ye that sing), 'for ye shall rejoice;' which rejoicing, if it may be applied to the present state of the church here, I conceive to be a grateful sense of the Lord's mercies: and showing forth his praises not only with our lips but in our lives. To con- clude, my friends, turn in to your own hearts. 'Behold,' says Christ, 'the kingdom of God is within you;' look not without for what I am persuaded is only to be found within. It is not much hearing or much speaking that brings true peace to the soul—the ear is never satisfied with hearing. As a proof of that, do not we see professors running hither and thither, as though the more they heard, the better they should be; encompassing themselves about with sparks of their own kindling; but what saith the Lord? 'Ye shall lie down in sorrow.' I am fully convinced it is for want of this looking in, and waiting to feel the power of the Lord there, judging and subduing sin, that there is so much talk, so much outward parade, and so little spirituality in the lives and conversation of the people. "J. S."

This I sent to the clerk, at the same time I sent som reasons for the apparent change in me, as, absenting from th sacrament, so called; and which I desired him to lay befor the minister and others, at a prayer meeting; which he seeme to object to, supposing me in error, and having a very un favourable opinion of Friends' principles. I soon after ha some conversation with him on the subject; which rathe confirmed me in my opinion than otherwise, his argument appeared so weak against Friends. Thus I went on som little time longer, still attending mornings and evenings; bu attending Friends' meetings in the afternoon. About this tim I read "Sewell's History of the Quakers," which I think re moved every objection, and confirmed me in my opinion o the truth of their principles. Their severe sufferings, the patience under them, and honest boldness before kings an rulers, convinced me that nothing but a divine power coul have supported them. I sought the company of some faithf Friends, as I could discover in some I had been with, littl more than the form. I desired to know their power in myself and to be truly taught of the Lord, that I might not do any thing by imitation, or because others did so : but retired ofte alone to be instructed of the Lord, what to do and what to leave; and glory to his name, he was found of me, and made those retirements precious and profitable to me, revealing his will unto me by degrees, as I was able to bear it. I now became acquainted with some solid Friends, and was occasionally in company with them, which excited the attention of my friends and neighbours; so that there was much talk about me, and various reports were propagated respecting it, most people thinking it very strange I should turn Quaker.

About this time I met with a considerable trial, the death of my father, whom I dearly loved. I had long been persuaded in some measure of the vanity and inconsistency of wearing black clothes on such occasions, knowing it to be only a worldly custom, and had often said to myself, during my father's illness, I would not put it on for any one except him; but there appeared so many reasons why I should conform on his account, that it was not till a very little time before his death that it pleased the Lord to remove my scruples respecting it, and strengthen me to bear such a public testimony as of necessity that event occasioned; and indeed, much opposition I met with on account of it, but the Lord supported me through all. I then constantly attended Friends' meetings.

About this time also I was concerned to write an address

o some who usually met on first-days, from different parts of the neighbouring country, to hear the minister, at a private house, where I had occasionally attended, with other professors of the town. I also wrote to the clerk, and sent him "No Cross, No Crown;" soon after, "Barclay's Apology;" and to another intimate friend, who was very zealous, I wrote and sent Beaven's "Primitive Christianity Restored." And though I desired in what I wrote to individuals, as well as the Society, it might be put about for the perusal of any, I found little notice taken by any—I thought they seemed rather to avoid me. One steady, experienced man, in a little conversation, observing, he hoped I did not look for that in myself, which was only to be found in Christ, I was concerned to write to him some little time after on the subject; and sent him at the same time, "No Cross, No Crown." While I was exercised towards the society I had left, I met with some more trials from other quarters—my relations complained of my silence, putting unfavourable constructions upon it. Indeed I had so much upon my mind, that I had little desire to speak much; for being often in my way of business, with people of consequence in the neighbourhood, most of whom had always shown me much attention and favour, now observing such a change, though only in dress at first, they began to look rather strangely upon me. The enemy of souls was not unmindful of my situation, and raised many difficulties in my way, as the loss of their favours, and, of course, my business; the great offence my conforming to other things not yet done would give them, such as the ceremony of the hat, the language, and their titles so highly valued; these seemed, indeed, so great discouragements, that my mind was at times sorely distressed.

I had some time felt an uneasiness respecting the performing some part of my business, such as nicking and cropping horses, &c., punishing them, for the sake of appearance, to please the fancies of men. When I began to mention my scruples, much opposition was made, as the consequence must, of course, be the loss of much business. I know not whether I was not too hasty in this matter, beginning in mine own strength, and not waiting the due time; for I found when I was required to do it, I gave way, which brought trouble upon me, till at last I was enabled to refuse several, among whom was one for whom I did much business, who, on my objecting and telling him my reasons, seemed very angry, and reproached my changing my religion, &c. He asked me to recommend some one to do it; but I told him I could not recommend another to do what I thought not right to do myself.

This event occasioned some uneasiness. I was blamed highly, on the supposition that I should soon lose my business; but I answered in the words of our Lord, "Except a man forsake all that he hath, he cannot be my disciple." I saw more and more how people could follow the ways customs, and fashions of the world, and use means not always the most honest to get its riches—so true is our Lord's saying "Where your treasure is, there will your hearts be also." Oh! how few really deny themselves, and take up the cross.

About this time came the quarterly meeting of a society I helped to establish, called "The Sick Man's Visitor," to relieve the wants of those in distress, conducted by the chief and most serious of the professors, a committee of whom met every week to transact the business of it, and to hold a prayer meeting, as they called it, at the same time singing, reading &c. Being the time I used to serve on the committee, I took the opportunity to write to them, giving my reasons why I could not join in the services performed at those times; also something more respecting the principles, &c., of Friends with what was upon my mind besides; observing, if any were desirous of more information on the subject, or had an objections to propose respecting Friends' principles, I was willing to receive them.

It was a great grief and concern to me to consider that, a it was a day of so great profession, many walking miles to hear what they supposed the gospel preached, our steeple house being generally crowded by people from the other parishes; I say it grieved me, that my leaving the fashions of the world, which they all professed to deny, should cause such amazement as it appeared to do even in professors which helped to confirm me in my opinion, that how much soever they could talk about religion, very little of the power thereof was known; indeed, had I not felt a want of the power of godliness, I should not have left them, as there were many ties which held me both to the priest and people. But it was that divine power I longed for, and nothing short of it could satisfy me, and sure nothing but that could have supported me in the different trials I soon had to encounter; but the battle was the Lord's, and his was the victory over every appearance of mine adversary, and to him be all the glory.

For several months my mind was much exercised on various occasions, the enemy assaulting me continually with reproaches from without and fears within. My business eemed to decline, and I was tempted to believe my conduct as the cause. I was reproved for over-acting my part, and informed that some of the Society had said so. It was great grief to me to observe some Friends, for whom I entertained great esteem, not so faithful against worldly titles, as Sir such a one; Mr., &c., as I believe was required and practised by ancient Friends. It gave the enemies much occasion against me.

About this time people's minds were much agitated on political subjects, the French having overturned all orders and distinctions, which gave great offence to people in general; they called their days, &c., as do Friends, instead of the old names. I mention this, because the adversary assailed me with the suggestion that I should be deemed of their spirit, influenced by such motives, and from the treatment of some who had evidenced such a spirit, I could expect little favour, though politics was a subject I thought little about, and spoke less, believing, as our blessed Lord said, "My kingdom is not of this world." Every true disciple being influenced by the same spirit, the attention as well as the affections will be engaged in things above, not of this world, more than needful; and it had been some time before a concern to me, to observe some of the Society of Friends meddling with such matters, more warmly than I thought consistent with their profession.

I was at times so sorely pressed, so burdened in spirit, that I seemed as though my strength was broken, and was ready to cry out, "The children are come to the birth, and there is not strength to bring forth:" but still my desires were to the Lord, who had hitherto supported me, that I might still experience him a God near at hand, and not afar off; for I felt how unable I was to move a step, without his divine assistance. So low was I reduced, that though I received several reviling letters, which were clearly against the truth, I had not power to answer them; being taught to leave the cause to the Almighty, and not be anxious to justify myself before men; but which may be an encouragement to any who may experience similar trials, I felt a secret upholding, a consoling assurance, that the Lord would plead his own cause, and in his own time bring forth judgment unto victory; and I desired that his hand might not spare, neither his eye pity, till his work was accomplished to his own glory, however it might be with me. Thus I continued some time, till it pleased the Lord to revive me; when, though I had little business in comparison to what I had heretofore, yet I

was abundantly satisfied with an enlivening sense of the
Lord's presence, which infinitely surpassed all worldly goods,
so that in measure I knew the truth of our dear Lord's
promise, that whoever may be enabled to leave anything for
his name's sake, shall receive an hundred fold even in this
life, either in kind or in kindness : and sure the comfortable
sense of the approbation of the Most High, is of infinitely
greater value than anything this world can afford. O! that
the people, particularly the Lord's professing people, may be
encouraged to be willing to part with everything, however
near and dear to flesh and blood, that stands in the way,
which obstructs that divine communion with him we are
taught to expect ; for true it is, except a man forsake all that
he hath, he cannot be Christ's disciple. And he is not a
hard master; doth not require anything to be parted with
but what would be really injurious to our spiritual welfare ;
though to man's carnal apprehension it may seem in some
cases in a different light. Man naturally loves ease. The
cross of Christ is not pleasant to flesh and blood ; but, my
friends, if ever we know true happiness, I believe we shall
first know the truth of what Paul declares, that "they who
are Christ's have crucified the flesh with its affections and
lusts ;" and the more readily we submit to the yoke, I am
persuaded we shall the sooner experience that subdued,
which dislikes the cross : then we shall know what our Lord
said, that his yoke is easy and his burden light.

A fear had arisen in my mind, lest I should be beholding
the mote in my brother's eye, and not attending sufficiently
to that power, which could alone remove the beam out of
my own : and though my spirit was frequently grieved on
hearing vain conversation, and often seemed to feel a desire
to reprove ; yet I was afraid to cast a stone, feeling myself
not without sin, and I had to remember and to desire to
practice what is recorded, to study to be quiet, and mind my
own business ; and I think I can truly say that, in stillness
and retiredness I experienced a greater degree of peace, and
I trust a growth in grace ; and I must acknowledge with
humble thankfulness the condescending kindness of my
Heavenly Father, in favouring me with much opportunity of
retirement, having comparatively but little worldly business :
for I sorrowfully found in those lawful engagements, a very
great difficulty of keeping in that straight line of duty, which
I believe was marked out for me. In the course of conversation words would occasionally drop, which afterwards, on
reflection, brought distress on my mind ; and I desired to be

ankful that I was enabled not to desire much of this world's
oods, but rather the reverse, and to be content with food and
iment. It was a concern to me to observe among Friends,
i a young man's beginning business for himself, a conformity
some things with the world, I thought, to gain their favour
ad custom; it appeared to me paying very dear for their
ssistance; and I believed I could prefer working hard as a
ervant, to the most profitable situation on such terms; and
fervent desire would frequently arise in my mind, that all
ho profess to be followers of Christ, particularly Friends,
ho profess more than most, would be concerned to practice
ur blessed Lord's advice, to seek first the kingdom of God
ad his righteousness; yea, and seek nothing else till they
ad found it; then I believed by attending to that, they
ould be divinely directed in temporal concerns, and pre-
erring it above all things, would be preserved from the too
revailing snare of flattering the world for their support. I
ave thought that people are often led to such practices, by
ngaging in concerns which bring extraordinary expense
pon them, which, requiring more of the things of this world,
greater difficulty is experienced in bearing a faithful testi-
iony against what they may be convinced is evil. These
onsiderations, through divine assistance, induced me to be
areful of confining my expenses in as narrow a compass as I
elieved consistent with my situation: and though for many,
ears I had strong inclinations to enter into the marriage
tate, I now experienced a check to every desire of the kind;
elieving it was my duty to keep myself as much as possible
rom the cumbers of this world, and as a faithful soldier, to
e ready for whatever my great Lord and Master should
equire of me.

Near the close of the year 1793, I wrote to the Friends
f the Monthly Meeting to be admitted a member of the
Society; which Friends in due season expressed their unity
nd compliance with: and here I would observe, that from
ny first acquaintance with Friends, I could not but approve
heir caution in not hastily admitting any into membership;
liffering from most societies, who, I have perceived, evince
i kind of exulting eagerness in adding to their numbers.
And I can say that I did not feel an anxiety to be received
nto membership; but rather to know that power which first
gathered Friends into a Society; to experience an union of
pirit with the faithful, than any name or outward relation-
hip: and though a little before I wrote to the Monthly
Meeting, I had some apprehension of being drawn for the

militia, which would probably have exposed me to some
severe trial, not being of the Society; yet convinced of the
necessity of bearing my testimony against wars and fightings
I was mercifully enabled to be still, and leave the event
whatever it might be, to the Lord, who had hitherto sup
ported me, and not apply for admission any sooner on that
account.

Being appointed by the parish overseer this year, I had
frequent opportunities of observing the difficulties many o
the poor laboured under, and was favoured to sympathise
with them therein; and I had often to consider the manne
of living among those in superior situations, as to outward
things, and it appeared to me not consistent with the graciou
designs of our Heavenly Father, that some should live luxu
riously and expend much upon superfluities, while so man
fellow-creatures were in want of the comforts and necessarie
of life. It seemed to me a great evil, and my spirit was ofter
bowed in consideration thereof: for I thought that the op
pression of the poor, and the extravagant living of others
was one cause of the judgments of the Most High being a
this time so awfully executed in the neighbouring kingdoms
And it was often the secret breathing of my spirit, that th
people of this land, instead of applying to carnal weapons
which was now pretty general throughout the kingdom, an
trusting to the multitude of their hosts, might endeavour to
avert the threatened indignation before it came home, b
turning every one from the evil of their ways, to serve th
Lord with their whole hearts, to relieve the distresses of th
poor, and content themselves with a moderate way of living
as becomes the followers of him who said, "My kingdom i
not of this world."

———

The above memorial of this devoted young man is extract
ed from "Some account of his convincement and religiou
progress," written by himself. It was published shortl
after his decease, on which occasion it was observed, in
short preface, that it was deemed "worthy of publication, a
an additional testimony to the cloud of witnesses we ar
favoured with, to the internal efficacy of the power and prin
ciple of Truth; the writer being remarkably distinguished b
a steady, uniform devotion, and dedication of heart to th
pure cause of truth and righteousness on the earth; whic

believed himself called to maintain, and to endeavour to promote by example and precept. His memory is, therefore, very precious; in particular to some who had an intimate acquaintance with him. To these more emphatically, he being dead, yet speaketh, in the remembrance of his solid, wise deportment, his fewness of words, and these seasoned with grace, and his steady firmness towards opposers of principles which he had not taken upon trust; and he was deeply engaged to exhibit an example of simplicity and uprightness." In a letter to a friend some months before his decease, after pointing out his great concern in observing the declensions amongst a highly professing and eminently favoured people, and making various remarks on the importance of preserving, as a wall of defence, the religious discipline established among them, he observed, " O, my friend, excuse my freedom; the cause of truth, I have to believe, though with a due proportion of fear I would express it, is so deeply impressed upon my mind, that neither the fear nor the love of any created being or thing can be permitted to obstruct or divert me from what may appear to be required of me." He was taken ill of a fever which continued about three weeks. In the forepart of his illness he expressed to a friend who visited him, "that there was no cause of discouragement to the right-minded." Being asked at another time if he had anything in particular to express to Friends, he replied, "No, only my love; all is well; nothing stands in my way." A few friends visited him near his solemn close, and though in the midst of mourning, were joyful witnesses and partakers of that solemnity and peace, which proved as a seal to his great religious concern and exercise. He died in the thirtieth year of his age, the 30th of the 1st month, 1795.

What is a true Christian?

Is it one who assents to and believes certain facts, as re
corded in Holy Writ, and forms certain principles and opinion
thereupon; producing perhaps a partial reformation, an ab
staining from the grosser pollutions of sin, but denying th
possibillity of a total cleansing and freedom from sin, in thi
world? Or is it one who knows, not in word only, but
deed and in truth, a death unto sin, and a new birth unt
righteousness: a being born again, not of blood, nor of th
will of the flesh, nor of man, but of God? "For," say
our blessed Lord, "except a man be born again, he canno
enter into the kingdom of God." A man may know wit
Nicodemus, and confess that Christ is a teacher sent fro
God: he may be able to talk much about the doctrines o
the Gospel, and fancy himself secure by imputation, but wha
has this to do with the new birth so essentially necessary?
What can all his wisdom and understanding teach him?
Nay, he cannot come into the new birth till all is parted with.
The very nature of the thing implies a beginning again, a
life as different from his former as light from darkness. "Ye
were sometimes darkness," says Paul, "but now are ye light
in the Lord." Now he who knows this new birth, not a
change of opinions, not a comprehending the truths of the
Gospel in his understanding, or joining this or that society,
but who knows the thing itself; not the name, not the imaginations concerning it, but the nature, the life, the essence
will such a man be like what he was before?

The forerunner of our Lord expressly told his hearers
when preparing them for the Gospel dispensation, "The axe
is laid to the root of the trees, and every tree that bringeth
not forth good fruit is hewn down and cast into the fire."
What tree and what root is there meant? Is it outward or
inward? Who can answer that, but he who hath felt the
axe, and the destruction, in a measure, of the corrupt tree?
"His fan is in his hand," he adds, "and he will thoroughly
purge his floor;" (mark, "thoroughly,") what will remain
then? that professors were concerned to know, and willing to
part with all that stands in the way, that they may know
indeed what it is to be thoroughly purged, instead of denying
the possibility of it: for it is a dreadful thing to oppose or
deny the power of Christ.

Christ said, "Blessed are the pure in heart;" but modern Christians, as they would be thought, say, there is
no purity of heart, but it is and must remain deceitful

ove all things, and desperately wicked. That the heart
every man is so by nature is allowed; but hath not
od promised a new heart and a new spirit; will that
, desperately wicked? Again, it is said, "who can bring
clean thing out of an unclean?" That the heart is na-
ally unclean is allowed; but hath not the Lord promised
leanse his people from all their uncleannesses; mark *all:*
at uncleannesses will then remain? Some attempt to
cuse themselves by what Paul once experienced; "The
sh lusteth against the spirit, and the spirit against the
sh: a law in the members warring against the law of
e mind." That Paul once felt that, is allowed, but did he
t after say, "There is no condemnation to them that are
Christ Jesus, who walk not after the flesh but after the
irit?" and did he not say, "the law of the spirit of life had
ade him free from the law of sin; and how could they who
ere dead unto sin live any longer therein?" Doth he not
ain say, "I am dead with Christ, nevertheless I live, yet
t I, (not natural, sinful self,) but Christ liveth in me?"
[will dwell in them, and walk in them, saith the Lord:"
d will the Lord dwell in an impure, an unholy place? As
on would light dwell with darkness. Satan can indeed
ansform himself into an angel of light, yea, he as God,
tteth in the temple of God, showing himself that he is
od. The imagining part in man is sure to be deceived,
nd worship the appearance instead of the reality, for the world
y wisdom, man by his natural or humanly acquired abilities,
new not, nor ever can know, God. "If any man," says
aul, "will be wise, let him first become a fool," that his
d eye may be closed, and the new eye, which can alone
iscern the things of God, may be opened.

Again, Christ saith, "Be ye perfect, even as your Father
hich is in heaven is perfect." But modern Christians, as
ey call themselves say, there is no such thing as perfection.
that they would consider whom they oppose by so saying.

Doth not Paul desire those he was writing to, to cleanse
emselves from all filthiness of flesh and spirit, perfecting
oliness in the fear of the Lord; and pray that others may
e perfect and complete in all the will of God? What does
ich plain, express language mean? O the subtilty of that
rpent, who can reason and argue the true meaning away;
nd O the lamentable state of those who are so deceived
y him, who are sitting down at ease, with the vain
nagination that what Christ hath done, as they suppose for
em will be sufficient; without experiencing the work in

REASONS, &c.

Amongst the striking characteristics of the Gospel dispensation, as revealed in former ages through prophetic
vision, and declared of by "holy men of God," who
"spake as they were moved by the Holy Ghost," there
is *one* which has a reference to some of the most precious
privileges of the christian covenant, the fulfilment of
which has been restricted, either by ecclesiastical domination, or by the prejudices and pre-conceived opinions
of many who profess the name of Christ.

When it pleased the Most High, through his prophet
Joel, to comfort his afflicted church with the promise
of future blessings, He graciously condescended to declare *what* should be the result of that more powerful
operation of his Spirit on the hearts of his people, which
should distinguish the dispensation that was to come,
in which types and shadows should be exchanged for
spiritual realities. And on that memorable day when the
company of disciples, consisting, as there appears good
reason to conclude, of both men and women, "were all
with one accord in one place, and were all filled with the
Holy Ghost, and began to speak with other tongues as
the Spirit gave them utterance," the Apostle Peter testified that, the period *had* commenced when the prediction
was to be fulfilled :* "This is that," said he, "which was
spoken by the prophet Joel; And it shall come to pass in
the last days, saith God, I will pour out of my Spirit
upon all flesh, and your sons and your daughters shall
prophesy, and your young men shall see visions, and your
old men shall dream dreams, and on my servants and on
my handmaidens I will pour out in those days of my
Spirit, and they shall prophesy." Let us mark the *period*
when this was to be acomplished—*in the last days.*
Now, this declaration of the apostle on the day of
Pentecost that it was *then* fulfilled, clearly indicates its

* In the previous chapter we are informed that the disciples "continued
with one accord with prayer and supplication, *with the women,*" &c.; and
we can scarcely doubt that the company assembled together on the day of
Pentecost consisted of the same persons ; and that it was in consequence
of the descent of the Holy Ghost on both men and women, that Peter
rehearsed the prediction of Joel, ii. 28, 29.

being a *feature* of the dispensation which was, on that
occasion, first preached to people of various climes and
nations, but which was to continue to the end of time,
being the one *everlasting* covenant between God and
his people, and therefore fitly spoken of as *the last days*.
It is also worthy of the reader's special attention, that
his outpouring of the Spirit, this gift of prophecy, was
as unequivocally declared to be bestowed on the *daughters*,
and on the *handmaidens*, as on the *sons* and the *servants*.
That women *did* continue to exercise this gift of prophecy, is sufficiently manifest.. The apostle Paul refers
particularly, in his Epistle to the Romans, to certain
women who were his fellow-workers in the Gospel, as
*Tryphena, and Tryphosa, and the beloved Persis, who la-
boured much in the Lord;* and, in that to the Philippians,
to those women who laboured with him in the Gospel speaking of them as *amongst his fellow-labourers, whose names
are in the book of life.*

In addressing the Corinthian church, the same apostle
in ch. xi. 4, 5, 6, gives some particular directions how both
men and *women* should behave themselves when engaged
in the holy assemblies, in the exercise of the gift of prophecy, or of prayer. These directions have an evident
allusion to certain irregularities in their manner of conducting public worship. He reprehends the practice of
the men who prayed or prophesied with their heads
covered, and that of the women who were engaged in
these sacred duties with their heads uncovered.

As the apostle thus decidedly recognises the public
praying and prophesying of females, giving these injunctions concerning their dress and deportment, when so
employed, it must surely be self-evident that some
women, as well as men, laboured in the ministry of the
word. In the 21st chapter of Acts, v. 9, there is an
incidental mention of Philip the evangelist, and the very
remarkable fact is then introduced, that "the same man
had four daughters which did prophesy." If the reader
be impressed with the belief that the gift of prophecy is
distinguishable from that of preaching the Gospel, we
would direct his attention to the definition of it, given
by the apostle (1 Cor. xiv. 3), "He that prophesieth
speaketh unto men to edification, exhortation, and com-

fort." That eminent writer, John Locke, in his "Para phrase and Notes on the Epistles of St. Paul," remark on Romans xii. 6—"Prophecy is enumerated in the New Testament among the gifts of the Spirit, and mean either the interpretation of Sacred Scripture, and ex plaining of prophecies already delivered, or foretelling things to come."* There is, however, another passage addressed to the Corinthian church, which has beer frequently adduced in proof that the apostle discouraged and even forbade, the preaching of women: "Let you women keep silence in the churches, for it is not per mitted unto them to speak, but they are commanded to be under obedience, as saith also the law: and if they will learn anything, let them ask their husbands at home: for it is a shame for women to speak in the church:" and also one in the first epistle to Timothy, "Let the women learn in silence with all subjection.—I suffer not a woman to teach, nor to usurp authority over the man, but to be in silence." That the practice which, in these injunctions is so strongly condemned, was not the exer cise of any spiritual gift is unquestionable; and from the context it appears evident that the whole was intended to correct certain abuses which had rendered their assem blies for worship unprofitable and disorderly. The learned Benson, in his commentary on the Epistles, vol. i. p. 628, says, "In the synagogues, any man who had a mind might ask questions of his teachers, and demand a further explanation of what had been said: and this custom was also transferred into the primitive christian church, and that with the approbation of St. Paul; only he would not permit the women to do so, as the Judaizers at Corinth would have had them. No: if they wanted to have any further instructions they were to ask their own parents or husbands at home, and not enter into such conferences publicly in the church." *In the Jewish synagogues it was customary for the hearers to question the ministers on such points of their doctrine as might require further explanation.*† But this liberty was not allowed to

* "That prophecy in the New Testament often means the gift of exhorting, preaching, or expounding the Scriptures, is evident from many places in the Gospels, Acts, and St. Paul's Epistles." Dr. Clarke on Rom. xii. 6.

† See Lightfoot, Hor. Heb. in loc.

omen.* On this passage the celebrated Hugo Grotius marks, "To teach was the office of the President or ishop, though he sometimes committed this branch of is duties to other persons, especially the elders. The ostle suffers not the women to perform such an office— at is to say, *unless* they have, and only *while* they ave the prophetical impulse. Prophecy is beyond the ach of positive laws."† "The apostolic rule," says enson, "was, that when they were under immediate spiration, the women might pray or prophecy in the urch, but when they were under no such inspiration, ey were not to speak, i. e., neither to pray nor read, ach nor ask questions there."‡

Can any serious reader of the New Testament suppose at the apostle Paul, after giving, in 1 Cor. xi., a plain irection in reference to the praying or prophesying of omen, could possibly design in the xiv. ch. to *forbid* such exercise? We must surely, on a calm, unbiassed review these passages, and on comparing them with other parts the epistolary writings of the same apostle be brought the conclusion, that the public speaking which he rohibited was not that inspired ministry which was im- ediately prompted by the Holy Spirit, and which it pears evident that he fully recognized and sanctioned.

In tracing the history of the christian church, we may bserve how very soon was the brightness of the Gospel ay eclipsed by the power of the "man of sin," who exalted

* "It was permitted to any man to ask questions, to object, to alter- te, attempt to refute, &c., in the synagogue; but this liberty was not lowed to any woman. St. Paul confirms this in reference also to the ristian church; he orders them to keep silence; and if they wished to arn anything let them enquire of their husbands at home, because it as perfectly indecorous for women to be contending with men in public semblies, on points of doctrine, cases of conscience, &c. But this by no eans intimated that, when a woman received any particular influence om God to enable her to teach, she was not to obey that influence: on e contrary, she *was* to obey it, and the apostle lays down directions .ch. ii. for regulating her personal appearance when thus employed." r. Adam Clarke on 1 Cor. xiv. 34.

† Com. in loc.—2. "Illustration of St. Paul's Epistles." Vol. 1, page 20.

‡ "Now, that the Spirit of God, and the gift of prophecy, should be ured out upon women, as well as men, in the time of the Gospel, is ain from Acts ii. 17, and then where could be a fitter place for them to ter their prophecies in, than the assemblies?" Locke's Paraphrase and otes on 1 Cor. xi. 4, 5.

himself above all that was called God, or that was worshipped, and who, in the persons of some who became as lords over God's heritage, was permitted to usurp that dominion over the church which belonged to Christ alone. Then, no longer was the choice and the qualification of the ministers referred to Him who is ordained to be the only " Head over all things to his church;" but men, swayed by temporal interests, appointed to this sacred office such as were the fit instruments for promoting or securing the wealth and power of worldly princes. And although the christian church has, to a considerable extent, emerged from the darkness of the apostacy; yet she has, perhaps, been in no respect more slow to avail herself of the blessings and privileges of this glorious Gospel day, than in allowing the free and unrestricted exercise of the ministry. How many of her members have yet to learn that in Christ Jesus "there is neither male nor female;" that as God is a Spirit, so his communications, through whatever medium conveyed, are directed to the *souls* of his rational creatures; that no external circumstances necessarily influence these communications; that to suppose they do so, is to estimate the dispensation of the Gospel as far below that of the law. Can we believe that the Holy Spirit is *now* more limited in its manifestations and in its requirements, than when, by its inspirations, Miriam prophesied and sang the praises of Jehovah?—when Deborah, under the palm-trees of Mount Ephraim, prophesied and judged Israel by the law and Spirit of the living God?—and when Huldah, the wife of Shallum, together with contemporary prophets, declared the judgments of the Most High as impending over a rebellious and gainsaying people? And when the Sun of Righteousness was about to arise on a benighted world, how remarkably were women employed to announce his coming and advent! when Elizabeth and Mary were filled with the Holy Ghost; and when Anna the prophetess "spake of" the infant Messiah "to all those that looked for redemption in Israel."

There is yet another argument sometimes brought forward to establish the supposition that the christian ministry is designed by our Lord Jesus Christ to devolve only on men, viz., that we do not find that He commissioned any females to preach the Gospel of the kingdom.

Iere again, there appears to be a misunderstanding, for
rant of sufficiently keeping in mind' the simplicity of
he message which was delivered by those whom he sent
)rth. His coming was effectually declared to the in-
abitants of Samaria through the instrumentality of a
roman;* and it was to women whose love to the cru-
ified Redeemer death and the grave could not weaken,
rhen they came early to the sepulchre, to embalm his
ody with sweet spices, that the unspeakably joyful tidings
rere communicated by the two men in shining garments:
He is not here but is risen." It was *they* who were
ommanded to "go quickly," and tell his sorrowing dis-
iples of his resurrection. It was a woman that received
hat most sacred commission, which expressed the fellow-
hip and oneness of his poor afflicted followers with their
isen Lord, and in language unutterably consoling, indi-
ate their ultimate participation in his glory: "Go to my
rethren and say unto them, I ascend unto my Father,
nd your Father, and to my God, and your God."
There is, however, in some sections of the christian
hurch, a recognition of the full and free agency and opera-
ion of that Holy Spirit which divideth to every man
everally as he will, and a thankful acceptance of that great
rospel truth, "There is neither Jew nor Greek, there is
either bond nor free, there is neither male nor female,"
ut "they are all one in Christ Jesus." Amongst such,
he preaching of women has been acknowledged to be a
pecial gift from Christ, who only has a right to appoint,
nd who alone can qualify his ministers effectually to pub-
sh the glad-tidings of salvation through Him. And so

* The earnestness which was manifested by the Samaritan woman, to
btain instruction as to the place divinely appointed for worship, her faith
the expected Messiah, and the great attention with which she listened
the sublime instructions of the stranger at Jacob's well, lead to the con-
usion, that He who "knew what was in man," beheld, in her heart, a
ncerity of desire for that which nourishes up the soul unto eternal life.
ow graciously did He condescend to impart to her truths most solemn,
d deeply important to his church; describing the spiritual nature of true
orship! This appears the more remarkable, when we consider that she
as one of that people who were the most inveterately opposed to the
ws, and who did not acknowledge allegiance to the same divine laws.
e sacred historian declares of the Samaritans, *they fear not the Lord,*
ither do they after the statutes, or after the ordinances, or after the law
d commandments, which the Lord commanded the children of Jacob,
om he named Israel. See 2 Kings xvii. 34.

effectually have these glad-tidings been declared by females, that many have been through their instrumentality
converted from the error of their way, and brought from
darkness to light; many hungry and thirsty souls have
been refreshed and strengthened; and many living members of the church edified together. And though this
preaching may not be "with excellency of speech or of
wisdom," but "in weakness and fear, and in much trembling," yet many can feelingly testify from heartfelt
experience, that it has often been exercised "in the
demonstration of the Spirit and of power." It may be remembered that, on the day of Pentecost, after the apostle
Peter had testified of that more abundant outpouring
of the Holy Spirit which characterises the dispensation of
the Gospel, he added this very striking and encouraging
declaration, in reference to its continued agency throughout the church of Christ: "The promise is to you, and to
your children, and *to all that are afar off, even to as many*
as the Lord our God shall call." Did professing Christians
with a more lively faith, appreciate their high privilege,
as offered through this most blessed gift—were they seeking to obey its teachings, and to live under its sanctifying
power—and with a true hunger and thirst after righteousness, thankfully accepting every medium, through which
the great Shepherd and Bishop of souls condescends to
feed and to instruct his people, there could be no disposition to dispute the authority of the instrument through
which He may, in his infinite compassion, extend to
sinners the invitations of His grace, and cause the glad-
tidings of his Gospel to be proclaimed.

May every sincere disciple of our Lord and Saviour
Jesus Christ cherish a desire to lay aside all prejudice,
and whatever may tend to obstruct the spreading of His
truth, not daring to limit the means by which he may
be graciously pleased to establish it in the hearts of men,
but humbly committing to Him *His own work*, fervently
unite in the prayer "Thy kingdom come, thy will be done
on earth, as it is done in heaven."

END.

Printed by E. Couchman & Co., 10, Throgmorton Street, London.

A SHORT ACCOUNT

OF

ROBERT SEARLES,

WITH

A FEW EXTRACTS FROM HIS DIARY.

" A highway shall be there—it shall be called the way of holiness
—the wayfaring men shall not err therein."—Isa. xxxv. 8.

The following account and some memorandums of one, who in his life and conduct adorned the station of a servant, are printed in the hope that the attentive perusal of them will be beneficial and animating, not only to those who may have to tread the same path, but to others who may be less exposed to outward toil and labour.

ROBERT SEARLES was born at Glatten, in Huntingdonshire, in the year 1764, of parents professing the religion of the Church of England. In his youth, he was a frequent associate with persons of irreligious characters, in the lowest ranks of life. When about twenty-three years of age, he became seriously disposed, and soon after joined the society of Calvinistic Baptists, amongst whom he was esteemed a highly valuable member.

The circumstances which gradually led to a change in his views on the most important subjects, are described by himself, nearly in the following words. After regretting that a difference in religious sentiments should produce so hostile a disposition in some serious minds, as at that period he had observed, he proceeds to remark :—" The great Leader and Pattern of Christianity said to his disciples, ' He that is not against us is on our part;' but some think, because another does not see as they do, and does not walk with them, he cannot be a disciple. Whereas it would be much better to endeavour to imitate our Holy Pattern, who was meek and lowly, kind and compassionate, willing to endure the cross, and despise the shame.

" I began to listen to what some of our neighbours said on this subject, that this was right and the other wrong.

No. 80.   [*Price* 6d. *per doz.*]

I left off going to the meetings of the General Baptists, who held salvation possible to all men; and went amongst the Calvinistic Baptists, who profess that salvation is provided for only a part of mankind; and that this part are sure of it, without any possibility of their missing; it being unalterably fixed from all eternity, so that the creature has nothing to do in it; for means and ends are so unalterably fixed, as surely to be accomplished on the part of mankind, so predestinated. But although they thus profess, how often do their ministers invite *all* to the Gospel Feast, to partake of that bread, of which, *according to their own doctrine*, there may be none provided for them! But O! what a favour that no one is excluded thence, but those who exclude themselves. Welcome the ignorant and polite; the learned and the rude.

"I constantly attended the meeting of these Calvinistic Baptists, was very earnest to be instructed, paid all the attention I possibly could, and was glad when meeting-day was near that I might go and hear another sermon. I also wanted to feel more of that power within, which was so much talked of amongst them; but in that I knew I fell short, although I greatly longed for it. The reason of this want I could not tell; it being so strongly held out by the minister, that the desire after it was life begun, meaning spiritual life; and then if begun, sure to be carried on.

"I well remember his saying many times, 'How do I know that I live naturally! Why, because I breathe: so I know I have spiritual life, because I feel breathing or desire to be saved.' But although it would encourage me a little, I felt that something more was wanting to satisfy me. I read much; prayed earnestly and constantly; endeavoured to get with those who I thought were spiritual; but all would not make me quite satisfied.

"I thought the people with whom I walked in a religious way were right, but that I was wrong myself. I thought I did not enter in at the right door; thus I went on until I became a member of their community; took part of the bread and wine; and was immersed in the river Ouse at Holywell; but I did not find myself so fully satisfied, as I thought others were who practised these things.

"My conduct all this time was steady and regular.—I
was respected as a servant or labourer; but felt a great
deal of that about me, which wanted doing away; yet
not applying rightly for the perfecting of the work, it
went slowly on.

"I think I went on in this way about eight or nine
years, and did not gain much spiritual ground, as I
thought. In process of time, an occurrence happened
which led to another change with me. My master who
employed me, died; and another came who professed
Quakerism, as it is called. He being observable of his
new set of men, and religiously inclined, left books in
our counting-house, which, being desirous of knowing
religious people and things, I used to get and read.

"One of these books was, Robert Barclay's Apology
for the Christian Faith, as held by the people called
Quakers. I thought myself a match for that, but was
mistaken; for whenever I read in it, it used to reach my
feelings.

"I cannot very well remember how it happened, but
I went to one of the Quarterly Meetings of Friends; and
there being a pretty many ministering Friends that day,
on an appointment from the Yearly Meeting, a great
many living testimonies were borne, in the power and
authority of Truth, to the tendering of my spirit; and a
refreshing meeting it was to me. On my returning home,
I thought, surely these must be the people who hold the
solemn meeting; and if I were clear of those other people, I should go to the meetings of Friends; but I did
not know what I must do, nor how the matter would end.
However, I was so far inclined to the Friends, that I
ventured the next first day to attend their meeting again,
and some of the same Friends were there, and bore living testimony to the power of Truth, and again refreshed
my spirit.

"One of these Friends, in the afternoon, was concerned to have a public meeting. I went, and had again
another good time. O! thought I, this is the way for
me to go in, and the language of my heart was, ' This is
the solemn assembly;' and I felt an increasing desire to
be united with Friends."

Our endeared Friend became an exemplary, and we

believe, constant attender of our religious meetings : and
in the course of a few years was, with the full unity of
Friends, joined to us in membership.

He was brought up to the trade of a miller, and for
about the last thirty years of his life, resided at Hough-
ton, in his native county, in the capacity of a servant.
His exemplary life and conduct, his unaffected simplicity
of manners, joined to deep humility, gained him the
love and esteem of all his friends. Private retirement
was his constant daily practice, and we doubt not but
these seasons were beneficial to his own growth in the
Truth, and increased his usefulness to others. Private
admonition was also a duty which he often performed,
though much in the cross to his own inclination. This
duty so strengthening to his own mind, was not confined
to the members of our own Society, but extended to
many others, by whom it was generally well received;
being accompanied by that love which breathes " Peace
on earth and good will to men."

: Thus dwelling near the fountain of Divine life, he
was, in due season, enabled to yield to an apprehension
of duty, to speak as a Minister in our religious meetings,
which was to the comfort and edification of Friends.
His first communications were short, but evidently accompanied with the savour of life. Careful to follow
his Divine Leader, his gift was much enlarged, and he
received renewed ability, frequently to labour amongst
those with whom his lot was cast. His offerings in the
ministry were clear and impressive, accompanied by the
baptizing power of the Spirit of Truth.·

In the spring of the year 1820, he was taken unwell,
but generally attended to his work. The following
extracts from two letters, written about that time,
describe the watchful state of his mind.

"21st of 1st month, 1820. I feel glad to find myself
at home again amongst the concerns relating to this
present life: although my service in this matter seems to
me on the decline: yet I am most easy to do what is
proper for me to do. I have thought much this day about
what an Apostle said of himself and his fellow-labourers
in the work of the Gospel: ' As deceivers, and yet true;
as unknown, and yet well known ; as dying, and behold

ve live.' 2 Cor. vi. 8, 9. O! how I have desired, under he same feelings, to endure all things for the Gospel's ake; and patiently to pass through evil report and good eport, with the same steady faith and confidence; and et none of these things move me; nor let me count any hing too dear to leave for the sake of that Gospel of life nd peace, for which the Apostle and his companions underwent so many hardships, and some of them even death for its sake.

"I cannot think that I have done anything, or suffered anything, worthy of the regard of Him, who so plentifully promises to reward in this life, and in the world to come with life everlasting; but I feel myself as a beginner, desiring to obtain a measure of strength to abide the day of trial, and to do the day's work in the day.

. "*7th of 4th month*, 1820. I long that I may be one of the subjects of Christ's kingdom, which He tells us is not of this world; so that I may be redeemed from the root of all striving, patiently submitting unto the Heavenly Father's will in all things. I hope I shall not complain, nor think my case hard. I am mortal, and must decay as to the outward, but am at times (although at some others very much discouraged) in the hope that the inward man gains a little strength; but more deepening is necessary, to come to a certainty of being prepared for an admittance into peace, when the spirit leaves the mortal tabernacle.

"I hope my dear friend is recruiting in strength, and growing in the life of Truth, so as to be able to work in the heritage of the Heavenly Husbandman, having a qualification to repair the waste places thereof. O! remember, dear friend, how frail man is! at best but a fading flower, which, whilst the day of sunshine and heavenly rain continues, *does* and *looks* well; but how soon may a blast nip it, or drought dry it up, and the freshness thereof fade. Therefore, learn more and more to cease from man, and trust in the Lord alone for help and strength to work whilst it is day, and vigour is left, before desire fail. O! fear not man; neither what he can do unto thee, any more than help thee; but look inward, have thy mind centred in the life alone, and as that moves, move with it."

On seventh day, the 15th of the 4th month, 1820, our dear friend became much worse. Although suffering under much debility of body, on the following day he attended the meeting at Ives, where, for the last time, he was favoured to labour in a remarkable manner; forcibly impressing on his hearers the necessity of a frequent recurrence to that Divine Power, which had called us to be a people in order to obtain instruction and direction, so to walk, as happily to be found of the number of those, who had not seen their Lord and Master naked, sick, or in prison, without ministering to Him.

He was confined to the house about a week. In a note to a friend, a few days before, he concludes thus: " O.! dear friend, what a happy escape, to be removed from these changing scenes to a state of uninterrupted tranquillity! but I desire first to bear patiently all that is needful, for a preparation for such a pure state."

On the 17th, a friend going to see him, in the course of conversation he instructively remarked:—" There is nothing will do but keeping in the cross;" and further observed, that he knew not how it might be, but in this illness he felt no condemnation. The same friend visited him again on the 21st, when under great suffering of body; but his mind was remarkably calm and tranquil: he had done his day's work in the day time, and having nothing now to do but to die, he again emphatically repeated, " I feel no condemnation."

Feeling a little revival of strength, he requested his wife and a few friends to sit with him awhile, when he said: ".Now what I want for us is, that we may be more fully dedicated, more resigned to follow the Lord, to follow Christ Jesus : there is no other way." And soon after he remarked: " I do not see but I may yet abide, though the petition of my mind is, ' O ! that I had wings like a dove, then would I flee away, and be at rest, and hasten my escape from the windy storm and tempest.' I have need of resignation to bear these sharp afflictions."

In this peaceful state of mind, was this dedicated servant of the Lord permitted to exchange time for immortality. This solemn event took place on the 24th of the 4th month, 1820. That Divine Power which had been so eminently his support in life, did not forsake

im in sickness; He who had been to him riches in
overty, was now a pleasant helper in the time of need:
vincing the truth of that declaration concerning our
Lord, that ": having loved his own, He loved them unto
he end."

SOME EXTRACTS FROM THE DIARY.

22nd of 6th Month, 1811. Endeavoured this morning
o feel after best help before I entered on my day's work;
and it has proved a pretty quiet day.

24th. Endeavoured this morning to get down to the
pring of Life, but found it hard work. O! for more
villingness to labour for daily bread, and for submission
of will to best direction. In the afternoon, suffered my
mind to get ruffled by trifling events, which left uneasiness. I wish more and more to turn to that which
miteth.

27th. Arose at four o'clock. Endeavoured to feel
after the springing up of that Life, which enliveneth the
pirit; and, though sensible to myself of little help at
his time, was enabled to get through the day without
condemnation.

1st of 7th month. Endeavoured to feel after good this
norning, and although I found myself heavy and dull,
yet find it good to seek daily for that, which when found,
does enliven and animate the soul to press forward.

4th. Sat alone this morning and read in the Bible
previously to entering upon my labour. Off my watch
in the course of this day, and used some unbecoming
expressions to a fellow-workman, which gave me uneasiness. O! for more of that love which is not easily
provoked, and thinketh no evil!

13th. Poor and low; but longing after a closer union
and communion with the Divine Life, got through this
lay pretty well.

16th. Went to meeting, in which I found a hard
combat between flesh and spirit. What a continual
warfare is a Christian life! and if it was not for a little
spiritual refreshment now and then mercifully vouchsafed, how difficult would it be to maintain it.

20th. Poor and low this morning, but wishing to learn, in whatsoever state, therein to be content; knowing what it is, in some degree, both to want and to abound. How precious is that life which brings the mind to the state of a little child!

21st. Experienced a little strength to my mind this day in solemn silence; although some trying matters occurred, in things pertaining to this transitory life. I wish for more of that love which is not easily provoked, and to manifest the same in conduct and conversation.

27th. My mind, like the parched ground, hard and dry. O! that I may wait willingly and attentively for the distilling of the heavenly rain, to soften and make it fruitful unto the Lord.

28th of 9th month. My mind preserved in quiet resignation through the day, in which I was concerned to admonish an individual to whom I had formerly been united in religious feeling, on some impropriety of conduct. He acknowledged my kind intention, which was relieving. I wish for myself and others to take up this part of the cross, when we see a friend or neighbour sliding away from the path of peace. It is written in Scripture: "Rebuke a wise man and he will love thee." Prov. ix. 8.

9th of 6th month, 1812. At meeting to-day derived a little spiritual strength. How precious is solemn silence and waiting upon God! I have many times thought in my solemn sittings in meetings, what a privilege it is to be disencumbered of the world, with the mind centred on that Power who humbleth the heart and contrites the spirit.

Having obtained mercy through many trials, and in much weakness, to be measurably faithful to that Light which shows the right way and good old path, I have continued to this day, desiring to be a witness both to small and great, that I am a disciple of Him who died and rose again for mankind, feeling in myself a dying daily to sin, but being alive unto God, through the virtues of Him who is the true Bread of Life, and will never leave nor forsake those who put their trust in

im ; although they may, at times, feel as if they were
it off for their part. If there be a struggling exercise
aintained : not giving up but pressing through the
owd of difficulties, the time will most assuredly come
hen a cure will be witnessed, and an evidence felt,
mewhat like what was said to the woman formerly :—
Daughter, be of good comfort, thy faith hath made thee
hole ; go in peace." This is and has been the happy
:perience of thousands, and will be that of all those
ho continue to seek that Power which works both to
ill and do of his good pleasure. O my soul ! keep
ar, keep near to that which alone can bear up under
ery weight, and make useful in the Church, until this
ortal must put on immortality, and the work be com-
eted to the praise of the Great Workman.

7th of 2nd month, 1814. More and more desirous to
now a communion with Him, who is our chiefest good,
id O ! that I may commit myself wholly to his guid-
ice ; He will not leave nor forsake those who trust in
im.

29th of 12th month. "The troubles of my heart are
ilarged. O, bring Thou me out of my distress !" In his
wn time, which is the best time, I trust He will. In
y present exercise, my dear children are very near to
y heart, and fearfulness attends lest they should not do
ell. I long for them to be witnesses for truth and
ghteousness upon the earth. "Gracious Father !" is
ie language of my heart, "draw them by the cords of
iy love, and allure them into the wilderness ; and there
ieak comfortably unto them ; that they may have
rength to cast all their care upon Thee, whose hand is
ot shortened that it cannot save, nor thine ear grown
eavy that it cannot hear ! O, that all the impediments
etween Thee and them may be removed ; and the
icomes of Divine consolation be poured into their
recious souls ! O ! that they may prize the favour of
ivine visitation, and improve the talent or talents
immitted to them, and not be of them who bury them
i the earth, or smother them amongst the vanities of
ie world to their own hurt, and religious ruin."

25th of 2nd month, 1815. This morning endeavoured
) seek after inward strength at first rising, but found the

enemy to all good striving against me. But what an
inestimable favour to experience, in such seasons, the
efficacy of the Divine Master's rebuke, when he arose
and said : " Peace, be still ; and the wind ceased, and
there was a great calm." Faith is hereby renewed, and
wisdom's ways are afresh seen to be ways of pleasantness,
and all her paths are peace. Favoured with great sweetness in our week-day meeting, where I was exercised to
express a few words ; but which, without the blessing,
could not feed any poor mind.

21st of 3rd month. This morning, great pain of body,
for three hours, caused close searching of heart, and
feeling after an evidence of acceptance, if removed out of
the body. O ! what need in time of health, to be preparing for the solemn change ! nothing had need be left
to be done when the pains are heavy on the body. May
this be my first and chief concern, to seek to the Helper
of Israel, for support to walk in the ways of salvation.

28th of 4th month. Was refreshed at a meeting to-day,
in silent waiting upon the Lord : precious feelings are at
times experienced in thus waiting on Him, who has
promised, that where two or three are met together
in his name, there will He be in the midst of them : and
his promises remain to be yea and amen for ever. His
ways are ways of pleasantness, and all his paths are
peace ! his right hand and his holy arm will, I believe,
give the victory over every besetment, to the watchful
mind ; and cause a song of praise to his holy name.

9th of 5th month. Very much tried the last two days
with a fear I should one day fall by the hand of the
enemy ; and it will be so, if not preserved from iniquity,
by the redeeming power of the Lord, which is able to do
all things in and for us.

4th of 10th month. Low and weak this morning,
feeling hardness and wandering of mind in retirement.—
In reading after breakfast, a little relief. How I wish I
could love the Lord my God with all my heart ; serve
Him, with a willing mind ; and seek him, so that he may
be found of me a poor creature ; and never forsake Him,
and incur the penalty of being cast off for ever.

15th. Felt condemned this morning, for speaking
something last evening, which would have been better

mitted. I entreated forgiveness, and have since known little quiet. What a favour it is to have an Advocate with the Father when poor, frail man offends! "He is the propitiation for our sins: and not for ours only, but also for the sins of the whole world."

18th. Refreshed this morning amongst my fellow workmen, at the house of my employer, before entering into the labour of the day. I wish it may be an increasing concern amongst masters, to instruct their dependants in the way of truth and righteousness; then, I believe, would servants be more diligent and faithful in their employ. "Masters, give unto your servants that which is just and equal; knowing that ye also have a Master in heaven." God is not unmindful of such a work and labour of love.

15th of 4th month, 1816. Renewed desires that it may please Infinite Wisdom and Goodness, to prepare my heart as a fit residence for his holiness: and that the God of my salvation may not leave me; but that his loving kindness and truth may continually preserve me.

8th of 5th month. Poor and needy, but sensible from whence help cometh. May I seek the Lord, and find Him a present help in the needful time.

11th of 1st month, 1817. Peace and quietness cover my mind this evening; feeling the blessing of the Lord, which maketh rich, and addeth no sorrow therewith. I desire to be more and more devoted in heart and life, to walk humbly with him the remainder of my days, that my footsteps slip not by the way. The Lord knoweth better than I do, what I am, and what is best for me; and I desire to cast all my care upon Him, and if He is pleased to uphold me by his free Spirit, I shall be safe from falling a prey to my own inclinations and weaknesses.

25th of 3rd month. A little unwatchfulness this day, brought to my mind by the good Remembrancer,) interrupted that serenity which I believe was designed for me this evening. When will all the old things be done away, and all things become new? I believe it is for

this good and gracious end that I am permitted to feel as
I now do; and O that I may profit thereby!

3rd of 6th month. I find great need to abide near that
which crucifies the affections and the lusts; which would
soon be uppermost, if we failed to look to that power
which keeps alive unto God. May I put my trust, and
cast all my care, on the All-sufficient Arm of help, that
He may not take his Holy Spirit from me!

8th. I want to feel yet more of the reduction of self
in every part, that the pure seed of the kingdom may
arise, and all its blessed fruits appear in life and conversation; and may I be united to the Unchangeable Source
of all blessedness, and experience fellowship with the
faithful, and an union with the Father and with the Son
Jesus Christ, our Lord and Saviour!

23rd of 3rd month, 1818. Satisfied that no other thing
than the power of God in man, is sufficient to serve
Him in holiness and righteousness; and, without fearing
man, I desire to impress on others, the importance
thereof.

26th of 7th month, 1819. How great are the tender
mercies of the Lord towards them that love and fear Him,
and great towards us, his frail creatures, is his compassion,
who knows all our weaknesses and our imperfections.
When we are desirous to walk in uprightness before
Him, He is, in the aboundings of his love and mercy
forgiving, cleansing, healing, and strengthening us to
hold on in that way, which he would have us to walk
in. May I be preserved humble, watchful, patient, and
resigned! May I pray without ceasing for preservation
through this world of snares, changes, and difficulties, so
that, in the end, I may have to sing, Hallelujah to the
Lord God and the Lamb; and that for evermore!

19th of 2nd month, 1820. Great is my desire that
through the remainder of my life, preservation may be
known in Christ Jesus the Lord of life and glory, so as
to bring forth fruit unto righteousness and peace.

London: Printed by Edward Couchman and Co., 10, Throgmorton Street; for
the Tract Association of the Society of Friends. Sold at the Depository
84, Houndsditch.—1861.

EXTRACTS

FROM

APPROVED DOCUMENTS

OF THE

RELIGIOUS SOCIETY OF FRIENDS,

RELATING TO THE

CHRISTIAN DOCTRINE.

~~~~~~~~~~~~~~~~~~~~~~~

LONDON:

Printed for the TRACT ASSOCIATION of the SOCIETY OF FRIENDS.

Sold at the DEPOSITORY, 12, Bishopsgate Street Without.

—

1862.

No. 81.   [*Price 4d. per dozen.*]

PREFACE.

THE original and immediate ground of the religious fellowship of the early members of the Society of Friends was union of sentiment in regard to Christ's inward teaching, a doctrine which they believe to have been too much neglected by others. They were at the same time firm believers in all that is revealed in Holy Scripture respecting the fall of man, and his redemption through our Lord and Saviour Jesus Christ; nor would they have allowed that any one held the truth who denied his coming in the flesh, or the benefit derived to man by his propitiatory sacrifice.

Our predecessors not only recognized the Bible as the standard of their religious doctrines; but were particularly careful to adhere to Scripture language in the statement of them. They adopted no creed or confession of faith to be subscribed by their members; yet when charged with false opinions, they did not hesitate to make a full declaration on any or all the points of the Christian faith.

The following extracts are taken from such declarations. Issued as they were at different periods, they exhibit the harmony which has prevailed in our religious Society, in reference to the doctrines of the Gospel—doctrines which are designed, through the power of the Holy Spirit, and the operation of a living faith to promote the happiness of man in this life, and to prepare him for eternal bliss in Christ's heavenly kingdom.

EXTRACTS.

Extract from George Fox's Epistle to the Governor of Barbadoes, 1671.

We own and believe in God, the only wise, omnipotent, and everlasting God, the Creator of all things in heaven and earth, and the Preserver of all that he hath made; who is God over all, blessed for ever; to whom be all honor, glory, dominion, praise, and thanksgiving, both now and for evermore! And we own and believe in Jesus Christ, his beloved and only begotten Son, in whom he is well pleased; who was conceived by the Holy Ghost, and born of the Virgin Mary; in whom we have redemption through his blood even the forgiveness of sins; who is the express image of the invisible God, the first-born of every creature, by whom were all things created that are in heaven and in earth, visible and invisible, whether they be thrones, dominions, principalities, or powers; all things were created by him. And we own and believe that he was made a sacrifice for sin, who knew no sin; neither was guile found in his mouth; that he was crucified for us in the flesh, without the gates of Jerusalem; and that he was buried, and rose again the third day by the power of his Father, for our justification; and that he ascended up into heaven, and now sitteth at the right hand of God. This Jesus, who was the foundation of the holy prophets and apostles, is our foundation; and we believe there is no other foundation to be laid but that which is laid, even Christ Jesus; who tasted death for every man, shed his blood for all men, is the propitiation for our sins, and not for ours only, but also for the sins of the whole world: according as John the Baptist testified of him, when he said, "Behold the Lamb of God that taketh away the sin of the world." John i. 29. We believe that he alone is our Redeemer and Saviour, the captain of our salvation, who saves us from sin, as well as from hell and the wrath to come, and destroys the devil and his works; he is the seed of the woman that bruises the serpent's head, to wit, Christ Jesus the Alpha and Omega, the First and the Last. He is (as the Scriptures of truth say of him) our wisdom, righteousness, justification, and redemption; neither is there salvation in any other, for there is no other name under heaven given among men, whereby we may be saved. He alone is the Shepherd and Bishop of our souls; he is our Prophet, whom Moses long since testified of, saying, "A Prophet shall the Lord your God raise up unto you of your brethren, like unto me; him shall ye hear in all things, whatsoever he shall say unto you: and it shall come to pass, that every soul which will not hear that Prophet shall be destroyed from among the people." Acts ii. 22, 23. He is now come in Spirit, "and hath given us an understanding, that we may know him that is true." He rules in our hearts by his law of love and life, and makes us free from the law of sin and death. We have no life, but by him; for he is the quickening Spirit, the second Adam, the Lord from heaven, by whose blood we are cleansed, and our consciences sprinkled from dead works, to serve the living God. He is our Mediator, who makes peace and reconciliation between God offended and us offending; he being the Oath of God, the new covenant of light, life, grace and peace; the author and finisher of our faith. This Lord Jesus Christ, the heavenly man, the Emanuel, God with us, we all own and believe in; he whom the high priest raged against and said, he had spoken blasphemy; whom the priests and elders of the Jews took counsel together against, and put to death; the same whom Judas betrayed for thirty pieces of silver, which the priests gave him as a reward for his treason; who also gave large money to soldiers to broach a horrible lie, namely, "That his disciples came and stole him away by night whilst they slept." After he was risen from the dead, the history of the acts of the apostles sets forth how the chief priests and elders persecuted the disciples of this Jesus, for preaching Christ and his resurrection. This, we say, is that Lord Jesus Christ, whom we own to be our life and salvation.

Concerning the Holy Scriptures, we believe they were given forth by the Holy Spirit of God, through the holy men of God, who (as the Scripture itself declares, 2 Pet.

21,) spake as they were moved by the Holy Ghost.
Te believe they are to be read, believed, and fulfilled, (he
ıat fulfils them is Christ;) and they are profitable for
ɔctrine, for reproof, for correction, for instruction in
ghteousness, that the man of God may be perfect,
ıroughly furnished unto all good works" (2 Tim. iii.
ɔ, 17); and are able to make wise unto salvation,
through faith in Christ Jesus."

---

*Extracts from a statement of Christian doctrine, issued
on behalf of the Society, in the year* 1693.

We sincerely profess faith in God by his only begotten
on Jesus Christ, as being our•light and life, our only
ay to the Father, and also our only Mediator and Advo-
ıte with the Father.

That God created all things, he made the worlds by
ıs Son Jesus Christ, he being that powerful and living
Tord of God, by whom all things were made; and that
ıe Father, the Word, and the Holy Spirit, are one, in
.vine being inseparable; one true, living, and eternal
od, blessed for ever.

Yet that this Word, or Son of God, in the fulness of
me, took flesh, became perfect man according to the
ɔsh, descended and came of the seed of Abraham and
avid; but was miraculously conceived by the Holy
host, and born of the virgin Mary: and also, farther,
ɔclared powerfully to be the Son of God, according to
ɔe spirit of sanctification, by the resurrection from the
ɔad.

That in the Word (or Son of God) was life, and the
me life was the light of men; and that he was that true
ɣht which enlightens every man coming into the world;
ɪd therefore that men are to believe in the light, that
ey may become the children of the light; hereby we
lieve in Christ the Son of God, as he is the light and
ɔe within us; and wherein we must needs have sincere
ɪspect and honour to (and belief in) Christ, as in his own
ıapproachable and incomprehensible glory and fulness;

as he is the fountain of life and light, and giver thereof
unto us; Christ, as in himself, and as in us, being not
divided. And that as man, Christ died for our sins, rose
again, and was received up into glory in the heavens. He
having, in his dying for all, been that one great universal
offering and sacrifice for peace, atonement, and reconciliation between God and man; and he is the propitiation
not for our sins only, but for the sins of the whole world.
We were reconciled by his death, but saved by his life.

That Jesus Christ who sitteth at the right hand of the
throne of the Majesty in the heavens, yet he is our King,
High Priest, and Prophet; in his church, a Minister of
the sanctuary, and of the true tabernacle which the Lord
pitched, and not man. He is Intercessor and Advocate with the Father in heaven, and there appearing in
the presence of God for us, being touched with the feeling
of our infirmities, sufferings, and sorrows. And also by
his Spirit in our hearts, he maketh intercession according
to the will of God, crying, Abba, Father.

That the Gospel of the grace of God should be preached
in the name of the Father, Son, and Holy Ghost, being
one in power, wisdom, and goodness, and indivisible, (or
not to be divided,) in the great work of man's salvation.
We sincerely confess (and believe in) Jesus Christ
both as he is true God, and perfect man, and that he is
the author of our living faith in the power and goodness
of God, as manifested in his Son Jesus Christ, and by his
own blessed Spirit (or divine unction) revealed in us,
whereby we inwardly feel and taste of his goodness, life,
and virtue: so as our souls live and prosper by and in
him: and the inward sense of this divine power of Christ,
and faith in the same, and the inward experience, are
absolutely necessary to make a true, sincere, and perfect
Christian in Spirit and life.

That divine honour and worship is due to the Son of
God; and that he is, in true faith, to be prayed unto, and
the name of the Lord Jesus Christ called upon (as the
primitive Christians did), because of the glorious union
or oneness of the Father and the Son, and that we cannot
acceptably offer up prayers and praises to God, nor receive
a gracious answer or blessing from God, but in and through
his dear Son Christ.

That Christ's body that was crucified was not the God-head,,yet by the power of God was raised from the dead; and that the same Christ that was therein crucified ascended into heaven and glory, is not questioned by us. His flesh saw no corruption; it did not corrupt, but yet, doubtless, his body was changed into a more glorious and heavenly condition than it was in when subject to divers sufferings on earth; but how and what manner of change it met withal, after it was raised from the dead, so as to become such a glorious body, (as it is declared to be,) is too wonderful for mortals to conceive, apprehend, or pry into (and more meet for angels to see); the Scripture is silent therein, as to the manner thereof, and we are not curious to enquire or dispute it; nor do we esteem it necessary to make ourselves wise above what is written, as to the manner or condition of Christ's glorious body, as in heaven: no more than to enquire how Christ appeared in divers manners or forms; or how he came in among his disciples the doors being shut; or how he vanished out of their sight, after he was risen. However, we have cause to believe his body, as in heaven, is changed into a most glorious condition, far transcending what it was in on earth, otherwise how should our low body be changed, so as to be made like unto his glorious body? for when he was on earth and attended with sufferings, he was said to be like unto us in all things, sin only excepted; which may not be so said of him as now in a state of glory, as he prayed for; otherwise where would be the change both in him and in us.

Concerning the resurrection of the dead, and the great day of judgment yet to come, beyond the grave, or after death, and Christ's coming without us, to judge the quick and the dead (as divers questions are put in such terms), what the Holy Scriptures plainly declare and testify in these matters, we have been always ready to embrace.

1. For the doctrine of the resurrection; if in this life only we have hope in Christ, we are of all men most miserable. 1 Cor. xv. 19. We sincerely believe not only a resurrection in Christ from the fallen sinful state here, but a rising and ascending into glory with him hereafter, that when he at last appears, we may appear with him in glory. Col. iii. 4; 1 John iii. 2.

But that all the wicked who live in rebellion against
the light of grace, and die finally impenitent, shall come
forth to the resurrection of condemnation.

And that the soul or spirit of every man and woman
shall be reserved in its own distinct and proper being, and
every seed (yea, every soul) shall have its proper body,
as God is pleased to give it. 1 Cor. xv. A natural body
is sown, a spiritual body is raised; that being first which
is natural, and afterwards that which is spiritual.—And
though it is said, this corruptible shall put on incorrup-
tion, and this mortal shall put on immortality : the change
shall be such, as flesh and blood cannot inherit the
kingdom of God, neither doth corruption inherit incor-
ruption. 1 Cor. xv. We shall be raised out of all
corruption and corruptibility, out of all mortality; and
the children of God and of the resurrection shall be
equal to the angels of God in heaven. And as the
celestial bodies do far excel terrestial, so we expect our
spiritual bodies in the resurrection shall far excel what
our bodies now are. Howbeit we esteem it very unnecessary to dispute or question how the dead are raised, or
with what body they come; but rather submit that to the
wisdom and pleasure of Almighty God.

2. For the doctrine of eternal judgment; God hath
committed all judgment unto his Son Jesus Christ; and
he is Judge both of quick and dead, and of the states
and ends of all mankind. John v. 22. 27; Acts x. 42;
2 Tim. iv. 1; 1 Pet. iv. 5.

That there shall be hereafter a great harvest, which
is the end of the world, a great day of judgment, and the
judgment of that great day, the Holy Scripture is clear.
Matt. xiii. 39, 40, 41; x. 15, and xi. 24; Jude 6.
"When the Son of Man cometh in his glory, and all the
holy angels with him, then shall he sit upon the throne
of his glory, and before him shall be gathered all nations,"
&c. Matt. xxv. 31, 32, to the end, compared with ch.
xxii. 31; Mark viii. 38; Luke ix. 26, and 1 Cor. xv. 52;
2 Thess. i. 7, 8, to the end, and 1 Thess. iv. 16: Rev.
xx. 12, 13, 14, 15.

Extract from the Minutes of the Yearly Meeting, 1829.

We feel ourselves called upon, at this time, to avow our belief in the inspiration and divine authority of the Old and New Testament.

We further believe, that the promise made after the transgression of our first parents, in the consequence of whose fall all the posterity of Adam are involved, that the seed of the woman shall bruise the head of the serpent; and the declaration unto Abraham, " In thy seed shall all the nations of the earth be blessed," had a direct reference to the coming in the flesh of the Lord Jesus Christ. To Him, also, did the prophet Isaiah bear testimony, when he declared, " Unto us a child is born, unto us a son is given; and the government shall be upon his shoulder: and his name shall be called Wonderful, Counsellor, the mighty God, the everlasting Father, the Prince of Peace: of the increase of his government and peace there shall be no end." And again, the same prophet spoke of him when he said, "Surely he hath borne our griefs, and carried our sorrows: yet we did esteem him stricken, smitten of God and afflicted; but he was wounded for our transgressions: he was bruised for our iniquities: the chastisement of our peace was upon him: and with his stripes we are healed." The same blessed Redeemer is emphatically denominated by the prophet Jeremiah, "The LORD OUR RIGHTEOUSNESS."

At that period, and in that miraculous manner which God in his perfect wisdom saw fit, the promised Messiah appeared personally upon earth, when " He took not on him the nature of angels; but he took on him the seed of Abraham." " He was in all points tempted like as we are, yet without sin." Having finished the work which was given him to do, he gave himself for us an offering and a sacrifice to God. He tasted death for every man. " He is the propitiation for our sins; and not for ours only, but also for the sins of the whole world." " We have redemption through his blood, even the forgiveness of sins." He passed into the heavens; and being the brightness of the glory of God, "and the express image of his person, and upholding all things by the word of his power, when he had by himself purged our sins, sat down on the right hand of the Majesty on high:" and ever liveth to make intercession for us.

It is by the Lord Jesus Christ that the world will be judged in righteousness. He is the mediator of the new covenant; "the image of the invisible God, the first-born of every creature: for by him were all things created that are in heaven and that are in earth, visible and invisible, whether they be thrones, or dominions, or principalities, or powers: all things were created by him, and for him; and he is before all things, and by him all things consist." "In him dwelleth all the fulness of the Godhead bodily:" and to him did the Evangelist bear testimony when he said, "In the beginning was the Word, and the Word was with God, and the Word was God. The same was in the beginning with God. All things were made by him; and without him was not anything made that was made. In him was life; and the life was the light of men." "He was the true light which lighteth every man that cometh into the world."

Our blessed Lord himself spoke of his perpetual dominion and power in his church, when he said, "My sheep hear my voice, and I know them, and they follow me: and I give unto them eternal life:" and, when describing the spiritual food which he bestoweth on the true believers, he declared, "I am the bread of life: he that cometh to me shall never hunger, and he that believeth on me shall never thirst." He spoke also of his saving grace, bestowed on those who come in faith unto him, when he said, "Whosoever drinketh of the water that I shall give him shall never thirst; but the water that I shall give him shall be in him a well of water, springing up into everlasting life."

Our religious Society, from its earliest establishment to the present day, has received these most important doctrines of Holy Scripture in their plain and obvious acceptation, and it is the earnest desire of this Meeting, that all who profess our name, may so live, and so walk before God, as that they may know these sacred truths to be blessed to them individually. We desire that, as the mere profession of sound Christian doctrine will not avail to the salvation of the soul, all may attain to a

ving efficacious faith, which, through the power of the
oly Ghost, bringeth forth fruit unto holiness; the end
hereof is everlasting life, through Jesus Christ our Lord.
Blessing, and honour, and glory, and power, be unto
[im that sitteth upon the throne, and unto the Lamb
r ever and ever."

Extract from the Epistle of the Yearly Meeting, 1830.

Dear friends, we are again made sensible that we
annot meditate on a subject more fraught with instruc-
on and comfort, than the coming of the Son of God in
ie flesh, and the many blessings which through him
ave been conferred on the human race,—the coming of
[im, who, being born of a virgin, "was made in the
keness of men:" "who, being in the form of God,
hought it not robbery to be equal with God; but made
imself of no reputation, and took upon him the form of
servant." He "was delivered for our offences, and
'as raised again for our justification." He ascended on
igh, he led captivity captive, he received gifts for men,
ea, for the rebellious also, that the Lord God might
well among them. He "sitteth on the right hand of
iod," making intercession for us. He "is made unto us
f God, wisdom, and righteousness, and sanctification,
nd redemption;". and unto him we must look as our
iediator and advocate with the Father. He emphati-
ally describes himself as "the good Shepherd." He is
ur Lawgiver; and solemn indeed is the declaration,
hat we must all appear before his judgment seat, to
eceive our reward, according to the deeds done in the
ody, whether they be good or bad.

We feel that it is not a light matter thus to advert
gain to the various offices of the Son and sent of the
'ather: and we beseech all whom we are addressing, to
ontemplate these solemn truths with due reverence: yet
:equently to meditate thereon, seeking for the assistance
f the grace of God to direct their understandings aright.
.s this is done with humble and believing hearts, the
nviction will increase, and ultimately become settled,
hat it is a great mercy to know individually that we

have not a High Priest who cannot be touched with a feeling of our infirmities, but who was in all points tempted like as we are, yet without sin.

But blessed be God, he has not only provided the means of reconciliation unto himself, through the sacrifice of Christ: he hath also through the same compassionate Saviour, granted unto us the gift of the Holy Spirit. By this the patriarchs, and the holy men of old who lived under the law, walked acceptably before God. Its more plenteous effusion and its powerful and lifegiving effects were distinctly foretold by the ancient prophets. Christ himself declared, that it was expedient that he should go away, that he might send the Comforter, the Spirit of Truth, who should guide into all truth; in allusion to whose coming he also said, "I will not leave you comfortless, I will come to you." To be guided by his Spirit is the practical application of the Christian religion. It is the light of Christ which enlightens the darkness of the heart of man; and by following this light, we are enabled to enjoy and maintain communion with him. The children of God are led by the Spirit of God; and this is the appointed means of bringing us into that state of "holiness, without which, no man shall see the Lord." It is not a doctrine of mysticism, but one of practical piety. The great office of the Holy Spirit, we firmly believe to be, to convince of sin, to bring the soul to a state of deep and sincere repentance, and to effect the work of sanctification. A holy and constant watchfulness is required, to preserve the mind alive to the guidance of this Divine Teacher; who, if diligently sought after and waited for, will be found to be a swift witness for God in the soul, producing that tenderness of spirit, and that quickness of understanding in the fear of the Lord, which are essential to our growth in grace.

It is through Him whom God hath sent forth to be a propitiation through faith in his blood, that we obtain pardon for sin: and it is through the power of his Spirit working mightily in us, that we come eventually to experience freedom from sin.

Printed by E. Couchman & Co., 10, Throgmorton Street, London.

THE UNLAWFULNESS

OF ALL

WARS AND FIGHTINGS

UNDER THE GOSPEL.

GIVEN FORTH BY THE RELIGIOUS SOCIETY OF FRIENDS.

FROM the earliest period of the history of our religious Society, we have maintained the principle, that all wars and fightings are wholly inconsistent with the Gospel dispensation; and we think it right at the present time thus to set forth the scriptural grounds of this principle.

We have ever accepted the Holy Scriptures as of divine authority, and being taught therein to honour the Lord Jesus Christ as our Lawgiver and our King, we have felt it to be an incumbent duty to obey His precepts. Among these precepts we have received in their full and comprehensive import those injunctions given forth by our Lord in His sermon on the Mount: "Love your enemies, bless them that curse you, do good to them that hate you, and pray for them which despitefully use you, and persecute you." Matt. v. 44. These commands of Christ are plain and unequivocal, and if we thus accept them, and are enabled through His grace to obey them without flinching and without compromise, we can take no part in war: for how can we destroy those whom we are taught to love, or injure those whom we are commanded to bless? How can we seek to kill those to whom we are required to do good; or treat with malevolence or cruelty those for whom we are enjoined to pray?

No lesson is more clearly taught in the Gospel than the forgiveness of injuries. This duty is repeatedly enjoined by our Lord Himself. It is even made the condition on which we are to ask for the pardon of our own offences: "Forgive us our debts, as we forgive our debtors." Matt. vi. 12. "If ye forgive not men their trespasses, neither will your Father forgive your

No. 82. [*Price 3d. per dozen.*]

trespasses." Matt. vi. 15. How solemn are His expressions when speaking of the punishment of the unmerciful servant! " So likewise shall my heavenly Father do also unto you, if ye from your hearts forgive not every one his brother their trespasses." Matt. xviii. 35. Thus does the law of Christ strike at the root of revenge : it forbids all vindictive feelings, even when an injury is committed or an insult is offered ; it prevents all animosities and strife ; it cuts off the exercise of retaliation ; it eradicates the very elements of war.

Nor is it by *precept* alone that our Lord has taught us that we are not to fight. He is Himself " The Prince o Peace" (Isa. ix. 6.) ; and in accordance with this blessed character He hath left us an *example* that we should follow His steps (1 Pet. ii. 21.)—an example which to the Christian ought of itself to be a conclusive authority against all war ; for if we are the disciples of Christ, we ought ourselves also so to walk even as He walked (1 John ii. 6.) : " Who, when He was reviled, reviled not again ; when He suffered, He threatened not ; but committed Himself to Him that judgeth righteously." 1 Pet. ii. 23. He rebuked His disciples when they sought to exercise revenge, saying, " Ye know not what manner of spirit ye are of ; for the Son of man is not come to destroy men's lives, but to save them." Luke ix. 55, 56. If we follow the example of Him who went about doing good, and who prayed even for His murderers, " Father, forgive them ; for they know not what they do" (Luke xxiii. 34.), how can we either directly or indirectly do violence or injury to others ? Neither will the Christian who rightly estimates the example of his Lord be disposed to elude or restrict it, or to weaken its force by any arguments of casuistry or expediency. He will not have one standard for his private, and another for his public duties. That which prescribes his conduct as a man, will regulate it also as a subject and a citizen, and even as a ruler. His demeanour in every relation of life will proclaim his undivided allegiance to the Prince of Peace, and will show that he is wholly redeemed from the spirit and the practice of wars and fightings.

Did the precepts and the example of their Lord thus regulate the lives of professing Christians, how would their consistent conduct exert its powerful influence over

heir fellow-countrymen, until the pure and peaceable
rinciples of the Gospel gave the impress of their own
lessed character to the community at large.—Thus would
he coming of that day be hastened when, according to
he language of ancient evangelical prophecy, men "shall
eat their swords into ploughshares and their spears into
runinghooks: nation shall not lift up sword against
iation, neither shall they learn war any more." Isa. ii. 4.

It is true that in the inscrutable wisdom of His provi-
lence, the Almighty was at times pleased, under a former
lispensation, to permit and to authorize war for the pun-
shment of nations for their wickedness: but this is no
varrant for *us* to fight. We can plead no such authority;
ve are living under that administration of grace and truth
vhich came by Jesus Christ. John i. 17. His advent
ipon earth was ushered in by a multitude of the heavenly
iost praising God, and saying, "Glory to God in the
iighest, and on earth peace, good will toward men." Luke
i. 14. It is the purpose of our heavenly Father that
nankind should be brought under the power of this grace
ind this truth. As this becomes the case, that love to
iur native land and that affection to our countrymen
vhich are natural to us, are enlarged, exalted, and purified.
Jnder the sacred and blessed influence of the love of
Christ, we not only seek to live in harmony with our
iwn countrymen, and in the performance of acts of
irotherly kindness towards them; but, under the expan-
iive power of the same heavenly principle, we acknow-
edge the people of every nation, of every colour, and of
ivery clime, as our brethren, the children of one and the
iame Almighty Parent, our Father in heaven. Regard-
ng them in this relation. we desire to serve them, to help
hem, and to do them good; we feel that to injure or to
lestroy them is to violate that brotherhood which God
ias established between us; is to transgress that holy law
if peace and goodwill which is the distinguishing charac-
eristic of the dominion of our Lord and Saviour.

We have observed with satisfaction and thankfulness,
hat the Holy Scriptures have been widely distributed in
Heathen and Mahomedan nations in the native languages
if the people, and that the truths of the Gospel have met
vith a ready acceptance by many who had been living in
iuperstition, idolatry, and vice. But it ought never to be

pleaded by any in justification of war and conquest, that these may prepare the way for the extension of the kingdom of our holy Redeemer over nations sunk in ignorance and darkness. In our apprehension it is highly displeasing in the sight of God for the inhabitants of a Christian country to pervert those talents which ought to have been devoted to His service, to the invention and exercise of means for the subjugation and oppression of less enlightened countries :—That naval and military armaments should have ever gone forth to any of those lands, spreading desolation, misery, and death among the unoffending inhabitants, we cannot but regard as a reproach to a people who profess to be the followers of Him who was holy, harmless, undefiled, and separate from sinners. Heb. vii. 26.

Even in times of outward tranquillity, military colleges and other establishments are maintained in nations professing the Gospel of Christ, in which men are trained for warriors, and designedly imbued with sentiments of human glory and ambition. For rational beings, possessing immortal souls, and all created by the same merciful Father, to be systematically instructed in the art of wounding and killing each other, and to exercise their skill to do this most effectually, is in itself so utterly opposed to the precepts of Christ, and therefore sinful, that nothing but the force of education and long familiarity with the practice and the history of war, can have reconciled sincere professors of faith in Christ, to the continuance of this practice.

We live at a time when the principles of inviolable peace are not generally embraced by either rulers or people; it therefore behoves those who maintain them to endeavour to be separated from the spirit and the policy of this world; and, in the exercise of a tender conscience, to be on their guard that they do not, in any of their transactions, act contrary to their high profession. They not only have to guard against being concerned in either offensive or defensive war, but against bearing arms for aggression or defence. On occasions of public excitement or party politics, they have especial need to watch unto prayer, and to let their communication be good to the use of edifying, that it may minister grace unto the hearers (Ephes. iv. 29.) : if civil tumults arise and military force

e resorted to, it is alike incumbent upon them to main-
ain this watchfulness, and to be careful that they do not
veaken themselves by trusting in this means of protection:
vhen war prevails, and battles are fought by sea and land.
t becomes the faithful subject of the Prince of Peace not
o place his dependence on fleets or armies; nor to allow
n himself, or countenance in others, anything at variance
vith the patience, the quietness, or the reliance of a
Christian. How forcible and how applicable on such
occasions is the declaration of Holy Scripture, "They
hat trust in the Lord shall be as Mount Zion, which
annot be removed!" Ps. cxxv. 1. To them He becomes
is a shield, and a wall of defence round about them; and
hey may humbly say, "The rock of my strength, and
ny refuge is in God!" Ps. lxii. 7.

We take comfort in the persuasion, that the peaceable
principles of the Gospel are spreading in the world: we
ire thankful in having been permitted to live in a day
vhen, under the cheering influence of peace, a friendly
ntercourse between nations, formerly enemies to each
other, has been long maintained. Their inhabitants have
ravelled from one country to another, in that confidence
ind security which a firm peace brings with it; exchang-
ng acts of friendship and kindness, and in many instances
eceiving and imparting that knowledge which would
promote the happiness one of another. The institutions
of nations have been improved, and the moral and reli-
;ious welfare of the people has been promoted. We
iave with great satisfaction observed that, in some
nstances of later times, disputes between nations of
professing Christendom have been peaceably settled by
eferring them to the arbitration of other powers. We
arnestly desire that this amicable method of adjusting
lifferences between governments may become more and
nore general, until it shall be invariably adopted.

Whilst advocating the views of the course of life which
. consistent Christian should adopt, and briefly adverting
o some of those practices which lead from the right way
of the Lord, we feel bound to declare our high value for
he benefits of civil government, and to acknowledge the
luty of cheerfully submitting to it, and yielding a ready
bedience to its authority, in all cases in which the law
f Christ is not compromised. But there are cases in

which we consider that this law is compromised. Amongst these, we have, as a religious Society, uniformly included the performance of military service, and the hiring of a substitute in the place of such requisition, and also the payment of military rates; when these are enforced we believe it right to submit to the consequences of a refusal in a meek and patient spirit.

We are very sensible that to live in the full observance of the law of righteousness and peace, is a high Christian attainment. In our fallen, unregenerate state, we cannot do this; we are by nature prone to malice and revenge; those lusts which give rise to wars and fightings do war in our members. It is only by submitting to the converting power of the Holy Spirit, and surrendering ourselves to the rule of Him who came to finish transgression, as well as to make reconciliation for iniquity (Dan. ix. 24.), that we are enabled to commend our principles to the favourable acceptance of others. We have, however, reverently to acknowledge that, in the mercy of God many have been strengthened, at different periods of time, thus to adorn their profession of the truth; and when surrounded by threatenings, persecutions, and imminent danger, to give proof that because they were Christians they could not fight. In the recent as well as in the earlier history of our own religious body, we have ample evidence of the all-sufficiency of the protecting, preserving power of the Most High, and of the blessedness o trusting in Him alone in such times of extremity.

With these views of the precepts and example of our Saviour, and of the character and requirements of the Gospel dispensation, we feel that it is our duty, not only to seek, through the help of the Holy Spirit, to be ourselves conformed to them, but to make them known to our neighbours, and to promote their universal reception. We would therefore affectionately entreat all our fellow-professors of the Gospel to be willing to examine and see these things for themselves, by the help of that light which maketh all things manifest—the light of the Spirit of God. In proportion as this light is received and followed in faith, the understanding is opened to behold the excellency and the fulness of the divine law: and many things are perceived to be contrary to it, which before were not so regarded. As the Scriptures are read with

single eye, and in dependence on that Spirit by which
ey were given forth, it will we believe be seen, that
ir, whatever form it may assume, is opposēd to the reli-
on of Jesus Christ, that it is a violation of his righteous
w, and hence that it is sin, "for sin is the transgression
the law." 1 John iii. 4. Pure and holy as are the
mmandments of God, they are not too pure for man-
nd to observe, otherwise they would not have been
joined. We are not commanded to do that which our
eavenly Father will not enable us to perform.
In the love of Christ, that love which desires the
esent and eternal happiness of the whole human race,
e earnestly commend these Gospel truths to all who
ar His name. Under a measure of the same love we
e bold to make our appeal, in an especial manner, to
e *rulers* of every nation professing the religion of our
ord and Saviour. We beseech them, in their delibera-
ns and councils, whether in the senate or the cabinet,
ntinually to bear in remembrance the righteousness, the
ve, and the forbearance inculcated by our Lord and His
ostles; and we entreat our fellow Christians of every
ime, and every description among men, seriously to
flect on those unchristian habits and dispositions which
e fostered and strengthened by a military life, and on
e sin of occupying the time, which is entrusted to us
r nobler purposes, in devising the means and acquiring
e art of distressing, and killing others—of cutting short
e earthly existence of those who are deemed the
iemies of their country, and thus hurrying them into
e presence of a just and righteous God.
We desire that religiously concerned parents may be
ought to see the evil of suffering their children to be
iined in the art and science of war. May all who are
itrusted with the education of the young be enabled, in
e fear of God, and under the influence of heavenly
sdom, to impress them with a sense of the miseries
d sinfulness of war; to guard them, especially when
ding history or biography, whether ancient or modern,
ainst those false principles of honour, which are often
quired in early life, and against an admiration of the
eds or renown of those who have been the destroyers
the human race. O that our fellow-professors of the
iristian religion would renounce the vain-glory and

pomp of military achievements, and that policy which leads to aggrandizement, retaliation, and enmity—that in national, not less than in individual intercourse, they would cherish a desire that all may be done in strict accordance with the precept, " All things whatsoever ye would that men should do to you, do ye even so to them," Matt. vii. 12. Then we reverently believe that He whose prerogative it is to bestow His blessing or to withhold it, would prosper the councils of those who thus acted in obedience to His law, would grant them national peace and happiness, and make them a blessing to all around them.

Living in love and good-will towards the whole family of man, the servants of the Lord Jesus would be found endeavouring, through His help, to lessen the mass of human misery, vice, and crime, to pull down the strongholds of sin and Satan, and to extend the peaceable reign of the Messiah. Exercising faith in Him whom they call their Lord, and fully acting up to His commands, they would, through the grace that is in them, be made instrumental in leavening those around them, by the force of Christian example, as with the leaven of the kingdom of our Holy Redeemer, that kingdom which is ultimately to pervade and prevail over all; when the heathen are to be given to Him for an inheritance, and the uttermost parts of the earth for a possession (Ps. ii. 8.); when the kingdoms of this world are to become the kingdoms of our Lord, and of his Christ (Rev. xi. 15.); when violence shall no more be heard in the land, wasting nor destruction within its borders (Isa. lx. 18.);—and when those memorable words of the prayer which our Lord taught his disciples shall be fulfilled, " Thy kingdom come. Thy will be done in earth, as it is in heaven." Matt. vi. 10. Amen.

END.

London : Printed by E. Couchman and Co., 10, Throgmorton Street; for the TRACT ASSOCIATION of the SOCIETY OF FRIENDS. Sold at the Depository 12, Bishopsgate Street Without.—1864.

REFLECTIONS

ON THE

WISDOM OF GOD

IN THE

CREATION,

AND ON

CHRISTIANITY.

'xtracted from an Address of *J. J. Gurney to the Mechanics
Manchester on Christianity, in* 1832.

LONDON:

Printed for the TRACT ASSOCIATION of the SOCIETY of FRIENDS.

Sold at the DEPOSITORY, 12, Bishopsgate Street Without.

—

1864.

No. 83.   [*Price 3d. per dozen.*]

THE WISDOM OF GOD

IN THE CREATION.

WHEN I contemplate the heavens and all their starr
host; when I take into view, as a complete system, th
planets, the moons which attend their course, and th
sun around which they move; when I behold in myriad
of fixed stars, the centres of as many more systems of th
same description; when I extend my conceptions to
countless number of these systems, moving round som
common centre of unspeakable magnitude—I am compelled to acknowledge that here is a stupendous *effect*
for which only one *cause* can by any possibility account
—I mean the FIAT of an intelligent and omnipotent
Being.

Constrained as we are, by the very structure of our
minds to rely on the uniformity of the operations of
nature, and taught by long and multiplied experience,
that every organized form of matter has a beginning, we
cannot, as it appears to me, avoid the conclusion, that
the vast machinery of the heavens once began to exist;
and being convinced of this truth, we are absolutely
certain that nothing could cause its existence but the
power of an eternal God. Thus do reason and philosophy
persuade and constrain our consent to a record of the
highest moment, contained only in Scripture—" IN THE
BEGINNING GOD CREATED THE HEAVEN AND THE EARTH."

But let us take some particular part of the created
universe—some single plant—some individual animal.
For example, let us occupy a few minutes in considering
the structure of any one individual man, whose existence
as we all know, can be traced to a beginning. Let us

amine him, body and mind. First, as to his body—it
full of contrivances—full of the evident results of
e most profound science, and of the nicest art. How
rfectly, for example, is the structure of his eye fitted
r the reception of those rays of light which are falling
on it in all directions from visible objects? How
cely are the rays refracted by its several lenses!
ow easily do they glide through the pupil! How
mprehensive, yet how perfect is the picture formed on
i retina—a picture reversed to inspection from without
t all in upright order to the percipient within! Here,
deed, is the science of optics diplayed in its perfection.
en turn to his ear. How finely does it illustrate the
inciples of acoustics! How nicely are its cavities fitted
r the reception and increase of sound? How accurately
es the drum in the centre respond to the undulation
om without!
Look at that most convenient of levers—the arm with
iich man is furnished; with what ease does he apply
forces! How nicely are its elbow and its shoulder
justed for their respective purposes; and how admir-
ly is the whole completed by the addition of a hand!
iink of the union of strength and pliancy which
stinguishes his spine—an effect produced by machinery
the most elaborate description! Contemplate his
nts—the hinge where a hinge is wanted—the ball
d socket where his comfort demands that peculiar
ucture; all lubricated by ever-flowing oil; all working
th a faultless accuracy! Think of his muscles, endued
th that curious faculty of contraction, by which he is
abled to move his members! Think of the studied
echanical adjustment by which, without ever interrupt-
g each other's functions, these muscles pull against
ch other, and keep his body even! Then consider
s blood; a fluid in perpetual motion—supplied with
re air, in one stage of its journey, and in another,
th the essence of his food; and conveying the elements
life, every few moments, to every part of his body;
iven from the heart by one set of vessels, and restored
it by another; those vessels most artificially supplied
th valves to prevent the backward motion of the fluid;
ile the pump in the centre is for ever at work, and

makes a *hundred thousand strokes in a day*, without eve
growing weary ! I will not now dwell particularly o
the still more complicated structure of his nerves, on th
chemistry of his stomach, on the *packing* of the whol
machinery, on the cellular substance which fills up it
cavities, on the skin which covers it, on the sightlines
and manly beauty which adorns the fabric. I will rathe
turn to the mind, which does, indeed, complete the ma
—its subtle powers of thought, memory, association
imagination—its passions and affections—its natural an
moral capacities. Surely we must all acknowledge tha
such a rational animal is a wonderful creature indeed
an effect for which it is utterly impossible to imagin
any adequate cause, but the *contriving intelligence* an
irresistible power of an all-wise Creator.

To look through nature up to nature's God, is indee
a profitable and delightful employment. While I woul
warmly encourage the cultivation of so desirable a habit
I wish again to remark that the wisdom and power o
God—displayed as they are in the outward creation
are inseparably connected with his *moral* government
Just in the degree in which we are obedient to that
government—just in the degree in which our faculties
both bodily and mental, are subjected to God's holy
law—will all the knowledge which we acquire be blessed
to our own happiness, and to that of our fellow men
Hence we may form some idea of the vast importance of
this subject, I mean *moral and religious knowledge.*

And where is *this* to be obtained ? Certainly we may
furnish our minds with some considerable portions of it
by reading the book of nature and providence : but there
is another book which must be regarded as its *depository*
—a book in which all things moral and spiritual, belonging to the welfare of man, are fully unfolded. True
indeed it is that natural science proclaims the power and
wisdom of God; that the perceptible *tendency* of his
government makes manifest his holiness; and lastly,
that the surplus of happiness bestowed on all living
creatures, demonstrates his goodness. I believe it is
also true that the law of God is written, in characters
more or less legible, on the hearts of all men. But for
a full account of his glorious attributes—for the know-

ledge of religion in all its beauty, and strength, and completeness—we must have recourse to the Bible—we must meditate on the sacred page, with minds under the influence of the same Spirit which gave it forth. There the whole moral law is delineated with a pencil of heavenly light. There man is described in his true character. "LIFE AND IMMORTALITY" are brought "to light by the Gospel." "This is LIFE ETERNAL, to know thee the only true God, and Jesus Christ whom thou hast sent!"

The religion of the Holy Scriptures will sweeten our sorrows, and sanctify our pleasures. It will keep not only our family circle, but *our own minds*, in right order; and while it will discountenance all vain notions and false speculations, it will enlarge and improve our faculties for every wise and worthy purpose.

ON CHRISTIANITY.

The doctrines of Christianity are founded on facts; and those facts are the subject of testimony. We are sure that the facts are true, and, therefore, that the doctrines resting on them are divine, because the testimony in question, is at once abundant in quantity, and sound in character. There are no facts whatsoever within the whole range of ancient history, of the truth of which we have more abundant and conclusive evidence, than of the DEATH AND RESURRECTION OF JESUS CHRIST. Indeed I know of no ancient events on record, of which the evidence is nearly so much accumulated, or nearly so strong.

The resurrection of Jesus Christ, together with the miracles of Christ himself and his apostles, are our sure vouchers that the Author of nature, who can alone suspend or reverse its order, was the Author of Christianity. These miracles bore no resemblance to the false pretences of the fanatical and superstitious. They were, for the most part, immediate in their operation; wrought in public; utterly incapable of being accounted for by second causes; and of so broad and conspicuous a character, that no deliberate eye-witness could be deceived respecting them. Nor were they, in point of fact, *improbable* events. Who will deny that the dark and degraded condition of mankind required an outward revelation of the Divine will? Who will not allow that miracles are a suitable test—the most suitable one which we can imagine—by which the truth of such a revelation might be established? Who does not perceive, that under such circumstances, it was credible—nay, highly *probable*—that God would permit or ordain them?

True indeed it is, that they were directly opposed to the course of nature. Otherwise they would not have been miracles—they would not have answered their purpose! But is it not equally opposed to the known order of things that an honest man in bearing witness to these facts, should tell a deliberate lie? Is it not yet more at variance with that order, that he should persevere in that lie through life, and sacrifice every worldly advantage, and even life itself, to the support of it? Is it not a far greater breach of every established probability, that *twelve* men, of the same virtuous character, should *all* tell this lie—should *all* persevere in it without deviation—should all sacrifice their property, their peace, and their reputation—should *all* be willing to lay down their lives, in its maintenance? Is it not, lastly, an actual *moral impossibility*, that this lie, accompanied by no temporal force and no worldly advantage, but by every species of loss and affliction, should triumph over the prejudices of the Jew, and the favourite habits of the Gentile—should be accepted and believed by myriads—and should finally, enthrone itself over the whole Roman empire?*

* Within a short period of our Saviour's death and resurrection, many thousands of persons were converted to Christianity at Jerusalem. Soon afterwards, Christian churches were settled in numerous parts of Syria, Lesser Asia, Macedonia, and Greece. The historian Tacitus declares that in the reign of Nero (A. D. 65), "great multitudes" of Christians were living at Rome. Pliny, when writing from his government in Bithynia to the Emperor Trajan (A. D. 107), describes our holy religion as "a contagion," which had seized the lesser towns as well as the cities, had spread among persons of all classes and descriptions, and had produced the utter neglect of the ancient idolatrous worship. During the reign of Constantine (A. D. 325), Christianity became the generally adopted and established religion of the whole Roman empire.

But the truth of Christianity does not depend solely n those miraculous facts to which we have now ad. erted. Prophecy duly fulfilled is itself a miracle, equally pplicable to the proof of religion; and the Scriptures bound in predictions, of which history has already ecorded the fulfilment. The events by which many f them have been fulfilled—for example the spread of 'hristianity, and the dispersion of the Jews—are familiar o us all.

Let us examine the prophecies scattered over the Old 'estament, and meeting us at every point in a most inartificial manner, respecting the Messiah who was to ome. Let us compare them with the history of his irth, life, character, ministry, death, resurrection, and scension, contained in the four Gospels. The prophecy nd the history are found to tally with a marvellous recision : and since the Old Testament can be *proved* o have been written long before the coming of Christ, ve find ourselves in possession of an evidence of which 10 cavils can deprive us, that Christianity is God's eligion. When a lock and a key are well fitted, a air presumption arises, even though they be of a simple haracter, that they were made for each other. If they re complex in their form, that presumption is consider- bly strengthened. But if the lock is composed of such trange and curious parts as to baffle the greatest skill— f it is absolutely novel and peculiar, differing from every hing which was ever before seen in the world—if no ey in the universe will enter it *except one;* and by hat one it is so easily and exactly fitted, that a child aay open it—then indeed are we absolutely certain that he lock and the key were made by the same master- and, and truly belong to each other. No less curiously iversified—no less hidden from the wisdom of man— o less novel and peculiar—are the prophecies contained a the Old Testament respecting Jesus Christ. No less asy—no less exact—is the manner in which they are tted by the Gospel history ! Who then can doubt that iod was the Author of these predictions—of the events y which they were fulfilled—and of the religion with hich they are both inseparably connected !

But independently of all outward testimony, and of

the evidence of miracles and prophecy, Christianity proclaims its own divine origin, by its character and its effects. This is a subject on which we may appeal to good sense, to practical feelings, to personal experience Christianity is the religion of *truth*, because it is the religion of *holiness*. In vain will the student search th pages of Plato and Aristotle—in vain will he examin the conversations of Socrates—in vain will he dive into the disputations of Cicero—for a moral system-so com plete, so simple, and so efficacious, as that of the Bible Where, within the whole range of uninspired ethics shall we find anything worthy even of a moment' comparison with that divine saying, in which the whol law of God is comprehended and concentrated? *" Tho shalt love the Lord thy God with all thy heart, and with all thy soul, and with all thy strength, and with all th mind; and thou shalt love thy neighbour as thyself."*

In the goodness of Christianity—in the purity of it law—in its display of the holy attributes of God—in it revelation of an awful and glorious eternity—in its actua efficiency for the moral restoration of our species—in the perfect fitness of that Saviour whom it unfolds to our spiritual need as sinners in the sight of God—we have abundant experimental proof of its truth and divine origin. Allow me, in conclusion, to bear my deliberate and solemn testimony in the words of an apostle—and may that testimony, by whomsoever borne, satisfy all understandings and imbue all hearts! May it be upheld and exalted on every side! May it surmount all opposition—may it pervade the whole land—may it spread from pole to pole—may it be as unrestrained and diffusive as the winds of heaven!—"OTHER FOUNDATION CAN NO MAN LAY THAN THAT IS LAID, WHICH IS JESUS CHRIST."

END.

Printed by E. Couchman & Co., 10, Throgmorton Street, London.

GOSPEL PRIVILEGES

EXEMPLIFIED IN

THE LIFE OF ANN SCOTT.

ANN SCOTT, the subject of the following account, was
an individual that moved in very humble life. She was
born at Aberford, in Yorkshire, but removed with her
parents, when about four years of age, to the village of
Bramham, where she was sent to a National School.
This School was conducted by pious teachers; and in
recurring to this period of her life in a Journal found
after her decease, she remarks, " The goodness of the
Lord planted in me very early in my life, pious and good
instruction, and I learned many good hymns."

There is reason to believe that this early religious
instruction was, through the divine blessing, the means
of bringing her gradually under the influence of religious
principle. No allusion is made in her memorandums to
such a time of awakening, as is often known in the experience of those who have grown up in forgetfulness of
God; and it seems probable that from an early period she
was made willing to surrender her heart to the government of Christ, and to accept him as her Saviour.

In 1825, being then in her eighteenth year, she went
to reside as a household servant with a family in York,
who were members of the Religious Society of Friends.
—In 1826, she attended a meeting for worship, appointed
by two ministers of that Society, in which she received
impressions that led her to adopt the principles of
Friends, under the conviction that they were in true
accordance with the Gospel. She became from this
period a constant attender of the meetings of Friends,
with whom she was joined in membership in 1831.

No. 84.   [*Price 3d. per dozen.*]

Ann Scott naturally possessed few talents, but through attention to the teaching of the Holy Spirit in the secret of her own heart, she became an encouraging example of the power of divine grace, in subduing the carnal mind, and bringing the will into conformity to the mind of Christ. Under the conviction that it is the duty of the Christian to take up his cross daily, and follow Christ, as well as his privilege to know past sins to be blotted out through faith in a crucified Lord, she was often brought into much mental conflict, by a deep sense of the natural corruption of her own heart. She longed for deliverance from the power of temptation, and often felt painfully the warring of the flesh against the Spirit; whilst she was favoured nevertheless to know the Spirit successfully to war against the flesh.

As a servant, she was remarkable for her fidelity and industry, and was much valued in the family into whose service she had entered, and in which she continued for nearly ten years. The delight which she took in reading the Holy Scriptures and a few other religious books, and the inclination which she felt to note down her thoughts, led her to improve herself much in the arts of reading and writing; and it was very observable, in her case, how powerful was the influence of true religion in the cultivation of the understanding and the affections, and in enlarging the sphere of refined enjoyment. It pleased Divine Providence to try her with an illness that was very afflictive to her, both in body and mind, and which was so protracted that she was obliged to quit her situation, in which she had received much Christian kindness. She never entirely recovered her health, but on her becoming considerably better, she found employment in a small family, where her worth was estimated, and due allowance made for her weakness. This provision for her, excited her lively gratitude to her Heavenly Father; and in one of her simple memorandums, after expressing this feeling, she notices that the kindly countenance of her mistress, and the love she felt for her, helped her to fulfil her duties. Her increasing debility, however, at length obliged her to quit this situation, and she subsequently supported herself chiefly by needlework, and by occasionally assisting in families. Her trials in connection with her indisposition were great, but these appear to have led her into more sympathy with others; and having occasionally the command of her own time, she often visited the sick and afflicted. In these visits, though of a peculiarly diffident disposition, and taking a very humble view of her own attainments, her desire for the spiritual welfare and encouragement of the visited, would often rise above every other feeling, and from her Bible or her Hymn Book, she would select and read to them, with much simplicity and feeling, such passages as she had herself derived consolation from. Often did these prove as a word in season to the weary ones who could appreciate the sweetness of her spirit and the love by which her labours were prompted.—By many of these, her visits are remembered with feelings of grateful affection.

The circle in which Ann Scott was known, was very limited, but in this she was esteemed and valued: and by her circumspect and humble deportment, and her simple reliance upon her Saviour, she was often made the means of instruction to those around her, evincing to them the blessed effects of having her attention turned to the guidance of the Spirit of Truth in her own heart, by obedience to the manifestations of which, she became " quick of understanding in the fear of the Lord."

The progress of divine grace in her soul, and the blessedness of which she partook in walking in simple faith, and in the fear of the Lord, will be best described by extracts from her own memorandums. These afford an instructive illustration of the power of religion, and of the wonderful adaptation of the Gospel to the wants of the poor and the afflicted.

5th month, 1835. "In my low condition, the Lord careth for me, though afflicted. When I contemplate the sufferings of our blessed Redeemer, I am strengthened to press forward, though sometimes faint and weary. 'There is a river, the streams whereof make glad the city of God!' O, how my soul feels to be watered, when I act in submission to the will of God! but the enemy of souls is suffered to entice me with his allurements: and the flesh likewise warreth against the spirit, so that I can adopt the language of the Apostle, 'When I would do good, evil is present with me.' In this situation I am led to lie prostrate in deep humility and self-abasement, at the throne of grace, till the Lord is pleased to appear and arise for my help.

10th of 9th month, 1836. "Yesterday, out of health and much exercised in mind. I remembered the saying, 'I had fainted unless I had believed to see the goodness of the Lord,' &c. And in the evening I found, after deep exercise of prayer, life and strength to arise, which caused me to rejoice in the Lord, and joy in the God of my salvation. I see more and more of my own infirmity, and of the all-sufficiency of the Lord. It is by trusting in Him alone that we find strength, not in ourselves. The Lord is good unto them that wait for Him, to the soul that seeketh Him. It is good to wait upon the Lord, to pour out the soul before Him.

29th. "Attended meeting this morning, felt much bowed down under a sense of my infirmities, and the help that I needed, for a growth in the knowledge and love of God. O! the earnestness of my soul for a nearer communion with my Heavenly Father! O! the deep conflicts which I do at times experience, yet how am I supported through them! I remember the merits of our Holy Redeemer,—the earnestness of his soul in holy exercise, which was poured forth in the garden of Gethsemane, when His sweat was as it were drops of blood falling down to the ground, for our sakes. Redeeming love! O! what an increase of light and strength do I ex_perience through deep baptisms of spirit. I find that self must be of no esteem, that the Lord alone may be exalted, and abiding in this exercise of mind, I find my way made plain before me.

12th month. "I have had to go weeping on my way. But I humbly trust I am doing the will of my Heavenly Father, and I can testify that, beyond all doubt, I am enabled to feel his extended love towards me. 'When thou passeth through the waters, I will be with thee; and through the rivers, they shall not overflow thee.'

3rd month, 1837. "O, the richness of Divine love to those that trust in the Lord! not leaning to their own understandings, but in all their ways acknowledging him; how is their way directed! mercy! rich mercy! unlimited love!

6th of 6th month. "I have been graciously permitted to draw near to the Fountain of all good, for that food which my soul needeth, and thirsteth after: for the Lord satisfieth the weary soul, and replenisheth the thirsty soul! O, the peace which I do at times experience in being resigned to my situation while travelling in this vale of tears. Obedience to the heavenly light is required, as our blessed Redeemer expressed: 'While ye have the light believe in the light, and walk in the light, lest darkness come upon you!' And though the Christian has at times much to bear, yet in endeavouring to keep to the light, the truth of the words 'my grace is sufficient for thee' will be experienced. O, saith my soul, may I not faint on my way, in waiting on, and suffering the will of God.

24th of 7th month. "Did not sufficiently attend to the simplicity of truth in my temporal concerns. Did

not stay to wait on the Lord, for a renewal of strength
against the powers of an unwearied enemy. O, how unworthy and poor I felt myself! but through the extended
love of God,—not any merit of my own,—I felt myself
enabled to draw near to the fountain of all good, for
deliverance.

18th of 10th month. " In self-examination, how needful I have felt it to be diligent in daily watching unto
prayer, keeping my eye single unto the Lord alone: I
have endeavoured to draw near unto the Lord, and to
pour out my complaints before Him; and my prayers
have been heard, and I have felt rest unto my soul. O,
the goodness of the Lord! How rich his mercies! my
heart overflows when I remember his extended love to so
unworthy a creature.—Although labouring under great
bodily weakness, I was enabled to cast all my burdens
on the Lord, and felt his sustaining arm underneath me.
Though my faith at times is weak, I have remembered
in my low estate the words of the dear Redeemer, ' Him
that cometh unto me, I will in no wise cast out;' O,
how encouraging are the precious promises!

10th of 12th month. " I feel myself weak in body.
Perhaps this tenement of clay is fast hastening to its
dissolution: I do not know how soon. I have felt this
evening great peace of mind.

21st of 12th month. " I trust I have been making
some progress in the way of truth. I feel the burden of
my weak body, yet my Heavenly Father deals very gently
with me. The Lord's goodness is great. I have this
afternoon felt such a fullness of heavenly bread! Glory
be alone ascribed unto the Giver of every good and perfect gift; My earnest cry to my Heavenly Father is, that
I may be faithful to what is required of me, however
humiliating.

5th of 1st month, 1838. " Surely the humble Christian
is kept from evil! O, to be faithful to that ' still small

oice,' which speaks within, saying, 'This is the way, ralk in it.'—What peace is extended to a true Christian! .nd for want of faithfulness, what langour arises! May . be willing to follow the Lamb whithersoever he eadeth; 'For our light affliction, which is but for a noment, worketh for us a far more exceeding and eternal reight of glory.'

14th of 2nd month. ' O, the riches of Divine love! ıow unworthy am I! poor and weak! and yet my faint‌ng soul is kept, I humbly trust, in the truth. I feel a abouring after that bread which endureth unto eternal ife, my soul thirsts after this inward life. O, may I ndeed be willing to suffer the loss of all things, that ‏. may win Christ!

15th of 9th month. "Felt the buffetings of an un‌vearied enemy during the night season, yet on rising ‌rom my pillow possessed a quiet frame of mind. What ‏v precious favour! After breakfast, these words arose in ny mind, 'Pray without ceasing.' How comfortable I ‌ave been this day! I have been enabled to tread upon he tempter's power. O! the fruits of true prayer! It is ‏;ood to retire and pour forth our complaints before the ‏.ord,—

> ' The feeblest worm he stoops to hear,
> Nor casts the meanest wretch away.'

29th of 6th month, 1839. "My soul has tasted the ich mercies of Christ. There doth indeed remain a rest ‏or the people of God. O! It is good to wait upon the ‏.ord for a renewal of our strength.

3rd of 4th month, 1840. "Have this day renewed ny covenant with my Heavenly Father; that I might nore obediently walk in the path cast up before me. I ‏el my spiritual strength renewed, my soul is filled with ‏.eavenly love. O, may I be more faithful!

29th of 6th month. "I have indeed fed upon the ‏.idden manna, that bread which endureth unto everlast-

ing life. Nothing but faithfulness and uprightness of
heart will do: though the conflict may at times be sore,
our Heavenly Parent is faithful, and mindful, over the
work of his own hands, not willing that any should
perish. The Gospel shines to give us light. Precious
indeed are the promises.

26th of 11th month. "Rose this morning between
six and seven. I was enabled to offer unto my Heavenly
Father, the tribute of thanksgiving for the mercies bestowed upon me. How precious the season. O, may I
be no more loitering, but endeavour day by day to grow
in grace."

Ann Scott's health had for some time been declining,
and in the early part of the 12th month, 1840, she had
a violent attack of inflammation of the chest, which
rapidly reduced her little remaining strength. Though
she was at times in much suffering, yet she expressed to
some friends who called to see her, that she felt in a most
remarkable manner, the condescension of the Most High
towards her,—that she could not have thought it possible, she could have witnessed such condescension. Her
weakness was so great that it was difficult for her to
express much; but her soul seemed filled with thanksgiving and praise; and when the final summons came,
it cannot be doubted that through the mercy of that
Saviour, "who, by one offering, hath perfected for ever
them that are sanctified," she was found among the
"pure in heart," of whom he declared, "blessed are
they, for they shall see God."—She died on the 9th of
the 12th month, 1840; aged 34 years.

END.

London: Printed by E. Couchman & Co., 10, Throgmorton Street, for the
TRACT ASSOCIATION of the SOCIETY OF FRIENDS. Sold at the Depository,
12, Bishopsgate Street Without.—1863.

THE POWER OF RELIGION,

EXEMPLIFIED IN THE LAST DAYS OF

A MOTHER.

THE writer of this little narrative being in the frequent practice of visiting the sick and the indigent, was requested some months since to visit the wife of F. B., who was sinking under that insidious disease—consumption. The family was previously unknown to her, but feeling much interested in the case, she was induced to make some memorandums, from which the following selections are made. They were penned without any view to publication : but as they present an instructive and encouraging instance of the efficacy of that faith by which this simple-hearted Christian was enabled to overcome the world, they are presented to the reader, with a sincere desire that they may prove useful.

"On my first introduction, I found the poor invalid in her room, which she had not left since her last confinement, a period of two months ; the infant had taken its mother's complaint ; but a more sweetly-intelligent countenance I never remember to have seen. She was sitting in a kind of easy chair, which by no means gave her the support her extreme weakness required. I made a few inquiries into her outward circumstances, but she was very careful and delicate in making any allusion to her necessities and privations, though everything indicated that she had gone through severe trials ; at the same time showing that, when in health, she had known how to manage with frugality, and valued those requisites to happiness, cleanliness and order.

"On the remark being made that she appeared very weak, 'I am,' she said, 'and my cough is dreadful, but everything is possible with God ; He has brought me low, and He can raise me up ; I do hope I shall get better ;

for what will my dear little babies do without a mother's
care? my husband could do better without me.' It was
painfully evident that her desire to live was very strong :
she was one in whom natural affections and sensibilities
were strikingly developed. I found in my subsequent
visits that she possessed some of those exquisitely fine
feelings which are only fully known when entire confidence is felt. Feeling deeply interested, and seeing how
closely she clung to the objects of her tender solicitude,
I found it difficult to tell her my views of her case. I
gently intimated that our Heavenly Father could indeed
restore her, for that all things were possible to Him : but
from the nature of her complaint it left but little ground
to build any hope that she would experience renewed
strength. Here was the touchstone—a deep and rather
prolonged silence ensued, when it was broken by the
remark, that a great change must be wrought in all of us
before we could enter into the kingdom of heaven; we
must have the mind of Christ : His Holy Spirit must
make us new creatures; old things must be done away;
and that which she now felt to be difficult would be
made easy, and a patient submissive spirit would be
effected in her by the operation of His Holy Spirit in her
heart; but in order to witness this change, we must
become passive clay in the hands of the mighty Potter.
She gave a look of earnest solicitude, and said, 'Oh!
there is a great work to be done before I shall be fit
to die; my ties as a wife and mother do bind me so
strong to this world, it is so hard to resign them : may
God grant me power to do it, and fit and prepare me for
Himself! I trust, I hope He will.' I now left her, with
being requested to come again soon. When I visited
her again, she told me she could sleep but little during
the night; that she had been engaged in deep thought;
'I do find there is much to be removed out of my heart
before I shall be able to

"———read my title clear
To mansions in the skies."

I have prayed that God may open my eyes and give me
understanding. Oh! He is very good to me, but His
hand is heavy upon me : my bodily sufferings are very

great, but I do try and pray to bear them patiently. I do not in my heart murmur at the affliction He has laid upon me; I shall not have one stroke too many; I deserve all, and more than all.' Her hope and confidence in the efficacy of Divine grace was now mercifully gaining strength; it was indeed truly instructive to witness the power of Divine love in bringing her mind into a state of passive obedience to the will of God; for in one of my earlier visits I found her low and depressed. She was sitting alone, with a sick child on her knee, the poor little suffering infant weeping and moaning in the cradle which she was endeavouring to rock by a string tied to the handle. She looked expressively up at me and said, 'I am *so ill*, and my poor, dear little baby is such a dreadful sufferer, I could die happier if I could see him go before me. I am sure I lose strength daily; do look at my hands; I am nothing but a frame. It is an awful thing to die: no one can tell what the feeling is, to know there can be *nothing* done; but to feel you are sinking, constantly sinking into the grave; not *one* ray of hope that you will ever recover; it is a lonely, a dull feeling, may the Lord help me!' She was encouraged to believe that He who had begun the good work would carry it on to His own glory and her salvation. 'I do *trust* He will, she replied. A great change had now been wrought, and she would frequently allude with cheerfulness to her declining strength, but would say with a smile, 'I still like to use the means God puts into my power; it is not for me to throw my life away; though I do not now think anything will do me any real good.' She derived great consolation and encouragement from hearing the Scriptures; and on reading the 14th of John's Gospel, she remarked, 'What comfort there is in that chapter for a poor soul like mine; I humbly trust I shall soon enter one of those many mansions. Oh! the Saviour is my meat and drink: I do live upon Christ: the bread and wine of the kingdom are spiritual. I have always thought it right to read the Bible; but I often closed it feeling no better than when I opened it, my mind was not enlightened to see its true meaning; nothing can give true light, I am now quite sure, but the Spirit of God; but it is a great blessing to have the help and

prayers of all such as are spiritually enlightened. Oh!
that God would in His mercy turn the hearts of all those
to Himself who undertake the spiritual instruction of
others.' She would often speak in the most grateful
manner of the ladies who visited and read to her; and
also frequently referred to the affection and devoted
attachment of her husband. 'Dear soul,' she said, 'he
is often afraid I shall want; but I tell him I believe God
will never let me; I hope his faith will increase, and
that he will be enabled to look as I have done, to the
" Rock of Ages" for strength to bear his separation from
me: he does feel it so keenly, poor fellow; I cannot now
shed a tear; I have done with them all.' It was remarked, what cause of thankfulness it was, that she had
been permitted to arrive at such a state of resignation;
'O yes,' she replied, 'one tie after another has given
way; my Redeemer has done the work for me, and it
has been done gradually; my sleepless nights have been
prayerful nights, and prayer has been heard and answered.' She had marked the following stanza of a
hymn which had been previously read to her:

"'If thou shouldst call me to resign,
What most I prized; it ne'er was mine;
I only yield thee what was thine;
Thy will be done.'

"In one of my late visits to her, she said, 'I have
been thinking so much about you, and I know you have
thought about me; I want you to read to me: can you
stay? but I know you are so engaged, I ought not, I
must not intrude so much on your time.' In this visit
she related many very interesting particulars of her early
life. She lost her mother when very young; and her
father was a very cruel and intemperate man, so that
her childhood was one of great temptation; but, to quote
her own words, 'God was very merciful, and watched
over me; He has been my protector and preserver; and
I humbly trust He will be so to my poor motherless
children;' adding, with great emphasis, 'dear little souls
I cannot any longer do anything for them; I tell my poor
Frank, I now deliver them up to him as their only
earthly friend; *poor little things*, they miss a mother's

are; but I pray that he may always do his duty by them; and I believe he will, he has always been so fond of his children.' She felt she had quite resigned them all, and herself also, into the hands of a faithful Creator, whom not having seen she loved, and in whom believing, she rejoiced with joy unspeakable and full of glory.

"In one of my calls on her, I remembered her telling me the severe conflict of mind she had suffered from giving way to impatience at a little want, as she thought, of consideration, of those about her: 'It was such a little thing,' she said, 'but I expressed myself *very* hastily: it made me so miserable; I felt my Saviour and all comfort had fled: I did grieve for my sinful temper; but I sought pardon, and, in His merciful goodness He returned again to me and peace was restored. It is of no use for us to say we will, or we will not do this or that; for unless we are helped by His Almighty power we shall never be able to do anything; if left but *one* moment we fall. It was satan that stirred me up to feel so impatient and ungrateful; I have so much kindness shown me; and I do think, if he could, my poor Frank would save me the trouble of wiping even my own lips.' She was told it was indeed very wrong, but that the enemy was a very cruel and busy one, and watched every opportunity to catch us off our guard; that he takes advantage of our weakness; but she had found that, as a 'father pitieth his children,' so the Lord had had pity on her, and had restored His good Spirit to her again, and she was once more permitted to feel Him to be her Light and Salvation; and having been thus humbled before Him for her transgressions, it was believed it would prove in the end a blessing, as it would lead her in future to be constantly praying to be kept on the watch-tower, waiting there with an attentive ear, listening to the voice of the true Shepherd in the secret of the soul, that witness for God in the conscience. Calling on her one day, near the close of her earthly course, she said, 'I have put by the dress you gave me, and have desired to be buried in it. I should so like you should be with me in my last moments.' This request was readily assented to, if it should be found practicable. The greater part of the body was laid for several days; and on being asked if she would

not like to have a bottle of water to her feet? she smiled
and very impressively said, 'No, I hope to be soon in
heaven.' The nurse said she had washed her early in
the morning to refresh her. 'Ah,' she sweetly answered,
'I shall soon be washed whiter, nurse, than anything
you can wash me with.' She continued to suffer great
pain: 'Even my nails ache,' she said, 'and my poor side
is in agony; none knows but my Saviour and myself
what I suffer; and this extreme weakness, it is past words
to express; if I am but moved, it feels as if I must be
smothered.' I sat quietly by her side, when she looked
at me and whispered, 'Will you read a little to me, I can
bear it?' I read the 39th Psalm; when it was finished,
she remarked, 'How suitable, how good it is; may I
know the fulfilment of the petitions!' After an interval
of silence prayer was offered, that if consistent with the
will of her Heavenly Father, she might be spared much
more bodily suffering, and that the passage to the grave
might be made easy: with great fervour she uttered,
'Lord have mercy upon me, and grant that this petition
with my own prayers, may reach thee in heaven, and be
answered!' The evening before she died, I saw her;
she was waiting, sweetly waiting for her change: the
following lines, which had been the experience of a devoted servant of the Lord, and which he had repeated a
short time before his death, were softly said to her:—

"'Down to the grave I sink by gradual decay,
Whilst resignation gently slopes the way;
With all my prospects brightening to the last,
My heaven commences ere this earth be passed.'

"'Yes, yes, this is my case; my prospects are all
brightening; but, Oh! how gradual has been my descent
into the grave.' Those about her remarked that it was
truly beautiful to witness her state of mind. The nurse
told me she was always afraid of death before, but it was
now a comfort and a pleasure to be with her. She
continued sensible to the last; and without a struggle
sweetly fell asleep in Jesus: being sprinkled with the
blood of the Everlasting Covenant, she is now, we consolingly believe, of that number of all nations, kindreds,
and people, and tongues, who stand before the Throne

d before the Lamb, clothed in white robes, and palms their hands, saying, 'Salvation to our. God which teth upon the Throne, and unto the Lamb.'

"Such was the end of M. B.'s earthly course, and es it not induce the prayer, 'Let me die the death of e righteous, and let my latter end be like his?'"

CHICHESTER, 1842.

~~~~~~~~~~~~

TO A DYING CHRISTIAN.

———

Parting soul! the flood awaits thee,
And the billows round thee roar:
Yet look on—the crystal city
Stands on yon celestial shore!
There are crowns and thrones of glory;
There the living waters glide;
There the just, in shining raiment,
Wander by Emmanuel's side.

Linger not—the stream is narrow,
Though its cold dark waters rise;
He who passed the flood before thee,
Guides thy path to yonder skies:
Hark! the sound of angels hymning
Rolls harmonious o'er thine ear;
See! the walls and golden portals
Through the mist of death appear.

Soul, adieu! this gloomy sojourn
Holds thy captive feet no more;
Flesh is dropp'd and sin forsaken,
Sorrow done, and weeping o'er:
Through the tears thy friends are shedding
Smiles of hope serenely shine;
Not a friend remains behind thee,
But would change his lot for thine.

FREEDOM FROM CARE.

While I liv'q' without the Lord,
   (If I might be said to live,)
Nothing could relief afford,
   Nothing satisfaction give.

Empty hopes and groundless fear,
   Mov'd by turns my anxious mind;
Like a feather in the air,
   Made the sport of every wind.

Now, I see, whate'er betide,
   All is well if Christ be mine;
He has promis'd to provide;
   I have only to resign.

"Cast," He says, "on me thy care,
   'Tis enough that I am nigh;
I will all thy burdens bear;
   I will all thy wants supply.

"Simply follow as I lead;
   Do not reason, but believe;
Call on me in time of need,
   Thou shalt surely help receive."

Lord, I would, I do submit,
   Gladly yield my all to thee;
What thy wisdom sees most fit
   Must be, surely, best for me.

Only, when the way is rough,
   And the coward flesh would start,
Let thy promise and thy love
   Cheer and animate my heart.

END.

London: Printed by E. Couchman & Co., 10, Throgmorton Street; fo
Tract Association of the Society of Friends. Sold at the Deposi
12, Bishopsgate Street Without.—1864.

THE

WAY OF SALVATION

BY

JESUS CHRIST.

———

.VATION is freely offered to mankind by JESUS CHRIST;
ertheless, multitudes are found disregarding the offers
mercy, and carelessly living in sin, or even pursuing
iestly a sinful course; notwithstanding sin always brings
ieasure of its own punishment in this world, and will
it certainly, if it be not forsaken, bring everlasting pun-
ment in the next. "For the Son of man shall come in
glory of his Father, with his angels, and then he shall
ard every man according to his works." Matt. xvi. 27.
he wicked is snared in the work of his own hands. The
ked shall be turned into hell, and all the nations that
et God." Ps. ix. 16, 17.
he Holy Scriptures assure us that all men shall perish
iss they repent. Luke xiii. 1. 3. Let none, therefore,
eive themselves by imagining that, because they receive
ortion of the punishment of sin in this world, they will
ipe the wrath of God in the next. For when God
iounced grievous judgments upon the Israelites by the
ihet Isaiah, because of their sins, he said, "For all
his anger is not turned away, but his hand is stretched
still." Isa. v. 25; ix. 12. 17. 21; x. 4. This was
iuse the people turned not to him that smote them,
her sought the Lord of Hosts. Isa. ix. 13. None
escape the just judgments of God without repentance;
none who truly repent can willingly continue in the
tice of sin. Sin becomes a grievous burden to the
tent; and, if through unwatchfulness they at any time
into it, they are deeply humbled before God under the
e of their transgression; and cannot rest till, through
wed repentance and faith in Christ, they know the
l to lift them up (Jas. iv. 10), by again giving them the
ence within themselves of the forgiveness of their sin.

o. 75.   [Price 5½d. per dozen.]

John the Baptist said to the multitude that came forth
be baptized of him, and thus made public profession
their belief in the doctrine of repentance,—"O generati
of vipers! Who hath warned you to flee from the wrath
come? Bring forth, therefore, fruits worthy of repentanc
and begin not to say within yourselves, We have Abrah
to our Father: for I say unto you, that God is able of the
stones to raise up children unto Abraham. And now a
the axe is laid unto the root of the trees; every tree, the
fore, which bringeth not forth good fruit, is hewn down a
cast into the fire." Luke iii. 7—9. As none, therefore,
that day, might hope to be saved because they were t
children of Abraham, unless they brought forth fruits m
for repentance, and thus did the works of Abraham; so
this day, none may hope to be saved because they c
themselves Christians, unless they bring forth fruits wort
of repentance, and follow Christ. Mark viii. 34.

Let not any, therefore, who do not forsake their sins, d
ceive themselves by supposing that their sins are forgiv
even though they may have confessed them, and had absol
tion pronounced upon them: for God never gave to any n
authority to pronounce absolution upon unrepented-of s
but he complained of such as assumed it, saying, "From
least of them even unto the greatest of them every one
given to covetousness; and from the prophet even unto
priest every one dealeth falsely: they have healed also
hurt of the daughter of my people slightly, saying, Pea
Peace, when there is no peace." "Therefore they s
fall among them that fall: at the time that I visit th
they shall be cast down, saith the Lord" (Jer. vi. 13.
viii. 10—12). Such are but "blind leaders of the blin
who, Christ has said, "shall both fall into the ditch." M
xv. 14.

Some persons profess to deny the being of a God;
the unbelief of such does not make the faith of those
do believe void, or alter the fact of the existence of G
any more than if a man were to shut his eyes and say the
was no such thing as the sun, this would blot the sun out
the heavens. It would, indeed, prove the man to be a fo
and it is "the fool who has said in his heart, There
no God." Ps. xiv. 1; liii. 1.

Others there are who assume that they are lost by
eternal decree, being predestinated to destruction, and
it is in vain for them to strive against sin. Thus, in th
folly, these charge their destruction upon God, and m

evere in the service of the devil. But the language of
Most High, to a people who turned to iniquity in former
s, was, "O Israel, thou hast destroyed thyself, but in
is thy help." Hosea xiii. 9. "Have I any pleasure at
hat the wicked should die? saith the Lord; and not that
should turn from his ways and live?" Ezek. xviii. 23.
he Lord is long-suffering to us-ward, not willing that
should perish, but that all should come to repentance."
et. iii. 9. Others, again, remain in a sinful course, who
acknowledge that sin makes them unhappy, and that it is
r duty to forsake it; but they say it is useless for them to
to do better while they are surrounded by evil example,
by persons who scoff at every thing good. But these
uses for not forsaking iniquity, and for remaining the
ants of Satan, are merely his temptations, by which he
ves to keep people in his service, in order that their por-
may be with him in that awful state of suffering which
l be the reward of the wicked in the world to come; and
ch is compared to a lake burning with fire and brimstone,
re the worm dieth not and the fire is not quenched.
r. xx. 10. Mark ix. 48. These excuses will not avail in
day of judgment; for God is willing to give grace to all
) seek to him for it, sufficient to enable them to resist
ptation. He "resisteth the proud, and giveth grace to
humble" (1 Pet. v. 5); and his "grace is sufficient" for
se who trust in him. 2 Cor. xii. 9. The exhortation of
ist, who "endured the contradiction of sinners against
self" (Heb. xii. 3), and who set us a righteous example,
"Fear not them which kill the body, but are not able to
the soul: but rather fear him, which is able to destroy
1 soul and body in hell:" and he likewise added,
Thosoever therefore shall confess me before men, him
I confess also before my Father which is in heaven;
whosoever shall deny me before men, him will I also
y before my Father which is in heaven." Matt. x. 28.
33.
'here is no doubt that all, on serious reflection, desire
ce to their immortal souls, both in this world and the
t. Let them be wise, then, and seek it where it is to be
nd. It is not to be found in sin; for, "the wicked are
the troubled sea when it cannot rest, whose waters cast
mire and dirt; there is no peace, saith my God, to the
ked." Isa. lvii. 20, 21. It is the same Almighty Being
) ordained that the sun should rise in the east and set in
west, who has ordained that there shall be no peace to

the wicked; and it would be just as rational to expect tl
course of nature to be changed in accommodation to ma
wishes, as to expect that peace can be attained while livi
in sin. Sin ever will bring trouble, and only trouble; i
" there is no peace saith the Lord, unto the wicked ?" I
xlviii. 22. May all constantly bear this in remembranc
and that " all unrighteousness is sin." 1 John v. 17.

" The fear of the Lord is the beginning of wisdom;
good understanding have all they that do his comman
ments." Ps. cxi. 10. " By the fear of the Lord m
depart from evil." " The fear of the Lord tendeth to lif
and he that hath it shall abide satisfied; he shall not
visited with evil." Prov. xvi. 6; xix. 23. Those who fe
the Lord regard his law, both as it is recorded in Ho
Scripture, and as it is revealed in their hearts; and obta
an inheritance in the new covenant of God: the covenant
life and of peace in Jesus Christ; for, " Behold the da
come, saith the Lord, that I will make a new covenant wi
the House of Israel, and with the House of Judah [with
who turn unto the Lord]. I will put my law in their inwa
parts, and write it in their hearts: and will be their Go
and they shall be my people; and they shall teach no mo
every man his neighbour, and every man his brother, sayin
Know the Lord; for they shall all know me, from the lea
of them to the greatest of them, saith the Lord, for I wi
forgive their iniquity, and I will remember their sin i
more." Jer. xxxi. 31—34. Heb. viii. 8—12.

This " Law of the Lord" is written in the hearts of mai
kind by the Holy Spirit or " Holy Ghost, whom " sa
Christ, " the Father will send in my name; he shall teac
you all things, and bring all things to your remembrand
whatsoever I have said unto you." John xiv. 26. " Whe
he, the Spirit of truth, is come, he will guide you into a
truth." " And when he is come he will reprove [or coi
vince] the world of sin, and of righteousness, and of judi
ment." John xvi. 8. 10. 13. The operation of this Spi
on the mind of man is continually referred to in the Scri
tures as essential to religion; and is described under a gre
variety of similitudes and terms, according to its diversifi
effects. The work of the Holy Spirit is ever to enlight
the mind, and to lead man in the paths of righteousness ai
peace. It is therefore called " Light." " All things th
are reproved," says the Apostle Paul, " are made manife
by the Light; for whatsoever doth make manifest is Lig
Wherefore, he saith. Awake thou that sleepest, and ari

the dead, and Christ shall give thee Light." Ephes. v. 14.

ow, all have, at times, known sin to be made manifest them, so that they have been convinced in their own ds that some things they were tempted to commit were nsive in the sight of God. And when they have ne. ted this warning, and have committed the sin, though no might know of its commission but themselves, they e felt an inward consciousness that it was known unto l; and a secret fear—a dread has attended them, that r "sin would find them out" (Numb. xxxii. 23), if not in world, at any rate in the next; and thus they have felt asy in their minds. All mankind may be boldly appealed s having felt thus, at one season or other, though they ' not hitherto have known what it was that thus secretly vinced them of sin: it may have been as a light shining arkness, and not comprehended; for, said the evangelist n, " The Light shineth in darkness, and the darkness prehended it not." Let all know, however, that that ch convinced them was the Light of the Holy Spirit, the ht which cometh by Jesus Christ. " In him was life, and life was the Light of men:"—This is the Light by ch He who is the " true Light, lighteth every man that eth into the world." John i. 5. 4. 9. he object for which Christ our Saviour thus enlightens kind, is clearly set forth by the Apostle Paul, in the sage already referred to (Eph. v. 13, 14), and again in e striking expressions: "God who commanded the light hine out of darkness hath shined in our hearts, to give light of the knowledge of the glory of God, in the of Jesus Christ." And, " If our Gospel be hid," he s, " it is hid to them that are lost: in whom the God of world hath blinded the minds of them which believe not, the light of the glorious Gospel of Christ, who is the ge of God, should shine unto them." 2 Cor. iv. 3. 6. cisely parallel to this testimony, is the spirit of the owing declaration of Christ himself: " This is the con- nation, that Light is come into the world, and men d darkness rather than light, because their deeds were ; for every one that doeth evil hateth the Light, neither eth to the Light, lest his deeds should be reproved: but that doeth truth cometh to the Light, that his deeds may made manifest that they are wrought in God." John iii. 21.

he term Grace is variously used in the Holy Scriptures,

in which the plan of salvation is spoken of as the " Gra
of God." It is so called, because this salvation is receive
through the mercy of God in Christ Jesus ; and for his sak
not for our own, " lest any man should boast." It
likewise declared, that it was by grace, through faith, th
the saints of old were saved; and that this grace came b
Jesus Christ. " By grace are ye saved, through faith, an
that not of yourselves ; it is the gift of God: not of work
lest any man should boast: for we are his workmanshi
created in Christ Jesus unto good works, which God hat
before ordained that we should walk in them." Ephe
ii. 8—10. " The law was given by Moses, but grace an
truth came by Jesus Christ." John i. 17.

The Holy Spirit is also alluded to under the appellatio
of Grace, and its teaching, as the teaching of the Grace
God; and it is declared that this " Grace of God, th
bringeth salvation, hath appeared to all men" (for all a
thereby convinced of sin); " teaching us that, denyii
ungodliness and worldly lusts, we should live soberl
righteously, and godly in this present world; looking f
that blessed hope, and the glorious appearing of the gre
God, and our Saviour Jesus Christ, who gave himself f
us, that he might redeem us from all iniquity, and purif
unto himself a peculiar people, zealous of good works.
Tit. ii. 11—14. This grace is sufficient to enable a ma
to overcome all evil. " My grace is sufficient for thee,
were the words of the Lord Jesus to Paul; and withou
this grace none can know Christ to be their Saviour, wh
came to " save his people from their sins" (Matt. i. 21
or know him to destroy the works of the devil in them
1 John iii. 8.

Let none, therefore, remain in blindness, hating the Ligh
and disregarding the grace of God; or continue at enmit
with God by wicked works: but may all believe in Chris
who is the " Light of the world," " the way, the truth, an
the life" (John xiv. 6), and come unto the revelation of hi
grace, or good Spirit, manifested in the heart, as unto the
without which they cannot be saved. The words of ou
gracious Redeemer himself are: " I am come a Light int
the world, that *whosoever* believeth on me *should not abia
in darkness.*" " I am the Light of the world, *he tha
followeth me shall not walk in darkness,* but shall have th
Light of life." " I am come *that they might have life,* an
that they might have it more abundantly." John xii. 46
viii. 12; x. 10.

He directed the attention of mankind to the " Light,"
" Grace," or " manifestation of the Spirit," by many
ailitudes, in order that this important doctrine might be
idered plain to all sincere inquirers after the truth. He
mpared the kingdom of heaven to " a grain of mustard
:d, which indeed is the least of all seeds, but when it is
)wn, it is the greatest among herbs, and becometh a tree,
that the birds of the air come and lodge in the branches
:reof." Matt. xiii. 31, 32. The seed of Divine Grace,
)ugh easily overlooked in its first appearances, when not
:isted, but suffered to remain in man's heart, not only
;ulates the affections and unruly passions of men, but
ngs " into captivity every thought to the obedience of
irist." 2 Cor. x. 5.

The kingdom of heaven is also declared by the Saviour,
be " like unto leaven, which a woman took and hid in three
:asures of meal till the whole was leavened" (Matt. xiii. 33);
cause, when the grace of God is suffered to work, it
idually leavens the heart of man into its own pure and
avenly nature, until the whole becomes leavened or
anged. This change is alluded to in Christ's conversation
th Nicodemus, as being " born again"—" born from
ove," without which, it is declared, " a man cannot see the
igdom of God." John iii. 3. It is that " treasure hid in
ield, which, when a man hath found"—when he has once
come convinced of its divine nature and origin, and the
)rious end for which it appears in his heart; viz., that
·ough this medium God may " work in him both to will
d to do of his good pleasure" (Phil. ii. 13)—" he hideth,
d for joy thereof goeth and selleth all that he hath, and
yeth that field" (Matt. xiii. 44. 46); he prizes it as some-
ng exceedingly precious, as " a pearl of great value;" and
llingly parts with every thing that may hinder his access
this inestimable treasure, or that may endanger its con-
.uance in his heart: in other words, he renounces all his
loved lusts, and denies himself of every sinful gratification,
it he " may win Christ." Phil. iii. 8.

Where Christ's dominion is thus established in the heart,
it sublime prophecy of Isaiah is fulfilled in the experience
the Christian : " unto us a child is born; unto us a son is
·en: and the government shall be upon his shoulder, and
; name shall be called Wonderful, Counsellor, the Mighty
)d, the everlasting Father, the Prince of Peace : of the
:rease of his government and peace there shall be no end."
ι. ix. 6, 7. This is that spiritual kingdom or government

for the coming of which Christ taught his disciples to pra
" thy kingdom come, thy will be done in earth as it is
heaven" (Matt. vi. 10): and which he declared, " come
not with observation." " The kingdom of God cometh n
with observation, neither shall men say, lo here; or, lo ther
behold the kingdom of God is within you." Luke xv
20, 21. "The kingdom of God is not in word, but in power
1 Cor. iv. 20. It " is not meat and drink, but righteou
ness and peace and joy in the Holy Ghost." Rom. xiv. 1

Salvation by Jesus Christ is, indeed, " the myste
which has been hid from ages and from generations, b
now is made manifest to his saints [and all are call
to be saints], to whom God will make known what
the riches of the glory of this mystery, which [sa
the Apostle Paul] is Christ in you, the hope of glory
Col. i. 26, 27. Those who rightly estimate this " unspea
able gift" (2 Cor. ix. 15), will be solicitous to have the
hearts made clean; for the heart in which Christ takes
his abode must be holy. " If a man love me," is t
language of our blessed Redeemer, " he will keep
words, and my Father will love him, and we will come un
him, and make our abode with him." John xiv. 23. It
thus that the Christian becomes " the temple of the livin
God." " Know ye not that ye are the temple of God, an
that the Spirit of God dwelleth in you; if any man defi
the temple of God, him shall God destroy; for the templ
of God is holy, which temple ye are." I Cor. iii. 16, 1
" For ye are the temple of the living God; as God hat
said, I will dwell in them and walk in them; and I will t
their God, and they shall be my people. Wherefore com
out from among them, and be ye separate, saith th
Lord, and touch not the unclean thing, and I will receiv
you, and will be a father unto you, and ye shall be m
sons and daughters, saith the Lord Almighty." 2 Co
vi. 16—18.

Thus, ever since the Gospel began to be preache
those who have believed in the Light—who have ha
faith in the Grace of God—who have been led by th
Spirit—have uniformly been enlightened thereby to pe
ceive their fallen and sinful state; have attained unto tru
repentance, and been enabled to look upon Jesus, " th
Lamb of God which taketh away the sin of the world," s
as to have peace with God through him; being strengthene
" to walk in the Spirit, not fulfilling the lust of the flesh
but glorifying God in their body and in their spirit, whic

God's." John xii. 36. Ephes. ii. 8—10. Rom. viii. 14.
an i. 29. Rom. v. 1. Gal. v. 16. 1 Cor. vi. 20.
May all strive to become of this happy number, who con-
ute " so great a cloud of witnesses" to the efficacy of
h in the power of Divine Grace ; that thus, " laying aside
ry weight, and the sin which doth so easily beset them,
y may run with patience the race that is set before them,
king unto Jesus, the Author and Finisher of [all true]
h ; who, for the joy that was set before him, endured the
ss, despising the shame, and is set down at the right
id of the throne of God." Heb. xii. 1, 2.
' God so loved the world that he gave his only begotten
n, that whosoever believeth in him should not perish, but
ve everlasting life : for God sent not his Son into the
rld to condemn the world, but that the world through
a might be saved." John iii. 16, 17. May all believe,
refore, in the mercy of God, which is freely offered to
m in the Lord Jesus Christ : for, as " God spared not his
n Son, but delivered him up for us all, how shall he not
h him also freely give us all things." Rom. viii. 32.
He was wounded for our transgressions ; he was bruised
our iniquities ; the chastisement of our peace was upon
a ; and with his stripes we are healed. All we, like
ep, have gone astray : we have turned every one to his
n way ; and the Lord hath laid on him the iniquity of us
." Isa. liii. 5, 6.
God is willing to forgive the sins of those who repent, for
rist's sake, who died for them, " the just for the unjust,
it he might bring us to God." 1 Pet. iii. 18. " Him hath
d exalted with his right hand, to be a prince and a
viour, for to give repentance and forgiveness of sins."
ts v. 31. Christ said, " No man can come to me, except
Father which hath sent me draw him." John vi. 44.
ive not all been thus drawn ? Have not all often felt con-
ced of sin, so as on many occasions clearly to distinguish
difference between right and wrong ? These convictions,
n, were the drawings of the Father, by his Eternal Spirit,
king to lead mankind unto the Son, that they might obtain
rnal life through him.
We read in the Scriptures, that under the law of Moses
en a man had sinned, he was to take his sin-offering to
priest, to lay his hand upon its head, and to slay it ; and
priest was to take of its blood, and to put it on the horns
the altar, and to pour out the rest at the bottom of the
ar and to burn its body upon the altar, to make an atone-

ment for him that his sin might be forgiven. Lev. iv. I
taking his sin-offering to the priest, the sinner thus confesse
that he had sinned; by laying his hand upon its head, h
made himself, as it were, one with his sacrifice: in slayin
it, pouring out its blood, and offering its body on the alta
he acknowledged the justice of God, in passing sentence
death on sin: "In the day thou eatest thereof thou shal
surely die." Gen. ii. 17. "The soul that sinneth it sha
die." Ezek. xviii. 4. "The wages of sin is death." Ron
vi. 23. Hereby the sinner offered the life of his sacrifice i
the stead of his own life—its blood in the place of his ow
blood: "for without shedding of blood there is no remis
sion." Heb. ix. 22.

This is a lively type or representation of the way of salva
tion under the Gospel. The sinner is to confess his sins t
God; to remember that the awful death which Christ, "wh
did no sin" (1 Pet. ii. 22), suffered on the cross, was due t
sin (2 Cor. v. 21); and that it is for his sake that forgivenes
of sin is offered to those who repent (Luke xxiv. 47. Ephes
iv. 32): for He is "the Lamb of God which taketh awa
the sin of the world." John i. 29. The conditions o
acceptance are, "repentance toward God, and faith towar
our Lord Jesus Christ." Acts xx. 21.

But he who truly repents and believes, or has faith i
Christ, believes in the truth of all his sayings, and feels the
necessity of obeying his precepts: he is baptised with the
baptism of Christ, even with the Holy Ghost and with fire
"I indeed baptise you with water," said John the Baptist
"but one mightier than I cometh, the latchet of whose shoe
I am not worthy to unloose: he shall baptise you with the
Holy Ghost and with fire: whose fan is in his hand, and he
will throughly purge his floor, and will gather the whea
into his garner, but the chaff he will burn with fire u
quenchable." Luke iii. 16, 17. Christ, who is the "Pow
of God" (1 Cor. i. 24), like a "consuming fire," (Deu
iv. 24. Heb. xii. 29) is revealed in the hearts of tr
believers, cleansing them from every corruption, even
gold is purified by fire, "for the trial of their faith is mu
more precious than of gold that perisheth." 1 Pet. i.
Such know, from heartfelt experience, that "the baptism
which now saveth is not the putting away the filth of th
flesh [not any outward washing] but the answer of a good
conscience toward God, by the resurrection of Jesu
Christ" (1 Pet. iii. 21): who cleanses them from every
defilement "by the spirit of judgment, and by the spiri

burning." Isa. iv. 4. And thus, " Zion is redeemed with
gment, and her converts with righteousness." Isa. i. 27.
Those who thus believe and are baptised, whatever name
y may bear as to religion among men, constitute that
one body"—"the Church," of which Christ is " the
ad" (Ephes. i. 22, 23. Colos. i. 18); " all such are the
ldren of God by faith in Christ Jesus." Gal. iii. 26.
For by one Spirit are we all baptised into one body,
ether we be Jews or Gentiles, whether we be bond or
e, and have all been made to drink into one Spirit."
Cor. xii. 13. " Through him they have access by one
irit unto the Father; they are no more strangers and
eigners, but fellow-citizens with the saints, and of the
usehold of God; and are built upon the foundation of the
ostles and prophets, Jesus Christ himself being the chief
ner-stone : in whom all the building fitly framed together
oweth unto an holy temple in the Lord: in whom they are
o builded together for an habitation of God through the
irit." Ephes. ii. 18—22.
Our heavenly Father is willing to give the Holy Spirit to
ose who sincerely ask it of him. " Ask," says Christ
and it shall be given you; seek, and ye shall find: knock,
l it shall be opened unto you; for every one that asketh
eiveth, and he that seeketh findeth, and to him that
ocketh it shall be opened. If a son shall ask bread of any
you that is a father, will he give him a stone? or, if
ask a fish, will he for a fish give him a serpent? or, if he
ll ask an egg, will he offer him a scorpion? If ye, then,
ng evil, know how to give good gifts unto your children,
w much more shall your heavenly Father give the Holy
irit to them that ask him?" Luke xi. 9—13. O, that all
uld believe, then, that God is willing to hear and to
swer the prayers of them that desire to be made what he
uld have them to be, how weak and unworthy soever they
y feel themselves! " Like as a father pitieth his children,
the Lord pitieth them that fear him; for he knoweth our
me, he remembereth that we are dust." Ps. ciii. 13, 14.
d he will regard the prayer of the heart, for " He knoweth
e secrets of the heart." Ps. xliv. 21. 1 Sam. i. 13.
Many persons have no private place, or closet, to retire
o, to " pray to their Father who is in secret;" but all
y pray in the closet of their own hearts, and the Lord
l hearken to the sincere breathings that arise from thence,
l will regard them as acceptable incense, whether they be
pressed with the tongue or not. Let all, therefore, lift up

their hearts unto him, whenever, and wherever, they ma
feel their necessities: whether it be by night or by day, i
the house or in the field. Let them pray unto their Fathe
which is in secret, and their Father which seeth in secre
will reward them openly. Matt. vi. 6. And let none b
discouraged from staying their souls upon God, by any sens
of their past delinquencies: for none are invited to pray i
their own names, but in the worthy name of Jesus (Joh
xiv. 13, 14; xv. 16), who "is able to save them to th
uttermost that come unto God by him, seeing he ever livet
to make intercession for them." Heb. vii. 25. Wherefore
all are invited to "come boldly to the Throne of Grac
that they may obtain mercy and find grace to help in time o
need." Heb. iv. 16. And they are encouraged to do so b
the assurance that Christ was "in all points tempted like a
we are, yet without sin" (Heb. iv. 15); that, therefore, h
"can have compassion on the ignorant, and on them tha
are out of the way" (Heb. v. 2); and "in that he himsel
hath suffered, being tempted, he is able to succour the
that are tempted." Heb. ii. 18. May all, therefore,
willing to seek reconciliation with God through him. 2 Co
v. 18—21.

Some persons have but few of the outward means o
religious instruction: but if such desire to learn righteousness, God is willing to teach them himself by th
Holy Spirit, the Spirit of Truth, who "will guide the
into all truth."

It is a profitable exercise to wait upon the Lord in still
ness, to feel after his presence, with the attention turned
the state of the heart before him, remembering that he
ever with his children: for "God that made the world, an
all things therein, seeing that he is Lord of heaven an
earth, dwelleth not in temples made with hands: neither i
worshipped with men's hands, as though he needed an
thing: seeing he giveth to all life, and breath, and a
things; and hath made of one blood all nations of men, fo
to dwell on all the face of the earth; and hath determine
the times before appointed, and the bounds of their habita
tion: that they should seek the Lord, if haply they migh
feel after him, and find him, though he be not far from ever
one of us: for in him we live, and move, and have ou
being." Acts xvii. 24. 28. And he has commanded us
saying: "Be still and know that I am God." Ps. xlvi. 10
"Keep silence before me, O islands, and let the peopl
renew their strength; let them come near, then let the

ιk; let us come near together to judgment." Isa. xli. 1.
is good for a man that he bear the yoke in his youth:
sitteth alone and keepeth silence, because he hath borne
ιpon him: he putteth his mouth in the dust, if so be
e may be hope." Lam. iii. 27—29. God will make
self known to those who thus wait upon him: and will
ver them: for it was declared by the prophet Isaiah, in
rring to the dispensation of the Gospel, that "it should
said in that day, Lo, this is our God, we have waited for
, and he will save us: this is the Lord; we have waited
him, we will be glad and rejoice in his salvation." Isa.
. 9.
hose who have the Holy Scriptures ought frequently to
l them: for "all Scripture is given by inspiration of
l, and is profitable for doctrine, for reproof, for correc-
, for instruction in righteousness: that the man of God
' be perfect, throughly furnished unto all good works."
im. iii. 16, 17. "They are they which testify of me,"
. Christ. As people give attention to his Light or Grace
heir hearts, thus coming unto Christ that they may have
(John v. 39, 40), he will open their understandings, and
ble them to understand these precious records aright;
such will know from happy experience that "the
iptures are able to make them wise unto salvation,
ough faith which is in Christ Jesus." 2 Tim. iii. 15.
ersons who diligently read the sacred volume, and attend
the Light of Christ, to which it directs them, cannot
tinue in bondage to Satan. But many who profess to be
istians are under his grievous yoke, as is too clearly
red by their sinful practices: "for of whom a man is
rcome, of the same is he brought in bondage" (2 Pet. ii.
; and by pride and avarice, cursing, swearing, and other
ane language, fornication and uncleanness, oppression and
rreaching, fraud and theft, and numerous other sins, it is
too plain that many are "taken captive by the devil at
will" (2 Tim. ii. 26); and thus by their sins dishonour
l, before whom they must shortly give account; for he
all judge the secrets of men by Jesus Christ" (Rom. ii.
; and "we must all appear before the judgment-seat of
ist; that every one may receive the things done in his
y, according to that he hath done, whether it be good or
." 2 Cor. v. 10.
et none defer the work of repentance, under the delusive
on that they will repent when drawing near unto death:
"this night," it may be said unto any man, "thy soul

shall be required of thee." Luke xii. 20. Many have gon
on in sin, thinking they would repent before they died, wh
have either been cut off suddenly, or prior to death hav
been given up to hardness of heart, so as to be wholly in
different about the state of their souls. These have, indeed
died "as the fool dieth" (2 Sam. iii. 33); the end of th
beasts that perish would have been infinitely preferable (
theirs. Ps. xlix. 18. 20. "For what shall it profit a ma
if he shall gain the whole world, and lose his own soul? C
what shall a man give in exchange for his soul?" —Mark vii
36, 37. Some who, in anticipation of death, have appeare
to be penitent, when unexpectedly to themselves, their live
have been prolonged, have failed to bring forth fruits mee
for repentance; and, on the contrary, have relapsed int
habitual sin. Hence it is to be inferred, that though possibl
some of these might be cases of sincere repentance, yet th
greater number deceived themselves, as well as others, wh
had hoped better things of them.

To defer, therefore, to the approach of death, to see
repentance and reconciliation with God, is but to make i
league with the devil to serve him as long as a man cai
and thus to wrong his own soul. All ought to remembe
with awe the declaration of the Most High; "My Spir
shall not always strive with man, for that he also is flesh.
Gen. vi. 3. And the emphatic expostulation of the Apostl
"Despisest thou the riches of his goodness and forbearanc
and long-suffering, not knowing that the goodness of Go
leadeth thee to repentance? But after thy hardness and im
penitent heart treasurest up unto thyself wrath, against th
day of wrath and revelation of the righteous judgment
God." Rom. ii. 4, 5. None know how short may be th
day of the Lord's merciful visitation to their souls. The
ought, therefore, to beware that they "do not frustrate th
Grace of God" (Gal. ii. 21); for if his grace be withdraw
they may seek "a place of repentance" when too lat
Heb. xii. 17. "To-day, therefore, to-day if ye will hea
his voice, harden not your hearts." Heb. iii. 7. 15.

Experience proves the truth of the Scriptural declaration
that "Man is born to trouble as the sparks fly upwards.'
Job v. 7. Now, as nothing happens but under the Provi
dence of God, without whose notice not a sparrow falls t
the ground, all ought to consider the cause and end fo
which God suffers them to be afflicted. The cause often is
that men cast the fear of the Lord behind them. Intempe
ance, lewdness, gaming, pride, avarice, neglect of the sab

h, or disregard of the Divine Law in some other respect,
often paves the way for affliction. This consideration,
ght to humble every one before God. For, how often
y it be said, "Hast thou not procured this unto thyself,
that thou hast forsaken the Lord thy God?" "Know,
refore, and see, that it is an evil thing and bitter, that
u hast forsaken the Lord thy God, and that my fear is
in thee, saith the Lord God of Hosts." Jer. ii. 17. 19.
d this conviction ought to make all watchful against the
s that "so easily beset them," and may already have
ught much suffering upon them, lest continued indul-
ice should become the means of plunging them into the
oths of degradation and misery.

A principal end for which affliction is dispensed to man,
ile in a state of probation, is, to turn him to the Lord:
o, though a God of judgment, in the midst of judgment
nembereth mercy: hence to the very people to whom the
guage quoted above was addressed, the following gracious
itation was at the same time extended: "Return thou,
cksliding Israel, saith the Lord, and I will not cause mine
er to fall upon you: for I am merciful, saith the Lord,
I will not keep anger for ever. Only acknowledge thine
quity, that thou hast transgressed against the Lord thy
d." "Return, ye backsliding children, and I will heal
ur backslidings." Jer. iii. 12, 13. 22.

It is a source of delight to the true Christian to see others
lking in the fear of the Lord: these he is glad to recognise
brethren in Christ, whatever may be their nation or colour
station in life: and he cannot but heartily desire their en-
iragement in every good word and work; and that by the
itinued exercise of faith and patience, they may inherit
promises, and know the consolations of the Gospel, to
nfort them in all their tribulations. 2 Cor. i. 4. But
ne can understand the joys of God's salvation until they
te of them in their own experience. "Eye hath not seen,
r ear heard, neither have entered into the heart of man,
an unregenerate state,] the things which God hath pre-
red for them that love him: but," added the Apostle Paul,
aking of those who were turned unto the Lord Jesus,
God hath revealed them unto us by his Spirit: for the
irit searcheth all things, yea, the deep things of God."
Cor. ii. 9, 10. There are no joys worthy to be compared
these, and all others must soon come to an end. "O
te, and see that the Lord is good. Blessed is the man
it trusteth in him." Ps. xxxiv. 8.

Let such as are not yet turned unto Christ, be encourag
to seek an acquaintance with him. " Seek the Lord wh
he may be found, call ye upon him while he is near.
the wicked forsake his way, and the unrighteous man
thoughts : and let him return unto the Lord, and he w
have mercy upon him, and to our God, for he will abun
antly pardon." Isa. lv. 6, 7.

And let all people "know assuredly that God hath
that same Jesus whom the Jews crucified, both Lord a
Christ ;" " neither is there salvation in any other :- for the
is none other name under heaven given among men where
we must be saved" but "the name of Jesus Christ
Nazareth." Acts ii. 36; iv. 10—12.

END.

London : Printed by E. Couchman & Co, 10, Throgmorton Street ; for l
TRACT ASSOCIATION of the SOCIETY OF FRIENDS. Sold at the DEPOSITOR
12, Bishopsgate Street Without.—1865.

MEMOIR

OF

DAVID FERRIS,

A Minister of the Society of Friends.

~~~~~~~~~~~~~~~~

.VID FERRIS was the son of Zachariah and Sarah
rris, and was born in Stratford, in Connecticut
vernment, New England, the 10th of the third
)nth, 1707.

He was a minister much esteemed in our religious
ciety; and, from some very interesting memoranda
ich he left of his life and of his Christian experience,
 following instructive account is compiled

His parents were Presbyterians, and educated him
that community. In reference to his early life, he
s, "My father, while I was very young, moved to
lace called New Milford. It being a newly settled
ce I had not the advantage of a school; but under
 care of my mother, I soon learned to read in the
ble, and understood that there was a Supreme Being,
o made all things, and preserved and upheld them
their order: and that, as the workmanship of his
d, I stood accountable to Him for every part of my
duct. About the eighth year of my age, I was
ormed that the Divine Being was self-existent,
hout beginning and without end; and not being
e to understand how that could be, I sometimes
ught so intensely on the subject that I became much
vildered. At length it was shown me, that the

proposition was too high for my comprehension, and
I received something like a reproof for searching into
things beyond my capacity. From that time I was
fearful of prying into such deep mysteries.

"My mother being a religious woman, and much
concerned for the good of her offspring, both temporally
and spiritually, was frequent in giving them good
advice and admonition; desiring that we might shun
the paths of error; and teaching us, by her own
example, as well as by precept, to walk in the ways of
virtue, which lead to peace. This was a great help to
us while young, and was not easily forgotten when
we came to maturity. Death was a frequent subject
of my thoughts; and, in the twelfth year of my age,
I was frequently called by the Holy Spirit to forsake
evil, and leave youthful vanities, which I then delighted in, and to be sober and circumspect in all my
ways."

He thus describes his experience in these days of
comparative childhood. "My mind was humbled
under a sense of my daily want of divine help : and
as I abode under a religious concern, attending to the
reproofs of instruction, which are the way to life, a
increase of light and life was communicated to me, so
that I came to delight in virtue. As my desires and
care for divine things increased, the knowledge of the
was unfolded. I could truly say, the Lord was my
delight. And for some years, as I dwelt in his fear
his yoke was easy, his burden light, and all childish
vanities were burdensome.

"While I kept near the spring of life, with my mind
fixed on the true object, the world and the thing
thereof lost all their lustre. But alas! not keeping
my eye single to the light, I lost my Leader; and then
by little and little, the world rose again with splendour
to my view. Earthly delights and vanity got such
hold of my affections, that I took great pleasure in airy
and vain company. This was an unspeakable loss to
me, and I mention it that others may take warning by
my harms. It seemed almost miraculous that I was

ever restored from this lapsed state. My mother
mourned over me, and often advised and urged my
return, showing me the danger of such a course of
vanity. Yet I was not wholly forsaken by my inward
Monitor and former Guide. At times it reproved me,
at other times called me, wooing and pleading with me
to return. Sometimes, in the midst of my vanity, I
saw that I was in the way to death; and that it would
land me in everlasting confusion if I did not forsake
it. Sometimes my concern was so great, that I was
obliged to leave my vain companions, and retire so
full of trouble and distress, that I had no satisfaction
until a considerable time afterward. During these
seasons of affliction, I was ready to promise to forsake
my vain course of life, and to covenant with the Lord
that I would do so no more, provided He would be
pleased to grant me his assistance. But my efforts,
being too much in my own strength, proved unavailing.
Vanity so prevailed that I took great delight in music,
dancing, and other vain amusements.

" In the twentieth year of my age, I was visited with
severe illness: so that I, and those about me, had very
little hope of my recovery. Then death stared me in
the face; and a dreadful scene of wo, anguish, and
misery opened to my view. It appeared clear to me,
that if I were then taken off the stage of action, I
should be unavoidably lost; and that evil spirits were
waiting round me, to convey my soul to the mansions
of misery and everlasting darkness; so that my horror,
anxiety, and distress were inexpressible. In the
utmost anguish of mind, I cried to the Lord for help;
promising amendment, if more time and ability were
afforded me: and it pleased a kind Providence to be
propitious to me, so that I was restored to health;
and in about a month, was able to walk about.

" After my recovery, I remembered the distress I had
been in, and the promise I had made, when under the
dreadful apprehension of everlasting misery and destruction; I saw the necessity of a faithful performance of my vows. I was sensible that there was a

work to be done; and that if I did not now comply with
my promise, I should have to pass through the same,
or rather a worse scene of misery and distress. It
appeared probable that a more convenient opportunity
for repentance than the present would not be afforded;
and I conluded that this was the time to turn from
vanity; forsake my evil ways; and renounce all my
sensual delights. But when I had resolved to begin
the necessary work of reformation, the adversary of all
good tempted me to believe that it was too late to
think of obtaining peace with my Maker; for this
plain reason, 'that, as there was a day, or time, in
which men might be saved; so, if they let that opportunity pass away unimproved, it would be in vain to
attempt it afterward.' He suggested that I had had
such a day of visitation, and had passed it by; that
I had been uncommonly favoured with help, and for
a time did not accept of it; that I had been made a
partaker of the Holy Ghost; that I had tasted of the
good word of God, and the powers of the world to
come, and had fallen from it; so now it was impossible that I should again be renewed unto repentance;
seeing I had crucified the Son of God afresh, and put
him to open shame. This reasoning appeared so
strong, and so consonant to the apostle's doctrine, that
I gave up the point; and concluded it was too late to
attempt a return, with hope of acceptance.

"From that time, during the space of about two
months, I never sought for mercy; but remained in
utter despair.

"My trouble continued and increased; so that I had
no satisfaction in life. On a certain day, in this
season of despair and deep distress, I concluded to
leave my native land and go into some foreign country,
to spend the residue of my days; where I purposed to
remain unknown, and that none of my relations or
acquaintance should know what was become of me.
Being in my own apprehension, a poor, lost, reprobate
creature, I was not willing to remain at home, to be a
disgrace to my relations and country people. This

was a day of the deepest affliction and distress that I had known. Towards evening, as I followed the plough, my attention was arrested, as it were, by a still, small voice, saying: 'The blood of Jesus Christ his Son cleanseth from all sin.' But I put it by: saying in my heart, 'It is too late; there has been a day wherein I might have been cleansed; but alas! I have let it pass over my head for ever.'

"Some time after this, (perhaps half an hour,) while I was musing on what land I should flee to, the same words passed through my mind again, with more authority than before, and commanded my attention rather more closely than they had done; but I again put them by; concluding I had lost all right to apply them to myself. So I resumed the consideration of my flight to a foreign land. In the mean time my sorrow and anxiety of mind increased so that I was not well able to support it, or go on with my business. But while I was still musing, the same words, unsought for, and unexpectedly, passed through my mind with greater power and authority than at any time before: 'The blood of Jesus Christ his Son cleanseth us from all sin.' At the sound of them my soul leaped for joy. I felt that a door of hope was opened, and said in my heart, 'If *all sin*, why not *mine?*' Then a living hope sprang in my soul. I saw the arms of mercy open to receive me, and the way cleared before me as a road through a thicket.

"I was now filled with joy unspeakable; thanksgiving and living praise to my Redeemer arose in my heart for the experience of so great and marvellous a deliverance. That my feet should be plucked out of the mire, and set upon a rock; that I who had no hope just before, should now be favoured with a well-grounded assurance of pardon and acceptance, was a mercy never to be forgotten.

"From this time I sought for Divine assistance; and in infinite kindness, a hand of help was extended for my restoration, and the healing of my backslidings. Then I was enabled to sing upon the banks of deliverance, and praise the name of Him who lives for ever. The Holy Spirit, that blessed Teacher, whom I had formerly been favoured with, but had forsaken, was now restored, as a Leader and Teacher, to direct and instruct me in the way to peace and rest.

"From this time my mind, after such great favour, was humbled and made subject to the cross of Christ, and heartily willing to take it up daily, and follow Him, my kind leader, in the narrow way of self-denial. And as I was obedient, He led me to forsake my vain course of life, and all those youthful delights and sensual pleasures which were displeasing to my dear Lord and Master; who in wonderful mercy had lifted me out of the dungeon, and heard my prayers in a time of deep affliction. He now became my director in all things; showing me clearly what my duties were, and enabling me to perform them in an acceptable manner. But if, at any time, I acted in my own will, I lost my strength, and found no acceptance or benefit by my performances; by which I gradually learnt, that I could do nothing acceptably, without the immediate assistance of the Spirit of Christ the Redeemer. Thus I found a necessity to apply continually to my only and all-sufficient Helper, and humbly to wait for his assistance and direction: and as I was faithful, He led me into the path of life, which, if continued in, will terminate in everlasting peace.

"Having gradually learned that nothing of a religious nature could be effectually done, without the immediate assistance of the Holy Spirit, I may humbly acknowledge that I was wonderfully favoured with Divine instruction, far beyond my expectation, and infinitely above my deserts. I was led, as it were, by the hand, and helped over every difficulty that attended me. But the adversary of my soul tried every stratagem to draw me aside from the path of virtue. He strove, night and day, to deter me from walking in the narrow way; representing the difficulties to be so great that I could never hold out to the end; and that all my attempts would be in vain. He seemed to be contin-

ally present, whether I was awake or asleep, dis.
quieting my mind as much as possible. – But my
prayer was incessant for Divine aid; that a stronger
than he might appear for my help, and dispossess him.
And, in about a year after I had been raised from the
pit of despair, as before related, I received a promise
that 'the God of peace would bruise Satan under my
feet shortly.' Faith was given me to believe in this
promise, and I hoped for a speedy deliverance. But
he continued to afflict me with his assaults, with temptations, and evil suggestions for some months afterward. Notwithstanding which, I still believed the
time would come, according to the promise, and I
prayed for its fulfilment in the Lord's time. At length,
a stronger than he did indeed come, and cast him out,
and wholly dispossessed him; and not only bruised
him under foot, but removed him far from me.

"The power of the enemy to assault, or in anywise
disquiet me, was now taken away; neither was he
able to lay any temptation before me. Now was my
soul daily filled with thanksgiving and living praise
for this deliverance: as well as for all the other manifold mercies and favours of God, from day to day
bestowed upon me 'a worm and no man.' To the
honour of his great name, who hath done marvellous
things for me, and to the praise of his grace, I may
say, that the adversary of all good was not only thus
prevented from troubling me, but the fountain of divine
love was opened, and the water thereof flowed so freely
and plentifully into my soul, that I was absorbed in it,
and so enamoured thereby, that all the riches, honours,
and vain pleasures of this world, had no place in my
affections. In this state I longed to be with Christ;
which, I was sensible, was better than to be here. I
do not know that there was one moment, whilst I was
awake, for the space of nearly two years, in which I
could not sing living praises to Him who liveth for
ever and ever. No losses, crosses, or disappointments
did, in any degree, disturb me: at least not percepti-
bly, either to myself or others; for my delight was in

objects very different from anything which this world can give or take away."

David Ferris possessed a strong and sound understanding, with considerable taste for literary pursuits. He had been well instructed in the Latin tongue; and wished to acquire a more extensive knowledge, especially in the languages. In order to accomplish this object, he entered as student in a college in New England.

At this period of his life he thus writes:—

"At my entrance into college my principles generally corresponded with those held by the Presbyterians. But I now began to think it was time to examine for myself, and no longer trust in the judgment of my forefathers. I found it necessary to subject my principles and practices to a strict scrutiny, because I began to be doubtful of some of them. But I was convinced that, as a rational creature, simply considered, without a Divine instructor I was not competent to the undertaking. Being very desirous to know the truth in all things, I made application to Him whom I believe to be the only Teacher of his people, and as I waited upon him for instruction, my understanding was gradually enlightened, so as to perceive many errors in my former creed, and to discover the truth in opposition to the doctrines of my education.

" That which stood most in my way, and appeared to be a grievous hardship to mankind, as well as a great dishonour to a just and righteous God, was their doctrine of *unconditional* election and reprobation; which would, according to their apprehension of it, shut out the chief part of mankind from all hope of mercy, as they believed they were the Lord's only people, and that but few of others were within the pale of election. Yet I believe there were some amongst them who had a more extensive charity. I was much concerned on this subject; and being earnestly desirous to discover the truth, it pleased the Lord to open my understanding, clearly to perceive the error of this doctrine; and I was enabled to believe that Christ, who ' gave him-

lf a ransom for all,' would, ' have all men to be
ived, and come to the knowledge of the truth.'

" I had before this period heard of a people called
luakers, but was unacquainted with any of them.
.s I had never seen any of their writings, I knew not
'hat doctrines they held, but ascribe all my knowledge
1 divine things to the inward manifestation of grace
nd truth, the teaching of the Holy Spirit. It was
'hrist, the light of the world, the life of men, who
pened to me the Scriptures, and gave me a discerning
f their meaning; and, as I was faithful and obedient
o the pointings of Truth, I was favoured with further
nd clearer discoveries thereof.

" I continued at the college until near the time for
aking my degrees; and being convinced of the errors
f my education relating to the doctrines we held, and
he worship we performed, I apprehended it was time
o consider what was best for me to do; and being
avoured to see that a qualification or commission
lerived from man was not sufficient for the Gospel
ninistry, I concluded not to take their degrees, nor
lepend upon their authority.

" I still continued a member of the Presbyterian
ociety: attended their meetings, and partook of their
iread and wine. But I was not free to sing with
hem, not having been for some time before in a con-
lition to sing; besides, it did not appear to me an
icceptable sacrifice, or anything like divine worship,
'or a mixed multitude to sing *that* of which they
cnew nothing by experience. My exercise of mind
laily increased, for now the time was near at hand in
which I must leave them. This was a day of trial:
'or although at the commencement of my religious
progress I had forsaken all the youthful delights and
vanities with which I had been diverted, and had been
inabled to trample them all under my feet, expecting
never again to encounter such difficulties, yet now I
found that self was not sufficiently mortified in me.
To be brought down from the pinnacle of honour; to
be esteemed a fool; be trampled under foot by high

and low, rich and poor, learned and unlearned, was hard to bear. As I observed before, I had been much esteemed; though, as I was sensible, more than I deserved. I knew the people had undue expectations of my future usefulness, and that if I left the college, as I thought it my duty to do, my credit would sink, and my honours be laid in the dust; and then, instead of being caressed and exalted, I must be neglected and despised.

" But I had other difficulties to encounter. My father looked forward with hope that I should be an honour to him and his family. He had promised to set me out in the world in the best manner his circumstances would admit. I knew that if I were obedient to my convictions of duty, he would regard it as a disgrace to my family and connections, and would be more likely to turn me out of his house, than in any way to assist me.

" Here, if I complied with my sense of duty, I must 'take up the cross,' and turn out unprovided for into the world; for I had very little property of my own, none to expect from my father, and no salary to support me.

" I laboured under a lively sense of all these difficulties. Poverty and disgrace stared me in the face; and, as I had none but the Lord to whom I could make known my distress and discouragements, nor any other of whom to ask counsel, I cried to Him incessantly for wisdom, strength, and fortitude, that I might be favoured with a clear discovery of my duty, and enabled faithfully to obey him in all things.

" It is difficult to conceive, and not in my power to express, the anxiety of my mind in this proving season; for everything valuable seemed in danger of being totally lost. Nevertheless, I cried unto the Lord for help; and covenanted with Him, that if he would be pleased to direct me in the way which would be safe for me to pursue, manifest his will therein, and afford me assistance to perform my duties, I would resign all to his disposal, obey his will, no longer reason with

sh and blood, but trust to his providence for support
d credit in the world, and for everything else He
ight deem best and most convenient for me.

" As soon as I was satisfied on these points, I rea.
ned not with flesh and blood but immediately gave
to the heavenly vision. I then went to the chief
ler of the college, and obtained his permission to
home; but I told no one my reasons for this pro.
lure.

" After I had parted from my companions, I went
to New Milford, where my parents and relations
ided. About three weeks afterwards, I went to a
arly Meeting of the people called Quakers, on Long
and; in order to discover whether they were a *living*
ople or not, for a living people I wished to find. I
d thought for several years before that there ought
be such a people, a people who had life in them,
d abounded in love to each other, as did the primi.
e Christians; a people who knew they had passed
m death unto life, by their love to the brethren.
re I gathered strength, and was more confirmed
at I was right in leaving the college;. for I found a
ing humble people, full of love and good works;
h a one-as I had never seen before. I rejoiced to
d *that* which I had been seeking, and soon owned
m to be of the Lord's people, and of the true
urch of Christ, according to his own description of
where he says, " By this shall all men know that
are my disciples, if ye love one another.'

" At the meeting before mentioned, there were
reral eminent ministers from Europe, both male and
nale. I there heard women preach the Gospel, in the
vine authority of truth, far exceeding all the learned
bbies I had known. This was not so strange to me
it might have been to others, for I had before seen,
the immediate manifestation of grace and truth,
at women, as well as men, might be clothed with
spel power; and that daughters, as well as sons,
der the Gospel dispensation, were to have the Spirit
ured upon them, that they might prophesy: and

though I had never before heard a woman preach,
I now rejoiced to see the prophecy fulfilled."

David Ferris now felt that he must separate hims
from the people amongst whom he had been educat
and he embraced the views which distinguish t
Society of Friends. He met with many close tri
of his faith and patience. For a time his father v
much displeased at the change which was manifest
his conduct and deportment; but becoming convin
of his son's sincerity, he was at length reconciled
him. In commemoration of the help which v
mercifully vouchsafed in this time of need,
writes thus :—

"I admire the boundless goodness, the infin
kindness, and tender mercy of a gracious God,
effecting my late deliverance; especially when I c
sider how tempestuous were the seas, and how i
billows rolled over me; how the mountains of oppo
tion raised their lofty heads to stop my passage;
again, in a short time, how the winds and seas w
hushed and still; and how the mountains becam
perfect plain! I truly found as great cause to s
upon the banks of deliverance, as Israel did of
when they had passed through the sea on dry grou
and had turned about and seen their enemies dead
the shore. I rejoiced in the Lord, and sang praise
Him, who had done marvellous things for me;
had made me acquainted with his blessed truth;
at length gave me ability to trample the world, and
its riches, honours, and pleasures, under my feet;
submit to the cross of Christ; and be willing to
accounted a fool of all men. For which favours I :
myself under great obligations to my gracious Be
factor."

In the sixth month, 1733, he removed to Ph
delphia, where he joined in religious fellowship w
Friends. In 1735, he married Mary, the daughter
Samuel and Sarah Massey; and in 1737 settled
Wilmington, in Newcastle county, where he li
during the remainder of his days.

'hilst he resided in Philadelphia, he was engaged
:aching the learned languages, and other branches
liberal education; but on removing to Wilmington
:mbarked in trade, in the pursuit of which he
:ed much watchfulness and Christian self-denial.
leased Divine Providence to bless his temporal
erns, and, as he gratefully acknowledged, to grant
plenty and peace.

bout a year after his admission into membership
Friends, he believed it to be his duty to speak as
inister in our religious meetings; and, as he ex-
:es it, "to excite the careless to a consideration of
· latter end." But it appears that, although he
been enabled, by closely adhering to the power of
ne grace, to renounce the pleasures, the profits,
the friendships of this world; and was made
ng to become as a fool and a by-word amongst his
:aintance, yet, at *this* requisition of his Lord, his
ι failed. He suffered a slavish fear, and the reason-
of fallen nature to prevail; and notwithstanding
the Divine will was, with remarkable clearness,
in a variety of ways, manifested to his mind, he
·nued to resist the impression. His disobedience
d him, he says, to be "full of sorrow, trouble,
)ain of heart;" and this increased until he was on
ery brink of despair. Respecting his spiritual
ition at this time, he writes, "I was so ungrateful
y heavenly Benefactor that it is a wonder I was
restored. And I have no doubt that thousands,
gh negligence, even after they have been called
f the world, and have run well for a season, have
finally lost. This I have written ·for a warning
hers."

e compassion of the Almighty was long extended
s soul, and the Holy Spirit continued to strive
him. "I then clearly saw," says he, "that if I
forsaken and left to myself, the consequences
d be death and darkness for ever! At the sight of
orrible pit that yawned for me, if I continued in
edience, my body trembled like an aspen leaf, and·

my soul was humbled within me ! Then I said, 'Lor
here am I : make of me what Thou wouldst have n
to be; leave me not in displeasure, I beseech thee.'

"After a time of great anxiety and distress of min
the Lord was graciously pleased to look upon me wi
compassion, and again offered to make me a pillar
his house, and I felt a renewed concern to appear
public for his name, and in the cause of Truth."

He first spoke as a minister in 1755, in the fort
eighth year of his age. "At that time," he remark
" I was made a real Quaker, and was not ashamed
be seen trembling before the Lord.   Under a sense
so great and merciful a deliverance, I saw and f
ample cause for it.   It was with me as with Israel
old, when the Lord caused their captivity to retur
saying, He would build them as at the first; and th
should fear and tremble for all his goodness, and
all the prosperity he would procure for them.   N
soul rejoiced in the Lord, and I magnified his excelle
name, who is worthy of all honour, glory, and e
nown, for ever.

"It appeared to me wonderful, that I should th
be lifted out of this horrible pit of my own diggin
and I was so absorbed in the love and mercy of n
heavenly Benefactor, that I was filled with thankf
ness and praise, attended with a desire that, in futu
I might diligently watch and wait for the pointing
his holy finger, to every service he might be plea
to allot me; that henceforth no opportunity mig
be lost of manifesting my gratitude by obedience t
his will."

During the remainder of his life he sought t
approve himself a diligent and faithful servant.   H
performed several extensive journeys in the service
the Gospel; and by certificates produced on his retur
home, it appeared that his conduct, conversation, an
labours abroad, were exemplary and edifying, tendin
to the advancement of truth and righteousness.   H
was very serviceable in meetings for discipline, which
with other meetings he diligently attended; not suffer

; his outward affairs to obstruct the fulfilment of
s duty to God.

He was hospitable and liberal in entertaining
iends; and remarkably charitable to the poor;
ely administering to their necessities.

Bodily weakness attended him during the last three
irs of his life, which he bore with much patience.
few months before his decease, he made the follow-
; very instructive memorandum.

"1779. I am now drawing towards the conclusion
life; being, this day, seventy-two years of age.
r the encouragement of others, I will now briefly
:apitulate some of the kind dealings of Providence
wards me. The God of my life, my Maker and
eserver, has been propitious to me, from youth to
l age. The fear of the Lord, which preserves from
il, was placed in my heart when I was but eight
ars old; so that I was afraid to offend Him. In the
·elfth year of my age, I was mercifully visited, and
lled out of the vanities of the world; at which time
:eceived a promise, that if I sought first the kingdom
God, all other necessary things should be added;
d I have found the promise true, for I never have
inted any of the good things of this life. I have
en blessed with sufficient for myself and friends,
d something to spare to the poor; and I esteem it
great favour, that I received a disposition to com-
unicate to those who stood in need.

"If all men would 'seek first the kingdom of heaven,
d the righteousness thereof,' and carefully attend to
e leadings of the Holy Spirit, with which all might
: favoured, I believe they would be blessed with a
fficient portion of wealth. O that mankind were
ise! and would early seek that treasure which cometh
om above; and which neither moth nor rust can cor-
.pt, nor thieves break through and steal! And may
e all beware of loving the world; and living at ease,
the enjoyment of its good and pleasant things!
ven those who have been favoured with remarkable
ivine visitations, and have been put in possession of

16

'the upper and the nether springs,' have great need to be on their guard. When we enjoy health and plenty, and all things seem pleasant around us, we are prone to forget the Lord, and neglect those 'things that belong to our peace.' "

Near the close of his days, he was much afflicted with sickness, which he bore with patience, often expressing his prospect of his approaching end, and his resignation therein, saying, "All is well." Several friends being present, after a time of silence, he in a lively manner repeated the expressions of the apostle, "To me, to live is Christ, and to die is gain."

He departed this life, the fifth of the twelfth month, 1779, aged upwards of seventy-two, a minister about twenty-four years.

 END.

London: Printed by E. Couchman & Co., 10, Throgmorton Street; for the TRACT ASSOCIATION *of the* SOCIETY OF FRIENDS. *Sold at the Depository,* *12, Bishopsgate Street Without.*—1865.

SELECTIONS

FROM A WORK ENTITLED

'IETY PROMOTED;

CONTAINING

RIEF MEMORIALS AND DYING EXPRESSIONS

OF SOME OF

THE SOCIETY OF FRIENDS.

~~~~~~~~~~~~~~~~~~

PART III.

~~~~~~~~~~~~~~~~~~

LONDON:

ted for the TRACT ASSOCIATION of the SOCIETY OF FRIENDS.

Sold at the DEPOSITORY, 84, Houndsditch.

—

1861.

No. 74.   [*Price 8d. per dozen.*]

SELECTIONS, &c.

In relating some particulars of the last days of sever
young persons, children of SAMUEL and REBECC
TREGELLES, of Falmouth, all of whom survived the
exemplary mother, it should awaken pious reflectio
thus to observe so many of one family early made meet fc
and removed to that city which hath foundations, who
maker and builder is God. The natural dispositions
these young persons were very different, consequentl
their besetments were so; but the great Physician i
whom they applied knew how to administer to all the
wants. The help of the Holy Spirit was not withhel
from these sincere suppliants for its renewing, sanctifj
ing influence; and it will be seen in the course of t
following narratives, that they were, in their differe
measures, enabled to witness a good confession, and t
lay down their heads in peace.

Although there is not much to record respectin
ROBERT TREGELLES, yet the lively faith and hop
which supported him, during the progress of a ver
gradual consumption, appear worthy of being briefl
noticed. In him the saying appears to have bee
exemplified, that "wisdom is the grey hair unto mer
and an unspotted life is old age." For though he ha
but just attained his sixteenth year, when he was re
moved from this state of existence, his discretion wa
remarkable; a strict attention to truth also, from ver
early childhood, stamped such frankness on his charactei
as gave additional lustre to every part of it.
As the disease gained ground, and he became sensibl
that it was not likely he would ever have to take a
active part in the concerns of this life, his mind wa
evidently more and more stayed on the immovable Rock
so that he could contemplate the approach of death with
out dismay, trusting in that infinite mercy which ha
reached, and was redeeming his soul. His views
himself were humble; but he appears, except on on

ısion to have had this blessed hope of eternal peace
haken.　Having at that time given way to some
ːulation, he evinced by his manner, that something
ressed him.　This led to an enquiry as to the cause,
ːn he replied, that he had been endeavouring to
ːom a great mystery: namely in what the joys of
ven could consist: and not being able to come to any
clusion, he felt tried.　He was answered: "Eye hath
 seen, nor ear heard, neither have entered into the
rt of man, the things which God hath prepared for
m that love Him."　After a short pause he expressed
ıself fully satisfied, and sensible that it was at least
ırofitable, thus to dwell on such subjects; saying,
·t he could entirely trust to divine mercy; for being
ːuch hands all must be well.

ːfter an almost imperceptible decline, for more than
ːear, he was at length taken off rather suddenly,
ːing only a few hours of increased illness.　He had
 up the usual time, on the 10th of the fifth month,
L5, and retired to bed without any symptoms of
mediate dissolution: but very early the following
rning the family were called up, and it was seen
ɪt life ebbed apace.　Being dressed and laid upon the
a, he remarked more than once, what a glorious
rning it was; which those around him considered
 emblematic of the more glorious one which was
ɪut to rise on his soul.　He desired one of his sisters
 read, and when he could no longer speak, showed
dent marks of being still able to understand; pressing
· hand, and looking at her with great emotion, on her
ding that passage of Holy Scripture, "Precious in
ː sight of the Lord is the death of his saints."　His
e beamed with heavenly peace; and as he gently
ːsed away, a sweet smile fixed on his countenance.

JOHN TREGELLES died at Ashfield, near Fal-
ɪuth, on the 8th of the eighth month, 1816, aged
ɪeteen years and a half.　His early youth was marked
 an unusual sweetness of natural disposition, which
ɪned him the love of those with whom he associated.

At the age of fifteen, he was placed as an apprenti at Wellington, where there is reason to believe that l was concerned to enter into covenant with the Lord, ar through his gracious assistance, was enabled to wa before him with uprightness and humility. At th place he continued until the autumn of 1815, whe a cough, to which he had been subject, increased t such a degree, that it was thought necessary to try h native air; but, contrary to the expectations of h friends, he became rapidly worse, so that a long voyag to a milder climate, during the remainder of the winte seemed the only expedient that could be tried with hor of benefit. This he almost immediately undertool accompanied by his brother Joseph.

They sailed for Jamaica, intending to touch at th Bermudas, to which place they had a stormy passag of ten weeks, and on their arrival were shipwreckec Staying some time there, they proceeded to Jamaica and thence returned to England, after an absence c twenty-four weeks: in which interval they had, fror various causes, undergone much suffering. Whilst i Jamaica, and on his return home he was greatly trie in spirit; but the arm of divine power was extende for his support, which he acknowledged as a peculi favour. On one of these occasions, when everythin outward looked discouraging, and his mind was muc bereft of consolation, a dream became the means comfort. It appeared as if he were alone on the wate in a small boat, exposed to a great storm, so that found it quite ineffectual to row: after much exertic he laid down the oars, concluding, that the only way w wholly to trust in divine help. When enabled so to d he soon found himself in safety, and was received on t shore by his beloved mother, who showed extreme jc and expressed her thankfulness that another of her so was safely landed.

On the 18th of the seventh month, 1816, in allusi to some matters which he had wished to attend to, said he had found, during the whole of his illness, a in the midst of many difficulties, that when he cou leave things entirely, and commit his cause to t Almighty, a way was made for him where the

eared to be none. At another time, being enquired
respecting the disposal of his books, he answered : " I
e not been so careful in the choice of my books as
ught to have been." On being told that none of
m appeared to be of a hurtful tendency, "No," he
lied, "I hope not; but now I should wish to have
h as would be really profitable." After this, he gave
ny clear directions respecting things which he wished
have done : saying, "These appear trifles now; but
hould not find them trifles on a death-bed." On the
h, he intimated that what had been said to him in
line of ministry, in a time of religious retirement
ich had occurred, was very suitable; "for," he added,
have many times felt great poverty; and sometimes,
ilst at sea, was tried beyond what I can express;
I can say, the Lord has delivered me out of all
troubles." And two days afterwards, conversing
h one of his sisters, he said, with great affection :
have a full hope; and I believe after a few years
past, we shall meet to part no more. I trust all
l conduct themselves so that we may meet again.
ave felt anxious about some; but it is taken from me,
ich is a great favour."
Early in the eighth month, a great alteration appeared,
d extreme bodily suffering attended. He once said,
t will only be a little longer :" and being reminded
it it was a great mercy, at such a time, to have
thing to contend with but the pains of the body, he
lied : "I find it so." He had expressed some solici-
le to see two of his brothers; and on their arrival,
cnowledged his thankfulness to his heavenly Father
permitting him to live to see them. After some
ier counsel, he thus addressed one of them; "When
ou meetest with difficulties, trust in that Power which
able to sustain thee : pray often to Him, and wait
his direction. I have always found that He helped
out of my troubles. I have settled my outward
airs to my satisfaction. I have had time, and reated of all my sins; and I believe they have been
ely forgiven, through the merits of my Redeemer;
we no man anything but love."
To an intimate friend, who was one of the family

during the last part of his illness, he said, "My de
Charles, farewell. I charge thee, obey that Pow
which is sufficient to direct thee in all thy ways."
the 7th, seeing some weeping, he said: "Do not wee
there is no cause for mourning: it is all thanksgiving
He took an affectionate leave of many of his frien
and sent messages of love to all he could think o
saying, he felt it abundantly. Between five and six t
next morning nature gave way, and in a few minut
his spirit was liberated, without a struggle, from
earthly tenement.

JOSEPH TREGELLES was removed from t
state of being at the age of twenty-six. He was
young man, whose general demeanour, and obligi
disposition, gained the affectionate regard and estee
of those around him, in no common degree. For sev
years he had been liable to occasional attacks of illnes
but it was not until within about six months of h
decease, that he became so ill, as to excite apprehensio
that his disorder, like that of his two brothers, wou
prove consumption.

At an early age he became sensible of the influence
the love of God upon his soul, and in the view of othe
his general conduct, appeared consistent with his rel
gious profession; yet, when the solemn prospect
death came before him, great was the distress of mi
in which he was involved, for a time refusing to be con
forted; and being afraid even to give sleep to his ey
lest he should be cut off, without feeling an eviden
that his sins were blotted out; his language often bein
"Oh, I have acted against conviction." In this sta
he passed several weeks, crying earnestly day and nig
before the Lord: for his soul could not feel satisfi
without an inward assurance that there was nothin
retained against him.

On the 22nd of the third month, 1817, some sympto
appeared to indicate that his change was approachi
On one of his sisters proposing his removal to a cham
where he would have more air than in his own apar

nt, he was much affected, and answered, that he did
deserve any of the comforts with which he was
rounded. She endeavoured to comfort him, and told
1 .there was yet hope, seeing he was sensible of the
tinued offers of mercy. He replied with great
nestness; "Oh; yes, I know that; but I have rejected
se offers so long, that I can expect nothing: I feel as
[had left it to the very last hour. If I could expect
live but a few weeks, what a. blessing I should con-
er it: but of .this there is no probability. The fever
ich I now have must soon wear me out. It is. the
easiness which I feel about myself, that prevents my
eping: if it were not for this, I could sleep soundly
ywhere.; but I have so long rejected what I knew
be right, that I.fear it is now too late." On his
ter's remarking, that she thought he had taken an
desirable view of _his past life, he replied, that it
l; been very different from what it ought to have
en; and that he had squandered his time, particu-
ly since his return from the West Indies with his
ther John. He would several times repeat, that he
t destitute of all help from above, and dared not
pe for mercy;—that he knew there was no way of
ing saved, except through the merciful intercession
the Redeemer; but that, as he had despised and
used Him whilst in health, he could not expect to
ve the invitation again extended. On his being re-
nded, that our blessed Lord came into the world to
ie sinners, and that his prayers and tears would not
disregarded by the Saviour of men, he seemed a
tle comforted.
He continued for some time in this tried state of
nd; but within a few days of his decease, he was
abled to feel an undoubted. evidence of acceptance
land through Christ, which, in much humility, he
ankfully acknowledged; impressively observing, that
short time before, he seemed to hear a voice, saying
[and my Father are one;" after which the mystery of
lemption appeared to open before him, which, he said,
had not before known, or rather, had not understood;
d now called on those around him to join in giving

praise where alone it was due, for they might truly sa
"This is 'the Lord's doing; and it is marvellous in o
eyes." Notwithstanding the comfort in which this d
was passed, he was fearful, the following morning, th
the enemy had been endeavouring to lull him into a sta
of security. In the evening, that part of Scripture w
read to him, which treats of our Lord's temptation
after he had been acknowledged as the beloved. So
and a remark being made to him thereon, that the
was no cause for him to be discouraged, though th
buffetted, he said, with great emphasis, " I know th
the Lord's hand is not shortened, that it cannot sav
neither his ear heavy that it cannot hear; but I al
know, that nothing short of the infinite mercy of a
all-merciful God can reach my case."

After this, he became tranquil, and remained so unt
the close of life, frequently expressing his great than
fulness. He was often fervent in supplication, and th
night before his departure, in these words: "Oh
Lord God Almighty, have mercy on me, and pardo
me, through thy beloved Son, our blessed Redeeme
who gave himself a ransom for the sins of the whol
world."

On the afternoon of the day preceding his death
great pain and distress on the lungs, for some hou
attended him, after which he became quite easy; an
as long as he could articulate, he continued to spe
of the mercy of the Most High, and was heard
supplication, when only a few words were distinguis
able. On taking something to drink, he said, "
believe this is the last; there is but one step betwe
me and eternity." He appeared to sink into a swe
sleep, and thus gently passed away, at midnight, o
the 26th of the seventh month, 1817; a remarkab
evidence being granted to some present, that he h
entered into that rest for which his soul had so ardentl
longed.

CATHERINE TREGELLES, daughter of Samuel
d Rebecca Tregelles, of Falmouth, through early
mission to the regulating power of the Lord's Spirit,
s a striking example in the discharge of social and
ative duties; she evinced a tender regard to the
lings of others, and manifested her humility by an
iable condescension to all.

When sixteen years of age she met with a very
se trial, in the death of her beloved twin brother
bert, during whose lingering illness she deeply ened into sympathy with him: and on his decease
r mind became much weaned from the things of time,
ugh she retained a true relish for its lawful enjoy-
nts. Soon after the completion of her nineteenth
ar, she took a cold, which terminated in a consump-
n. During the progress of her disease, she was much
posed to number her blessings, but made little
ntion of her sufferings. Indeed, such was her
bmission, that nothing like a murmur was known to
ape her lips. But she also passed through much
tress of mind, particularly in the early part of her
ness, in the remembrance of her secret sins and
ansgressions.

In the autumn of 1818, she became sensible that
e disorder was of a serious nature. At that time
e had so far overcome her natural diffidence, as to
l one of her sisters, that she was quite aware of the
certainty of her recovery; adding that, in whatever
y her illness might terminate, she knew it would be
. the best. And after some further conversation,
narked: "What I suffer every time you leave me,
ables me to form some idea of what my sufferings
uld be with the prospect of a final separation before
. Oh! the pang is indescribable." Gratitude seemed
be the clothing of her spirit, first towards her Heavenly
ther, for the immediate extension of his favour; and
en towards her friends, for their affectionate interest
her comfort and accommodation.

The prospect of death being very awful to her, she
us described her feelings, in a letter written about the
d of the eleventh month, to one of her sisters. "I
nnot be too thankful to my truly kind friends, for the

openness with which I have been treated respecting my
complaint: for so flattering is its nature, that I might
have been kept in ignorance to this day. It is not in
my power to express what I felt for some weeks after I
became aware of my danger, at the prospect of a separation from my beloved father, brothers, and sisters: and
inexpressibly awful was the reflection on my own utter
unworthiness. I am ready to believe, that had not been
help been afforded in this time of deep distress, I should
have sunk under it.: I believe no one was aware of my
sorrow, for I felt it my duty to endeavour to be cheerful
by day. I have often wished for bed-time, that I might
give vent to my feelings. My dear sister, do not suppose I am complaining, in telling thee what my feelings
have been since my indisposition; for I do hope I am
grateful in being able to feel, that although in myself
I am unworthy of the smallest of favours, yet I am
not forsaken."

Her health gradually declined for some months after
writing the foregoing; but she was at times favoured
with strong hopes of approaching bliss, and strengthened
to impart suitable counsel to her friends and relations. At

At one time she remarked, that she was abundantly
favoured with peace, and acknowledged that her cup
overflowed with blessings; and to a friend, who remarked that she had been preciously supported, her
reply was, "I have indeed been most mercifully dealt
with. I have none but bodily pains." Turning to one
of her sisters, she said: "I have yet one request to
make; daily retire to wait upon thy God: it has been
my practice for many years, and I have found strength
in so doing. Thou mayest perhaps feel discouraged
but persevere; and thou wilt in the end find thy strength
and comfort increased."

On the morning of the 16th of the fourth month, 1819,
she said that "she hoped very soon to be in paradise, with
her dear Redeemer; but that she desired to have no will
as to the time, being willing to wait the Lord's time, if
He saw good to detain her in suffering, either for her own
sake, or that of others." In the course of the same
day, she saw several of her friends, and took leave of
them with great composure; and one of them noticing

: great sweetness and quietude, replied, that if she
ce gave way to thinking of her bodily sufferings, she
uld soon be overwhelmed. The following day, she
s earnestly engaged in supplication on behalf of her
arest relations, particularly her nephew, desiring that
 might rather be taken out of the world, than suffered
 remain in it to dishonour the Almighty. In the
ernoon she took leave of him and her niece, and gave
em counsel suited to their ages, between six and eight
ars, concluding with warm desires that they might
re and serve the Almighty all the days of their lives.
On the 20th, after being greatly tried by weakness,
e was during part of the day much distressed, admit-
g deep discouragement, and saying to some who
sired that she might be strengthened to persevere, "If
had any access to the throne of grace I should hope,
t it seems denied me at present."
On the following day, the prospect brightened. She
oke impressively, of the solicitude she felt that not one
those most nearly connected with her, might be so
wise as to neglect the important business of knowing
eir peace made; that so they might be favoured to
n, her in those realms of bliss, into which, through
finite mercy, she was about to enter. She frequently
pressed her desire to be liberated, but always with
bmission; saying, she could leave all to divine dis-
sal.
On the morning of the 22nd of the fourth month, 1819,
e day on which she died, she spoke sweetly on death,
d enquired whether there was any probability of her
ing released that day: saying, the prospect of the
ins of death did not affright her, and earnestly suppli-
ting that the Almighty would be near her in the
proaching, trying hour. In the afternoon, within an
ur of her close, she called one of her younger brothers
her, and said: "My dear Henry, it is an awful thing
 die; and I desire thou mayest so live, that when the
lemn moment arrives, thou mayest have nothing to
ntend with but the pains of the body." After this
e spoke no more; but gently drew her last breath, at
e age of twenty, at Ashfield, near Falmouth.

Of this family, already so stripped, another ver
promising branch was soon taken away; for in abou
two years after the decease of Catherine,

HENRY TREGELLES, to whom her last word
were addressed, followed her. He was a boy of grea
spirit; but being early convinced of the excellency
that Divine instruction, which is in mercy offered 1
each of us, he was concerned to yield obedience to il
and a great portion of peace and comfort was his rewar
having often been known to acknowledge that he ha
not followed cunningly-devised fables, but living, sut
stantial Truth. This was proved by the patience, an
even cheerfulness, with which he was endued, during
painful illness, attributing all to the mercy of God i
Christ Jesus.

He spent about two years from home, the last
which was at Colchester, as an apprentice, where th
solidity of his deportment was observable, and where h
was much beloved amongst Friends, his conduct bein
such as to render him truly an example to others. Bu
decided symptoms of consumption appearing, he wa
removed home, in the fourth month, 1821.

In the course of his illness, as well as before, h
appeared to be very sensible of the privileges enjoyed b
the members of our Society, as they keep their places i
the Truth. He was particularly impressed with th
importance of a diligent attendance of meetings f
divine worship; and enforced the advice which he ga
on that subject, by going himself, when in a very wea
state; which, he said, proved strengthening to his min
He said but little respecting his religious feelings, excep
sometimes in allusion to the mercy which had made hi
sensible of the insignificance of everything, in compariso
with the love of his Heavenly Father; a convictio
which had induced a willingness to resign himself to b
formed according to his good pleasure. Some of hi
friends had entertained the pleasing hope that he migh
be spared for usefulness in that Society to which h
was so strongly attached; but Infinite Wisdom sa
meet to take him from the temptations of time, at th
age of sixteen years and a half: thus cutting short th
work in righteousness, and leaving a bright exampl
to the youth of one, who could say from experienc

odliness is profitable unto all things, having promise
the life that now is, and of that which is to come."
iongst other sources of virtuous enjoyment, the friend-
ps which he had formed were productive of much
d satisfaction; and many were the testimonies borne
persons of mature years, to the value of his society,
ich, although permitted for so short a time, had left
weet impression on their minds.

[n the latter part of his illness he was particularly
irous of great quietude, that there might be nothing
listract his attention from the Lord Jesus—from Him
whom he was enabled fully to cast himself, as having
hing, and yet possessing all things in Him. And in
s state of deep stillness, he passed gently away, on the
d of the eighth month, 1821.

MARY TREGELLES, fourth daughter of Samuel
1 Rebecca Tregelles, was born on the first of the eighth
nth, 1795.

For several years previous to her death, she had
t enjoyed robust health; but after an attack of fever,
the spring of 1826, consumptive symptoms became so
reasingly apparent that alarm for the result was soon
ited. She did, however, appear in some degree to
over: but disease was too deeply seated to be removed,
1 the whole of the following winter she was confined
one room.

In the second month, 1827, she tried change of air,
ich recruited her strength so much, that her friends
ttered themselves with the hope of seeing her entirely
tored to health. But this hope proved delusive, and
ain they witnessed a decline of her bodily powers, and
h a return of unfavourable symptoms, that short
ursions on the sea were recommended, as the means
st likely to benefit her.

In the fifth month she tried a voyage to Wales, where
e principally passed the summer, and did not return
l the tenth month; when, perceiving that the means
orted to had failed to produce the desired effect, she
came much more alive to her critical state.

Her passage home was tempestuous; but her mind
was kept in great quietness.' Often afterwards, she
spoke of this time with feelings of much gratitude,
observing, in allusion to this, and other proofs of the
providential care which was over her, that the word
"Be careful for nothing : but in everything give thanks,"
seemed very applicable to her. One evening, soon after
her return when one of her sisters, on taking leave of
her for the night, remarked her suffering countenance,
she told her that she had felt extremely anxious, from
the appearance of a new symptom of disease; that she
seemed as if she was only just awake to the reality
of life: that she had been living many years in the
world so differently from what she ought to have done,
that she had slighted the many advantages that had
been offered her, and had chosen her own path: this
was said with much feeling. Her sister endeavoured to
encourage her still to trust in that power which had
sustained her in many seasons of trial; and to believe
that, although she was cast down, she was not forsaken.
Once, when in a state of great weakness, she said, that
she felt her situation to be very awful: that she was
daily sensible of an increase of disease, but was
entirely unfit for the change that awaited her, that she
could not be otherwise than dismayed; such purity
being requisite, before we could be admitted into the
heavenly kingdom. She was reminded, that it is when
under such a sense of poverty and nothingness, that we
feel the need of the great mediatorial Sacrifice. Still, in
the midst of her anguish, she was permitted to derive a
little hope, from the assurance that "God is love ;" and
those who witnessed and measurably partook of the
conflicts of her soul, were enabled to believe, that one in
whose heart the love of God was so prevalent, could not
eventually be cast out.

On the evening of the 3rd of the twelfth month, she
asked one of her sisters to sit by her; when, in a very
feeling manner she described some of the conflict
through which she had had to pass during the interval
of their separation. She said, that some symptoms indicative of more disease in the lungs than she had been
aware of, had greatly afflicted her; that she felt as if she

ld have rejoiced in the prospect of annihilation; and
t it would not be possible to give an idea of her
'erings: adding, "Throughout one week, I seemed
the depth of despair; my sins, I was going to say all
;hem, were placed before me, but I believe not yet *all*
them; yet I trust that none may be permitted to be
ered, but that everything may be brought to judg-
nt. Amongst other things, it greatly distressed me
think of the irritability which I have often shown
'ards thee." Here her sister interrupted her by
ing, that she was scarcely sensible of it; and if
netimes there was an appearance of irritability, it
s attributable to the nature of her disease. She
ild not, however, admit the excuse. She afterwards
ke of the constant kind attentions of her friends
l relations; adding, "And how did I repay their
e and kindness? On my return home, I wished
make my sisters promise that I should go nowhere
l see no person: this was pride and ingratitude.
t after the time to which I allude, I can hardly
cribe the change: every one seemed to claim my
e, and all the creation appeared lovely: and should
iow return to health, I trust this time may never be
gotten." She then embraced her sister with much
rmth of affection; saying, she hoped she could forgive
ry unkind word, and every appearance of indifference.
During some part of her illness, she could scarcely
ir reading or conversation, lest it should divert her
ention from the one all-important subject which
upied her mind. She did indeed pass through deep
ters; but she could occasionally acknowledge, that
was not overwhelmed by the billows. About this
ie, she referred to a circumstance which occurred some
rs before, when she was addressed by a pious poor
man, to whom a remarkable sense of her state ap-
ired to be given. She told her, that a day would come
ien this language would be verified in her experience:
have heard of Thee by the hearing of the ear: but
w mine eye seeth Thee; wherefore I abhor myself and
ient in dust and ashes." This was inexplicable to
r, as she considered that she had more than heard with
s ear, and had understood with more than the natural

understanding; and it was not till now, when the secre
of her heart was, as it were, laid open before her, tha
the full force of this passage was explained to her.

On sixth-day morning, the 28th of the twelfth month
1827, her family perceived that her life was drawing to
close. She appeared about midnight to fall into a heavy
slumber, which they thought would terminate only witl
her earthly existence. Very earnestly had they desire
that, if consistent with the designs of that Wisdon
which is unerring, it might be permitted them to hea
from herself, that her doubts and fears were removed
Within about an hour of her departure, she appeare
quite sensible, spoke very clearly, and enquired whethe
she was not dying. One of her sisters told her that th
change appeared to be very near, and enquired whethe
all was peace within; to which she clearly answered
"It is all peace. I am ready to go, quite ready; do no
hold me." She then inquired for her father, and fo
other members of the family. She recognised them all
Very soon she said, "I sought the Lord." One wh
was near, answered, "and He has heard Thee." Sh
added, "Yes, and delivered me from all my fears. Oh
praise the Lord."

As she gradually, for a few minutes, breathed mor
gently, she was heard to say, "It is nearly over: it is
very pleasant prospect, and very near;" and almost i
the moment of death, those around her distinctly hear
the sound of "Hallelujah! Hallelujah!"

These were her last words; and about eight o'clocl
her purified spirit was released from its very sufferin
tenement, and we may humbly trust, entered into th
realms of light: there to know the fruition of that blis
of which so merciful a foretaste had been afforded her
it being literally verified in her experience, that, althoug
"weeping may endure for a night, yet joy cometh in th
morning."

END.

Printed by E. Couchman and Co., 10, Throgmorton Street, London.

ON THE

CHRISTIAN DOCTRINE

OF THE

ING OF THE HOLY SPIRIT,

AS HELD BY

THE SOCIETY OF FRIENDS.

LONDON:

ie TRACT ASSOCIATION of the SOCIETY OF FRIENDS.

the DEPOSITORY, 12, Bishopsgate Street Without.

—

1863.

[*Price 3d. per dozen.*]

TEACHING OF THE HOLY SPIRIT.

BEFORE proceeding to state the views of the Society
Friends, on the great doctrine which is the subject of t
Tract, it may be right to premise that they have alwa
maintained that the Holy Scriptures were given by ins
ration of God; and, believing them to convey to mar
declaration of the dealings of God with his people in p
ages—of his statutes, judgments, and mercy, and above
as containing the message of the covenant of grace and pea
through Jesus Christ—they have always taught that th
writings are to be reverently received, diligently read, a
their commands faithfully obeyed.

In full accordance with these writings they have e
believed—that there is one God and Father of all, of wh
are all things—that there is one Lord Jesus Christ, by wh
all things were made, who was glorified with the father befa
the world was, who is God over all, blessed for ever—and tl
there is one Holy Spirit, the promise of the Father and 1
Son; the leader, sanctifier, and comforter of his people : a
that these three are one God. And, though shunning sc
lastic terms and distinctions, or the attempt to be wise in 1
deep things of God beyond what he has plainly revealed, tl
have ever held, without any mystification, the real manho
as well as the deity of our Lord and Saviour Jesus Chri
that the Word which was in the beginning with God, and v
God, was made flesh and dwelt amongst us : that he was 1
Messiah of whom the Old Testament, from Genesis
Malachi, so largely speaks, and whose offices in the chui
were prefigured in various types under the Mosaic covena

They believe that man, as he stands in the fall is separat
alienated in his nature from God; that we have all sinn
and come short of the glory of God, and are theref
exposed to divine wrath; and that it is solely through 1
mercy of God in Jesus Christ that we are again brou;
into reconciliation with Him; receiving remission of our s

)ugh the one propitiatory offering of the Lamb of God,
sanctification of heart, through the influences of the
y Spirit.   They also believe that there shall be a great
of final account, in which all men shall be judged by
us Christ, when "all who are in the graves shall hear his
e, and shall come forth, they that have done good unto
resurrection of life; and they that have done evil unto
resurrection of damnation."   John v. 28, 29.

'he Society of Friends have from their origin declared
; they believed in no natural principle or power in man to
over divine truth, so as to enable him to turn effectually
}od; but they have not hesitated to declare their experi-
ital conviction, that by the immediate power of his Spirit
ı is convinced of sin; led to deep repentance for sin;
trust alone to the free mercy of God in Jesus Christ
the forgiveness of his sins; and to experience the puri-
tion of his heart by the baptism of the Spirit.

t is in reference to this great practical work that they
e urged so earnestly the doctrine of spiritual influence.
it they have appealed to men, whether they did not know
convictions for sin in their own hearts, and besought
m to attend to them as the monitions of the Holy Spirit
ing them unto Christ, that they might become partakers
the covenant of his grace, and know through Him true
on and peace with God.

They esteem it no derogation to the character of Holy
ipture, but that it is in the strictest accordance with its
pe and letter, to maintain that some measure of the light
the Spirit of God has been immediately granted to man
r since his fall, for the purpose of his restoration, and as
spring and principle of all true knowledge and holiness;
l that a larger measure of this grace—a fuller communi-
ion between God and his people, is the peculiar feature
l privilege of the Christian covenant.

Neither do they imagine that they withdraw one iota from
character of our blessed Lord as having been the sacrifice
our sins on the cross, and as still ever living at the right
ıd of the Father, as our high-priest and intercessor, when
y assert, as they believe on the full authority of Holy
ipture, that, as the "true light which lighteth every man
t cometh into the world," (John i. 9.) Christ has been
ritually present with mankind in every age; that with
ı in an especial manner the righteous patriarchs walked;
t he followed and instructed the children of Israel; and
t he is still present with the objects of his redeeming

love calling them by his grace, and when converted to Hin dwelling with them as their Bishop, Teacher, and King.

When the apostle John declares, that Christ "was th true light, which lighteth every man that cometh into th world," we apprehend that he speaks not only with referenc to that light which shone forth in himself when personall on earth, but also of his enlightening grace bestowed i measure upon all men as the objects of his redeeming lov in every age.

When our Lord, after his ascension, in the revelatio which he made to his servant John, declared "Behold, stand at the door and knock; if any man hear my voice, an open the door, I will come in to him, and will sup with hin and he with me;" (Rev. iii. 20.) we apprehend that he spol of those gracious visitations which, by his Spirit, he makes the souls of men, in their unregenerate state, to call the to repentance; and of that union with him which takes pla in, and is the unspeakable privilege of, the renewed so This privilege is spoken of, on another occasion, by o Lord, where he says, "If a man love me, he will keep m words: and my father will love him, and we will come unt him, and make our abode with him;" (John xiv. 23.) an again to his disciples, shortly before his ascension, "Lo, am with you alway, even unto the end of the world. (Matt. xxviii. 20.) This spiritual intercourse, the Socie of Friends do believe to be sensible and immediate, both it regards the first enlightenment of the soul, its spiritu discipline, and its fuller and more constant realization of t divine presence. And when our Saviour said, for t encouragement of his disciples, "Where two or three a gathered together in my name, there am I in the midst them" (Matt. xviii. 20.), we believe he spoke of his i mediate spiritual presence in the midst of his church, th is, not of a mere outward association of professors, but of t few or the many living spiritual disciples, in every plac under every name, and in every age.

In accordance with these declarations of our Lord a numerous passages in the epistolary writings of the Ne Testament. When the apostle Paul says, "Now if any m: have not the Spirit of Christ, he is none of his:" (Rom. vi 9.) and "Know ye not your ownselves, how that Jes Christ is in you, except ye be reprobates?" (2 Cor. xiii. 5 and when he says, "If Christ be in you, the body is de: because of (as regards) sin: but the Spirit is life because (as regards) righteousness; but if the Spirit of Him th

ed up Jesus from the dead dwell in you, He that raised
Christ from the dead shall also quicken your mortal
ies by his spirit that dwelleth in you;" (Rom. viii. 10,
and when in writing to the Collossian believers, he uses
e words, "Christ in you the hope of glory," we appre
d that he speaks of the presence of Christ by his Spirit,
ited for the purpose of drawing the soul to God, and
oing it in true union with him. We do not confound
ether the striving and convicting reproofs of the Holy
it in the soul, with that which may more especially be
ed his indwelling presence:—but we conceive that we
e apostolic authority for exhorting our young persons,
others, to mind the convictions of the Spirit of Christ in
n; and, upon the authority of the preceding as well as of
ous other passages of Holy Scripture, we apprehend that
are justified in holding, as we do, the doctrine of the
tinued presence of our Lord Jesus Christ with his people,
of the spiritual appropriation of all the benefits of his
ing, death, resurrection, and ascension, and of the partition in the soul, by living faith, of his body and blood.
t was this spiritual appropriation, this inward knowledge
Christ in all his gracious offices; not in opposition to the
ward knowledge; but certainly in opposition to the *resting*
he outward knowledge; which the early Friends pressed
arnestly. Strongly and frequently did they assert, that
r reference to the spiritual presence of Christ in the
t was not subversive of a simple unsophisticated belief
ll that is revealed in the Old and New Testament, relative
he character and offices of our blessed Saviour. It was
ed to Him, not in part, but in whole, that they called
; and whilst insisting on the actual necessity of a
ge of heart for acceptance with God, they undoubtedly
eved that it was only through his mercy in Christ as the
eemer of men, by the offering of his body on the cross,
they received the remission of their sins; and that it
alone to the power of that Holy Spirit which he had
chased for them by his blood, that they attributed their
ity to do any good work. Christ being thus the author
finisher of their faith, and their only hope of eternal life.
Ve apprehend, that whatever were the spiritual privileges,
sessed by the Jew, or symbolized in the economy of the
saic law, they are in the full possession of the Christian
rch. The sacrifices under the law set forth that one
bitiation, which, being applied by living faith to the
thened conscience, gives the remission of sins; and the

Divine Presence within the innermost vail (from which t
high priest received the special commands for the gover
ment of the people), is now we reverently believe, in t
midst of his church, ready to direct and guide it by
secret counsels, and to govern in the hearts of those w
truly wait on Him.

The prophecy of Jeremiah, in regard to the new covena
which was to supersede that of the law, appears to
strongly to support our views of the privileges of the Gos
day. "This is the covenant that I will make with t
house of Israel after those days saith the Lord; I will p
my laws into their mind, and write them in their heart
and I will be to them a God, and they shall be to me
people; and they shall not teach every man his neighbor
and every man his brother, saying, Know the Lord, for
shall know me from the least to the greatest." Heb.
10, 11.

When our blessed Lord said, "He that believeth on
as the Scripture hath said, out of his belly shall flow rive
of living water," (John vii. 36.) the apostle who records t
words, says, "but this spake he of the Spirit which th
that believe on him should receive;" (John vii. 39.) sign
fying, we apprehend, that the supply of their spiritual war
should be always at hand, and that the benefits of th
supply should be diffused around them. When our Lo
declared that it was expedient for his disciples that he shou
go away; for that if he went not away the Comforter wou
not come unto them; and when he spoke of the offices
that Comforter, we believe that he spoke of privileg
which were designed for all, according to their respect
needs, who should believe upon his name to the end of tim

We acknowledge that we do materially differ from tho
who assert that several of the divine promises, which
have just referred to, belong only to the apostles, and th
we derive the benefit of them *only* through their commu
cation: and we think that the stream of apostolic testimo
is in our favour, to the extent in which we understand t
doctrine of immediate revelation. When the apostle declar
"that no man can say that Jesus is the Lord, but by t
Holy Ghost;" (1 Cor. xii. 3.) when he declares that t
"Spirit itself beareth witness with our spirit that we a
the children of God;" (Rom. viii. 16.) we apprehend th
he sets forth the need of immediate spiritual teaching, for t
saving knowledge of Christ, and for becoming sons of God
And when he says, "the flesh lusteth against the Spiri

: the Spirit against the flesh;" (Gal. v. 17,) and when exhorts, "Walk in the Spirit, and ye shall not fulfil the :s of the flesh," (Gal. v. 16.) believing that these lusts are l those bonds and barriers which keep us from the peace. knowledge of God, and that the strivings of the Spirit are be known, as well as the strivings of the flesh: Friends ak they have apostolical authority for their so frequently ing the seeking of the Spirit, the minding of the Spirit, l the walking in the Spirit, that we may be kept from evils of the world, and be made subject to the law of Spirit of life in Christ Jesus. And in accordance, as y apprehend, with the scope of the preceding passages, l of the New Testament dispensation, and whilst fully ac- ting the authority of the whole revealed will of God, they e spoken of the spiritual law as constituting *the law* and *·liberty* of the true Christian : and, as the natural law in may fairly be called a *principle*, being the very element m which evil action springs, so have we spoken of the ewing grace of the Holy Spirit, as a *divine principle* in n, but not of man, which is the very element of all true iness, and which, if allowed free course, would prove alf to be like that "grain of mustard seed," spoken of in · Lord's parable, "which a man took and cast into his :den, and it grew and waxed a great tree."

When the apostle declares that the things of God are only own by the Spirit of God, and (addressing the Corinthians) s, "Now we have received, not the Spirit of the world, t the Spirit which is of God, that we might know the ngs that are freely given to us of God;"—"But the aural man receiveth not the things of the Spirit of God: they are foolishness unto him: neither can he know m, because they are spiritually discerned" (1 Cor. ii. 14.), we think that he speaks of those immediate percep- ns which the spiritually-minded man alone has of divine ngs, even of those which are externally revealed.

When the apostle John, writing to the church at large l speaking of those who seduced them, says, "But the inting which ye have received of him abideth in you, l ye need not that any man teach you: but as the same inting teacheth you of all things, and is truth, and is no :" (1 John ii. 27.) and where the apostle Paul writes so ticularly respecting spiritual gifts to the church of Corinth, think the position is clearly established, that immediate ritual gifts were not confined to the apostles ; and we can d no Scriptural authority which warrants us in denying

that immediate spiritual calls and qualifications for servi
in the church are still to be expected; but, on the contra
we believe the assertion, that they are the existing privil
of the church, is in strict accordance with the letter, and
the fullest harmony with the whole scope and spirit of t
New Testament.

Here, then, may be briefly enumerated the chief features
this fundamental Christian doctrine as held by the Socie
of Friends; set forth, as they apprehend it to be, in t
preceding and in many other passages of Holy Scripture.

1st. That the light of the Spirit of Christ enlighten
every man that cometh into the world.

2nd. That the dispensation of the Spirit in a larger a
fuller sense than had been heretofore witnessed, is the pe
liar privilege of the Christian covenant.

3rd. That the leading object of this gift is, and ev
has been, to quicken the soul, and raise man from a state
sin, which separates from God, to a state of holiness an
of acceptance with Him, through Jesus Christ.

4th. That some manifestation of the Spirit is given t
every true member of the church, to fit him for the pa
assigned him, and that the great Head of the Church do
immediately call some to, and qualify them for, those speci
services by which the body is edified.

5th. That, though not *looking* for any miraculous powe
or prophetic gifts in the sense of foretelling future event
they do not dare in these, or in any other respects, to se
limits to the divine agency in this day; believing that n
apprehension of danger authorises us to limit the power o
God, where he has not himself fully declared the limitation

Nevertheless, let it be remembered, that the Society o
Friends, fully unites with other Christians in believing, tha
there can be no other message and covenant of mercy an
peace to man, but that one everlasting Gospel of our Lor
and Saviour Jesus Christ, proclaimed by himself, and pro
mulgated by those men whom he so largely and special
endued for their work with the Spirit from on high; an
also, that they never looked for any other revelation of tha
message but that which is contained in the Holy Scriptures

Printed by E. Couchman, and Co., 10, Throgmorton Street, London.

)BSERVATIONS ON THE GREAT TRUTHS

OF THE

CHRISTIAN RELIGION.

~~~~~~~~~~~~~

ᴇ Almighty God in his Infinite wisdom and goodness
ʒ made every one of us. We are all the workmanship
his holy hands. He has formed us for a purpose of
glory: that we might live to his praise upon this earth,
ꭵ enjoy eternal happiness in the life which is to come.
In his unlimited power he has created the world and
that is therein. He formed the sea and the dry land,
ꭵ all that moveth on the face of the earth. He created
ᵉ sun to rule by day, and the moon to give her light by
ꞃht. He preserveth man and beast; his ever-watchful
ꞩvidence is over all: nothing is hid, or can be hid from
all penetrating eye. He knoweth the secret thoughts
ꭵ intents of every heart. He ruleth in the kingdoms
men, and giveth them to whomsoever he will.
Adam, the first man, was created after the image of
ꭨd: he fell from that holy and happy state in which he
s originally created, and in which he might have lived,
ꭵ he not disobeyed the righteous law of God: he became
ꭼtched and miserable, and was driven out of Paradise,
ᵉ garden of Eden, in which he had been placed. We
, the whole human race, are the children of Adam, and
ꞇake of the sad consequences of the sin of our first
ꞓnts: we are by nature the children of wrath, prone,
sin and wickedness.
Ɔur heavenly Father, in his infinite mercy, promised
our first parents a Deliverer who should rescue them
m the dreadful effects of their sin. He afterwards
.ewed this gracious assurance to Abraham, Isaac, and
ꞷob, promising that in their seed *all the families of the*

earth should be blessed. In after ages, the coming of a
Saviour and Redeemer, was more distinctly foretold, who
was to be wounded for our transgressions, to be bruised
for our iniquities, the chastisement of our peace was to be
upon him, and by his stripes we were to be healed :—He
was to be called, the Lord our Righteousness.

This great Deliverer, the Lord Jesus Christ, the Son
of God, has come to seek and to save that which was lost;
he was born of the Virgin Mary, and lived and died as a
man : he was crucified by the hands of wicked men : he
bare our sins in his own body upon the tree. He rose
from the dead the third day, showed himself alive after
his passion by many infallible proofs, being seen of his
apostles forty days. He ascended up into heaven, and
there sitteth on the right hand of God the Father. "He
was in the beginning with God, and was God. All things
were made by him, and without him was not any thing
made that was made." "He is over all, God blessed for
ever." "In him dwelleth all the fulness of the Godhead
bodily." "In him are hid all the treasures of wisdom
and knowledge."

Man is by nature dead in trespasses and sins. It is
the Holy Spirit, who proceeds from our heavenly Father,
and from his Son Christ Jesus, and who is God, that
quickens us, that enables us to cease from sin, and hate
sin, and to fulfil the first and great commandment;—
"Thou shalt love the Lord thy God with all thy heart,
with all thy mind, with all thy soul, and with all thy
strength;" and also the second which is like unto it,
"Thou shalt love thy neighbour as thyself."

These things are all true: they are recorded in the
Bible : which was written by inspiration of God, and is
profitable for doctrine, for reproof, for correction, for instruction in righteousness ; they were written for our
learning, that we, through patience and comfort of the
Scriptures, might have hope of everlasting rest and peace.

I earnestly entreat every one who reads these few lines,
seriously and deeply to meditate upon these and other
solemn truths of Holy Scripture : because they deeply
affect the present and future happiness or misery of each
of us. I invite you in Christian love to read the Bible

3

quently and diligently, and to pray to God that he will
e you a right understanding thereof.
[he Lord Jesus Christ calls upon us to repent and
ieve the Gospel. He declared, "Except ye be con-
ted and become as little children, ye shall not enter the
gdom of heaven." As we truly repent of our sins, we
ll be deeply sorry for them, be distressed because of
m, and strive to forsake them. We have all sinned,
l come short of the glory of God : we are therefore all
ler condemnation for sin. How are we to escape this
idemnation? We are to come in living faith unto
rist, the Lamb of God, who taketh away the sin of the
rld; and to pray for the forgiveness of our sins through
ms Christ, and for his sake.
The Gospel, or glad tidings, which we are to believe,
thus described by our Lord himself: "God so loved
world that he gave his only begotten Son, that
iosoever believeth in him should not perish, but have
rlasting life;" and the Lord Jesus holdeth out to us
is gracious invitation, "Come unto me all ye that la-
ur and are heavy-laden, and I will give you rest: take
y yoke upon you, and learn of me, for I am meek and
rly in heart; and ye shall find rest unto your souls."
hat blessed truths! how happy are those who receive
em in faith, and who live under the government of
rist!
That heavenly book already referred to, and more
iecially the New Testament, abounds with precious
iths about God, and Christ, and the Holy Spirit. It
iches us that our compassionate and ever merciful
viour, who is now glorified in the heavens, ever liveth
make intercession for us. It is through him that we
ve access unto the Father by one Spirit; it is through
s death on the cross that our transgressions are pardon-
; "We have redemption through his blood, even the
giveness of sins." It is a blessed thing to know, and
ought to be humbly thankful for this knowledge, that
n Jesus, the Son of God, we have not a High Priest
io cannot be touched with the feeling of our infirmities,
t who was in all points tempted like as we are, yet
thout sin : who himself having suffered, being tempted,
able to succour them that are tempted."

The devil, who tempted Adam and Eve in Paradis
tempts every one of us to sin, but our Heavenly Fathe
will give us power to resist him if we apply unto him i
faith.   If we yield to the devil, if we follow our own ev
inclinations, we do wickedly, we justly incur the displea
sure of a righteous God.   For all sin is highly offensiv
to Him who is a Being of infinite purity and holines
Our Lord himself declared, "If ye believe not that I a
He, ye shall die in your sins;" and if we die in our sins
where Christ is gone we cannot come.   He ascended u
into heaven, where all is joy and peace and love; bt
those who die in their sins, become the associates of non
but wicked spirits; they go to hell, where their wor
dieth not, and the fire is not quenched.   When, therefore
we are tempted to quarrel, to cheat, to lie, to swear, to b
angry, or to commit any other sin, let us turn immediatel
unto Christ, our Almighty Saviour, let us turn from th
temptation, and pray for the help of the Holy Spirit
forsake all manner of evil—to resist the devil.   We ar
assured that if we do resist him, he will flee from us
that if we draw nigh unto God, he will draw nigh unto us

It is a solemn truth, which we ought often to call t
mind, that we must all appear before the judgment-sea
of Christ, there to give an account of the deeds done in
the body. A distinction will be made between the righteous and the wicked.   "When the Son of man shal
come in his glory and all the holy angels with him, ther
shall he sit upon the throne of his glory, and before him
shall be gathered all nations; and he shall separate them
one from another, as a shepherd divideth his sheep from
the goats; and he shall set the sheep on his right hand
but the goats on the left.   And these shall go away into
everlasting punishment; but the righteous into life eternal."   This life is the only time allotted to us to prepare
for that solemn day, when Christ shall judge the world
We none of us know how long or how short our time
will be upon the earth—eternity is before us.   Let us
then be wise in time, that we may partake of the blessing
conferred on the righteous.

We cannot do this without the assistance of Divine
grace, for in us, that is, in our flesh, dwelleth no good
thing.   Our strength is in God, and this strength is in

at mercy offered to us. The Holy Spirit strives with
when we do wickedly; and if we yield to its convic-
s and obey them, if we follow the drawings of our
venly Father's love, we shall depart from evil and do
d. How very important then is it that we take heed
he grace of God, that we carefully watch what passes
ur own minds, that we thankfully accept the visitations
Divine love, and seek to become quick of understand-
, in the fear of the Lord,—that so we may, through the
er of his grace be established in righteousness, and
w the peace of God, which passeth all understanding,
keep our hearts and minds through Christ Jesus.

Our Lord taught his disciples to watch and pray.
is a great privilege to be permitted to pray unto
l in the name of Jesus Christ; and great will be our
if we do not avail ourselves of this privilege. We
ht always to offer up our petitions in true humility
in reverence of soul, never forgetting that He is in
ven, and we upon the earth: and under a deep sense
ur need of what we ask, and of his power and wil-
ness graciously to help us, if we ask in faith. If we
fess our sins, we ought to be earnest from the bottom
ur hearts to forsake our sins: if we ask for the help
he Holy Spirit, we ought to be ready to make use of
; help, and to follow the guidance of this Divine
cher, then shall we grow in grace and in the know-
ge of our Lord and Saviour Jesus Christ.

Our Saviour in the days of his flesh described himself
he light of the world, adding this gracious promise,
e that followeth me shall not walk in darkness, but
l have the light of life." It is as we follow him, the
d of life and glory, as we take heed to the light of his
rit shining upon the conscience, which illuminates the
r heart of man, that we come to see the evil of our own
rts, and the necessity, as well as the infinite value, of
aviour. The apostle John declares that, if we walk
he light, as God is in the light, we have fellowship one
1 another, and know the blood of Jesus Christ his Son
leanse us from all sin. "Come, and let us walk in
light of the Lord," that we may be children of the
t, and of the day of God's salvation.

Our Lord himself declares, "He that taketh not up his

cross, and followeth not after me, cannot be my discipl
According to this declaration; which is clear and positi
we are not to gratify our corrupt inclinations. We i
to deny ourselves, and not to fulfil the lust of the fle
the lust of the eye, nor the pride of life. He does i
call upon us to separate ourselves from mankind, l
in our daily intercourse in the world to let our lig
so shine before men, that others, seeing our good wor
may glorify our Father who is in heaven. Jesus furtl
said, "Whosoever shall confess me before men, him v
I confess also before my Father which is in heaven; l
whosoever shall deny me before men, him will I also de
before my Father who is in heaven."

In the New Testament of our Lord and Saviour,
have the purest law of morals that ever was taught
mankind since the creation of the world. All that is g
and excellent in the laws by which the human race
governed, may be traced to the law of Jesus Christ. :
that is defective in them, or contrary to pure justice a
equity, will be found to be contrary to the law of
Lord and Saviour. In his great goodness, he has not o
in his own heavenly discourses, and in the preaching a
epistles of his apostles, given us pure and holy laws
our individual conduct in the several relations of life, l
he has set us a perfect example that we should walk e
as he walked. He healed the diseases of men—his
was one continued course of benevolence and kindne
when he was reviled, he reviled not again—when agoni
on the cross for the sins of all mankind, he uttered i
Divine prayer, "Father, forgive them; they know
what they do!" He was holy, harmless, undefiled, se
rate from sinners.

The law of Christ teaches us to do strict justice on
another, in these comprehensive words, "All things wl
soever ye would that men should do to you, do ye e
so to them." As we obey the law of God, we sl
always speak the truth one to another, be kind on
another, help one another, and love one another—
shall not injure others, and we shall forgive the inju
we may receive from any—we shall not be covetous
speak evil one of another, nor render evil for evil, or
ing for railing, but contrariwise, blessing. Parents

n up their children in the nurture and admonition of
Lord. Children will honour their parents. Masters
give unto their servants that which is just and equal;
ants will obey their masters, not with eye-service, as
-pleasers, but in singleness of heart, fearing God.
evil communication will proceed out of our mouths—
filthy communication or jesting—there will be no
iviousness. Marriage will be esteemed honourable—
stity will be maintained—and a godly care exercised,
; impurity of thought, as well as of action, may be
lly shunned.

esus Christ is the ever present and glorified Head of
church. In his love to the children of men he has
ared himself to be the good shepherd. He says also,
y. sheep hear my voice, and I know them, and they
)w. me, and I give unto them eternal life." How gra-
is is our holy Redeemer, who thus offers to lead us
to guide us through the wilderness of this life, to
port and to comfort us amidst all our trials, per-
ities, and sorrows, and to bring us into one fold, to
tect us, and to keep us in it in time and in eternity.

Ie has spoken of one fold. All his true believers and
)wers, in every age of the world, whatever may be
r name as to religion, in every country on the face of
earth, are the sheep of his fold: they are brethren
sisters, and love one another. When the angels
ounced to the shepherds the birth of Christ, there was
nultitude of the heavenly host praising God, and
ing, "Glory to God in the highest, on earth peace,
good-will to man." His religion the only true
gion upon earth, teaches us to glorify God in our
ies and in our spirits, which are his. And as it brings
ce on earth, and good-will to men, if it prevailed in
world it would put an end to all wars and fightings,
h among nations, and between individuals; for wars
. fightings are wholly contrary to the religion of
us, they come from our lusts; the carnal mind is
ity with God. Those who maintain peace, and love
h other with a pure heart fervently, cannot fight, and
ind, and kill each other.

he faithful followers of our blessed Lord are at times
mitted to know for themselves, that the ways of

wisdom are ways of pleasantness, and all her paths ;
peace—that the fear of the Lord is indeed a fountain
life, which preserves from the snares of death—that t
kingdom of God is righteousness, peace, and joy
the Holy Ghost. How blessed are they to whom th
sacred truths are fulfilled in their own experience!

We are all fellow mortals, we are all fellow-travell
from time to eternity. We are all by creation t
children of one heavenly Father, redeemed by the bl
of one gracious Saviour, to be sanctified by the one H
Spirit. Let us then all keep the commandments
God, trust in Christ Jesus our Lord, and yield our hea
to the guidance of his Spirit. May we place our s
dependence upon Christ; may we know our sins to
washed away through living faith in his blood; and m
we finally unite with the redeemed out of every kindr
and tongue, and people, and nation, in the heavei
anthem, "Blessing, honour, glory, and power, be ui
Him that sitteth upon the throne, and unto the Lai
for ever and ever." J. F.

END.

London : Printed by E. Couchman and Co., 10, Throgmorton Street, for
TRACT ASSOCIATION of the SOCIETY OF FRIENDS. Sold at the Deposit
12, Bishopsgate Street Without.—1862.

OF

WISDOM

AND

THE FEAR OF GOD.

By Sir MATTHEW HALE,

LORD CHIEF JUSTICE OF ENGLAND.

'*And to man he said, behold the fear of the Lord, that wisdom, and to depart from evil is understanding.*"
Job. xxviii. 28.

The great pre-eminence that man hath over beasts is his *son ;* and the great pre-eminence that one man hath over ther is *wisdom ;* though all men have the privilege of son, yet all men have not the habit of wisdom. The atest commendation that we can give a man is, that he ι wise man ; and the greatest reproach that can be to ιan is to be called or esteemed a fool ; and yet as much wisdom is valued, and folly is despised, the generality mankind are in truth very fools, and make it a great t of their business to be so : and many that pretend to κ after wisdom, do either mistake the thing, or the way attain it. Commonly those that are the greatest preders to wisdom, place it in some little narrow concern, not in its true latitude commensurate to the nature nankind : and hence it is that one esteems it the only lom to be a wise politician or statesman ; another, to ι wise and knowing naturalist : another, to be a wise airer of health and the like : and all these are wisdom their kind, and the world perchance would be much er than it is if these kinds of wisdom were more in ion than they are ; but yet these are but partial wisdom ; wisdom that is most worth the seeking and finding, is

[*Price 4d. per dozen.*]

that which renders a man a wise man. And consonant to thi
David, a wise king, and Solomon, the wisest of men, affir
the same truth: "The fear of the Lord is the beginnin
of wisdom; a good understanding have all they that d
his commandments." Ps. cxi. 10. "The fear of the Lor
is the beginning of knowledge: but fools despise wisdo
and instruction." Prov. i. 7. "The fear of the Lord
the beginning of wisdom; and the knowledge of the hol
is understanding." Prov. ix. 10. And when the wise ma
had run all his long travel of experiments to attain th
which might be that good for the children of men, h
closeth up all with this saying, "Let us hear the conclusio
of the whole matter, fear God and keep his commandments
for this is the whole duty of man;" and he gives a shor
but effectual reason of it, "For God shall bring every wor
into judgment with every secret thing, whether it be goo
or whether it be evil." Eccles. xii. 13.

And yet it is strange to see how little this is thought of
believed in the world. Nay, for the most part he is thoug
the wisest man who hath the least of this principle of wisdo
appearing in him; that shakes off the fear of God, or t
sense of his presence, or the obedience to his will, a
the discipline of conscience, and by craft, or subtlety,
power, or oppression, or by whatsoever method may
most conducible, pursues his ends of profit, or power,
pleasure, or what else his own vain thoughts and the mi
taken estimate of the generality of men render desirable,
this world; and on the other side, he that governs himse
his life, his thoughts, words, actions, ends, and purpose
with the fear of Almighty God, with a sense and awe of h
presence, according to his Word, that drives at a nobler er
than ordinarily the world thinks of; namely, peace wil
Almighty God, and with his own heart and conscience, t
hope and expectation of eternity, such a man is counted
shallow, empty, inconsiderate, foolish man.

But upon a sound and true examination of this busines
we shall find that the man that feareth God is the wise
man, and he that upon that account departs from evil,
the man of greatest understanding. I shall show, therefor
these two things:—1st, What it is to fear God: 2nd, Th
this fear of God is most demonstratively the best wisdom
mankind, and makes a man truly and really a wise man.

1. A fear of reverence or awfulness; and this fear is rais
principally upon the sense of some object full of glory, m
jesty, greatness, though possibly there is no cause of expec

any hurt from the person or thing thus feared. Thus
ubject bears a reverential fear to his prince, from the
se of his majesty and grandeur: and thus much more
majesty and greatness of Almighty God excites reverence
l awfulness, though there were no other ingredient into
t fear. "Will ye not fear me, saith the Lord? Will
not tremble at my presence?" &c. Jer. v. 22. "Who
uld not fear thee, O King of Nations;" Jer. x. 7.

. A fear of caution or watchfulness. This is that which
wise man commends, "Blessed is the man that feareth
ays." Prov. xxviii. 14. And this fear of caution is a due
e and vigilancy not to displease that person from whom
enjoy or hope for good; the fear of a benefactor, or of
t person from whom we may, upon some just cause or
nerit, expect evil, as the fear of a just and righteous
ge. And these two kinds of fear, namely, the fear of
erence, and the fear of caution, are those that are the
ncipal ingredients, constituting this fear of God that these
ellent men commend to us as true wisdom.

Now this fear of God ariseth from right and true appre-
nsions concerning Almighty God; a true and deep sense,
owledge, and consideration of the majesty and glory of
d, at which the very angels of heaven, that are confirmed
an unchangeable estate of happiness, carry an inward,
l express an outward reverence; therefore the sense and
owledge of the almighty power of God is a great object of
fears. He doth whatsoever he pleaseth; all things had
ir being from him, and have their dependence on him.

The deep knowledge of the goodness of God is the noblest
iter of the noblest fear: a fear springing from love, and
t love fixing upon the eminent goodness of God which is
ogether lovely and perfect, and also upon the eminent and
nmunicative goodness of God, as he is our benefactor;
l wherever there is this love, there is the fear both of
erence and caution. We cannot choose but honour and
erence, and be careful to observe and please whatsoever
thus love; the intrinsic nature of that which we love for
own worth and perfection binds us by a kind of natural
nd or result to reverence and honour; and the extrinsic
anation of that goodness to us, binds us to reverence and
eem and honour it as our benefactor by a double bond.

A deep sense, knowledge, and consideration of the Divine
niscience. If there were all the other motives of fear
aginable, yet if this were wanting, the fear of God would
in a great measure abated; for what availeth reverence or

caution, if he to whom it is intended do not know it? what damage can be sustained by a neglect or omission that fear, if God Almighty know it not?

A deep sense of the holiness and purity of God, wh must needs cause in him an averseness unto and abhorre of whatsoever is simple or impure. Lastly, the sense of justice of God; not only an inherent justice, which is rectitude of his nature, but a transient or distributive justi that will most certainly distribute rewards to obedien observance, and the fear of his name; but punishments the disobedient and those that have no fear of him bef their eyes. The deep consideration and sense of th attributes of the divine perfection must needs excite b the fear of reverence and the fear of caution, or fear offending either by commission of what may displease G or of omitting of what is pleasing to him.

But although this knowledge of Almighty God and attributes may justly excite a fear both of reverence caution, yet without the knowledge of something else t fear will be extravagant and disorderly, and sometimes gets superstition or strange exorbitancy in this fear, or the expressions of it, and a want of regularity of duty obedience. If a man know that Almighty God is just, a will reward obedience and punish disobedience; yet if knows not what he will have done or omitted, he will inde fear to displease him, but he will not know how to please to obey him: therefore, besides the former, there must be knowledge of the will or law of God in things to be done omitted. This law of God hath a double inscription; 1 In nature, and that is again two-fold; first, the natu rudiments, or morality and piety written in the hea secondly, such as are deducible by the exercise of natu reason and light; for even from the notion of God the do result certain consequences of natural piety and religic as that he is to be prayed unto, to be praised, that he to be imitated as far as is possible by us; therefore, as is holy, beneficent, good, merciful, so must we be. 2nd But we have a more excellent transcript of the divi will, namely, the Holy Scriptures: which, therefore, a m that fears God will study, observe, and practice, as bei the best rule how to obey him. And the very fear of G arising upon the sense of his being and attributes w make that man very solicitous to know the will of Go and how he will be worshipped and served, and what would have to be done, or not to be done: and therefo

e the glorious God hath so far condescended as by his
vidence to send us a transcript of his mind, and will, and
, he will be very thankful for it, very studious of it, much
ighted in it, very curious to observe it, because it is the
e and direction how he may obey, and consequently please
t great God whom he fears. This Word he believes and
ees as his great charter, and in this Word he finds much
excite and regulate and direct his fear of God: he sees
mples of the divine justice against the offenders of his
, of the divine bounty in rewarding the obedience to it;
eatenings on one hand, promises on the other. Greater
aifestations of the divine goodness in the redemption of
akind by Christ Jesus, and therefore greater obligations
well to fear as to love such a benefactor.
And thus far of the kinds of the fear of God, and of the
ses or objects exciting it; now let us see how it doth
ear that this fearing man is the wise man, and how the
r of God discovers itself to be the true, and best, and
y, wisdom; which will appear in these particular con-
erations following:—
1. The fear of Almighty God is that which begetteth and
roveth justice. Hence it was that Moses, in his choice
udges, directs that they should be "Men fearing God,
l hating covetousness;" Jehoshaphat, in his charge to his
ges, thought this the best expedient to contain them
hin the bounds of justice, to put them in remembrance
ore whom, and for whom, they are to judge. And hence
is that Joseph could give no greater assurance to his
thren, of his just dealing with them, than this, "This
for I fear God." Gen. xlii. 18. And on the other side,
raham could have no greater cause of suspicion of ill and
ust dealing from the people with whom he conversed than
s, that they wanted the fear of God. "Because I thought
fear of God was not in this place," &c. Gen. xx. 11.
e sense of the greatness, and majesty, and power, and
tice, and all-seeing presence and command of Almighty
d lays a greater obligation and engagement upon a
rt fearing God, to deal justly and honestly, than all the
rors of death itself can do.
2. It is a great part of wisdom that concerns a person in the
rcise of the duties of his relations, and indeed it is a great
t of justice and righteousness. Now the fear of Almighty
d hath these two great advantages therein. First, the
l of God instructs exactly all relations in their reciprocal
ies, and this will of God is revealed in the Scriptures,

Secondly, the fear of God sets these directions close upon the heart, and is a severe and constant obligation to observe them; and so this fear of God doth effectually guide, and oblige a man to the duties of his several relations. It makes a good magistrate, a good subject, a good husband, a good wife, a good father, a good child, a good master, a good servant; in all those several kinds of goodness that are peculiar and proper to the several relations wherein a man stands.

3. Sincerity, uprightness, integrity, and honesty, are certainly true and real wisdom. Let any man observe it when he will, a hypocrite, or dissembler, or double-hearted man, though he may shuffle it out for a while, yet at the long run he is discovered, and disappointed, and betrays very much folly at the latter end; when a plain, sincere, honest man holds it out to the very last, so that the proverb is most true, that "Honesty is the best policy." Now the great privilege of the fear of God is that it makes the heart sincere and upright, and that will certainly make the words and actions so; for he is under the sense of the inspection of God that searches the heart, and therefore he dares not lie, nor dissemble, nor flatter, nor prevaricate; because he knows the all-seeing righteous God, that loves truth and integrity, and hates lying and dissimulation, observes him, and knows his thoughts, words, and actions. It is true that vain-glory and ostentation, and reputation, and designs and ends, may sometimes render the outward actions specious and fair, when the heart runs quite another way, and accordingly would frame the actions, if those ends and designs, and vain-glory and ostentation were not in the way: but the fear of God begins with the heart, and rectifies it, and from the heart thus rectified grows a conformity in the life, the words, the actions.

4. The great occasion and reason of the folly of mankind are—First, the unruliness and want of government of the sensual appetite or lusts: hence grows intemperance and excess in eating and drinking, unlawful and exorbitant lusts: and these exhaust the estate, waste and consume the health, embase and impoverish the mind, destroy the reputation, and render men unfit for industry and business. Secondly, the exorbitancy and unruliness, and irregularity of the passions: as excessive love of things that are either not lovely, or not deserving so much love; excess of anger, which oftentimes degenerates into malice and revenge; excess of joy in light, trivial, inconsiderable matters; excess of fear, where either no cause of fear, or not cause of so much fear is.

Now as we are truly told that the first degree and step of
dom is to put off folly, so it is the method of the fear
God (the beginning of all true wisdom), to disburthen
an of these originals and foundations of folly. It gives a
to the sensitive appetite, brings it in subjection, keeps it
hin the limits and bounds of reason, and of those instruc-
as and directions that the wise God hath prescribed: it
ps it under discipline and rule: it directs the passions to
ir proper objects, and keeps them within their due mea-
es, and within the due lines and limits of moderation, and
becomes a man that lives in the sight and observation
the God of Glory, Majesty, and Holiness; it cures those
eases and distempers of the mind by the presence of this
at preservative, the fear of God. If pride or vain-glory
ins to bud in the soul, he considers that the God he fears
ists the proud: this fear puts a man in remembrance of
glorious majesty of the most glorious God; and what is
oor worm, that he should be proud or vain-glorious in the
sence and sight of that mighty God! If ambition or
eteousness begin to appear, this fear of God presently
embers a man that the mighty God hath prohibited
m: that he hath presented unto us things of greater mo-
nt for our desires than worldly wealth or honour: that we
all of his household, and must content ourselves with
t portion he allots us, without pressing beyond the mea-
e of sobriety or dependence upon or submission unto
. If revenge stir in our hearts, this fear of God checks
tells a man that he usurps God's prerogative, who hath
erved vengeance to himself as part of his own sovereignty.
that vermin, envy, begins to live and crawl in our hearts,
s fear of God crusheth it by remembering us that the
ghty God prohibits it, that he is the Sovereign Lord and
spenser of all things: if he hath given me little, I ought to
contented; if he hath given another more, yet why should
eye be evil because his eye is good? Thus the fear of
Lord walks through the soul, and pulls up those weeds
l roots of bitterness and folly that infect, disquiet, dis-
ler, and befool it.
5. Another great cause of folly in the world is inadvert-
e, inconsiderateness, precipitancy, and over-hastiness, in
eches or actions. Now the fear of the Lord of heaven
l earth being actually present upon the soul and exerting
elf, is the greatest motive and obligation in the world to
sideration and attention touching things to be done or
d. When a man is to do anything, or speak in the pre-

sence of a great earthly prince, the very awe and fear of that
prince will give any man very much consideration touching
what he saith or doth, especially to see that it be conformable
to those laws and edicts that this prince hath made. Now
the great God of heaven and earth hath given us laws and
rules touching our words and actions; and what we are to
say or do, is to be said or done in no less a presence than the
presence of the ever glorious God, who observes every man
in the world, with the same advertence, as if there were no
thing else for him to observe; and certainly, there cannot be
imagined a greater engagement to advertence and consideration than this. And therefore, if the action or speech be of
any moment, a man that fears God will consider—1st, Is this
lawful to be done or not? If it be not, how shall I do this
great evil and sin against God? 2ndly, But if it be lawful,
yet is it fit?—is it convenient?—is it seasonable? If not,
then I will not do it, for it becomes not that presence before
whom I live. 3rdly, Again, if the thing be lawful and fit, yet
I will consider how it is to be done; what are the most
suitable circumstances to the honour and good pleasure of
that great God before whom I stand. And this advertence
and consideration doth not only qualify my actions and words
with wisdom and prudence, in contemplation of the duty I
owe to God, but it gives an excellent opportunity very many
times, by giving pause and deliberation in reference to my
duty to God, to discover many human ingredients of wisdom
and prudence requisite to the choice of actions and words,
and the manner of doing them.

6. It mightily advanceth and improveth the worth and excellency of most human actions in the world, and makes them
a nobler kind of a thing, than otherwise without it they would
be. Take a man that is much acquainted with the subtler
kind of learning, as philosophy, for instance, without the fear
of God upon his heart, it will carry him over to pride, arro-
gance, self-conceit, curiosity, presumption; but mingle it
with the fear of God, it will ennoble that knowledge, carry it
up to the honour and glory of that God that is the author of
nature, to the admiration of his power, wisdom, and goodness; it will keep him humble, modest, sober, and yet rather
with an advance than detriment to his knowledge. Take a
man industrious in his calling, without the fear of God with
it, he becomes a drudge to worldly ends, vexed when disappointed, overjoyed in success; mingle but the fear of God
with it, it will not abate his industry, but sweeten it; if he
prosper, he is thankful to God that gives him power to get

lth: if he miscarry, he is patient under the will and dis.
sation of the God he fears; it turns the very employment
.is calling into a kind of religious duty and exercise of his
gion without damage or detriment to it.

. The fear of God is certainly the greatest wisdom, be-
se it renders the mind full of tranquility and evenness in
states and conditions: for he looks up to the great Lord
he heavens and earth, considers what he commands and
aires, remembers that he observes and eyes all men,
.ws that his providence governs all things, and this keeps
i still, even, and square, without any considerable altera-
i, whatever his condition is. Is he rich, prosperous,
at?—yet he continues safe, because he continues humble,
.chful, advertent lest he should be deceived and trans-
ted: and he is careful to be the more thankful and the
.e watchful, because the command of his God and the
ure of his condition require it. Is he poor, neglected,
.uccessful?—yet he remains still patient, humble, con-
ted, thankful, dependent upon the God he fears. And
ely every man must needs agree, that such a man is a
er man than he who is ever changed and transported with
condition: that if he be rich or powerful, there is nothing
re vain, proud, insolent than he: and again let his condi-
i become poor, low, despised, there is nothing under
.ven more despondent, dispirited, heartless, discontented,
i tortured than such a man: and all for the want of the
: of Almighty God, which being once put into the heart,
: the tree put by Moses into the waters, cures the disorder
i uneasiness of all conditions.

. Inasmuch as the true fear of God is always mingled
h the knowledge of the will of God, and that will is
tained most fully in his written Word, it must needs
that a man that truly fears the Lord is instructed in
ly Scripture, the precepts thereof must needs be deeply
ested into his mind; and in these he shall assuredly
l the best directions in the world, for all kinds of moral
i divine wisdom.

. But besides all this, there is yet a secret, but a most
tain truth that highly improveth that wisdom, which the
: of the Lord bringeth, and that is this: that those that
ly fear God, have a secret guidance from a higher wisdom
n what is barely human, namely, by the spirit of truth
. wisdom, that doth really and truly, but secretly, prevent
direct them. And let no man think that this is a piece
fanaticism. Any man that sincerely and truly fears

Almighty God, relies upon him, calls upon him for his guid ance and direction, hath it as really as the son hath the counsel and direction of his father; and though the voice be no audible, nor the direction always perceptible to sense, yet it is equally as real as if a man heard the voice saying "This is the way, walk in it." And this secret direction of Almighty God is principally seen in matters relating to the good of the soul; but it may also be found in the great and momentous concerns of this life, which a good man that fears God and begs his direction, shall very often, if not at all times find. Besides this direction, a good man, fearing God, shall find his blessing upon him. It is true, that the portion of man fearing God is not in this life; oftentimes he meets with crosses, afflictions, and troubles in it, his portion is of a higher and more excellent state and condition than this life. Yet a man that fears God hath also his blessing in this life, even in relation to his very temporal condition for either his honest and just intentions and endeavours are blessed with success and comfort; or if they be not, yet even his crosses and disappointments are turned into a blessing, for they make him more humble and less esteeming this present world and setting his heart upon a better. For it is an everlasting truth, "That all things work together for good to them that love God" (Rom. viii. 28.) : and therefore certainly such a man is the wisest man.

10. But yet further: certainly it is one of the greatest evidences of wisdom to provide for the future, and to provide those things for the future that are of greatest moment, importance, and use. Upon this account, the wise man (Prov. xxx. 25.) admires the wisdom of the ant, that little creature that yet provides his meat in the summer; and we esteem it the folly of children and prodigals, that they have no prospect for the future how they shall subsist. Now the wisdom of man that feareth God discovereth itself in this, that it provides and lays up a good and safe store for the future, and that in respect of these three kinds of futurities. First, for the future part of his life; second for the future evil days; third, for the future life that is to take place after this present short, uncertain, and transitory life.

First, in respect of the future time of his life. It is true our lives in this world are but short at best, and together with that shortness, they are very uncertain; but yet the man fearing God makes a due and safe provision for that future portion of his life, how short or how long soever it be

By a constant walking in the fear of God, he transmits
he future part of his life, a quiet, serene, and fair con-
nce, and avoids those evil fruits and consequences which
nful life produceth, even in the after-time of man's life.
bruises and hurts we receive in youth are many times
'e painful in age than when we first received them. Our
s are like husbandmen's seed time; if we sow evil seeds
he time of our youth, it may be they may live five, ten,
nore years before they come up to a full crop, and possi.
then we taste the fruit of these evil ways in an unquiet
d or conscience, or some other sour effects of that evil
l. All this inconveniency a man fearing God prevents,
. instead thereof reaps a pleasing and comfortable fruit of
walk in the fear of God, namely, a quiet conscience, and
ven, settled, peaceable soul. 2ndly, But besides this, by
s means he keeps his interest in, and peace with Almighty
d, and makes sure of the best friend in the world for the
r-time of his life, to whom he is sure to have access at all
es and upon all occasions with comfort and acceptance:
it is an infallible truth, that God Almighty never for-
es any that forsake not him first.

The second futurity is the future evil day, which will most
tainly overtake every man, either the day of feeble and
repit age, or the day of sickness, or the day of death;
l against all those the true fear of God makes a safe and
ellent provision: so that although he may not avoid them,
may have a comfortable passage through them, and in the
lst of all these black clouds, the witness of a good con-
nce fearing God, and the evidence of the Divine favour,
l shine into the soul like a bright sun with comfort. This
l be a cordial under the faintness of old age, a relief under
pains of sickness, and cure of the fear of death itself,
ich to such a soul will be only a gate and passage to a life
t will be free from all pains and infirmities, a life of glory
l immortality.

The third futurity is the life and state after death. Most
tain it is that such a state there will be, and that it is but
two kinds: a state of everlasting happiness, or a state of
rlasting misery; and that all men in the world do most
tainly belong to one of these two states or conditions.
d as it is most just and equal, so it is most true that they
t truly fear God and obey him, through Jesus Christ
ll be partakers of that everlasting state of blessedness
l immortal happiness: and on the other side, they that
ect the fear of God, contemn and disobey his will, shall

without true repentance, be subject to a state of everlastin
misery.

Now herein the true wisdom of a man appears, that h
duly provides against the latter, and to obtain the former
all other wisdom of men, either to get human learnin;
wealth, honour, power—all wisdom of statesmen and pol
ticians, in comparison of this wisdom, is but vain and trivia
And this is the wisdom that the fear of God teacheth an
bringeth with it into the soul: 1st, it provides against th
greatest of evils, the everlasting state of misery and infel
city, and eternal death : 2ndly, it provides for, and attains a
everlasting estate of blessedness and happiness, of rest an
peace, of glory and immortality and eternal life ; a state c
that happiness and glory that exceeds expression and appre
hension; for "Eye hath not seen, nor ear heard, neithe
have entered into the heart of man, the things that God hat
prepared for them that love him" (1 Cor. ii.) ; and the
only, truly love God, that truly fear him: "And the
(namely, that fear God) shall be mine, saith the Lord, i
that day when I make up my jewels." Mal. iii. 17.

END.

London: Printed by E. Couchman & Co., 10, *Throgmorton Street; for t*
TRACT ASSOCIATION *of the* SOCIETY OF FRIENDS. *Sold. at the Depository,* 1
Bishopsgate Street Without.—1865.

A SKETCH

OF THE

LIFE AND CHARACTER

OF

DR. JOHN D. GODMAN.

DR. JOHN D. GODMAN was born in the year 1794, at
napolis, in the state of Maryland. His mother died before
was two years old, and his father did not long survive her.
the death of his mother he was placed under the care
an aunt; who, from her education, the sweetness of her
position, and elevated piety, was eminently qualified to
fold the youthful mind. Under such culture he received
first rudiments of his education, and his earliest moral
pressions; and when two years old, he was able to read in
Psalms. When only four years of age, he evinced so
ich sensibility, frankness, and sweetness of disposition, that
gained the affection and excited the admiration of all.
s reverence of truth was such, even from infancy, that he
s never known to equivocate. At the age of six his excel-
t aunt died, and he was left without any suitable protector
guide. It appears, however, that the moral and religious
pressions which had already been made upon his mind,
ugh obscured for a time, were never obliterated. During
last illness he often spoke of his aunt with feelings of
titude and affection. "If," said he, "I have ever been
to do any good, it has been through the influence of her
mple, instruction, and prayers." His father had lost the
ater part of his estate before his death, and that which
ained never came into the hands of his children. Young
dman, therefore, was apprenticed to a printer in Baltimore;
the occupation was not congenial to his taste, and after
w years, he left the business in disgust, and entered as a
or on board the flotilla which was then stationed in Chesa-
ke bay. While in this situation an incident occurred,
ich made a strong impression upon his mind. A raw sailor
o had been sent aloft by the captain, and was busy in per-
ming some duty which required him to stoop, was observed
falter and grow dizzy,—"*Look aloft*" cried the captain,
l the fainting landsman, as he instinctively obeyed the order
No. 70.   [*Price 4d. per dozen.*]

recovered his strength and steadiness. The young philosopher read a moral in this trifling incident, which he never forgot

At the close of the war, he was permitted to follow the strong bent of his mind, and commenced the study of medicine with a highly respectable physician, and pursued his studies with such eagerness and success, that some time before he graduated, he was selected to supply, for a few weeks, the place of his preceptor, who occupied the chair of anatomy in the University of Maryland, and was disabled by the fracture of a limb from completing his winter's course. The youthful deputy lectured with such eloquence, and was so clear and happy in his illustrations, as to gain universal applause; and at the time he was examined for his degree, the extent and accuracy of his knowledge were so apparent, that he was marked by the professors of the university, as one destined to confer honour upon the profession.

Soon after receiving his diploma, Dr. Godman settled on the Eastern shore of Maryland, at the spot described with so much truth and beauty in his "Rambles of a Naturalist." He there became engaged in laborious practice, and devoted all his intervals of leisure to the acquirement of general knowledge It was at this time that he commenced the study of Natural History, a science in which he became so distinguished.

But the place was too limited for the exercise of his powers; and not finding those advantages which he wished for the cultivation of his favourite pursuits, soon after his marriage he removed to Philadelphia, which he made his residence for four or five years. It was during this period that he published his celebrated work, the Natural History of American Quadrupeds. The fame of Dr. Godman as a teacher of anatomy was now widely spread, and he was solicited to accept the professorship of that branch of medicine, in the Rutgers' Medical College at New York.

His practice soon became extensive, and the affairs of the college prosperous, when in the midst of his second course of lectures, a severe cold settled on his lungs, accompanied by a copious hemorrhage, and compelled him to abandon his pursuits. He repaired with his family to one of the West India Islands, where he passed the remainder of the winter and the spring, and returned home, cheered, but not cured by the influence of that balmy climate. After his return, he settled in Germantown, and in this place and in Philadelphia, he spent the residue of his life. From the time Dr. Godman left New York, his disease advanced with so steady a pace, as to leave but little hope of his final recovery.

Dr. Godman's intellectual character was extraordinary. .is perception was quick and accurate; his memory exceed- ιgly retentive, for although his early education had been very mited, he had acquired such a knowledge of the Latin, ·reek, French, German, Danish, Spanish, and Italian lan- uages, as to read and translate them with fluency, and to rite several of them with elegance. His character and ac- uirements are justly portrayed by a distinguis. .d journalist, ι the extracts which follow. "The tributes," said he, which have been paid in the newspapers to the late Dr. todman, were especially due to the memory of a man, so ariously gifted by nature, and so nobly distinguished by indus- ry and zeal in the acquisition and advancement of science. Ie did not enjoy early opportunities of self-improvement, but e cultivated his talents, as he approached manhood, with a egree of ardour and success which supplied all deficiencies; nd he finally became one of the most accomplished general cholars and linguists, acute and erudite naturalists, ready, leasing, and instructive lecturers and writers of his country nd era. The principal subject of his study was anatomy in ts main branches, in which he excelled in every respect. His ttention was much directed also to physiology, pathology, nd natural history, with an aptitude and efficiency, abun- lantly proved by the merits of his published works, which ve need not enumerate.

· "We do not now recollect to have known any individual, vho inspired us with more respect for his intellect and heart, han Dr. Godman. Considering the decline of his health, for ι long period, and the pressure of adverse circumstances, vhich he frequently experienced, he performed prodigies, as ι student, an author, and a teacher;—he prosecuted exten- ive and diversified researches; composed superior disquisitions nd reviews, and large and valuable volumes; and in the reat number of topics, which he handled simultaneously or ι immediate succession, he touched none without doing him- elf credit. He lingered for years under consumption of the ungs; understood fully the incurableness of his melancholy tate; spoke and acted with an unfeigned and beautiful resig- ation, toiled at his desk to the last day of his thirty-five ears, still glowing with the love of science and the domestic ffections."

Such was the amiable individual whose history has been riefly sketched. We have, however, yet to view him in a ar more important relation; that which man, as an immortal eing, bears to his Almighty Creator.

Dr. Godman's enthusiastic devotion to science and learning commands our admiration : and, perhaps, no more ennobling pursuits can occupy the mind of him who looks not beyond the present state of existence ; but when these are brought into contrast with the concerns of eternity, they sink into utter insignificance. How then was the subject of this memoir influenced by *religious* considerations.

Unhappily the philosophical and religious opinions of Dr. Godman were formed in the school of the French naturalists of the last century. Many of the most distinguished of these men were avowed atheists, and others rejected absolutely the Christian revelation. Such is fallen human nature ! Surrounded by the most magnificent displays of Almighty wisdom, a purblind philosophy may devote herself to the study of his works, yet pass by the testimony they furnish of the existence of God. It was so with Dr. Godman ; for while assisted by such lights as these, he became as he tell us, *an infidel.* In the merciful providence of God, the light of truth at length beamed upon his understanding. In the winter of 1827, while engaged in his course of lectures in New York, an incident occurred, which led him to a candid perusal of the Gospels, as contained in the New Testament. It was a visit to the death-bed of a Christian ; the death-bed of a student of medicine. There he saw, what reason could not explain, nor philosophy fathom. He applied himself to the study of the New Testament. That this was made the means of his full conversion, will best appear from his own pen.—The following is an extract of a letter he addressed to a medical friend, Dr. Judson, a surgeon in the navy of the United States who was at that time in the last stage of consumption :

" *Germantown, December 25th,* 1828.

"In relation to dying, my dear friend, you talk like a sick man, and just as I used to do when very despondent. Death is a debt we all owe to nature, and must eventually ensue from a mere wearing out of the machine, if not from disease. Nature certainly has a strong abhorrence to this cessation of corporeal action, and all animals have a dread of death, who are conscious of its approach. A part of our dread of death is purely physical, and is avoidable only by a philosophical conviction of its necessity : but the greater part of our dread, and the terrors with which the avenues to the grave are surrounded, are from another, and a more potent source. "'Tis conscience that makes cowards of us all,'

l forces us by our terrors to confess, that we dread some.
ng beyond physical dissolution, and that we are terrified,
at merely ceasing to breathe, but that we have not lived
we ought to have done, have not effected the good that
s within the compass of our abilities, and neglected to
rcise the talents we possessed to the greatest advantage.
e only remedy for this fear of death, is to be sought by
roaching the Author of all things in the way prescribed
himself, and not according to our foolish imaginations.
miliation of pride, denial of self, subjection of evil tempers
l dispositions, and an entire submission to his will for
port and direction, are the best preparatives for such an
roach. A perusal of the Gospels, in a spirit of real inquiry
er a direction how to act, will certainly teach the way.
these Gospels, the Saviour himself has preached his own
ctrines, and he who runs may read. He has prescribed the
urse; he shows how the approval and mercy of God may be
n; he shows how awfully corrupt is man's nature, and how
idly his pride and stubbornness of heart, which cause him
try every subterfuge to avoid the humiliating confession
his own weakness, ignorance, and folly. But the same
ssed hand has stripped death of all the terrors which
oded around the grave, and converted the gloomy recep-
le of our mortal remains into the portal of life and light.
! let me die the death of the righteous; let my last end
l future state be like his.

" This is all I know on the subject. I am no theologian,
l have as great an aversion to priestcraft as one can enter-
n. I was once an infidel, as I told you in the West Indies.
ecame a Christian from conviction produced by the candid
quiry recommended to you. I know of no other way in
ich death can be stripped of its terrors; certainly none
ter can be wished. Philosophy is a fool, and pride a mad-
n. Many persons die with what is called *manly firm-*
s; that is, having acted a part all their lives according to
ir prideful creed, they must die *game.* They put on as
ooth a face as they can, to impose on the spectators, and
firmly. But this is all deception; the true state of their
nds at the very time, nine times out of ten, is worse than
most horrible imaginings even of hell itself. Some who
ve led lives adapted to sear their consciences, and petrify
the moral sensibilities, die with a kind of indifference
ilar to that with which a hardened convict submits to a
w infliction of disgraceful punishment. But the man who
s as a man ought to die, is the humble-minded believing,

Christian; one who has tasted and enjoyed all the blessi
of creation; who has had an enlightened view of the wis
and glory of his Creator: who has felt the vanity of me
worldly pursuits and motives, and been permitted to k
the mercies of a blessed Redeemer, as he approaches the
row house appointed for all the living. Physical death 1
cause his senses to shrink and fail at the trial; but his mi
sustained by the Rock of Ages, is serene and unwaveri
He relies not on his own righteousness, for that would
vain; but the arms of mercy are beneath him, the m
tering spirits of the Omnipotent are around him. He c
not die manfully, but he rests in Jesus; he blesses
friends; he casts his hope on One all-powerful to sust
and mighty to save, then sleeps in peace. He is dead—
liveth; for He who is the resurrection and the life
declared, 'Whoso believeth in me, though he were dead,
shall he live.' 'And whosoever liveth and believeth in
shall never die.'" * * * *

This letter, which so truly contrasts the death-bed sc
of the infidel with that of the Christian, and so beautif
portrays the history of the change which had been effec
in Dr. Goodman's own mind was not lost upon his frie1
It described his condition and it reached his heart.

Dr. Judson, though religiously instructed when you1
having a pious clergyman for his father, and another for 1
elder brother, had nevertheless long since freed himself fr(
what he called the prejudices of education. He had acquir
wealth and reputation; and was an estimable man in all t
domestic relations of life; but the self-denying doctrines
the Saviour were too humbling to his proud spirit, and
could not submit to their influence. At the time he receiv
Dr. Godman's letter, he was gloomy and despondent: lo(
ing forward with fearful forebodings to the period of 1
dissolution which seemed not far distant. He had no co1
dence but that of the sceptic—no hope but that of ceasi
to be. Aware of the fatal nature of the disease under whi
he had lingered for years, he had long been arming hims
to meet the king of terrors with composure, that he mig
die like a philosopher—"*with manly firmness;*" but as
drew nearer to the grave, he began to fear that there mig
be something beyond this narrow prison, and he inqui1
with solicitude, "Is there such a thing as the new birth, a
if so, in what does it consist?" He at length consented
make the investigation recommended by Dr. Godman. 1
took up the New Testament, and read it in the spirit

ndid inquiry. A conviction of the truth of its doctrines
stened upon him. The clouds which had so long enveloped
m were dissipated, light broke in upon his mind, and he
is enabled to lay hold of the promises. The remaining days
his life were devoted to fervent prayer, and the constant
idy of the Scriptures. Through the holy influences of
vine grace he was enabled to rely with confidence on the
erits of his Redeemer, his soul was filled with heavenly
mposure, and the last words he uttered were, " Peace
ace." If he did not die with "*manly firmness*," he
rested in Jesus."
The progress of Dr. Godman's disease was very gradual,
d allowed him many intervals of comparative ease. Per-
ctly aware of the fatal character of his disorder, he watched
progress, step by step, with the coolness of an anatomist;
ile he submitted to it with the resignation of a Christian.
is intellect was strong to the last, and almost the only
ange that could be observed in his mind was that which
longs to a being on the verge of eternity, in whose esti-
ate the concerns of this life are sinking in comparison with
e greater interests of that to which he is approaching. His
incipal delight was in the promises and consolations of the
ible, which was his constant companion. On one occasion,
few days before his death, while reading aloud from the
ew Testament to his family, his voice faltered, and he was
sired to read no longer, as it appeared to oppress him.
It is not that," replied he, " but I feel so in the immediate
esence of my Maker, that I cannot control my emotion!"
a manuscript volume which he sent to a friend, and which
intended to fill with original pieces of his own composition,
wrote as follows: " Did I not in all things feel most
oroughly convinced that the over-ruling of our plans by
all-wise Providence is always for good, I might regret
at a part of my plan cannot be executed. This was to
late a few curious incidents from among the events of my
ost singularly guided life, which, in addition to mere
ovelty or pecularity of character, could not have failed
ractically to illustrate the importance of inculcating correct
ligious and moral principles, and imbuing the mind there-
ith from the very earliest dawn of intellect, from the very
oment that the utter imbecility of infancy begins to disap-
ear. May his holy will be done, who can raise up abler
lvocates to support the truth!" " This is my first attempt
write in my Token—why may it not be the last? Oh!
ould it be, believe me, that the will of God will be most

acceptable. Notwithstanding the life of neglect, sinfulne
and perversion of heart, which I so long led, before it ple...
him to dash all my idols in the dust, I feel a humble ho]
in the boundless mercy of our blessed Lord and Saviour, wl
alone can save the soul from merited condemnation.   May
be in the power of those who chance to read these lines, i
say, Into thy hands I commend my spirit, for thou ha
redeemed me, O Lord! thou God of truth!"

A reliance on the mercies of God through Jesus Chri
became indeed the habitual frame of his mind; and imparte
to the closing scenes of his life a solemnity and a holy resi
nation, which robbed death of its sting, and the grave of i
victory.   The following extracts from some of his correspon
ence afford additional evidence of the glorious change whic
he had been permitted to experience.

"*Philadelphia, Feb.* 17*th*, 1829.

"My dear Friend,—Since my last to you my health h
suffered various and most afflicting changes."—"But than
to the mercies of Him who is alone able to save, the vall
and shadow of death were stripped of their terrors, and t
descent to the grave was smoothed before me.   Relying o
the mercies and infinite merits of the Saviour, had it please
God to call me then, I believe I should have died in a peace
ful, humble confidence.   But I have been restored to a stat
of comparative health, perhaps nearly to the condition i
which I was when I wrote to Dr. Judson; and I am agai
allowed to think of the education of my children, and th
support of my family."

In reply to a letter from Professor Sewall, giving a
account of the last moments of his friend Dr. Judson, h
responds in the following feeling manner.

"*Germantown, May* 21*st*, 1829.

"My dear Friend,—I feel very grateful for your attentid
in sending me an account of our dear Judson's last m
ments.   After all his doubts, difficulties, and mental co
flicts, to know that the Father of mercies was pleased to op
his eyes to the truth, and shed abroad in his heart the lo
and salvation offered through the Redeemer, is to me a sour
of the purest gratification, and a cause of the most since
rejoicing.   The bare possibility of my having been eve
slightly instrumental in effecting the blessed change of mir
he experienced, excites in me emotions of gratitude to th
source of all good which words cannot express."—"M
health has been in a very poor condition since my last to yo

warm weather now appears to have set in, and possibly
ay improve a little, otherwise it will not be long before
llow our lately departed friend. Let me participate in
prayers you offer for the sick and afflicted, and may God
it me strength to die to his honour and glory, in the
es and constancy derived from the merits and atonement
ae blessed Saviour."

"*Philadelphia, Oct. 6th*, 1829.

My dear Friend,—My health is, as for a considerable
e past, in a very tolerable condition; that is, I can sit up
eat part of the day writing or reading, without much
ry. My emaciation is great, and though not very rapid,
teady, so that the change in my strength takes place
ost imperceptibly. On the whole, though I suffer greatly
pared with persons in health, yet so gently have the
stenings of the Lord fallen upon me, that I am hourly
ed upon for thankfulness and gratitude for his unfailing
cies. Equal cause have I had for rejoicing, that I have
ned to put my whole trust in Him; as he has raised me
help and friends in circumstances which seemed to render
a hope impossible, and has blessed me and mine with
ee and content in the midst of all afflictions, trials, and
ersity."

a his last letter to Dr. Best of Cincinnati, with whom
aad long maintained an affectionate correspondence, he
es :—

It gives me great happiness to learn that you have been
ght as well as myself to fly to the Rock of Ages for shel-
against the afflictions of this life, and for hopes of eternal
ation. But for the hopes afforded me, by an humble reli-
e on the all-sufficient atonement of our blessed Redeemer,
ould have been the most wretched of men. But I trust,
, the afflictions I have endured have been sanctified to
awakening, and to the regeneration of my heart and life.
r we, my dear friend, persist to cling to the only sure
port against all that is evil in life, and all that is fearful
eath."

r. Best's circumstances were in several respects similar
hose of his Friend Godman; like him he had been a dis-
ever in the Christian religion, and like him had been
ight by a careful examination of its evidences to a percep-
and acknowledgment of the truth. He too was at this
e languishing in consumption—which brought him to the
e a few months after Dr. Godman,—and like him he

was supported and animated by the precious faith
Gospel, and yielded up his spirit in hope and peace.

Professor Sewall,* from whose account much of thi.
moir has been derived, remarks, "In the last letter \
I ever received from him, he observes, 'I have just concl
the publication of the translation of Levasseur's accou
Lafayette's progress through the United States, which
appear next week. My health has for the last week o:
been very good, for me, since, notwithstanding my r
excessive application during this time, I continue to do
My cough and expectoration are sufficiently troublesome
by light diet, and avoiding all irritation, I have but
little trouble from night sweats, and generally sleep tole
well. To-morrow I must resume my pen to complete
articles of Zoology for the Encyclopedia Americana,
preparing in Boston. It shall be my constant endeavo
husband my strength to the last; and by doing as mu
is consistent with safety, for the good of my fellow-creat
endeavour to discharge a mite of the immense debt I o\
the never-failing bounties of Providence.'

"He did husband his strength, and he toiled with his
almost to the last hours of his life; and by thus doin
furnished us with a singular evidence of the possibili
uniting the highest attainments of science, and the
ardent devotion to letters, with the firmest belief, an
purest practice of the Christian. But the period of hi
solution was not distant; the summons arrived; and con
that the messenger who had been long in waiting, coul
be bribed to tarry, he commended his little family in a fe
prayer to him who has promised to be the 'Father d
fatherless, and the widow's God,' and then with up
eyes and hands, and a face beaming with joy and confid
resigned his spirit into the arms of his Redeemer, o
morning of the 17th of April, 1830.

"A friend, who was his constant companion duri
sickness, and witnessed his last moments, writes me th
'You ask me to give you an account of his last mon
they were such as have robbed me of all terror of d
and will afford me lasting comfort through life. The
self-composure and entire resignation which were so re
able through his whole sickness, supported him to th
O it was not death——it was a release from mortal mi

* "An introductory Lecture, delivered Nov. 1st, 1830, by
Sewall, M.D., Professor of Anatomy and Physiology in the Colu
College, District of Columbia.

&sting happiness. Such calmness when he prayed for
ll, such a heavenly composure, even till the breath left
you would have thought he was going only a short
ey. During the day his sufferings had been almost
nd enduring. Frequently did he pray that the Lord
d give him patience to endure all till the end, knowing
it could not be many hours; and truly his prayers were
d, "*Lord Jesus, receive my soul*," were the last words
tered, and his countenance appeared as if he had a fore-
 of heaven even before his spirit left this world.' "

---

r. Godman's views of the authenticity and practical
ency of the Gospel, are expressed with singular force
beauty in the following extract from an essay written
long before his death.
Is proof wanting that these Gospels are true? It is only
ssary for an honest mind to read them candidly to be
inced. Every occurrence is stated clearly, simply, and
tentatiously. The narrations are not supported by assev-
ons of their truth, nor by parade of witnesses; the circum-
ces described took place in the presence of vast multitudes
are told in that downright, unpretending manner, which
d have called forth innumerable positive contradictions,
hey been untrue. Mysteries are stated without attempt
lanation, because *explanation* is not necessary to es-
sh, the *existence* of facts, however mysterious. Miracles,
attested by the presence of vast numbers are stated in
plainest language of narration, in which the slightest
 g of imagination cannot be traced. This very sim-
, this unaffected sincerity, and quiet affirmation, have
force than a thousand witnesses—more efficacy than
es of ambitious effort to support truth by dint of
entation.
What motive could the evangelists have to falsify? The
stian kingdom is not *of this world*, nor *in it*. Christian-
eaches disregard of its vanities; depreciates its honours
enjoyments; and sternly declares, that none can be Chris-
but those who escape from its vices and allurements.
re is no call directed to ambition—no gratification pro-
d to vanity: the sacrifice of self—the denial of all the
ensities which relate to the gratification of passion or
e, with the most humble dependence upon God, are
riably taught, and most solemnly enjoined, under penalty

of the most awful consequences! Is it then wonderful t
such a system should find revilers? Is it surprising t
sceptics should abound, when the slightest allowance of h
would force them to condemn all their actions? Or is 1
be wondered at that a purity of life and conversation
repugnant to human passions, and a humility so offensiv
human pride, should be opposed, rejected, and contemn
Such is the true secret of the opposition to *religion*—s
the cause inducing men who lead unchristian lives, to ar
the frailties, errors, weakness, and vices of individuals or se
against *Christianity*, hoping to weaken or destroy the
tem by rendering ridiculous or contemptible those who
fess to be governed by its influence, though their con
shows them to be acting under an opposite spirit.

"What is the mode in which this most extraordinary
trine of Christianity is to be diffused? By force—temp
power—temporal rewards—earthly triumphs? None of th
By earnest persuasion, gentle entreaty, brotherly moniti
paternal remonstrance. The dread resort of threatened p
ishment comes last—exhibited in sorrow, not in anger; t
as a fearful truth, not denounced with vindictive exultati
while to the last moment, the beamy shield of mercy is re
to be interposed for the saving of the endangered.

"Human doctrines are wavering and mutable: the d
trines of the blessed and adorable Jesus, our Saviour, i
fixed and immutable. The traditions of men are dissimi
and inconsistent: the declarations of the Gospel are harn
nious, not only with each other, but with the acknowledg
attributes of the Deity, and the well-known condition
human nature.

"What do sceptics propose to give us in exchange for t
system of Christianity, with its 'hidden mysteries,' 'mi
cles,' 'signs, and wonders?' Doubt, confusion, obscuri
annihilation! Life—without higher motive than selfishne
death—without hope! Is it for this that their zeal is
warmly displayed in proselyting? Is such the gain to acc1
for the relinquishment of our souls? In very deed, this
the utmost they have to propose, and we can only accou
for their rancorous efforts to render others like themsel
by reflecting, that misery loves company."

London: Printed by E. Couchman & Co., 10, Throgmorton Street; for
TRACT ASSOCIATION of the SOCIETY OF FRIENDS. Sold at the Deposit
12, Bishopsgate Street Without.—1862.

BRIEF MEMOIR

OF

SIR MATTHEW HALE.

⟨ MATTHEW HALE, Lord Chief Justice of England,
⟨s born in Gloucestershire, in the year 1609. Before
⟨ was six years old, he lost both his parents; but by
⟨ care of a judicious guardian, great attention was paid
his education. When he had completed his studies at
⟨ford, he quitted the University, with an intention of
⟨ing into the army; but on the persuasion of Sergeant
⟨anvill, he entered at Lincoln's Inn, and with great
⟨our, and almost unexampled application, bent his
⟨nd to the studies of his profession.

In early life he was fond of company, and fell into
⟨ny levities and extravagances; but this propensity
⟨d conduct were corrected by a circumstance that made
considerable impression on his mind during the rest of
⟨s life. Being one day in company with other young
⟨en, one of the party, through excess of wine, fell down,
⟨parently dead, at their feet. Young Hale was so
⟨fected on this occasion, that he immediately retired to
⟨other room; and shutting the door, fell on his knees,
⟨d prayed earnestly to God that his friend might be
⟨stored to life, and that he himself might be pardoned for
⟨ving given countenance to so much excess. At the
⟨me time he made a solemn vow, that he would never
⟨ain keep company in that manner, nor " drink a health"
⟨hile he lived. His friend recovered, and Hale religi-
⟨sly observed his vow. After this event there was an
⟨tire change in his disposition; he forsook all dissipated
⟨mpany, and was careful to divide his time between the
⟨ties of religion and the studies of his profession. He

became remarkable for a grave and exemplary deport
ment, great moderation of temper, and religious ten
derness of spirit; and these virtues appear to hav
accompanied him through the whole of his life.

The following extract from a diary which he regularl
kept, shows the piety of his mind, and how solicitous h
was to make the best use of his time.

"*Morning.*—1. To lift up the heart to God in thank
fulness for renewing my life.

"2. To renew my covenant with God in Christ
First, by renewed acts of faith receiving Christ, an
rejoicing in the height of that relation; secondly, by re
solving to be one of his people, and doing him allegiance

"3. Adoration and prayer.

"*Day Employment.*—There must be an employmen
of two kinds:

"1. Our ordinary calling. To serve God in it. It is
a service to Christ, though ever so mean. Here observe
faithfulness, diligence, cheerfulness. Not to overcharge
myself with more business than I can bear.

"2. Our spiritual employments. Mingle somewha
of God's immediate service in the day.

"*If Alone.*—1. Beware of wandering, vain, sensua
thoughts; fly from thyself rather than entertain these.

"2. Let thy solitary thoughts be profitable. View
the evidences of thy salvation, the state of thy soul, the
coming of Christ, and thy own mortality; this will make
thee humble and watchful.

"*Company.*—Do good to them. Use God's name
reverently. Beware of leaving an ill impression, or il
example. Receive good from them, if they are more
knowing.

"*Evening.*—Cast up the accounts of the day. If there
was ought amiss, beg pardon; resolve to be more vigilant
If thou hast done well, bless the mercy and grace of God
which have supported thee."

Thus did this excellent man occupy himself in the ser
vice of God, at the same time that he was making grea
progress in the study of the sciences, and particularl
that of the Law, in which he became a greater proficien
than any of his contemporaries.

In the duties of his office as a judge he conducted
nself with the greatest integrity. The motives which
luenced him to the faithful discharge of these duties,
re founded on the only firm basis—that of religion.
iis will appear by an extract from one of his papers,
titled "Things to be had in continual remembrance."
nong a numerous list of these are the following:—
[hat, in the administration of justice I am entrusted for
)d, the king, and the country: and therefore, that it be
ne uprightly, deliberately, resolutely. That I rest not
on my own direction and strength; but implore and
st upon the direction and strength of God.—That, in
e execution of justice, I carefully lay aside my own
ssions, and give not way to them, however provoked.
-That I be not biassed with compassion to the poor,
favour to the rich, in point of justice.—That popular
court applause, or dislike, have no influence in any-
ing I do in the distribution of justice.—That I be not
licitous about what men think or say, so long as I keep
yself exactly according to the rules of justice."
The writings of Sir Matthew Hale on religious sub-
cts, particularly his "Contemplations Moral and Divine,"
anifest a truly humble frame of mind; and contain a
riousness and fervency, well adapted to excite kindred
notions in the breast of the reader. We shall select a
w of these, as testimonies which this great and good
an bore to the power and efficacy of religion, as the
iide, support, and comfort of our lives.
"True religion," says he, "teaches the soul a high
neration for Almighty God; a sincere and upright
ilking, as in the presence of the invisible, all-seeing
od. It makes a man truly love, honour, and obey him,
id therefore careful to know what his will is. It ren-
rs the heart highly thankful to him, as his Creator,
edeemer, and Benefactor. It makes a man entirely
pend on him, seek him for guidance, direction, and pro-
ction, and submit to his will with patience, and resig-
tion of soul. It gives the law not only to his words
d actions, but to his very thoughts and purposes; so
at he dares not entertain any which are unbecoming the
esence of that God, by whom all our thoughts are

legible. It crushes all pride and haughtiness, both in man's heart and carriage, and gives him a humble stat of mind before God and men. It regulates the passion and brings them into due moderation. It ꞵ /es a ma a right estimate of this present world, and sets his hea and hopes above it; so that he never loves it more tha it deserves. It makes the wealth and the glory of thi world, high places, and great preferments, but of littl consequence to him; so that he is neither covetous, no ambitious, nor over solicitous, concerning the advantage of them. It makes him value the love of God and th peace of his own conscience above all the wealth an honour in the world, and to be very diligent in preservin them. He performs all his duties to God with sincerit and humility, and whilst he lives on earth, his conversa tion, his hope, his treasures, are in heaven; and h endeavours to walk suitably to such a hope."

Of the inward direction and assistance of the Spirit o God to the soul, he writes as follows:—

"Inasmuch as the true fear of God is always mingle(with the knowledge of the will of God, and that will i contained most fully in his written Word, it must need be, that a man that truly fears the Lord is instructed in Holy Scripture, and the precepts thereof must needs be deeply digested into his mind, and in these he will assur edly find the best directions in the world for all kind o moral and Divine Wisdom; but besides all this, there i yet a secret, but most certain truth that highly improvetl that wisdom which the fear of the Lord bringeth, and that is this, that they who truly fear God, have a secre guidance from a higher wisdom than what is barely human, namely, the Spirit of truth and wisdom; which does really, though secretly, prevent and direct them. And let no man think that this is a piece of fanaticism. And any man that sincerely and truly fears Almighty God, and calls and relies upon him for his direction, has it as really as a son has the counsel and direction of his father: and though the voice be not audible, nor discerni- ble by sense, yet it is equally as real as if a man heard a voice, saying, 'This is the way, walk in it.'"

"Though this secret direction of Almighty God is prin-

ally seen in matters relating to the good of the soul;
t even in the concerns of this life, a good man fearing
d, and begging his direction, will very often, if not
all times, find it. I can call my own experience to
tness, that even in the temporal affairs of my whole
e, I have never been disappointed of the best direction,
en I have, in humility and sincerity, implored it.

"The observance of the secret admonition of the Spirit
God in the heart, is an effectual means to cleanse
d sanctify us; and the more it is attended to, the more
will be conversant with our souls, for our instruction.
the midst of difficulties, it will be our counsellor; in
e midst of temptations, it will be our strength, and
ace sufficient for us; in the midst of troubles it will be
r life and our comforter."

" It is impossible for us to enjoy the influence of this
od Spirit, till we are deeply sensible of our own emp-
ess and nothingness and our minds are thereby brought
wn and laid in the dust. The Spirit of Christ is indeed
humbling spirit; the more we have of it, the more we
all be humbled; and it is a sign that either we have it
t, or that it is yet overpowered by our corruptions, if
r heart be still haughty."

" Attend, therefore, to the secret persuasions and dis-
asions of the Spirit of God, and beware of quenching
grieving it. This wind, that blows where it lists, if
ut out or resisted, may never breathe upon us again,
t leave us to be hardened in our sins. If observed and
eyed, it will, on all occasions, be our monitor and
ector. When we go out, it will lead us; when we
ep, it will keep us; and when we awake, it will talk
th us."

The following reflections on the vicissitudes of human
airs and on the benefits to be derived from duly consi-
ring them, are highly interesting and instructive.

" In the course of my life, I have been in as many sta-
ns and places as most men. I have experienced almost
ntinual motion; and although, of all earthly things, I
ve most desired rest, and a fixed private station, yet
various changes that I have seen and found, the pub-
employments that, without my seeking, and against

my inclination, have been put upon me, and many oth
interventions, as well private as public, have made
literally my experience, that I have here no continuin
city. When I had designed for myself a settled mansio
in one place, and had fitted it to my convenience and r
pose, I have been presently constrained, by my necessar
employments, to leave it, and repair to another: an
when again I thought to find repose there, and had suite
it to my convenience, some other necessary occurrenc
have diverted me from it. And thus my dwellings ha
been like so many inns to a traveller, of longer contint
ance, indeed, but of almost equal instability."

"This unsettledness of station, though troublesom
has given me a good and practical moral; namely, that
must not expect my rest in this lower world; but mu
consider it as the place of my journey and pilgrimag
and look further for complete happiness. And trul
when I reflect, that it has been the wisdom of Almigh
God, to exercise with this kind of discipline, those wo
thies whom he has exhibited as patterns to the rest
mankind, I have no reason to complain of it as a difficult
or an inconvenience; but to be thankful to him for it, a
an instruction and document to put me in remembranc
of a better home, and to incite me to make a due provi
sion for it: even that everlasting rest which he has pro
vided for them that love him; it is his gracious design
by pouring me thus from vessel to vessel, to keep m
from fixing myself too much upon this world below."

"But the truth is, did we consider this life as become
us even as wise men, we might easily find, without the
help of such discipline, that the world below neither wa
intended for, nor indeed can be, a place of rest: but tha
it is only a laboratory to fit and prepare the souls of th
children of men for a better and more abiding state;
school to exercise and train us up in habits of patienc
and obedience, till we are fitted for another station;
little narrow nursery, wherein we may be dressed an
pruned, till we are fit to be transplanted into paradise."

"The shortness of our lives, and the continual trouble
sicknesses, and calamities that attend them: and th
instances of mortality of all ages, sexes, and conditions

nkind, are sufficient to convince reasonable men, who
'e the seriousness and patience to consider and observe,
t we have no abiding city here. And on the other
:, if we will but give ourselves leisure to consider the
at wisdom of Almighty God, who adapts everything
the world to suitable ends; the excellence of the soul
l mind of man; the great advances and improvements
nature is capable of; the admirable means which the
rciful and wise God has afforded mankind, by his works
nature and providence, by his Word and instruments,
|ualify them for a nobler life than this world can yield,
   shall readily confess that there is another state,
ther city to come, which it becomes every good, and
e, and considerate man, to look after and fit himself
   And yet if we regard the generality of mankind
h due consideration, they will appear to be a company
distempered people. The greater part of them make
heir whole business to provide for rest and happiness
this world! they make the acquisition of wealth and
iour, and the preferments and pleasures of life their
at, if not their only business and happiness; and
ich is yet a higher degree of frenzy, they esteem this
 only wisdom, and think that the careful provision for
rnity is the folly of a few weak, melancholy, fanciful
n: whereas it is a truth, and in due time it will evi-
itly appear, that those men only, who are solicitous for
 attaining of their everlasting rest, are the truly wise
n, and shall be acknowledged to be so by those who
v despise them. 'We fools accounted his life madness,
l his end to be without honour; now is he numbered
|ong the children of God, and his lot is among the
nts!'"
This eminent and virtuous man possessed uninter-
ited health till near the sixty-sixth year of his age.
this period he was affected with an indisposition which,
a short time, greatly impaired his strength: and he
nd himself so unfit to discharge the duty of Justice of
 King's Bench, that he was obliged to resign the office.
He continued, however, (says Bishop Burnet,) to retire
quently for his devotions and studies. As long as he
ild go himself, he went regularly to his retirement;

and when his infirmities increased so that he was not able to walk to the place he made his servants carry him thither in a chair. At last as he winter came on, he saw with great joy his deliverance approaching: for besides his being weary of the world, and his longings for the blessedness of another state, his pains increased so much, that no patience inferior to his could have borne them without great uneasiness of mind. Yet he expressed to the last, such submission to the will of God, and so equal a temper, that the powerful effects of Christianity were evident, in the support which he derived from it under so heavy a load."

"He continued to enjoy the free use of his reason and senses to the latest moment of life. This he had often and earnestly prayed for during his last sickness. When his voice was so sunk that he could not be heard, his friends perceived, by the almost constant lifting up of his eyes and hands that he was still aspiring towards that blessed state, of which he was now to be speedily possessed. He had no struggles, nor seemed to be in any pangs in his last moments. He breathed out his righteous and pious soul in peace."

END.

London: Printed by E. Couchman & Co., 10, Throgmorton Street, for the TRACT ASSOCIATION of the SOCIETY OF FRIENDS. Sold at the Depository, 12, Bishopsgate Street Without.—1863.

HYMNS.

"THOU, GOD, SEEST ME."

Taylor.

AMONG the deepest shades of night
  Can there be one who sees my way?
Yes:—God is like a shining light,
  That turns the darkness into day.

When ev'ry eye around me sleeps,
  May I not sin without control?
No: for a constant watch He keeps,
  On ev'ry thought of ev'ry soul.

If I could find some cave unknown,
  Where human feet had never trod,
Yet there I could not be alone;
  On ev'ry side there would be God.

He smiles in Heav'n: he frowns in Hell:
  He fills the air, the earth, the sea;—
I must within his presence dwell;
  I cannot from his anger flee.

Yet I may flee—he shows me where:
  To *Jesus Christ* he bids me fly;
And while I seek for pardon there,
  There's only mercy in his eye.

THE CRUSE OF OIL.—2 KINGS iv. 4—7.

Newton.

By the poor widow's oil and meal
  Elijah was sustained;
Though small the stock, it lasted well,
  For God the store maintained.

It seemed as if from day to day,
  They were to eat and die;
But still, though in a secret way,
  He sent a fresh supply.

No. 71.   [*Price 4d. per dozen.*]

Thus to his poor he still will give
  Just for the present hour;
But for to-morrow they must live
  Upon his word and power.

No barn or storehouse they possess,
  On which they can depend;
Yet have no cause to fear distress,
  For Jesus is their friend.

Then let no fears your minds assail,
  Remember, God has said,
"The cruse aud barrel shall not fail;
  My people shall be fed."

THE BLASTED FIG TREE.—MARK xi. 20.

New

ONE awful word which Jesus spoke
  Against the tree which bore no fruit,
More piercing than the lightning's stroke,
  Blasted and dried it to the root.

But could a tree the Lord offend,
  To make him show his anger thus?
He surely had a further end,
  To be a warning word to us.

The fig tree by its leaves was known,
  But having not a fig to show,
It brought a heavy sentence down,
  " Let none hereafter on thee grow."

Too many, who the Gospel hear,
  Whom Satan blinds, and sin deceives,
We to this fig tree may compare,
  They yield no fruit, but only leaves.

Knowledge, and zeal, and gifts, and talk,
  Unless combin'd with faith and love,
And witness'd by a Gospel walk,
  Will not a true profession prove.

Without the fruit the Lord expects,
    Knowledge will make our state the worse,
The barren trees he still rejects,
    And soon will blast them with his curse.

O Lord, unite our hearts in prayer;
    On each of us thy Spirit send,
That we the fruits of grace may bear,
    And find acceptance in the end.

PRAISE FOR CREATION AND PROVIDENCE.

Watts.

I sing the almighty power of God,
    That made the mountains rise,
That spread the flowing seas abroad,
    And built the lofty skies.

I sing the wisdom that ordain'd
    The sun to rule the day;
The moon shines full at his command;
    And all the stars obey.

I sing the goodness of the Lord
    That filled the earth with food;
He form'd the creatures with his word,
    And then pronounced them good.

Lord, how thy wonders are display'd
    Where'er I turn mine eye!
If I survey the ground I tread,
    Or gaze upon the sky.

There's not a plant or flower below,
    But makes thy glories known:
And clouds arise and tempests blow
    By order from thy throne.

Creatures (as num'rous as they be)
    Are subject to thy care;
There's not a place where we can flee,
    But God is present there.

In heaven he shines with beams of love,
  With wrath in hell beneath,
'Tis on his earth I stand or move,
  And 'tis his air I breathe.

His hand is my perpetual guard,
  He keeps me with his eye ;
Why should I then forget the Lord,
  Who is for ever nigh.

HEAVEN AND EARTH.

Tay

COME, let us now forget our mirth,
  And think that we must die ;
What are our best delights on earth,
  Compared with those on high ?

A sad and sinful world is this,
  Although it seems so fair ;
But heaven is perfect joy and bliss,
  For God himself is there.

Here all our pleasures soon are past,
  Our brightest joys decay ;
But pleasures there for ever last,
  And cannot fade away.

Here many a pale and bitter groan
  Our feeble bodies tear ;
But pain and sickness are not known,
  And never shall be, there.

Here sins and sorrows we deplore,
  With many cares distress'd ;
But there the mourners weep no more,
  And there the weary rest.

Our dearest friends, when death shall call,
  At once must hence depart ;
But there we hope to meet them all,
  And never, never part.

Then let us love and serve the Lord
  With all our youthful powers ;
And we shall gain this great reward—
  This glory shall be ours.

THE REQUEST.

Father, whate'er of earthly bliss
  Thy sovereign will denies,
Accepted at thy throne of grace,
  Let this petition rise.

Give me a calm, a thankful heart,
  From every murmur free;
The blessings of thy grace impart,
  And make me live to thee.

Let the sweet hope that thou art mine,
  My life and death attend,
Thy presence through my journey shine,
  And crown my journey's end.

THE DANGER OF DELAY.

Watts.

Why should I say, " 'Tis yet too soon
  To seek for heaven or think of death?"
A flower may fade before 'tis noon,
  And I this day may lose my breath.

If this rebellious heart of mine
  Despise the gracious calls of heaven,
I may be hardened in my sin,
  And never have repentance given.

What, if the Lord grow wrath and swear,
  While I refuse to read and pray,
That he'll refuse to lend an ear
  To all my groans another day.

What, if his dreadful anger burn,
  While I refuse his offered grace;
And all his love to fury turn,
  And strike me dead upon the place!

'Tis dangerous to provoke a God!
  His power and vengeance none can tell;
One stroke of his Almighty rod,
  Shall send young sinners quick to hell.

Then 'twill for ever be in vain,
  To cry for pardon and for grace;
To wish I had my time again,
  Or hope to see my Maker's face.

WALKING WITH GOD.

Cowp

Oh! for a closer walk with God,
  A calm and heavenly frame;
A light to shine upon the road
  That leads me to the Lamb!

Where is the blessedness I knew,
  When first I saw the Lord?
Where is the soul-refreshing view
  Of Jesus and his word?

What peaceful hours I once enjoyed!
  How sweet their memory still!
But they have left an aching void,
  The world can never fill.

Return, O Holy Dove, return,
  Sweet messenger of rest;
I hate the sins that made thee mourn,
  And drove thee from my breast.

The dearest idol I have known,
  Whate'er that idol be,
Help me to tear it from thy throne,
  And worship only thee.

So shall my walk be close with God,
  Calm and serene my frame;
So purer light shall mark the road,
  That leads me to the Lamb.

LOVEST THOU ME?—John xxi. 16.

Cowp

Hark! my soul it is the Lord,
'Tis thy Saviour, hear his word;
Jesus speaks and speaks to thee,
 "Say, poor sinner, lov'st thou me?

"I deliver'd thee when bound,
And when bleeding, heal'd thy wound;
Sought thee wand'ring, set thee right;
Turn'd thy darkness into light.

"Can a woman's tender care
Cease towards the child she bare?
Yes, she may forgetful be,
Yet will I remember thee.

"Mine is an unchanging love,
Higher than the heights above;
Deeper than the depths beneath;
Free and faithful, strong as death.

"Thou shalt see my glory soon,
When the work of grace is done;
Partner of my throne shall be;
Say, poor sinner, lov'st thou me?"

Lord, it is my chief complaint,
That my love is weak and faint;
Yet I love thee and adore;
Oh, for grace to love thee more!

AGAINST LYING.

Watts.

O 'TIS a lovely thing for youth,
   To walk betimes in wisdom's way:
To fear a lie,—to speak the truth,
   That we may trust to all they say.

But liars we can never trust,
   Tho' they should speak the thing that's true;
And he that does one fault at first,
   And lies to hide it, makes it two.

Have we not known, nor heard, nor read,
   How God abhors deceit and wrong?
How Ananias was struck dead,
   Caught with a lie upon his tongue.

So did his wife Sapphira die,
  When she came in and grew so bold,
As to confirm that wicked lie,
  That just before her husband told.

The Lord delights in them that speak
  The words of truth; but every liar
Must have his portion in the lake
  That burns with brimstone and with fire.

Then let me always watch my lips,
  Lest I be struck to death and hell;
Since God a book of reck'ning keeps,
  For every lie that children tell.

———

ON SILENT WORSHIP.

J. J. Gurn

LET deepest silence all around
  Its peaceful shelter spread;
So shall that living word abound,
  The word that wakes the dead.

How sweet to wait upon the Lord,
  In stillness and in prayer!
What though no preacher speak the word!
  A minister is there.

A minister of wondrous skill
  True graces to impart,
He teaches all the Father's will,
  And preaches to the heart.

He dissipates the coward's fears,
  And bids the coldest glow;
He speaks, and, lo! the softest tears
  Of deep contrition flow.

He knows to bend the heart of steel,
  He bows the loftiest soul;—
O'er all we think, and all we feel,
  How matchless his control!

And, ah! how precious is his love,
  In tenderest touches given!
It whispers of the bliss above,
  And stays the soul on heaven.

From mind to mind, in streams of joy,
  The holy influence spreads ;—
'Tis peace, 'tis peace, without alloy;
  For God that influence sheds.

Dear Lord, to thee we still will pray,
  And praise thee as before ;
For this, thy glorious Gospel day,
  Teach us to praise thee more.

THE PREPARATION OF THE HEART.

Montgomery.

LORD, teach us how to pray aright,
  With rev'rence and with fear ;
Though dust and ashes in Thy sight,
  We may—we must draw near.

We perish if we cease from prayer.
  Oh! grant us power to pray !
And when to meet Thee we prepare,
  Lord, meet us by the way.

Burden'd with guilt, convinc'd of sin,
  In weakness, want, and wo ;
Fightings without, and fears within,
  Lord, whither shall we go ?

God of all grace we come to Thee
  With broken, contrite hearts :
Give what Thine eye delights to see—
  Truth in the inward parts.

Give deep humility; the sense
  Of godly sorrow give ;
A strong, desiring confidence
  To hear thy voice, and live.

Faith in the only sacrifice
  That can for sin atone :
To cast our hopes, to fix our eyes
  On Christ—on Christ alone ;—

Patience to watch, and wait, and weep,
  Though mercy long delay ;
Courage, our fainting souls to keep,
  And trust Thee though thou slay.

Give these—and then thy will be done :
  Thus strengthened with all might,
We, by thy Spirit and thy Son
  Shall pray, and pray aright.

PROVIDENCE.

Cowp

God moves in a mysterious way,
  His wonders to perform ;
He plants his footsteps in the sea,
  And rides upon the storm.

Deep in unfathomable mines
  Of never-failing skill,
He treasures up his bright designs
  And works his sov'reign will.

Ye fearful saints, fresh courage take,
  The clouds ye so much dread,
Are big with mercy, and shall break
  In blessings on your head.

Judge not the Lord by feeble sense,
  But trust him for his grace :
Behind a frowning providence
  He hides a smiling face.

His purposes will ripen fast,
  Unfolding every hour ;
The bud may have a bitter taste,
  But sweet will be the flower.

Blind unbelief is sure to err,
  And scan his work in vain ;
God is his own interpreter,
  And he will make it plain.

.SE FOR MERCIES, SPIRITUAL AND TEMPORAL.

Watts.

Whene'er I take my walks abroad,
  How many poor I see !
What shall I render to my God,
  For all his gifts to me.

No more than others I deserve,
  Yet God hath given me more,
For I have food while others starve,
  Or beg from door to door.

How many children in the street,
  Half naked I behold ;
While I am cloth'd from head to feet,
  And cover'd from the cold.

While some poor wretches scarce can tell
  Where they may lay their head,
I have a home wherein to dwell,
  And rest upon my bed.

While others early learn to swear,
  And curse, and lie, and steal ;
Lord, I am taught thy name to fear,
  And do thy holy will.

Are these thy favours day by day,
  To me above the rest ?
Then let me love thee more than they,
  And try to serve thee best.

CONFESSION.

Lord, when we bend before thy throne,
  And our confessions pour,
Teach us to feel the sins we own,
  And shun what we deplore.

Our contrite spirits pitying see,
  And penitence impart ;
And let a healing ray from thee
  Beam hope upon the heart

When we disclose our wants in prayer,
　May we our wills resign,
And not a thought our bosom share
　Which is not wholly thine.

Let faith each meek petition fill,
　And waft it to the skies;
And teach our hearts 'tis goodness still
　That grants it or denies.

THE ALL-SEEING GOD.

Watts.

ALMIGHTY God, thy piercing eye
　Strikes through the shades of night,
And our most secret actions lie
　All open to thy sight.

There's not a sin that we commit,
　Nor wicked word we say,
But in thy dreadful book 'tis writ,
　Against the judgment day.

And must the crimes that I have done
　Be read and published there;
Be all exposed before the sun,
　While men and angels hear?

Lord, at thy feet ashamed I lie;
　Upwards I dare not look:
Pardon my sins before I die,
　And blot them from thy book.

Remember all the dying pains
　That my Redeemer felt,
And let his blood wash out my stains,
　And answer for my guilt.

O may I now for ever fear
　T'indulge a sinful thought;
Since the great God can see and hear,
　And writes down every fault.

London: *Printed by E. Couchman & Co.*, 10, *Throgmorton Street; for the*
TRACT ASSOCIATION *of the* SOCIETY OF FRIENDS *Sold at the* DEPOSITORY,
12, *Bishopsgate Street Without.*—1863.